THE HANDBOOK
OF FIXED INCOME
SECURITIES

THE HANDBOOK OF FIXED INCOME SECURITIES

Fifth Edition

FRANK J. FABOZZI

Editor

McGraw-Hill
New York   San Francisco   Washington, D.C.   Auckland   Bogotá
Caracas   Lisbon   London   Madrid   Mexico City   Milan
Montreal   New Delhi   San Juan   Singapore
Sydney   Tokyo   Toronto

McGraw-Hill

A Division of The McGraw·Hill Companies

Library of Congress Cataloging in Publication Data

The handbook of fixed income securities / Frank J. Fabozzi, editor. --
5th ed.
   p. cm
  Includes bibliographical references and index.
  ISBN 0-7863-1095-2
  1. Bonds--Handbooks, manuals, etc. 2. Preferred stocks-
-Handbooks, manuals, etc. 3. Money market funds--Handbooks,
manuals, etc. 4. Mutual funds--Handbooks, manuals, etc. 5. Fixed
-income securities. I. Fabozzi, Frank J.
HG4651.H265 1997
332.63´2044—dc20   96-41065

PREFACE

This book is designed to provide extensive coverage of not only the wide range of fixed income products but also fixed income portfolio management strategies. Each chapter is written by an authority on the subject. Many of these authorities have written books, monographs, and/or articles on their topic. More than half of the chapters in this *Handbook* are either authored or co-authored by a Chartered Financial Analyst.

The fifth edition of the *Handbook* is divided into seven parts. Part 1 provides general information about the investment features of fixed income securities and the associated risks. Coverage of yield measures, spot rates, forward rates, total return, price volatility measures (duration and convexity), and bond market indexes is included in this part.

Parts 2 covers bonds (domestic and foreign) and money market instruments. Credit analysis of these instruments is explained in Part 3. Part 4 describes mortgage-backed securities (passthroughs, collateralized mortgage obligations, and stripped mortgage-backed securities) and asset-backed securities.

Part 5 builds on the analytical framework in Part 1. In this part, two methodologies for valuing fixed income securities are discussed: the binomial method and the Monte Carlo method. A byproduct of these methods is the option-adjusted spread. A methodology using the latest option technology for valuing convertible securities is explained. Also explained in this chapter are various risk measures beyond basic duration and convexity and the state-of-the art technology for modeling the term structure of interest rates.

The more popular fixed income portfolio management strategies are covered in Part 6. In addition to active strategies and structured portfolio strategies (indexing, immunization, and dedication), coverage includes the importance of selecting a performance bogey.

Part 7 covers derivative instruments and their portfolio management applications. Derivative instruments include futures/forward contracts, options, interest rate swaps, and interest rate agreements (caps and floors). The basic feature of each instrument is described as well as how it is used to control the risk of a fixed income portfolio.

The following 18 chapters are new:

ACKNOWLEDGMENTS

I would like to extend my deep personal appreciation to the contributing authors, the editorial advisory board, and the following individuals who provided various forms of assistance in this project:

Scott Amero (BlackRock Financial Management)

Keith Anderson (BlackRock Financial Management)

Cliff Asness (Goldman Sachs Asset Management)

Max Bublitz (Conesco)

Dwight Churchill (Fidelity Management and Research)

Robert Gerber (Sanford C. Bernstein & Co.)

David Germany (Miller Anderson & Sherrerd)

Laurie Goodman (PaineWebber)

Martin Leibowitz (TIAA-CREF)

Michael Marz (First Southwest)

Ed Murphy (Merchants Mutual Insurance Company)

Judith Otterman (Salomon Brothers)

Scott Pinkus (Goldman Sachs)

Robert Reitano (John Hancock Mutual Life Insurance Company)

Scott Richard (Miller Anderson & Sherrerd)

Ehud Ronn (University of Texas at Austin)

Ron Ryan (Ryan Labs)

Dexter Senft (Lehman Brothers)

Francis Trainer (Sanford C. Bernstein & Co.)

Frank J. Fabozzi

CONTRIBUTORS

Joseph V. Amato
Managing Director
Director of High Yield Bond Research
Lehman Brothers, Inc.

Chris Ames
Director
Asset-Backed Securities Trading
Lehman Brothers International (Europe)

David Audley
Director of Investment Systems and Technology
Tiger Management Corporation

David T. Beers
Managing Director
Sovereign Ratings Group
Standard & Poor's

Anand K. Bhattacharya, Ph.D.
Managing Director
Head of Fixed Income Research
Prudential Securities Inc.

Mihir Bhattacharya, Ph.D.
Managing Director, Capital Markets
UBS Securities, LLC.

Jane S. Brauer
Brady Bond Strategist
Emerging Markets Fixed Income Research
Merrill Lynch

Frank D. Campbell, CFA
Vice President
Conning & Company

Richard Chin
Fixed-Income Research
Goldman Sachs & Co.

Peter E. Christensen
Managing Director
ComTech, Incorporated

Leland E. Crabbe, Ph.D.
First Vice President
Merrill Lynch

Ravi E. Dattatreya, Ph.D.
Senior Vice President
Sumitomo Bank Capital Markets, Inc.

Andrew S. Davidson
President
Andrew Davidson & Co., Inc.

Chris P. Dialynas
Advisory Managing Director
Pacific Investment Management Company

John N. Dunlevy, CFA, CPA
Director and Senior Portfolio Manager
Hyperion Capital Management Inc.

Sylvan G. Feldstein, Ph.D.
Adjunct Lecturer
School of Management
Yale University

Michael G. Ferri, Ph.D.
Foundation Professor of Finance
George Mason University

H. Gifford Fong
President
Gifford Fong Associates

William J. Gartland, CFA
Vice President
Bloomberg Financial Market

Kevin E. Grant, CFA
Portfolio Manager
Fidelity Management & Research Company

Adam M. Greshin, CFA
Principal
Scudder, Stevens and Clark

Lakhbir S. Hayre, D. Phil.
Salomon Brothers Inc.

Michael D. Herskovitz
Morgan Stanley

David R. Howard
Senior Director, Asset Backed Securities
Fitch Investors Service, L.P.

Jane Tripp Howe, CFA
Vice President
Pacific Investment Management Company

Joseph C. Hu, Ph.D.
Managing Director
Director of Mortgage Research
Oppenheimer & Co., Inc.

James V. Jordan, Ph.D., CFA
Professor of Finance
The George Washington University

Ronald N. Kahn, Ph.D.
Director of Research
BARRA

Andrew J. Kalotay, Ph.D.
Director
Center for Finance and Technology
Polytechnic University

David T. Kim
Odyssey Partners, L.P.

Thomas E. Klaffky
Managing Director
Salomon Brothers Inc

Robert Kulason
Salomon Brothers Inc

Nicholas C. Letica
Associate Director
Bear Stearns & Co.

Anthony LoFaso, Ph.D.
Vice President
Union Bank of Switzerland

Jack Malvey, CFA
Managing Director
Lehman Brothers

Howard S. Marks, CFA
Chairman
Oaktree Capital Management

Elizabeth Mays, Ph.D.
Senior Economist
Federal Home Loan Mortgage Corporation

Richard W. McEnally, Ph.D., CFA
Meade Willis Professor of Investment Banking
University of North Carolina

Cyrus Mohebbi, Ph.D.
Director
Prudential Securities, Inc.

Ardavan Nozari
Vice President
Salomon Brothers Inc

Daralyn B. Peifer, CFA
Manager, Benefit Finance
General Mills, Inc.

Mark Pitts, Ph.D.
Principal
White Oak Capital Management Corp.

Sharmin Mossavar-Rahmani, CFA
Partner
Goldman Sachs Asset Management

Shrikant Ramamurthy
First Vice President
Fixed-Income Research
Prudential Securities

Frank R. Ramirez
Managing Director
Structured Capital Management

Chuck Ramsey
Managing Director
Structured Capital Management
and CEO
Mortgage Risk Assessment Corp.

Frank K. Reilly, Ph.D., CFA
Bernard J. Hank Professor of Finance
University of Notre Dame

John C. Ritchie, Jr., Ph.D.
Professor of Finance
Temple University

Michael R. Rosenberg, Ph.D.
First Vice President and Manager
International Fixed Income Research
Merrill Lynch Capital Markets

Andrew Shook
Associate
NationsBanc Capital Markets, Inc.

Christopher B. Steward, CFA
Vice President
Scudder, Stevens and Clark

Anthony V. Thompson
Director of ABS Research
Goldman, Sachs & Co.

Allen A. Vine
International Emerging Markets Specialist
Global High Yield Securities Research
Merrill Lynch

Michael Waldman
Director of Fixed Income Research
MacKay-Shields Financial Corp.

Kenneth L. Walker
President
T. Rowe Price Stable Asset Management, Inc.

George O. Williams, Ph.D.
Principal
Andrew Kalotay Associates

Richard S. Wilson
Executive Managing Director
Fitch Investors Service, L.P.

David J. Wright, Ph.D.
Associate Professor of Finance
University of Wisconsin—Parkside

David Yuen, CFA
Director of Research
Structured Capital Management

Yu Zhu, Ph.D.
Director, Risk Assessment and Control
Sakura Global Capital, Inc.

Thomas A. Zimmerman
Director—Fixed Income Research
Prudential Securities, Inc.

C O N T E N T S

Chapter 7

PART 2

GOVERNMENT AND PRIVATE DEBT OBLIGATIONS   147

Chapter 8

Chapter 9

Chapter 10

Chapter 11

Corporate Bonds   206
Frank J. Fabozzi, Richard S. Wilson, and John C. Ritchie, Jr.

Chapter 12

Medium-Term Notes   234
Leland E. Crabbe

Chapter 13

Domestic Floating-Rate and Adjustable-Rate Debt Securities   254
Richard S. Wilson

Chapter 14

Nonconvertible Preferred Stock   263
Richard S. Wilson

Chapter 15

Convertible Securities   287
John C. Ritchie, Jr.

Chapter 16

The High-Yield Bond Market   307
Joseph V. Amato

Chapter 17

International Bond Markets and Instruments   327
Christopher B. Steward and Adam M. Greshin

Chapter 25

High-Yield Analysis of Emerging Markets Debt   473
Allen A. Vine

PART 4

MORTGAGE-BACKED AND ASSET-BACKED SECURITIES   499

Chapter 26

Mortgages and Overview of Mortgage-Backed Securities   501
Frank J. Fabozzi and Chuck Ramsey

Chapter 27

Mortgage Pass-Through Securities   524
Lakhbir S. Hayre, Cyrus Mohebbi, and Thomas A. Zimmerman

Chapter 28

Collateralized Mortgage Obligations   569
Chris Ames

Chapter 29

Nonagency CMOs   598
Frank J. Fabozzi, David Yuen, Chuck Ramsey, and Frank R. Ramirez

Chapter 38

New Duration Measures for Risk Management   738
Thomas E. Klaffky, Ardavan Nozari, and Michael Waldman

Chapter 39

Interest-Rate Risk Models Used by Depository Institutions   751
Elizabeth Mays

Chapter 40

OAS and Effective Duration   763
David Audley, Richard Chin, and Shrikant Ramamurthy

Chapter 41

Fixed Income Risk Modeling   779
Ronald N. Kahn

Chapter 42

Chapter 43

PART 6

Chapter 44

Chapter 45

Chapter 46

A Sponsor's View of Benchmark Portfolios   896
Daralyn B. Peifer

Chapter 47

Indexing Fixed Income Assets   913
Sharmin Mossavar-Rahmani

Chapter 48

Bond Immunization: An Asset/Liability Optimization Strategy   925
Peter E. Christensen, Frank J. Fabozzi, and Anthony LoFaso

PART 7

DERIVATIVE INSTRUMENTS AND THEIR PORTFOLIO MANAGEMENT APPLICATIONS   1137

THE HANDBOOK OF FIXED INCOME SECURITIES

BACKGROUND

OVERVIEW OF THE TYPES AND FEATURES OF FIXED INCOME SECURITIES

Frank J. Fabozzi, Ph.D., CFA, CPA
Adjunct Professor of Finance
School of Management
Yale University

Michael G. Ferri, Ph.D.
Foundation Professor of Finance
George Mason University

This chapter will explore some of the most important features of bonds, preferred stock, and mortgage-backed securities, and provide the reader with a taxonomy of terms and concepts that will be useful in the reading of the specialized chapters to follow.

BONDS

Type of Issuer

One important characteristic of a bond is the nature of its issuer. Although foreign governments and firms raise capital in U.S. financial markets, the three largest issuers of debt are domestic corporations, municipal governments, and the federal government and its agencies. Each class of issuer, however, features additional and significant differences.

Domestic corporations, for example, include regulated utilities as well as unregulated manufacturers. Furthermore, each firm may sell different kinds of bonds: Some debt may be publicly placed, whereas other bonds may be sold directly to one or only a few buyers (referred to as a *private placement*); some debt is collateralized by specific assets of the company, whereas other debt may be unsecured. Municipal debt is also varied: "General obligation" bonds (GOs) are backed by the full faith, credit, and taxing power of the governmental unit issuing them; "revenue bonds," on the other hand, have a safety, or creditworthiness, that depends upon the vitality and success of the particular entity (such as toll roads, hospitals, or water systems) within the municipal government issuing the bond.

The U.S. Treasury has the most voracious appetite for debt, but the bond market often receives calls from its agencies. Federal government agencies include federally related institutions and government-sponsored enterprises.

It is important for the investor to realize that, by law or practice or both, these different borrowers have developed different ways of raising debt capital over the years. As a result, the distinctions among the various types of issuers correspond closely to differences among bonds in yield, denomination, safety of principal, maturity, tax status, and such important provisions as the call privilege, put features, and sinking fund. As we discuss the key features of fixed income securities, we will point out how the characteristics of the bonds vary with the obligor or issuing authority. A more extensive discussion is provided in later chapters in this book that explain the various instruments.

Maturity

A key feature of any bond is its *term-to-maturity,* the number of years during which the borrower has promised to meet the conditions of the debt (which are contained in the bond's indenture). A bond's term-to-maturity is the date on which the debt will cease and the borrower will redeem the issue by paying the face value, or principal. One indication of the importance of the maturity is that the code word or name for every bond contains its maturity (and coupon). Thus, the title of the Anheuser Busch Company bond due, or maturing, in 2016 is given as "Anheuser Busch $8^5/_8$s of 2016." In practice, the words *maturity, term,* and *term-to-maturity* are used interchangeably to refer to the number of years remaining in the life of a bond. Technically, however, *maturity* denotes the date the bond will be redeemed, and either *term* or *term-to-maturity* denotes the number of years until that date.

A bond's maturity is crucial for several reasons. First, maturity indicates the expected life of the instrument, or the number of periods during which the holder of the bond can expect to receive the coupon interest and the number of years before the principal will be paid. Second, the yield on a bond depends substantially on its maturity. More specifically, at any given point in time, the yield offered on a long-term bond may be greater than, less than, or equal to the yield offered on a short-term bond. As will be explained in Chapter 6, the effect of maturity on the yield depends on the *shape of the yield curve.* Third, the volatility of a bond's price is closely associated with maturity: Changes in the market level of rates will wrest much larger changes in price from bonds of long maturity than from otherwise similar debt of shorter life.[1] Finally, as explained in the next chapter, there are other risks associated with the maturity of a bond.

---

1. Chapter 5 discusses this point in detail.

When considering a bond's maturity, the investor should be aware of any provisions that modify, or permit the issuer to modify, the maturity of a bond. Although corporate bonds (referred to as "corporates") are typically *term bonds* (issues that have a single maturity), they often contain arrangements by which the issuing firm either can or must retire the debt early, in full or in part. Many corporates, for example, give the issuer a *call privilege,* which permits the issuing firm to redeem the bond before the scheduled maturity under certain conditions (these conditions are discussed below). Many municipal bonds have the same provision. Although the U.S. government no longer issues bonds that have a call privilege, there are outstanding issues with this provision. Many industrials and some utilities have *sinking-fund provisions,* which mandate that the firm retire a substantial portion of the debt, in a prearranged schedule, during its life and before the stated maturity. Typically, municipal bonds are *serial bonds* or, in essence, bundles of bonds with differing maturities. (Some corporates are of this type, too.)

Usually, the maturity of a corporate bond is between 1 and 30 years. This is not to say that there are not outliers. In fact, recently financially sound firms have begun to issue longer-term debt in order to lock in long-term attractive financing. Some examples are Tennessee Valley Authority (TVA), $8^{1}/_{4}$ maturing on 4/15/42 (callable on 4/15/12); and Conrail, $7^{7}/_{8}$ maturing on 5/15/43 (noncallable). Recently, Walt Disney Corporation issued a 100-year bond.

Although classifying bonds as "short-term," "intermediate-term," and "long-term" is not universally accepted, the following classification is typically used. Bonds with a maturity of 1 to 5 years are generally considered short-term; bonds with a maturity between 5 and 12 years are viewed as intermediate-term (and are often called *notes*). Long-term bonds are those with a maturity greater than 12 years.

Coupon and Principal

A bond's *coupon* is the periodic interest payment made to owners during the life of the bond. The coupon is always cited, along with maturity, in any quotation of a bond's price. Thus one might hear about the "ATT $5^{1}/_{8}$ due in 2001" or the "Ingersoll Rand 7.2 due in 2025" in discussions of current bond trading. In these examples, the coupon cited is in fact the *coupon rate,* that is, the rate of interest that, when multiplied by the *principal, par value,* or *face value* of the bond, provides the dollar value of the coupon payment. Typically, but not universally, for bonds issued in the United States the coupon payment is made in semiannual installments. In contrast, for bonds issued in some European bond markets and all bonds issued in the *Eurobond market,* the coupon payment is made once per year. Bonds may be *bearer bonds* or *registered bonds*. With bearer bonds, investors clip coupons and send them to the obligor for payment. In the case of registered issues, bond owners receive the payment automatically at the appropriate time. All new bond issues must be registered.

There are a few corporate bonds (mostly railroad issues), called *income bonds,* that contain a provision permitting the firm to omit or delay the payment of interest if the firm's earnings are too low. They have been issued as part of bankruptcy reorganizations or to replace a preferred-stock offering of the issuer.

Zero-coupon bonds have been issued by corporations and municipalities since the early 1980s. For example, Ford Motor Credit has a zero-coupon bond outstanding due 9/29/2000 that it issued on 9/17/1985. Although the U.S. Treasury does not issue zero-coupon debt with a maturity greater than one year, such securities have been created by government securities dealers. Merrill Lynch was the first to do this with its creation of Treasury Investment Growth Receipts (TIGRs) in August 1982. The most popular zero-coupon Treasury securities today are those created by government dealer firms under the Treasury's Separate Trading of Registered Interest and Principal Securities (STRIPS) program. Just how these securities are created will be explained in Chapter 8. The investor in a zero-coupon security typically receives interest by buying the security at a price below its principal, or maturity value, and holding it to the maturity date. The reason for the issuance of zero-coupon securities is explained in Chapter 8. However, some zeros are issued at par and accrue interest during the bond's life, with the accrued interest and principal payable at maturity.

There are securities that have a coupon rate that increases over time. These securities are called *step-up notes* because the coupon rate "steps up" over time. For example, a six-year step-up note might have a coupon rate that is 5 percent for the first two years, 5.8 percent for the next two years, and 6 percent for the last two years.

In contrast to a coupon rate that is fixed for the entire life of the bond or steps up, there are *floating-rate bonds.* The coupon rate on such securities is periodically reset based on some reference rate plus a spread. For example, the coupon rate may be reset every six months at a rate equal to the yield on a six-month Treasury security plus 50 basis points. The distinctions between a floating-rate bond and what is sometimes referred to as a *variable-rate bond* or *adjustable-rate bond* are the frequency at which the coupon rate is reset and the reference rate. A floating-rate bond resets more than once a year, and the reference rate is a short-term rate. In contrast, a variable-rate bond does not reset more than once a year, and the reference rate is a long-term interest rate. Institutional investors such as banks and thrifts have found floating-rate bonds indexed off an interest-rate benchmark attractive for asset/liability management.

Three last points about floating-rate securities. First, although the coupon rate on most floating-rate securities resets on the basis of some reference rate, some issues have a benchmark for the coupon rate that is a nonfinancial index, such as the price of a commodity. Second, whereas the coupon on floating-rate bonds benchmarked off a reference rate typically rises as the reference rate rises and falls as the reference rate falls, there are issues whose coupon rate moves in the opposite direction of the interest-rate change. Such issues are called *inverse floaters.* Finally, there are floating-rate securities whose coupon rate is equal to the reference rate as long as the reference rate is within a certain range at the reset date. However, if the reference rate is outside of the range, the coupon rate is zero for that period. Such issues are called *range notes.*

Structures in the *high-yield (junk bond)* sector of the corporate bond market have introduced variations in the way coupon payments are made. For example, in a leveraged buyout or recapitalization financed with high-yield bonds, the heavy interest payment burden the corporation must bear places severe cash-flow constraints on the firm. To reduce this burden, firms involved in leveraged buyouts (LBOs) and recapitalizations have issued deferred-coupon structures that permit the issuer to defer making cash interest payments for a period of three to seven years. There are three types of deferred-coupon structures: (1) deferred-interest bonds, (2) step-up bonds, and (3) payment-in-kind bonds. These structures are described in Chapter 16.

Another high-yield bond structure allows the issuer to reset the coupon rate so that the bond will trade at a predetermined price. The coupon rate may reset annually or reset only once over the life of the bond. Generally, the coupon rate will be the average of rates suggested by two investment banking firms. The new rate will then reflect the level of interest rates at the reset date and the credit spread the market wants on the issue at the reset date. This structure is called an *extendible reset bond.* Notice the difference between this bond structure and the floating-rate issue described earlier. With a floating-rate issue, the coupon rate resets based on a fixed spread to some benchmark, where the spread is specified in the indenture and the amount of the spread reflects market conditions at the time the issue is first offered. In contrast, the coupon rate on an extendible reset bond is reset based on market conditions suggested by several investment banking firms at the time of the reset date. Moreover, the new coupon rate reflects the new level of interest rates and the new spread that investors seek.

One reason that debt financing is popular with corporations is that the interest payments are tax-deductible expenses. As a result, the true after-tax cost of debt to a profitable firm is usually much less than the stated coupon interest rate. The level of the coupon on any bond is typically close to the level of yields for issues of its class at the time the bond is first sold to the public. Some bonds are initially issued at a price substantially below par value (called *original-issue discount bonds,* or *OIDs*), and their coupon rate is deliberately set below the current market rate. However, firms usually try to set the coupon at a level that will make the market price close to par value. This goal can be accomplished by placing the coupon rate near the prevailing market rate.

To many investors, the coupon is simply the amount of interest they will receive each year. However, the coupon has another major impact on an investor's experience with a bond. The coupon's size influences the volatility of the bond's price: The larger the coupon, the less the price will change in response to a change in market interest rates. Thus, the coupon and the maturity have opposite effects on the price volatility of a bond. This will be illustrated in Chapter 5.

The principal, par value, or face value of a bond is the amount to be repaid to the investor either at maturity or at those times when the bond is called or retired according to sinking-fund provisions. But the principal plays another role, too: It is the basis on which the coupon or periodic interest rests; the coupon is the product of the principal and the coupon rate. For most corporate issues, the face value is $1,000; many government bonds have larger principals starting with $10,000; and most municipal bonds come in denominations of $5,000.

Participants in the bond market use several measures to describe the potential return from investing in a bond: current yield, yield-to-maturity, yield-to-call for a callable bond, and yield-to-put for a putable bond. A *yield-to-worst* is often quoted for bonds. This is the lowest yield of the following: yield-to-maturity, yield to all possible call dates, and yield to all put dates. The calculation and limitations of these yield measures are explained and illustrated in Chapter 4.

The prices of most bonds are quoted as percentages of par or face value. To convert the price quote into a dollar figure, one simply multiplies the price by the par value. The following table illustrates this.

Par Value	Price Quote	Price as a Percentage of Par	Price in Dollars
$ 1,000	91 $^3/_4$	91.75	$ 917.50
5,000	102 $^1/_2$	102.5	5,125.00
10,000	87 $^1/_4$	87.25	8,725.00
25,000	100 $^3/_4$	100.875	25,218.75
100,000	71 $^9/_{32}$	71.28125	71,281.25

Treasury bonds and notes are quoted in 32nds of a percentage point, whereas corporate and municipal bonds are quoted in eighths of a percentage point. Care must be taken in translating quotes into dollar prices because the convention for Treasury bonds and notes is to quote, on dealer screens, the number of 32nds after the decimal. Specifically, for a Treasury note and bond, a quote of 91.24 means $91^{24}/_{32}$, or $91^3/_4$. A quote of 102.4 means $102^4/_{32}$, or $102^1/_8$.

Call and Refunding Provisions

If a bond's indenture contains a *call feature* or *call provision,* the issuer retains the right to retire the debt, fully or partially, before the scheduled maturity date. The chief benefit of such a feature is that it permits the borrower, should market rates fall, to replace the bond issue with a lower-interest-cost issue. The call feature has added value for corporations and municipalities. It may in the future help them to escape the restrictions that frequently characterize their bonds (about the disposition of assets or collateral). The call feature provides an additional benefit to corporations, which might want to use unexpectedly high levels of cash to retire outstanding bonds or might wish to restructure their balance sheets.

The call provision is detrimental to investors, who run the risk of losing a high-coupon bond when rates begin to decline. When the borrower calls the issue, the investor must find other outlets, which presumably would have lower yields than the bond just withdrawn through the call privilege. Another problem for the investor is that the prospect of a call limits the appreciation in a bond's price that could be expected when interest rates start to slip.

Because the call feature benefits the issuer and places the investor at a disadvantage, callable bonds carry higher yields than bonds that cannot be retired before maturity. This difference in yields is likely to grow when investors believe that market rates are about to fall and that the borrower may be tempted to replace a high-coupon debt with a new, low-coupon bond. (Such a transaction is called *refunding*.) However, the higher yield alone is often not sufficient compensation to the investor for granting the call privilege to the issuer. Thus, the price at which the bond may be called, termed the *call price,* is normally higher than the principal or face value of the issue. The difference between call price and principal is the *call premium,* whose value may be as much as one year's interest in the first few years of a bond's life and may decline systematically thereafter.

An important limitation on the borrower's right to call is the *period of call protection,* or *deferment period,* which is a specified number of years in the early life of the bond during which the issuer may not call the debt. Such protection is another concession to the investor, and it comes in two forms. Some bonds are *noncallable* (often abbreviated NC) for any reason during the deferment period; other bonds are *nonrefundable* (NF) for that time. The distinction lies in the fact that nonrefundable debt may be called if the funds used to retire the bond issue are obtained from internally generated funds, such as the cash flow from operations or the sale of property or equipment, or from nondebt funding such as the sale of common stock. Thus, although the terminology is unfortunately confusing, a nonrefundable issue may be refunded under the circumstances just described and, as a result, offers less call protection than a noncallable bond, which cannot be called for any reason except to satisfy sinking-fund requirements, explained later. Beginning in early 1986, a number of corporations issued long-term debt with extended call protection, not refunding protection. A number are noncallable for the issue's life, such as Dow Chemical Company's $8^5/_8$s due in 2006. The issuer is expressly prohibited from redeeming the issue prior to maturity. These *noncallable-for-life issues* are referred to as *bullet bonds.*

A key question is, When will the firm find it profitable to refund an issue? It is important for investors to understand the process by which a firm decides whether to retire an old bond and issue a new one. A simple and brief example will illustrate that process and introduce the reader to the kinds of calculations an issuer will make when trying to predict whether a bond will be refunded.

Suppose a firm's outstanding debt consists of $30 million par value of a bond with a coupon of 10 percent, a maturity of 15 years, and a lapsed deferment period. The firm can now issue a bond with a similar maturity for an interest rate of 7.8 percent. Assume that the issuing expenses and legal fees amount to $200,000. The call price on the existing bond issue is $105 per $100 par value. The firm must pay, adjusted for taxes, the sum of call premium and expenses. To simplify the calculations, assume a 30 percent tax rate. This sum is then $1,190,000.[2] Such a transaction would save the firm a yearly sum of $462,000 in interest (which equals the interest of $3 million on the existing bond less the $2.34 million on the new, adjusted for taxes) for the next 15 years.[3] The rate of return on a payment of $1,190,000 now in exchange for a savings of $462,000 per year for 15 years is about 38 percent. This rate far exceeds the firm's after-tax cost of debt (now at 7.8 percent times .7, or 5.46 percent) and makes the refunding a positive economic transaction.

In municipal securities, refunding often refers to something different, although the concept is the same. Municipal bonds can be prefunded prior to maturity (usually on a call date). Here, instead of issuing new bonds to retire the debt, the municipality will issue bonds and use the proceeds to purchase enough risk-free securities to fund all the cash flows on the existing bond issue. It places these in an irrevocable trust. Thus, the municipality still has two issues outstanding, but the old bonds receive a new label—they are *prerefunded.* If Treasury securities are used to prefund the debt, the cash flows on the bond are guaranteed by Treasury obligations in the trust. Thus, they become AAA rated and trade at higher prices than the underlying municipal bonds. Municipalities often find this an effective means of lowering their cost of debt.

Sinking-Fund Provision

The *sinking-fund provision,* which is typical for publicly and privately issued industrial bonds and not uncommon among certain classes of utility debt, requires the obligor to retire a certain amount of the outstanding debt each year. Generally, the retirement occurs in one of two ways. The firm may purchase the amount of bonds to be retired in the open market if their price is below par, or the company may make payments to the trustee who is empowered to monitor the indenture and who will call a certain number of bonds chosen by lottery. In the latter case, the investor would receive the prearranged call price, which is usually par value. The schedule of retirements varies considerably from issue to issue. Some issuers, particularly in the private-placement market, retire most if not all of their debt before maturity. In the public market, some companies may retire as little as 20 to 30 percent of the outstanding par value before maturity. Further, the indenture of many issues includes a deferment period that permits the issuer to wait five years or more before beginning the process of sinking-fund retirements. Government debt is generally free of this provision.

---

2. Both expenses are tax deductible for the firm. The total expense is the call premium of $1.5 million plus the issuing expenses and legal fees of $200,000. The after-tax cost is equal to the before-tax cost times (1 − tax rate). Hence, the after-tax cost is $1.7 million times (1 − .3), or $1,190,000.
3. The new interest expense would be $30 million times .078. The after-tax cost of the interest saving is $660,000 times (1 − .3).

There are four advantages of a sinking-fund provision from the investor's perspective. The sinking-fund requirement ensures an orderly retirement of the debt so that the final payment, at maturity, will not be too large. Second, the provision enhances the liquidity of some debt, especially for smaller issues with thin secondary markets. Third, the prices of bonds with this requirement are presumably more stable because the issuer may become an active participant on the buy side when prices fall. Fourth, because the issuer is under obligation to retire bonds even when interest rates are high, and the price below par, this provision can work to the benefit of the investor. For these reasons, the yields on bonds with sinking-fund provisions tend to be less than those on bonds without them.

The sinking fund, however, can work to the disadvantage of an investor. Suppose an investor is holding one of the early bonds to be called for a sinking fund. All of the time and effort put into analyzing the bond has now been wasted, and the investor will have to choose new instruments for purchase. Also, an investor holding a bond with a high coupon at the time rates begin to fall is still forced to relinquish the issue. For this reason, in times of high interest rates, one might find investors demanding higher yields from bonds with sinking funds than from other debt.

The sinking-fund provision may also harm the investor's position through the optional acceleration feature, a part of many corporate bond indentures. With this option, the corporation is free to retire more than the amount of debt the sinking fund requires (and often a multiple thereof) and to do it at the call price set for sinking-fund payments. Of course, the firm will exercise this option only if the price of the bond exceeds the sinking-fund price (usually near par), and this happens when rates are relatively low. If, as is typically the case, the sinking-fund provision becomes operative before the lapse of the call-deferment period, the firm can retire much of its debt with the optional acceleration feature and can do so at a price far below that of the call price it would have to pay in the event of refunding. The impact of such activity on the investor's position is obvious: The firm can redeem at or near par many of the bonds that appear to be protected from call and that have a market value above the face value of the debt.

Put Provisions

A *putable bond* grants the investor the right to sell the issue back to the issuer at par value on designated dates. The advantage to the investor is that if interest rates rise after the issue date, thereby reducing the value of the bond, the investor can force the issuer to redeem the bond at par. Some issues with put provisions may restrict the amount that the bondholder may put back to the issuer on any one put date. Put options have been included in corporate bonds to deter unfriendly takeovers. Such put provisions are referred to as "poison puts."

Put options can be classified as *hard puts* and *soft puts*. A hard put is one in which the security must be redeemed by the issuer only for cash. In the case of a soft put, the issuer has the option to redeem the security for cash, common stock, another debt instrument, or a combination of the three. Soft puts are found in convertible debt, which we describe next.

Convertible or Exchangeable Debt

A *convertible bond* is one that can be exchanged for specified amounts of common stock in the issuing firm: The conversion cannot be reversed, and the terms of the conversion are set by the company in the bond's indenture. The most important terms are *conversion ratio* and *conversion price*. The conversion ratio indicates the number of shares of common stock to which the holder of the convertible has a claim. For example, one convertible issue of Home Depot matures in 1997 (and is callable in 1995) and has a coupon rate of $4^1/_2$ percent; this bond has a conversion ratio of 25.8067 shares for one bond. Equivalently, this means at the time of issuance the conversion price was $38.75 per share ($1,000 par value divided by the conversion ratio 25.8067). The conversion price at issuance is also referred to as the *stated conversion price*.

The conversion privilege may be permitted for all or only some portion of the bond's life. The conversion ratio may decline over time. It is always adjusted proportionately for stock splits and stock dividends. Convertible bonds are callable by the issuer. This permits the issuer to force conversion of the issue. (Effectively, the issuer calls the bond, and the investor is forced to convert the bond or allow it to be called.) There are some convertible issues that have call protection. This protection can be in one of two forms: Either the issuer is not allowed to redeem the issue before a specified date, or the issuer is not permitted to call the issue until the stock price has increased by a predetermined percentage price above the conversion price at issuance.

An *exchangeable bond* is an issue that can be exchanged for the common stock of a corporation other than the issuer of the bond. For example, Ford Motor Credit exchangeable bonds can be exchanged for the common stock of its parent company, Ford Motor Company. There are a handful of issues that are exchangeable into more than one security.

One significant innovation in the convertible bond market is the "Liquid Yield Option Note" (LYON) developed by Merrill Lynch Capital Markets in 1985. A LYON is a zero-coupon, convertible, callable, and putable bond.

Techniques for analyzing convertible and exchangeable bonds are described in Chapters 15 and 42.

Warrants

A *warrant* is an option a firm issues that permits the owner to buy from the firm a certain number of shares of common stock at a specified price. It is not uncommon for publicly held corporations to issue warrants with new bonds.

A valuable aspect of a warrant is its rather long life: Most warrants are in effect for at least two years from issuance, and some are perpetual.[4] Another key feature of the warrant is the *exercise price,* the price at which the warrant holder can buy stock from the corporation. This price is normally set at about 15 percent above the market price of common stock at the time the bond, and thus the warrant, is issued. Frequently, the exercise price will rise through time, according to the schedule in the bond's indenture. Another important characteristic of the warrant is its detachability. *Detachable warrants* are often actively traded on the American Stock Exchange. Other warrants can be exercised only by the bondholder, and these are called *nondetachable warrants.* The chief benefit to the investor is the financial leverage the warrant provides.

PREFERRED STOCK

Preferred stock is a class of stock, not a debt instrument, but it shares characteristics of both common stock and debt. Like the holder of common stock, the preferred stockholder is entitled to dividends. Unlike those on common stock, however, preferred stock dividends are a specified percentage of par or face value.[5] The percentage is called the *dividend rate;* it need not be fixed, but may float over the life of the issue.

Failure to make preferred stock dividend payments cannot force the issuer into bankruptcy. Should the issuer not make the preferred stock dividend payment, usually made quarterly, one of two things can happen, depending on the terms of the issue. First, the dividend payment can accrue until it is fully paid. Preferred stock with this feature is called *cumulative preferred stock.* Second, if a dividend payment is missed and the security holder must forgo the payment, the preferred stock is said to be *noncumulative preferred stock.* Failure to make dividend payments may result in imposition of certain restrictions on management. For example, if dividend payments are in arrears, preferred stockholders might be granted voting rights.

Unlike debt, payments made to preferred stockholders are treated as a distribution of earnings. This means that they are not tax deductible to the corporation under the current tax code. Interest payments, on the other hand, are tax deductible. Although the after tax cost of funds is higher if a corporation issues preferred stock rather than borrowing, there is a factor that reduces the cost differential: A provision in the tax code exempts 70 percent of qualified dividends from

---

4. This long life contrasts sharply with the short life during which many exchange-traded call options on common stock, similar to warrants, are exercisable.

5. Almost all preferred stock limits the security holder to the specified amount. Historically, there have been issues entitling the preferred stockholder to participate in earnings distribution beyond the specified amount (based on some formula). Preferred stock with this feature is referred to as *participating preferred stock.*

federal income taxation if the recipient is a qualified corporation. For example, if Corporation A owns the preferred stock of Corporation B, for each $100 of dividends received by A, only $30 will be taxed at A's marginal tax rate. The purpose of this provision is to mitigate the effect of double taxation of corporate earnings. There are two implications of this tax treatment of preferred stock dividends. First, the major buyers of preferred stock are corporations seeking tax-advantaged investments. Second, the cost of preferred stock issuance is lower than it would be in the absence of the tax provision because the tax benefits are passed through to the issuer by the willingness of buyers to accept a lower dividend rate.

Preferred stock has some important similarities with debt, particularly in the case of cumulative preferred stock: (1) The returns to preferred stockholders promised by the issuer are fixed, and (2) preferred stockholders have priority over common stockholders with respect to dividend payments and distribution of assets in the case of bankruptcy. (The position of noncumulative preferred stock is considerably weaker than cumulative preferred stock.) It is because of this second feature that preferred stock is called a *senior security*. It is senior to common stock. On a balance sheet, preferred stock is classified as equity.

Preferred stock may be issued without a maturity date. This is called *perpetual preferred stock*. Almost all preferred stock has a sinking-fund provision, and some preferred stock is convertible into common stock. A trademark product of Morgan Stanley is the Preferred Equity Redemption Cumulative Stock (PERCS). This is a preferred stock with a mandatory conversion at maturity.

Historically, utilities have been the major issuers of preferred stock, making up more than half of each year's issuance. Since 1985, major issuers have been in the financial industry—finance companies, banks, thrifts, and insurance companies.

There are three types of preferred stock: (1) fixed-rate preferred stock, (2) adjustable-rate preferred stock, and (3) auction and remarketed preferred stock. The dividend rate on an adjustable-rate preferred stock (ARPS) is reset quarterly and based on a predetermined spread from the highest of three points on the Treasury yield curve. Most ARPS are perpetual, with a floor and ceiling imposed on the dividend rate of most issues. For auction preferred stock (APS) the dividend rate is reset periodically, as with ARPS, but the dividend rate is established through an auction process. In the case of remarketed preferred stock (RP), the dividend rate is determined periodically by a remarketing agent who resets the dividend rate so that any preferred stock can be tendered at par and be resold (remarketed) at the original offering price. An investor has the choice of dividend resets every 7 days or every 49 days.

MORTGAGE-BACKED SECURITIES

A *mortgage-backed security* (MBS) is an instrument whose cash flow depends on the cash flows of an underlying pool of mortgages. There are three types of mortgage-backed securities: (1) mortgage pass-through securities, (2) collateralized mortgage obligations, and (3) stripped mortgage-backed securities. This chapter provides an overview of these securities. A detailed discussion of the structure and analysis of these securities is presented in Part 4 of this book.

Mortgage Cash Flows

Because the cash flow for these securities depends on the cash flow from the underlying pool of mortgages, the first thing to define is a *mortgage*. A mortgage is a pledge of real estate to secure the loan originated for the purchase of that real property. The mortgage gives the lender *(mortgagee)* the right to foreclose on the loan and seize the property in order to ensure that the loan is paid off if the borrower *(mortgagor)* fails to make the contracted payments. The types of real estate properties that can be mortgaged are divided into two broad categories: residential and nonresidential (i.e., commercial and farm properties). The mortgage loan specifies the interest rate of the loan, the frequency of payment, and the number of years to maturity. Each monthly mortgage payment consists of the monthly interest, a scheduled amount in excess of the monthly interest that is applied to reduce the outstanding loan balance (this is called the *scheduled repayment of principal*), and any payments in excess of the mortgage payment. The latter payments are called *prepayments.*

In effect, the lender has granted the homeowner the right to prepay (or "call") all or part of the mortgage balance at any time. Homeowners prepay their mortgages for one of several reasons. First, they prepay the entire mortgage when they sell their home. Homes are sold for many reasons, among them a change of employment that requires moving or the purchase of a more expensive home. Second, if mortgage rates drop substantially after the mortgage loan was obtained, it may be beneficial for the homeowner to refinance the loan (even after paying all refinancing costs) at the lower interest rate. Third, if homeowners cannot meet their mortgage obligations, their property is repossessed and sold. The proceeds from the sale are used to pay off the mortgage loan. Finally, if the property is destroyed by fire or another insured catastrophe occurs, the insurance proceeds are used to pay off the mortgage.

Mortgage Pass-Through Securities

A *mortgage pass-through security* (or simply *pass-through*) is created when one or more holders of mortgages form a collection (pool) of mortgages and sell shares or participation certificates in the pool. A pool may consist of several thousand mortgages or only a few mortgages. The cash flow of a pass-through depends on the cash flow of the underlying mortgages, which, as just explained, consists of monthly mortgage payments representing interest, the scheduled repayment of principal, and any prepayments. Payments are made to security holders each month.

There are three major types of pass-through securities, guaranteed by the following organizations: Government National Mortgage Association ("Ginnie Mae"), Federal Home Loan Mortgage Corporation ("Freddie Mac"), and Federal

National Mortgage Association ("Fannie Mae"). The last two are government-sponsored entities. The Government National Mortgage Association is a wholly owned U.S. government corporation within the Department of Housing and Urban Development. The securities associated with these three entities are known as *agency pass-through securities*. There are also *nonagency pass-through securities,* issued by thrifts, commercial banks, and private conduits that are not backed by any agency.

While the preponderance of mortgage pass-through securities is backed by one to four family residential mortgages, there has been increased issuance of pass-throughs backed by other types of mortgages. These securities are called *commercial mortgage-backed securities.* The five major property types backing such securities are office space, retail property, industrial facilities, multifamily housing, and hotels.

Collateralized Mortgage Obligations

The *collateralized mortgage obligation (CMO)* structure was developed to broaden the appeal of mortgage-backed products to traditional fixed income investors. A CMO is a security backed by a pool of pass-throughs or a pool of mortgage loans. CMOs are structured so that there are several classes of bondholders with varying maturities. The different bond classes are also called *tranches.* The rules for the distribution of the principal payments and the interest from the underlying collateral among the tranches are specified in the prospectus. By redirecting the cash flow (i.e., principal payments and interest) from the underlying collateral, issuers have created classes of bonds that have different degrees of prepayment risk and are thereby more attractive to institutional investors to satisfy asset/liability objectives than a pass-through.

Numerous innovations in structuring CMOs have created classes of bonds with one or more of the following characteristics: (1) greater stability of cash flows over a wide range of prepayment speeds, (2) better matching of floating-rate liabilities, (3) substantial upside potential in a declining interest-rate environment but less downside risk in a rising interest-rate environment, or (4) properties that allow them to be used for hedging mortgage-related products.

The various types of bonds include sequential-pay bonds, planned amortization class (PAC) bonds, accrual (or Z) bonds, floating-rate bonds, inverse floating-rate bonds, targeted amortization class (TAC) bonds, support bonds, and very accurately determined maturity (VADM) bonds.

The most prevalent type of commercial mortgage-backed security is a CMO.

Stripped Mortgage-Backed Securities

A pass-through divides the cash flow from the underlying collateral on a pro rata basis to the security holders. *Stripped mortgage-backed securities,* introduced by

Fannie Mae in 1986, are created by altering the distribution of principal and interest from a pro rata distribution to an *unequal* distribution.

Why are stripped mortgage-backed securities created? It is sufficient to say at this juncture that the risk/return characteristics of these instruments make them attractive for the purpose of hedging a portfolio of pass-throughs and mortgage loans.

There are two types of stripped MBSs: synthetic-coupon pass-throughs and interest-only/principal-only securities. The first generation of stripped mortgage-backed securities were the synthetic-coupon pass-throughs because the unequal distribution of coupon and principal resulted in a synthetic coupon rate that is different from the underlying collateral. In early 1987, stripped MBSs began to be issued in which all of the interest is allocated to one class (the interest-only, or IO, class) and all of the principal to the other class (the principal-only, or PO, class). The IO class receives no principal payments, and the PO class receives no interest.

ASSET-BACKED SECURITIES

Asset-backed securities are securities collateralized by assets that are not mortgage loans. In structuring an asset-backed security, issuers have drawn from the structures used in the mortgage-backed securities market. Asset-backed securities have been structured as pass-throughs and as structures with multiple bond classes, just like CMOs. Credit enhancement is provided by letters of credit, recourse to the issuer, overcollateralization, or senior/subordination.

The four most common types of asset-backed securities are those backed by credit card receivables, home-equity loans, manufactured homes, and automobile loans. There are chapters in Part 4 dedicated to each of these securities. There are also asset-backed securities backed by Small Business Administration (SBA) loans, student loans, boat loans, equipment leases, recreational vehicle loans, and senior bank loans.

SUMMARY

This chapter has provided an overview of the types of fixed income securities and has explored the key features of these securities. It is our hope that this chapter will equip the reader with a general knowledge of the instruments and provide a conceptual and terminological background for the chapters that will investigate in more detail the features of these securities and the associated risks and returns.

2

⑥ RISKS ASSOCIATED WITH INVESTING IN FIXED INCOME SECURITIES

Ravi E. Dattatreya, Ph.D.
Senior Vice President
Sumitomo Bank Capital Markets, Inc.

Frank J. Fabozzi, Ph.D., CFA, CPA
Adjunct Professor of Finance
School of Management
Yale University

The return obtained from a fixed income security from the day it is purchased to the day it is sold can be divided into two parts: (1) the market value of the security when it is eventually sold and (2) the cash flows received from the security over the time period that it is held, plus any additional income from reinvestment of the cash flow. Several environmental factors affect one or both of these two parts. We can define the risk in any security as a measure of the impact of these market factors on the return characteristics of the security.

The different types of risk that an investor in fixed income securities is exposed to are as follows:

- Market, or interest-rate, risk.
- Reinvestment risk.
- Timing, or call, risk.
- Credit, or default, risk.
- Yield-curve, or maturity, risk.
- Inflation, or purchasing power, risk.
- Marketability, or liquidity, risk.
- Exchange rate, or currency, risk.
- Volatility risk.
- Political or legal risk.

- Event risk.
- Sector risk.

Each risk is described in this chapter. They will become more clear as the securities are described in more detail in other chapters of this book.

MARKET OR INTEREST-RATE RISK

The price of a typical fixed income security moves in the opposite direction of the change in interest rates: As interest rates rise (fall), the price of a fixed income security will fall (rise).[1] This property is illustrated in Chapter 4. For an investor who plans to hold a fixed income security to maturity, the change in its price before maturity is not of concern; however, for an investor who may have to sell the fixed income security before the maturity date, an increase in interest rates will mean the realization of a capital loss. This risk is referred to as *market risk,* or *interest-rate risk,* which is by far the biggest risk faced by an investor in the fixed income market.

It is customary to represent the market by the yield levels on Treasury securities. Most other yields are compared to the Treasury levels and are quoted as spreads off appropriate Treasury yields. To the extent that the yields of all fixed income securities are interrelated, their prices respond to changes in Treasury rates. As discussed in Chapter 5, the actual magnitude of the price response for any security depends on various characteristics of the security such as coupon, maturity, and the options embedded in the security (e.g., call and put provisions).

To control interest rate-risk, it is necessary to quantify it. The most commonly used measure of interest rate risk is *duration.* Duration is the approximate percentage change in the price of a bond or bond portfolio to a 100 basis point change in yields. This measure is explained in Chapter 5. Chapter 39 discusses how regulators of depository institutions have specified how interest-rate risk should be measured.

REINVESTMENT RISK

As explained in Chapter 4, the cash flows received from a security are usually (or are assumed to be) reinvested. The additional income from such reinvestment, sometimes called interest-on-interest, depends on the prevailing interest rate levels at the time of reinvestment as well as on the reinvestment strategy. The variability in the returns from reinvestment from a given strategy due to changes in market rates is called *reinvestment risk.* The risk here is that the

---

1. There are certain fixed income instruments whose price changes in the same direction as interest rates. Examples are put options and interest-only mortgage-backed securities.

interest rate at which interim cash flows can be reinvested will fall. Reinvestment risk is greater for longer holding periods. It is also greater for securities with large, early cash flows such as high-coupon bonds. This risk is analyzed in more detail in Chapter 4.

It should be noted that interest-rate risk and reinvestment risk oppose each other. For example, interest-rate risk is the risk that interest rates will rise, thereby reducing the price of a fixed income security. In contrast, reinvestment risk is the risk that interest rates will fall. A strategy based on these two offsetting risks is called "immunization" and is the topic of Chapter 48.

TIMING OR CALL RISK

As explained in the previous chapter, many bonds contain a provision that allows the issuer to retire, or "call," all or part of the issue before the maturity date. The issuer usually retains this right to refinance the bond in the future if market interest rates decline below the coupon rate.

From the investor's perspective, there are three disadvantages of the call provision. First, the cash flow pattern of a callable bond is not known with certainty. Second, because the issuer will call the bonds when interest rates have dropped, the investor is exposed to reinvestment rate risk. That is, the investor will have to reinvest the proceeds received when the bond is called at lower interest rates. Finally, the capital appreciation potential of a bond will be reduced because the price of a callable bond may not rise much above the price at which the issuer may call the bond.

Many agency, corporate, and municipal bonds, and all mortgage-backed securities, have embedded in them the option on the part of the borrower to call, or terminate, the issue before the stated maturity date. Even though the investor is usually compensated for taking the risk of call by means of a lower price or a higher yield, it is not easy to determine if this compensation is sufficient. In any case, the returns from a bond with call risk can be dramatically different from those obtained from a noncallable bond. The magnitude of this risk depends upon the various parameters of the call as well as on market conditions. Timing risk is so pervasive in fixed income portfolio management that many market participants consider it second only to interest-rate risk in importance. A framework for analyzing callable bonds and mortgage-backed securities is presented in Chapters 36 and 37, respectively.

In the case of mortgage-backed securities, the cash flow depends on prepayments of principal made by the homeowners in the pool of mortgages that serves as collateral for the security. The timing risk in this case is called *prepayment risk*. It includes *contraction risk*—the risk that homeowners will prepay all or part of their mortgage when mortgage interest rates decline. If interest rates rise, however, investors would benefit from prepayments. The risk that prepayments will slow down when mortgage interest rates rise is called *extension risk*.

Thus, timing risk in the case of mortgage-backed securities is called prepayment risk, which includes contraction risk and extension risk.

CREDIT RISK OR DEFAULT RISK

Credit risk, or *default risk,* refers to the risk that the issuer of a fixed income security may default (i.e., the issuer will be unable to make timely principal and interest payments on the security). Credit risk is gauged by quality ratings assigned by commercial rating companies such as Moody's Investor Service, Standard & Poor's Corporation, Duff & Phelps Credit Rating Co., and Fitch Investors Service.

Because of this risk, most bonds are sold at a lower price than, or at a yield spread to, comparable U.S. Treasury securities, which are considered free of credit risk. However, except for the lowest credit securities (known as "speculative grade" or"high-yield" or "junk bonds"), the investor is normally concerned more with the changes in the perceived credit risk and/or the cost associated with a given level of credit risk than with the actual event of default. This is so because even though the actual default of an issuing corporation may be highly unlikely, the impact of a change in perceived credit risk or the spread demanded by the market for any given level of risk can have an immediate impact on the value of a security.

YIELD-CURVE OR MATURITY RISK

In many situations, a bond of a given maturity is used as an alternative to another bond of a different maturity. An adjustment is made (see the discussion on duration in Chapter 5) to account for the differential interest-rate risks in the two bonds. However, this adjustment makes an assumption about how the interest rates (i.e., yields) at different maturities will move.[2] To the extent that the yield movements deviate from this assumption, there is *yield-curve* or *maturity risk.*

In general, yield-curve risk is more important in hedging situations than in pure investment decisions. For example, if a trader is hedging a position or if a pension fund or an insurance company is acquiring assets so as to enable it to meet a given liability, then yield-curve risk should be carefully examined. However, if a pension fund has decided to invest in the intermediate-term sector, then the fine distinctions in maturity are less important.

Another situation where yield-curve risk should be considered is in the analysis of bond swap transactions where the potential incremental returns are dependent entirely on the parallel shift (or other equally arbitrary) assumption for the yield curve.

---

2. Usually, a parallel shift assumption is made. That is, we assume that the yields at different maturities move by equal amounts.

INFLATION OR PURCHASING POWER RISK

Inflation risk, or *purchasing power risk,* arises because of the variation in the value of cash flows from a security due to inflation, as measured in terms of purchasing power. For example, if an investor purchases a five-year bond in which he or she can realize a coupon rate of 7 percent, but the rate of inflation is 8 percent, then the purchasing power of the cash flow has declined. For all but adjustable- or floating-rate bonds, an investor is exposed to inflation risk because the interest rate the issuer promises to make is fixed for the life of the security. To the extent that interest rates reflect the expected inflation rate, floating-rate bonds have a lower level of inflation risk.

MARKETABILITY OR LIQUIDITY RISK

Marketability risk, or *liquidity risk,* involves the ease with which an issue can be sold at or near its true value. The primary measure of marketability/liquidity is the size of the spread between the bid price and the offer price quoted by a dealer. The greater the dealer spread, the greater the marketability/liquidity risk. For an investor who plans to hold the bond until the maturity date, marketability/liquidity risk is less important.

EXCHANGE RATE OR CURRENCY RISK

A nondollar-denominated bond (i.e., a bond whose payments occur in a foreign currency) has unknown U.S. dollar cash flows. The dollar cash flows are dependent on the foreign-exchange rate at the time the payments are received. For example, suppose an investor purchases a bond whose payments are in Japanese yen. If the yen depreciates relative to the U.S. dollar, then fewer dollars will be received. The risk of this occurring is referred to as *exchange rate risk,* or *currency risk.* Of course, should the yen appreciate relative to the U.S. dollar, the investor will benefit by receiving more dollars.

In addition to the change in the exchange rate, an investor is exposed to the interest-rate, or market, risk in the local market. For example, if a U.S. investor purchases German government bonds denominated in deutsche marks, the proceeds received from the sale of that bond prior to maturity will depend on the level of interest rates in the German bond market, in addition to the exchange rate.

VOLATILITY RISK

As will be explained in later chapters, the price of a bond with an embedded option depends on the level of interest rates and factors that influence the value of the embedded option. One of the factors is the expected volatility of interest rates.

Specifically, the value of an option rises when expected interest-rate volatility increases. In the case of a callable bond or mortgage-backed security, because the investor has granted an option to the borrower, the price of the security falls because the investor has given away a more valuable option. The risks that a change in volatility will adversely affect the price of a security is called *volatility risk.*

POLITICAL OR LEGAL RISK

Sometimes the government can declare withholding or other additional taxes on a bond or declare a tax-exempt bond taxable. In addition, a regulatory authority can conclude that a given security is unsuitable for investment entities that it regulates. These actions can adversely affect the value of the security. Similarly, it is also possible that a legal or regulatory action affects the value of a security positively. The possibility of any political or legal actions adversely affecting the value of a security is known as *political* or *legal risk.*

To illustrate political or legal risk, consider investors who purchase tax-exempt municipal securities. They are exposed to two types of political risk that can be more appropriately called *tax risk.* The first type of tax risk is that the federal income tax rate will be reduced. The higher the marginal tax rate, the greater the value of the tax-exempt nature of a municipal security. As the marginal tax rates decline, the price of a tax-exempt municipal security will decline. For example, proposals for a flat tax with a low marginal tax rate significantly reduced the potential tax advantage of owning municipal bonds. As a result, tax-exempt municipal bonds began trading at lower prices. The second type of tax risk is that a municipal bond issued as tax-exempt will eventually be declared taxable by the Internal Revenue Service. This may occur because many municipal (revenue) bonds have elaborate security structures that could be subject to future adverse congressional actions and IRS interpretations. As a result of the loss of the tax exemption, the municipal bond will decline in value in order to provide a yield comparable to similar taxable bonds. For example, in June of 1980, the Battery Park City Authority sold $97.315 million in construction loan notes. At the time of issuance, the legal counsel thought that the interest on the note would be exempt from federal income taxation. In November of 1980, however, the IRS held that interest on these notes was not exempt, resulting in a lower price for the notes. The issue was not resolved until September 1981 when the Authority and the IRS signed a formal agreement resolving the matter so as to make the interest on the notes tax-exempt.

EVENT RISK

Occasionally, the ability of an issuer to make interest and principal payments is seriously and unexpectedly changed by (1) a natural or industrial accident or (2) a takeover or corporate restructuring. These risks are referred to as *event risk.* The cancellation of plans to build a nuclear power plant illustrates the first type of event in relation to the utility industry.

An example of the second type of event risk is the takeover in 1988 of RJR Nabisco for $25 billion via a financing technique known as a *leveraged buyout* (LBO). In such a transaction, the new company incurred a substantial amount of debt to finance the acquisition of the firm. Because the corporation was required to service a substantially larger amount of debt, its quality rating was reduced to noninvestment grade quality. As a result, the change in yield spread to a benchmark Treasury, demanded by investors because of the LBO announcement, increased from about 100 basis points to 350 basis points.

There are also spillover effects of event risk on other firms. For example, if there is a nuclear accident, this will affect all utilities producing nuclear power.

SECTOR RISK

Bonds in different sectors of the market respond differently to environmental changes because of a combination of some or all of the above risks, as well as others. Examples include discount versus premium coupon bonds, industrial versus utility bonds, and corporate versus mortgage-backed bonds. The possibility of adverse differential movement of specific sectors of the market is called *sector risk*.

OTHER RISKS

The various risks of investing in the fixed income markets reviewed in this chapter do not represent the entire range of risks. In the marketplace, it is customary to combine almost all risks other than market risk (interest-rate risk) and refer to it as *basis risk*.

SUMMARY

In this chapter, we have described 12 risks associated with investing in fixed income securities. Not all securities or investment strategies expose the investor to all of the risks we have discussed. As the instruments and portfolio management strategies are described in more detail throughout this book, these risks will be explained further.

3

⑥ A REVIEW OF THE TIME VALUE OF MONEY

Frank J. Fabozzi, Ph.D., CFA, CPA
Adjunct Professor of Finance
School of Management
Yale University

The notion that money has a time value is one of the basic concepts in the analysis of any financial instrument. Money has a time value because of the opportunities for investing money at some interest rate. In this chapter, we review the three fundamental concepts involved in understanding the time value of money: future value, present value, and yield. These concepts are applied in the next chapter, where we discuss bond pricing and yield measures.

FUTURE VALUE

Suppose an investor places $1,000 in a bank account and the bank agrees to pay interest of 7 percent a year. At the end of one year, the account will contain $1,070, or $1,000, the original principal, plus $70 interest. Suppose that the investor decides to let the $1,070 remain in the bank account for another year and that the bank agrees to continue paying interest of 7 percent a year. The amount in the bank account at the end of the second year will equal $1,144.90, determined as follows:

Principal at beginning of year 2	$1,070.00
Interest for year 2 ($1,070 × .07)	74.90
Total in bank account	$1,144.90

In terms of our original $1,000 investment, the $1,144.90 represents the following:

Original investment at beginning of year 1	$1,000.00
Interest for year 1 ($1,000 × .07)	70.00
Interest for year 2 based on original investment	70.00
Interest for year 2 earned on interest for year 1 ($70 × .07)	4.90
Total	$1,144.90

The additional interest of $4.90 in year 2 above the $70 interest earned on the original principal of $1,000 is the interest on the interest earned in year 1.

After eight years, $1,000 will grow to $1,718.19 if allowed to accumulate tax-free at an annual interest rate of 7 percent. We refer to the amount at the end of eight years as the *future value*.

Notice that the total interest at the end of eight years is $718.19. The total interest represents $560 of interest earned on the original principal ($70 × 8) plus $158.19 ($718.19 – $560) earned by the reinvestment of the interest.

Computing the Future Value of an Investment

To compute the amount to which $1,000 will grow by the end of eight years if interest is earned at an annual interest rate of 7 percent, the following formula is used:

$$\$1,000 \, (1.07)^8 = \$1,718.19$$

To generalize the formula, suppose $1,000 is invested for N periods at an annual interest rate of i (expressed as a decimal). Then, the future value N periods from now can be expressed as follows:

$$\$1,000 \, (1 + i)^N$$

For example, if $1,000 is invested for four years at an annual interest rate of 10 percent ($i = .10$), then it will grow to $1,464.10:

$$\$1,000 \, (1.10)^4 = \$1,000 \, (1.4641) = \$1,464.10$$

The expression $(1 + i)^N$ is the amount to which $1 will grow at the end of N years if an annual interest rate of i is earned. This expression is called the *future value of $1*. By multiplying the future value of $1 by the original principal, we can determine the future value of the original principal.

For example, we just demonstrated that the future value of $1,000 invested for four years at an annual interest rate of 10 percent is $1,464.10. The future value of $1 is $1.4641. Therefore, if instead of $1,000, $50,000 is invested, the future value is

$$\$50,000 \, (1.4641) = \$73,205.00$$

We can generalize the formula for the future value as follows:

$$FV = P(1 + i)^N$$

where

FV = Future value ($)
P = Original principal ($)
i = Interest rate (in decimal form)
N = Number of years

Most calculators have an option that computes this value. Alternatively, there are tables available that provide the value of $(1 + i)^N$. Exhibit 3–1 is an abridged future value table that provides the value of $(1 + i)^N$. Notice that at the intersection of the 10-percent column and four-period row, the value is 1.4641. This is the same value computed for $(1.10)^4$ in the above illustration.

The following three illustrations show how to apply the future value formula.

Illustration 1.   A pension fund manager invests $10 million in a financial instrument that promises to pay 8.7 percent per year for five years. The future value of the $10 million investment is $15,175,665, as shown below:

$$
\begin{aligned}
P &= \$10,000,000 \\
i &= .087 \\
N &= 5 \\
FV &= \$10,000,000\,(1.087)^5 \\
&= \$10,000,000\,(1.5175665) \\
&= \$15,175,665
\end{aligned}
$$

Illustration 2.   Suppose that a life insurance company has guaranteed a payment of $14 million to a pension fund four years from now. If the life insurance company receives a premium of $11 million and can invest the entire premium for four years at an annual interest rate of 6.5 percent, will it have sufficient funds from this investment to meet the $14 million obligation?

The future value of the $11 million investment at the end of four years is $14,151,130, as shown below:

$$
\begin{aligned}
P &= \$11,000,000 \\
i &= .065 \\
N &= 4 \\
FV &= \$11,000,000\,(1.065)^4 \\
&= \$11,000,000\,(1.2864664) \\
&= \$14,151,130
\end{aligned}
$$

Because the future value is expected to be $14,151,130, the life insurance company will have sufficient funds from this investment to satisfy the $14 million obligation to the pension fund.

EXHIBIT 3–1

Future Value of $1 at the End of N Periods

Interest Rate

Period	1%	2%	3%	4%	5%	6%	7%	8%	9%	10%	11%	12%	13%	14%	15%
1	1.0100	1.0200	1.0300	1.0400	1.0500	1.0600	1.0700	1.0800	1.0900	1.100	1.1100	1.1200	1.1300	1.1400	1.1500
2	1.0201	1.0404	1.0609	1.0816	1.1025	1.1236	1.1449	1.1664	1.1881	1.2100	1.2321	1.2544	1.2769	1.2996	1.3225
3	1.0303	1.0612	1.0927	1.1249	1.1576	1.1910	1.2250	1.2597	1.2950	1.3310	1.3676	1.4049	1.4429	1.4815	1.5209
4	1.0406	1.0824	1.1255	1.1699	1.2155	1.2625	1.3108	1.3605	1.4116	1.4641	1.5181	1.5735	1.6305	1.6890	1.7490
5	1.0510	1.1041	1.1593	1.2167	1.2763	1.3382	1.4026	1.4693	1.5386	1.6105	1.6851	1.7623	1.8424	1.9254	2.0114
6	1.0615	1.1262	1.1941	1.2653	1.3401	1.4185	1.5007	1.5869	1.6771	1.7716	1.8704	1.9738	2.0820	2.1950	2.3131
7	1.0721	1.1487	1.2299	1.3159	1.4071	1.5036	1.6058	1.7138	1.8280	1.9487	2.0762	2.2107	2.3526	2.5023	2.6600
8	1.0829	1.1717	1.2668	1.3686	1.4775	1.5938	1.7182	1.8509	1.9926	2.1436	2.3045	2.4760	2.6554	2.8526	3.0590
9	1.0937	1.1951	1.3048	1.4233	1.5513	1.6895	1.8385	1.9990	2.1719	2.3579	2.5580	2.7731	3.0040	3.2519	3.5179
10	1.1046	1.2190	1.3439	1.4802	1.6289	1.7908	1.9672	2.1589	2.3674	2.5937	2.8394	3.1058	3.3946	3.7072	4.0456
11	1.1157	1.2434	1.3842	1.5395	1.7103	1.8983	2.1049	2.3316	2.5804	2.8531	3.1518	3.4785	3.8359	4.2262	4.6524
12	1.1268	1.2682	1.4258	1.6010	1.7595	2.0122	2.2522	2.5182	2.8127	3.1384	3.4984	3.8960	4.3345	4.8179	5.3502
13	1.1381	1.2936	1.4685	1.6651	1.8856	2.1329	2.4098	2.7196	3.0658	3.4523	3.8833	4.3635	4.8980	5.4924	6.1528
14	1.1495	1.3195	1.5126	1.7317	1.9799	2.2609	2.5785	2.9372	3.3417	3.7975	4.3104	4.8871	5.5347	6.2613	7.0757
15	1.1610	1.3459	1.5580	1.8009	2.0789	2.3966	2.7590	3.1722	3.6425	4.1772	4.7846	5.4736	6.2543	7.1379	8.1371
16	1.1726	1.3728	1.6047	1.8730	2.1829	2.5404	2.9522	3.4259	3.9703	4.5950	5.3109	6.1304	7.0673	8.1372	9.3576
17	1.1843	1.4002	1.6528	1.9479	2.2920	2.6928	3.1588	3.7000	4.3276	5.0545	5.8951	6.8660	7.9861	9.2765	10.761
18	1.1961	1.4282	1.7024	2.0258	2.4066	2.8543	3.3799	3.9960	4.7171	5.5599	6.5435	7.6900	9.0243	10.575	12.375
19	1.2081	1.4568	1.7535	2.1068	2.5270	3.0256	3.6165	4.3157	5.1417	6.1159	7.2633	8.6128	10.197	12.055	14.231
20	1.2202	1.4859	1.8061	2.1911	2.6533	3.2071	3.8697	4.6610	5.6044	6.7275	8.0623	9.6463	11.523	13.743	16.366
21	1.2324	1.5157	1.8603	2.2788	2.7860	3.3966	4.1406	5.0388	6.1088	7.4002	8.9491	10.803	13.021	15.667	18.821
22	1.2447	1.5460	1.9161	2.3699	2.9253	3.6035	4.4304	5.4365	6.6586	8.1403	9.9335	12.100	14.714	17.861	21.644
23	1.2572	1.5769	1.9736	2.4647	3.0715	3.8197	4.7405	5.8715	7.2579	8.9543	11.026	13.552	16.627	20.361	24.891
24	1.2697	1.6084	2.0328	2.5633	3.2251	4.0489	5.0724	6.3412	7.9111	9.8497	12.239	15.178	18.788	23.212	28.625
25	1.2824	1.6406	2.0938	2.6658	3.3864	4.2919	5.4274	6.8485	8.6231	10.834	13.585	17.000	21.230	26.461	32.918
26	1.2953	1.6734	2.1566	2.7725	3.5557	4.5494	5.8074	7.3964	9.3992	11.918	15.080	19.040	23.990	30.166	37.856
27	1.3082	1.7069	2.2213	2.8834	3.7335	4.8223	6.2139	7.9881	10.245	13.110	16.739	21.324	27.109	34.389	43.535
28	1.3213	1.7410	2.2879	2.9987	3.9201	5.1117	6.6488	8.6271	11.167	14.421	18.580	23.883	30.633	39.204	50.065
29	1.3345	1.7758	2.3566	3.1187	4.1161	5.4184	7.1143	9.3173	12.172	15.863	20.624	26.749	34.616	44.693	57.575
30	1.3478	1.8114	2.4273	3.2434	4.3219	5.7435	7.6123	10.062	13.267	17.449	22.892	29.959	39.116	50.950	66.211

Illustration 3.   The portfolio manager of a tax-exempt fund is considering investing $400,000 in an instrument that pays an annual interest rate of 5.7 percent for four
years. At the end of four years, the portfolio manager plans to reinvest the proceeds
for three more years and expects that, for the three-year period, an annual interest
rate of 7.2 percent can be earned. The future value of this investment is $615,098.

The future value of the $400,000 investment for four years at 5.7 percent is
as follows:

$$
\begin{aligned}
P &= \$400{,}000 \\
i &= .057 \\
N &= 4 \\
FV &= \$400{,}000\,(1.057)^4 \\
&= \$400{,}000\,(1.248245) \\
&= \$499{,}298
\end{aligned}
$$

The future value of $499,298 reinvested for three years at 7.2 percent is
computed below:

$$
\begin{aligned}
i &= .072 \\
N &= 3 \\
FV &= \$499{,}298\,(1.072)^3 \\
&= \$499{,}298\,(1.231925) \\
&= \$615{,}098
\end{aligned}
$$

Fractional Periods
In our illustrations, we have computed the future value for whole years. The future value formula, however, is the same if an investment is made for part of a
year. Most pocket calculators can accommodate fractional exponents.

For example, suppose that $100,000 is invested for seven years and three
months. Because three months is 0.25 of one year, N in the future value formula
is 7.25. Assuming an annual interest rate of 5 percent, the future value of
$100,000 invested for seven years and three months is $142,437, as shown
below:

$$
\begin{aligned}
P &= \$100{,}000 \\
i &= .05 \\
N &= 7.25 \\
FV &= \$100{,}000\,(1.05)^{7.25} \\
&= \$100{,}000\,(1.424369) \\
&= \$142{,}437
\end{aligned}
$$

Compounding More than One Time per Year

An investment may pay interest more than one time per year. For example, interest may be paid semiannually, quarterly, monthly, weekly, or daily. Our future
value formula can handle interest payments that are made more than once per

year. This is done by adjusting the annual interest rate and the exponent. The annual interest rate is divided by the number of times that interest is paid per year. The exponent, which represents the number of years, is multiplied by the number of times interest is paid per year.

Mathematically, we can express the future value when interest is paid m times per year as follows:

$$FV = P(1 + i)n$$

where

i $=$ Annual interest rate divided by m
n $=$ Number of interest payments $(= N \times m)$

Illustration 4.   Suppose that a portfolio manager invests $1 million in an investment that promises to pay an annual interest rate of 6.4 percent for six years. Interest on this investment is paid semiannually. The future value is $1,459,340, as shown below:

$$
\begin{aligned}
P &= \$1,000,000 \\
m &= 2 \\
i &= .032 \,(= .064/2) \\
N &= 6 \\
n &= 12 \,(= 6 \times 2) \\
FV &= \$1,000,000 \,(1.032)^{12} \\
&= \$1,000,000 \,(1.459340) \\
&= \$1,459,340
\end{aligned}
$$

If interest is paid only once per year, this future value would be $1,450,941 instead of $1,459,340. The higher future value when interest is paid semiannually reflects the more frequent opportunity for reinvesting the interest paid.

Future Value of an Ordinary Annuity

Suppose that an investor expects to receive $10,000 a year from some investment for each of the next five years starting one year from now. Each time the investor receives the $10,000, he plans to invest it. Let's assume that the investor can earn an annual interest rate of 6 percent each time $10,000 is invested. How much money will the investor have at the end of five years?

Our future value formula makes it simple to determine to what amount each $10,000 investment will grow. This calculation is illustrated graphically in Exhibit 3–2. The total future value of $56,371.30 shown in Exhibit 3–2 is composed of the five payments of $10,000, or $50,000, plus $6,371.30 of interest earned by investing the $10,000 annual payments.

EXHIBIT 3–2

Future Value of an Ordinary Annuity of $10,000 per Year for 5 Years

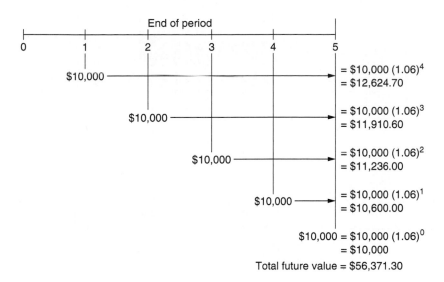

When the same amount of money is received (or paid) periodically, it is referred to as an *annuity*. When the first receipt occurs one period from now, it is referred to as an *ordinary annuity*.

The following formula can be used to calculate the future value of an ordinary annuity:

$$FV = A\left[\frac{(1+i)^N - 1}{i}\right]$$

where

A   = Amount of the annuity ($)
i   = Annual interest rate (in decimals)

The term in the square brackets is the *future value of an ordinary annuity of $1 per year.* Multiplying the future value of an ordinary annuity of $1 by the amount of the annuity produces the future value of an ordinary annuity of any amount.

For example, if $10,000 is invested at 6 percent each year for the next five years, starting one year from now, we have

A   = $10,000
i   = .06
N   = 5

EXHIBIT 3–3

Future Value of an Ordinary Annuity of $1 per Period for N Periods

Interest Rate

Number of Periods	1%	2%	3%	4%	5%	6%	7%	8%	9%	10%	11%	12%	13%	14%	15%
1	1.0000	1.0000	1.0000	1.0000	1.0000	1.0000	1.0000	1.0000	1.0000	1.0000	1.0000	1.0000	1.0000	1.0000	1.0000
2	2.0100	2.0200	2.0300	2.0400	2.0500	2.0600	2.0700	2.0800	2.0900	2.1000	2.1100	2.1200	2.1300	2.1400	2.1500
3	3.0301	3.0604	3.0909	3.1216	3.1525	3.1836	3.2149	3.2464	3.2781	3.3100	3.3421	3.3744	3.4069	3.4396	3.4725
4	4.0604	4.1216	4.1836	4.2465	4.3101	4.3746	4.4399	4.5061	4.5731	4.6410	4.7097	4.7793	4.8498	4.9211	4.9934
5	5.1010	5.2040	5.3091	5.4163	5.5256	5.6371	5.7507	5.8666	5.9847	6.1051	6.2278	6.3528	6.4803	6.6101	6.7424
6	6.1520	6.3081	6.4684	6.6330	6.8019	6.9753	7.1533	7.3359	7.5233	7.7156	7.9129	8.1152	8.3227	8.5355	8.7537
7	7.2135	7.4343	7.6625	7.8983	8.1420	8.3938	8.6540	8.9228	9.2004	9.4872	9.7833	10.089	10.405	10.730	11.066
8	8.2857	8.5830	8.8923	9.2142	9.5491	9.8975	10.259	10.636	11.028	11.435	11.859	12.299	12.757	13.232	13.726
9	9.3685	9.7546	10.159	10.582	11.026	11.491	11.978	12.487	13.021	13.579	14.164	14.775	15.416	16.085	16.785
10	10.462	10.949	11.463	12.006	12.577	13.180	13.816	14.486	15.192	15.937	16.722	17.548	18.420	19.337	20.603
11	11.566	12.168	12.807	13.486	14.206	14.971	15.783	16.645	17.560	18.531	19.561	20.654	21.814	23.044	24.649
12	12.682	13.412	14.192	15.025	15.917	16.869	17.888	18.977	20.140	21.384	22.713	24.133	25.650	27.270	29.001
13	13.809	14.680	15.617	16.626	17.713	18.882	20.140	21.495	22.953	24.522	26.212	28.029	29.985	32.088	34.851
14	14.947	15.973	17.086	18.291	19.598	21.015	22.550	24.214	26.019	27.975	30.095	32.392	34.883	37.581	40.504
15	16.096	17.293	18.598	20.023	21.578	23.276	25.129	27.152	29.360	31.772	34.405	37.729	40.418	43.842	47.580
16	17.257	18.639	20.156	21.824	23.657	25.672	27.888	30.324	33.003	35.949	39.190	42.753	46.672	50.980	55.717
17	18.430	20.012	21.761	23.697	25.840	28.212	30.840	33.750	36.973	40.544	44.501	48.883	53.739	59.117	65.075
18	19.614	21.412	23.414	25.645	28.132	30.905	33.999	37.450	41.301	45.599	50.396	55.749	61.725	68.394	75.836
19	20.810	22.840	25.116	27.671	30.539	33.760	37.379	41.446	46.018	51.159	56.940	63.439	70.749	78.969	88.211
20	22.019	24.297	26.870	29.778	33.066	36.785	40.995	45.762	51.160	57.275	64.203	72.052	80.947	91.024	102.44
21	23.239	25.783	28.676	31.969	35.719	39.992	44.865	50.422	56.764	64.002	72.265	81.698	92.470	104.76	118.81
22	24.471	27.299	30.536	34.248	38.505	43.392	49.005	55.456	62.873	71.402	81.214	92.502	105.49	120.43	137.63
23	25.716	28.845	32.452	36.617	41.430	46.995	53.436	60.893	69.531	79.543	91.148	104.60	120.20	138.29	159.27
24	26.973	30.421	34.426	39.082	44.502	50.815	58.176	66.764	76.789	88.497	102.17	118.15	136.83	158.65	184.16
25	28.243	32.030	36.459	41.645	47.727	54.864	63.249	73.105	84.700	98.347	114.41	133.33	155.62	181.87	212.79
26	29.525	33.670	38.553	44.311	51.113	59.156	68.676	79.954	93.323	109.18	128.00	150.33	176.85	208.33	245.71
27	30.820	35.344	40.709	47.084	54.669	63.705	74.483	87.350	102.72	121.09	143.08	169.37	200.84	238.49	283.56
28	32.129	37.051	42.930	49.967	58.402	68.528	80.697	95.338	112.96	134.20	159.82	190.69	227.95	272.88	327.10
29	33.450	38.792	45.218	52.966	62.332	73.639	87.346	103.96	124.13	148.63	178.40	214.58	258.58	312.09	377.16
30	34.784	40.568	47.575	56.084	66.438	79.058	94.460	113.28	136.30	164.49	199.02	241.33	293.20	356.78	434.74

therefore,

$$FV = \$10,000\left[\frac{(1.06)^5 - 1}{.06}\right]$$

$$= \$10,000\left[\frac{1.3382256 - 1}{.06}\right]$$

$$= \$10,000\,(5.63710)$$
$$= \$56,371$$

This value agrees with our earlier calculation.

Tables are available that provide the future value of an ordinary annuity of $1 per period. Exhibit 3–3 is an abridged version. The value from the table should be multiplied by the annuity payment to obtain the future value of the annuity. For example, from Exhibit 3–3 the future value of an ordinary annuity of $1 per period for 5 periods assuming a 6 percent interest rate per period is 5.6371. Hence, the future value of an ordinary annuity of $10,000 is $10,000 times 5.6371, or $56,371.

PRESENT VALUE

We illustrated how to compute the future value of an investment. Now we will illustrate how to work the process in reverse; that is, given the future value of an investment, we will illustrate how to determine the amount of money that must be invested today in order to realize that future value. The amount of money that must be invested today is called the *present value*.

Present Value of an Amount to Be Received in the Future

What we are interested in is how to determine the amount of money that must be invested today, earning an interest rate of i for N years, in order to produce a specific future value. This can be done by solving the future value formula given earlier for P, the original principal:

$$P = FV\left[\frac{1}{(1+i)^N}\right]$$

Instead of using P in the above formula, we shall denote the present value as PV. Therefore, the present value formula can be rewritten as

$$PV = FV\left[\frac{1}{(1+i)^N}\right]$$

The term in the square brackets is equal to the present value of $1; that is, it indicates how much must be set aside today, earning an interest rate of i, in order to have $1 N years from now. Present value tables are available. Exhibit 3–4 shows the present value of $1, which is found by dividing 1 by $(1 + i)^N$. The columns show the interest rate. The rows show the number of periods. The present value of $1 obtained from Exhibit 3–4 is then multiplied by the future value to determine the present value. For example, the present value of $1,000 seven years from now, assuming 12 percent interest compounded annually, is

$$\begin{aligned} PV &= \$1,000 \text{ (PV of \$1 from Exhibit 3–4)} \\ &= \$1,000 \, (.4523) \\ &= \$452.30 \end{aligned}$$

The process of computing the present value is also referred to as *discounting*. Therefore, the present value is sometimes referred to as the *discounted value*, and the interest rate is referred to as the *discount rate*.

There are two facts you should note about present value. Look again at Exhibit 3–4. Select any interest rate and look down the column. Notice that the present value decreases. That is, the greater the number of periods over which interest could be earned, the less must be set aside today for a given dollar amount to be received in the future. Next, select any period and look across the row. As you look across, the interest rate increases and the present value decreases. The higher the interest rate that can be earned on any amount invested today, the less must be set aside to obtain a specified future value.

The following two illustrations demonstrate how to compute the present value.

Illustration 5.   A pension fund manager knows that he must satisfy a liability of $9 million six years from now. Assuming that an annual interest rate of 7.5 percent can be earned on any sum invested today, the pension fund manager must invest $5,831,654 today in order to have $9 million six years from now, as shown below:

$$\begin{aligned} FV &= \$9,000,000 \\ i &= .075 \\ N &= 6 \end{aligned}$$

$$PV = \$9,000,000 \left[\frac{1}{(1.075)^6} \right]$$

$$= \$9,000,000 \left[\frac{1}{1.543302} \right]$$

$$= \$9,000,000 \, (.647961)$$

$$= \$5,831,654$$

Illustration 6.   Suppose a money manager has the opportunity to purchase a financial instrument that promises to pay $800,000 four years from now. The price

EXHIBIT 3-4

Present Value of $1

Interest (Discount) Rate

Period	1%	2%	3%	4%	5%	6%	7%	8%	9%	10%	11%	12%	13%	14%	15%	16%	18%	20%
1	.9901	.9804	.9709	.9615	.9524	.9434	.9346	.9259	.9174	.9091	.9009	.8929	.8850	.8772	.8696	.8621	.8475	.8333
2	.9803	.9612	.9426	.9246	.9070	.8900	.8734	.8573	.8417	.8264	.8116	.7972	.7831	.7695	.7561	.7432	.7182	.6944
3	.9706	.9423	.9151	.8890	.8638	.8396	.8163	.7938	.7722	.7513	.7312	.7118	.6931	.6750	.6575	.6407	.6086	.5787
4	.9610	.9238	.8885	.8548	.8227	.7921	.7629	.7350	.7084	.6830	.6587	.6355	.6133	.5921	.5718	.5523	.5158	.4823
5	.9515	.9057	.8626	.8219	.7835	.7473	.7130	.6806	.6499	.6209	.5935	.5674	.5428	.5194	.4972	.4761	.4371	.4019
6	.9420	.8880	.8375	.7903	.7462	.7050	.6663	.6302	.5963	.5645	.5346	.5066	.4803	.4556	.4323	.4104	.3704	.3349
7	.9327	.8706	.8131	.7599	.7107	.6651	.6227	.5835	.5470	.5132	.4817	.4523	.4251	.3996	.3759	.3538	.3139	.2791
8	.9235	.8535	.7894	.7307	.6768	.6274	.5820	.5403	.5019	.4665	.4339	.4039	.3762	.3506	.3269	.3050	.2660	.2326
9	.9143	.8368	.7664	.7026	.6446	.5919	.5439	.5002	.4604	.4241	.3909	.3606	.3329	.3075	.2843	.2630	.2255	.1938
10	.9053	.8203	.7441	.6756	.6139	.5584	.5083	.4632	.4224	.3855	.3522	.3220	.2946	.2697	.2472	.2267	.1911	.1615
11	.8963	.8043	.7224	.6496	.5847	.5268	.4751	.4289	.3875	.3505	.3173	.2875	.2607	.2366	.2149	.1954	.1619	.1346
12	.8874	.7885	.7014	.6246	.5568	.4970	.4440	.3971	.3555	.3186	.2858	.2567	.2307	.2076	.1869	.1585	.1372	.1122
13	.8787	.7730	.6810	.6006	.5303	.4688	.4150	.3677	.3262	.2897	.2575	.2292	.2042	.1821	.1625	.1452	.1163	.0935
14	.8700	.7579	.6611	.5775	.5051	.4423	.3878	.3405	.2992	.2633	.2320	.2046	.1807	.1597	.1413	.1252	.0985	.0779
15	.8613	.7430	.6419	.5553	.4810	.4173	.3624	.3152	.2745	.2394	.2090	.1827	.1599	.1401	.1229	.1079	.0835	.0649
16	.8528	.7284	.6232	.5339	.4581	.3936	.3387	.2919	.2519	.2176	.1883	.1631	.1415	.1229	.1069	.0930	.0708	.0541
17	.8444	.7142	.6050	.5434	.4363	.3714	.3166	.2703	.2311	.1978	.1696	.1456	.1252	.1078	.0929	.0802	.0600	.0451
18	.8360	.7002	.5874	.4936	.4155	.3503	.2959	.2502	.2120	.1799	.1528	.1300	.1108	.0946	.0808	.0691	.0508	.0376
19	.8277	.6864	.5703	.4746	.3957	.3305	.2765	.2317	.1945	.1635	.1377	.1161	.0981	.0829	.0703	.0596	.0431	.0313
20	.8195	.6730	.5537	.4564	.3769	.3118	.2584	.2145	.1784	.1486	.1240	.1037	.0868	.0728	.0611	.0514	.0365	.0261
21	.8114	.6598	.5375	.4388	.3589	.2942	.2415	.1987	.1637	.1351	.1117	.0926	.0768	.0638	.0531	.0443	.0309	.0217
22	.8034	.6468	.5219	.4220	.3418	.2775	.2257	.1839	.1502	.1228	.1007	.0826	.0680	.0560	.0462	.0382	.0262	.0181
23	.7954	.6342	.5067	.4057	.3256	.2618	.2109	.1703	.1378	.1117	.0907	.0738	.0601	.0491	.0402	.0329	.0222	.0151
24	.7876	.6217	.4919	.3901	.3101	.2470	.1971	.1577	.1264	.1015	.0817	.0659	.0532	.0431	.0349	.0284	.0188	.0126
25	.7798	.6095	.4776	.3751	.2953	.2330	.1842	.1460	.1160	.0923	.0736	.0588	.0471	.0378	.0304	.0245	.0160	.0105
26	.7720	.5976	.4637	.3607	.2812	.2198	.1722	.1352	.1064	.0839	.0663	.0525	.0417	.0331	.0264	.0211	.0135	.0087
27	.7644	.5859	.4502	.3468	.2678	.2074	.1609	.1252	.0976	.0763	.0597	.0469	.0369	.0291	.0230	.0182	.0115	.0073
28	.7568	.5744	.4371	.3335	.2551	.1956	.1504	.1159	.0895	.0693	.0538	.0419	.0326	.0255	.0200	.0157	.0097	.0061
29	.7493	.5631	.4243	.3207	.2429	.1846	.1406	.1073	.0822	.0630	.0485	.0374	.0289	.0224	.0174	.0135	.0082	.0051
30	.7419	.5521	.4120	.3083	.2314	.1741	.1314	.0994	.0754	.0573	.0437	.0334	.0256	.0196	.0151	.0116	.0070	.0042

of the financial instrument is \$572,000. Should the money manager invest in this financial instrument if she wants a 7.8 percent annual interest rate?

To answer this, the money manager must determine the present value of the \$800,000 to be received four years from now. The present value is \$592,400, as shown below:

$$FV = \$800,000$$
$$i = .078$$
$$N = 4$$

$$PV = \$800,000\left[\frac{1}{(1.078)^4}\right]$$

$$= \$800,000\left[\frac{1}{1.350439}\right]$$

$$= \$800,000\,(.740500)$$
$$= \$592,400$$

Because the price of the financial instrument is only \$572,000, the money manager will realize more than a 7.8 percent annual interest rate if the financial instrument is purchased and the issuer pays \$800,000 four years from now.

Fractional Periods

If a future value is to be received or paid over a fractional part of a year, the number of years is adjusted accordingly. For example, if \$1,000 is to be received nine years and three months from now and the interest rate is 7 percent, the present value is determined as follows:

$$F = \$1,000$$
$$i = .07$$
$$N = 9.25 \text{ years (3 months is .25 years)}$$

$$PV = \$1,000\left[\frac{1}{(1.07)^{9.25}}\right]$$

$$= \$1,000\left[\frac{1}{1.86982}\right]$$

$$= \$1,000\,(.53481)$$
$$= \$534.81$$

Present Value of a Series of Future Values

In most applications in investment management and asset/liability management, a financial instrument will offer a series of future values. To determine the present value of a series of future values, the present value of each future value must first be computed. Then the present values are added together to obtain the present value of the series of future values. This procedure is demonstrated in the following illustration.

Illustration 7.   An investor is considering the purchase of a financial instrument that promises to make the following payments:

Years from Now	Promised Payment by Issuer
1	$ 100
2	100
3	100
4	100
5	1,100

This financial instrument is selling for $1,243.83. Assume that the investor wants a 6.25 percent annual interest rate on this investment. Should he purchase this investment?

To answer this question, the investor first must compute the present value of the future amounts that will be received, as follows:

Years from Now	Future Value of Payment	Present Value of $1 at 6.25%	Present Value of Payment
1	$ 100	0.9412	$ 94.12
2	100	0.8858	88.58
3	100	0.8337	83.37
4	100	0.7847	78.47
5	1,100	0.7385	812.35
		Total present value =	$1,156.89

Because the present value of the series of future values promised by the issuer of this financial instrument is less than the price of $1,243.83, the investor would earn an annual interest rate of less than 6.25 percent. Thus, this financial instrument is unattractive.

Present Value of an Ordinary Annuity

One way to compute the present value of an ordinary annuity is to compute the present value of each future value and then total the present values. There is a formula that can be employed to compute—in one step—the present value of an ordinary annuity:

$$PV = A \left[\frac{1 - \dfrac{1}{(1+i)^N}}{i} \right]$$

where

A = amount of the annuity ($)

The term in the brackets is the *present value of an ordinary annuity of $1 for N years*. Exhibit 3–5 provides the present value of an ordinary annuity of $1 for N periods for selected interest rates. The present value of an ordinary annuity is computed by multiplying the value from Exhibit 3–5 by the annuity payment. The following illustration shows how to apply the formula.

Illustration 8.   An investor has the opportunity to purchase a financial instrument that promises to pay $500 a year for the next 20 years, beginning one year from now. The financial instrument is being offered for a price of $5,300. The investor seeks an annual interest rate of 5.5 percent on this investment. Should she purchase this financial instrument?

Because the first payment is to be received one year from now, the financial instrument is offering a 20-year annuity of $500 per year. The present value of this ordinary annuity is calculated as follows:

$$A = \$500$$
$$i = .055$$
$$N = 20$$

$$PV = \$500 \left[\frac{1 - \dfrac{1}{(1.055)^{20}}}{.055} \right]$$

$$= \$500 \left[\frac{1 - \dfrac{1}{2.917757}}{.055} \right]$$

$$= \$500 \left[\frac{1 - .342729}{.055} \right]$$

$$= \$500 \,(11.950382)$$
$$= \$5,975.19$$

Because the present value of an ordinary annuity of $500 per year when discounted at 5.5 percent exceeds the price of the financial instrument ($5,300), this financial instrument offers an annual interest rate greater than 5.5 percent. Therefore, it is an attractive investment for this investor.

EXHIBIT 3–5

Present Value of an Ordinary Annuity of $1 per Period for N Periods

Interest (Discount) Rate

Number of Periods	1%	2%	3%	4%	5%	6%	7%	8%	9%	10%	11%	12%	13%	14%	15%
1	0.9901	0.9804	0.9709	0.9615	0.9524	0.9434	0.9436	0.9259	0.9174	0.9091	0.9009	0.8929	0.8850	0.8772	0.8696
2	1.9704	1.9416	1.9135	1.8861	1.8594	1.8334	1.8080	1.7833	1.7591	1.7355	1.7125	1.6901	1.6681	1.6467	1.6257
3	2.9410	2.8839	2.8286	2.7751	2.7232	2.6730	2.6243	2.5771	2.5313	2.4869	2.4437	2.4018	2.3612	2.3216	2.2832
4	3.9020	3.8077	3.7171	3.6299	3.5460	3.4651	3.3872	3.3121	3.2397	3.1699	3.1024	3.0373	2.9745	2.9137	2.8550
5	4.8534	4.7135	4.5797	4.4518	4.3295	4.2124	4.1002	3.9927	3.8897	3.7908	3.6959	3.6048	3.5172	3.4331	3.3522
6	5.7955	5.6014	5.4172	5.2421	5.0757	4.9173	4.7665	4.6229	4.4859	4.3553	4.2305	4.1114	3.9976	3.8887	3.7845
7	6.7282	6.4720	6.2303	6.0021	5.7864	5.5824	5.3893	5.2064	5.0330	4.8684	4.7122	4.5638	4.4226	4.2883	4.1604
8	7.6517	7.3255	7.0197	6.7327	6.4632	6.2098	5.9713	5.7466	5.5348	5.3349	5.1461	4.9676	4.7988	4.6389	4.4873
9	8.5660	8.1622	7.7861	7.4353	7.1078	6.8017	6.5152	6.2469	5.9952	5.7590	5.5371	5.3282	5.1317	4.9464	4.7716
10	9.4713	8.9826	8.5302	8.1109	7.7217	7.3601	7.0236	6.7101	6.4177	6.1446	5.8892	5.6502	5.4263	5.2161	5.0188
11	10.3676	9.7876	9.2526	8.7605	8.3064	7.8869	7.4987	7.1390	6.8052	6.4951	6.2065	5.9377	5.6870	5.4527	5.2337
12	11.2551	10.5753	9.9540	9.3851	8.8633	8.3838	7.9427	7.5361	7.1607	6.8137	6.4924	6.1944	5.9177	5.6603	5.4206
13	12.1337	11.3484	10.6350	9.9856	9.3936	8.8527	8.3577	7.9038	7.4869	7.1034	6.7499	6.4235	6.1218	5.8424	5.5831
14	13.0037	12.1062	11.2961	10.5631	9.8986	9.2950	8.7455	8.2442	7.7862	7.3667	6.9819	6.6282	6.3025	6.0021	5.7245
15	13.3651	12.8493	11.9379	11.1184	10.3797	9.7122	9.1079	8.5595	8.0607	7.6061	7.1909	6.8109	6.4624	6.1422	5.8474
16	14.7179	13.5777	12.5611	11.6523	10.8378	10.1059	9.4466	8.8514	8.3126	7.8237	7.3792	6.9740	6.6039	6.2651	5.9542
17	15.5623	14.2919	13.1661	12.1657	11.2741	10.4773	9.7623	9.1216	8.5436	8.0216	7.5488	7.1196	6.7291	6.2739	6.0472
18	16.3983	14.9920	13.7535	12.6593	11.6896	10.8276	10.0591	9.3719	8.7556	8.2014	7.7016	7.2497	6.8399	6.4674	6.1280
19	17.2260	15.6785	14.3238	13.1339	12.0853	11.1581	10.3356	9.6036	8.9501	8.3649	7.8393	7.3658	6.9380	6.5504	6.1982
20	18.0456	16.3514	14.8775	13.5903	12.4622	11.4699	10.5940	9.8181	9.1285	8.5136	7.9633	7.4694	7.0248	6.6231	6.2593
21	18.8570	17.0122	15.4150	14.0292	12.8212	11.7641	10.8335	10.0168	9.2922	8.6487	8.0751	7.5620	7.1016	6.6870	6.3125
22	19.6604	17.6580	15.9369	14.4511	13.1630	12.0416	11.0612	10.2007	9.4424	8.7715	8.1757	7.6446	7.1695	6.7429	6.3587
23	20.4558	18.2922	16.4436	14.8568	13.4886	12.3034	11.2722	10.3711	9.5802	8.8832	8.2664	7.7184	7.2297	6.7921	6.3988
24	21.2434	18.9139	16.9355	15.2470	13.7986	12.5504	11.4693	10.5288	9.7066	8.9847	8.3481	7.7843	7.2829	6.8351	6.4338
25	22.0232	19.5235	17.4131	15.6221	14.0939	12.7834	11.6536	10.6748	9.8226	9.0770	8.4218	7.8431	7.3300	6.8729	6.4642
26	22.7952	20.1210	17.8768	15.9828	14.3752	12.0032	11.8258	10.8100	9.9290	9.1609	8.4881	7.8957	7.3717	6.9061	6.4906
27	23.5596	20.7069	18.3270	16.3296	14.6430	13.2105	11.9867	10.9352	10.0266	9.2372	8.5478	7.9426	7.4086	6.9352	6.5135
28	24.3164	21.2813	18.7641	16.6631	14.8981	13.4062	12.1371	11.0511	10.1161	9.3066	8.6016	7.9844	7.4412	6.9607	6.5335
29	25.0658	21.8444	19.1885	16.9837	15.1411	13.5907	12.2777	11.1584	10.1983	9.3696	8.7601	8.0218	7.4701	6.9830	6.5509
30	25.8077	22.3965	19.6004	17.2920	15.3725	13.7648	12.4090	11.2578	10.2737	9.4269	8.6938	8.0552	7.4957	7.0027	6.5660

YIELD (INTERNAL RATE OF RETURN)

The yield on any investment is computed by determining the interest rate that will make the present value of the cash flow from the investment equal to the price of the investment. Mathematically, the yield on any investment, y, is the interest rate that will make the following relationship hold:

$$p = \frac{C_1}{(1+y)^1} + \frac{C_2}{(1+y)^2} + \frac{C_3}{(1+y)^3} + \dots + \frac{C_N}{(1+y)^N}$$

where

C_t = Cash flow in year t
p = Price
N = Number of years

The individual terms that are being summed on the right-hand side of the above relationship are the present values of the cash flow. The yield calculated from the above relationship is also called the *internal rate of return.*

Solving for the yield (y) requires a trial-and-error procedure. The objective is to find the interest rate that will make the present value of the cash flows equal to the price. The following two illustrations demonstrate how it is carried out.

Illustration 9. A financial instrument offers the following annual payments:

Years from Now	Promised Annual Payments (Cash Flow to Investor)
1	$2,000
2	2,000
3	2,500
4	4,000

Suppose that the price of this financial instrument is $7,704. What is the yield, or internal rate of return, offered by this financial instrument?

To compute the yield, we must try different interest rates until we find one that makes the present value of the cash flows equal to $7,704 (the price of the financial instrument). Trying an annual interest rate of 10 percent gives the following present value:

Years from Now	Promised Annual Payments (Cash Flow to Investor)	Present Value of Cash Flow at 10%
1	$2,000	$1,818
2	2,000	1,652
3	2,500	1,878
4	4,000	2,732
	Total present value =	$8,080

Because the present value computed using a 10 percent interest rate exceeds the price of $7,704, a higher interest rate must be tried. If a 14 percent interest rate is assumed, the present value is $7,348, as shown below:

Years from Now	Promised Annual Payments (Cash Flow to Investor)	Present Value of Cash Flow at 14%
1	$2,000	$1,754
2	2,000	1,538
3	2,500	1,688
4	4,000	2,368
	Total present value =	$7,348

At 14 percent, the present value of the cash flows is less than the price of the financial instrument. Therefore, a lower interest rate must be tried. A 12 percent interest rate gives the following results:

Years from Now	Promised Annual Payments (Cash Flow to Investor)	Present Value of Cash Flow at 12%
1	$2,000	$1,786
2	2,000	1,594
3	2,500	1,780
4	4,000	2,544
	Total present value =	$7,704

The present value of the cash flow is equal to the price of the financial instrument when a 12 percent interest rate is used. Therefore, the yield is 12 percent.

Although the formula for the yield is based on annual cash flows, the formula can be generalized to any number of periodic payments in a year. The generalized formula for determining the yield is

$$p = \frac{C_1}{(1+y)^1} + \frac{C_2}{(1+y)^2} + \frac{C_3}{(1+y)^3} + ... + \frac{C_n}{(1+y)^n}$$

where

C_t = Cash flow in period t
n = Number of periods

Keep in mind that the yield computed is now the yield for the period. That is, if the cash flows are semiannual, the yield is a semiannual yield. If the cash flows are monthly, the yield is a monthly yield. The annual interest rate is computed by multiplying the yield for the period by the appropriate factor (the frequency of payments per year). We reconsider this procedure for annualizing yields later.

Illustration 10.   An investor is considering the purchase of a financial instrument that promises the following *semiannual* cash flows:

   10 payments of $50 every six months.

   $1,000 10 six-month periods (five years) from now.

Suppose that the price of this financial instrument is $1,243.88. What yield is this financial instrument offering?

   The yield can be computed by a trial-and-error procedure, as summarized in the table below:

Annual Interest Rate	Semi-annual Interest Rate	Present Value of 10 Six-Month Payments of $50[a]	Present Value of $1,000 10 Six-Month Periods from Now[b]	Total Present Value
6.000%	3.000%	$426.51	$744.09	$1,160.60
5.500	2.750	432.00	762.40	1,194.40
5.000	2.500	437.50	781.20	1,218.80
4.500	2.250	443.31	800.51	1,243.83

[a] $50 × present value of an ordinary annuity of $1 for 10 periods.
[b] $1,000 × present value of $1 10 periods from now.

   As can be seen from the calculation, when a semiannual interest rate of 2.250 percent is used to find the present value of the cash flows, the present value is equal to the price of $1,243.83. Hence, 2.250 percent is the six-month yield. Doubling this yield would give an annual interest rate of 4.5 percent.

Yield Calculation When There Is Only One Cash Flow

There is a special case when it is not necessary to go through the time-consuming trial-and-error procedure to determine the yield. This is the case where only one cash flow is provided by the investment. The formula to determine the yield is

$$y = (\text{Future value per dollar invested})^{1/n} - 1$$

where

   n = number of periods until the cash flow will be received

$$\text{Future value per dollar invested} = \frac{\text{Cash flow from investment}}{\text{Amount invested (or price)}}$$

Illustration 11.   An investment offers a payment 20 years from now of $84,957. The price of the investment is $20,000. The yield for this investment is

7.50 percent, as shown below:

$$\text{Future value per dollar invested} = \frac{\$84,957}{\$20,000} = 4.24785$$

$$y = (4.24785)^{1/20} - 1$$
$$= 1.07499 - 1$$
$$= .074999, \text{ or } 7.5\%$$

Annualizing Yields

We might want to annualize interest rates by simply multiplying by the frequency of payments per year. The resulting rate is called the *annual interest rate.* For example, if we computed a semiannual yield, we can annualize it by multiplying by 2. Alternatively, if we had an annual interest rate and wanted to determine a semiannual interest rate, we can divide by 2.

This procedure for computing the annual interest rate, given a periodic (weekly, monthly, quarterly, semiannual, etc.) interest rate is not correct. To see why, suppose that $100 is invested for one year at an annual interest rate of 8 percent. At the end of one year, the interest is $8. Suppose, instead, that $100 is invested for one year at an annual interest rate of 8 percent, but interest is paid semiannually at 4 percent (one-half the annual interest rate). The future value at the end of one year is $108.16. Interest is therefore $8.16 on a $100 investment. The interest rate, or yield, on the $100 investment is therefore 8.16 percent ($8.16/$100). The 8.16 percent is called the *effective annual yield.*

To obtain the effective annual yield associated with a periodic interest rate, the following formula can be used:

$$\text{Effective annual yield} = (1 + \text{Periodic interest rate})^m - 1$$

where

m = Frequency of payments per year

For instance, in the previous example, the periodic yield is 4 percent and the frequency of payments is twice per year. Therefore,

$$\text{Effective annual yield} = (1.04)^2 - 1$$
$$= 1.0816 - 1$$
$$= .0816, \text{ or } 8.16\%$$

If interest is paid quarterly, then the periodic interest rate is 2 percent (8%/4), and the effective annual yield is 8.24 percent, as shown below:

$$\text{Effective annual yield} = (1.02)^4 - 1$$
$$= 1.0824 - 1$$
$$= .0824, \text{ or } 8.24\%$$

We can also determine the periodic interest rate that will produce a given annual interest rate. For example, suppose we wanted to know what quarterly interest rate would produce an effective annual yield of 12 percent. The following formula can be used:

$$\text{Periodic interest rate} = (1 + \text{Effective annual yield})^{1/m} - 1$$

Applying this formula to determine the quarterly interest rate to produce an effective annual yield of 12 percent, we find that

$$\begin{aligned}
\text{Periodic interest rate} &= (1.12)^{1/4} - 1 \\
&= 1.0287 - 1 \\
&= .0287, \text{ or } 2.87\%.
\end{aligned}$$

SUMMARY

In this chapter, several basic mathematical concepts are presented—future value, present value, and yield (or internal rate of return). In the next chapter, we will see how these concepts can be applied to price fixed income securities and calculate various yield measures.

⑥ ## BOND PRICING AND RETURN MEASURES

Frank J. Fabozzi, Ph.D., CFA, CPA
Adjunct Professor of Finance
School of Management
Yale University

In this chapter, the pricing of fixed income securities and the various measures of computing return (or yield) from holding a fixed income security will be explained and illustrated. The chapter is organized as follows. In the first section, we extend the present value analysis reviewed in the previous chapter to explain how a bond's price is determined. Then we turn to yield measures, first focusing on conventional yield measures for a fixed-rate coupon bond (yield-to-maturity and yield-to-call in the case of a callable bond) and a floating-rate coupon bond. After highlighting the deficiencies of the conventional yield measures, a better measure of return—total return—is then presented.

BOND PRICING

The price of any financial instrument is equal to the present value of the expected cash flow. The interest rate or discount rate used to compute the present value depends on the yield offered on comparable securities in the market. In this chapter, we shall explain how to compute the price of a noncallable bond. The pricing of callable bonds is explained in Part 5.

Determining the Cash Flow

The first step in determining the price of a bond is to determine its cash flow. The cash flow of an option-free bond (i.e., noncallable/nonputable bond) consists of (1) periodic coupon interest payments to the maturity date and (2) the par (or maturity) value at maturity. Although the periodic coupon payments can be made over any time interval (weekly, monthly, quarterly, semiannually, or annually), most bonds issued in the United States pay coupon interest semiannually. In our illustrations, we shall assume that the coupon interest is paid semiannually. Also, to simplify the analysis, we shall assume that the next coupon payment for the bond will be made exactly six months from now. Later in this section, we explain how to price a bond when the next coupon payment is less than six months from now.

In practice, determining the cash flow of a bond is not simple, even if we ignore the possibility of default. The only case in which the cash flow is known with certainty is for fixed-rate coupon, option-free bonds. For callable bonds, the cash flow depends on whether the issuer elects to call the issue. In the case of a putable bond, it depends on whether the bondholder elects to put the issue. In either case, the date that the option will be exercised is not known. Thus, the cash flow is uncertain. For mortgage-backed securities, the cash flow depends on prepayments. The amount and timing of future prepayments are not known, and therefore the cash flow is uncertain. When the coupon rate is floating rather than fixed, the cash flow depends on the future value of the reference rate. The techniques discussed in Part 5 have been developed to cope with the uncertainty of cash flows. In this chapter, the basic elements of bond pricing, where the cash flow is assumed to be known, are presented.

The cash flow for an option-free bond consists of an annuity (that is, the fixed coupon interest paid every 6 months) and the par or maturity value. For example, a 20-year bond with a 9 percent (4.5 percent per 6 months) coupon rate and a par or maturity value of $1,000 has the following cash flows:

$$\text{Semiannual coupon interest} = \$1,000 \times .045$$
$$= \$45$$
$$\text{Maturity value} = \$1,000$$

Therefore, there are 40 semiannual cash flows of $45, and a $1,000 cash flow 40 six-month periods from now.

Notice the treatment of the par value. It is *not* treated as if it will be received 20 years from now. Instead, it is treated on a consistent basis with the coupon payments, which are semiannual.

Determining the Required Yield

The interest rate or discount rate that an investor wants from investing in a bond is called the *required yield.* The required yield is determined by investigating the yields offered on comparable bonds in the market. By comparable, we mean option-free bonds of the same credit quality and the same maturity.[1]

---

1. In Chapter 5, we introduce a measure of interest rate risk known as *duration.* Instead of talking in terms of a bond with the same maturity as being comparable, we can recast the analysis in terms of the same duration.

The required yield is typically specified as an annual interest rate. When the cash flows are semiannual, the convention is to use one-half the annual interest rate as the periodic interest rate with which to discount the cash flows. As explained at the end of the previous chapter, a periodic interest rate that is one-half the annual yield will produce an effective annual yield that is greater than the annual interest rate.

Although one yield is used to calculate the present value of all cash flows, there are theoretical arguments for using a different yield to discount the cash flow for each period. Essentially, the theoretical argument is that each cash flow can be viewed as a zero-coupon bond, and therefore the cash flow of a bond can be viewed as a package of zero-coupon bonds. The appropriate yield for each cash flow would then be based on the theoretical rate on a zero-coupon bond with a maturity equal to the time that the cash flow will be received. For purposes of this chapter, however, we shall use only one yield to discount all cash flows. In Chapters 6 and 36, this issue is reexamined.

Determining the Price

Given the cash flows of a bond and the required yield, we have all the necessary data to price the bond. The price of a bond is equal to the present value of the cash flows, and it can be determined by adding (1) the present value of the semiannual coupon payments and (2) the present value of the par or maturity value.

Because the semiannual coupon payments are equivalent to an ordinary annuity, the present value of the coupon payments and maturity value can be calculated from the following formula:[2]

$$c\left[\frac{1-\left[\dfrac{1}{(1+i)^n}\right]}{i}\right]+\frac{M}{(1+i)^n}$$

where

c = semiannual coupon payment ($)
n = number of periods (number of years times 2)
i = periodic interest rate (required yield divided by 2) (in decimals)
M = maturity value

Illustration 1.   Compute the price of a 9 percent coupon bond with 20 years to maturity and a par value of $1,000 if the required yield is 12 percent.

---

2. The formula is the same as the formula for the present value of an ordinary annuity for n periods given in the previous chapter. Instead of using A to represent the annuity, we have used c, the semiannual coupon payment.

The cash flows for this bond are as follows: (1) 40 semiannual coupon payments of $45 and (2) $1,000 40 six-month periods from now. The semiannual or periodic interest rate is 6 percent.

The present value of the 40 semiannual coupon payments of $45 discounted at 6 percent is $677.08, as shown below:

$$c = \$45$$
$$n = 40$$
$$i = .06$$

$$\$45\left[\dfrac{1-\left[\dfrac{1}{(1.06)^{40}}\right]}{.06}\right]$$

$$= \$45\left[\dfrac{1-\left[\dfrac{1}{10.28572}\right]}{.06}\right]$$

$$= \$45\left[\dfrac{1-.097222}{.06}\right]$$

$$= \$45\,(15.04630)$$
$$= \$677.08$$

The present value of the par or maturity value 40 *six-month periods* from now discounted at 6 percent is $97.22, as shown below:

$$M = \$1,000$$
$$n = 40$$
$$i = .06$$

$$\$1,000\left[\dfrac{1}{(1.06)^{40}}\right]$$

$$= \$1,000\left[\dfrac{1}{10.28572}\right]$$

$$= \$1,000\,(.097222)$$
$$= \$97.22$$

The price of the bond is then equal to the sum of the two present values:

Present value of coupon payments	$ 677.08
Present value of par (maturity) value	97.22
Price	$ 774.30

Illustration 2.   Compute the price of the bond in Illustration 1, assuming that the required yield is 7 percent.

The cash flows are unchanged, but the periodic interest rate is now 3.5 percent (7 percent/2).

The present value of the 40 semiannual coupon payments of $45 discounted at 3.5 percent is $960.98, as shown below:

$$c = \$45$$
$$n = 40$$
$$i = .035$$

$$\$45 \left[\frac{1 - \left[\dfrac{1}{(1.035)^{40}} \right]}{.035} \right]$$

$$= \$45 \left[\frac{1 - \left[\dfrac{1}{3.95926} \right]}{.035} \right]$$

$$= \$45 \left[\frac{1 - .252572}{.035} \right]$$

$$= \$45 \, (21.35509)$$
$$= \$960.98$$

The present value of the par or maturity value of $1,000 *40 six-month periods from now* discounted at 3.5 percent is $252.57, as shown below:

$$M = \$1,000$$
$$n = 40$$
$$i = .035$$

$$\$1,000 \left[\frac{1}{(1.035)^{40}} \right]$$

$$= \$1,000\left[\frac{1}{3.95926}\right]$$

$$= \$1,000\,(.252572)$$

$$= \$252.57$$

The price of the bond is then equal to the sum of the two present values:

Present value of coupon payments	$ 960.98
Present value of par (maturity) value	252.57
Price	$1,213.55

Relationship between Required Yield and Price at a Given Time

The price of an option-free bond changes in the direction opposite to the change in the required yield. The reason is that the price of the bond is the present value of the cash flows. As the required yield increases, the present value of the cash flows decreases; hence, the price decreases. The opposite is true when the required yield decreases: The present value of the cash flows increases and, therefore, the price of the bond increases.

We can see this by comparing the price of the 20-year, 9 percent coupon bond that we priced in Illustrations 1 and 2. When the required yield is 12 percent, the price of the bond is $774.30. If, instead, the required yield is 7 percent, the price of the bond is $1,213.55. Exhibit 4–1 shows the price of the bond for required yields from 5 percent to 14 percent for the 20-year, 9 percent coupon bond.

If we graphed the price/yield relationship for any option-free bond, we would find that it has the "bowed" shape shown in Exhibit 4–2. This shape is re-

E X H I B I T   4–1

Price/Yield Relationship for a 20-Year, 9 Percent Coupon Bond

Required Yield	Price of Bond
5%	$1,502.05
6	1,346.72
7	1,213.55
8	1,098.96
9	1,000.00
10	914.21
11	839.54
12	774.30
13	717.09
14	666.71

EXHIBIT 4–2

Price/Yield Relationship

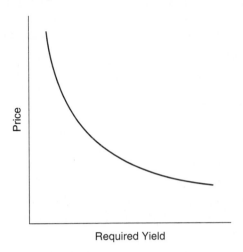

ferred to as *convex*. The convexity of the price/yield relationship has important implications for the investment properties of a bond. We've devoted Chapter 5 to examine this relationship more closely.

The Relationship between Coupon Rate, Required Yield, and Price

For a bond issue at a given point in time, the coupon rate and the term-to-maturity are fixed. Consequently, as yields in the marketplace change, the only variable that an investor can change to compensate for the new yield required in the market is the price of the bond. As we saw in the previous section, as the required yield increases (decreases), the price of the bond decreases (increases).

Generally, when a bond is issued, the coupon rate is set at approximately the prevailing yield in the market.[3] The price of the bond will then be approximately equal to its par value. For example, in Exhibit 4–1, we see that when the required yield is equal to the coupon rate, the price of the bond is its par value. Consequently, we have the following properties:

When the coupon rate equals the required yield, the price equals the par value.

When the price equals the par value, the coupon rate equals the required yield.

When yields in the marketplace rise above the coupon rate at *a given time,* the price of the bond has to adjust so that the investor can realize some additional interest. This adjustment is accomplished by having the bond's price fall below the par value. The difference between the par value and the price is a capital gain

---

3. The exception is an original-issue discount bond such as a zero-coupon bond.

and represents a form of interest to the investor to compensate for the coupon rate being lower than the required yield. When a bond sells below its par value, it is said to be selling at a *discount*. We can see this in Exhibit 4–1. When the required yield is greater than the coupon rate of 9 percent, the price of the bond is always less than the par value. Consequently, we have the following properties:

> *When the coupon rate is less than the required yield, the price is less than the par value.*

> *When the price is less than the par value, the coupon rate is less than the required yield.*

Finally, when the required yield in the market is below the coupon rate, the price of the bond must be above its par value. This occurs because investors who could purchase the bond at par would be getting a coupon rate in excess of what the market requires. As a result, investors would bid up the price of the bond because its yield is attractive. It will be bid up to a price that offers the required yield in the market. A bond whose price is above its par value is said to be selling at a *premium*. Exhibit 4–1 shows that for a required yield less than the coupon rate of 9 percent, the price of the bond is greater than its par value. Consequently, we have the following properties:

> *When the coupon rate is greater than the required yield, the price is greater than the par value.*

> *When the price is greater than the par value, the coupon rate is greater than the required yield.*

Time Path of a Bond

If the required yield is unchanged between the time the bond is purchased and the maturity date, what will happen to the price of the bond? For a bond selling at par value, the coupon rate is equal to the required yield. As the bond moves closer to maturity, the bond will continue to sell at par value. Thus, for a bond selling at par, its price will remain at par as the bond moves toward the maturity date.

The price of a bond will *not* remain constant for a bond selling at a premium or a discount. For all discount bonds the following is true: As the bond moves toward maturity, its price will increase if *the required yield* does not change. This can be seen in Exhibit 4–3, which shows the price of the 20-year, 9 percent coupon bond as it moves toward maturity, assuming that the required yield remains at 12 percent. For a bond selling at a premium, the price of the bond declines as it moves toward maturity. This can also be seen in Exhibit 4–3, which shows the time path of the 20-year, 9 percent coupon bond selling to yield 7 percent.

Reasons for the Change in the Price of a Bond

The price of a bond will change because of one or more of the following reasons:

- *A change in the level of interest rates in the economy.* For example, if interest rates in the economy increase (fall) because of Fed policy, the price of a bond will decrease (increase).

EXHIBIT 4–3

Time Paths of 20-Year, 9 Percent Coupon Discount and Premium Bonds

Years Remaining to Maturity	Price of Discount Bond[a]	Price of Premium Bond[b]
20	$774.30	$1,213.55
18	780.68	1,202.90
16	788.74	1,190.69
14	798.91	1,176.67
12	811.75	1,160.59
10	827.95	1,142.13
8	848.42	1,120.95
6	874.24	1,096.63
4	906.85	1,068.74
2	948.02	1,036.73
1	972.50	1,019.00
0	1,000.00	1,000.00

[a]Selling to yield 12 percent.
[b]Selling to yield 7 percent.

- *A change in the price of the bond selling at a price other than par as it moves toward maturity without any change in the required yield.* As we demonstrated, over time a discount bond's price rises in value if yields do not change; a premium bond's price declines over time if yields do not change.
- *For non-Treasury bonds, a change in the required yield due to changes in the spread to Treasuries.* If the Treasury rate does not change but the spread to Treasuries changes (narrows or widens), non-Treasury bond prices will change.
- *A change in the perceived credit quality of the issuer.* Assuming that interest rates in the economy and yield spreads between non-Treasuries and Treasuries do not change, the price of a non-Treasury bond will increase (decrease) if its perceived credit quality has improved (deteriorated).
- *For bonds with embedded options (e.g., callable bonds, putable bonds, and convertible bonds), the price of the bond will change as the factors that affect the value of the embedded options change.*

Pricing a Zero-Coupon Bond

So far, we have determined the price of coupon-bearing bonds. Some bonds do not make any periodic coupon payments. Instead, the investor realizes interest by the difference between the maturity value and the purchase price.

The pricing of a zero-coupon bond is no different from the pricing of a coupon bond: Its price is the present value of the expected cash flows. In the case of a zero-coupon bond, the only cash flow is the maturity value. Therefore, the price of a zero-coupon bond is simply the present value of the maturity value. The number of periods used to discount the maturity value is double the number of years to maturity. This treatment is consistent with the manner in which the maturity value of a coupon bond is handled.

Illustration 3.   The price of a zero-coupon bond that matures in 10 years and has a maturity value of $1,000 if the required yield is 8.6 percent, is equal to the present value of $1,000 20 periods from now discounted at 4.3 percent. That is,

$$\$1,000 \left[\frac{1}{(1.043)^{20}} \right] = \$430.83$$

Determining the Price When the Settlement Date Falls between Coupon Periods

In our illustrations, we assumed that the next coupon payment is six months away. This means that settlement occurs on the day after a coupon date. Typically, an investor will purchase a bond between coupon dates, so that the next coupon payment is less than six months away. To compute the price, we have to answer the following three questions:

- How many days are there until the next coupon payment?
- How should we determine the present value of cash flows received over fractional periods?
- How much must the buyer compensate the seller for the coupon interest earned by the seller for the fraction of the period that the bond was held?

The first question is the day count question. The second is the compounding question. The last question asks how accrued interest is determined. Below we address these questions.

Day Count
Market conventions for each type of bond dictate the answer to the first question: the number of days until the next coupon payment.

For Treasury coupon securities, a nonleap year is assumed to have 365 days. The number of days between settlement and the next coupon payment is therefore the actual number of days between the two dates. The day count convention for a coupon-bearing Treasury security is said to be "actual/actual," which means the actual number of days in a month and the actual number of days in the coupon period. For example, consider a Treasury bond whose last coupon payment was on March 1; the next coupon would be six months later on September 1. Suppose this bond is purchased with a settlement date of July 17. The actual number of days between July 17 (the settlement date) and September 1 (the date of the next coupon payment) is 46 days (the actual number of days in the coupon period is 184), as shown below:

July 17 to July 31	14 days
August	31 days
September 1	1 day
	46 days

In contrast to the actual/actual day count convention for coupon-bearing Treasury securities, for corporate and municipal bonds and agency securities, the day count convention is "30/360." That is, each month is assumed to have 30 days and each year 360 days. For example, suppose that the security in our previous example is not a coupon-bearing Treasury security but instead either a coupon-bearing corporate bond, a municipal bond, or an agency security. The number of days between July 17 and September 1 is shown below:

Remainder of July	13 days
August	30 days
September 1	1 day
	44 days

Compounding

Once the number of days between the settlement date and the next coupon date is determined, the present value formula must be modified because the cash flows will not be received six months (one full period) from now. The Street convention is to compute the price as follows:

1. Determine the number of days in the coupon period.

2. Compute the following ratio:

$$w = \frac{\text{Number of days between settlement and next coupon payment}}{\text{Number of days in the coupon period}}$$

For a corporate bond, municipal bond, and agency security, the number of days in the coupon period will be 180 because a year is assumed to have 360 days. For a coupon-bearing Treasury security, the number of days is the actual number of days. The number of days in the coupon period is called the *basis*.

3. For a bond with n coupon payments remaining to maturity, the price is

$$p = \frac{c}{(1+i)^w} + \frac{c}{(1+i)^{1+w}} + \frac{c}{(1+i)^{2+w}} + \dots + \frac{c}{(1+i)^{n-1+w}} + \frac{M}{(1+i)^{n-1+w}}$$

where

p = Price ($)
c = Semiannual coupon payment ($)
M = Maturity value
n = Number of coupon payments remaining
i = Periodic interest rate (required yield divided by 2)
       (in decimals)

The period (exponent) in the formula for determining the present value can be expressed generally as $t - 1 + w$. For example, for the first cash flow, the period is $1 - 1 + w$, or simply w. For the second cash flow, it is $2 - 1 + w$, or simply $1 + w$. If the bond has 20 coupon payments remaining, the last period is $20 - 1 + w$, or simply $19 + w$.

Illustration 4.   Suppose that a corporate bond with a coupon rate of 10 percent maturing March 1, 2003, is purchased with a settlement date of July 17, 1997. What would the price of this bond be if it is priced to yield 6.5 percent?

The next coupon payment will be made on September 1, 1997. Because the bond is a corporate bond, based on a 30/360 day count convention, there are 44 days between the settlement date and the next coupon date. The number of days in the coupon period is 180. Therefore,

$$w = \frac{\overline{44}}{180} = 0.24444$$

The number of coupon payments remaining, n, is 12. The semiannual interest rate is 3.25 percent (6.5 percent/2).

The calculation based on the formula for the price is given in Exhibit 4–4. The price of this corporate bond would be $120.0281 per $100 par value. The price calculated in this way is called the *full price* or *dirty price* because it reflects the portion of the coupon interest that the buyer will receive but that the seller has earned.

Accrued Interest and the Clean Price

The buyer must compensate the seller for the portion of the next coupon interest payment the seller has earned but will not receive from the issuer because the issuer will send the next coupon payment to the buyer. This amount is called *accrued interest* and depends on the number of days from the last coupon payment to the settlement date.[4] The accrued interest is computed as follows:

$$AI = c \left[\frac{\text{Number of days from last coupon payment to settlement date}}{\text{Number of days in coupon period}} \right]$$

---

4. Accrued interest is not computed for all bonds. No accrued interest is computed for bonds in default or income bonds. A bond that trades without accrued interest is said to be traded "flat."

EXHIBIT 4–4

Price Calculation When a Bond Is Purchased between Coupon Payments

Period	Cash Flow per $100 of Par	Present Value of $1 at 3.25%	Present Value of Cash Flow
0.24444	$ 5.000	$0.992212	$ 4.961060
1.24444	5.000	0.960980	4.804902
2.24444	5.000	0.930731	4.653658
3.24444	5.000	0.901435	4.507175
4.24444	5.000	0.873060	4.365303
5.24444	5.000	0.845579	4.227896
6.24444	5.000	0.818963	4.094815
7.24444	5.000	0.793184	3.965922
8.24444	5.000	0.768217	3.841087
9.24444	5.000	0.744036	3.720181
10.24444	5.000	0.720616	3.603081
11.24444	105.000	0.697933	73.283000
		Total	$120.028100

where

AI = Accrued interest ($)

c = Semiannual coupon payment ($)

Illustration 5.   Let's continue with the hypothetical corporate bond in Illustration 4. Because the number of days between settlement (July 17, 1997) and the next coupon payment (September 1, 1997) is 44 days and the number of days in the coupon period is 180, the number of days from the last coupon payment date (March 1, 1997) to the settlement date is 136 (180 – 44). The accrued interest per $100 of par value is

$$AI = \$5\left(\frac{136}{180}\right) = \$3.777778$$

The full or dirty price includes the accrued interest that the seller is entitled to receive. For example, in the calculation of the full price in Exhibit 4–4, the next coupon payment of $5 is included as part of the cash flow. The *clean price* or *flat price* is the dirty price of the bond minus the accrued interest.

The price that the buyer pays the seller is the dirty price. It is important to note that in calculation of the dirty price, the next coupon payment is a discounted value, but in calculation of accrued interest it is an undiscounted value. Because of this market practice, if a bond is selling at par and the settlement date is not a coupon date, the yield will be slightly less than the coupon rate. Only when the settlement date and coupon date coincide is the yield equal to the coupon rate for a bond selling at par.

In the U.S. market, the convention is to quote a bond's clean or flat price. The buyer, however, pays the seller the dirty price. In some non-U.S. markets, the dirty price is quoted.

CONVENTIONAL YIELD MEASURES

In the previous section, we explained how to compute the price of a bond given the required yield. In this section, we'll show how various yield measures for a bond are calculated given its price. First let's look at the sources of potential return from holding a bond.

An investor who purchases a bond can expect to receive a *dollar* return from one or more of the following sources:

- The coupon interest payments made by the issuer.
- Any capital gain (or capital loss—negative dollar return) when the bond matures, is called, or is sold.
- Income from reinvestment of the coupon interest payments.

This last source of dollar return is referred to as *interest-on-interest.*

Three yield measures are commonly cited by market participants to measure the potential return from investing in a bond—current yield, yield-to-maturity, and yield-to-call. These yield measures are expressed as a *percent* return rather than a dollar return. However, any yield measure should consider each of the three potential sources of return cited above. Below we discuss these three yield measures and assess whether they consider the three sources of potential return.

Current Yield

The current yield relates the *annual* coupon interest to the market price. The formula for the current yield is

$$\text{Current yield} = \frac{\text{Annual dollar coupon interest}}{\text{Price}}$$

Illustration 6.   The current yield for an 18-year, 6 percent coupon bond selling for $700.89 is 8.56 percent, as shown below:

$$\text{Annual dollar coupon interest} = \$1,000 \times .06$$
$$= \$60$$

$$\text{Current yield} = \frac{\$60}{\$700.89} = .0856, \text{ or } 8.56\%$$

The current yield considers only the coupon interest and no other source of return that will affect an investor's yield. For example, in Illustration 6, no consideration is given to the capital gain that the investor will realize when the bond matures. No recognition is given to a capital loss that the investor will realize when a bond selling at a premium matures. In addition, interest-on-interest from reinvesting coupon payments is ignored.

Yield-to-Maturity

In the previous chapter, we explained how to compute the yield or internal rate of return on any investment. The yield is the interest rate that will make the present value of the cash flows equal to the price (or initial investment). The yield-to-maturity is computed in the same way as the yield; the cash flows are those that the investor would realize by holding the bond to maturity. For a semiannual-pay bond, doubling the interest rate or discount rate gives the yield-to-maturity.

Recall from the previous chapter that the calculation of a yield involves a trial-and-error procedure. Although there is a *yield book* that contains tables that provide the yield-to-maturity given the price, coupon, and remaining time to maturity, practitioners usually use calculators or software to produce this number. The following illustration shows how to compute the yield-to-maturity for a bond.

Illustration 7.   In Illustration 6, we computed the current yield for an 18-year, 6 percent coupon bond selling for $700.89. The maturity value for this bond is $1,000. The yield-to-maturity for this bond is 9.5 percent, as shown in Exhibit 4–5. Cash flows for the bond are

- 36 coupon payments of $30 every six months.
- $1,000 36 six-month periods from now.

Different interest rates must be tried until one is found that makes the present value of the cash flows equal to the price of $700.89. Because the coupon rate on the bond is 6 percent and the bond is selling at a discount, the yield must be greater than 6 percent. Exhibit 4–5 shows the present value of the cash flows of the bond for semiannual interest rates from 3.25 percent to 4.75 percent (corresponding to annual interest rates from 6.5 percent to 9.50 percent). As can be seen, when a 4.75 percent interest rate is used, the present value of the cash flows is $700.89. Therefore, the yield-to-maturity is 9.50 percent ($4.75\% \times 2$).

The yield-to-maturity considers the coupon income and any capital gain or loss that the investor will realize by *holding the bond to maturity*. The yield-to-maturity also considers the timing of the cash flows. It does consider interest-on-interest; *however, it assumes that the coupon payments can be reinvested at an interest rate equal to the yield-to-maturity.* So, if the yield-to-maturity for a bond is 9.5 percent, to earn that yield, the coupon payments must be reinvested at an interest rate equal to 9.5 percent. The following example clearly demonstrates this.

EXHIBIT 4-5

Computation of Yield-to-Maturity for an 18-Year, 6 Percent Coupon Bond
Selling at $700.89

Objective: Find, by trial and error, the semiannual interest rate that will make the present value of the following cash flows equal to $700.89:

  36 coupon payments of $30 every six months
  $1,000 36 six-month periods from now

Annual Interest Rate	Semi-annual Rate	Present Value of 36 Payments of $30[a]	Present Value of $1,000 10 Periods from Now[b]	Present Value of Cash Flows
6.50%	3.25%	$631.20	$316.20	$947.40
7.00	3.50	608.71	289.83	898.54
7.50	3.75	587.42	265.72	853.14
8.00	4.00	567.25	243.67	810.92
8.50	4.25	548.12	223.49	771.61
9.00	4.50	529.98	205.03	735.01
9.50	4.75	512.76	188.13	700.89

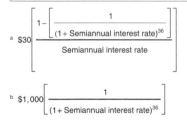

$$^a\ \$30 \left[\frac{1 - \left[\dfrac{1}{(1 + \text{Semiannual interest rate})^{36}} \right]}{\text{Semiannual interest rate}} \right]$$

$$^b\ \$1,000 \left[\frac{1}{(1 + \text{Semiannual interest rate})^{36}} \right]$$

Suppose an investor has $700.98 and places the funds in a certificate of deposit that pays 4.75 percent every six months for 18 years or 9.5 percent per year. At the end of 18 years, the $700.98 investment will grow to $3,726. Instead, suppose the investor buys a 6 percent, 18-year bond selling for $700.98. This is the same as the price of our bond in Illustration 7. The yield-to-maturity for this bond is 9.5 percent. The investor would expect that at the end of 18 years, the total dollars from the investment will be $3,726.

Let's look at what he will receive. There will be 36 semiannual interest payments of $30, which will total $1,080. When the bond matures, the investor will receive $1,000. Thus, the total dollars that he will receive is $2,080 if he holds the bond to maturity, but this is $1,646 less than the $3,726 necessary to produce a yield of 9.5 percent (4.75 percent semiannually). How is this deficiency supposed to be made up? If the investor reinvests the coupon payments at a semiannual interest rate of 4.75 percent (or a 9.5 percent annual rate), it is a simple exercise to demonstrate that the interest earned on the coupon payments will be $1,646. Consequently, of the $3,025 total dollar return ($3,726 – $701) necessary to produce a yield of 9.5 percent, about 54 percent ($1,646 divided by $3,025) must be generated by reinvesting the coupon payments.

Clearly, the investor will realize the yield-to-maturity stated at the time of purchase only if (1) the coupon payments can be reinvested at the yield-to-maturity and (2) if the bond is held to maturity. With respect to the first assumption, the risk that an investor faces is that future reinvestment rates will be less than the yield-to-maturity at the time the bond is purchased. This risk is referred to as *reinvestment risk*. If the bond is not held to maturity, the price at which the bond may have to be sold is less than its purchase price, resulting in a return that is less than the yield-to-maturity. The risk that a bond will have to be sold at a loss because interest rates rise is referred to as *interest rate risk*.

Reinvestment Risk

There are two characteristics of a bond that determine the degree of reinvestment risk. First, for a given yield-to-maturity and a given coupon rate, the longer the maturity, the more the bond's total dollar return is dependent on the interest-on-interest to realize the yield-to-maturity at the time of purchase. That is, the greater the reinvestment risk. The implication is that the yield-to-maturity measure for long-term coupon bonds tells little about the potential yield that an investor may realize if the bond is held to maturity. In high-interest-rate environments, the interest-on-interest component for long-term bonds may be as high as 80 percent of the bond's potential total dollar return.

The second characteristic that determines the degree of reinvestment risk is the coupon rate. For a given maturity and a given yield-to-maturity, the higher the coupon rate, the more dependent the bond's total dollar return will be on the reinvestment of the coupon payments in order to produce the yield-to-maturity at the time of purchase. This means that if maturity and yield-to-maturity are constant, premium bonds will be more dependent on interest-on-interest than bonds selling at par. For zero-coupon bonds, none of the bond's total dollar return is dependent on interest-on-interest; a zero-coupon bond carries no reinvestment risk if held to maturity.

Interest Rate Risk

As we explained in the previous section, a bond's price moves in the direction opposite to the change in interest rates. As interest rates rise (fall), the price of a bond will fall (rise). For an investor who plans to hold a bond to maturity, the change in the bond's price before maturity is of no concern; however, for an investor who may have to sell the bond prior to the maturity date, an increase in interest rates after the bond is purchased will mean the realization of a capital loss. Not all bonds have the same degree of interest-rate risk. In the next chapter, the characteristics of a bond that determine its interest-rate risk will be discussed.

Given the assumptions underlying yield-to-maturity, we can now demonstrate that yield-to-maturity has limited value in assessing the potential return of bonds. Suppose that an investor who has a five-year investment horizon is considering the following four option-free bonds:

Bond	Coupon Rate	Maturity	Yield-to-Maturity
W	5%	3 years	9.0%
X	6	20	8.6
Y	11	15	9.2
Z	8	5	8.0

Assuming that all four bonds are of the same credit quality, which one is the most attractive to this investor? An investor who selects Bond Y because it offers the highest yield-to-maturity is failing to recognize that the bond must be sold after five years, and the selling price of the bond will depend on the yield required in the market for 10-year, 11 percent coupon bonds at that time. Hence, there could be a capital gain or capital loss that will make the return higher or lower than the yield-to-maturity promised now. Moreover, the higher coupon rate on Bond Y relative to the other three bonds means that more of this bond's return will be dependent on the reinvestment of coupon interest payments.

Bond W offers the second highest yield-to-maturity. On the surface, it seems to be particularly attractive because it eliminates the problem faced by purchasing Bond Y of realizing a possible capital loss when the bond must be sold before the maturity date. In addition, the reinvestment risk seems to be less than for the other three bonds because the coupon rate is the lowest. However, the investor would not be eliminating the reinvestment risk because after three years, she must reinvest the proceeds received at maturity for two more years. The return that the investor will realize will depend on interest rates three years from now, when the investor must roll over the proceeds received from the maturing bond.

Which is the best bond? The yield-to-maturity doesn't seem to help us identify the best bond. The answer depends on the expectations of the investor. Specifically, it depends on the interest rate at which the coupon interest payments can be reinvested until the end of the investor's investment horizon. Also, for bonds with a maturity longer than the investment horizon, it depends on the investor's expectations about interest rates at the end of the investment horizon. Consequently, any of these bonds can be the best investment vehicle based on some reinvestment rate and some future interest rate at the end of the investment horizon. In the next section, we shall present an alternative return measure for assessing the potential performance of a bond.

Yield-to-Maturity for a Zero-Coupon Bond
In the previous chapter, we explained that when there is only one cash flow, it is much easier to compute the yield on an investment. A zero-coupon bond is char-

acterized by a single cash flow resulting from an investment. Consequently, the following formula, presented in the previous chapter, can be applied to compute the yield-to-maturity for a zero-coupon bond:

$$y = (\text{Future value per dollar invested})^{1/n} - 1$$

where

$$y = \text{One-half the yield-to-maturity}$$

$$\text{Future value per dollar invested} = \frac{\text{Maturity value}}{\text{Price}}$$

Once again, doubling y gives the yield-to-maturity. *Remember that the number of periods used in the formula is double the number of years.*

Illustration 8. The yield-to-maturity for a zero-coupon bond selling for $274.78 with a maturity value of $1,000, maturing in 15 years, is 8.8 percent, as computed below:

$$n = 15 \times 2 = 30$$

$$\text{Future value per dollar invested} = \frac{\$1,000.00}{\$274.78} = 3.639275$$

$$y = (3.639275)^{1/30} - 1$$
$$= (3.639275)^{.033333} - 1$$
$$= 1.044 - 1$$
$$= .044, \text{or } 4.4\%$$

Doubling 4.4 percent gives the yield-to-maturity of 8.8 percent.

Relationship between Coupon Rate, Current Yield, and Yield-to-Maturity
The following relationship should be recognized between the coupon rate, current yield, and yield-to-maturity:

Bond Selling at:	Relationship
Par	Coupon rate = Current yield = Yield-to-maturity
Discount	Coupon rate < Current yield < Yield-to-maturity
Premium	Coupon rate > Current yield > Yield-to-maturity

Problem with the Annualizing Procedure
As we pointed out at the end of the previous chapter, multiplying a semiannual interest rate by 2 will give an underestimate of the effective annual yield. The proper way to annualize the semiannual yield is by applying the following formula:

$$\text{Effective annual yield} = (1 + \text{Periodic interest rate})^k - 1$$

where

$$k = \text{Number of payments per year}$$

For a semiannual-pay bond, the formula can be modified as follows:

$$\text{Effective annual yield} = (1 + \text{Semiannual interest rate})^2 - 1$$

or

$$\text{Effective annual yield} = (1 + y)^2 - 1$$

For example, in Illustration 7, the semiannual interest rate is 4.75 percent, and the effective annual yield is 9.73 percent, as shown below:

$$\text{Effective annual yield} = (1.0475)^2 - 1$$
$$= 1.0973 - 1$$
$$= .0973, \text{ or } 9.73\%$$

Although the proper way for annualizing a semiannual interest rate is given in the formula above, the convention adopted in the bond market is to double the semi-annual interest rate. The yield-to-maturity computed in this manner—doubling the semiannual yield—is called a *bond-equivalent yield.* In fact, this convention is carried over to yield calculations for other types of fixed income securities.

Yield-to-Call

For a callable bond, investors also compute another yield (or internal rate of return) measure, the *yield-to-call.* The cash flows for computing the yield-to-call are those that would result if the issue were called on some assumed call date. Two commonly used call dates are the first call date and the first par call date. The yield-to-call is the interest rate that will make the present value of the cash flows if the bond is held to the assumed call date equal to the price of the bond (or total payment).

Illustration 9.   In Illustrations 6 and 7, we computed the current yield and yield-to-maturity for an 18-year, 6 percent coupon bond selling for $700.89. Suppose that this bond is callable in five years at $1,030. The cash flows for this bond if it is called in five years are

- 10 coupon payments of $30 every six months.
- $1,030 in 10 six-month periods from now.

The interest rate we seek is one that will make the present value of the cash flows equal to $700.89. From Exhibit 4–6, it can be seen that when the interest rate is 7.6 percent, the present value of the cash flows is $700.11, which is close enough to $700.89 for our purposes. Therefore, the yield-to-call on a bond-equivalent basis is 15.2 percent (double the periodic interest rate of 7.6 percent).

EXHIBIT 4–6

Computation of Yield-to-Call for an 18-Year, 6 Percent Coupon Bond Callable in 5 years at $1,030, Selling at $700.89

Objective: Find, by trial and error, the semiannual interest rate that will make the present value of the following cash flows equal to $700.89:

  10 coupon payments of $30 every six months
  $1,030 10 six-month periods from now

Annual Interest Rate	Semi-annual Rate	Present Value of 10 Payments of $30[a]	Present Value of $1,030 10 Periods from Now[b]	Present Value of Cash Flows
11.20%	5.60%	$225.05	$597.31	$822.36
11.70	5.85	222.38	585.35	805.73
12.20	6.10	219.76	569.75	789.51
12.70	6.35	217.19	556.50	773.69
13.20	6.60	214.66	543.58	758.24
13.70	6.85	212.18	531.00	743.18
14.20	7.10	209.74	518.73	728.47
14.70	7.35	207.34	506.78	714.12
15.20	7.60	204.99	495.12	700.11

[a] $\$30\left[\dfrac{1-\left[\dfrac{1}{(1+\text{Semiannual interest rate})^{10}}\right]}{\text{Semiannual interest rate}}\right]$

[b] $\$1,030\left[\dfrac{1}{(1+\text{Semiannual interest rate})^{10}}\right]$

According to the conventional approach, conservative investors will compute the yield-to-call and yield-to-maturity for a callable bond selling at a premium, selecting the lower of the two as a measure of potential return. It is the smaller of the two yield measures that investors would use to evaluate the yield for a bond. Some investors calculate not just the yield to the first call date and yield to first par call date, but the yield to all possible call dates. Because most bonds can be called at any time after the first call date, the approach has been to compute the yield to every coupon anniversary date following the first call date. Then, all calculated yields-to-call and the yield-to-maturity are compared. The lowest of these yields is called the *yield-to-worst*. The conventional approach would have us believe that this yield is the appropriate one an investor should use.

Let's take a closer look at the yield-to-call as a measure of the potential return of a callable bond. The yield-to-call does consider all three sources of potential return from owning a bond. However, as in the case of the yield-to-maturity, it assumes that all cash flows can be reinvested at the computed yield—in this case, the yield-to-call—until the assumed call date. As we noted earlier in this chapter, this assumption may be inappropriate. Moreover, the yield-to-call assumes that (1) the investor will hold the bond to the assumed call date and (2) the issuer will call the bond on that date.

The assumptions underlying the yield-to-call are often unrealistic. They do not take into account how an investor will reinvest the proceeds if the issue is called. For example, consider two bonds, M and N. Suppose that the yield-to-maturity for bond M, a five-year noncallable bond, is 10 percent, whereas for bond N the yield-to-call, assuming that the bond will be called in three years, is 10.5 percent. Which bond is better for an investor with a five-year investment horizon? It's not possible to tell from the yields cited. If the investor intends to hold the bond for five years and the issuer calls the bond after three years, the total dollars that will be available at the end of five years will depend on the interest rate that can be earned from reinvesting funds from the call date to the end of the investment horizon.

More will be said about the analysis of callable bonds in Part 5.

Yield (Internal Rate of Return) for a Portfolio

The yield for a portfolio of bonds is not simply the average or weighted average of the yield-to-maturity of the individual bond issues. It is computed by determining the cash flows for the portfolio and then finding the interest rate that will make the present value of the cash flows equal to the market value of the portfolio.[5]

Illustration 10.   Consider the following three-bond portfolio:[6]

Bond	Coupon Rate	Maturity	Par Value	Price Value	Yield-to-Maturity
A	7.0%	5 years	$ 10,000,000	$ 9,209,000	9.0%
B	10.5	7	20,000,000	20,000,000	10.5
C	6.0	3	30,000,000	28,050,000	8.5

---

5. In the next chapter, the concept of duration will be discussed. A good approximation to the yield for a portfolio can be obtained by using duration to weight the yield-to-maturity of the individual bonds in the portfolio.

6. To simplify the illustration, it is assumed that the coupon payment date is the same for each bond.

The portfolio's total market value is $57,259,000. The cash flow for each bond in the portfolio and for the whole portfolio is given below:

Period Cash Flow Received	Bond A	Bond B	Bond C	Portfolio
1	$ 350,000	$ 1,050,000	$ 900,000	$ 2,300,000
2	350,000	1,050,000	900,000	2,300,000
3	350,000	1,050,000	900,000	2,300,000
4	350,000	1,050,000	900,000	2,300,000
5	350,000	1,050,000	900,000	2,300,000
6	350,000	1,050,000	30,900,000	32,300,000
7	350,000	1,050,000	—	1,400,000
8	350,000	1,050,000	—	1,400,000
9	350,000	1,050,000	—	1,400,000
10	10,350,000	1,050,000	—	11,400,000
11	—	1,050,000	—	1,050,000
12	—	1,050,000	—	1,050,000
13	—	1,050,000	—	1,050,000
14	—	21,050,000	—	21,050,000

To determine the yield (internal rate of return) for this three-bond portfolio, the interest rate that makes the present value of the cash flows shown in the last column of the table above equal to $57,259,000 (the total market value of the portfolio) must be found. If an interest rate of 4.77 percent is used, the present value of the cash flows will equal $57,259,000. Doubling 4.77 percent gives 9.54 percent, which is the yield on the portfolio on a bond-equivalent basis.

Yield Measure for Floating-Rate Securities

The coupon rate for a floating-rate security changes periodically based on some reference rate (such as LIBOR).[7] Because the value for the reference rate in the future is not known, it is not possible to determine the cash flows. This means that a yield-to-maturity cannot be calculated.

A conventional measure used to estimate the potential return for a floating-rate security is the security's *discounted margin* or *effective margin*. This measure estimates the average spread or margin over the reference rate that the investor can expect to earn over the life of the security. The procedure for calculating the discounted margin is as follows:

1. Determine the cash flows assuming that the reference rate does not change over the life of the security.

---

7. Floating-rate securities are discussed in Chapter 13.

2. Select a margin (spread).

3. Discount the cash flows found in step (1) by the current value of the reference rate plus the margin selected in step (2).

4. Compare the present value of the cash flows as calculated in step (3) to the price. If the present value is equal to the security's price, the discounted margin is the margin assumed in step (2). If the present value is not equal to the security's price, go back to step (2) and try a different margin.

For a security selling at par, the discounted margin is simply the spread over the reference rate.

Illustration 11.   To illustrate the calculation, suppose that a six-year floating-rate security selling for 99.3098 pays a rate based on some reference rate index plus 80 basis points. The coupon rate is reset every six months. Assume that the current value for the reference rate is 10 percent. Exhibit 4–7 shows the calculation of the discounted margin for this security. The second column shows the current discounted

E X H I B I T   4–7

Calculation of the Discounted Margin for a Floating-Rate Security

Floating-rate security:			Maturity = 6 years				
			Coupon rate = Reference rate + 80 basis points				
			Reset every six months				

| | | | Present Value of Cash Flow: Assumed Annual Yield Spread (in bp) | | | | |
| | Reference | Cash | | | | | |
Period	Rate	Flow[a]	80	84	88	96	100
1	10%	5.4	5.1233	5.1224	5.1214	5.1195	5.1185
2	10	5.4	4.8609	4.8590	4.8572	4.8535	4.8516
3	10	5.4	4.6118	4.6092	4.6066	4.6013	4.5987
4	10	5.4	4.3755	4.3722	4.3689	4.3623	4.3590
5	10	5.4	4.1514	4.1474	4.1435	4.1356	4.1317
6	10	5.4	3.9387	3.9342	3.9297	3.9208	3.9163
7	10	5.4	3.7369	3.7319	3.7270	3.7171	3.7122
8	10	5.4	3.5454	3.5401	3.5347	3.5240	3.5186
9	10	5.4	3.3638	3.3580	3.3523	3.3409	3.3352
10	10	5.4	3.1914	3.1854	3.1794	3.1673	3.1613
11	10	5.4	3.0279	3.0216	3.0153	3.0028	2.9965
12	10	105.4	56.0729	55.9454	55.8182	55.5647	55.4385
Present value			100.0000	99.8269	99.6541	99.3098	99.1381

[a]For periods 1–11: Cash flow = 100 (Reference rate + Assumed margin) (0.5)
  For period 12: Cash flow = 100 (Reference rate + Assumed margin) (0.5) + 100

value for the reference rate (10 percent). The third column sets forth the cash flows for the security. The cash flow for the first 11 periods is equal to one-half the current value for the reference rate (5 percent) plus the semiannual spread of 40 basis points multiplied by 100. In the 12th six-month period, the cash flow is 5.4 plus the maturity value of 100. The top row of the last five columns shows the assumed margin. The rows below the assumed margin show the present value of each cash flow. The last row gives the total present value of the cash flows. For the five assumed yield spreads, the present value is equal to the price of the floating-rate security (99.3098) when the assumed margin is 96 basis points. Therefore, the discounted margin on a semiannual basis is 48 basis points and 96 basis points on an annual basis. (Notice that the discounted margin is 80 basis points, the same as the spread over the reference rate, when the security is selling at par.)

There are two drawbacks of the discounted margin as a measure of the potential return from investing in a floating-rate security. First, this measure assumes that the reference rate will not change over the life of the security. Second, if the floating-rate security has a cap or floor, this is not taken into consideration. Techniques described in Chapter 36 can allow interest rate volatility to be considered and can handle caps or floors.

TOTAL RETURN ANALYSIS

If conventional yield measures such as the yield-to-maturity and yield-to-call offer little insight into the potential return of a bond, what measure of return can be used? The proper measure is one that considers all three sources of potential dollar return over the investment horizon. This requires that an investor first project the total future dollars over an investment horizon. The return is then the interest rate that will make the bond's price (dirty price) grow to the projected total future dollars at the end of the investment horizon. The yield computed in this way is known as the *total return,* also referred to as the *horizon return.* In this section, we explain this measure and demonstrate how it can be applied in assessing the potential return from investing in a bond.

Calculating the Total Return

The total return requires that the investor specify

- An investment horizon.
- A reinvestment rate.
- A selling price for the bond at the end of the investment horizon (which depends on the assumed yield at which the bond will sell at the end of the investment horizon).

More formally, the steps for computing a total return over some investment horizon are as follows.

Step 1: Compute the total coupon payments plus the interest-on-interest based on an assumed reinvestment rate. The reinvestment rate is one-half the annual interest rate that the investor believes can be earned on the reinvestment of coupon interest payments.

The total coupon payments plus interest-on-interest can be calculated using the formula for the future value of an annuity (given in the previous chapter) as shown:

$$\text{Coupon plus interest-on-interest} = \text{Semiannual coupon}\left[\frac{[(1+r)^h - 1]}{r}\right]$$

where

h = Length of the investment horizon (in semiannual periods)
r = Assumed semiannual reinvestment rate

Step 2: Determine the projected sale price at the end of the investment horizon. The projected sale price will depend on the projected yield on comparable bonds at the end of the investment horizon.

Step 3: Add the values computed in steps 1 and 2. The sum is the *total future dollars* that will be received from the investment given the assumed reinvestment rate and projected required yield at the end of the investment horizon.

Step 4: To obtain the semiannual total return, use the following formula:[8]

$$\left(\frac{\text{Total future dollars}}{\text{Purchase price of bond}}\right)^{1/h} - 1$$

Step 5: Because coupon interest is assumed to be paid semiannually, double the interest rate found in step 4. The resulting interest rate is the total return expressed on a bond-equivalent basis. Alternatively, the total return can be expressed on an effective annual interest rate basis by using the following formula:

$$(1 + \text{Semiannual total return})^2 - 1$$

Illustration 12.   Suppose that an investor with a three-year investment horizon is considering purchasing a 20-year, 8 percent coupon bond for $828.40. The yield-to-maturity for this bond is 10 percent. The investor expects that he can reinvest the coupon interest payments at an annual interest rate of 6 percent and that at the end of the investment horizon the 17-year bond will be selling to offer a yield-to-maturity of 7 percent. The total return for this bond is computed in Exhibit 4–8.

Objections to the total-return analysis cited by some portfolio managers are that it requires them to make assumptions about reinvestment rates and future yields and forces a portfolio manager to think in terms of an investment horizon. Unfortunately, some portfolio managers find comfort in meaningless measures such as the yield-to-maturity because it is not necessary to incorporate any expectations. As explained below, the total-return framework enables the portfolio

8. This formula is the same formula as given in the previous chapter for calculating the yield on an investment when there is only one cash flow and, as expected, for calculating the yield on a zero-coupon bond given earlier in this chapter.

EXHIBIT 4–8

Illustration of Total Return Calculation

Assumptions:
Bond = 8 percent 20-year bond selling for $828.40 (yield-to-maturity is 10 percent)
Annual reinvestment rate = 6 percent
Investment horizon = 3 years
Yield for 17-year bonds at end of investment horizon = 7 percent

Step 1:   Compute the total coupon payments plus the interest-on-interest assuming an annual reinvestment rate of 6 percent, or 3 percent every six months. The coupon payments are $40 every six months for three years or six periods (the investment horizon). The total coupon interest plus interest-on-interest is

Coupon plus interest-on-interest =

$$\$40 \left[\frac{(1.03)^6 - 1}{.03} \right] = \$258.74$$

Step 2:   The projected sale price at the end of 3 years, assuming that the required yield-to-maturity for 17-year bonds is 7 percent, is found by determining the present value of 34 coupon payments of $40 plus the present value of the maturity value of $1,000, discounted at 3.5%. The price can be shown to be $1,098.51.

Step 3:   Adding the amount in steps 1 and 2 gives total future dollars of $1,357.25.

Step 4:   Compute the following:

$$\left(\frac{\$1,357.25}{\$828.40} \right)^{1/6} - 1$$

$$= (1.63840)^{.16667} - 1$$
$$= 1.0858 - 1$$
$$= .0858, \text{ or } 8.58\%$$

Step 5:   Doubling 8.58 percent gives a total return of 17.16 percent on a bond-equivalent basis. On an effective annual interest-rate basis, the total return is

$$(1.0858)^2 - 1$$
$$= 1.1790 - 1$$
$$= .1790$$
$$= 17.90\%$$

manager to analyze the performance of a bond based on different interest rate-scenarios for reinvestment rates and future market yields. By investigating multiple scenarios, the portfolio manager can see how sensitive the bond's performance is to each scenario. There is no need to assume that the reinvestment rate will be constant for the entire investment horizon.

For portfolio managers who want to use the market's expectations of short-term reinvestment rates and the yield on the bond at the end of the investment horizon, implied forward rates can be calculated from the yield curve. Implied forward rates are explained in Chapter 6, and are calculated based on arbitrage arguments. A total return computed using implied forward rates is called an *arbitrage-free total return*.

Scenario Analysis

Because the total return depends on the reinvestment rate and the yield at the end of the investment horizon, portfolio managers assess performance over a wide range of scenarios for these two variables. This approach is referred to as *scenario analysis*.

Illustration 13.   Suppose a portfolio manager is considering the purchase of bond A, a 20-year, 9 percent noncallable bond selling at $109.896 per $100 of par value. The yield-to-maturity for this bond is 8 percent. Assume also that the portfolio manager's investment horizon is three years and that the portfolio manager believes the reinvestment rate can vary from 3 percent to 6.5 percent and the yield at the end of the investment horizon from 5 percent to 12 percent.

The top panel of Exhibit 4–9 shows the total future dollars at the end of three years under various scenarios. The bottom panel shows the total return (based on the effective annualizing of the six-month total return). The portfolio manager knows that the maximum and minimum total return will be 16.72 percent and –1.05 percent, respectively, and the scenarios under which each will be realized. If the portfolio manager faces three-year liabilities guaranteeing, say, 6 percent, the major consideration is scenarios that will produce a three-year total return of less than 6 percent. These scenarios can be determined from Exhibit 4–9.

Illustration 14.   Suppose that the same portfolio manager owns bond B, a 14-year noncallable bond with a coupon rate of 7.25 percent and a current price of $94.553 per $100 par value. The yield-to-maturity is 7.9 percent. Exhibit 4–10 reports the total future dollars and total return over a three-year investment horizon under the same scenarios as Exhibit 4–9. A portfolio manager considering swapping from bond B to bond A would compare the relative performance of the two bonds as reported in Exhibits 4–9 and 4–10. Exhibit 4–11 shows the difference between the performance of the two bonds in basis points. This comparative analysis assumes that the two bonds are of the same investment quality and ignores the financial accounting and tax consequences associated with the disposal of bond B to acquire bond A.

Evaluating Potential Bond Swaps

Portfolio managers commonly swap an existing bond in a portfolio for another bond. Bond swaps can be categorized as pure yield pickup swaps, substitution swaps, intermarket spread swaps, or rate anticipation swaps. Total return analysis can be used to assess the potential return from a swap.

E X H I B I T   4–9

Scenario Analysis for Bond A

Bond A:	9 percent coupon, 20-year noncallable bond
Price:	$109.896
Yield to maturity:	8.00 percent
Investment horizon:	3 years

	Yield at end of horizon							
	5.00%	6.00%	7.00%	8.00%	9.00%	10.00%	11.00%	12.00%
	Horizon price							
	145.448	131.698	119.701	109.206	100.000	91.9035	84.763	78.4478
	Total future dollars							

Reinvestment rate	5.00%	6.00%	7.00%	8.00%	9.00%	10.00%	11.00%	12.00%
3.0%	173.481	159.731	147.734	137.239	128.033	119.937	112.796	106.481
3.5	173.657	159.907	147.910	137.415	128.209	120.113	112.972	106.657
4.0	173.834	160.084	148.087	137.592	128.387	120.290	113.150	106.834
4.5	174.013	160.263	148.266	137.771	128.565	120.469	113.328	107.013
5.0	174.192	160.443	148.445	137.950	128.745	120.648	113.508	107.193
5.5	174.373	160.623	148.626	138.131	128.926	120.829	113.689	107.374
6.0	174.555	160.806	148.809	138.313	129.108	121.011	113.871	107.556
6.5	174.739	160.989	148.992	138.497	129.291	121.195	114.054	107.739

	Total return (effective rate)							

Reinvestment rate	5.00%	6.00%	7.00%	8.00%	9.00%	10.00%	11.00%	12.00%
3.0%	16.44	13.28	10.37	7.69	5.22	2.96	0.87	−1.05
3.5	16.48	13.32	10.41	7.73	5.27	3.01	0.92	−0.99
4.0	16.52	13.36	10.45	7.78	5.32	3.06	0.98	−0.94
4.5	15.56	13.40	10.50	7.83	5.37	3.11	1.03	−0.88
5.0	16.60	13.44	10.54	7.87	5.42	3.16	1.08	−0.83
5.5	16.64	13.49	10.59	7.92	5.47	3.21	1.14	−0.77
6.0	16.68	13.53	10.63	7.97	5.52	3.26	1.19	−0.72
6.5	16.72	13.57	10.68	8.02	5.57	3.32	1.25	−0.66

• *Pure yield pickup swap:* Switching from one bond to another that has a higher yield is called a pure yield pickup swap. The swap may be undertaken to achieve either higher current coupon income or higher yield-to-maturity, or both. No expectation is made about changes in interest rates, yield spreads, or credit quality.

• *Rate anticipation swap:* A portfolio manager who has expectations about the future direction of interest rates will use bond swaps to position the portfolio to take advantage of the anticipated interest-rate move. These are known as rate anticipation swaps. If rates are expected to fall, for example, bonds with a greater

E X H I B I T   4–10

Scenario Analysis for Bond B

Bond B:	7.25 percent coupon, 14-year noncallable bond
Price:	$94.553
Yield to maturity:	7.90 percent
Investment horizon:	3 years

	Yield at end of horizon							
	5.00%	6.00%	7.00%	8.00%	9.00%	10.00%	11.00%	12.00%
	Horizon price							
	118.861	109.961	101.896	94.5808	87.9386	81.9009	76.4066	71.4012
	Total future dollars							

Reinvestment rate	5.00%	6.00%	7.00%	8.00%	9.00%	10.00%	11.00%	12.00%
3.0%	141.443	132.543	124.478	117.163	110.521	104.483	98.989	93.983
3.5	141.585	132.685	124.620	117.448	110.663	104.625	99.131	94.125
4.0	141.728	132.828	124.763	117.448	110.806	104.768	99.273	94.268
4.5	141.872	132.971	124.907	117.592	110.949	104.912	99.417	94.412
5.0	142.017	133.116	125.051	117.736	111.094	105.056	99.562	94.557
5.5	142.162	133.262	125.197	117.882	111.240	105.202	99.708	94.703
6.0	142.309	133.409	125.344	118.029	111.387	105.349	99.855	94.849
6.5	142.457	133.556	125.492	118.176	111.534	105.497	100.002	94.997

	Total return (effective rate)							

Reinvestment rate	5.00%	6.00%	7.00%	8.00%	9.00%	10.00%	11.00%	12.00%
3.0%	14.37	11.92	9.60	7.41	5.34	3.38	1.54	−0.20
3.5	14.41	11.96	9.64	7.45	5.38	3.43	1.59	−0.15
4.0	14.44	12.00	9.68	7.50	5.43	3.48	1.64	−0.10
4.5	14.48	12.04	9.72	7.54	5.48	3.53	1.69	−0.05
5.0	14.52	12.08	9.77	7.58	5.52	3.57	1.74	0.00
5.5	14.56	12.12	9.81	7.63	5.57	3.62	1.79	0.05
6.0	14.60	12.16	9.85	7.67	5.61	3.67	1.84	0.10
6.5	14.64	12.20	9.90	7.72	5.66	3.72	1.89	0.16

price volatility will be swapped for existing bonds in the portfolio with lower price volatility (to take advantage of the larger change in price that will result if interest rates do in fact decline). The opposite will be done if rates are expected to rise.

• *Intermarket spread swap:* These swaps are undertaken when the portfolio manager believes that the current yield spread between two bonds in the market is out of line with its historical yield spread and that the yield spread will realign by the end of the investment horizon. Yields spreads between bonds exist for the following reasons: (1) there is a difference in the credit quality of bonds (for exam-

EXHIBIT 4-11

Scenario Analysis Showing the Relative Performance of Bonds A and B

	Total Return for Bond A minus Total Return for Bond B (in basis points)							
Reinvestment rate	5.00%	6.00%	7.00%	8.00%	9.00%	10.00%	11.00%	12.00%
3.0%	207	136	77	28	−12	−43	−67	−85
3.5	207	136	77	28	−11	−42	−66	−84
4.0	207	136	77	28	−11	−42	−66	−84
4.5	207	136	77	29	−11	−42	−66	−83
5.0	207	137	78	29	−10	−41	−65	−83
5.5	208	137	78	29	−10	−41	−65	−82
6.0	208	137	78	30	−10	−41	−64	−82
6.5	208	137	78	30	−9	−40	−64	−81

ple, between Treasury bonds and double-A-rated public utility bonds of the same maturity), or (2) there are differences in the features of corporate bonds that make them more or less attractive to investors (for example, callable and noncallable bonds, and putable and nonputable bonds).

• *Substitution swap:* In a substitution swap, a portfolio manager swaps one bond for another bond that is thought to be identical in terms of coupon, maturity, price sensitivity to interest-rate changes, and credit quality but that offers a higher yield. This swap depends on a capital market imperfection. Such situations sometimes exist in the bond market because of temporary market imbalances. The risk that the portfolio manager faces is that the bond purchased may not be identical to the bond for which it is exchanged. For example, if credit quality is not the same, the bond purchased may be offering a higher yield because of higher credit risk rather than because of a market imbalance.

Comparing Municipal and Corporate Bonds

The conventional methodology for comparing the relative performance of a tax-exempt municipal bond and a taxable corporate bond is to compute the *taxable equivalent yield.* The taxable equivalent yield is the yield that must be earned on a taxable bond in order to produce the same yield as a tax-exempt municipal bond. The formula is

$$\text{Taxable equivalent yield} = \frac{\text{Tax-exempt yield}}{1 - \text{Marginal tax rate}}$$

For example, suppose an investor in the 39.6 percent marginal tax bracket is considering a 10-year municipal bond with a yield-to-maturity of 4.5 percent. The taxable equivalent yield is

$$\frac{4.5\%}{1 - .396} = 7.45\%$$

If the yield-to-maturity offered on a comparable quality corporate bond with 10 years to maturity is more than 7.45 percent, those who use this approach would recommend that the corporate bond be purchased. If, instead, a yield-to-maturity of less than 7.45 percent on a comparable corporate bond is offered, the investor should invest in the municipal bond.

What's wrong with this approach? The tax-exempt yield of the municipal bond and the taxable equivalent yield suffer from the same limitations we discussed with respect to yield-to-maturity. Consider the difference in reinvestment opportunities for a corporate and a municipal bond. For the former, coupon payments will be taxed; therefore, the amount to be reinvested is not the entire coupon payment but an amount net of taxes. In contrast, because the coupon payments are free from taxes for a municipal bond, the entire coupon can be reinvested.

The total return framework can accommodate this situation by allowing us to explicitly incorporate the reinvestment opportunities. There is another advantage to the total return framework as compared to the conventional taxable equivalent yield approach. Changes in tax rates (because the investor expects either his or her tax rate to change or the tax structure to change) can be incorporated into the total return framework.

SUMMARY

In this chapter, the pricing of bonds and the calculation of various yield measures have been described. The price of a bond is equal to the present value of the expected cash flow. For bonds with embedded options, the cash flow is difficult to estimate. The required yield used to discount the cash flow is determined by the yield offered on comparable securities.

The two most popular yield measures cited in the bond market are the yield-to-maturity and yield-to-call. Both yield measures consider the coupon interest and any capital gain (or loss) at the maturity date or call date in the case of the yield-to-call. The coupon interest and capital gain (or loss), however, are only two of the three components of potential dollar return from owning a bond until it matures or is called. The other component is the reinvestment of coupon income, commonly referred to as the interest-on-interest component. This component can be as large as 80 percent of a bond's total dollar return. The yield-to-maturity assumes that the coupon payments can be reinvested at the calculated yield-to-maturity. The yield-to-call assumes that the coupon payments can be reinvested at the calculated yield-to-call.

A better measure of the potential return from holding a bond over a predetermined investment horizon is the total return measure. This measure considers all three sources of potential dollar return and can be used to analyze bond swaps.

5

⑥ PRICE VOLATILITY CHARACTERISTICS OF FIXED INCOME SECURITIES

Frank J. Fabozzi, Ph.D., CFA, CPA
Adjunct Professor of Finance
School of Management
Yale University

Mark Pitts, Ph.D.
Principal
White Oak Capital Management Corp.

Ravi E. Dattatreya, Ph.D.
Senior Vice President
Sumitomo Bank Capital Markets, Inc.

To effectively employ fixed income portfolio strategies, it is necessary to understand the price volatility and convexity of bonds.[1] The purpose of this chapter is to explain and illustrate these concepts. First, we explain the characteristics of a bond that affect its price volatility. Second, we describe several measures of bond price volatility: price value of a basis point, yield value of a price change, and duration. We conclude this chapter with a discussion of the limitations of the duration and convexity measures. In later chapters, these measures are modified to overcome the limitations described in this chapter.

PRICE/YIELD RELATIONSHIP FOR OPTION-FREE BONDS

A fundamental property of an option-free bond (that is, a bond that does not have an embedded option) is that the price of a bond changes inversely to the change in the yield of the bond. This property follows from the fact that the price of an

---

1. For convenience, this discussion focuses on bonds. However, in most cases the discussion applies to fixed income securities in general.

E X H I B I T   5–1

Price/Yield Relationship for Four Hypothetical Bonds

Yield	6%/5-Year	6%/20-Year	9%/5-Year	9%/20-Year
4.00%	108.9826	127.3555	122.4565	168.3887
5.00	104.3760	112.5514	117.5041	150.2056
5.50	102.1600	106.0195	115.1201	142.1367
5.90	100.4276	101.1651	113.2556	136.1193
5.99	100.0427	100.1157	112.8412	134.8159
6.00	100.0000	100.0000	112.7953	134.6722
6.01	99.9574	99.8845	112.7494	134.5287
6.10	99.5746	98.8535	112.3373	133.2472
6.50	97.8944	94.4479	110.5280	127.7605
7.00	95.8417	89.3225	108.3166	121.3551
8.00	91.8891	80.2072	104.0554	109.8964

option-free bond is equal to the present value of its expected cash flows. An increase (decrease) in the yield decreases (increases) the present value of its scheduled cash flows, and, therefore, the bond's price. Exhibit 5–1 illustrates this property for the following four bonds: (1) a 9 percent coupon bond with five years to maturity, (2) a 9 percent coupon bond with 20 years to maturity, (3) a 6 percent coupon bond with five years to maturity, and (4) a 6 percent coupon bond with 20 years to maturity.

The graph of the price/yield relationship for any option-free bond exhibits the shape shown in Exhibit 5–2. Notice that, as the yield rises, the price of the option-free bond declines. However, the relationship is not linear. The shape of the price/yield relationship for any option-free bond is *convex,* meaning that it is bowed toward the origin. As we shall see, convexity implies that prices rise at an increasing rate as yields fall and that prices decline at a decreasing rate as yields rise. Obviously, convexity is a positive attribute of a bond.

Keep in mind that a given price/yield relationship may hold only at a given point in the life of the bond. As a bond moves toward maturity, two factors influence the price of any option-free bond. First, the bond's price changes as the yield changes, as we previously discussed. Second, for discount and premium bonds, the bond's price changes even if yields remain the same. In particular, with yields held constant, the price of a discount bond increases as it moves toward maturity, reaching par value at the maturity date; for a premium bond, the bond's price decreases as it approaches maturity, finally declining to par value at the maturity date.

BOND PRICE VOLATILITY

Although the prices of all option-free bonds move in the opposite direction of the change in yields, neither dollar price changes nor percentage price changes are

E X H I B I T 5–2

Graph of Price/Yield Relationship for an Option-Free Bond

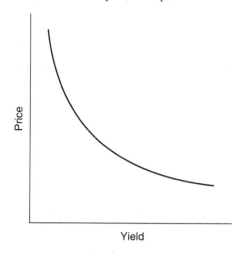

the same for all bonds. For our four hypothetical bonds, this can be seen in Exhibit 5–3. The top half of the exhibit shows the dollar price change and the bottom half shows the percentage price change for various changes in the yield, assuming that the initial yield for all four bonds is 6 percent. Note from Exhibit 5–3 that for a given bond, neither the absolute dollar price changes nor the absolute percentage price changes are the same for an equal increase and decrease in the yield, except for very small changes in the yield. Even for a small change in yield, the absolute dollar price change is less symmetric than the percentage price change. In general, the dollar price and percentage price increases that occur when the *upside* yield declines are greater than the dollar price and percentage price decreases that *downside* occur when the yield increases.

The fact that neither the absolute dollar nor the percentage price changes are equal for all bonds and the asymmetry in the absolute and percentage price changes for equal but opposite changes in yield are explained by the bond characteristics that determine the shape of the price/yield curve in Exhibit 5–2. The remainder of this section will explain the characteristics that account for the differences in absolute dollar and percentage price changes across bonds. Later in this chapter, we'll provide an explanation for the asymmetry in the absolute and percentage price changes. As the following sections show, two characteristics of an option-free bond are the primary determinants of its price volatility: coupon and term-to-maturity.[2]

2. The time to the first coupon payment as well as the frequency of payments (monthly, semiannual, or annual) also have a small effect.

EXHIBIT 5–3

Instantaneous Dollar and Percentage Price Changes for Four Hypothetical
Bonds (Initial yield for all four bonds is 6 percent)

	Dollar Price Change Per $100 Par			
New Yield	6%/5-Year	6%/20-Year	9%/5-Year	9%/20-Year
4.00%	8.9826	27.3555	9.6612	33.7165
5.00	4.3760	12.5514	4.7088	15.5334
5.50	2.1600	6.0195	2.3248	7.4645
5.90	0.4276	1.1651	0.4603	1.4471
5.99	0.0427	0.1157	0.0459	0.1437
6.01	−0.0426	−0.1155	−0.0459	−0.1435
6.10	−0.4254	−1.1465	−0.4580	−1.4250
6.50	−2.1056	−5.5521	−2.2673	−6.9116
7.00	−4.1583	−10.6775	−4.4787	−13.3171
8.00	−8.1109	−19.7928	−8.7399	−24.7758
	Percentage Price Change			
4.00%	8.98%	27.36%	8.57%	25.04%
5.00	4.38	12.55	4.17	11.53
5.50	2.16	6.02	2.06	5.54
5.90	0.43	1.17	0.41	1.07
5.99	0.04	0.12	0.04	0.11
6.01	−0.04	−0.12	−0.04	−0.11
6.10	−0.43	−1.15	−0.41	−1.06
6.50	−2.11	−5.55	−2.01	−5.13
7.00	−4.16	−10.68	−3.97	−9.89
8.00	−8.11	−19.79	−7.75	−18.40

Volatility in Terms of Percentage Price Change

First, let's look at bond price volatility in terms of percentage price change for a
change in yields.

For a given term-to-maturity and initial market yield, the percentage price
volatility of a bond is greater the lower the coupon rate. This property can be seen
by comparing the 9 percent and 6 percent coupon bonds with the same maturity
(see the bottom half of Exhibit 5–3). For example, if the initial market yield for
the two 20-year bonds is 6 percent and the yield rises to 8 percent (that is, a 200-
basis-point increase), the 9 percent coupon bond will fall in price from 134.6722
to 109.8964, a decline of 18.4 percent. However, the 6 percent 20-year bond will
fall by 19.8 percent, from 100.00 to 80.2072.

The second characteristic of a bond that affects its price volatility is its term-to-maturity. For a given coupon rate and initial yield, the longer the term-to-maturity, the greater the price volatility in terms of percentage price change.[3] This can be seen in the bottom half of Exhibit 5–3 by comparing the five-year bonds to the 20-year bonds with the same coupon. For example, if the yield increases 200 basis points from 6 percent to 8 percent, the 6 percent 20-year bond's price will fall by 19.8 percent (100 to 80.2072), whereas the 6 percent five-year bond will fall by only 8.11 percent (100 to 91.8891).

Volatility in Terms of Dollar Price Change

Do the same properties hold if volatility is measured in terms of dollar price change rather than percentage price change? The top half of Exhibit 5–3 demonstrates that holding all other factors constant, the dollar price change is greater the longer the term-to-maturity. However, the first characteristic concerning the effect of the coupon rate is not true when volatility is measured in terms of dollar price change instead of percentage price change. For a given maturity and initial market yield, the lower the coupon rate, the smaller the dollar price change.

The Effects of Yield-to-Maturity

We cannot ignore the fact that due to credit considerations, different bonds trade at different yields, even if they have the same coupon and maturity. How, then, does the yield-to-maturity affect a bond's price volatility? As it turns out, an increase in yield decreases the percentage price change and the absolute dollar price change. To see this, we can compare a 6 percent 20-year bond initially selling at a yield of 6 percent with a 6 percent 20-year bond initially selling at a yield of 10 percent. The former is initially at a price of 100, and the latter carries a price of 65.68. If the yields on both bonds increase by 100 basis points, the first bond trades down by 10.68 points (10.68 percent). After the assumed increase in yield, the second bond will trade at a price of 59.88, for a price decline of only 5.80 (or 8.83 percent). Thus, we see that the bond that trades at lower yields is more volatile in both percentage price changes and absolute price changes, as long as the other bond characteristics are the same.

A possibly more relevant comparison of bond price volatility is that of comparing bonds that trade at different yields but starting them all on the same footing (e.g., by comparing only bonds trading at par). For par bonds trading at different yields but with the same maturity, the lower-yielding bonds still exhibit both greater percentage price changes and absolute-price changes for a given change in yield.

---

3. There are exceptions for certain deep-discount, long-term coupon bonds.

MEASURES OF BOND PRICE VOLATILITY

Money managers, arbitrageurs, and traders need to have a way to measure a
bond's price volatility to implement hedging and trading strategies. Three measures that are commonly employed are price value of a basis point, yield value of
a price change, and duration.

Price Value of a Basis Point

The *price value of a basis point* (PVBP), also referred to as the *dollar value of an
01* (DV01), is the change in the price of the bond if the yield changes by one basis
point. Typically, the price value of a basis point is expressed as the absolute value
of the change in price; consequently, the greater the price value of a basis point,
the greater the dollar price volatility. As we saw earlier in this chapter, price
changes are almost symmetric for small changes in yield. Thus, it does not make a
great deal of difference whether we increase or decrease yields to calculate the
price value of a basis point. In practice, an average of the change resulting from
both an up and a down movement in yield is used.

   We will illustrate the calculation of the price value of a basis point using the
four bonds introduced in Exhibit 5–1. Exhibit 5–4 shows the initial price, the
price after decreasing the yield by one basis point (6 percent to 5.99 percent), and
the price after increasing the yield by one basis point (from 6 percent to 6.01 percent) for each bond. The dollar price change is then calculated and averaged to
get the price value of a basis point.

   Some investors calculate the price value of more than one basis point.[4] The
procedure for calculating the price value of any number of basis points is the
same. For example, the price value of 10 basis points is found by computing the
difference between the initial price and the price if the yield changed by 10 basis
points. This is shown in Exhibit 5–5 for our four hypothetical bonds. The relationship is still nearly symmetric for a 10-basis-point change in yield up or down, and
the price value of 10 basis points is approximately equal to 10 times the price
value of one basis point. However, for larger changes in yield, there will be a difference between the price value of a basis point if the yield is increased or decreased, and the price change for a large number of basis points can no longer be
approximated by the multiple times the price value of one basis point. Most investors who derive the price value of a basis point by calculating price changes
for large movements in yields (such as 100 basis points), will average the PVBPs
for an up move and a down move to get the final PVBP.

Yield Value of a Price Change

Another measure of the price volatility of a bond used by some investors is the
change in the yield for a specified price change. This is done by first calculating

---

4. For example, in the municipal bond market it is common to calculate the price value of five basis
   points.

EXHIBIT 5–4

Calculation of the Price Value of a Basis Point for Four Hypothetical Bonds

	Price			
Yield	6%/5-Year	6%/20-Year	9%/5-Year	9%/20-Year
6.00%	100.0000	100.0000	112.7953	134.6722
5.99	100.0427	100.1157	112.8412	134.8159
6.01	99.9574	99.8845	112.7494	134.5287
	Absolute Value of Dollar Price Change *for a Basis-Point Change in Yield*			
5.99%	0.0427	0.1157	0.0459	0.1437
6.01	0.0426	0.1155	0.0459	0.1435

EXHIBIT 5–5

Calculation of the Price Value of 10 Basis Points for Four Hypothetical Bonds

	Price			
Yield	6%/5-Year	6%/20-Year	9%/5-Year	9%/20-Year
6.00%	100.0000	100.0000	112.7953	134.6722
5.90	100.4276	101.1651	113.2556	136.1193
6.10	99.5746	98.8535	112.3373	133.2472
	Absolute Value of Dollar Price Change *for a 10-Basis-Point Change in Yield*			
5.90%	0.4276	1.1651	0.4603	1.4471
6.10	0.4254	1.1465	0.4580	1.4250
	Price Value of 10 Basis Points			
Average	0.4265	1.1558	0.4592	1.4361

the bond's yield-to-maturity, and then recalculating the yield if the bond's price is increased by X dollars. The difference between the initial yield and the new yield is the yield value of an X-dollar price change. The lower the yield value of an X-dollar price change, the greater the dollar price volatility. The reason for this is that it would take a smaller change in yield to produce a price change of X dollars.

As Treasury notes and bonds are quoted in $^1/_{32}$ of a percentage point of par, investors in these markets usually let X equal $^1/_{32}$ of a percentage point of par. The resulting calculation gives the yield value of a 32nd. Because corporate and municipal bonds are traded in $^1/_8$ increments of a percentage point of par, investors in this market are more concerned with the yield value of an 8th.

The calculation of the yield value of a 32nd and an 8th for the two hypothetical 6 percent coupon bonds is shown in Exhibit 5–6. In practice, the absolute changes in yield for an increase and decrease in price are calculated and then averaged to obtain the yield value of a price change.

E X H I B I T   5–6

Calculation of the Yield Value of a 32nd and the Yield Value of an 8th for the Two 6 Percent Coupon Bonds

Price	Price for a 32nd Change		Price for an 8th Change	
	6%/5-Year	6%/20-Year	6%/5-Year	6%/20-Year
Initial	100.0000	100.0000	100.0000	100.0000
Decrease	99.8750	99.8750	99.8750	99.8750
Increase	100.1250	100.1250	100.1250	100.1250

	New Yield if Price Changes by:			
	A 32nd		An 8th	
New Price	6%/5-Year	6%/20-Year	6%/5-Year	6%/20-Year
Decrease	6.007332%	6.002705%	6.029343%	6.010820%
Increase	5.992671	5.997297	5.970701	5.989193

	Absolute Value of Change in Yield from 6 Percent for:			
	A 32nd		An 8th	
Price	6%/5-Year	6%/20-Year	6%/5-Year	6%/20-Year
Decrease	0.007332%	0.002705%	0.029343%	0.010820%
Increase	0.007329	0.002703	0.029299	0.010807

	Yield Value of a 32nd		Yield Value of an 8th	
Average	0.007331%	0.002704%	0.029321%	0.010814%

Duration

Another measure of the price volatility of a bond is duration. In 1983, Frederick Macaulay defined duration as a weighted average term-to-maturity of a security's cash flows.[5] The weights are the present values of each cash flow as a percentage of the present value of all cash flows (i.e., the weights are the present value of each cash flow as a percentage of the bond's full price). As we shall see, the greater the duration of a bond, the greater its percentage price volatility and it is only in this context that duration is relevant.

Mathematically, Macaulay duration *on a coupon date* is computed as follows:

Macaulay duration (in years) =

$$\sum_{i=1}^{n} \frac{t \times PVCF_t}{k \times PVTCF}$$

or

$$\frac{1 \times PVCF_1 + 2 \times PVCF_2 + 3 \times PVCF_3 + \cdots + n \times PVCF_n}{k \times PVTCF}$$

where

k = Number of periods (payments) per year (e.g., $k = 2$ for semiannual payment bonds and $k = 12$ for monthly payment bonds)

n = Number of periods until maturity (years to maturity $\times k$)

t = Period in which the cash flow is expected to be received ($t = 1, \ldots, n$)

$PVCF_t$ = Present value of the cash flow in period t discounted at the yield-to-maturity

$PVTCF$ = Total present value of the cash flow of the bond where the present value is determined using the yield-to-maturity. This is simply the price of the bond on a coupon payment date.

For an option-free bond on a coupon date with semiannual payments, the cash flow for periods 1 through $n - 1$ is one-half the annual coupon interest. The cash flow in period n is the semiannual coupon interest plus the maturity value. The formula can be easily extended to fractional periods when a bond is not on its coupon date.

For a bond selling on its coupon date, the total present value of the cash flow is simply the quoted price (or flat price) of the bond. For a bond not selling on a coupon date, the total present value of the cash flows is the bond's quoted

---

5. Frederick Macaulay, *Some Theoretical Problems Suggested by the Movement of Interest Rates, Bond Yields, and Stock Prices in the U.S. Since 1856* (New York: National Bureau of Economic Research, 1938).

price plus accrued interest. The presence of k in the denominator adjusts for the frequency of payments per year.

Exhibits 5–7 and 5–8 show the details involved in calculating the Macaulay duration for the two 5-year bonds selling to yield 6 percent. The Macaulay duration for the four bonds is given below, assuming a yield-to-maturity of 6 percent for each bond:

Bond	Macaulay Duration
6 percent 5-year	4.39
6 percent 20-year	11.90
9 percent 5-year	4.19
9 percent 20-year	10.98

As shown in Exhibits 5–7 and 5–8, the Macaulay duration of a coupon bond is less than its maturity. For a zero-coupon bond, the Macaulay duration is equal to its maturity. With other factors held constant, the lower the coupon rate, the greater the duration of the bond.

E X H I B I T 5–7

Calculation of Duration and Convexity for a 6 Percent Five-Year Bond Selling to Yield 6 Percent

Period	Cash Flow	PV	PV $\times$ t	PV $\times$ t $\times$ (t + 1)
1	3.00	2.9126	2.9126	5.8252
2	3.00	2.8278	5.6556	16.9667
3	3.00	2.7454	8.2363	32.9451
4	3.00	2.6655	10.6618	53.3092
5	3.00	2.5878	12.9391	77.6348
6	3.00	2.5125	15.0747	105.5230
7	3.00	2.4393	17.0749	136.5994
8	3.00	2.3682	18.9458	170.5124
9	3.00	2.2993	20.6933	206.9325
10	103.00	76.6417	766.4167	8,430.5841
	Total	100.0000	878.6109	9,236.8324

$$\text{Macaulay duration} = \frac{878.6109}{2 \times 100} = 4.39$$

$$\text{Modified duration} = \frac{4.39}{(1.03)} = 4.27$$

$$\text{Convexity} = \frac{9,236.8324}{(1.03)^2 \times 2^2 \times 100} = 21.767$$

Notice the consistency between the properties of percentage price volatility discussed earlier and the properties of duration. We showed that with all other factors constant, the longer the maturity, the greater the percentage price volatility. With all other factors constant, the greater the maturity, the greater the duration.[6] We also showed that the lower the coupon rate, all other factors constant, the greater will be the percentage price volatility. As we just noted, the lower the coupon rate, the greater will be the duration. Thus, duration is telling us something about bond price volatility.

The relationship between Macaulay duration and bond price volatility is[7]

Percentage change in price =

$$-\frac{1}{1+(\text{Yield}/k)} \times \text{Macaulay duration} \times \text{Yield change} \times 100$$

E X H I B I T   5–8

Calculation of Duration and Convexity for a 9 Percent Five-Year Bond Selling to Yield 6 Percent

Period	Cash Flow	PV	PV × t	PV × t × (t + 1)
1	4.50	4.3689	4.3689	8.7379
2	4.50	4.2417	8.4834	25.4501
3	4.50	4.1181	12.3544	49.4176
4	4.50	3.9982	15.9928	79.9638
5	4.50	3.8817	19.4087	116.4522
6	4.50	3.7687	22.6121	158.2845
7	4.50	3.6589	25.6124	204.8991
8	4.50	2.5523	28.4187	255.7686
9	4.50	3.4489	31.0399	310.3988
10	104.50	77.7578	777.5781	8,553.3596
	Total	112.7953	945.8694	9,762.7321

$$\text{Macaulay duration} = \frac{945.8694}{2 \times 112.7953} = 4.19$$

$$\text{Modified duration} = \frac{4.19}{(1.03)} = 4.07$$

$$\text{Convexity} = \frac{9,762.7321}{(1.03)^2 \times 2^2 \times 112.7953} = 20.396$$

6. This property does not necessarily hold for long-maturity, deep-discount coupon bonds.
7. Mathematically, the relationship is obtained by taking the first derivative of the price function and then dividing it by price. See Frank J. Fabozzi, *Fixed Income Mathematics* (Chicago: Probus Publishing, 1988), Appendix A.

The relationship is exact for infinitesimal changes in yields, but is only approximate for larger yield changes.

Generally, the first two expressions on the right-hand side in this equation are combined into one term and called *modified duration;* that is,

$$\text{Modified duration } = \frac{\text{Macaulay duration}}{1 + (\text{Yield} / k)}$$

The relationship can then be expressed as follows:

$$\text{Percentage price change} = -\text{Modified duration} \times \text{Yield change} \times 100$$

Consider the 9 percent 20-year bond selling at 134.6722 to yield 9 percent. The Macaulay duration for this bond is 10.98 years. Modified duration is 10.66, as shown here:

$$\text{Modified duration } = \frac{10.98}{1 + (.06 / 2)} = 10.66$$

If yields increase instantaneously from 6.00 percent to 6.10 percent, a yield change in decimal form of + 0.0010, the formula above indicates that the percentage price change is as follows:

$$-10.66 \times (+.0010) \times 100 = -1.07\%$$

Notice from the bottom half of Exhibit 5–3 that the actual percentage price change is −1.06 percent. Similarly, if yields decrease instantaneously from 6.00 percent to 5.90 percent (a 10-basis-point decrease), the formula indicates that the percentage change in price is + 1.07 percent. From the bottom half of Exhibit 5–3, the actual percentage price change is + 1.07 percent. This example illustrates that for small changes in yield, duration does an excellent job of approximating the percentage price change.

Instead of a small change in yield, let's assume that yields increase by 200 basis points, from 6 percent to 8 percent (a yield change of + 0.02). The percentage change in price estimated using duration would be as follows:

$$-10.66 \times (+0.02) \times 100 = -21.32\%$$

How good is this approximation? As can be seen from the bottom half of Exhibit 5–3, the actual percentage change in price is only −18.40 percent. Moreover, if the yield decreased by 200 basis points from 6 percent to 4 percent, the approximate percentage price change based on duration would be + 21.32 percent, compared to an actual percentage price change of + 25.04 percent. Thus, not only is the approximation inaccurate, but we can see that duration estimates a symmetric percentage change in price. However, as we pointed out earlier in this chapter, this is not a property of the price/yield relationship for option-free bonds.

Exhibit 5–9 shows the approximate percentage change in price for various changes in yield for all four bonds estimated using duration.

EXHIBIT 5–9

Estimated Percentage Price Change Based on Duration (Initial Yield = 6 Percent)

New Yield	6%/5-Year	6%/20-Year	9%/5-Year	9%/20-Year
4.00%	8.54%	23.12%	8.14%	21.32%
5.00	4.27	11.56	4.07	10.66
5.50	2.14	5.78	2.04	5.33
5.90	0.43	1.16	0.41	1.07
5.99	0.04	0.12	0.04	0.11
6.01	−0.04	−0.12	−0.04	−0.11
6.10	−0.43	−1.16	−0.41	−1.07
6.50	−2.14	−5.78	−2.04	−5.33
7.00	−4.27	−11.56	−4.07	−10.66
8.00	−8.54	−23.12	−8.14	−21.32

Notice that for a 100-basis-point change in yield, the formula tells us that the percentage price change will be equal to the bond's modified duration. *Consequently, a useful working definition of modified duration is that it is the approximate percentage change in price for a 100-basis-point change in yield.* Thus, a bond with a modified duration of five will change by approximately 5 percent for a 100-basis-point change in yield. It is only an approximation because, as explained earlier, for large yield changes, modified duration does not provide a close estimate of the percentage price change.

Dollar Duration

Modified duration is related to percentage price change. However, for two bonds with the same modified duration, the dollar price change will not be the same. For example, consider two bonds, W and V. Suppose both bonds have a modified duration of five, but that W is trading at par while V is trading at 90. A 100-basis-point change for both bonds will change the price by approximately 5 percent. This means a dollar price change of 5 (5 percent times 100) for W and a dollar price change of 4.5 (5 percent times 90) for V.

Many of the strategies discussed in this book involve adjusting positions for dollar price changes. The dollar price volatility of a bond can be measured by multiplying modified duration by the full dollar price and the number of basis points (in decimal form), as follows:

Dollar price volatility =

Modified duration × Dollar price × Yield change (in decimals)

For a one-basis-point change in yield, the dollar price volatility will give the same result as the price value of a basis point.

When the dollar price volatility is calculated for a 100-basis-point change in yield, the resulting value is called *dollar duration*. Because 100 basis points is expressed as .01, the following equation holds:

$$\text{Dollar duration} = \text{Modified duration} \times \text{Dollar price} \times .01$$

So, for bonds W and V, the dollar duration is as follows:

$$\text{For bond W: Dollar duration} = 5 \times 100 \times .01 = 5.0$$
$$\text{For bond V: Dollar duration} = 5 \times 90 \times .01 = 4.5$$

Relationship between Price Volatility Measures

We have explained the relationship between the various bond price volatility measures. Exhibit 5–10 more formally summarizes the various measures of bond price volatility and their relationships to one another.

CONVEXITY

We are now ready to tie together the price/yield relationship and several of the properties of bond price volatility discussed in this chapter. Recall the shape of the price/yield relationship, as shown in Exhibit 5–2. We referred to that shape as convex.

In Exhibit 5–11, a tangent line is drawn to the price/yield relationship at yield y^*. The tangent shows the rate of change of price with respect to a change in interest rates at that point (yield level). The slope of the tangent line is closely related to the price value of a basis point. Consequently, for a given starting price, the tangent (which tells us the rate of absolute price changes) is closely related to the duration of the bond (which tells us about the rate of percentage price changes). The steeper the tangent line, the greater the duration; the flatter the tangent line, the lower the duration. Thus, for a given starting price, the tangent line and the duration can be used interchangeably and can be thought of as the same method of estimating the rate of price changes.

Notice what happens to duration (steepness of the tangent line) as yield changes: As yield increases (decreases), duration decreases (increases). This property holds for all option-free bonds.

If we draw a vertical line from any yield, as in Exhibit 5–12, the distance between the horizontal axis and the tangent line represents the price approximated by using duration starting with the initial yield y^*. The approximation will always understate the actual price. This agrees with what we demonstrated earlier about the relationship between duration (and the tangent line) and the approximate price change. When yields decrease, the estimated price change will be less than the actual price change. On the other hand, when yields increase, the estimated price change will be greater than the actual price change, resulting in an overestimate for the actual price change and an underestimate of the actual price.

EXHIBIT 5–10

Measures of Bond Price Volatility and Their Relationships to One Another

Notation:

D = Macaulay duration

D^* = modified duration

PVBP = price value of a basis point

YV32 = yield value of a 32nd

y = yield-to-maturity in decimal form

Y = yield-to-maturity in percentage terms ($Y = 100 \times y$)

P = price of bond

k = number of coupons per year

Relationships:

$D^* = \dfrac{D}{(1+y/k)}$	By definition
$\dfrac{\Delta P/P}{\Delta y} \approx D^*$	To a close approximation for small Δy
$\Delta P/\Delta Y \approx$ slope of price/yield curve	To a close approximation for small ΔY
PVBP $\approx \Delta P/(\Delta Y \times 100)$	To a close approximation for small ΔY
PVBP $\approx \dfrac{D^* \times P}{10,000}$	To a close approximation (also called dollar duration)
YV32 $\approx \dfrac{1}{3,200 \times \text{PVBP}}$	To a close approximation (when the yield is in percentage terms)
PVBP $\approx \dfrac{1}{3,200 \times \text{YV32}}$	To a close approximation (when the yield is in percentage terms)

For bonds at or near par:

PVBP $\approx D^*/100$	To a close approximation
$D^* \approx \Delta P/\Delta Y$	To a close approximation for small Δy

For small changes in yield, the tangent line, and thus duration, do a good job in estimating the actual price. However, the further away from the initial yield y^*, the worse the approximation. It should be apparent that the accuracy of the approximation depends on the convexity of the price/yield relationship for the bond.

The convexity of an option-free bond on a coupon date can be calculated using the following formula:

$$\text{Convexity (in years)} = \frac{1}{[1+(y/k)]^2} \sum_{i=1}^{n} \frac{t \times (t+1)\text{PVCF}_t}{k^2 \times \text{PVTCF}}$$

E X H I B I T   5–11

Price/Yield Relationship with Tangent Line

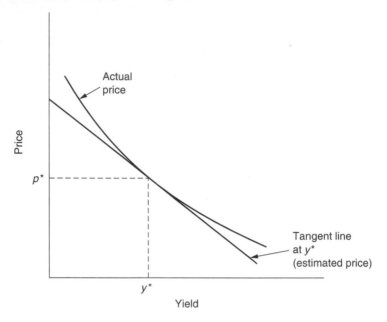

E X H I B I T   5–12

Price/Yield Showing Estimation Error

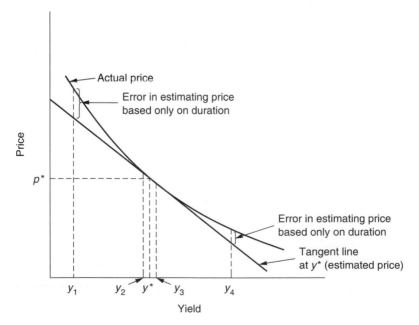

or

$$\frac{1\times 2 \times \text{PVCF}_1 + 2 \times 3 \times \text{PVCF}_2 + \cdots + n \times (n+1) \times \text{PVCF}_n}{[1+(\text{Yield}/2)]^2 \times k^2 \times \text{PVTCF}}$$

where all the terms are the same as in the Macaulay duration formula.

Exhibits 5–7 and 5–8 show the detailed calculations for the convexity of the two five-year bonds selling to yield 6 percent. The convexity values for our four hypothetical bonds are summarized below:

Bond	Convexity
6 percent 5-year	21.767
6 percent 20-year	186.827
9 percent 5-year	20.396
9 percent 20-year	164.106

Duration provides a first approximation to the percentage price change. Convexity provides a second approximation, based on the following relationship:[8]

Approximate percentage price change due to convexity =
$$0.5 \times \text{Convexity} \times (\text{Yield change})^2 \times 100$$

Here, the formula gives only an approximation of the part of the price change that is due solely to the curvature of the price/yield relationship. Some market participants and dealers refer to this approximation as the *percentage price change not explained by duration.*

The term *convexity* as used in the industry is confusing. On one hand, convexity refers to the shape (i.e., degree of curvature) of the price/yield relationship. On the other hand, the convexity measure as given by the previous formula is related to the second approximation of percentage price change that must be added to the approximation obtained by using duration.

In mathematical terms, any function can be estimated by a series of derivatives.[9] More specifically, the first approximation is obtained from the first derivative. To improve the approximation, the second derivative is used. A further improvement is obtained using the third derivative, and so on. We have used this mathematical principle. The price of a bond is a function of yield. The first approximation of this mathematical function is given by duration, which is related to the first derivative. The second approximation that is added to the first approximation is related to the convexity measure, which is related to the second derivative. The reason why additional derivatives are not used in the industry is because for most bonds and yield movements, two derivatives are sufficient to approximate the percentage price change.

---

8. Mathematically, this is derived from the second term of the Taylor series for the price function. See Appendix A in Fabozzi, *Fixed Income Mathematics.*

9. This is called a Taylor series.

For example, for the 9 percent coupon bond maturing in 20 years, the percentage price change due solely to convexity if the yield increases from 6 percent to 8 percent (+ 0.02 yield change) is approximated as follows:

$$0.5 \times 164.106 \times (0.02)^2 \times 100 = 3.28\%$$

If the yield decreases from 6 percent to 4 percent (–0.02 yield change), the approximate percentage price change due solely to convexity would also be 3.28 percent.

The approximate total percentage price change based on both duration and convexity is found by simply adding the two estimates. That is,

Estimated percentage price change =

$$- \text{Modified duration} \times \text{Yield change} \times 100$$
$$+ 0.5 \times \text{Convexity} \times (\text{Yield change})^2 \times 100$$

For example, if yields change from 6 percent to 8 percent, the estimated percentage price change would be

$$\text{Duration estimate} = -21.32\%$$
$$\text{Convexity adjustment} = +\ 3.28\%$$
$$\text{Total} = -18.04\%$$

Recall that the actual percentage price change is –18.40 percent. For a decrease of 200 basis points, from 6 percent to 8 percent, the approximate percentage price change would be as follows:

$$\text{Duration estimate} = +21.32\%$$
$$\text{Convexity adjustment} = +\ 3.28\%$$
$$\text{Total} = +24.60\%$$

The actual percentage price change is + 25.04 percent. Consequently, for large yield movements, a better approximation for bond price movement is obtained using both duration and convexity.

What does convexity measure? It measures the rate of change of duration as yields change. For all option-free bonds, duration increases as yields decline. This is a positive attribute of an option-free bond because as yields decline, price appreciation accelerates. When yields increase, the duration for all option-free bonds decreases. Once again, this is a positive attribute because as yields increase, this feature decelerates the price depreciation. This is the reason why the absolute and percentage price change is greater when yields decline than when they increase by the same number of basis points. Thus, an option-free bond is said to have *positive convexity*.

Although we have focused on the percentage price change due to convexity, a dollar price change can also be calculated. The practice is to calculate the *dollar convexity,* which is the dollar price change due to convexity (or not explained by duration) for a 100-basis-point change in yield. Dollar convexity is found as follows:

$$0.5 \times \text{Convexity} \times \text{Dollar price} \times (\text{Yield change})^2$$

LIMITATIONS OF DURATION

There are several limitations that portfolio managers should recognize when using duration. These limitations are discussed below.

Estimates Are Good Only for Small Yield Changes

Although we have not delved into the underlying mathematical theory behind the derivation of duration,we can see from the above discussion one clear limitation: It is a good approximation only for a small change in yields. Thus, two bonds with the same duration may perform differently for large changes in yields.

This difference can be seen in Exhibit 5–13. The two bonds in the exhibit, bonds G and H, are trading at the same price and yield. They also have the same duration. However, bond H has greater convexity than bond G. Thus, bond H has better price performance whether yields rise or fall from the yield shown in the exhibit. Obviously, the situation depicted in the exhibit cannot last in an actual market because investors would bid up the price (or, equivalently, drive down the yield) of bond H relative to bond G. Exhibit 5–13 illustrates why some analysts err in using duration as the sole measure of interest-rate risk when comparing yield spreads. Analysts can offset this limitation by recognizing that they must consider not only the duration measure, but also the convexity measure.

E X H I B I T   5–13

Comparison of Two Bonds with Different Convexities but the Same Duration

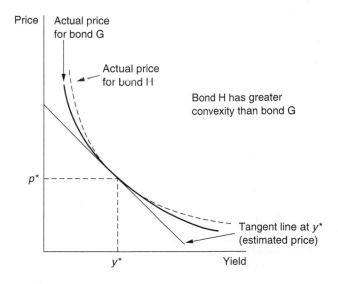

Portfolio Duration and Nonparallel Yield-Curve Shifts

A second limitation of duration arises when we calculate the duration of a portfolio. The duration of a portfolio is calculated as the weighted average duration of the portfolio. But how do we interpret the portfolio duration? It is the approximate percentage change in the portfolio's value when yield changes. But what yield changes? If the portfolio consists of bonds across the maturity spectrum, which yield is assumed to change? It is assumed that the yields for all maturities change by the same number of basis points. This assumption is commonly referred to as the "parallel yield-curve shift assumption." The problem is that yield curves typically do not shift in a parallel fashion. When they do not, two portfolios with the same duration can perform quite differently depending on the composition of the portfolio and how the yield curve shifts.

To illustrate this point, consider the three bonds shown in Exhibit 5–14 and the following two portfolios. Portfolio I consists of only bond C, a 10-year bond, and shall be referred to as the *bullet portfolio.* Portfolio II consists of 50.2 percent of bond A and 49.8 percent of bond B, and this portfolio shall be referred to as the *barbell portfolio.* The dollar duration of the bullet portfolio is 6.43409. Recall that dollar duration is the dollar price sensitivity for a 100-basis-point change in yield. As shown in Exhibit 15–14, the dollar duration of the barbell—which is just the weighted average of the dollar duration of the two bonds—is the same as the bullet portfolio. In fact, the barbell portfolio was designed to produce this result. However, the dollar convexity of the bullet portfolio is less than that of the barbell portfolio.

The yield for the two portfolios is not the same. The yield for the bullet is simply the yield-to-maturity of bond C, 9.25 percent. The traditional yield calculation for the barbell portfolio, which is found by taking a weighted average of the yield-to-maturity of the two bonds included in the portfolio, is 8.998 percent. This would suggest that the yield of the bullet portfolio is 25.2 basis points greater than that of the barbell portfolio. Alternatively, an internal rate of return or cash flow yield can be approximated for the barbell portfolio by calculating the dollar-duration market-weighted yield of the portfolio. As shown in Exhibit 5–14, the cash flow yield of the barbell portfolio is 9.187 percent, suggesting that the yield of the bullet portfolio is 6.3 basis points greater than that of the barbell portfolio. Thus, both portfolios have the same dollar duration but, using either yield measure, the yield of the bullet portfolio is greater than the yield of the barbell portfolio. However, the dollar convexity of the barbell portfolio is greater than that of the bullet portfolio. The difference in the two yields is sometimes referred to as the cost of convexity.

The second column of Exhibit 5–15 shows the difference in the total return over a six-month investment horizon for the two portfolios, assuming that the yield curve shifts in a parallel fashion.[10] By parallel, we mean that the yields for

---

10. Note that no assumption is needed for the reinvestment rate because the three bonds shown in Exhibit 5–14 are assumed to be trading right after a coupon payment has been made, and therefore there is no accrued interest.

EXHIBIT 5–14

Bullet-Barbell Analysis

Bond	Coupon	Maturity (Years)	Price Plus Accrued	Yield	Dollar Duration[a]	Dollar Convexity[a]
A	8.50%	5	100	8.50%	4.00544	19.8164
B	9.50	20	100	9.50	8.88151	124.1702
C	9.25	10	100	9.25	6.43409	55.4506

Bullet portfolio: Bond C

Barbell portfolio: Bonds A and B

Composition of barbell: 50.2 percent of Bond A; 49.8 percent of Bond B

$$\text{Dollar duration of barbell} = .502 \times 4.0054 + .498 \times 8.88151$$
$$= 6.434$$
$$\text{Average yield of barbell} = .502 \times 8.50 + .498 \times 9.5$$
$$= 8.998$$

$$\text{Cash flow yield of barbell}^{b} = \frac{(8.5 \times .502 \times 4.00544) + (9.5 \times .498 \times 8.88151)}{6.434}$$

$$= 9.187$$

Analysis based on duration, convexity, and average yield

$$\text{Dollar convexity of barbell} = .502 \times 19.8164 + .498 \times 124.1702$$
$$= 71.7846$$

$$\text{Yield pickup} = \text{Yield on bullet} - \text{Cash flow yield of barbell}$$
$$= 9.25 - 9.187 = .063, \text{ or } 6.3 \text{ basis points}$$

$$\text{Yield pickup} = \text{Yield on bullet} - \text{Average yield of barbell}$$
$$= 9.25 - 8.998 = .252, \text{ or } 25.2 \text{ basis points}$$

$$\text{Convexity give up} = \text{Convexity of barbell} - \text{Convexity of bullet}$$
$$= 71.7846 - 55.4506 = 16.334$$

[a]Per 100-basis-point change in yield

[b]The calculation shown is actually a dollar-duration-weighted yield, a very close approximation to cash flow yield.

the short-term bond (A), the intermediate-term bond (C), and the long-term bond (B) change by the same number of basis points, shown in the first column of the exhibit. The total return reported in the second column of Exhibit 5–15 is

Bullet portfolio's total return – Barbell portfolio's total return

Thus, a positive value in the second column means that the bullet portfolio outperformed the barbell portfolio, and a negative value means that the barbell portfolio outperformed the bullet portfolio.

Which portfolio is the better investment alternative if the yield curve shifts in a parallel fashion *and* the investment horizon is six months? The answer depends on the amount by which yields change. Notice in the second column that if the yields change by less than 100 basis points, the bullet portfolio will outperform the barbell portfolio. The reverse is true if yields change by more than 100 basis points.

Now let's look at what happens if the yield curve does not shift in a parallel fashion. The third and fourth columns of Exhibit 5–15 show the relative performance of the two portfolios for a nonparallel shift of the yield curve. Specifically, the third column assumes that if the yield on bond C (the intermediate-term bond) changes by the amount shown in the first column, bond A (the short-term bond) will change by the same amount plus 25 basis points, whereas bond B (the long-term bond) will change by the same amount shown in the first column less 25 basis points. That is, the nonparallel shift assumed is a flattening of the yield

E X H I B I T   5–15

Relative Performance of Bullet Portfolio and Barbell Portfolio over a Six-Month Investment Horizon[a]

Yield Change (bp)	Parallel Shift	Nonparallel Shift[b]	Nonparallel Shift[c]
−500 bp	−7.19%	−10.69%	−3.89%
−475	−6.28	−9.61	−3.12
−450	−5.44	−8.62	−2.44
−425	−4.68	−7.71	−1.82
−400	−4.00	−6.88	−1.27
−375	−3.38	−6.13	−0.78
−350	−2.82	−5.44	−0.35
−325	−2.32	−4.82	0.03
−300	−1.88	−4.26	0.36
−275	−1.49	−3.75	0.65
−250	−1.15	−3.30	0.89
−225	−0.85	−2.90	1.09
−200	−0.59	−2.55	1.25
−175	−0.38	−2.24	1.37
−150	−0.20	−1.97	1.47
−125	−0.05	−1.74	1.53
−100	0.06	−1.54	1.57
−75	0.15	−1.38	1.58
−50	0.21	−1.24	1.57
−25	0.24	−1.14	1.53
0	0.25	−1.06	1.48
25	0.24	−1.01	1.41
50	0.21	−0.98	1.32
75	0.16	−0.97	1.21

curve. For this yield-curve shift, the barbell will always outperform the bullet. In the last column, the nonparallel shift assumes that for a change in bond C's yield, the yield on bond A will change by the same amount less 25 basis points, whereas that on bond B will change by the same amount plus 25 basis points. That is, it assumes that the yield curve will steepen. In this case, the bullet portfolio will outperform the barbell portfolio as long as the yield on bond C does not rise by more than 250 basis points or fall by more than 325 basis points.

The key point here is that looking at measures such as yield (yield-to-maturity or some type of portfolio yield measure), duration, or convexity tells us little about performance over some investment horizon because performance depends on the magnitude of the change in yields and how the yield curve shifts.

Several measures have been suggested to determine the exposure of a portfolio to yield-curve shifts. One such measure is described in Chapter 38.

E X H I B I T   5–15 (*continued*)

Yield Change (bp)	Parallel Shift	Nonparallel Shift[b]	Nonparallel Shift[c]
100	0.09	−0.98	1.09
125	0.01	−1.00	0.96
150	−0.08	−1.05	0.81
175	−0.19	−1.10	0.66
200	−0.31	−1.18	0.49
225	−0.44	−1.26	0.32
250	−0.58	−1.38	0.14
275	−0.73	−1.46	−0.05
300	−0.88	−1.58	−0.24
325	−1.05	−1.70	−0.44
350	−1.21	−1.84	−0.64
375	−1.39	−1.98	−0.85
400	−1.57	−2.12	−1.06
425	−1.75	−2.27	−1.27
450	−1.93	−2.43	−1.48
475	−2.12	−2.58	−1.70
500	−2.31	−2.75	−1.92

[a]Performance is based on the difference in total return over a six-month investment horizon. Specifically:

Bullet portfolio's total return − Barbell portfolio's total return

Therefore, a negative value means that the barbell portfolio outperformed the bullet portfolio.

[b]Change in yield for bond C. Nonparallel shift as follows (flattening of yield curve):

Yield change for bond A = Yield change for bond C + 25 basis points

Yield change for bond B = Yield change for bond C − 25 basis points

[c]Change in yield for bond C. Nonparallel shift as follows (steepening of yield curve):

Yield change for bond A = Yield change for bond C − 25 basis points

Yield change for bond B = Yield change for bond C + 25 basis points

Yield Volatility Is Not Recognized

The third limitation of duration as a stand-alone measure of price sensitivity is that it does not account for the volatility of yields. This limitation is critical because the total potential price sensitivity of a portfolio depends not only on its duration but the volatility of yields. For example, the duration of a Treasury bond will be greater than that of a high-yield (or "junk") bond with the same maturity and issued at the same time. There are two reasons for this: The coupon rate is lower on the Treasury security, and it trades at a lower yield level. Does this mean that a Treasury security has a greater price volatility exposure? Not necessarily. It also depends on the relative volatility of yields of Treasury securities compared to high-yield bonds. The combination of the duration and yield volatility affects the portfolio's price volatility.

Applicable Only to Option-Free Bonds

The calculation of both modified and Macaulay duration assumes that when yields change, the cash flows of a bond will *not* change. This is an unrealistic assumption for callable and putable bonds. In the case of a callable bond, a decline in the market yield below or near the coupon rate will reduce the price appreciation. This is because investors will be reluctant to pay a price based on the cash flows for a noncallable bond because if the bond is called, the investor will receive only the cash flow up to the call date and the call price at this date.

For example, consider the 9 percent 20-year bond in Exhibit 5–1. If yields decline from 9 percent to 6 percent, the price of this bond will increase from 100 to 134.6722. Suppose that this bond is callable two years from now at 105. Investors would not be willing to pay 134.6722 because the bond can be called in two years at 105. No recognition is given to any embedded option when using Macaulay duration or modified duration.

Exhibit 5–16 shows the price/yield relationship for both an option-free bond and the same bond with a call option. The convex curve *a-a'* is the price/yield relationship for the option-free bond. The curve denoted by *a-b* is the price/yield relationship for the callable bond.

The reason for the unusual shape of the price/yield relationship for the callable bond is as follows: When the prevailing market yield for comparable bonds is much higher than the coupon rate on the bond, it is unlikely that the issuer will call the bond. In option terminology, the call option is deep out-of-the-money. Because the bond is unlikely to be called when it is deep out-of-the-money, a callable bond will have roughly the same price/yield relationship as an option-free bond. However, even when the option is near-the-money (the coupon rate is near the market yield) investors will not pay the same price for the bond if it is callable because there is still the chance the market yield may drop further, making it beneficial for the issuer to call the bond.

As yields in the market decline, the likelihood increases that the issuer will benefit from calling the bond. We may not know the exact yield level at which in-

EXHIBIT 5–16

Option-free and Callable Bond Price/Yield Relationship

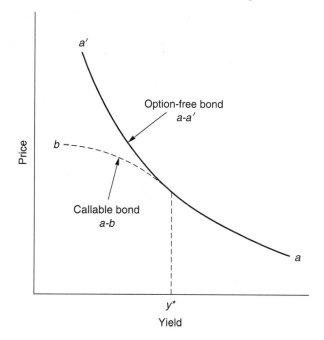

vestors begin to view the issue likely to be called, but we do know that there is some level. In Exhibit 5–16, at yield levels below y^*, the price/yield relationship for the callable bond departs significantly from the price/yield relationship for the option-free bond. Consequently, for a range of yields below y^*, there is significant price compression—that is, there is limited price appreciation as yields decline.

To understand the price volatility and the potential performance of callable bonds over some investment horizon, it is necessary to understand the components of the callable bond. A callable bond is a bond in which the bondholder has sold the issuer a call option[11] that allows the issuer to repurchase the bond.

Effectively, the owner of the callable bond enters into two separate transactions. First, he or she buys an option-free bond from the issuer, paying the issuer the bond price. Then, the buyer sells the issuer a call option, for which the issuer pays the option price. Therefore, we can summarize the position of a callable bondholder as follows:

Long a callable bond = Long an option-free bond + Short a call option

---

11. Call options are discussed in Chapter 56.

or equivalently,

Callable bond = Option-free bond − Call option

The minus sign in front of the call option means that the bondholder has sold (written) the call option.

The price of a callable bond is therefore equal to the price of the two component parts. That is,

Callable bond price = Option-free bond price − Call option price

The call option price is subtracted from the price of the option-free bond because, when the bondholder sells a call option, he or she receives the option price. Graphically, this can be seen in Exhibit 5–16. The difference between the price of the option-free bond and the callable bond at a given yield is the price of the embedded call option.

The price of a call option increases when the expected price volatility of the underlying instrument increases. Because the price of a call option on a bond depends on expected interest-rate volatility, the price of a callable bond will depend on expected interest-rate volatility.

The duration of a callable bond can also be expressed as the sum of its component parts. That is, the duration of a callable bond is equal to

Duration of callable bond =
                Duration of an option-free bond − Duration of the call option

Although we have focused on the duration of a callable bond, it can also be shown that the convexity of a callable bond is related to the convexity of an option-free bond and the convexity of the call option. Recall that convexity measures the rate of change of duration. For an option-free bond, convexity is always positive. Duration, which is related to the slope of the tangent to the price/yield relationship, increases when yield decreases, and decreases when yield increases. As can be seen in Exhibit 5–16, the slope of the line tangent to the price/yield relationship for a callable bond flattens when yield decreases. Thus, duration gets smaller as yield decreases. This feature of a callable bond is referred to as *negative convexity,* and causes the price compression that we referred to earlier.

APPROXIMATING DURATION AND CONVEXITY FOR ANY BOND

Unfortunately, market participants often confuse the main purpose of duration by referring to it as some measure of the weighted average life of a bond. This is because of the original use of duration by Macaulay. If you rely on this interpretation of duration, it will be difficult for you to understand why a bond with a maturity of 20 years can have a duration greater than 20. For example, there are certain collateralized mortgage obligation (CMO) bond classes that have a greater duration than the underlying mortgage loans. That is, a CMO bond class can have a duration of 50 whereas the underlying mortgage loans from which the CMO is created can have a maturity of 30 years. How can this happen?

The answer to this puzzle is that duration is the approximate percentage change in price for a small change in interest rates. In fact, a good way to remember duration is that it is the approximate percentage change in price for a 100-basis-point change in interest rates. Thus, subject to the drawbacks discussed in the previous section, a duration of 4 means that the price of the bond or portfolio will change by approximately 4 percent for a 100-basis-point change in yield. Certain CMO bond classes are leveraged instruments whose price sensitivity or duration, as a result, are a multiple of the underlying mortgage loans from which they were created. Thus, a CMO bond class with a duration of 50 does not mean it has some type of weighted average life of 50 years. Instead, it means that for a 100-basis-point change in yield, that bond's price will change by roughly 50 percent.

We interpret the duration of a call (or put) option in the same way. A call option can have a duration of 20 even though the call option expires in one year. This is confusing to someone who interprets duration as some measure of the life of an option. What this means is that if yields change by 100 basis points for the bond underlying the call option, the value of the call option will change by approximately 20 percent.

Once we understand that duration is related to percentage price change, none of the formulas given above are needed to calculate the approximate duration of a bond, or any other more complex derivative securities or options described throughout this book. All we are interested in is the percentage price change of a bond when interest rates change by a small amount. This can be found quite easily by the following procedure:

1. Increase the yield on the bond by a small number of basis points (Δy) and determine the new price at this higher yield level. We call this new price P_+.

2. Decrease the yield on the bond by the same number of basis points (Δy) and calculate the new price. We will call this new price P_-.

3. Letting P_0 be the initial price, duration can be approximated using the following formula:

$$\text{Approximate duration} = \frac{P_- - P_+}{2P_0(\Delta y)}$$

What the formula is measuring is the average percentage price change (relative to the initial price) per one basis-point change in yield.

To see how good this approximation is, let's apply it to the 9 percent coupon 20-year bond trading at 6 percent. The initial price (P_0) is 134.6722. The steps are given below:

1. Increase the yield on the bond by 20 basis points from 6 percent to 6.2 percent. Thus, Δy is 0.002. The new price (P_+) is 131.8439.

2. Decrease the yield on the bond by 20 basis points from 6 percent to 5.8 percent. Thus, Δy is 0.002. The new price (P_-) is 137.5888.

3. Because the initial price P_0 is 134.6722, the duration can be approximated as follows:

$$\text{Approximate duration} = \frac{137.5888 - 131.8439}{2(134.6722)(0.002)} = 10.66$$

How good is the approximation? The modified duration as calculated by formula is 10.66. Thus, the approximation formula does an excellent job.

If an investor is interested in the duration of an option, the same formula can be used. However, to use the formula, it is necessary to have an option-pricing model to get the new prices.

Similarly, the convexity of any bond can be approximated using the following formula:

$$\text{Approximate convexity} = \frac{P_+ + P_- - 2P_0}{2P_0(\Delta y)^2}$$

EFFECTIVE DURATION AND EFFECTIVE CONVEXITY

The approximation formula for duration and convexity are useful in estimating duration and convexity not only for option-free bonds, but also for bonds with embedded options. This can be done by estimating what the theoretical price of a bond with an embedded option will be after allowing for the change in the expected cash flow that occurs when yields change. Thus, the prices P_+ and P_- are theoretical prices. A valuation model is needed to obtain these prices.

In general, we refer to duration as the sensitivity of the bond's price to yield changes. Modified duration measures the price responsiveness assuming that changes in yield do not change the cash flow. This measure is appropriate for option-free bonds and bonds with embedded options where the embedded option is deep out-of-the-money (i.e., a yield environment in which the market yield is substantially higher than the coupon rate on the callable bond). In contrast, effective duration assumes that changes in yield can affect cash flow and takes this into account.

The distinction between modified duration and effective duration is shown in Exhibit 5–17.

EXHIBIT 5-17

Modified Duration versus Effective Duration

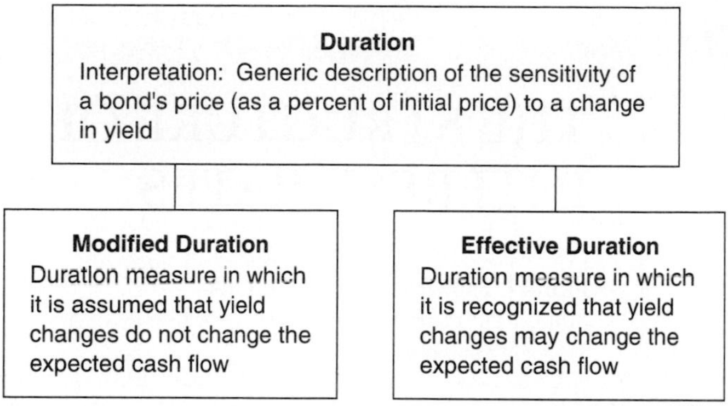

Duration
Interpretation: Generic description of the sensitivity of a bond's price (as a percent of initial price) to a change in yield

Modified Duration	Effective Duration
Duration measure in which it is assumed that yield changes do not change the expected cash flow	Duration measure in which it is recognized that yield changes may change the expected cash flow

SUMMARY

In this chapter, we reviewed the price volatility characteristics of option-free bonds. Several convenient measures, including price value of a basis point, duration, dollar duration, and convexity, were shown to summarize the important attributes of price volatility. The limitations of these measures were explored, and a better means of estimating the price volatility of bonds with embedded options—effective duration and convexity—was presented.

6

⑥ THE STRUCTURE OF INTEREST RATES

Frank J. Fabozzi, Ph.D., CFA, CPA
Adjunct Professor of Finance
School of Management
Yale University

There is no single interest rate for any economy; rather, there is an interdependent structure of interest rates. The interest rate that a borrower has to pay depends on a myriad of factors. In this chapter, we describe these factors. We begin with a discussion of the *base interest rate:* The interest rate on U.S. government securities. Next we explain the factors that affect the yield spread or risk premium for non-Treasury securities. Finally, we focus on one particular factor that affects the interest rate demanded in an economy for a particular security: maturity. The relationship between yield and maturity (or term) is called the *term structure of interest rates,* and this relationship is critical in the valuation of securities. Determinants of the *general* level of interest rates in the economy will not be discussed.

THE BASE INTEREST RATE

The securities issued by the U.S. Department of the Treasury are backed by the full faith and credit of the U.S. government. Consequently, market participants throughout the world view them as having no credit risk. Therefore interest rates on Treasury securities are the benchmark interest rates throughout the U.S. economy, as well as in international capital markets. The large sizes of Treasury issues have contributed to making the Treasury market the most active and hence the most liquid market in the world.

The minimum interest rate or *base interest rate* that investors will demand for investing in a non-Treasury security is the yield offered on a comparable maturity for an on-the-run Treasury security. For example, if an investor wanted to purchase a 10-year bond on March 8, 1996, the minimum yield he would seek is

EXHIBIT 6–1

Yields for On-the-Run Treasuries on March 8, 1996

Maturity	Yield
3 months	5.03%
6 months	5.21
1 year	5.40
2 years	5.77
3 years	5.92
5 years	6.09
10 years	6.43
30 years	6.74

Source: Lehman Brothers, *Relative Value Report,* Fixed Income Research, March 11, 1996, p. T-1.

6.43 percent, the on-the-run Treasury yield reported in Exhibit 6–1. The base interest rate is also referred to as the *benchmark interest rate.*

RISK PREMIUM

Market participants describe interest rates on non-Treasury securities as trading at a spread to a particular on-the-run Treasury security. For example, if the yield on a 10-year non-Treasury security is 7.43 percent and the yield on a 10-year Treasury security is 6.43 percent, the spread is 100 basis points. This spread reflects the additional risks the investor faces by acquiring a security that is not issued by the U.S. government, and therefore can be called a *risk premium.* Thus, we can express the interest rate offered on a non-Treasury security as

Base interest rate + Spread

or equivalently,

Base interest rate + Risk premium

The factors that affect the spread include: (1) the type of issuer, (2) the issuer's perceived creditworthiness, (3) the term or maturity of the instrument, (4) provisions that grant either the issuer or the investor the option to do something, (5) the taxability of the interest received by investors, and (6) the expected liquidity of the issue.

Types of Issuers

A key feature of a debt obligation is the nature of the issuer. In addition to the U.S. government, there are agencies of the U.S. government, municipal governments, corporations (domestic and foreign), and foreign governments that issue bonds.

The bond market is classified by the type of issuer. These are referred to as *market sectors.* The spread between the interest rate offered in two sectors of the bond market with the same maturity is referred to as an *intermarket-sector spread.*

Excluding the Treasury market sector, other market sectors have a wide range of issuers, each with different abilities to satisfy bond obligations. For example, within the corporate market sector, issuers are classified as utilities, transportations, industrials, and banks and finance companies. The spread between two issues within a market sector is called an *intramarket-sector spread.*

Perceived Creditworthiness of Issuer

Default risk or credit risk refers to the risk that the issuer of a bond may be unable to make timely principal or interest payments. Most market participants rely primarily on commercial rating companies to assess the default risk of an issuer. We discuss these rating companies in Chapter 11.

The spread between Treasury securities and non-Treasury securities that are identical in all respects except for quality is referred to as a *quality spread* or *credit spread.* For example, for the week of March 8, 1996 the yield on single-A 10-year industrial bonds was 7.01 percent and the corresponding yield for the 10-year on-the-run Treasury was 6.43 percent.[1] Therefore, the quality spread was 58 basis points.

Term-to-Maturity

As we explained in Chapter 5, the price of a bond will fluctuate over its life as yields in the market change. As demonstrated in that chapter, the volatility of a bond's price is dependent on its maturity. With all other factors constant, the longer the maturity of a bond, the greater the price volatility resulting from a change in market yields.

The spread between any two maturity sectors of the market is called a *yield curve spread* or *maturity spread.* The relationship between the yields on comparable securities with different maturities, as mentioned earlier, is called the term structure of interest rates. Exhibit 6–2 shows the various Treasury yield curve spreads on March 8, 1996.

The term-to-maturity topic is very important, and we have devoted more time to this topic later in this chapter.

---

1. These yields were estimated from Lehman Brothers, *Relative Value Report,* Fixed Income Research, March 11, 1996, T-3.

EXHIBIT 6–2

Treasury Yield Curve Spread on March 8, 1996

Maturity sector	Spread (in bp)
2–3 years	15
3–5 years	18
10–30 years	32
2–5 years	32
5–10 years	33
2–30 years	97

Source: Lehman Brothers, *Relative Value Report,* Fixed Income Research, March 11, 1996, p. T-1.

Inclusion of Options

It is not uncommon for a bond issue to include a provision that gives the bond-holder or the issuer an option to take some action against the other party. An option that is included in a bond issue is referred to as an *embedded option.* We discussed the various types of embedded options in Chapter 1. The most common type of option in a bond issue is the call provision, which grants the issuer the right to retire the debt, fully or partially, before the scheduled maturity date. The inclusion of a call feature benefits issuers by allowing them to replace an old bond issue with a lower-interest-cost issue when interest rates in the market decline. In effect, a call provision allows the issuer to alter the maturity of a bond. The exercise of a call provision is disadvantageous to the bondholder because the bond-holder must reinvest the proceeds received at a lower interest rate.

The presence of an embedded option affects both the spread of an issue relative to a Treasury security and the spread relative to otherwise comparable issues that do not have an embedded option. In general, market participants will require a larger spread to a comparable Treasury security for an issue with an embedded option that is favorable to the issuer (such as a call option) than for an issue without such an option. In contrast, market participants will require a smaller spread to a comparable Treasury security for an issue with an embedded option that is favorable to the investor (such as a put option or a conversion option). In fact, the interest rate on a bond with an option that is favorable to an investor may be less than that on a comparable Treasury security.

Taxability of Interest

Unless exempted under the federal income tax code, interest income is taxable at the federal level. In addition to federal income taxes, there may be state and local taxes on interest income.

The federal tax code specifically exempts the interest income from qualified municipal bond issues. Because of this tax exemption, the yield on municipal bonds is less than on Treasuries with the same maturity. The difference in yield between tax-exempt securities and Treasury securities is typically measured not in basis points but in percentage terms. More specifically, it is measured as the percentage of the yield on a tax-exempt security relative to a comparable Treasury security.

The yield on a taxable bond issue after federal income taxes are paid is equal to

$$\text{After-tax yield} = \text{Pretax yield} \times (1 - \text{Marginal tax rate})$$

For example, suppose a taxable bond issue offers a yield of 9 percent and is acquired by an investor facing a marginal tax rate of 39.6 percent. The after-tax yield would then be

$$\text{After-tax yield} = .09 \times (1 - 0.396) = 0.0544 = 5.44\%$$

Alternatively, we can determine the yield that must be offered on a taxable bond issue to give the same after-tax yield as a tax-exempt issue. This yield is called the *equivalent taxable yield* and is determined as follows:

$$\text{Equivalent taxable yield} = \frac{\text{Tax-exempt yield}}{(1 - \text{Marginal tax rate})}$$

For example, consider an investor facing a 39.6 percent marginal tax rate who purchases a tax-exempt issue with a yield of 6.21 percent. The equivalent taxable yield is then

$$\text{Equivalent taxable yield} = \frac{0.0544}{(1 - 0.396)} = .09 = 9\%$$

Notice that the lower the marginal tax rate, the lower the equivalent taxable yield. For example, in our previous example, if the marginal tax rate is 25 percent rather than 39.6 percent, the equivalent taxable yield would be 7.25 percent rather than 9 percent, as shown below:

$$\text{Equivalent taxable yield} = \frac{0.0544}{(1 - 0.25)} = .0725 = 7.25\%$$

State and local governments may tax interest income on bond issues that are exempt from federal income taxes. Some municipalities exempt interest income from all municipal issues from taxation, others do not. Some states exempt interest income from bonds issued by municipalities within the state but tax the interest income from bonds issued by municipalities outside of the state. The implication is that two municipal securities of the same quality rating and the same maturity may trade at some spread because of the relative demand for bonds of municipalities in different states. For example, in a high-income-tax state such as New York, the demand for bonds of municipalities will drive down their yield relative to municipalities in a low-income-tax state such as Florida, holding all credit issues aside.

Municipalities are not permitted to tax the interest income from securities issued by the U.S. Treasury. Thus, part of the spread between Treasury securities and taxable non-Treasury securities of the same maturity reflects the value of the exemption from state and local taxes.

Expected Liquidity of an Issue

Bonds trade with different degrees of liquidity. The greater the expected liquidity at which an issue will trade, the lower the yield that investors require. As noted earlier, Treasury securities are the most liquid securities in the world. The lower yield offered on Treasury securities relative to non-Treasury securities reflects the difference in liquidity as well as perceived credit risk. Even within the Treasury market, on-the-run issues have greater liquidity than off-the-run issues.

THE TERM STRUCTURE OF INTEREST RATES

In future chapters, we will see the key role that the term structure of interest rates plays in the valuation of bonds. For this reason, we devote a good deal of space to this important topic.

The Yield Curve

The graphical depiction of the relationship between the yield on the bonds of the same credit quality but different maturities is known as the *yield curve*. In the past, most market participants have constructed yield curves from the observations of prices and yields in the Treasury market. Two reasons account for this tendency. First, Treasury securities are free of default risk, and differences in creditworthiness do not affect yield estimates. Second, as the largest and most active bond market, the Treasury market offers the fewest problems of illiquidity or infrequent trading. Exhibit 6–3 shows the shape of four hypothetical Treasury yield curves that have been observed in the United States.

From a practical viewpoint, as we explained earlier in this chapter, the key function of the Treasury yield curve is to serve as a benchmark for pricing bonds and setting yields in many other sectors of the debt market, such as bank loans, mortgages, corporate debt, and international bonds. However, market participants are coming to realize that the traditionally constructed Treasury yield curve is an unsatisfactory measure of the relation between required yield and maturity. The key reason is that securities with the same maturity may actually carry different yields. As we will explain, this phenomenon reflects the impact of differences in the bonds' coupon rates. Hence, it is necessary to develop more accurate and

EXHIBIT 6-3

Four Hypothetical Yield Curves

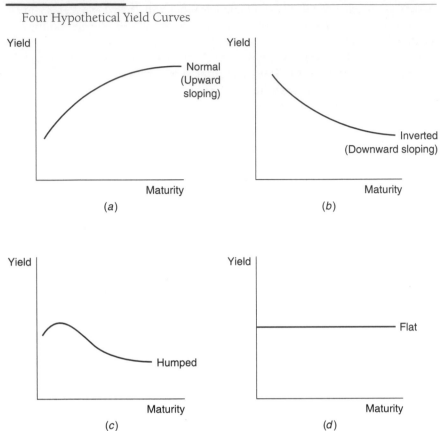

reliable estimates of the Treasury yield curve. We will show the problems posed by traditional approaches to the Treasury yield curve and we will offer an increasingly popular approach to building a yield curve. Our approach consists of identifying yields that apply to zero-coupon bonds and, therefore, eliminates the problem of nonuniqueness in the yield-maturity relationship.

Using the Yield Curve to Price a Bond

The price of a bond is the present value of its cash flows. However, in our previous discussion of the pricing of a bond, we have assumed that one interest rate should be used to discount all the bond's cash flows. The appropriate interest rate is the yield on a Treasury security with the same maturity as the bond, plus an appropriate risk premium or spread.

However, there is a problem with using the Treasury yield curve to determine the appropriate yield at which to discount the cash flow of a bond. To illustrate this problem, consider two hypothetical five-year Treasury bonds, A and B. The difference between these two Treasury bonds is the coupon rate, which is 12 percent for A and 3 percent for B. The cash flow for these two bonds per $100 of par value for the 10 six-month periods to maturity would be as follows:

Period	Cash Flow for A	Cash Flow for B
1–9	$ 6.00	$ 1.50
10	106.00	101.50

Because of the different cash flow patterns, it is not appropriate to use the same interest rate to discount all cash flows. Instead, each cash flow should be discounted at a unique interest rate that is appropriate for the time period in which the cash flow will be received. But what should be the interest rate for each period?

The correct way to think about bonds A and B is not as bonds but as packages of cash flows. More specifically, they are packages of zero-coupon instruments. Thus, the interest earned is the difference between the maturity value and the price paid. For example, bond A can be viewed as 10 zero-coupon instruments: One with a maturity value of $6 maturing six months from now, a second with a maturity value of $6 maturing one year from now, a third with a maturity value of $6 maturing 1.5 years from now, and so on. The final zero-coupon instrument matures 10 six-month periods from now, and has a maturity value of $106. Likewise, bond B can be viewed as 10 zero-coupon instruments: One with a maturity value of $1.50 maturing six months from now, one with a maturity value of $1.50 maturing one year from now, one with a maturity value of $1.50 maturing 1.5 years from now, and so on. The final zero-coupon instrument matures 10 six-month periods from now and has a maturity value of $101.50. Obviously, in the case of each coupon bond, the value or price of the bond is equal to the total value of its component zero-coupon instruments.

In general, any bond can be viewed as a package of zero-coupon instruments. That is, each zero-coupon instrument in the package has a maturity equal to its coupon payment date or, in the case of the principal, the maturity date. The value of the bond should equal the value of all the component zero-coupon instruments. If this does not hold, a market participant may generate riskless profits by stripping the security and creating stripped securities.

To determine the value of each zero-coupon instrument, it is necessary to know the yield on a zero-coupon Treasury with that same maturity. This yield is called the *spot rate,* and the graphical depiction of the relationship between the spot rate and its maturity is called the *spot-rate curve.* Because there are no zero-coupon Treasury debt issues with a maturity greater than one year, it is not possible to construct such a curve solely from observations of market activity. Rather, it is necessary to derive this curve from theoretical considerations as applied to the yields of actual Treasury securities. Such a curve is called a *theoretical spot-rate curve.*

Constructing the Theoretical Spot-Rate Curve

The theoretical spot-rate curve is constructed from the yield curve based on the observed yields of Treasury bills and Treasury coupon securities. The process of creating a theoretical spot-rate curve in this way is called *bootstrapping.*[2] To explain this process, we use the data for the hypothetical price, annualized yield (yield-to-maturity), and maturity of the 20 Treasury securities shown in Exhibit 6–4.

Throughout the analysis and illustrations to come, it is important to remember that the basic principle of bootstrapping is that the value of the Treasury coupon security should be equal to the value of the package of zero-coupon Treasury securities that duplicates the coupon bond's cash flow.

Consider the six-month Treasury bill in Exhibit 6–4. As explained in the next chapter, a Treasury bill is a zero-coupon instrument. Therefore, its annualized yield of 8 percent is equal to the spot rate. Similarly, for the one-year Treasury bill, the cited yield of 8.3 percent is the one-year spot rate. Given these two spot rates, we can compute the spot rate for a theoretical 1.5-year zero-coupon Treasury. The price of a theoretical 1.5-year Treasury should equal the present value of three cash flows from an actual 1.5-year coupon Treasury, where the yield used for discounting is the spot rate corresponding to the cash flow. Using $100 as par, the cash flow for the 1.5-year coupon Treasury is as follows:

0.5 years	$.085 \times \$100 \times .5$	$= \$ \ \ 4.25$
1.0 years	$.085 \times \$100 \times .5$	$= \$ \ \ 4.25$
1.5 years	$.085 \times \$100 \times .5 + 100$	$= \$ 104.25$

The present value of the cash flow is then

$$\frac{4.25}{(1+z_1)^1} + \frac{4.25}{(1+z_2)^2} + \frac{104.25}{(1+z_3)^3}$$

---

2. In practice, the securities used to construct the theoretical spot-rate curve are the most recently auctioned Treasury securities of a given maturity. Such issues are referred to as the *on-the-run Treasury issues.* As we explain in Chapter 8, there are actual zero-coupon Treasury securities with a maturity greater than one year that are outstanding in the market. These securities are not issued by the U.S. Treasury but are created by market participants from actual coupon Treasury securities. It would seem logical that the observed yield on zero-coupon Treasury securities can be used to construct an actual spot-rate curve. However, there are problems with this approach. First, the liquidity of these securities is not as great as that of the coupon Treasury market. Second, there are maturity sectors of the zero-coupon Treasury market that attract specific investors who may be willing to trade yield in exchange for an attractive feature associated with that particular maturity sector, thereby distorting the term structure relationship.

EXHIBIT 6–4

Maturity and Yield-to-Maturity for 20 Hypothetical Treasury Securities

Maturity	Coupon Rate	Yield-to-Maturity	Price
0.50 years	0.0000	0.0800	$ 96.15
1.00	0.0000	0.0830	92.19
1.50	0.0850	0.0890	99.45
2.00	0.0900	0.0920	99.64
2.50	0.1100	0.0940	103.49
3.00	0.0950	0.0970	99.49
3.50	0.1000	0.1000	100.00
4.00	0.1000	0.1040	98.72
4.50	0.1150	0.1060	103.16
5.00	0.0875	0.1080	92.24
5.50	0.1050	0.1090	98.38
6.00	0.1100	0.1120	99.14
6.50	0.0850	0.1140	86.94
7.00	0.0825	0.1160	84.24
7.50	0.1100	0.1180	96.09
8.00	0.0650	0.1190	72.62
8.50	0.0875	0.1200	82.97
9.00	0.1300	0.1220	104.30
9.50	0.1150	0.1240	95.06
10.00	0.1250	0.1250	100.00

where

z_1 = One-half the annualized six-month theoretical spot rate
z_2 = One-half the one-year theoretical spot rate
z_3 = One-half the 1.5-year theoretical spot rate

Because the six-month spot rate and one-year spot rate are 8.0 percent and 8.3 percent, respectively, we know that

$$z_1 = .04 \quad \text{and} \quad z_2 = .0415.$$

We can compute the present value of the 1.5-year coupon Treasury security as

$$\frac{4.25}{(1.0400)^1} + \frac{4.25}{(1.0415)^2} + \frac{104.25}{(1+z_3)^3}$$

Because the price of the 1.5-year coupon Treasury security (from Exhibit 6–4) is $99.45, the following relationship must hold:

$$99.45 = \frac{4.25}{(1.0400)^1} + \frac{4.25}{(1.0415)^2} + \frac{104.25}{(1+z_3)^3}$$

We can solve for the theoretical 1.5-year spot rate as follows:

$$99.45 = 4.08654 + 3.91805 + \frac{104.25}{(1+z_3)^3}$$

$$91.44541 = \frac{104.25}{(1+z_3)^3}$$

$$(1+z_3)^3 = 1.140024$$
$$z_3 = .04465$$

Doubling this yield, we obtain the bond-equivalent yield of .0893 or 8.93 percent, which is the theoretical 1.5-year spot rate. That rate is the rate that the market would apply to a 1.5-year zero-coupon Treasury security, if such a security existed.

Given the theoretical 1.5-year spot rate, we can obtain the theoretical two-year spot rate. The cash flow for the two-year coupon Treasury in Exhibit 6–4 is

0.5 years	$.090 \times \$100 \times .5$	$= \$ \quad 4.50$
1.0 years	$.090 \times \$100 \times .5$	$= \$ \quad 4.50$
1.5 years	$.090 \times \$100 \times .5$	$= \$ \quad 4.50$
2.0 years	$.090 \times \$100 \times .5 + 100$	$= \$104.50$

The present value of the cash flow is then

$$\frac{4.50}{(1+z_1)^1} + \frac{4.50}{(1+z_2)^2} + \frac{4.50}{(1+z_3)^3} + \frac{104.50}{(1+z_4)^4}$$

where

$$z_4 = \text{One-half the two-year theoretical spot rate}$$

Because the six-month spot rate, one-year spot rate, and 1.5-year spot rate are 8.0 percent, 8.3 percent, and 8.93 percent, respectively, then

$$z_1 = .04 \quad z_2 = .0415 \quad \text{and} \quad z_3 = .04465$$

Therefore, the present value of the two-year coupon Treasury security is

$$\frac{4.50}{(1.0400)^1} + \frac{4.50}{(1.0415)^2} + \frac{4.50}{(1.04465)^3} + \frac{104.50}{(1+z_4)^4}$$

Because the price of the two-year coupon Treasury security is $99.64, the following relationship must hold:

$$99.64 = \frac{4.50}{(1.0400)^1} + \frac{4.50}{(1.0415)^2} + \frac{4.50}{(1.04465)^3} + \frac{104.50}{(1+z_4)^4}$$

We can solve for the theoretical two-year spot rate as follows:

$$99.64 = 4.32692 + 4.14853 + 3.94730 + \frac{104.50}{(1+z_4)^4}$$

$$87.21725 = \frac{104.50}{(1+z_4)^4}$$

$$(1+z_4)^4 = 1.198158$$

$$z_4 = .046235$$

Doubling this yield, we obtain the theoretical two-year spot rate bond-equivalent yield of 9.247 percent.

One can follow this approach sequentially to derive the theoretical 2.5-year spot rate from the calculated values of z_1, z_2, z_3, and z_4 (the six-month, one-year, 1.5-year, and two-year rates), and the price and coupon of the bond with a maturity of 2.5 years. Further, one could derive theoretical spot rates for the remaining 15 half-yearly rates. The spot rates thus obtained are shown in Exhibit 6–5. They

E X H B I T   6–5

Theoretical Spot Rates

Maturity	Yield-to-Maturity	Theoretical Spot Rate
0.50 years	0.0800	0.08000
1.00	0.0830	0.08300
1.50	0.0890	0.08930
2.00	0.0920	0.09247
2.50	0.0940	0.09468
3.00	0.0970	0.09787
3.50	0.1000	0.10129
4.00	0.1040	0.10592
4.50	0.1060	0.10850
5.00	0.1080	0.11021
5.50	0.1090	0.11175
6.00	0.1120	0.11584
6.50	0.1140	0.11744
7.00	0.1160	0.11991
7.50	0.1180	0.12405
8.00	0.1190	0.12278
8.50	0.1200	0.12546
9.00	0.1220	0.13152
9.50	0.1240	0.13377
10.00	0.1250	0.13623

represent the term structure of interest rates for maturities up to ten years, at the particular time to which the bond price quotations refer.

Why Treasuries Must Be Priced Based on Spot Rates

Financial theory tells us that the theoretical price of a Treasury security should be equal to the present value of the cash flows where each cash flow is discounted at the appropriate theoretical spot rate. What we did not do, however, is demonstrate the economic force that ensures that the actual market price of a Treasury security does not depart significantly from its theoretical price.

To demonstrate this, we will use the 20 hypothetical Treasury securities introduced in Exhibit 6–4. The longest maturity bond given in that exhibit is the 10-year, 12.5 percent coupon bond selling at par with a yield-to-maturity of 12.5 percent. Suppose that a government dealer buys the issue at par and strips it, expecting to sell the zero-coupon Treasury securities at the yields-to-maturity indicated in Exhibit 6–5 for the corresponding maturity. (We will discuss stripping coupon Treasury securities in Chapter 8.)

Exhibit 6–6 shows the price that would be received for each zero-coupon Treasury security created. The price for each is the present value of the cash flow from the stripped Treasury discounted at the yield-to-maturity corresponding to the maturity of the security (from Exhibit 6–4). The total proceeds received from selling the zero-coupon Treasury securities created would be $104.1880 per $100 of par value of the original Treasury issue. This would result in an arbitrage profit of $4.1880 per $100 of the 10-year, 12.5 percent coupon Treasury security purchased.

To understand why the government dealer has the opportunity to realize this profit, look at the third column of Exhibit 6–6, which shows how much the government dealer paid for each cash flow by buying the entire package of cash flows (i.e., by buying the bond). For example, consider the $6.25 coupon payment in four years. By buying the 10-year Treasury bond priced to yield 12.5 percent, the dealer effectively pays a price based on 12.5 percent (6.25 percent semiannually) for that coupon payment, or, equivalently, $3.8481. Under the assumptions of this illustration, however, investors were willing to accept a lower yield-to-maturity, 10.4 percent (5.2 percent semiannually), to purchase a zero-coupon Treasury security with four years to maturity. Thus, investors were willing to pay $4.1663. On this one coupon payment, the government dealer realizes a profit equal to the difference between $4.1663 and $3.8481 (or $0.3182). From all the cash flows, the total profit is $4.1880. In this instance, coupon stripping shows that the sum of the parts is greater than the whole.

Suppose that, instead of the observed yield-to-maturity from Exhibit 6–4, the yields investors want are the same as the theoretical spot rates shown in Exhibit 6–5. If we use these spot rates to discount the cash flows, the total proceeds from the sale of the zero-coupon Treasury securities would be equal to $100, making coupon stripping uneconomic.

EXHIBIT 6–6

Illustration of Arbitrage Profit from Coupon Stripping

Maturity	Cash Flow	Present Value at 12.5%	Yield-to-Maturity	Present Value at Yield-to-Maturity
0.50 years	$6.25	5.8824	0.0800	$6.0096
1.00	6.25	5.5363	0.0830	5.7618
1.50	6.25	5.2107	0.0890	5.4847
2.00	6.25	4.9042	0.0920	5.2210
2.50	6.25	4.6157	0.0940	4.9676
3.00	6.25	4.3442	0.0970	4.7040
3.50	6.25	4.0886	0.1000	4.4418
4.00	6.25	3.8481	0.1040	4.1663
4.50	6.25	3.6218	0.1060	3.9267
5.00	6.25	3.4087	0.1080	3.6938
5.50	6.25	3.2082	0.1090	3.4863
6.00	6.25	3.0195	0.1120	3.2502
6.50	6.25	2.8419	0.1140	3.0402
7.00	6.25	2.6747	0.1160	2.8384
7.50	6.25	2.5174	0.1180	2.6451
8.00	6.25	2.3693	0.1190	2.4789
8.50	6.25	2.2299	0.1200	2.3210
9.00	6.25	2.0987	0.1220	2.1528
9.50	6.25	1.9753	0.1240	1.9930
10.00	106.25	31.6046	0.1250	31.6046
Total		100.0000		$104.1880

In our illustration of coupon stripping, the price of the Treasury security is less than its theoretical price. Suppose instead that the price of the Treasury security is greater than its theoretical price. In such cases, investors can purchase a package of zero-coupon Treasury securities such that the cash flow of the package of securities replicates the cash flow of the mispriced coupon Treasury security. By doing so, the investor will realize a yield higher than the yield on the coupon Treasury security. For example, suppose that the market price of the 10-year Treasury security we used in our illustration (Exhibit 6–6) is $106. By buying the 20 zero-coupon bonds shown in Exhibit 6–6 with a maturity value identical to the cash flow shown in the second column, the investor is effectively purchasing a 10-year Treasury coupon security at a cost of $104.1880 instead of $106.

The process of coupon stripping and reconstituting prevents the actual spot-rate curve observed on zero-coupon Treasuries from departing significantly from the theoretical spot-rate curve. As more stripping and reconstituting occurs, forces of demand and supply will cause rates to return to their theoretical spot-rate levels. This is what has happened in the Treasury market.

Forward Rates

Consider an investor who has a one-year investment horizon and is faced with the following two alternatives:

Alternative 1: Buy a one-year Treasury bill.
Alternative 2: Buy a six-month Treasury bill and when it matures in six months, buy another six-month Treasury bill.

The investor will be indifferent between the two alternatives if they produce the same return over the one-year investment horizon. The investor knows the spot rate on the six-month Treasury bill and the one-year Treasury bill. However, she does not know what yield will be available on a six-month Treasury bill that will be purchased six months from now. The yield on a six-month Treasury bill six months from now is called a *forward rate*. Given the spot rate for the six-month Treasury bill and the one-year bill, we wish to determine the forward rate on a six-month Treasury bill that will make the investor indifferent between the two alternatives. That rate can be readily determined.

At this point, however, we need to digress briefly and recall several present value and investment relationships. First, if you invested in a one-year Treasury bill, you would receive $100 at the end of one year. The price of the one-year Treasury bill would be

$$\frac{100}{(1 + z_2)^2}$$

where

z_2 is one-half the bond-equivalent yield of the theoretical one-year spot rate.

Second, suppose you purchased a six-month Treasury bill for X. At the end of six months, the value of this investment would be

$$X(1 + z_1)$$

where

z_1 is one-half the bond-equivalent yield of the theoretical six-month spot rate.

Let f represent one-half the forward rate (expressed as a bond-equivalent yield) on a six-month Treasury bill available six months from now. If the investor were to renew her investment by purchasing that bill at that time, then the future dollars available at the end of one year from the X investment would be

$$X(1 + z_1)(1 + f)$$

Third, it is easy to use that formula to find out how many $X the investor must invest in order to get $100 one year from now. This can be found as follows:

$$X(1 + z_1)(1 + f) = 100$$

which gives us

$$X = \frac{100}{(1 + z_1)(1 + f)}$$

We are now prepared to return to the investor's choices and analyze what that situation says about forward rates. The investor will be indifferent between the two alternatives confronting her if she makes the same dollar investment and receives $100 from both alternatives at the end of one year. That is, the investor will be indifferent if

$$\frac{100}{(1 + z_2)^2} = \frac{100}{(1 + z_1)(1 + f)}$$

Solving for f, we get

$$f = \frac{(1 + z_2)^2}{(1 + z_1)^1} - 1$$

Doubling f gives the bond-equivalent yield for the six-month forward rate six months from now.

We can illustrate the use of this formula with the theoretical spot rates shown in Exhibit 6–5. From that exhibit, we know that

Six-month bill spot rate $= .080$ so $z_1 = .0400$
One-year bill spot rate $= .083$ so $z_2 = .0415$

Substituting into the formula, we have

$$f = \frac{(1.0415)^2}{1.0400} - 1$$

$$= .043$$

Therefore, the forward rate on a six-month Treasury security, quoted on a bond-equivalent basis, is 8.6 percent ($.043 \times 2$). Let's confirm our results. The price of a one-year Treasury bill with a $100 maturity value is

$$\frac{100}{(1.0415)^2} = 92.19$$

If $92.19 is invested for six months at the six-month spot rate of 8 percent, the amount at the end of six months would be

$$92.19 \, (1.0400) = 95.8776$$

If $95.8776 is reinvested for another six months in a six-month Treasury offering 4.3 percent for six months (8.6 percent annually), the amount at the end of one year would be

$$95.8776\,(1.043) = 100$$

Both alternatives will have the same $100 payoff if the six-month Treasury bill yield six months from now is 4.3 percent (8.6 percent on a bond-equivalent basis). This means that, if an investor is guaranteed a 4.3 percent yield (8.6 percent bond-equivalent basis) on a six-month Treasury bill six months from now, she will be indifferent between the two alternatives.

We used the theoretical spot rates to compute the forward rate. The resulting forward rate is called the *implied forward rate.*

We can take this sort of analysis much further. It is not necessary to limit ourselves to implied forward rates six months from now. The yield curve can be used to calculate the implied forward rate for any time in the future for any investment horizon. For example, the following can be calculated:

- The two-year implied forward rate five years from now.
- The six-year implied forward rate two years from now.
- The seven-year implied forward rate three years from now.

Relationship between Spot Rates and Short-Term Forward Rates

Suppose an investor purchases a five-year zero-coupon Treasury security for $58.42 with a maturity value of $100. He could instead buy a six-month Treasury bill and reinvest the proceeds every six months for five years. The number of dollars that will be realized depends on the six-month forward rates. Suppose that the investor can actually reinvest the proceeds maturing every six months at the implied six-month forward rates. Let's see how many dollars would accumulate at the end of five years. The implied six-month forward rates were calculated for the yield curve given in Exhibit 6–5. Letting f_t denote the six-month forward rate beginning t six-month periods from now, the semiannual implied forward rates using the spot rates shown in that exhibit are as follows:

$$
\begin{array}{llll}
f_1 = .043000 & f_2 = .050980 & f_3 = .051005 & f_4 = .051770 \\
f_5 = .056945 & f_6 = .060965 & f_7 = .069310 & f_8 = .064625 \\
& f_9 = .062830 & &
\end{array}
$$

If he invests the $58.48 at the six-month spot rate of 4 percent (8 percent on a bond-equivalent basis) and reinvests at the above forward rates, the number of dollars accumulated at the end of five years would be

$$\$58.48(1.04)(1.043)(1.05098)(1.051005)(1.05177)(1.056945) \times$$
$$(1.060965)(1.069310)(1.064625)(1.06283) = \$100$$

Therefore, we see that if the implied forward rates are realized, the $58.48 investment will produce the same number of dollars as an investment in a five-year zero-coupon Treasury security at the five-year spot rate. From this illustration, we can see that the five-year spot rate is related to the current six-month spot rate and the implied six-month forward rates.

In general, the relationship between a t-period spot rate, the current six-month spot rate, and the implied six-month forward rates is as follows:

$$z_t = [(1 + z_1)(1 + f_1)(1 + f_2)(1 + f_3) \cdots (1 + f_{t-1})]^{1/t} - 1$$

Why should an investor care about forward rates? There are actually very good reasons for doing so. Knowledge of the forward rates implied in the current long-term rate is relevant in formulating an investment policy. In addition, forward rates are key inputs into the valuation of bonds with embedded options.

For example, suppose an investor wants to invest for one year (two six-month periods); the current six-month or short rate (z_1) is 7 percent, and the one-year (two-period) rate (z_2) is 6 percent. Using the formulas we have developed, the investor finds that by buying a two-period security, she is effectively making a forward contract to lend money six months from now at the rate of 5 percent for six months. If the investor believes that the second-period rate will turn out to be higher than 5 percent, it will be to her advantage to lend initially on a one-period contract, then at the end of the first period to reinvest interest and principal in the one-period contract available for the second period.

Determinants of the Shape of the Term Structure[3]

If we plot the term structure—the yield-to-maturity, or the spot rate, at successive maturities against maturity—what will it look like? Exhibit 6–3 shows four shapes that have appeared with some frequency over time. Panel (*a*) shows an upward-sloping yield curve; that is, yield rises steadily as maturity increases. This shape is commonly referred to as a *normal* or *upward-sloping yield curve.* Panel (*b*) shows a *downward-sloping* or *inverted yield curve,* where yields decline as maturity increases. Panel (*c*) shows a *humped yield curve.* Finally, panel (*d*) shows a *flat yield curve.*

Two major theories have evolved to account for these shapes: the *expectations theory* and the *market segmentation theory.*

There are three forms of the expectations theory: the *pure expectations theory,* the *liquidity theory,* and the *preferred habitat theory.* All share a hypothesis about the behavior of short-term forward rates and also assume that the forward rates in current long-term contracts are closely related to the market's expectations about future short-term rates. These three theories differ, however, on whether other factors also affect forward rates, and how. The pure expectations

---

3. For a more detailed discussion of the theories of the term structure of interest rates, see Chapter 43.

theory postulates that no systematic factors other than expected future short-term rates affect forward rates; the liquidity theory and the preferred habitat theory assert that there are other factors. Accordingly, the last two forms of the expectations theory are sometimes referred to as *biased expectations theories.*

The Pure Expectations Theory

According to the pure expectations theory, the forward rates exclusively represent the expected future rates. Thus, the entire term structure at a given time reflects the market's current expectations of future short-term rates. Under this view, a rising term structure, as shown in panel (*a*) of Exhibit 6–3, must indicate that the market expects short-term rates to rise throughout the relevant future. Similarly, a flat term structure reflects an expectation that future short-term rates will be mostly constant, and a falling term structure must reflect an expectation that future short-term rates will decline steadily.

We can illustrate this theory by considering how an expectation of a rising short-term future rate would affect the behavior of various market participants to result in a rising yield curve. Assume an initially flat term structure, and suppose that economic news leads market participants to expect interest rates to rise.

• Market participants interested in a long-term investment would not want to buy long-term bonds because they would expect the yield structure to rise sooner or later, resulting in a price decline for the bonds and a capital loss on the long-term bonds purchased. Instead, they would want to invest in short-term debt obligations until the rise in yield had occurred, permitting them to reinvest their funds at the higher yield.

• Speculators expecting rising rates would anticipate a decline in the price of long-term bonds and therefore would want to sell any long-term bonds they own and possibly to "short-sell" some they do not now own. (Should interest rates rise as expected, the price of longer-term bonds will fall. Because the speculator sold these bonds short and can then purchase them at a lower price to cover the short sale, a profit will be earned.) The proceeds received from the selling of long-term debt issues or the shorting of longer-term bonds will be invested in short-term debt obligations.

• Borrowers wishing to acquire long-term funds would be pulled toward borrowing now, in the long end of the market, by the expectation that borrowing at a later time would be more expensive.

All these responses would tend either to lower the net demand for, or to increase the supply of, long-maturity bonds, and two responses would increase demand for short-term debt obligations. This would require a rise in long-term yields in relation to short-term yields; that is, these actions by investors, speculators, and borrowers would tilt the term structure upward until it is consistent with expectations of higher future interest rates. By analogous reasoning, an unexpected event leading to the expectation of lower future rates will result in a downward-sloping yield curve.

Unfortunately, the pure expectations theory suffers from one serious shortcoming. It does not account for the risks inherent in investing in bonds and like instruments. If forward rates were perfect predictors of future interest rates, then the future prices of bonds would be known with certainty. The return over any investment period would be certain and independent of the maturity of the instrument initially acquired and of the time at which the investor needed to liquidate the instrument. However, with uncertainty about future interest rates and hence about future prices of bonds, these instruments become risky investments in the sense that the return over some investment horizon is unknown.

There are two risks that cause uncertainty about the return over some investment horizon. The first is the uncertainty about the price of the bond at the end of the investment horizon. For example, an investor who plans to invest for five years might consider the following three investment alternatives: (1) invest in a five-year bond and hold it for five years, (2) invest in a 12-year bond and sell it at the end of five years, and (3) invest in a 30-year bond and sell it at the end of five years. The return that will be realized for the second and third alternatives is not known because the price of each long-term bond at the end of five years is not known. In the case of the 12-year bond, the price will depend on the yield on seven-year debt securities five years from now; and the price of the 30-year bond will depend on the yield on 25-year bonds five years from now. Because forward rates implied in the current term structure for a future seven-year bond and a future 25-year bond are not perfect predictors of the actual future rates, there is uncertainty about the price for both bonds five years from now. Thus, there is price risk: The risk that the price of the bond will be lower than currently expected at the end of the investment horizon. As explained in the previous chapter, an important feature of price risk is that it increases as the maturity of the bond increases.

The second risk involves the uncertainty about the rate at which the proceeds from a bond that matures during the investment horizon can be reinvested, and is known as reinvestment risk. For example, an investor who plans to invest for five years might consider the following three alternative investments: (1) invest in a five-year bond and hold it for five years, (2) invest in a six-month instrument and, when it matures, reinvest the proceeds in six-month instruments over the entire five-year investment horizon, and (3) invest in a two-year bond and, when it matures, reinvest the proceeds in a three-year bond. The risk in the second and third alternatives is that the return over the five-year investment horizon is unknown because rates at which the proceeds can be reinvested are unknown.

Several interpretations of the pure expectations theory have been put forth by economists. These interpretations are not exact equivalents, nor are they consistent with each other, in large part because they offer different treatments of price risk and reinvestment risk.[4]

The broadest interpretation of the pure expectations theory suggests that investors expect the return for any investment horizon to be the same, regardless of

---

4. These formulations are summarized by John Cox, Jonathan Ingersoll, Jr., and Stephen Ross, "A Re-Examination of Traditional Hypotheses about the Term Structure of Interest Rates," *Journal of Finance*, September 1981, pp. 769–799.

the maturity strategy selected.[5] For example, consider an investor who has a five-year investment horizon. According to this theory, it makes no difference if a five-year, 12-year, or 30-year bond is purchased and held for five years because the investor expects the return from all three bonds to be the same over five years. A major criticism of this very broad interpretation of the theory is that, because of price risk associated with investing in bonds with a maturity greater than the investment horizon, the expected returns from these three very different bond investments should differ in significant ways.[6]

A second interpretation, referred to as the *local expectations* form of the pure expectations theory, suggests that the return will be the same over a short-term investment horizon starting today. For example, if an investor has a six-month investment horizon, buying a five-year, 10-year or 20-year bond will produce the same six-month return. It has been demonstrated that the local expectations formulation, which is narrow in scope, is the only interpretation of the pure expectations theory that can be sustained in equilibrium.[7]

The third interpretation of the pure expectations theory suggests that the return an investor will realize by rolling over short-term bonds to some investment horizon will be the same as holding a zero-coupon bond with a maturity that is the same as that investment horizon. (A zero-coupon bond has no reinvestment risk, so that future interest rates over the investment horizon do not affect the return.) This variant is called the *return-to-maturity expectations* interpretation. For example, let's once again assume that an investor has a five-year investment horizon. If he buys a five-year zero-coupon bond and holds it to maturity, his return is the difference between the maturity value and the price of the bond, all divided by the price of the bond. According to the return-to-maturity expectations, the same return will be realized by buying a six-month instrument and rolling it over for five years. At this time, the validity of this interpretation is subject to considerable doubt.

The Liquidity Theory
We have explained that the drawback of the pure expectations theory is that it does not account for the risks associated with investing in bonds. Nonetheless, we have just shown that there is indeed risk in holding a long-term bond for one period, and that risk increases with the bond's maturity because maturity and price volatility are directly related.

Given this uncertainty, and the reasonable consideration that investors typically do not like uncertainty, some economists and financial analysts have suggested a different theory. This theory states that investors will hold longer-term maturities if they are offered a long-term rate higher than the average of expected

5. F Lutz, "The Structure of Interest Rates," *Quarterly Journal of Economics,* 1940–41, pp. 36–63.
6. Cox, Ingersoll, and Ross, pp. 774–775.
7. Cox, Ingersoll, and Ross, p. 788.

future rates by a risk premium that is positively related to the term to maturity.[8] Put differently, the forward rates should reflect both interest rate expectations and a liquidity premium (which is really a risk premium), and the premium should be higher for longer maturities.

According to this theory, which is called the *liquidity theory of the term structure,* the implied forward rates will not be an unbiased estimate of the market's expectations of future interest rates because they include a liquidity premium. Thus, an upward-sloping yield curve may reflect expectations that future interest rates either will rise or will be flat (or even fall), but with a liquidity premium increasing fast enough with maturity so as to produce an upward-sloping yield curve.

The Preferred Habitat Theory

Another theory, known as the preferred habitat theory, also adopts the view that the term structure reflects the expectation of the future path of interest rates as well as a risk premium. However, the preferred habitat theory rejects the assertion that the risk premium must rise uniformly with maturity.[9] Proponents of the preferred habitat theory say that the latter conclusion could be accepted if all investors intend to liquidate their investment at the shortest possible date and all borrowers are anxious to borrow long. This assumption can be rejected because institutions have holding periods dictated by the nature of their liabilities.

The preferred habitat theory asserts that, to the extent that the demand and supply of funds in a given maturity range do not match, some lenders and borrowers will be induced to shift to maturities showing the opposite imbalances. However, they will need to be compensated by an appropriate risk premium that reflects the extent of aversion to either price or reinvestment risk.

Thus, this theory proposes that the shape of the yield curve is determined by both expectations of future interest rates and a risk premium, positive or negative, to induce market participants to shift out of their preferred habitat. Clearly, according to this theory, yield curves sloping up, down, flat, or humped are all possible.

Market Segmentation Theory

The market segmentation theory recognizes that investors have preferred habitats dictated by the nature of their liabilities. This theory also proposes that the major reason for the shape of the yield curve lies in asset/liability management constraints (either regulatory or self-imposed) and creditors (borrowers) restricting their lending (financing) to specific maturity sectors.[10] However, the market seg-

---

8. John R. Hicks, *Value and Capital,* second ed. (London: Oxford University Press, 1946), pp. 141–145.
9. Franco Modigliani and Richard Sutch, "Innovations in Interest Rate Policy," *American Economic Review,* May 1966, pp. 178–197.
10. This theory was suggested in J. M. Culbertson, "The Term Structure of Interest Rates," *Quarterly Journal of Economics,* November 1957, pp. 489–504.

mentation theory differs from the preferred habitat theory in that it assumes that neither investors nor borrowers are willing to shift from one maturity sector to another to take advantage of opportunities arising from differences between expectations and forward rates. Thus, for the segmentation theory, the shape of the yield curve is determined by supply of and demand for securities within each maturity sector.

SUMMARY

In all economies, there is not just one interest rate but a structure of interest rates. The difference between the yields on any two bonds is called the yield spread. The base interest rate is the yield on a Treasury security. The yield spread between a non-Treasury security and a comparable on-the-run Treasury security is called a risk premium. The factors that affect the spread include (1) the type of issuer (e.g., agency, corporate, municipality), (2) the issuer's perceived creditworthiness as measured by the rating system of commercial rating companies, (3) the term or maturity of the instrument, (4) the embedded options in a bond issue (e.g., call, put, or conversion provisions), (5) the taxability of interest income at the federal and municipal levels, and (6) the expected liquidity of the issue.

The relationship between yield and maturity is referred to as the term structure of interest rates. The graphical depiction of the relationship between the yield on bonds of the same credit quality but different maturities is known as the yield curve. Because the yield on Treasury securities is the base rate from which a nongovernment bond's yield often is benchmarked, the most commonly constructed yield curve is the Treasury yield curve.

There is a problem with using the Treasury yield curve to determine the one yield at which to discount all the cash payments of any bond. Each cash flow should be discounted at a unique interest rate that is applicable to the time period in which the cash flow is to be received. Because any bond can be viewed as a package of zero-coupon instruments, its value should equal the value of all the component zero-coupon instruments. The rate on a zero-coupon bond is called the spot rate. The theoretical spot-rate curve for Treasury securities can be estimated from the Treasury yield curve using a method known as bootstrapping.

Under certain assumptions, the market's expectation of future interest rates can be extrapolated from the theoretical Treasury spot-rate curve. The resulting forward rate is called the implied forward rate. Spot rates include the current six-month spot rate and the implied six-month forward rates.

Several theories have been proposed about the determinants of the term structure: the pure expectations theory, the biased expectations theories (the liquidity theory and the preferred habitat theory), and the market segmentation theory. All the expectation theories hypothesize that the one-period forward rates represent the market's expectations of future actual rates. The pure expectations theory asserts that these rates constitute the only factor. The biased expectations theories assert that there are other factors that determine the term structure.

⑥   # BOND MARKET INDEXES

Frank K. Reilly, Ph.D., CFA
Bernard J. Hank Professor of Finance
University of Notre Dame

David J. Wright, Ph.D.
Associate Professor of Finance
University of Wisconsin—Parkside

The value of nonmunicipal bonds outstanding in the United States at over $5 trillion exceeds the combined value of equity in the United States, and a similar comparison holds for world capital markets where the value of fixed income securities exceeds the total value of equity. The only instance where this capital comparison does not hold is in some emerging market countries where the bond markets have not yet developed. Given the economic dominance of fixed income markets, it is difficult to understand why there has not been greater concern and analysis of bond market indexes. Part of the reason for a lack of analysis of bond market indexes is the relatively short history of these indexes. Specifically, in contrast to stock market indexes that have been in existence for over 100 years, total rate-of-return bond indexes were not developed until the 1970s, and those created were limited to U.S. investment-grade bonds. For example, indexes for U.S. high-yield bonds, where the market has grown to over $200 billion, were not established until the mid-1980s, which is also when international government bond indexes were initially created.

There are four parts to this chapter. The first considers the major uses for bond market indexes. The second is concerned with the difficulty of building and maintaining a bond market index compared to the requirements for a stock market index. The third section contains a description of the indexes available in three major categories. Finally, we present the risk/return characteristics of the alternative bond market sectors and examine the correlations among the alternative indexes.

USES OF BOND INDEXES

An analysis of bond market indexes is important and timely for several reasons. First, the bond portfolios of both pension funds and individuals have grown substantially in recent years; sales of fixed income mutual funds exceeded equity mutual fund sales every year from 1985 to 1992. With the increase in the number and size of bond portfolios, investors and portfolio managers have increasingly come to rely on bond indexes *as benchmarks for measuring performance* and, in the case of those managing on a performance-fee basis, determining compensation. There are numerous indexes of differing construction that purport to measure the aggregate bond market and the major sectors of the market (government, corporate, and mortgages). An obvious concern is the choice of an appropriate index that will provide an accurate benchmark of bond market behavior.

Second, benchmarks for *bond index funds* have become increasingly popular because those who monitor the performance of bond portfolios have discovered that, similar to equity managers, most bond portfolio managers have not been able to outperform the aggregate bond market. The amount of money invested in bond index funds grew from $3 billion in 1984 to over $100 billion in 1995. Given the total size and growth of the bond market, it is estimated that bond index funds could grow to $200 billion by the end of the 1990s.

The behavior of a particular index is critical to fixed income managers who attempt to replicate its performance in an index fund. Clearly, if all indexes move together, one would be indifferent to the choice of a particular index. We examine the return correlations between the various indexes and their risk/return characteristics. The analysis of long-term risk/return and correlations is important because index numbers may differ markedly over short periods of time, yet still exhibit similar long-run movements.

Portfolio managers of a bond index fund need to rebalance their assets to replicate the composition, maturity, and duration of the bond market. As shown in Reilly, Kao, and Wright, the composition of the bond market changed dramatically during the 1980s and early 1990s.[1] It is possible to use the indexes to document the intertemporal changes in the makeup, maturity, and duration of the bond market that have influenced its risk and return characteristics.

Third, because of the size and importance of the bond market, there has been and will continue to be substantial fixed income research; the bond market indexes can provide accurate and timely measurement of the risk/return of these assets and the characteristics of the market, as noted above. For example, the time-series properties of equity index returns have been extensively examined, but these same tests were not applied to bond market returns. Our investigation indicated significant autocorrelation in bond market index returns, which were

---

1. Frank K. Reilly, Wenchi Kao, and David J. Wright, "Alternative Bond Market Indexes," *Financial Analysts Journal* 48, no. 3 (May/June 1992), pp. 44–58.

explained by examining the intertemporal behavior of U.S. Treasury securities with different maturities.[2]

BUILDING AND MAINTAINING A BOND INDEX

To construct a *stock* market index, you have to select a sample of stocks, decide how to weight each component, and select a computational method. Once you have done this, adjustment for stock splits is typically automatic, and the pricing of the securities is fairly easy because most of the sample stocks are listed on a major stock exchange or actively traded in the OTC market. Mergers or significant changes in the performance of the firms in an index may necessitate a change in the index components. Other than such events, a stock could continue in an index for decades. (On average, the DJIA has about one change per year.)

In contrast, the creation, computation, and maintenance of a bond market index is more difficult for several reasons. First, *the universe of bonds is broader and more diverse than that of stocks*. It includes U.S. Treasury issues, agency series, municipal bonds, and a wide variety of corporate bonds spanning several segments (industrials, utilities, financials) and ranging from high-quality, AAA-rated bonds to bonds in default. Furthermore, within each group, issues differ by coupon and maturity as well as sinking funds and call features. As a result of this diversity, an aggregate bond market series can be subdivided into numerous subindexes; the Merrill Lynch series, for example, contains over 150 subindexes.

Second, *the universe of bonds changes constantly*. A firm will typically have one common stock issue outstanding, which may vary in size over time as the result of additional share sales or repurchases. In contrast, a major corporation will have several bond issues outstanding at any point in time, and these issues will change constantly because of maturities, sinking funds, and call features. This change in the universe of bonds outstanding also makes it more difficult to determine the market value of bonds outstanding, which is necessary when computing market-value-weighted rates of return.

Third, *the volatility of bond prices varies across issues and over time*. As indicated in Chapter 5 bond price volatility is influenced by the *duration* and *convexity* of the bond. These factors change constantly with the maturity, coupon, market yield, and call features of the bond. As maturity changes constantly and market yields become more volatile, which in turn affects embedded call options, it becomes more difficult to estimate the duration, convexity, and implied volatility of an individual bond issue or an aggregate bond series.

Finally, *there can be significant problems in the pricing of individual bond issues*. Individual bond issues are generally not as liquid as stocks. While most

---

2. Ibid.

stock issues are listed on exchanges or traded in an active OTC market with an electronic quotation system (NASDAQ), most bonds are traded on a fragmented OTC market without a consolidated quotation system. This problem is especially acute for corporate bonds. Several studies have examined this problem and noted the significant effects of using alternative sources for prices.[3]

DESCRIPTION OF ALTERNATIVE BOND INDEXES

This section contains three subsections to reflect three major sectors of the global bond market: (1) U.S. investment grade bonds (including Treasury bonds), (2) U.S. high-yield bonds, and (3) international government bonds. In each case, we examine the overall constraints and computational procedures employed for the indexes in the three sectors.

Several characteristics are critical in judging or comparing bond indexes. First is the *sample of securities*, including the number of bonds as well as specific requirements for including the bonds in the sample, such as maturity and size of issue. It is also important to know what issues have been excluded from the index. Second is the *weighting of returns* for individual issues. Specifically, are the returns market-value weighted or equally weighted? Third, users of indexes need to consider the *quality of the price data* used in the computation. Are the bond prices used to compute rates of return based upon actual market transactions as they almost always are for stock indexes? Alternatively, are the prices provided by bond traders based upon recent actual transactions or are they the traders' current "best estimate"? Finally, are they based on "matrix pricing" that involves a computer model that estimates a price using current and historical relationships? Fourth, what *reinvestment assumption* does the rate of return calculation use for interim cash flows?

U.S. Investment-Grade Bond Indexes

Four firms publish ongoing rate-of-return investment-grade bond market indexes. Three of them publish a comprehensive set of indexes that span the universe of U.S. bonds: Lehman Brothers (LB), Merrill Lynch (ML), and Salomon Brothers (SB). The fourth firm, Ryan Labs (RL), concentrates on a long series for the government bond sector.

Exhibit 7–1 summarizes the major characteristics of the indexes created and maintained by these firms. Three of the four firms (LB, ML, and SB) include numerous bonds (over 5,000), and there is substantial diversity in a sample that includes

3. In this regard, see Kenneth P. Nunn, Jr., Joanne Hill, and Thomas Schneeweis, "Corporate Bond Price Data Sources and Return/Risk Measurement," *Journal of Financial and Quantitative Analysis* 21, no. 2 (June 1986), pp. 197–208; and Oded Sarig and Arthur Warga, "Bond Price Data and Bond Market Liquidity," *Journal of Financial and Quantitative Analysis* 24, no. 3 (September 1989), pp. 367–378.

EXHIBIT 7-1

Summary of Bond-Market Indexes

Name of Index	Number of Issues	Maturity	Size of Issues	Weighting	Pricing	Reinvestment Assumption	Subindexes Available
U.S. Investment-Grade Bond Indexes							
Lehman Brothers Aggregate	5,000+	Over 1 year	Over $100 million	Market value	Trader priced and model priced	No	Government, gov./corp., corporate, mortgage-backed, asset-backed
Merrill Lynch Composite	5,000+	Over 1 year	Over $50 million	Market value	Trader priced and model priced	In specific bonds	Government, gov./corp., corporate, mortgage
Ryan Treasury Composite	118	Over 1 year	All Treasury	Market value and equal	Market priced	In specific bonds	Treasury
Salomon Brothers Composite	5,000+	Over 1 year	Over $50 million	Market value	Trader priced	In one-month T-bill	Broad inv. grade, Treas.-agency, corporate, mortgage
U.S. High-Yield Bond Indexes							
Blume-Keim	233	Over 10 years	Over $25 million	Equal	Trader priced	Yes	Only composite
First Boston	423	All maturities	Over $75 million	Market value	Trader priced	Yes	Composite and by rating
Lehman Brothers	624	Over 1 year	Over $100 million	Market value	Trader priced	No	Composite and by rating
Merrill Lynch	735	Over 1 year	Over $25 million	Market value	Trader priced	Yes	Composite and by rating
Salomon Brothers	299	Over 7 years	Over $50 million	Market value	Trader priced	Yes	Composite and by rating
Global Government Bond Indexes (Initial Date of Index)							
Lehman Brothers (January 1987)	800	Over 1 year	Over $200 million	Market value	Trader priced	Yes	Composite and 13 countries, local and U.S. dollars
Merrill Lynch (December 1985)	9,736	Over 1 year	Over $100 million	Market value	Trader priced	Yes	Composite and 9 countries, local and U.S. dollars
J. P. Morgan (12/31/85)	445	Over 1 year	Over $200 million	Market value	Trader priced	Yes in index	Composite and 11 countries, local and U.S. dollars
Salomon Brothers (12/31/84)	525	Over 1 year	Over $250 million	Market value	Trader priced	Yes at local short-term rate	Composite and 14 countries, local and U.S. dollars

Source: Frank K. Reilly, Wenchi Kao, and David J. Wright, "Alternative Bond Market Indexes," *Financial Analysts Journal* 48, no. 3 (May–June, 1992); Frank K. Reilly and David J. Wright, "An Analysis of High Yield Bond Benchmarks," *Journal of Fixed Income* 3, no. 4 (March 1994); Frank K. Reilly and David J. Wright, "Global Bond Markets: An Analysis of Performance and Benchmarks," mimeo (March 1994).

Treasuries, corporates, and mortgage securities. In contrast, the Ryan series is limited to Treasury bonds and has a sample size that has varied over time, based upon the Treasury issues outstanding (i.e., from 26 to 118 issues). All of the indexes require bonds to have maturities of at least one year. The required minimum size of an issue varies from $25 million (ML and LB) to $50 million (SB); while the Treasury issues used by Ryan are substantially larger. All the series include only investment-grade bonds (rated BBB or better) and exclude convertible bonds and floating-rate bonds. The three broad-based indexes by LB, ML, and SB also exclude government flower bonds, while Ryan has included these bonds in its index because flower bonds were a significant factor in the government bond market during the 1950s.

The two major alternatives for weighting are *relative market value* of the issues outstanding and *equal weighting* (also referred to as *unweighted*). The justification for market-value weighting is that it reflects the relative economic importance of the issue and is a logical weighting for an investor with no preferences regarding asset allocation. Although this theoretical argument is reasonable, it is important to recognize that in the real world it is difficult to keep track of the outstanding bonds, given the possibility of calls, sinking funds, and redemptions. Alternatively, equal weighting is reasonable for an investor who has no prior assumptions regarding the relative importance of individual issues. Also, equal weighting is consistent if one is assuming the random selection of issues. Finally, an equally weighted index is easier to compute and the results are unambiguous because it is not necessary to worry about outstanding market value due to calls and so on. The three large-sample indexes are value-weighted, while Ryan Labs has created both a value-weighted and an equal-weighted series.

As noted, one of the major problems with computing returns for a bond index is that continuous transaction prices are not available for most bonds. Ryan can get recent transaction prices for its Treasury issues, while SB gets all prices from its traders. As noted, these trader prices may be based on a recent actual transaction, the trader's current bid price, or what the trader would bid if he or she made a market in the bond. Both LB and ML use a combination of trader pricing and matrix prices based on a computer model. It is contended that most of the individual issues are priced by traders, so most of the value of each index is based on trader prices.

The indexes also treat interim cash flows differently. Both ML and Ryan assume that cash flows are immediately reinvested in the bonds that generated the cash flows. SB assumes that flows are reinvested at the one-month T-bill rate, while LB does not assume any reinvestment of the funds. Obviously, immediate reinvestment in the same bond is the most aggressive assumption, while no reinvestment is the most conservative.

U.S. High-Yield Bond Indexes

There are two notable points about high-yield (HY) bond indexes. First, they have a shorter history than the investment-grade bond indexes. This is not surprising because, as shown in several studies, this market only became a recognizable factor in 1977 and its major growth began in about 1982.[4] Therefore, the fact that HY bond indexes began in about 1984 is reasonable.

Second, earlier we noted the general difficulty of creating and maintaining bond indexes because of the constant changes in the size and characteristics of the sample and the significant pricing problems. The fact is, these difficulties are magnified when dealing with the HY bond market because it experiences larger sample changes due to defaults and more frequent redemptions. In addition, the illiquidity and bond pricing problems in the HY bond market are a quantum leap above those faced in the government and investment-grade corporate bond market.

As shown in Exhibit 7–1, there are five creators of HY bond indexes, including an academic source (Professors Blume and Keim [BK]) and four investment firms (First Boston [FB], Lehman Brothers [LB], Merrill Lynch [ML], and Salomon Brothers [SB]).[5] The investment firms have also created indexes for rating categories within the HY bond universe: BB, B, and CCC bonds.

The summary of characteristics in Exhibit 7–1 indicates that there are substantial differences among the HY bond indexes. This contrasts with relatively small differences in the characteristics of investment-grade bond indexes. The number of issues in the alternative HY bond indexes varies from 233 HY bonds in the Blume-Keim (BK) series to 735 bonds in the Merrill Lynch High Yield Master (ML) series. Some of the differences in sample size can be traced to the maturity-size constraints of the particular index. The large number of bonds in the ML series can be partially explained by its maturity guideline, which includes all HY bonds with a maturity over one year compared to a 10-year maturity requirement for the BK series.

The minimum issue size is also important because ML and BK have a minimum issue size requirement of $25 million compared to $50 million (SB), $75 million (FB), and $100 million (LB). The only surprise is the large sample of bonds in the LB index (624) compared to the other HY bond indexes, which have much smaller size constraints than LB's $100 million.

Finally, there are significant differences in how the alternative indexes handle defaulted issues. The treatment varies, from dropping issues the day they default (ML) to retaining them for an unlimited period subject to size and other constraints (FB, LB).

Currently, only one index differs in how the returns are weighted. The four investment firm indexes have always been market-value weighted (FB, LB, ML, and SB). The BK index was originally equal-weighted, but currently is market-value weighted because it uses the market-weighted SB long-term HY index.

---

4. See, Edward I. Altman, "Revisiting the High Yield Bond Market," *Financial Management* 21, no. 2 (Summer 1992), pp. 78–92; Rayner Cheung, Joseph C. Bencivenga, and Frank J. Fabozzi, "Original-Issue High Yield Bonds: Historical Return and Default Experiences 1977-1989," *Journal of Fixed Income* 2, no. 2 (September 1992), pp. 58–76; Martin S. Fridson, "The State of the High Yield Bond Market: Overshooting or Return to Normalcy?" *Journal of Applied Corporate Finance* 7, no. 1 (Spring 1994), pp. 85–97.

5. Drexel Burnham also created an index before its demise in 1989. There is also an index of high-yield bond mutual funds created by Lipper Analytical.

All the bonds in the HY bond indexes are trader priced except for ML, which uses matrix pricing for a few of its illiquid issues. The difficulty with trader pricing is that when bond issues do not trade, the price provided is a trader's best estimate of what the price "should be." Matrix pricing is likewise a problem because each issue has unique characteristics that may not be considered by the computer program. Obviously, this means that it is possible to get significantly different prices from alternative traders or matrix pricing programs.

All the indexes except LB assume the reinvestment of interim cash flows, but at different rates—that is, the individual bond rate, the average portfolio rate, or a T-bill rate. Finally, the average maturity and the duration for the indexes are consistent with the constraints on the index: FB, LB, and ML have 1-year minimums and lower durations; while SB, with a 7-year minimum and BK, with a 10-year minimum, are at the high end.

In summary, there are significant differences in the characteristics of the alternative HY bond indexes in terms of the samples and pricing. One would expect these differences to have a significant impact on the risk/return performance and the correlations among indexes.[6]

Global Government Bond Market Indexes

Similar to the HY bond indexes, these global-based indexes are relatively new (beginning in 1985) because there was limited interest in these markets prior to the 1980s. The summary description in Exhibit 7–1 indicates numerous similarities among the indexes by the four investment firms (J. P. Morgan [JP], Lehman Brothers [LB], Merrill Lynch [ML], and Salomon Brothers [SB]) with the exception of minimum size that varied from $100 million (ML) to $250 million (SB). In turn, this issue size constraint had an impact on the sample sizes that ranged from JP at 445 to ML with over 9,000 bonds. Beyond this issue size and sample size difference, the indexes are the same regarding market-value weighting and trader pricing. All of them assume the reinvestment of cash flows with small differences in the reinvested security.

RISK/RETURN CHARACTERISTICS

The presentation of the risk/return results is divided into two subsections. The first subsection presents and discusses the results for the U.S. indexes, including government and investment-grade bonds as well as HY bonds. The second subsection provides a similar presentation for global bond indexes, including both domestic and U.S. dollar returns.

---

6. For a detailed analysis of the alternative HY bond indexes, see Frank K. Reilly and David J. Wright, "An Analysis of High-Yield Bond Benchmarks," *Journal of Fixed Income* 3, no. 4 (March 1994), pp. 6–25.

U.S. Investment-Grade and HY Bonds

The annual rates of return and risk measures are contained in Exhibit 7–2 for the period beginning in 1976, when the data are available. We show the Lehman Brothers index for U.S. investment-grade bonds because it has the earliest starting date and it has been shown that all of the investment-grade bond series are very highly correlated.[7] The SB broad investment-grade (BIG) index is provided because of its popularity, although it began in 1980. The FB high-yield indexes began in 1986, while the Altman Index of defaulted debt was created in 1987.

While some series are reported beginning in 1976, most comparisons will begin with 1986 to allow an analysis across the investment-grade and HY bond segments. When viewing the results in Exhibit 7–2 and Exhibit 7–3, one is struck by two factors. The first is the generally high level of mean returns over this 10-year period wherein the investment-grade bonds experienced average annual returns of approximately 10 percent and the HY bonds attained returns of almost 12 percent (the returns for the investment-grade bonds were slightly better for the 20-year period).

The second observation is that the relationship between return and risk (measured as the annualized standard deviation of returns) was generally consistent with expectations. The investment-grade bond indexes typically had lower returns and risk, while the HY bond indexes had higher returns and risk measures. The major deviations were the high-risk segments (CCC rated bonds and defaulted bonds), which experienced returns about in line with HY debt, but risk substantially above all other assets. The BB rated bonds experienced abnormally positive results because they experienced returns similar to other HY bonds but experienced risk similar to investment-grade debt.

Global Government Bonds

These results will be considered in two parts, involving results in local currency and in U.S. dollars. The results in Exhibits 7–4 and 7–5 show significant consistency between the risk and returns in local currency for the alternative countries. Germany experienced the lowest return and risk, while the U.K. had a much higher rate of return (12 percent versus about 7 percent) but also experienced higher risk (almost 8 percent for the U.K. versus 4 percent for Germany). The only country that deviated from the main security market line was Japan, which experienced relatively low risk but very low return.

The return/risk results in U.S. dollars are contained in Exhibits 7–4 and 7–6. The graph in Exhibit 7–6 makes it clear that the results change substantially with the conversion to U.S. dollars. Specifically, the U.S. is clearly the low risk/return market, followed by Canada, while the other four countries (France, Germany, Japan, and the U.K.) all experienced much higher returns (12 percent versus 15 percent) and larger risk (12 percent versus 16 percent). France had the best risk-adjusted returns during this time period.

---

7. Reilly, Kao, and Wright, *Op cit.*

EXHIBIT 7-2

Rates of Return and Risk for United States Bond Indexes (1976–1995)

	Lehman Bros. Govt/Corp	Lehman Bros. Government	Lehman Bros. Corporate	Lehman Bros. Mortgage	Lehman Bros. Aggregate	Salomon Bros. Broad Invest. Grade	First Boston High Yield Index	First Boston High Yield BB Grade	First Boston High Yield B Grade	First Boston High Yield CCC Grade	Altman Default Index
1976	15.58	12.36	19.34	16.31	15.60						
1977	2.98	2.80	3.16	1.89	3.03						
1978	1.19	1.80	0.35	2.41	1.40						
1979	2.29	5.41	-2.10	0.13	1.93						
1980	3.07	5.19	-0.29	0.65	2.71	2.73					
1981	7.26	9.36	2.95	0.07	6.25	6.70					
1982	31.10	27.75	39.20	43.04	32.62	31.78					
1983	7.99	7.39	9.27	10.13	8.36	8.21					
1984	15.02	14.50	16.62	15.79	15.15	14.98					
1985	21.30	20.43	24.06	25.21	22.10	22.23					
1986	15.62	15.31	16.53	13.43	15.26	15.45	13.65	12.70	14.77	6.58	
1987	2.29	2.20	2.56	4.29	2.76	2.60	0.39	13.33	1.61	-18.35	37.82
1988	7.58	7.03	9.22	8.72	7.89	7.98	-6.38	4.42	-3.27	-34.01	26.45
1989	14.24	14.23	14.09	15.35	14.53	14.44	43.76	26.84	45.06	100.15	-22.79
1990	8.28	8.72	7.05	10.72	8.96	9.09	16.65	13.86	18.73	40.42	-17.08
1991	16.13	15.32	18.51	15.72	16.00	15.97	18.91	16.09	18.32	38.85	43.10
1992	7.58	7.23	8.69	6.96	7.40	7.59	-0.98	-0.66	0.63	-15.44	15.40
1993	11.06	10.64	12.18	6.85	9.75	9.89	17.38	18.40	16.78	17.13	27.93
1994	-3.51	-3.38	-3.92	-1.61	-2.92	-2.85	-0.98	-0.66	0.63	-15.44	6.70
1995	19.25	18.34	22.25	16.80	18.48	18.55	17.38	18.40	16.78	17.13	11.26
Arithmetic Mean Return											
1976–1995	10.32	10.13	10.99	10.64	10.36	9.87	11.98	12.27	13.00	13.70	14.31
1986–1995	9.85	9.56	10.72	9.72	9.81						
Geometric Mean Return											
1973–1995	10.03	9.90	10.52	10.20	10.06	9.69	11.80	13.82	13.36	11.17	10.84
1986–1995	9.65	9.38	10.47	9.58	9.63						
Annualized Standard Deviation of Monthly Returns											
1976–1995	6.61	5.96	8.15	8.55	6.77	7.03	7.09	4.71	7.46	13.88	12.73
1986–1995	4.96	4.96	5.14	4.22	4.69	4.70					

All the computations with the Altman Default index were computed for the 1987–1995 time period only.

E X H I B I T   7–3

Geometric Mean Return versus the Standard Deviation of U.S. Bond Index Returns (1986–1995)

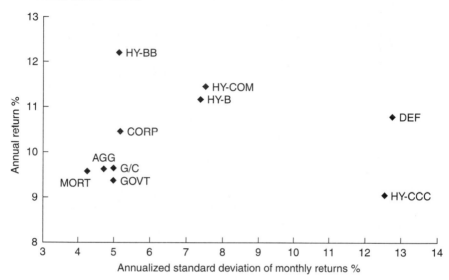

In addition to the individual countries, there is a global index with and without the U.S. Notably, both of these indexes are above the average line, which is probably because of the reduced risk due to global diversification.

CORRELATION RELATIONSHIPS

The correlations will likewise be presented in two parts: U.S. bond market results and global bond market results.

U.S. Investment-Grade and HY Bonds

The correlation results in Exhibit 7–7 confirm some expectations about relationships among sectors of the bond market but also provide some unique results. The expected relationships are those among the five investment-grade bond indexes. Because all of these are investment grade, which implies that there is a small probability of default, the major factor influencing returns is interest-rate changes based upon the Treasury yield curve. Therefore, since they have a common determinant, they are very highly correlated—that is, the correlations range from about 0.90 to 0.99, with the results for the mortgage bond sector at the low end because of the impact of the embedded call options.

The HY bond results show two distinct patterns. First, the correlations among the HY indexes are quite high, ranging from 0.74 to 0.99. Second, the

EXHIBIT 7-4

Annual Rates of Return and Risk Measures for Major Global Bond Markets in Local Currency and in U.S. Dollars (Merrill Lynch Indexes)

Year	In Local Currency						In U.S. Dollars							
	Canada	France	Germany	Japan	U.K.	U.S.	Canada	France	Germany	Japan	U.K.	U.S.	Global	Global w/o U.S.
1986	17.81	14.08	8.63	7.66	11.05	15.64	19.46	34.37	38.39	36.41	13.78	15.64	22.96	31.60
1987	3.89	5.40	5.08	8.32	15.97	2.11	10.35	27.63	28.60	41.38	47.67	2.11	17.97	35.93
1988	9.08	16.24	5.23	5.89	6.74	6.80	18.89	2.22	-6.64	2.63	2.47	6.80	4.42	2.27
1989	12.75	4.15	0.98	-1.50	8.01	14.41	16.12	8.91	5.57	-14.55	-3.72	14.41	4.80	-4.12
1990	7.42	7.33	1.09	0.78	9.53	8.53	7.22	22.36	14.79	7.19	31.31	8.53	11.31	14.35
1991	21.03	15.92	11.87	13.79	16.77	15.32	21.50	13.41	9.85	23.40	12.81	15.32	16.61	17.79
1992	9.44	11.29	13.34	11.31	18.83	7.27	-0.53	4.61	6.16	11.27	-3.94	7.27	7.42	7.79
1993	16.05	21.10	15.06	13.63	22.00	10.72	11.41	13.09	7.30	27.12	19.43	10.72	14.76	18.80
1994	-4.48	-5.49	-2.62	-3.03	-7.04	-3.32	-9.86	4.56	9.08	8.49	-1.68	-3.32	1.84	6.67
1995	19.30	17.12	16.78	14.14	16.65	18.59	22.71	27.81	26.49	10.42	15.77	18.59	17.31	16.74
Arithmetic Mean	11.23	10.71	7.54	7.10	11.85	9.61	11.73	15.90	13.96	15.38	13.39	9.61	11.94	14.78
Geometric Mean	10.97	10.45	7.36	6.92	11.56	9.42	11.26	15.40	13.27	14.26	12.36	9.42	11.74	14.18
Standard Deviation	6.64	5.26	3.99	5.17	7.58	5.10	9.30	12.28	13.36	15.14	14.82	5.10	7.06	11.66

EXHIBIT 7–5

Geometric Mean Return versus the Standard Deviation of Country Bond
Returns in Local Currency (1986–1995)

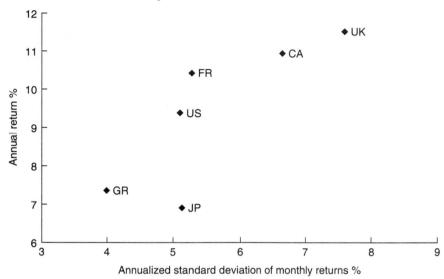

EXHIBIT 7–6

Geometric Mean Return versus the Standard Deviation of Country Bond
Returns in U.S. Dollars (1986–1995)

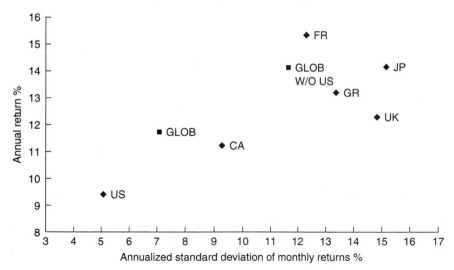

Correlation Coefficients of the U.S. Bond Index Monthly Returns (1986-1995)

	LB Govt./Corp.	LB Govt.	LB Corp.	LB Mort.	SB B.I.G.	LB HY Comp.	LB HY BB	LB HY B	LB HY CCC	Altman Default
LB Govt./Corp.	1.000									
LB Govt.	0.997	1.000								
LB Corp.	0.975	0.955	1.000							
LB Mort.	0.909	0.897	0.914	1.000						
SB B.I.G.	0.993	0.990	0.970	0.942	1.000					
LB HY Comp.	0.358	0.318	0.462	0.363	0.360	1.000				
LB HY BB	0.531	0.491	0.630	0.513	0.532	0.887	1.000			
LB HY B	0.348	0.309	0.448	0.358	0.350	0.989	0.866	1.000		
LB HY CCC	0.227	0.188	0.330	0.241	0.229	0.913	0.736	0.870	1.000	
Altman Default[a]	-0.054	-0.084	0.032	-0.034	-0.057	0.577	0.463	0.562	0.557	1.000

[a] All of the correlation coefficients with the Altman Default index were computed for the 1987–1995 time period only.

correlations among investment-grade bonds and HY bonds are significantly lower, generally ranging from about 0.20 to 0.40. Not surprising, the highest correlations are between BB rated bonds and investment-grade bonds, while the lowest correlations (several insignificant) are between investment-grade bonds and CCC rated bonds.

The correlations with defaulted debt were unique. The correlations between defaulted debt and investment-grade debt are generally negative but not significant. In contrast, the correlations among defaulted debt and various HY bonds are substantially higher and generally exceed the correlations between HY debt and investment-grade debt.

Global Government Bond Correlations

Again, the discussion is in two parts to consider the local currency and U.S. dollar results. Exhibit 7–8 contains correlations among returns in local currencies. The correlations of Canada with all non-U.S. countries indicate a similar relationship (about .45), while the U.S.-Canada correlation was about 0.70. In turn, France had fairly similar correlations with all the countries except a much higher

E X H I B I T   7–8

Correlation Coefficients Among Monthly Global Bond Index Returns in Local Currency 1986–1995

	Ryan U.S.	JPM Canada	JPM France	JPM Germany	JPM Japan	JPM U.K.	ML Global w/o U.S.	ML Global with U.S.
Ryan U.S.	—							
JPM Canada	0.746	—						
JPM France	0.514	0.439	—					
JPM Germany	0.472	0.435	0.734	—				
JPM Japan	0.386	0.378	0.370	0.506	—			
JPM U.K.	0.437	0.521	0.583	0.623	0.411	—		
ML Global w/o U.S.	0.304	0.262	0.250	0.430	0.584	0.336	—	
ML Global with U.S.	0.610	0.481	0.390	0.523	0.624	0.430	0.933	—

All of these correlations are significant at the 5% level.

The ML Global returns are expressed in U.S. dollars.

correlation with Germany—its major trading partner in Europe. Japan had correlations with the European countries between 0.40 and 0.55 but had lower correlations with the United States—about 0.38. This is even though Japan and the United States conduct significant trade.

Exhibit 7–9 contains correlations among returns in U.S. dollars. The results differ from local currency results as well as from normal expectations. Typically, correlations decline when one goes from local currency to U.S. currency. This is generally attributed to the effect of exchange-rate changes, which are somewhat random, thereby reducing the relationships. This is generally what happened for correlations among these countries and the United States: There were big differences with Canada and Japan but fairly small changes with France, Germany, and the U.K. In contrast, the correlations among the European countries and with Japan consistently experienced large *increases* when returns were in U.S. dollars—typically by about 0.20. For example, the correlations between France and Germany went from about 0.73 to about 0.93. This implies that during this period the exchange-rate correlations were quite high and became a cause for stronger return correlations.

E X H I B I T   7–9

Correlation Coefficients Among Monthly Global Bond Index Returns in U.S. Dollars 1986–1995

	Ryan U.S.	JPM Canada	JPM France	JPM Germany	JPM Japan	JPM U.K.	ML Global w/o U.S.	ML Global with U.S.
Ryan U.S.	—							
JPM Canada	0.604*	—						
JPM France	0.387*	0.169	—					
JPM Germany	0.322*	0.140	0.930*	—				
JPM Japan	0.218*	0.130	0.666*	0.694*	—			
JPM U.K.	0.307*	0.317*	0.652*	0.649*	0.581*	—		
ML Global w/o U.S.	0.304*	0.218*	0.812*	0.838*	0.937*	0.761*	—	
ML Global with U.S.	0.610*	0.395*	0.819*	0.815*	0.861*	0.739*	0.933*	—

*Significant at the 5% level.

CONCLUSION

Bond market indexes are a relatively new but important factor to those who analyze bonds or manage bond portfolios. They have several significant uses, including acting as performance benchmarks, as benchmarks for investors who want to invest through index funds, and as a means to determine risk/return characteristics and correlations as inputs into the asset-allocation decision. Clearly, although bond indexes are very difficult to create and maintain, they are worth the effort.

A brief analysis of the risk/return characteristics of alternative bond series indicated that most of the series had results in line with expectations. The outliers were the very risky securities (CCC bonds and defaulted bonds) and low-risk HY bonds (BB rated). The global bond results were heavily impacted by the currency effect. Local currency results were consistent except for Japan, which was below the market line. The U.S. dollar results were quite consistent in terms of risk and return, with almost all countries showing benefits from the weak dollar, especially France. The global indexes performed above the aggregate line, apparently due to the benefits of diversification.

The analysis of correlations for U.S. bond indexes confirmed prior studies that there is very high correlation among bond series within either the investment-grade or the HY bond sector (typically between 0.90 and 0.99). In contrast, there is significantly lower correlation between investment-grade and HY bonds. (The correlations were typically between 0.20 and 0.40.) Defaulted debt had no correlation with investment-grade debt but had fairly significant correlation with HY debt.

The correlations among the global indexes in local currencies typically showed fairly low relationships with other countries (about 0.40), except United States-Canada and France-Germany (about 0.70). The correlations changed when we considered returns in U.S. dollars. Specifically, all the correlations with the United States declined by about 0.20, while many of the correlations among non-U.S. countries increased by about 0.20 due to the weak U.S. dollar during this period, which affected these countries simultaneously.

Two final points. First, it is important to remember that the significance of many of the empirical results of risk/return and correlations are reduced because of the relatively short 10-year time period. Second, even though these results are not as powerful as one would want, the important point is that it is currently possible to do such analysis related to the bond market because there are a number of very well-constructed and diverse bond indexes available, as described herein. Such an analysis is critical for investors and portfolio managers making asset-allocation decisions.

GOVERNMENT AND PRIVATE DEBT OBLIGATIONS

⑥ TREASURY AND AGENCY SECURITIES

Frank J. Fabozzi, Ph.D., CFA, CPA
Adjunct Professor of Finance
School of Management
Yale University

Treasury securities are issued by the U.S. Department of the Treasury and are backed by the full faith and credit of the U.S. government. Consequently, market participants view them as having no credit risk. Interest rates on Treasury securities are the benchmark interest rates throughout the U.S. economy as well as in international capital markets. In this chapter, we will discuss Treasury securities and U.S. agency securities.

TREASURY SECURITIES

Two factors account for the prominent role of U.S. Treasury securities: volume (in terms of dollars outstanding) and liquidity. The Department of the Treasury is the largest single issuer of debt in the world, with Treasury securities accounting for more than $2.3 trillion (represented by over 180 different Treasury note and bond issues and 30 Treasury bill issues). The large volume of total debt and the large size of any single issue have contributed to making the Treasury market the most active, and hence the most liquid, market in the world. The spread between bid and ask prices is considerably narrower than in other sectors of the bond market, and most issues can be purchased easily. In contrast, many issues in the corporate and municipal markets are illiquid and thus cannot be traded readily.

The author is grateful to Michelle Monticciolo for helpful comments on the agency securities market.

Treasury securities are available in book-entry form at the Federal Reserve Bank. This means that the investor receives only a receipt as evidence of ownership instead of an engraved certificate. An advantage of book-entry is ease in transferring ownership of the security.

Interest income from Treasury securities is subject to federal income taxes but is exempt from state and local income taxes.

Types of Treasury Securities

There are two categories of government securities: *discount* and *coupon securities.* The fundamental difference between the two types lies in the stream of payments that the holder receives, which is reflected in how the securities are issued. Coupon securities pay interest every six months, plus principal at maturity. Discount securities pay only a contractually fixed amount at maturity, called maturity value or face value. Discount instruments are issued below maturity value. The return to the investor is the difference between the maturity value and the issue price.

Current Treasury practice is to issue all securities with maturities of one year or less as discount securities. These securities are called *Treasury bills.* All securities with maturities of two years or longer are issued as coupon securities. Treasury coupon securities issued with original maturities between 2 and 10 years are called *Treasury notes;* those with original maturities greater than 10 years are called *Treasury bonds.* Although there is a distinction between Treasury notes and bonds, in this chapter we refer to both simply as Treasury bonds.

The Primary Market

Treasury securities are typically issued on an auction basis according to regular cycles for securities of specific maturities. Three-month and six-month Treasury bills are auctioned every Monday. The amounts to be auctioned are ordinarily announced the previous Tuesday afternoon. The one-year (52-week) Treasury bills are auctioned in the third week of every month, with announcement on the preceding Friday. When the Treasury is temporarily short of cash, it issues *cash management bills.* The maturities of cash management bills coincide with the length of time that the Treasury anticipates the shortage of funds.

The Treasury regularly issues coupon securities with maturities of 2, 3, 5, 10, and 30 years. Two- and five-year notes are auctioned each month. At the beginning of the second month of each calendar quarter (February, May, August, and November), the Treasury conducts its regular refunding operations. At this time, it auctions 3-year, 10-year, and 30-year Treasury securities. On the last Wednesday of the month preceding, the Treasury announces (1) the amount that will be auctioned, (2) what portion of that amount is to replace maturing Treasury debt, (3) what portion of that amount is to raise new funds, and (4) the estimated cash needs for the balance of the quarter and how it plans to obtain the funds.

The auction for Treasury securities is conducted on a competitive bid basis. Competitive bids must be submitted on a yield basis. Noncompetitive tenders may also be submitted for up to a $1 million face amount. Such tenders are based only on quantity, not yield. The auction results are determined by first deducting the total noncompetitive tenders and nonpublic purchases (such as purchases by the Federal Reserve itself) from the total securities being auctioned. The remainder is the amount to be awarded to the competitive bidders.

At the time of this writing, there are two types of auctions held to determine the price that bidders will pay for the auctioned security: *multiple-price auctions* and *single-price auctions.* Single-price auctions are held for the two- and five-year notes; all other Treasury securities are held on a multiple-price auction basis.

In a single-price auction, all bidders are awarded securities at the highest yield of accepted competitive tenders. In a multiple-price auction, the lowest-yield (i.e., highest price) bidders are awarded securities at their bid price. Successively higher-yielding bidders are awarded securities at their bid price until the total amount offered (less noncompetitive tenders) is awarded. The highest yield accepted by the Treasury is referred to as the *stop yield*, and bidders at that price are awarded a percentage of their total tender offer. The price paid by noncompetitive bidders is the average price of the competitive bids.

The difference between the average yield of all the bids accepted by the Treasury and the stop yield is called the *tail.* Market participants use the tail as the measure of the success of the auction. The larger the tail, the less successful the auction. This is because the average price at which accepted bidders realized securities was considerably lower than the highest price paid.

Primary Dealers

Any firm can deal in government securities. In implementing its open market operations, however, the Federal Reserve will deal directly only with dealers that it designates as primary dealers. Primary dealers include large commercial banks and investment banking firms, both domestic and foreign.

Until 1991, primary dealers and large commercial banks that were not primary dealers would submit bids for their own accounts and for their customers. Others who wished to participate in the auction process could submit competitive bids only for their own accounts, not for their customers. Consequently, a broker-dealer in government securities that was not a primary dealer could not submit a competitive bid on behalf of its customers. Moreover, unlike primary dealers, non-primary dealers had to make large cash deposits or provide guarantees to ensure that they could fulfill their obligation to purchase the securities for which they bid.

Well-publicized violations of the auction process by Salomon Brothers in the summer of 1991 forced Treasury officials to scrutinize the activities of primary dealers more closely and also to reconsider the procedure by which Treasury securities are auctioned.[1] Specifically, the Treasury announced that it would

---

1. Salomon Brothers admitted that it repeatedly violated a restriction that limited the amount that any one firm could purchase at the Treasury auction. The firm also admitted that it submitted unauthorized bids for some of its customers.

allow qualified nonprimary broker-dealers to bid for their customers at Treasury auctions. If a qualified broker-dealer establishes a payment link with the Federal Reserve system, no deposit or guaranty would be required. Moreover, the auction would no longer be handled by the submission of hand-delivered sealed bids to the Federal Reserve. The new auction process will be a computerized auction system that can be electronically accessed by qualified broker-dealers.

The Secondary Market

The secondary market for Treasury securities is an over-the-counter market in which a group of U.S. government securities dealers offers continuous bid and ask prices on specific outstanding Treasuries.[2] The secondary market is the most liquid financial market in the world. Daily average trading volume for all Treasury securities by primary dealers for the week of March 20, 1996, was about $191.308 billion,[3] with the distribution among Treasury securities as follows:

Treasury bills	$52.050 billion
Coupon securities	
due in 5 years or less	94.691
due in more than 5 years	44.568

The most recently auctioned Treasury issues for each maturity are referred to as *on-the-run* or *current coupon* issues. Issues auctioned before the current coupon issues typically are referred to as *off-the-run* issues; they are not as liquid as on-the-run issues. That is, the bid-ask spread is larger for off-the-run issues relative to on-the-run issues.

Dealer profits are generated from one or more of three sources: (1) the bid-ask spread, (2) appreciation in the securities held in inventory or depreciation in the securities sold short, and (3) the difference between the interest earned on the securities held in inventory and the cost of financing that inventory. The last source of profits is referred to as *carry.*

Another component of the Treasury secondary market is the *when-issued,* or *wi,* market, where Treasury securities are traded before they are issued by the Treasury. When-issued trading for both Treasury bills and Treasury coupon issues extends from the day the auction is announced until the issue day. All deliveries on when-issued trades occur on the issue day of the Treasury security traded.

---

2. Some trading of Treasury coupon securities does occur on the New York Stock Exchange, but the volume of these exchange-traded transactions is very small when compared to over-the-counter transactions.

3. This figure represents immediate transactions of purchases and sales in the market as reported to the Federal Reserve Bank of New York on March 20, 1996. Immediate transactions are those scheduled for delivery in five days or less. The figure excludes all transactions under repurchase and reverse repurchase agreements. (These transactions are described in Chapter 10.)

Government Brokers

Treasury dealers trade with the investing public and with other dealer firms. When they trade with each other, it is through intermediaries known as *government brokers*. Dealers leave firm bids and offers with brokers, who display the highest bid and lowest offer in a computer network tied to each trading desk and displayed on a monitor. The dealer responding to a bid or offer by "hitting" or "taking" pays a commission to the broker. The size and prices of these transactions are visible to all dealers at once.

Treasury dealers use brokers because of the speed and efficiency with which trades can be accomplished through them. Brokers never trade for their own account, and they keep the names of the dealers involved in trades confidential. They include RMJ Securities Corp.; Garban Ltd.; Cantor, Fitzgerald Securities Corp.; Liberty; and Chapdelaine & Company Government Securities, Inc. These five firms service the primary government dealers and a dozen or so other large government dealers aspiring to be primary dealers.

Bid and Offer Quotes on Treasury Bills

The convention for quoting bids and offers is different for Treasury bills and Treasury coupon securities. Unlike bonds that pay coupon interest, Treasury bills are quoted on a *bank discount basis,* not on a price basis. The yield on a bank discount basis is computed as follows:

$$Y_d = \frac{D}{F} \times \frac{360}{t}$$

where

Y_d = Annualized yield on a bank discount basis (expressed as a decimal)
D = Dollar discount, which is equal to the difference between the face value and the price
F = Face value
t = Number of days remaining to maturity

As an example, a Treasury bill with 100 days to maturity and a face value of $100,000, selling for $97,569, would be quoted at 8.75 percent on a bank discount basis, calculated by first finding the dollar discount,

$$D = \$100,000 - \$97,569 = \$2,431$$

and then the yield on a bank discount basis:

$$Y_d = \frac{\$2,431}{\$100,000} \times \frac{360}{100} = 8.75\%$$

Given the yield on a bank discount basis, the price of a Treasury bill is found by first solving the formula for Y_d for the dollar discount (D), as follows:

$$D = Y_d \times F \times \frac{t}{360}$$

The price is then

$$\text{Price} = F - D$$

For the 100-day Treasury bill with a face value of $100,000, if the yield on a bank discount basis is quoted as 8.75 percent, D is equal to

$$D = 0.0875 \times \$100,000 \times \frac{100}{360} = \$2,431$$

Therefore

$$\text{Price} = \$100,000 - \$2,431 = \$97,569$$

The quoted yield on a bank discount basis is not a meaningful measure of the return from holding a Treasury bill for two reasons. First, the measure is based on a face-value investment rather than on the actual dollar amount invested. Second, the yield is annualized according to a 360-day rather than a 365-day year, making it difficult to compare Treasury bill yields with Treasury notes and bonds, which pay interest on a 365-day basis. Despite its shortcomings as a measure of return, this is the method dealers use to quote Treasury bills. Many dealer quote sheets and some reporting services provide two other yield measures that attempt to make the quoted yield comparable to that for a coupon bond and other money market instruments.

The measure that seeks to make the Treasury bill quote comparable to Treasury notes and bonds is called the *bond equivalent yield,* which was explained in Chapter 4. The *CD equivalent yield* (also called the *money market equivalent yield*) makes the quoted yield on a Treasury bill more comparable to yield quotations on other money market instruments that pay interest on a 360-day basis. It does this by taking into consideration the price of the Treasury bill rather than its face value. The formula for the CD equivalent yield is

$$\text{CD equivalent yield} = \frac{360 Y_d}{360 - t(Y_d)}$$

As an illustration, consider once again the hypothetical 100-day Treasury bill with a face value of $100,000, selling for $97,569, and offering a yield on a bank discount basis of 8.75 percent. The CD equivalent yield is as follows:

$$\text{CD equivalent yield} = \frac{360(0.0875)}{360 - 100(0.0875)}$$

$$= 8.97\%$$

Bid and Offer Quotes on Treasury Coupon Securities

Treasury coupon securities are quoted differently from Treasury bills. They trade on a dollar price basis in price units of $1/32$ of 1 percent of par (par is taken to be $100). For example, a quote of 92–14 refers to a price of 92 and $14/32$. If a Treasury coupon security has a $100,000 par value, then a change in price of 1 percent equates to $1,000, and $1/32$ equates to $31.25. A plus sign following the number of 32nds means that a 64th is added to the price. For example, 92–14 + refers to a price of 92 and $29/64$ or 92.453125 percent of par value.

On quote sheets and screens, the price quote is followed by some yield-to-maturity measure. We explained the yield-to-maturity calculation in Chapter 4.

Stripped Treasury Securities

The Treasury does not issue zero-coupon notes or bonds. In August 1982, however, both Merrill Lynch and Salomon Brothers created synthetic zero-coupon Treasury receipts. Merrill Lynch marketed its Treasury receipts as Treasury Income Growth Receipts (TIGRs), and Salomon Brothers marketed its receipts as Certificates of Accrual on Treasury Securities (CATS). The procedure was to purchase Treasury bonds and deposit them in a bank custody account. The firms then issued receipts representing an ownership interest in each coupon payment on the underlying Treasury bond in the account and a receipt for ownership of the underlying Treasury bond's maturity value. This process of separating each coupon payment, as well as the principal (called the corpus), and selling securities against them is referred to as *coupon stripping*. Although the receipts created from the coupon-stripping process are not issued by the U.S. Treasury, the underlying bond deposited in the bank custody account is a debt obligation of the U.S. Treasury, so the cash flow from the underlying security is certain.

As an illustration of the process, suppose $100 million of a Treasury bond with a 20-year maturity and a coupon rate of 10 percent is purchased to create stripped zero-coupon Treasury securities. The cash flow from this Treasury bond is 40 semiannual payments of $5 million each ($100 million × 0.10 ÷ 2) and the repayment of principal (corpus) of $100 million 20 years from now. This Treasury bond is deposited in a bank custody account. Receipts are then issued, each with a different single payment claim on the bank custody account. As there are 41 different payments to be made by the Treasury, a receipt representing a single payment claim on each payment is issued, which is effectively a zero-coupon bond. The amount of the maturity value for a receipt on a particular payment, whether coupon or corpus, depends on the amount of the payment to be made by the Treasury on the underlying Treasury bond. In our example, 40 coupon receipts each have a maturity value of $5 million, and one receipt, the corpus, has a maturity value of $100 million. The maturity dates for the receipts coincide with the corresponding payment dates by the Treasury.

Other investment banking firms followed suit by creating their own receipts. They all are referred to as *trademark zero-coupon Treasury securities* because they are associated with particular firms. (They are also called "animal products.") Receipts of one firm were rarely traded by competing dealers, so the secondary market was not liquid for any one trademark. Moreover, the investor was exposed to the risk—as small as it may be—that the custodian bank may go bankrupt.

To broaden the market and improve liquidity of these receipts, a group of primary dealers in the government market agreed to issue generic receipts that would not be directly associated with any of the participating dealers. These generic receipts are referred to as *Treasury Receipts* (TRs). Rather than representing a share of the trust as the trademarks do, TRs represent ownership of a Treasury security. A common problem with both trademark and generic receipts was that settlement required physical delivery, which is often cumbersome and inefficient.

In February 1985, the Treasury announced its Separate Trading of Registered Interest and Principal Securities (STRIPS) program to facilitate the stripping of designated Treasury securities. Specifically, all new Treasury bonds and all new Treasury notes with maturities of 10 years and longer are eligible. The zero-coupon Treasury securities created under the STRIPS program are direct obligations of the U.S. government. Moreover, the securities clear through the Federal Reserve's book-entry system.[4] Creation of the STRIPS program ended the origination of trademarks and generic receipts.

In Chapter 6, we explained that the price of a Treasury security should be equal to the present value of its cash flow, where each cash flow is discounted at its theoretical spot rate. It is the stripping of Treasury securities that ensures that the market price will be equal to the theoretical price. If the market price of a Treasury security is less than its theoretical price, a market participant could strip the Treasury security and sell the resulting zero-coupon instruments for more than the cost of buying the Treasury security.

FEDERAL AGENCY SECURITIES

The federal agency securities market can be divided into two sectors: the *government-sponsored enterprises securities market* and the *federally related institution securities market. Government-sponsored enterprises* (GSEs) are privately owned, publicly chartered entities. They were created by Congress to reduce the cost of capital for certain borrowing sectors of the economy deemed to be important enough to warrant assistance. These privileged sectors include farmers,

---

4. In 1987, the Treasury permitted the conversion of stripped coupons into book-entry form under its Coupons Under Book-Entry Safekeeping (CUBES) program.

homeowners, and students. Government-sponsored enterprises issue securities directly in the marketplace. The market for these securities, although smaller than that of Treasury securities, has in recent years become an active and important sector of the bond market.

Federally Related Institution Securities

Federally related institutions are arms of the federal government and generally do not issue securities directly in the marketplace (although they did before 1973). Instead, they typically obtain all or part of their financing by borrowing from the Federal Financing Bank, an entity created in 1973. The relatively small size of these issues made the borrowing cost for individual issues significantly greater than that of Treasury securities. Creation of the Federal Financing Bank was intended to consolidate and reduce the borrowing cost of federally related institutions.

Federally related institutions include the Export-Import Bank of the United States, the Commodity Credit Corporation, the Farmers Housing Administration, the General Services Administration, the Government National Mortgage Association, the Maritime Administration, the Private Export Funding Corporation, the Rural Electrification Administration, the Rural Telephone Bank, the Small Business Administration, the Tennessee Valley Authority, and the Washington Metropolitan Area Transit Authority. All federally related institutions are exempt from SEC registration. With the exception of securities of the Private Export Funding Corporation and the Tennessee Valley Authority, the securities are backed by the full faith and credit of the U.S. government.

Government-Sponsored Enterprise Securities

There are eight government-sponsored enterprises (GSEs). The enabling legislation dealing with GSEs is amended periodically. The Federal Farm Credit Bank System is responsible for the credit market in the agricultural sector of the economy. The Farm Credit Financial Association Corporation was created in 1987 to address problems in the existing Farm Credit System. Three federally sponsored agencies—the Federal Home Loan Bank, the Federal Home Loan Mortgage Corporation, and the Federal National Mortgage Association—are responsible for providing credit to the mortgage and housing sectors. The Student Loan Marketing Association provides funds to support higher education. The Financing Corporation was created in 1987 to recapitalize the Federal Savings and Loan Insurance Corporation. Because of continuing difficulties in the savings and loan association industry, the Resolution Trust Corporation (RTC) was created in 1989 to liquidate or bail out insolvent institutions.

GSEs issue two types of securities: discount notes and bonds. Discount notes are short-term obligations, with maturities ranging from overnight to 360 days. Bonds are sold with maturities greater than two years.

With the exception of the securities issued by the Farm Credit Financial Assistance Corporation, GSE securities are not backed by the full faith and credit of the U.S. government, as is the case with Treasury securities. Consequently, investors purchasing GSEs are exposed to some potential credit risk. The yield spread between these securities and Treasury securities of comparable maturity reflects differences in perceived credit risk and liquidity. The spread attributable to credit risk reflects financial problems faced by the issuing GSE and the likelihood that the federal government will allow the credit agency to default on its outstanding obligations.

The price quotation convention for GSE securities is the same as that for Treasury securities. That is, the bid and ask price quotations are expressed as a percentage of par plus 32nds of a point. Some GSE issues trade with almost the same liquidity as Treasury securities. Other issues that are supported by only a few dealers trade much like off-the-run corporate bonds.

Average daily trading in GSEs is a small fraction of trading in Treasury securities. For example, while average daily trading of Treasury securities for the week ending March 20, 1996, was $191.308 billion, the corresponding trading for federal agency securities (excluding federal agency mortgage-backed securities) was only $21.080 billion.

The following is a brief description of six of the eight federally sponsored agencies. The two agencies not discussed here—the Federal Home Loan Mortgage Corporation (Freddie Mac) and the Federal National Mortgage Association (Fannie Mae)—are covered in Chapter 27.

Federal Farm Credit Bank System

The purpose of the Federal Farm Credit Bank System (FFCBS) is to facilitate adequate, dependable credit and related services to the agricultural sector of the economy. The Farm Credit System consists of three entities: the Federal Land Banks, Federal Intermediate Credit Banks, and Banks for Cooperatives. Before 1979, each entity issued securities in its own name. Starting in 1979, they began to issue debt on a consolidated basis as "joint and several obligations" of the FFCBS. All financing for the FFCBS is arranged through the Federal Farm Credit Banks Funding Corporation, which issues consolidated obligations.

Farm Credit Financial Assistance Corporation

In the 1980s, the FFCBS faced financial difficulties because of defaults on loans made to farmers. The defaults were caused largely by high interest rates in the late 1970s and early 1980s and by depressed prices on agricultural products. To recapitalize the Federal Farm Credit Bank System, Congress created the Farm Credit Financial Assistance Corporation (FACO) in 1987. This GSE is authorized to issue debt to assist the FFCBS. FACO bonds, unlike the debt of other GSEs, are backed by the Treasury.

Federal Home Loan Bank System

The Federal Home Loan Bank System (FHLBS) consists of the 12 district Federal Home Loan Banks (which are instrumentalities of the U.S. government) and their member banks. An independent federal agency, the Federal Home Loan Bank Board was originally responsible for regulating all federally chartered savings and loan associations and savings banks, as well as state-chartered institutions insured by the Federal Savings and Loan Insurance Corporation. These responsibilities have been curtailed since 1989. The major source of debt funding for the Federal Home Loan Banks is the issuance of consolidated debt obligations, which are joint and several obligations of the 12 Federal Home Loan Banks.

Financing Corporation

The deposits of savings and loans were once insured by the Federal Savings and Loan Insurance Corporation (FSLIC), overseen by the Federal Home Loan Bank Board. When difficulties encountered in the savings and loan industry raised concerns about FSLIC's ability to meet its responsibility to insure deposits, Congress passed the Competitive Equality and Banking Act in 1987. This legislation included provisions to recapitalize FSLIC and establish a new GSE, the Financing Corporation (FICO), to issue debt in order to provide funding for FSLIC.

FICO is capitalized by the nonvoting stock purchased by the 12 regional Federal Home Loan Banks. On September 30, 1987, FICO issued its first bond—a 30-year noncallable $500 million issue. The issue was priced 90 basis points over the 30-year Treasury security at the time. The principal of these bonds is backed by zero-coupon Treasury securities. The legislation permits FICO to issue up to $10.825 billion but not more than $3.75 billion in any one year. FICO is legislated to be dismantled in 2026 or after all securities have matured, whichever comes sooner.

Resolution Trust Corporation

The 1987 legislation that created FICO did not go far enough to resolve the problems facing the beleaguered savings and loan industry. In 1989, Congress passed more comprehensive legislation, the Financial Institutions Reform, Recovery and Enforcement Act (FIRREA). This legislation has three key elements: (1) It transfers supervision of savings and loan institutions to a newly created Office of Thrift Supervision; (2) it shifts the FSLIC insurance function to a Savings Association Insurance Fund, placed under the supervision of the Federal Deposit Insurance Corporation; and (3) it establishes the Resolution Trust Corporation (RTC) as a GSE charged with the responsibility of liquidating or bailing out insolvent savings and loan institutions. The RTC obtained its funding from the Resolution Funding Corporation (REFCORP). The principal of this debt was backed by zero-coupon Treasury bonds. REFCORP has issued both 30-year and 40-year bonds. The RTC was dismantled in 1995.

Student Loan Marketing Association

Popularly known as Sallie Mae, the Student Loan Marketing Association provides liquidity for private lenders participating in the Federal Guaranteed Student Loan Program, the Health Education Assistance Loan Program, and the PLUS loan program (a program that provides loans to the parents of undergraduate students). Sallie Mae is permitted to purchase and offer investors participation in student loans. Sallie Mae issues unsecured debt obligations in the form of discount notes. In January 1982, Sallie Mae first issued floating-rate securities based on the bond equivalent yield on 91-day Treasury bills. Sallie Mae also has long-term fixed-rate securities and zero-coupon bonds outstanding.

SUMMARY

The U.S. Treasury market is closely watched by all participants in the financial markets because interest rates on Treasury securities are the benchmark interest rates throughout the world. The Treasury issues three types of securities: bills, notes, and bonds. Treasury securities are issued on a competitive bid auction basis according to a regular auction cycle. The secondary market for Treasury securities is an over-the-counter market, where dealers trade with the general investing public and with other dealers.

Although the Treasury does not issue zero-coupon Treasury securities with a maturity greater than one year, government dealers have created these instruments synthetically by a process called coupon stripping. Zero-coupon Treasury securities include trademarks (or animals products), Treasury receipts, and STRIPS. Creation of the first two types of zero-coupon Treasury securities has ceased; STRIPS now dominate the market.

Government-sponsored enterprise securities and federally related institution securities constitute the federal agency securities market. The former are privately owned, publicly chartered entities created to reduce the cost of borrowing for certain sectors of the economy. Federally related institutions are arms of the federal government whose debt is generally guaranteed by the U.S. government.

Ⓖ # MUNICIPAL BONDS

Sylvan G. Feldstein, Ph.D.
Adjunct Lecturer
School of Management
Yale University

Frank J. Fabozzi, Ph.D., CFA, CPA
Adjunct Professor of Finance
School of Management
Yale University

The U.S. bond market can be divided into two major sectors: the taxable bond market and the tax-exempt bond market. The former sector includes bonds issued by the U.S. government, U.S. government agencies and sponsored enterprises, and corporations. The tax-exempt bond market is one in which the interest from bonds that are issued and sold is exempt from federal income taxation. Interest may or may not be taxable at the state and local level. The interest on U.S. Treasury securities is exempt from state and local taxes, but the distinction in classifying a bond as tax-exempt is the tax treatment at the federal income tax level.

The majority of tax-exempt securities are issued by state and local governments and by their creations, such as "authorities" and special districts. Consequently, the terms *municipal market* and *tax-exempt market* are often used interchangeably. Although not all municipal bonds are tax-exempt securities, most are. Bonds are issued by as many as 50,000 municipal entities.

The major motivation for investing in municipal bonds is their tax advantage. With the increase in the marginal tax rates resulting from the 1993 tax act, more investors are purchasing municipal securities. The primary owners of municipal bonds are individual investors, who hold approximately 75 percent of all outstanding issues; the remainder of the investors consist of mutual funds, commercial banks, and property and casualty companies. Although certain institutional investors such as pension funds have no need for tax-advantaged investments, there have been instances where such institutional investors have crossed into the municipal bond market to take advantage of higher yields.

In the past, investing in municipal bonds has been considered second in safety only to that of U.S. Treasury securities; however, there have now developed among investors ongoing concerns about the credit risks of municipal bonds. This is true regardless of whether or not the bonds are given investment-grade credit ratings by the commercial rating companies. There are several reasons for this: (1) the financial crisis of several major municipal issuers beginning with the City of New York billion-dollar financial crisis in 1975 and more recently with the default of Orange County, California; (2) the federal bankruptcy law (which became effective October 1979) that makes it easier for municipal bond issuers to seek protection from bondholders by filing for bankruptcy; (3) the proliferation of innovative financing techniques and legally untested security structures, highlighted by the default of the Washington Public Power Supply System (WPPSS) in the early 1980s; (4) the cutbacks in federal grant and aid programs that will affect the ability of certain municipal issuers to meet their obligations; and (5) fundamental changes in the American economy that may cause economic hardship for municipal issuers in some regions of the country and thus difficulty in meeting their obligations.

FEATURES OF MUNICIPAL SECURITIES

In Chapter 1 the various features of fixed income securities were described. These include call and refunding provisions, sinking-fund provisions, and put provisions. Such provisions can also be included in municipal securities. In one type of municipal structure discussed below, a revenue bond, there is a special call feature wherein the issuer must call the entire issue if the facility is destroyed.

The coupon rate on a municipal issue can be fixed throughout the life of the issue or it can be reset periodically. When the coupon rate is reset periodically, the issue is referred to as a *floating-rate* or *variable-rate* issue. In general form, the coupon reset formula for a floating-rate issue is

$$\% \text{ of reference rate} \pm \text{Spread}$$

Typically, when the reference rate is a municipal index, the coupon reset formula is

$$\text{Reference rate} \pm \text{Spread}$$

Reference rates that have been used for municipal issues include the J.J. Kenny Municipal Index, the Municipal Bond Buyer Index, the Merrill Lynch Index, a Treasury rate, and the prime rate.

The coupon rate on a floating-rate issue need not change in the same direction as the reference rate. There are derivative municipal bonds whose coupon rate changes in the opposite direction to the change in the reference rate. That is, if the reference rate increases from the previous coupon reset date, the coupon rate on the issue declines. Such issues are referred to as *inverse floating-rate issues.*

Some municipal issues have a fixed coupon rate and are issued at a discount from their maturity value. Issues whose original-issue price is less than its maturity value are referred to as *original-issue discount bonds* (OIDs). The difference between the par value and the original-issue price represents tax-exempt interest that the investor realizes by holding the issue to maturity.

Two types of municipal issues do not distribute periodic interest to the investor. The first type is called a *zero-coupon bond.* The coupon rate is zero and the original issue price is below the maturity value. Zero-coupon bonds are therefore OIDs. The other type of issue that does not distribute periodic interest is one in which a coupon rate is stated but the coupon is not distributed to the investor. Instead, the interest is accrued and all interest is paid to the investor at the maturity date along with the maturity value.

Maturity Date

The maturity date is the date on which the issuer is obligated to pay the par value. Corporate issuers of debt generally schedule their bonds to mature in one or two different years in the future. Municipal issuers, on the other hand, frequently schedule their bonds to mature serially over many years. Such bonds are called *serial bonds.* It is common for a municipal issue to have 10 or more different maturities.

After the last of the serial maturities, some municipal issues lump together large sums of debt into one or two years—much the way corporate bonds are issued. These bonds, called *term bonds,* have become increasingly popular in the municipal market because active secondary markets for them can develop if the term issue is of sufficient size.

The Legal Opinion

Municipal bonds have legal opinions. The relationship of the legal opinion to the safety of municipal bonds for both general obligation and revenue bonds is three-fold. First, bond counsel should check to determine if the issuer is indeed legally able to issue the bonds. Second, bond counsel is to see that the issuer has properly prepared for the bond sale by having enacted the various required ordinances, resolutions, and trust indentures and without violating any other laws and regulations. This preparation is particularly important in the highly technical areas of determining if the bond issue is qualified for tax exemption under federal law and if the issue has not been structured in such a way as to violate federal arbitrage regulations. Third, bond counsel is to certify that the security safeguards and remedies provided for the bondholders and pledged either by the bond issuer or by third parties, such as banks with letter-of-credit agreements, are actually supported by federal, state, and local government laws and regulations.

The popular notion is that much of the legal work done in a bond issue is boilerplate in nature, but from the bondholder's point of view the legal opinions and document reviews should be the ultimate security provisions. The reason is that if all else fails, the bondholder may have to go to court to enforce his or her security rights. Therefore, the integrity and competence of the lawyers who review the documents and write the legal opinions that usually are summarized and stated in the official statements are very important.

TYPES OF MUNICIPAL OBLIGATIONS

Bonds

In terms of municipal bond security structures, there are basically two different types. The first type is the general obligation bond, and the second is the revenue bond.

General obligation bonds are debt instruments issued by states, counties, special districts, cities, towns, and school districts. They are secured by the issuer's general taxing powers. Usually, a general obligation bond is secured by the issuer's unlimited taxing power. For smaller governmental jurisdictions such as school districts and towns, the only available unlimited taxing power is on property. For larger general obligation bond issuers such as states and big cities, the tax revenues are more diverse and may include corporate and individual income taxes, sales taxes, and property taxes. The security pledges for these larger issuers such as states are sometimes referred to as being *full faith and credit obligations.*

Additionally, certain general obligation bonds are secured not only by the issuer's general taxing powers to create monies accumulated in the general fund but also from certain identified fees, grants, and special charges, which provide additional revenues from outside the general fund. Such bonds are known as being *double barreled* in security because of the dual nature of the revenue sources.

Also, not all general obligation bonds are secured by unlimited taxing powers. Some have pledged taxes that are limited as to revenue sources and maximum property-tax millage amounts. Such bonds are known as *limited-tax general obligation bonds.*

The second basic type of security structure is found in a revenue bond. Such bonds are issued for either project or enterprise financings in which the bond issuers pledge to the bondholders the revenues generated by the operating projects financed. Below are examples of the specific types of revenue bonds that have been issued over the years.

Airport Revenue Bonds

The revenues securing airport revenue bonds usually come from either traffic-generated sources—such as landing fees, concession fees, and airline apron-use and fueling fees—or lease revenues from one or more airlines for the use of a specific facility such as a terminal or hangar.

College and University Revenue Bonds

The revenues securing college and university revenue bonds usually include dormitory room rental fees, tuition payments, and sometimes the general assets of the college or university as well.

Hospital Revenue Bonds
The security for hospital revenue bonds is usually dependent on federal and state reimbursement programs (such as Medicaid and Medicare), third-party commercial payers (such as Blue Cross and private insurance), health maintenance organizations (HMOs), and individual patient payments.

Single-Family Mortgage Revenue Bonds
Single-family mortgage revenue bonds are usually secured by the mortgages and mortgage loan repayments on single-family homes. Security features vary but can include Federal Housing Administration (FHA), Federal Veterans Administration (VA), or private mortgage insurance.

Multifamily Revenue Bonds
These revenue bonds are usually issued for multifamily housing projects for senior citizens and low-income families. Some housing revenue bonds are usually secured by mortgages that are federally insured; others receive federal government operating subsidies, such as under section 8, or interest-cost subsidies, such as under section 236; and still others receive only local property-tax reductions as subsidies.

Industrial Development and Pollution Control Revenue Bonds
Bonds have been issued for a variety of industrial and commercial activities that range from manufacturing plants to shopping centers. They are usually secured by payments to be made by the corporations or businesses that use the facilities.

Public Power Revenue Bonds
Public power revenue bonds are secured by revenues to be produced from electrical operating plants. Some bonds are for a single issuer, who constructs and operates power plants and then sells the electricity. Other public power revenue bonds are issued by groups of public and private investor-owned utilities for the joint financing of the construction of one or more power plants. This last arrangement is known as a *joint power* financing structure.

Resource Recovery Revenue Bonds
A resource recovery facility converts refuse (solid waste) into commercially salable energy, recoverable products, and a residue to be landfilled. The major revenues for a resource recovery revenue bond usually are (1) the "tipping fees" per ton paid by those who deliver the garbage to the facility for disposal; (2) revenues from steam, electricity, or refuse-derived fuel sold to either an electric power company or another energy user; and (3) revenues from the sale of recoverable materials such as aluminum and steel scrap.

Seaport Revenue Bonds
The security for seaport revenue bonds can include specific lease agreements with the benefiting companies or pledged marine terminal and cargo tonnage fees.

Sewer Revenue Bonds

Revenues for sewer revenue bonds come from hookup fees and user charges. For many older sewer bond issuers, substantial portions of their construction budgets have been financed with federal grants.

Sports Complex and Convention Center Revenue Bonds

Sports complex and convention center revenue bonds usually receive revenues from sporting or convention events held at the facilities and, in some instances, from earmarked outside revenues such as local motel and hotel room taxes.

Toll Road and Gas Tax Revenue Bonds

There are generally two types of highway revenue bonds. The bond proceeds of the first type are used to build such specific revenue-producing facilities as toll roads, bridges, and tunnels. For these pure enterprise-type revenue bonds, the pledged revenues usually are the monies collected through the tolls. The second type of highway bond is one in which the bondholders are paid by earmarked revenues outside of toll collections, such as gasoline taxes, automobile registration payments, and driver's license fees.

Water Revenue Bonds

Water revenue bonds are issued to finance the construction of water treatment plants, pumping stations, collection facilities, and distribution systems. Revenues usually come from connection fees and charges paid by the users of the water systems.

Hybrid and Special Bond Securities

Though having certain characteristics of general obligation and revenue bonds, the following types of municipal bonds have more unique security structures as well.

Refunded Bonds

Although originally issued as either revenue or general obligation bonds, municipals arc sometimes *refunded*. A refunding usually occurs when the original bonds are escrowed or collateralized either by direct obligations guaranteed by the U.S. government, or by other types of securities. The maturity schedules of the securities in the escrow fund are such so as to pay when due the bond's maturity value, coupon, and premium payments (if any) on the refunded bonds. Once this cash flow match is in place, the refunded bonds are no longer secured as either general obligation or revenue bonds. The bonds are now supported by the securities held in the escrow fund. Such bonds, if escrowed with securities guaranteed by the U.S. government, have little if any credit risk. They are the safest municipal bond investments available.

Usually, an escrow fund is an irrevocable trust established by the original bond issuer with a commercial bank or state treasurer's office. Government securities are deposited in an escrow fund that will be used to pay debt service on the refunded bonds. A *pure* escrow fund is one in which the deposited securities are solely direct or guaranteed obligations of the U.S. government, whereas a *mixed* escrow fund is one in which the permitted securities, as defined by the trust indenture, are not exclusively limited to direct or guaranteed U.S. government securities. Other securities that could be placed in mixed escrow funds include federal agency bonds, certificates of deposit from banks, other municipal bonds, and even annuity policies from commercial insurance companies. The escrow agreement should indicate what is in the escrow fund and if substitutions of lower-credit-quality investments are permitted.

Still another type of refunded bond is a *crossover refunded bond*. Typically, proceeds from crossover refunding bonds are used to purchase securities that are placed in an escrow account. Usually, the crossover refunding bonds are secured by maturing principal and interest from the escrowed securities *only until the crossover date* and the bonds to be refunded continue to be secured by the issuer's own revenues until the crossover date, which is usually the first call date of the bonds to be refunded. On that date, the crossover occurs and the bonds to be refunded are redeemed from maturing securities in the escrow fund, which could include U.S. government securities or other investments, such as certificates of deposit. In turn, the security for the refunding bonds reverts back to the issuer's own revenues.

Here we focus primarily on the pure escrow-backed bonds, not the mixed escrow or crossover bonds. The escrow fund for a refunded municipal bond can be structured so that the refunded bonds are to be called at the first possible date or a subsequent call date established in the original bond indenture. The call price usually includes a premium of from 1 to 3 percent above par. This type of structure usually is used for those refundings that either reduce the issuer's interest payment expenses or change the debt maturity schedule. Such bonds are known in the industry as *prerefunded* municipal bonds.

Prerefunded municipal bonds usually are to be retired at their first or subsequent respective callable dates, but some escrow funds for refunding bonds have been structured differently. In such refundings, the maturity schedules of the securities in the escrow funds match the regular debt-service requirements on the bonds as originally stated in the bond indentures. Such bonds are known as *escrowed-to-maturity*, or ETM, bonds. It should be noted that under the Tax Reform Law of 1986 such ETM refundings still can be done. In the secondary market there are many ETM refunded municipal bonds outstanding. However, we note that the investor or trader should determine whether all earlier calls have been legally defeased before purchasing an ETM bond.

Insured Bonds

Insured bonds, in addition to being secured by the issuer's revenues, are also backed by insurance policies written by commercial insurance companies. The insurance, usually structured as an insurance contract, is supposed to provide prompt payment to the bondholders if a default should occur. These bonds are discussed in more detail later in this chapter.

Lease-Backed Bonds

Lease-backed bonds are usually structured as revenue-type bonds with annual payments. In some instances the payments may come only from earmarked tax revenues, student tuition payments, or patient fees. In other instances the underlying lessee governmental unit makes annual appropriations from its general fund.

Letter of Credit-Backed Bonds

Some municipal bonds, in addition to being secured by the issuer's cash flow revenues, also are backed by commercial bank letters of credit. In some instances the letters of credit are irrevocable and, if necessary, can be used to pay the bondholders. In other instances the issuers are required to maintain investment-quality worthiness before the letters of credit can be drawn upon.

Life Care Revenue Bonds

Life care, or Continuing Care Retirement Community (CCRC), bonds are issued to construct long-term residential facilities for older citizens. Revenues are usually derived from initial lump-sum payments made by the residents and operating revenues.

Moral Obligation Bonds

A moral obligation bond is a security structure for state-issued bonds that indicates that if revenues are needed for paying bondholders, the state legislature involved is legally authorized, though not required, to make an appropriation out of general state-tax revenues.

Municipal Utility District Revenue Bonds

Municipal utility district revenue bonds are usually issued to finance the construction of water and sewer systems as well as roadways in undeveloped areas. The security is usually dependent on the commercial success of the specific development project involved, which can range from the sale of new homes to the renting of space in shopping centers and office buildings.

New Housing Authority Bonds

New housing authority bonds are secured by a contractual pledge of annual contributions from HUD. Monies from Washington are paid directly to the paying agent for the bonds, and the bondholders are given specific legal rights to enforce the pledge. These bonds can no longer be issued.

Tax Allocation Bonds

These bonds are usually issued to finance the construction of office buildings and other new buildings in formerly blighted areas. They are secured by property taxes collected on the improved real estate.

"Territorial" Bonds

These are bonds issued by United States territorial possessions such as Puerto Rico, the Virgin Islands, and Guam. The bonds are tax-exempt throughout most of the country. Also, the economies of these issuers are influenced by positive special features of the United States corporate tax codes that are not available to the states.

"Troubled City" Bailout Bonds

There are certain bonds that are structured to appear as pure revenue bonds but in essence are not. Revenues come from general purpose taxes and revenues that otherwise would have gone to a state's or city's general fund. Their bond structures were created to bail out underlying general obligation bond issuers from severe budget deficits. Examples are the New York State *Municipal Assistance Corporation for the City of New York Bonds* (MAC) and the state of Illinois *Chicago School Finance Authority Bonds*.

Money Market Products

Tax-exempt money products include notes, commercial paper, variable-rate demand obligations, and a hybrid of the last two products.

Notes

Municipal notes include tax anticipation notes (TANs), revenue anticipation notes (RANs), grant anticipation notes (GANs), and bond anticipation notes (BANs). These are temporary borrowings by states, local governments, and special jurisdictions. Usually, notes are issued for a period of 12 months, though it is not uncommon for notes to be issued for periods of as short as 3 months and for as long as three years. TANs and RANs (also known as TRANs) are issued in anticipation of the collection of taxes or other expected revenues. These are borrowings to even out the cash flows caused by the irregular flows of income into the treasuries of the states and local units of government. BANs are issued in anticipation of the sale of long-term bonds.

Tax-exempt money market products generally have some type of credit support. This may come in the form of an irrevocable letter of credit, a line of credit, a municipal bond insurance policy, an escrow agreement, a bond purchase agreement, or a guaranteed investment contract. With a bond purchase agreement, a bank obligates itself to purchase the debt if the remarketing agent cannot resell the instrument or make a timely payment. In the case of a guaranteed investment contract, either an insurance company or a bank invests sufficient proceeds so that the cash flow generated from a portfolio of supporting assets can meet the obligation of the issue.

Commercial Paper

As with commercial paper issued by corporations, tax-exempt commercial paper is used by municipalities to raise funds on a short-term basis ranging from 1 day to 270 days. The dealer sets interest rates for various maturity dates and the investor then selects the desired date. Thus the investor has considerable choice in selecting a maturity to satisfy investment objectives. Provisions in the 1986 tax act, however, have restricted the issuance of tax-exempt commercial paper. Specifically, this act limits the new issuance of municipal obligations that is tax exempt, and as a result, every maturity of a tax-exempt commercial issuance is considered a new debt issuance. Consequently, very limited issuance of tax-exempt commercial paper exists. Instead, issuers use one of the next two products to raise short-term funds.

Variable-Rate Demand Obligations (VRDOs)

Variable-rate demand obligations are floating-rate obligations that have a nominal long-term maturity but have a coupon rate that is reset either daily or every seven days. The investor has an option to put the issue back to the trustee at any time with seven days notice. The put price is par plus accrued interest.

Commercial Paper/VRDO Hybrid

The commercial paper/VRDO hybrid is customized to meet the cash flow needs of an investor. As with tax-exempt commercial paper, there is flexibility in structuring the maturity, because the remarketing agent establishes interest rates for a range of maturities. Although the instrument may have a long nominal maturity, there is a put provision as with a VRDO. Put periods can range from 1 day to over 360 days. On the put date, the investor can put back the bonds, receiving principal and interest, or the investor can elect to extend the maturity at the new interest rate and put date posted by the remarketing agent at that time. Thus the investor has two choices when initially purchasing this instrument: The interest rate and the put date. Interest is generally paid on the put date if the date is within 180 days. If the put date is more than 180 days forward, interest is paid semiannually. Commercial paper dealers market these products under a proprietary name. For example, the Merrill Lynch product is called Unit Priced Demand Adjustable Tax-Exempt Securities, or UPDATES. Lehman markets these simply as money market municipals. Goldman Sachs refers to these securities as flexible rate notes, and Smith Barney Shearson markets them as BITS (Bond Interest Term Series).

Municipal Derivative Securities

In recent years, a number of municipal products have been created from the basic fixed-rate municipal bond. This has been done by splitting up cash flows of newly issued bonds as well as bonds existing in the secondary markets. These products have been created by dividing the coupon interest payments and principal payments into two or more bonds classes, or *tranches*. The resulting bond classes may have far different yield and price volatility characteristics than the underlying fixed-rate municipal bond from which they were created. By expanding the risk/return profile available in the municipal marketplace, institutional investors have more flexibility in structuring municipal bond portfolios either to satisfy a specific asset/liability objective or to make an interest rate or yield curve bet more efficiently.

The name *derivative securities* has been attributed to these bond classes because they derive their value from the underlying fixed-rate municipal bond. Much of the development in this market has paralleled that of the taxable, and specifically the mortgage-backed securities, market. The ability of investment bankers to create these securities has been enhanced by the development of the municipal swap market.

A common type of derivative security is one in which two classes of securities, a *floating-rate security* and an *inverse floating-rate bond,* are created from a fixed-rate bond. The coupon rate on the floating-rate security is reset based on the results of a Dutch auction. The auction can take place anywhere between 7 days and 35 days. The coupon rate on the floating-rate security changes in the same direction as market rates. The inverse floating-rate bond receives the residual interest; that is, the coupon interest paid on this bond is the difference between the fixed-rate on the underlying bond and the floating-rate security. Thus the coupon rate on the inverse floating-rate bond changes in the opposite direction of interest rates.

The sum of interest paid on the floater and inverse floater (plus fees associated with the auction) must always equal the sum of the fixed-rate bond from which they were created. A floor (a minimum interest rate) is established on the inverse floater. Typically the floor is zero. As a result, a cap (maximum interest rate) will be imposed on the floater such that the combined floor of zero on the inverse floater and the cap on the floater is equal to the total interest rate on the fixed-rate bond from which they were created.

Several investment banking firms active in the municipal bond market have developed proprietary derivative products. Merrill Lynch's institutional floating-rate securities are called *FLOATS* and its inverse floaters are called *RITES* (Residual Interest Tax Exempt Securities). Goldman Sachs's proprietary products are called *PARS* (Periodic Auction Reset Securities), which are floaters, and *INFLOS,* which are inverse floaters. Lehman's proprietary products are called *RIBS* (Residual Interest Bonds) and *SAVRS* (Select Auction Variable Rate Securities). Merrill Lynch also sells institutional *Short RITES* by creating an inverse floater via the swaps market. Its retail inverse floating-rate product is called *TEEMS* (Tax Exempt Enhanced Municipal Securities). Goldman Sachs markets these as *Index Floaters.* Lehman markets similar products as *Yield Curve Enhanced Notes.* These are also created by means of the municipal swap market.

The investment banker may create *putable floating-rate securities* with inverse floaters. This is an example of a senior/subordinated class of securities. The structure is the same as with floating-rate and inverse floating-rate securities. However, if the remarketing agent fails to sell out the floating-rate class or the underlying bond falls below a minimum collateral value and the investors in the inverse floaters do not purchase the floating-rate securities, the floating-rate investor will put the bond. Here the trustee terminates the trust and liquidates the bonds. The proceeds of the liquidation are used first to pay the par value of the floating-rate instrument and any accrued interest. The inverse floating-rate investor receives the residual. Merrill Lynch markets these securities as *Putable Floats/Rites.*[1]

THE COMMERCIAL CREDIT RATING
OF MUNICIPAL BONDS

Of the municipal bonds that were rated by a commercial rating company in 1929 and plunged into default in 1932, 78 percent had been rated double-A or better, and 48 percent had been rated triple-A. Since then the ability of rating agencies to assess the creditworthiness of municipal obligations has evolved to a level of general industry acceptance and respectability. In most instances, they adequately describe the financial conditions of the issuers and identify the credit-risk factors. However, a small but significant number of recent instances have caused market participants to reexamine their reliance on the opinions of the rating agencies.

As an example, the troubled bonds of the Washington Public Power Supply System (WPPSS) should be mentioned. Two major commercial rating companies—Moody's and Standard & Poor's—gave their highest ratings to these bonds in the early 1980s. Moody's gave the WPPSS Projects 1, 2, and 3 bonds its very highest credit rating of Aaa and the Projects 4 and 5 bonds its rating of A1. This latter investment-grade rating is defined as having the strongest investment attributes within the upper medium grade of creditworthiness. Standard & Poor's also had given the WPPSS Projects 1, 2, and 3 bonds its highest rating of AAA and Projects 4 and 5 bonds its rating of A + . While these high-quality ratings were in effect, WPPSS sold over $8 billion in long-term bonds. By 1990, over $2 billion of these bonds were in default.

In fact, since 1975 all of the major municipal defaults in the industry initially had been given investment-grade ratings by these two commercial rating companies. Of course, it should be noted that in the majority of instances ratings of the commercial rating companies adequately reflect the condition of the credit. However, unlike 25 years ago when the commercial rating companies would not rate many kinds of revenue bond issues, today they seem to view themselves as assisting in the capital formation process. The commercial rating

---

1. For a description of other types of municipal derivative securities and their roles in municipal bond portfolio management, see Chapters 4 and 15 in Frank J. Fabozzi, T. Dessa Fabozzi, and Sylvan G. Feldstein, *Municipal Bond Portfolio Management* (Burr Ridge, IL: Irwin Professional Publishing, 1994).

companies now receive fairly substantial fees from issuers for their ratings, and they are part of large, growth-oriented conglomerates. Moody's is an operating unit of the Dun & Bradstreet Corporation and Standard & Poor's is part of the McGraw-Hill Corporation.

Today, many large institutional investors, underwriters, and traders rely on their own in-house municipal credit analysts for determining the creditworthiness of municipal bonds. However, other investors do not perform their own credit-risk analysis but instead rely upon credit-risk ratings by Moody's and Standard & Poor's. In this section, we discuss the rating categories of these two commercial rating companies.

We note that there is also a third, and smaller, commercial rating company, Fitch. It has enhanced its market presence and is particularly known in the industry for its health care and Continuing Care Retirement Community ratings, among others.

Moody's Investors Service

The municipal bond rating system used by Moody's grades the investment quality of municipal bonds in a nine-symbol system that ranges from the highest investment quality, which is Aaa, to the lowest credit rating, which is C. The respective nine alphabetical ratings and their definitions are found in Exhibit 9–1.

Municipal bonds in the top four categories (Aaa, Aa, A, and Baa) are considered to be of investment-grade quality. Additionally, bonds in the Aa through B

EXHIBIT 9–1

Moody's Municipal Bond Ratings

Rating	Definition
Aaa	Best quality; carry the smallest degree of investment risk.
Aa	High quality; margins of protection not quite as large as the Aaa bonds.
A	Upper medium grade; security adequate but could be susceptible to impairment.
Baa	Medium grade; neither highly protected nor poorly secured—lack outstanding investment characteristics and sensitive to changes in economic circumstances.
Ba	Speculative; protection is very moderate.
B	Not desirable investment; sensitive to day-to-day economic circumstances.
Caa	Poor standing; may be in default but with a workout plan.
Ca	Highly speculative; may be in default with nominal workout plan.
C	Hopelessly in default.

categories that Moody's concludes have the strongest features within the respective categories are designated by the symbols Aa1, A1, Baa1, Ba1, and B1, respectively. Moody's also may use the prefix *Con.* before a credit rating to indicate that the bond security is dependent on (1) the completion of a construction project, (2) earnings of a project with little operating experience, (3) rentals being paid once the facility is constructed, or (4) some other limiting condition. Moody's applies numerical modifiers 1, 2, and 3 in each generic rating classification from Aa through B to municipal bonds that are issued for industrial development and pollution control. The modifier 1 indicates that the security ranks in the higher end of its generic rating category; the modifier 2 indicates a midrange ranking; and the modifier 3 indicates that the bond ranks in the lower end of its generic rating category.

The municipal note rating system used by Moody's is designated by four investment-grade categories of Moody's Investment Grade (MIG), as shown in Exhibit 9–2.

Moody's also provides credit ratings for tax-exempt commercial paper. These are promissory obligations (1) not having an original maturity in excess of nine months and (2) backed by commercial banks. Moody's uses three designations, all considered to be of investment grade, for indicating the relative repayment capacity of the rated issues, as shown in Exhibit 9–3.

E X H I B I T 9–2

Moody's Municipal Note Ratings[a]

Rating	Definition
MIG 1	Best quality
MIG 2	High quality
MIG 3	Favorable quality
MIG 4	Adequate quality

[a]A short issue having a "demand" feature (i.e., payment relying on external liquidity and usually payable upon demand rather than fixed maturity dates) is differentiated by Moody's with the use of the symbols VMIG1 through VMIG4.

E X H I B I T   9–3

Moody's Tax-Exempt Commercial Paper Ratings

Rating	Definition
Prime 1 (P-1)	Superior capacity for repayment
Prime 2 (P-2)	Strong capacity for repayment
Prime 3 (P-3)	Acceptable capacity for repayment

Standard & Poor's

The municipal bond rating system used by Standard & Poor's grades the invest-ment quality of municipal bonds in a 10-symbol system that ranges from the highest investment quality, which is AAA, to the lowest credit rating, which is D. Bonds within the top four categories (AAA, AA, A, and BBB) are considered by Standard & Poor's as being of investment-grade quality. The respective 10 alpha-betical ratings and definitions are shown in Exhibit 9–4.

Standard & Poor's also uses a plus (+) or minus (–) sign to show relative standing within the rating categories ranging from AA to BB. Additionally, Stan-dard & Poor's uses the letter p to indicate a provisional rating that is intended to be removed upon the successful and timely completion of the construction pro-ject. A double dagger (‡) on a mortgage-backed revenue bond rating indicates that the rating is contingent upon receipt by Standard & Poor's of closing documenta-tion confirming investments and cash flows. An asterisk (*) following a credit rat-ing indicates that the continuation of the rating is contingent upon receipt of an executed copy of the escrow agreement.

The municipal note rating system used by Standard & Poor's grades the in-vestment quality of municipal notes in a four-symbol system that ranges from highest investment quality, SP-1 + , to the lowest credit rating, SP-3. Notes within the top three categories (i.e., SP-1 + , SP-1, and SP-2) are considered by Standard & Poor's as being of investment-grade quality. The respective ratings and sum-marized definitions are shown in Exhibit 9–5.

EXHIBIT 9–4

Standard & Poor's Municipal Bond Ratings

Rating	Definition
AAA	Highest rating; extremely strong security.
AA	Very strong security; differs from AAA in only a small degree.
A	Strong capacity but more susceptible to adverse economic effects than two above categories.
BBB	Adequate capacity but adverse economic conditions more likely to weaken capacity.
BB	Lowest degree of speculation; risk exposure.
B	Speculative; risk exposure.
CCC	Speculative; major risk exposure.
CC	Highest degree of speculation; major risk exposure.
C	No interest is being paid.
D	Bonds in default with interest and/or repayment of principal in arrears.

EXHIBIT 9–5

Standard & Poor's Municipal Note Ratings

Rating	Definition
SP-1	Very strong or strong capacity to pay principal and interest. Those issues determined to possess overwhelming safety characteristics will be given a plus (+) designation.
SP-2	Satisfactory capacity to pay principal and interest.
SP-3	Speculative capacity to pay principal and interest.

Standard & Poor's also rates tax-exempt commercial paper in the same four categories as taxable commercial paper. The four tax-exempt commercial paper rating categories are shown in Exhibit 9–6.

How the Rating Agencies Differ

Although there are many similarities in how Moody's and Standard & Poor's approach credit ratings, there are certain differences in their respective approaches as well. As examples, we shall present below some of the differences in approach between Moody's and Standard & Poor's when they assign credit ratings to general obligation bonds.

The credit analysis of general obligation bonds issued by states, counties, school districts, and municipalities initially requires the collection and assessment of information in four basic categories. The first category includes obtaining information on the issuer's debt structure so that the overall debt burden can be determined. The debt burden usually is composed of (1) the respective direct and overlapping debts per capita as well as (2) the respective direct and overlapping debts as percentages of real estate valuations and personal incomes. The second category of needed information relates to the issuer's ability and political discipline for maintaining sound budgetary operations. The focus of attention here is usually on the issuer's general operating funds and whether or not it has maintained at least balanced budgets over the previous three to five years. The third category involves determining the specific local taxes and intergovernmental revenues available to the issuer, as well as obtaining historical information on both tax collection rates, which are important when looking at property tax levies, and on the dependency of local budgets on specific revenue sources, which is important when looking at the impact of state and federal revenue sharing monies. The fourth and last general category of information necessary to the credit analysis is an assessment of the issuer's overall socioeconomic environment. Economic indexes that must be determined include the local employment distribution and composition, population growth, and real estate property valuation and personal income trends, among others.

EXHIBIT 9–6

Standard & Poor's Tax-Exempt Commercial Paper
Ratings

Rating	Definition
A-1+	Highest degree of safety
A-1	Very strong degree of safety
A-2	Strong degree of safety
A-3	Satisfactory degree of safety

Although Moody's and Standard & Poor's rely on these same four informational categories in arriving at their respective credit ratings of general obligation bonds, what they emphasize among the categories can result at times in dramatically different credit ratings for the same issuer's bonds. The objective here is to outline the actual differences between Moody's and Standard & Poor's. Furthermore, although the rating agencies have stated in their publications what criteria guide their respective credit-rating approaches, the conclusions here about how they go about rating general obligation bonds are derived not only from these sources, but also from reviewing their credit reports and rating decisions on individual bond issues.

How Do Moody's and Standard & Poor's Differ in Evaluating the Four Basic Informational Categories?

Simply stated, Moody's tends to focus on the debt burden and budgetary operations of the issuer, whereas Standard & Poor's considers the issuer's economic environment as the most important element in its analysis. Although in most instances these differences of emphasis do not result in dramatically split credit ratings for a given issuer, there are at least two recent instances in which major differences in ratings on general obligation bonds have occurred.

The general obligation bonds of the Chicago School Finance Authority in 1994 rated only A by Moody's, but Standard & Poor's rates the same bonds AA. In assigning the credit rating of A, Moody's bases its rating on the following debt- and budget-related factors: (1) The deficit-funding bonds are to be retired over a 30-year period, an unusually long time for such an obligation; (2) the overall debt burden is high; and (3) the school board faces long-term difficulties in balancing its operating budget because of reduced operating taxes, desegregation program requirements, and uncertain public employee union relations.

Standard & Poor's credit rating of AA appears to be based primarily upon the following two factors: (1) Chicago's economy is well diversified and fundamentally sound; and (2) the unique security provisions for the bonds in the opinion of the bond counsel insulate the pledged property taxes from the school board's creditors in the event of a school-system bankruptcy.

How Do the Credit-Rating Agencies Differ in Assessing the Moral Obligation Bonds?

In more than 20 states, state agencies have issued housing revenue bonds that carry a potential state liability for making up deficiencies in their one-year debt service reserve funds (backup funds), should any occur. In most cases if a drawdown of the debt reserve occurs, the state agency must report the amount used to its governor and the state budget director. The state legislature, in turn, may appropriate the requested amount, though there is no legally enforceable obligation to do so. Bonds with this makeup provision are the so-called moral obligation bonds.

Below is an example of the legal language in the bond indenture that explains this procedure.

> In order to further assure the maintenance of each such debt service reserve fund, there shall be annually apportioned and paid to the agency for deposit in each debt service reserve fund such sum, if any, as shall be certified by the chairman of the agency to the governor and director of the budget as necessary to restore such fund to an amount equal to the fund requirement. The chairman of the agency shall annually, on or before December first, make and deliver to the governor and director of the budget his certificate stating the sum or sums, if any, required to restore each such debt service reserve fund to the amount aforesaid, and the sum so certified, if any, shall be apportioned and paid to the agency during the then current state fiscal year.

Moody's views the moral obligation feature as being more literary than legal when applied to legislatively permissive debt service reserve makeup provisions. It therefore does not consider this procedure a credit strength. Standard & Poor's, to the contrary, does. It views moral obligation bonds as being no lower than one rating category below a state's own general obligation bonds. Its rationale is based upon the implied state support for the bonds and the market implications for that state's own general obligation bonds should it ever fail to honor its moral obligation.

Several municipal bonds have split ratings as a result of these two different opinions of the moral obligation. As examples, in mid-1996 the Nonprofit Housing Project Bonds of the New York State Housing Finance Agency, and the General Purpose Bonds of the New York State Urban Development Corporation had the Moody's credit rating of Ba, which is a speculative investment category. Standard & Poor's, because of the moral obligation pledge of the state of New York, gave the same bonds a credit rating of BBB–, which is an investment-grade category.

How Do the Credit Rating Agencies Differ in Assessing the Importance of Withholding State Aid to Pay Debt Service?

Still another difference between Moody's and Standard & Poor's involves their respective attitude toward state-aid security-related mechanisms. Since 1974, it has been the policy of Standard & Poor's to view as a very positive credit feature the automatic withholding and use of state aid to pay defaulted debt service on local government general obligation bonds. Usually the mechanism requires the respective state treasurer to pay debt service directly to the bondholder from monies due the local issuer from the state. Seven states have enacted security mechanisms that in one way or another allow certain local government general obligation bondholders to be paid debt service from the state-aid appropriations, if necessary. In most instances the state-aid withholding provisions apply to general obligation bonds issued by school districts.

Although Standard & Poor's does review the budgetary operations of the local government issuer to be sure there are no serious budgetary problems, the assigned rating reflects the general obligation credit rating of the state involved, the legal base of the withholding mechanism, the historical background and long-term state legislative support for the pledged state-aid program, and the specified coverage of the state-aid monies available to maximum debt-service requirements on the local general obligation bonds. Normally, Standard & Poor's applies a blanket rating to all local general obligation bonds covered by the specific state-aid withholding mechanism. The rating is one or two notches below the rating of that particular state's general obligation bonds. Whether the rating is either one notch below or two notches below depends on the coverage figures, the legal security, and the legislative history and political durability of the pledged state-aid monies involved. It should also be noted that, although Standard & Poor's stated policy is to give blanket ratings, a specified rating is granted only when an issuer or bondholder applies for it.

Although Moody's recognizes the state-aid withholding mechanisms in its credit reviews, it believes that its assigned rating must in the first instance reflect the underlying ability of the issuer to make timely debt-service payments. Standard & Poor's, to the contrary, considers a state-aid withholding mechanism that provides for the payment of debt service equally as important a credit factor as the underlying budget, economic, and debt-related characteristics of the bond issuer.

What Is the Difference in Attitudes toward Accounting Records?

Another area of difference between Moody's and Standard & Poor's concerns their respective attitudes toward the accounting records kept by general obligation bond issuers. In May 1980, Standard & Poor's stated that if the bond issuer's financial reports are not prepared in accordance with generally accepted accounting principles (GAAP) it will consider this a "negative factor" in its rating process. Standard & Poor's has not indicated how negative a factor it is in terms of credit rating changes but has indicated that issuers will not be rated at all if either the financial report is not timely (i.e., available no later than six months after the fiscal year-end) or it is substantially deficient in terms of reporting. Moody's policy here is quite different. Because Moody's reviews the historical performance of an issuer over a three- to five-year period, requiring GAAP reporting is not necessary from Moody's point of view, although the timeliness of financial reports is of importance.

Fitch

A third, and smaller, rating company is Fitch. The alphabetical ratings and definitions used by Fitch are given in Exhibit 9–7. Plus (+) and minus (–) signs are used

E X H I B I T   9–7

Fitch Municipal Bond Ratings

Rating	Definition
AAA	Highest credit quality
AA	Very high credit quality
A	High credit quality
BBB	Satisfactory credit quality
BB	Speculative
B	Highly speculative
CCC	May lead to default
CC	Default seems probable
C	In imminent default
DDD, DD, D	In default

with a rating to indicate the relative position of a credit within the rating category. Plus and minus signs are not used for the AAA category.

MUNICIPAL BOND INSURANCE

Using municipal bond insurance is one way to help reduce credit risk within a portfolio. Insurance on a municipal bond is an agreement by an insurance company to pay debt service that is not paid by the bond issuer. Municipal bond insurance contracts insure the payment of debt service on a municipal bond to the bondholder. That is, the insurance company promises to pay the issuer's obligation to the bondholder if the issuer does not do so.

The insurance usually is for the life of the issue. If the trustee or investor has not had his bond paid by the issuer on its due date, he notifies the insurer and presents the defaulted bond and coupon. Under the terms of the insurance contract, the insurer is generally obligated to pay sufficient monies to cover the value of the defaulted insured principal and coupon interest when they come due.

Because municipal bond insurance reduces the credit risk for the investor, the marketability of certain municipal bonds can be greatly expanded. Municipal bonds that benefit most from the insurance would include lower-quality bonds, bonds issued by smaller governmental units not widely known in the financial community, bonds that have a sound though complex and difficult-to-understand security structure, and bonds issued by infrequent local-government borrowers who do not have a general market following among investors.

Of course, a major factor for an issuer to obtain bond insurance is that its creditworthiness without the insurance is substantially lower than what it would be with the insurance. That is, the interest cost savings are only of sufficient magnitude to offset the cost of the insurance premium when the underlying creditworthiness of the issuer is lower. There are two major groups of municipal bond insurers. The first includes the "monoline" companies that are primarily in the business of insuring municipal bonds. Almost all of the companies that are now insuring municipal bonds can be characterized as monoline in structure. The second group of municipal bond insurers includes the "multiline" property and casualty companies that usually have a wide base of business, including insurance for fires, collisions, hurricanes, and health problems. Most new issues in the municipal bond market today are insured by the insurers described below. By mid-1996 over 50 percent of all new issues came with bond insurance.

The monoline companies are primarily in the business of insuring municipal bonds, and their respective assets, as determined in various state statutes and administrative rulings, are dedicated to paying bond principal and interest claims. The active insurers are: AMBAC Indemnity Corporation (AMBAC); Connie Lee Insurance Company; Financial Guaranty Insurance Company (FGIC); Financial Security Assurance, Inc. (FSA); and Municipal Bond Investors Assurance Corporation (MBIA Corp.).

EQUIVALENT TAXABLE YIELD

An investor interested in purchasing a municipal bond must be able to compare the promised yield on a municipal bond with that of a comparable taxable bond. The following general formula is used to determine the equivalent taxable yield for a tax-exempt bond:

$$\text{Equivalent taxable yield} = \frac{\text{Tax-exempt yield}}{(1 - \text{Marginal tax rate})}$$

For example, suppose an investor in the 40 percent marginal tax bracket is considering the acquisition of a tax-exempt bond that offers a tax-exempt yield of 6 percent. The equivalent taxable yield is 10 percent, as shown below.

$$\text{Equivalent taxable yield} = \frac{.06}{(1 - .40)} = .10 = 10\%$$

When computing the equivalent taxable yield, the traditionally computed yield-to-maturity is not the tax-exempt yield if the issue is selling below par (i.e., selling at a discount) because only the coupon interest is exempt from federal income taxes. Instead, the yield-to-maturity after an assumed capital gains tax is computed and used in the numerator of the formula.

The yield-to-maturity after an assumed capital gains tax is calculated in the same manner as the traditional yield-to-maturity. However, instead of using the redemption value in the calculation, the net proceeds after an assumed tax on any capital gain are used.

There is a major drawback in employing the equivalent taxable yield formula to compare the relative investment merits of a taxable and tax-exempt bond. Recall from the discussion in Chapter 4 that the yield-to-maturity measure assumes that the entire coupon interest can be reinvested at the computed yield. Consequently, taxable bonds with the same yield-to-maturity cannot be compared because the total dollar returns may differ from the computed yield. The same problem arises when attempting to compare taxable and tax-exempt bonds, especially because only a portion of the coupon interest on taxable bonds can be reinvested, although the entire coupon payment is available for reinvestment in the case of municipal bonds. The total return framework that should be employed to compare taxable and tax-exempt bonds is discussed in Chapter 4.

TAX PROVISIONS AFFECTING MUNICIPALS

Federal tax rate levels affect municipal bond values and strategies employed by investors. There are two additional provisions in the Internal Revenue Code that investors in municipal securities should recognize. These provisions deal with the alternative minimum tax and the deductibility of interest expense incurred to acquire municipal securities. Moreover, there are state and local taxes that an investor must be aware of.

Alternative Minimum Tax

Alternative minimum taxable income (AMTI) is a taxpayer's taxable income with certain adjustments for specified tax preferences designed to cause AMTI to approximate economic income. For both individuals and corporations, a taxpayer's liability is the greater of (1) the tax computed at regular tax rates on taxable income and (2) the tax computed at a lower rate on AMTI. This parallel tax system, the alternative minimum tax (AMT), is designed to prevent taxpayers from avoiding significant tax liability as a result of taking advantage of exclusions from gross income, deductions, and tax credits otherwise allowed under the Internal Revenue Code.

There are different rules for determining AMTI for individuals and corporations. The latter are required to calculate their minimum tax liability using two methods. Moreover, there are special rules for property and casualty companies.

One of the tax preference items that must be included is certain tax-exempt municipal interest. As a result of the AMT, the value of the tax-exempt feature is reduced. However, the interest of some municipal issues is not subject to the AMT. Under the current tax code, tax-exempt interest earned on all private activity bonds issued after August 7, 1986, must be included in AMTI. There are two exceptions. First, interest from bonds that are issued by 501(c)(3) organizations (i.e., not-for-profit organizations) is not subject to AMTI. The second exception is interest from bonds issued for the purpose of refunding if the original bonds were issued before August 7, 1986. The AMT does not apply to interest on governmental or nonprivate activity municipal bonds. An implication is that those issues that are subject to the AMT will trade at a higher yield than those exempt from AMT.

Deductibility of Interest Expense Incurred to Acquire Municipals

Some investment strategies involve the borrowing of funds to purchase or carry securities. Ordinarily, interest expense on borrowed funds to purchase or carry investment securities is tax deductible. There is one exception that is relevant to investors in municipal bonds. The Internal Revenue Service specifies that interest paid or accrued on "indebtedness incurred or continued to purchase or carry obligations, the interest on which is wholly exempt from taxes," is not tax deductible. It does not make any difference if any tax-exempt interest is actually received by the taxpayer in the taxable year. In other words, interest is not deductible on funds borrowed to purchase or carry tax-exempt securities.

Special rules apply to commercial banks. At one time, banks were permitted to deduct all the interest expense incurred to purchase or carry municipal securities. Tax legislation subsequently limited the deduction first to 85 percent of the interest expense and then to 80 percent. The 1986 tax law eliminated the deductibility of the interest expense for bonds acquired after August 6, 1986. The exception to this nondeductibility of interest expense rule is for *bank-qualified issues.* These are tax-exempt obligations sold by small issuers after August 6, 1986, and purchased by the bank for its investment portfolio.

An issue is bank qualified if (1) it is a tax-exempt issue other than private activity bonds, but including any bonds issued by 501(c)(3) organizations, and (2) it is designated by the issuer as bank qualified and the issuer or its subordinate entities reasonably do not intend to issue more than $10 of such bonds. A nationally recognized and experienced bond attorney should include in the opinion letter for the specific bond issue that the bonds are bank qualified.

State and Local Taxes

The tax treatment of municipal bonds varies by state. There are three types of taxes that can be imposed: (1) an income tax on coupon income, (2) a tax on realized capital gains, and (3) a personal property tax.

A majority of the states levy an individual income tax. Several of these states exempt coupon interest on *all* municipal bonds, whether the issue is in state or out of state. Coupon interest from obligations by in-state issuers is exempt from state individual income taxes in most states. A few states levy individual income taxes on coupon interest whether the issuer is in state or out of state.

State taxation of realized capital gains is often ignored by investors when making investment decisions. In many states, a tax is levied on a base that includes income from capital transactions (i.e., capital gains or losses). In many states where coupon interest is exempt if the issuer is in state, the same exemption will not apply to capital gains involving municipal bonds.

Some states levy a personal property tax on municipal bonds. The tax resembles more of an income tax than a personal property tax.

In determining the effective tax rate imposed by a particular state, an investor must consider the impact of the deductibility of state taxes on federal income taxes. Moreover, in some states, *federal* taxes are deductible in determining state income taxes.

YIELD RELATIONSHIPS WITHIN THE MUNICIPAL BOND MARKET

Differences within an Assigned Credit Rating

Bond buyers primarily use the credit ratings assigned by the commercial rating companies, Standard & Poor's and Moody's, as a starting point for pricing an issue. The final market-derived bond price is determined by the assigned credit rating and adjustments by investors to reflect their own analysis of creditworthiness and perception of marketability. For example, insured municipal bonds tend to have yields that are substantially higher than noninsured superior-investment-quality municipal bonds even though most insured bonds are given triple-A ratings by the commercial rating companies. Additionally, many investors have geographical preferences among bonds, in spite of identical credit quality and otherwise comparable investment characteristics.

Differences between Credit Ratings

With all other factors constant, the greater the credit risk perceived by investors, the higher the return expected by investors. The spread between municipal bonds of different credit quality is not constant over time. Reasons for the change in spreads are (1) the outlook for the economy and its anticipated impact on issuers, (2) federal budget financing needs, and (3) municipal market supply-and-demand factors. During periods of relatively low interest rates, investors sometimes increase their holdings of issues of lower credit quality in order to obtain additional yield. This narrows the spread between high-grade and lower-grade credit issues. During periods in which investors anticipate a poor economic climate, there is often a "flight to quality" as investors pursue a more conservative credit-risk exposure. This widens the spread between high-grade and lower-grade credit issues.

Another factor that causes shifts in the spread between issues of different quality is the temporary oversupply of issues within a market sector. For example, a substantial new-issue volume of high-grade state general obligation bonds may tend to decrease the spread between high-grade and lower-grade revenue bonds. In a weak market environment, it is easier for high-grade municipal bonds to come to market than for weaker credits. Therefore, it is not uncommon for high grades to flood weak markets at the same time there is a relative scarcity of medium- and low-grade municipal bond issues.

Differences between In-State and General Market

Bonds of municipal issuers located in certain states (for example, New York, California, Arizona, Maryland, and Pennsylvania) usually yield considerably less than issues of identical credit quality that come from other states that trade in the "general market." There are three reasons for the existence of such spreads. First, states often exempt interest from in-state issues from state and local personal income taxes, and interest from out-of-state issues is generally not exempt. Consequently, in states with high income taxes (e.g., New York and California), strong investor demand for in-state issues will reduce their yields relative to bonds of issues located in states where state and local income taxes are not important considerations (e.g., Illinois and Florida). Second, in some states, public funds deposited in banks must be collateralized by the bank accepting the deposit. This requirement is referred to as pledging. Acceptable collateral for pledging will typically include issues of certain in-state issuers. For those issues qualifying, pledging tends to increase demand (particularly for the shorter maturities) and reduce yields relative to nonqualifying comparable issues. The third reason is that investors in some states exhibit extreme reluctance to purchase issues from isuers outside of their state or region. In-state parochialism tends to decrease relative yields of issues from states in which investors exhibit this behavior.

Differences between Maturities

One determinant of the yield on a bond is the number of years remaining to maturity. As explained in Chapter 6, the yield curve depicts the relationship at a given point in time between yields and maturity for bonds that are identical in every way except maturity. When yields increase with maturity, the yield curve is said to be *normal* or have a *positive slope*. Therefore, as investors lengthen their maturity, they require a greater yield. It is also possible for the yield curve to be "inverted," meaning that long-term yields are less than short-term yields. If short-, intermediate-, and long-term yields are roughly the same, the yield curve is said to be *flat*.

In the taxable bond market, it is not unusual to find all three shapes for the yield curve at different points in the business cycle. However, in the municipal bond market the yield curve is typically normal or upward sloping. Consequently, in the municipal bond market, long-term bonds generally offer higher yields than short- and intermediate-term bonds.

Insured Municipal Bonds

In general, although insured municipal bonds sell at yields lower than they would without the insurance, they tend to have yields higher than other Aaa/AAA-rated bonds such as deep-discount refunded bonds. Of course, supply-and-demand forces and in-state taxation factors can distort market trading patterns from time to time. Insured bonds as a generic group may not be viewed as having the same superior degree of safety as either refunded bonds secured with escrowed U.S. Treasuries or those general obligation bonds of states that have robust and growing economies, fiscally conservative budgetary operations, and very low debt burdens.

PRIMARY AND SECONDARY MARKETS

The municipal market can be divided into the primary market and the secondary market. The primary market is where all new issues of municipal bonds are sold for the first time. The secondary market is the market where previously issued municipal securities are traded.

Primary Market

A substantial number of municipal obligations are brought to market each week. A state or local government can market its new issue by offering bonds publicly to the investing community or by placing them privately with a small group of investors. When a public offering is selected, the issue usually is underwritten by investment bankers or municipal bond departments of commercial banks. Public offerings may be marketed by either competitive bidding or direct negotiations with underwriters. When an issue is marketed via competitive bidding, the issue is awarded to the bidder submitting the best bid.

Most states mandate that general obligation issues be marketed through competitive bidding, but generally this is not required for revenue bonds. Usually state and local governments require a competitive sale to be announced in a recognized financial publication, such as *The Bond Buyer,* which is the trade publication for the municipal bond industry. *The Bond Buyer* also provides information on upcoming competitive sales and most negotiated sales, as well as the results of previous weeks.

An official statement describing the issue and the issuer is prepared for new offerings.

Secondary Market

Municipal bonds are traded in the over-the-counter market supported by municipal bond dealers across the country. Markets are maintained on smaller issuers (referred to as *local credits*) by regional brokerage firms, local banks, and some of the larger Wall Street firms. Larger issuers (referred to as *general market names*) are supported by the larger brokerage firms and banks, many of whom have investment banking relationships with these issuers. There are brokers who serve as intermediaries in the sale of large blocks of municipal bonds among dealers and large institutional investors. In addition to these brokers and the daily offerings sent out over *The Bond Buyer*'s "munifacts" teletype system, many dealers advertise their municipal bond offering for the retail market in what is known as *The*

Blue List. This is a 100-plus-page booklet published every weekday by the Standard & Poor's Corporation that gives municipal securities offerings and prices.

In the municipal bond markets, an odd lot of bonds is $25,000 or less in par value for retail investors. For institutions, anything below $100,000 in par value is considered an odd lot. Dealer spreads depend on several factors. For the retail investor, the spread can range from as low as one-quarter of one point ($12.50 per $5,000 of par value) on large blocks of actively traded bonds to four points ($200 per $5,000 of par value) for odd-lot sales of an inactive issue. For institutional investors, the dealer spread rarely exceeds one-half of one point ($25 per $5,000 of par value).

The convention for both corporate and Treasury bonds is to quote prices as a percentage of par value with 100 equal to par. Municipal bonds, however, generally are traded and quoted in terms of yield (yield-to-maturity or yield-to-call). The price of the bond in this case is called a *basis price.* Certain long-maturity revenue bonds are exceptions. A bond traded and quoted in dollar prices (actually, as a percentage of par value) is called a *dollar bond.*

REGULATION OF THE MUNICIPAL SECURITIES MARKET[2]

As an outgrowth of abusive stock market practices, Congress passed the Securities Act of 1933 and the Securities Exchange Act of 1934. The 1934 act created the Securities and Exchange Commission (SEC), granting it regulatory authority over the issuance and trading of *corporate* securities. Congress specifically exempted municipal securities from both the registration requirements of the 1933 act and the periodic-reporting requirements of the 1934 act. However, antifraud provisions did apply to offerings of or dealings in municipal securities.

The exemption afforded municipal securities appears to have been due to (1) the desire for governmental comity, (2) the absence of recurrent abuses in transactions involving municipal securities, (3) the greater level of sophistication of investors in this segment of the securities markets (i.e., institutional investors dominated the market), and (4) the fact that there were few defaults by municipal issuers. Consequently, from the enactment of the two federal securities acts in the early 1930s to the early 1970s, the municipal securities market can be characterized as relatively free from federal regulation.

In the early 1970s, however, circumstances changed. As incomes rose, individuals participated in the municipal securities market to a much greater extent. As a result, public outcries over selling practices occurred with greater frequency. For example, in the early 1970s, the SEC obtained seven injunctions against 72 defendants for fraudulent municipal trading practices. According to the SEC, the

---

[2] Parts of this discussion are drawn from Thomas F. Mitchell, "Disclosure and the Municipal Bond Industry," Chapter 40, and Nancy H. Wojtas, "The SEC and Investor Safeguards," Chapter 42 in *The Municipal Bond Handbook,* eds. Frank J. Fabozzi, Sylvan G. Feldstein, Irving M. Pollack, and Frank G. Zarb (Homewood, IL: Dow Jones-Irwin, 1983).

abusive practices involved both disregard by the defendants as to whether the particular municipal bonds offered to individuals were in fact appropriate investment vehicles for the individuals to whom they were offered and misrepresentation or failure to disclose information necessary for individuals to assess the credit risk of the municipal issuer, especially in the case of revenue bonds. Moreover, the financial problems of some municipal issuers, notably New York City, made market participants aware that municipal issuers have the potential to experience severe and bankruptcy-type financial difficulties.

Congress passed the Securities Act Amendment of 1975 to broaden federal regulation in the municipals market. The legislation brought brokers and dealers in the municipal securities market, including banks that underwrite and trade municipal securities, within the regulatory scheme of the Securities Exchange Act of 1934. In addition, the legislation mandated that the SEC establish a 15-member Municipal Securities Rule Making Board (MSRB) as an independent, self-regulatory agency, whose primary responsibility is to develop rules governing the activities of banks, brokers, and dealers in municipal securities.[3] Rules adopted by the MSRB must be approved by the SEC. The MSRB has no enforcement or inspection authority. This authority is vested with the SEC, the National Association of Securities Dealers, and certain regulatory banking agencies such as the Federal Reserve Bank.

The Securities Act Amendment of 1975 does *not* require that municipal issuers comply with the registration requirement of the 1933 act or the periodic-reporting requirement of the 1934 act. There have been, however, several legislative proposals to mandate financial disclosure. Although none has been passed, there is clearly pressure to improve disclosure. Even in the absence of federal legislation dealing with the regulation of financial disclosure, underwriters began insisting upon greater disclosure as it became apparent that the SEC was exercising stricter application of the antifraud provisions. Moreover, underwriters recognized the need for improved disclosure to sell municipal securities to an investing public that has become much more concerned about credit risk by municipal issuers.

On June 28, 1989, the Securities and Exchange Commission formally approved the first bond disclosure rule, effective January 1, 1990. The following paragraphs summarize its contents.

The rule applies to all new issue municipal securities offerings of $1 million or more. Exemptions have been added for securities offered in denominations of $100,000 or more, if such securities

- Are sold to no more than 35 "sophisticated investors," or
- Have a maturity of 9 months or less, or
- Are variable-rate demand instruments.

---

3. For a detailed discussion of the MSRB, see Frieda K. Wallison, "Self-Regulation of the Municipal Securities Industry," Chapter 41 in *The Municipal Bond Handbook.*

Before bidding or purchasing an offering, underwriters must obtain and review official statements that are deemed final by the issuer, with the omission of no more than the following information:

- Offering price;
- Interest rate;
- Selling compensation;
- Aggregate principal amount;
- Principal amount per maturity;
- Delivery dates; and
- Other terms or provisions required by an issuer of such a security to be specified in a competitive bid, ratings, other terms of the securities depending on such matters, and the identity of the underwriters.

The underwriters shall contract with an issuer or its designated agent to receive copies of a final official statement within seven business days after any final agreement to purchase, offer, or sell any offering and in sufficient time to accompany any confirmation that requests payment from any customer.

Except for competitively bid offerings, the underwriters shall send, no later than the next business day, to any potential customer, on request, a single copy of the most recent preliminary official statement, if any.

Underwriters are required to distribute the final official statement to any potential customer, on request, within 90 days, or 25 days if the final official statement is available from a repository.

Material Event Disclosure under SEC Rule 15c2-12

The first phase of the implementation of amendments to Rule 15c2-12, that took effect on July 3, 1995, required dealers to determine that issuers before issuing new municipal bonds made arrangements to disclose in the future financial information *at least* annually as well as notices of the occurrence of any of 11 material events as specified in the Rule. This resulted in the creation of state information depositories ("SIDs") and municipal securities information repositories ("NRMSIRs") to which issuers are to deliver annual information and notices. The SIDs and NRMSIRs make this information available to the public. The second phase went into effect on January 1, 1996 and required dealers to have in-house procedures in place to provide reasonable assurance that they will receive prompt notice of the any material that is required to be disclosed by the issuers.

⑥ PRIVATE MONEY MARKET INSTRUMENTS

Frank J. Fabozzi, Ph.D., CFA, CPA
Adjunct Professor of Finance
School of Management
Yale University

Historically, the money market has been defined as the market for assets maturing in one year or less. The assets traded in this market include Treasury bills, commercial paper, some medium-term notes, bankers acceptances, federal agency discount paper, short-term municipal obligations, certificates of deposit, repurchase agreements, floating-rate instruments, and federal funds. Although several of these assets have maturities greater than one year, they are still classified as part of the money market.

In Chapter 8, Treasury bills are discussed. In this chapter, we will cover private money market instruments: commercial paper, bankers acceptances, certificates of deposit, repurchase agreements, and federal funds. Medium-term notes have maturities ranging from nine months to 30 years. These securities are discussed in Chapter 12.

COMMERCIAL PAPER

A corporation that needs long-term funds can raise those funds in either the equity or bond market. If, instead, a corporation needs short-term funds, it may attempt to acquire those funds via bank borrowing. An alternative to bank borrowing for large corporations with strong credit ratings is commercial paper. Commercial paper is short-term unsecured promissory notes issued in the open market as an obligation of the issuing entity.

The commercial paper market once was limited to entities with strong credit ratings, but in recent years some lower-credit-rated corporations have issued commercial paper by obtaining credit enhancements or other collateral to allow them to enter the market as issuers. Issuers of commercial paper are not restricted to U.S. corporations. Foreign corporations and sovereign issuers also issue commercial paper.

Although the original purpose of commercial paper was to provide short-term funds for seasonal and working capital needs, it has been issued for other purposes in recent years, frequently for "bridge financing." For example, suppose that a corporation needs long-term funds to build a plant or acquire equipment. Rather than raising long-term funds immediately, the issuer may elect to postpone the offering until more favorable capital market conditions prevail. The funds raised by issuing commercial paper are used until longer-term securities are sold. Commercial paper has been used as bridge financing to finance corporate takeovers.[1]

The maturity of commercial paper is typically less than 270 days; the most common maturity range is 30 to 50 days or less.[2] There are reasons for this. First, the Securities Act of 1933 requires that securities be registered with the SEC. Special provisions in the 1933 act exempt commercial paper from registration so long as the maturity does not exceed 270 days. To avoid the costs associated with registering issues with the SEC, issuers rarely issue commercial paper with a maturity exceeding 270 days. To pay off holders of maturing paper, issuers generally issue new commercial paper. Another consideration in determining the maturity is whether the paper would be eligible collateral by a bank if it wanted to borrow from the Federal Reserve Bank's discount window. In order to be eligible, the maturity of the paper may not exceed 90 days. Because eligible paper trades at a lower cost than paper that is not eligible, issuers prefer to issue paper whose maturity does not exceed 90 days.

The risk that the investor faces is that the borrower will be unable to issue new paper at maturity. As a safeguard against this, commercial paper is typically backed by unused bank credit lines.

Investors in commercial paper are institutional investors. Money market mutual funds purchase roughly one-third of all the commercial paper issued. Pension funds, commercial bank trust departments, state and local governments, and nonfinancial corporations seeking short-term investments purchase the balance. The minimum round-lot transaction is $100,000. Some issuers will sell commercial paper in denominations of $25,000.

Issuers of Commercial Paper

Corporate issuers of commercial paper can be divided into financial companies and nonfinancial companies. The majority of commercial paper outstanding was issued by financial companies.

---

1. Commercial paper has also been used as an integral part of an interest rate swap transaction. We discuss interest-rate swaps in Chapter 61.
2. *Money Market Instruments* (New York: Merrill Lynch Money Markets, Inc., 1989), p. 16.

There are three types of financial companies: captive finance companies, bank-related finance companies, and independent finance companies. Captive finance companies are subsidiaries of equipment-manufacturing companies. Their primary purpose is to secure financing for the customers of the parent company. The three major U.S. automobile manufacturers, for example, have captive finance companies: General Motors Acceptance Corporation (GMAC), Ford Credit, and Chrysler Financial. GMAC is by the far the largest issuer of commercial paper in the United States. Bank holding companies may have a finance company subsidiary that provides loans to individuals and businesses to acquire a wide range of products. Independent finance companies are those that are not subsidiaries of equipment-manufacturing firms or bank holding companies.

Although the typical issuers of commercial paper are those with high credit ratings, smaller and less well-known companies with lower credit ratings have been able to issue paper in recent years. They have been able to do so by means of credit support from a firm with a high credit rating (such paper is called *credit-supported commercial paper*) or by collateralizing the issue with high-quality assets (such paper is called *asset-backed commercial paper*). An example of credit-supported commercial paper is an issue supported by a letter of credit. The terms of such a letter of credit specify that the bank issuing it guarantees that the bank will pay off the paper when it comes due, if the issuer fails to. Banks charge a fee for letters of credit. From the issuer's perspective, the fee enables it to enter the commercial paper market and obtain funding at a lower cost than bank borrowing. Paper issued with this credit enhancement is referred to as *LOC paper*. The credit enhancement may also take the form of a surety bond from an insurance company.[3]

Directly Placed versus Dealer-Placed Paper

Commercial paper is classified as either direct paper or dealer paper. *Direct paper* is sold by the issuing firm directly to investors without using a securities dealer as an intermediary. A large majority of the issuers of direct paper are financial companies. Because they require a continuous source of funds in order to provide loans to customers, they find it cost-effective to establish a sales force to sell their commercial paper directly to investors.

In the case of dealer-placed commercial paper, the issuer uses the services of a securities firm to sell its paper. Commercial paper sold in this way is referred to as *dealer paper.* Competitive pressures have forced dramatic reductions in the underwriting fees charged by dealer firms.

Historically, the dealer market has been dominated by large investment banking firms because commercial banks were prohibited from underwriting

---

3. A surety bond is a policy written by an insurance company to protect another party against loss or violation of a contract.

commercial paper by the Glass-Steagall Act. In June 1987, however, the Fed granted subsidiaries of bank holding companies permission to underwrite commercial paper. Although investment banking firms still dominate the dealer market, commercial banks are making inroads.

The Secondary Market

Despite the fact that the commercial paper market is larger than markets for other money market instruments, secondary trading activity is much smaller. The typical investor in commercial paper is an entity that plans to hold it until maturity, given that an investor can purchase commercial paper with the specific maturity desired. Should an investor's economic circumstances change such that there is a need to sell the paper, it can be sold back to the dealer, or, in the case of directly placed paper, the issuer will repurchase it.

Yields on Commercial Paper

Like Treasury bills, commercial paper is a discount instrument. That is, it is sold at a price less than its maturity value. The difference between the maturity value and the price paid is the interest earned by the investor, although some commercial paper is issued as an interest-bearing instrument. For commercial paper, a year is treated as having 360 days.

The yield offered on commercial paper tracks that of other money market instruments. The commercial paper rate is higher than that on Treasury bills for three reasons. First, the investor in commercial paper is exposed to credit risk. Second, interest earned from investing in Treasury bills is exempt from state and local income taxes. As a result, commercial paper has to offer a higher yield to offset this tax advantage. Finally, commercial paper is less liquid than Treasury bills. The liquidity premium demanded is probably small, however, because investors typically follow a buy-and-hold strategy with commercial paper and so are less concerned with liquidity. The rate on commercial paper is higher by a few basis points than the rate on certificates of deposit, which we discuss later in this chapter. The higher yield available on commercial paper is attributable to the poorer liquidity relative to certificates of deposit.

BANKERS ACCEPTANCES

Simply put, a bankers acceptance is a vehicle created to facilitate commercial trade transactions. The instrument is called a bankers acceptance because a bank accepts the ultimate responsibility to repay a loan to its holder. The use of bankers acceptances to finance a commercial transaction is referred to as *acceptance financing*.

The transactions in which bankers acceptances are created include (1) the importing of goods into the United States, (2) the exporting of goods from the

United States to foreign entities, (3) the storing and shipping of goods between two foreign countries where neither the importer nor the exporter is a U.S. firm,[4] and (4) the storing and shipping of goods between two entities in the United States.

Bankers acceptances are sold on a discounted basis just as Treasury bills and commercial paper. The major investors in bankers acceptances are money market mutual funds and municipal entities.

Illustration of the Creation of a Bankers Acceptance

The best way to explain the creation of a bankers acceptance is by an illustration. Several entities are involved in our transaction:

- Car Imports Corporation of America ("Car Imports"), a firm in New Jersey that sells automobiles
- Germany Autos Inc. ("GAI"), a manufacturer of automobiles in Germany
- Hoboken Bank of New Jersey ("Hoboken Bank"), a commercial bank in Hoboken, New Jersey
- Berlin National Bank ("Berlin Bank"), a bank in Germany
- High-Caliber Money Market Fund, a mutual fund in the United States that invests in money market instruments

Car Imports and GAI are considering a commercial transaction. Car Imports wants to import 15 cars manufactured by GAI. GAI is concerned with the ability of Car Imports to make payment on the 15 cars when they are received.

Acceptance financing is suggested as a means for facilitating the transaction. Car Imports offers $300,000 for the 15 cars. The terms of the sale stipulate payment to be made to GAI 60 days after it ships the 15 cars to Car Imports. GAI determines whether it is willing to accept the $300,000. In considering the offering price, GAI must calculate the present value of the $300,000 because it will not be receiving the payment until 60 days after shipment. Suppose that GAI agrees to these terms.

Car Imports arranges with its bank, Hoboken Bank, to issue a letter of credit. The letter of credit indicates that Hoboken Bank will make good on the payment of $300,000 that Car Imports must make to GAI 60 days after shipment. The letter of credit, or time draft, will be sent by Hoboken Bank to GAI's bank, Berlin Bank. Upon receipt of the letter of credit, Berlin Bank will notify GAI, who will then ship the 15 cars. After the cars are shipped, GAI presents the shipping documents to Berlin Bank and receives the present value of $300,000. GAI is now out of the picture.

---

4. Bankers acceptances created from these transactions are called *third-country acceptances.*

Berlin Bank presents the time draft and the shipping documents to Hoboken Bank. The latter will then stamp "accepted" on the time draft. By doing so, the Hoboken Bank has created a bankers acceptance. This means that Hoboken Bank agrees to pay the holder of the bankers acceptance $300,000 at the maturity date. Car Imports will receive the shipping documents so that it can procure the 15 cars once it signs a note or some other type of financing arrangement with Hoboken Bank.

At this point, the holder of the bankers acceptance is the Berlin Bank. It has two choices. It can retain the bankers acceptance as an investment in its loan portfolio, or it can request that the Hoboken Bank make a payment of the present value of $300,000. Let's assume that Berlin Bank requests payment of the present value of $300,000.

Now the holder of the bankers acceptance is Hoboken Bank. It has two choices: retain the bankers acceptance as an investment as part of its loan portfolio or sell it to an investor. Suppose that Hoboken Bank chooses the latter, and that High-Caliber Money Market Fund is seeking a high-quality investment with the same maturity as that of the bankers acceptance. The Hoboken Bank sells the bankers acceptance to the money market fund at the present value of $300,000. Rather than sell the instrument directly to an investor, Hoboken Bank could sell it to a dealer who would then resell it to an investor such as a money market fund. In either case, at the maturity date, the money market fund presents the bankers acceptance to Hoboken Bank, receiving $300,000, which the bank in turn recovers from Car Imports.

Credit Risk

Investing in bankers acceptances exposes the investor to credit risk. This is the risk that neither the borrower nor the accepting bank will be able to pay the principal due at the maturity date.

Eligible Bankers Acceptance

An accepting bank that has decided to retain a bankers acceptance in its portfolio may be able to use it as collateral for a loan at the discount window of the Federal Reserve. The reason we say it "may" is that bankers acceptances must meet certain eligibility requirements established by the Federal Reserve. One requirement for eligibility is maturity, which with few exceptions cannot exceed six months. The other requirements for eligibility are too detailed to review here, but the basic principle is simple: The bankers acceptance should be financing a self-liquidating commercial transaction.

Eligibility is also important because the Federal Reserve imposes a reserve requirement on funds raised via bankers acceptances that are ineligible. Bankers acceptances sold by an accepting bank are potential liabilities of the bank, but no reserve requirements are imposed for eligible bankers acceptances. Consequently, most bankers acceptances satisfy the various eligibility criteria. Finally, the Federal Reserve also imposes a limit on the amount of eligible bankers acceptances that may be issued by a bank.

Rates Banks Charge on Bankers Acceptances

To calculate the rate to be charged the customer for issuing a bankers acceptance, the bank determines the rate for which it can sell its bankers acceptance in the open market. To this rate it adds a commission. In the case of ineligible bankers acceptances, a bank will add an amount to offset the cost of the reserve requirements imposed.

LARGE-DENOMINATION NEGOTIABLE CDS

A *certificate of deposit* (CD) is a certificate issued by a bank or thrift that indicates a specified sum of money has been deposited at the issuing depository institution. CDs are issued by banks and thrifts to raise funds for financing their business activities. A CD bears a maturity date and a specified interest rate, and it can be issued in any denomination. CDs issued by banks are insured by the Federal Deposit Insurance Corporation but only for amounts up to $100,000. As for maturity, there is no limit on the maximum, but by Federal Reserve regulations CDs cannot have a maturity of less than seven days.

A CD may be nonnegotiable or negotiable. In the former case, the initial depositor must wait until the maturity date of the CD to obtain the funds. If the depositor chooses to withdraw funds prior to the maturity date, an early withdrawal penalty is imposed. In contrast, a negotiable CD allows the initial depositor (or any subsequent owner of the CD) to sell the CD in the open market prior to the maturity date.

Negotiable CDs were introduced in the early sixties. At that time, the interest rate that banks could pay on various types of deposits was subject to ceilings administered by the Federal Reserve (except for demand deposits, defined as deposits of less than one month that by law could pay no interest). For complex historical reasons, these ceiling rates started very low, rose with maturity, and remained below market rates up to some fairly long maturity. Before introduction of the negotiable CD, those with money to invest for, say, one month had no incentive to deposit it with a bank because they would get a below-market rate, unless they were prepared to tie up their capital for a much longer period of time. When negotiable CDs came along, those investors could buy a three-month or longer negotiable CD yielding a market interest rate and recoup all or more than the investment (depending on market conditions) by selling it in the market.

This innovation was critical in helping banks to increase the amount of funds raised in the money market, a position that had languished in the earlier postwar period. It also motivated competition among banks, ushering in a new era. There are now two types of negotiable CDs. The first is the large-denomination CD, usually issued in denominations of $1 million or more. These are the negotiable CDs whose history we described above.

In 1982, Merrill Lynch entered the retail CD business by opening up a primary and secondary market in small-denomination (less than $100,000) CDs.

While it made the CDs of its numerous banking and savings institution clients available to retail customers, Merrill Lynch also began to give these customers the negotiability enjoyed by institutional investors by standing ready to buy back CDs prior to maturity. Today, several retail-oriented brokerage firms offer CDs that are salable in a secondary market. These are the second type of negotiable CD. Our focus in this chapter, though, is on the large-denomination negotiable CD, and we refer to them simply as CDs throughout the chapter.

The largest group of CD investors comprises investment companies, and money market funds make up the bulk of them. Far behind are banks and bank trust departments, followed by municipal entities and corporations.

CD Issuers

CDs can be classified into four types, based on the issuing bank. First are CDs issued by domestic banks. Second are CDs that are denominated in U.S. dollars but are issued outside of the United States. These CDs are called *Eurodollar CDs* or *Euro CDs*. Euro CDs are U.S. dollar–denominated CDs, issued primarily in London by U.S., Canadian, European, and Japanese banks. Branches of large U.S. banks once were the major issuers of Euro CDs. A third type of CD is the *Yankee CD*, which is a CD denominated in U.S. dollars and issued by a foreign bank with a branch in the United States. Finally, *thrift CDs* are those issued by savings and loan associations and savings banks.

Yields on CDs

Unlike Treasury bills, commercial paper, and bankers acceptances, yields on domestic CDs are quoted on an interest-bearing basis. CDs with a maturity of one year or less pay interest at maturity. For purposes of calculating interest, a year is treated as having 360 days. Term CDs issued in the United States normally pay interest semiannually, again with a year taken to have 360 days.

The yields posted on CDs vary depending on three factors: (1) the credit rating of the issuing bank, (2) the maturity of the CD, and (3) the supply and demand for CDs. With respect to the third factor, banks and thrifts issue CDs as part of their liability management strategy, so the supply of CDs will be driven by the demand for bank loans and the cost of alternative sources of capital to fund these loans. Moreover, bank loan demand will depend on the cost of alternative funding sources such as commercial paper. When loan demand is weak, CD rates decline. When demand is strong, the rates rise. The effect of maturity depends on the shape of the yield curve.

Credit risk has become more of an issue. At one time, domestic CDs issued by money center banks traded on a no-name basis. Recent financial crises in the banking industry, however, have caused investors to take a closer look at issuing banks. Prime CDs (those issued by high-rated domestic banks) trade at a lower yield than nonprime CDs (those issued by lower-rated domestic banks). Because of the unfamiliarity investors have with foreign banks, generally Yankee CDs trade at a higher yield than domestic CDs.

Euro CDs offer a higher yield than domestic CDs. There are three reasons for this. First, there are reserve requirements imposed by the Federal Reserve on CDs issued by U.S. banks in the United States that do not apply to issuers of Euro CDs. The reserve requirement effectively raises the cost of funds to the issuing bank because it cannot invest all the proceeds it receives from the issuance of a CD, and the amount that must be kept as reserves will not earn a return for the bank. Because it will earn less on funds raised by selling domestic CDs, the domestic issuing bank will pay less on its domestic CD than a Euro CD. Second, the bank issuing the CD must pay an insurance premium to the FDIC, which again raises the cost of funds. Finally, Euro CDs are dollar obligations that are payable by an entity operating under a foreign jurisdiction, exposing the holders to a risk (referred to as *sovereign risk*) that their claim may not be enforced by the foreign jurisdiction. As a result, a portion of the spread between the yield offered on Euro CDs and domestic CDs reflects what can be termed a *sovereign risk premium.* This premium varies with the degree of confidence in the international banking system.

CD yields are higher than yields on Treasury securities of the same maturity. The spread is due mainly to the credit risk that a CD investor is exposed to and the fact that CDs offer less liquidity. The spread due to credit risk will vary with economic conditions and confidence in the banking system, increasing when there is a flight to quality or when there is a crisis in the banking system.

At one time, there were more than 30 dealers who made markets in CDs. The presence of that many dealers provided good liquidity to the market. Today, fewer dealers are interested in making markets in CDs, and the market can be characterized as an illiquid one.

REPURCHASE AGREEMENTS

A *repurchase agreement* is the sale of a security with a commitment by the seller to buy the security back from the purchaser at a specified price at a designated future date. Basically, a repurchase agreement is a collateralized loan, where the collateral is a security. The agreement is best explained with an illustration.

Suppose a government securities dealer has purchased $10 million of a particular Treasury security. Where does the dealer obtain the funds to finance that position? Of course, the dealer can finance the position with its own funds or by borrowing from a bank. Typically, however, the dealer uses the repurchase agreement or "repo" market to obtain financing. In the repo market, the dealer can use the $10 million of the Treasury security as collateral for a loan. The term of the loan and the interest rate that the dealer agrees to pay (called the "repo rate") are specified. When the term of the loan is one day, it is called an *overnight repo;* a loan for more than one day is called a *term repo.*

The transaction is referred to as a repurchase agreement because it calls for the sale of the security and its repurchase at a future date. Both the sale price and the purchase price are specified in the agreement. The difference between the purchase (repurchase) price and the sale price is the dollar interest cost of the loan.

Let us return to the dealer who needs to finance $10 million of a Treasury security that it purchased and plans to hold overnight. Suppose that a customer of the dealer has excess funds of $10 million. (The customer might be a municipality with tax receipts that it has just collected, and no immediate need to disburse the funds.) The dealer would agree to deliver ("sell") $10 million of the Treasury security to the customer for an amount determined by the repo rate and buy ("repurchase") the same Treasury security from the customer for $10 million the next day. Suppose that the overnight repo rate is 6.5 percent. Then, as will be explained below, the dealer would agree to deliver the Treasury securities for $9,998,194 and repurchase the same securities for $10 million the next day. The $1,806 difference between the "sale" price of $9,998,194 and the repurchase price of $10 million is the dollar interest on the financing. From the customer's perspective, the agreement is called a *reverse* repo.

The formula following is used to calculate the dollar interest on a repo transaction:

$$\text{Dollar interest} = (\text{Dollar principal}) \times (\text{Repo rate}) \times \left(\frac{\text{Repo term}}{360} \right)$$

Notice that the interest is computed on a 360-day basis. In our example, at a repo rate of 6.5 percent and a repo term of one day (overnight), the dollar interest is $1,806, as we show below:

$$= \$10,000,000 \times 0.065 \times \frac{1}{360}$$
$$= \$1,806$$

The advantage to the dealer of using the repo market for borrowing on a short-term basis is that the rate is less than the cost of bank financing. We will explain why later in this section. From the customer's perspective, the repo market offers an attractive yield on a short-term secured transaction that is highly liquid.

The example illustrates financing a dealer's long position in the repo market, but dealers can also use the market to cover a short position. For example, suppose a government dealer sold $10 million of Treasury securities two weeks ago and must now cover the position—that is, deliver the securities. The dealer can do a reverse repo (agree to buy the securities and sell them back). Of course, the dealer eventually would have to buy the Treasury security in the market in order to cover its short position.

There is a good deal of Wall Street jargon describing repo transactions. To understand it, remember that one party is lending money and accepting security as collateral for the loan; the other party is borrowing money and giving collateral to borrow money. When someone lends securities in order to receive cash (i.e., borrow money), that party is said to be *reversing out* securities. A party that lends money with the security as collateral is said to be *reversing in* securities. The expressions *to repo securities* and *to do repo* are also used. The former means that someone is going to finance securities using the security as collateral; the latter means that the party is going to invest in a repo. Finally, the expressions *selling collateral* and *buying collateral* are used to describe a party financing a security with a repo on the one hand, and lending on the basis of collateral on the other.

The collateral in a repo is not limited to government securities. Money market instruments, federal agency securities, and mortgage-backed securities are also used.

Credit Risks

Despite the fact that there may be high-quality collateral underlying a repo transaction, both parties to the transaction are exposed to credit risk. The failure of a few small government securities dealer firms involving repo transactions in the 1980s has made market participants more cautious about the creditworthiness of the counterparty to a repo.[5]

Why does credit risk occur in a repo transaction? Consider our initial example, in which the dealer used $10 million of government securities as collateral to borrow. If the dealer cannot repurchase the government securities, the customer may keep the collateral; if interest rates on government securities have increased subsequent to the repo transaction, however, the market value of the government securities will decline, and the customer will own securities with a market value less than the amount it loaned to the dealer. If the market value of the security rises instead, the dealer firm will be concerned with the return of the collateral, which then has a market value higher than the loan.

Repos are now more carefully structured to reduce credit risk exposure. The amount loaned is less than the market value of the security used as collateral, which provides the lender with some cushion should the market value of the security decline. The amount by which the market value of the security used as collateral exceeds the value of the loan is called *margin*.[6] The amount of margin is generally between 1 percent and 3 percent. For borrowers of lower creditworthiness or when less liquid securities are used as collateral, the margin can be 10 percent or more.

Another practice to limit credit risk is to mark the collateral to market on a regular basis. When market value changes by a certain percentage, the repo position is adjusted accordingly. Suppose that a dealer firm has borrowed $20

---

5. Failed firms include Drysdale Government Securities, Lion Capital, RTD Securities, Inc., Belvill
     Bressler & Schulman, Inc., and ESM Government Securities, Inc.
6. Margin is also referred to as the "haircut."

million using collateral with a market value of $20.4 million. The margin is 2 percent. Suppose further that the market value of the collateral drops to $20.1 million. A repo agreement can specify either (1) a margin call or (2) repricing of the repo. In the case of a margin call, the dealer firm is required to put up additional collateral with a market value of $300,000 in order to bring the margin up to $400,000. If repricing is agreed upon, the principal amount of the repo will be changed from $20 million to $19.7 million (the market value of $20.1 million divided by 1.02). The dealer would then send the customer $300,000.

One concern in structuring a repo is delivery of the collateral to the lender. The most obvious procedure is for the borrower to deliver the collateral to the lender. At the end of the repo term, the lender returns the collateral to the borrower in exchange for the principal and interest payment. This procedure may be too costly, though, particularly for short-term repos, because of the costs associated with delivering the collateral. The cost of delivery would be factored into the transaction by a lower repo rate offered by the borrower. The risk of the lender not taking possession of the collateral is that the borrower may sell the security or use the same security as collateral for a repo with another party.

As an alternative to delivering the collateral, the lender may agree to allow the borrower to hold the security in a segregated customer account. Of course, the lender still faces the risk that the borrower uses the collateral fraudulently by offering it as collateral for another repo transaction.

Another method is for the borrower to deliver the collateral to the lender's custodial account at the borrower's clearing bank. The custodian then has possession of the collateral that it holds on behalf of the lender. This practice reduces the cost of delivery because it is merely a transfer within the borrower's clearing bank. If, for example, a dealer enters into an overnight repo with Customer A, the next day the collateral is transferred back to the dealer. The dealer can then enter into a repo with Customer B for, say, five days without having to redeliver the collateral. The clearing bank simply establishes a custodian account for Customer B and holds the collateral in that account.

There have been a number of well-publicized losses by nondealer institutional investors—most notably Orange County, California—that have resulted from the use of repurchase agreements. Such losses did not occur as a result of credit risk. Rather, it was the use of repos to make a leverage bet on the movement of interest rates. That is, the repo was not used as a money market instrument but as a leveraging vehicle.

Participants in the Market

Because it is used by dealer firms (investment banking firms and money center banks acting as dealers) to finance positions and cover short positions, the repo market has evolved into one of the largest sectors of the money market. Financial and nonfinancial firms participate in the markets as both sellers and buyers, depending on the circumstances they face. Thrifts and commercial banks are typically *net sellers* of collateral (i.e., net borrowers of funds); money market funds, bank trust departments, municipalities, and corporations are typically *net buyers* of collateral (i.e., providers of funds).

Although a dealer firm uses the repo market as the primary means for financing its inventory and covering short positions, it will also use the repo market to run a matched book where it takes on repos and reverse repos with the same maturity. The firm will do so to capture the spread at which it enters into the repo and reverse repo agreement. For example, suppose that a dealer firm enters into a term repo of 10 days with a money market fund and a reverse repo rate with a thrift for 10 days in which the collateral is identical. This means that the dealer firm is borrowing funds from the money market fund and lending money to the thrift. If the rate on the repo is 7.5 percent and the rate on the reverse repo is 7.55 percent, the dealer firm is borrowing at 7.5 percent and lending at 7.55 percent, locking in a spread of 0.05 percent (five basis points).

Another participant is the repo broker. To understand the role of the repo broker, suppose that a dealer firm has shorted $50 million of a security. It will then survey its regular customers to determine if it can borrow via a reverse repo the security it shorted. Suppose that it cannot find a customer willing to do a repo transaction (repo from the customer's point of view, reverse repo from the dealer's). At that point, the dealer firm will use the services of a repo broker. When the collateral is difficult to acquire, it is said to be a *hot* or *special* issue.

The Fed and the Repo Market

The Federal Reserve influences short-term interest rates through its open market operations—that is, by the outright purchase or sale of government securities. This is not the common practice followed by the Fed, however. It uses the repo market instead to implement monetary policy by purchasing or selling collateral. By buying collateral (i.e., lending funds), the Fed injects money into the financial markets, thereby exerting downward pressure on short-term interest rates. When the Fed buys collateral for its own account, this is called a *system repo*. The Fed also buys collateral on behalf of foreign central banks in repo transactions that are referred to as *customer repos*. It is primarily through system repos that the Fed attempts to influence short-term rates. By selling securities for its own account, the Fed drains money from the financial markets, thereby exerting upward pressure on short-term interest rates. This transaction is called a *matched sale*.

Note the language that is used to describe the transactions of the Fed in the repo market. When the Fed lends funds based on collateral, we call it a *system* or *customer repo*, not a reverse repo. Borrowing funds using collateral is called a *matched sale*, not a repo. The jargon is confusing, which is why we used the terms of *buying collateral* and *selling collateral* to describe what parties in the market are doing.

Determinants of the Repo Rate

There is no one repo rate; rates vary from transaction to transaction, depending on several factors:

Quality. The higher the credit quality and liquidity of the collateral, the lower the repo rate.

Term of the repo. The effect of the term of the repo on the rate depends on the shape of the yield curve.

Delivery requirement. As noted earlier, if delivery of the collateral to the lender is required, the repo rate will be lower. If the collateral can be deposited with the bank of the borrower, a higher repo rate is paid.

Availability of collateral. The more difficult it is to obtain the collateral, the lower the repo rate. To understand why this is so, remember that the borrower (or equivalently, the seller of the collateral) has a security that is a hot or special issue. The party that needs the collateral will be willing to lend funds at a lower repo rate in order to obtain the collateral.

The factors above determine the repo rate on a particular transaction; the federal funds rate discussed below determines the general level of repo rates. The repo rate will be a rate below the federal funds rate. The reason is that a repo involves collateralized borrowing, whereas a federal funds transaction is unsecured borrowing.

FEDERAL FUNDS

The rate determined in the federal funds market is the major factor that influences the rate paid on all the other money market instruments described in this chapter.

Depository institutions (commercial banks and thrifts) are required to maintain reserves. The reserves are deposits at their district Federal Reserve Bank, which are called federal funds. The level of the reserves that a bank must maintain is based on its average daily deposits over the previous 14 days. Of all depository institutions, commercial banks are by far the largest holders of federal funds.

No interest is earned on federal funds. Consequently, a depository institution that maintains federal funds in excess of the amount required incurs an opportunity cost—the loss of interest income that could be earned on the excess reserves. At the same time, there are depository institutions whose federal funds are less than the amount required. Typically, smaller banks have excess reserves, whereas money center banks find themselves short of reserves and must make up the shortfall. Banks maintain federal funds desks whose managers are responsible for the bank's federal funds position.

One way that banks with less than the required reserves can bring reserves to the required level is to enter into a repo with a nonbank customer. An alternative is for the bank to borrow federal funds from a bank that has excess reserves. The market in which federal funds are bought (borrowed) by banks that need these funds and sold (lent) by banks that have excess federal funds is called the *federal funds market*. The equilibrium interest rate, which is determined by the supply and demand for federal funds, is the federal funds rate.

The federal funds rate and the repo rate are tied together because both are a means for a bank to borrow. The federal funds rate is higher because the lending of federal funds is done on an unsecured basis; this differs from the repo, in which the lender has a security as collateral. The spread between the two rates varies depending on market conditions; typically the spread is around 25 basis points.

The term of most federal funds transactions is overnight, but there are longer-term transactions that range from one week to six months. Trading typically takes place directly between the buyer and seller—usually between a large bank and one of its correspondent banks. Some federal funds transactions require the use of a broker.

SUMMARY

Money market instruments are debt obligations that at issuance have a maturity of one year or less. Commercial paper is a short-term unsecured promissory note issued in the open market that represents the obligation of the issuing entity. It is sold on a discount basis. To avoid SEC registration, the maturity of commercial paper is less than 270 days. Generally, commercial paper maturity is less than 90 days so that it will qualify as eligible collateral for the bank to borrow from the Federal Reserve Bank's discount window. Financial and nonfinancial corporations issue commercial paper, with the majority issued by the former. Direct paper is sold by the issuing firm directly to investors without using a securities dealer as an intermediary; with dealer-placed commercial paper, the issuer uses the services of a securities firm to sell its paper. There is little liquidity in the commercial paper market.

A bankers acceptance is a vehicle created to facilitate commercial trade transactions, particularly international transactions. They are called bankers acceptances because a bank accepts the responsibility to repay a loan to the holder of the vehicle created in a commercial transaction in case the debtor fails to perform. Bankers acceptances are sold on a discounted basis, as are Treasury bills and commercial paper.

Certificates of deposit (CDs) are issued by banks and thrifts to raise funds for financing their business activities. Unlike Treasury bills, commercial paper, and bankers acceptances, yields on domestic CDs are quoted on an interest-bearing basis. A floating-rate CD is one whose coupon interest rate changes periodically in accordance with a predetermined formula.

A repurchase agreement is a lending transaction in which the borrower uses a security as collateral for the borrowing. The transaction is referred to as a repurchase agreement because it specifies the sale of a security and its subsequent repurchase at a future date. The difference between the purchase (repurchase) price and the sale price is the dollar interest cost of the loan. An overnight repo is for one day; a loan for more than one day is called a term repo. The collateral in a repo may be a Treasury security, money market instrument, federal agency security, or mortgage-backed security. The parties to a repo are exposed to credit risk, limited by margin and mark-to-market practices included in a repo agreement. Dealers use the repo market to finance positions and cover short positions, and to run a matched book so that they can earn spread income. The Fed uses the repo market to implement monetary policy. Factors that determine the repo rate are the federal funds rate, the quality of the collateral, the term of the repo, the delivery requirement, and the availability of the collateral.

The federal funds market is the market where depository institutions borrow (buy) and sell (lend) federal funds. The federal funds rate, which is the rate at which all money market interest rates are anchored, is determined in this market. The federal funds rate is higher than the repo rate because borrowing done in the federal funds market is unsecured borrowing.

11

⑥ CORPORATE BONDS

Frank J. Fabozzi, Ph.D., CFA, CPA
Adjunct Professor of Finance
School of Management
Yale University

Richard S. Wilson
Executive Managing Director
Fitch Investors Service, L.P.

John C. Ritchie, Jr., Ph.D.
Professor of Finance
Temple University

A corporate bond is a debt instrument setting forth the obligation of the issuer to satisfy the terms of the agreement. Essentially an IOU, it can be quite a complex instrument, although the essential features may be relatively simple. The maker, or issuer, agrees to pay a certain amount or a percentage of the face, or principal, value (also known as par value) to the owner of the bond, either periodically over the life of the issue or in a lump sum upon the bond's retirement or maturity. Failure to pay the principal and/or interest when due (and to meet other of the debt's provisions) in accordance with the terms of the instrument constitutes legal default and court proceedings can be instituted to enforce the contract. Bondholders, as creditors, have a prior legal claim over common and preferred stockholders as to both income and assets of the corporation for the principal and interest due them and may have a prior claim over other creditors if liens or mortgages are involved. It is important to recognize, however, that a superior legal status will not prevent bondholders from suffering financial loss when the ability of a corporation to generate cash flow adequate to pay its obligations is seriously eroded.

Bond prices can and do undergo sizeable changes as the general level of interest rates changes, reflecting changing supply-and-demand conditions for loanable funds. Bonds can be acquired for income, emphasizing the relative sureness and attractiveness of periodic interest receipts and tending to ignore price fluctuations. On the other hand, fixed income securities can be among the most speculative investment vehicles available when bought on margin or when a low-quality issue is purchased.

Previous versions of this chapter were coauthored with Harry Sauvain.

Corporate bonds are usually issued in denominations of $1,000 and multiples thereof. In common usage, a corporate bond is assumed to have a par value of $1,000 unless otherwise explicitly specified. A security dealer who says he or she has five bonds to sell means five bonds each of $1,000 principal amount. If the promised rate of interest (coupon rate) is 6 percent, the annual amount of interest on each bond is $60 and the semiannual interest is $30.

Although there are technical differences between bonds, notes, and debentures, we will use Wall Street convention and call fixed income debt by the general term—*bonds.*

THE CORPORATE TRUSTEE

The promises of corporate bond issuers and the rights of investors who buy them are set forth in great detail in contracts generally called *indentures.* If bondholders were handed the complete indenture, some may have trouble understanding the legalese and have even greater difficulty in determining from time to time if the corporate issuer is keeping all the promises made. These problems are solved for the most part by bringing in a *corporate trustee* as a third party to the contract. The indenture is made out to the corporate trustee as a representative of the interests of bondholders; that is, the trustee acts in a fiduciary capacity for investors who own the bond issue.

A corporate trustee is a bank or trust company with a corporate trust department and officers who are experts in performing the functions of a trustee. This is no small task. The corporate trustee must, at the time of issue, authenticate the bonds issued—that is, keep track of all the bonds sold and make sure that they do not exceed the principal amount authorized by the indenture. It must then be a watchdog for the bondholders by seeing to it that the issuer complies with all the covenants of the indenture. These covenants are many and technical, and they must be watched during the entire period that a bond issue is outstanding. We will describe some of these covenants in subsequent pages.

It is very important that corporate trustees be competent and financially responsible. To this end, there is a federal statute known as the Trust Indenture Act, which requires that for all corporate bond offerings in the amount of more than $5 million sold in interstate commerce there must be a corporate trustee. The indenture must include adequate requirements for performance of the trustee's duties on behalf of bondholders; there must be no conflict between the trustee's interest as a trustee and any other interest it may have, especially if it is also a creditor of the issuer; and there must be provision for reports by the trustee to bondholders. If a corporate issuer fails to pay interest or principal, the trustee may declare a default and take such action as may be necessary to protect the rights of bondholders. If the corporate issuer has promised in the indenture to always maintain an amount of current assets equal to two times the amount of current liabilities, the trustee must watch the corporation's balance sheet and see that the promise is kept. If the issuer fails to maintain the prescribed amounts, the trustee must take action on behalf of the bondholders. However, it must be emphasized that the trustee is paid by the debt issuer and can only do what the indenture provides. The indenture may contain a clause stating that the trustee undertakes to perform such duties and only such duties as are specifically set forth in the indenture, and no implied covenants or obligations shall be read into the indenture against the trustee. Also, the trustee is usually under no obligation to exercise the rights or powers under the indenture at the request of bondholders unless it has been offered reasonable security or indemnity. The trustee is not bound to make investigations into the facts surrounding documents delivered to it, but it may do so if it sees fit.

The terms of bond issues set forth in bond indentures are always a compromise between the interests of the bond issuer and those of investors who buy bonds. The issuer always wants to pay the lowest possible rate of interest and to be tied up as little as possible with legal covenants. Bondholders want the highest possible interest rate, the best security, and a variety of covenants to restrict the issuer in one way or another. As we discuss the provisions of bond indentures, keep this opposition of interests in mind and see how compromises are worked out in practice.

SOME BOND FUNDAMENTALS

Bonds can be classified by a number of characteristics, which we will use for ease of organizing this section.

Bonds Classified by Issuer Type

The five broad categories of corporate bonds sold in the United States based on the type of issuer are public utilities, transportations, industrials, banks and finance companies, and international or Yankee issues. Finer breakdowns are often made by market participants to create homogeneous groupings. For example, public utilities are subdivided into telephone or communications, electric companies, gas distribution and transmission companies, and water companies. The transportation industry can be subdivided into airlines, railroads, and trucking companies. Like public utilities, transportation companies often have various degrees of regulation or control by state and/or federal government agencies. Industrials are a catchall class, but even here, finer degrees of distinction may be needed by analysts. The industrial grouping includes manufacturing and mining concerns, retailers, and service-related companies. Even the Yankee or international borrower sector can be more finely tuned. For example, one might classify the issuers into categories such as supranational borrowers (International Bank for Reconstruction and Development and the European Investment Bank), sovereign issuers (Canada, Australia, United Kingdom), and foreign municipalities and agencies.

Corporate Debt Maturity

A bond's maturity is the date on which the issuer's obligation to satisfy the terms of the indenture is fulfilled. On that date the principal is repaid with any premium and accrued interest that may be due. However, as we shall see later when discussing debt redemption, the final maturity date as stated in the issue's title may or may not be the date when the contract terminates. Many issues can be retired prior to maturity.

Thus, although we often talk about long-term and short-term bonds, our long-term holdings may turn out to be relatively short. Also, investors' perceptions of what constitutes short- and long-term maturity for bonds has undergone considerable change over time. A half-century ago some experts viewed bonds with maturities of 5 to 15 years as short-term issues and those with maturities from 15 to 40 years as intermediate-term paper. Such is not the case today. Issues maturing within a year are usually viewed as the equivalent of cash items. Debt maturing more than one year from the reference date to five years later is generally thought of as short-term. Intermediate-term debt matures in 5 to 12 years, whereas long-term debt obviously matures in more than 12 years. These are not hard-and-fast classifications. Some think short-term bonds mature within 2 to 3 years and intermediate-term issues not longer than 8 to 10 years.

Before the Great Depression, there were a number of long-term bond issues with maturities of 100 or more years. Many were issued by railroads and others came out of corporate reorganizations. In a few cases, maturities were as long as 999 years from the date of issue. Today, only a few such issues are around. Investors prefer bonds to mature within their lifetime, not during the lifetime of some progeny centuries away.

Since the early 1970s, the average maturity of domestically issued new corporate debt shortened distinctly. Investor preference for shorter maturities is attributed to the increased volatility of bond prices caused by higher interest rates. All other things being the same, shorter maturity means reduced price risk. However, the shorter maturity structure of corporate debt increases pressures on corporate financial managers. It becomes more difficult to match long-lived assets with long-term liabilities. Years ago, a matching of assets and liabilities was deemed the proper course for corporations to follow. Now that isn't necessarily so. The more frequent refinancings necessary to replace a heavier volume of maturing debt also add to the burden of the corporate financial officer and to the pressures on the corporate bond market. More of a company's cash flow might have to be directed to paying off these obligations as they become due.

Interest Payment Characteristics

The three main interest payment classifications of domestically issued corporate bonds are straight-coupon bonds, zero-coupon bonds, and floating-rate, or variable-rate, bonds. Floating-rate issues are discussed in Chapter 13 and the other two types are examined below.

However, before we get into interest-rate characteristics, let us briefly discuss bond types. We refer to the interest rate on a bond as the coupon. This is technically wrong, as bonds issued today do not have coupons attached. Instead, bonds are represented by a certificate, similar to a stock certificate, with a brief description of the terms printed on both sides. These are called *registered bonds*. The principal amount of the bond is noted on the certificate, and the interest-paying agent or trustee has the responsibility of making payment by check to the registered holder on the due date. Years ago, bonds were issued in *bearer,* or *coupon,* form with coupons attached for each interest payment. However, the registered form is considered safer and entails less paperwork. As a matter of fact, the registered bond certificate is on its way out as more and more issues are sold in *book-entry* form. This means that only one master or global certificate is issued. It is held by a central securities depository that issues receipts denoting interests in this global certificate. U.S. Treasury issues are sold in this form.

Straight-coupon bonds have an interest rate set for the life of the issue, however long or short that may be; they are also called *fixed-rate* bonds. Most fixed-rate bonds pay interest semiannually and at maturity. For example, a bond with an interest rate of 9 percent maturing on June 15, 2000, will pay $45 per $1,000 par amount each June 15 and December 15, including June 15, 2000. Of course, at maturity the par amount is also paid. Bonds with interest payable once a year are uncommon among domestic issues but are the norm for issues sold overseas. From time to time, investors may encounter bonds with other payment patterns such as quarterly or even monthly.

Interest payments due on Sundays or holidays are normally paid on the next business day without additional interest for the extra day or two the company has use of the monies. Interest on corporate bonds is based on a year of 360 days made up of twelve 30-day months. It does not matter whether the month is February, April, or May; all months for this purpose are of the same length. The 9 percent bond pays interest of $90 per year per $1,000 face value. Interest accrues at the rate of $7.50 a month or $0.25 per day. The corporate calendar day count convention is referred to as *30/360.*

Most fixed-rate corporate bonds pay interest in a standard fashion. However, there are some variations of which you should be aware. Most domestic bonds pay interest in U.S. dollars. However, starting in the early 1980s, issues were marketed with principal and interest payable in other currencies such as the Australian, New Zealand, or Canadian dollar or the European Currency Unit (ECU). Generally, interest and principal payments are converted from the foreign currency to U.S. dollars by the paying agent unless it is otherwise notified. The bondholders bear any costs associated with the dollar conversion. Foreign currency issues provide investors with another way of diversifying a portfolio, but not without risk. The holder bears the currency, or exchange, risk in addition to all of the other risks associated with debt instruments.

There are a few issues of bonds that can participate in the fortunes of the issuer over and above the stated coupon rate. These are called *participating bonds,* as they share in the profits of the issuer or the rise in certain assets over and above certain minimum levels. Another type of bond rarely encountered today is the *income bond.* These bonds promise to pay a stipulated interest rate, but the payment is contingent on sufficient earnings and is in accordance with the definition of available income for interest payments contained in the indenture. Repayment of principal is not contingent. Interest may be cumulative or noncumulative. If payments are cumulative, unpaid interest payments must be made up at some future date. If noncumulative, once the interest payment is past, it does not have to be repaid. Failure to pay interest on income bonds is not an act of default and is not a cause for bankruptcy. Income bonds have been issued by some financially troubled corporations emerging from reorganization proceedings.

Zero-coupon bonds are, just as the name implies, bonds without coupons or an interest rate. Essentially, zero-coupon bonds pay only the principal portion of a complete bond at some future date. These bonds are issued at discounts to par; the difference constitutes the return to the bondholder. The difference between the face amount and the offering price when first issued is called the *original-issue discount* (OID). The rate of return depends on the amount of the discount and the period over which it accretes. For example, a 5-year zero-coupon bond yielding 9 percent on a semiannual basis must be priced at 64.39 percent of par. If due in 7 years, the price would be 59 percent; in 10 years, 41.46 percent; and in 15 years, only 26.70 percent.

Zeros were first publicly issued in the corporate market in the spring of 1981 and were an immediate hit with investors. The rapture only lasted a couple of years because of changes in the income tax laws that made ownership more costly on an after-tax basis. Also, these changes reduced the tax advantages to issuers. However, tax-deferred investors, such as pension funds, could still take advantage of zero-coupon issues. One important risk is eliminated in a zero-coupon investment—the reinvestment risk. Because there is no coupon to reinvest, there isn't any risk. Of course, although this is beneficial in declining interest-rate markets, the reverse is true when interest rates are rising. The investor will not be able to reinvest an income stream at rising reinvestment rates. Investors tend to find zeros less attractive in lower interest-rate markets because compounding is not as meaningful as when rates are higher. Also, the lower the rates are, the more likely that they will rise again, making a zero-coupon investment worth less in the eyes of potential holders.

In bankruptcy, a zero-coupon bond creditor can claim the original offering price plus accrued and unpaid interest to the date of the bankruptcy filing, but not the principal amount of $1,000. Zero-coupon bonds have been sold at deep discounts and the liability of the issuer at maturity may be substantial. The accretion of the discount on the corporation's books is not put away in a special fund for debt retirement purposes. There are no sinking funds on most of these issues. One hopes that corporate managers properly invest the proceeds and run the corporation for the benefit of all investors so that there will not be a cash crisis at maturity. The potentially large balloon repayment creates a cause for concern among investors. Thus, it is most important to invest in higher-quality issues so as to reduce the risk of a potential problem. If one wants to speculate in lower-rated bonds, then that investment should throw off some cash return.

Finally, a variation of the zero-coupon bond is the deferred-interest bond (DIB), also known as a zero/coupon bond. These bonds have generally been subordinated issues of speculative-grade issuers, also known as *junk* issuers. Most of the issues are structured so that they do not pay cash interest for the first five years. At the end of the deferred-interest period, cash interest accrues, generally between 13 percent and 18 percent, and is paid semiannually until maturity, unless the bonds are redeemed earlier. The deferred-interest feature allows newly restructured, highly leveraged companies and others with less-than-satisfactory cash flows to defer the payment of cash interest over the early life of the bond. Hopefully, when cash interest payments start, the company will be able to service the debt. If it has made excellent progress in restoring its financial health, the company may be able to redeem or refinance the debt rather than have high interest outlays.

An offshoot of the deferred-interest bond is the pay-in-kind (PIK) debenture. With PIKs, cash interest payments are deferred at the issuer's option until some future date. Instead of just accreting the original-issue discount as with DIBs or zeros, the issuer pays out the interest in additional pieces of the same security. The option to pay cash or in-kind interest payments rests with the issuer, but in many cases the issuer has little choice because provisions of other debt instruments often prohibit cash interest payments until certain indenture or loan tests are satisfied. The holder just gets more pieces of paper, but these at least can be sold in the market without giving up one's original investment; PIKs, DIBs, and zeros do not have provisions for the resale of the interest portion of the instrument. An investment in this type of bond, because it is issued by speculative-grade companies, requires careful analysis of the issuer's cash flow prospects and ability to survive.

SECURITY FOR BONDS

Shylock demanded a pound of flesh as his security. Investors who buy corporate bonds don't go quite that far, but they do like some kind of security. Either real property (using a mortgage) or personal property may be pledged to offer security beyond that of the general credit standing of the issue. In fact, the kind of security or the absence of a specific pledge of security is usually indicated by the title of a bond issue. However, the best security is a strong general credit that can repay the debt from earnings.

Mortgage Bond

Readers of *The Wall Street Journal* may have seen an advertisement for "$50,000,000 issue of Metropolitan Edison, First Mortgage Bonds, 9 percent Series, due December 1, 2008." That title says several things about this bond issue.

It says that the issuer has granted the bondholders a first-mortgage lien on substantially all of its properties. That is good from the viewpoint of bondholders.

But in return the issuer got a lower rate of interest on the bonds than if the issue were unsecured. A debenture issue (i.e., unsecured debt) of the same company might have carried an interest rate of 9.25 percent to 9.375 percent. A *lien* is a legal right to sell mortgaged property to satisfy unpaid obligations to bondholders. In practice, foreclosure of a mortgage and sale of mortgaged property is unusual. If a default occurs, there is usually a financial reorganization on the part of the issuer, in which provision is made for settlement of the debt to bondholders. The mortgage lien is important, though, because it gives the mortgage bondholders a very strong bargaining position relative to other creditors in determining the terms of a reorganization.

Often first-mortgage bonds are issued in series with bonds of each series secured equally by the same first mortgage. The title of the bond issue mentioned above includes "9 percent Series," which says that the issue is one of a series. Many companies, particularly public utilities, have a policy of financing part of their capital requirements continuously by long-term debt. They want some part of their total capitalization in the form of bonds because the cost of such capital is ordinarily less than that of capital raised by sale of stock. So, as a principal amount of debt is paid off, they issue another series of bonds under the same mortgage. As they expand and need a greater amount of debt capital, they can add new series of bonds. It is a lot easier and more advantageous to issue a series of bonds under one mortgage and one indenture than it is to create entirely new bond issues with different arrangements for security. This arrangement is called a *blanket mortgage*. When property is sold or released from the lien of the mortgage, additional property or cash may be substituted or bonds may be retired in order to provide adequate security for the debtholders.

When a bond indenture authorizes the issue of additional series of bonds with the same mortgage lien as those already issued, the indenture imposes certain conditions that must be met before an additional series may be issued. Bondholders do not want their security impaired; these conditions are for their benefit. It is common for a first-mortgage bond indenture to specify that property acquired by the issuer subsequent to the granting of the first-mortgage lien shall be subject to the first-mortgage lien. This is termed the *after-acquired clause*. Then the indenture usually permits the issue of additional bonds up to some specified percentage of the value of the after-acquired property, such as 60 percent. The other 40 percent, or whatever the percentage may be, must be financed in some other way. This is intended to ensure that there will be additional assets with a value significantly greater than the amount of additional bonds secured by the mortgage. Another customary kind of restriction on the issue of additional series is a requirement that earnings in an immediately preceding period must be equal to some number of times the amount of annual interest on all outstanding mortgage bonds including the new or proposed series (1.5, 2, or some other number). For this purpose, *earnings* are usually defined as earnings before income tax. Still another common provision is that additional bonds may be issued to the extent that earlier series of bonds have been paid off.

You seldom see a bond issue with the term *second mortgage* in its title. The reason is that this term has a connotation of weakness. Sometimes companies get around that difficulty by using such words as *first and consolidated, first and refunding,* or *general and refunding mortgage bonds.* Usually this language means that a bond issue is secured by a first mortgage on some part of the issuer's property but by a second or even third lien on other parts of its assets. A general and refunding mortgage bond is generally secured by a lien on all of the company's property *subject* to the prior lien of first mortgage bonds, if any are still outstanding.

Collateral Trust Bonds

Some companies do not own fixed assets or other real property and so have nothing on which they can give a mortgage lien to secure bondholders. Instead, they own securities of other companies; they are *holding companies,* and the other companies are *subsidiaries.* To satisfy the desire of bondholders for security, they pledge stocks, notes, bonds, or whatever other kind of obligations they own. These assets are termed *collateral* (or personal property), and bonds secured by such assets are *collateral trust bonds.* Some companies own both real property and securities. They may use real property to secure mortgage bonds and use securities for collateral trust bonds.

The legal arrangement for collateral trust bonds is much the same as that for mortgage bonds. The issuer delivers to a corporate trustee under a bond indenture the securities pledged, and the trustee holds them for the benefit of the bondholders. When voting common stocks are included in the collateral, the indenture permits the issuer to vote the stocks so long as there is no default on its bonds. This is important to issuers of such bonds because usually the stocks are those of subsidiaries, and the issuer depends on the exercise of voting rights to control the subsidiaries.

Indentures usually provide that, in event of default, the rights to vote stocks included in the collateral are transferred to the trustee. Loss of the voting right would be a serious disadvantage to the issuer because it would mean loss of control of subsidiaries. The trustee may also sell the securities pledged for whatever prices they will bring in the market and apply the proceeds to payment of the claims of collateral trust bondholders. These rather drastic actions, however, are not usually taken immediately on an event of default. The corporate trustee's primary responsibility is to act in the best interests of bondholders, and their interests may be served for a time at least by giving the defaulting issuer a proxy to vote stocks held as collateral and thus preserve the holding company structure. It may also defer the sale of collateral when it seems likely that bondholders would fare better in a financial reorganization than they would by sale of collateral.

Collateral trust indentures contain a number of provisions designed to protect bondholders. Generally, the market or appraised value of the collateral must be maintained at some percentage of the amount of bonds outstanding. The percentage is greater than 100 so that there will be a margin of safety. If collateral value declines below the minimum percentage, additional collateral must be provided by the issuer. There is almost always provision for withdrawal of some collateral provided other acceptable collateral is substituted.

Collateral trust bonds may be issued in series in much the same way that mortgage bonds are issued in series. The rules governing additional series of bonds require that adequate collateral must be pledged, and there may be restrictions on the use to which the proceeds of an additional series may be put. All series of bonds are issued under the same indenture and have the same claim on collateral.

Equipment Trust Certificates

The desire of borrowers to pay the lowest possible rate of interest on their obligations generally leads them to offer their best security and to grant lenders the strongest claim on it. Many years ago, the railway companies developed a way of financing purchase of cars and locomotives, called *rolling stock,* that enabled them to borrow at just about the lowest rates in the corporate bond market.

Railway rolling stock has for a long time been regarded by investors as excellent security for debt. This equipment is sufficiently standardized that it can be used by one railway as well as another. And it can be readily moved from the tracks of one railroad to those of another. There is generally a good market for lease or sale of cars and locomotives. The railroads have capitalized on these characteristics of rolling stock by developing a legal arrangement for giving investors a legal claim on it that is different from, and generally better than, a mortgage lien.

The legal arrangement is one that vests legal title to railway equipment in a trustee, which is better from the standpoint of investors than a first-mortgage lien on property. A railway company orders some cars and locomotives from a manufacturer. When the job is finished, the manufacturer transfers the legal title to the equipment to a trustee. The trustee leases it to the railroad that ordered it and at the same time sells *equipment trust certificates* (ETCs) in an amount equal to a large percentage of the purchase price, normally 80 percent. Money from sale of certificates is paid to the manufacturer. The railway company makes an initial payment of rent equal to the balance of the purchase price, and the trustee gives that money to the manufacturer. Thus the manufacturer is paid off. The trustee collects lease rental money periodically from the railroad and uses it to pay interest and principal on the certificates. These interest payments are known as dividends. The amounts of lease rental payments are worked out carefully so that they are enough to pay the equipment trust certificates. At the end of some period of time, such as 15 years, the certificates are paid off, the trustee sells the equipment to the railroad for some nominal price, and the lease is terminated.

Railroad ETCs are usually structured in serial form; that is, a certain amount becomes payable at specified dates until the final installment. For example, a $15 million ETC might mature $1 million on each June 15 from 1990 through 2004. Each of the 15 maturities may be priced separately to reflect the shape of the yield curve, investor preference for specific maturities, and supply-and-demand considerations. The advantage of a serial issue from the investor's point of view is that the repayment schedule matches the decline in the value of the equipment used as collateral. Hence, principal repayment risk is reduced. From the issuer's side, serial maturities allow for the repayment of the debt periodically over the life of the issue, making less likely a crisis at maturity due to a large repayment coming due at one time.

The beauty of this arrangement from the viewpoint of investors is that the railroad does not legally own the rolling stock until all the certificates are paid. In case the railroad does not make the lease rental payments, there is no big legal hassle about foreclosing a lien. The trustee owns the property and can take it back because failure to pay the rent breaks the lease. The trustee can lease the equipment to another railroad and continue to make payments on the certificates from new lease rentals.

This description emphasizes the legal nature of the arrangement for securing the certificates. In practice, these certificates are regarded as obligations of the railway company that leased the equipment and are shown as liabilities in its balance sheet. In fact, the name of the railway appears in the title of the certificates. In the ordinary course of events, the trustee is just an intermediary who performs the function of holding title, acting as lessor, and collecting the money to pay the certificates. It is significant that even in the worst years of depression, railways have paid their equipment trust certificates, though they did not pay bonds secured by mortgages. Although railroads have issued the largest amount of equipment trust certificates, airlines have also utilized this form of financing.

Debenture Bonds

After all the emphasis upon security, you might think that usury-minded investors would not buy bonds without something to secure them. But not so! Investors often buy large issues of unsecured bonds just as they buy first-mortgage bonds. These unsecured bonds are termed *debentures*. As a matter of fact, with the exception of the utility industry and specifically structured special purpose financings, nearly all other corporate debt sold is unsecured.

Debentures are not secured by a specific pledge of designated property, but that does not mean that they have no claim on property of issuers or on their earnings. Debenture bondholders have the claim of general creditors on all assets of the issuer not pledged specifically to secure other debt. And they even have a claim on pledged assets to the extent that these assets have value greater than necessary to satisfy secured creditors. In fact, if there are no pledged assets and no secured creditors, debenture bondholders have first claim on all assets along with other general creditors.

These unsecured bonds are sometimes issued by companies that are so strong financially and have such a high credit rating that to offer security would be gilding the lily. Such companies can simply turn a deaf ear to investors who want security and still sell their debentures at relatively low interest rates. But debentures are sometimes issued by companies that have already sold mortgage bonds and given liens on most of their property. These debentures rank below the mortgage bonds or collateral trust bonds in their claim on assets, and investors may regard them as relatively weak. This is the kind that bears the higher rates of interest.

Even though there is no pledge of security, the indentures for debenture bonds may contain a variety of provisions designed to afford some protection to investors. Frequently the amount of a debenture bond issue is limited to the amount of the initial issue. This limit is to keep issuers from weakening the position of debenture holders by running up additional unsecured debt. Sometimes additional debentures may be issued a specified number of times in a recent accounting period, provided that the issuer has earned its bond interest on all existing debt plus the additional issue.

If a company has no secured debt, it is customary to provide that debentures will be secured equally with any secured bonds that may be issued in the future. This is known as the *negative pledge clause*. Some provisions of debenture bond issues are intended to give the corporate trustee early warning of deterioration in the issuer's financial condition. The issuer may be required to always maintain a specified minimum amount of net working capital—the excess of current assets over current liabilities—equal to not less than the amount of debentures outstanding. The corporate trustee must watch the issuer's balance sheets and, on failure to maintain the required amount of net working capital, take whatever action is appropriate in the interest of debenture holders. Another common restriction is one limiting the payment of cash dividends by the issuer. Another restriction limits the proportion of current earnings that may be used to pay dividends. However, the trend in recent years, at least with investment-grade companies, is away from indenture restrictions.

Subordinated and Convertible Debentures

You might think that debenture bonds have about the weakest possible claim on the assets and earnings of a corporate issuer, but that is not so. Many companies have issued *subordinated debenture bonds*. The term *subordinated* means that such an issue ranks after secured debt, after debenture bonds, and often after some general creditors in its claim on assets and earnings. Owners of this kind of bond stand last in line among creditors when an issuer fails financially.

Because subordinated debentures are weaker in their claim on assets, issuers would have to offer a higher rate of interest unless they also offer some special inducement to buy the bonds. The inducement can be an option to convert bonds into stock of the issuer at the discretion of bondholders. If the issuer prospers and the market price of its stock rises substantially in the market, the bondholders can convert bonds to stock worth a great deal more than what they paid for the bonds. This conversion privilege may also be included in the provisions of debentures that are not subordinated. Convertible securities are discussed in Chapter 15.

The bonds may be convertible into the common stock of a corporation other than that of the issuer. Such issues are called *exchangeable bonds.* There are also issues indexed to a commodity's price or its cash equivalent at the time of maturity or redemption.

Guaranteed Bonds

Sometimes a corporation may guarantee the bonds of another corporation. Such bonds are referred to as guaranteed bonds. The guarantee, however, does not mean that these obligations are free of default risk. The safety of a guaranteed bond depends upon the financial capability of the guarantor to satisfy the terms of the guarantee, as well as the financial capability of the issuer. The terms of the guarantee may call for the guarantor to guarantee the payment of interest and/or repayment of the principal. A guaranteed bond may have more than one corporate guarantor. Each guarantor may be responsible for not only its pro rata share but also the entire amount guaranteed by the other guarantors.

PROVISIONS FOR PAYING OFF BONDS

What would you pay for a bond that promises to pay interest in the amount of $50 or $60 a year from now to eternity but never promises to repay the principal? The right to receive interest in perpetuity may very well be worth $1,000, depending upon the current level of interest rates in the market, but investors generally dislike the absence of a promise to pay a fixed amount of principal on some specified date in the future; therefore, there is no such thing as a perpetual bond in the U.S. financial markets.

Call and Refund Provisions

One important question in the negotiation of terms of a new bond issue is whether the issuer shall have the right to redeem the bonds before maturity, either as a whole or in part. Issuers generally want to have this right, and investors do not want them to have it. Both sides think that at some time in the future the general level of interest rates in the market may decline to a level well below that prevailing at the time bonds are issued. If so, issuers want to redeem all of the bonds outstanding and replace them with new bond issues at lower interest rates. But this is exactly what investors do not want. If bonds are redeemed when interest rates are low, investors have to take their money back and reinvest it at a low rate.

The usual practice is a provision that denies the issuer a right to redeem bonds during the first 5 or 10 years following the date of issue if the proceeds from the redemption are from lower-cost funds obtained with issues ranking equally with or superior to the debt to be redeemed. This type of redemption is called *refunding*. However, although most long-term issues have these refunding bars, or prohibitions, they are usually immediately callable, in whole or in part, if the source of funds is not lower-interest-cost money. Such sources may include retained earnings, the proceeds from a common stock sale, or funds from the disposition of property. Although the redemption price is often at a premium, there are many cases where the call price is 100 percent of par.

Many short- to intermediate-term bonds and notes are not callable for the first three to seven years (in some cases, not callable for the life of the issue). Thereafter, they may be called for any reason. Bond market participants often confuse refunding protection with call protection. Call protection is much more absolute in that bonds cannot be redeemed for any reason. Refunding restrictions only provide protection against one type of redemption, as mentioned above. Failure to recognize this difference has resulted in unnecessary losses for some investors.

Long-term industrial issues generally have 10 years of refunding protection but are immediately callable. Electric utilities most often have 5 years of refunding protection, although during times of high interest rates, issues with 10 years of refunding protection have been sold. Long-term debt of the former members of the Bell Telephone System has 5 years of call protection.

As a rule, corporate bonds are callable at a premium above par. Generally, the amount of the premium declines as the bond approaches maturity. The initial amount of the premium may be as much as one year's interest or as little as interest for half a year. When less than the entire issue is called, the specific bonds to be called are selected randomly or on a pro rata basis. If the bonds selected on a random basis are bearer bonds, the serial numbers of the certificates are published in *The Wall Street Journal* and major metropolitan dailies.

Outright Redemptions

For lack of a better term, we will use *outright redemptions* to describe the call of debt at general redemption prices. In the spring of 1973, Bristol-Myers Company called for redemption at 107.538 one-third, or $25 million, of its $8^5/_8$ percent debentures due 1995. Trading as high as 111 in 1972 and about 108–109 when the call was announced, there were obviously some losses involved. Some market participants were confused by the call as they did not know the difference between nonrefundable and currently callable.

In 1977, NCR Corporation redeemed $75 million of its $9^3/_4$ percent debentures due 2000 at 107.88. The bonds were trading at 111–111$^1/_2$. The company was in a strong cash position and projected cash flow was substantially in excess of expected capital spending plans. Thus, NCR took action to improve its balance sheet and to reduce leverage through the call of this debt.

In 1983, a good example of an industrial redemption involved Archer Daniels Midland Company 16 percent sinking-fund debentures due May 15, 2011. The bonds were sold May 12, 1981, at $99^1/_2$ and had the standard redemption/refunding provisions (i.e., currently callable but nonrefundable prior to May 15, 1991). On June 1, 1983, the company announced the call of the bonds for August 1 at 113.95 plus accrued interest. On May 31, the bonds traded at 120. The source of the funds, according to the company, was from the two common stock offerings in January and June. Bondholders brought legal action, but the court allowed the redemption to proceed. On August 6, 1984, Archer Daniels Midland sold $100 million of 13 percent sinking-fund debentures due 8/1/2014 at 97.241, for a yield of 13.375 percent. The financial press reported that the investor reception was lukewarm. Would you like to guess one of the reasons for this?

Sinking-Fund Provision

Term bonds may be paid off by operation of a *sinking fund.* Those last two words are often misunderstood to mean that the issuer accumulates a fund in cash, or in assets readily sold for cash, that is used to pay bonds at maturity. It had that meaning many years ago, but too often the money supposed to be in a sinking fund was not all there when it was needed. In modern practice, there is no fund, and *sinking* means that money is applied periodically to redemption of bonds before maturity. Corporate bond indentures require the issuer to retire a specified portion of an issue each year. This kind of provision for repayment of corporate debt may be designed to liquidate all of a bond issue by the maturity date, or it may be arranged to pay only a part of the total by the end of the term. If only a part is paid, the remainder is called a *balloon maturity.*

The issuer may satisfy the sinking-fund requirement in one of two ways. A cash payment of the face amount of the bonds to be retired may be made by the corporate debtor to the trustee. The latter then calls the bonds by lot for redemption. Bonds have serial numbers, and numbers may be randomly selected for redemption. Owners of bonds called in this manner turn them in for redemption; *interest payments stop at the redemption date.* Alternatively, the issuer can deliver to the trustee bonds with a total face value equal to the amount that must be retired. The bonds are purchased by the *issuer* in the open market. This option is elected by the issuer when the bonds are selling below par. A few corporate bond indentures, however, prohibit the open market purchase of the bonds by the issuer.

Many electric utility bond issues can satisfy the sinking fund requirement by a third method. Instead of actually retiring bonds, the company may certify to the trustee that it has utilized unfunded property credits in lieu of the sinking fund. That is, it has made property and plant investments that have not been utilized for issuing bonded debt. For example, if the sinking-fund requirement is $1 million, it may give the trustee $1 million in cash to call bonds; it may deliver to the trustee $1 million of bonds it purchased in the open market; or it may certify that it made additions to its property and plant in the required amount, normally $1,667 of plant for each $1,000 sinking-fund requirement. In this case, it could satisfy the sinking fund with certified property additions of $1,667,000.

The issuer is granted a special call price to satisfy any sinking-fund requirement. Usually, the sinking-fund call price is the par value if the bonds were originally sold at par. When issued at a price in excess of par, the sinking-fund call price generally starts at the issuance price and scales down to par as the issue approaches maturity.

There are two advantages of a sinking-fund requirement from the bondholder's perspective. First, default risk is reduced because of the orderly retirement of the issue before maturity. Second, if bond prices decline as a result of an increase in interest rates, price support may be provided by the issuer or its fiscal agent, because it must enter the market on the buy side in order to satisfy the sinking-fund requirement. However, the disadvantage is that the bonds may be called at the special sinking-fund call price at a time when interest rates are lower than rates prevailing at the time of issuance. In that case, the bonds will be selling above par but may be retired by the issuer at the special call price that may be equal to par value.

Usually, the periodic payments required for sinking-fund purposes will be the same for each period. Gas company issues often have increasing sinking-fund requirements. However, a few indentures might permit variable periodic payments, where the periodic payments vary based upon prescribed conditions set forth in the indenture. The most common condition is the level of earnings of the issuer. In such cases, the periodic payments vary directly with earnings. An issuer prefers such flexibility; however, an investor may prefer fixed periodic payments because of the greater default risk protection provided under this arrangement.

Many corporate bond indentures include a provision that grants the issuer the option to retire more than the amount stipulated for sinking-fund retirement. This option, referred to as an *accelerated sinking-fund provision,* effectively reduces the bondholder's call protection because, when interest rates decline, the issuer may find it economically advantageous to exercise this option at the special sinking-fund call price to retire a substantial portion of an outstanding issue.

With the exception of finance companies, industrial issues almost always include sinking-fund provisions. Finance companies, on the other hand, almost always do not. The inclusion or absence of a sinking-fund provision in public utility debt obligations depends upon the type of public utility. Pipeline issues almost always include sinking-fund provisions, whereas telephone issues do not. Electric utility companies have varying sinking-fund provisions. There can be a mandatory sinking fund where bonds have to be retired or, as mentioned above, a nonmandatory sinking fund in which it may utilize certain property credits for the sinking-fund requirement. If the sinking fund applies to a particular issue, it is called a *specific* sinking fund. There are also nonspecific sinking funds (also known as funnel, tunnel, blanket, or aggregate sinking funds) where the requirement is based upon the total bonded debt outstanding of an issuer. Generally, it might require a sinking-fund payment of one percent of all bonds outstanding as of year-end. The issuer can apply the requirement to one particular issue or to any other issue or issues. Again, the blanket sinking fund may be mandatory (where bonds have to be retired) or nonmandatory (whereby it can utilize unfunded property additions). Companies with blanket sinking funds include Alabama Power Company, Georgia Power Company, Consumers Power Company, and Pacific Gas and Electric Company, among others. In some years, they might actually retire bonds, whereas in other years they may certify unfunded property additions. The blanket sinking fund of Baltimore Gas and Electric Company is mandatory.

Maintenance and Replacement Funds

Calls under maintenance and replacement fund (M&R) provisions first occurred in 1977–78. They shocked bondholders, as calls were thought to be unlikely under these provisions, which were little known and used. However, due to the steep decline in interest rates in 1985 and early 1986, some electric utility companies decided to make use of the M&R calls again. Now investors recognize this type of redemption, but because the calls were around the par level and the bonds with above-market-level coupons were trading at higher prices, the results still hurt.

Florida Power & Light Company retired $63.7 million out of $125 million of its $10^{1}/_{8}$ percent bonds due March 1, 2005, at 100.65 on September 2, 1977, through the M&R provisions. The regular redemption price at the time was 110.98 and the issue was well within the refunding period, which expired on February 28, 1980 (call price starting March 1, 1980, was 109.76).

In 1977 and 1978, Carolina Power & Light deposited nearly $79 million with its trustee under the M&R fund provisions. The company, on June 2, 1978, called $46 million of its privately held $11^{1}/_{8}$ percent bonds due 1994 and $32.7 million of the public 11 percent bonds of 1984 at the special redemption price of par. The company's announcement stated the following:

> The funds deposited were derived at the time from cash flow; however, if it is assumed that the eventual result is the replacement of the interest cost of the bonds to be redeemed with bonds at a probable interest cost of about 9 percent for 30 years, it is apparent that there will be a significant reduction of interest costs with an attendant improvement in fixed-charge coverages. The security of the total body of bondholders is improved and the maturities lengthened. These debt management actions are a positive demonstration to customers, stockholders and regulators that the management of the company continues to exercise appropriate cost control measures.

Of course, some bondholders objected to the retirements, claiming that, as the calls were within the refunding protected periods, the companies were barred from these special debt redemptions. They also claimed that the prospectuses and offering statements were unclear. However, a *careful* reading of the prospectuses revealed that the debt could be redeemed at the special redemption prices for the replacement fund or from certain other deposited cash. The general redemption prices applied to other redemptions, provided that none of the bonds could be redeemed *at the general redemption price* before the end of the refunding protected period if such redemption was for the purpose or in anticipation of refunding the bonds through the use of borrowed funds at a lower interest cost. The M&R provisions were allowed exceptions, and the courts have upheld companies' rights to redeem bonds in accordance with their terms.

Not all electric utility companies provide maintenance and replacement fund requirements for all of their mortgage debt. Some of the more recent issues lack the M&R provisions, although, as long as some of the older issues are still outstanding with these clauses, the M&R provisions apply. A number of issues subject to M&R clauses may be retired at the higher general redemption price and not the lower special call price. Others are protected from M&R redemption through the end of the refunding protected period, and in some cases certain property credits *must* be used before cash could be deposited with the trustee.

Redemption through the Sale of Assets and Other Means

Because mortgage bonds are secured by property, bondholders want the integrity of the collateral to be maintained. Bondholders would not want a company to sell a plant (which has been pledged as collateral) and then to use the proceeds for a distribution to shareholders. Therefore, release-of-property and substitution-of-property clauses are found in most bond indentures.

Wisconsin Michigan Power retired $9.9 million of its $9^1/_4$ percent bonds due 2000 on February 28, 1977, through the release-of-property clause at a redemption price of 100.97. On June 30, 1976, the company sold its gas business for $16,920,000 to an affiliate, Wisconsin Natural Gas. Of the proceeds, $16,520,000 was deposited with the trustee under the mortgage per the release and substitution-of-property clause, and a portion of these funds was released to the company against certified property additions. The balance was used to redeem the $9^1/_4$'s as interest rates dropped to a level where the company thought it was to its advantage to retire high-coupon debt.

On December 7, 1983, Virginia Electric and Power Company said it would redeem its $100 million $15^3/_4$ percent bonds due April 1, 1989 (the highest public coupon), with the proceeds (so-called release moneys) from the sale of ownership interests in some nuclear facilities. Property sales are not unusual for electric utility companies and a number have been negotiated in recent years.

Many utility bond issues contain provisions regarding the confiscation of assets by a governmental body through the right of eminent domain or the disposition of assets by order of or to any governmental authority. In a number of cases, bonds *must* be redeemed if the company receives more than a certain amount in cash. Washington Water Power Company must apply the proceeds of $15 million or more to the retirement of debt in the case of government takeover of its property. The redemption price may be either the special or regular, depending on the issue. In 1984, Pacific Power & Light Company sold an electric distribution system to the Emerald People's Utility District for $25 million. It applied these proceeds to the redemption of half of the outstanding $14^3/_4$ percent mortgage bonds due 2010 at the special redemption price of 100. This issue was not the highest-coupon bond outstanding in the company's capitalization. There were some 18s of 1991, but these were exempt from the special provisions for the retirement of bonds with the proceeds from property sold to governmental authorities. More recently, in April 1988, Utah Power & Light company retired some 13 percent bonds due 2012 with funds obtained from the condemnation of some of its property in Kaneb, Utah, and the sale of electric assets to a couple of other cities.

On December 13, 1983, InterNorth, Inc., announced the call on February 1, 1984, of $90.5 million out of $200 million of its $17^1/_2$ percent debentures due August 1, 1991, at the regular redemption price of 112.32. The refunding protected period expired September 30, 1988. However, the proceeds were obtained from the sale of its Northern Propane Gas Co. unit. Because these are unsecured debentures and not mortgage bonds, there was no release and substitution of property clause and no special call price. On October 1, 1984, it redeemed another $23,875,000 of these $17^1/_2$ percent debentures at 109.86 with funds obtained from the December 1983 sale of two tanker ships.

SOURCES OF INFORMATION ABOUT CORPORATE BOND OFFERINGS

For a new corporate bond offering, an investor can obtain a prospectus. The prospectus is a statement filed by the issuer with the Securities and Exchange Commission and containing all of the pertinent information about the security being offered and the company offering the security.

Summary information about a new offering is provided in *Moody's Credit Survey.* This service is published weekly and provides selected information on the business of the issuer, how the issuer will use the proceeds, the quality rating of the issue as assigned by Moody's, denominations available, the form of the security (registered or bearer), exchange options, security for the bonds, guarantees, call provisions, sinking-fund requirements, restrictions on management, and statistical highlights about the issuer. This service provides information not only on new offerings but also on proposed offerings. *CreditWeek,* published weekly by Standard & Poor's, provides similar information. These weekly publications are usually carried by local libraries.

For seasoned issues, major contractual provisions are provided in *Moody's Manuals* or Standard & Poor's *Corporation Records.* To obtain basic information about a seasoned corporate issue, the investor can check the monthly publication by either Moody's (*Moody's Bond Record*) or Standard & Poor's (*Standard & Poor's Bond Guide*).

CORPORATE BOND RATINGS

At any one time, the yields that investors obtain by purchasing bonds in the market may vary according to how investors estimate the uncertainty of future payment of dollar amounts of interest and principal exactly as set forth in bond indentures. This uncertainty is often called *financial risk* because it depends upon the financial ability of issuers to make those payments. If an issuer can pay, it will. Failure by a company to pay usually means intervention of a court of law on behalf of bondholders and court supervision of the conduct of business. In any event, a default is a disaster for an issuer.

Professional bond investors have ways of analyzing information about companies and bond issues to estimate the uncertainty of future ability to pay. These techniques are explained in Part 3 of this book. However, most individual bond investors and some institutional bond investors make no such elaborate studies. In fact, they rely largely upon bond ratings published by several organizations that do the job of bond analysis and express their conclusions by a system of ratings. The four major nationally recognized statistical rating organizations (NRSROs) in the United States are Duff & Phelps Credit Rating Co. (D&P); Fitch Investors Service, Inc. (Fitch); Moody's Investors Service, Inc. (Moody's); and Standard & Poor's Corporation (S&P). These ratings are used by market participants as a factor in the valuation of securities on account of their independent and unbiased nature.

Rating definitions are released by these firms in their various publications. Investors are urged to read these definitions. It should be remembered that they are not "buy," "hold," or "sell" indicators. They do not state whether an issue is "cheap" or "dear" among the multitude of bond issues. They do not point to the direction of the market. Although only a guide to the issuer's ability and willingness to meet the terms of the issue, they are a very important factor in the bond investment decision.

The rating systems use similar symbols, as shown in Exhibit 11–1. The bonds in the four highest rating categories are known as *high grade*, or *investment grade*, meaning that financial risk is relatively low and the probability of future payment relatively high. Lower-rated bonds have speculative elements, and the repayment of principal and interest in accordance with the terms of the issue is not ensured.

EVENT RISK

In recent years, one of the more talked-about topics among corporate bond investors is *event risk*. Over the last couple of decades, corporate bond indentures have become less restrictive, and corporate managements have been given a free rein to do as they please without regard to bondholders. Management's main concern or duty is to enhance shareholder wealth. As for the bondholder, all a company is required to do is to meet the terms of the bond indenture including the payment of principal and interest. With few restrictions and the optimization of

E X H I B I T   11–1

Summary of Rating Symbols and Definitions

Moody's	S&P	Fitch	D&P	Brief Definition
Investment Grade—High Creditworthiness				
Aaa	AAA	AAA	AAA	Gilt edge, prime, maximum safety
Aa1	AA+	AA+	AA+	
Aa2	AA	AA	AA	Very high grade, high quality
Aa3	AA–	AA–	AA–	
A1	A+	A+	A+	
A2	A	A	A	Upper medium grade
A3	A–	A–	A–	
Baa1	BBB+	BBB+	BBB+	
Baa2	BBB	BBB	BBB	Lower medium grade
Baa3	BBB–	BBB–	BBB–	
Distinctly Speculative—Low Creditworthiness				
Ba1	BB+	BB+	BB+	
Ba2	BB	BB	BB	Low grade, speculative
Ba3	BB–	BB–	BB–	
B1	B+	B+		
B2	B	B	B	Highly speculative
B3	B–	B–		
Predominantly Speculative—Substantial Risk or in Default				
	CCC+			
Caa	CCC	CCC	CCC	Substantial risk, in poor standing
	CCC–			
Ca	CC	CC		May be in default, extremely speculative
C	C	C		Even more speculative than those above
	CI			CI = Income bonds—no interest is being paid
		DDD		Default
		DD	DD	
	D	D		

Source: Richard S. Wilson and Frank J. Fabozzi, *Corporate Bonds: Structures and Analysis* (New Hope, PA : Frank J. Fabozzi Associates, 1996).

shareholder wealth of paramount importance for corporate managers, it is no wonder that bondholders became concerned when merger mania and other events swept the nation's boardrooms. Events such as decapitalizations, restructurings, recapitalizations, mergers, acquisitions, leveraged buyouts, and share repurchases, among other things, often caused substantial changes in a corporation's capital structure, namely, greatly increased leverage and decreased equity. Bondholders' protection was sharply reduced and debt quality ratings lowered, in many cases to speculative-grade categories. Along with greater risk came lower bond valuations. Shareholders were being enriched at the expense of bondholders.

In reaction to the increased activity of corporate raiders and mergers and acquisitions, some companies incorporated "poison puts" in their indentures. These are designed to thwart unfriendly takeovers by making the target company unpalatable to the acquirer. The poison put provides that the bondholder can require the company to repurchase the debt under certain circumstances arising out of specific designated events such as a change in control. Poison puts may not deter a proposed acquisition but could make it more expensive. In some cases if the board of directors approves the change in control—a "friendly" transaction (and all takeovers are friendly if the price is right)—the poison put provisions will not become effective. The designated event of change in control generally means either that continuing directors no longer constitute a majority of the board of directors or that a person, including affiliates, becomes the beneficial owner, directly or indirectly, of stock with at least 20 percent of the voting rights. Many times, in addition to a designated event, a rating change to below investment grade must occur within a certain period for the put to be activated. Some issues provide for a higher interest rate instead of a put as a designated event remedy.

Event risk has caused some companies to include other special debt retirement features in their indentures. An example is the *maintenance of net worth clause* included in the indentures of some lower-rated bond issues. In this case, an issuer covenants to maintain its net worth above a stipulated level, and if it fails to do so, it must begin to retire its debt at par. Usually the redemptions affect only part of the issue and continue periodically until the net worth recovers to an amount above the stated figure or the debt is retired. In other cases, the company is required only to *offer to redeem* a required amount. An offer to redeem is not mandatory on the bondholders' part; only those holders who want their bonds redeemed need do so. In a number of instances in which the issuer is required to call bonds, the bondholders may elect not to have bonds redeemed. This is not much different from an offer to redeem. It may protect bondholders from the redemption of the high-coupon debt at lower interest rates. However, if a company's net worth declines to a level low enough to activate such a call, it would probably be prudent to have one's bonds redeemed.

Protecting the value of debt investments against the added risk caused by recent corporate management activity is not an easy job. Investors should carefully analyze the issuer's fundamentals to determine if the company may be a candidate for restructuring. Attention to news and equity investment reports can make the task easier. Also, the indenture should be reviewed to see if there are any protective features. However, even these can often be circumvented by sharp legal minds. Toward this end, some of the debt rating services issue commentary on indenture features of corporate bonds, noting the degree of protection against event risk. Of course, large portfolios can reduce risk with broad diversification among industry lines, but price declines do not always affect only the issue at risk; they also can spread across the board and take the innocent down with them. This happened in the fall of 1988 with the leveraged buyout of RJR Nabisco, Inc. The whole industrial bond market suffered as buyers and traders withdrew from the market, new issues were postponed, and secondary market activity came to a standstill. This can be seen in Exhibits 11–2 and 11–3. Exhibit 11–2 shows the impact of the initial leveraged buyout bid announcement on yield spreads for RJR Nabisco's debt. The yield spread to a benchmark Treasury increased from about 100 basis points to 350 basis points. The RJR transaction showed that size was not an obstacle. Therefore, other large firms that investors previously thought were unlikely candidates for a leveraged buyout were fair game. To see the spillover effect, look at Exhibit 11–3, which shows how event risk fears caused yield spreads to widen for three large firms.

E X H I B I T   11–2

RJR Nabisco—The Impact of the Initial LBO Bid Announcement on Yield Spreads

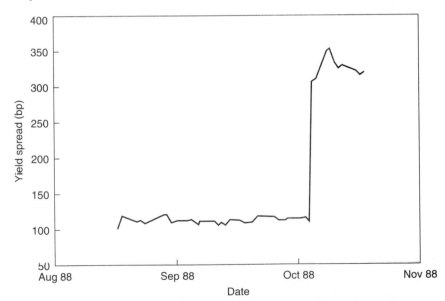

Source: N.R. Vijayarghavan and Randy Snook, "Takeover Event Risk and Corporate Bond Portfolio Management," in Frank J. Fabozzi (ed.), *Advances and Innovations in Bond and Mortgage Markets* (Chicago: Probus Publishing, 1989), p. 55.

E X H I B I T   11–3

Anheuser Busch, Sara Lee, & Union Pacific—Event Risk Fears and Widening Yield Spreads—The Impact of the Initial LBO Bid Announcement on Yield Spreads

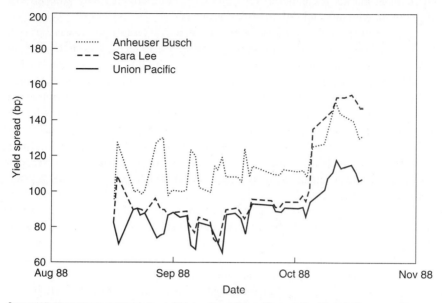

Source: N.R. Vijayarghavan and Randy Snook, "Takeover Event Risk and Corporate Bond Portfolio Management," in Frank J. Fabozzi (ed.) *Advances and Innovations in Bond and Mortgage Markets* (Chicago: Probus Publishing, 1989), p.

THE BOND MARKETS

It is easy to buy bonds. The minimum you need to know is the telephone number of a broker-dealer firm with whom you have established an account. It is better, though, if you know something about the bond markets and how they operate. Familiarity with markets may affect your choice of bond issues and enable you to minimize the cost of buying and selling.

Billions of dollars of new corporate bonds are sold each year in the primary market—the market for new issues. As soon as a new bond issue is publicly offered, investors begin to buy and sell in the secondary market—the market for outstanding issues.

The secondary market for bonds is a big one. You may not hear as much about it as about the stock markets, but there are more corporate bond issues listed on the New York Stock Exchange (NYSE) than there are stock issues. The dollar value of daily bond trading on the exchanges and in the over-the-counter market appears to be not too much less than the value of trading in stocks on the exchanges. The reason the bond market is inconspicuous to the public is that it is mostly an institutional market wherein life insurance companies, pension funds, and savings institutions quietly buy and sell large amounts of bonds with little or no publicity.

There are really two bond markets. One is the *exchange market,* where certain members may make a market in listed issues. The other is the *over-the-counter market,* which is a market made by dealer firms in their offices. The exchange market for bonds is chiefly the New York Stock Exchange. The over-the-counter market is chiefly in New York City, but there are many firms all over the country who buy and sell securities as dealers.

In discussing the bond markets, one must differentiate clearly between brokers and dealers. Brokers execute orders for accounts of customers; they are agents and get a commission for their services. Dealers buy and sell for their own accounts. When they buy, they take the risk of reselling at a loss. Dealers "make a market" when they quote a bond continuously. A *quote* is a bid and an offer. The *bid* is the price a dealer will pay for bonds of an issue to whoever may want to sell to the dealer, and the *offer* is the price at which a dealer will sell bonds to whoever may want to buy from the dealer. The offer is always higher than the bid; that is, the dealer buys at a lower price than that at which he or she sells, and so makes a profit. The difference between bid and offer prices is the dealer's *spread.*

A very large percentage of all bond trading, including listed issues, is over the counter. The over-the-counter (OTC) market is hard to describe in precise language because it does not exist in a particular place, it has no listed issues, and there is no published information about the prices at which bonds are traded or about the volume of trading. Any dealer can make a market for a bond issue without having to be a member of an exchange or even a member of the National Association of Securities Dealers (the organization to which most broker-dealer firms belong).

The heart of the over-the-counter market is a group of perhaps a dozen large dealer firms located in New York City that make *wholesale* markets in large numbers of bond issues. Their market is called wholesale because for the most part they deal only with other wholesalers and with broker-dealer firms that have *retail* orders from their own customers to execute as brokers. Wholesalers also deal directly with large institutional investors, who buy and sell in large lots, such as 500 bonds or more.

Some years ago, the National Association of Securities Dealers (NASD)-which is both a trade association and a governing organization-developed a computerized system by which dealers may enter their bids and offers for issues in which they make a market; subscribers can read these quotations on terminals in their offices. The system is called *NASDAQ* (for National Association of Securities Dealers Automated Quotation service). A broker-dealer firm with an order to execute for a customer can learn instantly the highest bid and lowest offer for the issue in which he or she is interested and then execute the order by telephone. This is much more efficient than the old system of telephoning around to several dealers for quotes.

DIFFERENCES IN THE QUALITY OF MARKETABILITY

Any bond that is quoted continually by a dealer is a *marketable bond;* there is a market for it. But sophisticated investors want to know much more than that; they want to know how good the market is. It may be inferred that a bond quoted by only one dealer in Kansas City has a poor market and that one quoted by half a dozen large wholesalers in New York City has an excellent market. There are gradations between poor and excellent. It is useful to recognize differences in the quality of markets for different bond issues.

The principal basis for grading securities in marketability is the size of the spread between dealers' bid and asked prices. A narrow spread—say, one fourth to one half of 1 percent—indicates an excellent market. A wide spread—such as 2 or 3 percent—means a poorly marketable issue. The principal determinant of the size of spread is not so much the number of dealers, as suggested above, but the usual volume of trading in an issue. The number of dealers is more or less proportionate to the volume of trading. If there is a lot of business in a bond issue, there are more dealers seeking the business. The size of the spread is also related to the volume of trading. A large volume of trading and a large number of dealers make a highly competitive market in which spreads narrow. In the actively traded issues, dealers take less risk when they buy bonds and carry them in inventory. Usually, price changes in any short period are small, and a dealer who wishes to do so can unload bonds. In addition, active trading distributes the dealer's costs over many transactions.

The reason for differentiating between bond issues in grades of marketability is that high marketability costs money. Other things being equal, investors prefer the highly marketable issues and accordingly will pay slightly more for them. A slightly higher price means a slightly lower yield. An investor who buys in the bond market and expects to sell in the market after some period of time needs high marketability. Only by trading in highly marketable issues can the investor minimize transaction costs. Consider, for example, the cost of buying and selling a bond that is usually quoted with a spread of one half of 1 percent. The cost of a *round trip*—that is, a purchase and a sale—is only 1 percent for the dealer. In addition, a broker's commission on a round trip is likely to be about one half of 1 percent. The sum is about 1.5 percent. In comparison, the cost of a round trip in a poorly marketable issue might be twice as much.

Many investors do not need high marketability. They buy new corporate bond issues when the issues are first offered to the public at the public offering price. The cost of public distribution is paid by the issuer. Then they usually hold bonds until they are redeemed at par or a premium over par when bonds are called before maturity. Thus they pay no dealer's spread and no commission. The round trip is free. On exceptional occasions such investors elect to sell bonds in the market and have to pay for a one-way trip back.

EXHIBIT 11–4

Actual versus Required Corporate Bond Yield Premium: 1983–1992[a]

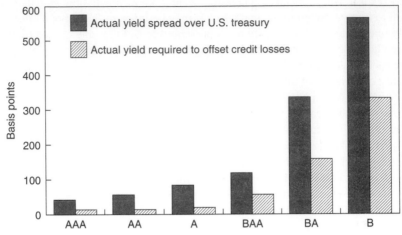

[a]Data obtained from Salomon Brothers, Moody's Investors Service, and Miller, Anderson & Sherrerd.

Source: Thomas L. Bennett, Stephen F. Esser, and Christian G. Roth, *Corporate Credit Risk and Reward* (West Conshohocken, PA: Miller, Anderson & Sherrerd).

EXHIBIT 11–5

Annualized Total Returns and Return Spreads—U.S. Treasuries, Investment-Grade Corporates, and S & P 500 (Periods Ended December 1992)

	20 Years	10 Years	5 Years
Treasuries	9.13%	11.63%	10.85%
Corporates	9.64%	12.53%	11.46%
Spread vs. Treasuries	+51 basis points	+90 basis points	+61 basis points
AAA	9.20%	11.89%	11.04%
Spread vs. Treasuries	+7 basis points	+27 basis points	+27 basis points
AA	9.35%	12.18%	11.33%
Spread vs. Treasuries	+23 basis points	+55 basis points	+48 basis points
A	9.63%	12.58%	11.54%
Spread vs. Treasuries	+50 basis points	+95 basis points	+69 basis points
BBB	10.37%	13.45%	11.68%
Spread vs. Treasuries	+124 basis points	+182 basis points	+83 basis points
S&P 500	11.33%	16.18%	15.88%

Data obtained from Lehman Brothers and Miller, Anderson & Sherrerd.

Source: Thomas L. Bennett, Stephen F. Esser, and Christian G. Roth, *Corporate Credit Risk and Reward* (Miller, Anderson & Sherrerd, 1993).

There is also another category of corporate bond investors, which includes those who buy in the secondary market and seek to realize capital gains by sale in the market at a higher price; there is speculation in bonds just as there is in stocks. Clearly this category of investors needs highly marketable issues in order to minimize the transaction costs.

RISK AND RETURN IN THE CORPORATE BOND MARKET

A study by Thomas Bennett, Stephen Esser, and Christian Roth reported the risk and reward relationship in the corporate bond market.[1] Exhibit 11–4 shows for the four investment grade ratings and the first two non-investment grading ratings the actual yield spread over U.S. Treasuries for the 10 years ending 1992. Also shown in the exhibit is the yield spread required to offset credit losses for each quality rating. As indicated in the exhibit, investors have been rewarded for accepting corporate credit risk.

Exhibit 11–5 shows the annualized total returns and return spreads versus U.S. Treasuries for investment-grade corporates and the Standard & Poor's 500 for various periods ending 1992. The reported results are based on a duration-matched return series for Treasuries and the corporates. The two key findings of Exhibit 11–5 are that (1) corporate bonds outperformed Treasuries and (2) the lower the credit rating, the better was the performance relative to Treasuries. Thus the ratings appear to do a good job of differentiating the credit risk associated with investing in corporate bonds.

---

1. Thomas L. Bennett, Stephen E. Esser, and Christian G. Roth, *Corporate Credit Risk and Reward* (West Conshohocken, PA: Miller, Anderson & Sherrer, 1993).

⑥ MEDIUM-TERM NOTES*

Leland E. Crabbe, Ph.D.
First Vice President
Merrill Lynch

Over the past decade, medium-term notes (MTNs) have emerged as a major source of funding for U.S. and foreign corporations, federal agencies, supranational institutions, and sovereign countries. U.S. corporations have issued MTNs since the early 1970s. At that time, the market was established as an alternative to short-term financing in the commercial paper market and long-term borrowing in the bond market; hence the name *medium term*. Through the 1970s, however, only a few corporations issued MTNs, and by 1981 outstandings amounted to only about $800 million. In the 1980s, the U.S. MTN market evolved from a relatively obscure niche market dominated by the auto finance companies into a major source of debt financing for several hundred large corporations. In the 1990s, the U.S. market has continued to attract a diversity of new borrowers, and outside the United States, the Euro-MTN market has grown at a phenomenal rate. By year-end 1995, outstanding MTNs in domestic and international markets stood at an estimated $975 billion (Exhibit 12–1).

Most MTNs are noncallable, unsecured, senior debt securities with fixed coupon rates and investment-grade credit ratings. In these features, MTNs are similar to investment-grade corporate bonds. However, they have generally differed from bonds in their primary distribution process. MTNs have traditionally been sold on a best-efforts basis by investment banks and other broker-dealers acting as agents. In contrast to an underwriter in the conventional bond market, an agent in the MTN market has no obligation to underwrite MTNs for the

---

*This chapter is adapted from Leland E. Crabbe, "Anatomy of the Medium-Term Note Market," *Federal Reserve Bulletin,* August 1993, pp. 751–768.

EXHIBIT 12–1

Size of the Worldwide Medium-Term Note Market Year-End 1995

Market Sector	Amount Outstanding Year-End 1995 (Billions of dollars)
Total	975
U.S. market	479
Public MTNs of U.S. corporations	267
Federal agency and others	167
Private placements	45
International markets	495
Euro-MTNs	470
Foreign domestic markets	25

issuer, and the issuer is not guaranteed funds. Also, unlike corporate bonds, which are typically sold in large, discrete offerings, MTNs are usually sold in relatively small amounts either on a continuous or on an intermittent basis.

Borrowers with MTN programs have great flexibility in the types of securities they may issue. As the market for MTNs has evolved, issuers have taken advantage of this flexibility by issuing MTNs with less conventional features. Many MTNs are now issued with floating interest rates or with rates that are computed according to unusual formulas tied to equity or commodity prices. Also, many include calls, puts, and other options. Furthermore, maturities are not necessarily "medium term"—they have ranged from nine months to 30 years and longer. Moreover, like corporate bonds, MTNs are now often sold on an underwritten basis, and offering amounts are occasionally as large as those of bonds. Indeed, rather than denoting a narrow security with an intermediate maturity, an MTN is more accurately defined as a highly flexible debt instrument that can easily be designed to respond to market opportunities and investor preferences.

The emergence of the MTN market has transformed the way that corporations raise capital and that institutions invest. In recent years, this transformation has accelerated because of the development of derivatives markets, such as swaps, options, and futures, that allow investors and borrowers to transfer risk to others in the financial system who have different risk preferences. A growing number of transactions in the MTN market now involve simultaneous transactions in a derivatives market.

This chapter discusses the history and economics of the MTN market, analyzes statistics on MTNs collected by the Federal Reserve, and reviews recent developments in the U.S. and Euro-MTN markets.[1]

BACKGROUND OF THE MTN MARKET[2]

General Motors Acceptance Corporation (GMAC) created the MTN market in the early 1970s as an extension of the commercial paper market. To improve their asset/liability management, GMAC and the other auto finance companies needed to issue debt with a maturity that matched that of their auto loans to dealers and consumers. However, underwriting costs made bond offerings with short maturities impractical, and maturities on commercial paper cannot exceed 270 days. The auto finance companies therefore began to sell MTNs directly to investors. In the 1970s, the growth of the market was hindered by illiquidity in the secondary market and by securities regulations requiring approval by the Securities and Exchange Commission (SEC) of any amendment to a registered public offering. The latter, in particular, increased the costs of issuance significantly because borrowers had to obtain the approval of the SEC each time they changed the posted coupon rates on their MTN offering schedule. To avoid this regulatory hurdle, some corporations sold MTNs in the private placement market.

In the early 1980s, two institutional changes set the stage for rapid growth of the MTN market. First, in 1981 major investment banks acting as agents committed resources to assist in primary issuance and to provide secondary market liquidity. By 1984, the captive finance companies of the three large automakers had at least two agents for their MTN programs. The ongoing financing requirements of these companies and the competition among agents established a basis for the market to develop. Because investment banks stood ready to buy back MTNs in the secondary market, investors became more receptive to adding MTNs to their portfolio holdings. In turn, the improved liquidity and consequent reduction in the cost of issuance attracted new borrowers to the market.

Second, the adoption by the SEC of Rule 415 in March 1982 served as another important institutional change. Rule 415 permits delayed or continuous issuance of so-called shelf-registered corporate securities. Under shelf registrations, issuers register securities that may be sold for two years after the effective date of the registration without the requirement of another registration

---

1. The Federal Reserve Board conducts a survey of borrowing by U.S. corporations in the public MTN market, the largest sector of the worldwide market. The Federal Reserve collects these data to improve its estimates of new securities issues of U.S. corporations, as published in the *Federal Reserve Bulletin,* and to improve estimates of corporate securities outstanding, as shown in the flow of funds accounts.

2. Material in this and the next two sections was originally presented in Leland Crabbe, "Corporate Medium-Term Notes," *The Continental Bank Journal of Applied Corporate Finance,* Winter 1992, pp.90–102.

statement each time new offerings are made. Thus shelf registration enables issuers to take advantage of brief periods of low interest rates by selling previously registered securities on a moment's notice. In contrast, debt offerings that are not made from shelf registrations are subject to a delay of at least 48 hours between the filing with the SEC and the subsequent offering to the public.

The ability of borrowers to sell a variety of debt instruments with a broad range of coupons and maturities under a single prospectus supplement is another advantage of a shelf-registered MTN program. Indeed, a wide array of financing options have been included in MTN filings.[3] For example, MTN programs commonly give the borrower the choice of issuing fixed- or floating-rate debt.[4] Furthermore, several "global" programs allow for placements in the U.S. market or in the Euromarket. Other innovations that reflect the specific funding needs of issuers include MTNs collateralized by mortgages issued by thrift institutions, equipment trust certificates issued by railways, amortizing notes issued by leasing companies, and subordinated notes issued by bank holding companies. Another significant innovation has been the development of asset-backed MTNs, a form of asset securitization used predominantly to finance trade receivables and corporate loans. This flexibility in types of instruments that may be sold as MTNs, coupled with the market timing benefits of shelf registration, enables issuers to respond readily to changing market opportunities.

In the early and mid-1980s, when finance companies dominated the market, most issues of MTNs were fixed rate, noncallable, and unsecured, with maturities of five years or less. In recent years, as new issuers with more diverse financing needs have established programs, the characteristics of new issues have become less generic. For example, maturities have lengthened as industrial and utility companies with longer financing needs have entered the market. Indeed, in July 1993, Walt Disney Company issued a note with a 100-year maturity off its medium-term note shelf registration. A growing volume of placements of notes with long maturities have made the designation *medium term* something of a misnomer.

MECHANICS OF THE MARKET

The process of raising funds in the public MTN market usually begins when a corporation files a shelf registration with the SEC.[5] Once the SEC declares the registration statement effective, the borrower files a prospectus supplement that

---

3. For example, MTNs have been callable, putable, and extendible; they have had zero coupons, step-down or step-up coupons, or inverse floating rates; and they have been foreign-currency denominated or indexed, and commodity indexed.
4. The most common indexes for floating-rate MTNs are the following: the London interbank offered rate (LIBOR), commercial paper, Treasury bills, federal funds, and the prime rate. MTN programs typically give the issuer the option of making floating-rate interest payments monthly, quarterly, or semiannually.
5. SEC-registered MTNs have the broadest market because they have no resale or transfer restrictions and generally fit within an investor's investment guidelines.

describes the MTN program. The amount of debt under the program generally ranges from $100 million to $1 billion. After establishing an MTN program, a borrower may enter the MTN market continuously or intermittently with large or relatively small offerings. Although underwritten corporate bonds may also be issued from shelf registrations, MTNs provide issuers with more flexibility than traditional underwritings in which the entire debt issue is made at one time, typically with a single coupon and a single maturity.

The registration filing usually includes a list of the investment banks with which the corporation has arranged to act as agents to distribute the notes to investors. Most MTN programs have two to four agents. Having multiple agents encourages competition among investment banks and thus lowers financing costs. The large New York-based investment banks dominate the distribution of MTNs.

Through its agents, an issuer of MTNs posts offering rates over a range of maturities: for example, 9 months to a year, a year to 18 months, 18 months to 2 years, and annually thereafter (see Exhibit 12–2). Many issuers post rates as a yield spread over a Treasury security of comparable maturity. The relatively at-

EXHIBIT 12–2

An Offering Rate Schedule for a Medium-Term Note Program

Medium-Term Notes			Treasury Securities	
Maturity Range	Yield (percent)	Yield Spread of MTN over Treasury Securities (basis points)	Maturity	Yield (percent)
9 months to 12 months	([a])	([a])	9 months	3.35
12 months to 18 months	([a])	([a])	12 months	3.50
18 months to 2 years	([a])	([a])	18 months	3.80
2 years to 3 years	4.35	35	2 years	4.00
3 years to 4 years	5.05	55	3 years	4.50
4 years to 5 years	5.60	60	4 years	5.00
5 years to 6 years	6.05	60	5 years	5.45
6 years to 7 years	6.10	40	6 years	5.70
7 years to 8 years	6.30	40	7 years	5.90
8 years to 9 years	6.45	40	8 years	6.05
9 years to 10 years	6.60	40	9 years	6.20
10 years	6.70	40	10 years	6.30

[a]No rate posted.

tractive yield spreads posted at the maturities of three, four, and five years shown in Exhibit 12–2 indicate that the issuer desires to raise funds at these maturities. The investment banks disseminate this offering rate information to their investor clients.

When an investor expresses interest in an MTN offering, the agent contacts the issuer to obtain a confirmation of the terms of the transaction. Within a maturity range, the investor has the option of choosing the final maturity of the note sale, subject to agreement by the issuing company. The issuer will lower its posted rates once it raises the desired amount of funds at a given maturity. In the example in Exhibit 12–2, the issuer might lower its posted rate for MTNs with a five-year maturity to 40 basis points over comparable Treasury securities after it sells the desired amount of debt at this maturity. Of course, issuers also change their offering rate scales in response to changing market conditions. Issuers may withdraw from the market by suspending sales or, alternatively, by posting narrow offering spreads at all maturity ranges. The proceeds from primary trades in the MTN market typically range from $1 million to $25 million, but the size of transactions varies considerably.[6] After the amount of registered debt is sold, the issuer may "reload" its MTN program by filing a new registration with the SEC.

Although MTNs are generally offered on an agency basis, most programs permit other means of distribution. For example, MTN programs usually allow the agents to acquire notes for their own account and for resale at par or at prevailing market prices. MTNs may also be sold on an underwritten basis. In addition, many MTN programs permit the borrower to bypass financial intermediaries by selling debt directly to investors.

THE ECONOMICS OF MTNS AND CORPORATE BONDS

In deciding whether to finance with MTNs or with bonds, a corporate borrower weighs the interest cost, flexibility, and other advantages of each

---

6. Financing strategies vary among the borrowers. Some corporate treasurers prefer to "go in for size" on one day with financings in the $50 million to $100 million range, reasoning that smaller offerings are more time-consuming. Furthermore, a firm may be able to maintain a "scarcity value" for its debt by financing intermittently with large offerings, rather than continuously with small offerings. Other treasurers prefer to raise $50 million to $100 million over the course of several days with $2 million to $10 million drawdowns. These corporate treasurers argue that a daily drawdown of $50 million is an indication that they should have posted a lower offering rate. In regard to the posting of offering rates, some treasurers post an absolute yield, whereas others post a spread over Treasuries, usually with a cap on the absolute yield. A few active borrowers typically post rates daily in several maturity sectors; less active borrowers post only in the maturity sector in which they seek financing and suspend postings when they do not require funds.

security.[7] The growth of the MTN market indicates that MTNs offer advantages that bonds do not. However, most companies that raise funds in the MTN market have also continued to issue corporate bonds, suggesting that each form of debt has advantages under particular circumstances.

Offering Size, Liquidity, and Price Discrimination

The amount of the offering is the most important determinant of the cost differential between the MTN and corporate bond markets. For large, standard financings (such as $300 million of straight debt with a 10-year maturity) the all-in interest cost to an issuer of underwritten corporate bonds may be lower than the all-in cost of issuing MTNs. This cost advantage arises from economies of scale in underwriting and, most important, from the greater liquidity of large issues. As a result, corporations that have large financing needs for a specific term usually choose to borrow with bonds. From an empirical point of view, the liquidity premium, if any, on small offerings has yet to be quantified. Nevertheless, the sheer volume of financing in the MTN market suggests that any liquidity premium that may exist for small offerings is not a significant deterrent to financing. According to market participants, the interest cost differential between the markets has narrowed in recent years as liquidity in the MTN market has improved. Many borrowers estimate that the premium is now only about 5 to 10 basis points.[8]

Furthermore, many borrowers believe that financing costs are slightly lower in the MTN market because its distribution process allows borrowers to price discriminate. Consider an example of a company that needs to raise $100 million. With a bond offering, the company may have to raise the offering yield

---

7. Apart from the distribution process, MTNs have several less significant features that distinguish them from underwritten corporate bonds. First, MTNs are typically sold at par, whereas traditional underwritings are frequently sold at slight discounts or premiums to par. Second, the settlement for MTNs is in same-day funds, whereas corporate bonds generally settle in next-day funds. Although MTNs with long maturities typically settle five business days after the trade date (as is the convention in the corporate bond market), MTNs with short maturities sometimes have a shorter settlement period.

Finally, semiannual interest payments to noteholders are typically made on a fixed cycle without regard to the offering date or the maturity date of the MTN; in contrast, corporate bonds typically pay interest on the first or fifteenth day of the month at six-month and annual intervals from the date of the offering. The interest payment convention in the MTN market usually results in a short or a long first coupon and in a short final coupon. Consider, for example, an MTN program that pays interest on March 1 and September 1 and at maturity of the notes. A $100,000 MTN sold on May 1 with a 9 percent coupon and a 15-month maturity from such a program would distribute a "short" first coupon of $3,000 on September 1, a full coupon of $4,500 on March 1, and a "short" final coupon of $3,750 plus the original principal on August 1 of the following year. Like corporate bonds, interest on fixed-rate MTNs is calculated on the basis of a 360-day year of 12 30-day months.

8. Commissions to MTN agents typically range from 0.125 percent to 0.75 percent of the principal amount of the note sale, depending on the stated maturity and the credit rating assigned at the time of issuance. Fees to underwriters of bond offerings are somewhat higher.

significantly, for example, from 6 percent to 6.25 percent, to place the final $10 million with the marginal buyer. In contrast, with MTNs the company could raise $90 million by posting a yield of 6 percent; to raise the additional $10 million, the company could increase its MTN offering rates or issue at a different maturity. Consequently, because all of the debt does not have to be priced to the marginal buyer, financing costs can be lower with MTNs.

The Flexibility of MTNs

Even if conventional bonds enjoy an interest cost advantage, this advantage may be offset by the flexibility that MTNs afford. Offerings of investment-grade straight bonds are clustered at standard maturities of 2, 3, 5, 7, 10, and 30 years. Also, because the fixed costs of underwritings make small offerings impractical, corporate bond offerings rarely amount to less than $100 million. These institutional conventions tend to keep corporations from implementing a financing policy of matching the maturities of assets with those of liabilities. By contrast, drawdowns from MTN programs over the course of a month typically amount to $30 million, and these drawdowns frequently have different maturities and special features that are tailored to meet the needs of the borrower. This flexibility of the MTN market allows companies to match more closely the maturities of assets and liabilities.

The flexibility of continuous offerings also plays a role in a corporation's decision to finance with MTNs. With MTNs, a corporation can "average out" its cost of funds by issuing continuously rather than coming to market on a single day. Therefore, even if bond offerings have lower average yields, a risk-averse borrower might still elect to raise funds in the MTN market with several offerings in a range of $5 million to $10 million over several weeks, rather than with a single $100 million bond offering.

The flexibility of the MTN market also allows borrowers to take advantage of funding opportunities. By having an MTN program, an issuer can raise a sizable amount of debt in a short time; often, the process takes less than half an hour. Bonds may also be sold from a shelf registration, but the completion of the transaction may be delayed by the arrangement of a syndicate, the negotiation of an underwriting agreement, and the "preselling" of the issue to investors. Furthermore, some corporations require that underwritten offerings receive prior approval by the president of the company or the board of directors. In contrast, a corporate treasurer may finance with MTNs without delay and at his or her discretion.[9]

---

9. The administrative costs may be lower with MTNs than with bonds. After the borrower and the investor have agreed to the terms of a transaction in the MTN market, the borrower files a one-page pricing supplement with the SEC, stating the sale date, the rate of interest, and the maturity date of the MTN. In contrast, issuers of corporate bonds sold from shelf registrations are required to file a prospectus supplement.

Discreet Funding with MTNs

The MTN market also provides corporations with the ability to raise funds discreetly because the issuer, the investor, and the agent are the only market participants that have to know about a primary transaction. In contrast, the investment community obtains information about underwritten bond offerings from a variety of sources.

Corporations often avoid the bond market in periods of heightened uncertainty about interest rates and the course of the economy, such as the period after the 1987 stock market crash. Underwritings at such times could send a signal of financial distress to the market. Similarly, corporations in distressed industries, such as commercial banking in the second half of 1990, can use the MTN market to raise funds quietly rather than risk negative publicity in the high-profile bond market. Thus, during periods of financial turmoil, the discreet nature of the MTN market makes it an attractive alternative to the bond market.

Reverse Inquiry in the MTN Market

Another advantage of MTNs is that investors often play an active role in the issuance process through the phenomenon known as *reverse inquiry.* For example, suppose an investor desires to purchase $15 million of A-rated finance company debt with a maturity of six years and nine months. Such a security may not be available in the corporate bond market, but the investor may be able to obtain it in the MTN market through reverse inquiry. In this process, the investor relays the inquiry to an issuer of MTNs through the issuer's agent. If the issuer finds the terms of the reverse inquiry sufficiently attractive, it may agree to the transaction even if it was not posting rates at the maturity that the investor desires.

According to market participants, trades that stem from reverse inquiries account for a significant share of MTN transactions. Reverse inquiry not only benefits the issuer by reducing borrowing costs but also allows investors to use the flexibility of MTNs to their advantage. In response to investor preferences, MTNs issued under reverse inquiry often include embedded options and frequently pay interest according to unusual formulas. This responsiveness of the MTN market to the needs of investors is one of the most important factors driving the growth and acceptance of the market.

THE FEDERAL RESERVE BOARD'S SURVEY OF U.S. CORPORATE MTNS

The Federal Reserve surveys U.S. corporations with MTN programs. These companies provide data on a confidential basis about the amount of MTNs they issue; respondents report monthly, quarterly, or annually, depending on how active they are in the market. At year-end, all MTN issuers are asked to provide data on the amount of their outstandings. The data on gross issuance began in January 1983, and the data on outstandings have been collected since year-end 1989. The Federal Reserve obtains information on new programs from announcements of SEC Rule 415 registrations and contacts with MTN agents.

Because the participation rate in the Federal Reserve survey is 100 percent, it provides an accurate measure of the volume of MTN financing by U.S. corporations in the U.S. public market. However, although the U.S. corporate sector is the largest segment of the MTN market, MTNs have been issued in other markets and by non-U.S. corporations. For example, several U.S. corporations have issued MTNs in the Euromarket. Also, the survey does not include MTNs issued in the U.S. public market by government-sponsored agencies such as the Federal National Mortgage Association, by supranational institutions, and by non-U.S. corporations. Furthermore, although the database includes MTNs issued by bank holding companies, it does not include deposit notes and bank notes offered by banks because these securities are exempt from SEC registration. Perhaps most important, the database does not include privately placed MTNs. The private-placement market is particularly attractive to issuers who wish to gain access to U.S. investors without having to obtain SEC approval for a public offering. According to MTN agents, non-U.S. corporations are the largest borrowers in the market for privately placed MTNs. Because the financing costs are usually lower in the public market than in the less-liquid private market, most U.S. corporations choose to issue public, SEC-registered MTNs.

Issuance Volume and Industry of the Issuers

From 1983 through 1995, the volume of MTN issuance in the public market increased in each year, rising from $5.5 billion in 1983 to $98.7 billion in 1995, and totaled $603 billion over the 13-year period (Exhibit 12–3). Similarly, the number of borrowers increased from 12 in 1983 to 192 in 1995 and totaled 504 corporations for the period.

Borrowers in the MTN market span a wide array of industry groups. In the financial sector, major borrowers include auto finance companies, bank holding companies, business and consumer credit institutions, and securities brokers. In the nonfinancial sector, participants in the MTN market include utilities, telephone companies, manufacturers, service firms, and wholesalers and retailers. Within industry groups, the auto finance companies have been the heaviest borrowers, raising $122 billion over the period. In relative terms, however, issuance by auto finance companies declined from an 87 percent share of the MTN market in 1983 to 12 percent in 1995.

In the early to mid-1980s, financial companies dominated the MTN market. Indeed, in 1983, only two nonfinancial companies issued MTNs, and they accounted for less than 1 percent of the issuance volume. In recent years, however, nonfinancial companies have increased their share of the market, and in the 1990s, they have accounted for about 30 percent of MTN issuance.

The increase in the volume of MTN issuance reflects a dramatic increase in the number of new borrowers in the market. In each year from 1984 through 1992, at least 20 companies issued MTNs for the first time, and most of the new entrants have been nonfinancial companies. In 1991, for example, 66 new borrowers entered the market, of which 55 were nonfinancial companies. As a result of this trend, in each year beginning in 1990, the total number of nonfinancial firms issuing MTNs has exceeded the total number of financial issuers.

EXHIBIT   12–3

Gross Borrowing by U.S. Corporations in the U.S. Medium-Term Note
Market, 1983–95

Type of Issuer	1991	1992	1993	1994	1995
	Amount in Millions of Dollars				
All U.S. Corporations	72,018	74,539	86,037	87,845	98,721
Financial corporations	45,773	50,626	57,817	70,074	79,384
Auto finance companies	12,380	13,450	10,755	11,219	11,631
Banking firms	11,157	6,603	7,536	8,103	13,869
Finance Companies	14,802	18,635	19,306	30,086	34,017
Real estate	1,027	1,129	1,422	846	1,671
Savings and loans	0	67	861	500	1,285
Securities brokers	6,408	10,741	17,937	19,320	16,912
Nonfinancial corporations	26,245	23,913	28,220	17,771	19,337
Electric, gas, and water	5,143	7,535	10,858	2,524	2,710
Manufacturing	12,503	9,190	8,394	6,818	7,531
Services	2,409	1,747	3,079	3,529	4,691
Telephone and communi-cations	1,373	1,635	2,729	1,492	1,493
Transportation	1,800	1,068	1,740	920	512
Wholesale and retail trade	3,018	2,738	1,420	2,489	2,400
	Number of Issuers				
All U.S. corporations	224	211	209	171	192
Financial	76	66	70	68	77
Nonfinancial	148	145	139	103	115

The Volume of Corporate MTNs Outstanding
and the Components of Net Borrowing

Outstanding MTNs and issuer use of MTN programs have increased sharply since
1989. In the aggregate, outstanding MTNs increased from $76 billion in 1989 to
$267 billion in 1995. Over this period, outstandings of nonfinancial firms increased
from $18.5 billion to $96.3 billion, while outstandings of financial corporations increased from $57.5 billion to $171 billion. For individual firms, outstandings of
MTNs averaged $672 million in 1995, compared with $350 million in 1989.

The data on net borrowing, that is, the year-over-year change in outstandings, can be dissected to determine the sources of growth in the market. For the
market as a whole, new entrants accounted for about one-third of net borrowing
in 1990, one-fourth of net borrowing in 1991, and less than one-fifth in 1992.
Thus, firms that had already issued MTNs accounted for most of the recent
growth in the market. In the financial sector, in particular, new entrants accounted

for only a small proportion of the growth, simply because a large share of the financial firms that could enter the MTN market did so in the 1980s. Among nonfinancial firms, in contrast, new entrants have continued to fuel a significant share of the growth in the market.

Credit Ratings

The corporations issuing MTNs have had high credit ratings. Since 1983, 99 percent of MTNs have been rated investment grade (Baa or higher) at the time of issuance. In 1995, $65 billion of the $99 billion in MTN offerings were rated single A, and five firms, issuing a total of $701 million, had ratings of Ba or lower. Outstanding MTNs also tend to have high credit ratings, but not as high as the ratings on new offerings because of the preponderance of rating downgrades in recent years. Nevertheless, 98 percent of outstanding MTNs were rated investment grade at year-end 1995.

Maturities and Yield Spreads

Maturities on MTNs reflect the financing needs of the borrowers. Financial firms tend to issue MTNs with maturities matched to the maturity of loans made to their customers. Consequently, in the financial sector, maturities are concentrated in a range of 1 to 5 years, and only a small proportion are longer than 10 years (Exhibit 12–4). Nonfinancial firms, in contrast, often use MTNs to finance long-lived assets, such as plant and equipment. As a result, maturities on MTNs issued by nonfinancial corporations cover a wider range, and in 1992, 25 percent to 30 percent were longer than 10 years.

Yields on fixed-rate MTNs, commonly quoted as a yield spread over a Treasury security of comparable maturity, reflect the credit risk of the borrower. Other factors held constant, Baa-rated MTNs have higher yield spreads than A-rated MTNs, which in turn have higher yield spreads than Aa-rated MTNs (Exhibit 12–5). Yield spreads also vary over time, particularly over the course of the business cycle. Spreads on A-rated MTNs increased from 60 basis points over Treasury securities in July 1990, a cyclical peak, to 140 basis points in January 1991.[10]

The Relative Size of the MTN Market

The MTN market accounts for a significant share of borrowing by U.S. corporations. One measure of the size of the market is the ratio of outstanding MTNs to the amount of outstanding public debt (MTNs plus public corporate bonds). According to this definition of market share, MTNs accounted for 19 percent of public corporate debt in 1995, compared with 9 percent in 1989. This ratio

---

10. These yield spreads are estimated using the model presented in Leland E. Crabbe and Christopher M. Turner, "A Dynamic Linear Model of the Determinants of Yield Spreads on Fixed-Income Securities" (Board of Governors of the Federal Reserve System, working paper, June 1993).

EXHIBIT   12–4

Distribution of Maturities of Corporate Medium-Term Notes, 1992

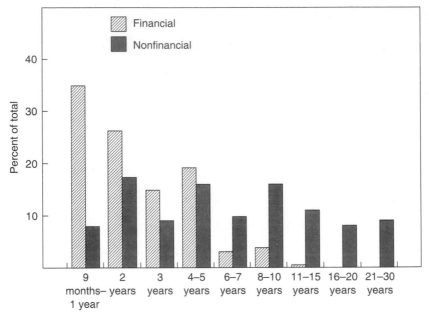

Source: Merrill Lynch.

understates the size of the MTN market, however, because the market is still relatively new, and outstandings are growing rapidly.

An alternative measure of the size of the market is the volume of investment-grade MTN issuance as a percentage of total investment-grade debt issuance (MTNs plus underwritten straight bonds). By this definition, the share of investment-grade debt issued as MTNs rose from 18 percent in 1983 to 47 percent in 1995, after peaking at 54 percent in 1994. This ratio of debt issuance may overestimate the size of the MTN market because MTNs typically have shorter maturities than corporate bonds.

MTNs represent an increasingly important source of credit to nonfinancial corporations, as companies have shifted funding from alternative credit markets. In general, nonfinancial corporations that borrow in the MTN market have access to other major credit markets: corporate bonds, commercial paper, bank loans, and privately placed bonds. From 1989 through 1992, net borrowing by nonfinancial corporations in the MTN market increased $49 billion, while borrowing in the other four markets increased an estimated $102 billion. Notably, corporate borrowing in the public bond market rose $100 billion, while borrowing at banks fell $35 billion. The shift to long-term financing (MTNs and bonds) over this period is a typical, cyclical phenomenon that occurs in periods of slow economic growth and falling long-term interest rates. However, some of the growth of the MTN market reflects a decline in the role of banks as financial intermediaries.

EXHIBIT 12–5

Yield Spreads between Two-Year Medium-Term Notes of Financial Companies and Two-Year Treasury Notes, Selected Ratings. October 1987–December 1992

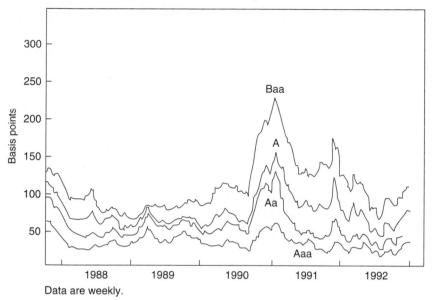

Data are weekly.

RECENT DEVELOPMENTS IN THE MTN MARKET

In recent years, several changes have occurred in the MTN market as a result of innovations in other capital markets. Among the most important changes in the MTN market are the increasing use of "structured" MTNs, the increasing participation by banking organizations in the market, and the development of a system for book-entry clearing and settlement of MTN transactions. Also, foreign corporations have begun to use the MTN market more frequently since the adoption of SEC Rule 144A in April 1990. The first two changes are discussed below.[11]

Structured MTNs

In recent years, an increasing share of MTNs have been issued as part of structured transactions. In a structured MTN, a corporation issues an MTN and simultaneously enters into one or several swap agreements to transform the cash flows that it is obligated to make. The simplest type of structured MTN involves a "plain

---

11. For a discussion of the development of the book-entry clearing and settlement of MTN transactions and Rule 144A, see Leland E. Crabbe, "Anatomy of the Medium-Term Note Market," *Federal Reserve Bulletin,* August 1993, pp. 751–768.

vanilla" interest rate swap.[12] In such a financing, a corporation might issue a three-year, floating-rate MTN that pays LIBOR plus a premium semiannually. At the same time, the corporation negotiates a swap transaction in which it agrees to pay a fixed rate of interest semiannually for three years in exchange for receiving LIBOR from a swap counterparty. As a result of the swap, the borrower has synthetically created a fixed-rate note because the floating-rate payments are offsetting.

At first glance, structured transactions seem needlessly complicated. A corporation could simply issue a fixed-rate MTN. However, as a result of the swap transaction, the corporation may be able to borrow at a lower rate than it would pay on a fixed-rate note. Indeed, most MTN issuers decline to participate in structured financings unless they reduce borrowing costs at least 10 or 15 basis points. Issuers demand this compensation because, compared with conventional financings, structured financings involve additional expenses, such as legal and accounting costs and the cost of evaluating and monitoring the credit risk of the swap counterparty. For complicated structured transactions, most issuers require greater compensation.

Many structured transactions originate with investors through a reverse inquiry. This process begins when an investor has a demand for a security with specific risk characteristics. The desired security may not be available in the secondary market, and regulatory restrictions or bylaws prohibit some investors from using swaps, options, or futures to create synthetic securities. Through a reverse inquiry, an investor will use MTN agents to communicate its desires to MTN issuers. If an issuer agrees to the inquiry, the investor will obtain a security that is custom-tailored to its needs. The specific features of these transactions vary in response to changes in market conditions and investor preferences. For example, in 1991 many investors desired securities with interest rates that varied inversely with short-term market interest rates. In response to investor inquiries, several corporations issued "inverse floating-rate" MTNs that paid an interest rate of, for example, 12 percent minus LIBOR. At the time of the transaction, the issuers of inverse floating-rate MTNs usually entered into swap transactions to eliminate their exposure to falling interest rates.

Although structured transactions in the MTN market often originate with investors, investment banks also put together such transactions. Most investment banks have specialists in derivative products who design securities to take advantage of temporary market opportunities. When an investment bank identifies an opportunity, it will inform investors and propose that they purchase a specialized security. If an investor tentatively agrees to the transaction, the MTN agents in the investment bank will contact an MTN issuer with the proposed structured transaction.

Most investors require that issuers of structured MTNs have triple-A or double-A credit ratings. By dealing with highly rated issuers, the investor reduces the possibility that the value of the structured MTN will vary with the credit quality of the issuer. In limiting credit risk, the riskiness of the structured MTN

---

12. Interest rate swaps are described in Chapter 61.

mainly reflects the specific risk characteristics that the investor prefers.[13] Consequently, federal agencies and supranational institutions, which have triple-A ratings, issue a large share of structured MTNs. The credit quality profile of issuers of structured MTNs has changed slightly in recent years, however, as some investors have become more willing to purchase structured MTNs from single-A corporations. In structured transactions with lower-rated borrowers, the investor receives a higher promised yield as compensation for taking on greater credit risk.

Market participants estimate that structured MTNs accounted for 20 percent to 30 percent of MTN volume in the first half of 1993, compared with less than 5 percent in the late 1980s. The growth of structured MTNs highlights the important role of derivative products in linking various domestic and international capital markets. Frequently, the issuers of structured MTNs are located in a different country from that of the investors.

The increasing volume of structured transactions is testimony to the flexibility of MTNs. When establishing MTN programs, issuers build flexibility into the documentation that will allow for a broad range of structured transactions. Once the documentation is in place, an issuer is able to reduce borrowing costs by responding quickly to temporary opportunities in the derivatives market.

The flexibility of MTNs is also evident in the wide variety of structured MTNs that pay interest or repay principal according to unusual formulas. Some of the common structures include the following: (1) floating-rate MTNs tied to the federal funds rate, LIBOR, commercial paper rates, or the prime rate, many of which have included caps or floors on rate movements; (2) step-up MTNs, the interest rate on which increases after a set period; (3) LIBOR differential notes, which pay interest tied to the spread between, say, deutsche mark LIBOR and French franc LIBOR; (4) dual-currency MTNs, which pay interest in one currency and principal in another; (5) equity-linked MTNs, which pay interest according to a formula based on an equity index, such as the Standard & Poor's 500 or the Nikkei; and (6) commodity-linked MTNs, which have interest tied to a price index or to the price of specific commodities such as oil or gold. The terms and features of structured MTNs continue to evolve in response to changes in the preferences of investors and developments in financial markets.

Bank Notes

Banking organizations are major participants in the MTN market. Like other corporations, bank holding companies must file registration documents with the SEC when issuing public securities. Consequently, the Federal Reserve survey captures MTNs issued by bank holding companies. From 1983 to 1995, 45 bank

---

13. An additional reason for the high credit quality of structured MTNs is that some investors, such as money market funds, face regulatory restrictions on the credit ratings of their investments. See Leland Crabbe and Mitchell A. Post, "The Effect of SEC Amendments to Rule 2a-7 on the Commercial Paper Market," *Finance and Economics Discussion Series 199* (Board of Governors of the Federal Reserve System, May 1992).

holding companies raised funds in the MTN market, and from 1989 to 1995, outstanding MTNs of bank holding companies increased from $9.3 billion to $28 billion. Although most of these MTNs have senior status in relation to other debt outstanding, a few bank holding companies have issued subordinated MTNs. Subordinated MTNs of bank holding companies typically have long maturities of about 10 years. Under regulatory capital requirements, subordinated debt with a maturity of 5 years or longer qualifies as tier 2 capital.

In contrast to public offerings by bank holding companies, securities issued by banks are exempt from registration under section 3(a)2 of the Securities Act of 1933. In recent years, a growing number of banks have issued exempt securities, called *bank notes,* that have characteristics in common with certificates of deposit (CDs), MTNs, and short-term bonds.

Like CDs, most bank notes are senior, unsecured debt obligations issued by the bank. However, in the event of the insolvency of the issuing institution, insured and uninsured deposits have priority over bank notes. As with institutional CDs, nearly all bank notes are sold to institutional investors in minimum denominations of $250,000 to $1 million. Bank notes are not covered by FDIC insurance, nor are they subject to FDIC insurance assessments. CDs, in contrast, are insured for $100,000 per depositor. Furthermore, in the event of a bank failure, the FDIC could choose to protect the financial interests of some or all depositors or other creditors without treating bank notes in the same manner.

Like MTNs, bank notes may be offered continuously or intermittently in relatively small amounts that typically range from $5 million to $25 million. In addition, as with MTNs, most medium-term bank notes have maturities that range from one to five years.[14] However, ratings on senior bank notes are typically one notch higher than the ratings on senior MTNs, which are issued at the holding company level. Reflecting these differences in ratings and priority in the firms' capital structures, the yields on banks notes usually are significantly lower than the yields on MTNs of comparable maturity.

Some bank notes, which are similar to corporate bonds, are sold in large, underwritten, discrete offerings that range from $50 million to $1 billion. However, they differ from corporate bonds in that they are not registered with the SEC. From 1988 through 1992, banks issued $14.3 billion of underwritten, senior bank notes, including $7.8 billion in 1992. In the first half of 1993, they issued $6.3 billion.

EURO-MTNS

MTNs have become a major source of financing in international financial markets, particularly in the Euromarket. Like Eurobonds, Euro-MTNs are not subject

---

14. Banks also issue bank notes with shorter maturities that range from seven days to one year. These short-term bank notes are sold to money market investors with interest calculated on a CD basis or discount basis. As with medium-term bank notes, short-term bank notes are issued at the bank level, and they are not insured. Short-term bank notes differ from commercial paper in that commercial paper is an obligation of the bank holding company.

to national regulations, such as registration requirements.[15] Although Euro-MTNs and Eurobonds can be sold throughout the world, the major underwriters and dealers are located in London, where most offerings are distributed.

Although the first Euro-MTN program was established in 1986, the market represented a minor source of financing throughout the 1980s. In the 1990s, the Euro-MTN market has grown at a phenomenal rate, with outstandings increasing from less than $10 billion in early 1990 to $470 billion year-end 1995. New borrowers account for most of this growth, as a majority of the 560 entities that have established Euro-MTN programs did so in the 1990s. As in the U.S. market, flexibility is the driving force behind the rapid growth of the Euro-MTN market. Under a single documentation framework, an issuer with a Euro-MTN program has great flexibility in the size, currency denomination, and structure of offerings. Furthermore, reverse inquiry gives issuers of Euro-MTNs the opportunity to reduce funding costs by responding to investor preferences.

The characteristics of Euro-MTNs are similar, but not identical, to MTNs issued in the U.S. market. In both markets, most MTNs are issued with investment-grade credit ratings, but the ratings on Euro-MTNs tend to be higher. In 1992, for example, 68 percent of Euro-MTNs had Aaa or Aa ratings, compared with 13 percent of U.S. corporate MTNs. In both markets, most offerings have maturities of one to five years. However, offerings with maturities longer than 10 years account for a smaller percentage of the Euromarket than of the U.S. market. In both markets, dealers have committed to provide liquidity in the secondary market, but by most accounts the Euromarket is less liquid.

In many ways, the Euro-MTN market is more diverse than the U.S. market. For example, the range of currency denominations of Euro-MTNs is broader, as would be expected. The Euromarket also accommodates a broader cross-section of borrowers, both in terms of the country of origin and the type of borrower, which includes sovereign countries, supranational institutions, financial institutions, and industrial companies. Similarly, Euro-MTNs have a more diverse investor base, but the market is not as deep as the U.S. market.

In several respects, the evolution of the Euro-MTN market has paralleled that of the U.S. market. Two of the more important developments have been the growth of structured Euro-MTNs and the emergence of large, discrete offerings. Structured transactions represent 50 percent to 60 percent of Euro-MTN issues, compared with 20 percent to 30 percent in the U.S. market. In the Euro-MTN

---

15. Bonds and MTNs may be classified as either domestic or international. By definition, a domestic offering is issued in the home market of the issuer. For example, MTNs sold in the United States by U.S. companies are domestic MTNs in the U.S. market. Similarly, MTNs sold in France by French companies are domestic MTNs in the French market. Bonds and MTNs sold in the international market can be further classified as foreign or Euro. Foreign offerings are sold by foreign entities in a domestic market of another country. For example, bonds sold by foreign companies and sovereigns in the U.S. market are foreign bonds, known as "Yankee bonds." Eurobonds and Euro-MTNs are international securities offerings that are not sold in a domestic market. As a practical matter, statisticians, tax authorities, and market participants often disagree about whether particular securities should be classified as domestic, foreign, or Euro.

market, many of the structured transactions involve a currency swap in which the borrower issues an MTN that pays interest and principal in one currency and simultaneously agrees to a swap contract that transforms required cash flow into another currency. Most structured Euro-MTNs arise from investor demands for debt instruments that are otherwise unavailable in the public markets. To be able to respond to investor-driven structured transactions, issuers typically build flexibility into their Euro-MTN programs. Most programs allow for issuance of MTNs with unusual interest payments in a broad spectrum of currencies with a variety of options.

Large, discrete offerings of Euro-MTNs first appeared in 1991, and about 40 of these offerings occurred in 1992. They are similar to Eurobonds in that they are underwritten and are often syndicated using the fixed-price reoffering method. As a result of this development, the distinction between Eurobonds and Euro-MTNs has blurred, just as the distinction between corporate bonds and MTNs has blurred in the U.S. market.

The easing of regulatory restrictions by foreign central banks has played an important role in the growth of the Euro-MTN market. For example, in recent years MTNs denominated in deutsche marks have emerged as a major sector in the Euromarket as a result of regulatory changes made by the Bundesbank in August 1992. Under the previous rules, foreign borrowers could only issue debt denominated in deutsche marks through German subsidiaries or other German financial firms, and maturities could not be shorter than two years. Debt denominated in deutsche marks also had to be listed on a German exchange, and these offerings were subject to German law, clearing, and payment procedures. These rules effectively precluded issuers from establishing multicurrency Euro-MTN programs with a deutsche mark option.

In the August 1992 deregulation, the Bundesbank removed the minimum maturity requirement on debt denominated in deutsche marks issued by foreign nonbanks, and it eliminated or simplified issuance procedures for all issuers. Although the new rules require that a "German bank" act as an arranger or dealer, the definition is broad enough to include German branches and subsidiaries of foreign banks. The arranger is required to notify the Bundesbank monthly of the volume and frequency of issues denominated in deutsche marks. As a result of the Bundesbank's deregulation, from 1991 to 1993, the share of Euro-MTN offerings denominated in deutsche marks increased from 1.4 percent to 13.5 percent, while the volume of issuance in deutsche marks rose from $268 million to $10.66 billion. Other central banks have instituted similar liberalizations that may result in rapid growth of MTNs denominated in other currencies, such as the Swiss franc and the French franc.

OUTLOOK FOR THE MTN MARKET

Few innovations in finance have been as successful as the medium-term note. Its success derives from its remarkable adaptability to the needs of both borrowers and investors. The success can be measured by the number of borrowers, the diversity of note structures, and the amount of outstanding MTNs, all of which have increased dramatically over the past decade.

The adoption of SEC Rule 415 in 1982 was the key event that removed the regulatory impediments to continuous offerings of corporate notes. Other regulatory changes, such as SEC Rule 144A and liberalizations by European central banks, have been instrumental in the development of new sectors in the MTN market. As a result of these regulatory changes, financial markets have become more efficient. In 1992, the SEC eased restrictions on the types of securities eligible for shelf registration. As a result of this ruling, asset-backed MTNs may emerge as the next major growth sector in the public MTN market.

ⓖ   # DOMESTIC FLOATING-RATE AND ADJUSTABLE-RATE DEBT SECURITIES

Richard S. Wilson
Executive Managing Director
Fitch Investors Services, L.P.

This chapter discusses the many varieties of *floating-rate* and *adjustable-rate* debt. It reviews the market for domestic instruments, which have coupons or interest rates that adjust periodically over their stated life span, with adjustments occurring as often as once a week to as infrequently as every 11 years.

CLASSIFICATION OF FLOATING-RATE DEBT INSTRUMENTS AND SUMMARY OF TERMS

Floating-rate notes (FRNs) is a phrase that embraces different types of securities with a similar feature—a coupon or interest rate that is adjusted periodically because of changes in a base or benchmark rate.[1] Although the jargon of the investment world will continue to utilize this term to cover all manner of variable-rate debt issues (although there are more than 85 phrases and acronyms describing the different types of debt, ranging from annual adjustable-rate notes to yield-curve notes), they could very well be classified in two very broad (and at times overlapping) categories.

Thus, floating-rate notes are those instruments with coupons based on a short-term rate index (such as the prime rate or the three-month Treasury bill) and that are reset more than once a year.

Adjustable-rate notes or variable-rate notes (or debentures, bonds, and the like) are debt securities with coupons based on a longer-term index. Coupons are

---

1. The U.S. government issues a form of floating-rate debt, namely, the Series EE Savings Bonds. The semiannual interest rate is announced each May 1 and November 1. For the first five years, the Series EE bonds issued on or after May 1, 1995, earn interest at 85 percent of the average of six-month Treasury yields. For bonds held more than 5 years to redemption or maturity, the rate will be 85 percent of the average of 5-year Treasury yields.

usually redetermined no more than once a year, but often a longer time elapses between changes in the interest rates. For example, the base rate might be the two-year Treasury yield, and the coupon would then change every two years to reflect the new level of the Treasury security.

HISTORICAL OVERVIEW

Floating-rate notes originated in Europe and made their appearance in this country in the early 1970s. To the best of our knowledge, the first publicly offered issue in the United States was $15 million Mortgage Investors of Washington Floating Rate (8 percent to 12 percent) Senior Subordinated Notes due November 1, 1980, offered on November 1, 1973. This was quickly followed by $20 million First Virginia Mortgage and Real Estate Investment Trust with similar terms.

The big impetus to the market was the June 30, 1974 offering of Citicorp (a bank holding company) $650 million floating-rate notes. The issue was originally structured with the individual investor in mind (Citicorp would be obligated to repurchase any notes offered to it every six months after issuance), and the initial demand was such that it probably could have sold close to $1 billion of the notes. However, opposition from the thrift industry, Congress, and others caused Citicorp to modify the proposed terms so that the date of the first put[2] was June 1, 1976, and semiannually thereafter. It also reduced the size of the final offering. The interest rate on the notes was to be redetermined or readjusted each June and December at 1 percent higher than the Treasury bill rate, except that the minimum rate for the first year was 9.7 percent. The Treasury bill rate at the date of the offering was 7.7 percent.

Citicorp's offering was followed quickly by an issue of Chase Manhattan Corporation. Other corporate borrowers flocked to the trough over the next few months—by year-end, 13 issues were outstanding, amounting to $1.36 billion. Issuance of floaters disappeared as rapidly as they made their mark on the investment community, and not one issue was offered for the next three years. Again, in mid-1978, Citicorp tapped the market with a $200 million, 20-year note issue. This time it did not give the holder the right to put the notes back to the company, and the interest rate was set at a spread above the six-month Treasury bill rate.

In 1979, 18 issues similar to Citicorp's (except that some could be converted into long-term fixed-rate debt) were sold. This was followed by only six offerings for $912 million over the next two years. However, increased market volatility and high interest rates whetted investors' appetites for variable-rate securities, and the market started to mushroom in 1982; now they are an accepted part of the market, issued by all types of corporations, ranging from electric utilities to government sponsored enterprises. Outstanding issues range in quality from triple-A down to single-D (the issuer is in default). Although most are tied in

---

2. A put is a provision of the debt instrument that gives the holder the right to require the issuer to repurchase the security at certain prices (generally 100 percent of face value) at specific dates before the stated maturity.

one way or another with various interest-rate bases, several have been linked to nonfinancial benchmarks, such as the price of West Texas crude oil or the share volume on the New York Stock Exchange. There have also been a few issues convertible into common shares.

BACKGROUND OF THE ISSUES

Banks and financial service companies have been the largest issuers of variable-rate securities. This is understandable considering the floating-rate nature and turnover of their assets. In effect, they are trying to provide a matching of floating-rate assets with floating-rate liabilities. One study of the new-issue volume for the 1973 through 1988 period showed that 69.5 percent of the dollar volume of the offerings came from banks, thrifts, and other financial firms; 29 percent from industrial, transportation, and similar issuers; and about 1.5 percent from utility companies.

According to the corporate bond database of Fitch Information Services, Inc., at the end of 1992 there were 221 issues totaling approximately $26.7 billion of corporate floating-rate debt outstanding in the United States. Excluded from this figure are issues in default, floaters of international and foreign type issuers sold in the domestic market, and variable-rate debt of government-sponsored enterprises. Of this amount, 64.3 percent is from financially oriented firms, 32.8 percent from industrial and transportation companies, and 2.9 percent from utilities.

Some of the issues provide the holder with the option of putting the debt back to the borrower at par at certain dates before maturity. Generally, to exercise a put option, the holder must notify the issuer or its trustee some time before the put date (usually notice of 30 to 60 days is required). Often, the put, once exercised, is irrevocable, but a few of the note indentures make it possible for one to withdraw the notification of redemption. This is usually found in issues for which a company might wish to forestall early redemption by increasing the interest rate above what is determined by the interest-rate-setting mechanism. For example, an issuer might wish to delay or prevent the early redemption of the debt if it has determined that it needs the funds for business activities or other purposes. By doing so, it will not have to borrow the funds from other sources, thus possibly eliminating expenses associated with another borrowing.

Also, call provisions[3] are not constant among the issues. Some are not optionally redeemable by the issuer for the life of the notes, whereas other issues can be called two or three years after sale. In some cases, the call provision applies to only part of the time that the issue is outstanding.

Denominations vary among the issues, ranging from a minimum of $1,000 to as large as $100,000, with increments of $1,000 to $100,000. In cases of large minimum denominations where a put is provided, it may be exercised in whole or

---

3. Call provisions are included in bond contracts to allow the issuer to retire the debt at its convenience. This usually occurs when the general level of interest rates is below the coupon of the subject debt security.

in part, and, if the latter, the remaining outstanding holding must be at least equal to the required minimum denomination.

There are also some issues that are exchangeable either automatically at a certain date (often five years after issuance) or at the option of the issuer into fixed-rate securities. Many of these are rated below investment grade. Generally, the fixed-rate note that is issued on exchange will mature no later than five years after the exchange or, in some cases, at the maturity date of the variable-rate note. The fixed-rate notes will bear interest based on a premium to the comparable Treasury constant maturity.[4]

In 1984, Chrysler Financial Corporation issued subordinated exchangeable variable-rate notes due in 1994 that were exchangeable, at Chrysler Financial's option, into fixed-rate notes maturing August 1, 1994. The interest rate on the fixed-rate notes was based on a rate equal to 124 percent of the 10-, 7-, or 5-year Treasury constant maturity, depending on when the exchange occurred, but no later than August 1, 1989. The company exchanged the variable-rate notes in 1986 for 9.30 percent fixed-rate notes with the coupon rate based on the 10-year TCM benchmark.

COUPON CHARACTERISTICS

Financial engineers worked overtime on floating-rate securities and have created debt instruments with a variety of terms and features different from those of conventional fixed-coupon bonds. Market participants are urged to carefully review the prospectuses and offering documents to ensure that they are familiar with all of the particular features.

The coupons or interest rates of floaters are based on various benchmarks, ranging from short-term rates, such as the prime rate and one-month commercial paper, to one-year and longer Treasury rates, as well as nonfinancial determinants. There are also issues where the rates are arbitrarily set by the issuer, and others where the interest rate is determined by a Dutch auction procedure. In many cases, the basic data can be quite easily obtained, with few calculations required. Federal Reserve Release H.15(519), "Selected Interest Rates," is one important source of this needed data. For other issues, the coupon-setting data are more difficult to obtain, and the investor must rely on the trustee or agent bank to announce the rates. The revised rates are often published in a newspaper of general circulation in New York City. However, many note agreements do not require the publication of the new rates but state only that such notice must be mailed to the registered holder of the security.

---

4. The Treasury constant maturity series is described in the Federal Reserve Statistical Release H.15(519). Yields on Treasury securities at "constant maturity" are estimated from the Treasury's daily yield curve. The curve, which relates a yield on a security to its time to maturity, is based on the closing market bid yields on actively traded Treasury securities. The constant-yield values are read from the yield curve at fixed maturities, currently 1, 2, 3, 5, 7, 10, and 30 years. This method permits estimation of the yield for a 10-year maturity, for example, even if no outstanding security has exactly 10 years remaining to maturity.

Most of the issues sold in the United States are payable in U.S. dollars. But there are also issues denominated in the European Currency Unit (ECU) and Australian and New Zealand dollars, among others. In most cases, the interest rate is set at a certain premium to the base or benchmark rate. For issues based on the Treasury maturity, it might be at a minimum percentage to the base rate (and may be higher at the issuer's discretion). An example is Primerica Corporation's Extendible Notes due August 1, 1996, which were scheduled for an interest rate change on August 1, 1987. The coupon was 13.25 percent, but because interest rates were considerably lower, the company set the rate for the period from August 1, 1987, through July 31, 1992, at 8.4 percent, about 105 percent of the five-year Treasury constant maturity of 8 percent. The minimum percentage under the indenture was 102.5 percent. Apparently this rate was not satisfactory to the holders; many holders put back their notes to the company during the first two weeks of July, and many others threatened to do so. In any event, several days before the commencement of the new rate and interest period, a notice appeared in *The Wall Street Journal* announcing that the company "is exercising its option under the terms of the extendible notes due 1996 to establish an interest rate higher than the rate previously announced." The rate was increased to 8.875 percent, equal to 110.9 percent of the Treasury constant maturity. The notice further stated, "Holders of the Notes who have previously elected repayment of their Notes may revoke such election (and thereby become entitled to receive the increased interest rate)" by notice "to the company or Trustee no later than 5:00 PM, New York City time on the first business day following publication of this Notice."

In other cases, the rate might be set at a certain number of basis points above or below the base rate. Many three-month LIBOR-based[5] issues have the rate set at LIBOR plus 12.5 or 25 basis points, and some three-month Treasury-bill-based issues are spread from 100 basis points to as much as 450 basis points over the base rate. The spread over the base rate tends to be higher for relatively low-yielding indexes and lower for higher-yielding ones, all other things being equal. For some issues, the spread may be a discount from the base rate. In general, the progression of the benchmark rates from the lowest to the highest starts with the prime rate, followed by LIBOR, federal funds, commercial paper, certificates of deposit, the 11th District cost of funds,[6] and Treasury bills, which often have the widest spreads. Of course, the spread is also a function of the credit quality of the issue.

Some issues provide for a change in the spread from the base rate at certain intervals over the life of the floater. For instance, the coupon for Citicorp's floater due September 1, 1998, was based on the interest yield equivalent of the market discount rate for six-month Treasury bills plus 120 basis points from March 1, 1979, through August 31, 1983, and then 100 basis points over the base rate to August 31,

---

5. LIBOR stands for London interbank offered rate, the rate at which the major banks in London lend Eurodollar deposits of specific maturities. There are also LIBOR rates for other currencies, such as the 6–month Swiss franc LIBOR.
6. The 11th District index is a weighted average of interest costs for thrift liabilities in the 11th District of the Federal Home Loan Bank System.

1988, and the 75 basis points to maturity. Step-down floaters have the same characteristic of a lower spread as maturity approaches. Chemical Banking Corporation's two-year step-down floating-rate notes due July 18, 1990, have a 25-basis-point premium to the one-month commercial paper index for the first year, declining to a 20-basis-point premium in the second year. Some issues are on an "either or" basis. One such example is BarclaysAmerican Corporation floating-rate subordinated notes due November 1, 1990. Interest is payable quarterly and calculated monthly at the higher of (1) the prime rate minus 125 basis points or (2) the 30-day commercial paper rate plus 25 basis points. Other issues have their coupon rates determined through a Dutch auction procedure or remarketing process, with the applicable interest rate the one at which all sell orders and all buy orders are satisfied.

One usually expects that when interest rates rise, the coupon on the floater increases, and as rates fall, the coupon decreases. This makes sense to most people, but some issues can be confusing. With yield-curve notes, the interest rate is reset and payable twice a year based on a certain percentage rate (depending on the issue) minus the six-month LIBOR rate. For example, the General Motors Acceptance Corporation's yield-curve notes due April 15, 1993, are based on 15.25 percent minus the six-month LIBOR rate. If LIBOR is at 7 percent, the rate on the notes would be 8.25 percent. If LIBOR increases to 9 percent, the rate falls to 6.25 percent, and if LIBOR declines to 5 percent, the yield-curve notes would have a 10.25 percent interest coupon. Only investors who are bullish on the direction of short-term interest rates would like these issues. Another type of issue for interest-rate bulls are the maximum reset notes and debentures. The two issues (one of each), which came to market in late 1985, were not well received by investors. The initial coupon rates were 10.625 percent. Interest was adjusted quarterly and payable quarterly, and if, at the interest determination date, six-month LIBOR exceeds 10.50 percent, then the interest rate for the period is reduced from 10.625 percent by the excess over 10.50 percent, with the minimum rate no less than zero percent. With LIBOR at 12 percent, the rate on these securities would decline to 9.125 percent. At least if LIBOR exceeds $21\frac{1}{8}$ percent, the holder will not have to pay the issuer anything.

Some issues have floors below which the interest rate cannot go. Some floors may be fixed at one rate for their duration, whereas others may have a declining minimum. An example of the latter is again the Citicorp floaters due September 1, 1998. From the date of issue through August 31, 1983, the minimum rate was 7.50 percent. Then it declined to 7 percent from September 1, 1983, through August 31, 1988, and then at 6.50 percent to maturity. Certain issues have ceilings or maximum rates. For many, the maximum is 25 percent because of the New York State usury law. In 1974, Crocker National Corporation sold $40 million of floating-rate notes due 1994 with a 10 percent maximum rate owing to uncertainties with California law. For several years, the coupon rate was below the ceiling, but in 1979 interest rates shot up, restricting the coupon to 10 percent. As the notes had a put feature, smart investors put the bonds back to the company and reinvested the proceeds in more attractive instruments. Had there been no put feature, those investors would have been out of pocket for a number of years.

Some issues have both a floor and a ceiling, which together are called *collars*. An example is a 1985 issue of Baltimore Gas & Electric Company with the interest rate set at 110 basis points over the bond-equivalent basis of the 91-day Treasury bill auction rate subject to a relatively narrow collar of an 8 percent lower limit and a 12 percent maximum rate. Student Loan Marketing Association's multi-index floating-rate notes, series T due May 15, 1996, has a wider collar, zero percent on the downside and 24 percent on the upside. For each semiannual interest rate period, the coupon is set at 9.125 percent plus 1.5 times the result of 6-month Swiss franc LIBOR less 6-month U.S. dollar LIBOR less 3.125 percent.

LOOKING AT YIELDS—EVALUATION METHODS

Bonds with coupons that remain constant to the next put date should be looked at on a yield-to-put basis, whether the put is five months or five years away. Instead of using the maturity date in the calculations, the optional put date is used. This method takes into account any premium or discount amortized or accreted over the remaining term to the put.

More complex are those issues where the coupon varies over the time to put or maturity. There are numerous calculations used by investors in evaluating relative attractiveness, and we will briefly discuss several of them. It is important when comparing issues to make sure that they have similar coupon redetermination *bases* and to be consistent with the method used so as to reduce distortions that could occur if issues with dissimilar features are analyzed. Comparing a weekly certificate of deposit-based floater with quarterly interest payments to a six-month Treasury bill secondary market-based floater paying interest semiannually would not be acceptable, nor would using one method of calculation for issue A and another for issue B be valid. The issue used in this discussion is a hypothetical one, and the terms and results are shown in Exhibit 13–1. It should be noted that there are cases where one bond might appear to be the more attractive value under one method or set of assumptions and less attractive under another method and circumstances. Market participants will have to live with these complications.

The current-yield method (current interest rate divided by market price) is not a satisfactory measurement for floaters, because it only reflects the present point in time, assuming that both the coupon and the price remain unchanged. When comparing two similar issues with each other, the current yield would not provide much help in determining relative values, especially when there are different coupon reset dates involved. However, if we were to readjust or reset the coupon as of the present time, we would get a better guide to the relative attractiveness (all other things being equal). Thus, the simple current yield for issue A is 5.05 percent, and the adjusted reset current yield is 6.57 percent.

Although the contractual reset spread to the base rate is plus 100 basis points, the notes are selling at a discount and we are really getting a greater spread or margin. Subtracting the assumed reset rate (5.50 percent) from the adjusted reset current yield (6.57 percent) gives us the adjusted spread to base 107 basis points. If the notes were selling at par, the adjusted reset spread would be 100 basis points (6.50 percent – 5.50 percent).

EXHIBIT 13–1

Hypothetical Issue A

Coupon/maturity	5.00% September 1, 1999
Coupon reset and payment dates	March 1 & September 1
Reset spread	+100 basis points (1.00%)
Base rate	6-month U.S. Treasury bill, interest yield equivalent of the secondary market rate
Price	99
Today's assumed based rate	5.50%
Adjusted reset coupon	6.50%
Time remaining to maturity (assuming today is 9/1/95)	4 years
Simple current yield	5.05%
Adjusted reset current yield	6.57%
Adjusted spread to base	107 basis points
Zero-coupon basis—spread from base	125 basis points
Reset or adjusted yield-to-maturity	6.79%
Spread or reset yield-to-maturity over base rate	129 basis points

However, floating-rate notes are not perpetual securities, as are preferred stocks. For issues selling below par, we pick up the discount at maturity (or put date), and for issues selling above par we lose the premium. Therefore, other calculations are used to analyze floaters. For example, one can view the bond as a zero-coupon issue, obtain the yield-to-maturity on that basis, and add it to the reset spread to arrive at the zero-coupon basis-spread from base measurement. Of course, in relative value analysis, the investor must take into consideration the quality of the debt as well as other factors such as call, sinking-fund, and subordination provisions, if any.

MARKET COMMENT

The first series of floating-rate notes issued in 1974 met with good investor reception. The two-year delay until the put feature became operative was a small negative, but it was used to mollify the thrift interests that feared an outflow of deposits to these new securities. From the investor's viewpoint, they were, at worst, two-year instruments and then six-month instruments once the puts became effective. Price volatility was relatively modest because of the put. Investors also flocked to the second round of floaters, which came to market in 1979. Many did not care that the new generation of floating-rate paper did not have any puts. They thought that as long as the coupon rate was adjusted every six months the bonds would naturally stay around par. However, there was nothing to keep them trading around par when all others around them were changing. The spread was fixed at market levels that existed at the time the issues were originally offered. They did not have puts, and as interest-rate movements became increasingly more volatile later in the year, their prices sank. These new issues were just intermediate- to longer-term securities with a coupon that happened to fluctuate. If the credit quality of the issue deteriorated, prices would be reduced. Because of rapid movements in interest rates, the coupon rates, when reset, were often below market rates. Prices had to adjust for this gap between the floater rate and the market rate. The semiannual coupon change did not provide the needed support. In the January 1980 to June 1981 period, based on end-of-week prices on the New York Stock Exchange, Citicorp's June 1, 1989, floater with a put had a price range of only 96 to $103^{1}/_{4}$. In comparison, floaters without puts had wider price fluctuations. Manufacturers Hanover's floating-rate notes of May 1987 moved between $86^{1}/_{4}$ and $101^{1}/_{2}$, while Chase Manhattan's due in 2009 had a low of 82 and a high of $100^{1}/_{2}$.

In early 1980, interest rates fell sharply. The floaters that were hurt the most in the preceding few months moved rapidly from the low 80s and 90s to the par area. For example, Chase Manhattan's 2009s went from 86 to about 100 in 15 weeks. But restraining some prices were the investors who wanted to get even; they wanted to get rid of an investment that had not measured up to their initial unreal performance expectations. After the rally, prices tumbled again as rates rose once more. This history shows how important the put feature can be. Of course, it also helps to know the risks and rewards of the various instruments one happens to be investing in.

Many floating-rate note investors are financial institutions with floating-rate liabilities of one sort or another. Other investors use floaters as substitutes for money market instruments, although those without put features are not perfect substitutes for short-dated instruments. Money market funds are large buyers of floaters with puts within one year. They have been used as hedges against rising interest-rate markets. If interest rates are thought to be on the increase, floaters with frequent resets should provide increasing income. Their defensive characteristics ought to lend them price stability. A mismatched floater might be suitable. Resetting weekly to increasingly higher levels with interest payable quarterly or semiannually, the holder is not locked into one rate for three or six months. LIBOR has historically been at higher levels than Treasury bill rates, and the relationship between the two should be analyzed prior to investing. If the spread between the two is relatively narrow and one's interest-rate outlook is cautious, then LIBOR-based floaters might be considered so as to take advantage of a possible widening of the spread relationship.

Investors looking for a decline in interest rates may prefer floaters with less frequent resets (such as extendible notes) and deferred resets (so as to maintain the higher coupon for as long as possible). Of course, large investors don't have to limit themselves to just what is available in the domestic market; the supply of floating-rate paper in the foreign markets is considerable. The major investment firms with their worldwide trading capabilities participate in these markets 24 hours a day. But floaters are complex instruments, and investors who don't understand them should stay away. This applies to individuals as well as institutional portfolio managers.

14

⑥   # NONCONVERTIBLE PREFERRED STOCK

Richard S. Wilson
Executive Managing Director
Fitch Investors Services, L.P.

This chapter reviews fixed-rate and variable-rate nonconvertible preferred stock. Preferred stock that is convertible into common shares is discussed in Chapter 15.

THE ESSENTIAL NATURE OF PREFERRED STOCKS

Preferred stock is a class of stock entitling the holder to certain preferences over the common stock of the issuer. It is an equity-type security and not a debt instrument. These preferred-equity instruments can be traced back to the mid-16th century in England and to before 1850 in the United States. However, they first came into prominence in the 1890s during the formation of the giant trusts and industrial combinations. At first, preferences concerned dividend rights, but later other provisions were added, giving the shares additional features and priorities over the common equity. Preferred shares have some of the characteristics of debt securities (although ranking below debt in the capital structure of a corporation), including priority over common shares in liquidation of the issuer. For the sake of convenience, the term *preferred* will refer to all classes of senior equity securities unless specifically noted.

PROFILE OF THE PREFERRED STOCK MARKET

Fixed-dividend, adjustable-rate, and auction market and remarketed preferreds are the three main types of nonconvertible preferred stocks. More will be said later about the specifics of these issues; we will review in this space the size and makeup of the public nonconvertible preferred market.

Issue Types and Issuers

One of the major structural changes in the preferred stock market over the last 15 years is characterized by the trend away from fixed-rate dividends toward variable-rate dividends. Although the total volume of nonconvertible preferred stock issuance in the public markets is greater than a decade ago, the growth has come in variable-rate issues, not the conventional preferreds. Before 1982, the only dividend a public preferred had was fixed-rate—that is, the same dividend applied throughout the life of the issue. In May of that year, Chemical Bank issued the first adjustable-rate preferred stock (ARPS) in the public market. The private market had a few variable-rate issues such as AMAX Inc.'s LIBOR-based stock issued in 1978 and Citibank and Chemical New York Corporation's three-year adjustable-rate shares.

The market's romance with adjustable-rate preferreds did not last long as a better, less volatile mousetrap was invented. Two years later, in 1984, Dutch auction market preferreds appeared. The next year, ARPS issuance started its descent, and auction market and remarketed preferreds became the new hot items. Thus, although the public market before 1982 was 100 percent fixed-dividend issues, in 1982 only 45 percent of the volume was conventional preferreds. In 1984, less than 13 percent of the dollar volume was in fixed-rate shares, and in 1986 only 26 percent. In 1988, straight-dividend preferreds accounted for less than 16 percent of total issuance. But in the four years 1989 through 1992, the issuance trend has reversed, with fixed-dividend issues accounting for 60 percent of issuance. Exhibit 14–1 shows the new issue nonconvertible preferred stock financing volume by dividend type for 1982 through 1992.

The second major structural change of the 1980s has been the shift in the industrial classification of the issuers. Historically, utility companies have been the largest issuers of preferred stock. Prior to 1982, electric, gas, water, and telephone companies accounted for well over half of any one year's volume, and, in some cases, nearly all. However, in 1982 the pattern changed, as less than 44 percent of the dollar volume came from utility issuers. Because of the lower financing needs of utilities, issuance fell off on an absolute and relative basis. In 1985, utility preferred stock issuance amounted to $655 million, or only 10 percent out of some $6.5 billion of preferred offerings. In 1987, utility volume was 29 percent of the total, and in 1992 only 22 percent.

Of the more than $81 billion raised in the nonconvertible public preferred market during the 1982 to 1992 period, some 62 percent was from financially oriented companies—banks, thrifts, finance and insurance companies, and investment funds. A number of these were structured, asset-related transactions of special purpose, bulletproof, bankruptcy remote issuer subsidiaries of thrift institutions. This type of issuer was new to the 1980s. In that 11-year period, utilities accounted for 21.3 percent, and industrial companies a little more than 17 percent. Exhibit 14–2 shows the financing volume by industry type in the 1982 to 1992 period.

EXHIBIT 14–1

Nonconvertible Preferred Stock Financing Volume by Dividend Type, 1982–1992

Type of Issue	Total[a]	1992	1991	1990	1989	1988	1987	1986	1985	1984	1983	1982
Fixed dividend	$33,587.57	$11,429.70	$3,295.80	$3,416.00	$3,719.60	$1,122.50	$2,896.50	$2,259.63	$1,066.60	$463.00	$1,609.50	$2,308.74
Number of issues	368	88	27	28	26	18	41	36	10	11	33	50
Variable dividend	$48,037.40	$3,989.00	$6,740.20	$1,366.60	$2,480.20	$5,977.96	$5,325.56	$6,292.50	$5,483.34	$3,182.89	$4,375.94	$2,823.21
Number of issues	551	36	52	19	21	82	71	83	75	40	48	24
Total volume	$81,624.97	$15,418.70	$10,036.00	$4,782.60	$6,199.80	$7,100.46	$8,222.06	$8,552.13	$6,549.94	$3,645.89	$5,985.44	$5,131.95
Number of issues	919	124	79	47	47	100	112	119	85	51	81	74

[a]Dollar figures are in millions.

EXHIBIT 14-2

Nonconvertible Preferred Stock Financing Volume by Industry Type, 1982–1992

Industry Type	Total[a]	1992	1991	1990	1989	1988	1987	1986	1985	1984	1983	1982
Bank and financial	$41,110.46	$5,476.90	$4,317.30	$1,641.60	$2,993.80	$3,999.96	$4,989.06	$5,717.50	$4,258.84	$2,185.06	$3,132.23	$2,398.21
# of issues	409	31	28	14	21	49	62	73	54	26	32	19
Investment companies	$9,151.40	$2,204.00	$2,995.80	$1,365.00	$1,254.60	$1,332.00						
# of issues	88	24	25	12	7	20						
Utilities	$17,378.28	$3,353.00	$1,347.90	$950.00	$985.00	$763.50	$2,408.00	$1,649.60	$655.00	$1,019.29	$2,003.25	$2,243.74
# of issues	319	54	23	16	11	16	42	32	13	21	42	49
Industrials and transportation	$13,984.83	$4,384.80	$1,375.00	$826.00	$966.40	$1,005.00	$825.00	$1,185.03	$1,636.10	$441.54	$849.96	$490.00
# of issues	103	15	3	5	8	15	8	14	18	4	7	6
Total volume	$81,624.97	$15,418.70	$10,036.00	$4,782.60	$6,199.80	$7,100.46	$8,222.06	$8,552.13	$6,549.94	$3,645.89	$5,985.44	$5,131.95
# of issues	919	124	79	47	47	100	112	119	85	51	81	74

[a]Dollar figures are in millions.

In October 1990, Merrill Lynch's fixed income research reported that the public nonconvertible preferred stock market consisted, in round numbers, of some 1,038 fixed-dividend issues with a par value of $30.3 billion. To this we can add about 360 or so variable-rate issues with a par value of approximately $28 billion. In total, the preferred market approximated 1,400 issues with a par value around $58 billion. In comparison, the Federal Reserve System reported that the amount of U.S. corporate bonds outstanding at the end of 1990 was $1.3 trillion. U.S. Treasury debt at the same time was $2.5 trillion. Thus, the preferred market is "small change" when compared to the considerably larger bond markets.

PREFERRED-STOCK RATINGS

A preferred-stock rating is an indicator or assessment of the issuer's ability to meet the terms of the issue, including dividend payments and sinking-fund requirements, if any, in accordance with the appropriate legal document authorizing such shares. These documents include the certificate of incorporation, the certificate of designation, or the charter, among others. Preferred-stock ratings are issued by four nationally recognized statistical rating organizations (NRSROs). The four NRSROs are Duff and Phelps Credit Rating Co., Fitch Investors Service, LP, Moody's Investors Service, Inc., and Standard & Poor's Ratings Group. These are agencies whose ratings are generally accepted by the vast majority of investment professionals and by regulatory authorities.

Rating agencies help to bridge the gap between issuers and investors by issuing preferred-stock quality rating opinions. Because of their independent and unbiased nature, ratings are used by market participants as a factor in the valuation of securities and the assessment of the risk of the particular issue. Investors should be cautioned that although some agencies' preferred-stock ratings may have symbols similar to their debt-rating symbols, preferred ratings should be viewed within the universe of preferred equity, separate and distinct from debt.

Ratings are defined by these firms in their various publications. Investors are urged to read these definitions. It should be remembered they are not "buy," "hold," or "sell" indicators. They do not state whether or not an issue is "cheap" or "dear" among the multitude of preferred issues. They do not point to the direction of the market. Although only a guide to the issuer's ability and willingness to meet the terms of the issue, they are a most important factor in the preferred-stock investment decision.

THE TERMS OF THE BARGAIN WITH INVESTORS

The agreement or authorizing document between a corporate issuer and the preferred shareowners has numerous provisions governing the rights and duties of the two parties. Similar to a bond indenture, the preferred-stock document sets forth the terms and dividend preferences, redemption and sinking-fund provisions, and rights in liquidation, among other things.

Preferred-Stock Terms and Features

The chief difference between preferred and common stock lies with the treatment of dividends. Preferred-stock dividends either are fixed rate or variable rate. As mentioned before, the total public preferred market is now about evenly divided between fixed-rate and variable-rate issues. Fixed-rate preferred stock is entitled to dividends at a predetermined rate based on the par value, stated value, or fixed dollar amount per share annually before any dividend can be paid on the issuer's common stock. For example, such dividend may be stated as $2.50 per share ($25.00 par or stated value) or 10.00 percent based on some predetermined value. In the latter case, if the par value were $25.00, the annual dividend would amount to $2.50 per share; if the par value were $50.00 per share, the annual dividend would be $5.00; and if the par value were $100.00 per share, the annual dividend would be $10.00. Dividends on fixed-rate shares are normally paid quarterly, although there are a few issues with semiannual dividend payments. The amount of the dividend on straight preferred stock is ordinarily limited to that fixed amount or rate of dividend stated in the description of the issue. It is as though the preferred stockholders say to the common stockholders, "Let us have dividends up to the stipulated amount per share before you receive dividends, and, regardless of whether you receive them, we will agree that our dividends shall be limited to the stipulated amount per share. You common shareholders can have dividends in an amount limited only by the financial ability of the company to pay them."

Most fixed-rate shares pay their dividends in cash. However, in the speculative 1980s there appeared preferreds paying dividends in kind. They are known as *PIKs*. This printing-press paper dividend is a device used by weak companies to conserve their limited cash resources to pay higher-ranked security holders. Although some advocates say that PIKs resemble compounding instruments—shares issued on shares—compounding can work in reverse. After all, if the issuer doesn't succeed, the investor will take a greater loss without having received any cash. True, the PIK dividends can be sold, but this is certainly not the same as a cash dividend. Taxable investors also have to pay income taxes on these paper dividends. If the issuer succeeds, the shares get called and the promoters get the gravy. Also, the number of shares received as dividends is calculated on the par or stated value, not the market value of the preferred. If the preferred shares decline in price, the dividend will be worth less. If this were a cash dividend–paying security and the market for the shares declined, an investor, having confidence in the outlook for the company, would at least be able to reinvest the dividends at the reduced market price for a greater number of shares. In the opinion of many observers, investors in speculative-grade securities would do better receiving a cash return, not funny money.

In contrast to fixed-dividend preferreds, there are adjustable-rate preferred stocks (ARPS). In general, these issues have dividends that are adjusted or reset quarterly at a fixed spread (dividend reset spread) above, at, or below the highest of three points on the Treasury yield curve. These benchmark rates are (1) the per annum market discount rate for three-month Treasury bills, (2) the 10-year

Treasury constant maturity, and (3) the 20–year or 30–year Treasury constant maturity (TCM), as the case may be. The Treasury constant maturity yields are calculated by the Federal Reserve and relate the yield on a government bond to its maturity. This dividend-setting structure has an advantage as it is not tied to either a short-term or long-term rate. A fixing based on only one rate could prove to be a disadvantage when the shape or slope of the yield curve changes. Most of the dividends are subject to minimum levels called *collars*. The maximum rate is the cap and the minimum rate is the floor.

ARPS are neither money market instruments nor substitutes for short-dated securities. They possess more of the characteristics of equities than of debt. They do not enjoy the "magical drawing power," or "magnetism," of an approaching maturity as is the case with floating-rate debt. Preferred-stock investors needing an investment in a money market type of equity are advised to turn to remarketed preferred stock or auction market preferred, described below.

Some market participants might be under the impression that ARPS should trade around the par level at the dividend adjustment date, no matter what the direction of interest rates is. However, it should be remembered that the dividend determination spreads were set in place when the shares were first issued. Interest-rate levels, the creditworthiness of the issuer, and/or the tax laws could change, with the result that investors may demand a different relationship to the base rate. Securities do not trade in a vacuum but in the marketplace, which constantly scrutinizes relative values. Values are placed on securities, taking into account many factors, including the terms of the particular issue, other alternative investments, market conditions, and investors' perceptions of quality and liquidity, among others.

Auction preferred stock (*APS*), an offshoot of adjustable-rate preferred stock, was first publicly issued in 1984, when the American Express Company offered $150 million of Money Market Preferred Stock (*MMP*). This evolution in the preferred market has been warmly received by market participants. Investment bankers have given proprietary names and acronyms to the many issue varieties. The instrument is designed for corporate cash managers seeking tax-advantaged money market type income. Most of the shares or units of trading are priced at $100,000. A few issues even have shares with stated values as high as $500,000 or even $1 million each. The dividends, most of which are payable every seven weeks (there are some exceptions) and determined by auction bids from current holders and potential buyers, are reflective of current money market conditions (both taxable and tax-exempt) and perceived credit risks.

In addition to auction preferred shares, there are remarketed preferred stocks (RP), which have the dividend rate determined by a remarketing agent. The dividend is set at a rate designed to enable the agent to remarket all of the tendered shares at the original offering price. The remarketed preferred offers the holder the choice of dividend resets and payments every seven days or every 49 days. In some cases, other dividend periods may also be offered. The portfolio manager of "temporarily" idle corporate funds should find these auction and remarketed issues attractive alternatives to money market debt instruments, including short-term tax-exempts and other types of preferred stocks.

The more frequent dividend-setting mechanism of APS and RP shares, along with the fact that the rate is determined through an auction or remarketing process as opposed to being fixed at a predetermined spread from a base rate, as is the case with adjustable-rate preferreds, allows the dividends (subject to certain minimum and maximum rates) to be based on the current credit standing and perceptions of the issuer as well as conditions in the marketplace. Thus, the price of auction and remarketed preferred shares does not normally fluctuate, as all purchases and sales conducted through the auction or remarketing are at the original issue price. Therefore, an important difference between ARPS and APS/RP stock involves principal protection. ARPS do not provide it, whereas APS/RPs do. The latter issues are designed so that the issuer, not the investor, generally bears the credit risk as well as the risks associated with supply imbalances.

Nonparticipating Preferred Stock

Almost all preferred stocks in today's public market are nonparticipating. This means that the owners of preferred are entitled to no more than the rate or amount of dividend stipulated in the legal provisions describing the class of stock. A company may become very profitable and realize earnings many times the amounts necessary to pay the regular preferred dividend. However, this does preferred stockholders little good except perhaps to boost the rating for the shares. The big earnings over and above those needed for preferred dividends go to the common stockholders to be reinvested in the firm or to be distributed as common dividends.

In the history of preferreds, there have been instances of participating preferred stocks. The terms have varied, but the general idea may be illustrated by a single provision: After the preferred has received its stipulated dividend and the common has received the same amount of dividend per share as the preferred, funds remaining available for dividend payments are distributed in equal amounts per share between both the common and preferred stocks. From the standpoint of corporate management, such an arrangement is too good for preferred stock because it permits preferred stockholders to have their cake and eat it, too. Their cake is the preference to dividends; the eating of it is participation with common in larger dividends per share.

Cumulative Preferred Stock

A lopsided deal in favor of corporate management is noncumulative preferred stock. The language would say, in effect, "If the issuer does not pay the preferred dividend in any dividend period, you just forget about it because you are not going to get paid." That would be a very weak preference because management could skip a dividend payment at its discretion. In our financial history, there have been few noncumulative preferred stocks of this type, and most of these have probably been the result of corporate reorganizations.

An example of noncumulative preferred stock was Wabash Railway's 5 percent Series A shares. Between 1915 and 1926, no dividends (or less than the stated amount) were paid even though earnings were available for payment at times. The company reinvested earnings in plant and equipment. When the Board of Directors later wanted to pay dividends on the Series B preferred and the common shares, the Series A holders brought legal action to obtain back and unpaid dividends, as they were earned even though not paid. In 1930, the Supreme Court decided in favor of the company, holding that, as the earnings were reinvested in plant and equipment and as no dividends were declared, the preferred holders had no right to receive a share of the earnings. Some state statutes (New Jersey for one) provide that preferred dividends are cumulative if there are earnings and no dividends are declared.

There have been a few more issues of noncumulative preferreds where the dividends are paid *only* if earned; if the company records a loss for a year, the dividend is not paid and it is not made up or left to accumulate for payment in future years. The right to the dividend is gone forever and the company has no obligation to make future payment. These are known as *cumulative-to-the-extent-earned* preferreds.

However, although there have been few noncumulative preferreds, they reappeared in 1988 when The Bank of New York Company, Inc., issued a couple of series of fixed/adjustable-rate noncumulative preferreds. Investors thought this relic of the past had gone the way of the dodo bird, but someone saw the need for it. *Barron's* financial weekly, in its April 18, 1988, issue, refers to this type of preferred as "a relic of the horse-and-buggy era, a device of the robber barons." These preferred shares are contingently convertible into common stock with a market value equal to the preferreds' stated value in the event of a dividend omission or a downgrading below investment grade. However, this contingent conversion feature doesn't provide full principal protection, as there is a maximum number of common shares that can be issued for each preferred share. If the common gets low enough in price, the preferred shareholder could take a hit. Of course, the pricing of the shares theoretically takes into account the noncumulative and contingent conversion features, at least at the initial offering.

One must be wary and make sure to read prospectuses for the correct basic information since some electronic news and security information display screens may not have complete information. Even though the issuer may be highly rated, that is not sufficient reason for an investor to let his or her guard down. Highly rated companies have been known to fall from their lofty status. Federal National Mortgage Association issued "aa3" preferred stock in April 1996. This Series B, 6.50 percent, $50 stated value stock is noncumulative. Even if the dividend is earned, it doesn't have to be paid. Page 10 of the offering circular states, "Dividends on shares of the Preferred Stock will not be mandatory. Holders of record of

Preferred Stock . . . will be entitled to receive, when, as, and if declared by the Board of Directors of the Corporation . . . in its sole discretion out of funds legally available therefore, non-cumulative, quarterly cash dividends which will accrue . . . ."

Cumulative means that when a preferred dividend is not paid (whether or not earned) it accumulates, and no dividend may be paid on shares ranking on a parity with or junior to the preferred until all dividend arrearages have been paid on the particular preferred issue. The prohibition of dividend payments on common stock when dividends on preferred stock are in arrears is a serious restriction. Common stockholders like their dividends, and when common dividends are stopped and cannot be resumed until preferred dividend arrearages are paid, they can direct some very sharp questions to management. This dissatisfaction is also expressed in the stock market by lower share prices.

Usually failure to pay preferred dividends results in other financial restrictions on management. It is common to provide that while preferred dividends are in arrears the issuer may not redeem any shares of stock junior to the preferred. Generally, the terms of preferred stocks also provide that when dividends are in arrears, sinking-fund payments on the preferred and on any junior preferred are suspended and no money may be used to redeem preferred or common stock. The company may not purchase any shares of the preferred except through a purchase offer made to all preferred shareholders. Consumers Power Company is an exception because its corporate charter does not contain any restrictions on the repurchase or redemption of its preferred and preference shares while there are arrearages of dividends on such stock.

A thorough study of a preferred stock includes an examination of the terms of any bond issues and bank loans of the issuer and of any class of preferred senior to the one being studied. Sometimes these senior securities have provisions prohibiting payment of dividends on junior securities when the issuer's financial condition falls below standards set in these agreements, such as a minimum current ratio or a minimum amount of surplus available for the payment of dividends. In 1984, Long Island Lighting Company, as part of its revolving credit agreement with 14 banks, agreed to suspend the declaration of preferred stock dividends payable on and after October 1, 1984. Dividends were resumed in 1989 after reaching agreement with the authorities over rate matters and the disposition of the politically sensitive Shoreham nuclear generating plant.

In early 1985, the LTV Corporation sought approval from the holders of its 5 percent subordinated debentures due January 15, 1988, to the declaration and payment of regular quarterly cash dividends to January 15, 1988, on its preferred stock then outstanding or to be outstanding. The indenture under which the debentures were issued prohibited the payment of dividends and certain other distributions to the aggregate of $15 million plus LTV's accumulated net income subsequent to December 31, 1966. Because of asset write-downs, losses, and expected losses, there would be a deficiency in retained earnings under this provision, which would preclude the payment of dividends. Declaration of dividends due for payment in the first quarter of 1985 was deferred.

In the proxy statement sent to debentureholders, the Company stated the following:

> The Board of Directors and management of the Company strongly recommend that Debentureholders give their approval [to pay cash dividends on the preferred stock]. The Company believes that such approval is in the best interests of Debentureholders and the Company because it would enhance the Company's ability to refinance existing debt and raise additional capital in the market place. The ability to pay preferred dividends will also enhance the Company's ability to issue additional preferred stock instead of debt, which, under certain circumstances, may be more beneficial to both the Company and its debentureholders.

On February 6, 1985, the debentureholders approved the company's request and received a payment of $2.50 per $100 principal amount of debentures outstanding. Preferred dividends were declared on February 7 for payment on March 1; regular declaration and payments continued thereafter on the normal quarterly schedule until they were again omitted in the fall of the year. In July 1986, LTV sought protection from creditors under Chapter 11 of the bankruptcy laws.

Preference to Assets

At the time a preferred stock is issued, hardly anyone thinks about the possibility that the issuing corporation may be liquidated or reorganized, except perhaps the lawyers who draw up the terms of security issues. They write in provisions about what happens to a preferred stock in the event the issuer is liquidated either voluntarily or involuntarily in financial failure. A simple preference is that after settlement has been made with creditors, the preferred stockholders are entitled to receive the par, stated, or liquidation value of the preferred before any distribution is made to common stock or to any junior preferred issue. In the case of stock without par value, an amount per share is stipulated. In addition, an amount equal to all accumulated and unpaid dividends to the date of liquidation must also be paid. Sometimes preferred holders are entitled to a larger amount in voluntary liquidation than in involuntary liquidation.

For example, Jersey Central Power & Light Company's 7.52 percent Series K cumulative preferred has an involuntary liquidation value of $100 per share and a voluntary liquidation value of the amount equal to the optional redemption price applicable at the time of liquidation. In the case of Consumers Power Company's $7.76 preference stock, the involuntary liquidation value is $100 per share and the voluntary liquidation value $101.43 a share (the initial offering price).

There are some issues that may participate with the common stock in the event of liquidation. Public Service Electric & Gas Company had a $1.40 cumulative dividend preference common entitling the holder to receive, upon the company's liquidation, twice the amount per share distributed on each share of common. Holders of Southern California Edison's 5 percent original cumulative participating preferred stock, par value 8\frac{1}{3}$, were entitled to the par value in the event of liquidation before payment on preferred, preference, or common stock. It was also entitled to participate with the common stock in any balance remaining after the preferred and preference shares have been paid in full (including dividends) and par (4^1/_6$) had been paid on the common. Finally, Southern California Gas Co. has an issue of 6 percent, $25 par value preferred with asset participation rights. In liquidation or dissolution of the company, holders of the outstanding preferred stock would be entitled to receive no more than the par value for their shares and any accrued dividends. However, the subject preferred will receive the $25 par value and accrued and unpaid dividends; then it shall participate on a pro rata basis with the common in the remaining assets after the par value has been paid on the common.

Seldom are corporations voluntarily liquidated, but City Investing Company is one such exception. On June 28, 1985, it called for redemption at the liquidation values plus accrued dividends three series of publicly issued convertible preference stock. Two of the issues were converted by their holders into common shares, as the conversion values were substantially in excess of the redemption price. However, holders of the third issue—$ 2.875 convertible/exchangeable preference series E—turned their shares in for the $25 redemption price because the conversion worth was only about $17.50 a share.

Wickes Companies and its subsidiary, Gamble-Skogmo, Inc., emerged from reorganization in early 1985. Wickes $8.75 Series A preferred, $100 par value, received 7.459 shares of the new company's common stock. The new common shares were worth $3.53125 per share, or a total of $26.34 per share of old preferred. Gamble-Skogmo's $1.75 preferred ($40 par value) received 4.321 shares of the new Wickes common, and the $1.60 preferred ($35 par value) received 3.779 shares. The total market values of these two distributions were $15.26 and $13.34 a share, respectively. If the company had liquidated instead of reorganizing, the distribution to all security holders probably would have been smaller.

Another example of a distribution to preferred holders of a company coming out of bankruptcy proceedings is Itel Corporation. Itel had an issue of $1.44 preferred with a liquidation price of $15.00 per share. Each 100 shares of preferred (total liquidation value of $1,500) received 38.7 shares of common stock of the newly reorganized company. With the new common initially valued at $7.25 a share, the holder received $280.58 worth of stock, or about 18.70 percent of the claim.

Voting Rights

Preferred-stock issuers are inclined toward the view that as long as preferred shareholders receive their dividends regularly, there is no need for them to have voting rights. Generally, preferred shares do not carry standard voting privileges, but in some cases each preferred share has the same voting rights as the common equity. Southern California Edison's preferred issues have varying degrees of voting power. Shares of cumulative preferred stock are entitled to six votes per share, whereas the $100 cumulative preferred has two votes per share. All of these votes may be cumulative in electing directors.

However, when preferred dividends have been in arrears for a certain period (usually four or six dividend payments), it is common practice to give non-voting stock the right to elect some number of directors. This is *contingent voting stock*; the voting right is contingent upon the preferred stockholders' lack of dividends. In some cases, the preferred class may elect only two directors (e.g., Southern California Edison); in other cases, they may elect a majority of the board. Thus, preferred holders are assured of representation on the board of a company experiencing financial difficulties. This kind of provision has become common because the New York Stock Exchange requires it as a condition for listing nonvoting preferred stocks. Another kind of contingent voting provision gives preferred stockholders one vote per share, the same as common stock, when dividends are in arrears. When arrears of dividends on contingent voting stock have been paid or settled, the conditional voting right ceases. In 1985, preferred holders elected members to the Board of Directors of Eastern Air Lines and Public Service Company of New Hampshire. In Eastern's case, they elected two members of the Board. In the case of Public Service Company of New Hampshire, the preferred stockholders, voting as a class, elected seven members to serve on the Board, while the common shareholders elected six.

The terms of some preferreds state that certain corporate acts must be approved by preferred shareholders voting as a class whenever dividends have been in arrears for some period of time. For example, agreement by two-thirds of the preferred stock voting as a class may be required for approval of such management proposals as (1) increasing the authorized amount of any class or series of stock that ranks ahead of the preferred as to dividends or as to assets upon liquidation, (2) altering the provisions of the issuer's articles of incorporation, or (3) merging or consolidating with another company in such manner as to adversely affect the rights and preferences of the preferred stock. Preferred stock with such a provision is called *vetoing stock* because it can veto action proposed by management. The power to veto ceases when dividend arrears are paid.

Redemption Provisions

Circumstances often change while a preferred stock is outstanding, and a time may come when an issuer finds it desirable to eliminate the shares from its capitalization. Preferred-stock voting rights might present an obstacle for control of a corporation by its common shareholders. Or it may become economical to refund a preferred stock with bonds to increase earnings for the common stock. Interest is a deductible expense in calculating corporate income subject to income taxes, but preferred dividends are not. Such a refunding would change a nondeductible expense (preferred dividends) to a tax-deductible expense (bond interest). Or an issuer might want to restructure its capitalization. In 1985, Pacificorp and Atlantic Richfield Co. redeemed preferreds for these reasons. The most important reason for a senior security to be redeemed is that financing costs have declined, thereby making it possible for the issuing company to save money through the replacement of high-cost issues with lower-cost issues. Virtually all issuers of preferred stock make provisions for (1) periodic redemption by a sinking fund, (2) redemption of stock in whole or in part by call, or (3) conversion into common stock.

Preferreds without any redemption provisions are quite rare. These are truly perpetual issues because there is no way other than through reorganization that the issuer can retire the stock against the will of the owner. Of course, it could make open market purchases or ask for tenders of the shares, but the stock cannot be involuntarily lost by the investor. There are a few other issues that do not appear to be callable, but they contain sinking-fund features providing for the periodic retirement of the shares.

Nearly all preferreds are redeemable in one way or another. A majority of the outstanding public issues are currently callable at any time, in whole or in part, at the option of the issuer and at preset prices plus accrued and unpaid dividends up to the call date. Generally, the initial call price is par or the offering price plus the annual dividend or rate. The call price is then reduced periodically to par or the initial offering price. For example, Duke Power Company's 7.12 percent Series Q preferred stock ($100 par value) is callable at $107.12 for its first five years through March 15, 1992, then at $104.75 for the next five years, then at $102.38 for the next five years, and finally at $100.00 on and after March 16, 2002. A few other issues have redemption schedules with call prices declining each year by generally equal amounts.

Most new issues provide some type of deferred call or redemption provision. Some might not be callable under any circumstance for the first 5 to 10 years, whereas others might be currently callable but protected against lower-cost refunding for a certain period. This is similar to provisions found in corporate debt issues. Noncallable is far more absolute than nonrefundable, and yet many investors are confused and treat refunding protection the same as call protection. This could prove to be costly.

Many currently callable issues cannot be called for a certain period if the company sells debt or equity securities ranking equal or superior to the preferred at a lower cost of capital than the outstanding preferred. This is refunding protection; it does not allow the issuer to take advantage of lower money costs on senior issues for a certain number of years following the initial public offering of the stock. However, if the issuer sells junior preferred or common equity prior to the expiration of the refunding protected period, the proceeds may be used to retire or refund the higher-cost preferred.

Commonwealth Edison Company issued 1 million shares of 9.44 percent cumulative prior preferred stock in June 1970. Less than two years later, it redeemed the shares at $110; just prior to the redemption announcement, the stock was trading at about $119 to $120 a share. The funds for the redemption came from the sale of common stock and common stock purchase warrants, clearly junior securities. The preferred prospectus stated the following:

> Prior to August 1, 1980, none of the shares . . . may be redeemed through refunding, directly or indirectly, by or in anticipation of the incurring of any debt or the issuance of any shares of the Prior Preferred Stock or of any other stock ranking prior to or on a parity with the Prior Preferred Stock, if such debt has an interest cost . . . or such shares have a dividend cost . . . less than the dividend cost . . . of the 9.44 percent . . . Stock.

The company was sued by some institutional holders, but the judge decided the redemption provision did not prohibit redemption directly out of an issue of common shares. Since then, other companies have done similar redemptions.

In the decision concerning the Florida Power & Light Company's maintenance and replacement fund redemption,[1] the judge stated that

> The terms "redemption" and "refunding" are not synonymous. A "redemption" is simply a call of bonds. A "refunding" occurs when the issuer sells bonds in order to use the proceeds to redeem an earlier issue of bonds . . . The refunding bond issue being sold is closely linked to the one being redeemed by contractual language and proximity in time so that the proceeds will be available to pay for the redemption. Otherwise, the issuer would be taking an inordinate risk that market conditions would change between the redemption of the earlier issue and the sale of the later issue.

This principle can also be applied to preferred stock redemptions.

Sinking-fund provisions for preferred stocks are similar to those of bonds. They provide for the periodic retirement of stock, usually on an annual basis. Often commencing on or after the call or refunding protected period has expired, there are instances where the sinking fund operates before such expiration. A specific number of shares or a certain percentage of the original issue is specified for retirement periodically. Often it will amount to about 2 to 8 percent of the original number of shares, with 5 percent being the more common requirement. Commonwealth Edison had an issue of $10.875 preference stock that required all of the shares to be retired at one time at par through the sinking fund on November 1, 1989, the date the call-protected period terminated. Thus, this issue had another feature that most bonds have—that is, a maturity of sorts. Most sinking funds have provisions allowing the issuer the noncumulative option to increase payments (usually to double the amount at any one time). Sinking-fund payments may be made in shares of stock purchased in the open market or by the call of the required number of shares at the sinking-fund call price, normally par or stated value. There are instances in which a company wishing to retire an entire issue of sinking-fund preferred will call the maximum number of shares allowed for the sinking fund at the lower sinking-fund redemption price and

---

1. *Lucas et al.* v. *Florida Power & Light Company,* Final Judgement, 77-4009-CIV-SMA, United States District Court, Southern District of Florida, October 31, 1983.

redeem the balance at the normal call price. Failure to make sinking-fund payments is not an act of default, as it would be in the case of debt; the company cannot be placed in bankruptcy.

Many preferred stock market participants refer to issues without sinking funds as perpetual preferreds, but this is a misuse of that term. Non-sinking-fund issues need not be perpetual, yet they do not have a date at which they must be retired. Sinking-fund operations can provide some measure of market support if the issuer can come into the open market and purchase stock at less than the redemption price. However, in periods of lower interest and dividend rates and higher preferred prices, a call below market prices can result in capital losses to investors. Shares to be redeemed for the sinking fund are usually selected randomly by lot and not pro rata, or in proportion, to one's holdings.

An important consideration for insurance companies is a rule by the National Association of Insurance Commissioners allowing qualifying sinking-fund preferred stocks to be valued on the books at cost rather than to be marked to the current market price. This accounting or valuation treatment, at least for regulatory or reserve purposes, reduces the impact of market fluctuations on the company's portfolio to the extent that it utilizes sinking-fund preferreds.

Some preferred issues have purchase funds. These are, to some extent, optional on the part of an issuer because it will have to use its best efforts to retire a portion of the shares periodically if such shares can be purchased in the open market, or through tender, at less than the redemption or liquidation price. If the stock is selling above the applicable price, the purchase fund cannot be put into operation. Again, the purchase fund may provide some market support to the issue in a higher dividend rate environment, but when rates are lower it is inoperative. In the case of Occidental Petroleum's $15.50 cumulative preferred stock issued in connection with the acquisition of Cities Service Company in 1982, Occidental was required to use its best efforts to purchase shares in the open market at or below the liquidation value with the proceeds derived from certain asset sales in excess of $100 million. Any shares so purchased would then be credited against any sinking-fund payments when the sinking fund became operational.

It is important to read prospectuses carefully. Although preferreds are not bonded securities, unlike mortgage debt with its release and substitution-of-property clauses, there have been instances of preferred stock retirement prior to the end of the refunding protected period because of asset sales. A case in point is Crown Zellerbach Corporation's $3.05 cumulative preferred stock, Series B, issued May 19, 1982, at $20 per share. It was protected against refunding before April 15, 1987, and had the normal call schedule starting immediately at $23.05 and declining to $20 a share in 1997. However, it also had a special provision for its retirement prior to April 15, 1997, if the company sold certain assets aggregating at least $100 million in any 12-month period. The redemption premium under this circumstance was one-half the regular redemption premium. It started at $21.52 per share and declined to $20 in 1997. On May 20, 1983, Crown Zellerbach redeemed this stock at the special redemption price of $21.42 a share; the regular call price at that time was $22.85. The proceeds came from the sale of its interests in Crown Zellerbach Canada Ltd. and a small steamship company. In late October 1982, it announced it had a preliminary agreement for the sale of these assets; the use of the proceeds for share redemption should not have come as any surprise to the preferred holders. The shares sold at $21^7/_8$ at the end of December and rose as high as $23^7/_8$ in 1983 before the retirement of the stock.

MULTIPLE ISSUES OF ONE CLASS OF PREFERRED

Some companies may have multiple classes of preferred stock. The terms of the two or more classes are determined separately at the times of their respective issuance. When there is more than one class, investors may wonder which stock is senior to another in claim to dividends, and assets upon liquidation. A senior preferred may receive dividends whereas a junior preferred does not. Other rights and limitations of the two or more classes of preferred may differ. Generally speaking, preferred shares are senior to preference shares. Some companies have only one class of senior equity outstanding, whereas others might have two classes with different priorities. Consolidated Edison has only preferred shares, whereas Consumers Power and a number of other utilities have preferred and preference shares.

Companies using preferred stocks in their capitalizations usually authorize a class of preferred stock with a defined preference as to dividends. This class may be issued in series from time to time; there may be Series A, Series B, and so on, with each series of the same class ranking equally with each other as to dividend preference. It is not uncommon for public utility companies to have six, eight, or more series of one class of preferred outstanding. One series may have one stipulated rate of dividends and another series a different rate. For example, on December 31, 1994, the Southern Company, an electric utility holding company, listed 54 different issues of subsidiary preferred stocks in its annual report. The 50 fixed-dividend preferred issues had $25 par and stated values and $100 par and stated values with dividends ranging from 4.20 percent to 11.36 percent. There were also two adjustable rate and two auction rate series. The total outstanding par and stated values was $1.43 billion.

Just as with bonds, the other terms of a class of preferred stock may differ among the series. One series may be voting and another nonvoting. The terms for sinking-fund redemption and for redemption in whole or in part may vary. One series may be convertible and another not. Each series is tailored to conditions in the securities markets at the time of issue.

In the early 1970s, electric utility companies made increased use of preference stock. Some companies were unable to issue preferred shares because of restrictions contained in their preferred-stock agreements or articles of incorporation; they simply could not meet the required earnings tests for issuance of additional preferred stock. As there are usually no similar restrictions on the issuance of shares junior to the preferred, classes of preference shares were authorized and issued. Also, many corporate charters restricted preferred shares to $100 par or stated value. To broaden the market for their stock, some utilities offered preference stock with lower par values, such as $10, $20, and $25. The lower prices appealed to many individual and less sophisticated investors because they could buy round lots of 100 shares each instead of odd lots of one to 99 shares. Although primarily of psychological value only to the small investor (100 shares at $25 is the same as 25 shares at $100 each), this allowed companies to take advantage of a pool of capital that was previously not too interested in preferred stocks.

Another device used by some issuers to bring the price of their shares down to a level at which individual investors would buy them is the depositary preferred share. The depositary share represents a fractional interest in a whole preferred share that has been deposited with a bank under legal depositary agreements. It entitles the holder proportionately to all of the rights and preferences of the underlying preferred stock. For example, in 1992 the Bank of New York Company issued 4 million depositary shares at $25 each representing a one-twenty-fifth interest in a share of 8.60 percent Cumulative Preferred Stock ($6.25 per share stated value). In 1985, Harnischfeger Corporation issued 3 million shares of Series B $3.402 depositary preferred shares at $25.00 a share. Each represented a one-fiftieth ownership in the Series B sinking-fund exchangeable preferred stock (60,000 shares deposited with the depositary bank). The company used this financing method because it did not have enough authorized shares of preferred stock to permit a broad distribution. Only 132,500 shares of authorized but unissued stock were available.

TAXABILITY OF PREFERRED STOCK DIVIDENDS

Tax laws should always be considered when making investment decisions, and preferred stock is no different. Currently a corporation may exclude from gross income 70 percent of the qualified dividends received from other *domestic* corporations subject to federal income taxes. It does not matter whether the dividends are from preferred, preference, or common stock. This exclusion is justified on the ground that it mitigates double taxation of dividends paid by one company to another and then paid to the stockholders of the second company. Dividends by one company are paid after its earnings have been taxed under the federal corporate income tax. Then when received by a second company they would be taxed again as income to that company. This 70 percent exclusion, or dividends-received deduction (DRD), leaves only 30 percent to be taxed in the hands of a corporate owner of preferred stock. This rule applies only to preferreds of banks, utility holding companies, railroads, and industrial and financial concerns. Dividends from registered investment companies are treated differently, depending on the source of the income used to pay dividends. Closed-end investment companies with portfolios of tax-exempt municipal and state bonds receive tax-exempt interest income, and that tax exemption is passed along with the dividends paid on these shares. Because of this tax-exempt status, there is no dividend-received deduction and no minimum holding period.

For utility operating companies, the deduction is applicable to "new money" issues—those preferreds sold after October 1, 1942, for purposes other than refunding. Preferreds sold before that date and those issued afterward for debt and preferred refunding purposes are "old money" issues, with the dividends-received deduction only 42 percent. There are some 100 to 125 utility old money issues and 25 or so "partly new money" issues out of nearly 1,000 fixed-dividend preferred-stock issues outstanding. Partly new money issues are those where only a portion of the proceeds were used for refunding purposes.

In order to qualify for the dividends-received deduction, a corporation must hold the preferred shares at least 46 days. Days on which the stock is held after the dividend is received, as well as before its receipt, are counted for purposes of this minimum holding period. The deduction is increased to 80 percent for investors holding at least 20 percent of a dividend-paying corporation (by the dividend payer's voting power and value). For "debt-financial portfolio stock," the dividends-received deduction must be reduced by the percentage related to the amount of debt incurred to purchase the stock.

The effective tax rate on dividends for qualified investors in the 35 percent marginal corporate tax bracket and a 70 percent dividends-received deduction is 10.5 percent ($.30 \times .35$). Taxes are paid on only 30 percent of the dividends, with the investor keeping 89.5 percent of the dividend. Exhibit 14–3 summarizes the intercorporate dividends-received deduction for new money and old money stock for corporations in the 35 percent tax bracket.

EXHIBIT   14–3

Summary of Intercorporate Dividends-Received Deduction

	New Money	Old Money
Dividends received	$1,000.00	$11,000.00
Dividend exclusion:		
Percent	70.00%	42.00%
Amount	$700.00	$420.00
Amount subject to taxes	$300.00	$580.00
Marginal tax rate	35.00%	35.00%
Taxes paid	$105.00	$203.00
Effective tax rate	10.50%	20.30%
Dividends retained:		
Percent	89.50%	79.70%
Amount	$895.00	$797.00

Exhibit 14–4 shows the pretax and the after-tax yields at the 35 percent corporate tax rate for preferred stocks and fully taxable alternative investments such as commercial paper, certificates of deposit, and corporate debts, as well as the pretax yields needed on alternative fully taxable investments in order to equal the preferred's after-tax return. Thus, a preferred with a dividend of 8.00 percent will provide an after-tax yield of 7.16 percent under current tax rates and the new money dividends-received deduction. In order to equal these yields, a fully taxable investment must yield 11.02 percent (after-tax preferred yield divided by 1 minus the tax rate, or 7.16/.15). A fully taxable instrument with an 8.00 percent nominal rate yields only 5.20 percent to a corporate investor in the 35 percent tax bracket.

Yields on preferreds and most debt instruments are calculated using a day count basis of a 360-day year as the denominator and either the actual number of days or 30-day months as the numerator. When comparing after-tax yields with most other investments, the second column of Exhibit 14–4 is the appropriate

EXHIBIT 14–4

Comparison of New Money Preferred and Other Yields

	Preferred Stock After-Tax Yield Comparison to:			Pretax Yield Needed to Equal After-Tax Return on Preferred	
Nominal Yield	Taxable and Other Debt 30/360	Short-Term Tax-Exempts Actual/ Actual	After-Tax Yield on a Fully Taxable Investment	Taxable Securities	Tax-Exempt Securities
4.00%	3.58%	3.63%	2.60%	5.51%	3.58%
4.50	4.03	4.08	2.93	6.20	4.03
5.00	4.48	4.54	3.25	6.88	4.48
5.50	4.92	4.99	3.58	7.57	4.92
6.00	5.37	5.44	3.90	8.26	5.37
6.50	5.82	5.90	4.23	8.95	5.82
7.00	6.27	6.35	4.55	9.64	6.27
7.50	6.71	6.81	4.88	10.33	6.71
8.00	7.16	7.26	5.20	11.02	7.16
8.50	7.61	7.71	5.53	11.70	7.61
9.00	8.06	8.17	5.85	12.39	8.06
9.50	8.50	8.62	6.18	13.08	8.50
10.00	8.95	9.07	6.50	13.77	8.95
10.50	9.40	9.53	6.83	14.46	9.40
11.00	9.85	9.98	7.15	15.15	9.85
11.50	10.29	10.44	7.48	15.83	10.29
12.00	10.74	10.89	7.80	16.52	10.74

one to use. However, some tax-exempt short-term instruments such as variable-rate demand obligations (VRDOs) and unit priced demand adjustable tax-exempt securities (UPDATES), have yields calculated on the basis of the actual number of days per month and actual number of days per year. This basis is called *actual/actual* and overstates the yield for comparison purposes. The auction market and remarketed preferred yields are understated in comparison to these short-term municipals. Therefore, adjustments have to be made to the auction preferred yield to put it on the same footing as the comparable short-term tax-exempt investment.

Instead of multiplying the nominal preferred yield by 89.5 percent to get the after-tax return, the preferred yield should be multiplied by 90.7 percent to get the adjusted after-tax basis equivalent for VRDO/UPDATES comparisons. The nominal preferred yield must be grossed up to account for the actual 365-day count instead of 360 days. Thus, an 8.00 percent dividend is multiplied by the fraction 365/360 resulting in 8×1.0139, or 8.1111. This adjusted pretax yield is then multiplied by 89.5 to obtain the adjusted after-tax yield, which in this case is 7.26 percent, or 90.7 percent of the 8 percent nominal rate. These adjusted after-tax yields are found in the table's third column of Exhibit 14–4.

The breakeven or indifference level between preferreds and the pretax yield needed from a fully taxable instrument to match the preferred's net yield is 72.6 percent. As long as the preferred's pretax yield is greater than 72.6 percent of the required return from a fully taxable investment, the preferred shares are the more attractive. When it is less than the breakeven rate percent, the alternative investment will provide a greater yield.

Our discussion to this point has centered on corporations and the dividends-received deduction. Of interest is the issuance of *American Depositary Shares (ADS)*, representing preference shares of British companies. Dividends paid by these companies to American shareholders, whether corporations or individuals, although not eligible for the dividends-received deduction, are considered dividends for federal income tax purposes. Under the income tax treaty between the United Kingdom and the United States, the dividend payments carry an imputed tax credit, which in 1992 equaled one-third of the nominal dividend. In the United Kingdom, it is called the advance corporation tax (ACT). Eligible corporate U.S. holders receive an effective after-tax equivalent of 87 percent of the nominal dividend as compared with 89.5 percent for qualified dividends subject to the DRD. Individual investors in the 28 percent tax bracket effectively keep 96 percent of the nominal dividend.

The ACT payment or imputed tax credit is designed to lessen the burden of double taxation on qualified holders. Exhibit 14–5 shows how the effective tax rates are calculated for dividends received from British corporations. The United Kingdom imposes a 15 percent withholding tax on the sum of the nominal dividend and the ACT.

E X H I B I T   14–5

Comparison of Dividends with Imputed Tax Credits Received from United Kingdom Corporations

	Marginal Tax Rate	Corporation 35%	Individual 28%
(a)	Nominal dividend	$9.00	$9.00
(b)	Plus imputed tax credit (1/3 of nominal)	3.00	3.00
(c)	Total dividend and ACT credit	$12.00	$12.00
(d)	Less 15% U.K. withholding tax on (c) above	1.80	1.80
(e)	Dividend paid to eligible U.S. holder	$10.20	10.20
(f)	Cash tax outlay to the IRS on (c) above (marginal income tax rate less tax credit for the 15% U.K. withholding tax)	2.40	1.56
(g)	Net after-tax dividend to U.S. holder	$7.80	$8.64
(h)	Effective tax-free dividend rate (g)/(a)	86.7%	96%

THE MARKET FOR PREFERREDS

Publicly distributed preferred stocks are marketable in the sense that they may be traded on the stock exchanges and in the over-the-counter market. There is usually a dealer or a stock exchange specialist willing to quote a bid price (what he or she will pay if you want to sell) and an offered price (what he or she will sell it for if you want to buy). But there are marked differences in the marketability of preferred stocks, and these differences are important to investors who buy and sell these stocks.

Less than half of the publicly issued preferred shares are listed on the New York or the American Stock Exchanges; the rest trade in the over-the-counter market. This is similar to the situation with corporate bonds. The normal unit of trading is 100 shares on the major stock exchanges, but some issues trade in round lots of 10 shares. Investors who wish to buy or sell odd lots (i.e., less than the standard unit of trading) will pay a fraction more or receive a fraction less per share than a round-lot transaction. These 10-share issues are indicated in the stock exchange transaction tables with the letter z next to the trading volume.

Exchange listings generally improve an issue's marketability, but other factors include the size and the quality ratings. Larger unlisted issues might be more marketable and trade in greater volume than smaller listed issues. The better marketability of larger and higher-rated issues is attributed to the fact that many preferred investors are restricted to what they can hold in their portfolios. There are generally more buyers for shares with these characteristics, and trades can take place far more easily than for small and noninvestment-grade issues. The spread between the bid and the ask prices is often smaller for highly marketable securities because the volume of trading is greater and the trader or specialist will usually have little trouble in selling the shares to a willing buyer at market prices close to the price at which the shares just previously traded. If it looks as though the trader would experience difficulty in quickly moving the shares, the bid price would likely be lower and the ask price would likely be higher.

SOURCES OF INFORMATION ABOUT PREFERRED STOCKS

The best source of information about a specific preferred stock is the prospectus published at the time it is first issued. Prospectuses contain fairly complete information about the terms of the new preferred issues; however, in many cases (but not all), the information about the operations of the issuers leaves much to be desired. This is due to the shortened prospectus form used by many corporations under the streamlined shelf-registration procedures introduced by the Securities and Exchange Commission in 1982.

Information about preferred stocks is available from many of the sources for common stocks and bonds. Manuals issued by financial publishers provide detailed information about corporate issuers and their securities. They are particularly useful for information about the provisions of preferred stocks that we have examined here. They also publish monthly guides to senior securities, which contain condensed information about many preferred-stock issues. You can compare a number of preferreds quickly by using them. They provide in abbreviated form the ratings, issues, information about the principal terms, current and historical price data, and shares outstanding, among other things. Also, corporate annual reports will often contain valuable information. In addition, a number of investment brokers provide research about issuers and issues.

The major daily and weekly financial newspapers have stock tables that include trading and dividend data on common and preferred shares. One newspaper, *Investors Business Daily*, has a separate table for listed preferred stocks, which is quite a convenience for preferred-stock investors.

SUMMARY

A preferred stock is a peculiar kind of security. It is senior to common stock and junior to debt. Although preferred may have many features similar to debt, it is not debt. Preferred stock is a right of ownership in a company. There are many possible variations in the terms of the different preferred issues. They are distinctly unlike common stock in that dividends not paid usually accumulate and generally must be paid before dividends may be paid on the common. But unlike bonds, failure to pay dividends on preferred is not a default, as is failure to pay bond interest. Although not a default, dividend omissions may result in the imposition of serious financial restrictions upon the issuer. Like bonds, many preferred issues have no voting power as long as dividends are being paid, but they usually gain some limited voting power when dividends are in arrears. A company may have one class of preferred stock and issue it in series with different terms for different series of stock. Preferred stock is peculiar because it has some of the characteristics of bonds and some of the characteristics of common equity. It is also peculiar because the exclusion from taxable income of most of the amount of preferred dividends received by corporations from qualified issuers causes it to be owned very largely by corporate investors rather than individuals.

⑥ CONVERTIBLE SECURITIES

John C. Ritchie, Jr., Ph.D.
Professor of Finance
Temple University

Convertible securities are fixed income securities that permit the holder the right to acquire the common stock of the issuing corporation under specified conditions rather than by direct purchase in the stock market.[1] The terms at which the security can be exchanged for the issuer's common stock are set forth in the bond indenture. The option to convert is solely at the discretion of the holder and will only be exercised when and if the holder finds such an exchange desirable.

There are typically other embedded options in a convertible security, the most common being the right of the issuer to call the issue at its discretion in accordance with the terms set forth in the indenture. An example of a convertible bond with a call and a put option is the Liquid Yield Option Notes (LYONs), a product of Merrill Lynch.[2] Because of the multiple embedded options in a convertible security, the valuation of these securities is not a simple task. The

---

1. A few bond issues grant the security holder the right to convert to the common stock of a company other than the issuer. Such issues are referred to as *exchangeable bonds*.
2. LYONs will be discussed in Chapter 42.

valuation of convertible securities has been advanced significantly in recent years with the development of option pricing theory for both equity options and interest-rate options.

In this chapter, the fundamental characteristics of convertible securities, their risk and return characteristics, and the basic principles of how they should be valued are described. In Chapter 42, the application of the state-of-the-art option technologies to the valuation of these securities is presented.

GENERAL CHARACTERISTICS OF CONVERTIBLES

Convertible bonds are often subordinated debentures; this means that the claims of "senior" creditors must be settled in full before any payment will be made to holders of subordinated debentures in the event of insolvency or bankruptcy. Senior creditors typically include all other long-term debt issues and bank loans. Subordinated debentures do, of course, have a priority over common and preferred stock. Convertible preferred stocks are equity securities with a priority to dividend payments over common stock that offer the opportunity to share in corporate growth.

A convertible security will reflect changes in the value of the underlying common stock, when the value of the underlying stock is greater than the value of the convertible as a fixed income instrument. Moreover, convertible securities will also reflect interest-rate movements.

New convertible bonds typically have a maturity of 25 to 30 years and carry a coupon (or dividend, in the case of preferred stock) rate below that of a comparable-quality nonconvertible bond. The underlying stock typically costs 20 percent to 30 percent more if acquired through the convertible than if purchased directly in the stock market, though this premium will vary over the life of the issue.[3]

Although our discussion will consistently refer to convertible bonds, the comments and the approach to analysis of such securities are generally also applicable to convertible preferred stocks.

Yearly issues of Euroconvertibles and U.S. domestic convertibles were provided by Goldman Sachs and are presented in Exhibit 15–1. Exhibit 15–2 offers a

---

3. The statistics quoted in this paragraph are taken from Luke Knecht and Mike McCowin, "Valuing Convertible Securities," in Frank J. Fabozzi (ed.), *Advances and Innovations in the Bond and Mortgage Markets* (Chicago: Probus Publishing Company, 1989), p. 98.

E X H I B I T   15–1

Breakdown of U.S. and Euroconvertible Markets by Currency of Issue
(measured in U.S. Dollars)

United States (in U.S. dollars)		$ 52 billion
Europe		$ 58 billion
U.S. dollars	$ 40.0 billion	
British pounds	11.5	
French francs	3.0	
Other currencies	3.0	
Total		$ 110 billion

Source: Goldman Sachs & Co., New York, NY. Used with permission.

E X H I B I T   15–2

Breakdown of U.S. and Euroconvertible Markets by Issuer Nationality
(in billions of U.S. Dollars)

United States (in U.S. dollars)		$ 52 billion
Europe		$ 58 billion
Japan	$ 24 billion	
U.S.	11	
U.K.	10	
France	4	
Others	9	
Total		$ 110 billion

Source: Goldman Sachs & Co., New York, NY. Used with permission.

breakdown of U.S. and Euroconvertible markets by issuer nationality. The United States is the largest issuer of convertible securities, and foreign issuers denominate a significant amount of their issues in dollars. Historically, utility issues account for a large portion of total bond issues outstanding in the United States, but the utilities chose to issue practically no convertibles during the later 1970s and offered a relatively small proportion of new convertible issues in the 1980s. Industrial corporations have been the main issuers of convertible bonds.

New cash offerings of convertibles tend to be greater during periods of rising stock prices, such as in 1972, 1975–76, 1980–81, 1983, 1985–87, and 1991. For example, the rapid rise in common-stock prices beginning in 1985 and peaking in October 1987 (before the sharp break in stock prices) fueled a sharp increase in the amount of convertibles issued. The right to share in future price rises for the common stock is likely to be most highly valued during a period of bullish expectations for common stocks, allowing corporations to issue convertible securities on favorable terms.

Convertible securities are often employed as deferred common-stock financing. The issuing companies expect them to be converted in the future. For example, a smaller and more speculative firm may issue subordinated convertible debenture bonds. The company incurs less dilution in earnings per share both at issue and typically in the future, thus benefiting existing owners. This occurs because the conversion price of a convertible issue typically exceeds the issuing price that could be realized on a sale of common stock. Conversion can later be forced through call, assuming company success, thus allowing the issuer to sell common stock at a higher price than could have been realized through an immediate issue. This point is illustrated in the discussion of advantages and disadvantages of convertibles that follows. Moreover, cost is lowered while the convertible issue remains outstanding.

ADVANTAGES AND DISADVANTAGES
TO ISSUING FIRMS

Convertible issues offer two basic potential advantages to the issuer. First, a lower interest cost is incurred and generally less restrictive covenants need be included in the indenture than for a nonconvertible bond issue. In other words, the investor pays for the privilege of speculating on future favorable price changes in the underlying common stock by accepting a lower interest return and a less restrictive debt agreement.

The required yield to sell a convertible relative to that of a nonconvertible issue varies over time and with the issuer. A nonconvertible issue will require a yield-to-maturity that is higher than that offered by a convertible issue. Convertible bonds, moreover, are typically subordinated debt issues. The rating agencies, therefore, have usually rated convertible issues one class below that of a straight debenture issue.[4] This would suggest even higher relative interest-cost savings than suggested by the differentials noted above. The interest-cost savings to a firm will, of course, be highly related to market expectations for the common stock.

Second, a firm may be able to sell common stock at a better price through a convertible bond than by a direct issue. For example, assume a firm is currently earning $5 a common share and that the common stock is selling at $50 per share. The firm believes it can utilize new capital effectively and that it would be preferable to raise equity rather than debt capital. The firm foresees, however, a potential fall in earnings per share if common stock is sold directly because it will take time to bring the new facilities, acquired with the funds raised, on stream. The market might well also fear potential dilution of earnings per share and might not be as optimistic as management about the future of the planned investments. For these reasons, the firm might have to sell new common stock at less than $50 a share. On the other hand, the firm might be able to sell a convertible bond issued at par that can be converted into 20 shares of the firm's common stock. The required interest rate might result in less dilution in earnings per share currently than would a direct stock issue, because the number of shares outstanding would not increase. Further assume that the bonds would be callable at 105 ($1,050 per bond).

If the new capital investments raised earnings per share to $6.50 two years hence, the price of the common stock in the market would increase to $65 a share, assuming that a price-earnings ratio of 10 continued to exist. The firm could then call the bonds, forcing conversion. The value of stock received in conversion is $1,300 ($65 per share times 20 shares), which is greater than the cash ($1,050) that would be received by allowing the issuer to call the stock. In effect, the firm sold stock for $50 a share, less issuance costs, through the convertible bonds. The firm, therefore, received a greater price per share than by a direct issue of com-

---

4. George E. Pinches and Kent A. Mingo, "A Multivariate Analysis of Industrial Bond Ratings," *Journal of Finance,* March 1973, pp. 1–18.

mon stock at that time, because the market price for a direct issue is expected to be lower and the issuance cost of a common issue is typically higher than for a convertible bond issue. The firm, in other words, would have to issue fewer common shares to raise a given amount by selling convertibles and forcing conversion than by directly selling common stock. Interest cost is also lowered, sometimes substantially, by offering the conversion privilege.

Convertible securities do have possible disadvantages to the issuer. If the underlying common stock does increase markedly in price, the issuer might have been better off had the financing been postponed and a direct issue made. Moreover, if the price of the common stock drops after the issue of the convertible instrument, conversion cannot be forced and will not occur. The firm, therefore, cannot be sure it is raising equity capital when a convertible issue is made.

ADVANTAGES TO THE INVESTOR

An investor purchasing a convertible security supposedly receives the advantages of a senior security: the safety of principal in terms of a prior claim to assets over equity security holders and relative income stability at a known rate. Furthermore, if the common stock of the issuer rises in price, the convertible instrument will usually also rise to reflect the increased value of the underlying common stock. Upside potential can be realized through sale of the convertible bond, without conversion into the stock. On the other hand, if the price of the underlying common stock declines in the market, the bond can be expected to decline only to the point where it yields a satisfactory return on its value as a straight bond. A convertible offers the downside protection that bonds can offer during bad economic times, while allowing one to share in the upside potential for the common stock of a growing firm.

In terms of their yield, convertible bonds also typically offer higher current yield than do common stocks. If the dividend yield on the underlying common stock surpassed the current yield on the convertible bond, conversion would tend to be attractive.

Convertible bonds may have special appeal for financial institutions, notably commercial banks. Commercial banks are not permitted to purchase common stocks for their own account and, therefore, lose the possibility of capital gains through participation in corporate earnings growth. In 1957, approval was given for the purchase of eligible convertible issues by commercial banks if the yield obtained is reasonably similar to nonconvertible issues of similar quality and maturity and they are not selling at a significant conversion premium. Admit-

tedly, commercial banks hold relatively few convertibles, and convertibles typically do sell at a conversion premium.

Convertible bonds have good marketability, as shown by active trading in
large issues on the New York Exchange, whereas nonconvertible issues of similar
quality are sometimes difficult to follow, because they are traded over the counter.
Moreover, Goldman Sachs has noted that convertibles offer greater liquidity than
stock in emerging markets, such as Southeast Asia.

DISADVANTAGES TO THE INVESTOR

The investor pays for the conversion privilege by accepting a significantly lower
yield-to-maturity than that currently offered by nonconvertible bonds of equivalent quality. Also, a call clause can lessen the potential attractiveness of a convertible bond because the firm may be able to force conversion into the common
stock, as previously discussed. The possibility of forced conversion limits the
speculative appeal.

If anticipated corporate growth is not realized, the purchaser will have sacrificed current yield and may well see the market value of the convertible instrument fall below the price paid to acquire it. A rise in the price of the underlying
common stock is necessary to offset the yield sacrifice. For example, prices of
convertible bonds rose to very high levels in 1965, but in 1966, when both stock
and bond markets declined, many convertible issues declined even more than the
stocks into which they were convertible. It appears a speculative premium was
built into the price of convertibles in 1965, and the market no longer believed that
this premium was justified in 1966.

Investor risk can be markedly heightened by purchasing convertibles on
margin. If interest rates rise after purchase, bondholders may receive margin
calls, reflecting falling prices of convertible bonds, as happened during the
1966–70 period. Many bonds had to be sold, depressing the market further than
purchasers had thought possible based on their estimate of a floor price at which
the bonds would sell on a pure yield or straight investment basis.

ALTERNATIVE FORMS OF CONVERTIBLE FINANCING

Exhibit 15–3, prepared by Goldman Sachs and used with permission, lists seven
convertible types and notes how each differs from a traditional convertible. The
wide variety of convertibles issued widen investor alternatives, meeting a variety
of portfolio objectives.

EXHIBIT 15–3

Characteristics of Nontraditional Convertible Bonds

Convertible type	Difference with traditional convertible
High coupon/ high premium	• Higher guaranteed return • Lower conversion probability
Premium put convertible	• Guaranteed capital appreciation • Lower coupon • Higher premium • One-time right to put bond back to issuer • Provides investor protection for speculative stocks
Rolling put convertible	• Guaranteed capital appreciation • Lower coupon • Higher premium • Right to put bond back to issuer on multiple dates • Higher incentive to hold bond beyond first put
Zero coupon convertible	• Guaranteed capital appreciation • Issued at deep discount • No current income • Low likelihood of conversion
Discount convertible	• Guaranteed capital appreciation • Likelihood of conversion higher than zero convertible, lower than traditional convertible
Exchangeable structure	• Bond issued by one company, converted into shares of another • Credit quality of issuer combined with stock story of third party
Bond with warrant	• Lower coupon • Higher premium • Warrant embedded within convertible may be detached and traded as separate instrument

Source: Goldman Sachs & Co., New York, NY. Used with permission.

TYPES OF CONVERTIBLE INVESTORS

Following are brief descriptions of some of the types of convertible investors typically found in the market.

1. *Defensive equity managers*—Some managers of common stock portfolios may wish to be defensive at times. Convertible securities offer the possibility of being defensive through their downside protection, while still pursuing the growth potential associated with common-stock investment.

2. *Equity managers seeking income*—Some portfolios may desire a higher level of income than currently being provided by common stocks, while maintaining the potential of sharing in the growth of the firm through the embedded warrant on the underlying equity. Some growth potential is sacrificed because convertibles typically sell at a premium.

3. *Convertible specialists*—There are investment managers who deal exclusively in the management of convertible securities.

4. *Bond portfolio managers*—Some bond portfolio managers are willing to sacrifice income to obtain a limited exposure to the growth potential and risks associated with an option on the underlying common stock.

5. *Arbitrageurs and hedgers*—There are investors who attempt to exploit perceived disparities in the relationship between the underlying common stock and convertible securities.

ANALYSIS OF CONVERTIBLE SECURITIES

The following factors must be considered when evaluating convertible securities:

1. The appreciation in price of the common stock that is required before conversion could become attractive; measured by the *conversion premium ratio*

2. The prospects for growth in the price of the underlying stock

3. The downside potential in the event that the conversion privilege proves valueless

EXHIBIT 15-4

Comparative Data for Two Convertible Securities as of January 1993

	Advanced Micro Devices $3 Preferred	Carnival Cruise Lines $4^{1}/_{2}$s of 7/1/97
Known Data		
Conversion ratio	1.987	28.78
Market price of convertible	$48.50	$1,112.50
Market price of common stock	$19.875	$34.25
Dividend per common share	0	$0.56
Call price	$51.20	$1,009.00
First call date	Immediately	7/3/96
Yield-to-maturity for equivalent quality nonconvertible[a]	7.9%	8.2%
Calculated Data		
Market conversion price[b]	$24.409	$38.66
Conversion premium per share	$4.534	$4.41
Conversion premium ratio[c]	22.81%	12.88%
Current yield—convertible	6.19%	4.04%
Yield-to-maturity—convertible	No maturity	1.85%
Dividend yield—common	0	1.64%
Yield sacrifice on convertible[d]	1.91%	6.35%
Income differential—total[e]	$3	$28.88
Income differential—per share	$1.51	$1.00
Breakeven time	3 years	4.534 years
Estimated floor price	$37.97	$871.50

[a] The average yield-to-maturity for bonds or preferred stocks of companies of equivalent quality, mediated by the writer's judgment.

[b] Market price of the convertible instrument divided by the conversion ratio.

[c] The conversion premium per common share divided by the market price of the common stock.

[d] The yield-to-maturity offered by equivalent nonconvertible securities less the yield offered by the convertible security.

[e] The interest income paid by the converting instrument less the annual dividend income that would be received by converting into the underlying common shares. This figure expresses the income advantage in holding the convertible bond, rather than the equivalent number of shares of the underlying common stock.

4. The yield sacrifice required to purchase the convertible

5. The income advantage offered through acquiring the convertible bond, rather than the number of common shares that would be obtained through conversion

6. The quality of the security being offered

7. The number of years over which the conversion premium paid to acquire the convertible will be recouped by means of the favorable income differential offered by the convertible relative to the underlying common stock; called the *breakeven time*

The following material will concentrate on calculations typically used by analysts to evaluate points 1, 3, 4, 5, and 7. Valuation of convertibles will also be examined. The grading of bonds in terms of quality, both by the rating agencies and in terms of financial analysis and assessing the prospects for growth in the price of the underlying common stock is the work of fundamental analysis.[5]

An Illustrative Analysis

Exhibit 15–4 contrasts the $3 convertible preferred stock issued by Advanced Micro Devices with the $4^{1}/_{2}$ percent convertible debenture issued by Carnival Cruise Lines that mature on July 1, 1997. Pertinent calculations contained in the exhibit are explained below.

A few basic definitions are in order before Exhibit 15–4 is examined. The convertible security contract will state either a conversion ratio or a conversion price. A *conversion ratio* directly specifies the number of shares of the issuing firm's common stock that can be obtained by surrendering the convertible security. Alternatively, the conversion rate may be expressed in terms of a *conversion price*—the price paid per share to acquire the underlying common stock through conversion. The conversion ratio may then be determined by dividing the stated conversion price into the par value of the security:

$$\text{Conversion ratio} = \frac{\text{Par value of security}}{\text{Conversion price}}$$

5. See, for example, John C. Ritchie, Jr., *Fundamental Analysis* (Burr Ridge, IL: Irwin Professional Publishing, 1996).

For example, if the conversion price were $20, a holder of such a bond would receive 50 shares of common stock in conversion, assuming a typical par value of $1,000 for the bond.

In some cases, the security contract may provide for changes in the conversion price over time. For example, a conversion price of $20 might be specified for the first five years, $25 for the next five years, $30 for the next five years, and so on. This, of course, means that a holder of the instrument will be able to obtain fewer shares through conversion each time the conversion price increases. For example, 50 shares can be obtained when the conversion price is $20, but only 40 shares when the conversion price rises to $25. Such a provision forces investors to emphasize early conversion if they intend to convert, and the provision would be reasonable if corporate growth generally leads to a rising value for the common stock over time.

Conversion Premium

The *market conversion price* of a convertible instrument represents the cost per share of the common stock if obtained through the convertible instrument, ignoring commissions. For example, the market conversion price of $38.66 calculated for the Carnival Cruise Lines convertible bond is obtained by dividing the market price of the convertible bond ($1,112.50) by the number of common shares that could be obtained by converting that bond (28.78 shares). Because the market conversion price is higher than the current market price of a common share, the bond is selling at a *conversion premium,* represented by the excess cost per share to obtain the common stock through conversion.

The *conversion premium ratio* shows the percentage increase necessary to reach a *parity price* relationship between the underlying common stock and the convertible instrument. *Conversion parity* is that price relationship between the convertible instrument and the common stock at which neither a profit nor a loss would be realized by purchasing the convertible, converting it, and selling the common shares that were received in conversion, ignoring commissions. At conversion parity, the following condition would exist:

$$\frac{\text{Par value of security}}{\text{Conversion price}} = \frac{\text{Market price of the convertible}}{\text{Market price of the common}}$$

When the price of the common stock exceeds its conversion parity price, one could feel certain that the convertible security would fluctuate directly with changes in the market price of the underlying common stock. In other words, gains in value of the underlying common stock should then be able to be realized by the sale of the convertible instrument, rather than conversion and sale of the stock itself. The market conversion price, incidentally, is the parity price for a share of common stock obtainable through the convertible instrument.

At the time of this comparative analysis, both instruments sold at premium, but the premium on the Advance Micro Devices convertible preferred was greater both in relative and absolute terms. If one assumes that the appreciation potentials of the common stocks of both companies were equal (a feeling the market appeared not to hold), the Carnival Cruise Lines bond had a substantial advantage. An increase of only 12.88 percent in the price of the common stock of Carnival Cruise Lines was needed to insure that further increases in the underlying common would be reflected in the price of the convertible instrument. Advance Micro Devices common stock, however, would have to rise 22.81 percent before the convertible had an ensured value. Analysts do begin to question when the premium exceeds 20 percent.

There is usually, although not always, some conversion premium present on convertible instruments, which reflects the anticipation of a possible increase in the price of the underlying common stock beyond the parity price. Professional arbitrageurs are constantly looking for situations in which the stock can be obtained more cheaply (allowing for commissions) by buying the convertible instrument than through direct purchase in the market. For example, assume that a bond is convertible into 20 shares and can be purchased for $1,000. If the common stock was currently selling at $55 a share, an arbitrageur would buy the convertible and simultaneously short sell the common stock. The arbitrageur would realize a gross profit (before transaction costs) of $100 calculated as follows:

Short sale of 20 shares at $55/share	$1,100
Less purchase cost of bond	1,000
	$ 100

The demand by arbitrageurs for the convertible would continue until the resultant rise in the price of the convertible no longer made such actions profitable.

Yield Sacrifice

At the time of this analysis, nonconvertible bonds of equivalent quality to the convertible issued by Carnival Cruise Lines offered a yield-to-maturity of 8.20 percent, or 635 basis points higher than the yield-to-maturity offered by the convertible. The yield sacrifice suggested by this would have to be overcome by an equivalent rise in the price of the underlying common stock, assuming the bond was held to maturity, or the investor would have been better advised to purchase the nonconvertible instrument. This differential is possibly misleading in this case, as the sacrifice relative to the current yield is significantly less. The current yield would seem more significant if the rise in the common stock were realized well before maturity.

The yield sacrifice (on a yield-to-maturity basis) is substantially greater for the Carnival Cruise Line bonds than for the Advanced Micro Devices preferred, thereby requiring more appreciation potential for its common stock during the holding period to make the convertible attractive. In the final analysis, it is the price appreciation potential for the underlying common stock that is most important.

Downside Risk Potential

The floor price for a convertible is estimated as that value at which the instrument would sell in the market to offer the yield of an equivalent nonconvertible instrument. Carnival Cruise Line bonds were rated BBB by Standard & Poor's Corporation at the time of this analysis, and the yield paid by BBB bonds was used as the basis for estimating the required market yield for present-value calculations for the nonconvertible bond. Nonconvertible preferreds, felt to be of equivalent quality to those issued by Advanced Micro Devices, were used as a basis for estimating the required yield for that company.

The floor price of the Advanced Micro Devices convertible preferred was calculated by dividing the annual dividend ($3 per share) by 7.9 percent (.079), because a preferred is a perpetuity. The sum of the present values of the cash flows (discounting at 8.2 percent) that would be generated by a nonconvertible $4^1/_2$ percent bond maturing in 4 years and 2 months determined the floor price of $871.50 for Carnival Cruise Lines.

The analysis suggests a 21.67 percent (241/1112.50) downside risk for Carnival Cruise Line bonds, and a 21.71 percent (10.53/48.50) downside risk for the Advanced Micro Devices preferred stock. There is no real difference suggested for the two instruments in terms of downside risk.

One should not, however, place too much emphasis on the estimated floor prices. The calculations assume that current-yield levels will continue, and this may well not be correct. On the one hand, if market yields rise to higher levels and the conversion privilege proves worthless, the price of the bonds could fall below the estimated floor price. On the other hand, if market yield levels fall, the loss will not be as great as suggested. More importantly, one should not be purchasing convertibles (remember the yield sacrifice) unless one believes the probability is relatively high that the market price of the underlying common stock will rise and eventually exceed the parity price for that common stock.

Breakeven Time

Breakeven time represents the number of years it will take for the favorable income differential over the common stock offered by the convertible instrument to equal the total dollar conversion premium paid to acquire that convertible instrument on a per share basis. For example, the breakeven time for the Carnival Cruise Lines convertible bonds is 4.41 years, calculated as follows:

Interest paid on each $1,000 bond at $4^1/_2$%	$45.00
Dividend income offered by 28.78 shares into which each bond is convertible (28.78×0.56)	16.12
Favorable bond income differential	$28.88
Favorable income differential per common share (28.88/28.78)	1.00
Breakeven time equals conversion premium per share divided by favorable income differential per share ($4.41/1.00)	4.41 years

Professional investors in convertible bonds consider breakeven times of three years or less as desirable and question longer payback times. Breakeven times up to five years can be acceptable, however, where justified by strong expectations for favorable growth in the underlying common stock and a favorable yield differential while holding the convertible. The Advanced Micro Devices preferred has a desirable breakeven time, and the Carnival Cruise Lines bond was acceptable to many analysts because growth prospects were considered good and there was a considerable current yield advantage in holding the convertible rather than the underlying common stock. Some analysts did question the future growth potential for Advanced Micro Devices because of a recent adverse legal decision.

Call Risk

Advanced Micro Devices is immediately callable, but at a call price in excess of the market price of the convertible. The call risk is not, therefore, high. However, call could still limit the potential gain on the convertible.

The convertible of Carnival Cruise Lines offered call protection through July 3, 1996, ensuring that up to that date would be available to allow growth in the common that would translate into meaningful gain for the convertible. The low premium, call protection, and the 240-basis-point current yield advantage over the common are attractive features of this convertible.

Putable Convertibles

Some convertibles offer a put option, adding a possible further attractive feature to the instrument. For example, AMR Corporation convertibles were putable to the corporation after March 15, 1996, at 54.041, offering downside protection with a 6.25 percent yield to the 1996 put. Automatic Data convertibles were putable on February 20, 1997, at 45.463 for a 4.06 percent yield to put.

Neither of the convertibles contrasted in this chapter was putable.

Dilution of the Conversion Privilege

A large common-stock split or stock dividend could markedly dilute the value of the conversion privilege, unless adjustment of the number of shares received in conversion is made. For example, assume that a bond is convertible into 20 shares and that the company undergoes a two-for-one stock split. Recognizing this, the conversion privilege is typically protected by terms in the bond indenture providing for a pro rata adjustment of the conversion price and/or the conversion ratio so that the exchange ratio would increase to 40 shares after the stock split.

VALUATION OF CONVERTIBLES

An investor in a convertible security effectively owns a nonconvertible fixed income security and a call option on the issuer's common stock. The value of a convertible security is therefore the sum of these two values—disregarding any other options that may be embedded in the convertible security (e.g., the issuer's right to call the issue).

The value of a convertible bond disregarding the conversion feature is called its *straight value*. This is found by discounting the cash flow for the bond at a yield equal to the yield-to-maturity of an equivalent nonconvertible bond.

The value of a convertible bond if it is converted immediately into the common stock of the issuer is called its *conversion value*. This value is found by multiplying the conversion ratio by the current market price of the common stock. The conversion value for Carnival Cruise Lines in our illustration is $985.72 (28.78 × $34.25).

The minimum value of a convertible bond is the *greater* of its (1) straight value and (2) conversion value. Arbitrage ensures that this will occur. For example, suppose that the straight value of the Carnival Cruise Lines issue is $800 when its conversion value is $985.72 and that the issue is trading at $800. Investors would buy the issue for $800 and convert it for 28.78 shares worth $34.25 each, resulting in a riskless arbitrage profit of $185.72 less transaction costs. Suppose, instead, the straight value is $1,050 at the time the conversion value is $985.72 but the issue is trading at $985.75. In this case, investors would be buying a bond offering a higher-than-market yield.

A convertible bond will trade at a premium above the minimum value just described because of the value of the option the security holder has. The exception is when the issue is maturing or the market is convinced that the option has no value.

Exhibit 15–5 shows the typical price response of a convertible bond at different stock price levels. The solid line in the exhibit shows the conversion value.

E X H I B I T   15–5

Convertible Bond Price versus Stock Price

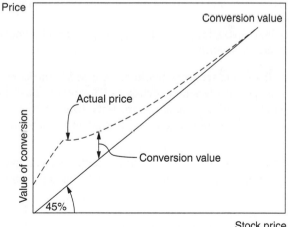

The dashed curve is the actual price of the convertible bond. At any common stock price, the difference between the actual price and the minimum price is the value of the option.

Determining the worth of the option to buy the common stock embedded in a convertible bond is complicated. Here is where equity option pricing models are typically used. The Black-Scholes option pricing model might be used for a quick approximation of the value of the equity option. Unfortunately, this model entails a number of assumptions regarding dividend policy, the stock's volatility, and the possibility of the issuer exercising its call option that limits its use.[6] Other equity option pricing models have been developed that can cope with some of these assumptions. A more comprehensive model that takes into consideration these nuances as well as other options that might be embedded in a convertible bond is explained in Chapter 42.

SUMMARY

Some fixed income securities are convertible into common stock, offering the basic advantages of a senior security (bond or preferred stock) while allowing the holder to participate in potential corporate growth. The investor pays for the conversion privilege by accepting a significantly lower yield than could be obtained by purchasing nonconvertible bonds or preferred stocks. A convertible, moreover, usually sells at a premium over the value of the underlying common stock. If the anticipated growth in the value of the common stock is not realized, the purchaser will have sacrificed yield and may well also see the value of the convertible instrument fall sharply.

There are three distinct areas of analysis that should be undertaken when evaluating a convertible security:

1. The quality of the security should be assessed in the same way as for other nonconvertible senior securities. This requires assessing the ability of the issuing company to meet the fixed charges mandated by the issue under reasonably conceivable adverse economic circumstances.

2. The growth potential for the underlying common stock must be evaluated, because that growth potential offers the basis for generating the

---

6. Knecht and McCowin, "Valuing Convertible Securities."

added yield necessary to offset the yield sacrifice incurred at the time of purchase and provides a return that makes purchase attractive.

3. Special calculations developed in the illustrative analysis in this chapter should be used to assess the relative attractiveness of the many convertible securities available in the market.

Conversion should be considered when the annual total dividends that would be received from the common shares obtained through conversion exceed the annual coupon payments offered by the convertible bond. Sale of the convertible security should also be considered when the price of that security exceeds the estimated value of the underlying stock into which it is convertible and/or the prospects for favorable growth in the underlying common stock deteriorate.

ⓖ   # THE HIGH-YIELD BOND MARKET

Joseph V. Amato
Managing Director
Director of High Yield Bond Research
Lehman Brothers, Inc.

INTRODUCTION

The high-yield market, once regarded as the renegade of the corporate bond market, has matured over the past several years and become a large, relatively stable market for providing capital to noninvestment-grade companies. This chapter will describe the various types of high-yield securities that have been issued over the past decade and provide a review of the market and its historical return experience.

TYPES OF SECURITIES

During the market's developmental stage, numerous types of debt instruments were used to meet investor and issuer objectives. These instruments ranged from the simple fixed-rate, cash-paying debt to payment-in-kind and increasing-rate debt. Increasing-rate securities, for example, were introduced during the LBO boom of the mid-1980s as an interim financing vehicle. More recently, however, the market has gone "back to basics" and the old "plain vanilla" cash-pay, fixed-rate debt has been the dominant instrument used to raise capital. However, several nontraditional types of securities continue in use due to specific issuer needs. For example, deferred-pay securities have been frequently used to raise capital for fast-growing industries, such as wireless telecommunications, that require heavy capital investment and that lack near-term free cash flow.

Plain Vanilla Fixed-Rate, Cash-Pay Securities

This is by far the most popular debt instrument used in the high-yield market. Approximately 90 percent of all debt currently outstanding in the market has a fixed-rate coupon and pays cash interest. These securities typically have original maturities of 7 to 12 years and are callable 3 to 5 years after issuance. The callability is intended to give the issuer flexibility to repay higher coupon debt as its credit quality improves. Callable bonds represent 72 percent of the total high-yield market (see Exhibit 16–1). The bond covenants may also provide the issuer a special call option in the event that equity capital is raised. This "equity clawback" typically allows the issuer to call some portion (typically 24 percent to 35 percent) of the issue during the first three years after issuance at a relatively steep call price notwithstanding the standard call provisions pertaining to the remaining 65 percent to 75 percent of the issue.

Rule 144A Securities

Issuing securities pursuant to SEC Rule 144A has become a very popular financing technique in the high-yield market over the past several years. This technique can and has been used for all types of high-yield securities. The technique allows issuers quick access to the market by initially selling the securities in a private placement transaction to underwriters acting as the initial buyers of the securities. The underwriters then resell these securities to qualified institutional investors under the safe harbor resale provisions of Rule 144A. The issuer agrees to register

E X H I B I T   16–1

Outstanding High-Yield Debt by Structure* as of December 31, 1995

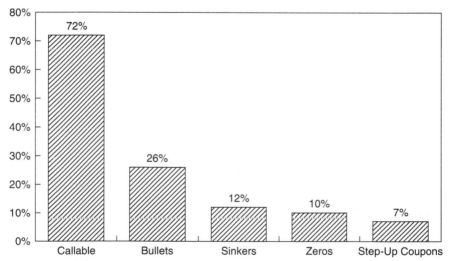

*Some structures overlap.

Source: Lehman Brothers High-Yield Research.

the securities within a relatively short period of time, typically 30–90 days after issuance. The ability to avoid a typical four-week review period by the SEC prior to coming to market has enabled issuers to refrain from obtaining costly bridge loans to fund acquisitions quickly. One occasional drawback of 144A transactions pertains to the investment charters of certain high-yield investors. Mutual funds, for example, typically have some limit on the percentage of their assets that may be invested in unregistered securities.

Split-Coupon Securities

Split-coupon securities begin as zero-coupon bonds and pay no cash interest for an initial period, which typically lasts for three to seven years, after which cash interest is payable at the stated fixed rate until maturity. These securities are issued at a discounted price calculated by using a discounted cash flow analysis with the stated coupon as the discount rate. Split-coupon securities allow issuers time to increase cash flows to fund interest requirements. Companies in rapidly expanding industries or that are in the midst of significant operating turnarounds have been the most common issuers of this type of security. One alternative to issuing a split-coupon security is to overfund the required proceeds to allow the issuer to pay cash interest during the first several years out of the overfunded proceeds. For example, instead of raising $100 million of proceeds from the issuance of split-coupon securities, the issuer may choose to raise $135 million with the "extra" $35 million going towards paying cash interest for the first three years. From the issuer's perspective, the economics are essentially the same. The advantage to the technique (or "gimmick" depending on one's perspective) is to broaden the appeal of the security to investors who do not or cannot purchase noncash-paying securities.

Payment-in-Kind Securities

Payment-in-kind securities (PIKs) allow the issuer the option to pay interest at the designated rate either in cash or in like-kind securities. The PIK option is allowed for only a specified period of time that typically runs three to five years. As the issuer chooses the PIK option, the principal amount of the debt increases and the future cash interest obligation rises. PIK securities trade in a manner different from that of the typical high-yield security. Since during the PIK period the interest payment is at the issuer's option, a PIK security will trade without accrued interest, and the coupon payment is reflected in the accreted price of the security, similar to how preferred stocks trade.

Step-Up Coupon Securities

Step-up coupon securities are a variation of the split-coupon security. In this case, the initial coupon is a relatively low cash interest rate for the first three to five years that increases on a specified date to a higher predetermined rate. This rate change occurs one time only, and the new interest rate remains in effect until maturity. The reduced interest burden in the first several years allows the issuer time to increase its cash flow to meet the higher stepped-up rate.

Bond and Stock Units

Issuance of units consisting of bonds and some form of equity has increased substantially for companies with rapid growth potential but significant business risk. For these types of issuers, investors have demanded more upside participation given the equity-like risks being incurred. To satisfy investor demands, issuers have packaged equity with their debt securities to give bondholders a "piece of the action." The equity participation has typically been anywhere from 5 percent to 25 percent of the issuer's equity ownership in the form of warrants (with a nominal exercise price) or shares of straight common stock. Investors can usually strip the equity portion of the unit to realize its value and thus lower their effective price of the debt security. Alternatively, the holder can keep the equity upside while selling the debt portion of the unit.

Extendible/Reset Securities

Issuers of these securities have the option to reset the coupon or extend the maturity of the bonds at designated times. In general, the coupons for reset securities must be reset to levels that will cause the bonds to trade at a certain price or have a certain market value, as determined by one or more investment banks. In some cases, coupons are subject to floors and caps. Although extendible bonds, at issue, have a specified final maturity date, an issuer may choose to have the bonds mature at one of a number of predetermined dates before the final maturity date. The majority of reset and extendible securities also have put features, which can be exercised at the option of the bond holders. Usually, holders may require an issuer to repurchase securities (at specified prices) if a bond's maturity is extended and, in some cases, when a coupon is reset. Issuers of reset and extendible securities can benefit from declining interest rates and improved credit quality. For investors, the reset feature can be attractive in environments with rising interest rates and can be used as a hedge against an issuer's deteriorating credit quality. This feature, however, can have unintended consequences by actually accelerating credit problems since the issuer's interest burden increases just as its credit quality is deteriorating. Very few extendible or reset securities remain outstanding in the high-yield market.

Increasing-Rate Notes (IRNs)

Increasing-rate notes were issued primarily in the mid- to late 1980s as interim financing for acquisitions and leveraged buyouts. The coupon on these securities would usually increase quarterly at predetermined rates, usually 25 to 50 basis points. In order to complete these transactions quickly, IRNs were generally issued as private placements with registration rights. The increasing interest payments on these securities provided issuers with a strong incentive to retire IRNs before the stated maturities. IRNs were ultimately replaced as a financing vehicle by other, more cost-effective alternatives, such as secured bank loans, subordinated bridge loans, or 144A financings. Virtually no IRNs remain outstanding in the high-yield market.

High-Yield Bank Loans

Over the last several years, the lines have been blurring between bank loans and securities, particularly in the high-yield market. The lenders' desire for liquidity, breakdowns of regulatory barriers, and standardization of the loan documentation have led to a growing, actively traded market for noninvestment-grade bank loans. Trading activity increased dramatically as secondary loan trading volume rose from only $7.9 billion in 1991 to almost $34 billion in 1995 (see Exhibit 16–2). These increases in trading followed the surge in leverage lending that occurred in the 1988–1990 time frame when much of the funding for leveraged companies was done via the bank loan market. In 1990, for example, as the high-yield market essentially shut down any new issuance, leveraged bank loans comprised 98 percent of all funds provided to leveraged companies (see Exhibit 16–3). Furthermore, the development of the "B loan" market for longer maturity bank loans with little near-term amortization looks remarkably like a securities

E X H I B I T   16–2

Bank Loan Trading Volume: 1991–1995

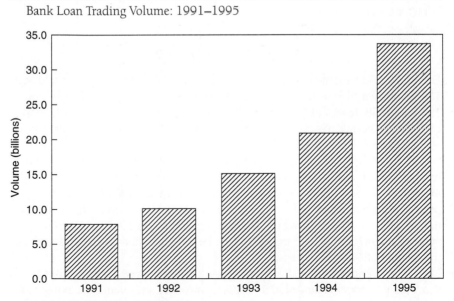

Source: LPC, Lehman Brothers High-Yield Research.

EXHIBIT 16–3

Leveraged Bank Lending versus High-Yield Issuance: 1987–1995

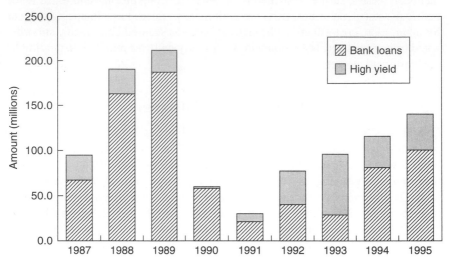

Source: LPC, Lehman Brothers High-Yield Research.

market. There remain, however, significant differences between the typical high-yield security and high-yield bank loan. Bank loans, for example, carry floating interest rates, are callable at any time, and are usually secured by the issuer's assets. Almost all high-yield securities, on the other hand, carry fixed rates, have call protection, and are unsecured. Furthermore, bank loans carry much more restrictive covenants by which the issuer must abide.

MARKET OVERVIEW

Driven by a surge in new issuance in the early to mid-1990s, the high-yield market has grown in size to approximately $300 billion, up from $200 billion in 1990. Exhibits 16–4 and 16–5 depict the size and growth of the high-yield market over the last decade. As opposed to the mid- to late 1980s when 40 percent of new issuance was used for acquisition and LBO financings, the dominant use of new issuance over the past several years has been for growth capital and existing debt refinancings. Exhibit 16–6 shows a breakdown of the use of proceeds for high-yield debt issued over the past several years. Financing for LBOs fell to just 4 percent of new issuance in 1995. New issuance for general refinancings and internal growth made up 76 percent of new issue volume in 1995, up from only 21 percent in 1987. From 1993 through 1995, new issue volume included a substantial amount of 144A financings.

The overall credit quality of the market has improved over the past several years as investors demanded higher quality product and as an improving economy helped existing issuers improve their credit quality. Exhibit 16–7 categorizes

EXHIBIT 16-4

Outstanding High-Yield Debt: 1983–1995

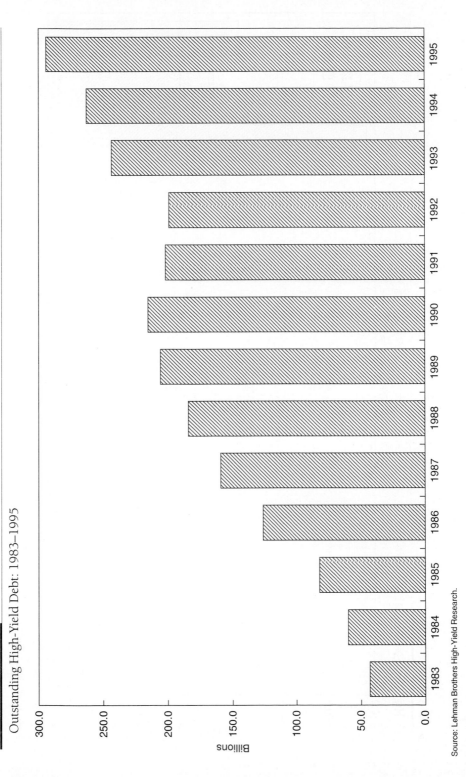

Source: Lehman Brothers High-Yield Research.

High-Yield New Issuance: 1983–1995

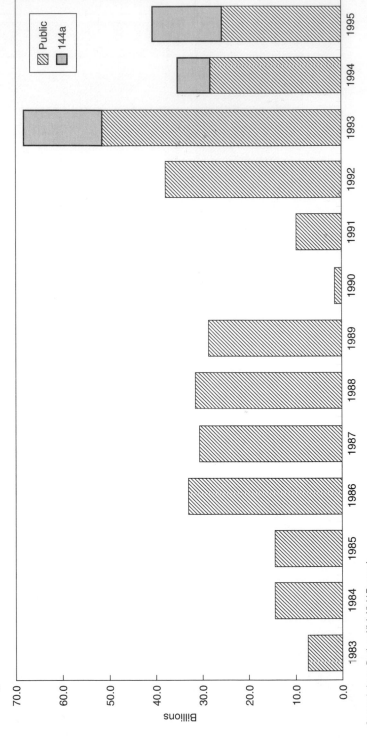

Source: Lehman Brothers High-Yield Research.

EXHIBIT 16–6

High-Yield Securities Use of Proceeds

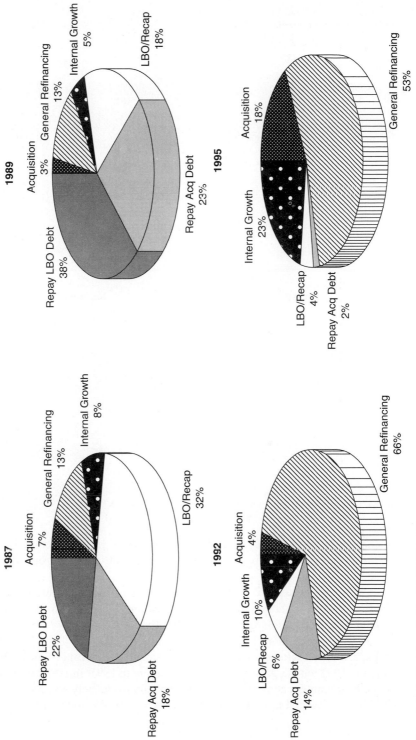

1987

Acquisition
7%

General Refinancing
13%

Internal Growth
8%

Repay LBO Debt
22%

LBO/Recap
32%

Repay Acq Debt
18%

1989

Acquisition
3%

General Refinancing
13%

Internal Growth
5%

Repay LBO Debt
38%

LBO/Recap
18%

Repay Acq Debt
23%

1992

Acquisition
4%

Internal Growth
10%

LBO/Recap
6%

Repay Acq Debt
14%

General Refinancing
66%

1995

Acquisition
18%

Internal Growth
23%

LBO/Recap
4%

Repay Acq Debt
2%

General Refinancing
53%

Source: In Depth Data, Lehman Brothers High-Yield Research.

E X H I B I T   16-7

High-Yield Market Rating Composition: 1987–1995

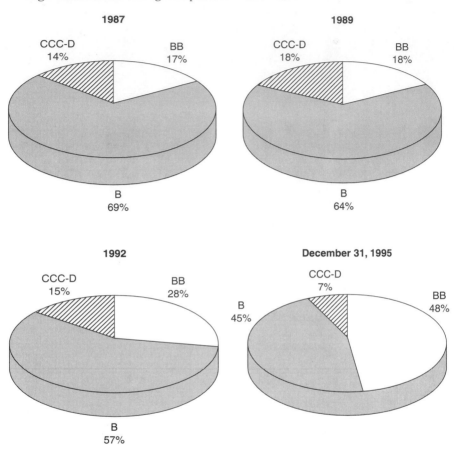

Source: Lehman Brothers High-Yield Research.

the changes in the market by rating quality since 1987. In 1995, double-B issuers represented 48 percent of the high-yield market, up substantially from 18 percent in 1989.

With respect to industry concentrations, high-yield debt raised to finance growth in the media, cable, and telecommunications industries has been the most dramatic change over the past several years. Exhibit 16–8 shows the breakdown by industry concentrations as reflected in the Lehman Brothers High-Yield Index. Media, cable, and telecommunications represented 9.6 percent of the high-yield market in 1992 but has grown to almost 14 percent in 1995. In 1994 and 1995, the media/telecommunications sector represented approximately 33 percent of total new-issue volume. Improving fundamentals in certain other industries have

EXHIBIT   16–8

High-Yield Market Composition by Industry: 1992 vs. 1995

	Percent		Par-Weighted Average Coupon		Average Maturity		Market-Weighted Average Rating	
	Dec-92	Dec-95	Dec-92	Dec-95	Dec-92	Dec-95	Dec-92	Dec-95
Composite	**100.00%**	**100.00%**	**10.78**	**8.63**	**8.67**	**8.51**	**B1/B2**	**BA3/B1**
Industrial	*80.70%*	*82.80%*	*10.92*	*8.87*	*8.61*	*8.21*	*B1/B2*	*BA3/B1*
Basic industry	7.20	13.00	11.34	9.82	8.96	7.19	B1/B2	BA3/B1
Chemicals	2.30	3.30	11.48	9.02	13.69	7.60	B1/B2	BA3/B1
Metals	2.40	3.50	12.22	10.73	6.73	6.93	B1/B2	BA3/B1
Paper	2.50	6.20	10.26	9.72	6.80	7.12	B1/B2	BA3/B1
Other	0.00	0.00	0.00	0.00	0.00	0.00	NA	NA
Capital goods	16.10	10.40	11.29	8.57	8.09	8.06	B2/B3	B1/B2
Aerospace	1.00	0.70	11.97	11.33	9.23	8.13	B1/B2	B1/B2
Building								
materials	2.60	2.30	11.95	5.62	8.89	8.28	CAA1/CAA2	BA3/B1
Conglomerates	3.80	2.10	9.95	8.78	8.23	10.44	B3/CAA1	BA3/B1
Constr.								
machinery	0.50	0.00	11.55	0.00	7.31	0.00	BA3/B1	NA
Packaging	4.80	2.40	11.04	9.52	8.5	7.23	B1/B2	B1/B2
Defense	0.20	0.40	12.13	10.05	6.7	6.19	BA3/BA3	BA3/B1
Environmental	0.00	0.50	0.00	10.47	0.00	7.08	NA	B2/B3
Others	3.30	2.00	12.12	9.12	6.54	6.93	B3/CAA1	B1/B2
Consumer cyclical	28.80	36.60	11.04	8.47	9.36	8.92	B1/B2	BA3/B1
Automotive	5.10	1.80	12.91	9.87	13.38	6.88	B1/B2	B1/B2
Entertainment	1.50	6.50	11.28	8.46	10.94	12.26	BA3/B1	BA1/BA2
Gaming	3.50	3.90	11.01	11.31	6.94	7.20	B2/B3	BA3/B1
Home								
construction	0.60	1.50	11.86	10.52	8.08	6.74	B1/B2	B1/B2
Lodging	1.90	1.10	10.01	9.93	7.95	8.44	BA2/BA3	BA3/B1
Media—cable	6.30	9.60	10.57	6.51	9.39	10.11	BA3/B1	BA3/B1
Media—noncable	3.30	4.40	10.32	6.95	9.52	8.32	BA3/B1	B1/B2
Retailers	3.30	3.50	11.07	9.99	7.36	6.89	B2/B3	B1/B2
Services	1.50	2.10	7.52	10.19	9.25	6.70	B1/B2	B1/B2
Textile	1.50	1.50	12.19	10.11	6.46	7.25	B2/B3	B1/B2
Others	0.40	0.60	13.70	3.62	7.13	5.51	B2/B3	BA3/B1
Consumer								
noncyclical	18.30	12.20	9.66	9.16	8.4	7.48	B1/B2	B1/B2
Beverage	0.70	0.70	5.19	8.79	7.63	6.66	B2/B3	B2/B3
Consumer								
products	1.40	1.50	12.66	5.6	4.25	5.05	B3/CAA1	B2/B3
Food	2.20	2.50	11.47	9.62	7.34	9.12	BA3/B1	BA3/B1
Health care	3.60	3.10	10.92	10.02	9.84	7.71	B1/B2	B1/B2
Pharmaceuticals	0.30	0.10	14.25	6.75	6.76	8.08	B2/B3	BA1/BA1

continued

EXHIBIT 16-8

(Continued)

	Percent		Par-Weighted Average Coupon		Average Maturity		Market-Weighted Average Rating	
	Dec. 92	Dec. 95	Dec. 92	Dec. 95	Dec. 92	Dec. 95	Dec. 92	Dec. 95
Composite	100.00%	100.00%	10.78	8.63	8.67	8.51	B1/B2	BA3/B1
Consumer								
noncyclical (cont.)	18.30	12.20	9.66	9.16	8.4	7.48	B1/B2	B1/B2
Supermarkets	7.60	4.10	9.63	9.8	9.2	7.25	B1/B2	BA3/B1
Tobacco	1.90	0.00	3.62	0.00	8.16	0.00	BA1/BA2	NA
Others	0.50	0.30	12.87	9.13	5.41	8.3	CAA1/CAA2	BA2/BA3
Energy	4.30	5.70	10.65	8.95	9.38	7.11	BA3/B1	BA3/B1
Independent	2.60	3.10	9.85	9.82	9.85	6.85	BA3/B1	BA3/B1
Integrated	0.00	0.00	0.00	0.00	0.00	0.00	NA	NA
Oil field services	0.50%	0.70%	12.44	11.04	8.27	6.32	BA3/B1	B1/B2
Refining	0.80%	0.90%	10.65	6.50	8.68	7.54	BA2/BA3	BA3/B1
Others	0.50%	1.10%	12.47	7.71	9.01	7.93	CAA1/CAA2	BA3/B1
Technology	3.50%	1.90%	11.94	8.95	6.40	8.38	B2/B3	BA3/B1
Transportation	2.50%	3.00%	13.2	9.77	5.74	9.65	B1/B2	B1/B2
Airlines	0.30%	1.60%	12.83	9.68	2.26	11.29	CAA1/CAA2	B1/B2
Railroads	1.20%	0.30%	13.88	9.38	6.76	9.62	B1/B2	BA3/BA3
Services	0.90%	0.90%	12.68	10.19	5.50	6.45	BA3/B1	B2/B3
Others	0.00%	0.20%	0.00	8.96	0.00	10.44	NA	BA1/BA2
Utilities	*8.60*	*12.20*	*10.10*	*6.58*	*10.73*	*10.98*	*BA3/B1*	*BA3/B1*
Electric	2.90	6.70	9.71	8.88	11.79	13.61	BA2/BA3	BA2/BA3
Telecommunication	1.20	4.60	13.26	3.42	5.40	7.56	B3/CAA1	B2/B3
Natural gas	4.50	0.90	9.60	9.34	11.40	9.00	BA3/B1	BA1/BA2
Distributors	0.20	0.20	9.54	10.09	17.37	6.18	BA2/BA2	BA2/BA3
Pipelines	4.30	0.70	9.6	9.12	11.14	9.82	BA3/B1	BA1/BA1
Water	0.00	0.00	0	0	0	0	NA	NA
Finance	*9.50%*	*3.70%*	*10.25*	*8.75*	*7.12*	*7.48*	*BA3/B1*	*BA2/BA3*
Banking	2.40	0.60	10.60	4.40	7.09	11.40	BA3/B1	BA2/BA3
Brokerage	0.00	0.00	0.00	0.00	0.00	0.00	NA	NA
Financial Cos.	4.90	0.50	9.83	10.29	7.34	5.13	B1/B2	B2/B3
Captive	4.40	0.00	10.22	0.00	7.78	0.00	B1/B2	NA
noncaptive	0.60	0.50	7.60	10.29	3.82	5.13	BA2/BA3	B2/B3
Consumer	0.00	0.20	0.00	10.09	0.00	5.79	NA	D/D
Diversified	0.60	0.30	7.60	10.50	3.82	4.69	BA2/BA3	BA2/BA3
Insurance	1.80	1.90	11.50	10.05	7.15	7.11	BA3/B1	BA2/BA3
Others	0.40	0.80	6.00	9.64	4.22	6.81	B2/B2	BA2/BA3
Yankees	*0.70%*	*1.20%*	*9.76*	*9.33*	*10.50*	*8.38*	*BA1/BA2*	*BA2/BA3*
Canadians	0.00	0.00	0.00	0.00	0.00	0.00	NA	NA
Corporates	0.70	1.20	10.38	9.33	10.94	8.38	BA1/BA2	BA2/BA3

Source: Lehman Brothers High-Yield Research.

opened previously closed financing windows. In the paper sector, for example, improved industry profitability led to a dramatic rise in new issuance as the sector increased from 2.5 percent of the market to 6.2 percent. The capital goods sector, on the other hand, fell to 10.4 percent of the market from 16.1 percent over the same time period, driven by upgrades and debt repayment.

HISTORICAL RETURN EXPERIENCE

The annual returns of the high-yield market over the past decade have been affected by the overall interest-rate environment, the macroeconomic situation, and certain exogenous events. In the 1989–1990 time frame, for example, restrictions on investing in high-yield securities imposed by Congress and regulators on the thrift and insurance industries caused a severe supply/demand imbalance that exacerbated the problems in the market caused by the overall slowdown in economic activity. In 1990, Lehman's index declined 9.6 percent, the worst performance in the past decade. In 1991 and 1992, however, with an improving economy providing the significant boost, the high-yield market performed spectacularly, with total returns of 46.1 percent and 15.8 percent, respectively. In the economic climate of the 1992–1995 period, marked by a favorable combination of moderate growth and low interest rates, the market has continued to perform well, with total returns in the 16 percent to 19 percent range (excluding the 1 percent decline in 1994 when the dramatic increase in overall interest rates caused nearly every segment of the bond market to perform poorly).

The performance of the high yield market compares very favorably to that of other financial asset classes. Exhibit 16–9 summarizes the performance since 1984 of the Lehman Brothers High Yield Index and other indices of major asset classes. From 1984 to 1995, Lehman's High Yield index returned 307.5 percent while Lehman's Government Bond Index increased 237.9 percent. Only the 455.1 percent return of the S&P 500 outperformed the high yield market. Lehman Brothers' Investment-Grade Corporate Index generated a 291.4 percent return over the same period. The results since 1990 are particularly noteworthy as the high yield sector outperformed all asset classes that were analyzed. High yield was up 111.3 percent, well above the investment-grade return of 81.6 percent and even above the S&P 500 return of 106.7 percent. We have also included the standard deviations for the various returns to point out the relative volatility. As one would expect, high yield returns have had the most volatility over the 1984–1995 period among all the sectors measured.

Exhibit 16–10 further breaks down the returns of the market by credit quality. Lower rated credits, indicating greater risk of default, presumably should provide higher total returns than less risky securities. Historical returns by credit rating quality demonstrate this clearly. From 1990 to 1995, Lehman's index of triple-C rated credits provided a total return of 124.2 percent, while the double-B index returned 97.2 percent. However, when looking at the 1984–1995 period, the triple-C sector performed worst, as the high default experienced took its toll on

EXHIBIT 16–9

High-Yield Total Returns versus Other Asset Classes, 1984–1995

	Lehman High-Yield Corporate	Lehman Inv. Grade Corporate	S&P 500	Lehman Eurobond	Lehman Government	Lehman Mortgage
1984	9.70%	16.62%	6.27%	N/A	14.50%	15.79%
1985	25.64	24.06	32.16	N/A	20.43	25.21
1986	17.45	16.53	18.47	N/A	15.31	13.43
1987	4.99	2.56	5.23	1.35%	2.20	4.29
1988	12.53	9.22	16.81	9.12	7.03	8.72
1989	0.83	14.09	31.49	13.54	14.23	15.35
1990	−9.59	7.05	−3.15	8.84	8.72	10.72
1991	46.08	18.51	30.45	16.49	15.32	15.72
1992	15.75	8.69	7.61	8.17	7.23	6.95
1993	17.12	12.16	10.08	10.30	10.66	6.84
1994	−1.03	−3.93	1.32	−2.41	−3.37	−1.61
1995	19.17	22.25	37.58	16.91	18.34	16.80
Total return (1984–1995)	307.52	291.35	455.06	NA	237.92	261.95
Total return (1984–1989)	92.84	115.47	168.48	NA	98.66	115.09
Total return (1990–1995)	111.33	81.63	106.74	72.59	70.10	68.28
Annualized (1984–1995)	12.42	12.04	15.35	NA	10.68	11.32
Annualized (1984–1989)	11.57	13.65	17.89	NA	12.12	13.62
Annualized (1990–1995)	13.28	10.46	12.87	9.52	9.26	9.06
Mean (1984–1995)	13.22%	12.32%	16.19%	9.14%	10.88%	11.52%
Mean (1984–1989)	11.86%	13.85%	18.41%	8.00%	12.28%	13.80%
Mean (1990–1995)	14.58%	10.79%	13.98%	9.72%	9.48%	9.24%
Standard deviation (1984–1995)	14.35%	8.11%	13.75%	6.42%	6.89%	7.04%
Standard deviation (1984–1989)	8.89%	7.32%	11.69%	6.17%	6.53%	7.11%
Standard deviation (1990–1995)	19.23%	9.25%	16.36%	7.05%	7.55%	6.78%

Source: Lehman Brothers High-Yield Research.

the total return. As expected, the standard deviation of the triple-C index was considerably higher than the double-B index.

Another way of measuring and analyzing the high-yield market is to examine the relative yield spread over the risk-free yield of the Treasury market. As logic (and history) would dictate, investors demand higher yield and thus wider

EXHIBIT 16–10

High-Yield Total Returns by Credit Quality: 1984–1995

	High-Yield	BB	B	CCC	S&P 500
1984	9.70%	9.67%	10.75%	−5.39%	6.27%
1985	25.64	27.06	22.94	17.19	32.16
1986	17.45	23.33	16.80	9.37	18.47
1987	4.99	6.12	4.85	3.95	5.23
1988	12.53	13.77	12.92	9.25	16.81
1989	0.83	7.81	0.86	−14.26	31.49
1990	−9.59	0.07	−8.62	−22.64	−3.15
1991	46.08	24.43	43.34	83.17	30.45
1992	15.75	12.07	15.91	22.88	7.61
1993	17.12	15.86	16.91	20.01	10.08
1994	−1.03	−0.39	0.15	−11.93	1.32
1995	19.17	21.84	16.57	21.82	37.58
Total return (1984–1995)	307.52	341.17	293.38	164.72	455.06
Total return (1984–1989)	92.84	123.71	89.92	18.09	168.48
Total return (1990–1995)	111.33	97.20	107.13	124.16	106.74
Annualized (1984–1995)	12.42	13.17	12.09	8.45	15.35
Annualized (1984–1989)	11.57	14.36	11.28	2.81	17.89
Annualized (1990–1995)	13.28	11.98	12.90	14.40	12.87
Mean (1984–1995)	13.22%	13.47%	12.78%	11.12%	16.19%
Mean (1984–1989)	11.86%	14.63%	11.52%	3.35%	18.41%
Mean (1990–1995)	14.58%	12.31%	14.04%	18.88%	13.98%
Standard deviation (1984–1995)	14.35%	9.30%	13.22%	27.31%	13.75%
Standard deviation (1984–1989)	8.89%	8.65%	7.99%	11.40%	11.69%
Standard deviation (1990–1995)	19.23%	10.60%	17.79%	36.97%	16.36%

Source: Lehman Brothers High-Yield Research.

spreads to compensate them for investing in riskier securities. Over the past decade, with the notable exception of the 1989–1990 period, yield spreads on high securities have been in a relatively consistent band. As shown in Exhibit 16–11, spreads for single-B rated securities have been between 400 and 600 basis points over the Treasury curve, excluding the 1989–1990 period. During the

EXHIBIT 16–11

Spreads by Credit Quality: 1987–1995

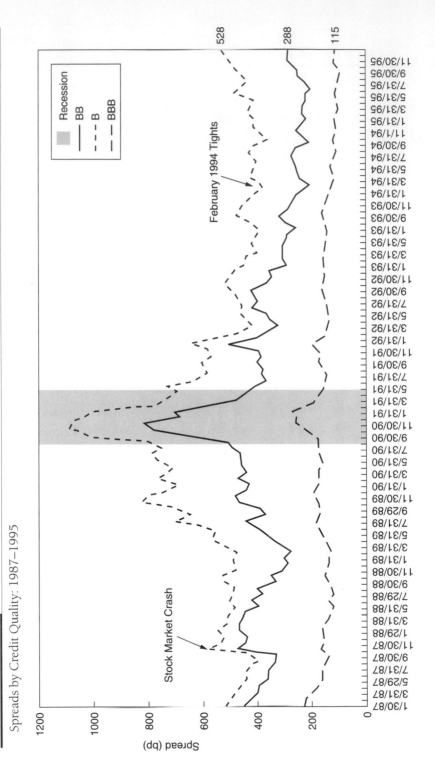

E X H I B I T   16-12

Estimated Ownership of Liquid High-Yield Securities

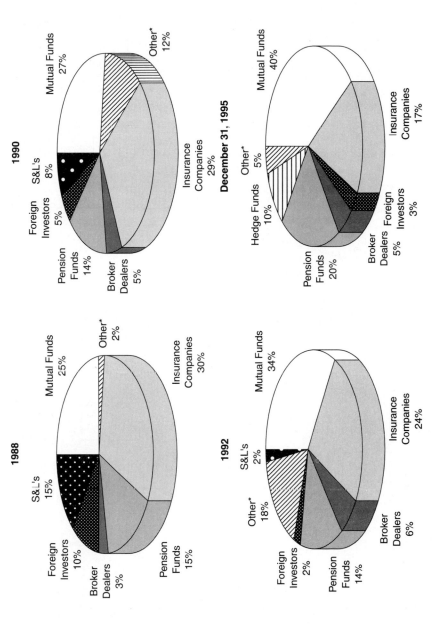

*Other includes equity mutual funds, households, and other.

Source: Lehman Brothers Estimates.

High-Yield Mutual Fund Flows vs. Total Return: 1994–1995

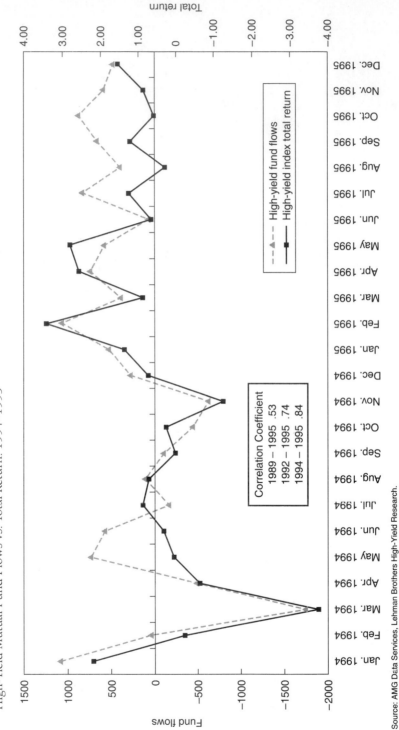

Source: AMG Data Services, Lehman Brothers High-Yield Research.

Defauts as a Percent of Outstanding High-Yield Debt: 1983–1995

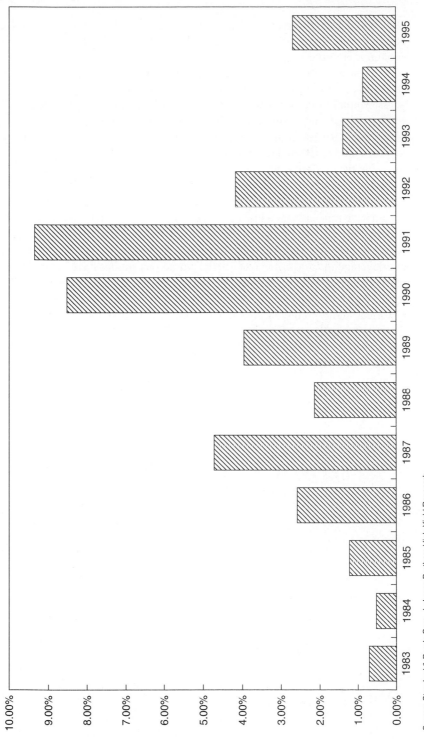

Source: Standard & Poor's Corp., Lehman Brothers High-Yield Research.

1989–1990 period, spreads widened out to over 1,000 basis points over the curve due to the previously discussed supply/demand imbalance and also to the weak economic environment at that time.

Historical returns have developed a high correlation to mutual funds flow of cash as the investor profile of the high-yield market has changed over the past five years. Mutual funds are now the dominant holder of high-yield securities, representing approximately 40 percent of the total market, up from 25 percent in 1988 (see Exhibit 16–12). Exhibit 16–13 charts the remarkably close correlation of the market's total return and mutual funds flow data.

No discussion of the high-yield market is complete without a word about historical default rates. Exhibit 16–14 shows the historical defaults as a percentage of total debt outstanding over the past 13 years. Annual default rates over this period have ranged from a low of 0.5 percent in 1984 to a high of just over 9 percent in 1991. The surge in defaults in the 1990–1991 time period was driven by several factors including the overall economic recession and the numerous large, overleveraged LBOs of the late 1980s. Numerous studies have been done on the market's historical default rates that have concluded an average default rate of roughly 3 percent per year. Several factors have limited the usefulness of these historical studies in predicting future default rates. These factors include the relatively brief history of the "mature" high-yield market, the exogenous events of the late 1980s, and finally the overall credit quality improvement of the market in the past five years.

17

⑥ INTERNATIONAL BOND MARKETS AND INSTRUMENTS

Christopher B. Steward, CFA
Vice President
Scudder, Stevens and Clark

Adam M. Greshin, CFA
Principal
Scudder, Stevens and Clark

INTRODUCTION

International bond investing is hardly a new activity. Cross-border investments in government bonds were common before the first World War. By 1920, Moody's was providing credit ratings on some 50 sovereign borrowers. However, most of these foreign investments ended badly for U.S. investors. Hyperinflation under the German Weimar Republic of the 1920s rendered the Reichsmark worthless. Similarly, during the 1920s U.S. investors saw their foreign investments decline in U.S. dollar terms by 86 percent in France, 70 percent in Italy, and 50 percent in Spain. Interestingly, some of the countries which avoided sharp devaluations during this period (including the U.K., Sweden, and surprisingly, Argentina) have lost much of their value since the collapse of the Bretton Woods system of fixed exchange rates in the 1970s. Between 1930 and 1970, capital controls and domestic regulations sharply curtailed cross-border bond investment. The offshore markets and banks led the way toward greater cross-border investment flows in the early 1980s, prompting governments to introduce domestic market reforms liberalizing capital flows in money, bond, and equity markets. However, some foreign bond markets, such as Italy's, were closed to foreign investors until 1990.[1]

---

1. See Michael Mussa and Morris Goldstein, "The Integration of World Capital Markets," in *Changing Capital Markets: Implications for Monetary Policy* (Federal Reserve Bank of Kansas, 1993) for a more complete discussion.

An explosion in international bond trading has occurred over the past 10 years, driven by reductions in capital controls, spectacular technological advances in the dissemination of information, and in computing power to track portfolios and forecast capital market trends. A large rise in debt issuance, primarily by governments running large budget deficits, has contributed to a fourfold increase in the nominal value of developed county debt outstanding, from $4.6 trillion in 1984 to $18.5 trillion in 1994.[2] The United States still has the largest bond market, although its share of total debt outstanding has decreased from over 50 percent in 1984 to 43.4 percent in 1994. If Eurodollar bond issues, which are traded offshore, are stripped out, nearly two-thirds of the world's bonds are traded outside of the U.S. market. The variety of borrowers in the international bond markets has increased dramatically, and financing techniques in these markets now rival the U.S. domestic market in their sophistication. Although the sheer size of the U.S. economy ensures a central role for U.S. bonds in world capital markets, the growth in volume and turnover in international bonds suggests that a general understanding of their characteristics is in order.

This chapter will attempt to provide a broad overview of the instruments, markets, and players in international bond investing. First, the instruments and markets for the U.S.-pay sector of the international bond market are described, including emerging market debt. Then the foreign-pay sectors of the international bond market are described, with emphasis placed on the contribution of currency to returns for U.S. dollar-based investors. The rationale for international bond investing and the impact of including international bonds in a U.S. bond portfolio, are discussed in Chapter 54.

Do international bonds have a role for U.S. dollar-based investors? Domestic bonds are often included in diversified portfolios because their price movements are generally less volatile than equities, they pay a known amount of interest at regular intervals, and they mature; that is, with high credit bonds, you are nearly certain to get your money back. U.S. dollar-denominated international bonds behave much like domestic U.S. bonds. But foreign-pay bonds, because of the currency component, are much more volatile. How should foreign-pay bonds be used in diversified portfolios? How should their performance be judged? Does currency hedging eliminate the diversification benefit of holding international bonds? These are some of the questions addressed below.

THE INSTRUMENTS: EURO, FOREIGN, AND GLOBAL

International bonds are divided into three general categories: domestic, Euro, and foreign, depending on the domicile of the issuer, the nature of the underwriting syndicate, the domicile of the primary buyers, and the currency denomination.

---

2. This, and other data on the size of the international bond market is from data published by Salomon Brothers, Inc. in *How Big Is the World Bond Market—1995 Update* (August 1995) and *Eurobond Market Trends* (various dates).

Domestic bonds are issued, underwritten, and traded under the currency and regulations of a country's bond market by a borrower located within the country. Eurobonds are underwritten by an international syndicate and traded outside of any one domestic market. Foreign bonds are issued under the regulations of a domestic market and are intended primarily for that country's domestic investors by a foreign-domiciled borrower. Global bonds are a hybrid, designed to trade and settle in both the Euro, and U.S. foreign or Yankee markets.

The most decisive influence on the price or yield of a bond is currency denomination. Thus, for U.S. investors, the pertinent division is between those international bonds that are denominated in U.S. dollars and those denominated in other currencies. Regardless of the domicile of the issuer, the buyer, or the trading market, prices of issues denominated in U.S. dollars (U.S.-pay) are affected principally by the direction of U.S. interest rates, whereas prices of issues denominated in other currencies (foreign-pay) are determined primarily by movement of interest rates in the country of the currency denomination. Thus, analysis of international bond investing must be separated into two parts: U.S.-pay and foreign-pay.

Most U.S.-pay international bonds can be included in a domestic bond portfolio with little change to the management style and overall risk profile of the portfolio. In most cases, a marginal extra effort is all that is required to analyze the credits of a few new unfamiliar issuers and to learn the settlement procedures for Eurodollar bonds. The notable exception in the U.S.-pay area is in emerging market debt, which, as detailed below, can be far more volatile than most other U.S.-pay bonds. The currency component of foreign-pay bonds, however, entails a fair degree of volatility of returns and has a far different risk profile than domestic U.S., and U.S.-pay international bonds. The question of currency hedging (either passive, active, or not at all), plus considerations of trading hours, settlement procedures, withholding taxes, and other nuances of trading foreign-pay international bonds, require much greater training and effort to manage them effectively.

U.S.-PAY INTERNATIONAL BONDS

The U.S.-pay international bond market consists of Eurodollar bonds, which are issued and traded outside any one domestic market, and Yankee bonds, which are issued and traded primarily in the United States. Global bonds are issued in both the Yankee and Eurodollar markets simultaneously, but domestic investors are generally indifferent between global and straight Yankee issues except where liquidity differs. Before examining the instruments in depth, some of the more basic questions regarding U.S.-pay international bonds need to be addressed.

Why do foreign-domiciled issuers borrow in the U.S.-dollar markets? First, the U.S. bond market is the largest, most liquid, and most sophisticated of the world's bond markets. By issuing in the U.S. market, foreign entities diversify their sources of funding. Also, as companies have become more global in production and distribution, they have assets and liabilities in many different currencies and hence are less tied to their domestic bond markets. Financial innovations, particularly the advent of the interest-rate and currency swap markets, have greatly expanded the diversity of borrowers, notably in the corporate sector. Companies in need of floating-rate finance have been able to combine a fixed-coupon bond with an interest-rate swap to create a cheaper means of finance than a traditional floating-rate note. Similarly, when currency swap terms are favorable, a company in need of, say, deutschemark funds could issue a Eurodollar bond and combine it with a currency swap to create a cheaper source of deutschemark funds than a traditional deutschemark bond.

Why should U.S. dollar-based investors be interested in U.S.-pay international bonds? Yankee bonds are SEC registered and trade like any other U.S. domestic bond. The credit quality of issuers in the Yankee market is very high, although the credit quality of new issuers has been declining in recent years. Eurobonds are generally less liquid than Yankee bonds but can sometimes offer more attractive yields and a broader list of available credits. As most international bond issues are rated by the major rating agencies, for a little additional credit work, investors may be able to find a higher yield on a U.S.-pay international bond than on other comparably rated issues, especially where the credit may be less familiar to United States investors.

What is the difference between a Yankee and a Eurodollar bond? The primary difference is SEC registration. Yankee bonds are registered with the SEC, and issued, and traded in the United States; Eurodollar bonds are issued outside the United States and traded primarily by foreigners. Eurodollar bonds are issued mostly by corporate issuers; Yankees are issued mostly by high credit-quality sovereign and sovereign-guaranteed issuers. The size of the Eurodollar market, measured at $620 billion in bonds outstanding in 1994, is more than four times the size of the Yankee market of $138 billion. In addition, Yankees are registered securities; Eurodollar bonds are issued in unregistered, or bearer, form. Yankees pay interest semiannually; Eurodollar bonds carry annual coupons.

Eurodollar Bonds

The prefix "Euro" has come to mean offshore. The Eurodollar banking market began during the cold war as the Soviets, wary that the United States might freeze their dollar deposits, preferred to hold their dollar-denominated bank deposits outside the reach of the U.S. authorities. The Eurodollar market grew as banks sought to avoid domestic banking restrictions such as Regulation Q, which set a ceiling on interest levels paid on deposits, and the Glass-Steagall Act, which prohibited banks from engaging in underwriting and brokerage. Restrictions placed on direct investment overseas by U.S. companies in 1968 encouraged companies to raise capital offshore, thus increasing the size of the Eurobond market. However, the most significant growth in the Eurodollar market occurred in the late 1970s as the recycling of large dollar surpluses by OPEC countries (as oil is denominated in dollars) injected huge amounts of liquidity into the market.

Balance-of-payments deficits, due to higher oil prices, also increased sovereign and sovereign-guaranteed Eurodollar issuance.

Eurodollar bonds are the largest single component of the Eurobond market, which encompasses securities of all different currency denominations. Eurodollar bonds are:

1. Denominated in U.S. dollars.

2. Issued and traded outside the jurisdiction of any single country.

3. Underwritten by an international syndicate.

4. Issued in bearer (unregistered) form.

Since Eurodollar bonds are not registered with the SEC, as U.S. domestic new issues are required to be, underwriters are legally prohibited from selling new issues to the U.S. public until the issue has "come to rest" and a seasoning period has expired. An issue is usually considered seasoned 40 days after it has been fully distributed.[3] This seasoning requirement effectively locks U.S. investors out of the primary market. Even though a portion of Eurodollar outstandings end up in U.S.-based portfolios after the seasoning period expires, the lack of participation of U.S. investors in new offerings ensures that the Eurodollar market will remain dominated by foreign-based investors. Although no single location has been designated for Eurodollar market making, London is the de facto primary trading center for all Eurobonds.

The Eurodollar bond market has grown dramatically from its humble beginnings in the early 1960s, although the vast majority of growth has occurred in only the past 10 years. In 1980, total Eurodollar new issuance was a still modest $16 billion. By 1994, new-issue volume had grown by a factor of 10 as $156.4 billion of new issues were brought to market — more than 49 percent of total Eurobond new issuance. Marketability of Eurodollar bonds has improved as the market has grown, but there are still many examples of straight fixed-coupon bonds that trade infrequently, particularly among the older issues, which may be only $50 million or less in individual issue size. Normal issue size today is $100–300 million. Despite the increase in market size, liquidity will remain somewhat constrained by the popularity of Eurodollar bonds among European retail investors, who are likely to buy bonds and tuck them away until maturity. Since Eurobonds are held in bearer (unregistered) form, details about major holders of Eurodollar bonds are often unreliable, but market participants estimate retail investors account for 40 to 50 percent of the market.

Borrowers in the Eurodollar bond market may be divided into four major groups: sovereign, supranational agency, corporate, and financial. Supranational agencies, such as the World Bank and the European Investment Bank, are consis-

---

3. The Securities and Exchange Commission's revised Regulation S reduced the seasoning period from 90 to 40 days. Other changes in SEC regulations, notably Regulation 144A, make the Euromarkets and the U.S. domestic bond markets more fungible.

tently among the top borrowers, reflecting their constant need for development financing and their lack of "home" issuance market. Sovereign and sovereign-backed borrowers are also prominent, although the growth in sovereign Eurodollar issuance slowed in the late 1980s as governments either cut back on their external borrowing in favor of their domestic bond markets, or chose to borrow in the nondollar markets to diversify their currency exposure. Fiscal retrenchment in most developed countries and the growth of domestic bond markets have served to reduce the role that sovereign issuers play in the primary Eurobond market. Governments, which were a major force in 1992 and 1993, issued far fewer Eurobonds in 1994 and 1995.

The future of the Eurodollar bond market is largely a function of the domestic regulatory environment in the major issuer countries. The dominating presence of Japanese companies among Eurodollar borrowers in the late 1980s has diminished in recent years. This reflects both the opening up of the Japanese domestic bond market (thus diminishing the relative attractiveness of issuing in the offshore market) and intense fiscal retrenchment by Japanese companies as evidenced by an astounding 21 percent decline in real Japanese private nonresidential investment in the three years through 1994. Japan, which may have accounted for as much as 50 percent of new-issue volume in the Eurodollar bond market in 1989, has trailed behind issuance by both U.S. and German borrowers in total Eurobond issuance in 1994 and 1995. In addition, as many countries have sought to develop and expand their local domestic markets, issuance has shifted to local currency.

The course of the U.S. dollar and U.S. interest rates have the greatest short-term impact on the growth of the Eurodollar bond market. The strength in the dollar from 1987 to 1990, particularly against the yen, increased investor appetite for dollar-denominated securities and encouraged dollar bond issuance. Similarly, the dollar's weakness in 1994 and 1995 led to less issuance of Eurodollar bonds by Japanese borrowers. The relative and absolute level of U.S. interest rates also has a substantial impact on Eurodollar bond issuance. For example, the rally in the U.S. bond market in 1986, which brought interest rates down toward 7 percent, their lowest level of the decade, resulted in a sharp expansion of corporate borrowing, despite a rapidly depreciating dollar.

The direction of U.S. interest rates and the value of the dollar will continue to have an impact on the size and liquidity of the Eurodollar bond market. Over the long term, however, the survivability of the market will be decided by the global trend toward financial deregulation. To the extent that national governments continue to dismantle the laws that hobble the development of domestic bond markets, the attraction of Eurodollar bonds, and all Eurobonds, to issuers and investors will diminish. Running counter to this trend, the growth of global bonds (discussed below), which allows for access to a broad array of investors across national and offshore markets, has served to increase the attractiveness of the Eurobond market.

Yankee Bonds

The other portion of the U.S.-pay international bond market, referred to as the Yankee bond market, encompasses those foreign-domiciled issuers who register with the SEC and borrow dollars via issues underwritten by a U.S. syndicate for delivery in the United States.[4] The principal trading market is in the United States, although foreign buyers can and do participate. Unlike Eurodollar bonds, Yankee bonds pay interest semiannually.

The Yankee market is much older than the Eurodollar market. Overseas borrowers first issued Yankee bonds in the early 1900s, when the U.S. became the world's preeminent creditor nation. The repayment record of these early issues was not good; as much as one-third of the outstanding "foreign" bonds in the United States were in default on interest payments by the mid-1930s. After years of slow growth the market expanded rapidly after the abolition of the interest-equalization tax in 1974.[5] Between 1989 and 1995, total bonds outstanding in the Yankee market more than doubled, from $66 billion to $137.5 billion, a figure rivaling other sectors of the U.S. corporate market in size.

Supranational agencies and Canadian provinces (including provincial utilities) have historically been the most prominent Yankee issuers, comprising well over half the total market (see Exhibit 17–1 and Exhibit 17–2). The corporate sector, which is a major borrower in the Eurodollar bond market, is of only minor importance in the Yankee bond market. The increased use of global bonds, however, has confused the distinction between the Yankee and Eurodollar bond markets. The rankings of top issuers in the Yankee market change, depending upon whether global bonds are included or excluded. For example, Exhibit 17–1 excludes U.S. agency-issued global bonds, which have increased in recent years.

The credit quality of the Yankee market has changed dramatically over the past 11 years, along with its composition, as shown in Exhibit 17–2. Issuance by Canadian Provinces, which had dominated the Yankee market, dropped dramatically, while issuance by financial institutions and corporates has risen. Also, lower quality issuers have made substantial inroads into the Yankee market. Whereas in 1985 all of the Yankee bond issuers were rated AA or better, by 1995 that figure had dropped to 58.9 percent.

---

4. A small portion of outstanding Yankee bonds are foreign-currency denominated. These are not included in this analysis.
5. The interest equalization tax was imposed on purchases of foreign securities by U.S. residents during the years 1963–1974. The intent and effect of the tax was to discourage foreign borrowing in the United States by increasing the cost of capital. To make returns after the IET competitive with rates on domestic issues, gross rates on foreign borrowings had to be higher than would otherwise have been the case.

E X H I B I T   17–1

Top U.S. Dollar Global and Yankee Borrowers by Issuance Volume
January 1992 through December 1995

Issuer	Total New Issuance Volume ($ Billion)
Province of Ontario	$ 11.0
Republic of Italy	5.5
Republic of Finland	4.5
BCH Cayman Island (subordinated)	3.3
Province of Quebec	3.2
Hydro Quebec	3.2
Canada	3.0
Korea Development Bank	3.0
Province of Saskatchewan	2.5
Grand Metropolitan	2.4
Hanson Overseas B.V.	2.0
Kingdom of Sweden	2.0
Korea Electric Power Corp.	2.0
Province of Manitoba	2.0
Total	**$49.6**

Source: Salomon Brothers.

The Market for Eurodollar and Yankee Bonds

Foreign investors play a major role in the Yankee market, although the market's
location in the United States prevents foreigners from having as dominating a
presence as they have in the Euromarkets. Prior to 1984, foreign investors had a
preference for U.S.-pay international bonds, which include both Yankees and Eurodollar issues, because they were not subject to the 30 percent withholding tax
imposed by the U.S. government on all interest paid to foreigners. When the withholding tax exception was abolished in July 1984, a major advantage of U.S.-pay
international bonds over U.S. Treasuries and domestic corporate bonds was removed. The result was a cheapening of Yankees and Euros relative to the U.S. domestic market, but foreign investor support remained strong. U.S.-pay
international bonds offer a yield advantage over U.S. government bonds, usually
due to the lesser liquidity and credit quality of international issues, and foreign
buyers are often more familiar with Yankee and Eurodollar credits than they are
with U.S. domestic credits. Finally, Yankee and Eurodollar issuers sometimes
compensate for their "foreign" status in the U.S.-pay market by offering bonds

E X H I B I T   17–2

Changing Issuer Composition and Credit Quality of the Yankee Market

Issuers

	Corporates	Sovereigns	Supernationals	Financials	Canadian Provinces
1985	2.0%	32.0%	19.0%	4.0%	43.0%
1989	18.8	18.3	8.4	20.8	33.7
1991	32.9	15.1	6.3	9.8	35.9
1993	29.1	30.8	1.1	5.5	33.5
1995	32.9	23.9	8.6	27.0	7.6

Credit Quality

	AAA	AA	A	BBB	BB
1985	83.0%	17.0%			
1989	28.0	37.0	35.0%		
1991	14.5	44.1	36.7	4.7%	
1993	7.4	37.9	36.8	11.1	6.8%
1995	9.3	49.6	30.1	9.0	2.0

Source: Salomon Brothers.

with shorter maturities and greater call protection—structures that traditionally appeal to overseas investors.

For these reasons, when foreign buyers seek exposure to U.S.-pay bonds, they often buy U.S.-pay international bonds—Eurodollar or Yankee—instead of domestic issues. The degree of interest of foreign buyers in U.S.-pay securities, or lack thereof, is reflected in narrowing or widening of the yield spread to U.S. Treasury bonds. This is particularly true of Eurodollar bonds, since foreign interest governs this market to a greater extent than the Yankee market, which is more attuned to U.S. investor preferences. The fact that the Eurodollar market and the Yankee market have different investor bases occasionally leads to trading disparities between the two markets. For example, similarly structured Canadian Yankee bonds often trade at lower yields than Canadian Eurodollar bonds because U.S. investors tend to be more comfortable with Canadian credits due to the close proximity of the two countries.

The globalization of the investment world has brought the Yankee and Eurodollar bond markets closer together, and it is not uncommon for investors to arbitrage the two markets when yield disparities appear. The dividing line between the two markets has become increasingly blurred with the advent of the "global bond." The World Bank issued the first global bond in 1989, with a $1.5 billion issue that was placed simultaneously in both the Yankee and the Eurodollar markets. The idea was to create an instrument that had attributes of both a Yankee bond and a Eurodollar bond and thereby do away with the market segmentation that inhibited liquidity and created yield disparities. The success of global bond issues is further evidence of the melding of the Euro and domestic markets that has accelerated as barriers to cross-border capital movements have been lowered.

The global bond market has been primarily utilized by central governments and supranational organizations. However, as many governments have endeavored to increase the depth and liquidity of their domestic bond markets and lower their borrowing requirements through deficit reduction policies, U.S. borrowers have begun to dominate global bond issuance. U.S. agencies, especially the Federal Mortgage Credit Agencies, have become frequent global bond issuers, with the Tennessee Valley Authority bringing two deals in the second half of 1995 worth $3.6 billion. The OECD has speculated that "on the basis of recent trends, it would appear that the market for global bonds is, for the time being, evolving into an extension of the domestic United States market and an additional source of funds for United States borrowers."[6] According to OECD estimates, the issuance of bonds with "global characteristics" in 1994 totaled $49 billion, or 11 percent of all international bond offerings.

Two other recent developments in the offshore market are worthy of mention: the sharp increase in the use of Euro medium-term note (EMTN) programs, and the success of Regulation 144A. The volume of newly arranged EMTN agreements more than doubled to $243 billion in 1994, up from only $18 billion in 1990. EMTNs allow for issuance in different currencies and maturities under one umbrella agreement. Thus borrowers can use EMTNs to tap the markets more quickly and efficiently than with traditional Eurodollar bonds, which require separate documentation for each bond issue. In fact, although EMTNs were originally used only for nonunderwritten private placements, since 1992 EMTNs have been used for underwritten deals as well, further blurring the distinction between EMTNs and traditional Eurobonds. As the majority of all Eurobond issues are swapped into floating-rate debt and market opportunities to obtain favorable swap terms can be fleeting, borrowers appreciate the flexibility of EMTN programs.

Regulation 144A was enacted in 1990 to allow professional investors greater liquidity in trading private placement issues[7] while continuing to restrict access by the general public. According to Moody's, annual issuance of 144A paper has risen to $80 billion; roughly 50 percent from foreign borrowers. Approximately 90 percent of the issues in 1995 were rated by the major credit-rating

---

6. *Financial Market Trends,* OECD Paris, June 1995, p.79.
7. Regulation 144A also provided foreign borrowers with greater access to institutional investors by allowing issuers to provide only the documentation required by their home-market regulators rather than undergo the more cumbersome SEC registration process.

agencies. Historically, 144A securities, due to the somewhat smaller issuance size, have been geared more toward buy-and-hold accounts; however, liquidity has been increasing relative to registered securities.

Bradys, Aztecs, and FLIRBs: The Emerging Markets

Emerging market bonds have been increasingly used in global bond portfolios. Most of these bonds are U.S. dollar-denominated; however, local currency instruments, such as Mexican Cetes, are often available to international investors as well. The majority of secondary market trading is in Brady bonds, named after Treasury Secretary Nicholas Brady, who fostered a market-oriented approach to the Latin American debt crisis by repackaging nonperforming bank loans into marketable securities in the late 1980s.

The first Brady agreement was reached with Mexico, and the bonds were issued in March 1990; however, Aztec bonds, a similar privately arranged restructuring of Mexican debt by J.P. Morgan, were issued two years earlier. The Mexican Brady plan offered the commercial banks two options in return for their Mexican loans: a *discount* bond issued at 65 percent of face value paying a floating market coupon of LIBOR+13/16, and a *par* bond issued at full face value, but paying a below-market fixed coupon of 6.25 percent. Both discount and par bonds have their principal repayment backed by zero-coupon U.S. Treasuries plus a rolling interest guarantee covering 18 months of interest payments. The banks were also given a third alternative, allowing them to carry existing loans on their books at face value if they agreed to provide new lending to Mexico of at least 25 percent of their existing exposure over the next three years. Today, 12 countries have issued Brady bonds, although Latin American countries still dominate the Brady market, with 86 percent of debt outstanding. The size of the Brady market has grown from $30 billion in 1990 to $136 billion in 1995, with the debt divided evenly between fixed- and floating-rate bonds.

There is no generally accepted delineation between an emerging and a developed market. Mexico and the Czech Republic, considered by many to be emerging markets, are now members of the OECD. Some emerging markets have issued bonds in the Eurobond market. Generally, the distinction is left up to the credit rating agencies, who determine whether a country is investment grade: Moody's Baa3, Standard & Poor's BBB−, or better. Even the credit rating agencies sometimes cannot agree. For example, South Africa has a split rating of Baa3/BB+, meaning that Moody's regards the credit as investment grade, whereas Standard & Poor's does not.

Needless to say, regardless of currency denomination, the market risk of holding emerging market securities is generally much higher than holding developed country credits. The turmoil in the emerging markets that began in December 1994 and lasted through the first quarter of 1995 serves as a vivid reminder of the risks associated with holding emerging market debt. Concerns about the Mexican peso's ability to stay within its stated devaluation band in the face of extremely large current account deficits and declining reserves prompted many Mexican residents to move money out of the country. When the sentiment of international investors turned as well, the reaction was quick and harsh. On December 19, 1994 the Mexican peso was devalued. By the following March, the peso had lost half of its value against the dollar, and Mexican par bonds had also fallen by 50 percent. By the end of 1995, market prices had recovered substantially as investor confidence improved and liquidity returned to the emerging markets.

FOREIGN-PAY INTERNATIONAL BONDS

From the standpoint of the U.S. investor, foreign-pay international bonds encompass all issues denominated in currencies other than the dollar. A variety of issues are available to the U.S. investor, but in practically all cases the primary trading market is outside the United States. The currency component introduces a significant source of volatility; hence, the most important question facing U.S. investors in foreign-pay international bonds is whether or not to hedge the currency. The theoretical underpinnings of the currency hedge question are explored in detail below, but first the instruments require some explanation. The three types of instruments, just as in the United States bond market, are determined by the domicile of the issuer and the location of the primary trading market: the domestic market; the foreign market (like the Yankee market), where the issuer is domiciled outside of the country of issuance; and the Euro market, which trades outside of any national jurisdiction.

The Non-U.S. Domestic Markets

Securities issued by a borrower within its home market and in that country's currency are typically termed domestic issues. These may include bonds issued directly by the government; government agencies, sometimes called semi-governments; or corporations. In most countries, the domestic bond market is dominated by government-backed issues. Central governments have directly issued or guaranteed approximately 56 percent of the world's outstanding bonds. Another 7 percent of outstandings is accounted for by state (provincial) or local government issues, meaning nearly 63 percent of the publicly issued bonds outstanding are government credits. The United States is the only country with a well-developed, actively-traded corporate bond market. Other countries have discourage private-sector bond issuance in favor of bank loans or equity financing, or companies themselves have chosen to raise funds in the Euromarkets, where they have had access to a wider investor audience with fewer issuing restrictions. Recent progress in international credit-rating procedures and greater cross-border capital flows have helped to develop domestic corporate bond markets outside the United States, but liquidity remains spotty, and the number of issuers in each country is limited.

Bulldogs, Samurais, and other Foreign Bonds

The *foreign bond market* includes issues sold primarily in one country and currency by a borrower of a different nationality. The Yankee market is the U.S.-dollar version of this market. Other examples are the Samurai market, which consists of yen-denominated bonds issued in Japan by non-Japanese borrowers, and the Bulldog market, which is composed of United Kingdom sterling-dominated bonds issued in the United Kingdom by non-British entities. Relative to the size of the domestic bond markets, these foreign bond markets are quite small, and liquidity can be limited. For borrowers, the major advantage of the foreign bond markets is the access they provide to investors in the country in which the bonds are issued. The Samurai market, for example, allows borrowers directly to tap the huge pools of investment capital in Japan. For investors, foreign bonds offer the convenience of domestic trading and settlement, and often additional yield.

The Offshore Foreign-Pay Market

Securities issued directly into the international ("offshore") markets are called Eurobonds. Eurodollar bonds are the U.S.-pay version; however, Eurobonds can be issued in a variety of currencies including deutsche marks, Japanese yen, Italian lira, even South African rand and Czech koruna. These securities are typically underwritten by international syndicates and are sold in a number of national markets simultaneously. They may or may not be obligations of, or guaranteed by, an issuer domiciled in the country of currency denomination, and the issuer may be a sovereign government, a corporation, or a supranational agency. The Eurobond market encompasses any bond not issued in a domestic market, regardless of issuer nationality, or currency denomination. Eurodollar bonds consistently have been the largest sector of this market, although their share of total Eurobond debt outstanding has declined from about 65 percent in 1984 to about 50 percent in 1989, and 38 percent in 1994. The decline of the share of the U.S. dollar in Eurobond issuance can be traced to three general trends: A trend depreciation of the dollar from its peak in 1984, a desire to diversify currency exposure and funding sources as the deutschemark and yen have become more important as reserve currencies, and the liquidity of the swaps and other derivatives markets. Eurodeutschemark and Euroyen bonds are the next largest sectors, with a 15 and 14 percent share, respectively.[8] Thus, the G3 account for two-thirds of the currency denomination of the Eurobond market. As with the foreign bond markets, liquidity of Eurobonds is typically less than the liquidity of domestic government issues.

Components of Return

To the dollar-based investor, there are two components of return in actively managed U.S.-pay bond portfolios: coupon income and capital change. Capital change

---

8. Germany's actual market share is probably slightly less than Japan's as Germany doesn't distinguish between foreign and Eurobond issues.

can result from either interest-rate movements or a change in the perceived creditworthiness of the issuer. In foreign-pay investing, a third component of return must be considered: foreign currency movements. The U.S. investor must couple the domestic or internal price movement with income and then translate the total domestic return into dollars to assess the total return in U.S. dollars.

For the U.S. investor in foreign currency bonds, the prospects for return should not only be viewed in an absolute sense but should also be analyzed relative to returns expected in the U.S. market. The analysis can be separated into three questions.

What Is the Starting Yield Level Relative to Yield Levels on U.S. Bonds?

Where this spread is positive, the income advantage will, over time, provide a cushion against adverse movements of the foreign bond price relative to U.S. bonds, or against deterioration in the value of the foreign currency. The longer the time horizon, the greater the cushion provided by this accumulating income advantage. If, on the other hand, the starting income level of the foreign currency issue is below that provided by U.S. bonds, this income deficiency must be offset continually by an appreciating currency or positive internal price movement relative to U.S. bonds to provide comparable returns. This may appear to be a difficult challenge, but the decade of the 1970s as a whole saw the best U.S. dollar total returns accruing to the bond investments with the lowest income levels. This same result was achieved in the 1980s, when Japanese yen bonds had the world's best total returns in U.S. dollar terms despite the fact that yen bonds offered the lowest interest rates of the world's major bond markets. The underlying rationale for this result is that bonds with low yields are denominated in currencies of countries with low inflation rates, which theoretically translates into currency appreciation relative to the U.S. dollar.[9]

What Are the Prospects for Internal Price Movements Relative to Expectations for U.S. Bond Prices?

This factor can be broadly discussed in terms of changing yield spreads of foreign-pay bonds versus U.S. issues in the same way that changing yield spreads within the domestic U.S. market are discussed in describing changes in relative prices. However, several points should be considered in regard to this analogy. First, in the U.S. market, all bond prices generally move in the same direction, although not always to the same extent, whereas domestic price movements of foreign-pay bonds may move in the direction opposite to that of the U.S. market. Second, although yield spread relationships within the U.S. market may fluctuate broadly, in many cases there is a normal spread that has some repetitive meaning.

---

9. See Exhibit 54–14 in Chapter 54, which shows the long-term relationship between currency movements and inflation.

However, changing economic, social, and political trends between the United States and other countries suggest that there are few normal relationships to serve as useful guidelines.

Third, investors must be aware that similar interest rate shifts may result in significantly different capital price changes. Both U.S. and international investors are very familiar with the concept of duration; that is, that equal yield movements will result in differing price movements depending upon the individual security's current yield, maturity, coupon, and call structure. However, as international bond investors are focused on the spread relationship to the benchmark market (explained in detail below), they often pay less attention to the consequences of duration on similar maturity bonds across markets. For example, the low yield on Japanese long bonds, currently around 3 percent, makes Japanese 10-year bond prices about 25 percent more sensitive to changes in yield than Italian bonds, where yields are above 10 percent. Thus, a 20-basis-point (0.2 percent) decline in the yield of a 10-year Italian fixed coupon government issue starting at a 10-percent yield results in a 1.14 percent price change, whereas the same 20-basis-point move equates to a 1.42 percent price change for a 10-year Japanese issue with a starting yield of 3 percent. When the more commonly analyzed effects of varying maturities and differing yield changes are added to the impact of different starting yield levels, the resulting changes in relative price movements are not intuitively obvious. For example, the various combinations of starting yield, maturity, and yield change shown in Exhibit 17–3 all result in the same 10 percent capital price increases.

Finally, changes in credit quality can have dramatic influences on bond prices. The most spectacular recent example is the sharp drop in Mexican asset prices in the first quarter of 1995. However, credit concerns have also influenced developed country debt premia. During the sharp rise in global bond yields in 1994, there was much discussion over whether highly indebted countries such as Italy, Belgium, Sweden, and Canada could find themselves in a "debt trap," where they would not be able to service their existing debt. As can be seen in Exhibit 17–4, the rise in bond yields during 1994 was highly correlated with budget

EXHIBIT 17–3

Impact of Maturity and Starting Yield on Yield and Price Change Relationships

Starting Yield	Maturity (Years)	Yield Change	Price Change
10%	10	−1.50%	+10%
10	5	−2.44	+10
6	10	−1.27	+10
6	5	−2.21	+10

EXHIBIT 17–4

Budget Deficit and 1994 10-Year Yield Change

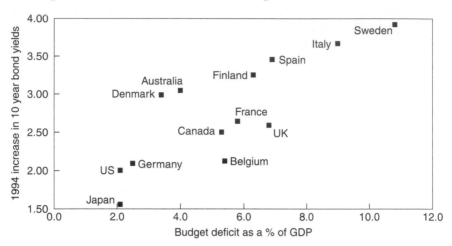

Source: OECD Economic Outlook and Scudder, Stevens and Clark data.

deficits and national debt levels.[10] As the bond market rally got underway in 1995, concerns over the debt trap faded into the background.

What Are the Prospects for Currency Gain versus the U.S. Dollar?
Winston Churchill reportedly said, "There is no sphere of human thought in which it is easier to show superficial cleverness and the appearance of superior wisdom than in discussing currency and exchange." This demonstrates that the debate as to whether or not foreign currency changes can be predicted and, if so, what factors determine such changes, is an old one. In many ways, this debate is little different from that regarding the predictability of stock market movements or interest rates. Like the stock and bond markets, a number of factors exert a direct influence on foreign exchange rates. The common problems faced by forecasters are whether these factors have already been fully discounted in prices—be they stock, bond, or foreign exchange—and which factor will predominate at any given time. Those

---

10. The debt trap is a condition where the national debt has become so large that a country cannot fully service its existing debt without recourse to new borrowing, which creates a self-perpetuating dynamic of higher future debt service costs and a larger national debt. As the debt grows, the market will demand a higher risk premium, driving up interest rates on new debt and adding further to debt service costs, until credit concerns prompt the market to halt lending altogether and default, or debt restructuring, becomes inevitable. For a more complete discussion of the dynamics of the debt trap, see the *OECD Economic Outlook* no. 58, OECD, Paris (December 1995) pp. 19–23.

factors generally regarded as affecting foreign currency movements include the following:

1. The balance of payments and prospective changes in that balance.
2. Inflation and interest-rate differentials between countries.
3. The social and political environment, particularly with regard to the impact on foreign investment.
4. Relative changes in the money supply.
5. Central bank intervention in the currency markets.

Part of the reason that exchange rates have become more difficult to forecast is that they are decreasingly governed by end-user transactions. The ratio of foreign-exchange transactions relative to world-trade flows has skyrocketed, from 10:1 in 1983 to more than 60:1 in 1992. The latest estimate of average daily turnover in the foreign exchange markets, based on a 1995 survey conducted by the Bank for International Settlements, is $1.3 trillion. This is nearly twice the $754 billion in foreign exchange reserves held by what the IMF terms the *industrialized countries,* and only slightly smaller than the annual outlays of the U.S. federal government of some $1.6 trillion.

A common question is whether international bond returns are almost entirely a function of currency movements. Exhibit 17–5[11] shows that for the 11-year

E X H I B I T   17–5

Average Annual Returns of International Bond Index by Components

	Contribution to Return			
	Income	**Domestic Capital Gain**	**Foreign Currency**	**Total Dollar-converted Average Annual Return**
1985–86	+7.7%	+3.2%	+19.8%	+33.2%
1987–89	+7.5	−1.7	+4.2	+10.1
1990–92	+8.1	+2.3	+1.3	+12.0
1993–95	+7.4	+2.2	+3.4	+13.4
1985–95	+7.7	+1.3	+5.8	+15.4

The Salomon Brothers Non-U.S. Dollar World Government Bond Index—Market-weighted in the government bonds of Australia, Austria, Belgium, Canada, Denmark, France, Germany, Italy, Japan, the Netherlands, Spain, Sweden, and the United Kingdom.

---

11. Monthly total returns in Exhibits 17–5 and 17–6 were taken from Salomon Brothers' International Market Indexes, published monthly; particularly the Salomon Brothers' Non-U.S. Dollar World Government Bond Index. The income component of total return was computed from principal local market returns provided by Salomon Brothers.

E X H I B I T   17–6

Average Annual Returns of International Bond Index by Components

| | | **Contribution to Return** | | |
	Income	Domestic Capital Gain	Foreign Currency	Total Dollar-Converted Average Annual Return
1985	8.1%	2.7%	21.6%	35.0%
1986	7.3	3.6	18.1	31.4
1987	7.2	0.4	25.6	35.1
1988	7.6	–0.5	–4.4	2.3
1989	7.7	–4.9	–5.7	–3.4
1990	8.3	–3.5	10.2	15.3
1991	8.1	5.8	1.7	16.2
1992	7.9	4.8	–7.2	4.8
1993	7.6	9.3	–2.0	15.1
1994	7.4	–10.0	9.6	6.0
1995	7.1	8.5	3.0	19.6

The Salomon Brothers Non-U.S. Dollar World Government Bond Index—market-weighted in the government bonds of Australia, Austria, Belgium, Canada, Denmark, France, Germany, Italy, Japan, the Netherlands, Spain, Sweden, and the United Kingdom.

period from 1985 to 1995, and for three of the four interim periods, the income component of return proved to be the largest of the three components, as measured by the Salomon Brothers Non-U.S. World Government Bond Index.

Over a shorter time horizon, however, foreign currency or domestic capital changes can be significantly more important. Exhibit 17–6 breaks down the 1985–1995 period into annual returns to demonstrate the influence domestic capital changes and movements in exchange rates can have on total returns over the short term. Domestic capital changes ranged from –10.0 percent in 1994 to 9.3 percent in 1993, and currency returns varied from –6.3 percent in 1992 to 25.6 percent in 1987. (Recall that negative foreign currency returns for dollar-based investors correspond to a strengthening in the dollar versus other currencies, and vice versa.) The income component of return varied in a much narrower range throughout the period, from a low of 7.1 percent in 1995 to a high of 8.1 percent in 1985 and 1991.

For individual countries, the variation in components of return was even greater. The greatest capital price changes were +15.5 percent in Italy in 1982 and –14.8 percent in Australia in 1994. Currency changes for specific countries ranged from +31.8 percent in Japan in 1987 to –22.3 percent in Italy in 1992. The least variable component of return—income—still ranged widely, from 13.5 percent in Australia in 1990 to just 2.9 percent in Japan in 1994. These data show clearly that all three factors of return—income, capital change, and currency movement—are important and must be considered both absolutely and relative to U.S. alternatives.

CONCLUSION

International bonds, both U.S.-pay and foreign-pay, represent a significant portion of the world's fixed-income markets, and an understanding of their characteristics is important for all bond investors. U.S.-pay international bonds generally have very similar characteristics to domestically issued bonds and can offer opportunities to enhance returns in domestic bond portfolios with a little additional credit analysis and education. The risks—and potential returns—however, are much greater in foreign-pay international bonds, which require far more expertise and support to effectively handle the currency, settlement, and custodial risks unique to global bond investing.

U.S.-pay international bonds make up roughly 9 percent of the U.S.-dollar bond market. Issuance and liquidity in these instruments have increased dramatically in the past decade, although continued growth in the Eurodollar and Yankee bond markets is subject to regulatory policies in the domestic markets as well as the vagaries of the dollar and U.S. interest rates. Foreign investors will continue to have a large presence in the U.S.-pay international bond market. Successful utilization of the Eurodollar and Yankee bond markets requires an ongoing familiarity with foreign investor preferences and issuer motivations.

Investors in foreign-pay bonds must consider income levels and prospective price movements both in absolute terms and relative to U.S.-pay alternatives. The outlook for foreign currency changes must also be evaluated. The evidence indicates that over the 1978–1995 period, converted U.S. dollar returns for foreign-pay bonds were somewhat better than returns in the U.S. bond market, although during shorter time periods within that 18-year interval, foreign-pay bonds sometimes provided inferior returns. Although these facts by themselves have little repetitive significance, many of the factors leading to the low correlation in returns between the U.S. and foreign-pay markets can be expected to continue making foreign-pay international bonds an effective diversifier for U.S. dollar-based portfolios.

⑥ BRADY BONDS

Jane S. Brauer
Brady Bond Strategist
Emerging Markets Fixed Income Research
Merrill Lynch

The term *Brady bond* refers to a series of sovereign bonds issued by several developing countries in exchange for their rescheduled bank loans. The term comes from a U.S. government program, which combined U.S. government and official multilateral support in obtaining debt and debt-service relief from foreign commercial bank creditors for those countries that successfully implemented comprehensive structural reforms supported by the International Monetary Fund and the World Bank. Thus far, 13 countries have taken advantage of the program, with a cumulative face value of $156 billion of Brady bonds issued. Currently, the majority of debt is from Latin America, with Brazil, Mexico, Argentina, and Venezuela representing 82 percent of the outstanding Brady bond market. (See Exhibit 18–1.)

The Brady market is unique in two respects. First, the yields are very high, ranging from 9 percent to 25 percent. Second, some issues are extremely large and liquid, especially compared to typical sovereign Eurobonds. The high liquidity also provides support to an active over-the-counter derivatives market. Investors can take views on country risk, bond spreads, or volatility, as well as hedge portfolios through the use of options. In addition, investors can buy calls on Brady bonds that they expect will outperform the market without having to buy the bonds outright.

TYPES OF BRADY BONDS

Countries typically issue several types of Brady bonds covering the outstanding principal amount of their bank loans and one or more bonds covering past-due interest. The particular bond types are chosen by creditors to provide debt and debt-service relief to sovereign debtors.

EXHIBIT   18–1

Total Brady/Exchange Debt Issued (in US$B)*

Country	Pars	Discounts	Other Principal Bonds	Past Due Interest	Exchange Bonds	Total Debt Issued	Percent
Latin America							
Argentina	12.7	4.3	na	7.1	na	24.1	15.4%
Brazil	9.0	7.3	12.5	11.5	8.9	49.1	34.1
Costa Rica	na	na	0.4	.01	na	0.5	0.3
Dominican							
Republic	na	0.3	na	0.2	na	0.5	0.3
Ecuador	1.9	1.4	na	2.6	na	6.0	3.8
Mexico	22.4	11.8	na	na	2.6	36.7	23.5
Uruguay	0.5	na	0.5	na	na	1.1	0.7
Venezuela	7.3	1.3	10.0	na	na	18.5	11.8
Non-Latin							
Bulgaria	na	1.9	1.7	1.6	na	5.1	3.3%
Jordan	0.5	0.2	0.1	na	na	0.7	0.5
Nigeria	2.1	na	na	na	na	2.1	1.3
Philippines	1.9	na	1.5	na	0.9	4.2	2.7
Poland	0.9	3.0	1.3	2.7	na	7.8	5.0
Total	59.2	31.4	27.9	25.8	12.3	156.6	100%
Percent	37.8%	20.1%	17.8%	16.5%	7.8%	100%	

*These totals refer to the amounts issued. The current amount outstandings of these Issues is less, due to buybacks by some governments or governmental agencies.

Two principal bonds, par and discount bonds, are 25–30 year registered bullet bonds and represent the largest, most common, and most liquid issues in the Brady bond market. Pars and discounts represent 58 percent of the Brady bond market. Issue size ranges from $90 million to $22.4 billion, in some cases larger than the most liquid U.S. Treasury issues. Par bonds are issued at "par" in exchange for the original face value of the rescheduled loans but carry a fixed, below-market interest rate. Discount bonds, on the other hand, carry a floating market interest rate but are exchanged for fewer bonds than the original loan amount, or at a discounted face value of the previously rescheduled loans.

Pars and discounts also generally have principal collateralized by a U.S. Treasury zero coupon bond and interest collateralized by cash maintained at the Federal Reserve Bank of New York to cover a specific number of months of coupon payments (usually 12 to 18 months). In the event that the country misses an interest payment, the trustee will pay the investor out of the interest guarantee until the number of coupon payments guaranteed has been exhausted. Default on an interest payment does not mean that the debtor will never pay interest on the bond; instead, the country could continue to make payments in arrears after the interest guarantee has been depleted, or the country may try to renegotiate the terms of the bond. The trustee will pay the principal, as needed, from the collateral at the time the principal is due.

Certain par and discount bonds carry "value recovery" rights or warrants, which give bondholders the opportunity to "recapture" some of the debt and debt-service reduction provided in the exchange if future economic performance and the debt-servicing capacity of the sovereign debtor improves. The warrants are linked to indexes of oil export prices, or the country's oil export receipts in the case of Mexico, Venezuela, and Nigeria, or the level of a terms-of-trade index in the case of Uruguay.

The type of bonds included in a given plan is determined during the debt-restructuring negotiations between a consortium of creditors and the debtor country. The bonds often have varying coupon schedules, amortizations, and sometimes capitalization of interest. Each plan may also include principal types other than par and discount bonds, such as debt-conversion bonds (DCBs), the related new-money bonds (NMBs), front-loaded interest-reduction bonds (FLIRBs), and capitalization bonds (C-Bonds). The DCBs, NMBs, and FLIRBs are typically noncollateralized amortizing bearer instruments with a significantly shorter final maturity and average life and are generally less liquid than the pars or discounts. DCBs are issued at full face value and carry a floating market interest rate, but creditors who choose the DCB option must also extend new funds to the sovereign debtor by buying short-term, floating-rate NMBs. FLIRBs carry collateral-securing interest payments, generally for 12 months, and the guarantee is available for the first five to six years of the life of the bond. C-bonds are capitalization bonds, which first appeared in the Brazil plan. Brazil agreed to an 8 percent interest accrual but only pays out 4 percent for the first six years; the remaining 4 percent capitalizes, increasing the par amount outstanding at the end of the first year, for example, to 104 percent of the original amount.

Past-due interest on several Brady plans has also been consolidated into past-due interest bonds (PDI), interest due and unpaid bonds (IDU), eligible interest bonds (EI), interest arrears bonds (IAB), or floating-rate past-due interest bonds (FRB), usually a noncollateralized, 10–20 year amortizing floating rate bond. Ecuador has the option in its PDI bonds to capitalize several of the early interest payments, and Panama is negotiating a similar feature on its soon-to-be Brady PDI bond.

Other Exchange Bonds

A number of other bonds with characteristics similar to those of the Brady bonds were exchanged for restructured loans prior to the creation of the Brady plan: Mexico issued 20-year "Aztecs," United Mexican States collateralized floating rate bonds; Brazil issued IDUs, NMBs, and exit bonds; and the Philippines issued NMBs. These bonds are often included in Brady/exchange references due to their similar characteristics and liquidity.

What Does the Restructuring Package Do for the Sovereign Country?

Typically, a country negotiating a Brady restructuring has significant external debt outstanding and cannot meet the debt payment schedule. By restructuring its debt, the country obtains some debt forgiveness while simultaneously deferring some principal and interest payments for a few years to allow time for reforms to ripple through the economy and improve cash flow and the balance of payments.

Assessing Value in Brady Bonds

A bond with collateral requires a somewhat different method of assessing value than merely calculating yield-to-maturity based on price. Investors can think of a discount or par bond as having three components: the U.S. Treasury fully collateralized principal, the collateralized rolling interest guarantee, and the risky remainder of the bond's cash flows. The yield-to-maturity of a collateralized bond is lower than that of a bond with no collateral because it has some credit enhancement. The country risk factor, or yield spread, should be applied to the risky cash flows only. Typically, investors will calculate present values of both the principal and interest collateral components and subtract them from the price of the bond. This stripped price is used to calculate an internal rate of return (IRR) of the noncollateralized portion of the cash flows. The IRR of the stripped price is called the *stripped yield.* A common measure of value, the stripped yield spread (the stripped yield less the interpolated U.S. Treasury yield) is perceived as a representation of the "market's" view of that country's level of sovereign risk. By stripping out the collateral, investors can more easily compare yields of collateralized and noncollateralized sovereign bonds.

Unlike most corporate bonds, many Brady bonds amortize and may bear floating-rate coupons for some or all of the coupon periods. A common way to compare fixed-rate and floating-rate coupons is to "swap" the floating rate to a fixed rate, or assume that the floating-rate coupon resets at forward LIBOR, based on the LIBOR swap curve or on the Eurodollar futures curve. The yields of the resulting cash flows, without the collateral, can be compared to U.S. Treasuries to identify cheap bonds (wide-stripped spreads) versus rich bonds (tight-stripped spreads).

"Pre-Brady" Loans

Perhaps the most speculative segment of an already high-risk, high-yielding market are bank loans (generally nonperforming and available only through assignment or participation agreements with extended 21-day settlement). They are often off-limits to investors. The principally traded types of bank loans are the "pre-Brady" claims of countries expected to obtain debt and debt service relief under the auspices of the Brady initiative in the future. Ecuadorian creditors recently exchanged approximately $6 billion (face value) of previously rescheduled loans and accrued interest claims on these loans. Panama recently reached a preliminary agreement and is expected to issue about $3.5 billion face value of Brady bonds early in 1996. Peru and the Ivory Coast may receive similar treatment somewhat later, and Russia is negotiating a similar, but non-Brady, restructuring.

Progress in negotiations (or lack thereof) and speculation of eventual bond issuance dates drives the price volatility of this segment of international emerging markets (IEM). In some cases, prices of these loans have gone above levels that fully reflect sovereign risk, deal completion risk, and the time value of holding nonperforming claims for one or two years and as such are highly speculative and vulnerable to significant volatility and downside risk. Bank loans of better credit risks such as Chile and Colombia, both viewed as investment-grade, are rarely traded.

High Yields Have Drawn New Investors

One key element to investing in Brady bonds is an understanding of supply-and-demand conditions. The debt supply in IEM comes from a broad range of asset classes, including Brady bonds, bank loans, new medium-term Eurobond issues, dollar-denominated money market instruments, local currency fixed-income instruments, and derivative and structured products. However, only Brady bonds provide a combination of high yield, price appreciation potential, and collateralized securities, with size and liquidity large enough to accommodate the increasingly dominant source of demand—institutional investors.

In recent years, these attributes have encouraged successive waves of institutional investors to enter the Brady market for the first time. Originally, the principal investors in the market were high-net-worth individuals from emerging market countries themselves. They were the first to realize that these countries had begun to "turn the corner" in the late 1980s and began repatriating their funds by buying distressed assets. This, in turn, triggered a steady recovery in asset values, which was further supported by the subsequent issuance of Brady bonds. The high returns on these assets increasingly drew institutional interest. The first institutional investors were the more aggressive fund managers (hedge funds, global growth funds, dedicated emerging market funds, etc.) and broker/dealers (including major Wall Street houses and some of the banks who were original lenders of the claims that were later converted into Brady bonds). Then came "crossover"

Total Return Index for Brady Bonds
December 1989–July 1995

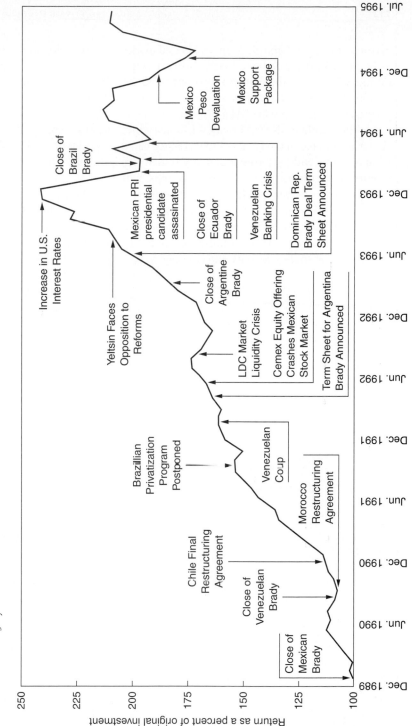

investors from the domestic high-yield bond market (where yields were no longer as high). With the U.S. bond market still rallying in 1993 and U.S. interest rates hitting a 25-year low, demand also appeared from the most conservative investors: Insurance companies and pension funds, driven by the need for higher yields, began investing in IEM.

The profile of the IEM market is transforming from sovereign debt ownership concentrated in the hands of few creditor banks and dealers to ownership distributed more widely through actively traded Brady bonds. The new investors require more research and risk-analysis tools, which enhance the ability of new players to enter the market. Despite poor performance over the last year and a half due to the decline in the U.S. market and subsequent devaluation of the Mexican peso, prices have recently improved, approaching the predevaluation levels (see Exhibit 18–2 on page 351.) At this point, dedicated money managers account for the majority of trading activity and continue to be very active investors.

19

⑥ STABLE VALUE INVESTMENTS

Kenneth L. Walker
President
T. Rowe Price Stable Asset Management, Inc.

Investment professionals have created an efficient marketplace for traditional equity, bond, and short-term cash equivalents. External influences, including the Employee Retirement Income Security Act of 1974, as amended, tax legislative changes, and union negotiations spurred the growth of the pension industry. Today this industry controls a significant component of the capital markets.

The volatile financial markets of the 1970s and 1980s and the shift in focus from defined benefit to defined contribution plans created the demand for a new investment alternative: the stable value investment. This demand for stability of returns was met by the life insurance industry in the early to mid-1970s with the guaranteed investment contract (GIC), an investment generally supported by the general account of the insurer. Recent statistics indicate that the stable value market, including 401(k), 403(b), and 457 plans, has in excess of $300 billion, accounting for approximately one-third of all defined contribution assets.

TYPES OF CONTRACTS AND STRATEGIES

The cornerstone of most stable value funds has been the GIC; an obligation of the insurance company, typically issued through the insurer's general account, and providing a fixed rate and fixed maturity. Banks also had been active in this market, issuing bank investment contracts (BICs) generally as a deposit obligation with a fixed rate and fixed maturity. In recent years, new stable-value investment

The author acknowledges the contributions to this chapter of his colleagues at T. Rowe Price.

contracts have been developed by banks and insurance companies in response to plan sponsors' desire for added diversification, credit enhancement, and greater control over the underlying assets. Most of these contracts fall into two broad categories: separate account contracts (SACs) offered by insurance companies, where a separate portfolio of assets is owned and managed by the insurance company for the benefit of the plan (or group of plans), and "synthetic investment contracts" (SICs) offered by both insurance companies and banks, where a separate portfolio of securities is owned by the plan and "wrapped" by a third-party financial institution to provide book-value accounting treatment. Characteristics of these contracts are compared in Exhibit 19–1.

Stable value investment contracts[1] differ from traditional fixed income instruments in two ways. Those issued to qualified plans by insurance companies and banks generally are exempt from registration as a security with the Securities and Exchange Commission. The majority of investment contract products enjoy amortized cost (book value) accounting treatment. This accounting basis provides an investment whose principal value remains stable and does not fluctuate with changes in interest rate levels.

E X H I B I T   19–1

Key Points	Separate Account Contracts	Synthetic GICs
Assets held by	Insurance company in a separate account	Plan in custody account
Assets selected by	Issuer, within guidelines approved by plan sponsor	Issuer, plan sponsor, or manager
Assets actively managed?	Yes	Yes; for constant duration strategy
Assets credit risk borne by	Plan	Plan
Credit exposure to issuer	Lower than to general account products	Lower than to general account products
Fully benefit-responsive	Yes; benefit liquidations may affect future returns	Depending on contract type, benefit liquidation may not affect future returns

---

1. Throughout the chapter, GICs, SACs, and SICs will be referred to as *investment contracts*. However, the term *investment contracts* may have certain regulatory meanings and connotations that are not necessarily applied to GICs, SACs, and SICs.

Coincident with the introduction of a new generation of SIC stable-value alternatives has been the development of appropriate alternative investment strategies. The buyer now has the opportunity to choose along a risk spectrum from a single security strategy, often referred to as a "buy/hold" SIC, which most closely resembles the fixed-rate GIC, to a more active and diversified strategy, including immunization, constant duration, and other "controlled volatility" investment strategies.

These new alternatives are in response to the changing mood of the marketplace. The desire on the part of many plan sponsors is to move away from the *explicit guarantee* to stable value.

Where are these changes leading? Buyers of the traditional GIC portfolio of bullet and window contracts are modifying their investment objectives and communicating to participants a change in investment philosophy. Dependence on the insurance industry as the sole provider of stable value products is changing, as witnessed with the entry of multinational banks as wrappers of SICs.

The marketplace has witnessed almost 15 years of declining interest rates (see Exhibits 19–2 through 19–5). This decline has produced a positive lag effect

EXHIBIT   19–2

GIC Returns Compared to Bond Returns

Year	Lehman Brothers Immediate Government/Corporate Index			GIC Average Rates (4-Year Maturity)		
	Total Return	Yield	Average Maturity	High	Low	Average
1982	26.11%	12.03%	3.7–3.9	16.53%	11.52%	14.31%
1983	8.60	10.93	3.8–3.9	12.37	10.83	11.69
1984	14.37	11.33	3.8–3.9	13.87	11.09	12.56
1985	18.00	10.64	3.9–4.1	11.80	8.84	10.40
1986	13.13	9.29	4.0–4.2	9.11	7.39	8.03
1987	3.66	8.70	4.1–4.2	9.87	7.35	8.34
1988	6.67	9.39	4.2–4.3	9.30	7.84	8.60
1989	12.77	8.25	4.2–4–3	9.88	8.13	8.89
1990	9.16	7.94	4.2–4.3	9.61	8.12	8.86
1991	14.62	5.77	4.2–4.3	8.24	6.05	7.61
1992	7.17	5.67	4.2–4.3	7.22	5.21	6.24
1993	9.79	6.59	4.2–4.3	6.13	4.69	5.20
1994	−1.93	7.11	4.2–4.3	8.12	5.10	6.84
1995	15.35	5.50	4.1–4.2	8.18	5.55	6.58

Source: GIC rate data obtained from The Laughlin Group and the T. Rowe Price GIC Index. Bond data obtained from Lehman Brothers, *Bond Market Report.*

EXHIBIT 19–3

GIC Rates Compared to Money Market Rates

GIC Average Rates (2-Year Maturity)

Year	High	Low	Average	Money Market Yields	Spread Average
1982	16.00%	10.67%	14.00%	12.23%	1.77
1983	11.86	9.95	10.85	8.58	2.27
1984	13.23	10.26	11.94	10.04	1.90
1985	11.02	8.01	9.58	7.71	1.87
1986	8.43	6.10	7.30	6.26	1.04
1987	9.17	6.58	7.55	6.12	1.43
1988	9.02	7.07	7.98	7.10	0.88
1989	9.73	7.73	8.63	8.90	−0.27
1990	9.26	7.57	8.40	7.90	0.50
1991	7.51	5.04	6.76	5.71	1.05
1992	6.08	4.01	5.03	3.36	1.67
1993	4.93	3.97	4.27	2.70	1.57
1994	7.84	4.27	6.14	3.83	2.31
1995	7.82	5.30	6.24	5.53	0.71

Source: GIC rate data obtained from The Laughlin Group and the T. Rowe Price GIC Index. Bond data obtained from Lehman Brothers, *Bond Market Report.*

EXHIBIT 19–4

GIC Yield Spreads (Three-Year Maturity)

Year	High Rate	Low Rate	High Spread	Low Spread
1982	16.25%	11.17%	1.86%	0.71%
1983	12.14	10.57	1.78	0.39
1984	13.56	10.75	0.82	0.06
1985	11.46	8.57	0.64	0.18
1986	8.84	7.14	1.02	0.27
1987	9.52	6.99	0.68	−0.13
1988	9.15	7.54	0.34	−0.11
1989	9.85	8.01	0.65	−0.02
1990	9.52	7.90	0.63	0.29
1991	7.90	5.58	0.61	0.28
1992	6.75	4.60	0.58	0.18
1993	5.57	4.35	0.49	0.20
1994	8.04	4.69	0.32	0.16
1995	8.09	5.42	0.30	−0.19

Source: Yield spreads reflect spreads over equivalent maturity U.S. Treasury issues unadjusted for semiannual versus annualized yields. GIC rate data obtained from The Laughlin Group and T. Rowe Price GIC Index.

EXHIBIT 19–5

GIC Yield Spreads (1982–1995)

Maturity (years)	High	Low	Average
1	2.40%	−0.65%	0.19%
2	2.24	−0.53	0.31
3	1.86	−0.13	0.46
4	2.25	0.06	0.56
5	2.28	0.06	0.72
7	2.48	0.05	0.69
10	2.77	−0.17	0.76

Source: Yield spread reflects spreads over equivalent maturity U.S. Treasury issues adjusted for semiannual versus annualized yields. GIC rate data obtained from The Laughlin Group and T. Rowe Price GIC Index.

EXHIBIT 19–6

Alternative Strategies

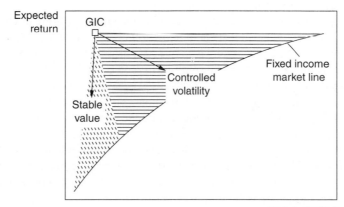

for investors in stable value funds as rates declined below the portfolio's blended yield. Should rates begin to trend significantly upward, the positive lag effect in the stable value portfolio could be replaced with a negative one.

As illustrated in Exhibit 19–6, the plan sponsor is being faced in the current environment with one of several alternative strategies. The traditional GIC historically has produced a competitive yield with little or no perceived real risks over time. Going forward, the decision could encompass a trade-off of general account risk for return. Stable value will be able to be maintained, but possibly at lower returns compared to other fixed income alternatives.

What are the current alternatives facing the plan sponsor?

- *Stable-value strategy.* Investment media include GICs, SACs, SICs, money market securities, and other book-value instruments.

- *Controlled volatility strategy.* Investment media include traditional GICs, SACs, SICs, money market instruments, other book-value instruments, and marketable fixed income securities.

- *Conventional fixed income strategy.* Investment media include money market instruments and marketable fixed income securities.

NEW STABLE VALUE INVESTMENT CONTRACTS

The creation of new types of investment contracts has been the next natural step in the evolution of the "GIC" market. The history of every securities market is characterized by increasing efficiency, better liquidity, and improved risk-management opportunities (e.g., credit and interest-rate risks) at each step in its evolution. The stable value market has been no exception.

The objective of a SAC or SIC is to diversify the credit exposure of the plan away from the unsecured general account or deposit obligation of the issuer. This is accomplished in several different ways. In SACs offered by insurance companies, separate accounts holding bonds, mortgages, and other fixed income instruments are established. Assets in such accounts appear to be protected by state laws against liabilities arising out of the insurance company's other business.[2] Often the insurer will pool accounts together into the separate account or, dollar size permitting, a plan may negotiate its own separate account. Securities are selected for the separate account by the insurance company within investment guidelines approved by the plan and the insurance company managing those assets. The insurance company provides a "wrap," which serves to amortize capital gains and losses in the portfolio, and provides a zero floor crediting rate and a "guarantee" that if an investing plan has a need for liquidity for normal course events, it can liquidate amounts needed to pay participants at book value.

SICs offered by both banks and insurers have emerged as another popular alternative. The plan sponsor or the plan's manager selects a portfolio of assets that are purchased and held in custody for the plan.[3] The bank or insurance com-

---

2. The buyer is cautioned to perform independent research to determine the rights of the plan in the event of issuer insolvency. The buyer also is cautioned to research both accounting and ERISA issues as they relate to SACs and SICs. See A.I.C.P.A. Statement of Position 94–4 released in September of 1994 for more information on book-value eligibility.

3. These types of contracts are drafted so that the plan actually owns the securities.

pany, as with a SAC, provides a zero-floor crediting rate and provides a wrap that gives the plan the right to liquidate the securities and receive book value in the event of participant-initiated liquidity needs.

The following description provides a summary of generic SACs and SICs.

Separate Account Contracts: Key Features

- Contract is typically a modified ("participating") group annuity contract.
- Securities are segregated from other liabilities of the issuer in a separate account.
- Securities are selected and managed by the insurance company within guidelines approved by the plan.
- Contract earnings rate usually is reset periodically (1-, 3-, 6-, or 12-month intervals) to reflect:
  - Gains and losses on individual securities.
  - Variance in performance from targeted return.
  - Changes in reinvestment rate.
  - Securities defaults.
  - Impact of deposits or withdrawals that alter the ratio of market value to book value or the average yield or duration of the portfolio.
- Differences between book value and market value due to the above factors are amortized, typically over the duration of the portfolio, and reflected in future credited rates, resulting in low volatility of returns. (See the appendix to this chapter for an explanation of crediting rate methodologies.)

Synthetic Investment Contracts: Key Features

- "Wrapped" structure can be either a single-security, immunized strategy or a constant-duration strategy.
- Contract may be fully participating, like SACs, where the impact of withdrawals is reflected in credited rates, or the contract may provide that the issuer absorb ordinary participant withdrawal risks.
- Securities usually held in a custody account in plan's name.
- Securities selected by plan or investment manager with issuer approval.
- Various levels of securities cash flow/return risk can be covered by a wrap contract.

Decisions regarding which type(s) of stable value products to use and in what proportions depend on the plan sponsor's objectives and analysis of many factors that relate the characteristics of the products to attainment of these objectives, all within the framework of the existing structure of the fund. For example, high-quality GICs still meet the credit, return, and cash flow needs of many plan sponsors. Single-security SICs may provide credit enhancement and diversification, but the return may be lower than for traditional GICs or other alternatives. Also, the plan may have to assume cash flow risks associated with asset-backed and mortgage-backed securities (the two most popular assets used for single-security strategies) if not assumed by the wrap provider. Constant-duration SICs may provide credit enhancement, added diversification, and the potential for higher return (due to exposure on the longer end of the yield curve) but might not provide future cash flows necessary for optimum liquidity since all cash flow is typically reinvested. Management fees and wrap charges are also important factors in evaluating alternatives.

Decisions are also heavily influenced by the structure of the total investment, which includes contract provisions and investments and how they interrelate. The contract must address questions such as: Does the contract meet all applicable ERISA, tax, and book value accounting requirements? How often is the crediting rate reset, and what method is used to calculate crediting rates? What options does the plan sponsor or investment manager have for terminating the contract, and what are the financial and accounting implications of termination? How are downgraded and defaulted securities handled? What happens in the event of default or breach of contract by the parties? GIC alternatives usually are purchased on an opportunistic basis only after evaluating the relative advantages and disadvantages of both the asset and liability components of each structure.

TYPES OF SICS

The three predominant strategies that have emerged in the marketplace, as illustrated in Exhibit 19–7, are the single-security, immunized, and constant-duration. The decision as to which strategy is best suited for a fund depends on the particular fund's investment objectives. As illustrated in Exhibit 19–8, returns can differ significantly, depending on market factors, including yield-curve positioning and slope, wrap fees, asset classes utilized, sector allocation, etc.

Single-Security SIC

A single-security SIC usually is structured with one fixed-income security; typically a U.S. agency issued mortgage-backed security or AAA-rated asset-backed security. Because both types of securities provide cash flows from a pool of liquidating collateral, many buyers choose to purchase a form of insurance from the wrapper in order to provide certainty as to the cash flows. Mortgages are subject to prepayment or refinancing and, as such, their cash flows are hard to predict. Asset-backed securities are typically structured around credit card receivables— their cash flows are more predictable, yet default rates are higher. Cash-flow protection at the front end is referred to as *prepayment coverage;* at the tail end it is referred to as *extension coverage.*

EXHIBIT 19–7

Features of Principal Types of Stable Value Investments

Feature	GICs	Single Security SICs* with Extension Coverage Only	Immunized SICs	Constant Duration SICs
Credit exposure	100% to issuer	Securities (Avg–agency). Minimal to SIC issuer.	Securities (Avg–AAA/AA). Minimal to SIC issuer.	Securities (Avg–AAA/AA). Minimal to SIC issuer.
Securities types	N/A–issuer general account	Treasuries, Agencies, CMOs, ABSs.	Treasuries, agencies, CMOs, ABSs, corporates, foreign governments.	Treasuries, agencies, CMOs, ABSs, corporates, foreign governments.
Return pattern	Fixed rate	Based on YTM at purchase. Varies, based on changes in securities repayment.	Achieve target rate over investment horizon. Relatively stable crediting rate but will change each reset based on performance.	Crediting rate changes each reset, based on performance. Will track but lag trend in market interest rates.
Investment cash flows	Fixed repayment as negotiated in contract	As securities repay, or at contract fixed maturity, whichever occurs first.	Scheduled dates. Amounts based on portfolio performance.	No set maturity. Perpetual until payout elected. Payment made "duration" years from election.
Investment management	Issuer's general account	Buy-and-hold. Replaced if necessary.	Periodic rebalancing (more passive than active). Emphasize scenario analysis and horizon returns.	Managed to maintain target duration. Emphasize sector rotation, credit research, quantitative techniques.
Deposit types	Lump sum or periodic	Lump sum or periodic.	Lump sum or periodic.	Lump sum or periodic crediting rate reset with each deposit.

Single-security SICs are structured to provide for a final maturity date. The interest rate may be fixed during the investment's life (if prepayment and extension risk coverage are purchased) or can change if no such coverage is purchased to reflect the cash-flow payment behavior of the underlying security(s).

Single-security SICs are often used to provide a future source of cash for benefit payments or reinvestment, or to complement the existing in-force portfolio ladder of traditional GICs.

EXHIBIT 19-8

Historical Spreads versus U.S. Treasury for GICs and SICs

	Benchmark		Spreads-Model Portfolios		
	5 Year Treasury Yields	5 Year GIC	5 Year Buy-and-Hold SIC	5 Year Immunized SIC	Constant Duration SIC
31-Jan-95	7.54	.48	.36	.36	.76
28-Feb-95	7.06	.40	.33	.35	.56
31-Mar-95	7.08	.40	.29	.40	.58
30-Apr-95	6.88	.32	.24	.46	.62
31-May-95	6.08	.38	.22	.37	.74
30-Jun-95	5.98	.39	.22	.40	.81
31-Jul-95	6.16	.40	.21	.43	.76
31-Aug-95	6.07	.37	.24	.39	.73
30-Sep-95	6.01	.42	.24	.31	.66
31-Oct-95	5.81	.35	.23	.44	.76
30-Nov-95	5.53	.39	.24	.46	.86
31-Dec-95	5.38	.33	.20	.30	.94

Immunized SIC Portfolio:		CDSIC Portfolio:	
26%	Agencies	17%	Treasuries
49%	A–AAA corporates	19%	Agencies
0%	Mortgages	29%	A–AAA corporates
25%	ABS	35%	Mortgages
Effective duration—4.92 years		Effective duration—5.01 years	
Average life—5.99 years		Average life—8.19 years	

All SICs net of wrap and custody fees.

Source: GIC rate data obtained from The Laughlin Group and the T. Rowe Price GIC Index. Bond data obtained from Lehman Brothers, *Bond Market Report.*

Immunized SIC

An immunized SIC, like a single-security SIC, has a final maturity date. It differs in that the strategy involves a portfolio of securities managed to a selected maturity date. The contract's maturity date and future payment amount establishes the contract liability. During the course of the investment term, the manager matches the underlying securities with the liability to ensure that sufficient funds are available on the payment date. The rate is subject to change as the manager rebalances the portfolio to correct for duration drifts and to reflect the amortization of both realized and unrealized gains and losses.

Constant-Duration SIC

Constant-duration SICs do not have a predetermined maturity date and will continue in force until the plan sponsor elects termination. (The wrap contract can be terminated by the plan at market value, usually upon payment of a penalty, or can be converted to a fixed-maturity contract with a maturity date approximately equal to the portfolio duration at the time of termination.) This open-ended arrangement permits the investment manager to position the portfolio continuously on the longer end of the yield curve which, with a normally positive slope to the curve, may increase investment returns over time. For example, the duration of the Lehman Brothers Aggregate Bond Index, generally in the 4.5–5.5 year range, is a common target duration for a portfolio supporting a constant duration strategy. (Duration of the supporting portfolio is rarely "constant," but will be managed within a narrow range around the target.)

Because of the higher returns potentially available from a constant-duration SIC, this type of contract often is used as a way to diversify investments and reduce exposure to a single industry while providing the opportunity for increased yields. One drawback to this type of investment is that the contracts do not throw off cash for possible future needs.

The constant-duration SIC, like other SICs, is available in various structures for providing benefit responsiveness. Generally, three types of liquidity for benefit responsiveness can be negotiated: a "put," where the wrapper absorbs the book-to-market differential if assets are sold; an "advance," where the wrapper advances funds to the plan and is repaid with cash flows arising from income from the assets and/or new contributions; and a "participating" feature, where all gains and losses are amortized over the portfolio's duration and reflected in the next crediting-rate reset.

The interaction of the constant-duration investment strategy and the crediting-rate mechanism produces a change in the crediting rate that will follow trends in market interest rates. This tracking ability is considered a positive feature of this contract type. When a constant duration contract is included in a portfolio comprised of different types of contracts, the crediting rate for the entire portfolio should be modeled to assess the incremental impact of the constant duration strategy.

EMERGING ALTERNATIVES: DERIVATIVE-BASED TRANSACTIONS

Given the broad-based financial dealings of wrappers, including derivative-based transactions, new strategies are emerging that incorporate swaps and other hedging strategies into the investment structure.

An emerging, fixed-maturity GIC/SIC alternative is the Alpha GIC (Alpha). Similar to a SIC, Alpha allows a plan to own and manage supporting securities, which a third-party wraps to provide benefit responsiveness. The securities typically are managed in an open-ended strategy, but the terms of the wrap generally are finite. This ensures that the contract matures at a predetermined point in the future.

The supporting securities are usually managed to a given index, and the index's return is paid to the wrap in exchange for a rate that resets periodically.[4] The Alpha rate generated is a base rate plus (minus) any outperformance (underperformance) of the securities versus the index.

To the extent the manager outperforms relative to the index, the opportunity for yield enhancement exists. However, the plan must be aware of and be comfortable with risks inherent in Alpha, including credit risks of the underlying securities, underperformance relative to the index, and the risk that the wrapper (or counterparty) will not meet its financial obligation.

A plan can employ multiple Alpha strategies, each wrapped by its own wrapper and supported by its separate pool of securities. Conversely, a plan can establish one pool of securities and have multiple wrappers wrap pieces of the pool. This conceptually enables a plan to employ a laddered series of fixed-maturity Alpha investments and an open-ended constant-duration component, if chosen, using a single pool of securities.

INVESTMENT CONSIDERATIONS

With SACs and constant-duration SICs, the plan sponsor often will depend on an investment manager or consultant to recommend investment guidelines consistent with the plan sponsor's overall investment philosophy and tolerance for risk. Typically, wrap providers are more flexible with respect to managed programs since credit and investment performance risks, as well as potential for higher return, are borne by the plan through the rate-reset mechanism. Accordingly, corporate bonds with credit ratings ranging from BBB to AAA are used in these portfolios in addition to the asset classes mentioned above.

To control risks at reasonable levels, investment guidelines generally specify types of permissible investments, credit parameters, and diversification limits by issuer and industry. There must be a clear understanding on the degree of market timing permitted in the management of the assets. This can range from a conservative strategy, where the duration of the portfolio is maintained at the duration of an agreed benchmark index, to a more aggressive strategy, where the duration may be varied within specified ranges around the duration of an index. Typically, portfolio durations will be maintained within a range of plus or minus six months of the duration of the benchmark index.

---

4. Certain Alphas include a counterparty to meet the terms of the swap.

SUMMARY

The new emerging alternatives to traditional GICs greatly expand opportunities for better meeting the needs and desires of plan sponsors and participants in managing stable value funds. At the same time, these alternatives create new challenges in understanding and communicating the new structures. Rarely has a segment of the financial markets exhibited such rapid and dramatic change. Most practitioners expect continuing developments in the foreseeable future.

APPENDIX

Crediting Rate Theory and Methodology

The managed SIC crediting rate is initially set approximately equal to the expected rate of return on the portfolio. The rate is then periodically reset to reflect changes in the portfolio, investment performance, changes in market interest rates, and, for some contracts, benefit payments. While there are at least three mathematically different methods for determining crediting rates, they are all conceptually consistent; that is, the crediting rate is the rate that will amortize differences between book value and market value over the duration of the portfolio. The various methods produce generally consistent crediting rates under most circumstances.

The crediting rate may be reset as frequently as monthly and generally not less than semiannually. Wrap fees and investment management fees are usually subtracted from the gross crediting rate to arrive at the net rate, which is credited to participant accounts.

Which method is preferred? The issuer and the investment manager usually decide on the crediting-rate method that best meets their needs. All three methods described below are in use, and all produce acceptable results.

METHOD 1—INTERNAL RATE OF RETURN

Using this method, the gross crediting rate is the internal rate of return (or discount rate) that equates projected future inflows of principal and interest to the current book value (present value).

Internal rate of return differs from "weighted average yield-to-maturity," defined as the sum of products of market value times yield-to-maturity for each individual security in the portfolio divided by total market value. In the examples below, the weighted average yield-to-maturity of the sample portfolio is 4.82 percent, while the internal rate of return is 5.30 percent. Since the yield curve is positively sloped, IRR is higher than weighted average yield-to-maturity because IRR gives proportionately greater weight to longer maturities.

The IRR formula is:

$$BV = \sum \frac{Cn}{(1+i)^n}$$

Where

BV = Book value
Cn = Cash flow in year n
n = Number of years to receipt of cash flow
i = Crediting rate (IRR)

Calculations for a sample portfolio are shown below.

Securities	Face Amount	Coupon	Maturity in Years	Current Market Value	Current Market Yield-to-Maturity	Duration
(A) Treasury note	100.00	4.875%	1.0	101.344	3.526%	0.99
(B) Treasury note	100.00	7.500	3.0	107.156	4.966	2.75
(C) Treasury note	100.00	7.875	5.0	108.906	5.882	4.27
Total market value of portfolio:				317.406	4.821%	2.71
Book value of portfolio:				317.406		

Time in years	Expected cash flows			(Book Value) Total Inflows
	(A)	(B)	(C)	(317.406)
0.5	2.4375	3.7500	3.9375	10.1250
1.0	102.4375	3.7500	3.9375	110.1250
1.5		3.7500	3.9375	7.6875
2.0		3.7500	3.9375	7.6875
2.5		3.7500	3.9375	7.6875
3.0		103.7500	3.9375	107.6875
3.5			3.9375	3.9375
4.0			3.9375	3.9375
4.5			3.9375	3.9375
5.0			103.9375	103.9375

IRR (annualized) of total cash flow on book value if book and market are equal:	**5.30%**
IRR if book value is 1% less than market value:	**5.69%**
IRR if book value is 1% greater than market value:	**4.91%**

METHOD 2—DISCOUNT RATE WHICH EQUATES CURRENT BOOK VALUE TO THEORETICAL FUTURE VALUE

First, a theoretical future market value is calculated by taking the current market value of the portfolio and compounding it forward at the average yield-to-maturity of the portfolio. The next step is to find the discount rate which equates this future value to the current book value of the portfolio. This is the gross crediting rate, as illustrated by the following formula:

$$MV(1 + YTM)^{DUR} = BV(1 + i)^{DUR}$$

where

   MV = Market value of portfolio
   YTM = Dollar-duration weighted yield-to-maturity
   DUR = Duration of portfolio.

The yield-to-maturity used in the above formula may be either dollar-duration weighted or dollar weighted. Dollar-duration weighting closely approximates IRR. In a constant-duration portfolio where cash flow is reinvested at longer maturities, dollar-duration weighting gives the best approximation of expected total return. In the case of an immunized portfolio where duration is collapsing, it is preferable to use dollar-weighted yield-to-maturity. In the example below, dollar-duration weighted yield-to-maturity is used. Dollar-duration weighted yield-to-maturity is 5.29 percent, whereas dollar weighted yield-to-maturity is 4.82 percent.

   Where the terms *yield-to-maturity* and *duration* are used in this discussion, the appropriate measures in the case of mortgages and optionable securities are effective or option-adjusted yield and effective duration.

   For the sample portfolio the calculations are as follows:

Securities	Face Amount	Coupon	Maturity in Years	Current Market Value	Current Market Yield-to-Maturity	Duration	Dollar Duration	Dollar Duration Times Yield-to-Maturity
(A) Treasury note	100.00	4.875%	1.0	101.344	3.526%	0.99	100.3306	3.5377
(B) Treasury note	100.00	7.500	3.0	107.156	4.966	2.75	294.6790	14.6338
(C) Treasury note	100.00	7.875	5.0	108.906	5.882	4.27	465.0286	27.3530
Total market value of portfolio:				317.406	4.821%	2.71	860.0381	45.5244
Book value of portfolio:				317.406			(a)	(b)

Dollar duration weighted yield to maturity [(b)/(a)] =   5.29%

Calculation of estimated future value: $317.406 * (1.0529)^{2.71} =$ 365.016

Discount rate which equates estimated future value to current book value:

   Gross crediting rate if book and market are equal $[(365.016/317.406)^{1/2.71} - 1]$:   **5.29%**

   Gross crediting rate if book value is 1% less than market value =   **5.68%**

   Gross crediting rate if book value is 1% greater than market value =   **4.91%**

METHOD 3—DIFFERENCE BETWEEN MARKET VALUE AND BOOK VALUE DIVIDED BY DURATION

The percentage difference between market value and book value is divided by the weighted average duration of the portfolio and added to the current dollar-duration weighted (or dollar weighted if appropriate) market yield-to-maturity. This method involves no exponentiation.

This formula is suitable only if the weighted average duration is greater than one year. If the duration is less than one year, particularly during a wind-down phase where market and book value must converge at termination, IRR should be used to calculate the crediting rate.

The formula is expressed as

$$i = YTM + \left[\frac{(MV - BV)}{MV} \right]^{\left[\frac{1}{DUR} \right]}$$

Example of Calculations for Sample Portfolio

Securities	Face Amount	Coupon	Maturity in Years	Current Market Value	Current Market Yield-to-Maturity	Duration	Dollar Duration	Dollar Duration Times Yield-to-Maturity
(A) Treasury note	100.00	4.875%	1.0	101.344	3.526%	0.99	100.3306	3.5377
(B) Treasury note	100.00	7.500	3.0	107.156	4.966	2.75	294.6790	14.6338
(C) Treasury note	100.00	7.875	5.0	108.906	5.882	4.27	465.0286	27.3530
Total market value of portfolio:				317.406	4.821%	2.71	860.0381	45.5244
Book value of portfolio:				317.406			(a)	(b)

Dollar-duration weighted yield to maturity [(b)/(a)] =   5.29%
Percent difference between market and book divided by weighted average duration:
     If book and market are equal   0.00%
     If book value is 1% less than market value   0.37%
     If book value is 1% greater than market value   −0.37%
Gross crediting rate:
     If book and market are equal   **5.29%**
     If book is 1% less than market   **5.66%**
     If book is 1% greater than market   **4.92%**

P A R T

3

CREDIT ANALYSIS

⑥ CREDIT ANALYSIS FOR CORPORATE BONDS*

Jane Tripp Howe, CFA
Vice President
Pacific Investment Management Company

Traditionally, credit analysis for corporate bonds has focused almost exclusively on the default risk of the bond—the chance that the bondholder will not receive the scheduled interest payments and/or principal at maturity. This one-dimensional analysis concerned itself primarily with straight ratio analysis. This approach was deemed appropriate when interest rates were stable and investors purchased bonds with the purpose of holding them to maturity. In this scenario, fluctuations in the market value of the bonds due to interest-rate changes were minimal, and fluctuations due to credit changes of the bond issuer were mitigated by the fact that the investor had no intention of selling the bond before maturity. During the past two decades, however, the purpose of buying bonds has changed dramatically. Investors still purchase bonds for security and thereby forgo the higher expected return of other assets such as common stock. However, an increasing number of investors buy bonds to actively trade them with the purpose of making a profit on changes in interest rates or in absolute or relative credit quality. The second dimension of corporate bond credit analysis addresses the latter purpose of buying a bond. What is the likelihood of a change in credit quality that will affect the price of the bond? This second dimension deals primarily with the ratios and profitability trends, such as return on equity, operating margins, and asset turnover, generally associated with common stock analysis. In practice, both dimensions should be applied in corporate bond analysis. In a sense, both dimensions are addressing the same issue—default or credit risk.

---

*The author wishes to thank Richard S. Wilson, Fitch Investors Service, Inc., for his helpful comments and suggestions.

However, only by using both dimensions of credit analysis will the analyst address the dual purpose of bond holding: security of interest and principal payments and stability or improvement of credit risk during the life of the bond.

Historically, common stock and bond research areas have been viewed as separate. However, with the development of options theory, the two disciplines are beginning to be viewed as complementary.

The value of the option is a direct function of the company's aggregate equity valuation. As the market value of a company's stock increases, the value of the option increases. Conversely, as the market value of a company's stock declines, so does the value of the option. The practical implication of this theory for corporate bond analysis is that the perceptions of both markets should be compared before a final credit judgment is rendered. For the analyst who believes that there is a higher level of efficiency in the stock market than in the bond market, particular attention should be paid to the stock price of the company being analyzed. Of interest will be those situations in which the two markets are judged to differ substantially.

For example, in early 1981 the market to book values of the major chemical companies ranged from .77 to 2.15. The bond ratings of these same companies ranged from Baa/BBB to Aaa/AAA. The interesting point is not the range of either the market to book values or bond ratings, but rather the fact that although there was some correlation between the market/book ratios and bond ratings, there were instances in which there was little or no correlation. Options theory would suggest that there should be more of a relationship between the two. When the relative valuation of the bond as measured by the rating is low compared with the equity valuation as measured by market/book, one or both markets may be incorrectly valuing the company. Given the evidence that bond-rating changes generally lag behind market moves, it is likely in this case that the bond market is undervaluing the company.

Although there are numerous types of corporate bonds outstanding, three major issuing segments of bonds can be differentiated: industrials, utilities, and finance companies. This chapter will primarily address industrials in its general description of bond analysis, and then discuss the utility and finance issues.

INDUSTRY CONSIDERATIONS

The first step in analyzing a bond is to gain some familiarity with the industry. Only within the context of an industry is a company analysis valid. For example, a company growing at 15 percent annually may appear attractive. However, if the industry is growing at 50 percent annually, the company is competitively weak. Industry considerations can be numerous. However, an understanding of the following eight variables should give the general fixed income analyst a sufficient framework to properly interpret a company's prospects.

Several of these variables should be considered in a global context. For example, it is not sufficient to consider the competitive position of the automobile industry without considering its global competitive position. As trade barriers fall, the need to become globally competitive increases. International competition is also an important factor in an analysis of the paper industry. Although U.S. firms had no plans to significantly increase capacity in 1996, global supply would be affected by capacity increases in several parts of the world, including Southeast Asia and Latin America.

Economic Cyclicality

The economic cyclicality of an industry is the first variable an analyst should consider in reviewing an industry. Does the industry closely follow GNP growth, as does the retailing industry, or is it recession-resistant but slow-growing, like the electric utility industry? The growth in earnings per share (EPS) of a company should be measured against the growth trend of its industry. Major deviations from the industry trend should be the focus of further analysis. Some industries may be somewhat dependent on general economic growth but be more sensitive to demographic changes. The nursing home industry is a prime example of this type of sensitivity. With the significant aging of the U.S. population, the nursing home industry is projected to have above-average growth for the foreseeable future. Other industries, such as the banking industry, are sensitive to interest rates. When interest rates are rising, the earnings of banks with a high federal funds exposure underperform the market as their loan rates lag behind increases in the cost of money. Conversely, as interest rates fall, banking earnings outperform the market because the lag in interest change works in the banks' favor.

In general, however, the earnings of few industries perfectly correlate with one economic statistic. Not only are industries sensitive to many economic variables, but often various segments within a company or an industry move countercyclically, or at least with different lags in relation to the general economy. For example, the housing industry can be divided between new construction and remodeling and repair. New construction historically has led GNP growth, but repair and remodeling have exhibited less sensitivity to general trends. Therefore, in analyzing a company in the construction industry, the performance of each of its segments must be compared with the performance of the subindustry.

Growth Prospects

A second industry variable related to economic cyclicality is the growth prospects for an industry. Is the growth of the industry projected to increase and be maintained at a high level, such as in the nursing industry, or is growth expected to decline, as in the defense industry? Each growth scenario has implications for a company. In the case of a fast-growth industry, how much capacity is needed to meet demand, and how will this capacity be financed? In the case of slow-growth industries, is there a movement toward diversification and/or a consolidation within the industry, such as in the trucking industry? A company operating within a fast growing industry often has a better potential for credit improvement than does a company whose industry's growth prospects are below average. However, barriers to entry and the sustainability of growth must be considered along with growth prospects for an industry. If an industry is growing rapidly, many new participants may enter the business, causing oversupply of product, declining margins, and possible bankruptcies.

Research and Development Expenses

The broad assessment of growth prospects is tempered by the third variable—the research and development expenditures required to maintain or expand market position. The technology field is growing at an above-average rate, and the companies in the industry should do correspondingly well. However, products with high-tech components can become dated and obsolete quickly. Therefore, although a company may be well situated in an industry, if it does not have the financial resources to maintain a technological lead or at least expend a sufficient amount of money to keep technologically current, its position is likely to deteriorate in the long run. In the short run, however, a company whose R&D expenditures are consistently below industry averages may produce above-average results because of expanded margins.

Evaluation of research and development is further complicated by the direction of technology. Successful companies must not only spend an adequate amount of resources on development, they must also be correct in their assessment of the direction of the industry. Deployment of significant amounts of capital may not prevent a decline in credit quality if the capital is misdirected. For example, computer companies that persisted in spending a high percentage of their capital expenditures on the mainframe component of their business suffered declines in credit quality because the mainframe business is declining.

Competition

Competition is based on a variety of factors. These factors vary depending on the industry. Most competition is based on quality and price. However, competition is also derived from other sources, such as airlines operating in bankruptcy that are able to lower their costs by eliminating interest on debt and rejecting high-cost leases and thereby gain a cost advantage.

Increasingly, all forms of competition are waged on an international basis and are affected by fluctuations in relative currency values. Companies that fare well are those that compete successfully on a global basis and concentrate on the regions with the highest potential for growth. Consumers are largely indifferent to the country of origin of a product as long as the product is of high quality and reasonably priced.

Competition within an industry directly relates to the market structure of an industry and has implications for pricing flexibility. An unregulated monopoly is in an enviable position in that it can price its goods at a level that will maximize profits. Most industries encounter some free market forces and must price their goods in relation to the supply and demand for their goods as well as the price charged for similar goods. In an oligopoly, a pricing leader is not uncommon. Philip Morris, for example, performs this function for the tobacco industry. A concern arises when a small company is in an industry that is moving toward oligopoly. In this environment, the small company's costs of production may be higher than those of the industry leaders, and yet it may have to conform to the pricing of the industry leaders. In the extreme, a price war could force the smaller companies out of business. This situation has occurred in the brewing industry. For the past two decades, as the brewing industry has become increasingly concentrated, the leaders have gained market share at the expense of the small local brewers. Many small local brewers have either been acquired or gone out of business. These local brewers have been at a dual disadvantage: They are in an industry whose structure is moving toward oligopoly, and yet their weak competitive position within the industry largely precludes pricing flexibility.

A concern also arises when there is overcapacity in the industry. Often, overcapacity is accompanied by price wars. This has periodically occurred in the airline industry. Generally, price wars result in an industrywide financial deterioration as battles for market share are accompanied by declining profits or losses.

Sources of Supply

The market structure of an industry and its competitive forces have a direct impact on the fifth industry variable—sources of supply of major production components. A company in the paper industry that has sufficient timber acreage to supply 100 percent of its pulp is preferable to a paper company that must buy all or a large percentage of its pulp.

The importance of self-sufficiency in pulp has increased over the past few years because of environmental restrictions related to the spotted owl. As a result of the spotted owl situation, over half of the timber provided by the federal forests in the Northwest was removed from the market. The removal caused pulp prices to skyrocket. As a result, companies with low self-sufficiency in the Northwest, such as Boise Cascade, have experienced significant losses in their paper segments. Affected companies were unable to pass along the increased costs because of the commodity nature of the business.

A company that is not self-sufficient in its factors of production but is sufficiently powerful in its industry to pass along increased costs is in an enviable position. RJR Nabisco is an example of the latter type of company. Although RJR Nabisco has major exposure to commodity prices for ingredients, its strong market position has historically enabled it to pass along increased costs of goods sold.

Degree of Regulation

The sixth industry consideration is the degree of regulation. The electric utility industry is the classic example of regulation. Nearly all phases of a utility's operations have historically been regulated. However, the industry has a federal mandate to deregulate. Initially, it was thought that deregulation would proceed rapidly. However, the complexity of the process suggests that the deregulation of the electric utility industry will take longer than originally thought. This change in time frame was the result of change in perceptions. Originally, legislators focused on the fact that deregulation would result in lower aggregate rates. More recently, legislators have focused on the fact that the benefit of lower rates will be offset in large part by a loss of control over rates.

The analyst should not be concerned with the existence or absence of regulation per se but rather with the direction of regulation and the effect it has on the profitability of the company. For the electric utility industry, the transition to deregulation will still be largely controlled by the regulatory authorities in a given state. In particular, regulatory commissions will have to deal with the treatment of stranded costs. These are costs that are unlikely to be recouped in future rates. Stranded costs include such items as generating plants whose cost/KW is above current market costs, and contracts with independent power producers to purchase power at above market prices. Although all electric utilities will transition to deregulation over the next decade, companies whose regulatory authorities assist in this effort will be better positioned than companies with unsupportive regulatory authorities.

Other industries, such as the drug industry, also have a high, though less pervasive, degree of regulation. In the drug industry, however, the threat of increased regulation has been a negative factor in the industry for some time. This risk was heightened periodically with the Clinton administration's health care proposals. The anticipation of increased regulation leading to lower profits in the pharmaceutical industry has contributed periodically to a major sell-off in these securities.

Labor

The labor situation of an industry should also be analyzed. Is the industry heavily unionized? If so, what has been the historical occurrence of strikes? What level of flexibility does management have to reduce the labor force? When do the current contracts expire, and what is the likelihood of timely settlements? The labor situation is also important in nonunionized companies, particularly those whose labor situation is tight. What has been the turnover of professionals and management in the firm? What is the probability of a firm's employees, such as highly skilled engineers, being hired by competing firms?

The more labor intensive an industry, the more significance the labor situation assumes. This fact is evidenced by the domestic automobile industry, in which overcapacity and high unionization have contributed to high fixed costs and cyclical record operating losses.

Many think that the power of unions has weakened over the past decade as membership has declined. Unfortunately for managements negotiating contracts, this decline in power attributable to a decline in membership has been offset in part by the ability of unions to easily disrupt production because of "just-in-time" inventory management. Because corporations inventory small amounts of parts, a strike at a critical parts plant can halt production at an entire corporation in a short time.

Accounting

A final industry factor to be considered is accounting. Does the industry have special accounting practices, such as those in the insurance industry or the electric utility industry? If so, an analyst should become familiar with industry practices before proceeding with a company analysis. Also important is whether a company is liberal or conservative in applying the generally accepted accounting principles. The norm of an industry should be ascertained, and the analyst should analyze comparable figures.

Care should also be taken when dealing with historical data. Frequently, companies adjust prior years' results to adjust for discontinued operations and changes in accounting. These adjustments can mask unfavorable trends. For example, companies that regularly dispose of underperforming segments and then highlight the more profitable continuing operations may be trying to hide poor management. In order to fully appreciate all trends, both the unadjusted and the adjusted results should be analyzed.

FINANCIAL ANALYSIS

Having achieved an understanding of an industry, the analyst is ready to proceed with a financial analysis. The financial analysis should be conducted in three phases. The first phase consists of traditional ratio analysis for bonds. The second phase, generally associated with common stock research, consists of analyzing the components of a company's return on equity (ROE). The final phase considers such nonfinancial factors as management and foreign exposure, and includes an analysis of the indenture.

Traditional Ratio Analysis

There are numerous ratios that can be calculated in applying traditional ratio analysis to bonds. Of these, eight will be discussed in this section. Those selected are the ratios with the widest degree of applicability. In analyzing a particular industry, however, other ratios assume significance and should be considered. For example, in the electric utility industry, allowance for funds used in construction as a percent of net income as well as the total amount of stranded assets as a percentage of equity are important ratios that are inapplicable to the analysis of industrial or financial companies.

Pretax Interest Coverage

Generally, the first ratio calculated in credit analysis is pretax interest coverage. This ratio measures the number of times interest charges are covered on a pretax basis. Fixed-charge coverage is calculated by dividing pretax income plus interest charges by total interest charges. The higher the coverage figure, the safer the credit. If interest coverage is less than 1X, the company must borrow or use cash flow or sale of assets to meet its interest payments. Generally, published coverage figures are pretax as opposed to after-tax because interest payments are a pretax expense. Although the pretax interest coverage ratio is useful, its utility is a function of the company's other fixed obligations. For example, if a company has other significant fixed obligations, such as rents or leases, a more appropriate coverage figure would include these other fixed obligations. An example of this is the retail industry, in which companies typically have significant lease obligations. A calculation of simple pretax interest coverage would be misleading in this case because fixed obligations other than interest are significant. The analyst should also be aware of any contingent liabilities such as a company's guaranteeing another company's debt. For example, there has been a dramatic increase in the insurance industry's guaranteeing of other company's debt. Today, this guaranteed debt exceeds the debt of the industry. Although the company being analyzed may never have to pay interest or principal on the guaranteed debt, the existence of the guarantee diminishes the quality of the pretax coverage. In addition, the quality of the guaranteed debt must be considered.

Once pretax interest coverage and fixed-charge coverage are calculated, it is necessary to analyze the ratios' absolute levels and the numbers relative to those of the industry. For example, pretax interest coverage for an electric utility of 4.0 is consistent with a AA rating, whereas the same coverage for a drug company would indicate a lower rating.

Standard & Poor's 1992–1994 median ratios of pretax interest coverage ranges for the senior debt of industrial companies were as follows:

Rating Classification	Pretax Interest Coverage
AAA	17.99
AA	9.74
A	5.35
BBB	2.91

Leverage

A second important ratio is *leverage,* which can be defined in several ways. The most common definition, however, is long-term debt as a percent of total capitalization. The higher the level of debt, the higher the percentage of operating income that must be used to meet fixed obligations. If a company is highly leveraged, the analyst should also look at its margin of safety. The margin of safety is defined as the percentage by which operating income could decline and still be sufficient to allow the company to meet its fixed obligations. Standard & Poor's 1992–1994 median ratios of leverage for the senior debt of industrial companies were as follows:

Rating Classification	Long-Term Debt/Capitalization
AAA	13.2
AA	19.7
A	33.2
BBB	44.8

The most common way to calculate leverage is to use the company's capitalization structure as stated in the most recent balance sheet. In addition to this measure, the analyst should calculate capitalization using a market approximation for the value of the common stock. When a company's common stock is selling significantly below book value, leverage will be understated by the traditional approach.

Occasionally, stockholders' equity can be negative, as was the case with FMC after it issued significant debt to repurchase its own stock in a leveraged recapitalization. Although FMC's equity was negative after the recapitalization, its stock market capitalization correctly indicated that the equity of FMC was valuable.

The degree of leverage and margin of safety varies dramatically among industries. Finance companies have traditionally been among the most highly leveraged companies, with debt to equity ratios of 10:1. Although such leverage is tolerated in the finance industry, an industrial company with similar leverage would have a difficult time issuing debt.

In addition to considering the absolute and relative levels of leverage of a company, the analyst should evaluate the debt itself. How much of the debt has a fixed rate, and how much has a floating rate? A company with a high component of debt tied to the prime rate may find its margins being squeezed as interest rates rise if there is no compensating increase in the price of the firm's goods. Such a debt structure may be beneficial during certain phases of the interest-rate cycle, but it precludes a precise estimate of what interest charges for the year will be. In general, a company with a small percentage of floating-rate debt is preferable to a similarly leveraged company with a high percentage of floating-rate debt.

The maturity structure of the debt should also be evaluated. What is the percentage of debt that is coming due within the next five years? As this debt is refinanced, how will the company's embedded cost of debt be changed? In this regard, the amount of original-issue discount (OID) debt should also be considered. High-quality OIDs were first issued in sizable amounts in 1981, although lower quality OIDs have been issued for some time. This debt is issued with low or zero coupons and at substantial discounts to par. Each year, the issuing company expenses the interest payment as well as the amortization of the discount. At issuance, only the actual bond proceeds are listed as debt on the balance sheet. However, as this debt payable will increase annually, the analyst should consider the full face amount due at maturity when evaluating the maturity structure and refinancing plans of the company.

The existence of material operating leases can understate the leverage of a firm. Operating leases should be capitalized to give a true measure of leverage. This approach is particularly enlightening in industries such as the airline industry, where leverage for the three major carriers increases from approximately 70 percent to 90 percent when leases are considered.

A company's bank lines often comprise a significant portion of a company's total long-term debt. These lines should be closely analyzed in order to determine the flexibility afforded to the company. The lines should be evaluated in terms of undrawn capacity as well as security interests granted. In addition, the analyst should determine whether the line contains a Material Adverse Change (MAC) clause under which the line could be withdrawn. For example, a company that has drawn down its bank lines completely and is in jeopardy of activating its MAC clause may have trouble refinancing any debt.

Cash Flow

A third important ratio is cash flow as a percent of total debt. Cash flow is often defined as net income from continuing operations plus depreciation, depletion, amortization, and deferred taxes. In calculating cash flow for credit analysis, the analyst should also subtract noncash contributions from subsidiaries. In essence, the analyst should be concerned with cash from operations. Any extraordinary sources or uses of funds should be excluded when determining the overall trend of cash flow coverage. Cash dividends from subsidiaries should also be questioned in terms of their appropriateness (too high or too low relative to the subsidiary's earnings) and also in terms of the parent's control over the upstreaming of dividends. Is there a legal limit to the upstreamed dividends? If so, how close is the current level of dividends to the limit? Standard & Poor's 1992–1994 Median Ratios of Funds From Operations/Long-Term Debt for the senior debt of industrial companies were as follows:

Rating Classification	Funds from Operations/ Total Debt
AAA	97.5
AA	68.5
A	43.8
BBB	29.9

Net Assets

A fourth significant ratio is net assets to total debt. In analyzing this facet of a bond's quality, consideration should be given to the liquidation value of the assets. Liquidation value will often differ dramatically from the value stated on the balance sheet. At one extreme, consider a nuclear generating plant that has had operating problems and has been closed down and whose chance of receiving an operating license is questionable. This asset is probably overstated on the balance sheet, and the bondholder should take little comfort in reported asset protection. The issue of overstated values on the balance sheet of an electric utility will be increasingly highlighted as the electric utility industry deregulates and has to explicitly deal with stranded investments. At the other extreme is the forest products company whose vast timber acreage is significantly understated on the balance sheet. In addition to the assets' market value, some consideration should also be given to the liquidity of the assets. A company with a high percentage of its assets in cash and marketable securities is in a much stronger asset position than a company whose primary assets are illiquid real estate.

The wave of takeovers, recapitalizations, and other restructurings has increased the importance of asset coverage protection. Unfortunately for some bondholders, mergers or takeovers may decimate their asset coverage by adding layers of debt to the corporate structure that is senior to their holdings. While the analyst may find it difficult to predict takeovers, it is crucial to evaluate the degree of protection from takeovers and other restructurings that the bond indenture offers.

In extreme cases, the analyst must consider asset coverage in the case of bankruptcy. This is particularly important in the case of lease obligations because the debtor has the ability to reject leases in bankruptcy. In the case of lease rejections, the resulting asset protection may depend on a legal determination of whether the underlying lease is a true lease or a financing arrangement. Even if the lease if determined to be a true lease, the determination of asset protection is further complicated by a determination of whether the lease relates to nonresidential real property or to personal property. The difference in security (i.e., recovery in a bankruptcy) is significant. Damages under a lease of nonresidential real property are limited to three years of lease payments. Damages under a lease of personal property are all due under the lease.

Standard & Poor's offers some assistance in this regard through its Event Risk Covenant Rankings, which assess the protection offered by the indenture to such restructurings. Standard & Poor's ranks this protection on a scale of E-1 (strong protection) to E-5 (little or no protection). The analyst must be mindful that indenture protection will vary significantly among the bonds of the same issuer.

Change of control covenants must be read carefully with particular attention to the definitions of change of control and whether the change of control has to be hostile in order to trigger the provisions.

In addition to the major variables discussed above, the analyst should also consider several other financial variables including intangibles, or unfunded pension liabilities, the age and condition of the plant, and working capital adequacy.

Intangibles

Intangibles often represent a small portion of the asset side of a balance sheet. Occasionally, particularly with companies that have or have had an active acquisition program, intangibles can represent a significant portion of assets. In this case, the analyst should estimate the actual value of the intangibles and determine whether this value is in concert with a market valuation. A carrying value significantly higher than market value indicates a potential for a write-down of assets. The actual write-down may not occur until the company actually sells a subsidiary with which the intangibles are identified. However, the analyst should recognize the potential and adjust capitalization ratios accordingly.

Unfunded Pension Liabilities

Unfunded pension liabilities can also affect a credit decision. Although a fully funded pension is not necessary for a high credit assessment, a large unfunded pension liability that is 10 percent or more of net worth can be a negative. Of concern is the company whose unfunded pension liabilities are sufficiently high to interfere with corporate planning. For example, a steel company with high unfunded pension liabilities might delay or decide against closing an unprofitable plant because of the pension costs involved. The analyst should also be aware of a company's assumed rate of return on its pension funds and salary increase assumptions. The higher the assumed rate of return, the lower the contribution a company must make to its pension fund, given a set of actuarial assumptions. Occasionally, a company having difficulty with its earnings will raise its actuarial assumption and thereby lower its pension contribution and increase earnings. The impact on earnings can be dramatic. In other cases, companies have attempted to "raid" the excess funds in an overfunded retirement plan to enhance earnings.

In periods of declining interest rates, the analyst must also consider the discount rate companies use to discount their future obligations. Companies generally use the yield of AA corporate bonds as a discount factor. Companies that persist in using a higher rate may be understating their unfunded pension obligations dramatically. General Motors announced in May 1993 that the drop in long-term interest rates could result in a $5 billion increase in its unfunded pension obligations because of a potential drop in its discount rate.

Age and Condition of Plant

The age of a company's plant should also be estimated, if only to the extent that its age differs dramatically from industry standards. A heavy industrial company whose average plant age is well above that of its competitors is probably already paying for its aged plant through operating inefficiencies. In the longer term, however, the age of the plant is an indication of future capital expenditures for a more modern plant. In addition, the underdepreciation of the plant significantly increases reported earnings.

The Financial Accounting Standards Board Statement Number 33 requires extensive supplementary information from most companies on the effect of changing prices. This information is generally unaudited, and there is still no consensus on the best presentation of such data. However, the supplementary information provision does give the analyst an indication of the magnitude of the effects of inflation on a given company. The effects differ dramatically from industry to industry. At one extreme are the high-technology and financial firms, where the effects are nominal. At the other extreme are the capital intensive industries, where the effects are major.

Working Capital

A final variable in assessing a company's financial strength concerns the strength and liquidity of its working capital. Working capital is defined as current assets less current liabilities. Working capital is considered a primary measure of a company's financial flexibility. Other such measures include the current ratio (current assets divided by current liabilities) and the acid test (cash, marketable securities, and receivables divided by current liabilities). The stronger the company's liquidity measures, the better it can weather a downturn in business and cash flow. In assessing this variable, the analyst should consider the normal working capital requirements of a company and industry. The components of working capital should also be analyzed. Although accounts receivable are considered to be liquid, an increase in the average days a receivable is outstanding may be an indication that a higher level of working capital is needed for the efficient running of the operation.

The state of contraction or expansion should also be considered in evaluating working capital needs. Automobile manufacturers typically need increased working capital in years when automobile sales increase.

Analysis of the Components of Return on Equity

Once the above financial analysis is complete, the bond analyst traditionally examines the earnings progression of the company and its historical return on equity (ROE). This section of analysis often receives less emphasis than the traditional ratio analysis. It is equally important, however, and demands equal emphasis. An analysis of earnings growth and ROE is vital in determining credit quality because it gives the analyst necessary insights into the components of ROE and indications of the sources of future growth. Equity analysts devote a major portion of their time examining the components of ROE, and their work should be recognized as valuable resource material.

A basic approach to the examination of the components of return on equity is presented in a popular investment textbook by Jerome B. Cohen, Edward D. Zinbarg, and Arthur Zeikel.[1] Their basic approach breaks down return on equity into four principal components: pretax margins, asset turnover, leverage, and one minus the tax rate. These four variables multiplied together equal net income/stockholders' equity, or return on equity.

$$\left(\frac{\text{Nonoperating pretax income}}{\text{Sales}} + \frac{\text{Operating pretax income}}{\text{Sales}} \right)$$
$$\times \frac{\text{Sales}}{\text{Assets}} \times \frac{\text{Assets}}{\text{Equity}} \times (1 - \text{Tax rate}) = \text{Net income/Equity}$$

---

1. *Investment Analysis and Portfolio Management* (Homewood, IL: Richard D. Irwin, 1977).

In analyzing these four components of ROE, the analyst should examine their progression for a minimum of five years and through at least one business cycle. The progression of each variable should be compared with the progression of the same variables for the industry, and deviations from industry standards should be further analyzed. For example, perhaps two companies have similar ROEs, but one company is employing a higher level of leverage to achieve its results, whereas the other company has a higher asset-turnover rate. As the degree of leverage is largely a management decision, the analyst should focus on asset turnover. Why have sales for the former company turned down? Is this downturn a result of a general slowdown in the industry, or is it that assets have been expanded rapidly and the company is in the process of absorbing these new assets? Conversely, a relatively high rise in asset-turnover rate may indicate a need for more capital. If this is the case, how will the company finance this growth, and what effect will the financing have on the firm's embedded cost of capital?

The analyst should not expect similar components of ROE for all companies in a particular industry. Deviations from industry norms are often indications of management philosophy. For example, one company may emphasize asset turnover, and another company in the same industry may emphasize profit margin. As in any financial analysis, the trend of the components is as important as the absolute levels.

In order to give the analyst a general idea of the type of ratios expected by the major rating agencies for a particular rating classification, Standard & Poor's medians of key ratios for 1992–1994 by rating category are outlined in Exhibit 20–1. The analyst should use this table only in the most general applications, however, for three reasons. First, industry standards vary considerably. Second, financial ratios are only one part of an analysis. Third, major adjustments often need to be made to income statements and balance sheets to make them comparable with the financial statements of other companies.

The importance of adjusting financial statements to capture differences among firms was highlighted in November 1993 by S&P's introduction of "adjusted key industrial financial ratios." In calculating its adjusted ratios, S&P eliminates nonrecurring gains and losses. In addition, S&P includes operating leases in all of its calculations.

Analysts interested in financial ratios for specific industries should consult Standard & Poor's CreditStats Service. This service, introduced in October 1989, presents key financial ratios organized into 53 industry groups as well as ratio analysis by long-term rating category for utility companies.

Nonfinancial Factors

After the traditional bond analysis is completed, the analyst should consider some nonfinancial factors that might modify the evaluation of the company. Among these factors are the degree of foreign exposure and the quality of management. The amount of foreign exposure should be ascertainable from the annual report.

E X H I B I T   20–1

Three-Year (1992–1994) Medians of Key Ratios by Rating Category

Adjusted key industrial financial ratios
Industrial long-term debt

Three-year (1992–1994) medians	AAA	AA	A	BBB	BB	B
Pretax interest cov. (x)	17.99	9.74	5.35	2.91	2.09	1.01
EBITDA interest cov. (x)	22.63	12.82	8.00	4.82	3.50	1.90
Funds from operations/total debt (%)	97.5	68.5	43.8	29.9	17.1	9.9
Free operating cash flow/total debt (%)	51.0	29.7	20.2	6.2	3.4	1.1
Pretax return on perm. capital (%)	28.2	20.6	16.7	12.7	11.6	8.3
Operating income/sales (%)	22.0	17.7	15.2	13.2	13.6	11.6
Long-term debt/capital (%)	13.2	19.7	33.2	44.8	54.7	65.9
Total debt/cap. incl. short-term debt (%)	25.4	32.4	39.7	49.5	60.1	73.4

Three-year (1991–1993) medians	AAA	AA	A	BBB	BB	B
Pretax interest cov. (x)	16.39	8.26	4.31	2.69	1.61	0.99
EBITDA interest cov. (x)	20.29	11.41	6.82	4.35	2.85	1.77
Funds from operations/total debt (%)	109.3	68.8	40.5	26.6	15.8	9.9
Free operating cash flow/total debt (%)	46.1	31.3	16.7	7.1	3.4	0.3
Pretax return on perm. capital (%)	27.1	19.9	15.3	11.5	10.4	7.6
Operating income/sales (%)	21.7	16.6	14.6	12.7	12.6	11.9
Long-term debt/capital (%)	11.9	22.8	33.6	44.6	56.5	68.0
Total debt/cap. incl. short-term debt (%)	24.9	29.5	41.0	50.2	61.3	77.1

Glossary

Pretax income from continuing operations.   Net income from continuing operations before (1) special items, (2) minority interest, (3) gains on reacquisition of debt, plus income taxes.

Eight times rents.   Gross rents paid multiplied by capitalization factor of eight.

Equity.   Shareholders' equity (including preferred stock) plus minority interest.

Free operating cash flow.   Funds from operations minus capital expenditures and minus (plus) the increase (decrease) in working capital (excluding changes in cash, marketable securities, and short-term debt).

Funds from operations (or funds flow).   Net income from continuing operations plus depreciation, amortization, deferred income taxes, and other noncash items.

Gross interest.   Gross interest incurred before subtracting (1) capitalized interest, (2) interest income.

Gross rents.   Gross operating rents paid before sublease income.

Interest expense.   Interest incurred minus capitalized interest.

Long-term debt.   As reported, including capitalized lease obligations on the balance sheet.

Operating income.   Sales minus cost of goods manufactured (before depreciation and amortization), selling, general and administrative, and research and development costs.

Total debt.   Long-term debt plus current maturities, commercial paper, and other short-term borrowings.

E X H I B I T   20–1

(Continued)

Formulas for Key Ratios

Pretax interest coverage = $\dfrac{\text{Pretax income from continuing operations} + \text{Interest expense}}{\text{Gross interest}}$

Pretax interest coverage including rents =

$$\dfrac{\text{Pretax income from continuing operations} + \text{Interest expense} + \text{Gross rents}}{\text{Gross interest} + \text{Gross rents}}$$

EBITDA interest coverage =

$$\dfrac{\text{Pretax income from continuing operations} + \text{Interest expense} + \text{Depreciation and amortization}}{\text{Gross interest}}$$

Funds from operations (or funds flow) as a % of total debt = $\dfrac{\text{Funds from operations}}{\text{Total debt}} \times 100$

Free operating cash flow as a % of total debt = $\dfrac{\text{Free operating cash flow}}{\text{Total debt}} \times 100$

Pretax return on permanent capital =

$$\dfrac{\text{Pretax income from continuing operations} + \text{Interest expense}}{\begin{array}{c}\text{Sum of (1) the average of the beginning of year and end of}\\ \text{year current maturities, long-term debt, noncurrent deferred}\\ \text{taxes, minority interest, and shareholders' equity and}\\ \text{(2) average short-term borrowings during year per footnotes}\\ \text{to financial statements}\end{array}} \times 100$$

Operating income as a % of sales = $\dfrac{\text{Operating income}}{\text{Sales}} \times 100$

Long-term debt as a % of capitalization = $\dfrac{\text{Long-term debt}}{\text{Long-term debt} + \text{Equity}} \times 100$

Total debt as a % of capitalization + short-term debt = $\dfrac{\text{Total debt}}{\text{Total debt} + \text{Equity}} \times 100$

Total debt + 8 times rents as a % of capitalization + short-term debt + 8 times rents =

$$\dfrac{\text{Total debt} + 8 \text{ times gross rentals paid}}{\text{Total debt} + \text{Equity} + 8 \text{ times gross rentals paid}} \times 100$$

Source: "Great Comments," Standard & Poor's Credit Week, November 8, 1993, pp. 41–42.

Sometimes, however, specific country exposure is less clear because the annual report often lists foreign exposure by broad geographic divisions. If there is concern that a major portion of revenue and income is derived from potentially unstable areas, the analyst should carefully consider the total revenue and income derived from the area and the assets committed. Further consideration should be given to available corporate alternatives should nationalization of assets occur. Additionally, the degree of currency exposure should be determined. If currency fluctuations are significant, has management hedged its exposure?

The internationalization of the bond markets and the ability of countries to issue debt in other countries highlights the importance of understanding the effect of currency risks. For example, many Mexican companies issued U.S. dollar de-nominated debt in the early 1990s. This issuance positively impacted the finan-cials of these Mexican companies because of the generally lower interest rates available in the United States relative to Mexico. However, when the peso was significantly devalued in December 1994, the ability of some of these companies to meet their U.S. dollar denominated obligations was questioned. Of particular concern were the companies whose revenues were largely denominated in pesos but whose interest expense was denominated in U.S. dollars.

The quality and depth of management is more difficult to evaluate. The best way to evaluate management is to spend time with management, if possible. Earnings progress at the firm is a good indication of the quality of management. Negative aspects would include a firm founded and headed by one person who is approaching retirement and has made no plan for succession. Equally negative is the firm that has had numerous changes of management and philosophy. On the other hand, excessive stability is not always desirable. If one family or group of investors owns a controlling interest in a firm, they may be too conservative in re-acting to changes in markets. Characteristics of a good management team include depth, a clear line of succession if the chief officers are nearing retirement, and a diversity of age within the management team.

INDENTURE PROVISIONS

An indenture is a legal document that defines the rights and obligations of the borrower and the lender with respect to a bond issue. An analysis of the indenture should be a part of a credit review in that the indenture provisions establish rules for several important spheres of operation for the borrower. These provisions, which can be viewed as safeguards for the lender, cover such areas as the limita-tion on the issuance of additional debt, sale and leasebacks, and sinking-fund provisions.

The indentures of bonds of the same industry are often similar in the areas they address. Correlation between the quality rating of the senior debt of a com-pany and the stringency of indenture provisions is not perfect. For example, sometimes the debt test is more severe in A securities than in BBB securities. However, subordinated debt of one company will often have less restrictive pro-visions than will the senior debt of the same company. In addition, more restric-tive provisions are generally found in private placement issues. In analyzing a company's indenture, the analyst should look for the standard industry provi-sions. Differences in these provisions (either more or less restrictive) should be examined more closely. In this regard, a more restrictive nature is not necessarily preferable if the provisions are so restrictive as to hinder the efficient operation of the company.

Bond indentures should be analyzed in conjunction with the covenants of bank lines. Frequently, bank lines can be more restrictive than bond indentures. The analyst should focus on the most restrictive covenants.

Outlined below are the provisions most commonly found in indentures. These provisions are categorized by industry because the basic provisions are fairly uniform within an industry. A general description of the indenture is found in a company's prospectus. However, notification is generally given that the indenture provisions are only summarized. A complete indenture may be obtained from the trustee who is listed in the prospectus.

Careful attention should be paid to the definitions in indentures as they vary from indenture to indenture. Frequently, the definitions of terms specify carveouts, or excluded items, that are material. For example, the definition of consolidated net assets may carve out or exclude changes resulting from unfunded pension liabilities.

Utility Indentures

Security
The security provision is generally the first provision in a utility indenture. This provision specifies the property upon which there is a mortgage lien. In addition, the ranking of the new debt relative to outstanding debt is specified. Generally, the new bonds rank equally with all other bonds outstanding under the mortgage. This ranking is necessary, but it has created difficulty for the issuing companies because some mortgage indentures were written more than 40 years ago. Specifically, because all bondholders must be kept equal, companies must often retain antiquated provisions in their indentures. Often these provisions hinder the efficient running of a company due to structural changes in the industry since the original writing of the indenture. Changes in these provisions can be made, but changes have occurred slowly because of the high percentage of bondholders who must approve a change and the time and expense required to locate the bondholders. Occasionally, a company may retire certain old issues in order to eliminate a covenant that has not been included in recent offerings.

Issuance of Additional Bonds
The "Issuance of Additional Bonds" provision establishes the conditions under which the company may issue additional first mortgage bonds. Often this provision contains a debt test and/or an earnings test. The debt test generally limits the amount of bonds that may be issued under the mortgage to a certain percentage (often 60 percent) of net property or net property additions, the principal amount of retired bonds, and deposited cash. The earnings test, on the other hand, restricts the issuance of additional bonds under the mortgage unless earnings for a particular period cover interest payments at a specified level.

Although both of these tests may appear straightforward, the analyst must carefully study the definitions contained in the tests. For example, net property additions may be defined as plant that has operating licenses. This was a particular concern during the 1980s. During that time, there was a great deal of nuclear construction, but operating licenses were slow to be granted. As a result, there was a significant backlog of construction work in progress (CWIP) that had to be financed, but which was not operational for some time. This situation presented problems for companies whose indentures require net plant additions to be licensed and/or used and useful assets. In the extreme case, a company may find itself unable to issue bonds under the mortgage indenture.

In a similar circumstance, a company whose regulatory commission requires a substantial write-down related to nuclear construction may find itself unable to meet a debt test for several years if the write-down is taken in one quarter.

The potential for such write-downs has become more visible since the implementation of SFAS 90. SFAS 90 requires utilities to record a loss against income for any portion of an investment in an abandoned plant for which recovery has been disallowed. It further requires all costs disallowed for ratemaking purposes to be recognized as a loss against income as soon as the loss becomes probable with respect to disallowances of new plant costs resulting from a cap on expenditures. These losses may be reported by either restating financial statements for prior fiscal years or by recording the cumulative loss the year SFAS 90 is adopted.

The application of FAS 71 may similarly affect electric utilities. Continued use of FAS 71 requires that (1) rates be designed to recover specific costs of regulated service and (2) it is reasonable to assume that rates are set to continue to recover such costs. In the current environment of a transition to deregulation, utilities may be required to partially or totally write down assets that are to be recovered in rates. Such write-downs may affect these companies' ability to issue first mortgage bonds.

Maintenance and Replacement Fund

The purpose of a maintenance and replacement fund (M&R) is to ensure that the mortgaged property is maintained in good operating condition. To this end, electric utility indentures generally require that a certain percentage of gross operating revenues, a percentage of aggregate bonded indebtedness, or a percentage of the utility's property account be paid to the trustee for the M&R fund. A major portion of the M&R requirement has historically been satisfied with normal maintenance expenditures. To the extent there is a remaining requirement, the company may contribute cash, the pledge of unbonded property additions, or bonds.

The rapid escalation of fuel costs during the 1970s has greatly raised the required levels of many M&R funds that are tied to operating revenues. This situation precipitated a number of bond calls for M&R purposes. Bonds can still be called for this purpose, but investors are more cognizant of this risk and are less likely to pay a significant premium for bonds subject to such a call. Furthermore,

M&R requirements are slowly being changed toward formulas that exclude the large portion of operating income attributable to increases in fuel costs. Finally, a number of companies have indicated that they have no intention of using M&R requirements for calling bonds because of the original intent of the provision and also because of the disfavor such an action would generate among bondholders. However, the intent of companies in this regard would certainly be secondary if a call for M&R requirements were ordered by a commission.

Redemption Provisions

The redemption, or call, provision specifies during what period and at what prices a company may call its bonds. Redemption provisions vary. Refunding is an action by a company to replace outstanding bonds with another debt issue sold at a lower interest expense. (Refunding protection does not protect the bondholder from refunding bonds with equity or short-term debt.) The refunding protection is a safeguard for bondholders against their bonds being refunded at a disadvantageous time.

Declines in long-term interest rates have motivated corporate treasurers to investigate all methods of redeeming high-coupon debt. For example, some indentures allow bonds to be called in the event of municipalization or in the event that the majority of assets are sold to a government agency. Careful attention to these possibilities is required to avoid an untimely redemption.

Sinking Fund

A sinking fund is an annual obligation of a company to pay the trustee an amount of cash sufficient to retire a given percentage of bonds. This requirement can often be met with actual bonds or with the pledge of property. In general, electric utilities have 1 percent sinking funds that commence at the end of the refunding period. However, there are several variations of the sinking fund provision with which the analyst (and bondholder) should be familiar because they could directly affect the probability of bonds being called for sinking fund purposes. Some companies have nonspecific, or funnel, sinkers. This type of sinker often entails a 1 or 1.5 percent sinking fund applicable to all outstanding bonds. The obligation can be met by the stated percentage of each issue outstanding, by cash, or by applying (or funneling) the whole requirement against one issue or several issues.

Other Provisions

In addition to the provisions discussed above, the indenture covers the events of default, modification of the mortgage, security, limitations on borrowings, priority, and the powers and obligations of the trustee. In general, these provisions are fairly standard. However, differences occur that should be evaluated.

Indentures of electric utilities must be scrutinized as part of the analysis during the deregulation process. In specific, attention must be paid to the ability of a company to remove assets from under its mortgage indenture. Some companies require that removal of assets must be made at fair market value, while other indentures are silent on this point. In addition, some companies may effectively remove assets through the use of purchased money mortgages.

Industrial Indentures

Many of the provisions of an industrial indenture are similar to those of a utility's indenture, although specific items may be changed. In general, there are five indenture provisions that have historically been significant in providing protection for the industrial bondholder.

Negative Pledge Clause

The negative pledge clause provides that the company cannot create or assume liens to the extent that more than a certain percentage of consolidated net tangible assets (CNTA) is so secured without giving the same security to the bondholders. This provision is important to the bondholders because their security in the specific assets of the company establishes an important protection for their investment. The specific percentage of CNTA that is exempted from this provision is referred to as exempted indebtedness, and the exclusion provides some flexibility to the company.

Limitation on Sale and Leaseback Transactions

The indenture provision limiting sale and leaseback parallels the protection offered by the negative pledge clause, except that it provides protection for the bondholder against the company selling and leasing back assets that provide security for the debtholder. In general, this provision requires that assets or cash equal to the property sold and leased back be applied to the retirement of the debt in question or used to acquire another property for the security of the bondholders.

Sale of Assets or Merger

The sale of assets or merger provision protects the bondholder in the event that substantially all of the assets of the company are sold or merged into another company. Under these circumstances, the provision generally states that the debt be retired or be assumed by the merged company. It should be noted that the merged company that assumes the debt may have a different credit rating.

Dividend Test

The dividend test provision establishes rules for the payment of dividends. Generally, it permits the company to pay dividends to the extent that they are no greater than net income from the previous year plus the earnings of a year or two prior. Although this provision allows the company to continue to pay dividends when there is a business decline, it assures the bondholders that the corporation will not be drained by dividend payments.

Debt Test

The debt test limits the amount of debt that may be issued by establishing a maximum debt/assets ratio. This provision is generally omitted from current public offerings. However, there are numerous indentures outstanding that include this provision. In addition, private placements often include a debt test. When present, the debt test generally sets a limit on the amount of debt that can be issued per dollar of total assets. This limitation is sometimes stated as a percentage. For example, a 50 percent debt/asset limit restricts debt to 50 percent of total assets.

Financial Indentures

Sinking-Fund and Refunding Provisions

Like industrial indentures, indentures for finance issues specify sinking fund and refunding provisions. In general, finance issues with a short maturity are non-callable, whereas longer issues provide 10-year call protection. Occasionally, an issue can be called early in the event of declining receivables. Sinking funds are not as common in finance issues as they are in industrial issues, although they are standard for some companies.

Dividend Test

Perhaps the most important indenture provision for a bondholder of a finance subsidiary is the dividend test. This test restricts the amount of dividends that can be upstreamed from a finance subsidiary to the parent and thereby protects the bondholder against a parent draining the subsidiary. This provision is common in finance indentures, but it is not universal. (One notable exception is International Harvester Credit, now Navistar.)

Limitation on Liens

The limitation on liens provision restricts the degree to which a company can pledge its assets without giving the same protection to the bondholder. Generally, only a nominal amount may be pledged or otherwise liened without establishing equal protection for the bondholder.

Restriction on Debt Test

The debt test limits the amount of debt the company can issue. This provision generally is stated in terms of assets and liabilities, although an earnings test has occasionally been used.

UTILITIES

Historically, utilities have been regulated monopolies. These companies generally operate with a high degree of financial leverage and low fixed-charge coverage (relative to industrial companies). These financial parameters have been historically accepted by investors due to the regulation of the industry and the belief that there is minimal, if any, bankruptcy risk in those securities because of the essential services they provide. The changing structure of the electric utility industry brought about by significant investment in nuclear generating units and their inherent risk as well as the transition to deregulation has changed this belief. Initially, the faltering financial position of General Public Utilities precipitated by the Three Mile Island nuclear accident and the regulatory delays in making a decision regarding the units highlighted the default risk that exists in the industry. More recently, the defaults of several Washington Public Power Supply System issues, the restructuring of Tucson Electric Company, and the bankruptcies of Public Service Company of New Hampshire and El Paso Electric Company and the transition to deregulation reemphasized the default risk. In addition, the industry is faced with the acid rain issue and increased uncertainty in construction costs and growth rates. In 1985, Standard & Poor's developed more conservative financial benchmarks for a given rating to reflect the increased risk in the industry.

Segments within the Utility Industry

There are three major segments within the utility industry: electric companies, gas companies, and telephone companies. This chapter will deal primarily with the electric utilities.

Nonfinancial Factors

Although financial factors are important in analyzing any company, nonfinancial factors are particularly important in the electric utility industry and may alter a credit assessment. The six nonfinancial factors outlined below are of particular importance to the utility industry.

The importance of nonfinancial factors led S & P to revise its financial ratios for electric utilities to explicitly take these nonfinancial factors into consideration. Specifically, in October 1993, S & P divided the electric utility universe into three groups according to business profile. These business profiles are: above average, average, and below average. Accordingly, the median financial parameters in the Financial Analysis section are segmented according to business risk as well as rating category.

Regulation is perhaps the most important variable in the electric utility industry because regulatory commissions largely determine how much profit an electric utility generates. All electric companies are regulated, most by the state or states in which they operate. If a company operates in more than one state, the analyst should weigh the evaluation of the regulatory atmosphere by revenues generated in each state.

The evaluation of regulatory commissions is a dynamic process. The composition of commissions changes because of retirements, appointments, and elections. The implications of personnel changes are not clear until decisions have been made. For example, it is not always the case that elected commissioners are pro-consumer and appointments by a conservative governor are pro-business. Several brokerage firms can assist in evaluations of commissions.

In addition, the Federal Energy Regulatory Commission (FERC) regulates interstate operations and the sale of wholesale power. Currently, FERC regulation is considered to be somewhat more favorable than that of the average state regulatory commission.

Utilities that are constructing or operating nuclear reactors are also subject to the regulation of the Nuclear Regulatory Commission (NRC). The NRC has broad regulatory and supervisory jurisdiction over the construction and operation of nuclear reactors. Importantly, the NRC approves licensing of nuclear reactors.

Regulation by state commissions, FERC, and the NRC is most visible. However, regulation by congressional action also has potential financial impact. For example, passage of acid rain legislation mandated the reduction of sulfur dioxide and nitrogen oxide emissions. In order to reduce these emissions, utilities can either install scrubbers or switch to low-sulfur coal. Either option is costly.

Utilities may be affected by the decisions of state commissions even if the commissions are located in a different state. For example, California has imposed significant penalties on long-term purchases of coal-fired energy by publicly owned California utilities. Therefore, non-California utilities that have historically sold coal-fired energy to California may find their energy priced too high.

Regulation is best quantified by recent rate decisions and the trend of these decisions. Although a company being analyzed may not have had a recent rate case, the commission's decisions for other companies operating within the state may be used as a proxy. Regulatory commissions are either appointed or elected. In either case, the political atmosphere can have a dramatic effect on the trend of decisions.

The regulators determine innumerable issues in a rate decision, although analysts often mistakenly focus only on the allowed rate of return on equity or the percentage of request granted. In particular, the commissions determine how much of construction work in progress (CWIP) is allowed into the rate base. A company may appear to have a favorable allowed ROE but be hurt by the fact that only a small portion of the company's capital is permitted to earn that return, and the CWIP earns nothing. Allowance of CWIP in the rate base was of critical importance during the 1980s because of the high construction budgets for nuclear generating plants and the length of time these plants are under construction. Some companies have had more than half of their capital in CWIP that is not permitted to earn a return.

The importance of whether CWIP is allowed in the rate base is highlighted by the financial distress and January 1988 bankruptcy filing of Public Service Company of New Hampshire (PSNH). PSNH's Seabrook Nuclear Unit I was virtually complete in 1986. However, licensing delays and New Hampshire's statutory prohibition of CWIP in the rate base were major contributing factors in the bankruptcy filing.

In addition, regulators have a high degree of control over the cash flow of a company through the allowance or disallowance of accounting practices and the speed with which decisions are made on cases.

The source of a company's energy is a second important variable. Currently, a company with a heavy nuclear exposure is viewed less favorably than a company with natural gas or coal units. Not only are nuclear assets subject to licensing procedures, but they will also require material decommissioning expenses. The energy source variable relates to a third variable—the growth and stability of the company's territory. Although above-average growth is viewed positively in an industrial company, it may be viewed negatively with respect to an electric utility. An electric utility with above-average growth may face construction earlier than its competitors. To the extent that CWIP is disallowed or only partially allowed in the company's rate base, the company is likely to have declining financial parameters until the unit is operational.

Slow growth is not necessarily positive if it places a utility in a position of excess capacity. The increase in cogeneration and the mergers executed in order to better match supply and demand can place a utility at risk. This could result if Utility A were selling power to Utility B. If the expiration of the contract coincides with Utility B's ability to purchase power for less and results in Utility B's nonrenewal of the contract, Utility A could be negatively affected unless it can sell the power to a third utility.

A fourth variable, whether or not a company is a subsidiary of a holding company, should also be considered. Holding company status permits nonutility subsidiaries, but these subsidiaries (even if successful) will not necessarily improve the overall credit quality of the company. This depends on the regulatory atmosphere. Furthermore, when there are several electric utility subsidiaries, the parent is more likely to give relatively large equity infusions to the relatively weak subsidiaries. The stronger subsidiary may have to support the other subsidiaries. Finally, holding companies should be analyzed in terms of consolidated debt. Although a particular subsidiary may have relatively strong financial parameters, off balance sheet financing may lower the overall assessment.

A final nonfinancial factor is the rate structure of a utility. An electric utility with a comparatively low rate structure is generally in a stronger position politically to request rate increases or to request a rate freeze than one with rates higher than national averages, and particularly one with rates higher than regional averages.

The competitive position of an electric utility is increasingly important as the possibility of retail wheeling increases. Those companies with high overall rates, and particularly those with high commerical rates, may find themselves losing customers as access to transmission and distribution lines increases.

In addition, those utilities with high stranded investments are vulnerable to competition. In the transition period to deregulation, many utilities have negotiated rates with their large industrial customers in order to retain them as customers. This negotiation is only a short-term solution if a utility's embedded costs are higher than those of utilities who have access to their service territory.

At best, negotiated rates for industrial customers will buy time for utilities with high costs to lower their costs to make them more in line with the rates of their competitors.

Financial Analysis

There are four major financial ratios that should be considered in analyzing an electric utility: leverage, pretax interest coverage, cash flow/spending, and cash flow/capital.

Leverage in the electric utility industry is high relative to industrial concerns. This degree of leverage is accepted by investors because of the historical stability of the industry. The expected ranges for AA, A, BBB, and BB companies are outlined below. No electric utility companies are currently rated AAA by Standard & Poor's.

Business Position	Total Debt/Total Capitalization			
	AA	A	BBB	BB
Above average	47%	52%	59%	65%
Average	42	47	54	60
Below average	—	41	48	54

In calculating the debt leverage of an electric utility, long-term debt/capitalization is standard. However, the amount of short-term debt should also be considered because this is generally variable-rate debt. A high proportion of short-term debt may also indicate the possibility of the near-term issuance of long-term bonds. In addition, several companies guarantee the debt of subsidiaries (regulated or nonregulated). The extent of these guarantees should be considered in calculating leverage.

Fixed-charge coverage for the electric utilities is also low relative to coverage for industrial companies. Standard & Poor's expected ranges for coverage are as follows:

Business Position	Pretax Interest Coverage (x)			
	AA	A	BBB	BB
Above average	4.0x	3.25x	2.25x	1.75
Average	4.5	4.0	3.0	2.0
Below average	—	5.0	4.0	2.75

These ranges are accepted by investors because of the stability of the industry. However, due to the changing fundamentals of the industry as discussed above, perhaps less emphasis should be placed on the exact coverage figures and more on the trend and quality of the coverage.

The utility industry is unique in that its earnings include an allowance for funds used during construction (AFUDC). AFUDC is an accounting treatment that allows utilities to recognize income (at a rate determined by individual regulatory commissions) on the amount of funds employed in construction. The percentage that AFUDC represents of total earnings varies significantly from almost zero to more than 70 percent of earnings. Obviously, the higher the percentage that AFUDC represents of net earnings, the lower the quality of earnings. This becomes evident when the cash flow of a utility is calculated. Often, the cash flow of a utility with substantial AFUDC is less than the dividend requirements of the company. In this instance, the company is returning the capital of the shareholders!

In calculating fixed-charge coverage, the analyst should calculate two sets of coverage figures—fixed-charge coverage including AFUDC and fixed-charge coverage excluding AFUDC, with the latter being more important.

A third important ratio is net cash flow/spending. This ratio should be approximated for three years (the typical electric company's construction forecast). The absolute level as well as the trend of this ratio gives important insights into the trend of other financial parameters. An improving trend indicates that construction spending is probably moderating, whereas a low net cash flow/spending ratio may indicate inadequate rates being approved by the commissions and a heavy construction budget. Estimates for construction spending are published in the company's annual reports. Although these are subject to revision, the time involved in building a generator makes these forecasts reasonably reliable. In 1985, Standard & Poor's deemphasized this ratio primarily due to its volatility. Although it will still be considered, Standard & Poor's now emphasizes funds from operations/total debt as a preferable indicator of cash flow adequacy.

Standard & Poor's benchmarks for net cash flow/capital expenditures and for funds from operations/total debt are as follows:

	Net Cash Flow/Capital Expenditures (%)			
Business Position	**AA**	**A**	**BBB**	**BB**
Above average	90%	70%	45%	30%
Average	110	85	60	40
Below average	—	105	80	60

	Funds from Operations/Total Debt (%)			
Business Position	**AA**	**A**	**BBB**	**BB**
Above average	26%	19%	14%	11%
Average	32	25	19	13
Below average	—	34	29	20

In calculating cash flow, the standard definition outlined above should be followed. However, AFUDC should also be subtracted, and any cash flow from nonregulated subsidiaries should be segregated and analyzed within the total context of the company. The regulatory commissions take divergent views on nonutility subsidiaries. Some commissions do not regulate these subsidiaries at all, whereas other commissions give inadequate rate relief to an electric utility with a profitable nonutility subsidiary under the premise that the company should be looked at as a whole. In the extreme, the latter view has encouraged companies to sell or spin off some subsidiaries.

FINANCE COMPANIES

Finance companies are essentially financial intermediaries. Their function is to purchase funds from public and private sources and to lend them to consumers and other borrowers of funds. Finance companies earn revenue by maintaining a positive spread between what the funds cost and the interest rate charged to customers. The finance industry is highly fragmented in terms of type of lending and type of ownership. This section will briefly outline the major sectors in the industry and then discuss the principal ratios and other key variables used in the analysis of finance companies.

Segments within the Finance Industry

The finance industry can be segmented by type of business and ownership. Finance companies lend in numerous ways in order to accommodate the diverse financial needs of the economy. Five of the major lending categories are (1) sales finance, (2) commercial lending, (3) wholesale or dealer finance, (4) consumer lending, and (5) leasing. Most often, companies are engaged in several of these lines rather than one line exclusively. Sales finance is the purchase of third-party contracts that cover goods or services sold on a credit basis. In most cases, the sales finance company receives an interest in the goods or services sold. Commercial finance is also generally on a secured basis. However, in this type of financing, the security is most often the borrower's accounts receivable. In factoring, another type of commercial lending, the finance company actually purchases the receivables of the company and assumes the credit risk of the receivables.

Dealer or wholesaler finance is the lending of funds to finance inventory. This type of financing is secured by the financed inventory and is short-term in nature. Leasing, on the other hand, is intermediate to long-term lending—the lessor owns the equipment, finances the lessee's use of it, and generally retains the tax benefits related to the ownership.

Consumer lending has historically involved short-term, unsecured loans of relatively small amounts to individual borrowers. In part because of the more lenient bankruptcy rules and higher default rates on consumer loans, consumer finance companies have dramatically expanded the percentage of their loans for second mortgages. The lower rate charged to individuals for this type of loan is offset by the security and lower default risk of the loan.

There are numerous other types of lending in addition to those described above. Among these are real estate lending and export/import financing.

The ownership of a finance company can significantly affect evaluation of the company. In some instances, ownership is the most important variable in the analysis. There are three major types of ownership of finance companies: (1) captives, (2) wholly-owned, and (3) independents.

Captive finance companies, such as General Motors Acceptance Corporation, are owned by the parent corporation and are engaged solely or primarily in the financing of the parent's goods or services. Generally, maintenance agreements exist between the parent and the captive finance company under which the parent agrees to maintain one or more of the finance company's financial parameters, such as fixed-charge coverage, at a minimum level. Because of the overriding relationship between a parent and a captive finance subsidiary, the financial strength of the parent is an important variable in the analysis of the finance company. However, captive finance companies can have ratings either above or below those of the parent.

A wholly owned finance company, such as Associates Corporation of North America prior to its IPO, differs from a captive in two ways. First, it primarily finances the goods and services of companies other than the parent. Second, maintenance agreements between the parent and the subsidiary are generally not as formal. Frequently, there are indenture provisions that address the degree to which a parent can upstream dividends from a finance subsidiary. The purpose of these provisions is to prevent a relatively weak parent from draining a healthy finance subsidiary to the detriment of the subsidiary's bondholders.

Independent finance companies are either publicly owned or closely held. Because these entities have no parent, the analysis of this finance sector is strictly a function of the strengths of the company.

Financial Analysis

In analyzing finance companies, several groups of ratios and other variables should be considered. There is more of an interrelationship between these ratios and variables than for any other type of company. For example, a finance company with a high degree of leverage and low liquidity may be considered to be of high investment quality if it has a strong parent and maintenance agreements. Variables should be viewed not in isolation but rather within the context of the whole finance company/parent company relationship.

Asset Quality

The most important variable in analyzing a finance company is asset quality. Unfortunately, there is no definitive way to measure asset quality. However, there are several variables which in the aggregate present a good indication of asset quality.

Diversification is one measure of portfolio quality. Is the portfolio diversified across different types of loans? If the company is concentrated in or deals exclusively in one lending type, is there geographic diversification? A company that deals exclusively in consumer loans in the economically sensitive Detroit area would not be as favorably viewed as a company with broad geographic diversification. Accounting quality is also an important factor in assessing portfolio quality. The security for the loans is also an important variable in portfolio quality. The stronger the underlying security, the higher the loan quality. The analyst should be primarily concerned with the level of loans compared with levels of similar companies and the risk involved in the type of lending. For example, the expected loan loss from direct unsecured consumer loans is higher than for consumer loans secured by second mortgages. However, the higher fees charged for the former type of loan should compensate the company for the higher risk.

Numerous ratios of asset quality such as loss reserves/net charge-offs, net losses/average receivables, and nonperforming loans/average receivables give good indications of asset quality. However, finance companies have a high level of discretion in terms of what they consider and report to be nonperforming loans and what loans they charge off. Therefore, unadjusted ratios are not comparable among companies. In addition, companies periodically change their charge-off policies. For example, in April 1990, ITT Financial Corporation liberalized its charge-off policy for consumer loans by changing to a modified recency basis from a present contractual basis. (Under a recency basis, delinquencies are measured from the date of last payment, regardless of payment history.) ITT reduced the implications of this change by eliminating "curing" activities under which the terms of the contractual loan are modified.

In spite of the drawbacks of the asset quality ratios, they are useful in indicating trends in quality and profitability. Of these ratios, loss reserves/net charge-offs is perhaps the most important ratio in that it indicates how much cushion a company has. A declining ratio indicates that the company may not be adding sufficient reserves to cover future charge-offs. Such a trend may lead to a future significant increase in the reserves and therefore a decrease in earnings as the increase is expensed. Net losses/average receivables and nonperforming loans/average receivables are other indicators of asset quality. An increasing ratio indicates a deterioration in quality. Declines may be exacerbated by an overall contraction or slow growth in the receivables. On the other hand, because of different accounting treatments, a stable net losses/average receivables ratio under deteriorating economic conditions may indicate a delay in loss recognition.

Leverage
Leverage is a second important ratio used in finance company analysis. By the nature of the business, finance companies are typically and acceptably more highly leveraged than industrial companies. The leverage is necessary to earn a sufficient return on capital. However, the acceptable range of leverage is dependent on other factors such as parental support, portfolio quality, and type of business. The principal ratio to determine leverage is total debt to equity, although such variations as total liabilities to equity may also be used. In a diversified company with high portfolio quality, a leverage ratio of 5 to 1 is acceptable. On the other hand, a

ratio of 10 to 1 is also acceptable for a captive with a strong parent and mainte-nance agreements. The analyst should always view the leverage of a finance com-pany in comparison with similar companies.

Liquidity

The third important variable in finance company analysis is liquidity. Because of the capital structure of finance companies, the primary cause of bankruptcies in this industry is illiquidity. If for some reason a finance company is unable to raise funds in the public or private market, failure could quickly result. This inability to raise funds could result from internal factors, such as a deterioration in earnings, or from external factors such as a major disruption in the credit markets. What-ever the cause, a company should have some liquidity cushion. The ultimate liq-uidity cushion, selling assets, is only a last resort because these sales could have long-term, detrimental effects on earnings. The traditional liquidity ratio is cash, cash equivalents, and receivables due within one year divided by short-term lia-bilities. The higher this ratio, the higher the margin of safety. Also to be consid-ered are the liquidity of the receivables themselves and the existence of bank lines of credit to provide a company with short-term liquidity during a financial crisis. In general, the smaller and weaker companies should have a higher liquidity cushion than companies with strong parental backing who can rely on an interest-free loan from the parent in times of market stress.

Liquidity considerations were heightened with the implementation of the SEC's rule 2a-7 in June 1991. This rule limits to 5 percent of assets the amount of medium-grade securities that a money market fund can purchase. As a result, companies whose commercial paper was downgraded to medium-grade are ex-cluded to a large extent from the commercial paper market. A company can avoid a liquidity crisis stemming from lack of access to the commercial paper market by retaining bank lines to back up their commercial paper. Westinghouse Credit was able to replace its commercial paper with bank financing in 1992, despite down-grades, because of the adequacy of its bank lines.

Asset Coverage

A fourth important variable in the analysis of finance companies that is related to the three variables discussed above is the asset coverage afforded the bondholder. In assessing asset protection, the analyst should consider the liquidation value of the loan portfolio.

A definitive assessment of the value of assets is difficult because of the flex-ibility finance companies have in terms of valuing assets. A finance company can value real estate assets on a number of bases. For example, a finance company that plans to liquidate its commercial real estate portfolio over twelve months in a depressed real estate environment will value its assets much lower than if it planned to systematically sell the same assets over a three- to five-year period. Westinghouse Credit's $2.6 billion write-off in the fourth quarter of 1992 demon-strates this difference.

Earnings Record

The fifth variable to be considered is the finance company's earnings record. The industry is fairly mature and is somewhat cyclical. The higher the annual EPS growth, the better. However, some cyclicality should be expected. In addition, the analyst should be aware of management's response to major changes in the business environment. The recent easing of personal bankruptcy rules and the fact that personal bankruptcy is becoming more socially acceptable have produced significantly higher loan losses in direct, unsecured consumer loans. Many companies have responded to this change by contracting their unsecured personal loans and expanding their portfolios invested in personal loans secured by second mortgages.

Size

A final factor related to the finance company or subsidiary is size. In general, larger companies are viewed more positively than smaller companies. Size has important implications for market recognition in terms of selling securities and of diversification. A larger company is more easily able to diversify in terms of type and location of loan than is a smaller company, and thereby to lessen the risk of the portfolio.

In addition to an analysis of the financial strength of the company according to the above variables, the analyst must incorporate the net effect of any affiliation the finance company has with a parent. If this affiliation is strong, it may be the primary variable in the credit assessment. The affiliation between a parent company and a finance subsidiary is straightforward; it is captive, wholly-owned, or independent. However, the degree to which a parent will support a finance subsidiary is not as straightforward. Traditionally, the integral relationship between a parent and a captive finance subsidiary has indicated the highest level of potential support. However, it is becoming increasingly clear that a wholly-owned finance subsidiary can have just as strong an affiliation. For example, General Electric Credit Corporation (GECC) finances few or no products manufactured by its parent, General Electric Company. However, General Electric receives substantial tax benefits from its consolidation of tax returns with GECC. Additionally, General Electric has a substantial investment in its credit subsidiary. Therefore, although there are no formal maintenance agreements between General Electric and GECC, it can be assumed that General Electric would protect its investment in GECC if the finance subsidiary were to need assistance. In other instances, it may be that the affiliation and maintenance agreements are strong but that the parent itself is weak. In this case, the strong affiliation would be discounted to the extent that parent profitability is below industry standards.

In addition to affiliation, affiliate profitability, and maintenance agreements, the analyst should also examine any miscellaneous factors that could affect the credit standing of the finance company. Legislative initiatives should be considered to determine significant changes in the structure or profitability of the industry.

THE RATING AGENCIES AND BROKERAGE HOUSES

There is no substitute for the fundamental analysis generated by the fixed income analyst. The analyst has many sources of assistance, however. The major sources of assistance are the public rating agencies and brokerage houses that specialize in fixed income research.

Rating Agencies

Four rating agencies provide public ratings on debt issues: Standard & Poor's Corporation, Moody's Investors Service, Fitch Investors Service, and Duff & Phelps.

Standard & Poor's (S&P) and Moody's are the most widely recognized and used of the services, although Duff & Phelps and Fitch are frequently cited. Fitch was revitalized in 1989 by a new investor group. S&P and Moody's are approximately the same size, and each rates the debt securities of approximately 2,000 companies. If a company desires a rating on an issue, it must apply to the rating agency. The agency, in turn, charges a one-time fee of generally $5,000 to $20,000. For this fee, the issue is reviewed periodically during the life of the issue, and at least one formal review is made annually.

All of the rating agencies designate debt quality by assigning a letter rating to an issue. Standard & Poor's ratings range from AAA to D, with AAA obligations having the highest quality investment characteristics and D obligations being in default. In a similar fashion, Moody's ratings extend from Aaa to C, and Fitch's from AAA to D. Duff & Phelps' ratings currently extend from AAA to CCC.

Public ratings are taken seriously by corporate managements because a downgrade or an upgrade by a major agency can cost or save a corporation thousands of dollars in interest payments over the life of an issue. In the event of downgrade below the BBB– or Baa3 level, the corporation may find its bonds ineligible for investment by many institutions and funds, by either legal or policy constraints. Corporations therefore strive to maintain at least an investment-grade rating (Baa3 or higher) and are mindful of the broad financial parameters that the agencies consider in deriving a rating.

Many factors promote the use of agency ratings by investors, bankers, and brokers. Among these strengths are the breadth of companies followed, the easy access to the ratings, and the almost universal acceptance of the ratings. On the other hand, the ratings are criticized for not responding quickly enough to changes in credit conditions and for being too broad in their classifications.

The slow response time of the agencies to changes in credit conditions is certainly a valid criticism. There are few instances in which the lag is significant in terms of a dramatic change, but the market generally anticipates rating changes. The rating agencies have become increasingly sensitive to this criticism and have been quicker to change a rating in light of changing financial parameters. On the other hand, the agencies recognize the financial impact of their ratings and their obligation to rate the long-term (as opposed to the short-term) prospects of companies. They therefore have a three- to five-year perspective and deliberately do not change a rating because of short-term fluctuations.

Standard & Poor's has addressed this criticism directly by creating *Creditwatch,* a weekly notice of companies whose credit ratings are under surveillance for rating changes. These potential rating changes can be either positive or negative. The basis for potential change can emanate from a variety of sources, including company and industry fundamentals, changes in the law, and mergers. Duff & Phelps also has a "Watch List" of companies that are potential upgrades or downgrades. Additionally, subscribers to the agencies' services have access to agency analysts to discuss individual companies or industries.

Investors who are concerned that the ratings are too broad in their classifications have several options among the brokerage-house services that offer more continuous ratings.

Brokerage-House Services

Numerous brokerage houses specialize in fixed income research. Generally, these services are available only to institutional buyers of bonds. The strength of the research stems from the in-depth coverage provided, the statistical techniques employed, and the fine gradations in rating. On the other hand, the universe of companies that these firms follow is necessarily smaller than that followed by the agencies.

In spite of the numerous services available, the market continues to demand more fixed income research. To partially satisfy this demand, many independent analysts are evaluating segments of the market previously not covered or inadequately covered.

CONCLUSION

This chapter has emphasized a basic method for analyzing corporate bonds. A format for analysis is essential. However, analysis of securities cannot be totally quantified, and the experienced analyst will develop a second sense about whether to delve into a particular aspect of a company's financial position or to take the financial statements at face value. All aspects of credit analysis, however, have become increasingly important as rapidly changing economic conditions and increasingly severe business cycles change the credit quality of companies and industries.

@ # CREDIT CONSIDERATIONS IN EVALUATING HIGH-YIELD BONDS

Jane Tripp Howe, CFA
Vice President
Pacific Investment Management Company

INTRODUCTION

Many analysts shy away from the analysis of high-yield bonds. Perhaps their reticence is a function of the security's lack of a rating or of a rating that is "below investment grade" and therefore publicly documented as having varying degrees of investment risk or elements of speculation. Although the comfort of an investment-grade rating is missing or its assignment is often enough to prohibit the security's inclusion in a portfolio, the potential rewards of this area of credit analysis are well worth the time invested.

The analysis of high-yield bonds, or junk bonds as they are unfortunately nicknamed, is similar to the complete analysis of any other corporate bond, but the emphasis of the analysis must change. Both high-yield and junk bonds are securities that trade primarily on their creditworthiness, as opposed to the level of interest rates. However, an important difference exists between junk and high-yield securities. Both classifications generate high yields. Although the yield of junk bonds reflects the poor quality of the underlying issuer, the yield of many high-yield securities reflects a variety of circumstances such as the small size of a firm or the lack of a credit history. Although rating agencies often penalize such a firm by giving it a low rating, the firm may exhibit good credit quality in many areas. It is this difference that presents the challenge to the credit analyst.

The recent expansion of the high-yield market presents an opportunity for the analyst to identify quality in issues that the majority of analysts have ignored. This process involves in-depth research. Because many high-yield bonds have short histories, the analyst must necessarily make more projections. Overall, the analysis will be heavily weighted to the second dimension of credit analysis discussed in Chapter 20—the aspects that are most commonly associated with the analysis of common stock. In addition, the analyst is often faced with innovative characteristics of the security, such as options exercisable only under certain circumstances. These features must be evaluated within the context of the total valuation process.

The artificial differentiation between bonds and the associated technique of credit analysis stem perhaps from some investors' segmentation of the market, whereby the bond portion is the "safe" area in which no risk should be taken. In this framework, potential rewards from bonds are probably not considered. Recent academic papers and numerous studies generated by the securities industry show the fallacy of such reasoning. These studies suggest that the historical risk/return relationship is consistent with what is expected from capital market theory: Although high-yield bonds have greater risk than Treasury securities and high-grade corporate bonds, they have provided higher returns.

If this is the case, why have these credits been historically so carefully ignored by most analysts? There are four major reasons for this inefficient behavior. First, institutional and legal constraints are often imposed on money managers, confining investments to "investment-grade" securities (i.e., those rated BBB– or higher by the rating agencies). Interestingly, these same money managers often buy the equity of a company whose debt they would not buy. Second, the high-yield market has been well developed for only a few years. Previously, the high-yield market lacked liquidity and stability. Portfolio managers hesitated to invest in this market for portfolios that required liquidity. Third, diversification in the low-grade market has historically been difficult. Until recently, the market has been heavily weighted in the railroad industry, as potential issuers relied primarily on bank financing and private placements. Finally, the lack of significant buyers restricted young growth companies from issuing public debt. High-yield securities were therefore associated with junk securities and the behavior was reinforced. A further discussion of these points is given in Chapter 16, along with a history of the high-yield market.

The analysis of high-yield bonds is essentially the same as the complete analysis of investment-grade bonds. However, because of the nature of the company, more time will generally be involved. Extensive market projections are often required, as well as possible explanations for inconsistencies in growth patterns. In addition, the commitment involved in the analysis of high-yield bonds cannot be made to merely analyze a single credit or even several credits. Because the prices of high-yield bonds change more as a function of changes in creditworthiness (nonmarket risk) than as a function of interest-rate changes (market risk), any commitment to high-yield bonds must be made within the context of a portfolio in order to help it benefit from diversification and lowering of specific risk. The analyst must be familiar with a number of industries to accomplish this.

The importance of diversification and its ability to increase expected return per unit of risk is an accepted tenet of portfolio management. Even portfolio managers who invest solely in high-grade securities will lower their risk by diversifying across industries, coupons, and maturities. The addition of a diversified portfolio of high-yield bonds may add more to a portfolio than the generally perceived higher rate of return. A study by Blume and Keim found that lower quality bonds experienced less volatility or risk than high-grade bonds or equities over the period studied, when risk was defined as the standard deviation of monthly returns.[1] Blume and Keim suggest that this result may be explained by the fact that much of the risk associated with high-yield bonds is nonmarket or firm specific and can therefore be eliminated by diversification.

The implications of this result are far reaching. Many investors, particularly institutional investors, are leery of the high-yield bonds because of the added risk they attribute to these bonds. This avoidance behavior is reinforced by the occasional well-publicized default or bankruptcy. The evidence shows, however, that the investor would be better off in terms of return and possible reduction of risk by including a diversified portfolio of high-yield bonds in a total portfolio. The avoidance behavior may in fact enhance yields. It is unfortunate that well-intentioned bureaucrats occasionally seek to protect the public by trying to legislate that certain types of high-yield securities be avoided. They may be increasing the rewards to the investors who do participate in the high-yield market.

As in any other bond analysis, the analyst's purpose here is to determine the value of the security. Will the issuing company be able to meet its interest and principal payments? Will the credit quality of the bond change over the life of the issue?

The progression of analysis for a high-yield bond should also be the same as that for any bond as discussed in Chapter 20. The analysis must be rigorous, however, as the margin of safety is generally more narrow. In addition, several areas of analysis should be expanded.

Competition

The size of a company has important credit implications. It is well known that many "small" firms file for bankruptcy each year. It should be noted, however, that these firms are not the same "small" firms that are issuing high-yield debt. The firms labeled small by investors are generally small only in relation to the giants of the industry. As the rating agencies favor the very large, well-established firms, the "small" firms suffer by comparison.

In an industry where the leader or leaders can set pricing, a small firm could be at a significant disadvantage. In the scenario where the pricing is set, the small

---

1. Marshall E. Blume and Donald B. Keim, *Risk and Return Characteristics of Lower-Grade Bonds* (Philadelphia: Rodney L. White Center for Financial Research, 1984), p. 4.

firm must have unit costs approaching, equal to, or lower than the pricing leaders. The small firm that is inefficient cannot withstand a prolonged pricing war. The leaders in this case could launch a pricing war to gain market share and effectively drive the inefficient producers out of business. In certain circumstances, the small firm may be able to differentiate its product and thereby control a certain segment of the market. However, there is always the threat of competition. The company with a market niche must be monitored to ensure that the niche remains the domain of the company in question.

Cash Flow

One of the most important elements in analyzing a high-yield security is cash flow. In such an analysis, cash flow/long-term debt is not as important as cash flow/total cash requirements. Does the company have enough cash flow to meet its interest payments and to fund necessary research and growth? Does the company have sufficient cash flow to tide it over during a period of weak economic activity? What borrowing capacity is available? The ability to borrow enabled several large firms such as Chrysler and Ford Motor to meet their debt obligations when these companies were experiencing significant losses. As a result, the companies were granted time to reformulate products and reposition themselves for an upturn in the economy and industry. The smaller firm may not have this advantage. On the other hand, the larger firms, which often have the luxury of expanding borrowings during weak markets, may be trading on their market name long after their credit quality has deteriorated.

The evaluation of cash flow coverage of fixed charges should not be conducted to the exclusion of total fixed-charge coverage. Some high-yield issuers have a high percentage of interest that is paid-in-kind. The identification of a clear path (or lack thereof) for meeting these obligations when they become cash payments is an integral part of an analysis of a high-yield bond. Future asset sales to meet these obligations may not materialize at the anticipated prices.

The analyst must particularly focus on cash flow in certain leveraged buyout situations. Although the purchaser may have a specific plan for selling assets to reduce debt and related payments, time may be critical. Can the company meet its cash obligations if the sale of assets is delayed? How liquid are the assets that are scheduled for sale? Are the appraised values of these assets accurate? What financial flexibility does the company have in terms of borrowing capacity? Are indenture covenants being met?

Net Assets

In analyzing a bond, the analyst must ascertain or at least approximate the liquidation value of the assets. Are these assets properly valued on the balance sheet? Of particular interest may be real estate holdings. For example, in analyzing the gaming companies, a market assessment of land holdings should be included. On the other hand, one should also consider the likelihood of those assets being available for liquidation, if necessary. To whom do they belong? Are they mortgaged or being used as collateral? Assets are occasionally spun off to the equity owners of the company. In such a circumstance, the bondholders may experience a sudden and dramatic deterioration of credit quality. Other bondholders are secured by specific assets such as railroad cars or a nuclear power station. In these circumstances, the value and marketability of the collateral must be ascertained. Collateral by definition must be specific and so must be the analysis. Ten railroad engines may appear to be secure until it is discovered that the engines are not only obsolete but have not been maintained for a number of years.

Particular attention must be paid to the asset protection in a takeover situation. In this instance, assets that originally provided protection for your holdings could be used to secure new debt senior to your holding.

The analyst must also focus on the location of the assets. If the assets are in a foreign country, the analyst should be familiar with that country's laws regarding expatriation of funds. In the extreme case, the analyst should be familiar with that country's laws regarding bankruptcy proceedings.

Management

Management is a critical element in the assessment of any firm. Given enough time, poor management can bankrupt the most prosperous firm. Conversely, good management is essential to the long-term survival of all firms. Many successful firms were started by employees of the leaders in an industry. The high-technology area is an example of this. Often, employees decide to start their own firms for personal profit. Very often the firms are founded by some of the leading engineers or salesmen. While the creative talents and profit motive in these firms may be high, the whole management team must be evaluated. Is there a strong financial manager? Is there a strong marketing manager? Where are the controls? Start-up operations provide high incentives for success. The ownership of a significant portion of the company by management is generally positive. Too often, employees of a large firm relate only to their personal paychecks and not to the overall profitability of the firm.

Leverage

Companies that issue high-yield bonds are generally highly leveraged. Leverage per se is not harmful and in many circumstances is beneficial to growth. However, the degree of leverage should be evaluated in terms of its effect on the financial flexibility of the firm. As pointed out in Chapter 20, leverage should be calculated on absolute and market-adjusted bases. The most common approach to market adjustment is to calculate a market value for the equity of the firm. To the extent that the common stock is selling below book value, leverage will be understated by a traditional approach. Some firms also adjust the market value of debt in calculating leverage. This approach is interesting, but a consistent approach must be employed when convertibles are considered in the equity equation. The benefit of adjusting the equity side of the leverage equation is clear. As the market values a company's equity upward, the market is indicating a willingness to support more leverage. A similar increase in the market adjustment of a firm's debt may indicate an upward appraisal of creditworthiness or an overall lowering of interest rates. In either case, the company would probably have the opportunity to refinance at a lower cost and thereby increase profitability.

SPECIAL TYPES OF HIGH-YIELD SECURITIES

In addition to the special circumstances involved in analyzing a high-yield security, the analyst is faced with nontraditional forms of financing. This is not surprising. Over the past ten years, the high-yield market has provided the majority of innovative financing. A thorough understanding of the type of security is necessary to complete an evaluation. Some modifications of the security have important implications for the analysis. The modifications and refinements to high-yield securities have been numerous. Several of these modifications are outlined below.

Exchangeable Variable-Rate Notes (EVRNs)

EVRNs are subordinated, intermediate-term obligations that pay interest quarterly. The interest rate is fixed for a short period. This period is called the "teaser" because the fixed rate is generally set above the rate dictated by the formula. After the fixed-rate period, the rate is adjusted quarterly and is tied to certain benchmarks such as the prime rate or 90-day Treasury bills. Generally, the issuer has the option to exchange the notes for fixed-rate notes with predetermined features such as maturity and call price. Generally, the issuer must exchange the securities after five years.

Usable Bonds

Usable bonds are securities that are issued with a warrant to purchase the issuing company's common stock. When the warrants are exercised, the bonds can be used at par in lieu of cash. (These bonds are also called synthetic convertibles when they are considered with their respective warrants.) The market value of these securities is sometimes highly correlated to the value of the company's stock and amount of usable bonds outstanding in relation to the amount required for exercise of the warrants.

Springing Issues

Springing securities are issues that will change one or more of their characteristics if a certain event occurs. One such issue was a note with springing warrants that would be exercisable only if someone tried to acquire the issuer. Another springing security was originally issued as subordinated debt but would become senior indebtedness when an old outstanding debenture had been discharged, as long as the issuing company was able to create the additional senior indebtedness without violating any covenants of a third outstanding issue. In evaluating springing issues, the analyst must determine the likelihood of the issue's changing form and the value of the change.

Pay-in-Kind Securities

Pay-in-kind securities (PIKs) give the issuer the option to pay interest in either cash or additional securities for a specified period of time. This option gives the issuer flexibility in terms of its cash-flow management. The PIK market has grown significantly in recent years. Many PIK securities are issued in Chapter 11 reorganizations.

In evaluating PIK securities, the analyst must use a discounted cash-flow technique if the security is trading at either a discount or a premium. This approach is required because the value of the payments-in-kind is equal to the current market value of the security.

Other Issues

In recent years, the assortment of high-yield securities has proliferated. Issues that offer a share of the firm's profits in addition to a stated interest rate, as well as issues backed by commodities, have been floated. Other firms have issued private placements with registration rights.

The variety of financing alternatives is likely to continue to expand. The analyst must evaluate the characteristics of each issue to determine how much, if any, value it adds to the credit. The analysis of low-grade securities often requires additional work. The investor is rewarded for this effort in two ways. The first benefit is enhanced yield. This yield advantage has been significant. Historically, low-grade securities have yielded 300 to 500 basis points more than comparable Treasury issues. The yield advantage over high-grade corporates has almost been as great. When this advantage is compounded annually, the performance benefit to individuals as well as institutional investors is significant. The advantage is only slightly reduced when default risk is considered. The second benefit of high-yield credit analysis is the likelihood of identifying credits that are improving. These credits will provide not only enhanced yield but also capital appreciation relative to the market. This benefit is familiar to the credit analyst who seeks to identify improving as well as deteriorating credits.

PERFORMANCE OF HIGH-YIELD SECURITIES
AND DEFAULT RISK

Historically, defaults and bankruptcies have been nominal in relation to outstanding U.S. debt. W. Braddock Hickman's study, *Corporate Bond Quality and Investor Experience*, concluded that, on average during the period 1900–1943, 1.7 percent of all straight public and private debt defaulted.[2] More recent studies have found historic default rates of only approximately .5 percent annually, with several years producing no defaults.

Recently, several default studies have been published. These studies address various time frames between 1970 and 1992. Although the studies vary in their methodologies and definitions of default, the consensus annual default figure is approximately 2–4 percent of all high-yield issues outstanding.

A recent Moody's study of default rates in the speculative grade securities calculated the weighted average one-year default rate for 1970 to 1992 at 4.58 percent.[3] This figure was influenced by the high default rates of 8.8 percent and 9.5 percent in 1990 and 1991, respectively. Although the level of defaults has declined since 1991, the possibility of another period of high defaults reinforces the need for in-depth credit research.

Any study of defaults must pay particular attention to the industry source of the default. When defaults are analyzed by industry, it becomes evident that close to 50 percent of the high-yield defaults during 1977–1987 were in the oil and steel industries. This fact clearly emphasizes the potential reward of credit research.

Regardless of how low default rates are in a given year, investors who own defaulted issues will be greatly affected if the defaulted issues represent a significant portion of their portfolios. A portfolio must be well diversified to prevent such losses.

In spite of careful analysis, the investor may be faced with a default or bankruptcy. In such a circumstance, analysis must continue. There have been situations where a defaulting issuer has subsequently resumed payments or issued stock to bondholders that eventually was worth more than the original debt.

The potential for defaults in the high-yield area has discouraged some investors from participating in this market. For some investors, this may not have been a rational decision. To fully evaluate the decision whether to participate in the high-yield market, investors must balance the potential for default with the potential for gain.

---

2. W.B. Hickman, *Corporate Bond Quality and Investor Experience* (Princeton University Press and the National Bureau of Economic Research, 1958).
3. "Corporate Bond Defaults and Default Rates 1970–1992," *Moody's Special Report,* January, 1993.

BROKERAGE HOUSES AND
THE RATING AGENCIES

As with high-grade securities, there is no substitute for sound fundamental analysis. The rating agencies can provide some help. In addition, more in-depth research in this area is being conducted by brokerage firms. Even *The Wall Street Journal,* in response to investors' demand for more information about the high-yield bond market, initiated coverage of junk bonds in 1991.

CONCLUSION

Analysts often classify themselves according to the type of security they analyze. This classification is misleading. An analyst who understands the principles of accounting and credit analysis should feel equally comfortable with high- or low-grade securities. Analysis will never be a rote process. It is only the good analyst who knows when to delve into a specific area exhaustively and when to quickly assess other areas of a company. This intuitive aspect of credit analysis is particularly important in analyzing low-grade credits. It can usually be developed with experience.

⑥ INVESTING IN CHAPTER 11 AND OTHER DISTRESSED COMPANIES*

Jane Tripp Howe, CFA
Vice President
Pacific Investment Management Company

Investors and analysts often shy away from distressed and Chapter 11 companies. On the surface, this hesitancy is understandable. Most investors would not
willingly invest in bankrupt companies, which the Random House Dictionary defines as "at the end of one's resources" or in the state of "utter ruin, failure, depletion, or the like." Most analysts believe that analysis directed at healthy
companies is more likely to be profitable. This avoidance of bankrupt and distressed companies is unwise for several reasons. First, investing in Chapter 11
companies can be highly profitable. Many companies use the bankruptcy process
to reorganize. Often, reorganization gives companies a new start that can provide
rewarding investment opportunities. The key to success is to differentiate between the companies that are truly depleted and those that will reorganize successfully. Second, a total avoidance of bankrupt companies may induce an
investor to sell a holding of a bankrupt company at its lowest price. The prices of
securities of companies that have filed for Chapter 11 often plummet when the filing is made. These prices often recover somewhat with time. Investors who immediately sell their securities upon news of a filing will suffer a more significant
loss than would occur if they were patient.

Historically, most investors who owned companies in bankruptcy did so by
default. Today, many investors actively invest in companies in reorganization.
These investors intend to profit by taking advantage of the substantial inefficiencies in this market. This chapter gives the investor an understanding of the bankruptcy process and outlines a method for evaluating securities in bankruptcy.

---

*The author wishes to thank George Putnam III, publisher of *Bankruptcy Datasource,* for his helpful
    comments and suggestions.

The methodology outlined here can also apply to companies that are distressed but have not filed for bankruptcy. In the case of distressed companies, the analyst should value the company as an ongoing business as well as a business that has filed for bankruptcy. With these two valuations in hand, the analyst will be able to weigh the potential benefit/cost of investing in the security.

THE IMPORTANCE OF A BASIC UNDERSTANDING

Most investors believe that they will never have to deal with a company that has filed for protection under the Bankruptcy Code. Although this may be true for the majority of investors, as long as there are bankruptcies, there will be investors who own the securities of the bankrupt companies. The possibility of owning the securities of one of these companies is increasing as the number of companies filing for protection under the Bankruptcy Code has been increasing in recent years. A basic understanding of bankruptcy analysis is also important in order to evaluate the potential rewards of this market.

OVERVIEW OF BANKRUPTCY

There are two types of investors who deal with the securities of companies in bankruptcy. The first type is the investor who owns the security by default. This investor purchases the security with the intention of profiting from a healthy company. The second type of investor buys the securities of bankrupt companies after the company has filed for protection. Regardless of how you came to own the security, the analysis of the holding is similar.

Investors who analyze their investment holdings carefully are unlikely to be surprised if one of their investments petitions for bankruptcy protection. The decline of a company into bankruptcy generally takes several years and is often the result of illiquidity and deteriorating operating performance. Although most bankruptcies can be predicted in advance with sound credit analysis, occasionally companies that are financially sound file for protection. For example, Johns Manville was profitable when it declared bankruptcy in August 1982. Manville filed for bankruptcy because of the contingent liabilities arising from claims of individuals who had contracted asbestos-related diseases as well as claims from property owners who incurred costs for the removal of asbestos materials from their property. Although bankruptcy filings for nonfinancial reasons are less easy to predict, they should not be complete surprises. For example, sometime in the future, tobacco companies could be faced with a similar situation regarding their contingent liabilities for illnesses caused by smoking. The astute analyst should always be mindful of footnotes that outline contingent liabilities.

All companies that file for bankruptcy are governed by the Bankruptcy Reform Act of 1978, which then-President Carter signed into law on November 6, 1978. The Act became law on October 1, 1979. The purpose of the law is twofold:

(1) to provide consistency to the companies filing for protection under the law and (2) to provide a framework under which a company can either reorganize or liquidate in an orderly fashion. Perhaps the most important facet of bankruptcy law is the protection it affords companies in distress. Filing for protection triggers the automatic stay provisions of the Code. This provision precludes attempts of creditors to collect prepetition claims from the debtor or otherwise interfere with its property or business. This provision gives the debtor breathing room to formulate a plan of reorganization or to formulate a plan for orderly liquidation. Creditors are necessarily discouraged from racing to the court to dismember the debtor.

The current Bankruptcy Code consists of 15 chapters. Each chapter deals with a different facet and/or type of bankruptcy. For most investors, an understanding of Chapters 7 and 11, which deal with corporate liquidation and corporate reorganization, respectively, is sufficient.

When a Company Files for Protection

When a company files for protection under the bankruptcy law, it can do so either voluntarily or involuntarily. A voluntary petition is filed by the company declaring bankruptcy. In an involuntary bankruptcy, the petition is filed by three or more creditors of the company whose claims are neither contingent nor subject to dispute.

When a company files for bankruptcy, the filing may include only the parent company and exclude one or more subsidiaries. For example, when Southmark filed for protection in July 1989, several of its subsidiaries were not included in the filing. These nonfiling subsidiaries included NACO Finance, Thousand Trails, Southmark California (Carlsberg Corp.), and Servico. In a similar manner, when Lomas Financial filed for Chapter 11 in September 1989, many of its operating subsidiaries were not included. In an effort to educate the investing public as to which of its subsidiaries filed and which did not file, Lomas Financial placed a full page advertisement in the New York Times to outline the difference.

When a company files for bankruptcy, it files in the appropriate circuit and the appropriate district within that circuit. (There are 11 circuits and 93 districts.) The "appropriate" court cannot necessarily be predicted. Appropriate can mean the court with jurisdiction over the company's headquarters location or perhaps the court with jurisdiction over its principal place of business. Companies have some flexibility in their choice of geographic location for filing. Eastern Airlines, for instance, filed in New York even though its corporate headquarters was in Miami. The airline stated it filed in New York because it had substantial operations in New York, and its financial efforts and lawyers were there. In addition, many of Eastern's creditors were also in New York, which facilitated meetings.

When a company petitions for protection, its petition is accompanied by several items, including basic administrative information and a listing of the 20 largest creditors. These creditors will be contacted by the court and called for a meeting. Other financial information is required within 15 days of filing. Sometimes, the financial information accompanies the filing. Other times, it is delayed. Included in this financial information is a listing of assets and liabilities as of the petition date. This listing represents the company's best estimate of its assets and liabilities. Often, this listing of assets and liabilities can cover several hundred pages.

Significant adjustments are often made to the assets and liabilities by the time a company completes its reorganization process. These adjustments are noticeable when assets are sold during the reorganization process and also when the asset values are compared with estimates of the liquidation value of the assets. This is principally because the values are based on the company as an ongoing business in its prepetition form. Revco's February 1989 sale of 113 sites exemplifies the discrepancy between listed asset values and realizable value. In its February 1989 sale, Revco was enabled (with bankruptcy court approval) to sell 14 sites. What is more significant, however, is the fact that no bids were made on several sites. The difference between listed market value of assets and the liquidation value of these assets can be even more dramatic. For example, in its September 5, 1989, Second Amended Plan of Reorganization, Cardis Corporation estimated that its inventory would be discounted by 52 percent. Cardis further estimated that its net plant, property, and equipment would be discounted by 23 percent in a liquidation. In fact, the only asset that will not suffer a discount will be cash.

Although the assets and liabilities filed with the Bankruptcy Court are not precise, they are useful because they give an indication of the overall picture of the company. For example, when Manville filed for protection in 1982, it had more assets than liabilities and was a profitable company. On the other hand, when Worlds of Wonder filed on December 22, 1987, it listed $271.6 million in debts and $222.1 million in assets.

Once a company files for protection under the Bankruptcy Code, the company becomes a "debtor-in-possession." As such, the company continues to operate its business under the supervision of the court. Usually, the debtor-in-possession needs to obtain court approval only for major and unusual transactions (such as the sale of property). Generally, the United States Trustee for the particular district is assigned to the proceeding. The U.S. Trustee's duties are essentially administrative. The appointment of the U.S. Trustee has become fairly routine.

The increasing complexity of bankruptcies has resulted in the increased frequency of a second appointment to a bankruptcy case. This appointment is usually an examiner but can also be a trustee. The requirements for the appointment of an examiner are fairly broad. An examiner can be appointed if the appointment serves the interests of the creditors, equity holders, or other interests. For example, an examiner was appointed in the case of A. H. Robbins because management had shown an inability to follow the bankruptcy rules. An examiner was also appointed in the case of Eastern Airlines, whose slide into bankruptcy was at least partially caused by striking unions. Shortly after Eastern Airlines filed for protection, the unions petitioned the court to have a trustee appointed to run the company. Eastern management petitioned the court to have an examiner appointed rather than a trustee so that it would have more flexibility in running its business. The federal bankruptcy judge in the Eastern case ordered the appointment of a "powerful" examiner, who was given a broad mandate to end the strike. Sometimes, if there are allegations of negligence or mismanagement, then an examiner will be appointed to investigate the allegations and report to the court. Occasionally, a trustee will be appointed by the court to take control of the business if there is gross negligence or mismanagement. This is relatively unusual. A recent case where a trustee was appointed was Sharon Steel, where there were allegations of fraud.

Proceeding toward a Plan

The purpose in filing for protection under the Bankruptcy Code is to give the debtor time to decide whether it should reorganize or liquidate and time to formulate a plan for the chosen action. The intent generally is to successfully reorganize. The first step in formulating a plan of reorganization is the appointment of committees. Generally, only a committee of unsecured creditors is appointed by the U.S. Trustee. Frequently, this committee is comprised of an elected subcommittee of the 20 largest creditors. The committee represents a particular class of claimants. Its principal function is to help formulate a plan of reorganization that is equitable to all classes and that will be confirmed (approved) by the court and the claimants. The committee approach is necessary because plans are negotiated.

Although only one committee is usual, there has been a growing incidence of multiple committees, each representing a different class of creditors. For example, in the Revco D.S. bankruptcy, there were two committees: the Noteholders Committee and the Unsecured Creditors Committee. In the Allegheny bankruptcy, there were four committees: the Equity Holders Committee, the Secured Creditors Committee, the Unsecured Creditors Committee, and the Sunbeam Corporation Creditors Committee. Often, the existence of multiple committees slows the bankruptcy process as factions can develop that undermine the spirit of cooperation necessary to formulate a plan. Cooperation is necessary because plans of reorganization rarely work under the premise of absolute priority; that is, the most senior classes are paid in full before a less senior class receives anything. The negotiation process inherent in a reorganization generally grants all classes some token distribution in order to obtain their acceptance of the plan. This is the reason why shareholders often receive some percent of the equity of the reorganized company. (The percentage distributed to the equity holders varies considerably. In recent plans of reorganization, equity holders of Po Folks were proposed to receive 0 percent, while equity holders of Allis Chalmers were proposed to receive 19 percent.)

This is also the reason why secured creditors accept less than a full recovery even if there are sufficient assets in the debtor's estate to satisfy the claim.

There are several theories that explain the high incidence of reorganizations that do not adhere to the absolute priority rule. These include the fact that junior creditors and holders of equity interests can significantly delay the reorganization process unless they are given a distribution in order to obtain their acceptance of the plan. Other plans are confirmed that do not adhere to the rule of absolute priority in order to preserve valuable net operating loss carryforwards that may be lost if a plan is confirmed according to strict absolute priority.

After the committee of unsecured creditors has been appointed, the debtor generally makes specific decisions whether to assume or to reject its executory contracts (contractual commitments entered prior to bankruptcy for the provision of future goods or services). In many bankruptcies, the rejection of high-priced contracts has been beneficial to the debtor. For example, when LTV declared bankruptcy, it was able to reject several high-priced contracts for raw materials. Several debtors have also rejected high-priced labor contracts. For example, in 1984, a bankruptcy judge upheld Continental Airlines' decision to break its labor agreements with its pilots union. The laws have changed for the rejection of labor contracts. Currently, collective bargaining agreements cannot be rejected so easily. Although many executory contracts can be rejected, specific rules may apply to the rejection of certain contracts. For example, Chapter 11 companies may reject leases with the approval of the Bankruptcy Court, only after they have made efforts to sell the sites. This was the case with Revco. After Revco had held an auction for 113 of its sites, the Bankruptcy Court was likely to grant Revco permission to reject the leases of sites for which no bids were received.

Formulation of a Plan

Once the committees are in place, the formulation of a plan begins. The debtor has the exclusive right to file a plan of reorganization for 120 days. The length of the exclusive period is determined by the court and can be extended or shortened. (Generally, the exclusive period tends to be longer than 120 days.) No other plan can be filed during this period, but this exclusive period does not stop other parties from formulating plans. In the case of Allegheny International, the unsecured creditors formulated a plan during the exclusive period (which had been repeatedly extended) because of their frustration with what they perceived to be lack of progress in the Allegheny bankruptcy. Generally, the first plan of reorganization is not the final plan. It is common to see the first amended and second amended plans of reorganization. (During August 1989, Allegheny International filed its Sixth Amended Plan of Reorganization.) Sometimes, even the debtor knows that its first formulation of a plan is not its final formulation. For instance, Allegheny actually labeled its August 30, 1988 Disclosure Statement "Preliminary." It is important to remember that a plan is commonly amended at least once before it is confirmed. Amended plans often entail significant changes in the funding of the plan, terms of the reorganization securities, and distributions to classes. Investors must be certain that they are working with the most recent plan of reorganization.

Investors must also be aware of plans of reorganization filed by others. For example, in September 1989, four plans of reorganization were filed for Public Service Company of New Hampshire. These plans were filed by (1) Public Service Company of New Hampshire (the debtor), (2) New England Power Company on behalf of itself and New England Electric System, (3) The United Illuminating Company, and (4) Northeast Utilities Service Company. A potential investor in Public Service Company of New Hampshire's securities would have to be familiar with each of these plans.

Historically, bankruptcy courts have allowed competing plans to be filed simultaneously. Recently, however, courts are more active in exercising their authority to determine which plans are distributed. This authority is most notably exercised in the court's extension of the period of exclusivity. The Integrated Resources reorganization exemplifies this new activism. The court refused to consider any plans that competed with the debtors' plan until the court determined whether the debtors' plan was confirmable. Once the debtors' plan was judged nonconfirmable by the court, the court authorized the filing of a competing plan by Steinhardt Management Company.

There are several ways to ensure that the investor is working with the most recent plan. One way is to keep in contact with the debtor. A second way is to subscribe to a bankruptcy service such as *Bankruptcy Datasource* in Boston, which has the advantage of being timely and convenient. A third way to is monitor the docket of the case with the bankruptcy court in which the petition was filed. A docket for a bankruptcy case lists all of the filings made with respect to the case. Therefore, the docket is an excellent source to alert the investor to new filings. Access to dockets varies significantly among bankruptcy courts. If an investor is interested in only one bankruptcy and happens to be located in the city in which the bankruptcy case was filed, monitoring the specific docket can be as simple as walking to the court and xeroxing the docket. More likely, investors will be following numerous bankruptcies filed in a variety of cities. In these circumstances, investors are dependent on the accessibility of the court. Fortunately for investors, electronic access to dockets is becoming more common. In addition, many courts are able to provide the names of copy services that are able to quickly access dockets and related filings and mail them for a fee. Unfortunately, some courts persist in requiring a written request for any document. Access to documents is thus more limited. Although documents are available for viewing, at specific courts documents are not available electronically. Copy services are usually the most expedient way of obtaining documents from such courts.

In filing a plan of reorganization, a debtor with one or more subsidiaries must decide if the plan will incorporate substantive consolidation of the subsidiaries. Under substantive consolidation, all of the assets and liabilities of the entities in question are pooled and used collectively to pay debts. Substantive consolidation must be approved by the court. The approval is not granted lightly.

In order for substantive consolidation to be granted, proponents must prove that the parent and the subsidiaries in question operated as a single unit. This can be proved by such means as intercompany guarantees and transfers of assets. The issue of substantive consolidation can have important ramifications for the investor. For example, in the case of LTV, the aerospace/defense subsidiary was profitable and had assets in excess of its liabilities. On the other hand, the steel subsidiary was unprofitable at the time of filing and had liabilities significantly in excess of its assets. If LTV is reorganized without substantive consolidation, investors owning the securities guaranteed by the aerospace/defense subsidiary will receive generous distributions. On the other hand, if substantive consolidation is granted, the distributions to these investors will be decreased as the assets of the aerospace/defense subsidiary are pooled to pay the debts of the entire corporation.

In fact, LTV eventually confirmed a plan premised on the substantive consolidation of LTV into five cases: LTV (Parent), LTV Steel, LTV Aerospace, AM General, and LTV Energy. The recoveries of the five cases varied significantly.

Disclosure Statement

Once a plan of reorganization has been finalized (and generally has been informally approved by the major creditors), the debtor produces and files for approval a disclosure statement about the plan with the court. The disclosure statement provides enough information to allow reasonable investors to make informed judgments. Approval of the disclosure statement is premised on the court's opinion that the disclosure statement contains sufficient information to allow reasonable investors to make informed judgments. Approval of a disclosure statement does not reflect an opinion of the court regarding the plan's merits.

A disclosure statement summarizes the plan. It also contains fairly detailed financial information about the debtor, including the company's five-year pro forma statements, which are required by statute. It also presents a liquidation analysis of the company that supports the company's contention that creditors will receive a higher distribution under the plan than they would if the debtor were to be liquidated. The disclosure statement also provides a brief history of the company, including reasons for filing and significant events since filing. The disclosure statement is generally more understandable and readable than the legal plan.

If the court approves the disclosure statement, the plan and the disclosure statement are mailed to the impaired classes for approval. Holders of claims that are not impaired (i.e., claims that are paid in full or whose interests are not adversely affected by the proceeding) are not entitled to vote because unimpaired classes are conclusively presumed to have accepted the plan. Classes that are entitled to vote are generally given 30 days to do so.

In order for a plan to be accepted, at least two thirds of the amount and more than one half of the number of claims actually voting of each impaired class and at least two thirds of the outstanding shares of each class of interests must accept the plan. If the plan is approved by the voting classes, it is sent to the court for confirmation. When the court confirms the plan, it approves the transactions specified in the plan and a date for the reorganization to take effect.

Cram-Down

It is interesting to note that a plan can be confirmed under the cram-down provisions even if the required number of creditors do not approve the plan. The confirmation of a plan under the cram-down provisions must meet several specific requirements. First, the plan must be shown not to discriminate unfairly against any impaired class. Such a determination includes the requirement that no class shall receive more than 100 percent of the amount of its claim. In addition, each dissenting class must receive as much as they would be entitled to receive under a liquidation. Often, plans state that the Bankruptcy Court will confirm the plan under the cram-down provisions if all the requirements are met except for the requirement that each class has accepted the plan. Second, a plan must be shown to be fair and equitable to a nonaccepting class. Under the Bankruptcy Code, a plan is fair and equitable to a nonaccepting class if, among other things, it provides that the nonaccepting class either (a) receives property of a present value equal to the allowed amount of such claims, or (b) if the class is to receive property of any lesser value, no class junior to the nonaccepting class receives or retains any property under the plan. Third, the plan must be accepted by at least one impaired class.

ANALYSIS OF COMPANIES IN REORGANIZATION

There are several different approaches that can be used to invest in the bankruptcy market. Large and aggressive investors buy a substantial block of the debtor's bonds and try to become a significant factor in the reorganization plan. Often these investors pool their resources in vulture funds, which invest in the securities of bankrupt companies. Such funds frequently operate by acquiring large blocks of a particular class of securities and use their leverage in the reorganization process to formulate a plan favorable to their position. Not all such strategies are profitable. In one case, a vulture fund acquired a large percentage of the subordinated debentures of a Chapter 11 company, hoping that it would receive a controlling equity interest in the reorganized company. Unfortunately for the vultures, more than 90 percent of the equity in the reorganized company was distributed to secured creditors.

Investing in Individual Securities

Another approach to investing in Chapter 11 companies, more suited to individual investors, is to buy specific securities in a bankrupt company. This approach has the advantage of not requiring a large investment, thereby allowing investors to diversify their investments. It does require a significant commitment to analysis of the company, but has the potential to be extremely profitable.

In buying the securities of a bankrupt company, the investor has the choice of investing for a general improvement in the overall condition of the company or of investing in situations (such as secured bonds) where the return is more quantifiable because of the assets.

Selecting the Universe

Selection of a universe of potential acquisition candidates is the initial step in investing in bankrupt securities. Thousands of corporations file Chapter 11 petitions yearly. However, many of these filings represent corporations whose securities are inappropriate for individual investment because the securities are not publicly traded or because the corporations are very small. In these cases, the individual investor could have difficulty obtaining sufficient financial information for analysis or purchasing the securities if analysis could be accomplished. Individual investors should confine their universe to companies that are publicly traded and have assets of at least $25 million. Potential candidates fitting this description can be collected from a variety of sources. An individual investor will probably find a sufficient universe from which to select simply by consulting the business section of newspapers. All listed bankruptcies are identified by a symbol. All bankruptcies listed on the New York, American, and the National Association of Securities Dealers Automated Quotations system's over-the-counter have a "vj" preceding the name of the stock. For example, BASIX Corporation was listed on the New York Stock Exchange Composite Transactions as of September 26, 1989, as vjBasix. The NASDAQ National Market Issue listings include an additional indication of bankruptcy. These listings are identified by a four- or five-letter symbol. The fifth letter indicates the issues that are subject to restrictions or special conditions. Securities that are in bankruptcy have a "Q" as the fifth letter of their symbol. For example, American Carriers was listed on the NASDAQ National Market Issues as of April 6, 1989, as vjAmCarriers ACIXQ. A reading of the business section of a major newspaper should keep investors current on recent bankruptcy listings.

OBTAINING FINANCIAL INFORMATION

Perhaps the most difficult aspect of investing in Chapter 11 companies is obtaining financial and trading information. Trading in the securities of small companies that have filed for bankruptcy can present problems if the companies are delisted. (If a company is delisted, its price can often be found on the National Daily Quotation Service Pink Sheets, published by the National Quotation Bureau. The Pink Sheets also provide potential market makers for the issues listed on the sheets.) More importantly, financial information can be difficult to obtain after a filing. Although SEC filing requirements are not suspended for Chapter 11 companies, filing requirements are often neither strictly observed nor enforced. Therefore, a potential investor may want to limit his or her universe of investment candidates to Chapter 11 companies whose filings are current. This is not always necessary, however, if the investor uses other sources of information and invests only in those securities that are clearly undervalued, employing alternative methods of evaluation.

Once a list of potential candidates has been selected, the collection of financial information should begin. For each company, the investor should obtain the most recent annual report, 10-K, and quarterly report. In addition, the investor should obtain the 8-K that reports on the bankruptcy because this document may have useful facts about the filing. These documents will give the investor some indication of how the company has performed historically and perhaps why it declared bankruptcy. (Old copies of *Value Line* are also useful for obtaining historical perspectives on companies.) The investor should also collect information on the company's publicly traded securities. For stock, such data would include current shares outstanding, par value, and current price.

The information that should be gathered for bonds is more substantial. Bond data should include a complete description of the bond, the amount of bonds outstanding including the amount of original-issue discount, price, and security (i.e., the specific assets supporting the bond). If the value of the security is known or can be estimated, this should also be listed. All bonds should be listed in order of seniority. Sometimes the securities data is found in the 10-K. More often, the investor needs to consult the appropriate *Moody's Manual* (industrial, public utility, etc.). These are found in most libraries.

It is also important to stay current on the news items that affect each of the companies being considered. An easy way to accomplish this is to use a computer news retrieval service such as the Dow Jones News Retrieval, which lists all news stories from the past 90 days from the Dow Jones News Service (the Broad Tape), *The Wall Street Journal,* and *Barron's*. Finally, one should attempt to be placed on the mailing list of the companies being considered. This is sometimes difficult, particularly for those who do not own any securities.

Investing Without a Plan of Reorganization

Perhaps the most important documents for the analysis of bankrupt securities are the most recent plan of reorganization and the accompanying disclosure statement. These documents specify what each class of claimants (including each class of security holders) will receive in a reorganization. If a plan of reorganization has not been filed, investors must speculate on the distributions to the classes. Because it does not lend itself to thorough analysis, investing without a plan of reorganization is not generally recommended for the individual investor. Although investors can make intelligent decisions regarding some of the more senior debt of the Chapter 11 company, the inability to analyze thoroughly causes trouble in the area of common stock. An analysis of distributions for numerous bankruptcies quickly reveals the variance of distributions for similar classes of claimants. This is most noticeable in the distributions made to holders of common equity interests who have received from zero percent to a major portion of the equity in the reorganized company.

Potential distributions to common stockholders can be further complicated if the "new value" principle is applied. This principle contends that the equity holders who contribute new money and/or management expertise to the reorganization should receive a substantial equity position in the reorganized company. Unfortunately for the holders of subordinated debt, the increased distribution to equity holders translates into a decreased equity distribution to them. Although this principle has been applied in some small bankruptcies, it is infrequently applied in the larger cases. This may change. Revco filed a preliminary proposal that grants 55 percent of the new Revco stock to its stockholders in exchange for $150 million. Under the proposal, secured creditors would have been paid in full, but subordinated debt holders received stock and bonds valued at only 25 percent of their claims.

The valuation of the securities of a debtor that has not filed a plan of reorganization is similar to a liquidation analysis with one important exception. The company is assumed to be an ongoing business, and therefore no substantial discount is applied to the value of its assets. Under this approach, the assets of the company are totaled and the liabilities are systematically subtracted from this total to give an approximation of how many assets are available to repay each class of claimants. Each class is subtracted in order of seniority. For example, the fully secured claims will be among the first to be subtracted. Although this approach is a quick valuation technique, it is imprecise. It can, however, be used even with somewhat dated financials. Furthermore, this methodology can be usefully applied to both a full value and a liquidation value of the company. This application would serve to bracket the value of the company with a worst case (liquidation value) as well as an optimistic case (full valuation). The application of this technique is outlined below.

Estimated Valuations of Securities

Total Assets		$xxx
Less:	Collateralized debt	
	Banks	−xxx
	Other	−xxx
Equals:	Amount remaining for distribution to other creditors	xxx
Less:	Amount due to other creditors (in order of seniority)	−xxx
Equals:	Amount remaining for distribution to equity holders	xxx

This approach is generally not applicable to the valuation of common stock simply because the assets are depleted before the common stockholders are eligible for a distribution. In order to estimate a value for common stock, one must make assumptions regarding the plan of reorganization and the percentage of the equity of the reorganized company that the old shareholders will receive. If this approach is used, the valuation of the common stock should follow the methodology presented under "Investing with a Plan of Reorganization."

Secured Bonds

A major exception to the premise that investors should generally wait until a plan of reorganization is filed relates to secured bonds. When a company petitions for protection, it is subject to the automatic stay provisions of the Bankruptcy Code. These provisions generally disallow the accrual of interest during bankruptcy, except in the case of secured debt. Secured claims are allowed to accrue postpetition interest during bankruptcy to the extent of the value of the collateral. (Although postpetition interest is accrued, the Code does not generally require that it be paid.) Given these provisions, an astute investor could conceivably purchase a secured bond whose collateral exceeds the principal amount of the bond at a substantial discount to par, knowing that eventually the bond will either be reinstated or be paid off at par plus postpetition interest. An example of how this provision of the Bankruptcy Code could have been beneficial to investors is provided by the LTV bankruptcy. When LTV filed for bankruptcy on July 1, 1986, all of its securities declined significantly. The overall decline overlooked the intrinsic value of the Youngstown Sheet & Tube First Mortgage bonds, whose collateral exceeded the value of the bonds. These bonds, therefore, were entitled to the continuation of their interest.

The recent significant declines in real estate values have focused attention on secured debt in bankruptcies. Because of the decline, the secured debt of many investors exceeds the value of the underlying collateral. In this scenario, investors have a secured claim only to the extent of their collateral. Any deficiency will be treated as an unsecured claim. These creditors are not entitled to postpetition interest. Given the major difference in treatment of secured versus unsecured claims, the debtor and the creditor frequently have major disputes regarding the value of a property. Generally, the creditor and the proponent of the plan negotiate a value for the collateral. If the creditor and the proponent are unable to negotiate a value, the bankruptcy court determines a value. Sometimes, the debtor satisfies its obligation to a secured creditor by simply transferring the collateral to the creditor. However, even the transfer of collateral in satisfaction of the debt can be complicated by the imposition of high taxes associated with such a transfer.

An additional exception to the automatic stay provisions relates to certain equipment trust financing. Much airline equipment debt and railroad equipment debt is exempt from the automatic stay provisions of the Code and the power of the court to repossess the equipment due to §§1110 and 1168 of the Bankruptcy Code, respectively. Instead, the court gives the debtor 60 days to reaffirm the lease on the equipment or return the equipment to the lessor. The debtor is unlikely to cancel the lease because the company cannot operate without the equipment represented by the lease. Airlines cannot operate without airplanes! Generally, in cases of §1110 equipment trusts, the debtor assumes the lease and resumes current interest payments, including interest payable during the 60-day period. Recent examples of §1110 equipment trusts are Eastern Airlines' 16.125 percent Secured Equipment Trust Certificates due 10/15/02 and Eastern's 17.5 percent Secured Equipment Certificates, Series A, due 1/1/98, and Series B, due 7/1/97. The fact that a particular equipment certificate is covered under §1110 is not part of the general description of the certificate. The investor must refer to the "Events of Default, Notice, and Waiver" section of the prospectus or indenture of a given issue to ensure that a particular trust certificate is covered.

Although secured claims are afforded special treatment in bankruptcy, investors must be studious in their appraisal of the underlying collateral and the fundamentals of the debtor. Even leases on airline equipment can be rejected if the bankrupt carrier is forced to liquidate or downsize dramatically.

Fraudulent Conveyance

Investors cannot rely blindly on the secured status of particular bonds. In some instances, fraudulent conveyance or transfer may become an issue. If fraudulent conveyance is proved, the seniority of debt may be reordered.

Fraudulent conveyance can become an issue when a company is restructured and security interests are granted in the stock or assets of a company. For example, assume that company A acquires company B in a leveraged buyout for $550 million. Before the buyout, company B's capital structure consisted of equity and $300 million in subordinated debt.

Assume further that the transaction was financed by $50 million in equity and $500 million in debt secured by the assets of company B. Company A subsequently filed for bankruptcy within six months of the LBO. At first glance, one would assume that the secured bonds issued by company A would be paid in full with company B's bonds receiving a share in the remaining assets. In fact, company B's bonds could be deemed senior to company A's bonds if it can be proved that a fraudulent conveyance occurred. Fraudulent conveyance can be proven if fraud was involved. It can also be proved if, at the time of the transfer, company B received less than fair or less than reasonably equivalent value for the transfer and either (1) it was insolvent or rendered insolvent by the transfer, (2) its remaining unencumbered property constituted unreasonably small capital, or (3) it is believed that it incurred debts beyond its ability to pay as such debt matured.

Investing with a Plan of Reorganization

The analysis of companies in bankruptcy that have filed plans of reorganization should be approached in the same systematic way that the analysis of any security is approached. However, there are two important differences. First, the analyst must place more emphasis on pro formas and less emphasis on historical results. This emphasis is necessary because a reorganized company is generally significantly different from the company that filed for protection. Second, the analyst must be a combination equity/fixed income securities analyst. It is not always clear which of the securities of the reorganized debtor are the most attractive. Often, the relative rates of return among old securities are substantially reordered under the plan. The analyst must therefore be willing to value all securities of the debtor and purchase those that offer the highest potential returns.

Evaluation of the Plan

The first step in analyzing a company in bankruptcy that has filed a plan is to carefully read the plan and determine the distribution each class will receive upon reorganization. This effort should be conducted on a per share or per bond basis. Terms of new securities that are to be issued under the plan should be examined carefully so that they can be valued properly. Often, securities issued in reorganization have unique characteristics. For example, the senior notes proposed under Texas International's April 28, 1989, Plan of Reorganization provided for an initial coupon payment 39 months after issuance. The notes proposed under Delta U.S.'s May 1989 plan provided that interest and principal repayments could be deferred for a specific period if cash flow and rig count, respectively, were below certain levels. Furthermore, an increasing number of issues proposed under plans of reorganization are bonds whose interest may be paid-in-kind at the option of the reorganized debtor.

The analysis of a plan should begin with a listing of each class of creditor, the amount of the claim, the proposed distribution, the proposed distribution per security (where applicable), and the value of the distribution. This part of the analysis could take the form of the hypothetical ABC Incorporated shown in Exhibit 22–1.

EXHIBIT 22–1

Plan of Reorganization—ABC Incorporated

Class	Amount of Claim	Total Distribution	Distribution per Security	Valuation per Security
1st mortgage bonds	$100 million	$100 million plus pre- and post-petition interest in cash	100%	100%
Debentures	$100 million	$100 million face value of debentures of reorganized debtor	100%	90%[a]

[a]The amount of discount attributable to the new debentures is a function of coupon, credit considerations, etc.

Frequently, there are only 6 to 12 classes of creditors. These can be individually listed. Sometimes, as in the case of Allegheny International, there are over 50. In these instances, it is wise to itemize only the relevant classes or consolidate the classes to make them more manageable. The classes that should be listed are those that contain publicly traded securities or that receive securities to be publicly traded. By consolidating the proposed distribution in this manner, the investor can easily focus on the relevant securities.

It is also advisable at this point to chart the proposed equity ownership per class. This chart allows the investor to quickly convert changes in the valuation of the company into tangible values. A chart of equity ownership could take the form shown in Exhibit 22–2.

Western Company of North America's equity ownership is fairly straightforward. The only dilution that has to be considered is the possible exercise of employee options. Frequently, the distribution of equity in plans of reorganization is more complex, with warrants and options affecting the fully diluted stock ownership of several classes. In such cases, it is helpful to include additional columns that outline the fully diluted common stock ownership. This chart could take the form of Exhibit 22–3, which outlines the equity ownership proposed under Heck's Second Amended Plan.

Determining a Price per Share for the Debtor

Once the specifics of the plan of reorganization are known, including potential dilution, the valuation of the company can proceed. In this chapter, Cardis Corporation will be used for our analysis.

EXHIBIT 22–2

Distribution of New Common Stock of Western Company of North America: Second Amended Plan of Reorganization

Class	Number of Shares	% of Common
Senior unsecured claims	8,750,000	70.00
Senior subordinated claims	1,285,438	10.28
Junior subordinated claims	1,120,812	8.97
Old preferred stock	562,500	4.50
Old common stock	406,250	3.25
Management incentive compensation plan	375,000	3.00
Total	12,500,000	100.00
Reserved for employee option plans	956,250	7.1

Source: Western Company of North America's Second Amended Plan of Reorganization and Disclosure Statement dated January 19, 1989, *Bankruptcy Datasource,* Boston, MA.

E X H I B I T   22–3

Proposed Equity Ownership of Heck's

	Number of Shares	% of Common	Fully Diluted Number of Shares	% of Common
Unsecured claims and PNB	2,000,000	79%	2,000,000	68%
Shareholder actions	22,222	1	22,222	1
Old common	200,000 60,000 warrants	8	260,000	9
Key employees	225,000 warrants	0	225,000	7
Hallwood	294,967 147,484 warrants	12	442,451	15
Total	2,517,189 shares	100%	2,949,673	100%

Source: Heck's Second Amended Joint Plan of Reorganization and Disclosure Statement dated March 24, 1989, *Bankruptcy Datasource*, Boston, MA.

Often, disclosure statements provide a valuation or a valuation range for the stock of the reorganized debtor. This valuation is generally provided by the financial advisor to the debtor. The use of the disclosure statement's valuation would speed the valuation process. However, an independent analysis that is later compared with the disclosure statement's appraisal is recommended for two reasons. First, an independent analysis may be more accurate. Secondly, an independent analysis that is later compared with the official appraisal will eliminate bias.

Cardis Corporation filed for bankruptcy on May 25, 1988. It has been engaged in the wholesale and retail distribution of automotive parts, supplies, tools, and accessories since 1917. Cardis also owns Tune-Up Masters, which operates 242 company-owned service centers principally in the western and southwestern United States.

Cardis's Second Amended Plan of Reorganization and Disclosure Statement were filed on August 11, 1989. The plan is premised on the sale of Tune-Up Masters (TUM) and the reorganization of the company around its remaining warehouse distribution centers and 29 retail stores. Importantly, however, the plan may be confirmed without the sale. Under the Second Amended Plan of Reorganization, Security Pacific National Bank (SPNB) will receive $15 million in cash, a $29 million seven-year secured note, a $20 million secured revolving credit note, and $8 million from the sale of stock or assets of TUM. The plan provides that if TUM is not sold within three months of the confirmation date, the debtor will issue 80,000 shares of new preferred stock to SPNB with a face amount of $8 million. The reorganized debtor will then convey its right and interests to the TUM stock to a trust for the benefit of SPNB and the reorganized

E X H I B I T   22–4

Proposed Equity Ownership of Cardis: Second Amended Plan of
Reorganization

Class	Number of Shares	Percent of Common[a]
Unsecured creditors	7,540,000	65%
Subordinated debentures	1,740,000	15
Present equity security holders	1,160,000	10
Reserved for management	1,160,000	10
Total	11,600,000	100

[a]The percentages are subject to a potential dilution of 13 percent if the reorganized debtor exercises its right under certain circumstances to put 1,800,691 common shares in exchange for the new preferred stock.

Source: Cardis Corporation's Second Amended Plan of Reorganization and Disclosure Statement dated August 11, 1989, *Bankruptcy Datasource,* Boston, MA.

debtor. The general unsecured creditors will receive 65 percent of the stock of reorganized Cardis, debenture holders will receive 15 percent of the stock, old equity holders will receive 10 percent of the stock, and a final 10 percent of the stock will be reserved for management. This allocation of common stock is presented in Exhibit 22–4.

The analysis of Cardis should begin with the debtor's pro forma income statements, balance sheets, and cash flow statements, which are provided in the disclosure statement. Care should be taken to evaluate the debtor's assumptions in formulating these pro formas. Modifications should be made to the pro formas where the assumptions look doubtful. After the pro formas have been adjusted, an estimate of the company's value (in terms of price per share) should be calculated. One way of approaching this task is to apply valuation multiples. The analyst should estimate what range of multiples the stock should command in terms of earnings, sales, book value, and cash. The analyst can use the traditional approach of averaging the appropriate multiples of comparable companies and then applying these multiples to the company being analyzed.

In the case of Cardis, the analyst must first determine the market multiples of the auto parts (replacement) industry. To estimate the auto parts industry multiples, one should first select an industry sample of companies. In this case, SPX Corp., Echlin, Federal Mogul, and Genuine Parts are used as the representative sample. These four companies were selected in part because they are all followed by *Value Line,* and therefore consistent projections of earnings, sales, book value, and cash flow were readily available. Once the sample was selected, *Value Line's* estimates for 1992–1994 for each of the companies were listed. These estimates are listed in Exhibit 22–5.

Once the estimates of these values have been logged, the range of valuations relative to price/share can be calculated for each sample company by divid-

E X H I B I T   22–5

Auto Parts (Replacement) Industry (1992–1994 *Value Line* Estimates)

	Price Range	Sales/ Share	BV/ Share	EPS	Cash/ Share
Cardis[a]		10.43	.26	.16	.45
Echin	20–31	32.75	13.50	1.80	2.75
Federal Mogul	40–48	73.90	18.95	3.70	6.30
Genuine Parts	56–72	60.00	18.80	3.85	4.25
SPX Corp.	46–64	69.65	25.95	4.65	6.90

[a]Company estimates from the disclosure statement.

ing each estimate by the estimated prices. Because *Value Line* gives a range for estimated prices, it is necessary to divide the appropriate per share figure by both the high and the low price estimates. Once these calculations are made, the numbers should be averaged to generate an average range of valuations for the industry, as shown below.

Price Sales/Share	.69 to .92
Price BV/Share	2.09 to 2.78
Price Earnings/Share	11.59 to 15.68
Price Cash/Share	8.37 to 11.28

To arrive at an estimated value for the common stock of Cardis, multiply the above multiples (or, more realistically, some discount of the multiples so as to reflect the problems associated with the debtor) times the appropriate variable for Cardis. When these valuations are multiplied times the pro forma estimates of Cardis's sales/share, book value/share, EPS, and cash/share, a value of $.54 to $9.56 per share is estimated for Cardis. If the multiples are discounted by 50 percent to reflect problems associated with Cardis, the valuation declines to $.27 to $4.78. This looked attractive compared to a September 1989 price of $0.06. However, this price assumes that each old share of Cardis will own the same proportionate share of the new company. In fact, Cardis's August 1989 Plan of Reorganization provides that each old share will receive the equivalent of .20 new shares. Therefore, these prices must be discounted by a factor that reflects that a share purchased at current prices may only be worth .20 shares if the plan is confirmed. When the estimated valuation is discounted by 80 percent as required, the estimated value declines to $.05 to $.96. At these levels, the stock is valued at the low end of the projections. The projected prices must be discounted once more, however, to reflect the potential dilution of 13 percent should reorganized Cardis exercise its put. If this potential dilution is considered, the projected range for Cardis becomes $.04 to $.83.

Once the valuation of the debtor's stock is complete, the analyst should proceed to investigate the other securities of the debtor, if any, to determine whether another security is attractive. Frequently, this is where value is found.

Cardis has outstanding $25.16 million (as of 4/30/88) 12.5 percent Senior Subordinated Debentures due 6/30/97. To determine whether the bonds are undervalued or overvalued, the relationship between the current price of each bond and the valuation of its proposed distribution must be compared. In the case of Cardis, debenture holders are proposed to receive 69.6 shares per $1,000 of face value of debenture. The analyst must value these distributions to see if the debentures represent an undervalued or an overvalued situation. If the valuation of Cardis common stock outlined above is used, then the debentures should be worth between $2.78 and $57.77 per bond. This compares with a market estimate of $15 per bond. The bonds appear to be within the same relative range as the common stock (i.e., at the low end of the projections).

Both the common stock and the debentures of Cardis appear to have more upside potential than downside risk. The risk/reward trade-off will be a function of the price the investor actually pays for the securities. Frequently, securities of bankrupt companies are thinly traded and the offering price of a security may differ substantially from the most recent quotation.

CONCLUSION

The analysis of bankrupt securities involvés several variables. The investor must analyze both the plan of reorganization and the pro forma projections of the reorganized company. The analysis should not stop once these two analyses are complete, however. Companies should be monitored in order to keep current on changes in the plan as well as on company prospects. Significant changes in this market can occur quickly. The likelihood of such changes must be factored into the analysis. They also signal the need for diversification in bankruptcy investing. The time element must also be factored into the analysis. Most bankrupt securities do not accrue interest during reorganization. Therefore, the investor must estimate when the company will emerge from bankruptcy to fully estimate (and discount) values. Because most bankrupt companies take at least a year to reorganize and some have taken over seven years (Manville), the time element can be significant.

ⓖ
GUIDELINES IN THE CREDIT ANALYSIS OF GENERAL OBLIGATION AND REVENUE MUNICIPAL BONDS

Sylvan G. Feldstein, Ph.D.
Adjunct Lecturer
School of Management
Yale University

INTRODUCTION

Historically, the degree of safety of investing in municipal bonds has been considered second only to that of U.S. Treasury bonds, but beginning in the 1970s, ongoing concerns have developed among many investors and underwriters about the potential default risks of municipal bonds.

The First Influence: Defaults and Bankruptcies

One concern resulted from the well-publicized, billion-dollar general obligation note defaults in 1975 of New York City. Not only did specific investors face the loss of their principal, but the defaults sent a loud and clear warning to the municipal bond investors in general. The warning was that regardless of the supposedly ironclad legal protections for the bondholder, when issuers have severe budget-balancing difficulties, the political hues, cries, and financial interests of public employee unions, vendors, and community groups may be dominant forces in the initial decision-making process.

This reality was further reinforced by the new federal bankruptcy law that took effect on October 1, 1979, which makes it easier for municipal bond issuers to seek protection from bondholders by filing for bankruptcy. One byproduct of the increased investor concern is that since 1975, the official statement, which is the counterpart to a prospectus in an equity or corporate bond offering and is to contain a summary of the key legal and financial security features, has become more comprehensive. As an example, before 1975 it was common for a city of New York official statement to be only 6 pages long, whereas for a bond sale in 1996 it was over 150 pages long.

The Second Influence: Strong Investor Demand for Tax Exemption

The second reason for the increased interest in credit analysis was derived from the changing nature of the municipal bond market. It is now characterized by strong buying patterns by private investors and institutions. The patterns were caused in part by high federal, state, and local income tax rates. Tax-exempt bonds increasingly have become an important and convenient way to shelter income. One corollary of the strong buyers' demand for tax exemption has been an erosion of the traditional security provisions and bondholder safeguards that had grown out of the default experiences of the 1930s. General obligation bond issuers with high tax and debt burdens, declining local economies, and chronic budget-balancing problems had little difficulty finding willing buyers. Also, revenue bonds increasingly were rushed to market with legally untested security provisions, modest rate covenants, reduced debt reserves, and weak additional-bond tests. Because of this widespread weakening of security provisions, it has become more important than ever before that the prudent investor carefully evaluate the creditworthiness of a municipal bond before making a purchase.

In analyzing the creditworthiness of either a general obligation or revenue bond, the investor should cover five categories of inquiry: (1) legal documents and opinions, (2) politics/management, (3) underwriter/financial advisor, (4) general credit indicators and economics, and (5) red flags, or danger signals.

The purpose of this chapter is to set forth the general guidelines that the investor should rely upon in asking questions about specific bonds.

THE LEGAL OPINION

Popular opinion holds that much of the legal work done in a bond issue is boilerplate in nature, but from the bondholder's point of view the legal opinions and document reviews should be the ultimate security provisions because, if all else fails, the bondholder may have to go to court to enforce his or her security rights. Therefore, the integrity and competency of the lawyers who review the documents and write the legal opinions that usually are summarized and stated in the official statements are very important.

The relationship of the legal opinion to the analysis of municipal bonds for both general obligation and revenue bonds is threefold. First, the lawyer should check to determine whether the issuer is indeed legally able to issue the bonds. Second, the lawyer is to see that the issuer has properly prepared for the bond sale by enacting the various required ordinances, resolutions, and trust indentures and without violating any other laws and regulations. This preparation is particularly important in the highly technical areas of determining whether the bond issue is qualified for tax exemption under federal law and whether the issue has been structured in such a way as to violate federal arbitrage regulations. Third, the lawyer is to certify that the security safeguards and remedies provided for the bondholders and pledged by either the bond issuer or third parties (such as banks with letter-of-credit agreements) are actually supported by federal, state, and local government laws and regulations.

General Obligation Bonds

General obligation bonds are debt instruments issued by states, counties, towns, cities, and school districts. They are secured by the issuers' general taxing powers. The investor should review the legal documents and opinion as summarized in the official statement to determine what specific *unlimited* taxing powers, such as those on real estate and personal property, corporate and individual income taxes, and sales taxes, are legally available to the issuer, if necessary, to pay the bondholders. Usually for smaller governmental jurisdictions, such as school districts and towns, the only available unlimited taxing power is on property. If there are statutory or constitutional taxing power limitations, the legal documents and opinion should clearly describe how they affect the security of the bonds.

For larger general obligation bond issuers, such as states and big cities that have diverse revenue and tax sources, the legal opinion should indicate the claim of the general obligation bondholder on the issuer's general fund. Does the bondholder have a legal claim, if necessary, to the first revenues coming into the general fund? This is the case with bondholders of state of New York general obligation bonds. Does the bondholder stand second in line? This is the case with bondholders of state of California general obligation bonds. Or are the laws silent on the question altogether? This is the case for most other state and local governments.

Additionally, certain general obligation bonds, such as those for water and sewer purposes, are secured in the first instance by user charges and then by the general obligation pledge. (Such bonds are popularly known as being double barreled.) If so, the legal documents and opinion should state how the bonds are secured by revenues and funds outside the issuer's general taxing powers and general fund.

Revenue Bonds

Revenue bonds are issued for project or enterprise financings that are secured by the revenues generated by the completed projects themselves, or for general public-purpose financings in which the issuers pledge to the bondholders tax and revenue resources that were previously part of the general fund. This latter type of revenue bond is usually created to allow issuers to raise debt outside general obligation debt limits and without voter approvals. The trust indenture and legal opinion for both types of revenue bonds should provide the investor with legal comfort in six bond-security areas:

- The limits of the basic security.
- The flow-of-funds structure.
- The rate, or user-charge, covenant.
- The priority of revenue claims.
- The additional-bonds test.
- Other relevant covenants.

Limits of the Basic Security

The trust indenture and legal opinion should explain what the revenues for the bonds are and how they realistically may be limited by federal, state, and local laws and procedures. The importance of this is that although most revenue bonds are structured and appear to be supported by identifiable revenue streams, those revenues sometimes can be negatively affected directly by other levels of government. For example, the Mineral Royalties Revenue Bonds that the state of Wyoming sold in December 1981 had most of the attributes of revenue bonds. The bonds had a first lien on the pledged revenues, and additional bonds could only be issued if a coverage test of 125 percent was met. Yet the basic revenues themselves were monies received by the state from the federal government as royalty payments for mineral production on federal lands. The U.S. Congress was under no legal obligation to continue this aid program. Therefore, the legal opinion as summarized in the official statement must clearly delineate this shortcoming of the bond security.

Flow-of-Funds Structure

The trust indenture and legal opinion should explain what the bond issuer has promised to do concerning the revenues received. What is the order of the revenue flows through the various accounting funds of the issuer to pay for the operating expenses of the facility, payments to the bondholders, maintenance and special capital improvements, and debt-service reserves? Additionally, the trust indenture and legal opinion should indicate what happens to excess revenues if they exceed the various annual fund requirements.

The flow of funds of most revenue bonds is structured as *net revenues* (i.e., debt service is paid to the bondholders immediately after revenues are paid to the basic operating and maintenance funds, but before paying all other expenses). A *gross revenues* flow-of-funds structure is one in which the bondholders are paid even before the operating expenses of the facility are paid. Examples of gross revenue bonds are those issued by the New York Metropolitan Transportation

Authority. However, although it is true that these bonds legally have a claim to the fare-box revenues before all other claimants, it is doubtful that the system could function if the operational expenses, such as wages and electricity bills, were not paid first.

Rate or User-Charge Covenants

The trust indenture and legal opinion should indicate what the issuer has legally committed itself to do to safeguard the bondholders. Do the rates charged only have to be sufficient to meet expenses, including debt service, or do they have to be set and maintained at higher levels to provide for reserves? The legal opinion should also indicate whether or not the issuer has the legal power to increase rates or charges of users without having to obtain prior approvals by other governmental units.

Priority of Revenue Claims

The legal opinion as summarized in the official statement should clearly indicate whether or not others can legally tap the revenues of the issuer even before they start passing through the issuer's flow-of-funds structure. An example would be the Highway Revenue Bonds issued by the Puerto Rico Highway Authority. These bonds are secured by the revenues from the Commonwealth of Puerto Rico gasoline tax. However, under the commonwealth's constitution, the revenues are first applied to the commonwealth government's own general obligation bonds if no other funds are available for them.

Additional-Bonds Test

The trust indenture and legal opinion should indicate under what circumstances the issuer can issue additional bonds that share equal claims to the issuer's revenues. Usually, the legal requirement is that the maximum annual debt service on the new bonds as well as on the old bonds be covered by the projected net revenues by a specified minimum amount. This can be as low as one times coverage. Some revenue bonds have stronger additional-bonds tests to protect the bondholders. For example, the state of Florida Orlando–Orange County Expressway Bonds have an additional-bonds test that is twofold. First, under the Florida constitution the previous year's *pledged historical revenues* must equal at least 1.33 times maximum annual debt service on the outstanding and to-be-issued bonds. Second, under the original trust indenture, *projected revenues* must provide at least 1.50 times the estimated maximum annual debt service on the outstanding and to-be-issued bonds.

Other Relevant Covenants

Lastly, the trust indenture and legal opinion should indicate whether there are other relevant covenants for the bondholder's protection. These usually include pledges by the issuer of the bonds to insure the project (if it is a project-financing revenue bond), to have the accounting records of the issuer annually audited by an outside certified public accountant, to have outside engineers annually review the condition of the capital plant, and to keep the facility operating for the life of the bonds.

In addition to the above aspects of the specific revenue structures of general obligation and revenue bonds, two other developments over the recent past make it more important than ever for the investor to carefully review the legal documents and opinions summarized in the official statements. The first development involves the mushrooming of new financing techniques that may rest on legally untested security structures. The second development is the increased use of legal opinions provided by local attorneys who may have little prior municipal bond experience. (Legal opinions have traditionally been written by experienced municipal bond attorneys.)

Legally Untested Security Structures and New Financing Techniques

In addition to the more traditional general obligation bonds and toll road, bridge, and tunnel revenue bonds, there are now more nonvoter-approved, innovative, and legally untested security mechanisms. These innovative financing mechanisms include lease-rental bonds, moral obligation housing bonds, take-and-pay power bonds with step-up provisions requiring the participants to increase payments to make up for those that may default, commercial bank-backed letter-of-credit "put" bonds, and tax-exempt commercial paper. What distinguishes these newer bonds from the more traditional general obligation and revenue bonds is that they have no history of court decisions and other case law to firmly protect the rights of the bondholders. For the newer financing mechanisms, the legal opinion should include an assessment of the probable outcome if the bond security were challenged in court. Note, however, that most official statements do not provide this to the investor.

The Need for Reliable Legal Opinions

For many years, concern over the reliability of the legal opinion was not as important as it is now. As the result of the numerous bond defaults and related shoddy legal opinions in the 19th century, the investment community demanded that legal documents and opinions be written by recognized municipal bond attorneys. As a consequence, over the years a small group of primarily Wall Street-based law firms and certain recognized firms in other financial centers dominated the industry and developed high standards of professionalism.

Now, however, more and more issuers have their legal work done by local law firms, a few of whom have little experience in municipal bond work. This development, along with the introduction of more innovative and legally untested financing mechanisms, has created a greater need for reliable legal opinions. An example of a specific concern involves the documents the issuers' lawyers must complete so as to avoid arbitrage problems with the Internal Revenue Service. On negotiated bond issues, one remedy has been for the underwriters to have their own counsels review the documents and to provide separate legal opinions.

THE NEED TO KNOW WHO *REALLY* IS THE ISSUER

Still another general question to ask before purchasing a municipal bond is just what kind of people are the issuers? Are they conscientious public servants with clearly defined public goals? Do they have histories of successful management of public institutions? Have they demonstrated commitments to professional and fiscally stringent operations? Additionally, issuers in highly charged and partisan environments in which conflicts chronically occur between political parties or among political factions or personalities are clearly bond issuers to scrutinize closely and possibly to avoid. Such issuers should be scrutinized regardless of the strength of the surrounding economic environment.

For General Obligation Bonds

For general obligation bond issuers, focus on the political relationships that exist among chief executives such as mayors, county executives, and governors, and among their legislative counterparts. Issuers with unstable political elites are of particular concern. Of course, rivalry among politicians is not necessarily bad. What is undesirable is competition so bitter and personal that real cooperation among the warring public officials in addressing future budgetary problems may be precluded. An example of an issuer that was avoided because of such dissension is the city of Cleveland. The political problems of the city in 1978 and the bitter conflicts between Mayor Kucinich and the city council resulted in a general obligation note default in December of that year.

For Revenue Bonds

When investigating revenue bond issuers, it is important to determine not only the degree of political conflict, if any, that exists among the members of the bond-issuing body, but also the relationships and conflicts among those who make the appointments to the body. Additionally, the investor should determine whether the issuer of the revenue bond has to seek prior approval from another governmental jurisdiction before the user-fees or other charges can be levied. If this is the case, then the stability of the political relationships between the two units of government must be determined.

An important example involves the creditworthiness of the water and electric revenue bonds and notes issued by Kansas City, Kansas. Although the revenue bonds and notes were issued by city hall, it was the six-member board of public utilities, a separately elected body, that had the power to set the water and electricity rates. In the spring of 1981, because of a political struggle between a faction on the board of public utilities and the city commissioners (including the city's finance commissioner), the board refused to raise utility rates as required by the covenant. The situation came under control only when a new election changed the makeup of the board in favor of those supported by city hall.

In addition to the above institutional and political concerns, for revenue bond issuers in particular, the technical and managerial abilities of the staff should be assessed. The professional competency of the staff is a more critical factor in revenue bond analysis than it is in the analysis of general obligation bonds. The reason is that, unlike general obligation bonds, which are secured in the final instance by the full faith and credit and unlimited taxing powers of the issuers, many revenue bonds are secured by the ability of the revenue projects to be operational and financially self-supporting.

The professional staffs of authorities that issue revenue bonds for the construction of nuclear and other public power-generating facilities, apartment complexes, hospitals, water and sewer systems, and other large public works projects, such as convention centers and sports arenas, should be carefully reviewed. Issuers who have histories of high management turnovers, project cost overruns, or little experience should be avoided by the conservative investor, or at least considered higher risks than their assigned commercial credit ratings may indicate. Additionally, it is helpful, although not mandatory, for revenue bond issuers to have their accounting records annually audited by outside certified public accountants so as to provide the investor with a more accurate picture of the issuer's financial health.

ON THE FINANCIAL ADVISOR AND UNDERWRITER

Shorthand indications of the quality of the investment are (1) who the issuer selected as its financial advisor, if any, (2) its principal underwriter if the bond sale was negotiated, and (3) its financial advisor if the bond issue came to market competitively. Additionally, since 1975 many prudent underwriters will not bid on competitive bond issues if there are significant credit-quality concerns. Therefore, it is also useful to learn who was the underwriter for the competitive bond sales as well.

Identifying the financial advisors and underwriters is important for two reasons.

The Need for Complete, Not Just Adequate, Investment Risk Disclosures

The first reason relates to the quality and thoroughness of information provided to the investor by the issuer. The official statement, or private placement papers if the issue is placed privately, is usually prepared with the assistance of lawyers and a financial advisor or by the principal underwriter. There are industrywide disclosure guidelines that are generally adhered to, but not all official statements provide the investor with complete discussions of the risk potentials that may result from either the specific economics of the project or the community settings and the operational details of the security provisions. It is usually the author of this document who decides what to emphasize or downplay in the official statement. The more professional and established the author is in providing unbiased and complete information about the issuer, the more comfortable the investor can be with information provided by the issuer and in arriving at a credit-quality conclusion.

The Importance of Firm Reputation for Thoroughness and Integrity

By itself, the reputation of the issuer's financial advisor and/or underwriter should not be the determinant credit-quality factor, but it is a fact the investor should consider, particularly in the case of marginally feasible bond issues that have complex flow-of-funds and security structures. The securities industry is different from other industries, such as real estate, in that trading and investment commitments are usually made over the phone with a paper trail following days later. Many institutional investors, such as banks, bonds funds, and property and casualty insurance companies, have learned to judge issuers by the company they keep. Institutions tend to be conservative, and they are more comfortable with financial information provided by established financial advisors and underwriters who have recognized reputations for honesty. Individual investors and analysts would do well to adopt this approach.

GENERAL CREDIT INDICATORS AND ECONOMIC FACTORS IN THE CREDIT ANALYSIS

The last analytical factor is the economic health or viability of the bond issuer or specific project financed by the bond proceeds. The economic factors cover a variety of concerns. When analyzing general obligation bond issuers, one should look at the specific budgetary and debt characteristics of the issuer, as well as the general economic environment. For project-financing, or enterprise, revenue bonds, the economics are primarily limited to the ability of the project to generate sufficient charges from the users to pay the bondholders. These are known as pure revenue bonds.

For revenue bonds that rely not on user charges and fees but instead on general purpose taxes and revenues, the analysis should take basically the same approach as for the general obligation bonds. For these bonds, the taxes and revenues diverted to the bondholders would otherwise go to the state's or city's general fund.

As examples of such bonds, both the New York State Municipal Assistance Corporation for the City of New York Bonds (MAC), secured by general New York City sales taxes and annual state-aid appropriations, and the state of Illinois Chicago School Finance Authority Bonds, secured by unlimited property taxes levied within the city of Chicago, are bonds structured to appear as pure revenue bonds; but in essence they are not. They both incorporate bond structures created to bail out the former, New York City, and the latter, Chicago's board of education, from severe budget deficits. The creditworthiness of these bonds is tied to that of their underlying jurisdictions, which have had portions of their taxing powers and general fund revenues diverted to secure the new revenue-type bailout bonds. Besides looking at the revenue features, the investor therefore must look at the underlying jurisdictions.

For General Obligation Bonds

For general obligation bonds, the economic concerns include questions in four specific areas: debt burden, budget soundness, tax burden, and the overall economy.

Debt Burden

In relation to the debt burden of the general obligation bond issuer, some of the more important concerns include the determination of the total amount of debt outstanding and to be issued that is supported by the general taxing powers of the issuer as well as by earmarked revenues.

For example, general obligation bonds issued by school districts in New York State are general obligations of the issuer and are also secured by state-aid payments due the issuer. If the issuer defaults, the bondholder can go to the state comptroller and be paid from the next state-aid payment due the local issuer. An example of another earmarked-revenue general obligation bond is the State of Illinois General Obligation Transportation, Series A Bond. For these state general obligations, debt service is secured by gasoline taxes in the state's transportation fund.

The debt of the general obligation bond issuer includes, in addition to the general obligation bonds outstanding, leases and "moral obligation" commitments. Additionally, the amount of the unfunded pension liabilities should be determined. Key debt ratios that reveal the burden on local taxpayers include determining the per capita amount of general obligation debt as well as the per capita debt of the overlapping or underlying general obligation bond issuers. Other key measures of debt burden include determining the amounts and percentages of the outstanding general obligation bonds as well as the outstanding general obligation bonds of the overlapping or underlying jurisdictions to real estate valuations. These numbers and percentages can be compared with most recent year medians, as well as with the past history of the issuer, to determine whether the debt burden is increasing, declining, or remaining relatively stable.

Budgetary Soundness

Concerning the budgetary operations and budgetary soundness of the general obligation bond issuer, some of the more important questions include how well the issuer over at least the previous five years has been able to maintain balanced

budgets and fund reserves. How dependent is the issuer on short-term debt to finance annual budgetary operations? How have increased demands by residents
for costly social services been handled? That is, how frugal is the issuer? How
well have the public-employee unions been handled? They usually lobby for
higher salaries, liberal pensions, and other costly fringe benefits. Clearly, it is undesirable for the pattern of dealing with the constituent demands and public-
employee unions to result in raising taxes and drawing down nonrecurring budget
reserves. Last, another general concern in the budgetary area is the reliability of
the budget and accounting records of the issuer. Are interfund borrowings reported? Who audits the books?

Tax Burden

Concerning the tax burden, it is important to learn two things initially. First, what
are the primary sources of revenue in the issuer's general fund? Second, how dependent is the issuer on any one revenue source? If the general obligation bond issuer relies increasingly upon a property tax, wage and income taxes, or a sales tax
to provide the major share of financing for annually increasing budget appropriations, taxes could quickly become so high as to drive businesses and people away.
Many larger northern states and cities with their relatively high income, sales, and
property taxes appear to be experiencing this phenomenon. Still another concern
is the degree of dependency of the issuer on intergovernmental revenues, such as
federal or state revenue sharing and grants-in-aid, to finance its annual budget appropriations. Political coalitions on the state and federal levels that support these
financial transfer programs are not permanent and could undergo dramatic change
very quickly. Therefore, a general obligation bond issuer that currently has a relatively low tax burden but receives substantial amounts of intergovernmental
monies should be carefully reviewed by the investor. If it should occur that the aid
monies are reduced, as has been occurring under many federal legislative programs, certain issuers may primarily increase their taxes, instead of reducing their
expenditures to conform to the reduced federal grants-in-aid.

Overall Economy

The fourth and last area of general obligation bond analysis concerns the issuer's
overall economy. For local governments, such as counties, cities, towns, and
school districts, key items include learning the annual rate of growth of the full
value of all taxable real estate for the previous 10 years and identifying the 10
largest taxable properties. What kinds of business or activity occur on the respective properties? What percentage of the total property tax base do the 10 largest
properties represent? What has been the building permit trend for at least the previous five years? What percentage of all real estate is tax-exempt, and what is the
distribution of the taxable ones by purpose (such as residential, commercial, industrial, railroad, and public utility)? Last, who are the five largest employers?
Concerning the final item, communities that have one large employer are more
susceptible to rapid adverse economic change than communities with more diver-

sified employment and real estate bases. For additional information that reveals economic health or decline, one must determine whether the population of the community over the previous 10 years has been increasing or declining by age, income, and ethnicity and how the monthly and yearly unemployment rates compare with the national averages as well as with the previous history of the community.

For state governments that issue general obligation bonds, the economic analysis should include many of the same questions applied to local governments. In addition, the investor should determine on the state level the annual rates of growth for the previous five years of personal income and retail sales and how much the state has had to borrow from the Federal Unemployment Trust Fund to pay unemployment benefits. This last item is particularly significant for the long-term economic attractiveness of the state because under current federal law, employers in states with large federal loans in arrears are required to pay increased unemployment taxes to the federal government.

For Revenue Bonds

Airport Revenue Bonds

For airport revenue bonds, the economic questions vary according to the type of bond security involved. There are two basic security structures.

The first type of airport revenue bond is one based upon traffic-generated revenues that result from the competitiveness and passenger demand of the airport. The financial data on the operations of the airport should come from audited financial statements going back at least three years. If a new facility is planned, a feasibility study prepared by a recognized consultant should be reviewed. The feasibility study should have two components: (1) a market and demand analysis to define the service area and examine demographic and airport use trends and (2) a financial analysis to examine project operating costs and revenues.

Revenues at an airport may come from landing fees paid by the airlines for their flights, concession fees paid by restaurants, shops, newsstands, and parking facilities, and from airline apron and fueling fees.

Also, in determining the long-term economic viability of an airport, the investor should determine whether or not the wealth trends of the service area are upward; whether the airport is dependent on tourism or serves as a vital transfer point; whether passenger enplanements and air cargo handled over the previous five years have been growing; whether increased costs of jet fuel would make other transportation such as trains and automobiles more attractive in that particular region; and whether the airport is a major domestic hub for an airline, which could make the airport particularly vulnerable to route changes caused by schedule revisions and changes in airline corporate management.

The second type of airport revenue bond is secured by a lease with one or more airlines for the use of a specific facility such as a terminal or hangar. The lease usually obligates them to make annual payments sufficient to pay the expenses and debt service for the facility. For many of these bonds, the analysis of the airline lease is based upon the credit quality of the lessee airline. Whether or not the lease should extend as long as the bonds are outstanding depends on the specific airport and facility involved. For major hub airports, it may be better not to have long-term leases because without leases, fees and revenues can be increased as the traffic grows, regardless of which airline uses the specific facility. Of course, for regional or startup airports, long-term leases with trunk (i.e., major airline) carriers are preferred.

Highway Revenue Bonds
There are generally two types of highway revenue bonds. The bond proceeds of the first type are used to build specific revenue-producing facilities such as toll roads, bridges, and tunnels. For these pure enterprise revenue bonds, the bondholders have claims to the revenues collected through the tolls. The financial soundness of the bonds depends on the ability of the specific projects to be self-supporting. Proceeds from the second type of highway revenue bond generally are used for public highway improvements, and the bondholders are paid by earmarked revenues such as gasoline taxes, automobile registration payments, and driver's license fees.

Concerning the economic viability of a toll revenue bond, the investor should ask a number of questions.

1. What is the traffic history, and how inelastic is the demand? Toll roads, bridges, and tunnels that provide vital transportation links are clearly preferred to those that face competition from interstate highways, toll-free bridges, or mass transit.

2. How well is the facility maintained? Has the issuer established a maintenance reserve fund at a reasonable level to use for such repair work as road resurfacing and bridge painting?

3. Does the issuer have the ability to raise tolls to meet covenant and debt-reserve requirements without seeking approvals from other governmental actors such as state legislatures and governors? In those few cases where such approvals are necessary, the question of how sympathetic these other power centers have been in the past in approving toll-increase requests should be asked.

4. What is the debt-to-equity ratio? Some toll authorities have received substantial nonreimbursable federal grants to help subsidize their costs of construction. This, of course, reduces the amount of debt that has to be issued.

5. What is the history of labor-management relations, and can public-employee strikes substantially reduce toll collections?

6. When was the facility constructed? Generally, toll roads financed and constructed in the 1950s and 1960s tend now to be in good financial condition because the cost of financing was much less than it is today.

Many of these older revenue bond issuers have been retiring their bonds ahead of schedule by buying them at deep discounts to par in the secondary market.

7. If the facility is a bridge that could be damaged by a ship and made inoperable, does the issuer have adequate use-and-occupancy insurance?

Those few toll revenue bonds that have defaulted have done so because of either unexpected competition from toll-free highways and bridges, poor traffic projections, or substantially higher than projected construction costs. An example of one of the few defaulted bonds is the West Virginia Turnpike Commission's Turnpike Revenue Bonds, issued in 1952 and 1954 to finance the construction of an 88-mile expressway from Charleston to Princeton, West Virginia. The initial traffic-engineering estimates were overly optimistic, and the construction costs came in approximately $37 million higher than the original budgeted amount of $96 million. Because of insufficient traffic and toll collections, between 1956 and 1979 the bonds were in default. By the late 1970s with the completion of various connecting cross-country highways, the turnpike became a major link for interstate traffic. Since 1979, the bonds became self-supporting in terms of making interest coupon payments. It was not until 1989 that all the still-outstanding bonds were finally redeemed.

Concerning the economics of highway revenue bonds that are not pure enterprise type but instead are secured by earmarked revenues, such as gasoline taxes, automobile registration payments, and driver's license fees, the investor should ask the following questions.

- Are the earmarked tax revenues based on state constitutional mandates, such as the state of Ohio's Highway Improvement Bonds, or are they derived from laws enacted by state legislatures, such as the state of Washington's Chapters 56, 121, and 167 Motor Vehicle Fuel Tax Bonds? A constitutional pledge is usually more permanent and reliable.

- What has been the coverage trend of the available revenues to debt service over the previous 10 years? Has the coverage been increasing, stable, or declining?

- If the earmarked revenue is gasoline tax, is it based on a specific amount per gallon of gasoline sold or as a percentage of the price of each gallon sold? With greater conservation and more efficient cars, the latter tax structure is preferred because it is not as susceptible to declining sales of gasoline and because it benefits directly from any increased gasoline prices at the pumps.

- What has been the history of statewide gasoline consumption through recessions and oil shocks?

Hospital Revenue Bonds

Two unique features of hospitals make the analysis of their debt particularly complex and uncertain. The first concerns their sources of revenue, and the second concerns the basic structure of the institutions themselves.

During the past 30 years, the major sources of revenue for most hospitals have been (1) payments from the federal (Medicare) and combined federal-state (Medicaid) hospital reimbursement programs and (2) appropriations made by local governments through their taxing powers. It is not uncommon for hospitals to receive at least two thirds of their annual revenues from these sources. How well the hospital management markets its service to attract more private-pay patients, how aggressive it is in third-party collections, such as from Blue Cross and HMOs, and how conservatively it budgets for the governmental reimbursement payments are key elements for distinguishing weak from strong hospital bonds.

Particularly for community-based hospitals (as opposed to teaching hospitals affiliated with medical schools), a unique feature of their financial structure is that their major financial beneficiaries, physicians, have no legal or financial liabilities if the institutions do not remain financially viable over the long term. An example of the problems that can be caused by this lack of liability is found in the story of the Sarpy County, Nebraska, Midlands Community Hospital Revenue Bonds. These bonds were issued to finance the construction of a hospital three miles south of Omaha, Nebraska, that was to replace an older one located in the downtown area. Physician questionnaires prepared for the feasibility study prior to the construction of the hospital indicated strong support for the replacement facility. Many doctors had used the older hospital in downtown Omaha as a backup facility for a larger nearby hospital. Unfortunately, once the new Sarpy hospital opened in 1976, many physicians found that the new hospital could not serve as a backup because it was 12 miles further away from the major hospital than the old hospital had been. Because these physicians were not referring their patients to the new Sarpy hospital, it was soon unable to make bond principal payments and was put under the jurisdiction of a court receiver.

The above factors raise long-term uncertainties about many community-based hospitals, but certain key areas of analysis and trends reveal the relative economic health of hospitals that already have revenue bonds outstanding. The first area is the liquidity of the hospital as measured by the ratio of dollars held in current assets to current liabilities. In general, a five-year trend of high values for the ratio is desirable because it implies an ability by the hospital to pay short-term obligations and thereby avoid budgetary problems. The second indicator is the ratio of long-term debt to equity, as measured in the unrestricted end-of-year fund balance. In general, the lower the long-term debt to equity ratio, the stronger the finances of the hospital. The third indicator is the actual debt-service coverage of the previous five years, as well as the projected coverage. The fourth indicator is the annual bed-occupancy rates for the previous five years. The fifth is the percentage of physicians at the hospital who are professionally approved (board certified), their respective ages, and how many of them use the hospital as their primary institution.

For new or expanded hospitals, much of the above data is provided to the investor in the feasibility study. One item in particular that should be determined for a new hospital is whether the physicians who plan to use the hospital actually live in the area to be served by the hospital. Because of its importance in providing answers to these questions, the feasibility study must be prepared by reputable, experienced researchers.

Housing Revenue Bonds

For housing revenue bonds, the economic and financial questions vary according to the type of bond security involved. There are two basic types of housing revenue bonds, each with a different type of security structure. One is the housing revenue bond secured by *single-family* mortgages, and the other is the housing revenue bond secured by mortgages on *multifamily* housing projects.

Concerning single-family housing revenue bonds, the strongly secured bonds usually have four characteristics.

- The single-family home loans are insured by the Federal Housing Administration (FHA), Federal Veterans Administration (VA), or an acceptable private mortgage insurer or its equivalent. If the individual home loans are not insured, then they should have a loan-to-value ratio of 80 percent or less.

- If the conventional home loans have less than 100 percent primary mortgage insurance coverage, an additional 5–10 percent mortgage-pool insurance policy or its equivalent would be required. The private mortgage insurer should be of high quality in terms of company capitalization and in terms of conservative underwriting standards and limits.

- In addition to a debt reserve with monies equal at least to six months of interest on the single-family housing revenue bonds, there is a mortgage reserve fund equal at least to 1 percent of the mortgage portfolio outstanding.

- The issuer of the single-family housing revenue bonds is in a region of the country that has stable or strong economic growth as indicated by increased real estate valuations, personal income, and retail sales, as well as low unemployment rates.

In the 1970s, state agency issuers of single-family housing revenue bonds assumed certain prepayment levels in structuring the bond maturities. In recent years, most issuers have abandoned this practice but investors should review the retirement schedule for the single-family mortgage revenue bonds to determine whether or not the issuer has assumed large, lump-sum mortgage prepayments in the early year cash-flow projections. If so, how conservative are the prepayment assumptions, and how dependent is the issuer on the prepayments to meet the annual debt-service requirements?

It should be noted that single-family housing revenue bonds issued by local governments such as towns, cities, and counties usually have conservative bond-retirement schedules that have not included any home mortgage prepayment assumptions. Single-family housing revenue bonds issued by state agencies sometimes include prepayment assumptions. This positive feature of local government-issued bonds is balanced somewhat by the facts that state-issued bonds generally no longer include prepayment assumptions and usually are secured by home mortgages covering wider geographic areas. Additionally, the state issuing agencies usually have professional in-house staffs that closely monitor the home mortgage portfolios, whereas the local issuers do not. Finally, many state issuing agencies have accumulated substantial surplus funds over the years that can be viewed as an additional source of bondholder protection.

For multifamily housing revenue bonds, there are four specific, though overlapping, security structures. The first type of multifamily housing revenue bond is one in which the bonds are secured by federally insured mortgages. Usually, the federal insurance covers all but the difference between the outstanding bond principal and collectible mortgage amount (usually 1 percent), and all but the *nonasset* bonds (i.e., bonds issued to cover issuance costs and capitalized interest). The attractiveness of the federal insurance is that it protects the investor against bond default within the limitations outlined. The insurance protects the bondholders regardless of whether the projects are fully occupied and generating rental payments.

The second type of multifamily housing revenue bond is one in which the federal government subsidizes, under the HUD Section 8 program, all annual costs (including debt service) of the project not covered by tenant rental payments. Under Section 8, the eligible low-income and elderly tenants pay only 15 to 30 percent of their incomes for rent. Because the ultimate security comes from the Section 8 subsidies, which escalate annually with the increased cost of living in that particular geographic region, the bondholder's primary risks concern the developer's ability to complete the project, find tenants eligible under the federal guidelines to live in the project, and then maintain high occupancy rates for the life of the bonds. The investor should carefully review the location and construction standards used in building the project, as well as the competency of the project manager in selecting tenants who will take care of the building and pay their rents. In this regard, state agencies that issue Section 8 bonds usually have stronger in-house management experience and resources for dealing with problems than do the local development corporations that have issued Section 8 bonds. It should be noted that the federal government has eliminated appropriations for new Section 8 projects. Since 1995 the federal government has restricted automatic rent increases under the Section 8 program. This has introduced financial pressure.

The third type of multifamily housing revenue bond is one in which the ultimate security for the bondholder is the ability of the project to generate sufficient monthly rental payments from the tenants to meet the operating and debt-service expenses. Some of these projects may receive governmental subsidies (such as interest-cost reductions under the federal Section 236 program and property tax abatements from local governments), but the ultimate security is the economic viability of the project. Key information includes the location of the project, its occupancy rate, whether large families or the elderly will primarily live in the project, whether or not the rents necessary to keep the project financially sound are competitive with others in the surrounding community, and whether or not the project manager has a proven record of maintaining good service and of establishing careful tenant selection standards.

A fourth type of multifamily housing revenue bond is one that includes some type of private credit enhancement to the underlying real estate. These credit enhancements can include guarantees or sureties of an insurance company, securitization by the Federal National Mortgage Association (FNMA), or a bank letter of credit.

Other financial features desirable in all multifamily housing bonds include a debt-service reserve fund, which should contain an amount of money equal to the maximum annual debt service on the bonds, a mortgage reserve fund, and a capital repair and maintenance fund.

Another feature of many multifamily housing revenue bond programs, particularly those issued by state housing agencies, is the state moral obligation pledge. Several state agencies have issued housing revenue bonds that carry a potential state liability for making up deficiencies in their one-year debt-service reserve funds, should any occur. In most cases, if a drawdown of the debt reserve occurs, the state agency must report the amount used to its governor and state budget director. The state legislature, in turn, may appropriate the requested amount, although there is no legally enforceable obligation to do so. Bonds with this makeup provision are called moral obligation bonds.

The moral obligation provides a state legislature with permissive authority—*not mandatory authority*—to make an appropriation to the troubled state housing agency. Therefore, the analysis should determine (1) whether the state has the budgetary surpluses for subsidizing the housing agency's revenue bonds; and (2) whether there is a consensus within the executive and legislative branches of that particular state's government to use state general fund revenues for subsidizing multifamily housing projects.

Industrial Revenue Bonds

Generally, industrial revenue bonds are issued by state and local governments on behalf of individual corporations and businesses. The security for the bonds usually depends on the economic soundness of the particular corporation or business involved. If the bond issue is for a subsidiary of a larger corporation, one question to ask is whether or not the parent guarantees the bonds. Is it obligated only through a lease, or does it not have any obligation whatsoever for paying the bondholders? If the parent corporation has no responsibility for the bonds, then the investor must look very closely at the operations of the subsidiary in addition to those of the parent corporation. The investor must also determine whether the bond is guaranteed by the company or is a lease obligation.

For companies that have issued publicly traded common stock, economic data are readily available either in the annual reports or in the 10-K reports that must be filed annually with the Securities and Exchange Commission. For privately held companies, financial data are more difficult to obtain.

In assessing the economic risk of investing in an industrial revenue bond, another question to ask is whether the bondholder or the trustee holds the mortgage on the property. Although holding the mortgage is not an important economic factor in assessing either hospital or low-income, multifamily housing bonds where the properties have very limited commercial value, it can be an important strength for the holder of industrial development revenue bonds. If the bond is secured by a mortgage on a property of either a fast-food retailer, such as McDonald's, or an industrial facility, such as a warehouse, the property location and resale value of the real estate may provide some protection to the bondholder, regardless of what happens to the company that issued the bonds. Of course, the investor should always avoid possible bankruptcy situations regardless of the economic attractiveness of the particular piece of real estate involved. The reason is that the bankruptcy process usually involves years of litigation and numerous court hearings, which no investor should want to be concerned about.

Lease-Rental Bonds

Lease-rental bonds are usually structured as revenue bonds, and annual payments, paid by a state or local government, cover all costs including operations, maintenance, and debt service. It should be noted that Certificate of Participation Bonds, or COPs, are similar in security structure in that they too are dependent on the annual legislative appropriation process. The public purposes financed by these bond issues include public office buildings, fire houses, police stations, university buildings, mental health facilities, and highways, as well as office equipment and computers. In some instances, the payments may come from student tuition, patient fees, and earmarked tax revenues, and the state or local government is not legally obligated to make lease-rental payments beyond the amount of available earmarked revenues. However, for many lease-rental bonds, the underlying lessee state, county, or city is to make payment from its general fund subject to annual legislative appropriation. For example, the Albany County, New York, Lease Rental South Mall Bonds were issued to finance the construction of state office buildings. Although the bonds arc technically general obligations of Albany County, the real security comes from the annual lease payments made by the state of New York. These payments are annually appropriated. For such bonds, the basic economic and financial analysis should follow the same guidelines as for general obligation bonds.

Public Power Revenue Bonds

Public power revenue bonds are issued to finance the construction of electrical generating plants. An issuer of the bonds may construct and operate one power plant, buy electric power from a wholesaler and sell it retail, construct and operate several power plants, or join with other public and private utilities in jointly financing the construction of one or more power plants. This last arrangement is known as a joint-power financing structure. Although there are revenue bonds that can claim the revenues of a federal agency (e.g., the Washington Public

Power Supply System's Nuclear Project No. 2 Revenue Bonds, which if necessary can claim the revenues of the Bonneville Power Administration) and many others that can require the participating underlying municipal electric systems to pay the bondholders whether or not the plants are completed and operating (i.e., the Michigan Public Power Agency Revenue Bonds), the focus here is how the investor determines which power projects will be financially self-supporting without these backup security features.

There are at least five major questions to ask when evaluating the investment soundness of a public power revenue bond.

- Does the bond issuer have the authority to raise its electric rates in a timely fashion without going to any regulatory agencies? This is particularly important if substantial rate increases are necessary to pay for new construction or plant improvements.

- How diversified is the customer base among residential, commercial, and industrial users?

- Is the service area growing in terms of population, personal income, and commercial/industrial activity so as to warrant the electrical power generated by the existing or new facilities?

- Are rates competitive with neighboring IOUs? This is a significant credit factor resulting from the competitive provisions contained in the Energy Policy Act of 1992.

- What are the projected and actual costs of power generated by the system, and how competitive are they with other regions of the country? Power rates are particularly important for determining the long-term economic attractiveness of the region for industries that are large energy users.

- How diversified is the fuel mix? Is the issuer dependent on one energy source such as hydro dams, oil, natural gas, coal, or nuclear fuel?

Concerning electrical generating plants fueled by nuclear power, the aftermath of the Three Mile Island nuclear accident in 1979 has resulted in greater construction and maintenance reviews and costly safety requirements prompted by the Federal Nuclear Regulatory Commission (NRC). The NRC oversees this industry. In the past, although nuclear power plants were expected to cost far more to build than other types of power plants, it was also believed that, once the generating plants became operational, the relatively low fuel and maintenance costs would more than offset the initial capital outlays. However, with the increased concern about public safety brought about by the Three Mile Island accident, repairs and design modifications are now expected to be made even after plants begin to operate. Of course, this increases the ongoing costs of generating electricity and reduces the attractiveness of nuclear power as an alternative to the oil, gas, and coal fuels.

Resource Recovery Revenue Bonds

A resource recovery facility converts refuse (solid waste) into commercially salable energy, recoverable products, and a residue to be landfilled. The major revenues for a resource recovery bond usually are the tipping fees per ton paid by those who deliver the garbage to the facility for disposal; revenues from steam, electricity, or refuse-derived fuel sold to an electric power company or another energy user; and revenues from the sale of recoverable materials such as aluminum and steel scrap.

Resource recovery bonds are secured in one of two ways or a combination thereof. The first security structure is one in which the cost of running the resource recovery plant and paying the bondholders comes from the sale of the energy produced (steam, electricity, or refuse-derived fuel) as well as from fees paid by the haulers, both municipal and private, who bring the garbage to the facility. In this financing structure, the resource recovery plant usually has to be operational and self-supporting for the bondholders to be paid. The second security structure involves an agreement with a state or local government, such as a county or municipality, that contractually obligates the government to haul or to have hauled a certain amount of garbage to the facility each year for the life of the facility and to pay a tipping fee sufficient to operate the facility. The tipping fee must include amounts sufficient to pay bondholders whether or not the resource recovery plant has become fully operational.

When deciding to invest in a resource recovery revenue bond, one should ask the following questions. First, how proven is the system technology to be used in the plant? *Mass burning* is the simplest method, and it has years of proven experience. In mass burning, the refuse is burned with very little processing. Prepared fuels and shredding, the next most proven method, requires the refuse to be prepared by separation or shredding so as to produce a higher quality fuel for burning. More innovative approaches require the most detailed engineering evaluations by qualified specialists. Second, how experienced and reliable are the construction contractors and facility operators (vendors)? Third, are there adequate safeguards and financial incentives for the contractor/vendor to complete and then maintain the facility? Fourth, what are the estimated tipping fees that will have to be charged, and how do they compare with those at nearby landfills? In 1994 the U.S. Supreme Court in the *Carbone* decision struck down "flow control" ordinances which had been used to require all garbage within a local region to be delivered to designated plants regardless of economically attractive alternatives. As a result of *Carbone* the competitiveness of the tipping fee will be a critical credit factor. Fifth, is the bondholder protected during the construction stage by reserves and by fixed-price construction contracts? Sixth, are the prices charged for the generated energy fixed, or are they tied to the changing costs of the fuel sources such as oil and gas in that particular marketplace?

Because of the uniqueness of the resource recovery technology, there are additional questions that should be asked. First, even if the plant-system technology is a proven one, is the plant either the same size as others already in operation or a larger scale model that would require careful investor review? Second, if the system technology used is innovative, is there sufficient redundancy, or low-utilization assumptions in the plant design to absorb any unforeseen problems once the plant begins production? Last, in addition to the more routine reserves (such as debt, maintenance, and special capital improvement reserves) and covenants (such as covenants that commercial insurance be placed on the facility and that the contractor pledge to maintain the plant for the life of the bonds) there should also be required yearly plant reviews by independent consulting engineers. The vendor should be required to make the necessary repairs so that the facility will be operational for the life of the bonds.

For resource recovery revenue bonds that have a security structure involving an agreement with a local government, additional questions for the investor to ask are the following: Is the contractual obligation at a fixed rate, or is the tipping fee elastic enough to cover all the increasing costs of operations, maintenance, and debt service? Would strikes or other *force majeure* events prevent the contract from being enforceable or preclude the availability of an adequate supply of garbage? Last, the investor should determine the soundness of the budgetary operations and general fund reserves of the local government that is to pay the tipping or service fee. For these bonds, the basic economic analysis should follow the same guidelines as for general obligation bonds.

Student Loan Revenue Bonds

Student loan revenue bonds are usually issued by state agencies and are used for purchasing new guaranteed student loans for higher education or existing guaranteed student loans from local banks.

The student loans are 100 percent guaranteed. They are guaranteed either directly by the federal government—under the Federal Insured Student Loan (FISL) program for 100 percent of principal and interest—or by a state guaranty agency under a more recent federal insurance program, the Federal Guaranteed Student Loan (GSL) program. This latter program provides federal reimbursement for a state guaranty agency on an annual basis for 100 percent of the payment on defaulted loans up to approximately 5 percent of the amount of loans being repaid, 90 percent for claims in excess of 5 percent but less than 9 percent, and 80 percent for claims exceeding 9 percent. The federal commitments are not dependent on future congressional approvals. Loans made under the FISL and GSL programs are contractual obligations of the federal government.

Although most student loans have federal government support, the financial soundness of the bond program that issues the student loan revenue bonds and monitors the loan portfolio is of critical importance to the investor because of the unique financial structure of a student loan portfolio. Although loan repayments from the student or, in the event of student default, repayments from the guaranty agency are contractually insured, it is difficult to precisely project the actual loan repayment cash flows. The reason is that the student does not begin repaying the loan until he or she leaves college or graduate school and all other deferments, such as military service, have ended. Before the student begins the loan repayments, the federal government pays the interest on the loans under pre-scribed formulas. Therefore, the first general concern of the investor should be to determine the strength of the cash-flow protection.

The second general concern is the adequacy of the loan guaranty. Under all economic scenarios short of a depression, in which the student loan default rate could be 20 percent or greater, the GSL sliding federal reinsurance scale of 100–90–80 should provide adequate cash-flow and bond default protection as long as the student loan revenue bond issuer effectively services the student loan repayments, has established and adequately funded loan-guaranty and debt-reserve funds, employs conservative loan-repayment assumptions in the original bond-maturity schedule, and is required to call the bonds at par if the student loan repayments are accelerated. This latter factor presents a reinvestment risk for the bondholder.

There are eight specific questions for the investor to ask:

- What percentage of the student loans are FISL- and GSL-backed?
- Has a loan-guarantee fund been established and funded? Usually, a fund that is required to have an amount equal to at least 2 percent of the loan principal outstanding is desirable.
- Is the issuer required to maintain a debt-reserve fund? Usually, for notes, a fund with at least six-months interest, and for bonds, a fund with a one-year maximum annual debt-service, are desirable.
- If the bond issuer has purchased portfolios of student loans from local banks, are the local lenders required to repurchase any loans if there are either defaults or improperly originated loans?
- What in-house capability does the issuer have for monitoring and servic-ing the loan repayments?
- What is the historical loan-default rate?
- How are the operating expenses of the agency met? If federal operating subsidies are received under the "Special Allowance Payment Rate" pro-gram, what are the rate assumptions used? In this program, the issuer re-ceives a supplemental subsidy, which fluctuates with the 91-day U.S. Treasury bill rate.
- If a state agency is the issuer, is it dependent on appropriations for cover-ing operating expenses and reserve requirements?

Water and Sewer Revenue Bonds

Water and sewer revenue bonds are issued to provide for a local community's basic needs and as such are not usually subject to general economic changes. Be-cause of the vital utility services performed, their respective financial structures are usually designed to have the lowest possible user charges and still remain fi-nancially viable. Generally, rate covenants requiring that user charges cover oper-ations, maintenance, and approximately 1.2 times annual debt-service and reserve requirements are most desirable. On one hand, a lower rate covenant provides a smaller margin for unanticipated slow collections or increased operating and plant maintenance costs caused by inflation. On the other hand, rates that generate revenues more than 1.2 times the annual debt-service and reserve requirements could cause unnecessary financial burdens on the users of the water and sewer systems. A useful indication of the soundness of an issuer's operations is to compare the water or sewer utility's average quarterly customer billings to those of other water or sewer systems. Assuming that good customer service is given, the water or sewer system that has a relatively low customer billing charge generally indicates an efficient operation and therefore strong bond-payment prospects.

Key questions for the investor to ask include the following:

- Has the bond issuer, through local ordinances, required mandatory water or sewer connections? Also, local board of health directives against well water contamination and septic tank usage can often accomplish the same objective as the mandatory hookups.

- Does the issuer have to comply with an EPA consent decree and thereby issue significant amounts of bonds?

- What is the physical condition of the facilities in terms of plant, lines, and meters, and what capital improvements are necessary for maintaining the utilities as well as for providing for anticipated community growth?

- For water systems in particular, it is important to determine if the system has water supplies in excess of current peak and projected demands. An operating system at less than full utilization is able to serve future customers and bring in revenues without having to issue additional bonds to enlarge its facilities.

- What is the operating record of the water or sewer utility for the previous five years?

- If the bond issuer does not have its own distribution system but instead charges other participating local governments that do, are the charges or fees based upon the actual water flow drawn (for water revenue bonds) and sewage treated (for sewer revenue bonds) or upon gallonage entitlements?

- For water revenue bonds issued for agricultural regions, what crop is grown? An acre of oranges or cherries in California will provide the grower with more income than will an acre of corn or wheat in Iowa.

- For expanding water and sewer systems, does the issuer have a record over the previous two years of achieving net income equal to or exceeding the rate covenants, and will the facilities to be constructed add to the issuer's net revenues?

- Has the issuer established and funded debt and maintenance reserves to deal with unexpected cash-flow problems or system repairs?

- Does the bond issuer have the power to place tax liens against the real estate of those who have not paid their water or sewer bills? Although the investor would not want to own a bond for which court actions of this nature would be necessary, the legal existence of this power usually provides an economic incentive for water and sewer bills to be paid promptly by the users.

Additional bonds should be issued only if the need, cost, and construction schedule of the facility have been certified or sureties an independent consulting engineer and if the past and projected revenues are sufficient to pay operating expenses and debt service. Of course, for a new system that does not have an operating history, the quality of the consulting engineer's report is of the uppermost importance.

RED FLAGS FOR THE INVESTOR

In addition to the areas of analysis described above, certain red flags, or negative trends, suggest increased credit risks.

For General Obligation Bonds

For general obligation bonds, the signals that indicate a decline in the ability of a state, county, town, city, or school district to function within fiscally sound parameters include the following:

- Declining property values and increasing delinquent taxpayers.
- An annually increasing tax burden relative to other regions.
- An increasing property tax rate in conjunction with a declining population.
- Declines in the number and value of issued permits for new building construction.
- Actual general fund revenues consistently falling below budgeted amounts.
- Increasing end-of-year general fund deficits.
- Budget expenditures increasing annually in excess of the inflation rate.
- The unfunded pension liabilities are increasing.
- General obligation debt increasing while property values are stagnant.
- Declining economy as measured by increased unemployment and declining personal income.

For Revenue Bonds

For revenue bonds, the general signals that indicate a decline in credit quality include the following:

- Annually decreasing coverage of debt service by net revenues.
- Regular use of debt reserve and other reserves by the issuer.
- Growing financial dependence of the issuer on unpredictable federal and state-aid appropriations for meeting operating budget expenses.
- Chronic lateness in supplying investors with annual audited financials.
- Unanticipated cost overruns and schedule delays on capital construction projects.
- Frequent or significant rate increases.
- Deferring capital plant maintenance and improvements.
- Excessive management turnovers.
- Shrinking customer base.
- New and unanticipated competition.

⑥ STANDARD & POOR'S SOVEREIGN RATINGS CRITERIA

David T. Beers
Managing Director
Sovereign Ratings Group
Standard & Poor's

Standard & Poor's sovereign credit ratings—which as of August 1996 cover obligations denominated in local currency as well as foreign currency issued by 59 countries (see Exhibit 24–1)—are an assessment of each national government's ability and willingness to repay debt according to its terms. The ratings are based on an appraisal of the country's overall creditworthiness that is both quantitative and qualitative. The quantitative aspects of the analysis incorporate a number of measures of economic and financial performance outlined below. The analysis is qualitative because Standard & Poor's ratings indicate future debt service capacity.

The analytical framework is divided into several categories so that all important variables are considered in turn (see Exhibit 24–2). Each category is related to two key aspects of sovereign credit risk: economic risk and political risk. Economic risk addresses the government's ability to repay its obligations on time and is a function of both quantitative and qualitative factors. Political risk addresses the sovereign's willingness to repay debt.

Willingness to pay is a qualitative issue distinguishing sovereigns from other types of borrowers. Partly because creditors have only limited legal redress, a government may choose to default due to political considerations, even when it possesses the financial capacity to service debt in a timely manner. In practice, of course, political risk and economic risk are related. A government that is unwilling to repay debt usually has in place economic policies that weaken its ability to do so. Willingness to pay therefore encompasses the range of economic and political factors influencing government economic policy.

As part of the committee process Standard & Poor's uses to assign credit ratings to all issuers, each sovereign is scored on a scale of one (representing the

E X H I B I T   24-1

Standard & Poor's Sovereign Credit Ratings

Issuer	Local Currency	Foreign Currency	Issuer	Local Currency	Foreign Currency
Austria	AAA	AAA	Slovenia	AA	A
France	AAA	AAA	Thailand	AA	A
Germany	AAA	AAA	Hong Kong	A+	A
Japan	AAA	AAA	Chile	AA	A–
Luxembourg	AAA	AAA	Israel	AA–	A–
Netherlands	AAA	AAA			
Norway	AAA	AAA	China	N.R.	BBB
Singapore	AAA	AAA	Indonesia	A+	BBB
Switzerland	AAA	AAA	Qatar	N.R.	BBB
United			Colombia	A+	BBB–
Kingdom	AAA	AAA	Greece	N.R.	BBB–
United States	AAA	AAA	Slovak Rep.	A	BBB–
			Oman	N.R.	BBB–
Belgium	AAA	AA+	Poland	A–	BBB–
Canada	AAA	AA+			
Denmark	AAA	AA+	Hungary	N.R.	BB+
New Zealand	AAA	AA+	India	N.R.	BB+
Sweden	AAA	AA+	South Africa	BBB+	BB+
Taiwan	N.R.	AA+	Trinidad &		
Australia	AAA	AA	Tobago	BBB+	BB+
Bermuda	N.R.	AA	Uruguay	BBB	BB+
Ireland	AAA	AA			
Italy	AAA	AA	El Salvador	BBB+	BB
Spain	AAA	AA	Mexico	BBB+	BB
Finland	AAA	AA–	Philippines	BBB+	BB
Korea	N.R.	AA–	Argentina	BBB–	BB–
Portugal	AAA	AA–	Paraguay	BBB–	BB–
Cyprus	AA+	AA–	Romania	BBB–	BB–
Iceland	AA+	A+	Jordan	BBB–	B+
Malaysia	AA+	A+	Pakistan	N.R.	B+
Malta	AA+	A+	Brazil	BB	B+
Czech Republic	N.R.	A	Turkey	N.R.	B+
			Venezuela	N.R.	B

Ratings as of 8/31/96.

N.R.—Not rated.

E X H I B I T   24–2

Sovereign Ratings Methodology Profile

ECONOMIC RISK

Economic system and structure

- Market or nonmarket economy
- Resource endowments, degree of diversification
- Size, composition of savings and investment
- Rate, pattern of economic growth

Fiscal policy and public debt

- Public sector fiscal balances
- Currency composition, structure of public debt
- Public debt and interest burdens
- Contingent liabilities

Monetary policy and inflation

- Trends in price inflation
- Rates of money and credit growth
- Exchange-rate policy
- Degree of central bank autonomy

Balance of payments flexibility

- Impact on external accounts of fiscal and monetary policies
- Structure, performance, and responsiveness of the current account
- Adequacy, composition of capital flows

External financial position

- Size and currency composition of public and private external debt
- Maturity structure and debt-service burden
- Level, composition of reserves and other assets

POLITICAL RISK

Political system

- Form of government and adaptability of institutions
- Degree of popular participation
- Orderliness of leadership succession
- Degree of consensus on economic policy objectives
- Debt-service track record

Social environment

- Living standards, income and wealth distribution
- Labor market conditions
- Cultural, demographic characteristics

International relations

- Integration in global trade and financial system
- Security risks

highest score) to five (the lowest) for each analytical category in relation to the universe of rated sovereigns. There is, however, no exact formula combining the scores to determine ratings. The analytical variables are interrelated, and the emphasis can change when, for example, differentiating the degree of credit risk between the sovereign's local and foreign currency debt.

Because the default frequency of sovereign local currency debt differs significantly from foreign currency debt, both types of debt are analyzed. The same political, social, and economic factors affect the government's ability and willingness to honor local currency and foreign currency debt, though in varying degrees. A sovereign government's ability and willingness to service local currency debt is supported by its taxing power and control of the domestic financial system, which gives it potentially unlimited access to local currency resources. To service foreign currency debt, however, the sovereign also must secure foreign exchange, usually by purchasing it in the currency markets. That can be a binding constraint, as reflected in the higher frequency of foreign than local currency debt default. The primary focus of Standard & Poor's local currency credit analysis, therefore, is on the fiscal, monetary, and inflation outcomes of government policies that support or erode incentives for timely debt service. Standard & Poor's places somewhat more weight on the interaction of fiscal and monetary policies with the balance of payments, their impact on changes in the external debt burden, and the degree of each country's integration in the global trade and financial system when assessing a sovereign's capacity and willingness to honor foreign currency debt.

SOVEREIGN RATING CEILING

Compared with foreign currency debt, the historical frequency of local currency debt default is significantly lower among both rated and unrated sovereigns (see Exhibits 24–3 and 24–4). Surveying the credit performance of local and foreign currency debt of 113 governments since 1970, Standard & Poor's has identified eight sovereigns—Angola, Argentina, Brazil, Ghana, Myanmar (Burma), Russia, Venezuela and Vietnam—that recorded defaults on their local currency obligations. A total of 69 defaulted on their foreign currency debt. At least two successive local currency defaults were noted in both Argentina and Brazil over the period. Defaulted local currency debt included bank notes (Myanmar, Ghana, Russia, and Vietnam), bonds (Angola, Argentina, Brazil, and Venezuela), and bank deposits (Argentina, Brazil, and Vietnam). Default on bank notes typically took the form of partial conversion into new currency; in the case of bonds, it typically took the form of the abrogation of foreign exchange- or inflation-linked indexes embedded in the terms of the issues, and the unilateral extension of maturities.

Among the 69 sovereigns defaulting on foreign currency debt, rescheduling of bank debt featured in 68 cases, bonds in 7, and both types of debt in 6. Reschedulings were counted as defaults even where, legally speaking, the extension of principal was deemed to be voluntary by bank creditors—as was generally the case during the 1980s Latin American debt crisis. Of the eight countries identified as defaulting on their local currency debt, five (Angola, Argentina, Brazil, Russia, and Venezuela) had previously also defaulted on their foreign currency debt; the other three (Ghana, Myanmar, and Vietnam) had no foreign currency bonds and little commercial bank debt outstanding at the time of their local currency defaults. On the other hand, a sizable majority (62) continued servicing local currency debt without interruption after defaulting on their foreign currency debt.

E X H I B I T   24–3

Rated Sovereigns: Years in Default Since 1975

Issuer	LC/FC Ratings	Local Currency Debt	Foreign Currency Bond Debt	Foreign Currency Bank Debt
Slovenia	AA/A			1992–95
Chile	AA/A–			1983–90
Poland	A–/BBB–			1981–94
South Africa	BBB+/BB+			1985–87,89,93
Trinidad & Tobago	BBB+/BB+			1988–89
Uruguay	BBB/BB+			1983,87,90–91
Mexico	BBB+/BB			1982–86,88–90
Philippines	BBB+/BB			1983–92
Argentina	BBB–/BB–	1982,89–90	1989	1982–93
Paraguay	BBB–/BB–			1985–92
Romania	BBB–/BB–			1981–82,86
Jordan	BBB-/B+			1989–93
Brazil	N.R./B+	1986–87,90		1983–94
Turkey	N.R./B+			1978–81
Venezuela	N.R./B+	1995		1983–88,90

LC—Local currency, FC—Foreign currency, N.R. —Not rated.

Standard & Poor's ratings as of 8/31/96

Among the handful of sovereigns defaulting on foreign currency bonds during the period, Zimbabwe and Panama attract special attention because their defaults lasted for extended periods. Zimbabwe's default occurred initially in 1965, when Southern Rhodesia, as the country then was known, unilaterally ended its colonial links with Britain. After its independence was legally recognized, Zimbabwe's new government settled with its creditors in 1980. Panama's bond default began in 1987, a few years after its bank debt went into default, and was cured through an exchange in 1994.

No sovereign issuer defaulted on any local currency or foreign currency debt rated by Standard & Poor's during this period. Venezuela defaulted on a portion of its unrated local currency debt in 1995, while maintaining debt service on its rated (B+) Eurobonds. Also, a number of issuers have been assigned credit ratings subsequent to their defaults. Two such issuers (Argentina and Brazil) previously defaulted on both its local currency and foreign currency debt, while 12 others had previously defaulted on their foreign currency debt. The remaining local and foreign currency defaults were by issuers not yet rated by Standard & Poor's. This group includes six issuers that defaulted on foreign currency bonds, 53 that defaulted on foreign currency bank loans, and five that defaulted on local currency debt.

E X H I B I T   24–4

Unrated Issuers: Years in Default Since 1975

Issuer	Local Currency Debt	Foreign Currency Bond Debt	Foreign Currency Bank Debt
Albania			1991–95
Algeria			1992–1995
Angola	1992		1985–95
Bolivia			1980–81,84–93
Bosnia & Herzegovina			1992–95
Bulgaria			1990 94
Cameroon			1989–95
Congo			1986–95
Costa Rica		1984–85	1981,83–90
Cote d'Ivoire			1983,86–95
Croatia			1992–95
Cuba			1982–95
Dominican Republic			1982–83,89–94
Ecuador			1983–95
Egypt			1984
Ethiopia			1991–95
Gabon			1986–94
Gambia			1986–90
Ghana	1979		1987
Guatemala		1989	1986
Guinea			1986–88,91–95
Guyana			1979,82,84,86–92
Haiti			1982–95
Honduras			1981,86–95
Iran			1978,92–95
Iraq			1990–95
Jamaica			1978,81,87–93
North Korea			1986–95
Liberia			1981–95
Macedonia			1992–95
Madagascar			1981–04,86–95
Malawi			1982,88
Morocco			1983,86–90
Mozambique			1984–91
Myanmar (Burma)	1984		
Nicaragua			1979–82,86–95
Niger			1983,86–91
Nigeria		1986–88,92	1982–92
Panama		1987–94	1983–95
Peru			1976,78,80,84–95

* Bonds initially defaulted in 1965.   *continued*

Source: Standard & Poor's.

E X H I B I T   24–4

(continued)

Issuer	Local Currency Debt	Foreign Currency Bond Debt	Foreign Currency Bank Debt
Sao Tome & Principe			1987–94
Senegal			1981,90,92–95
Serbia			1992–95
Sierra Leone			1983,86–95
Sudan			1979–81,83–95
Tanzania			1984–95
Togo			1979–80,88,90–95
Uganda			1980–93
USSR/Russia	1993		1991–95
Vietnam	1975		1985–95
Yemen			1990–95
Yugoslavia		1992–95	1983–91
Zaire			1979–80,85–95
Zambia			1982, 86–94
Zimbabwe		1975–80*	

* Bonds initially defaulted in 1965.

Source: Standard & Poor's.

With the possible exception of foreign currency bonds, this compilation of sovereign defaults may not be exhaustive. Local and foreign currency debt defaults may have passed unnoticed (except by creditors) in a few countries. Defaults on foreign currency bank debt certainly did occur among a larger number of sovereigns than the ones listed.

LOCAL CURRENCY DEBT-RATING FACTORS

The following are some of the key economic and political risk factors Standard & Poor's considers when rating sovereign debt:

- Stability of political institutions and degree of popular participation in the political process.
- Economic system and structure.
- Living standards and degree of social and economic cohesion.
- Fiscal policy and budgetary flexibility.
- Public debt burden and debt service track record.
- Monetary policy and inflation pressures.

More than any others, these factors directly determine the ability and willingness of governments to ensure timely local currency debt service. And because fiscal and monetary policies ultimately influence the country's external balance sheet, these factors also influence the ability and willingness of governments to service foreign currency debt. The stability and perceived legitimacy of a country's form of government are important considerations because they set the parameters for economic policy making, including whether and when policy errors are corrected. A country's economic structure comes into play since the decentralized decision making of a market economy, with legally enforceable property rights, is generally less vulnerable to policy error and more respectful of the interests of creditors than one where the state dominates. A country with a relatively high and growing standard of living and income distributions regarded as broadly equitable can more readily support even high levels of public debt, and withstand unexpected economic shocks, than can one with a poor or stagnant economy. And a sovereign with a recent history of default generally must manage with lower levels of leverage to rebuild credibility than one that has maintained an unblemished debt record.

These factors, in turn, influence the conduct of fiscal and monetary policies and their impact on future changes in the public debt burden. When considering the impact of fiscal policy on local currency creditworthiness, Standard & Poor's focuses on three interrelated issues: the purpose of public sector borrowing, its impact on the growth of public indebtedness, and its implications for inflation. Deficit financing can be an appropriate policy tool for any government. Public sector infrastructure projects, for example, are prudently financed by borrowing when they generate revenues sufficient to cover debt service. More typically, however, governments borrow to finance combinations of consumption and investment that raise public debt. While sovereign creditworthiness is not correlated closely with the public debt burden, high levels of government borrowing can adversely affect it if left unchecked.

Analysis of public finance factors is complicated by the fact that the taxing and monetary powers unique to sovereigns permit them to manage often widely varying debt levels over time. Depending on their political support, governments can raise taxes to meet their obligations. But a growing tax burden can adversely affect the economy's growth prospects. Moreover, public opinion often favors the lowest possible fiscal burden, so much so that proposals to raise tax rates can occasionally drive governments from office. Efforts to cut spending frequently are stymied by powerful interests that benefit from government programs. Unless there is a well-entrenched political consensus favoring conservative fiscal principles, sovereigns can succumb to the temptation to print money owing to their monopoly over the currency and control of the banking system.

INFLATION AND PUBLIC DEBT

However, significant monetization of budget deficits fuels price inflation, which can undermine popular support for governments. As a result, policy makers usually respond with measures to contain it; if they do not, and price increases accelerate, serious economic damage and an erosion of public trust in political institutions can result. Such conditions are fertile ground for a sovereign default.

EXHIBIT 24-5

Sovereigns: Inflation Ranges

LC Rating Category	Annual Inflation (%)
BB	25–100
BBB	10–50
A	7–25
AA	4–15
AAA	0–10

For these reasons, Standard & Poor's regards the rate of inflation as the single most important leading indicator of sovereign local currency credit trends. Related indicators include the level of public debt, the impact of fiscal policy on its trend rate of growth, and the rate of money and credit expansion. Inflation benchmarks and their relationship to different local currency rating categories are shown in Exhibit 24–5.

In evaluating price pressures in each country, Standard & Poor's considers their behavior in past economic cycles and makes a conservative assessment of average inflation, as measured by the consumer price index, over the next cycle. The analysis is based in part on the level and maturity structure of the public debt burden—total borrowings of central, regional, and local governments in relation to GDP—together with the likely extent of future borrowing. Off-balance-sheet and contingent liability items—such as public sector pensions, banks, and other enterprises—are also scrutinized for their possible contribution to fiscal and monetary pressures.

In addition, Standard & Poor's looks at institutional factors affecting inflation. For example, an autonomous central bank with a public mandate to ensure price stability can be a strong check on fiscal imbalances; less so a central bank tied closely to the government. The depth and breadth of the country's capital markets can also act as an important discipline. The sovereign has fewer incentives to default on its local currency obligations when they are held by a broad cross-section of investors rather than concentrated in the hands of local banks. For this reason, the establishment of mandatory, privately funded pension funds in a number of developing countries may help bolster their credit standing by creating an influential new class of bondholders. The experience of many OECD countries suggest that, even when public debt reaches high levels, creditworthiness can be sustained over long periods when policy makers are responsive to constituencies such as these with vested interests in safeguarding the value of money.

FOREIGN CURRENCY DEBT-RATING FACTORS

The same economic and political factors affecting a sovereign's local currency credit standing also affect its ability and willingness to honor foreign currency debt—often to a greater degree because of the binding constraints the balance of payments can impose. As a result, Standard & Poor's analysis of foreign currency debt focuses on how government economic policies are likely to influence trends in the external debt burdens of both the public and private sectors over time. From a political-risk perspective, the extent of each country's integration in the global trade and financial systems is also considered. A high degree of integration in the world economy generally gives the government strong incentives to meet its external obligations because of the correspondingly high diplomatic and political as well as economic costs of default. At the same time, the nature of relations with neighboring countries is also examined to highlight potential security risks. National security is a concern when military threats place significant burdens on fiscal policy, reduce the flow of investment, and put the balance-of-payments under stress.

BALANCE OF PAYMENTS

Standard & Poor's analysis of the balance of payments focuses on the adequacy and sustainability of the country's future flows of foreign exchange in relation to the risks they might pose to the government's debt-service position. It is important to emphasize that the size of a country's current account deficit, if one exists, by itself may not be a significant rating consideration. The tendency for some countries to run current account surpluses, and others current account deficits, is the product of many economic factors, not all of them negative, and not all related to government policies. But, as Mexico's debt-servicing crisis in 1994–95 well illustrated, current account deficits are a concern when the government's fiscal and monetary policies increasingly influence balance of payments trends, and the structure of public external debt makes it vulnerable to sudden changes in investor confidence.

With these considerations in mind, merchandise trade and other current account transactions are examined both alone and in the context of accompanying flows of capital and international reserves to judge whether access to foreign exchange is reliable. Balance of payments flexibility depends on an economy's vulnerability to changes in the domestic and foreign environments and the authorities' ability to respond quickly with appropriate policy measures. The current account's degree of responsiveness to internal and external developments partly depends on the structure of merchandise trade, services, and transfers. The product and geographic market composition of merchandise exports and imports is therefore examined for concentrations that may limit the external trade sector's capacity to adjust. The economic characteristics of traded products are studied to determine their sensitivity to changes in prices and incomes. Wage and price movements relative to major trading partners are compared to exchange rate changes to assess international competitiveness. Services and transfers are scrutinized for items that pose a potential vulnerability, with special emphasis on the size and composition of investment income, notably interest, receipts, and payments.

Analysis of the capital account focuses on the adequacy of current account financing and the degree of vulnerability of the government's foreign exchange position. Capital flows are categorized as being either equity or debt. In contrast to the interest-bearing nature of debt-related inflows, the direct investment in plant and equipment and other forms of equity can impart greater flexibility to the balance of payments. Debt flows are examined by type of borrower and lender, as well as by maturity and currency, to assess the country's exposure to interest, exchange rate, and liquidity risks.

When assessing a government's capacity to implement effective balance of payments adjustment policies, Standard & Poor's studies a range of factors, such as living standards and labor market conditions, that indicate a society's tolerance for austerity. A country's historical experience in dealing with balance of payments pressures can be an important indicator of the likelihood that policy makers will correctly identify, and move forcefully to correct, future imbalances. For corrective action may still be impeded by political constraints, conflicting policy objectives, and institutional rigidities, which slow implementation.

EXTERNAL FINANCIAL POSITION

Along with its analysis of the balance of payments, Standard & Poor's examines the structure of each country's external balance sheet. Not surprisingly, this analysis focuses on the burden of public external debt, the magnitude of any contingent liabilities of the government, and the adequacy of its foreign exchange reserves to service the public sector's foreign currency debt. Public external debt generally includes the direct and guaranteed debt of the central government, obligations of other levels of government, and the nonguaranteed debt of other public entities. Claims on the private sector are also important because, in certain circumstances, they can represent contingent liabilities of the state that must ultimately be serviced from the same limited supply of foreign exchange earnings. Measurement of gross external debt includes both long-term and short-term debt.

Although excluded from external debt calculations, Standard & Poor's also estimates nondebt liabilities, including inward direct and portfolio equity investment. Equity investment can represent a burden for the balance of payments but most often is an important source of financial flexibility. Foreign assets include the central bank's international reserves, other public sector assets, overseas assets of the banking system, and assets of the nonbank private sector. The latter can include holdings of foreign securities and direct and portfolio equity investment abroad. International reserves consist of holdings of foreign currencies and gold, with the latter valued at market prices.

Standard & Poor's focuses on three key measures of a country's external position: net public external debt, total net external debt, and net external liabilities. The country's net public external debt equals total public sector debt less public sector financial assets. Total net external debt equals the stock of total public and private sector external debt less the stock of public and private foreign assets, including official international reserves, commercial bank assets, and other private sector loans. Net external liabilities is a broader measure of a country's external financial position, which adds to net external debt the net balance of inward and outward direct and portfolio equity investment, as well as government loans abroad.

To evaluate the burden these liabilities place on a country's economy, Standard & Poor's compares them against gross domestic product (GDP) and exports of goods and services, plus net public and private transfers where they are positive. The net external indebtedness of financial institutions and the nonfinancial private sector are also separately measured in this way as possible contingent liabilities of the sovereign. The debt burden also is a function of the debt's maturity profile, currency composition, and interest-rate sensitivity. These factors influence future debt-service payments and are compared to projected exports. Related to the net external debt and liability measures, Standard & Poor's also monitors the ratios of net interest and investment payments to total exports.

International reserves are another important indicator since they usually provide the government with a cushion during periods of temporary balance-of-payments difficulties. Official reserves are adjusted for the net short-term external position of the banking system. Reserve adequacy is measured by comparing the level of adjusted reserves to total imports and nonbank, short-term debt. The adequacy of a given level of reserves depends on the country's vulnerability to sudden swings in export receipts and import payments, and on the volatility of capital flows. Related considerations include the convertibility of the country's currency, its exchange-rate policy, and its access to concessional and market-related types of foreign credit.

ECONOMIC AND POLITICAL PROSPECTS

It cannot be stressed often enough that, because credit ratings measure future debt service capacity, the evaluation of each country's economic and political prospects is the most important aspect of sovereign risk assessment. Current economic and financial indicators of debt-service capacity alone do not determine sovereign ratings. The economic future of a country depends largely on the structure and management of the economy, as outlined above. From a foreign currency rating perspective, emphasis is placed on the outlook for the export sector since expanding foreign exchange earnings are a critical aspect of a country's future ability to meet its external debt-service requirements. The government's medium- and long-term economic plans are reviewed, when available, to gain a better understanding of the likely direction of economic development. These plans are evaluated in terms of internal and external resource constraints, as well as in comparison with independent economic forecasts, with special emphasis on the impact of such plans on a country's likely future external borrowing requirements.

To assess the potential vulnerability of a country's external position, Standard & Poor's sovereign credit evaluation includes consideration of reasonable worst-case scenarios. In such an analysis, Standard & Poor's examines the sensitivity of major external indicators, such as exports, the current account balance, and external debt service to a pessimistic evaluation of key variables, including international trade growth, import and export prices, and international interest rates.

LOCAL AND FOREIGN CURRENCY RATING DISTINCTIONS

The divergence, if any, between a sovereign's local and foreign currency ratings reflects the distinctive credit risks of each type of debt. For example, long-standing political stability, fiscal and monetary policies resulting in relatively low inflation, and a high degree of international economic integration are characteristics of sovereign issuers of AAA-rated local currency debt. The manageable public external debt burdens of these issuers, in turn, are generally reflected in foreign currency debt ratings at the upper end of the investment-grade spectrum.

Differences between local and foreign currency debt ratings can widen to some degree further down the ratings scale. Such sovereigns typically fall into one of two categories: sovereigns in the first have long records of timely service on both local currency and foreign currency debt. Inflationary pressures are moderate, public finances are relatively sound, but foreign currency indebtedness may be relatively high or likely to become so over time. Sovereigns in the second category also have unblemished local currency debt-servicing track records but relatively recent histories of foreign currency default. The local currency and foreign currency debt ratings assigned to them balance often substantial improvements in inflation and public finances with the risks inherent to still heavy foreign currency debt burdens. At the lower end of the rating scale, however, such rating differences tend to narrow. Some sovereigns in this category have emerged from local and/or foreign currency debt default quite recently and still carry the risk of policy reversals that result in renewed default. Other sovereigns in this category have also not defaulted but face high inflation, sharp declines in per capita income, and other forms of social and political stress, which carry a material risk of local currency default after payment of foreign currency debt can no longer be assured.

Belgium and Canada (local currency debt rated AAA, foreign currency debt rated AA+) are examples of governments shouldering public debt burdens on the order of 100 percent of GDP—well above the OECD country average—but where the political commitment to low or moderate rates of inflation seems well entrenched. Conversely, when public finances are weak and inflation is left unchecked, the stage can be set for an accelerating spiral that leads to default. Government-inspired indexation of debt and other contracts to price inflation often abets the process, as in the defaults of Argentina and Brazil. But not all countries that have experimented with indexation suffer hyperinflation and default. Chile (peso debt rated AA, foreign currency debt rated A–) and Colombia (peso debt rated A+, foreign currency debt rated BBB–) are countries with long records of timely local currency debt service whose general credit standing has been bolstered in recent years by conservative fiscal policies helping to unwind inflation and contain the burden of external debt.

⑥ # HIGH-YIELD ANALYSIS OF EMERGING MARKETS DEBT

Allen A. Vine
International Emerging Markets Specialist
Global High Yield Securities Research
Merrill Lynch

INTRODUCTION

The distinct strength of high-yield investors is fundamental orientation and ability to translate credit quality into relative pricing. Few markets in the world today can make this activity more rewarding than international emerging markets (IEM). The similarities between high-yield analysis commonly applied to domestic issuers and the type of analysis required for emerging markets, in our view, position U.S. high-yield investors as among the best prepared to take full advantage of the many opportunities emerging markets present. We are not suggesting speculation. Rather, we are suggesting a thorough and conservative analysis of the fundamentals, committed conclusions, and exploitation of market inefficiencies. Toward this end, this chapter examines the variables that determine values in emerging markets and issues of sovereign, technical, and fundamental analysis.

For purposes of this chapter, we define emerging markets as all of Latin America, Eastern Europe, Russia, and Asia (with the exception of Japan). Major product categories available to high-yield investors in emerging markets include Brady bonds, newly issued bonds, tradable performing loans, local currency instruments, and derivatives. Brady bonds are restructured bank loans of governments. They are described in detail in Chapter 18 but the key characteristics include large size, relatively high liquidity, and generally high volatility. Newly issued bonds refer to Eurobond and Yankee obligations of governments, quasi-sovereigns, and corporations, which are primarily dollar-denominated, but also include a growing issuance in currencies such as the Deutsche mark and the yen. Tradable performing loans can offer high yield but are generally the least liquid market instrument with many logistical difficulties in terms of settlement. Local currency instruments include domestic treasuries, bank certificates of deposit, and bonds. These instruments can provide yields substantially in excess of those on hard currency instruments of the same issuer, but they carry full currency risk. Derivatives include a range of options, forwards, and warrants. In light of the high market volatility, these instruments tend to be expensive but can provide very high returns.

BACKGROUND ON EMERGING MARKETS

The value of emerging markets debt fell sharply in February 1994 after two years of rapid appreciation. Events that followed, including the Mexican financial crisis and the subsequent collapse of the Latin American markets in 1995, have all contributed to a profound discomfort still being experienced by many investors. The sustained high volatility throughout the period, especially the episodes of extreme over- and undervaluation, have all exposed the vast complexity of IEM and the need for a new set of effective tools to deal with it. Perhaps as a result of these conditions, U.S. high-yield investors have continued to largely stay away from emerging markets despite the tight domestic spreads and the still attractive valuation of many IEM issuers. Notwithstanding the likelihood of continued high volatility in emerging markets for the foreseeable future, our view of market dynamics leads us to propose that (1) already in the medium term, U.S. high-yield investors have *no* choice but to develop expertise in emerging markets, (2) these markets offer *unique* profit potential, and (3) tools exist to effectively assess the relative risk of these markets and to transform them into a more stable trading environment.

No Choice

Emerging markets have now become an indelible part of the global capital arena. First, because of the sheer size. The total amount of the outstanding Brady bonds alone now exceeds $155 billion. With bank debt and the new sovereign and corporate Euro and Yankee issues, the total market size exceeds $500 billion. Second, because of future issuance. The significant capital needs of emerging economies position them as potentially the largest issuers of debt and equity for the foreseeable future. Third, assessment of relative values. A growing number of money managers around the world now view emerging markets as part of the global investment continuum. In valuing domestic issuers, they look abroad for comparison of credit fundamentals and prices. Also, the increasing speed and freedom of international capital flows are creating an environment in which domestic bond values in any country can be affected by a reaction of investors to developments in another nation halfway around the world.

A Unique Opportunity

Emerging markets today present an unmatched profit potential. Inefficient markets have always offered significant rewards to those willing to brave them. Yet, only a few periods in history can rival conditions today, when in the space of merely five years two-thirds of the world became one big marketplace for investors willing to explore. Reforms in Latin America and Asia, the opening of Russia and Eastern Europe, and privatizations in Western Europe have produced a multitude of new investment opportunities. Direct and portfolio equity investment, debt, local instruments, and derivatives from over 20 countries have now become a part of the investment continuum. However, the international financial community has just begun developing analytical tools adequate to evaluate these opportunities. It has just entered into what is likely to be a long maturation cycle for the emerging markets, whereby a more systematic risk analysis will replace speculations and theories that often drove pricing in the past (see Exhibit 25–1).

E X H I B I T   25–1

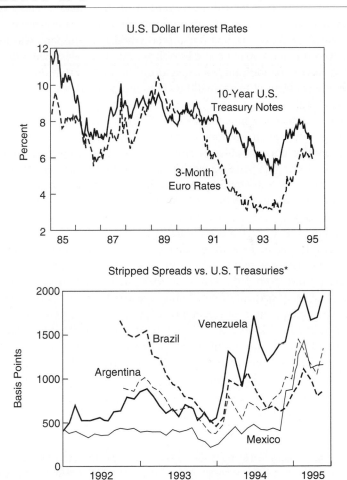

Source: Merrill Lynch Fixed Income Research.
*Par Bonds except Brazil (IDUs). End-of-month data through May 1995; latest data June 21.

Improved Credit Quality

It can be argued today that the emerging markets boom of the 1990s is qualitatively different from the numerous speculative bubbles that first elated and then crushed investors in the past. While not minimizing the structural problems yet to be addressed by emerging countries, we believe that fundamentally many situations have improved substantially from a decade ago. Going forward, these countries' firm commitment to market reforms suggests a high probability of continued and accelerating fundamental improvement.

THE VALUE TRIANGLE

The key question to be addressed with regard to any new market is how values are determined. This may sound like an obvious point, yet many people were surprised in early 1995 to learn that it mattered whether a company was located in Mexico, even if that company could have been rated double-A were it located in the United States. In addition, understanding the factors that drive values in a given market is essential to evaluating whether a particular analytical approach can be successful.

Three factors determine values of emerging markets debt: (1) cross-border/sovereign risk, (2) global capital formation/technical conditions, and (3) fundamental quality of individual issuers.[1] While solid empirical data are not available to assign exact percentages to each category, we estimate that *at present* cross-border risk accounts for 50 percent of how prices are determined, domestic yields and capital availability account for 30 percent, and issuer-specific fundamentals represent 20 percent. Clearly, these percentages vary from country to country and in times of high market volatility.

We emphasize *at present* because the change in relative weightings of each category signifies maturation of the market. For example, it is arguable that in the period from 1992 through 1993, strong technical conditions accounted for over 50 percent of how values were determined, sovereign risk for less than 40 percent, and fundamental risk for less than 10 percent (see Exhibit 25–2). As a result of losses dealt to investors since 1994, these proportions have changed to reflect more of the fundamental risk. We anticipate that this adjustment will continue. Importantly, the increasing role of fundamentals in the determination of values plays directly to the analytical strengths of high-yield investors.

---

1. Factors (1) and (2) apply in the case of sovereign issuers. For issuers that do not have the explicit full faith and credit of the sovereign, such as banks, corporates, and quasi-sovereigns, factors (1), (2), and (3) apply.

E X H I B I T   25–2

The Value Triangle

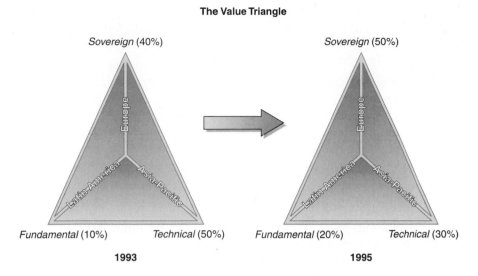

The Value Triangle

1993

1995

ANALYSIS OF CROSS-BORDER RISK

Cross-border risk (CBR) embodies all issues that arise as a consequence of investing in a foreign country. Political and social stability, economic conditions, legal and regulatory environment, and bilateral relations are all elements of CBR. A subset of CBR commonly used in the market for analysis of foreign investments is sovereign risk, which includes most key components of CBR. We define *sovereign risk* as a probability of default and pricing volatility which arise as a consequence of actions by a foreign government. There are two components of sovereign risk: (1) *willingness* to pay, which historically has been driven by ideological considerations, and (2) *ability* to pay, which is driven by economic considerations. The conceptual difference between the two defines the degree to which each can be analyzed and predicted.

The issue of willingness to pay has been rare, but hard to predict. History indicates that attempts to forecast credit events driven strictly by political considerations of foreign governments have not been successful. Fortunately, such events have happened rarely. In this century, there have been only four major cases of sovereign default motivated primarily by politics and/or ideology. In 1917, the Bolshevik government of Russia repudiated foreign obligations of the czar. In 1934, Hitler repudiated much of Germany's obligations under the Versailles treaty. Japan followed a similar path in 1941, as did communist China in

1949. In all of these cases, extreme internal conditions and/or ideological considerations were at the core of a country's unwillingness to honor obligations.

The issue of ability to pay is predominant, but predictable. The majority of
events wherein a country failed to service debt were caused by economic inability
to pay, which was then followed by a political act of default. Although history is
replete with sovereign defaults, most of them could have been predicted and
many were. The following are recent examples:

- The 1980s debt crisis in Latin America was caused primarily by the
  countries' economic inability to pay, which became apparent well before Mexico set in motion a chain of defaults.

- High volatility in pricing of Venezuelan debt in 1994 was due to the
  country's economic difficulties.

- The Mexican debacle in 1995 had its origin in the country's poor economic policies.

Again, the distinction we draw is between *unwillingness* to pay as the sole cause
of default and *inability* to pay, which leads to default. The former is generally unpredictable. The latter can be predicted effectively.

Cash flow is a good predictor. Sovereign investment analysis is different
from pure political or economic analysis of a country in one key dimension. With
investments, at issue is not the *absolute* creditworthiness of a country, although it
is obviously important, but the country's creditworthiness *relative* to other sovereign issuers. Thus, an adequate system for analysis of sovereign risk must provide
a solid basis for establishing relative value of countries. Such a system needs to
incorporate quantitative indicators that can be applied consistently to *all* issuers
and that lend themselves to a *meaningful* qualitative interpretation. We propose
such indicators to be foreign exchange reserves, exports, and the balance of payments (see Exhibit 25–3).

Foreign Exchange Reserves

Foreign exchange (FX) reserves represent the money with which investors get
paid. In high-yield terms, their function is similar to earnings before interest,
taxes, depreciation, and amortization (EBITDA). Some of the analytical tests that
can be performed on this indicator are discussed below.

Percentage of Reserves Obtained through Exports versus Foreign Investment

A country that obtains a high percentage of FX reserves through foreign investment perpetuates its dependence on capital inflows while limiting its ability to
deleverage.

Dependence on foreign capital inflows is likely to be symptomatic of an undeveloped or uncompetitive industrial base and/or low domestic saving rates,

EXHIBIT 25-3

Analysis of Sovereign Risk

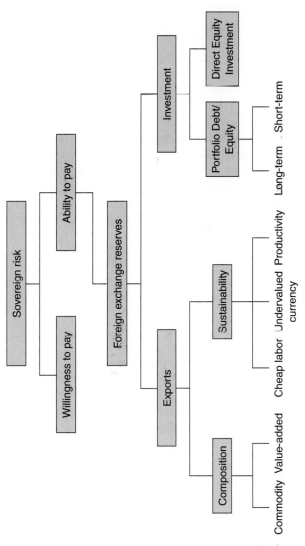

whereby domestic spending outstrips investment, as was the case with Mexico prior to devaluation. Prices on debt of countries with this characteristic will likely become more volatile going forward relative to countries that derive a higher percentage of FX generation from exports.

Proportion of Portfolio to Direct Investment within the Foreign Investment Category

Portfolio investment tends to be short term and can leave a country as fast as it comes in. *Direct* investment tends to be long term and has an added benefit of improving productivity in a country's private sector. Therefore, countries with a higher proportion of direct to portfolio investment should present a more stable credit profile over the longer term.

Proper Sterilization of Flows of Foreign Capital by the Central Bank

A large change in FX reserves that is not sterilized by the central bank poses high risks to the long-term prospects of an economy. For example, assume a significant capital inflow into a country. Unless the central bank sells an amount of assets to domestic banks matching the FX reserves it received, the inflow will increase money supply and possibly fuel inflation. To persuade domestic banks to buy its assets, the central bank would likely need to raise interest rates. Rising real interest rates make the country more attractive to foreign investors and could induce further capital inflows. This can lead to appreciating currency, which could hamper exports. A deteriorating trade balance can produce a current account deficit. If the government then resorts to devaluing currency to boost exports and curtail inflow, it risks a loss of confidence of international investors. This problem is magnified when a high percentage of the inflow is short-term portfolio investment. Given the complex nature of sterilizations, their success usually can be judged only over the long term.

Ratio tests that can be performed with FX reserves include FX reserves to debt service and months of imports of goods, services, and interest covered by FX reserves.

Exports

Exports are a "blood test" for an economy. The analysis of exports can provide perhaps the most meaningful insight into the state of a country's economy and its long-term outlook.

1. Exports are a key source for building FX reserves. In high-yield terms, it is similar to operating income. A country for which exports represent a high percentage of FX generation is generally a lower and more stable credit risk than a country that relies primarily on capital inflows. Also, export revenues can provide an opportunity to deleverage.

EXHIBIT 25-4

Foreign Exchange Reserves

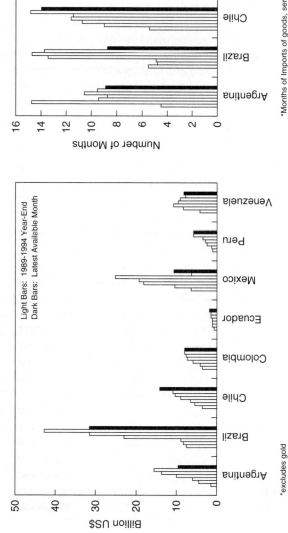

International Reserves, Billions US$*

Light Bars: 1989-1994 Year-End
Dark Bars: Latest Available Month

Billion US$

Argentina, Brazil, Chile, Colombia, Ecuador, Mexico, Peru, Venezuela

*excludes gold

International Reserves, Import Coverage Ratio*

Light Bars: 1989-1994 Year-End
Dark Bars: Latest Available Month

Number of Months

Argentina, Brazil, Chile, Colombia, Ecuador, Mexico, Peru, Venezuela

*Months of Imports of goods, services, and income; excludes gold

2. Analysis of the *composition* and *sustainability* of exports can provide reliable insight into the economic *and* political fundamentals of a country.

Composition addresses whether a country exports value-added goods or commodities. Reliance on commodities with prices subject to sharp fluctuations adds to the volatility of a country's credit profile. One example would be a contrast between Mexico and Brazil. The bulk of Mexico's exports through the 1970s was oil. When in the early 1980s oil prices declined while interest rates rose and many developed economies went into recession, most Mexican issuers, including the sovereign, encountered great difficulty paying debt. Brazil, however, enjoyed a developed export sector that was well integrated into many major economies of the world. At least partly as a result, there were almost no defaults in the Brazilian private sector in the 1980s, and Brazilian corporate issuers could have continued to service debt were it not for the exchange controls imposed by the government.

Sustainability addresses whether a country exports because of high productivity or cheap labor and/or undervalued currency. One of the key points of the Uruguay round of the General Agreement on Tariffs and Trade (GATT) was an implied message from the developed countries that they can no longer afford to allow their developing counterparts to compete primarily on the basis of undervalued currency or cheap labor. With high labor and social costs, the developed world has no choice but to seek productivity as a means to competitiveness. Therefore, those countries that have invested in productivity should outperform in terms of exports.

3. *Purchasing power parity* (PPP) is a useful way to reconcile inflation to export competitiveness. Closed economies and high inflation have been a common characteristic of many developing countries. Inefficient domestic enterprises and import restrictions endemic to such economies have generally produced high inflation. In the absence of foreign exchange controls, a country with high inflation would need to devalue its currency to regain competitiveness and/or raise interest rates to attract foreign capital. A depreciating currency is disadvantageous to foreign investors because (1) it makes it more difficult for domestic issuers to raise the same amount of hard currency with their local currency earnings, and (2) it reduces the value of returns on local financial instruments. Conversely, rising real interest rates can lead to appreciation of the currency through capital inflows, which can hamper exports through an unfavorable exchange rate. In general, knowledge and application of the interrelationships implicit in PPP should enable investors to anticipate changes in a country's interest and exchange rate policies on the basis of inflation and trade balance data. (See the discussion of fundamental valuation later in this chapter.)

EXHIBIT 25–5

External Debt Service, % of Exports**
1989 - 1994

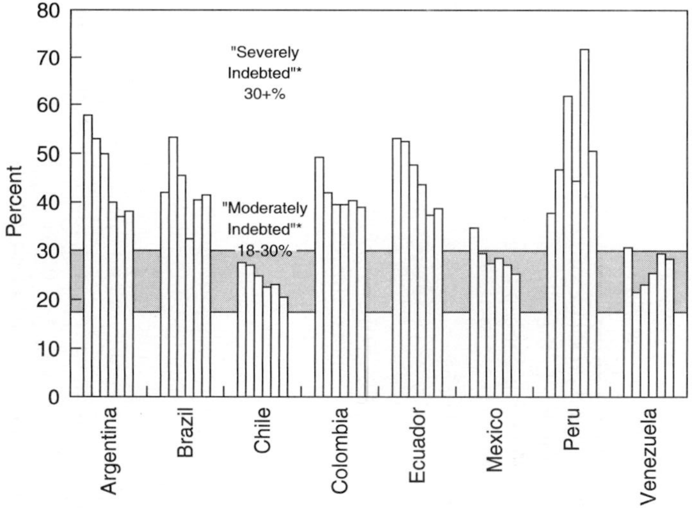

Source: IIF. *World Bank definition **Exports of goods, services, and income

External Debt, % of Exports**
1989 - 1994

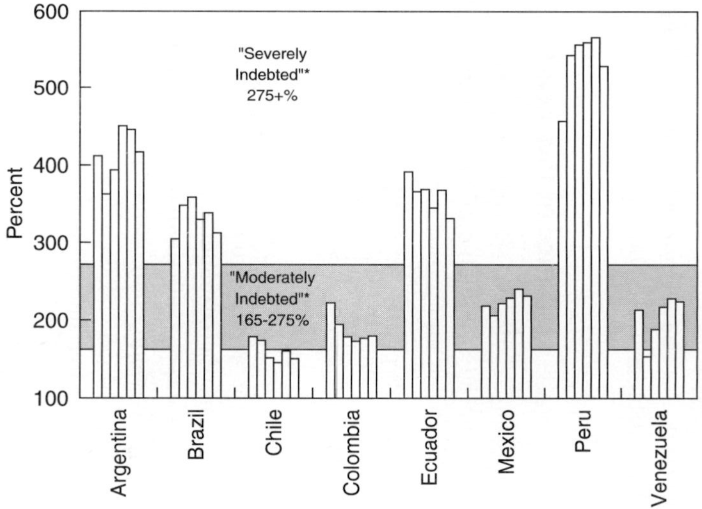

Source: IIF. *World Bank definition **Exports of goods, services, and income

Ratio tests that can be performed with exports include total external debt/exports, and total debt service/exports.

Balance of Payments

Balance of payments (BOP) presents the overall picture. Defined as exports – imports + capital inflows – capital outflows + change in exchange reserves, the BOP contains important information such as the *current account* (CA) and the composition of foreign capital flows. Since the Mexican financial crisis in early 1995, the investor community has placed great emphasis on the current account balance. Although it is certainly alarming to see a country running a large CA deficit, that alone should not be the basis for judging a country's credit quality because of different natures of CA deficits. Analysis of two other components in the BOP can provide for a more complete evaluation: (1) the composition of imports—proportions of consumption, intermediate and capital goods—and (2) how the deficit is financed—with short- or long-term portfolio money or direct investment. The credit condition of a country that imports primarily capital goods financed with long-term money (e.g., Asian tigers) would be generally stronger than that of a country that imports primarily consumption goods financed with short-term money (e.g., Mexico in 1994).

An added benefit of looking at the BOP is the ability to gauge in broad terms a country's liquidity, that is, credit lines with the International Monetary Fund, World Bank, and other official creditors, and access to global capital markets. Finally, the BOP contains what could be viewed as a leading indicator of a country's credit quality: the flight capital. Consisting primarily of the money of a country's wealthy residents, and often difficult to identify, flight capital empirically has been a good predictor of imminent changes in a country's political and economic conditions. In the discussion of fundamental valuation, we present a formula that captures flight capital as a forecasting tool.

Other Indicators

Inflation, money supply, and gross domestic product are among other useful indicators available to investors. However, when using these indicators, it is important to keep in mind their handicaps. For example, inflation can be a short-term indicator. Countries that are forced to perform a balancing act between bringing down inflation and keeping the trade deficit in check will likely have intermittent success with both. Judging credit quality by one or even three months worth of inflation or trade data may result in missing the big picture. Gross domestic product, another potential indicator, needs to be adjusted to reflect compositional differences between countries and thus lacks easy comparability in many cases. Overall, the short-term nature and/or lack of comparability of most economic indicators in IEM require that to be useful they must be viewed against the backdrop of a long-term fundamental judgment on a country.

LIMITATIONS OF SOVEREIGN ANALYSIS

In considering IEM, we believe it is *essential* to differentiate between events that can and cannot be predicted. In general, past evidence suggests that many integral components of sovereign risk do not lend themselves to effective prediction. Such components include political stability, short-term economic policies, and outcomes of major policy initiatives. And it is precisely the events that cannot be anticipated effectively, such as devaluations, that have historically had the greatest impact on market values.

Even if cultural differences are excepted from credit analysis, the number of remaining variables is considerable. Key among them is how a country secures money to pay debt. If it relies mostly on capital inflows, the question is whether its creditors will continue lending. If it primarily earns money through exports, an analysis of its industrial base is needed, though predicting competitiveness and economic cycles is less than a precise science. Finally, assuming a sound assessment on the ability to raise funds is achievable, local political judgment needs to be considered. For example, it is unlikely that the Mexican government expected the violent reaction it received to the devaluation in December 1994. Thus, a government's miscalculation of how others may react to its actions can bring a country to the brink of collapse, even if such an event may not be warranted by the country's credit fundamentals.

A phenomenon worth mentioning in this context is the value of promises. The American public is among the more skeptical electorates in the world. Domestic politicians are commonly afforded limited trust and campaign promises are generally not expected to be totally fulfilled. This skepticism has been in sharp contrast to the firm trust the market has placed in foreign politicians on numerous occasions, no matter how counterintuitive their pronouncements seemed. Recent evidence suggests that this trust was misplaced in many cases, and predictions made on the basis of such promises were equally misplaced, e.g. the well-known pledge of the Mexican government not to devalue the peso.

The fact that sovereign predictions of the past have had a wide margin for improvement has not deterred many current experts from undertaking to forecast exactly what will happen where and when. Often, these forecasts impact or even drive the short-term pricing of securities, but inevitably, reality catches up. Once again, Mexico is a good example. In 1994, despite a skyrocketing current account deficit, dwindling FX reserves, rising political instability, and other loud indicators of trouble, the predicting consensus was that Mexico would become investment grade in 1995. The reality could not have been more different. Investors who were paying attention to the country's fundamentals got out in time. Those who believed in promises and predictions were less fortunate.

Going forward, to succeed in emerging markets, we believe it is critical for investors to recognize (1) the great number of variables that compose sovereign risk, (2) the very limited ability of *anyone* to predict accurately most of these variables, and (3) even less ability to predict their interplay. As a consequence, we view selecting a group of fundamental indicators that are quantifiable, comparable from country to country, and that lend themselves to a meaningful qualitative interpretation as the optimal way for assessing sovereign risk.

ANALYSIS OF CAPITAL FORMATION/TECHNICAL CONDITIONS

Technicals can drive the market. Technical factors play a principal role in determining values in IEM. In fact, it is arguable that the significant flow of portfolio investment to emerging markets in 1992–1993 was driven primarily by the strong technical pressures on U.S. institutional investors. At their peak, these pressures created a market in which the concept of sovereign risk was often ignored, flexible accounting practices and spotty financial disclosure were dismissed as "cultural differences," and bankruptcy protection was barely contemplated. This environment allowed many IEM issuers to enter the U.S. bond market at the same spreads, or even tighter, than domestic high-yield issuers. Ultimately, the minimal absolute yields, strong correlation with U.S. Treasuries, and the lack of a fundamental basis behind prices created a situation where a mere 25-basis-point increase in interest rates by the Federal Reserve in February 1994 caused a precipitous drop in all emerging market values.

Despite a substantial improvement in the general credit quality of emerging markets, significant risk remains. Because of the magnitude and nature of this risk, we believe a large percentage of emerging market issuers should *not* be priced in terms of spread to Treasuries, but in terms of *absolute yield*, like domestic high-yield issuers. Pricing off the U.S. Treasuries curve in 1993 led to yield compression well in excess of fundamental improvement in emerging markets, causing some investors large losses in 1994. Losing sight of the absolute yield level and whether that level reflects the fundamental risk of an issuer will inevitably lead to losses again as the U.S. Federal Reserve adjusts its policies. Once again, capital formation and technical conditions *are* an indelible part of the forces that determine values. However, in certain circumstances, investors may be better served playing these forces directly, rather than through emerging markets debt. (In the 1970s, commercial banks might have been better off betting directly that oil prices would continue to go up, rather than betting that oil prices would continue to go up and thus Mexico's credit quality would continue to improve.) Cognizance of absolute yield can be an effective means for keeping a perspective on the fundamental risk and avoiding technical traps.

Establishing the Appropriate Absolute Yield Level

The lack of a long track record, limited liquidity, high volatility, and a number of other risks do not allow us at this time to provide a precise recipe for how to establish the appropriate absolute yield level for the emerging market issuers. However, we can suggest two benchmarks. The first one is the general risk profile of a portfolio. Baskets dedicated to quality assets are not suitable for a large percentage of IEM issues. The second benchmark can be calculated through the application of the classic arbitrage theory, described in detail in the section on fundamental valuation. The argument there is that, in equilibrium, the following parity should hold:

$$R_{\text{external bond}} = R_{\text{domestic bond}} - \text{Currency hedge} \pm \frac{\text{Material difference in}}{\text{asset characteristics}}$$

Where

$R_{\text{external bond}}$ = Yield on a foreign currency-denominated debt of an entity A
$R_{\text{domestic bond}}$ = Yield on a domestic currency-denominated debt of
                an entity A
Material difference in asset characteristics = Collateral, duration,
guarantees, structure, etc.

At present, the second benchmark is still largely a conceptual point for the same reasons that a precise recipe on how to establish the appropriate absolute yield level does not exist. However, the grasp of interrelationships implicit in this formula is positively key to understanding the forces that drive values in emerging markets. Incidentally, flight capital, which we view as the leading indicator of a country's credit quality, is captured in this formula. We believe that when the parity described above can be calculated with precision, a new level of stability and efficiency in IEM will emerge.

A New Dimension of Technical Complexity

An added complexity of emerging markets is attributable to participation by a large number of investors from different parts of the world, mainly Asia and Europe. This has had the effect of materially altering the way values are determined. American investors derive relative value of emerging markets debt primarily on the basis of comparing it to U.S. domestic debt and in relation to U.S. Treasury rates. Investors from other parts of the world derive relative value of IEM debt primarily on the basis of comparing it to *their* own domestic debt and treasury rates. As a result, a change in local conditions in any one of the large investing countries may prompt a buying/selling spree in emerging markets, regardless of whether a fundamental change occurred with any of the issuers. Theoretically, a proper recommendation to address this issue would be to suggest a global portfolio approach, whereby investors would look at markets as a continuum—the United States, Europe, Asia, Latin America—on the basis of credit quality. Realistically, it may not be feasible for anyone to maintain awareness of so many variables and to continuously formulate correct judgments as these variables change. Therefore, a feasible solution comes back to developing a fundamental view on the countries, which should enable investors to wait out technical storms.

Another angle on the same problem is the pricing of new issues. For example, in August 1995, Mexico was able to price a sovereign yen deal almost 180 basis points tighter than its Eurobond deal of a few weeks earlier. This tightening of spread was *not* a result of a material improvement in the credit quality of Mexico in the period between the two deals. Rather, it reflected the fact that the Japanese treasury bonds yielded 1.91 percent in the week when the yen deal was priced versus 6 percent for the European LIBOR rate at the time of the Eurobond transaction. Yet, Mexico presents the same fundamental risk to all investors, regardless of the currency in which the debt is held; that is, all investors will see the same FX reserves, inflation, trade and other data as they pertain to the country. Logically, because an issuer presents the same fundamental risk to all investors, the real interest rate charged on its debt should also be the same in efficient markets, regardless of the currency in which the debt is issued. In reality, market efficiency is yet to be achieved in IEM. Because of differences in technical conditions among the United States, Europe, and Asia and differences in investing criteria among investor bases, investors may see inefficiencies in the pricing of new deals as issuers access countries with the most favorable technical conditions. While this is clearly advantageous for issuers, it is not advantageous for investors who may end up *not* being compensated fairly for the intrinsic issuer risks they assume.

Conceptually, technical conditions in a country are largely a product of the country's monetary policy, which in turn is usually reflective of the country's economic cycle. When a country's central bank lowers domestic cost of capital, the goal generally is to stimulate the domestic economy, not to provide cheap capital for foreign issuers. Domestic investors who opt for foreign securities in search of yield, and who reflexively benchmark that yield by the domestic yield curve, may set themselves up for losses as the economic cycle and technical conditions change in their countries. That is why we strongly urge investors to keep in mind absolute yield and not feel compelled to translate every move in treasuries into pricing of emerging markets debt. The absolute yield should reflect an issuer's fundamental risk. The parity that can help investors establish the appropriate absolute yield level was introduced earlier and is discussed in detail in the section on fundamental valuation. We believe that as emerging markets evolve, developed markets integrate further, and fundamentals become the driving force in valuation of IEM debt, the discrepancies in pricing described above will diminish.

Technicals Can Produce Excess in Secondary Trading

There are two patterns worth mentioning here. First, the "lumping effect," wherein bad news in one country drags down market values in all others. This effect was particularly common while Mexico was the bellwether, since at the time it seemed reasonable that a problem with the "best" should be extrapolated onto the rest. Recent advances in fundamental analysis are making this pattern less prevalent as investors begin to differentiate better between issuers. Second is the "pendulum effect." For example, bad news in a country leads to a sell-off of its securities. This sell-off is often accompanied by the taking of short positions by traders expecting more bad news, which may lead to overselling and price declines in excess of the significance of the news. Then, the pendulum may swing the other way as traders begin to cover their shorts, giving impetus to price appreciation. Of course, what goes down precipitously can come up sharply as well. As a result, investors may see wild swings in prices, until a new equilibrium is found.

On the negative side, these swings have contributed to the staggering losses dealt to many investors in emerging markets. As recently as in the first three months of 1995, some investors saw the value of their IEM portfolios decline by more than 30 percent. On the positive side, these swings provided many extraordinary trading opportunities for investors who either had the ability to hang on or held a fundamental view on the countries. By mid-June 1995, emerging markets were up almost 40 percent from the lows of March 1995.

Rumors Are Not Your Friends
On Friday, May 26, 1995, right before the Memorial Day weekend in the United States, the emerging markets were hit with speculation that Mexico was about to default. In the wake of the debacle earlier in the year, a concern that "things look darkest right before they go pitch black" sent traders and investors heading for the exit, and prices of Latin American instruments dove south. However, a close analysis of the situation showed that there was no new material information released that week to indicate any change in the credit condition of Mexico. The entity that was discussing default was Aeromexico, the country's beleaguered trunk airline. Our recommendation for dealing with such situations is to inquire first whether any new *material* information has become available that would change an issuer's outlook.

New Players, New Risks
The high returns available in emerging markets have attracted many different types of investors. Highly consequential to market volatility have been hedge funds. Armed with significant capital access and a diverse arsenal of trading strategies, these institutions have demonstrated repeatedly the ability to affect markets and even countries. With regard to IEM, declining interest rates in the United States, Europe, and Japan in 1992 and 1993 made available to hedge funds an unprecedented amount of cheap capital. At the same time, tight liquidity in emerging markets enabled them to move markets by merely shifting capital or using derivatives. Subsequently, an increase in U.S. interest rates in February 1994 caused significant losses to many hedge funds, and their ability to influence markets was subsequently curtailed at least temporarily. Nonetheless, fundamental investors need to keep in mind that any future price storms may be caused artificially. Once again, a determination for whether material new information was released to alter the outlook for issuers can help investors make the right decision.

ISSUES OF FUNDAMENTAL RISK

A large number of emerging markets issuers are not sovereign but are either quasi-sovereign or private. Quasi-sovereigns include issuers with some form of government ownership but *not* the explicit full faith and credit of the sovereign.

Privately owned entities include banks and industrial and service companies. There are obvious reasons why additional credit analysis is required for corporates and banks and compelling reasons why it is required for quasi-sovereigns.

Quasi-Sovereigns: What You See May Not Be What You Get

At present, fundamental analysis is rarely applied to quasi-sovereigns because of the argument, "the government owns them." Yet, unless the government provides an explicit guarantee for an entity's debt, it should not be assumed that in a case of financial difficulty it will definitely compensate debt holders. Another danger comes from privatizations. Although they are generally good for a country's economy, they may be bad for bondholders because the privatized entity may present greater credit risk as a stand-alone entity than when evaluated as part of the government structure. Specifically, a key risk that arises as a result of privatizations is access to hard currency. A good example would be utilities that earn revenues in domestic currency and rely on the government to supply them with hard currency. Once privatized, they may face difficulty competing and generating sufficient revenues to cover their debt service. Importantly, the ill-defined legal and regulatory frameworks and the general lack of precedents regarding effective bankruptcy protection in foreign countries suggest the absence of an effective exit strategy for investors if a government sells its stake in a quasi-sovereign and that entity does not prove viable on a stand-alone basis.

Banks Are Difficult to Value

To assess credit quality of a bank, an analysis of its asset quality and duration of its assets and liabilities is required. Banks generally do not disclose who they lend to and how they finance loan portfolios, so neither piece of information is generally available (or reliable when available) in emerging markets. As a result, there is often little indication of trouble with a bank until it is too late, and when it is too late, there are generally no assets to compensate investors. In this context, banks that are not explicitly sovereign but that have government ownership are particularly risky because they are often forced by the government to finance state-run companies, some of which may be insolvent. In the end, such banks may accumulate loan portfolios of poor quality, while their own debt still does not have a sovereign guarantee and investors may have difficulty getting their money back.

Corporates Present a Favorable Risk-Return Relationship

Corporates are the only product in emerging markets for which the extent of risk can be assessed with a reasonable degree of certainty. Traditional credit analysis of industry cycle, competitiveness, revenue composition, cost structure, and capitalization can be performed with most emerging market companies just as effectively as with domestic issuers. In addition, a majority of foreign corporate issuers fall into the same industry categories that dominate the domestic U.S. high-yield market: telecommunications, oil and gas, steel, paper, bottling, building materials, and so on. As a result, U.S. domestic industry expertise clearly applies. This is especially true for industries like oil, paper, and steel, which have product prices generally determined in the global marketplace. The ability to analyze key variables that exist with corporates is in sharp contrast to the situation with sovereigns and quasi-sovereigns. Going forward, this characteristic should make corporates increasingly attractive to fundamental investors vis-à-vis sovereign debt.

Sovereign Credit Quality Still Dominates the Pricing of Corporates

Presently, sovereign instruments account for the largest portion of IEM trading. This is reasonable, given the dominant size of Brady bonds outstanding in the marketplace. Also, information flow related to countries and the number of analysts following sovereigns far exceeds information flow and the number of analysts following corporates. As a result of these conditions, fundamentals still play a small role in determining the bond prices of IEM corporate issuers. Rather, these prices often reflect more of sovereign risk, and there tends to be high correlation between prices of sovereign and corporate debt (see Exhibit 25–6). Great opportunities often arise as a consequence of this.

Corporates can present better credit quality than the countries where they are located. While conditions in a country are clearly important, there are compelling reasons why some corporate issuers can and should trade through the sovereign ceiling. These reasons exist *only* when there is a low probability that the sovereign will impose foreign exchange controls and *mainly* when a company earns a high percentage of its external debt service through hard currency exports. In the absence of FX controls, a company with a high percentage of export earnings in its revenue mix, low leverage, and competitive cost structure can present a

EXHIBIT 25–6

Price Correlation of Latin American Eurobonds and Corporates to Brady Bond Index 1992–First Half 1995

	Euro/Brady Correlation	Corporate/Brady Correlation
1992	0.998	0.997
1993	0.984	0.980
1994	0.905	0.830
1995*	0.939	0.920
1992–1995*	0.957	0.964

*First six months

Source: Merrill Lynch Strategy.

more attractive credit profile than its home country. One such example is YPF in Argentina, which in addition to export earnings, low leverage, and an improving cost structure has assets in the United States worth over $700 million. The combination of these attributes, at present, arguably makes YPF a better credit risk than Argentina. Thus, provided the country's government does not impose currency controls, a corporation can often present a better credit risk than the sovereign if it commands a more stable and diversified hard currency revenue base, lower leverage, and assets in a stable, developed country. Keeping this thought in mind should allow fundamental investors to identify and exploit multiple market inefficiencies that are bound to arise when sovereign events depress the prices of premier corporates.

FUNDAMENTAL VALUATION

The increased use of forward and option products in IEM is making the classic arbitrage pricing theory increasingly applicable to these markets. Key economic relationships implied in the theory are as follows:[2]

- The interest rate parity (IRP) relationship, also referred to as the law of one price, links national money market rates to foreign exchange rates and states that the difference in national interest rates for securities of similar risk and maturity should be equal to but opposite in sign to the forward exchange rate discount or premium.

- The purchasing power parity (PPP) relationship states that a country with higher inflation will have a depreciating currency.

- The Fisher effect states the nominal interest rates in each country are equal to the required real rate of return to the investor plus compensation for expected inflation. Consequently, in equilibrium, the difference in expected inflation between two countries must equal the difference in nominal interest rates.

- The International Fisher effect (IFE) describes the theoretical difference in nominal interest rates across national boundaries. The difference is linked to expectations of relative real interest rates and inflation. For example, investors in foreign securities must be rewarded with a higher interest rate to offset the expected rate of depreciation of the foreign currency when they attempt to convert principal and interest back into the home currency.

On the basis of these relationships, with regard to establishing the appropriate absolute yield level for IEM securities, we propose for the following to hold in theory:

---

2. For a more detailed discussion of the concepts presented here, see David K. Eiteman and Arthur I. Stonehill, *Multinational Business Finance* (Reading, MA:Addison-Wesley, 1989), pp.71–78, 105–109.

$$R_{\text{external bond}} = R_{\text{domestic bond}} - \text{Currency hedge} \pm \frac{\text{Material difference in asset}}{\text{characteristics (IRP)}}$$

$$\text{Currency hedge} = \text{Forward discount/Premium}$$

$$\text{Forward discount/Premium} = \text{Domestic anticipated inflation} - \frac{\text{Foreign}}{\text{anticipated}}\text{ inflation (PPP)}$$

Where

$R_{\text{external bond}}$ = Yield on a foreign currency-denominated debt of an entity A
$R_{\text{domestic bond}}$ = Yield on a domestic currency-denominated debt of an
    entity A
Material difference in asset characteristics = Collateral, duration,
guarantees, structure, etc.

The Concept

A country presents the same fundamental risk regardless of the currency denomination of its debt; that is, local and foreign investors will see the same inflation, trade, and currency reserve data for the country regardless of what type of security they own. Therefore, in theory, the real rate of return on debt of the same issuer in any currency should also be the same, adjusted for currency risk and differences in product characteristics.

The product characteristics component includes duration, guarantees, collateral value, convertibility risks, taxes, put/call options, and so on. Most of these characteristics cannot be valued with a reasonable degree of precision in emerging markets today due to the lack of product comparability, limited liquidity, and other factors. Yet, we believe that eventually most of these characteristics will become quantifiable, introducing a new measure of efficiency to IEM.

The currency risk component represents a microcosm of many key risks confronting investors in the emerging markets. It is through currency that the state of a country's economy relative to other economies can be established. Under the PPP, a depreciating currency signals future inflation. Under a derivative of the IFE, a depreciating currency may also signify such pressures as excessive imports and substantial capital outflows. The former is usually an effect and a cause of serious imbalances in an economy. The latter may primarily comprise the money of foreign investors or of a country's wealthy residents. In the first case, the outflow will likely be a lagging indicator; in the second case, it is likely to be a leading indicator. It either case, capital outflows are likely to be the result of rising political instability or other causes that convey the loss of investor confidence. In all cases, most of the causes under PPP and IFE deal with fundamental risks, which must be equally reflected in values of both local and foreign currency debt instruments.

The practical significance of using currency as a microcosm for fundamental risks is that the cost of a currency hedge subtracted from the rate of return on local currency instruments can provide investors with the first indication of what the required absolute yield level for the hard currency debt of the same issuer should be. This level then needs to be adjusted for different characteristics of debt instruments and risks that do not exhibit themselves through currency fluctuations. As was mentioned above, at present this is not entirely feasible. However, when it does become feasible, investors will have a solid benchmark by which to check whether they are being compensated adequately for the risks they take investing in a foreign country and which will help them avoid technical traps.

FINANCIAL DISCLOSURE, CONTRACTS, AND BANKRUPTCY

The key purpose of accounting and its main difference from bookkeeping is the ability to achieve a more precise matching of revenues and expenses. Unlike U.S. GAAP, accounting standards in Latin America generally have been so flexible that a host of manipulative practices have been possible, and the numbers produced under these standards have left much to be desired. An example of this flexibility can be found in the treatment of capital expenditures: Companies in Latin America are able to expense or capitalize at their discretion and are not required to follow a consistent practice from year to year. With regard to Asia, there have been few corporate issuers but enough to exhibit equally lacking accounting standards. While this is understandable given the recent entry of these countries into the international capital markets, we believe it is critical for investors to demand more consistent accounting practices from the emerging market issuers if credit analysis is to become valid and the markets more stable.

In general, the value of contracts has not been high in emerging markets, and there are few signs of this changing. Recent noteworthy examples of a "respectful" treatment of contracts include China's decision to change the location of the largest McDonald's in the world from its premier spot in Beijing to another location in 1994 and, in August 1995, the cancellation of a multibillion dollar Enron project in India. This disregard for binding agreements at the government level can generally be found at other levels of society as well. The basic concept here is that a contract or a pledge mean different things in different places, with very limited enforcement available to the injured parties in most cases.

In terms of financing, "a dollar borrowed is a dollar earned" may not be so much the attitude to raising capital today, but neither is responsible conduct. For example, one of the first news items out of Mexico in January 1995 was a decision by Grupo Sidek not to service a part of its debt, which was later reversed. Had it not been reversed, the cross-default covenant could have put most of the company's debt in default. Given the company's eagerness not to pay, it is not clear how the investors would have gotten their money back.

A bankruptcy code exists in the majority of emerging countries. Its value to investors has been very limited in the past and is likely to remain so at least in the foreseeable future. In looking at IEM companies, high-yield investors need to keep in mind that traditional liquidation analysis generally does not apply. Just as with quasi-sovereigns, the ill-defined legal and regulatory frameworks and the general lack of precedents when investors received effective bankruptcy protection should indicate that liquidation will remain an unlikely option for some time. As a result, instead of doing an EBITDA multiple-asset valuation, a more practical approach may be to try to figure out what kind of package a bankrupt company will offer investors in return for the defaulting securities. Evidence to date indicates that these packages have *not* been generous, which should be all the more reason to scrutinize company-specific risks beforehand and *not* expect protection under the law.

In order to scrutinize company-specific risks, investors need financial information. It would seem intuitive that issuers that are new to the market, be it sovereign or corporate, would go an extra mile in trying to get investors comfortable with their credit profiles. However, IEM issuers from countries with a great deal of uncertainty, who are not subject to the U.S. jurisdiction, have been allowed to get away with no or minimal disclosure. By getting away, we mean trading at the same spreads or tighter than domestic U.S. issuers. Many arguments have been used to justify this situation, including cultural sensitivity. It may be the case that in the initial stages of market opening it was somehow reasonable for the emerging market issuers to feel uncomfortable with the "prying" analysts. However, if anything, the Mexican debacle has demonstrated vividly the absolute legitimacy of requests for better disclosure. It is arguable that if information about Mexican FX reserves and other pertinent economic data had been released on a consistent basis, the market might have been better prepared for the action, and great losses might have been avoided. Therefore, we believe that the time of justifying inadequate disclosure has passed. At present, a number of Brazilian companies are preparing financial statements in the U.S. GAAP. Major Russian companies have retained U.S. accounting firms to do the same in advance of their attempts to enter global capital markets. Long-established German automobile manufacturer Daimler Benz recently announced plans to have U.S. GAAP financials as well. The concept here is that if an issuer has no reason to withhold information, "cultural sensitivity" should not prevent it from providing investors with accurate financial statements and straight answers to legitimate questions.

SUMMARY

We believe the following can be done to succeed in emerging markets: (1) assessment of cross-border/sovereign risk with emphasis on quantifiable variables such as foreign exchange reserves, exports, and the balance of payments; (2) analysis of what part technicals play in determining prevailing bond values; (3) complete credit analysis of quasi-sovereign and corporate issuers; and (4) evaluation of bond values on the basis of absolute yield, not spread to treasuries. In the case of new issues, quality of structure, distribution, and ability of underwriters to support their deals need to be taken into consideration. In terms of corporate issuers, we believe that investors will find optimal values in companies with an export business generating sufficient hard currency to service a high percentage of the company's foreign debt, adequate liquidity to weather an economic downturn, and familiar industry fundamentals so that qualified credit analysis can be performed. A select group of corporate issuers can and should trade through the sovereign ceiling.

APPENDIX

Framework for Analysis

Below, we provide a list of questions and issues that we believe investors need to feel comfortable with before making an investment decision on sovereign, quasi-sovereign, and private issuers in emerging markets. This list is not exhaustive but is meant as a general guide.

A. Sovereign Analysis

1. Amount of foreign exchange (FX) reserves a country has. Coverage ratios:
   - FX reserves/debt service.
   - Months of imports of goods, services, and interest covered by FX reserves.
2. Percentage of FX reserves obtained through exports versus investment.
3. Effectiveness of a country's central bank in sterilizing capital flows.
4. Composition of investment: official creditors; direct versus portfolio capital; short or long term.
5. Trade balance (exports – imports). Coverage ratios:
   - Total external debt/export revenues.
   - Total debt service/export revenues.
6. Composition of exports: commodities versus value-added goods.
7. Sustainability of exports: Is the driving force behind exports cheap labor, undervalued currency, or productivity?
8. Impact of inflation on the value of currency and export competitiveness; application of the purchasing power parity.

9. Composition of imports: proportions of consumption, intermediate and capital goods.

10. How the imports are financed: portfolio/direct investment; if portfolio investment, short- or long-term (imports include goods, services, and debt service).

11. Interrelationship between inflation and the current account: Is a country striving to achieve low inflation while trying to maintain export competitiveness?

12. Capital flows: Do local residents keep money in domestic banks, "under the mattress" in local currency, or invest in hard currency instruments—a leading indicator? Does a country attract direct investment—a less-leading indicator? Does a country attract portfolio investment (short or long term)—an ambiguous indicator?

13. Impact of capital flows on the value of currency and export competitiveness.

14. Political and social stability in a country: unemployment; law and order; cooperation between the branches of government; fiscal prudence; distribution of wealth.

15. History of honoring debt obligations.

16. Respect for foreign investors and international law.

17. Relationship with the United States.

B. Technical Analysis

1. Domestic interest rates in the United States, Germany, and Japan.

2. Domestic yield levels in secondary markets in the United States, Europe, and Japan.

3. Availability of capital and receptiveness of international investors to emerging market issuers.

4. The size of forward calendar in domestic markets of the United States, Europe, and Japan.

5. Absolute yield levels on domestic and emerging market securities in secondary markets.

6. Domestic interest rates in emerging market countries.

7. What accounts for the difference between domestic yields and yields in developed markets for the same emerging market issuers?

8. Are the yields on emerging market issuers driven by fundamental changes in the quality of issuers or changes in treasury rates in the United States, Europe, or Japan?

9. What happens to prices of the outstanding emerging market issues when the Federal Reserve in the United States or central banks in

Germany or Japan change short-term rates? By how much will the change in prices of emerging market issues exceed the change in prices of domestic debt?

10. At times of high-market volatility, what percentage of price movements can be accounted for by fundamental news about the issuer? Could the changes have been caused by rumors, large capital movements by certain players, or trading strategies of certain market participants?

C. Fundamental Analysis

1. All standard questions about industry cycle, competitiveness, revenue base, cost structure, and capitalization.

2. Percentage of export earnings in the revenue mix.
   - Are exports a product of cheap currency, cheap labor, or productivity?

3. Percentage of foreign currency costs in the cost structure.

4. Percentage of foreign currency debt in the capitalization.

5. Ability to get through an economic downturn.
   - Internal liquidity.
   - Banking relationships, access to capital markets.

6. Past payment history.

7. Quality of financial disclosure.

MORTGAGE-BACKED AND ASSET-BACKED SECURITIES

⑥　MORTGAGES AND
OVERVIEW OF
MORTGAGE-BACKED
SECURITIES

Frank J. Fabozzi, Ph.D., CFA, CPA
Adjunct Professor of Finance
School of Management
Yale University

Chuck Ramsey
Managing Director
Structured Capital Management
and CEO
Mortgage Risk Assessment Corp.

A mortgage loan is a loan secured by the collateral of some specified real estate property, which obliges the borrower to make a predetermined series of payments. The mortgage gives the lender (the *mortgagee*) the right of foreclosure on the loan if the borrower (the *mortgagor*) defaults. That is, if the borrower fails to make the contracted payments, the lender can seize the property in order to ensure that the debt is paid off.

The types of real estate properties that can be mortgaged are divided into two broad categories: residential and nonresidential properties. The former category includes houses, condominiums, cooperatives, and apartments. Residential real estate can be subdivided into single-family (one- to four-family) structures and multifamily structures (apartment buildings in which more than four families reside). Nonresidential property includes commercial and farm properties.

The market where these funds are borrowed is called the *mortgage market*. This sector of the debt market is by far the largest in the world. The mortgage market has undergone significant structural changes since the 1980s. Innovations have occurred in terms of the design of new mortgage instruments and the development of products that use pools of mortgages as collateral for the issuance of a security. Such securities are called *mortgage-backed securities*. When a mortgage is used as collateral for the issuance of a security, the mortgage is said to be *securitized*.

Some mortgage-backed securities are backed implicitly or explicitly by the U.S. government. These securities are not rated by commercial rating companies. However, for the wide range of mortgage-backed securities that do not carry an implicit or explicit government guarantee, the securities are rated using the same rating systems as for corporate bonds.

In this chapter, our focus is on the structure of the mortgage market, the risks associated with investing in mortgages, and the different types of mortgage design. We then provide an overview of mortgage-backed securities. Later chapters discuss these securities in much more detail.

PARTICIPANTS IN THE MORTGAGE MARKET

In addition to the ultimate investor of funds, there are three groups involved in the mortgage market: mortgage originators, mortgage servicers, and mortgage insurers.

Mortgage Originators

The original lender is called the *mortgage originator*. Mortgage originators include commercial banks, thrifts, mortgage bankers, life insurance companies, and pension funds. The three largest originators for all types of residential mortgages are commercial banks, thrifts, and mortgage bankers, originating more than 95 percent of annual mortgage originations.

Originators may generate income for themselves in one or more ways. First, they typically charge an *origination fee*. This fee is expressed in terms of points, where each point represents 1 percent of the borrowed funds. For example, an origination fee of two points on a $100,000 mortgage represents $2,000. Originators also charge application fees and certain processing fees.

The second source of revenue is the profit that might be generated from selling a mortgage at a higher price than it originally cost. This profit is called *secondary marketing profit*. Of course, if mortgage rates rise, an originator will realize a loss when the mortgages are sold in the secondary market. Finally, the mortgage originator may hold the mortgage in its investment portfolio.

A potential homeowner who wants to borrow funds to purchase a home will apply for a loan from a mortgage originator. Upon completion of the application form, which provides financial information about the applicant, and payment of an application fee, the mortgage originator will perform a credit evaluation of the applicant. The two primary factors in determining whether the funds will be lent are the *payment-to-income* (PTI) ratio and the *loan-to-value* (LTV) ratio.

The PTI, the ratio of monthly payments (both mortgage and real estate tax payments) to monthly income, is a measure of the ability of the applicant to make monthly payments. The lower this ratio, the greater the likelihood that the applicant will be able to meet the required payments.

The difference between the purchase price of the property and the amount borrowed is the borrower's down payment. The LTV is the ratio of the amount of the loan to the market (or appraised) value of the property. The lower this ratio, the more protection the lender has if the applicant defaults and the property must be repossessed and sold.

After a mortgage loan is closed, a mortgage originator can do one of three things: (1) hold the mortgage in its portfolio, (2) sell the mortgage to an investor who wishes to hold the mortgage or who will place the mortgage in a pool of mortgages to be used as collateral for the issuance of a mortgage-backed security, or (3) use the mortgage as collateral for the issuance of a mortgage-backed security.

When a mortgage originator intends to sell the mortgage, it will obtain a commitment from the potential investor (buyer). Two federally sponsored credit agencies and several private companies buy mortgages. As these agencies and private companies pool these mortgages and sell them to investors, they are called *conduits*. The two agencies, the Federal Home Loan Mortgage Corporation and the Federal National Mortgage Association (discussed further below), purchase only *conforming mortgages*. A conforming mortgage is one that meets the underwriting standards established by these agencies for being in a pool of mortgages underlying a security that they guarantee. Three underwriting standards established by these agencies in order to qualify as a conforming mortgage are (1) a maximum PTI, (2) a maximum LTV, and (3) a maximum loan amount. If an applicant does not satisfy the underwriting standards, the mortgage is called a *nonconforming mortgage*. Loans that exceed the maximum loan amount are called *jumbo mortgages*.

Mortgages acquired by the agency may be held as investments in their portfolio or securitized. The securities offered are discussed in Chapter 27. Private conduits typically will securitize the mortgages purchased rather than hold them as an investment. Both conforming and nonconforming mortgages are purchased. Examples of private conduits are the Residential Funding Corporation, GE Capital Mortgage Services, Prudential Home, and Chase Mortgage Finance Corporation. When evaluating mortgage-backed securities issued by private conduits, the commercial rating companies assess the underwriting standards and procedures of the originator.

Mortgage Servicers

Every mortgage loan must be serviced. Servicing of a mortgage loan involves collecting monthly payments and forwarding proceeds to owners of the loan, sending payment notices to mortgagors, reminding mortgagors when payments are overdue, maintaining records of principal balances, administering an escrow balance for real estate taxes and insurance purposes, initiating foreclosure proceedings if necessary, and furnishing tax information to mortgagors when applicable.

Servicers include bank-related entities, thrift-related entities, and mortgage bankers. The servicer receives a servicing fee. This fee is a fixed percentage of the outstanding mortgage balance. Consequently, the revenue from servicing declines over time as the mortgage balance amortizes.

Servicers play a critical role for mortgage-backed securities and asset-backed securities.[1] In rating securities that do not have government guarantees, the commercial rating companies assess the quality of the operations of the servicer.

Mortgage Insurers

When the lender makes the loan based on the credit of the borrower and on the collateral for the mortgage, the mortgage is said to be a *conventional mortgage*. The lender may require the borrower to obtain mortgage insurance to insure against default by the borrower. It is usually required by lenders on loans with loan-to-value (LTV) ratios greater than 80 percent. The amount insured will be some percentage of the loan and may decline as the LTV ratio declines. While the insurance is required by the lender, its cost is borne by the borrower, usually through a higher mortgage rate.

There are two forms of this insurance: insurance provided by a government agency and by a private mortgage insurance company. The federal agencies that provide this insurance to qualified borrowers are the Federal Housing Administration (FHA), the Veterans Administration (VA), and the Federal Farmers Administration (FmHA). Private mortgage insurance can be obtained from a mortgage insurance company such as Mortgage Guaranty Insurance Company and PMI Mortgage Insurance Company.

Another form of insurance may be required for mortgages on property that is located in geographical areas where the occurrence of natural disasters such as floods and earthquakes is higher than usual. This type of insurance is called *hazard insurance*.

When mortgages are pooled by a private conduit and a security is issued, additional insurance for the pool is typically obtained to enhance the credit of the security. This is because the major commercial rating agencies of such securities require external credit enhancement for the issuer to obtain a particular investment-grade rating. The credit rating of the mortgage insurer is an important factor considered by commercial rating companies. The factors that the commercial rating agencies assess to judge the credit quality of a pool of mortgages are the credit quality of the individual mortgages, the credit rating of the mortgage insurer, the underwriting standards and procedures of the originator, and the quality of the operations of the servicer.

ALTERNATIVE MORTGAGE INSTRUMENTS

There are many types of mortgage loans from which a borrower can select. We review several of the more popular mortgage designs here.

The interest rate on a mortgage loan (called the *contract rate*) is greater than the risk-free interest rate, in particular the yield on a Treasury security of

---

1. For a discussion of the role of servicers, see Galia Gichon, "The Role of Servicers," in *The Handbook of Commercial Mortgage-Backed Securities,* eds. Frank J. Fabozzi and David P. Jacob (New Hope, PA: Frank J. Fabozzi Associates, 1996).

comparable maturity. The spread reflects the higher costs of collection, the costs associated with default, which are not eliminated despite the collateral, poorer liquidity, and uncertainty concerning the timing of the cash flow (which we explain later). The frequency of payment is typically monthly, and the prevailing term of the mortgage is 20–30 years, although in recent years an increasing number of 15-year mortgages have been originated.

Level-Payment, Fixed-Rate Mortgage

The basic idea behind the design of the level-payment, fixed-rate mortgage is that the borrower pays interest and repays principal in equal installments over an agreed-upon period of time, called the *maturity* or *term* of the mortgage. Thus, at the end of the term, the loan has been fully amortized. Each monthly mortgage payment for a level-payment mortgage is due on the first of each month and consists of the following:

1. Interest of $1/12$th of the fixed annual interest rate times the amount of the outstanding mortgage balance at the beginning of the previous month.

2. A repayment of a portion of the outstanding mortgage balance (principal).

The difference between the monthly mortgage payment and the portion of the payment that represents interest equals the amount that is applied to reduce the outstanding mortgage balance. The monthly mortgage payment is designed so that after the last scheduled monthly payment of the loan is made, the amount of the outstanding mortgage balance is zero (i.e., the mortgage is fully repaid).

To illustrate a level-payment mortgage, consider a 30-year (360-month), $100,000 mortgage with a 9.5 percent mortgage rate. The monthly mortgage payment would be $840.85.[2] Exhibit 26–1 shows how each monthly mortgage payment is divided between interest and repayment of principal. At the beginning of month 1,

---

2. The formula for obtaining the monthly mortgage payment is

$$MP = MB_0 \left[\frac{i(1+i)^n}{(1+i)^n - 1} \right]$$

where

MP = monthly mortgage payment ($)
  n = number of months
MB_0 = original mortgage balance ($)
  i = simple monthly interest rate (annual interest rate/12)

For our hypothetical mortgage:

  n = 360
MB_0 = $100,000
  i = .0079167 (=.095/12)

$$MP = \$100,000 \left[\frac{.0079167 \, (1.0079167)^{360}}{(1.0079167)^{360} - 1} \right] = \$840.85$$

E X H I B I T   26–1

Amoritization Schedule for a Level-Payment, Fixed-Rate Mortgage
(Mortgage Loan: $100,000; Mortgage Rate: 9.5%; Monthly Payment: $840.85;
Term of Loan: 30 Years [360 Months])

Month	Beginning Mortgage Balance	Monthly Mortgage Payment	Interest for Month	Principal Repayment	Ending Mortgage Balance
1	$100,000.00	$840.85	$791.67	$49.19	$99,950.81
2	99,950.81	840.85	791.28	49.58	99,901.24
3	99,901.24	840.85	790.88	49.97	99,851.27
4	99,851.27	840.85	790.49	50.37	99,800.90
5	99,800.90	840.85	790.09	50.76	99,750.14
6	99,750.14	840.85	789.69	51.17	99,698.97
7	99,698.97	840.85	789.28	51.57	99,647.40
8	99,647.40	840.85	788.88	51.98	99,595.42
9	99,595.42	840.85	788.46	52.39	99,543.03
10	99,543.03	870.85	788.05	52.81	99,490.23
...	...	...	...	...	...
...	...	...	...	...	...
...	...	...	...	...	...
98	92,862.54	840.85	735.16	105.69	92,756.85
99	92,756.85	840.85	734.33	106.53	92,650.32
100	92,650.32	840.85	733.48	107.37	92,542.95
101	92,542.95	840.85	732.63	108.22	92,434.72
102	92,434.72	840.85	731.77	109.08	92,325.64
103	92,325.64	840.85	730.91	109.94	92,215.70
104	92,215.70	840.85	730.04	110.81	92,104.89
105	92,104.89	840.85	729.16	111.69	91,993.20
106	91,993.20	840.85	728.28	112.57	91,880.62
...	...	...	...	...	...
...	...	...	...	...	...
...	...	...	...	...	...
209	74,177.40	840.85	587.24	253.62	73,923.78
210	73,923.78	840.85	585.23	255.62	73,668.16
211	73,668.16	840.85	583.21	257.65	73,410.51
212	73,410.51	840.85	581.17	259.69	73,150.82
...	...	...	...	...	...
...	...	...	...	...	...
...	...	...	...	...	...
354	5,703.93	840.85	45.16	795.70	4,908.23
355	4,908.23	840.85	38.66	802.00	4,106.24
356	4,106.24	840.85	32.51	808.35	3,297.89
357	3,297.89	840.85	26.11	814.75	2,483.14
358	2,483.14	840.85	19.66	821.20	1,661.95
359	1,661.95	840.85	13.16	827.70	834.25
360	834.25	840.85	6.60	834.25	0.00

the mortgage balance is $100,000, the amount of the original loan. The mortgage payment for month 1 includes interest on the $100,000 borrowed for the month. The interest rate is 9.5 percent, so the monthly interest rate is 0.0079167 (.095 divided by 12). Interest for month 1 is therefore $791.67 ($100,000 times 0.0079167). The $49.18 difference between the monthly mortgage payment of $840.85 and the interest of $791.67 is the portion of the monthly mortgage payment that represents repayment of principal. This $49.18 in month 1 reduces the mortgage balance.[2]

The mortgage balance at the end of month 1 (beginning of month 2) is then $99,950.81 ($100,000 minus $49.19). The interest for the second monthly mortgage payment is $791.28—the monthly interest rate (0.0079167) times the mortgage balance at the beginning of month 2 ($99,950.81). The difference between the $840.85 monthly mortgage payment and the $791.28 interest is $49.57, representing the amount of the mortgage balance paid off with that monthly mortgage payment. Notice in Exhibit 26–1 that the last monthly mortgage payment is sufficient to pay off the remaining mortgage balance. When a loan repayment schedule is structured in this way, so that the payments made by the borrower will completely pay off the interest and principal, the loan is said to be *fully amortizing*. Exhibit 26–1 is then referred to as an *amortization schedule.*

As Exhibit 26–1 clearly shows, *the portion of the monthly mortgage payment applied to interest declines each month, and the portion applied to reducing the mortgage balance increases.* The reason for this is that as the mortgage balance is reduced with each monthly mortgage payment, the interest on the mortgage balance declines. Because the monthly mortgage payment is fixed, a larger part of the monthly payment is applied to reduce the principal in each subsequent month.

What was ignored in the amortization is the portion of the cash flow that must be paid to the servicer of the mortgage. The servicing fee is a specified portion of the mortgage rate. The monthly cash flow from a mortgage loan, regardless of the mortgage design, can therefore be decomposed into three parts:

1. The servicing fee.
2. The interest payment net of the servicing fee.
3. The scheduled principal repayment.

For example, consider once again the $100,000 30-year level-payment, fixed-rate mortgage with a contract rate of 9.5 percent. Suppose the servicing fee is 0.5 percent per year. Exhibit 26–2 shows the cash flow for the mortgage with this servicing fee. The monthly mortgage payment is unchanged. The amount of the principal repayment is the same as in Exhibit 26–1. The difference is that the interest is reduced by the amount of the servicing fee. The amount of the servicing fee, just like the amount of interest, declines each month because the mortgage balance declines.

Adjustable-Rate Mortgage

An adjustable-rate mortgage (ARM) is a loan in which the contract rate is reset periodically in accordance with some appropriately chosen reference rate.

---

2. Slight differences are due to rounding.

EXHIBIT 26-2

Cash Flow for a Mortgage with Servicing Fee
(Mortgage Loan: $100,000; Mortgage Rate: 9.5%; Servicing Fee: 0.5%; Monthly Payment: $840.85; Term of Loan: 30 Years [360 Months])

Month	Beginning Mortgage Balance	Monthly Mortgage Payment	Net Interest for Month	Servicing Fee	Principal Repayment	Ending Mortgage Balance
1	$100,000.00	$840.85	$750.00	$41.67	$49.19	$99,950.81
2	99,950.81	840.85	749.63	41.65	49.58	99,901.24
3	99,901.24	840.85	749.26	41.63	49.97	99,851.27
4	99,851.27	840.85	748.88	41.60	50.37	99,800.90
5	99,800.90	840.85	748.51	41.58	50.76	99,750.14
6	99,750.14	840.85	748.13	41.56	51.17	99,698.97
7	99,698.97	840.85	747.74	41.54	51.57	99,647.40
8	99,647.40	840.85	774.36	41.52	51.98	99,595.42
9	99,595.42	840.85	749.97	41.50	52.39	99,543.03
10	99,543.03	870.85	746.57	41.48	52.81	99,490.23
...	...	...	...	...	...	...
...	...	...	...	...	...	...
...	...	...	...	...	...	...
98	92,862.54	840.85	696.47	38.96	105.69	92,756.85
99	92,756.85	840.85	695.68	38.65	106.53	92,650.32
100	92,650.32	840.85	694.88	38.60	107.37	92,542.95
101	92,542.95	840.85	694.07	38.56	108.22	92,434.72
102	92,434.72	840.85	693.26	38.51	109.08	92,325.64
103	92,325.64	840.85	692.44	38.47	109.94	92,215.70
104	92,215.70	840.85	691.62	38.42	110.81	91,104.89
105	92,104.89	840.85	690.79	38.38	111.69	91,993.20
106	91,993.20	840.85	689.95	38.33	112.57	91,880.62
...	...	...	...	...	...	...
...	...	...	...	...	...	...
...	...	...	...	...	...	...
209	74,177.40	840.85	556.33	30.91	253.62	73,923.78
210	73,923.78	840.85	554.43	30.80	255.62	73,668.16
211	73,668.16	840.85	552.51	30.70	257.65	73,410.51
212	73,410.51	840.85	550.58	30.59	259.69	73,150.82
...	...	...	...	...	...	...
...	...	...	...	...	...	...
...	...	...	...	...	...	...
354	5,703.93	840.85	42.78	2.28	795.70	4,908.23
355	4,908.23	840.85	36.81	2.05	802.00	4,106.24
356	4,106.24	840.85	30.80	1.71	808.35	3,297.89
357	3,297.89	840.85	24.73	1.37	814.75	2,483.14
358	2,483.14	840.85	18.62	1.03	821.20	1,661.95
359	1,661.95	840.85	12.46	0.69	827.70	834.25

Outstanding ARMs call for resetting the contract rate either every month, six months, year, two years, three years, or five years. In recent years, ARMs typically have had reset periods of six months, one year, or five years. The contract rate at the reset date is equal to a reference rate plus a spread. The spread is typically between 125 and 200 basis points, reflecting market conditions, the features of the ARM, and the increased cost of servicing an ARM compared to a fixed-rate mortgage.

Reference Rate

Two categories of reference rates have been used in ARMs: (1) market-determined rates and (2) calculated rates based on the cost of funds for thrifts. Market-determined rates have been limited to Treasury-based rates. The reference rate will have an important impact on the performance of an ARM and how it is priced.

Cost of funds for thrifts indexes are calculated based on the monthly weighted average interest cost for liabilities of thrifts. The two more popular indexes are the Eleventh Federal Home Loan Bank Board District Cost of Funds Index (COFI) and the National Cost of Funds Index, the former being the most popular.

The Eleventh District includes the states of California, Arizona, and Nevada. The cost of funds is calculated by first computing the monthly interest expenses for all thrifts included in the Eleventh District. The interest expenses are summed and then divided by the average of the beginning and ending monthly balance. The index value is reported with a one-month lag. For example, June's Eleventh District COFI is reported in July. The contract rate for a mortgage based on the Eleventh District COFI is usually reset based on the previous month's reported index rate. For example, if the reset date is August, the index rate reported in July will be used to set the contract rate. Consequently, there is a two-month lag by the time the average cost of funds is reflected in the contract rate. This obviously is an advantage to the borrower when interest rates are rising, and a disadvantage to the investor. The opposite is true when interest rates are falling.

The National Cost of Funds Index is calculated based on all federally insured S&Ls. A median costs of funds is calculated rather than an average. This index is reported with about a one and one-half month delay. The contract rate is typically reset based on the most recently reported index value.

Features of Adjustable-Rate Mortgages

To encourage borrowers to accept ARMs rather than fixed-rate mortgages, mortgage originators generally offer an initial contract rate that is less than the prevailing market mortgage rate. This below-market initial contract rate, set by the mortgage originator based on competitive market conditions, is commonly referred to as a *teaser rate*. At the reset date, the reference rate plus the spread determines the new contract rate. For example, suppose that one-year ARMs are typically offering a 100-basis-point spread over the reference rate. Suppose also that the reference rate is 6.5 percent, so that the initial contract rate should be 7.5 percent. The mortgage originator might set an initial contract rate of 6.75 percent, a rate 75 basis points below the current value of the reference rate plus the spread.

A pure ARM is one that resets periodically and has no other terms that affect the monthly mortgage payment. However, the monthly mortgage payment, and hence the investor's cash flow, are affected by other terms. These are due to (1) periodic caps and (2) lifetime rate caps and floors. Rate caps limit the amount that the contract rate may increase or decrease at the reset date. A lifetime cap sets the maximum contract rate over the term of the loan.

Balloon Mortgage

In a *balloon mortgage*, the borrower is given long-term financing by the lender, but at specified future dates the contract rate is renegotiated. Thus, the lender is providing long-term funds for what is effectively a short-term borrowing, how short depending on the frequency of the renegotiation period. Effectively, it is a short-term balloon loan in which the lender agrees to provide financing for the remainder of the term of the mortgage. The balloon payment is the original amount borrowed less the amount amortized. Thus, in a balloon mortgage, the actual maturity is shorter than the stated maturity.

"Two-Step" Mortgage

Akin to the idea of a balloon loan with a refinancing option for the borrower is a fixed-rate mortgage with a single rate reset at some point prior to maturity. Unlike a refinancing option, this rate reset occurs without specific action on the part of the borrower.

Unlike in balloon mortgages, the rate reset on the two-step mortgage does not consist of a repayment of the initial loan and the origination of a new one; thus, a 30-year two-step mortgage has a 30-year final maturity, rather than the shorter final maturity of a balloon mortgage. Essentially, then, the two-step mortgage is an adjustable-rate mortgage with a single reset.

Graduated Payment Mortgage

With a *graduated payment mortgage* (GPM), both the interest rate and the term of the mortgage are fixed, as they are with a level-payment mortgage. However, the monthly mortgage payment for a GPM is smaller in the initial years than for a level-payment mortgage with the same contract rate but larger in the remaining years of the mortgage term. Origination of GPMs has faded in popularity in recent years with the growing popularity of the other mortgage instruments discussed in this section.

The terms of a GPM plan include (1) the mortgage rate, (2) the term of the mortgage, (3) the number of years over which the monthly mortgage payment will increase (and when the level payments will begin), and (4) the annual percent increase in the mortgage payments.

The monthly mortgage payments in the earlier years of a GPM are generally not sufficient to pay the entire interest due on the outstanding mortgage balance. The difference between the monthly mortgage payment and the accumulated interest (based on the outstanding mortgage balance) is added to the outstanding mortgage balance, so that in the earlier years of a GPM there is *negative amortization*. The higher-level mortgage payments in the later years of the GPM are designed to fully amortize the outstanding mortgage balance, which is by then greater than the original amount borrowed.

Growing Equity Mortgage

A *growing equity mortgage* (GEM) is a fixed-rate mortgage whose monthly mortgage payments increase over time. Unlike a GPM, there is no negative amortization. The initial monthly mortgage payment is the same as for a level-payment mortgage. The higher monthly mortgage payments are applied to paying off the principal. As a result, the principal of a GEM is repaid faster. For example, a 30-year $100,000 GEM loan with a contract rate of 8.125 percent might call for an initial monthly payment of $742.50 (the same as a level-payment 8.125 percent 30-year mortgage loan). However, the GEM payment would gradually increase, and the GEM might be fully paid in only 15 years. Pools of GEMs have been securitized.

Tiered-Payment Mortgage

Another mortgage design with a fixed rate and a monthly payment that graduates over time is the *tiered-payment mortgage* (TPM). The initial monthly mortgage payments are below that of a traditional mortgage, as with a GPM. However, unlike a GPM, there is no negative amortization because withdrawals are made from a buydown account to supplement the initial monthly payments to cover the shortfall of interest. The buydown account is established at the time the loan is originated by the borrower, lender, or a third party such as a relative or business associate.

Fixed/Adjustable-Rate Mortgage Hybrids

Another type of mortgage loan structure that has experienced growing popularity is the *fixed/adjustable-rate mortgage hybrid*. Typically, these mortgages are originated with fixed rates for their first 5, 7, or 10 years, after which the interest rate on the loan begins floating, with contractual characteristics similar to those of current ARM structures. For instance, a hybrid structure may have a fixed rate for five years, and thereafter have a floating rate that resets every six months at a margin over the six-month CD index. Like many other ARMs the coupon is subject to both periodic and lifetime limitations on the rate change. Other fixed/ARM hybrids turn into one-year Treasury ARMs or monthly Eleventh District COFI

ARMs after their fixed period. In many cases, the first coupon reset is not subject to any periodic caps that may apply to later coupon resets, and instead is subject only to the lifetime cap.

PREPAYMENT RISK

The investor in a mortgage grants the homeowner the option to prepay the mortgage in whole or in part at any time. No penalty is imposed on the homeowner for prepaying the mortgage. That is, the loan is repaid at par value at any time. Any amount paid in excess of the contractual mortgage payments is called a *prepayment*. For example, suppose the monthly mortgage payment is $800 and the mortgage balance is $110,000. Any mortgage payment in excess of $800 would be a prepayment. The prepayment could be sufficient to pay off the mortgage completely. Or the prepayment could be less than the remaining mortgage balance. In our example, a mortgage payment of $2,800 would mean a prepayment of $2,000. The mortgage balance would then be reduced by that amount. The effect of this partial prepayment is to reduce the mortgage's life. A partial prepayment of a mortgage is called a *curtailment*.

Because of the right granted to the homeowner to prepay, called the *prepayment option*, an investor in a mortgage cannot be certain of the cash flow. A 30-year mortgage could turn out to have a maturity of one year or a maturity of 30 years. The uncertainty about the cash flow due to the prepayment option granted the homeowner is called *prepayment risk*.

An investor is exposed to prepayment risk for an individual mortgage and for a pool of mortgages. Consequently, any security backed by a pool of mortgages exposes an investor to prepayment risk.

Prepayments occur for one of several reasons. First, homeowners prepay the entire mortgage when they sell their home. The sale of a home can result from (1) a change of employment that necessitates moving, (2) the purchase of a more expensive home ("trading up"), or (3) a divorce in which the settlement requires sale of the marital residence, among other reasons. Second, in the case of homeowners who cannot meet their mortgage obligations, the property is repossessed and sold. The proceeds from the sale are used to pay off the mortgage in the case of a conventional mortgage. For an insured mortgage, the insurer will pay off the mortgage balance. Third, if property is destroyed by fire or another insured catastrophe occurs, the insurance proceeds are used to pay off the mortgage. Finally, the borrower will have an incentive to refinance the mortgage when the current mortgage rate falls by a sufficient amount below the contract rate after taking into account refinancing costs.

The key in analyzing an individual mortgage or a pool of mortgages is the projection of prepayments. All primary dealers and several vendors have developed prepayment models. While a discussion of these models is beyond the scope of this chapter, suffice it to say that there is not one prepayment model for all of the mortgage designs that we reviewed in the previous section. While a good deal of data on the prepayment activity of certain types of mortgage designs is available, the same cannot be said of some of the newer mortgage designs.

Prepayment risk also has implications for the performance of a mortgage. The performance is similar to that of a callable bond, a fact that should not be surprising, given that a mortgage is nothing more than a callable security. Specifically, the investor in a mortgage is exposed to negative convexity when interest rates decline below the loan's contract rate. In addition, the investor is exposed to reinvestment risk.

DEFAULT RISK

Default or credit risk is the risk that the homeowner/borrower will default. For FHA, VA, and FmHA insured mortgages, this risk is minimal. For privately insured mortgages, the risk can be gauged by the credit rating of the private insurance company that has insured the mortgage. For conventional mortgages without private insurance, the credit risk depends on the borrower. In recent years, the market for securities backed a pool of nonconforming mortgage loans that are not backed by a government agency has grown dramatically. An understanding of default risk is critical to investors in such securities.

One of the key characteristics of a mortgage loan that affects defaults is the LTV ratio at origination. This ratio is called the *original LTV*. The higher the original LTV or, equivalently, the less equity the borrower has in the property, the higher the probability of default. This finding was supported by studies of default rates.[3]

Unfortunately, looking at the original LTV underestimates the level of delinquencies because of the mismeasurement of the amount of equity that borrowers have in their home. Such mismeasurement is due to two factors. First, there may be a decline in the price of a home. Second, the homeowner can remove some equity via second mortgages or home equity lines of credit.

A study by Bendt, Ramsey, and Fabozzi examined not just the original LTV and its impact on default rates but also the *current LTV*.[4] The current LTV considers the loan value to the estimated current market price. Exhibit 26–3 shows the effects of changing property values on the distribution of LTVs. Almost all original LTVs fall under 80 percent in a large pool of nonconforming mortgage loans (100,000 plus) analyzed, and none are above 90 percent. Adjusted for declines in property values, however, nearly 40 percent have current LTVs above 80 percent, and about 15 percent have current LTVs above 90 percent.

---

3. See Robert Van Order, "The Hazards of Default," *Secondary Mortgage Markets* (Fall 1990), pp. 29–32; Helen F. Peters, Scott M. Pinkus, and David J. Askin, "Default: The Last Resort," *Secondary Mortgage Markets* (August 1984), pp. 16–22; and Scott Brown, et al. *Analysis of Mortgage Servicing Portfolios* (New York: Financial Strategies Group, Prudential-Bache Capital Funding, December 1990). The last study analyzed FHA/VA loans as well as conventional loans.
4. Douglas L. Bendt, Chuck Ramsey, and Frank J. Fabozzi, "The Rating Agencies' Approach: New Evidence," in *Whole-Loan CMOs,* eds. Frank J. Fabozzi, Chuck Ramsey, and Frank Ramirez (New Hope, PA: Frank J. Fabozzi Associates 1995).

E X H I B I T   26–3

Percentage of Loans Without Second Mortgages within LTV Ranges

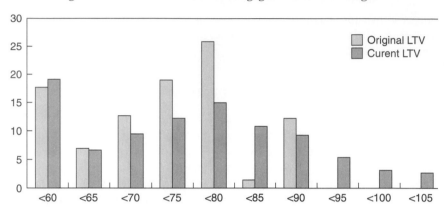

Data source: Mortgage Risk Assessment Corporation.

Source: Frank J. Fabozzi, Chuck Ramsey, and Frank Ramirez, *Collateralized Mortgage Obligations: Structures and Analysis* (Buckingham, PA: Frank J. Fabozzi Associates, 1994).

The Bendt-Ramsey-Fabozzi study also examined defaults, taking into consideration second mortgages. Exhibit 26–4 shows that borrowers with second mortgages behind their first mortgage become delinquent twice as often as borrowers without second mortgages. As Exhibit 26–5 shows, even adjusting for the higher LTVs, which take into account second mortgages, borrowers with second mortgages have higher delinquency rates compared to borrowers with the same LTV without any seconds. On average, delinquency rates are about 25 percent higher—possibly because the combined monthly payments on a first and second mortgage would be higher than the same-size first mortgage.

Empirical studies also suggest there is a seasoning effect for default rates. That is, default rates tend to decline as mortgage loans become seasoned.[5] The reason for the seasoning effect on default rates is twofold. First, since a borrower typically knows shortly after moving into a home whether or not he or she can afford to make the mortgage payments, default rates are higher in the earlier years. Second, the longer a borrower remains in a home, the lower the LTV ratio (i.e., the greater the equity in the home), and therefore the incentive to default declines.

Van Order examined several characteristics of the borrower that he hypothesized would affect default rates. For example, as explained earlier in this chapter, the payment-to-income (PTI) ratio is a measure of the burden of the mortgage payments. It is expected that the higher this ratio at origination, the greater the probability of default. Van Order found that the probability of default increased only slightly the higher this burden. As he notes, this conclusion is only tentative

---

5. For conventional mortgage loans, the maximum default rate appears to be three to four years after origination. For FHA/VA mortgage loans, it seems to be two to three years after origination.

EXHIBIT 26–4

Percentage Delinquencies

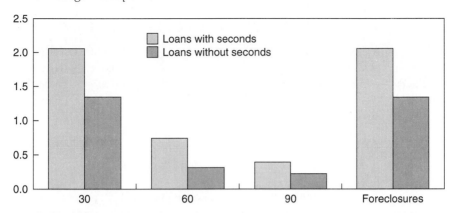

Data source: Mortgage Risk Assessment Corporation.

Source: Frank J. Fabozzi, Chuck Ramsey, and Frank Ramirez, *Collateralized Mortgage Obligations: Structures and Analysis* (Buckingham, PA: Frank J. Fabozzi Associates, 1994).

EXHIBIT 26–5

Percentage Delinquencies by LTV Range

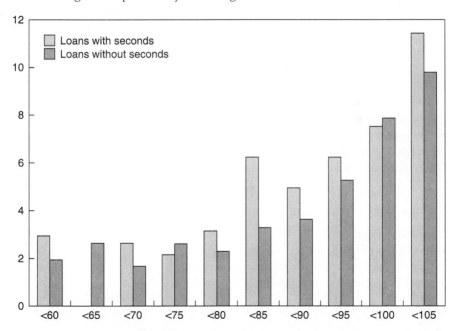

Data source: Mortgage Risk Assessment Corporation.

Source: Frank J. Fabozzi, Chuck Ramsey, and Frank Ramirez, *Collateralized Mortgage Obligations: Structures and Analysis* (Buckingham, PA: Frank J. Fabozzi Associates, 1994).

because his sample did not include many observations with high PTIs. None of the other borrower characteristics appeared to significantly affect default rates.

OVERVIEW OF MORTGAGE-BACKED SECURITIES

We close this chapter with an overview of mortgage-backed securities. There is one basic product—a *mortgage pass-through security*—and two derivative products—*collateralized mortgage obligations* and *stripped mortgage-backed securities.* Mortgage-backed securities can be created in which the underlying mortgages are one- to four-family residential mortgages. Or the underlying mortgages can be created by other property types. Five major property types backing such securities are office space, retail property, industrial facilities, multifamily housing, and hotels. These securities are called *commercial mortgage-backed securities.*

Securities guaranteed by the full faith and credit of the U.S. government or a government-sponsored enterprise are commonly referred to as *agency mortgage-backed securities.* Those securities that do not carry such a guarantee are referred to as *nonagency mortgage-backed securities.*

We will illustrate the creation of mortgage-backed securities using Exhibit 26–6 through 26–9. It is assumed that the underlying mortgages are one- to four-family residential mortgages. Exhibit 26–6 shows 10 mortgage loans (each loan depicted as a home) and the cash flows from these loans. For simplicity, we will assume that the amount of each loan is $100,000 so that the aggregate value of all 10 loans is $1 million. The cash flows are monthly and consist of three components: (1) interest, (2) scheduled principal repayment, and (3) prepayments.

An investor who owns one of the mortgage loans shown in Exhibit 26–6 faces prepayment risk. For an individual loan, it may be difficult to predict prepayments. If an individual investor purchased all 10 loans, then the investor might be better able to predict prepayments. In fact, if there were 500 mortgage loans in Exhibit 26–6 rather than 10, the investor might be able to use historical prepayment experience to improve predictions about prepayments. But an investor would have to invest $1 million to buy 10 loans and $50 million to buy 500 loans, assuming each loan is for $100,000.

Mortgage Pass-Through Securities

Suppose, instead, that some entity purchases all 10 loans in Exhibit 26–6 and pools them. The 10 loans can be used as collateral for the issuance of a security, with the cash flow from that security reflecting the cash flow from the 10 loans, as depicted in Exhibit 26–7. Suppose there are 40 units of this security issued. Thus, each unit is initially worth $25,000 ($1 million divided by 40). Each unit would be entitled to 2.5 percent (1/40) of the cash flow. The security created is called a *mortgage pass-through security*, or simply a *pass-through.*

EXHIBIT 26–6

Ten Mortgage Loans

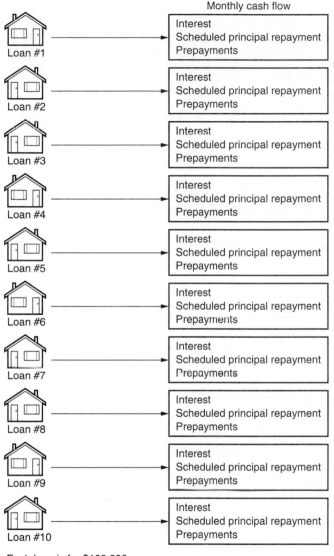

Each loan is for $100,000

Total loans: $1 million

EXHIBIT 26-7

Creation of a Pass-Through Security

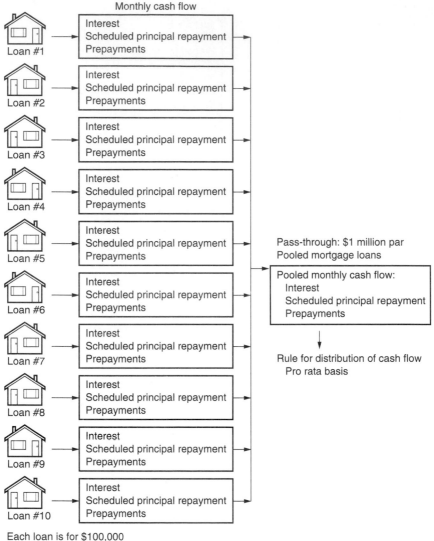

Each loan is for $100,000

Total loans: $1 million

Let's see what has been accomplished by creating the pass-through. The total amount of prepayment risk has not changed. However, now with an amount of less than $1 million, the investor can be exposed to the total prepayment risk of all 10 loans rather than face the risk of an individual mortgage loan.

So far, this financial engineering has not resulted in the creation of a totally new instrument since an individual investor could have accomplished the same outcome by purchasing all 10 loans. In addition to being able to acquire a proportionate share of all 10 loans with less than $1 million by buying a pass-through, the liquidity of a pass-through is greater than individual loans. Moreover, by selling a pass-through, the investor can dispose of all 10 loans rather than having to dispose of each loan one by one. Thus, a pass-through can be viewed as a more transactionally efficient vehicle for investing in mortgages than is the purchasing of individual mortgages.

Collateralized Mortgage Obligations

An investor in a pass-through is still exposed to the total prepayment risk associated with the underlying pool of mortgage loans. Suppose that instead of distributing the monthly cash flow on a pro rata basis, as in the case of a pass-through, the distribution of the principal (both scheduled and prepayments) are done on some prioritized basis. How this is done is illustrated in Exhibit 26–8.

Exhibit 26–8 shows the cash flow of our original 10-mortgage loan and the pass-through. Also shown are three classes of bonds, the par value of each class, and a set of rules indicating how the principal from the pass-through is to be distributed to each. Note the following. The sum of the par value of the three classes is equal to $1 million. While not shown in the exhibit, for each of the three classes, there will be units representing a proportionate interest in a class. For example, suppose that for Class A, which has a par value of $400,000, there are 50 units of Class A issued. Each unit would receive a proportionate share (2 percent) of what is received by Class A.

The rule for the distribution of principal shown in Exhibit 26–8 is that Class A will receive all principal (both scheduled and prepayments) until that class receives its entire par value of $400,000. Then, Class B receives all principal payments until it receives its par value of $350,000. After Class B is completely paid off, Class C receives principal payments. The rule for the distribution of cash flow in Exhibit 26–8 indicates that each of the three classes will receive interest based on the amount of par value outstanding.

The mortgage-backed security that has been created is called a *collateralized mortgage obligation* (CMO). The collateral for a loan may be either one or more pass-throughs or a pool of mortgage loans that have not been securitized. In the latter case, when the underlying mortgages are not guaranteed by an agency, the CMO structure is referred to as a *whole-loan CMO*. The ultimate source for the CMO's cash flow is the pool of mortgage loans.

Let's look at what has been accomplished. Once again, the total prepayment risk for the CMO is the same as the total prepayment risk for the 10 mortgage loans. However, the prepayment risk has been distributed among the three classes

EXHIBIT 26-8

Creation of a Collateralized Mortgage Obligation

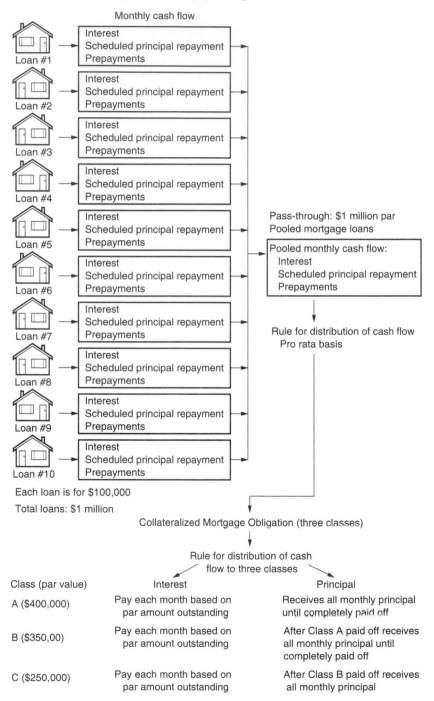

Monthly cash flow

Loan #1	Interest / Scheduled principal repayment / Prepayments
Loan #2	Interest / Scheduled principal repayment / Prepayments
Loan #3	Interest / Scheduled principal repayment / Prepayments
Loan #4	Interest / Scheduled principal repayment / Prepayments
Loan #5	Interest / Scheduled principal repayment / Prepayments
Loan #6	Interest / Scheduled principal repayment / Prepayments
Loan #7	Interest / Scheduled principal repayment / Prepayments
Loan #8	Interest / Scheduled principal repayment / Prepayments
Loan #9	Interest / Scheduled principal repayment / Prepayments
Loan #10	Interest / Scheduled principal repayment / Prepayments

Pass-through: $1 million par
Pooled mortgage loans

Pooled monthly cash flow:
  Interest
  Scheduled principal repayment
  Prepayments

Rule for distribution of cash flow
Pro rata basis

Each loan is for $100,000
Total loans: $1 million

Collateralized Mortgage Obligation (three classes)

Rule for distribution of cash
flow to three classes

Class (par value)	Interest	Principal
A ($400,000)	Pay each month based on par amount outstanding	Receives all monthly principal until completely paid off
B ($350,00)	Pay each month based on par amount outstanding	After Class A paid off receives all monthly principal until completely paid off
C ($250,000)	Pay each month based on par amount outstanding	After Class B paid off receives all monthly principal

of the CMO. Class A absorbs prepayments first, then Class B, and then Class C. The result of this is that Class A will effectively be a shorter-term security than the other two classes; Class C will have the longest maturity. Institutional investors will be attracted to the different classes given the nature of their liability structure and the effective maturity of the CMO class. Moreover, the uncertainty about the maturity of each class of the CMO is far less than the uncertainty about the maturity of the pass-through.

Thus, by redirecting the cash flow from the underlying mortgage pool, classes of bonds have been created that are more attractive to institutional investors to satisfy asset/liability objectives than a pass-through. In theory, a CMO is not a new market instrument since it simply represents the redirecting of the cash flow. However, it is a more transactionally efficient instrument for distributing prepayment risk.

The CMO we depicted in Exhibit 26–8 has a simple set of rules for prioritizing the distribution of principal. Today, much more complicated CMO structures exist. The purpose is to provide certain CMO classes with less uncertainty about prepayment risk. However, this can occur only if the reduction in prepayment risk for such classes is absorbed by other classes in the CMO structure.

Stripped Mortgage-Backed Securities

Consider once again the 10 mortgage loans in Exhibit 26–6. In the CMO, there was a set of rules for prioritizing the distribution of the principal payments amongst the various classes. In a stripped mortgage-backed security, the principal and interest are divided among two classes unequally. For example, one class may be entitled to receive all of the principal and the other class all of the interest. This is depicted in Exhibit 26–9. This distribution for the interest and principal is the most common type of stripped mortgage-backed securities. The class that receives all the interest is called the *interest-only*, or IO, class. The class that receives all the principal is called the *principal only*, or PO, class. The IO class receives no principal payments.

The PO security is purchased at a substantial discount from par value. The return an investor realizes depends on the speed at which prepayments are made. The faster the prepayments, the higher the investor's return. In the extreme case, if all homeowners in the underlying mortgage pool decide to prepay their mortgage loans immediately, PO investors will realize the entire principal immediately. At the other extreme, if all homeowners decide to remain in their homes for the life of the mortgage and make no prepayments, the return of principal will be spread out over the life of the underlying mortgages, which would result in a lower return for PO investors.

Let's look at how the price of the PO would be expected to change as mortgage rates in the market change. When mortgage rates decline below the coupon rate, prepayments are expected to speed up, accelerating payments to the PO holder. Thus, the cash flow of a PO improves (in the sense that principal repayments are received earlier). The cash flow will be discounted at a lower interest rate because the

EXHIBIT 26–9

Creation of a Stripped-Mortgage-Backed Security

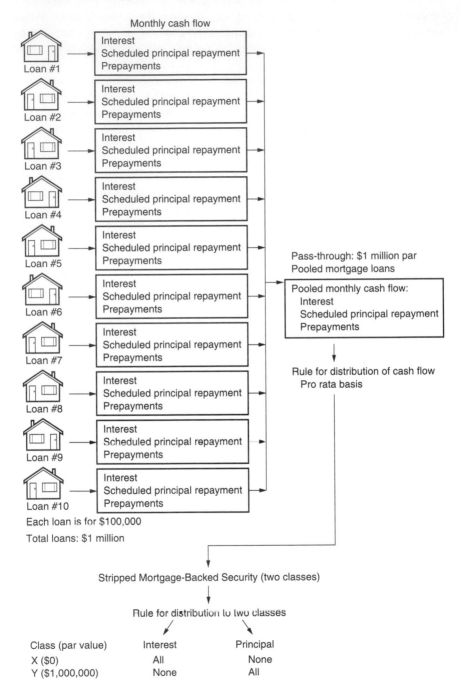

mortgage rate in the market has declined. The result is that the PO price will increase when mortgage rates decline. When mortgage rates rise above the coupon rate, prepayments are expected to slow down. The cash flow deteriorates (in the sense that it takes longer to recover principal repayments). Couple this with a higher discount rate, and the price of a PO will fall when mortgage rates rise.

An IO has no par value. In contrast to the PO investor, the IO investor wants prepayments to be slow. The reason is that the IO investor receives interest only on the amount of the principal outstanding. When prepayments are made, less dollar interest will be received as the outstanding principal declines. In fact, if prepayments are too fast, the IO investor may not recover the amount paid for the IO. This occurs despite the fact that the interest is guaranteed by a government agency.

Let's look at the expected price response of an IO to changes in mortgage rates. If mortgage rates decline below the coupon rate, the prepayments are expected to accelerate. This would result in a deterioration of the expected cash flow for an IO. While the cash flow will be discounted at a lower rate, the net effect typically is a decline in the price of an IO. If mortgage rates rise above the coupon rate, the expected cash flow improves, but the cash flow is discounted at a higher interest rate. The net effect may be either a rise or fall for the IO. Thus, we see an interesting characteristic of an IO: Its price tends to move in the same direction as the change in mortgage rates: (1) when mortgage rates fall below the coupon rate and (2) for some range of mortgage rates above the coupon rate. Both POs and IOs exhibit substantial price volatility when mortgage rates change. The greater price volatility of the IO and PO compared to the pass-through is due to the fact that the combined price volatility of the IO and PO must be equal to the price volatility of the pass-through.

What may be confusing is why stripped mortgage-backed securities are created. We explained the motivation for the creation of pass-throughs and CMOs but not for a stripped mortgage-backed security. For now, it is sufficient to say that when properly used the risk/return characteristics of these instruments make them attractive for purposes of hedging a portfolio of pass-throughs and hedging other assets such as mortgage servicing rights.

Home Loan Asset-Backed Products

In other chapters in this part of the book, asset-backed securities are described. These securities are backed by loans or receivables. In the U.S. capital market, an artificial distinction is made between mortgage-backed securities and asset-backed securities. Technically, mortgage-backed securities are part of the asset-backed securities market, where the underlying collateral is a first mortgage lien on the real estate property.

There are asset-backed securities backed by loans in which the underlying collateral is real estate. The two primary examples are home equity loans and manufactured housing loans. These two asset-backed securities are discussed in Chapters 32 and 33, respectively.

⑥ MORTGAGE PASS-THROUGH SECURITIES

Lakhbir S. Hayre, D. Phil.*
Salomon Brothers Inc.

Cyrus Mohebbi, Ph.D.
Director
Prudential Securities, Inc.

Thomas A. Zimmerman
Director—Fixed Income Research
Prudential Securities, Inc.

INTRODUCTION

Few markets in recent years have experienced the rapid growth and innovations of the secondary mortgage markets. Issuance of mortgage-backed securities (MBSs) reached a record level of $667 billion in 1993 at the peak of the refinancing boom and has since returned to a more typical level of around $400 billion. There also has been a rapid expansion in the issuance of derivative mortgage securities, such as Collateralized Mortgage Obligations (CMOs)[1] and stripped MBSs (STRIPS), which have broadened the range of investors in MBSs. The secondary mortgage market is now comparable to the corporate bond market in terms of size and constitutes a major segment of the fixed income markets. It also has potential for substantial continued growth; one-to-four family mortgage debt in the United States currently exceeds $3.7 trillion, of which only about 49 percent has been securitized.[2]

However, the mortgage market can present challenges to the investor. The typical fixed income investor has developed valuation standards based on the rel-

---

*Dr. Hayre was employed by Prudential Securities, Inc. when this chapter was written.

1. For a discussion of CMOs, see Chapter 21, and Lakhbir Hayre, "Floating-Rate Collateralized Mortgage Obligation," Chapter 13 in *The Handbook of Mortgage-Backed Securities*, ed. Frank J. Fabozzi (Chicago: Probus Publishing, 1992).
2. Data in this chapter have been obtained from GNMA, FNMA, FHLMC, and the *Bulletin of the Federal Reserve Board*.

atively simple cash flow patterns of standard bond investments, such as Treasury or corporate securities. The cash flow patterns of mortgage securities are more complex. Mortgage securities are self-amortizing—principal is returned gradually over the term of the security, rather than in one lump sum at maturity. A more fundamental complexity arises from the homeowner's right to prepay part or all of a mortgage at any time. Prepayment levels, which fluctuate with interest rates and a number of other economic and mortgage variables, play a major role in determining the size and timing of cash flows. In evaluating the characteristics of an MBS, it is necessary to project prepayment rates for the remaining term of the security. This introduces an element of subjectivity into MBS analysis.

Why Mortgage-Backed Securities?

Although mortgage securities are relatively complex, they should be seriously considered by fixed income investors who seek both high credit quality and high yields. The benefits of mortgage securities include the following.

High returns: The complexity and uncertainty associated with MBSs have resulted in pricing at significantly higher yields than other securities of comparable quality. Consequently, in the last 15 years pass-throughs have typically performed better than comparable Treasuries and corporates. Recent yields on MBSs have been between 100 to 200 basis points higher than yields on comparable-maturity Treasuries. The recent yield spread for AAA-rated corporates over Treasuries has averaged between 30 and 50 basis points.

Wide range of product: The mortgage pass-through markets include 15- and 30-year securities with a wide range of coupons, as well as adjustable-rate mortgage (ARM) securities, balloon securities, and graduated-payment mortgage (GPM) securities.[3] Recent innovations have expanded the type of MBSs that are available. CMOs have created short-, intermediate-, and long-maturity securities by sequentially segmenting mortgage cash flows. STRIPS separate the interest and principal components of mortgage cash flows to create synthetic securities with a wide range of investment profiles as interest rates change.

High credit quality: Agency pass-throughs have a government or quasi-government guarantee as to payment of interest and principal and therefore can be considered to be of higher credit quality than corporate AAA-rated bonds. Nonagency pass-throughs typically have AA or AAA ratings, depending on the level of credit support.

Liquidity: There is an active and liquid market in pass-throughs. The major agency pass-through coupons are as liquid as Treasuries and more liquid than most corporates.

Monthly income: An important consideration for the retail investor may be the regular monthly income from pass-through securities.

Overview of the Chapter

This chapter attempts to provide a comprehensive introduction to the investment characteristics of pass-throughs. It provides an overview of the pass-through market, discussing its history and growth and the three agency

---

3. See Chapter 26 for a review of mortgage instruments.

pass-through programs. It discusses prepayments and their effect on pass-through cash flows, and it discusses methods of measuring the investment life of a pass-through. It describes the effect of interest-rate, and hence prepayment-rate, changes on the price and yield of a pass-through security and introduces the use of option-adjusted spread (OAS) in MBS pricing. Finally, it provides an introduction to duration and convexity and their calculation and an interpretation for MBSs, and it examines holding-period returns.

OVERVIEW OF THE MARKET

The Advent of the Secondary Mortgage Market

A secondary market for whole loans, or unsecuritized mortgages, existed long before the creation of mortgage pass-through securities. The secondary whole-loan market helped to reduce imbalances between lenders in capital-deficit areas and lenders in capital-surplus areas. Even though the servicing often remained with the originator of the mortgage, buyers of whole loans faced many of the legal complications and paperwork of mortgage ownership. More importantly, there was little liquidity in the whole-loan market, and buyers ran the risk of potential losses if forced to sell their mortgages quickly. The extensive details, paperwork, and cost involved in these types of transactions prevented many small buyers from entering the market. The introduction of the mortgage pass-through created a means of buying and selling mortgages that was more convenient and in many ways more efficient than the whole-loan market. Pass-through certificates represent pro rata shares of the interest (after subtraction of a servicing fee) and principal cash flow from a pool of mortgages. The cash flows from the mortgages are "passed through," after subtraction of a service fee, to the holders of the pass-through securities on a monthly basis, typically with a delay. The payments made to the investor consist of scheduled principal and interest and any unscheduled payments of principal (resulting from prepayments and defaults) that may occur.

The great majority of pass-throughs have been issued by three agencies that were created by Congress to increase liquidity in the secondary mortgage markets and thus increase the supply of capital available for residential housing loans. The Federal National Mortgage Association (FNMA, or "Fannie Mae"), the oldest of these agencies, was established by the federal government in 1938 to help solve some of the housing finance problems brought on by the Depression. FNMA's original mandate allowed it to buy Federal Housing Administration (FHA) and Veterans Administration (VA) loans from lenders. In 1968, Congress divided the original FNMA into two organizations: the current FNMA and the Government National Mortgage Association (GNMA, or "Ginnie Mae"). GNMA remains a government agency within the Department of Housing and Urban Development (HUD), helping to finance government-assisted housing programs. FNMA became a private corporation rechartered by Congress with a mandate to establish a secondary market for conventional mortgages, that is, loans not FHA insured or VA guaranteed. Established in 1970, the Federal Home Loan Mortgage Corporation (FHLMC, or "Freddie Mac") initially was a government-chartered corporation owned by the 12 Federal Home Loan Banks and the federally insured savings institutions, which in turn owned stock in the Federal Home Loan Banks. In 1989, as part of the Financial Institutions Reform Recovery and Enforcement Act (FIRREA), FHLMC became a private corporation much like FNMA. Like FNMA, FHLMC seeks to enhance liquidity for residential mortgage investments, primarily by assisting in the development of secondary markets for conventional mortgages.

Growth in Pass-Through Issuance

The first pass-throughs were issued by GNMA in 1970. FHLMC issued its first pass-throughs in 1971. FNMA, which traditionally financed its mortgage purchases through debenture offerings, began issuing pass-throughs at the end of 1981. In recent years, a growing fraction of the total pass-through volume has consisted of nonagency pass-throughs from private issuers. Exhibit 27–1 shows

EXHIBIT   27–1

Pass-Through Issuance from 1985–1995

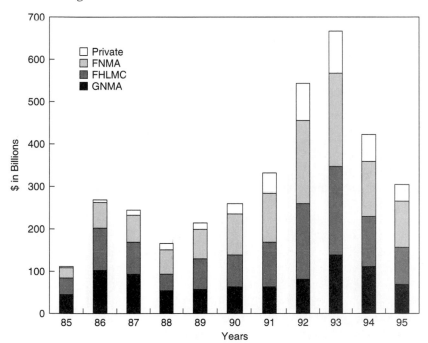

the yearly volume of pass-through issuance from 1985–1995. Notice the dramatic surge in pass-through issuance during the major refinancing episodes of 1986–1987 and 1992–1993.

Issuance has shown a major increase since 1985, partly because a larger proportion of mortgage originations is now securitized. Mortgage lenders, after their experiences of the early 1980s, are now more likely to sell their fixed-rate mortgages in order to avoid losses if rates rise. The increased participation of agency and private issuers in this market has facilitated the increase in mortgage securitization.

The growth in pass-through issuance has occurred not only in absolute terms, but also relative to other sectors of the fixed income market. Exhibit 27–2 shows the sizes of the pass-through, Treasury, corporate, and agency markets from year-end 1990 to year-end 1995.

As Exhibit 27–2 shows, the pass-through market is now comparable to the corporate market in size and is substantially larger than the agency market.

A striking aspect of the secondary mortgage markets is their potential for growth. Residential debt alone is nearly $3.7 trillion in the United States, a figure comparable to the total Treasury market. When commercial debt, farm mort-

E X H I B I T   27–2

Sizes of the Pass-Through, Treasury, Corporate, and Agency Markets: Year-End 1990 through Year-End 1995

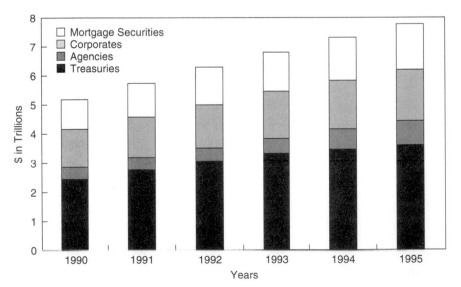

gage debt, and home equity loans are considered, the potential for growth is substantial.

Comparisons of GNMA, FNMA, and FHLMC Pass-Throughs

Although all pass-throughs basically have the same structure—cash flows from the mortgages in the pool are passed through to the security holders after subtraction of a servicing fee—there are a number of generally minor differences among the pass-throughs issued by the three agencies. Exhibit 27–3 gives basic information about the GNMA, FNMA, and FHLMC pass-through programs.

The following are some of the important features of the agency pass-through programs:

Guarantees
GNMA pass-throughs are guaranteed directly by the U.S. government as to timely payment of interest and principal. FNMA and FHLMC pass-throughs carry agency guarantees only; however, both agencies can borrow from the U.S. Treasury, and it is not likely that the U.S. government would allow the agencies to default. FNMA guarantees the timely payment of interest and principal, on all its securities. FHLMC guarantees the timely payment of interest and principal on its Gold program, originated in 1990, but on its 75-day program it guarantees the timely payment of interest and the ultimate (within one year) payment of principal. From the investor's point of view, because of the guarantees, a default is essentially equivalent to a prepayment.

Payment Delay
Pass-throughs pay interest after a specified delay. For example, interest for the month of August would be paid on September 15 for GNMAs (September 20 for GNMA II pass-throughs), on September 15 for Gold FHLMCs (October 15 for 75-day FHLMCs), and on September 25 for FNMAs. On these dates, the security holder would also receive any principal payments made by the mortgage holders during the month of August. The delay is said to be 45 days for GNMAs and Gold FHLMCs, 55 days for FNMAs, and 75 days for 75-day FHLMCs. However, because interest for the month of August would be paid on September 1 if there were no delay, the actual delays are 14, 24, and 44 days, respectively.

Pool Composition
GNMA pools consist of VA- and FHA-insured mortgages that are assumable, whereas FNMA and FHLMC pools generally consist of conventional loans that are not assumable. FNMA and FHLMC pools also tend to be much larger than GNMA pools and hence are less regionally concentrated.

EXHIBIT 27-3

Characteristics of GNMAs, FNMAs, and FHLMCs[a]

	GNMA	FNMA	FHLMC 75-day	FHLMC Gold
Types of mortgage	FHA/VA	Conventional (some FHA/VA)	Conventional (some FHA/VA)	Conventional (some FHA/VA)
Main payment types	Level payment	Level payment	Level payment	Level payment
	Graduated payment	ARM	ARM	Balloon
	ARM	Balloon	Balloon	
			Tiered payment	
Maximum loan size	$184,000[b,c]	$203,150	$203,150	$203,150
Mortgage age at securitization	New origination	New or seasoned	New or seasoned	New or seasoned
Main term	30- and 15-year	30-, 20-, and 15-year fixed	30- and 15-year fixed	30-, 20-, and 15-year fixed
	(some 40-yr. project loans)	7-year balloons	7- and 5-year balloons	7- and 5-year balloons
		30-year ARMs	30-year ARMs	
Number of pools:				
Issued	GNMA I: 251,831	181,071	114,165	66,460
	GNMA II: 13,606			
Outstanding	GNMA I: 241,085	177,226	110,452[d]	66,373
	GNMA II: 12,258			
Amount ($bb):				
Issued	825.36	786.75	512.60	359.41
Outstanding	427.51	458.54	157.97[d]	293.83
Mortgage coupon	GNMA I: 0.50	0.25–2.50, range 2.00	Cash: 0–2.00, range 1.00	Cash: 0.50–1.00
Allowed (%) over pass-through rate	GNMA II: 0.50–1.50		Swap: 0–2.50	Swap: 0–2.50
Delays (days):				
Stated	45 (GNMA II: 50)	55	75	45
Actual	14 (GNMA II: 19)	24	45	14

[a] Data current as of May 1993.
[b] Maximum FHA loan size is $151,725.
[c] GNMA limit for VA Interest Rate Reduction Refinancing Loans (IRRL) is $200,000.
[d] Does not include 1,417 pools ($19.35 bb) of converted 75-day FHLMC PCs included in Outstanding Gold PCs.

Liquidity

The growth in the size of the pass-through markets has led to greater liquidity, with FNMAs and FHLMCs now generally as liquid as GNMAs. Bid–ask spreads for the major coupons (currently in the $6\frac{1}{2}$ percent to $9\frac{1}{2}$ percent range) are generally about $\frac{1}{8}$ of a point, which is similar to Treasuries and less than most corporates. Thus, liquidity for the major coupons is comparable to that for Treasuries and greater than that for most corporates. Exhibit 27–4 shows total pass-through issuance by the three agencies for coupons from $6\frac{1}{2}$ percent to 13 percent (only 30-year securities are included). Also shown is the amount outstanding. Two points are clearly indicated by Exhibit 27–4. First, the market for high-premium securities (with coupons of 12 percent or higher) has virtually disappeared because of the massive refinancings of high-coupon mortgages. Second, although historically GNMA played the largest role in the secondary market, today FNMA and FHLMC have much larger annual issuance and their amounts outstanding approach or surpass the outstanding GNMAs.

PREPAYMENT AND CASH FLOW BEHAVIOR

The timing and amounts of the cash flows received from a pass-through are greatly affected by the prepayment of the mortgages in the underlying pool. This makes the choice of a projected prepayment rate critical in evaluating and pricing an MBS. Prepayment rates tend to fluctuate with interest rates and other economic variables and depend on mortgage characteristics such as coupon and age. There is also a strong seasonal effect on prepayment, which reflects the well-known seasonal variations in housing turnover. This section addresses the prepayment conventions and models used in pricing and trading MBSs, as well as the effect of prepayments on pass-through cash flows.

Prepayment Models and Conventions

Twelve-Year Prepaid Life

At one time, the standard approach to prepayments was 12-year prepaid life, which assumes no prepayments for the first 12 years of the pass-through life and then full prepayment at the end of the 12th year. This was based on FHA data that showed that on the average mortgages terminated in their 12th year. It is now generally realized that the 12-year prepaid life assumption can often give misleading results; prepayment rates tend to vary with interest rates and mortgage characteristics and are higher for premium coupons than for discounts. This method is now rarely used in the pricing and trading of MBSs, although quoted mortgage yields are sometimes based on it.

Constant Prepayment Rate (CPR)

A commonly used method is to assume a constant prepayment rate (CPR) for a pool of mortgages. If one thinks of the pool as consisting of a large number of

E X H I B I T   27–4

Total Pass-Through Issuance for Major 30-Year Coupons
(Data as of June 1996)

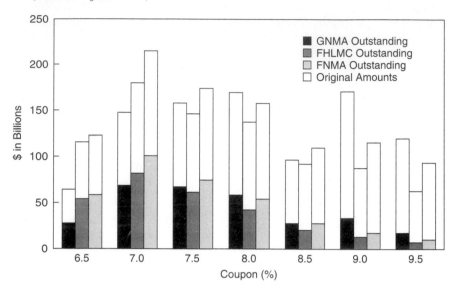

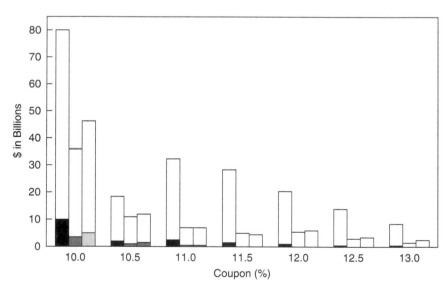

$1 mortgages, then the CPR for a period is the percentage of mortgages out-standing at the beginning of the period that terminate during that period. The CPR is usually expressed on an annualized basis, whereas the terms *single monthly mortality* (SMM) or *constant monthly prepayment* (CMP) refer to monthly prepayment rates.

For example, if a pool of mortgages is prepaying at a constant rate of 1 per-cent per month, then 1 percent of the outstanding balance, after subtraction of the scheduled principal, will be prepaid in each month. Thus, if the outstanding prin-cipal balance at the beginning of the month is $100,000 and the scheduled princi-pal payment is $1,000, then an SMM of 1 percent means that 1 percent of $99,000 (the remaining balance after the scheduled principal payment), or $990, will be prepaid that month. (Because the scheduled principal payments for a 30-year mortgage are generally small until the latter part of the mortgage term, one can, as a good approximation, multiply the outstanding balance by the SMM to obtain the amount of principal prepayment.)

The effective annual prepayment rate, or CPR, corresponding to a given monthly prepayment rate is almost, but not quite, equal to 12 times the monthly rate. For a 1 percent monthly rate, the CPR is 11.36 percent. The reason that the annual rate is less than 12 percent is that the monthly prepayment rate of 1 percent is being applied to a decreasing principal balance each month. Hence, a 1 percent SMM in month 10, say, means less principal prepayment in dollar terms than a 1 percent SMM in month 1. (See the appendix to this chapter for a formula for con-verting a monthly rate to an annual rate and vice versa.)

FHA Experience

At one time, FHA experience was a widely used prepayment model. However, it is not often used today. FHA experience projects the prepayment rate of a mort-gage pool relative to the historical prepayment and default experience of FHA-insured, 30-year mortgage loans. FHA periodically publishes a table of 30 numbers that represent the annual survivorship rates of FHA-insured mortgages. The table indicates the probability for survival of a mortgage and reports the per-centage of mortgages expected to terminate for any given policy year.

A mortgage pool's prepayment rates are expressed as a percentage of FHA experience. For example, if a pool of mortgages prepays at 100 percent FHA, then in each mortgage year the loans in the pool will terminate at the rate given by FHA statistics. A rate of 200 percent FHA means that the mortgages terminate twice as fast as 100 percent FHA experience would predict, and 50 percent FHA means that the mortgages terminate half as fast as 100 percent FHA experience would predict.

The major advantage of FHA experience over CPR is that it reflects the ef-fect of age on prepayments and, in particular, the low prepayment levels typical of newer mortgages. Its major disadvantages are its complexity and the fact that periodic updates of the FHA data mean that the prepayment rates implied by a given percentage of FHA experience also change periodically.

Public Securities Association (PSA) Model

The current industry standard is the Public Securities Association (PSA) prepayment model, which was developed to describe mortgage prepayment behavior by combining the information in the FHA survivorship schedules with the simplicity of the CPR method. The PSA benchmark (denoted 100 percent PSA) assumes a series of CPRs that begin at 0.2 percent in the first month and increase by 0.2 percent thereafter, until leveling 30 months after mortgage origination, when the CPR is 6 percent, as shown in Exhibit 27–5. Also shown in Exhibit 27–5 is the FHA curve on which the PSA model is based.

Interpreting multiples of PSA is simpler than interpreting multiples of FHA. For example, a projected prepayment rate of 200 percent PSA means that the CPR in any month will be twice the CPR corresponding to 100 percent PSA; thus, for 200 percent PSA the CPR will be 0.4 percent in month one, 0.8 percent in month two, and so on, until it levels off at 12 percent in month 30. Exhibit 27–6 illustrates this for 50 percent PSA, 100 percent PSA, and 150 percent PSA.

Econometric Prepayment Models

Many major Wall Street firms have developed econometric models that project prepayment rates as a function of specified economic and mortgage variables. In the most general case, an econometric prepayment model will project SMMs for each remaining month of the mortgage security. This vector of monthly prepayment

E X H I B I T   27–5

FHA and PSA Prepayment Models

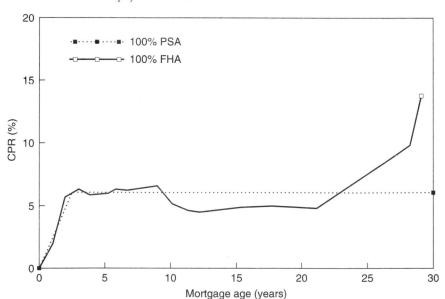

EXHIBIT 27-6

Multiples of PSA

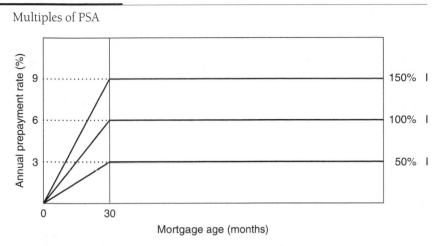

rates will reflect seasonal and age variation in prepayments, as well as changing patterns of housing turnover and refinancing over time for a given pool of mortgages. For trading and sales purposes, however, using a vector of monthly prepayments is sometimes impractical. Hence, the vector is usually presented as an equivalent averaged CPR or percentage of PSA. For example, the Prudential Securities Prepayment Model calculates the PSA rate that produces the same weighted average life as the vector of monthly prepayment rates. Using econometric models is often preferable to using recent prepayment levels as a means of choosing a projected CPR or PSA rate because changing economic factors may have made recent prepayment levels an unreliable indicator of future prepayments.

Effect of Prepayments on Cash Flows

Exhibit 27–7 shows the cash flows generated by the pool of mortgages backing a new current-coupon GNMA at various prepayment rates. At a zero prepayment level, the monthly dollar cash flows from the mortgage loans are constant. Notice, however, that the composition of principal, interest, and servicing that constitute each of the monthly cash flows changes as the mortgages amortize. As principal payments increase and the remaining principal balance declines, the dollar amount of interest due declines proportionally. Servicing fees, like interest payments, are calculated based on the remaining principal balance of the mortgage loan. For the current-coupon GNMA in Exhibit 27–7(a), the servicing fee is 50 basis points of interest. Pass-through investors will experience the effect of a decrease in servicing fees (as the remaining principal balance declines) in terms of slightly increasing monthly dollar cash flows.

At more realistic prepayment levels, the cash flows are more concentrated early in the pass-through term. Exhibit 27–7(b) shows the cash flows at a prepay-

EXHIBIT 27-7

Current-Coupon GNMA Cash Flows at Various Prepayment Rates

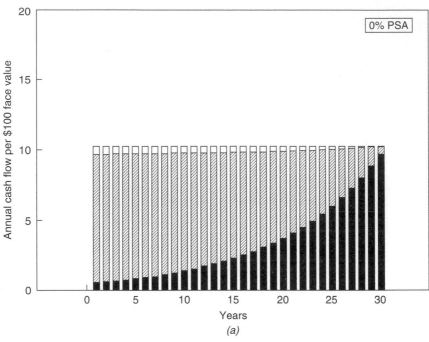

(a)

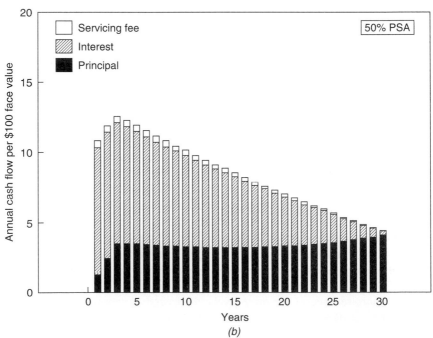

(b)

E X H I B I T   27–7

(Continued)

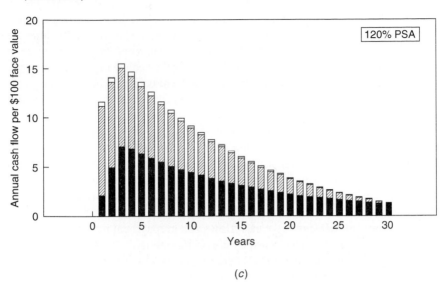

(c)

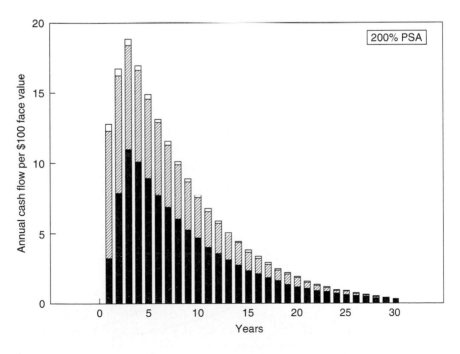

(d)

ment rate of 50 percent PSA—historically a slow speed for current-coupon GNMA prepayment levels. The principal paydowns increase for the first two and one-half years, as the prepayment rate increases according to the PSA pattern until month 30. The prepayment rate then remains constant at 3 percent per year. Note that the total amount of principal received by the pass-through investor is fairly constant after the first two years. At an assumed prepayment rate of 50 percent PSA, the increase in the scheduled principal payment each period offsets the decline in prepaid principal, which is approximately a constant percentage of the remaining principal balance.

Exhibit 27–7(c) shows the cash flows at a prepayment rate of 120 percent PSA, an average prepayment speed for a current coupon. Again, the amount of principal increases for the first two and one-half years, as the prepayment rate increases for 30 months before leveling off at 7.2 percent (1.20 × 6 percent) per year after month 30. The total principal payments gradually decrease after month 30, because at 120 percent PSA the principal balance has declined to the point at which the scheduled principal payments are much less significant than they are at 50 percent PSA.

Exhibit 27–7(d) shows the cash flows at a prepayment rate of 200 percent PSA, which is considered to be fast by historical standards for a current coupon. The prepayment rate levels off at 12 percent per annum after month 30, and the principal paydown is concentrated in the early years.

The outstanding principal balances at 0 percent, 50 percent, 120 percent, and 200 percent PSA are shown in Exhibit 27–8. These reflect the principal payment patterns shown in Exhibit 27–7.

E X H I B I T   27–8

Outstanding Balances of a Current-Coupon GNMA at Various Prepayment Rates

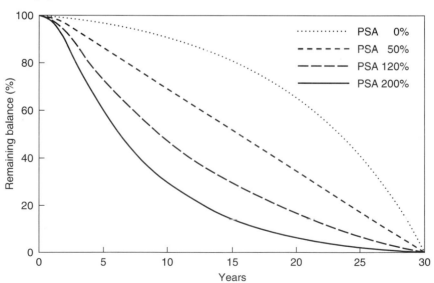

MEASURES OF PASS-THROUGH LIFE

A pass-through is a self-amortizing security that returns principal throughout its term. In comparing pass-throughs (or any MBS) with other bonds, such as a Treasury that returns all its principal at maturity, it is necessary to determine some reasonable measure of the investment life of the pass-through.

The selection of a reasonable measure of mortgage life is important. Measures of investment life are used in several ways when assessing the investment's value:

- They suggest the effective span of time during which a mortgage security provides a stated yield or return.

- They suggest how to compare the mortgage security to other, more familiar bond investments—in particular, they suggest the maturity on the Treasury yield curve against which to compare a pass-through.

- They can indicate the pass-through's volatility in a shifting-interest-rate environment.

Average Life

Average life, or weighted-average life (WAL), is defined as the weighted-average time to the return of a dollar of principal. It is calculated by multiplying each portion of principal received by the time at which it is received, and then summing and dividing by the total amount of principal. (See the appendix for the mathematical formula for average life.) For example, consider a simple annual-pay, four-year bond with a face value of $100 and principal payments, as in Exhibit 27–9. As the exhibit illustrates, each time point at which principal is returned is weighted by the percentage of principal returned at that time point, so that the average life in this example could be calculated as

$$\text{Average life} = .4 \times 1 \text{ year} + .3 \times 2 \text{ years} + .2 \times 3 \text{ years} + .1 \times 4 \text{ years}$$
$$= 2 \text{ years}$$

E X H I B I T   27–9

Calculation of Average Life

Time	Principal	Time × Principal
1 year	$40	1 year × $40 = 40
2	30	2 years × 30 = 60
3	20	3 years × 20 = 60
4	10	4 years × 10 = 40
	$100	200

$$\text{Average life} = \frac{\text{Sum of (Time} \times \text{Principal)}}{\text{Total Principal}} = \frac{200}{100} = 2 \text{ years}$$

Average life is commonly used as the measure of investment life for MBSs, and the yield of an MBS is typically compared against a Treasury with maturity close to the average life of the MBS.

Exhibit 27–10 plots the average life of a new current-coupon GNMA at prepayment speeds of 50 percent PSA, 120 percent PSA, and 200 percent PSA. The exhibit shows that the average life of an MBS depends heavily on the prepayment rate. An interesting graphical interpretation of average life is obtained if one thinks of the principal payments as weights, with each weight equal to the amount of principal. The average life is the point at which the weights on each side of the point are exactly balanced. In other words, if in Exhibit 27–10 the horizontal axis were a seesaw, then the seesaw would have to be balanced at the average life for it not to tilt to one side.

Exhibit 27–11 shows the variation of average life with respect to coupon and prepayment rate. Specifically, it indicates that, for a given remaining term and prepayment rate, the average life of an MBS increases with the coupon. This is true because a higher coupon means that the interest portion is a higher percentage of the monthly payments in the early years of the mortgage term, with the principal payments being more concentrated toward the later years.

Macaulay Duration

An alternative to average life as a measure of investment life is duration. Duration, or Macaulay duration (named after Frederick Macaulay, who introduced the concept in 1938), is defined as the weighted-average time to return of a dollar of price. It is calculated by multiplying the present value of each cash flow by the time at which it is received, summing and then dividing by the price. (See the appendix for the mathematical formula for Macaulay duration.) Exhibit 27–12 illustrates the calculation of Macaulay duration for an annual-pay, four-year bond with cash flows of $30 each year and an assumed discount rate of 8 percent.

This example shows that one can obtain Macaulay duration if, in the formula for average life, the total principal is replaced by the price and the principal payments at each point in time are replaced by the present values of the cash flows. Thus, Macaulay duration can be thought of as the average life of a dollar of price of the security.

Macaulay duration is often considered to be a better measure of investment life than average life. It considers the total cash flow, not just the principal component. Thus, it can be applied to derivative MBSs, such as CMO residuals and interest-only STRIPS, that have no principal payments. It also recognizes the time value of money by giving greater weight to earlier cash flows.

Exhibit 27–13 shows the Macaulay durations of a new current-coupon GNMA at prepayment rates of 50 percent PSA, 120 percent PSA, and 200 percent

EXHIBIT 27–10

Average Life of a New Current-Coupon GNMA at 50 percent, 120 percent, and 200 percent PSA

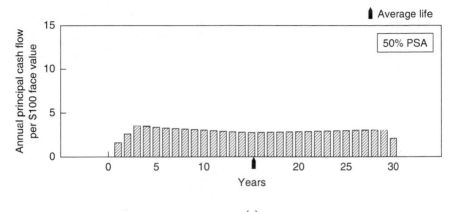

(a)

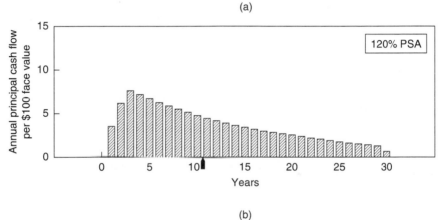

(b)

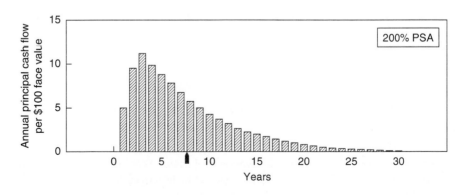

(c)

EXHIBIT 27–11

Average Life of New GNMA 6s, 9s, and 14s

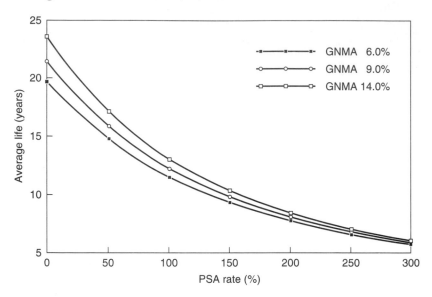

EXHIBIT 27–12

Calculation of Macaulay Duration

Time	Cash Flow	Present Value at 8%	Present Value × Time
1 year	$30	$27.78	27.78
2	30	25.72	51.44
3	30	23.81	71.43
4	30	22.05	88.20
		Price = $99.36	238.85

$$\text{Duration} = \frac{\text{Sum of (Present values} \times \text{Time)}}{\text{Price}} = \frac{238.5}{99.36} = 2.40 \text{ years}$$

PSA. A comparison of Exhibit 27–10 and Exhibit 27–13 shows that the later cash flows are less significant in the calculation of duration than in the calculation of average life. Consequently, the duration tends to be less than the average life.

Macaulay duration (or a slight variation on it called *modified duration*, which is defined later) is often used as a measure of the volatility of price with

EXHIBIT 27–13

Macaulay Duration for a New Current-Coupon GNMA at 50 percent, 120 percent, and 200 percent PSA

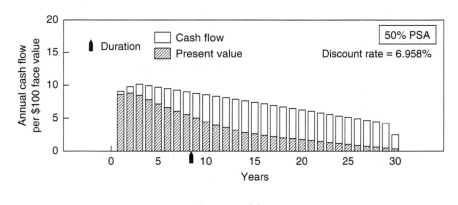

(a)

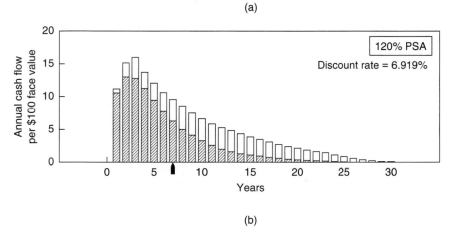

(b)

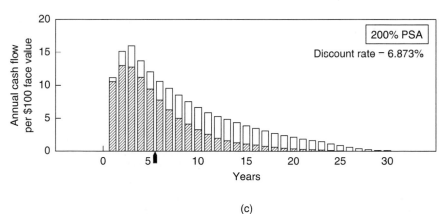

(c)

Priced at 100–08.

respect to changes in yield. This is appropriate as long as the cash flows are not a function of interest rates. However, the cash flows of an MBS depend on prepayments, which are driven to a large extent by interest rates. In the case of interest-rate-dependent cash flows, great care must be taken in using Macaulay duration as a measure of price volatility.

PRICE AND YIELD BEHAVIOR

This section will examine how the price and yield-to-maturity of pass-through securities vary as interest rates vary. As discussed earlier, the cash flows from an MBS are affected by changes in interest rates because of the resulting changes in prepayment levels. This makes the price and yield characteristics of an MBS more complex than those of a standard fixed income security such as a Treasury.

Calculation of Yield-to-Maturity

The yield-to-maturity, or yield, of a security is defined as the discount rate that makes the present value of the security's cash flows equal to its current price. (See the appendix for a mathematical formula for calculating yield.) For a noncallable bond, the calculation of yield is straightforward, given the price, coupon, and timing of cash flows. Even for a standard callable bond, one can calculate a yield-to-call or estimate the probability of calls at different points in time. However, for an MBS there is a separate call option on each dollar of mortgage because in general a homeowner can prepay part or all of a mortgage at any time. Furthermore, because mortgages are self-amortizing, the amount redeemed if a homeowner "exercises a call" will depend on the original term, coupon, and age of the mortgage.

To calculate a yield for an MBS, a prepayment rate must be specified for each remaining month of the MBS's term. Once the prepayment rate has been chosen, cash flows can then be obtained for each month, and the yield (and other security characteristics, such as average life) can be calculated. The necessity of specifying a prepayment rate introduces an element of subjectivity into the calculation of an MBS's yield; there is no consensus on the projected prepayment rate of an MBS and hence no consensus on the yield.

An earlier approach to prepayments was to assume a 12-year prepaid life, but this method is not used today. MBSs are now usually priced at a specified CPR or percentage of PSA. The CPR or percentage of PSA to be used for a given MBS should be chosen using relevant mortgage characteristics and economic variables.

Exhibit 27–14 shows the projected yields-to-maturity of various GNMAs plotted against average lives. These are calculated using prepayment projections from the Prudential Securities Prepayment Model. This graph can be thought of as a GNMA yield curve. For comparison, the graph also shows the Treasury curve and an agency yield curve based on the averages of the yields of selected agencies of various maturities. Pass-throughs have essentially the same credit quality and

EXHIBIT 27–14

GNMA, Agency, and Treasury Yield Curves

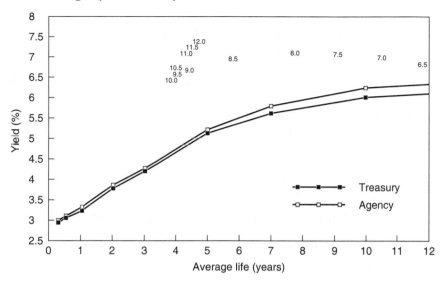

GNMA coupon	6.5	7.0	7.5	8.0	8.5	9.0
Remaining term (years-months)	29-10	29-09	29-10	29-06	28-10	24-08
Price	97-21	100-08	102-24	104-31	106-12	107-15
Projected prepayment rate (% PSA)	94	116	146	177	260	299
Average life (years)	11.8	10.7	9.5	8.2	5.8	4.6
Yield-to-maturity (bond equivalent)	6.89	7.02	7.11	7.14	7.01	6.90

GNMA coupon	9.5	10.0	10.5	11.0	11.5	12.0
Remaining term (years-months)	25-05	25-08	25-08	23-01	21-07	22-01
Price	108-25	110-09	111-25	113-05	115-04	116-24
Projected prepayment rate (% PSA)	336	348	334	302	286	281
Average life (years)	4.2	4.1	4.2	4.6	4.8	4.9
Yield-to-maturity (bond equivalent)	6.81	6.77	6.92	7.23	7.29	7.41

Source: Data are based on closing prices and projected prepayments from the Prudential Securities Prepayment Model on April 30, 1993. The base mortgage rate is 7.4 percent.

liquidity as agencies, so the pass-through spread over the agencies can be thought of as compensation for prepayment uncertainty and for the relative complexity of pass-throughs compared with agencies.

Mortgage Yield and Bond-Equivalent Yield

Mortgage pass-through cash flows typically are paid monthly. The yield calculated from these monthly cash flows is called the *mortgage yield;* it implicitly assumes monthly compounding of interest. To make the yield of an MBS comparable to semiannual-pay Treasuries or corporates, the mortgage yield must be converted to a semiannual compounding basis, or bond-equivalent yield. (See the appendix for the mathematical formula for bond-equivalent yield.) The bond-equivalent yield is higher than the mortgage yield because monthly compounding generates a higher annual yield than semiannual compounding. Hence, to be equivalent to the mortgage yield, the semiannual yield must be higher.

Price Behavior as Interest Rates Vary

The prepayment of principal affects price in different ways for different coupon mortgage securities. Discount coupon securities—those with coupon rates lower than the current coupon rate—trading below par benefit from the early return of principal at par. On the other hand, premium securities trading above par experience a negative effect from early principal prepayment. As an extreme example, if a premium MBS is bought for a price of 105 and a full prepayment of principal is made the next month, 100 is received for 105 paid a month earlier.

Exhibit 27–15 shows closing prices on April 30, 1993, for GNMA, FNMA, and FHLMC pass-throughs. Note that the slope of the graph is less steep for the higher-premium coupons. The price compression in premium-coupon mortgage securities can be explained by the fact that prepayments tend to increase the further the coupon is above the current coupon. The higher the coupon rate on the underlying security, the greater is the likelihood that the homeowner will refinance at the lower prevailing mortgage rates. Exhibit 27–15 indicates that in the opinion of the market, the extra coupon income earned from the FNMAs and FHLMCs with higher coupons is partially canceled by faster expected prepayment levels.

Changes in the prevailing level of interest rates affect the prepayment rates of mortgage securities. As interest rates increase, prepayments tend to slow down, and as interest rates decrease, prepayments tend to increase. The interaction of interest-rate and prepayment-rate changes on the price of an MBS can be illustrated by looking at projected price paths when interest rates change. Exhibit 27–16 shows the projected prices of GNMA $6^1/_2$s and $8^1/_2$s as interest rates change, assuming the yield spread to the Treasury curve remains constant. (A more complicated method of calculating price change as interest rates change will be described later, but it is useful to first understand the basic price/yield relationship described here.)

As interest rates increase, the slowdown in prepayments has an adverse price effect on the GNMA $6^1/_2$, which is priced below par. As interest rates continue to increase, prepayments on the GNMA $6^1/_2$ bottom out and become

EXHIBIT 27–15

Prices of Pass-Through Securities

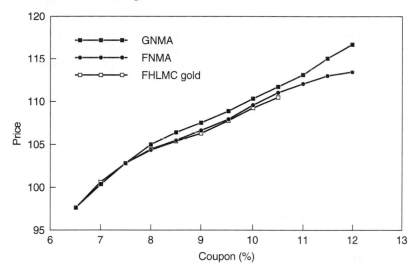

Source: Data are based on closing prices on April 30, 1993. The base mortgage rate is 7.41 percent.

EXHIBIT 27–16

Projected Price Paths of GNMA 6.5s and 8.5s

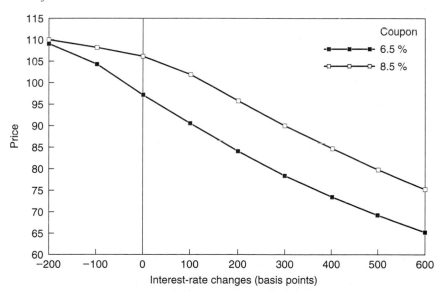

Source: Data are based on assumptions of a parallel shift in interest rates. Projected prices are calculated using prepayment projections from the Prudential Securities Prepayment Model. The no-change prices are the closing prices on May 3, 1993, and the base mortgage rate is 7.34 percent.

relatively insensitive to interest rates, and its price behavior is similar to that of a Treasury or corporate security. For the GNMA $8^1/_2$, which is priced above par, the slowdown in prepayments is beneficial. It reduces the size of the price decline if rates increase 100 basis points. If rates continue to increase, any further slowdown in the prepayment rate for the GNMA $8^1/_2$ is minor, and the GNMA $8^1/_2$, like the GNMA $6^1/_2$, behaves like a Treasury or corporate security. If interest rates decline, there is a sharp increase in projected prepayment rates for the GNMA $8^1/_2$ and consequently very little price appreciation for interest-rate declines of up to 200 basis points. However, if rates decline further, prepayments level off, and there is more price appreciation. For the GNMA $6^1/_2$, the drag on price appreciation does not occur unless interest rates decline by 200 or more basis points. The GNMA $6^1/_2$ then becomes a premium security, and there is a sharp increase in prepayments. If interest rates continue to decline, prepayments on the GNMA $6^1/_2$ begin to level off, and its price behavior is like that of the GNMA $8^1/_2$.

Yield Behavior as Interest Rates Vary

Exhibit 27–17 illustrates the effect of various interest-rate changes on the yields-to-maturity of GNMA $6^1/_2$ and GNMA $8^1/_2$ when price is held constant.

As interest rates increase and prepayments slow down, the yield on the discount GNMA $6^1/_2$ decreases slightly, while the yield on the premium GNMA $8^1/_2$

E X H I B I T   27–17

Projected Yields-to-Maturity for GNMA 6.5s and 8.5s

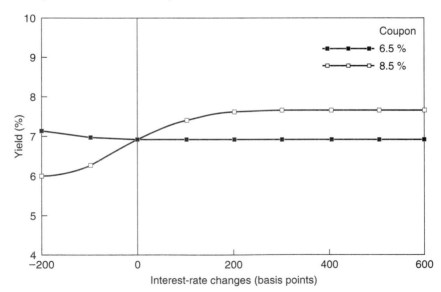

Source: Yields are calculated using projections from the Prudential Securities Prepayment Model.

increases sharply and then levels off. As interest rates decrease and prepayments accelerate, there is a sharp drop in the yield of the GNMA $8\frac{1}{2}$ and a slight rise in the yield of the GNMA $6\frac{1}{2}$. The yield fluctuations are much less for the GNMA $6\frac{1}{2}$, which is priced near par, than for the premium GNMA $8\frac{1}{2}$.

Prepayment Volatility

In general, prepayment volatility is greatest for MBSs whose underlying mortgages have coupons between 100 and 300 basis points above current mortgage rates. At the lower end of this range, a decrease in interest rates may trigger a surge in refinancings, while at the upper end, an increase in interest rates may slow down prepayments substantially. The effect of prepayments on yield will depend on the magnitude of the MBS price discount or premium; for an MBS priced at par with no payment delay, the yield-to-maturity does not depend on the level of prepayments. Exhibit 27–18 illustrates the yield and average-life volatility of several GNMA coupons if interest rates decline or increase by 50 basis points when price is held constant. For all five coupons in Exhibit 27–18, average life increases with interest rates. The GNMA $8\frac{1}{2}$ has the highest prepayment volatility and thus experiences the largest increase in average life as mortgage rates rise. The GNMA $8\frac{1}{2}$ also has the highest yield volatility, with its

E X H I B I T   27–18

Yield and Average-Life Volatility of GNMAs

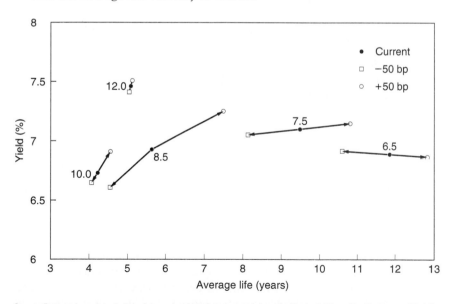

Source: Data are based on closing prices and projected prepayments from the Prudential Securities Prepayment Model on April 30, 1993. The base mortgage rate is 7.41 percent.

higher prepayment volatility outweighing the greater differences from par of the GNMA 10 and the GNMA 12. The yield change of the GNMA $6^1/_2$ is slight because it is priced close to par.

Option-Adjusted Spread—Stochastic Valuation of Mortgage Securities

The volatility of a mortgage security's yield and average life typically works against the investor who owns the mortgage security. That is, the actual yield realized on the security has a high probability of being less than the yield projected on the basis of a single prepayment forecast. In essence, homeowners exercise their option to prepay their mortgages at the time least favorable to the investor. For example, if rates fall, prepayments increase, which means that the homeowner calls away a portion of the investor's principal, and that principal can only be reinvested at a lower rate.

In an attempt to measure this risk, various option models have been developed. The approach most commonly used is the option-adjusted spread (OAS) model. In this approach the cost of the homeowner's prepayment option is calculated in terms of a basis-point penalty that must be subtracted from the expected yield spread on the security. The OAS method involves simulating hundreds of future interest rate paths and calculating the average impact on the security's expected yield spread. (OAS is not precisely comparable to yield spread because a different discounting method is used. OAS discounts the cash flow in each period by a yield based on the forward Treasury rate plus a constant, i.e., the OAS. In a yield-spread calculation the cash flows are all discounted by a single yield, i.e., the security's yield-to-maturity. Hence, OAS is a spread added to the entire Treasury curve, whereas yield spread is a spread added to a single point on the Treasury curve.)

Because OAS takes into account the option component of a mortgage security, it will change less than a security's yield spread as interest rates change. In a flat yield curve one can think of the OAS/yield spread relationship as

$$\text{OAS} = \text{Yield spread} - \text{Option cost}$$

This relationship helps to explain the fact that during market rallies yield spreads on current coupon mortgages often widen. As rates fall, the option cost on a current coupon increases. That is, it moves closer to being in the money. Traders and investors adjust for this increased option cost by demanding wider spreads, which in turn keeps the OAS relatively unchanged.

We can use the concept of OAS to create a price/interest rate graph similar to the one shown in Exhibit 27–16. In that earlier graph, the yield spread on the security was held constant; in Exhibit 27–19, OAS is held constant. Although constant OAS is a better standard than constant yield spread for estimating price movements in mortgage securities, market sentiment often causes OASs to widen and tighten, so even a constant OAS price chart is only a projection of likely price changes and should not be confused with a similar graph for a noncallable Treasury, where there

EXHIBIT 27–19

Projected Price Paths of GNMA 6.5s and 8.5s for Constant OASs

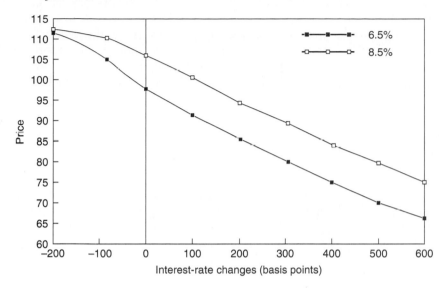

is a simple mathematical relationship between price and yield. (The OAS approach to valuing mortgage securities is described in Chapters 37 and 40 of this book.)

DURATION AND CONVEXITY

Modified and Effective Durations

Earlier, Macaulay duration was defined as a commonly used measure of maturity for MBSs. Macaulay duration, or a slightly adjusted version known as *modified duration,*[4] is often used as a measure of the sensitivity of price to small changes in yields. This is based on the fact that if cash flows are not dependent on interest rates, then modified duration is equal to the rate of percentage change of price with respect to changes in yield.

For an MBS, however, a key characteristic is the dependence of cash flows, via prepayments, on interest rates. This can make Macaulay or modified duration an inadequate or even misleading measure of price sensitivity. To examine the price effect for changes in interest rates, an "effective duration" is often calculated as an alternative measurement of price sensitivity. Effective duration incorporates the changes in prepayment levels that may occur as a result of interest-rate changes. (See the appendix for a mathematical definition of effective duration.)

---

4. Formally, Modified duration = Macaulay duration/$(1 + y/200)$ where y is the bond-equivalent yield.

The calculation of effective duration involves the use of our OAS model because we assume that the OAS on the security remains unchanged as interest rates move. This requirement means that the yield on the security may change by a different amount than the change in the reference Treasury curve. In essence, effective duration measures the percentage change in the price of the security for a small change in the Treasury curve. The effective durations in this report are based on a 25-basis-point parallel shift in the Treasury curve.

Exhibit 27–20 illustrates the calculation of effective duration for a FNMA 9, using the closing price on May 7, 1993. The FNMA 9 had underlying mortgages with coupons 150 to 200 basis points above prevailing mortgage rates and hence had very high prepayment volatility.

The exhibit shows the expected price change for a 25-basis-point parallel shift in the yield curve when OAS is held constant. For an upward shift in the curve, the simulated interest-rate paths from the OAS calculation will be higher on average, and hence prepayment speeds will be slower than in the case of a constant prepayment speed. Because premium pass-throughs such as the FNMA 9s benefit from slower speeds, the price decline under the constant OAS scenario is less than under the constant prepayment scenario used to calculate modified duration. In a similar fashion, faster prepayments will restrain the expected price rise

E X H I B I T   27–20

Calculation of Effective Duration for a FNMA 9

| | Interest-Rate Change (Basis Points) | | |
	–25	**–0**	**+25**
Pricing yield (%)	6.31	6.56	6.81
Projected prepayment rate (% PSA)	438	411	379
Price at 411% PSA	107.2813	106.5313	105.7813
Price at projected prepayment rate	107.0938	106.5313	105.9375

Modified duration = Price volatility assuming no change in prepayments

$$= \frac{-100}{\text{Price}} \times \frac{\text{Change in price}}{\text{Change in yield}} = \frac{-1}{106.5313} \times \frac{(105.7813 - 107.2813)}{0.50}$$

= 2.82% per 100 bp change in yield

Effective duration = Price volatility assuming no change in OAS

$$= \frac{-100}{\text{Price}} \times \frac{\text{Change in price}}{\text{Change in yield}} = \frac{-1}{106.5313} \times \frac{(105.9375 - 107.0938)}{0.50}$$

= 2.17% per 100 bp change in yield

Source: Data are based on FNMA 9s priced at 106-17 on May 7, 1993. Underlying mortgage coupons were 150 to 200 basis points above prevailing mortgage rates.

in the premium FNMA 9 when the curve shifts. In the example in Exhibit 27–21, the FNMA 9 is projected to have an effective duration, or price volatility, of 2.17 percent per 100 basis points. This means that at current interest-rate levels, a one-basis-point change in Treasury yields will lead to a percentage change in price of 0.0217 percent. This is much lower than the price volatility of 2.82 percent per 100 basis points given by the traditional modified duration calculation, which does not take into account changes in prepayments.

The example in Exhibit 27–20 indicates that while the usual duration calculation may be adequate for discount or high-premium MBSs whose prepayment levels are unlikely to change much for small changes in interest rates, it can be inadequate or even misleading for low-premium coupons, which have high prepayment volatility. An effective-duration calculation is more appropriate in such cases. This is borne out by historical studies that have shown that price volatilities do tend to follow the pattern suggested by effective durations.[5] Exhibit 27–21 shows modified and effective durations for several seasoned FNMA securities. The effective durations are calculated by using 25-basis-point moves in interest rates in each direction. The exhibit indicates that modified duration overestimates the price volatility of low-premium

E X H I B I T   27–21

Modified and Effective Durations for FNMAs

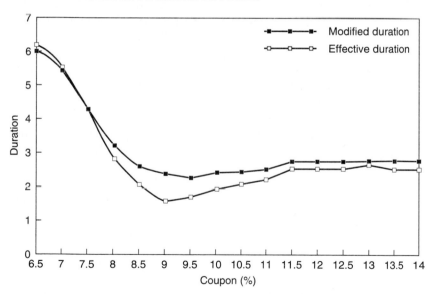

Source: Data are based on closing prices and prepayment projections on May 7, 1993. Effective durations are calculated using 25-basis-point moves in interest rates in each direction.

5. Scott M. Pinkus and Marie A. Chandoha, "The Relative Price Volatility of Mortgage Securities," in *Mortgage-Backed Securities: New Strategies, Applications and Research,* ed. Frank J. Fabozzi (Chicago: Probus Publishing, 1987).

coupons. This has important implications for hedging strategies. Hedge ratios based on the use of Macaulay or modified duration to estimate price volatility will fail for mortgage coupons with high prepayment volatility. (This has been a painful lesson for many participants in the MBS markets.) It is important to look at changes in both yield and prepayment rates when calculating price volatility; effective duration provides a means for doing this. Another useful analytic tool in this context is convexity, which measures the rate of change of price volatility.

Convexity

In mortgage analysis, considerable attention is given to the concept of convexity and in particular to the so-called negative convexity of MBSs. Convexity refers to the curvature of the price/yield curve. (See the appendix for a mathematical definition of convexity.) In other words, convexity is the rate of change of duration, that is, price volatility. If one considers duration to be the speed of price changes, then convexity can be thought of as acceleration. The projected price paths shown in Exhibit 27–19 illustrate positive, zero, and negative convexity.

A straight line has zero convexity. Thus, because the price/yield curve of the GNMA $6\frac{1}{2}$ in Exhibit 27–19 is essentially a straight line at the no-change point on the horizontal axis, then the GNMA $6\frac{1}{2}$ has almost zero convexity at prevailing interest rates. This means that for small equal changes in interest rates the price of the GNMA $6\frac{1}{2}$ will increase or decrease approximately the same amount.

Discount and high-premium MBSs, like Treasuries, tend to have positive convexity. Positive convexity implies that for small, equal, and opposite changes in interest rates, the price increase if rates decline will be more than the price decrease if rates increase. This means that the rate of decrease in price slows down as interest rates increase; that is, the curve has a downward "bulge" in the middle. When interest rates rise by several hundred basis points, the GNMA $6\frac{1}{2}$ will become a deep-discount coupon and have positive convexity.

Negative convexity means that the price/yield curve flattens as interest rates decline. This is characteristic of slight-premium MBSs for which increasing prepayments place a drag on price increases as interest rates decline. Thus, for small equal changes in rates, the price is likely to decline more than it will increase. Exhibit 27–19 shows that at prevailing interest rates the GNMA $8\frac{1}{2}$ has a high degree of negative convexity, whereas the GNMA $6\frac{1}{2}$ has large negative convexity if interest rates decline by between 100 to 200 basis points. On the other hand, if rates rise by 100 to 200 basis points, the GNMA $8\frac{1}{2}$ will then have positive convexity. Hence, negative convexity is a characteristic of low-premium MBSs.

Calculation of Convexity

Convexity can be estimated by considering small positive and negative shifts in yield curve (while holding OAS constant) and calculating the changes in price in both cases. Exhibit 27–22 illustrates the calculation of the convexities of a FNMA $6\frac{1}{2}$ and a FNMA 8 using 25-basis-point changes in interest rates.

EXHIBIT 27–22

Calculation of Convexity

Change in Rates (Basis Points)	FNMA $6^1/_2$			FNMA 8		
	Projected Prepayment Rate	Yield	Price	Projected Prepayment Rate	Yield	Price
−25 bp	154% PSA	6.67%	99-13$^1/_4$	378% PSA	6.37%	105-07
0	140	6.87	97-28	336	6.71	104-15
25	134	7.12	96-10$^3/_4$	290	7.08	103-17$^1/_2$

$$\text{Convexity} = \frac{100}{\text{Price}} \times \frac{(\text{Change in price if rates go down}) - (\text{Change in price if rates go up})}{(\text{Change in rates})^2}$$

$$= \frac{100}{97.8750} \times \frac{(99.4141 - 97.8750) - (97.8750 - 96.3359)}{(.25)^2} = 0.00 \text{ for FNMA } 6^1/_2$$

$$= \frac{100}{104.4688} \times \frac{(105.2188 - 104.4688) - (104.4688 - 103.5469)}{(.25)^2} = -2.63 \text{ for FNMA } 8$$

The no change-case prices are closing prices on May 7, 1993.

The discount FNMA $6\frac{1}{2}$ has zero convexity, whereas the low-premium FNMA 8 has large negative convexity. This can be explained by considering the likely magnitudes and effects of prepayment changes for the two coupons. For the FNMA $6\frac{1}{2}$, the change in interest rates causes a small change in prepayments, just enough so that the positive impact of faster prepayments on the discount when rates fall offsets the negative impact of slower prepayments when rates rise. However, the FNMA 8 has high prepayment volatility; the increasing prepayments as interest rates decline put a drag on price increases. The benefits of a slowdown in prepayments if interest rates increase are not sufficient to offset this price compression.

Exhibit 27–23 shows the convexities of various FNMA pass-throughs based on prices and prepayment projections on May 7, 1993. It can be seen that convexity reaches a low at the $7\frac{1}{2}$ coupon and then starts increasing again. This happens because high-premium coupons, like deep-discounts, have low prepayment volatility and, hence, positive convexity.

Investment Implications of Convexity

Positive convexity is generally a desirable characteristic in a fixed income security. However, this does not mean that securities with negative convexity, such as low-premium pass-throughs, should be avoided. The market may have adjusted the prices of such securities to compensate investors for the negative convexity,

E X H I B I T   27–23

Convexities of FNMA Pass-Throughs

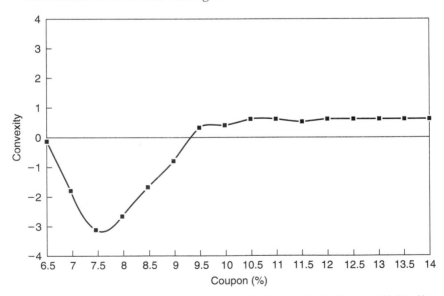

Source: Data are based on prices and prepayment projections from the Prudential Securities Prepayment Model on May 7, 1993, with the base mortgage rate equal to 7.30 percent.

making their yields sufficiently high so that they offer better value than many securities with positive convexity.

Another point that should be kept in mind is that for a given security, convexity changes with interest rates. In other words, negative convexity is a "local" property of low-premium pass-throughs; if there are substantial changes in interest rates, the low-premium pass-through will become a discount or high-premium pass-through and may then have positive convexity. This is a relevant consideration if one plans to hold the security for a year or more, when the length of the holding period makes large interest-rate changes possible. In general, securities should be evaluated and compared by calculating total holding-period returns under a range of projected interest-rate changes. The total return incorporates such factors as initial price and convexity (through the change in the price over the period) and hence will give a good indication of the value of the security.

A Comment on the Units Used to Measure Duration and Convexity

Traditionally, duration has been measured in units of years, and convexity in $(years)^2$. This is so because Macaulay duration, which is a measure of investment life, is measured in years. Modified duration, which is used as a measure of price volatility, is closely related to Macaulay duration and therefore is also measured in years. The units of convexity result from the fact that it has been defined as a weighted (the weights being the present values of the cash flows) average of the squares of the times-to-receipt of all cash flows. However, years and $(years)^2$ are not appropriate measures of price volatility and convexity. As discussed previously, duration (or effective duration) is the percentage change in price for a given change in yield. In the example in Exhibit 27–20, the price volatility of the FNMA 9 was 2.17 percent per 100 basis points, or 0.0217 percent per basis point. The appropriate units for duration when it is used as a measure of price volatility are change per basis point or per 100 basis points.

Convexity is the rate of change of price volatility. The convexity of the FNMA 8 in Exhibit 27–22 was –2.63. Analysis of the calculation in Exhibit 27–22 shows that this can be expressed as –2.63 percent per 100 basis points. In other words, the price volatility, expressed as a percentage price change per 100 basis points, increases by –2.63 for each 100-basis-point change in yield.

TOTAL HOLDING-PERIOD RETURNS

Fixed income securities are generally priced and traded by yield-to-maturity. However, from the investor's point of view, yield-to-maturity can be an unsatisfactory measure of the likely return from the security for two important reasons:

- The yield-to-maturity assumes that all cash flows are reinvested at a rate equal to the yield.

- It assumes that the security is held until maturity, thus ignoring the capital gain or loss from selling the security at the end of a holding period.

The total return (or the horizon or holding-period return) measures the actual return over a specified holding period. This return is composed of three elements:

- The cash flows from the security during the holding period.
- The reinvestment income from the cash flows from the time each cash flow is received to the end of the holding period for specified levels of reinvestment rates that prevailed during the holding period.
- The gain or loss from selling the security at the end of the period. The proceeds from the sale are equal to the price at the end of the period multiplied by the amount of principal still outstanding at the time, plus any accrued interest.

Calculation of Total Return

Exhibit 27–24 illustrates the calculation of the total return from holding a new GNMA 7 for six months. The security is purchased on May 14 at a price of 100-14, that is, $100 $^{14}/_{32}$ or $100.4375 is paid for each $100 of face value, with settlement on June 16. The security is sold on December 10 for a price of 100-17, with settlement on December 16. Because the security is actually transferred between the buyer and seller and cash is exchanged on the settlement dates, these dates should be used as the beginning and end of the holding period. The first cash flow is received on July 15 and constitutes interest and principal for the month of June. The sixth and final cash flow is received on December 15. All cash flows (including reinvestment income) are assumed to be reinvested each month at a reinvestment rate of 3 percent. A prepayment rate of 120 percent PSA is assumed.

With these assumptions, the actual return from holding the security over the six months is 3.570 percent or, stated as an annual rate, 7.140 percent. The effective annual return, with a six-month compounding frequency, is 7.267 percent. The corresponding bond-equivalent (semiannual compounding) rate of return is 7.140 percent.

Assumptions Used in Calculating Total Returns

The calculation of a projected rate of return over a holding period requires assumptions about the values of three major determinants of the holding-period return: prepayment rates, reinvestment rates, and the selling price at the end of the holding period. The question of prepayment assumptions was addressed in the prepayment behavior and cash flow section. Here the other two assumptions are discussed.

EXHIBIT 27–24

Calculation of Total Return for a GNMA 7

Buy: $1 million face of GNMA 7s, with a remaining term of 29 years–9 months on May 14 at 100-14.
       Settlement is June 16.

Amount paid: $1MM x 100-14 = $1,004,375
                      + 15 days of accrued interest = $ 2,917
                                            Total $1,007,292

Cash Flows

Date	Remaining Balance	Interest	Scheduled Principal	Prepaid[a] Principal	Reinvestment[b] Income	Total Cash Flow
7/15	998,266	5,833	758	976	1	7,568
8/15	996,404	5,824	762	1,100	20	7,706
9/15	994,280	5,812	765	1,359	40	7,976
10/15	991,999	5,800	770	1,511	59	8,140
11/15	989,439	5,787	773	1,787	82	8,429
12/15	986,846	5,771	777	1,816	100	8,464
Totals:	986,846	34,827	4,605	8,549	302	48,283

Sell: Remaining $986,846 face value of GNMA 7 on December 10 for settlement on December 16.

Sale proceeds: Remaining balance x Price = $ 992,089
                     + 15 days of accured interest = $ 2,878
                                        Total $ 994,967

$$\text{Total return over holding period} = \frac{\text{Sale proceeds} - \text{Price paid} + \text{Total cash flows}}{\text{Price paid}}$$

$$= \frac{994,967 - 1,007,292 + 48,283}{1,007,292}$$

$$= 0.3570 \text{ or } 3.570\%$$

Total return of an annualized basis = 3.570% × (12/6) = 7.140%

$$\text{Effective annual return with six-month compounding frequency} = \left(1 + \frac{.0714}{12/6}\right)^{12/6} - 1 = 7.26\%$$

$$\text{Total return on a semiannual compounding basis} = 2\left[\left(1 + \frac{7,267}{100}\right)^{12/6} - 1\right] = 7.140\%$$

[a]Constant prepayment rate of 120% PSA is assumed.
[b]Assumed reinvestment rate is 3%.

Reinvestment Rates

There are several approaches for determining appropriate reinvestment rates. The calculation in Exhibit 27–24 uses a constant reinvestment rate of 3 percent with monthly rollover of accumulated cash flows. This method is similar to assuming that all cash flows are deposited in a short-term cash or money market account. Under this method, the money market reinvestment rate can be allowed to change over the course of the holding period in line with projected changes in the yield level used in calculating the selling price of the security. For example, if the initial reinvestment rate is 3 percent, and it is assumed that yield levels will increase by 100 basis points over the holding period, then the reinvestment rate could be allowed to increase gradually to 4 percent over the holding period.

A second approach that is sometimes used is to reinvest each cash flow from the time it is received to the end of the holding period at a rate chosen according to the length of the reinvestment period. For example, if a cash flow is received one year before the end of the holding period, it may be reinvested at the one-year Treasury rate, rather than at a short-term money market rate. However, this assumes that the end of the holding period is known from the start. In practice, an investor does not generally know the exact time at which the security will be sold.

A third approach is to assume that all cash flows are reinvested in securities of the same type and to assume a reinvestment rate close to the yield of the security. However, this approach raises questions about the meaning of the holding-period return because at the end of the period some of the cash flow received is tied up in new securities.

Selling Price at End of the Holding Period

Choosing the price of an MBS at the end of the holding period is perhaps the assumption most open to question. In the example in Exhibit 27–24, a known horizon selling price was assumed for illustrative simplicity. The standard approach in calculating projected returns is to assume a given change in yield levels and then calculate the price at the end of the holding period by discounting future cash flows at the assumed horizon yield. However, in projecting prepayment and reinvestment rates and in comparing the total return of an MBS with a Treasury, assumptions must be made about the relationship between changes in the yield levels of MBSs and changes in interest rates in general. A common assumption is a parallel shift in interest rates, so that short-term, MBS, and Treasury yields all change by the same amount. It is important to realize that this is just an assumption, and that yield spreads of MBSs to Treasuries may widen or narrow. A more recent approach that has become popular is to hold the OAS of the security constant throughout the holding period.

As this discussion suggests, the calculation of a holding period return requires important assumptions about reinvestment rates and yields used to calculate the redemption value at the end of the period. This is true for all securities, not just MBSs. However, for MBSs there is the additional assumption concerning prepayment levels. These assumptions can have a strong impact on the value of the projected return, so it is important that these assumptions be understood when evaluating securities on a total-return basis over a holding period.

Variation of Total Returns with Holding Period and Rate Changes

Exhibit 27–25 shows the total returns for one-year and five-year holding periods under various interest-rate changes for a GNMA 7 and a GNMA 9. A parallel shift in the Treasury curve and a constant OAS is assumed. The initial reinvestment rate is assumed to be 3.125 percent with all cash flows reinvested monthly. Interest rates are assumed to change uniformly over the year for the one-year horizon and at a rate of 100 basis points per year for the five-year horizon.

As indicated in Exhibit 27–25, the one-year returns depend on interest-rate changes to a greater degree than do the five-year returns. There are two reasons for this:

- The coupon and reinvestment income constitutes a much larger proportion of the total return over the five-year holding period, thus reducing the importance of the change in price of the security due to changes in interest rates.

EXHIBIT 27–25

One-Year and Five-Year Holding-Period Returns for GNMA 7s and 9s

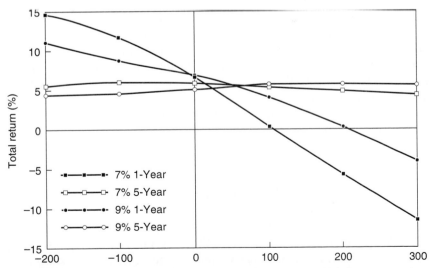

Source: The GNMA 7 is bought at a price of 100-25 and the GNMA 9 at a price of 107-19 with the base mortgage rate equal to 7.27 percent. The following assumptions are made: (1) a parallel shift in interest rates and yield spreads; (2) initial reinvestment rate is 3.125 percent with all cash flows reinvested monthly; (3) interest rates change uniformly over the year for the one-year horizon and at a rate of 100 basis points per year for the five-year horizon.

- A larger proportion of the principal will pay down over the five-year period, because of both scheduled payments and prepayments. This also reduces the importance of price changes, particularly in a declining-interest-rate environment when prepayments will be high.

The lackluster performance of both securities over the five-year period in the declining interest-rate scenarios is explained by the second point. The high prepayment levels result in a low remaining balance at the time of the sale. This reduces the benefits from price appreciation, which in any case has become compressed by the high prepayments (as illustrated in Exhibit 27–19).

Over the one-year holding period, the GNMA 7, like other fixed income securities, performs poorly if interest rates increase and performs well if interest rates decline (although there is some effect of price compression and high prepayments if interest rates decline by 200 basis points). The GNMA 9 does slightly better than the GNMA 7 if rates increase, due to the benefits of a slowdown in prepayments for the premium GNMA 9. In the declining-interest-rate scenarios, the high prepayments and the resulting price compression cause the GNMA 9 return to increase much more slowly than the GNMA 7 return after interest rates have declined by more than 100 basis points.

SUMMARY

The secondary mortgage market has grown tremendously in recent years and now constitutes a major sector of the fixed income market, comparable in size to the corporate market and greater than the agency market. The huge amount of mortgage debt in the United States and the fact that less than one-half of this debt has been securitized to date indicate substantial potential for growth.

This chapter has attempted to provide a full discussion of mortgage-backed pass-throughs, which constitute the largest sector of the secondary mortgage markets. Pass-throughs, like all MBSs, are more complex in their investment characteristics and behavior than standard Treasury or corporate securities. Their cash flows are unpredictable; they are self-amortizing; their price/yield relationship is complicated by prepayments; and consequently, the usual interpretations of duration and convexity may be misleading.

Despite their complexity, or rather because of it, the mortgage markets provide opportunities for astute fixed income investors seeking high yields without sacrificing high quality. The complexity of pass-throughs has resulted in pricing at significantly higher yields than comparable-quality securities. Recent yields have been between 100 and 200 basis points higher than comparable-maturity Treasuries, compared with yield spreads of 30 to 50 basis points over Treasuries for AAA-rated corporates. The credit quality of agency pass-throughs is clearly higher, however, than even AAA-rated corporates, because of U.S. government or quasi-government guarantees concerning payment of interest and principal. Historical studies have shown that, as a result of their higher yields, pass-throughs typically have provided higher returns than Treasuries or high-quality corporates.

In sum, pass-throughs provide investors with a large and liquid market in securities that combine very high credit quality with yields that are substantially higher than other comparable-quality securities. Mortgage securities have complex investment characteristics and require a more careful analysis than a plain-vanilla Treasury or corporate security. The higher potential returns of mortgage pass-through securities, however, suggest that the extra effort may well be worthwhile for fixed income investors.

APPENDIX

Mortgage Mathematics

MORTGAGE CASH FLOW WITHOUT PREPAYMENTS

Monthly Payment

For a level-payment mortgage, the constant monthly payment is

$$M_n = \frac{B_0 \left(\dfrac{G}{1200} \right) \left(1 + \dfrac{G}{1200} \right)^N}{\left(1 + \dfrac{G}{1200} \right)^N - 1}$$

where

M_n = Monthly payment for month n
B_0 = Original balance
G = Gross coupon rate (%)
N = Original term in months (e.g., 360)

Remaining Balance

The remaining balance after n months is

$$B_n = \frac{B_0 \left[\left(1 + \dfrac{G}{1200} \right)^N - \left(1 + \dfrac{G}{1200} \right)^n \right]}{\left(1 + \dfrac{G}{1200} \right)^N - 1}$$

where B_n = Remaining balance at the end of month n.

Principal Payment

The amount of principal paid in month n is given by

$$P_n = \frac{B_0 \left(\dfrac{G}{1200}\right)\left(1 + \dfrac{G}{1200}\right)^{n-1}}{\left(1 + \dfrac{G}{1200}\right)^{N} - 1}$$

where P_n = Principal paid in month n.

Interest Payment

The amount of interest paid in month n can be written as

$$I_n = \frac{B_0 \left(\dfrac{G}{1200}\right)\left[\left(1 + \dfrac{G}{1200}\right)^{N} - \left(1 + \dfrac{G}{1200}\right)^{n-1}\right]}{\left(1 + \dfrac{G}{1200}\right)^{N} - 1} = B_{n-1}\left(\dfrac{G}{1200}\right)$$

where I_n = Interest paid in month n.

It should be noted that

$$G = S + C$$

where

S = Service fee (%) and
C = Security coupon rate (%), so Servicing Amount $= [S/(C + S)]I_n$.

Therefore, the cash flow to the security holder in month n is given by

$$\text{CF}_n = P_n + I_n - \text{Servicing amount} = P_n + \left(\frac{C}{C + S}\right)I_n$$

PREPAYMENT MEASURING CONVENTIONS

For a given pool of mortgages, let

B_n = Remaining principal balance per dollar of mortgage at the end of month n if there are no prepayments
C_n = Pool factor (i.e., actual remaining principal balance per dollar of mortgage) at the end of month n

Let $Q_n = C_n/B_n$. If one thinks of the pool as consisting of a very large number of $1 mortgages, each of which can terminate separately, then Q_n represents the percentage of mortgages remaining at the end of month n. Then

$$\text{Percentage of initial balance that has been prepaid} = 1 - Q_n$$

For month n, the single monthly mortality, or SMM, stated as a decimal, is given by

$$\text{SMM} = \text{Proportion of \$1 mortgages outstanding at the beginning of}$$
$$\text{the month that are prepaid during the month}$$

$$= \frac{Q_{n-1} - Q_n}{Q_{n-1}} = 1 - \frac{Q_n}{Q_{n-1}}$$

For the period from month m to month n, the constant SMM rate that is equivalent to the actual prepayments experienced is given by

$$\left(1 - \text{SMM}\right)^{n-m} = \frac{Q_n}{Q_m}$$

That is,

$$\text{SMM} = 1 - \left(\frac{Q_n}{Q_m}\right)^{1/(n-m)}$$

The conditional prepayment rate, or CPR (also expressed as a decimal), is the SMM expressed as an annual rate, and is given by

$$1 - \text{CPR} = (1 - \text{SMM})^{12}$$
$$\text{CPR} = 1 - (1 - \text{SMM})^{12}$$

The SMM can therefore be expressed as

$$\text{SMM} = 1 - (1 - \text{CPR})^{1/12}$$

Percentage of PSA

If a mortgage prepays at a rate of 100 percent of PSA, the CPR for the month when the mortgage is n months old is

$$\text{CPR} = 6\% \times \frac{n}{30} \qquad\qquad \text{if } n \le 30$$
$$= 6\% \qquad\qquad\qquad \text{if } n > 30$$
$$= 6\% \times \min\left(1, \frac{n}{30}\right) \qquad \text{for any } n$$

For a general prepayment rate of x percent of PSA, for age n,

$$\text{CPR} = 6\% \times \frac{x}{100} \times \frac{n}{30} \qquad\qquad \text{if } n \le 30$$

$$= 6\% \times \frac{x}{100} \qquad\qquad \text{if } n > 30$$

$$= 6\% \times \frac{x}{100} \times \min\left(1, \frac{n}{30}\right) \quad \text{for any } n$$

Conversely, if a mortgage of age n months prepays at a given CPR, the PSA rate for that month is given by

$$\% \text{ of PSA} = \text{CPR} \times \frac{100}{6} \times \frac{30}{n} \qquad\qquad \text{if } n \le 30$$

$$= \text{CPR} \times \frac{100}{6} \qquad\qquad \text{if } n > 30$$

$$= \text{CPR} \times \frac{100}{6} \times \max\left(1, \frac{30}{n}\right) \quad \text{for any } n$$

MORTGAGE CASH FLOW WITH PREPAYMENTS

Let $\hat{M}_n$, $\hat{P}_n$, $\hat{I}_n$, and $\hat{B}_n$ denote the monthly scheduled payment, scheduled principal, interest, and remaining (end-of-month) balance for month n when prepayments are included. Let SMM_n be the prepayment rate in month n, stated as a decimal, and let

$$Q_n = (1 - \text{SMM}_n)(1 - \text{SMM}_{n-1}) \ldots (1 - \text{SMM}_1)$$

The *total scheduled monthly payment* in month n is given by

$$\hat{M}_n = \frac{\hat{B}_{n-1}\left(\dfrac{G}{1200}\right)\left(1 + \dfrac{G}{1200}\right)^{N-n+1}}{\left(1 + \dfrac{G}{1200}\right)^{N-n+1} - 1} = M_n Q_{n-1}$$

The *scheduled principal* portion of this payment is given by

$$\hat{P}_n = \frac{\hat{B}_{n-1}\left(\dfrac{G}{1200}\right)}{\left(1 + \dfrac{G}{1200}\right)^{N-n+1} - 1} = P_n Q_{n-1}$$

The *interest* portion is given by

$$\hat{I}_n = \hat{B}_{n-1}\left(\frac{G}{1200}\right) = I_n Q_{n-1}$$

The *unscheduled principal payment* in month n is written as

$$\text{PR}_n = (\hat{B}_{n-1} - \hat{P}_n)\text{SMM}_n$$

The *remaining balance* is given by

$$\hat{B}_n = \hat{B}_{n-1} - \hat{P}_n - \mathrm{PR}_n = B_n Q_n$$

The total cash flow to the investor is

$$\hat{CF}_n = \hat{P}_n + \mathrm{PR}_n + \left(\frac{C}{C+S}\right)\hat{I}_n$$

AVERAGE LIFE

Average life assigns weights to principal paydowns according to their arrival dates.

$$\text{Average Life (in years)} = \frac{1}{12}\sum_{t=1}^{N}\frac{(t+\alpha-1)(\text{Principal}_t)}{\sum_{t=1}^{N}\text{Principal}_t}$$

where

$$
\begin{aligned}
t &= \text{Time subscript, } t = 1, \dots N \\
\text{Principal}_t &= \text{Principal arriving at time } t \\
N &= \text{Number of months until last principal cash flow comes in} \\
\alpha &= \text{Days between settlement date and first cash flow date,} \\
&\quad \text{divided by 30 (i.e., the fraction of a month between} \\
&\quad \text{settlement date and first cash flow date)}
\end{aligned}
$$

MACAULAY DURATION

Duration assigns time weights to the present values of all cash flows.

$$\text{Maculay duration (in years)} = \frac{1}{12}\sum_{t=1}^{N}\frac{\dfrac{(t+\alpha-1)C(t)}{(1+r/1200)^{t+\alpha-1}}}{\sum_{t=1}^{N}\dfrac{C(t)}{(1+r/1200)^{t+\alpha-1}}}$$

where

$$
\begin{aligned}
C(t) &= \text{Cash flow at time } t \\
r &= \text{Cash flow yield of mortgage (\%)}
\end{aligned}
$$

CASH FLOW YIELD

To obtain the cash flow yield, equate the present value of the security's cash flows on the settlement date to its initial price P plus its accrued interest I.

$$P + I = \sum_{t=1}^{N}\frac{C(t)}{(1+r/1200)^{t+\alpha-1}}$$

This equation is solved iteratively for r. The solution is called the *mortgage yield*.

BOND-EQUIVALENT YIELD

The interest on a mortgage security is compounded monthly, whereas the interest on bonds such as Treasuries and corporates is compounded semiannually. The compounding frequency is reflected in the yield of a security. Therefore, to make mortgage yields and bond yields comparable, the yield of a mortgage is normally converted to a bond-equivalent yield, that is, a yield based on semiannual compounding of the mortgage's interest payments.

A yield based on monthly compounding can be converted to a bond-equivalent yield and vice versa as follows:

r = Mortgage yield based on monthly compounding (%)
y = Bond-equivalent yield (%)

$$y = 200\left[\left(1+\frac{r}{1200}\right)^6 - 1\right]$$

$$r = 1200\left[\left(1+\frac{y}{200}\right)^{1/6} - 1\right]$$

TOTAL RETURN

The total return over a holding period h (percent) is calculated as

$$y_h = \frac{\begin{array}{c}\text{Sales} \\ \text{proceeds}\end{array} - \begin{array}{c}\text{Total} \\ \text{price} \\ \text{paid}\end{array} + \begin{array}{c}\text{Total net cash flow} \\ \text{received during} \\ \text{the holding period}\end{array} + \begin{array}{c}\text{Total reinvestment} \\ \text{income during} \\ \text{the holding period}\end{array}}{\text{Total price paid}} \times 100$$

The bond-equivalent total return rate y_{BE} is given by

$$\left(1+\frac{y_h}{100}\right)^{12/h} = \left(1+\frac{y_{BE}}{200}\right)^2$$

MODIFIED DURATION

Modified duration is given by

$$\text{Modified duration} = \frac{\text{Macaulay duration}}{1 + y/200}$$

where y = Bond-equivalent yield (%).

⑥ COLLATERALIZED MORTGAGE OBLIGATIONS

Chris Ames
Director
Asset-Backed Securities Trading
Lehman Brothers International (Europe)

INTRODUCTION

The U.S. mortgage-backed securities (MBS) market has grown significantly in the last 15 years. At the end of 1980, approximately $111 billion MBS were outstanding; by the end of 1995, the amount had grown nearly 16-fold to $1.8 trillion. Much of this growth has come in the form of collateralized mortgage obligations (CMOs) and real estate mortgage investment conduits (REMICs),[1] structures that significantly broadened the investor base for mortgage-backed securities by offering near-U.S. Treasury credit quality, customized performance characteristics, attractive yields across a range of maturities, and a variety of risk/return profiles to fit investors' needs. CMOs currently account for 50 percent of all fixed-rate mortgage-backed securities outstanding.

Throughout the 1970s and early 1980s, most mortgage-backed securities were issued in pass-through form. Pass-throughs, which are participations in the cash flows from pools of individual home mortgages, have long final maturities and the potential for early partial repayment of principal. These securities primarily appeal to investors willing to accept long and uncertain investment horizons in exchange for relatively high yields and credit quality.

---

1. Although CMOs and REMICs have different tax and regulatory characteristics for issuers, there is little difference between them for the investor. In practice, the market uses the terms interchangeably, and the term CMO is used generically in this chapter. A detailed discussion of the differences between the two is described later in this chapter.

In 1983, a dramatic fall in mortgage rates and a surging housing market caused mortgage originations to double. Much of this production was sold in the capital markets; pass-through issuance jumped from $53 billion in 1982 to $84 billion. To accommodate this surge in supply, financial innovators designed a security that would broaden the existing MBS investor base. In mid-1983, the Federal Home Loan Mortgage Corporation (Freddie Mac, or FHLMC) issued the first CMO, a $1 billion, three-class structure that offered short-, intermediate-, and long-term securities produced from the cash flows of a pool of mortgages. This instrument allowed more investors to become active in the MBS market. For instance, banks could participate in the market more efficiently by buying short-term mortgage securities to match their short-term liabilities (deposits).

The CMO market evolved rapidly, growing in size and complexity. Annual issuance of agency CMOs rose steadily, from $5 billion in 1983 to a peak of $324 billion in 1993. Exhibit 28–1 shows CMO issuance from 1983 to 1995. CMO issuance fell in 1994 and 1995 for a variety of reasons. Sharply higher mortgage rates curtailed refinancing activity and resulted in lower MBS collateral issuance. With lower prepayment volatility, many mortgage securities investors chose to hold pass-throughs instead of CMOs. At the same time, bank demand for CMOs softened as lending activity finally began to rise after the credit crunch years of 1991–93. Finally, many of the hedge funds that had been buyers of the more high-risk and high-yielding tranches turned to other investments. Currently over 50% of all 30-year FHLMC and Federal National Mortgage Association (Fannie Mae or FNMA) pass-throughs are pledged as collateral for CMOs. More recently, CMOs backed by individual mortgages and issued by nonagency entities (known as whole-loan or private label CMOs) have become a significant market in their own right, and today the balance of whole-loan CMOs outstanding is approximately $195 billion.[2]

The thrust in the CMO market has been the development of innovative structures to meet the needs of institutional investors and broaden the investor base for mortgage-backed securities. For example, demand from traditional corporate bond investors for CMO bonds with insulation from prepayment volatility led to the creation of planned amortization classes (PACs) and targeted amortization classes (TACs). Regulatory pressures on banks and thrifts led to the creation of very accurately defined maturity (VADM) bonds that were guaranteed not to extend past a given date. Growing interest from overseas investors gave rise to floating-rate bonds indexed to the London interbank offered rate (LIBOR). Increased investor sophistication and technological breakthroughs have created a large market for derivative securities: interest- and principal-only bonds (IOs, POs), inverse floaters, and others. A broad range of products is now available to suit almost any investor preference (see Exhibit 28–2).

---

2. Lehman Brothers, *Inside Mortgage Securities,* February 2, 1996, p. 2.

E X H I B I T   28–1

CMO Issuance
($ Billion)

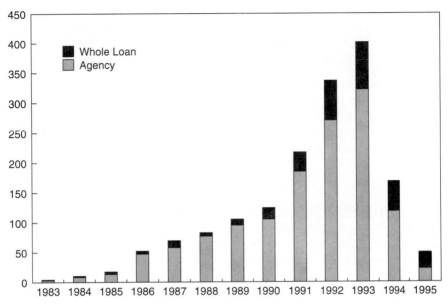

Source: Lehman Brothers, *Inside Mortgage Securities.*

E X H I B I T   28–2

Agency CMOs Outstanding by Class at Year-End 1995
($ Billion)

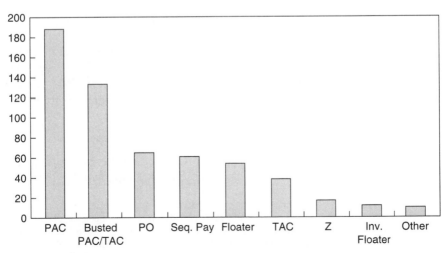

Source: Lehman Brothers.

This chapter explains how CMOs are structured and defines the major types of securities available. It also describes the evolving CMO regulatory environment, PAC band drift, the pricing relationship between CMOs and collateral, some valuation techniques employed by CMO investors, and trading conventions.

PASS-THROUGHS AND WHOLE LOANS: THE BUILDING BLOCKS OF CMOS

In order to develop realistic expectations about the performance of a CMO bond, an investor must first evaluate the underlying collateral, since its performance will determine the timing and size of the cash flows reallocated by the CMO structure. Agency and whole-loan CMOs have distinct collateral, credit, and prepayment characteristics.

Collateral

Individual home mortgages are the underlying collateral and source of cash flow for CMOs. In the case of agency CMOs, these mortgages are already pooled and securitized in pass-through form. The mortgages backing an agency pass-through are of similar size, age, and underwriting quality and have similar rates. All principal and interest cash flows generated by the underlying mortgages, including any prepayments, are channeled to investors, net of a servicing spread (a small portion of each month's interest payment paid to the institution that collects and distributes the mortgage payments). Pass-through investors share in the cash flows on a pro rata basis.

Whole-loan CMO issuers do not take the interim step of creating a pass-through security from a pool of individual mortgages; instead, they create a structure directly based on the cash flows of a group of mortgages. Whole-loan pools, like agency pass-throughs, usually contain mortgages of similar underwriting quality, age, and rate (the range of ages and rates is often somewhat wider for whole-loan pools than for agency pass-throughs). The most common distinguishing characteristic of whole loans is their size. The agencies accept only mortgages below a certain size (currently $207,000 for FNMA and FHLMC and $155,250 for GNMA); larger loans, known as jumbo loans, make up the primary collateral for whole-loan CMOs.

Credit

GNMA is a U.S. government agency, and FHLMC and FNMA are government-sponsored enterprises. All three entities guarantee the full and timely[3] payment of

---

3. Early FHLMC pass-throughs, known as 75-day delay pass-throughs, carry a guarantee of full and timely payment of interest and eventual payment of principal (after disposal of the foreclosed property). FHLMC CMOs backed by these securities carry the same guarantee as the underlying pass-throughs.

all principal and interest due from pass-throughs issued under their names. GNMA securities, like U.S. Treasury securities, are backed by the full faith and credit of the U.S. government. FNMA and FHLMC, although not government agencies, are federally chartered corporations, and the market assumes an implicit U.S. government guarantee backing the agency guarantee. Securities issued by all three entities are called *agency securities.*

Although whole loans do not carry agency guarantees against default, they generally adhere to agency underwriting standards for types of documentation required, loan-to-value ratios, and income ratios. In addition, the rating agencies require significant levels of credit enhancement[4] to obtain a triple- or double-A rating. The combination of collateral quality and structural features make it highly unlikely that investors in senior classes of whole-loan CMOs will sustain credit-related losses.

Prepayments

Expected prepayment behavior is a critical factor in evaluating CMO collateral. Three collateral characteristics are necessary for evaluating collateral from a prepayment perspective: issuer/guarantor, gross weighted average coupon (WAC), and weighted average loan age (WALA) or weighted average maturity (WAM). The issuer/guarantor is important because of the details known about borrowers within different programs. For example, GNMAs are backed by loans insured by the Federal Housing Administration (FHA) or guaranteed by the Veterans Administration (VA). Borrowers under these programs tend to be less mobile than non-FHA/VA (conventional[5]) borrowers, and therefore GNMA prepayments have been slower and more stable than conventional prepayments. Whole loans, on the other hand, tend to be larger and therefore represent more wealthy or sophisticated borrowers: in falling rate environments, they have prepaid approximately 1.5–2 times faster than comparable coupon conventionals.

Gross WAC is the average of the interest rates of the mortgages backing a structure before adjusting for the servicing fee. Since the actual mortgage rate determines a borrower's refinancing incentive, gross WAC is a better indicator of prepayment potential than the net coupon of the collateral. Finally, loan age is important in determining short-term prepayments. The best measure of age is WALA, which tracks the age of the underlying mortgages. If WALA is not available, then taking the original term of the mortgages and subtracting the WAM will give an approximation.

---

4. Common whole-loan CMO credit enhancements are senior/subordinated structures and third-party pool insurance. These are described in Chapter 23.

5. A conventional mortgage is any mortgage not FHA-insured or VA-guaranteed. In practice, the market uses the term *conventional* to group loans eligible for securitization under FHLMC and FNMA programs since securities from these agencies are usually backed by non-FHA/VA mortgages.

CMO STRUCTURES

In a CMO, cash flows from one or more mortgage pass-throughs or a pool of mortgages are reallocated to multiple classes with different priority claims. The CMO is self-supporting, with the cash flows from the collateral always able to meet the cash-flow requirements of the CMO classes under any possible prepayment scenario. The CMO creation process is a dynamic one. This chapter describes the most common types of CMO classes, but dealers will frequently tailor bonds to fit investors' specific needs.

The following general points are important for any discussion of CMO structures:

- CMOs issued by FNMA and FHLMC (known collectively as conventional CMOs) carry the same guarantee as conventional pass-throughs, and CMOs issued by GNMA carry the same guarantee as GNMA pass-throughs. Both FNMA and FHLMC are authorized to issue CMOs with GNMA pass-throughs as collateral. The guarantee for a FNMA- or FHLMC-issued CMO backed by GNMA collateral is the same as that for a conventional CMO. Since credit risk is not an issue for agency CMOs, there is no need for credit enhancements in the structures.

- Whole-loan CMOs do not carry government default guarantees and are therefore usually rated by the bond rating agencies. A variety of credit enhancement techniques are employed so that most or all bonds in a structure receive a AAA rating. The most common technique today is the senior/subordinated structure, with senior bonds generally rated AAA and layers of subordinated bonds receiving lower investment- or noninvestment-grade ratings.

- Most CMO classes pay interest monthly, based on the current face amount of the class, even if it is not currently paying down principal.

- Most CMO classes have a principal lockout period during which only interest payments are received. The payment window is the period during which principal payments are received. In most cases, the lockout period and the payment window are not absolute but are affected by prepayments on the underlying collateral.

- CMO classes are structured with specific cash flow profiles and investment terms based on an assumed prepayment rate. This assumed rate, which represents the market's current expectation of future prepayments on the collateral, is known as the pricing speed.

- CMOs can be structured from collateral of any maturity. The examples that follow focus on 30-year collateral, but in the last few years CMOs have been backed by 20- and 15-year fixed-rate and 5-and 7-year balloon collateral, depending on the supply and cost of the collateral and the demand for CMOs with the particular characteristics imparted by the collateral.

CMO structures are of two major types: One provides for the redirection of principal payments only, and the other for redirection of interest as well as principal. Sequential-pay, PAC/companion, and TAC/companion structures redirect principal and are the starting point for all CMOs.

Sequential-Pay Classes

The primary purpose of the first CMOs was to bring a broader range of maturity choices to the MBS market. These CMOs—called sequential-pay, plain vanilla, or clean structures—reallocate collateral principal payments sequentially to a series of bonds. All initial principal amortization and prepayments from the collateral are paid to the shortest maturity class, or tranche, until it is fully retired; then principal payments are redirected to the next shortest class. This process continues until all classes are paid down. Exhibit 28–3 demonstrates how the principal flows of a $1 million pool of FNMA 7.5s would be distributed in a sequential-pay structure if the collateral prepaid consistently at 185 percent PSA. In this example, owners of the first class, identified as a three-year class due to its weighted average life of 3.0 years, receive all principal flows from month 1 until month 64, when their principal balance is $0. Investors who own the second class (the seven-year) receive principal flows from month 65 to month 107. Owners of the 10-year class receive principal from month 108 to month 134, and investors in the final class receive the remaining principal flows. The amount of time that each class is outstanding, as well as the months that principal payments begin and end, vary as actual prepayment experience varies from the assumed prepayment rate.

E X H I B I T   28–3

Principal Flows from a Four-Tranche Sequential-Pay Structure
($1 Million 7.5% Pool at 185% PSA)

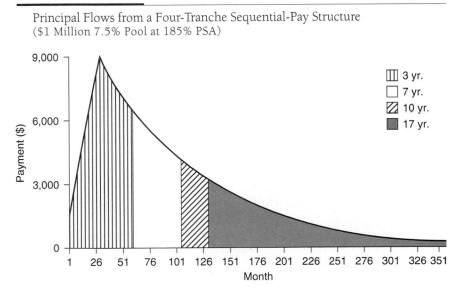

With the creation of the sequential-pay structure, capital market participants with short investment horizons were able to enter the MBS market because they could buy bonds that more closely matched their desired terms. Investors with long-term horizons also benefited because they were insulated from prepayments during the early years of a pool's life.

Planned Amortization Classes

In 1986, after a period of substantial interest-rate declines and the resulting surge of mortgage refinancing activity and prepayments, issuers began producing prepayment-protected bonds called *planned amortization classes* (PACs). These structures offered substantial protection from the reinvestment risk and weighted average-life volatility associated with prepayments.

PACs have a principal payment schedule (similar to a sinking fund mechanism) that can be maintained over a range of prepayment rates. This schedule is based on the minimum amount of principal cash flow produced by the collateral at two prepayment rates known as the *PAC bands*. For example, if the PAC bands were 95 percent PSA and 240 percent PSA, a PAC principal payment schedule could be constructed equal to the shaded area in Exhibit 28–4. The minimum amount of principal produced in the early months follows the principal payment path of the lower band (95 percent PSA), and after 116 months (where the two lines on the graph intersect), the schedule is constrained by the upper band (240 percent PSA) because principal has paid off more quickly under this scenario.

E X H I B I T   28–4

Determining the PAC Schedule
Principal Flows from $1 Million 7.5% Pool

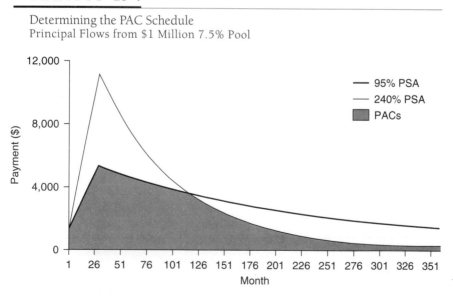

The total principal flow available under the PAC schedule determines the original amount of PACs in a structure. (In this example, PACs represent 70 percent of the structure.) If wider bands are chosen, the derived PAC schedule will be smaller; that is, there will be fewer PACs in the structure.

The PAC schedule is maintained by redirecting cash flow uncertainty to classes called *companions*. In times of fast prepayments, companions support PACs by absorbing principal payments in excess of the PAC schedule. In times of slow prepayments, amortization of the companions is delayed if there is not enough principal for the currently paying PAC. As a result of this support mechanism, faster-than-expected prepayments cause companions to pay off sooner, or contract in weighted average life. Conversely, slower-than-expected prepayments cause companions to remain outstanding longer, or extend. Exhibit 28–5 shows how the companions support the PACs at both ends of the protected prepayment range.

Total PAC and companion principal flows can be divided sequentially, much like a sequential-pay structure. Exhibit 28–6 illustrates a possible PAC/companion structure. Exhibit 28–7 shows the WALs of the PACs and companions compared to a sample sequential-pay structure and to the collateral across a range of prepayment rates. In relation to the sequential-pay bonds, the PACs are completely stable at prepayment rates within the bands and less volatile when prepayments fall outside the bands because the companions continue to provide stability. As a result, PACs are generally priced at tighter spreads to the Treasury curve, and companion bonds at wider spreads, than sequential-pay bonds with the same average lives.

E X H I B I T   28–5

PAC/Companion Profile at PAC Band Limits
Principal Flows from $1 Million 7.5% Pool

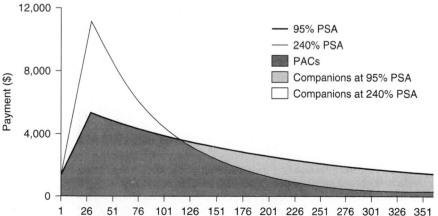

EXHIBIT 28–6

PAC/Companion Structure at 185% PSA
Principal Flows from $1 Million 7.5% Pool

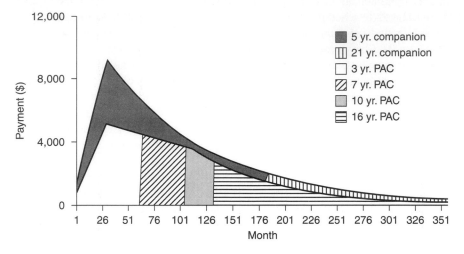

EXHIBIT 28–7

Weighted Average Lives of Alternative CMO Structures under Selected Prepayment Assumptions
Backed by 30-Year, 7.5% Pass-Throughs
        Pricing Speed: 185% PSA
        PAC Bands: 95%–240% PSA

PSA	50%	95%	185%	240%	300%
Pass-through	15.4	12.2	8.3	6.9	5.9
Sequential-pay					
A	6.6	4.5	3.0	2.6	2.3
B	16.0	11.3	7.0	5.7	4.8
C	20.9	15.9	10.0	8.1	6.7
D	26.3	23.3	17.1	14.2	11.9
PAC/Companion					
PAC A	4.3	3.0	3.0	3.0	2.9
PAC B	10.4	7.0	7.0	7.0	6.1
PAC C	14.4	10.0	10.0	10.0	8.3
PAC D	19.1	16.2	16.2	16.2	13.6
Companion E	24.6	19.2	5.0	2.8	2.2
Companion F	29.2	28.2	21.5	6.6	4.2

Effective PAC bands are important in evaluating PACs. These bands define the actual range of collateral prepayment rates over which a particular PAC class can remain on its payment schedule. An example of this distinction can be seen in the first class of the sample PAC structure. Even though the structure was constructed with bands of 95 percent to 240 percent PSA, this class is actually protected from WAL changes over a broader range of prepayment rates: The effective PAC bands are 95 percent to 288 percent PSA. All the companions in a structure must be paid off before the WAL of a PAC will shorten, so the earlier PACs in a structure generally have higher upper effective bands than the later PACs since there are more companions outstanding. The effective bands of a PAC will change over time, depending on the prepayment experience of the collateral. As discussed later, most of the time, this change (drift) is small and gradual.

PACs have been structured with varying protection levels and yield trade-offs. The most common variants are Type II/Type III PACs and super/subordinate PACs.

Type II and Type III PACs

As the CMO marketplace grew more sophisticated, investors sought bonds that would offer some prepayment protection and earn higher cash-flow yields than generic PACs. The resulting innovation was the Type II PAC, structured from companion cash flows in a PAC/companion structure. These bonds have narrower prepayment protection bands than standard PACs, but as long as prepayments stay within the bands, they pay down according to a schedule, much like regular PACs. Because Type II PACs are second in priority to PACs, the remaining companion bonds provide support even if prepayments are outside the bands. If extended periods of high prepayments cause the companions in a structure to be paid off, the remaining Type II PACs become companions to the PACs, with the potential WAL volatility of companion bonds.

Exhibit 28–8A shows the addition of Type II PACs (125 percent –220 percent PSA bands) to the PAC/companion structure illustrated in Exhibit 28–5. The PAC principal flow has not changed, and the Type II PACs are layered on top of the PACs.

Another layer of PACs, with narrower bands, is sometimes created as well. These securities, known as Type III PACs, act as support for PACs and Type II PACs in a structure but retain some stability because of the companions that remain.

Super/Subordinate PACs

The prepayment experience of 1992–1993 caused many investors to view MBSs as more callable than they had previously thought and to demand significantly higher levels of prepayment protection. In early 1993, Lehman Brothers responded by issuing the first super/subordinated PAC structure. In this structure, standard PACs are divided into super and subordinate (sub-) PACs. By rearranging the cash flow priorities within the total PAC class, the super PACs receive additional prepayment stability from the sub-PACs and therefore have much wider protection bands.

E X H I B I T   28–8

PAC/Companion Structure
Principal Flows from $1 Million 7.5% Pool

A. With Type II PACs

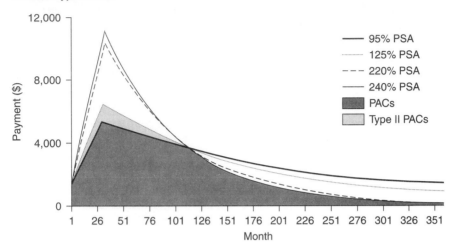

B. With Super and Sub-PACs

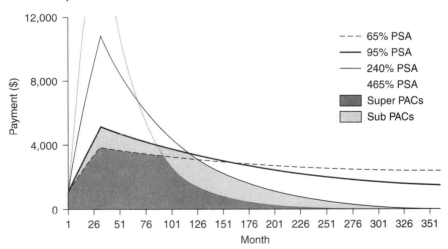

Since both super- and sub-PAC classes are created from the total PAC cash flows and generally have all the structure's companions available to support them, sub-PACs offer more protection from average-life volatility than similar average-life Type II or Type III PACs in the same structure. This relationship can be seen in FHLMC 1499, which has three-year super, sub-, and Type III PACs. The effective bands are 70 percent to 625 percent PSA on the super PAC, 100 percent to 250 percent PSA on the sub-PAC, and 140 percent to 220 percent PSA on the Type III PAC. Sub-PACs trade at higher yields than PACs because they can have more average-life volatility at prepayment rates outside their protection bands.

Exhibit 28–8B shows super and sub-PACs in the example PAC/companion structure. The combined principal flows of the super and sub-PACs are equivalent to the original PAC principal flows.

Targeted Amortization Classes

Targeted amortization classes (TACs) were introduced to offer investors a pre-payment-protected class at wider spreads than PACs. Like PACs, TACs repay principal according to a schedule as long as prepayments remain within a range. If the principal cash flow from the collateral exceeds the TAC schedule, the excess is allocated to TAC companion classes. Unlike PACs, TACs do not provide protection against WAL extension if prepayments fall below the speed necessary to maintain the TAC schedule. Therefore, the typical TAC can be viewed as a PAC with a lower band equal to the CMO pricing speed and an upper band similar to that of PACs backed by comparable collateral. In falling/low interest-rate environments, investors are primarily concerned that increasing prepayments will shorten average life due to increasing prepayments. Many investors are willing to forego the protection against extension offered by PACs in exchange for the higher yields of TACs.

Companions

Companion is a general term in the CMO market for a class that provides prepayment protection for another class. In evaluating companions (also known as *support classes*), it is important to review the rest of the CMO structure; the behavior of a particular companion class is influenced by the class(es) it supports. For instance, if the companion is supporting a TAC, it will have less extension risk than a PAC companion because the TAC is not protected from extension. In addition, other bonds in the structure may affect the companion's potential performance. For example, the presence of Type II PACs in a structure indicates that part of the original companions is being traded in a more stable form, leaving the remaining companions more volatile. Another important consideration for companions is the collateral backing the CMO. If the pass-throughs have a shorter maturity than 30 years, such as 15-year or balloon MBSs, the PACs in the structure will require less extension protection. Therefore, there will be fewer companions in the structure than in a 30-year structure with the same PAC bands, and the companions will have less extension risk. Finally, a class's sensitivity to prepayments should be viewed in a yield or total return context. Because prepayments are paid at par, faster-than-expected prepayments will have a positive effect on a discount bond's yield, and slower-than-expected prepayments will have a positive effect on a premium bond's yield. On a total return basis (see Evaluating CMOs below for details on total return calculation), these generalizations will usually apply as well, although the interaction between prepayments, average life, and reinvestment rate may offset the effects of being repaid at par.

The CMO classes that have been reviewed (sequential-pay, PAC, TAC, and companion) are structures that provide for the redirection of principal payments. The classes that follow address the redirection of interest payments as well. These classes usually rely on one of the above structures to reallocate principal payments.

Z Bonds

The Z bond is a CMO class with a period of principal and interest lockout. It typically takes the place of a coupon-bearing class at or near the end of a CMO structure. When the CMO is originally issued, the Z bond has a face amount significantly lower than it would have if it were an interest-bearing class. Each month that the Z is outstanding, it generates coupon cash flows, like any other bond in the structure; however, as long as the Z class is not paying out principal, this coupon flow is used to pay down other classes. The Z gets credit for the foregone interest payments through increases to its principal balance, known as *accretion*. Once the classes preceding the Z bond are fully paid down, it begins to receive principal and interest.

The Z bond in Exhibit 28–9 begins with a face amount of $118,000. The coupon in the first month ($118,000 × 7.5%/12 = $737.50) is paid as a prepayment

E X H I B I T   28–9

Sample Z-Bond Cash Flows
In Sequential-Pay/Z Bond Structure
Backed by 30-Year, 7.5% Pass-Throughs($)

Month	Beginning Balance	Coupon Accretion	Coupon Cash Flow	Amortiz./ Prepay.	Ending Balance	Total Cash Flows
1	118,000.00	737.50	0.00	0.00	118,737.50	0
2	118,737.50	742.11	0.00	0.00	119,479.61	0
3	119,479.61	746.75	0.00	0.00	120,226.36	0
.	.	.	.	.	.	0
.	.	.	.	.	.	0
131	265,245.57	1,657.78	0.00	0.00	266,903.35	0
132	266,903.35	1,668.15	0.00	0.00	268,571.50	0
133	268,571.50	1,678.57	0.00	47.44	270,202.63	47.44
134	270,202.63	0.00	1,688.77	3,131.55	267,071.08	4,820.31
135	267,071.08	0.00	1,669.19	3,099.51	263,971.57	4,768.70

to the first class in the structure, and the Z bond accretes that amount. The accretion amounts increase as the principal amount (on which coupon cash flows are calculated) grows. In month 133, the final sequential-pay class receives its last principal payment, which includes $1,678.57 from the Z coupon. The collateral has produced an additional $47.44 in principal cash flows that month, and since the Z is the only outstanding class, it receives the principal payment. The Z bond balance has grown to $270,203. Since the Z is the only remaining class from month 134 on, it receives all principal and interest payments generated by the collateral.

In a simple sequential-pay/Z bond structure, the Z accelerates the principal repayments of the sequential-pay bonds. As a result, restructuring a sequential-pay bond as a Z allows for larger sequential-pay classes with the same WALs as the original classes. Since a portion of the principal payments of these sequential-pay bonds is coming from the Z coupon flows (which do not vary until the Z begins amortizing), average-life volatility is decreased in the sequential-pay classes. In fact, in the sample structure, all bonds including the Z have less average-life volatility when the Z is introduced to the structure (see Exhibit 28–10). The Z's impact is clearest in the scenario where prepayments fall from 185 percent PSA to 95 percent PSA: The change in average life is 10 percent to 23 percent lower for all bonds than in the basic sequential-pay structure.

Although the Z structure appears to have reduced uncertainty across the board, it is important to look at the effective durations of the bonds as well.

EXHIBIT 28–10

Weighted Average Lives of Alternative Sequential-Pay Structures under Selected Prepayment Assumptions
Backed by 30-Year, 7.5% Pass-Throughs
Pricing Speed: 185% PSA

PSA	95%	185%	240%
Sequential-Pay			
A	4.5	3.0	2.6
B	11.3	7.0	5.7
C	15.9	10.0	8.1
D	23.3	17.1	14.2
Sequential-Pay/Z			
A	4.2	3.0	2.6
B	10.1	7.0	5.9
C	13.5	9.9	8.5
Z	21.5	17.0	14.8

EXHIBIT 28-11

Effective Durations of Alternative Sequential-Pay
Structures
Backed by 30-Year, 7.5% Pass-Throughs

Class	Sequential-Pay	Sequential-Pay with Z
A	1.53 years	1.69 years
B	6.80	6.47
C	8.58	8.16
D/Z	10.19	18.47

Exhibit 28–11 shows that the durations of the first three sequential-pay bonds do not change substantially when the last class is replaced with a Z. The Z bond, on the other hand, has almost twice the effective duration of the sequential-pay bond that it replaced, moving from 10.2 years to 18.5 years. The price of the Z is highly sensitive to interest-rate movements and the resulting changes in prepayment rates because its ultimate principal balance depends on total accretions credited by the time it begins to pay down. Although WAL volatility has decreased, the price sensitivity of the last class is increased dramatically by making it a Z.

Z bonds offer much of the appeal of zero coupon Treasury strips: There is no reinvestment risk during the accretion phase. In addition, Z bonds offer higher yields than comparable WAL Treasury zeros.

Accretion-Directed Classes

In the falling interest-rate environment that has characterized most of the CMO era, many structures have been developed to protect investors from higher-than-anticipated prepayments. *Accretion-directed* (AD) bonds are designed to protect against extension in average life if rates rise and prepayments are lower than expected. These bonds, also known as *very accurately defined maturity* (VADM) *bonds,* derive all their cash flows from the interest accretions of a Z class. Because there is no deviation in Z accretions until the Z bond begins to pay down, VADMs do not extend even if there are no prepayments. VADMs are also protected from prepayment increases because the Z bonds that support them tend to be the last classes to begin repaying principal.

Floaters and Inverse Floaters

The first floating-rate CMO class was issued by Shearson Lehman Brothers in 1986. These classes are created by dividing a fixed-rate class into a floater and an inverse floater. The bonds take their principal paydown rules from the underlying fixed-rate class. A floater/inverse combination can be produced from a sequential-pay class, PAC, TAC, companion, or other coupon-bearing class. The coupon of the floater is reset periodically (usually monthly) at a specified spread, or margin, over an index. Typical indices include LIBOR, the Federal Home Loan Bank 11th District Cost of Funds Index (COFI), and various maturities of the constant maturity Treasury (CMT) series. The coupon of the inverse floater moves inversely with the index. Floaters and inverses have caps and floors that set the maximum and minimum coupons allowable on the bonds. These caps and floors may be explicit (e.g., a floater cap of 10 percent) or implicit (a floater's floor would equal the floater's margin if the underlying index fell to 0 percent) and may either be constant throughout the life of the bond or change according to a predetermined schedule.

Floaters are usually designed to be sold at par; their caps and margins are dictated by the option and swap markets and by expectations about the performance of the underlying fixed-rate CMO class. Floaters have many natural buyers, such as banks, which prefer the limited interest-rate risk that an adjustable-rate security provides. Since inverse floater coupons move in the opposite direction from their index, investors generally require higher yields for inverses than for floaters or the underlying fixed-rate classes. To increase the yield, cap, and initial coupon, inverses are often structured with multipliers in the coupon formulas that magnify movements in the underlying index.

Exhibit 28–12 shows how a floater and an inverse can be created from a fixed-rate bond. Both floater and inverse have coupon formulas tied to COFI; the

E X H I B I T   28–12

Creating a Floater and Inverse
$120MM 5-Year, 7.5% Companion Becomes . . .
$80MM 5-Year Companion COFI Floater (Coupon = COFI + 65 bp, 10% Cap)
$40MM 5-Year Companion COFI Inverse (Coupon = 21.20% – 2 × COFI, 2.50% Floor)

| | Coupon | | Wt. Avg. |
COFI Index	Floater	Inverse	Coupon
0.00%	0.65%	21.20%	7.50%
2.00	2.65	17.20	7.50
4.00	4.65	13.20	7.50
6.00	6.65	9.20	7.50
8.00	8.65	5.20	7.50
9.35	10.00	2.50	7.50
10.00	10.00	2.50	7.50
12.00	10.00	2.50	7.50

floater coupon adjusts at COFI + 65 basis points with a 10 percent interest-rate cap, and the inverse coupon, which has a multiplier of 2, adjusts at $21.20 - 2 \times$ COFI with a 2.50 percent floor. In this example, the floater class is twice the size of the inverse floater. When a multiplier greater than 1 is used to set the inverse floater's coupon, the face amount of the inverse must be smaller than the floater to keep the weighted average of the two coupons equal to the fixed-rate bond coupon.

Interest- and Principal-Only Strips

Any pool of coupon-bearing collateral can be stripped into interest-only (IO) and principal-only (PO) segments and sold separately. Exhibit 28–13A illustrates the interest cash flows for 7.5 percent collateral at various prepayment rates. The total amount of interest flow varies depending on the prepayment rate. Since interest cash flows exist only if principal remains outstanding, IOs benefit from slowing prepayments. POs represent a stream of principal payments purchased at a discount. If prepayments rise, discounted principal flows are received at par earlier than expected, improving the security's performance. Exhibit 28–13B illustrates principal cash flows from the collateral. Here the total flows will always equal the face amount of the collateral, but the prepayment rate affects the timing and value of the flows. IOs are bearish securities and usually have negative durations (their prices rise as rates rise); POs are bullish securities with long positive durations.

The same principles for stripping pools of collateral can be applied to individual CMO classes or to blocks of classes within a single structure. CMO strips may represent 100 percent of the interest or principal flows; or, more commonly, only a portion of the interest may be stripped, resulting in an IO and a reduced-coupon fixed-rate bond. For example, if a dealer is structuring a PAC class with a 7.5 percent coupon but investors are more willing to buy the class if it has a 7 percent coupon, a 50-bp PAC IO can be stripped from the class and sold separately.[6] Structurers may also strip part of the coupon flows from the entire block of collateral before dividing it into classes. This method produces an IO-ette security and is employed to lower the coupons on all bonds in a structure.

---

6. Until recently, all REMIC IO classes had to be sold with some small amount of principal, called a *nominal balance*. To generate the cash flows for bonds with this structure, the nominal balance is amortized and prepaid according to the type of bond. Since the balance is small, the coupon is extremely large. IOs sold this way tend to have multiple-digit coupons (e.g., 1183 percent) and high dollar prices (e.g., 3626-12). Alternatively, IOs may be based on a notional balance. Here, the IO tranche has no principal balance and its coupon flows are calculated on the declining balance of the underlying principal-bearing tranche. No principal cash flows are paid to the IO holder. This procedure results in MBS-like coupons (7.5 percent, 8 percent, etc.) or in basis-point coupons (e.g., 100 bps) and below-par prices. These two techniques result in equivalent investment amounts and cash flows. The difference in prices (3626-12 versus 18-02, for example) does not denote any relative value difference between IOs priced with one method or the other.

E X H I B I T   28–13

A. Interest Flows from $1 Million 7.5% Pool

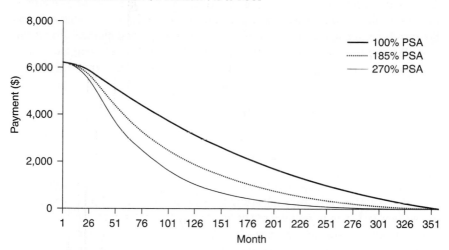

B. Principal Flows from $1 Million 7.5% Pool

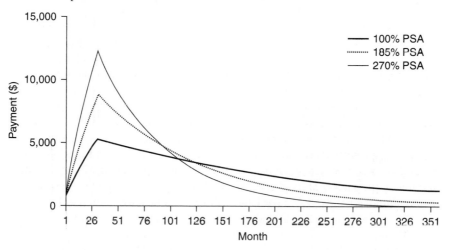

Strips made from CMO bonds require more analysis than regular IOs and POs. In the above example, since the IO has been stripped from a PAC class, it will be insulated from cash flow changes as long as prepayments remain within the PAC bands. Only if the PAC begins to pay down principal early will the holder of the PAC IO experience the negative effects of prepayments. An investor should look to the underlying class that defines the rules for principal paydown. Since prepayments are the primary consideration in evaluating stripped securities, the behavior of the underlying class plays a significant role in the overall analysis.

Another type of strip results from the creation of whole-loan CMOs. For agency CMOs, the coupon of the collateral (the pass-throughs) is fixed; for whole-loan CMOs, the collateral coupon is a weighted average of all the individual mortgage coupons (which may vary by 100 bps or more). As loans prepay, the weighted-average coupon (WAC) of the collateral can change. To be sure that all fixed-rate bonds in a structure receive their allotted coupons, issuers often split off part of the principal or interest cash flow from individual mortgages in a pool, leaving a block of collateral with a stable WAC. These strips of principal or interest are combined into WAC POs or WAC IOs and trade much like trust POs and IOs.

PAC BAND DRIFT

Effective PAC bands change (drift) over time, even if prepayments remain within the initial bands. Band drift results from the interaction of actual prepayments and the current PAC bands, and the resulting changes in collateral balance and relative PAC and companion balances. The band drift of a particular PAC can be viewed under three scenarios: when prepayments are within the current effective bands, when prepayments are above the current upper band, and when prepayments are below the current lower band.

If prepayments are within the bands, the currently paying PAC will pay on schedule. Any additional prepayments will go to the currently paying companion. Over time, both upper and lower bands will drift up. This happens because any prepayment within the bands is also lower than the upper band and higher than the lower band. From the point of view of the upper band, prepayments have been slower than expected and more companions are available to absorb high prepayments in the future. Thus, the upper band rises. From the point of view of the lower band, prepayments have been faster than expected and less collateral is outstanding to produce principal flows. If prepayments slow to the original lower band, there may not be enough principal coming in to pay the PACs on schedule, and they will extend. Thus, the lower band rises as well. For most prepayment rates within the bands, the upper band will rise at a faster rate than the lower, so prepayments within the bands tend to cause the bands to widen over time.

If prepayments are above the current upper band, the PAC will continue to pay on schedule until all companions are retired. If the fast prepayments are only temporary, there will probably be little impact on the bands. If prepayments remain above the upper band, however, the upper and lower bands will begin to converge. This happens because there are fewer companions available to absorb fast prepayments and less collateral outstanding to generate principal cash flows if prepayments slow. The bands will converge once all companions have been retired, and the PAC will pay like a sequential-pay class from that point.

If prepayments are below the current lower band, the currently paying PAC will not be able to pay according to its schedule since there will be no other principal flows coming into the structure that can be redirected to the PAC. This is typically a temporary situation because the lower band is usually substantially lower than the base prepayment rate expected from simple housing turnover and because most PACs have priority over all subsequent cash flows until they are back on schedule. Prepayments below the current lower band cause the upper band to rise (more companions are available to absorb faster prepayments in the future) and may cause the lower band to rise slightly (since most PACs have catch-up features, a higher future prepayment rate is necessary to put the PAC back on schedule).

Most band drift is small and gradual. Large changes to PAC bands will occur only if prepayments are significantly outside the bands, or if they remain near either of the bands for a long period of time. Effective bands represent the range of prepayment rates that the collateral can experience for its remaining life and still maintain the payment schedule for a specific PAC. Temporary movements outside the bands will not affect PAC cash flows as long as companion cash flows and principal balances are available to support them.

CMO STRUCTURING EXAMPLE

In this section, we follow a structurer through the process of creating a multiclass CMO. Diagrams (not drawn to scale) are included to illustrate the structures.

The structurer begins with a block of collateral—in this case FNMA 7.5s (Exhibit 28–14a). If the market expects interest rates and prepayments to be stable, the structurer may construct a sequential-pay CMO (Exhibit 28–14b). If investors are concerned about rates rising and prepayments slowing (e.g., extension risk), the structurer may produce the last class as a Z bond (Exhibit 28–14c). This allows him to apply the Z coupon flows as principal payments to the early sequential-pay classes or to create VADMs that offer the strongest extension protection (Exhibit 28–14d). If the collateral is priced at a premium, the structurer may strip some interest cash flows before creating the rest of the classes. This allows the creation of discount or par bonds. Figure 28–14e shows the FNMA 7.5s after a 50-bp IO-ette is stripped and sold separately. The remaining collateral now has a 7 percent coupon and can be structured in any way that the original 7.5s could have been.

If the market expects high interest-rate and prepayment volatility, the structurer will likely create PAC/companion or TAC/companion CMOs. Exhibit 28–14f illustrates the initial allocation of cash flows to PACs and companions. Once the amount of principal that can be attributed to PACs or companions is identified, these classes go through the sequential-pay structuring process to create PACs and companions of various average lives (Exhibit 28–14g). Individual classes from any of these structures can be further divided. If a foreign bank wants to purchase a LIBOR-based floater with a relatively high margin and a five-year average life, for example, the structurer can produce a bond with the desired characteristics from the five-year companion class (Exhibit 28–14h) that will offer a higher yield than noncompanion tranches. At the same time, the structurer

E X H I B I T   28–14

CMO Structuring Example
FNMA 7.5% Collateral

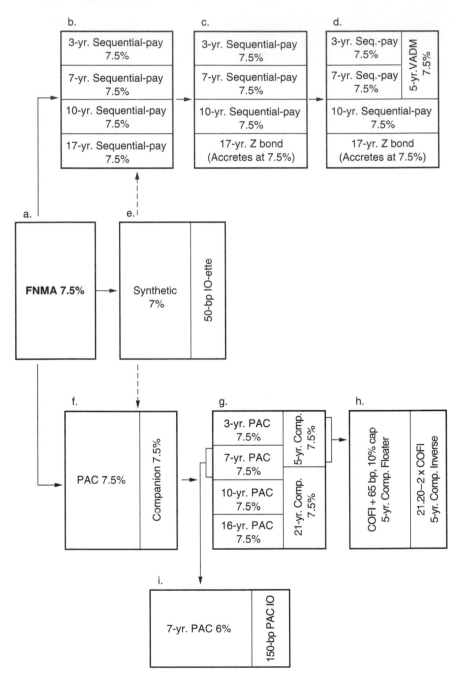

will look at the inverse floater market to determine yield and coupon (set by adjusting the multiplier) for the resulting LIBOR inverse floater. On the PAC side, there may be an investor who wants to purchase a seven-year PAC with a 6 percent coupon (and therefore a lower price) as protection from the risk of high prepayments on premium-priced bonds. If so, the structurer can split the seven-year PAC into a 150-bp PAC IO and a 6 percent PAC (Exhibit 28–14i). These are a few examples of the flexibility in the structuring process. The customizable nature of many CMO classes is a key to the popularity of these bonds.

REGULATORY DEVELOPMENTS AFFECTING CMOS

When FHLMC issued the first CMO in 1983, multiclass mortgage securities were subject to various regulatory constraints. For example, federal tax law treated payments from a multiclass trust as equity dividends. Unlike debt payments, dividend payments are not tax deductible. Therefore, the issuer who established a multiclass trust was unable to claim a tax deduction for interest paid to security holders to offset taxes on interest received from the underlying collateral. The resulting double taxation—interest income was taxed at both the trust and investor level—made the transaction economically impractical.

The CMO avoided this problem because it was an offering of collateralized debt. Therefore, tax deductions for interest paid to certificate holders offset the tax liability on interest received from the underlying collateral. However, CMOs were subject to other constraints to ensure that they were treated as debt instead of equity for tax purposes. Issuers had to maintain a portion of residual interests, record CMOs as liabilities in their financial statements, and satisfy minimum capital requirements. Issuers also had to include a call provision, forcing them to price longer maturity bonds at a wider spread to the Treasury curve. In addition, issuers had to structure a mismatch between receipts on the underlying mortgages and payments to the CMO bondholders; generally they passed monthly collateral payments through to bondholders on a quarterly basis. These constraints made it difficult to issue CMOs efficiently.

Toward the end of 1985, issuers overcame some of these obstacles by issuing CMOs through an owner's trust. This mechanism allowed issuers to sell their residual interests and remove the debt from their books. The owner's trust, however, was not conducive to a liquid market because residual buyers became personally liable for the CMO: If the cash flow from the collateral was insufficient to pay regular interest holders, residual owners had to cover the shortage. As a result, issuers could sell residual interests only to investors capable of meeting ongoing net worth tests. Although these tests were different for each transaction, they all effectively limited potential buyers to institutional investors with adequate net worth.

The 1986 Tax Reform Act addressed these problems by defining a new issuance vehicle: the real estate mortgage investment conduit (REMIC). To qualify for REMIC status, a multiclass offering can have multiple classes of regular interests but only one class of residual interest. The legislation defines a regular interest as a fixed principal amount with periodic interest payments or accruals on the outstanding principal balance. Buyers of regular interests are taxed as holders of debt obligations. A residual interest consists entirely of pro rata payments (if any). Buyers of residual interests are taxed based on the taxable income of the REMIC. Taxable income is the excess collateral and reinvestment income over REMIC regular interest and servicing expenses.

REMIC legislation was a milestone in the development of multiclass mortgage securities because it allowed issuers to adopt whatever structure best exploited particular economic, financial, or accounting considerations. For tax purposes, all conduits qualifying for REMIC status are treated equally whether they structure a multiclass mortgage transaction as a borrowing collateralized by mortgages or as a sale of the underlying mortgages. In either case, only the investors and residual holders are subject to tax, not the conduit itself. REMIC legislation also allows issuers to sell the entire residual class, and since 1987 it has permitted issuers to sell floating-rate classes. This flexibility has allowed issuers to develop new products, particularly since repeated interest-rate declines since 1982 have led investors to seek products with either improved call protection or higher risk/reward opportunities.

Following a five-year phaseout of all previous structures that ended in 1991, all issuers of multiclass mortgage securities must now use REMICs. However, from the investor's perspective, there is little difference between CMO and REMIC products; in either case, the investor is buying multiclass mortgage securities. Consequently, the terms *CMO* and *REMIC* are often used interchangeably, even though they are crucially different tax vehicles from the issuer's perspective.

Until 1988, private issuers (primarily investment bankers and home builders) accounted for almost the entire supply of multiclass mortgage securities. These issuers generally used agency collateral to obtain the highest ratings from the nationally recognized rating agencies. However, the credit quality of the issuer was also important insofar as cash flows from the underlying collateral might be insufficient to cover obligations to all bondholders. Therefore, issuers had to take extra measures, such as overcollateralizing the bonds or buying insurance, to obtain high investment-grade credit ratings.

In 1988, FHLMC and FNMA gained full authorization to issue REMICs. Their REMICs automatically obtained government agency status, regardless of the underlying collateral. Therefore, FHLMC and FNMA were not subject to the credit-enhancing constraints imposed on private issuers, giving them a crucial market advantage. Agency CMOs jumped from only 2 percent of total CMO issuance in 1987 to 33 percent in 1988 and 83 percent in 1989. In 1992, agencies issued 85 percent of CMOs.

By 1988, regulatory and market developments had stimulated demand for multiclass mortgage securities. In July 1988, the Basle Committee on Banking Regulations and Supervisory Practices set forth risk-based capital guidelines to ensure the fiscal stability of the international banking infrastructure by requiring minimum capital levels as a percentage of assets—loans made and securities purchased—weighted according to risk classification. Since agency-issued REMICs offer high yields in relation to their 20% risk weighting, they became increasingly popular with banks and thrifts. Less volatile REMIC products, such as floaters and short and intermediate maturity PACs and TACs, were most appropriate since banks and thrifts needed to match assets with liabilities of similar maturities.

Since about 1988, insurance companies have looked to the REMIC market for assets to offset intermediate to long-term liabilities. Given the poor performance of real estate holdings and commercial mortgages, insurance companies needed to diversify their portfolios, and REMICs offered an attractive alternative because of their credit quality and spread levels. At year-end 1993, life insurance companies implemented their own risk-based capital requirements, which provided an additional incentive to hold mortgages in securitized form.

EVALUATING CMOS

The most common way to communicate the value and performance expectations of a CMO bond is the yield table, showing cash flow yields under a series of prepayment rate assumptions. Computer models that produce yield tables take price(s) and prepayment rates as inputs (and index levels, in the case of floaters and inverse floaters), and calculate yields and spreads, average lives, durations, and payment windows for each prepayment assumption. With this information, the investor can determine the level of prepayment protection offered by the bond, the average life volatility for given changes in collateral prepayment rates, the impact of prepayments on yields, and the time over which principal is likely to be received. Exhibits 28–15 and 28–16 are yield tables for the three-year sequential-pay and PAC bonds in the earlier examples. The yield changes for the sequential-pay bond under each prepayment scenario, but the PAC yield is stable from 95 percent PSA to 285 percent PSA. The average life and duration of the PAC are more stable at prepayment rates outside the PAC bands as well. The payment windows show when the bonds will begin to pay principal and when the final payment will occur under each prepayment scenario. Finally, a comparison of the two tables shows that in the base case the sequential-pay bond is

E X H I B I T   28–15

Yield Table for 3-Year Sequential-Pay Class (Price—104-04)

| PSA | Base Case | | | | | | | |
	35%	95%	135%	185%	200%	240%	285%	335%
Yield(%)/Spread(bp)	6.79/105	6.37/111	6.13/127	5.86/140	5.79/133	5.61/114	5.42/143	5.24/125
Avg. life (yr.)	7.85	4.54	3.64	3.00	2.86	2.57	2.33	2.13
Mod. dur. (yr.)	5.54	3.67	3.06	2.60	2.49	2.27	2.08	1.92
Windows (yr.)	0.1–14.7	0.1–8.6	0.1–6.7	0.1–5.3	0.1–5.1	0.1–4.4	0.1–3.9	0.1–3.5
Benchmark Tsy.	7-yr.	5-yr.	4-yr.	3-yr.	3-yr.	3-yr.	2-yr.	2-yr.

E X H I B I T   28–16

Yield Table for 3-Year PAC (Price—106-04)

	Base Case							
PSA	35%	95%	135%	185%	200%	240%	285%	335%
Yield(%)/Spread (bp)	6.04/78	5.31/85	5.18/72	5.18/72	5.18/72	5.18/72	5.18/72	5.13/67
Avg. life (yr.)	5.07	3.00	3.00	3.00	3.00	3.00	3.00	2.92
Mod. dur. (yr.)	4.04	2.62	2.62	2.62	2.62	2.62	2.62	2.56
Windows (yr.)	0.1–9.3	0.1–5.2	0.1–5.2	0.1–5.2	0.1–5.2	0.1–5.2	0.1–5.2	0.1–4.7
Benchmark Tsy.	5-yr.	3-yr.	3-yr.	3-yr.	3-yr.	3-yr.	3-yr.	3-yr.

being offered at nearly double the spread of the PAC to compensate investors for its additional average-life volatility.

Total return scenario analysis may also be used to evaluate CMOs. It addresses two drawbacks of the cash-flow yield approach: Many investors do not expect to hold their securities to maturity, and the reinvestment assumption in the cash flow yield analysis—that all cash flows are reinvested at the security's yield—is usually unrealistic. Total return calculations cover a specific investment period and make an assumption about the bond's price at the end of the period (the horizon). They further assume a reinvestment rate and prepayment rate for the period to generate cash flows. Total return is the change in market value of the bond (reflecting price changes and principal paydown) plus the cumulative value of all cash flows and reinvestment proceeds as of the horizon date, divided by the initial market value. Although total return scenario analysis involves several assumptions, it is often a desirable addition to the yield tables, especially if the investment period is expected to be relatively short.

Option-adjusted spread (OAS) analysis is another relative value measurement tool used by fixed income market participants. Based on multiple interest-rate simulations and the resulting prepayments predicted by a prepayment model, the cash flows of a callable bond are analyzed to calculate the average spread to the Treasury spot curve implied by the security's current price. Since this process nets out the impact of prepayments (partial calls) of MBSs, OAS allows direct comparisons among MBSs and other callable and noncallable fixed income securities. Using current OAS to calculate the horizon price of a CMO is a common method in total return analysis. This allows the investor to avoid making a direct horizon price assumption and incorporates more information (such as the shape of the yield curve) into the analysis.

THE CMO/COLLATERAL PRICING RELATIONSHIP

Because of strong investor demand for CMOs, a large percentage of newly issued pass-throughs and jumbo mortgages has gone into CMO structures in recent years. Investor preference for structured mortgage securities has led to a highly efficient pricing relationship between the CMO and collateral sectors.

The source of the CMO/collateral pricing relationship is the interplay between the yield curve and spreads on collateral and CMOs. Exhibit 28–17 shows the projected yields and payment windows of each bond in a four-class, sequential-pay CMO and the yield of the collateral. Each bond's yield is quoted as a spread to the on-the-run Treasury with a maturity closest to the bond's average life. In this example, the three-year CMO class has a lower yield than the collateral. The 7-year yield is about equal to, and the 10- and 17-year yields are higher than, the yield of the collateral. When the yield curve is positively sloped, earlier classes are generally offered at lower yields than later classes. Assuming that spreads remain constant, a steepening of the yield curve results in a greater difference between the yields of shorter and longer classes.

By definition, the price of an individual CMO bond represents the present value of the bond's projected cash flows, using the bond's yield as the discount rate. Therefore, the cash flows of any class with a lower yield than the collateral will be priced using a lower discount rate than the single discount rate used to price all the collateral cash flows. This means that this portion of the pass-through's cash flows will have a higher value when structured as part of a CMO. Likewise, the cash flows of bonds with yields higher than the collateral yield will be priced with a higher discount rate than the collateral, leading to lower valuations in relation to collateral cash flows.

Over time, as CMOs are created using a particular collateral type and coupon, supply and demand forces cause the collateral spread to tighten and/or the spreads of the CMO classes to widen until there is no profit in issuing the CMO. If collateral is too expensive (rich) to make the creation of CMO bonds

EXHIBIT 28–17

Yields on Collateral and Sequential-Pay CMO Tranches

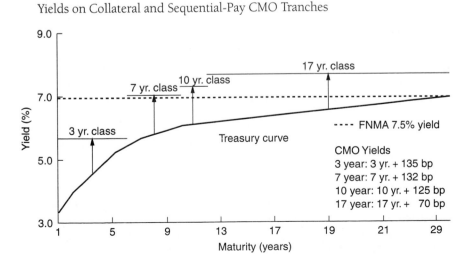

economic, CMO issuance will slow until pass-through spreads widen and/or CMO spreads tighten. Because of temporary changes in market preference for structured products, collateral can trade at levels too rich to create CMOs. However, in equilibrium, it is rare for CMOs to trade rich to collateral, since collateral spreads will quickly tighten as more CMOs are issued.

CMO TRADING AND CLEARING

Generally, CMO bonds are offered on the basis of a yield (more accurately, a spread over the yield of a benchmark Treasury) and a prepayment assumption. A price is calculated from this information and is agreed upon by both parties to the trade. The CMO market convention is corporate settlement (three business days after the trade date) unless the CMO is a new issue. In the case of a new issue, the settlement date for all the CMO classes is usually one to three months after the CMO is initially offered for sale. This period allows dealers to accumulate the collateral that will back the CMO. Whether the CMO bond is a new offering or a previously traded security, interest begins accruing on the first day of the settlement month. An exception to this rule is that most floating-rate CMO bonds begin accruing interest on the previous month's payment date so that they more closely resemble floating-rate notes.

Because of their credit quality, most CMOs can be used in repurchase and reverse repurchase agreements.

Most agency CMO trades are cleared through electronic book-entry transfers such as Fedwire, a clearing system maintained by the Federal Reserve. This system also handles monthly principal and interest payments, which are paid to the investor who holds the security on the record date (generally the last calendar day of the month). Whole-loan CMO trades are cleared through physical delivery or electronic book entry, depending on the issuer. Most MBSs pay with a delay—the cash flows earned during one month are paid out a fixed number of days after the end of the month to give mortgage servicers time to collect payments. Exhibit 28–18 identifies payment delays for the various combinations of CMO issuers and collateral types.

E X H I B I T   28–18

Payment Delays for CMO Issuers and Collateral Types

CMO Issuer	Collateral Type	Payment Delay
GNMA	GNMA	15 days after the record date
FHLMC	FHLMC 75-day	45 days after the record date*
FHLMC	FHLMC Gold	15 days after the record date
FHLMC	GNMA	25 days after the record date
FNMA	FNMA	25 days after the record date
FNMA	GNMA	15 days after the record date
Nonagency	Whole loans	25 days after the record date**

*Record date is the last calendar day of each month.
**May vary by issuer.

CONCLUSION

A consistent theme in the CMO market throughout the past decade has been innovation in response to investor needs. As the CMO market has grown more liquid, larger structures have become feasible, providing the flexibility to develop new products. These products have refined the distribution of prepayment uncertainty and risk/reward opportunities to meet the increasingly specialized needs and objectives of investors. The range of options in the CMO market will continue to grow as both originators and investors adapt to a continually changing marketplace.

⑥   # NONAGENCY CMOS*

Frank J. Fabozzi, Ph.D., CFA
Adjunct Professor of Finance
School of Management
Yale University

David Yuen, CFA
Director of Research
Structured Capital Management

Chuck Ramsey
Managing Director
Structured Capital Management
and CEO
Mortgage Risk Assessment Corp.

Frank R. Ramirez
Managing Director
Structured Capital Management

All the cash flow structures found in agency CMOs as described in the previous chapter are also applicable to nonagency or whole-loan CMO structures. The major additional element in structuring nonagency CMOs is credit enhancement. The investor in a whole-loan CMO is exposed to both prepayment risk and credit risk. Other elements include compensating interest payments, weighted average coupon dispersions, and clean-up call provisions. In this chapter, we will discuss various credit enhancement structures, compensating interest payments, clean-up call provisions, and the impact of coupon dispersions. In addition, we will discuss the PSA standard default assumption benchmark and whole-loan prepayment behavior.

CREDIT ENHANCEMENTS

Four nationally recognized statistical rating organizations rate whole-loan CMOs: Standard & Poor's Corporation, Moody's Investors Service, Fitch Investors Ser-

---

*This chapter is adapted from chapters by Frank J. Fabozzi, Chuck Ramsey, and Frank R. Ramirez (with the assistance of David Yuen); *Collateralized Mortgage Obligations: Structures & Analysis* (New Hope, PA; Frank J. Fabozzi Associates, 1994).

vice, and Duff & Phelps Credit Rating Company. The primary factors these rating organizations consider in assigning a rating are the type of property (single-family residences, condominiums), the type of loan (fixed-rate level payment, adjustable rate, balloon), the term of the loans, the geographical dispersion of the loans, the loan size (conforming loans, jumbo loans), the amount of seasoning of the loan, and the purpose of the loan (purchase or refinancing). Typically, a double-A or triple-A rating is sought for the most senior tranche. The amount of credit enhancement necessary depends on rating agency requirements.

There are two general types of credit enhancement structures: external and internal. We will describe each type below.

External Credit Enhancements

External credit enhancements come in the form of third-party guarantees that provide for first loss protection against losses up to a specified level, for example, 10 percent. The most common forms of external enhancements are (1) a corporate guarantee, (2) a letter of credit, (3) pool insurance, and (4) bond insurance.

Pool insurance policies cover losses resulting from defaults and foreclosures. Policies are typically written for a dollar amount of coverage that continues in force throughout the life of the pool. However, some policies are written so that the dollar amount of coverage declines as the pool seasons as long as two conditions are met: (1) The credit performance is better than expected and (2) the rating agencies that rated the issue approve. The three major providers of pool insurance are GEMICO, PMI Mortgage Insurance Corp., and United Guarantee Insurance. Since only defaults and foreclosures are covered, additional insurance must be obtained to cover losses resulting from bankruptcy (i.e., court mandated modification of mortgage debt), fraud arising in the origination process, and special hazards (i.e., losses resulting from events not covered by a standard homeowner's insurance policy).

Bond insurance provides the same function as in municipal bond structures. The major insurers are FGIC, AMBAC, and MBIA. Typically, bond insurance is not used as primary protection but to supplement other forms of credit enhancement.

A CMO issue with external credit support is subject to the credit risk of the third-party guarantor. Should the third-party guarantor be downgraded, the CMO issue itself could be subject to downgrade even if the structure is performing as expected. For example, in the early 1990s, mortgage-backed securities issued by Citibank Mortgage Securities Inc. were downgraded when Citibank, the third-party guarantor, was downgraded. This is the chief disadvantage of third-party guarantees. Therefore, it is imperative that investors perform credit analysis on both the collateral (the loans) and the third-party guarantor.

External credit enhancements do not materially alter the cash flow characteristics of a CMO structure except in the form of prepayment. In case of a default resulting in net losses within the guarantee level, investors will receive the principal amount as if a prepayment has occurred. If the net losses exceed the guarantee level, investors will have a shortfall in the cash flow.

Internal Credit Enhancements

Internal credit enhancements come in more complicated forms than external credit enhancements and may alter the cash flow characteristics of the loans even in the absence of default. The most common forms of internal credit enhancements are reserve funds (cash reserve funds or excess servicing spread accounts) and senior/subordinated structures.

Reserve Funds

Reserve funds come in two forms, cash reserve funds and excess servicing spread accounts. *Cash reserve funds* are straight deposits of cash generated from issuance proceeds. In this case, part of the underwriting profits from the deal are deposited into a hypothecated fund which typically invests in money market instruments. Cash reserve funds are typically used in conjunction with letters of credit or other kinds of external credit enhancements. For example, a CMO may have 10 percent credit support, 9 percent of which is provided by a letter of credit and 1 percent from a cash reserve fund.

Excess servicing spread accounts involve the allocation of excess spread or cash into a separate reserve account after paying out the net coupon, servicing fee, and all other expenses on a monthly basis. For example, suppose that the gross weighted average coupon (gross WAC) is 7.75 percent, the servicing and other fees is 0.25 percent, and the net weighted average coupon (net WAC) is 7.25 percent. This means that there is excess servicing of 0.25 percent. The amount in the reserve account will gradually increase and can be used to pay for possible future losses.

The excess spread is analogous to the guarantee fee paid to an agency, except that this is a form of self-insurance. This form of credit enhancement relies on the assumption that defaults occur infrequently in the initial stages of the loans but gradually increase in the following two to five years. This assumption is consistent with the PSA's Standard Default Assumption (SDA) curve that we will describe later in the chapter.

Senior/Subordinated Structure

The most widely used internal credit support structure is by far the senior/subordinated structure. The subordinated class is the first loss piece absorbing all losses on the underlying collateral, thus protecting the senior class. For example, a $100 million deal can be divided into two classes: a $92.25 million senior class and a $7.75 million subordinated class. The subordination level in this hypothetical structure is 7.75 percent. The subordinated class will absorb all losses up to $7.75 million, and the senior class will start to experience losses thereafter. So, if there is $5 million of losses, the subordinated class will realize this loss. Thus, it would realize a 64.5 percent loss ($5/$7.75). If, instead, there is $10 million of losses, the subordinated class will experience $7.75 million of losses or a 100 percent loss, and the senior class will experience a loss of $2.25 million ($10 million minus $7.75 million) or a 2.4 percent loss ($2.25/$92.25). Exhibit 29–1 is a loss severity table showing various percentage losses in principal on both senior and subordinated classes at different loss levels.

EXHIBIT 29–1

Loss Severity Table
$100MM Deal, 7.75% Subordination

Loss Amount	Senior Class	Subordinated Class
$5.00 MM	0.0%	64.5%
7.75	0.0	100.0
10.00	2.4	100.0
20.00	13.3	100.0

EXHIBIT 29–2

Average Life for Senior/Subordinated Structure
Assuming No Defaults

Structure Gross WAC = 8.125% New WAC = 7.50% WAM = 357 Months	Average Life at 165 PSA Assuming No Defaults
No Shifting Interest Senior class (92.25%) Subordinate class (7.75%)	8.77 8.77
With Shifting Interest Senior class (92.25%) Subordinate class (7.75%)	8.41 13.11
With Shifting Interest Senior class (84.5%) Subordinate class (15.5%)	7.98 13.11

The subordinated class holder would obviously require a yield premium to take on the greater default risk exposure relative to the senior class. This setup is another form of self-insurance wherein the senior class holder is giving up yield spread to the subordinated class holder. This form of credit enhancement does not affect cash flow characteristics of the senior class except in the form of prepayment. To the extent that losses are within the subordination level, the senior class holder will receive principal as if a prepayment has occurred. Exhibit 29–2 shows the average life of both classes at 165 PSA before any default assumption for a hypothetical $100 million structure with a 7.75 percent subordination level.

Almost all existing senior/subordinated structures also incorporate a *shifting interest structure*. A shifting interest structure redirects prepayments disproportionally from the subordinated class to the senior class according to a specified schedule. An example of such a schedule would be as follows:

Months	Percentage of Prepayments Directed to Senior Class
1–60	100
61–72	70
73–84	60
85–96	40
97–108	20
109 +	pro rata

The rationale for the shifting interest structure is to have enough insurance outstanding to cover future losses. Because of the shifting interest structure, the subordination amount may actually grow in time, especially in a low default and fast prepayment environment. This is sometimes referred to as "riding up the credit curve."

Using the same example of our previous $100 million deal with 7.75 percent initial subordination and assuming a cumulative principal paydown of $16 million ($6 million of regular repayments and $10 million of prepayments) by year five and no losses, the subordination will actually increase to 9.5 percent. The subordinated class principal balance will be reduced by the pro rata share of regular repayments (7.75 percent of $6 million) and none of the prepayments to $7.29 million. The senior class principal balance will be reduced by the pro rata share of regular repayments (92.25 percent of $6 million) and all of the $10 million prepayments to $76.71. The new subordination level will increase to 9.5 percent ($7.29/$76.71). Exhibit 29–3 shows the new subordination levels, given various combinations of prepayments and losses. Holding net loss at zero, the faster the prepayments, the higher the subordination grows. Even in the case of losses, fast prepayments can sometimes offset the effect of principal losses to maintain the initial subordination.

While the shifting interest structure is beneficial to the senior class holder from a credit standpoint, it does alter the cash flow characteristics of the senior class even in the absence of defaults. As Exhibit 29–2 indicates, a 7.75 percent subordination with the shifting interest structure will shorten the average life of the senior class to 8.41 years at the same 165 PSA, assuming no default. The size of the subordination also matters. A larger subordinated class redirects a higher proportion of prepayments to the senior class, thereby shortening the average life even further. A 15.5 percent subordination in the same example shortens the average life to 7.98.

It may be counterintuitive that the size of the subordination should affect the average life and cash flow of the senior class more than the credit quality. This is because the size of the subordination is already factored into the rating. The rating agency typically requires more subordination for lower credit quality loans to obtain a triple-A rating and less subordination for better credit quality loans. From a credit standpoint, the investor may be indifferent between a 5 percent sub-

EXHIBIT 29–3

Subordination Level Drift
$100 MM Deal, 7.751% Subordination, 5 Years Out

Regular Paydown	Prepayment	Loss	Size of Senior Class	Size of Sub.Class	Sub. Level
$6 MM	$10 MM	$0 MM	$76.71 MM	$7.29 MM	9.50%
$6	$20	$0	$66.71	$7.29	10.93
$6	$40	$0	$46.71	$7.29	15.61
$6	$10	$2	$76.71	$5.29	6.90
$6	$20	$2	$66.71	$5.29	7.93
$6	$40	$2	$46.71	$5.29	11.33
$6	$10	$5	$76.71	$2.29	2.99
$6	$20	$5	$66.71	$2.29	3.43
$6	$40	$5	$46.71	$2.29	4.90

ordination on a package of good quality loans and a 10 percent subordination on a package of lower quality loans as long as the rating agency gives them the same rating. However, the quality of the underlying loans will determine the default rate and therefore the timing of the cash flow.

COMPENSATING INTEREST

An additional factor to consider, which is unique to whole-loan CMO structures, is compensating interest. Mortgage pass-throughs and CMOs pay principal and interest on a monthly basis (with the exception of some early quarterly-pay CMOs), and principal paydown factors are also calculated only once a month. While homeowners may prepay their mortgage on any day throughout the month, the agencies guarantee and pay the investors a full month of interest as if all the prepayments occur on the last day of the month. Unfortunately, this guarantee does not apply to whole-loan mortgages and, consequently, not to whole-loan CMOs. If a homeowner pays off a mortgage on the 10th day of the month, he or she will stop paying interest for the rest of the month. Because of the payment delay (for example, 25 days) and the once-a-month calculation of principal paydown, the investor will receive full principal but only 10 days of interest on the 25th of the following month.

This phenomenon is known as *payment interest shortfall* or *compensating interest* and is handled differently by different issuers and services. Some issuers will only pay up to a specified amount, and some will not pay at all. Exhibit 29–4 is a list of issuers who generally pay and those who do not generally pay compensating interest. The economic value of compensating interest depends on the level of prepay-

EXHIBIT 29–4

Treatment of Compensating Interest by Some
Issuers

Issuers Who Generally Pay Compensating Interest	Issuers Who Generally Do Not Pay Compensating Interest
Chase	GE
Citicorp	RFC
Capstead	Ryland
PruHome	SecPac
RTC	Sears

ment and the types of CMO tranches. Generally, the faster the prepayment and the higher the coupon tranche, the higher the economic value of compensating interest.

WEIGHTED AVERAGE COUPON DISPERSION

The pooling standard on whole loans is also looser than that on agency deals. Therefore, most whole-loan CMOs have wider gross coupon and maturity dispersions given any WAC and WAM. While the agency would strip off variable amounts of servicing and guarantee fees to bring the net coupon of a pool down to 50 bps increments, whole loans have fixed servicing fees, and the net coupons can vary. Using Exhibit 29–5 and 29–6 as examples, an agency CMO may contain four pools with gross coupons of 8.7 percent, 8.6 percent, 8.5 percent, and 8.4 percent to yield a GWAC of 8.55 percent. Seventy bps are stripped off the first pool to yield an 8 percent net coupon. Sixty bps will be stripped off the second pool to also yield an 8 percent coupon. Fifty bps and 40 bps will be stripped off the third and fourth pools, respectively. Since all the pools have net coupons of 8 percent, the weighted average net coupon is also 8 percent. Conversely, a whole-

EXHIBIT 29–5

Agency CMO

Pools	GWAC	Net Coupon	IO-ette	Stripped-Down Coupon
1	8.70%	8.00%	100 bps	7.00%
2	8.60	8.00	100	7.00
3	8.50	8.00	100	7.00
4	8.40	8.00	100	7.00
Average	8.55%	8.00%	100 bps	7.00%

EXHIBIT 29–6

Whole Loan CMO

Pools	GWAC	Servicing	Net Coupon	WAC IO	Stripped-Down Coupon
1	8.70%	55 bps	8.15%	115 bps	7.00%
2	8.60	55	8.05	105	7.00
3	8.50	55	7.95	95	7.00
4	8.40	55	7.85	85	7.00
Average	8.55%	55 bps	8.00%	100 bps	7.00%

EXHIBIT 29–7

Whole-Loan CMO After Paydown

Pools	GWAC	Servicing	Net Coupon	WAC IO	Stripped-Down Coupon
3	8.50%	55 bps	7.95%	95 bps	7.00%
4	8.40	55	7.85	85	7.00
Average	8.45%	55 bps	7.90%	90 bps	7.00%

loan CMO containing four pools with the exact GWACs will have a constant servicing fee of 55 bps. The net coupons on these four pools will then be 8.15 percent, 8.05 percent, 7.95 percent, and 7.85 percent to yield the same weighted average net coupon of 8 percent. To create fixed-rate (e.g., 7 percent coupon) tranches from the whole-loan CMO regardless of which pool prepays, a WAC IO (weighted average coupon interest only) tranche must be created to absorb the variability of net coupons on the underlying pools. The WAC IO tranche will receive a weighted average coupon of 100 bps off the whole deal. The WAC IO is equivalent in structure to an IO strip or IO-ette in an agency deal. However, as soon as prepayments start to occur, the WAC IO strip may change. Hypothetically and intuitively, Pools 1 and 2, with the higher WACs, prepay first. Exhibit 29–7 shows that this will leave the WAC IO strip with only 90 bps of coupon, one-tenth less in cash flow going forward. This is extremely important in the anaylsis of WAC IO since whole loan CMOs tend to have wider WAC dispersion.

CLEAN-UP CALL PROVISIONS

All whole-loan CMO structures are issued with "clean-up" call provisions. The clean-up call provides the servicers or the residual holders (typically the issuers) the right, but not the obligation, to call back all the outstanding tranches of the

CMO structure when the CMO balance is paid down to a certain percentage of the original principal balance. The servicers typically find it more costly than the servicing fee to service the CMO when the balance is paid down to a small amount. For example, suppose a $100 million CMO was originally issued with a 10 percent clean-up call. When the entire CMO balance is paid down to $10 million or less, the servicer can exercise the call to pay off all outstanding tranches like a balloon payment regardless of the percentage balance of the individual tranches.

The call provision, when exercised, shortens the principal payment window and the average life of the back-end tranches of a CMO. This provision is not unique to whole-loan CMO structures. It is mandatory, however, for all whole-loan CMO structures while agency CMOs may or may not have clean-up calls. Typically, FHLMC CMOs have 1 percent clean-up calls, and FNMA CMOs do not have clean-up calls.

ASSESSING PREPAYMENT RATES OF WHOLE-LOAN CMOS

Prepayment conventions are discussed in Chapter 27 using both the PSA and CPR models. While analyzing whole-loan prepayments is beyond the scope of this chapter, there are implications for using the PSA and CPR conventions on whole loans. Traditionally, the agencies only reported the WAM of the CMO with the implied age being the loan term minus the WAM. For example, a group of 30-year loans is assumed to be 10 months old if they have a reported WAM of 350 months, and a group of 15-year loans is assumed to be 10 months old if they have a reported WAM of 170.

Recently, the agencies started to report loan age as well as WAM. FHLMC calls it WALA (weighted average loan age), and FNMA calls it CAGE (calculated loan age). These are critical measures because WALA and WAM may not add up to 360 or 180 months. This is due to partial prepayments (curtailments). Partial prepayments do not impact the age of the loans but shorten the WAM of the loans.

Partial prepayment is not a new phenomenon but is more noticeable recently for two reasons. The first reason is the steepness of the yield curve. Homeowners find that partial prepayment on a 7 percent mortgage is a higher yielding investment than a 3 percent certificate of deposit. The second reason is the recent changes in the Internal Revenue Code that limit tax deductions on mortgage interest payments for higher income taxpayers. Both reasons impact jumbo mortgages more than conforming mortgages.

Partial prepayment can distort the reported prepayment speeds. For example, if the loan age is not available and the loans backing the whole loan have a WAM of 350 and the prepayment speed is 2 percent CPR, this converts to 100 PSA.[1] If the

---

1. This is found as follows when the seasoning is assumed to be 10 months:

$$\frac{2\% \text{ CPR} \times 100 \text{ PSA}}{10 \,(0.2\% \text{ CPR})} = 100 \text{ PSA}$$

WALA is known to be three months due to partial prepayments, 2 percent CPR converts to 333 PSA.[2]

PSA STANDARD DEFAULT ASSUMPTION BENCHMARK

In Chapter 26, defaults on residential mortgages were explained. With the increase in whole-loan CMO issuance, the Public Securities Association introduced a standardized benchmark for default rates. The PSA standard default assumption (SDA) benchmark gives the annual default rate for a mortgage pool as a function of the seasoning of the mortgages. The PSA SDA benchmark, or 100 SDA, specifies the following:

1. The default rate in month 1 is 0.02 percent and increases by 0.02 percent up to month 30 so that in month 30 the default rate is 0.60 percent.
2. From month 30 to month 60, the default rate remains at 0.60 percent.
3. From month 61 to month 120, the default rate declines linearly from 0.60 percent to 0.03 percent.
4. From month 120 on, the default rate remains constant at 0.03 percent.

This pattern is illustrated in Exhibit 29–8.

E X H I B I T   29–8

PSA Standard Default Assumption Benchmark (100 SDA)

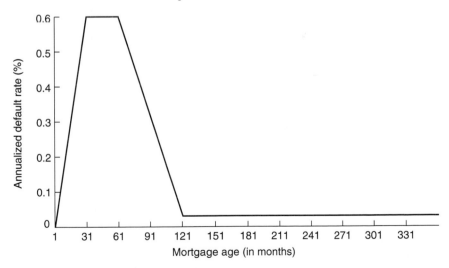

2. This is found as follows when the seasoning is three months:

$$\frac{2\% \text{ CPR} \times 100 \text{ PSA}}{3 \,(0.2\% \text{ CPR})} = 333 \text{ PSA}$$

As with the PSA prepayment benchmark, multiples of the benchmark are found by multiplying the default rate by the assumed multiple. For example, 200 SDA means the following pattern:

- The default rate in month 1 is 0.04 percent and increases by 0.04 percent up to month 30 so that in month 30 the default rate is 1.20 percent.
- From month 30 to month 60, the default rate remains at 1.20 percent.
- From month 61 to month 120, the default rate declines from 1.20 percent to 0.06 percent.
- From month 120 on, the default rate remains constant at 0.06 percent.

A 0 SDA means that no defaults are assumed.

⑥ # COMMERCIAL MORTGAGE-BACKED SECURITIES*

John N. Dunlevy, CFA, CPA
Director and Senior Portfolio Manager
Hyperion Capital Management Inc.

INTRODUCTION

In previous chapters in this section of the book, underlying loans for the mortgage-backed securities are for one- to four-family residence properties. In this section, we look at securities backed by other property types. These securities are called *commercial mortgage-backed securities.* The five major property types backing such securities are office space, retail property, industrial facilities, multifamily housing, and hotels.

Commercial mortgage-backed securities (CMBS) are a rapidly growing segment of the fixed income market. This growth has been spurred by the ability of Wall Street to securitize real estate and loans of real estate, and to transform equity into real estate investment trusts (REITs) and debt into CMBS (see Exhibit 30–1). This chapter will focus on the structural considerations impacting CMBS investments. While there are five basic types of CMBS transactions, we will concentrate on the three types of CMBS deals that are greatly impacted by structure.

BASIC CMBS STRUCTURE

A CMBS transaction is formed when an issuer places commercial loans into a trust that then issues classes of bonds backed by the interest and principal of the underlying mortgages. The basic building block of the CMBS transaction is a

---

*This chapter is adapted from John N. Dunlevy, "Structural Considerations Impacting CMBS," in *The Handbook of Commercial Mortgage-Backed Securities,* eds. Frank J. Fabozzi and David P. Jacob (New Hope, PA: Frank J. Fabozzi Associates, 1996).

E X H I B I T   30–1

Transformation of Real Estate and Real Estate Loans

	Equity	**Debt**
Private	Direct investments Commingled funds	Whole loans
Public	REITs	CMBS

commercial loan that was originated either to finance a commercial purchase or to refinance a prior mortgage obligation.

Many types of commercial loans can be either sold by the originator as a commercial whole loan or structured into a CMBS transaction (see Exhibit 30–2). The whole-loan market, which is largely dominated by insurance companies and banks, is focused on loans between $10 and $50 million issued on traditional property types (multifamily, retail, office, and industrial). CMBS transactions, on the other hand, can involve loans of virtually any size (from conduit loans as small as $1 million to single-property transactions as large as $200 million) and/or property type.

The CMBS transaction structure takes shape when the owner of the commercial loans has a potential transaction "sized" by the rating agencies. This sizing will determine the necessary level of credit enhancement to achieve a desired rating level. For example, if certain *debt-service coverage* (DSC) and *loan-to-value* (LTV) ratios are needed and these ratios cannot be met at the loan level, subordination is used to achieve these levels. In Exhibit 30–3, a simple example demonstrates how a CMBS transaction can be structured to meet the rating agencies' required DSC and LTV ratios. For example, Duff & Phelps requires a 1.51× coverage to achieve a single-A rating on a regional mall deal. Since that level cannot be obtained at the collateral level (coverage of 1.25×) a CMBS structure with 17.2 percent subordination is created.

Paydown Priority

The rating agencies will require that the CMBS transaction be retired sequentially with the highest rated bonds paying off first. Therefore, any return of principal caused by amortization, prepayment, or default will be used to repay the highest rated tranche.

Interest on principal outstanding will be paid to all tranches. In the event of a delinquency resulting in insufficient cash to make all scheduled payments, the transaction's servicer will advance both principal and interest. Advancing will continue from the servicer for as long as these amounts are deemed recoverable.

Losses arising from loan defaults will be charged against the principal balance of the lowest rated CMBS bond tranche outstanding. The total loss charged

EXHIBIT 30–2

Commercial Loan Disposition after Origination

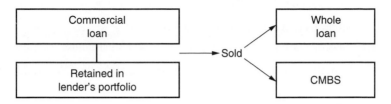

EXHIBIT 30–3

How a CMBS Transaction Can Be Structured to Satisfy Required DSC and LTV Ratios of Duff & Phelps

Loan Information

Assume $100 million

Regional mall loan	DSC 1.25×*
	LTV 75%*
Market value	$133.3 million
Debt service	$10.0 million
NOI	$12.5 million

CMBS Structure	Required Subordination (%)*	Tranche Size	Tranche LTV (%)	Tranche DSC
AAA	31.4	68.6	51.5	1.82×
AA	23.3	8.1	57.5	1.63×
A	17.2	6.1	62.1	1.51×
BBB	12.0	5.2	66.0	1.42×
BB	6.6	5.4	70.1	1.34×
B	2.6	4.0	73.1	1.28×
NR	0.0	2.6	75.0	1.25×
		100.0		

* Source: Duff & Phelps.

will include the amount previously advanced as well as the actual loss incurred in the sale of the loan's underlying property.

Finally, the investor must be sure to understand the cash flow priority of any prepayment penalties and/or yield-maintenance provisions, as this can impact a particular bond's average life and overall yield.

Structural Call Protection

The degree of call protection available to a CMBS investor is a function of the following two characteristics:

1. Call protection available at loan level.
2. Call protection afforded from the actual CMBS structure.

At the commercial loan level, call protection can take the following forms:

1. Prepayment lockout.
2. Prepayment penalty.
3. Yield maintenance penalties.

The strongest type of prepayment protection is prepayment lockout. A lockout is a contractual agreement that prohibits all prepayments during the period of the lockout.

Prepayment penalties are predetermined penalties that must be paid by the borrower if the borrower wishes to refinance. For example, 5-4-3-2-1 is a common prepayment penalty structure. That is, if the borrower wishes to prepay during the first year, he or she must pay a 5 percent penalty for a total of $105 rather than $100 (which is the norm in the residential market). Likewise, during the second year, a 4 percent penalty would apply, and so on.

Yield maintenance penalties, in their simplest terms, are designed to make investors indifferent to the timing of prepayments. The yield maintenance provision makes it uneconomical to refinance solely to get a lower mortgage rate. The simplest and most restrictive form of yield maintenance (Treasury flat-yield maintenance) penalizes the borrower based on the difference between the mortgage coupon and the prevailing Treasury rate.

The other type of call protection available in CMBS transactions is structural. That is, because the CMBS bond structures are sequential-pay (by rating) the AA-rated tranche cannot pay down until the AAA is completely retired, and the AA-rated bonds must be paid off before the A-rated bonds, etc. (see Exhibit 30–4).

E X H I B I T   30–4

Sequence of Principal Paydowns

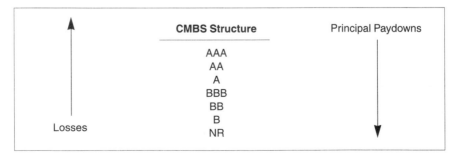

However, as mentioned earlier, principal losses due to defaults are impacted from the bottom of the structure upward.

Balloon Maturity Provisions

Many commercial loans backing CMBS transactions are balloon loans, which require substantial principal payment on the final maturity date. Although many investors like the "bullet bond-like" paydown of the balloon maturities, it does present difficulties from a structural standpoint. That is, if the deal is structured to completely pay down on a specified date, an event of default will occur if any delays occur. However, how such delays impact CMBS investors is dependent on the bond type (premium, par, or discount) and whether or not the servicer will advance to a particular tranche after the balloon default. Another concern for CMBS investors in multitranche transactions is the fact that all loans must be refinanced to pay off the most senior bondholders. Therefore, the balloon risk of the most senior tranche (i.e., AAA) may be equivalent to that of the most junior bond class (i.e., B).

Currently, three types of structural provisions can be present in CMBS transactions. The provisions are summarized in Exhibit 30–5.

The first provision—*time matched method*—is no longer used in CMBS transactions because it often results in actual defaults upon balloon maturity. This method was common prior to the real estate recession that began in the late 1980s. Prior to this national real estate downturn, extension risk was not a primary concern for traditional lenders (i.e., insurance companies and banks). However, the real estate recession caused a rapid decline in property values, which in turn caused many loans to be nonrefinanceable under the original loan terms. Many of these deals did contain default rate provisions. That is, an extension

E X H I B I T   30–5

Types of CMBS Balloon Provisions

Method	Description	Examples
Time matched	Balloon maturity and bond maturity are the same	CMBS deals pre-RTC
Internal tail	Balloon maturity and bond maturity are the same but provisions for refinancing begin 1 to 2 years prior to maturity	DLJ 1992 and 1993 "M" series
External tail	Balloon maturity occurs before bond maturity	Most 1995 conduit deals and secured REIT debt transactions

could be granted in exchange for an increase in the interest rate. Further, many deals of this type also had a "cash-trap" mechanism that captured all excess cash flow and used it to pay down debt.

The second type of balloon loan provision is the *internal tail*. The internal tail requires the borrower to provide ongoing evidence of her or his efforts to refinance the loan. For example, the following procedures would have to be undertaken within one year of the balloon date:

- Appraisals on all properties.
- Phase I environmental reports.
- Engineering reports.

Finally, within six months prior to balloon maturity, the borrower must obtain a refinancing commitment.

The third type of balloon loan provision is the *external tail*. This method is preferred by the major rating agencies since it gives the borrower the most time to arrange refinancing while avoiding default on the bond obligations. The external tail method, as shown in Exhibit 30–6, sets the maturity date of the CMBS issue longer than that of the underlying loans. The difference between these two dates acts as a buffer to arrange loan refinancing. Further, the CMBS investor does not suffer an interruption in cash flow during this period since the servicer advances any missing interest and scheduled principal (but not the balloon payment).

Evaluating the Timing of Cash Flows

Similar to mortgage-backed and asset-backed securities, CMBS structures can experience principal amortization throughout the life of the underlying loans.

As shown in Exhibit 30–7, the investor must evaluate CMBS cash flows occurring across the varying principal payment windows. The traditional evaluation uses yield-to-maturity to evaluate a bond's relative attractiveness. However, yield-to-maturity assumes each cash flow received over the life of a security can be reinvested at a constant rate. This implies that the yield curve also remains unchanged, or flat, over time. The "flat" scenario is highly unlikely over extended

E X H I B I T   30–6

External Tail Time Line

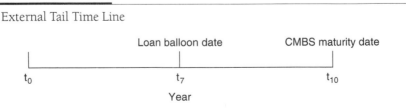

E X H I B I T   30–7

Diagram of Principal Payment Windows

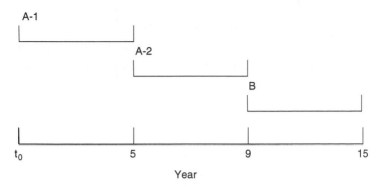

periods of time. When, for example, the yield curve is steep, the actual total return to maturity should be less than the yield-to-maturity for amortizing classes.

This is the case because in a steep yield-curve environment it is not possible to reinvest at a yield-to-maturity level without sharply increasing duration. Therefore, a better way to evaluate these securities is to use the bond's *Z spread*. Z spread refers to the bond's option-adjusted spread (OAS) at a zero interest-rate volatility. Z spread allows the investor to quantify the cost of the amortization period and achieve an apples-to-apples comparison between a bullet bond and an amortizing security.

Another key component in evaluating a security's overall attractiveness is the bond's default-adjusted yield. This calculation can only be performed after the necessary time and resources have been committed to building a default model. The recently announced Equitable Real Estate/Hyperion Capital joint venture has built such a model. The key elements to building such a model are as follows:

- Twenty-plus years experience captured with regard to all *actual whole loan experience.*
- Database of actual *NOI volatility* by property type, geographic location, and point in real estate cycle.
- Generation of 1,000 interest rate and NOI paths to estimate foreclosure frequency.
- Ability to use actual experience as RTC servicer to generate loss severity estimates by property type and state.
- Ability to estimate losses and calculate yield impact on tranches by overlying deal structure.
- Ability to calculate standard deviation of defaults and estimate confidence intervals.

- Ability to calculate above on a loan-by-loan basis rather than using simplifying assumptions.

Servicer's Role

The servicer on a CMBS deal can play a key role in the overall success of the transaction. The key responsibilities of the servicer are to do the following:

- Collect monthly loan payments.
- Keep records relating to payments.
- Maintain property escrows (taxes and insurance).
- Monitor condition of underlying properties.
- Prepare reports for trustee.
- Transfer collected funds to trustee for payment.

There are different types of servicers, and their roles can vary from deal to deal. In general, we will discuss three types of servicers: the subservicer; the master servicer; and the special servicer. These different servicers are highlighted in Exhibit 30–8.

The *subservicer* is usually the originator of the loan in a conduit deal who has decided to sell the loan but retain the servicing. All payments and property information will then be sent by the subservicer to the *master servicer*. The master servicer oversees the deal and makes sure the servicing agreements are maintained. In addition, the master servicer must facilitate the timely payment of interest and principal. That is, when a loan goes into default, the master servicer has the responsibility to provide for servicing advances. This role is critical to the

EXHIBIT 30–8

Types of Servicers

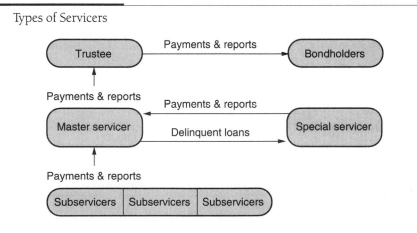

success of a deal; therefore, it is important for an investor to be comfortable with both the financial strength and the overall experience of the master servicer.

A *special servicer* also plays a vital role within a CMBS transaction. The special servicer is usually engaged whenever a loan becomes more than 60 days past due. The special servicer usually has the power to do the following:

- Extend the loan.
- Make loan modifications.
- Restructure the loan.
- Foreclose on the loan and sell the property.

The special servicer is important to subordinated buyers because the timing of the loss can significantly impact the loss severity, which in turn can greatly impact subordinated returns. Therefore, first-loss investors usually want to either control the appointment of the special servicer or perform the role themselves.

DIFFERENT TYPES OF CMBS DEALS

Exhibit 30–9 shows the five types of CMBS deal structures. The first three types—liquidating trusts, multiproperty single-borrower, and multiproperty conduit—will be discussed in detail in this section. These three deal types, which allow investors to focus more attention on structural aspects, have been the focus of most fixed income money manager's CMBS activity. The latter two deal types—multiproperty nonconduit and single-property single-borrower—have been the focus of real estate money manager activity within CMBS. The recently announced Equitable Real Estate/Hyperion Capital joint venture will combine the

E X H I B I T   30–9

CMBS Deal Structures

	Liquidating Trusts (Nonperforming)	Multiproperty Single-Borrower	Multiproperty Conduit	Multiproperty Nonconduit	Single-Property Single-Borrower
Sample deals	-RTC N-Series -Lennar -SKW -Kearny Street	-Belaire -Factory stores -Kranzco	-Nomura -Megadeal -DLJ Conduit	-RTC C-Series -New England -Confid Life	-Danbury Mall -Freehold Mall
Key risks	Structural	Structural/Credit	Structural/Credit	Credit	Credit
Loan age	Seasoned	New	New	Seasoned	New
Available ratings	AA-B	AAA-NR	AAA-NR	AAA-B	AAA-NR

structural skills (Hyperion) necessary to invest in the first three deal types with the real estate skills (Equitable) necessary to invest in the later two deal types.

Liquidating Trusts (Nonperforming CMBS)

A small but interesting segment of the CMBS market is the nonperforming, or liquidating, trusts. This segment, as the name implies, represents CMBS deals backed by nonperforming mortgage loans. This market segment contains several structural nuances that must be analyzed when deciding upon the relative attractiveness of a particular bond tranche. Some of the features are discussed below.

Fast-Pay Structure

The so-called *fast-pay* structure requires that all cash flows from both asset sales and ongoing debt service, after bond interest payments, be used to retire the most senior bond class outstanding. The fast pay structure prevents the equity holder from receiving any cash flow until all bond classes are retired. Since equity holders are highly sensitive to internal rate of return (i.e., they want to retire the bond classes quickly), the bondholder's interests are aligned with those of the equity holder.

Overcollateralization

Liquidating trusts are structured so that the debt obligations (bond classes) are less than the actual receivables outstanding (loan note amount). This creates a level of overcollateralization that can be used to offer discounted payoffs in order to accelerate the retirement of the bond classes. As an example, the first nonperforming CMBS transaction—RTC 1992-N1—had the following attributes:

- Estimated market value: $155.3 million (DIV).
- Bond classes issued: $110.0 million.
- Original loan balances: $345.8 million.
- Equity contribution: $61.8 million.

These transactions have proven to work well since structurally the acquisition price or derived investment value (DIV) is often 60 percent or less of the current balance of the mortgage collateral. In this case, the DIV was 45 percent of the original loan balances ($155.3/$345.8), while the bond classes issued were only 71 percent of the estimated market value or DIV.

Servicer Flexibility

Liquidating trust structures generally allow the servicer maximum flexibility to liquidate the pool's underlying assets. Nonperforming loans are generally grouped into three categories: performing, subperforming, and real estate owned (REO).

As shown in Exhibit 30–10, the servicer (who is often also the transaction's equity holder) will work to carry out an asset-disposition strategy that was designed at the deal's inception. The servicer's ability to dispose of property is paramount to maximizing value for bondholders. To help ensure that bondholder values are maximized, incentives are built in for the servicer.

E X H I B I T   30–10

Asset-Disposition Strategy by Servicer

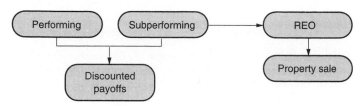

Generally, the servicer can use one of two disposal strategies: discounted payoffs, or taking title of a property through foreclosure and then selling the property from REO. The method employed is a function of where the loans are currently situated. That is, if a high percentage of loans are already in REO, the investor will expect a shorter average life and less potential extension risk. Deals with a higher percentage of performing loans are expected to have longer average lives and more extension risk.

Furthermore, performing loans can only be liquidated using the discounted payoff method, as they have the right to continue through the maturity of the loan. The subperforming loans can be liquidated either by using the discounted payoff method or by initiating foreclosure proceedings. Foreclosure can be a difficult and expensive undertaking, but when it is successful and the title to the property is obtained, the trust can then liquidate the underlying property to retire the mortgage debt.

Reserve Funds

Another important structural feature found in liquidating trust transactions are reserve funds. Reserve funds are necessary in these transactions since it is difficult to project the timing of asset dispositions and their resulting cash flows. These reserve funds are established at the time of closing and are used to protect bondholders. The two common types of reserve funds are summarized in Exhibit 30–11.

Usually the asset-expenditure reserve can be used to back up the liquidity reserve and make interest payments in the event of interest shortfalls to the investment-grade bonds. However, the asset-expenditure reserve is not used to accelerate bond class paydown after the investment-grade bonds are retired.

Required Principal Payments

Nonperforming CMBS are structured with relatively short average lives that receive cash flows from some loans while others are being disposed of. Therefore, the deal will be structured to achieve certain principal paydown targets. In the event these targets are not achieved, often the fixed rate coupon is scheduled at a preset date (i.e., increased from 10 percent to 12 percent). This motivates the borrower not to allow extension on the lower-rated bond classes.

E X H I B I T   30–11

Types of Reserve Funds

	Liquidity	**Asset-Expenditure**
Purpose	Cash flow used to prevent interest shortfalls to investment-grade bonds	Cash flow used to pay taxes, legal fees, and property maintenance
Used for acceleration	Yes	No

Single-Borrower/Multiproperty Deals

The second type of CMBS deal that contains important structural considerations is the single-borrower/multiproperty transaction. The following are important structural features that are often contained in these deals:

- Cross-collateralization and cross-default feature.
- Property-release provisions.
- Lock-box mechanism.
- Cash-trap features.

Each of these features are discussed below.

Cross-Collateralization and Cross-Default

Cross-collateralization is a mechanism whereby the properties that collateralize the individual loans are pledged against each loan. Cross-default, on the other hand, allows the lender to call each loan within the pool, when any one defaults. Thus, by tying the properties together, the cash flow is available to meet the collective debt on all the loans. Therefore, from a credit standpoint, an individual loan should not become delinquent as long as there is sufficient excess cash flow available from the pool to cover this shortfall.

Exhibits 30–12 and 30–13 show a simplified example of the power of the cross-collateralization cross-default mechanism. In our example, we assume that all properties have the same debt-service coverage (DSC) ratio and loan-to-value (LTV) ratio, except for one distressed loan. In Exhibit 30–12, we calculate the breakeven DSC ratio possible before a default would be likely to occur.

For example, if a single loan pool had a DSC ratio of 1.30× (that is, it can cover debt service by 1.30 times), the coverage ratio could decline by 23 percent before a breakeven level is reached. A further decline could lead to a loan default. However, if the same loan was within a pool of five cross-collateralized, cross-defaulted loans, it could experience a complete loss of cash flow (100 percent), and a second loan could also experience a 15 percent decline in the cash flow before a

EXHIBIT 30–12

Breakeven DSC Ratio

Number of Properties	DSC Ratio (%)				
	1.15 ×	1.25 ×	1.30 ×	1.35 ×	1.50 ×
1	13	20	23	26	33
3	39	60	69	78	100
5	65	100	115	130	167
10	130	200	230	259	333
15	196	300	345	389	500

EXHIBIT 30–13

Breakeven LTV Ratio

Number of Properties	LTV Ratio (%)				
	90%	80%	75%	70%	60%
1	10	20	25	30	40
3	30	60	75	90	120
5	50	100	125	150	200
10	100	200	250	300	400
15	150	300	375	450	600

similar breakeven point is reached. As can be seen from Exhibit 30–12, the stronger the overall DSC of the pool and the larger the overall pool, the greater the cushion against a single distressed loan. Similarly, Exhibit 30–13 shows the buffer of protection available on cross-collateralized, cross-defaulted pools by LTV.

As shown in Exhibits 30–12 and 30–13, a five-loan pool with an initial LTV of 75 percent could have a single distressed loan decline in value to zero and have a second loan decline in value by 25 percent before a zero-equity position in the pool is reached.

Property Release Provisions

Another structural feature often present in single-borrower/multiproperty transactions is property-release mechanisms. The investor should be concerned about the ability of the lender to prepay or otherwise remove the stronger properties from the pool. Various property-release provisions will protect the investor against this risk. These provisions usually take the following form:

- If any properties are sold, the borrower must retire *125 percent of the initial allocatable mortgage amount.*
- Resulting *DSC ratios cannot be lower than before sale.*
- No collateral substitutions are permitted.

These property release provisions are important in order to maintain adequate structural protection in single-borrower transactions. Again, these provisions are to protect the investor from the borrower stripping the pool of its best properties.

Lock-Box Structures

Another structural feature often found in single-borrower transactions is the lock-box mechanism. The lock-box mechanism gives the trustee control over the gross revenues of the properties (see Exhibit 30–14).

Just as the cash flow of a CMBS deal flows through a waterfall payment mechanism, the property cash flow in a lock-box structure flows through a waterfall. As shown in Exhibit 30–14, the owner only has claim to excess cash flow after taxes, insurance, debt service, operating expenses, and property reserves. Likewise, management fees are often subordinate to debt service and operating expenses. The intent of the lock-box structure is not only to insure payment of debt service but also to provide a strong incentive for owners and property managers to operate the properties efficiently since they have a subordinate claim on cash flow.

E X H I B I T   30–14

Lock-Box Structure

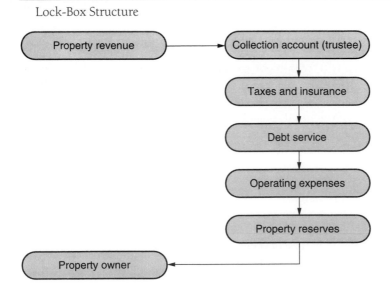

Cash-Trap Feature

Another structural feature sometimes found in single-borrower/multiproperty transactions is the "cash-trap." The cash-trap is the CMBS equivalent of "early amortization" within the asset-backed market. The intent is to penalize the borrower for something he or she has failed to do by amortizing the CMBS debt ahead of schedule. In the process, the cash-trap prevents the borrower from receiving excess cash flow. The most common triggers—which would cause all of the excess cash flow to be trapped for debt reduction—are as follows:

- Failure to maintain predetermined DSC ratio.
- Failure to maintain required minimum debt ratings.
- Failure to maintain adequate property reserves.

The cash-trap feature works particularly well with a lock-box structure since the trustee can easily "trap" all of the deal's excess cash. Cash-trap features have not been that common in recent deals (i.e., 1995 vintage) since borrowers have had more funding options (i.e., traditional lenders have returned and REITs that issue this type of debt have recently used unsecured debt issuance).

Multiborrower/Conduit Deals

Another growing segment of the CMBS is conduit-originated transactions. Conduits are commercial-lending entities that are established for the sole purpose of generating collateral to securitize. Most Wall Street houses have established conduits to originate collateral to be used in CMBS transactions. Some important factors when analyzing conduit deals are origination standards, number of originators, pool diversification, and degree of loan standardization. Each of these considerations will be further discussed below.

Origination Standards

A key consideration in analyzing a conduit CMBS product is understanding how the loans were originated. This analysis must address the following standards:

- Key DSC and LTV ratios.
- Cash flow assumptions used in underwriting.
- Standards for property reserves.
- Method of arriving at appraised values.
- Loan terms offered (i.e., amortizing/balloon and call protection terms).
- Geographic and property type diversification.
- Timing of loan originations (i.e., month and year of origination).

Analyzing the origination standards is important in understanding how the loans were originated.

Number of Originators

Many conduit deals have had more than one originator. This is usually done to speed up the funding period and to accumulate a larger critical mass. Most analysts agree that a minimum issue size of $100 to $125 million is desirable to effectively price a CMBS deal (given the fixed expenses of issuance). However, because multiple lenders may have originated the product, the investor has to get comfortable with the fact that a different lender underwrote the loans in a consistent manner. This can be determined only by carefully analyzing the mortgage loan files. It is for this reason that most investors prefer conduit deals originated by a single entity.

Pool Diversification

Another important factor to consider in conduit-originated deals is the diversification of the underlying loans. That is, how geographically and numerically diversified are the loans? Most investors like to see loan originations across several states without any major loan concentrations. One recent conduit deal had a single loan that comprised nearly 15 percent of the pool. A concentration such as this or a group of similar loans could severely impact the default-adjusted yields of the underlying securities.

Furthermore, the rating agencies have recently given lower overall levels of credit-enhancement to deals that contain diversification across property types. The theory is that because one cannot predict which property type will enjoy the best performance going forward, it is better to be adequately diversified.

Degree of Loan Standardization

It is important to analyze just how "cookie-cutter" a particular mortgage pool is. The higher the homogeneity, the greater the comfort that investors will be able to look to the deal's structural features. For example, if a deal has a large concentration of 10-year balloon maturities with seven years of prepayment lockout, the deal will usually appeal to crossover corporate buyers. Moreover, a highly standardized deal will more easily accept tranches such as bond-IOs (interest only strips). However, a deal that enjoys a high degree of standardization with regard to loan terms may not appeal to below investment-grade buyers. This is because the rating agencies have tended only to upgrade deals due to retirement of debt or deleveraging. In the example above, the balloon term usually implies interest only (i.e., no debt amortization), while the long lockout period would prevent voluntary prepayments. Thus, the below investment-grade bonds would not be candidates for upgrade.

SUMMARY

This chapter has focused on the structural considerations impacting MBS investments. We first looked at the basic CMBS structure: paydown priority, structural call protection, balloon maturity provisions, cash flows, and servicers' role. We then discussed the different types of CMBS deals, focusing on three types: liquidating trusts, single-borrower/multiproperty deals, and multiborrower/conduit deals.

⑥ # AUTO-LOAN-BACKED SECURITIES*

Thomas A. Zimmerman
Director—Fixed Income Research
Prudential Securities Inc.

INTRODUCTION

Auto-loan-backed securities represent one of the largest and most mature sectors of the ABS market. The first auto-loan deal was issued in May 1985, a scant two months after the first ABS securitization—the Sperry computer-lease issue of March 1985. Auto loans were a natural follow-up to the large-scale securitization that was already under way in the mortgage market at the time. Like home mortgages, auto loans are an amortizing consumer asset, but they have virtually none of the negative prepayment characteristics of mortgages. As such, auto ABSs compete with credit cards and Treasuries as stable, short average-life investments for banks, money managers, and other investors. Because of their straightforward structure, they are often one of the first securities investors turn to when they contemplate entering the ABS market. Issuance in the early years of the ABS auto market was dominated by commercial banks and the captive-finance subsidiaries of the Big Three U.S. auto makers. In recent years, independent finance companies have become equally important in terms of issuance.

Some major changes underway in the auto-finance industry are having a significant impact on the auto ABS market. For example, leasing continues to grow in importance and now accounts for about 30 percent of new-car financing. While it is likely that auto-lease backed securities eventually will become a major part of the auto ABS market, only a few auto lease-backed deals have been

---

*This chapter is adapted from Anand K. Bhattacharya and Frank J. Fabozzi (eds.), *Asset-Backed Securities* (New Hope, PA: Frank J. Fabozzi Associates, 1996).

completed to date. Hence, so far, at least, the growth of leasing has acted to restrain the volume of auto ABS issuance, not expand it. Also, the sub-prime sector has grown rapidly in recent years. However, the sub-prime sector differs from the prime sector in that its high level of defaults make it a totally separate product category. Because both auto-lease-backed securities and sub-prime auto securities have their own unique characteristics, they will not be discussed in this chapter.

The Auto-Finance Industry

The amount of auto financing originated each year is a function of new- and used-car sales, new- and used-car prices, and the percent of the purchase price that is financed. Sales of new cars and light trucks in the U.S. run around 14.5 to 15.0 million units per year. A noteworthy trend is that the share accounted for by light trucks, which typically are more expensive than cars, has increased from 32.9 percent in 1990 to 41.3 percent in 1995.

The average new price increased from $12,022 in 1985 to around $19,750 in 1995, an annual increase of 5.09 percent—a rate substantially greater than the increase in median family income during that period. Because of this, fewer families can afford to buy new cars and a growing percentage are buying used ones. Abetting this trend has been a large number of "almost" new cars coming off of lease. These developments have caused an increase in the sale of used cars, and today the dollar value of used-car sales is about 33 percent of the dollar value of new-car sales.

These sales and price trends can be used to estimate the annual volume of auto financing in the United States. Sales of 15 million units and an average sales price of $20,000 mean that around $300 billion is spent each year on new cars and light trucks. Furthermore, with about 90 percent of new sales financed and the average amount financed around 100 percent (including taxes, financing fees, preparation charges, etc.), new-car financing accounts for approximately $270 billion. Adding another 33 percent to that estimate for used cars yields a total new and used-car financing requirement of around $360 billion. This estimate agrees with the data compiled by CNW Marketing/Research, which puts total auto financing in 1995 at $369 billion. CNW breaks down the total as $226 billion for new and used prime loans, $67 billion for prime leasing, and $76 billion for sub-prime loans. According to the Federal Reserve Board, commercial banks control 43.8 percent of the auto-finance market, followed by finance companies at 31.0 percent and others, mainly credit unions, at 25 percent.

Auto-Loan Terms

Auto receivables take two forms: (1) installment-sales contracts and (2) consumer loans, made or purchased by banks, captive finance subsidiaries of the major auto manufacturers, and independent finance companies. The typical maturity ranges from three to six years, with most loans written for four or five years. The average maturity of a new-car loan at finance companies has stayed in a narrow range of 55.1 months to 54.1 months from 1991 to 1995. During that period, the average maturity of a used-car loan increased from 47.2 months to 52.2 months. The average auto loan at finance companies had an interest rate of around 150 basis points greater than the rate at commercial banks, and used-car loan rates averaged 300 to 350 basis points greater than new-car loan rates.

AUTO-LOAN SECURITIES

The first auto-loan securities were issued by Valley National Bank and Marine Midland in May 1985. From then to mid-June 1996, 355 deals representing $162 billion of auto securities have been issued. On a year-to-year basis, this sector has been either the largest or second largest sector of the ABS market. However, auto-security issuance has fluctuated a fair amount in recent years, rising to $26 billion in 1993, falling to $16 billion in 1994, and then recovering to $25.8 billion in 1995.

Major Issuers

The fluctuations in annual issuance reflect the varying degrees to which the major originators of auto loans have chosen to utilize the ABS market. For example, following the 1990/1991 recession—which severely impacted earnings and balance sheets—the long-term debt of all Big Three auto makers was downgraded. In the next two years, 1992 and 1993, GMAC found it beneficial to securitize a large number of their auto receivables. However, the strong expansion in the economy in recent years, coupled with major productivity improvements and other restructurings have led to rating upgrades for all of the Big Three. Chrysler Financial's rating fell to Ba3 and has recovered to A3, GMAC bottomed out at Baa1 and is now rated A3, and Ford Motor Credit fell to A2 and is now rated A1.

As GMAC's fortunes recovered in 1994 and 1995 and their ratings improved, they reduced their reliance on term securitization and turned to other funding mechanisms, including asset-backed commercial paper. In recent years, they have been only marginal participants in the auto ABS market, but they continue to issue a deal or two per year to maintain their access to the ABS market. The impact of GMAC's changing use of the ABS market is illustrated in Exhibit 31–1, which shows auto ABS issuance by major sector since 1990. Chrysler and Ford made more consistent use of securitization during those years.

Commercial banks also have been variable issuers of auto ABSs. After a three-year period of little issuance, 1992 to 1994, commercial banks issued $6.3 billion in 1995. In part, this was a result of balance-sheet adjustments that accompanied several large-scale bank mergers, but it also reflected the emergence of several new bank issuers, such as NationsBank and Banc One, and a decision by Chase Manhattan to securitize a major portion of its auto portfolio.

EXHIBIT 31–1

Annual Auto ABS Issuance by Sector

	GMAC $ (BB)	Ford and Chrysler $ (BB)	Comm. Banks $ (BB)	Other $ (BB)	Total $ (BB)	% Big 3	% Comm. Banks & Other
1990	1.2	6.4	2.8	2.5	12.9	58.9	44.1
1991	3.2	7.8	2.1	3.7	16.8	65.5	34.5
1992	12.0	4.0	0.4	5.3	21.7	73.7	26.3
1993	10.2	9.3	0.7	6.3	26.5	73.6	26.4
1994	1.2	8.6	0.1	6.5	16.4	59.8	40.2
1995	1.1	8.3	6.2	10.3	25.9	36.3	63.7

Source: Prudential Securities' IMPACT database.

The third major sector of the auto ABS market, and the fastest growing, consists of the independent finance companies and small financial institutions that specialize in auto loans. These include such companies as Olympic Financial, Western Financial, and Union Acceptance Corporation. These firms differ from commercial banks and the captive finance subsidiaries in that they do not look upon the ABS market as an alternative source of funding, but rather they literally exist because of the ABS market. Because of securitization, these smaller capitalized institutions can create triple-A securities and fund themselves at much lower rates than if they had to rely on traditional funding sources.

Structure

Exhibit 31–2 contains the structural elements common to most auto-loan securitizations. As indicated, the receivables are purchased or originated by a finance company and then transferred to a bankruptcy-remote special-purpose corporation (SPC) through a true sale. The receivables are then sold to a trust that issues asset-backed securities to investors. Payments made by consumers flow through the structure to investors.

Auto securities are structured both as pass-throughs and pay-throughs. In the pass-through structure, payments of principal and interest flow through the trust to certificate holders on a pro-rata basis. In the pay-through structure, the SPC allocates cash flows to note holders.

Most auto structures are pass-throughs in which a grantor trust retains legal title to the assets. The trust is a passive entity that holds the self-liquidating receivables for the benefit of the certificate holders. The grantor trust is not taxed on the entity level. This tax status is a result of the fixed nature of the trust. The only allocations of cash flows permitted in a grantor trust are credit tranching and into

E X H I B I T   31–2

Auto ABS Structure

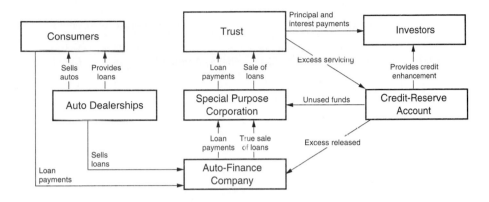

senior and subordinate classes. Maturity tranching is not permitted. The pass-through grantor-trust structure is appropriate for most auto-loan securities because auto-loan maturities range from four to five years and the average life of a pool of auto loans is usually two years or less. Unlike the mortgage market, where asset maturities stretch to 30 years, there is less of an incentive to tranche auto-backed cash flows.

The early 1990s saw an increase in both the size and quantity of auto-backed security issuance. With the flood of pass-through paper, issuers began to tailor their bonds' cash flows to investor demand. They achieved tighter execution by issuing pay-through securities that allow for varied payment characteristics. Pay-through securities generally are issued in multiple tranches by an owner trust. The owner trust is structured for tax purposes as a partnership. The SPC retains a 1% interest in the owner trust to maintain its characterization as a partnership for tax, while the remaining 99% is sold to outside investors. Unlike the grantor trust, the owners trust issues both debt and equity securities (in the form of partnership interest). The owners of the "equity certificates" are taxed as partnership holders and the owners of the notes, which are issued under an indenture, are taxed as creditors.

Typically, more deals are issued as pass-throughs than as tranched deals, but since tranched deals are often larger than the average pass-through deal, about 35 percent to 45 percent of each year's issuance comes in the form of tranched securities. Exhibit 31–3 shows the typical structure of a tranched auto and a passthrough auto.

The Financial Asset Securitization Investment Trust (FASIT) legislation that currently is before Congress at the time of this writing would simplify the structuring of auto-loan securities in the same way that the Real Estate Mortgage

E X H I B I T   31–3

Pass-Through versus Tranched Structure

Pass-Throughs				Tranched			
Class	Amount ($)	Avg. Life (Yrs.)	Spread (BPs.)	Class	Amount ($)	Avg. Life (Yrs.)	Spread (BPs.)
A	187,050,000	1.87	52	A1	250,000,000	0.2	Pvt.
B	18,499,000	1.87	60	A2	545,000,000	0.8	1-Mo. L+7
IO	6,000,000	1.46	84	A3	400,000,000	1.9	34
				A4	248,760,000	3.0	35
				B	56,240	3.3	53

Source: Prudential Securities' IMPACT database.

Investment Conduit (REMIC) provided greater tax certainty in the structuring of mortgage-backed securities.

Credit Support

Most auto securities use a senior/subordinate structure for credit enhancement, often coupled with one or more other types of enhancement, such as over collateralization or a cash-reserve account. Total support usually runs in the 8 percent to 12 percent range, with the lower enhancement levels reserved for the larger, more secure issuers. Some of the new and smaller issuers have chosen to use a super-senior structure. This type of credit support utilizes subordination to bring the senior tranches to a triple-A level and then the entire deal, including the subordinate bonds, is wrapped by a monoline insurer. In the unlikely event of an insurer default the senior bonds would be protected by the support bonds.

CREDIT PERFORMANCE

In general, cumulative losses over the life of most auto issues average about 1 percent to 2 percent, but there is a good deal of variation from company to company depending on underwriting and servicing standards. Exhibit 31–4 shows annual portfolio loss data for several of the major ABS auto-loan issuers. The data was taken from company prospectuses and shows a fairly wide variation. The Big Three U.S. auto companies have fairly comparable loss rates, running roughly between 0.5 percent and 1.5 percent. In contrast, some of the foreign-car companies, such as Volvo and Daimler Benz, have much lower loss experiences. This appears to reflect the higher credit characteristics of the typical buyer of those upscale cars. However, even though Honda, Toyota, and Nissan all have similar customer

E X H I B I T   31–4

Net Portfolio Losses for Major Auto-Loan ABS Issuers
(As Percent of Outstanding Receivables at Year-End)

	1988	1989	1990	1991	1992	1993	1994
Chrysler	0.57	0.83	0.98	1.21	0.97	0.75	0.73p
GMAC	0.93	1.13	1.11	1.08	0.89	0.64	0.57p
Ford	1.40	1.57	1.31	1.29	0.90	0.69	0.59p
Daimler Benz		0.30	0.54	0.55	0.90	0.46	
Volvo	0.12	0.06	0.19	0.51	0.26p		
Honda		0.24	0.43	0.51	0.40	0.41	
Nissan	1.18	2.42	3.19	1.99	2.40	2.78	0.99p
Toyota	1.30	1.33	1.01	0.85	0.69	0.49p	
World Omni	1.60	1.82	1.68	1.87	1.22	0.93	
Olympic					0.22	0.52	0.66
USFB	0.63	1.29	0.80	0.71	0.64	0.69	1.08
RCSB	1.19	1.29	1.02	0.95	1.33p		
Western Fin.			1.21	1.40	1.73	1.53	1.09

P = preliminary.
Source: Moody's Asset Credit Evaluations.

profiles, they have very different average loss rates, which suggests their under-writing and collection standards vary considerably. Auto-loan losses also are sensitive to economic cycles. As shown in Exhibit 31–4, losses mounted during the last recession only to decline in recent years as the economy recovered.

While portfolio data can give a general picture of overall losses it is also important to look at losses on individual pools of auto loans. Exhibit 31–5 shows cumulative losses for a number of individual auto-loan pools through the third quarter of 1995. The pools range in age from a few months (pool factors greater than 0.800) to nearly three years (pool factors less than 0.200).

The pool data in Exhibit 31–5 show a slightly different picture than the portfolio data in Exhibit 31–4. The portfolio data show that the Big Three have roughly the same level of losses, but the cumulative pool data show that Chrysler pools have had larger losses than Ford pools and GMAC pools have had the smallest losses of the Big Three. It should be noted, however, that the relatively low loss experience on the GMAC pools is due, in part, to GMAC using more seasoned loans in some of their securitizations. Since the largest loss rates occur on auto loans in the second year, a pool made up largely of loans seasoned for two years or more will show a lower loss rate than a pool of mainly new loans.

E X H I B I T   31–5

Cumulative Losses for Selected Auto-Loan Deals as a Percent of Original Balances

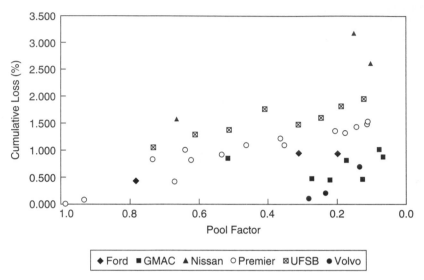

Source: Moody's Asset Credit Evaluations

It is important to understand that loss rates are driven by company-specific underwriting and servicing standards, as well as by the overall economy, and that these factors change over time. Historical data, such as the data shown in Exhibits 31–4 and 31–5, can give only a rough estimate of likely losses. Developing a sound projection of losses for a particular deal requires a careful examination of the latest information available with respect to the issuer, the industry, and the general economy.

PREPAYMENTS

Prepayments are much less of a concern in auto securities than in mortgage related securities. However, speed is still an issue— i.e., pools from certain issuers or with certain characteristics will prepay faster than others, but auto ABSs have virtually no prepayment response to changes in interest rates. In other words, these securities have no discernible negative convexity.

There are several reasons for this lack of response to changes in interest rates. Since autos are a depreciating asset, after a short time, the amount of the loan oftentimes is more than the value of the auto, so a refinancing of the loan would mean putting up cash to pay off the old loan. Also, used-car loans have much higher rates than do new-car loans, as much as 300 basis points or more.

Interest rates would have to fall a great deal before refinancing into a used loan would make economic sense. Finally, the size of the average car loan, at around $20,000, is far less than the average home-mortgage loan. This means a reduced interest rate will not make a great difference in monthly payments. For all of these reasons auto prepayments are largely interest-rate insensitive.

Non–interest sensitive prepayments occur for several reasons. including theft, accidents, and the desire to trade up to a newer car. Prepayments from theft and accidents do not vary significantly with the age of the loan, but the desire to trade up increases as the loan seasons. Hence, prepayments on autos, measured in CPR terms, show a rising trend as the loans age. This is illustrated in Exhibit 31–6, which plots average prepayment speeds for 15 auto deals originated in 1993. The top half of the exhibit shows speeds in terms of CPR, the traditional speed measure for MBSs.[1] However, because there is no one CPR speed that adequately describes this pattern of prepayments, a new measure of prepayment speed, called ABS, was developed for auto-loan securities.

E X H I B I T   31–6

Average Prepayment Speeds on 1993 Auto Deals

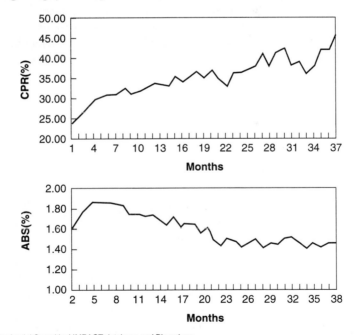

Source: Prudential Securities' IMPACT database and Bloomberg.

---

1. CPR means conditional prepayment rate. For a further discussion see Chapter 27.

ABS versus CPR as Speed Measures

The ABS measure calculates prepayments by comparing actual prepayments each month with the original outstanding balance in the pool. CPR, the traditional prepayment measure in the mortgage market, is calculated by comparing actual prepayments each month with the remaining balance in the pool. A constant ABS curve translates into a continuously rising CPR curve. Exhibit 31–7 shows the CPR equivalent to a 1.5 percent ABS speed. In reality, auto-loan prepayment speeds do not increase continually in CPR terms as a constant ABS implies, but rather level off after three or so years and then turn down. Hence, in ABS terms speeds do not remain constant but, after holding stable for several years, decline in the last years of a pool's life. However, there is very little principal remaining by then, so the use of a constant ABS does not lead to any significant error in calculating yields or average lives. The speeds for the 1993 auto deals in ABS terms are shown in the bottom half of Exhibit 31–6.

Historical Prepayment Speeds

While prepayment speeds vary slightly from issuer to issuer and also vary slightly with weighted-average coupon (WAC), weighted-average maturity (WAM), and percentage of used cars, these influences have only a minor impact. Prepayments on most auto-loan-backed ABSs are quite similar. This is shown in Exhibit 31–8, which presents the pricing speeds and actual lifetime speeds for a number of auto issues originated in 1992 and 1993. Those issuance years were chosen because

E X H I B I T   31–7

CPR Equivalent of 1.5% ABS

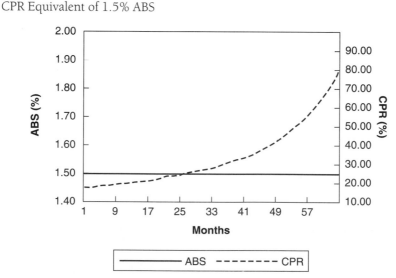

Source: Prudential Securities' IMPACT database.

EXHIBIT 31-8

Actual Auto Prepayment Speeds Versus Pricing

		Pricing ABS (%)	Actual Lifetime ABS (%)*	Diff. (%)
1992 Issuance				
UAC	1992-A	1.40	1.51	+0.11
	1992-B	1.40	1.53	+0.13
	1992-C	1.40	1.52	+0.12
GMAC	1992-A	1.30	1.49	+0.19
	1992-C	1.30	1.60	+0.30
	1992-D	1.30	1.60	¡0.30
	1992-E	1.30	1.56	+0.26
	1992-F	1.30	1.79	+0.49
CARAT	1992-1	1.30	1.66	+0.36
Nissan	1992-A	1.30	1.48	+0.18
	1992-B	1.30	1.63	+0.33
Volvo	1992-A	1.30	1.49	+0.19
	1992-B	1.30	1.60	+0.30
World Omni	1992-A	1.30	1.56	+0.26

		Pricing ABS (%)	Actual Lifetime ABS (%)*	Diff. (%)
1993 Issuance				
GMAC	1993-A	1.50	1.71	+0.21
	1993-B	1.50	1.78	+0.28
Ford	1993-A	1.30	1.63	+0.33
	1993-B	1.30	1.47	+0.17
UAC	1993-A	1.40	1.52	+0.12
	1993-B	1.50	1.48	−0.02
	1993-C	1.50	1.53	+0.03
Olympic	1993-A	1.30	1.90	+0.60
	1993-B	1.50	1.86	+0.36
	1993-C	1.50	1.73	+0.23
	1993-D	1.50	1.64	+0.14
Toyota	1993-A	1.40	1.56	+0.16
Hyundai	1993-A	1.30	1.52	+0.22
World Omni	1993-A	1.30	1.60	+0.30

Summary Statistics

		Pricing ABS (%)		Actual ABS (%)		
Issues	#	Range	Avg.	Range	Avg.	Std. Dev.
1992	14	1.30–1.50	1.35	1.48–1.79	1.57	0.08
1993	14	1.30–1.50	1.41	1.47–1.90	1.64	0.13
1996**	11	1.30–1.80	1.51			

* Most deals in Exhibit 31–7 have been paid down fully or will be paid down fully in the near future.

** For the first six months of 1996.

Source: Prudential Securities' IMPACT database and Bloomberg.

the deals from those years have either recently paid down fully or will in the near future, so the lifetime speeds for the entire life, or almost the entire life, of each deal are available.

As the data in Exhibit 31–7 show, actual speeds for issues from both 1992 and 1993 fell in a fairly narrow range of 1.47 percent ABS to 1.90 percent ABS. The actual average speeds for 1992 and 1993 were 1.57 percent ABS and 1.64 percent ABS, respectively. The standard deviations in those years were 0.08 percent ABS and 0.13 percent ABS, respectively. If we use an average speed of 1.60 percent ABS and a standard deviation of 0.10 percent ABS to represent the overall population of auto loans, then 95 percent of all auto speeds would be expected to fall within a range of 1.40 percent ABS to 1.80 percent ABS. A prepayment variation of 1.4 percent ABS to 1.8 percent ABS would cause the average life of a typical auto-loan security to shift from 1.6 years to 1.9 years. For a 95 percent confidence range this is relatively small and because of this, prepayment speed on autos is not a major concern for most investors.

Having said that, however, the data in the exhibit also show that, in 1992 and 1993, most issuers used pricing speeds that proved to be slower than actual speeds. For the 1992 issues in Exhibit 31–7, the average pricing speed was 1.35 percent ABS, compared with an actual speed of 1.57 percent ABS; for 1993, the average pricing speed was 1.41 percent ABS compared with an actual average of 1.64 percent ABS. In response to this underestimation, issuers have begun to use slightly faster pricing speeds. In the first five months of 1996, more 1.5 percent ABS and 1.6 percent ABS speeds were used in pricing than in prior years and the average climbed to 1.51 percent, not far from the average actual speeds recorded for the 1992 and 1993 origination-year deals.

SPREADS—AUTOS VERSUS OTHER ABSS

In the ABS market, auto securities, next to credit cards, have the simplest structure. As noted earlier, they are amortizing securities but they have virtually no negative convexity. Hence, they trade only slightly behind credit cards, but tighter than mortgage related products, such as manufactured-housing and home-equity-loan (HELs) securities. Exhibit 31–9 shows the typical spread relationship between autos and other ABSs. Most pass-through autos have average lives of 1.8 to 2.2 years—with 4- to 5-year windows. Tranched deals include bonds with average lives that range from 1 to 5 years, with the majority having average lives of 1 to 3 years. Only a small percentage of the tranched bonds have average lives as long as 4 or 5 years. Windows on tranched deals run from 1 to 3 years.

Exhibit 31–10 shows historical spreads on 2-year autos compared with 2-year credit cards and HELs. In late-1991/early-1992, auto spreads and credit-card spreads were virtually the same. In part, this reflected the credit concerns of the 1990/1991 recession and the fear that increasing defaults on credit cards would lead to early amortization events. Since then, auto spreads have fluctuated in a

EXHIBIT 31–9

Auto Spreads versus Other ABS Spreads*

Spread	2-Year	3-Year
Credit Cards	26	28
Autos—Tranched	34	36
Autos—PTs	40	–
Manufactured Housing	45	47
HELs	68	75

* As of 5/8/96.

Source: Prudential Securities' IMPACT database.

EXHIBIT 31–10

Spread Comparison—2-Year Auto versus 2-Year HEL and Credit-Card Bullet

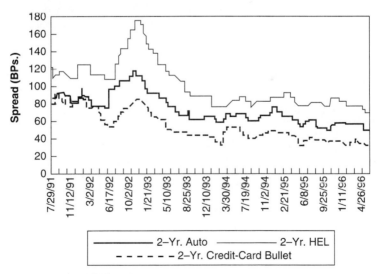

Source: Prudential Securities' IMPACT database.

more typical range of 10 to 25 basis points wider than cards. The current difference of around 15 basis points in mid-June 1996 is roughly in the middle of that historical range.

Finance-Company Spreads

One pricing aspect of the auto market that investors should be aware of is that issues from the independent finance companies and smaller issuers such as Olympic and Union Acceptance Corporation (UAC) typically trade 5 to 10 basis points wider than the issues from the Big Three or the major commercial banks. This is illustrated in Exhibit 31–11, which shows spreads on a group of auto deals issued in February/March 1996. In the tranched section, the 2-year bonds from Olympic 1996-A and Western Financial 1996-A were priced 6 and 8 basis points, respectively, wider than the 2-year from the Premier 1996-1. In a like manner, the UAC 1996-A pass-through was priced 6 to 8 basis points wider than the auto pass-throughs from the three major commercial banks shown in the exhibit.

The wider spreads exist because of liquidity and credit concerns. However, since the bonds from the finance companies are rated triple-A just as are the bonds from the Big Three, there seems little reason to view the securities from the finance companies as any less credit worthy. There is a question of liquidity because the finance companies typically have smaller issues than the Big Three, but this does not seem to be worth the 6 to 8 basis-point differential, especially for buy-and-hold investors. Hence, we believe that the wide spreads on the independent finance-company auto ABSs often represent an opportunity for investors.

EXHIBIT 31–11

Recent Auto ABS Issues

Tranched	Date	Amt. (MM)	Avg. Life (yrs.)	Spread (Bps)
Premier 1996-1	3/21/96	1,250	2.0	34
Olympic 1996-A	3/7/96	600	2.0	40
Western Fin 1996-A	3/21/96	484	2.0	42
Pass-Throughs				
Chase 1996-A	2/14/96	1,474	1.6	41
Banc One 1996-A	3/15/96	537	1.6	42
Fifth Third 1996-A	3/19/96	408	1.7	43
UAC 1996-A	2/9/96	203	1.9	49

Source: Prudential Securities' IMPACT database.

RELATIVE VALUE AND THE SHAPE
OF THE YIELD CURVE

Autos, as amortizing assets, have wider payment windows than many competing securities, such as credit cards and Treasuries. Because of this, the relative value of autos versus credit cards and other short-term securities can be impacted significantly by the shape of the yield curve. In general, bullet-like securities, such as cards, perform better with a steep yield curve because they roll down the curve faster than wide-window bonds. This can be seen by comparing autos to cards under two scenarios, one when the curve is flat and another when the curve is relatively steep. The first quarter 1996 was an excellent period to make this comparison because the short end of the curve went from slightly inverted to steeply positive in a few weeks between mid-February and the end of March.

Exhibit 31–12 shows how the steepening of the curve impacted the total return on a pass-through auto (UAC 1996-C) and a controlled-amortization credit

EXHIBIT 31–12

The Impact of Curve Steepening on Total Return

	2/14/96	
Type	Pass-Through Auto	Credit Card
Issue	UAC 1995-C	Advanta 1992-3
Class	A	A
Price (32nds)	101–09+	101–08
Average Life (Yrs.)	1.49	1.40
Yield (%)	5.43	5.08
Spread/Coupon (BPs.)	50	28
Spread/WAL (BPs.)	62	28
6-Mo. Total Return (%)	5.45	5.08
Total-Return Advantage (BPs.)	37	
	3/28/96	
Type	Pass-Through Auto	Credit Card
Issue	UAC 1995-C	Advanta 1992-3
Class	A	A
Price (32nds)	100–04	100–05
Average Life (Yrs.)	1.49	1.40
Yield (%)	6.28	5.91
Spread/Coupon (BPs.)	50	28
Spread/WAL (BPs.)	62	28
6-Mo. Total Return (%)	6.38	6.26
Total-Return Advantage (BPs.)	12	

Source: Prudential Securities' IMPACT database.

EXHIBIT 31-13

Impact of Curve Steepening on Z-Spreads

	Window* (Yrs.)	Average Life (Yrs.)	Price (32nds)	Spread to Cpn. (BPs.)	Spread to WAL (BPs.)	Z-Spread (BPs.)	Diff. (BPs.)	Date
Tranched Autos								
Olympic 1995-E A2	0.2–1.3	0.66	100–09+	46	57	56	1	2/14/96
			100–01	46	57	48	9	3/12/96
Pass-Through Autos								
UFSB 1994-C 1A	0.1–2.4c	1.11	101–10+	50	59	55	4	2/14/96
			100–21	50	59	44	15	3/12/96
UAC 1995-D A	0.1–3.5c	1.74	100–29+	49	59	51	8	2/14/96
			99–19	49	59	48	11	3/12/96
Cards								
Discover 1992-B A	1.3–2.2	1.78	102–19+	28	35	35	0	2/14/96
			101–06+	28	35	31	4	3/12/96
Standard 1993-1 A	2.6	2.60	100–05+	28	31	31	0	2/14/96
			97–31	28	31	29	2	3/12/96

* The UFSB 1994-C and UAC 1995-D autos are priced to their cleanup calls.

Source: Prudential Securities' IMPACT database.

card (Advanta 1992-3). Prior to the curve steepening, the auto had a spread advantage of 34 basis points (62 versus 28) and all of that advantage was passed on in its total-return advantage of 37 basis points (5.45 percent versus 5.08 percent). That is, the auto was not penalized for having a wide window and rolling down the curve at a slower speed than the card. However, after the front end of the curve steepened, the total-return advantage of the auto declined to 12 basis points, even though its nominal spread advantage remained at 34 basis points.

During this period, a similar change took place with the Z-spreads on auto issues.[2] A Z-spread calculation differs from the traditional yield-spread calculation in that it uses the entire curve to discount a bond's cash flows rather than just one point. Because of this, a Z-spread gives a more accurate representation of value when the yield curve is sloped than does yield spread. The impact of the February/March 1996 steepening on auto and credit-card Z-spreads is shown in Exhibit 31–13. The Z-spreads on the shortest autos, Olympic 1995-E and UFSB 1994-C, tightened by 8 and 11 basis points, respectively, even though nominal spreads were unchanged. On the cards, the Z-spreads tightened by only 2 to 4 basis points. For the Z-spread buyer, the autos suddenly had become 6 to 7 basis points more expensive.

SUMMARY

Auto-loan securities have long played a leading role in the ABS market and occasionally have vied with credit cards for the largest ABS issuance sector. Like most other ABS securities, autos typically carry a triple-A rating based on expected losses, structure, and credit support. They are either structured as pass-throughs, with a single senior class, or as an owners' trust, when they are tranched into different average-life securities. Their prepayment seasoning pattern shows an ever increasing speed in CPR terms but, when translated to ABS—the speed metric for autos—they show roughly a constant speed, with slightly faster ABSs in the first two years. Prepayment speeds vary little from issuer to issuer or over the economic cycle and generally fall within a small range of 1.4 percent ABS to 1.8 percent ABS. The stable prepayments and short average lives make auto ABSs attractive to short-term investors. Spreads usually run 10 to 25 basis points wider than credit cards.

---

2. Z-spread is also referred to as a *zero-volatility spread* and *static spread.* For a discussion of this measure, see Chapter 35.

⑥ HOME EQUITY LOANS (HELS) AND HEL-BACKED SECURITIES

Joseph C. Hu, Ph.D.
Managing Director
Director of Mortgage Research
Oppenheimer & Co., Inc.

Home equity loans (HELs) are the third most significant collateral of asset-backed securities (ABSs), next only to credit card receivables and auto loans. This chapter provides basic information about HELBSs in five areas. First, it describes the nature, the type, the growth, the underwriting criteria, the various credit quality of borrowers, and the delinquency and default experience of HELs. Second, it describes important elements of securitizing HELs: the pool characteristics, the credit enhancement, and the maturity tranching of HELBSs. Third, it provides a discussion of the unique patterns of HELBS prepayments versus those of first-lien mortgage pools. Fourth, it presents yield spreads and relative value of HELBSs. The final section looks into the potential growth of HELs and HELBSs in the near term.

ESSENCE OF HOME EQUITY LOANS*

A HEL is essentially a second-lien (or in a limited number of cases, a third-lien) mortgage on a house that has already been pledged to secure a first-lien mortgage. In case of a default on the second mortgage, the lender of the second mortgage (second mortgagee) is entitled to initiate the foreclosure proceedings and

---

*The author is grateful for the valuable comments by Spencer Kowal of Duff & Phelps Credit Rating Co. and Michele Loesch of Fitch Investors Service, L.P.

liquidate the house in order to satisfy the claim. Proceeds from liquidation, however, are first to satisfy the claim of the lender of the first mortgage (first mortgagee). The second mortgagee is not entitled to receive anything until the first mortgagee is paid in full.

Lending on a second mortgage therefore is riskier than a first mortgage. A lender, however, would still be willing to finance the homeowner with a second mortgage if there is a significant build-up of equity on the house. The equity build-up can be the result of (1) substantial paydown of the first mortgage through amortization over time and partial prepayments (curtailments) and/or (2) significant price appreciation of the house.

RECENT GROWTH OF SECOND MORTGAGES

While HELs have existed nearly as long as first mortgages, their annual originations began to expand significantly only in the 1980s. This rapid expansion was made possible by a decade of phenomenal house price appreciation in the 1970s. As the post–World War II baby boomers first reached home-buying age in the early 1970s, demand for housing rose sharply. As a result, house prices on average jumped 10 percent annually during the 1970s. Recognizing this substantial accumulation of equity, homeowners resorted to second mortgages to finance their various big-ticket expenses.

After the mid-1980s, the incentive to rely on second mortgages as a major financing vehicle was strengthened even more by the enactment of the Tax Reform Act of 1986. The Act phased out the income tax deductibility of nonmortgage interest expenses. It greatly encouraged homeowners to consolidate their debts through second mortgages to reduce the after-tax interest expenses. (However, the Act specified that mortgage interest costs are deductible only if the loan proceeds are used for home improvement, and educational and medical expenses.) The subsequent Omnibus Budget Reconciliation Act of 1987 furthered the expansion of second mortgages as it allowed homeowners to fully deduct the interest expenses of second mortgages up to a maximum balance of $100,000 with no restrictions on the use of the proceeds.

In recent years, lenders have become more active in soliciting homeowners to explore second mortgage financing. They are doing so to offset the sharp drop of first-mortgage originations from the 1992–93 period. During this period, refinancing was at record strong pace and it ballooned originations of first mortgages to nearly $1 trillion annually. Now that refinancing activity has slowed considerably and first-mortgage originations are running only at an annualized rate of $600 to $650 billion, lenders have resorted to second mortgages to sustain their origination activity. This is particularly true among lenders who greatly expanded their underwriting staff and facilities during the refinancing wave. As will be mentioned later, many lenders are not only actively marketing HELs to homeowners with favorable credit histories but to those with less desirable histories as well.

Origination and Outstanding Volumes

Various research reports citing different sources have estimated that, as of year-end 1993, the outstanding volume of HELs ranged between $255 and $275 billion.[1] A period of rapid growth of HELs was between 1986 and 1991, when the estimated outstanding volume expanded from $100 to $160 billion to around $275 billion. However, the growth of the outstanding balance of HELs appears to have either leveled off or even contracted after 1991.

Given that the estimated outstanding volume has leveled off since 1991, the annual originations of HELs in recent years can be approximated. As will be discussed later, prepayments of pools of securitized HELs average much faster than those of first-lien mortgages underlying FNMA/FHLMC-guaranteed pass-throughs. Throughout this chapter, first-lien mortgages that are eligible for securitization programs of FNMA/FHLMC are referred to as *conforming mortgages*. Roughly, HEL pools prepay between 20 percent and 30 percent CPR annually. Assume that the outstanding balance of HELs has leveled off at $275 billion since 1991 and that the annual prepayment rate has been constantly 25 percent, then annual HEL originations during 1991–93 are just under $70 billion. However, given the anecdotal evidence, annual originations during 1994–95 could far exceed $70 billion.

Two Types of HELs

HELs can be originated in the form of either closed- or open-end. A *closed-end HEL* is structured similarly to a first mortgage. It usually has a 10- to 15-year maturity with a fixed interest rate and a full amortization schedule. An *open-end HEL* has a revolving line of credit. It can be a fully amortized loan or a loan with an interest-only period for the first few years. A fully amortized open-end HEL calls for the drawn amount of the credit line to be paid over a fixed period. If there are any additional draws, the monthly payment will then be adjusted so that the loan will be fully repaid within a specified amortization period. The interest-only period of an open-end HEL can be as long as 15 years. At the end of the interest-only period, the loan can be repaid either in full with a balloon payment or in an amortized manner according to a specified schedule. The interest rate on an open-end HEL is usually adjustable, indexed to the prime rate, the Treasury bill rate, or LIBOR.

---

1. There are several excellent reference articles on home equity loans that have estimated the outstanding volume of HELs. See Glenn B. Canner and Charles A. Luckett, "Home Equity Lending: Evidence from Recent Surveys," *Federal Reserve Bulletin* (July 1994), pp. 571–83; Suzanne Mistretta, Kathleen Haas, and Bruce Kramer, "An Introduction to Home Equity Loans," *Asset-Backed Securities Special Report,* Bear Stearns, December 5, 1994; "Fixed-Rate Home Equity Loan Market Summary," First Boston, April 1991; "Home Equity Loans," *Structured Finance Special Report,* Duff & Phelps Credit Rating Co., February 1992; and Paul Jablansky, "HELs and HELOCs: The Market for Securitized Home Equity Loans and Lines of Credit," *Fixed Income Research*, Goldman Sachs, April 1991.

Prior to the mid-1980s, HELs were mostly closed-end. In 1985, closed-end accounted for over 85 percent of the estimated outstanding HELs. In recent years, however, open-end has become increasingly popular among borrowers. As of year-end 1993, open-end almost caught up with closed-end, representing 43 percent of the outstanding HELs. In general, banks and thrifts, being depository institutions, are mostly lenders of open-end HELs. Finance companies and mortgage bankers, on the other hand, originate primarily closed-end HELs.

Financial Characteristics of Borrowers

A nationwide survey of households conducted jointly by the Survey Research Center of the University of Michigan and the Federal Reserve Board for November 1993 through March 1994 found that homeowners with open-end HELs have an average income of $61,234.[2] This income is 33 percent higher than the average of closed-end borrowers and 18 percent higher than those with only first mortgages. Further, the open-end borrowers on average own more expensive homes ($165,838) than closed-end ($113,282) and first-mortgage borrowers ($129,174). Open-end borrowers have an average of $109,564 home equity—2.5 times the average equity of closed-end and 1.9 times that of first-mortgage borrowers.

Underwriting Criteria—Three Ratios

Unlike first mortgages, where there are long-established FNMA/FHLMC underwriting standards, HELs are originated with varying underwriting criteria. However, all lenders examine three ratios along with the credit quality of borrowers when underwriting HELs: combined loan-to-value ratio (CLTV), second-lien ratio, and debt-to-income ratio.

The *CLTV* is derived by dividing the total amount of the outstanding liens on the house (mostly just the balance of the first mortgage and the loan balance of the second mortgage) by the appraised value of the house. For example, as shown in Exhibit 32–1, the outstanding balance of the first-lien mortgage is $100,000 and the amount of the to-be-originated HEL1 is $25,000. The combined mortgage debt is $125,000. If the house is appraised at $135,000, the CLTV is 92.6 percent. The *second-lien ratio* is obtained by dividing the balance of the HEL1 by the combined debt. From the above example, the second-lien ratio is 20 percent. If the homeowner has no debt other than the two mortgages, the monthly payment on the mortgages will be $1,002 (assuming a 30-year 8 percent first mortgage and a 15-year 10 percent HEL). If the homeowner has an after-tax monthly income of $3,125, the *debt-to-net income ratio,* a quotient of the monthly mortgage payment divided by the monthly income, netting out income taxes, is 32 percent (not counting expenses on the property tax and various types of insurance).

---

2. See Canner and Luckett, p. 574.

E X H I B I T   32–1

Risk Analysis of Three Hypothetical Home Equity Loans with Different
Second-Lien Ratios and Combined Loan-to-Value Ratios

	Second -Lien Ratio		
	HEL1	**HEL2**	**HEL3**
I. Market Value of House			
Appraised value of house	$135,000	$135,000	$135,000
Less: price depreciation	$15,000	$15,000	$15,000
Less: foreclosure expenses & carrying costs	$15,000	$15,000	$15,000
Equal: available proceeds for claims	$105,000	$105,000	$105,000
II. Status of Mortgage Lien			
First lien	$100,000	70,000	$56,000
Second lien	$25,000	55,000	$44,000
Equal: total lien	$125,000	125,000	$100,000
Second lien ratio	**20%**	**44%**	**44%**
Combined loan-to-value ratio	**92.6%**	**92.6%**	**74.1%**
III. Recoveries			
Available proceeds for claims	$105,000	105,000	$105,000
Less: first lien	$100,000	70,000	$56,000
Equal: proceeds available for second lien	$5,000	35,000	$49,000
Minus: second lien	$25,000	55,000	$44,000
Equal: (loss of second lien)	($20,000)	(20,000)	$5,000
Percent of loss of second lien	**(80%)**	**(36.4%)**	**None**

Notes:

1. At the origination of HEL, the house was appraised at $100,000. Later on, when default occurs, the house price may appreciate or depreciate. In the present example, it has depreciated 15 percent.

2. The format of this spreadsheet analysis is essentially derived from a report by Michele J. Loesch and Mary Sue Lundy, "Home Equity Loan Criteria," *Structured Finance Special Report,* Fitch Investors Service, Inc., October 31, 1994.

In general, given the debt-to-net income ratio and the CLTV, a HEL is riskier if its second-lien ratio is lower. Alternatively, holding the debt-to-net income and the second-lien ratio constant, a HEL is riskier if its CLTV is higher. As Exhibit 32–1 shows, HEL1 is riskier than HEL2 because it has a lower second-lien ratio (25 percent versus 44 percent), although both have the same CLTV of 92.6 percent. In foreclosure, the lender of HEL1 has an 80 percent loss, substantially greater than the 36.4 percent loss of HEL2. However, HEL2 is riskier than HEL3 even though both have the same 44 percent second-lien ratio. It is the higher CLTV that makes HEL2 riskier relative to HEL3. The lower CLTV of HEL3 protects the lender completely in foreclosure so that it has no loss from default.

Four Credit Quality Groups of Homeowners

In addition to the three ratios, the credit quality of the homeowner is an important element in underwriting HELs. In fact, recent default history of HELBSs suggests that the credit quality is probably more important than the three ratios. In general, the credit quality of homeowners falls into four groups: A, B, C, and D. However, there are no industry-defined standards to describe these groups. Lenders, under the pressure of intensive competition to originate loans, may very well have a flexible "working definition" to classify borrowers with respect to their credit history in conjunction with their debt-to-net-income ratio and CLTV. Thus, a "B" borrower defined by one lender may very well be classified as "A–" by another lender. With that in mind, Exhibit 32–2 shows the general description of the four credit quality groups that fits the working definition of most of lenders.

E X H I B I T   32–2

Description of Borrowers of Home Equity Loans by Credit Quality Group

	Credit Quality Group		
Credit Profile	A/A–	B & C	D
Quality Definition	Excellent/Good	Satisfactory/Fair	Unsatisfactory/Poor
Credit History	• No more than two 30-day delinquencies in past 12 months • No prior bankruptcies	• No more than four 30-, day 60-day, and one 90-day delinquencies in past 12 months • No bankruptcies in past 2 to 3 years	• More than four 30-day, two 60-day, and one 90-day delinquencies in past 12 months • No bankruptcies in past 2 years
Originators	Mainly banks, some finance companies	Mainly finance companies, some banks	Finance companies
Underwriting Decisions	Strong capacity to pay with emphasis on property value	Ability to pay and property value	Property value with little emphasis on ability to pay
Maximum CLTV	80%–85%	65%–80%	65%–70%
Debt/Income Ratio	Less than 45%	45%–55%	No higher than 60%
Mortgage Rate	Equal to or slightly higher than first lien	150 to 400 bps higher than first lien	300 to 600 bps higher than first lien

Sources:

1. Michele J. Loesch and Mary Sue Lundy, "Home Equity Loan Criteria," *Structured Finance Special Report,* Fitch Investors Service, Inc., October 31, 1994.

2. Catherine E. Needham, "B & C Programs: Are They Making the Grade?" *Structured Finance Special Report,* Moody's Investors Service, October 1994.

3. Suzanne Mistretta, Kathleen Haas, and Bruce Kramer, "An Introduction to Home Equity Loans," *Asset-Backed Securities Special Report,* Bear Stearns, December 5, 1994.

Delinquencies and Defaults

According to the American Bankers Association, the delinquency rate of open-end HELs is markedly lower than closed-end. Both, however, have lower delinquencies than other consumer loans. Between 1987 and 1995 (first two quarters), the quarterly delinquency rates (for 30 days or more, measured in terms of number of loans) of open-end HELs ranged between 0.57 percent and 0.98 percent. For the same period, the range of the comparable delinquency rates of closed-end HELs was between 1.20 percent and 2.06 percent. The delinquency rates of credit cards, auto loans, and other personal loans during this period were minimally 1.45 percent, ranging mostly between 2.3 percent and 3.3 percent. The primary reason for the excellent track record of HELs, open-end in particular, is that these loans are secured by the borrowers' principal residence. Just as with first mortgages, the borrowers will try their best to keep up the scheduled monthly payments.

Delinquency rates of HELs are even lower than those of first-lien conforming mortgages. The Mortgage Bankers Association of America indicated that the comparable delinquency rate of conforming mortgages ranged between 2.4 percent and 3.2 percent during the 1987–95 period.[3] However, conforming mortgages are less prone to default than HELs. The default rate of the former generally ranges between 0.2 percent and 0.3 percent, less than one-half to one-third of the latter.[4]

The fact that conforming mortgagors are more frequently delinquent, but less prone to default than HEL borrowers is interesting but easy to explain. Both become delinquent, as they are occasionally in financial stress. And a long period of delinquency of both loans will result in foreclosure. Thus, they have equally strong incentive to cure the delinquency. But first mortgagors are better able to do so because they are less burdened with debt than HEL borrowers. Having to service both the first- and the second-mortgage debt, HEL borrowers are more likely to eventually default when they become delinquent.

STRUCTURING HELBSs

While HELs have been securitized in significant volume only in the 1990s, they are the third most significant collateral for ABSs—next to credit cards and auto loans. As shown in Exhibit 32–3, HELBSs made their capital-market debut in 1989 with an annual issuance of $2.7 billion. Between 1990 and 1994, annual issuance of HELBSs ranged between $5.6 and $10.4 billion. They represented 13 percent to 21 percent of all ABSs. Based on data of the first nine months, the 1995 issuance of HELBSs is expected to grow to $12 billion, or 12 percent of the ex-

---

3. See quarterly issues of American Bankers Association's *Consumer Credit Delinquency Bulletin* and Mortgage Bankers Association of America's *National Delinquency Survey.*
4. See Lakhbir Hayre, Charles Huang, and Tom Zimmerman, *Analysis of Home-Equity Securities*, Financial Strategy Group, Prudential Securities, August 1993.

EXHIBIT   32–3

Issuance Volume of Asset-Backed Securities and Home Equity Loan-Backed Securities, 1989–1995

	ABSs	*HELBSs*	
	Issuance ($ Billions)	**Issuance ($ Billions)**	**Percent of ABSs (%)**
1989	24.6	2.7	11
1990	42.7	5.6	13
1991	50.5	10.4	21
1992	51.2	6.0	12
1993	59.7	7.0	12
1994	75.6	10.1	13
1995	100	12	12

Source: CS First Boston (1989–1994) and Bloomberg (1995 projection based on data of first nine months).

pected $100 billion ABS issuance. Annual originations of HELs in recent years were estimated to be $70 billion. Thus, the securitization ratio of newly originated HELs is 17 percent. This ratio is far below the 60 percent of conforming mortgages when they were in the early years of securitization.

Although originations of open-end HELs have grown rapidly in recent years, closed-end loans have been mostly collateralized for HELBSs. This is particularly true when their respective shares in securitization are measured by the number of transactions rather than in the dollar amount of issuance. Exhibit 32–4 shows that during the 1990–95 period, closed-end accounted for 55 percent of all newly issued HELBSs measured in dollar amount. In number of transactions, however, the share of closed-end HELs was 78 percent. In the past three years, closed-end loans represented at least 60 percent in dollar amount and 79 percent in number of transactions of all HELBSs. One reason is that closed-end loans are mechanically easier to structure. The system requirements for cash flow allocation among various entities of open-end transactions are much more onerous than those of closed-end. Also, closed-end loans are mainly originated by finance companies. Without their own steady source of funding, finance companies (who normally obtain funds from banks with interest rates pegged to the prime rate) have to sell their originations.

Securitizing HELs

To securitize HELs, the lender pools its newly originated HELs and sells them to a trust. By selling these loans, *the lender* (now, *the seller*) transfers all the right, title, and interest in and to the loans to the trust. *The trust* (now, *the issuer*) then

EXHIBIT 32-4

Shares of Closed- and Open-End Loans Backing HELBSs by Dollar Amount of Issuance and Number of Transactions

Time Period/ Type of Loans	Dollar Amount		Transactions	
	($ millions)	Share (%)	Number	Share (%)
1990–95	46,567		209	
Closed-end	23,172	55	146	78
Open-end	18,871	45	42	22
Undetermined	4,524	—	21	—
1993	6,733		41	
Closed-end	4,028	60	35	85
Open-end	2,705	40	6	15
Undetermined	0	—	0	—
1994	9,378		58	
Closed-end	5,538	63	41	84
Open-end	3,226	37	8	16
Undetermined	614	—	9	—
1995	6,317		38	
Closed-end	3,352	76	23	79
Open-end	1,044	23	6	21
Undetermined	1,921	—	9	—

Note: This table was compiled by Oppenheimer's Mortgage Research according to Bloomberg's collateral description of all publicly offered HELBSs at issuance since inception. Some early transactions have already been paid off. A few transactions where collateral description is not provided are classified as *undetermined*. The share computation excludes the undetermined. For the compilation of this table, Oppenheimer now has collateral information of all publicly offered HELBSs.

Sources: Bloomberg and Oppenheimer & Co., Inc.

issues a HELBS with the stipulated payment of interest and principal of the security backed by the cash flow of the pooled HELs. For income-tax purposes, the issuer normally elects the REMIC (Real Estate Mortgage Investment Conduit) status that allows the cash flow of HELs (income to the issuer) to pass through the trust to the investor without taxation.[5] Because of this arrangement, HELBSs are "pass-throughs," not debt securities of their issuers.

Also, from an accounting point of view, the transfer of loans from the seller to the issuer constitutes a sale of assets rather than financing. On behalf of the trust, the seller normally acts as *the servicer* of the HELBS to manage, administer, ser-

5. Although virtually all ABSs and mortgage-backed securities (MBSs) are now issued with the issuers electing the REMIC status for reasons of taxation, the term *REMICs* conventionally refers to multiclass MBSs. Further, since the original cash flow structure of REMICs came from collateralized mortgage obligations (CMOs), REMICs are often colloquially called CMOs.

vice, and make collection on the loans. If there are several lenders pooling and selling their HELs to a trust, a master servicer would be needed. Depending on the financial strength of the sellers, one of them may or may not be the master servicer.

Pool Characteristics

In structuring a HELBS, the most important consideration for the issuer is the credit rating of the security. Although rating agencies also pay a great deal of attention to the operation quality of the originator and the servicer, the quality of the underlying HELs in the pool ultimately determines the risk of a HELBS. Exhibit 32–5 lists the statistics that generally characterize a pool of HELs at issuance of HELBSs.

From the two randomly selected transactions shown in Exhibit 32–5, it is clear that each HELBS is backed by a unique pool of loans. The mix of first- and second-lien loans in a pool varies from an extreme of 100 percent first-lien to 64 percent second-lien. Other transactions have virtually the other extreme, with 95 percent second-lien loans. By definition, a HEL is a second-lien mortgage secured by the equity of a house already pledged as collateral for the first-lien mortgage. The very term *equity* implies that the value of the house far exceeds the first-lien balance. But in reality, the HEL lender may provide the homeowner a large loan to pay off the first lien so that the supposedly HEL becomes the first-lien. This type of lending is prevalent and explains why most HELBSs are to some degree backed by first-lien mortgages. The UCFC transaction is the best example that the term *HEL* has become a misnomer. It no longer necessarily implies a second-lien status.

The uniqueness of each HELBS can be demonstrated by the characteristics of its pool. For example, the average size of a HEL pool ranges roughly between $25,000 and $40,000. (The average size of $91,394 of UCFC's Pool Group II is exceptionally large.) The CLTV varies from 75 percent to 79 percent. (For a larger sample of transactions, this range widens to 60 percent to 80 percent.) There is always wide variation of mortgage rates among HELs in a pool. The difference between the highest and the lowest mortgage rates could be as much as 800 basis points. While most closed-end HELs carry a fixed mortgage rate, open-end mortgages carry an adjustable rate. The adjustable rate can be pegged to the 1-, 3-, or 6-month Treasury bill rate or LIBOR. Still, there are exceptions: Closed-end mortgages in UCFC's Pool Group II have an adjustable rate. Although over 90 percent of the houses securing HELs are owner occupied, there is a wide geographic spread in their location. In terms of dollar amount, the top three states usually account for 30 percent to 50 percent of the pool's balance.

Credit Enhancement

Despite their low rates of delinquency and default, HELs by themselves are inadequate for securities backed by their cash flows to obtain the top credit rating without credit enhancement. The following three types of credit enhancement—bond

EXHIBIT 32–5

Original Pool Characteristics of Two Randomly Selected HELBSs

Pool Characteristics	Household Revolving Home Equity Loan Trust 1994-1	UCFC Home Equity Loan Trust 1995-A1 & 1995-A2		
		Pool Group I	Pool Group II	Pool Group III
Size ($ millions)	$731,292	$129,484	$20,655	$15,399
Type of loans	Open-end, ARM	Closed-end, FRM	Closed-end, ARM	Closed-end, FRM
Total loans	21,736	3,269	226	589
Average loan size	$34,329	$39,610	$91,394	$26,144
CLTV	79%	78%	76%	75%
First-lien	36%	100%	100%	26%
Second-lien	64%	0%	0%	74%
Owner occupancy	98%	94%	92%	92%
WAM	168 months	223 months	316 months	166 months
WAC	ARM	12.85%	10.6%	12.75%
Rate range	8%–16%	9.75%–17.75%	7.95%–13.99%	10%–15.5%
Index for ARMs	The prime rate or the 6-month T-bill rate	n. a.	The 6-month LIBOR	n. a.
State concentration	CA: 17.4% NY: 10.6% OH: 8.5%	OH: 12.8% NC: 9.4% LA: 7.7%	MI: 16.4% CA: 13.94% OH: 12.1%	FL: 12.1% LA: 10.7% IL: 9.9%
Credit enhancement	1. Seller subordinated interest 2. O/C 3. CapMAC insurance	1. Reserve account 2. Cross-collateralization 3. MBIA insurance		

Sources:

1 Household Revolving Home Equity Loan Trust, Duff & Phelps Credit Rating Co.

2 UCFC Home Equity Loan Trust, Moody's Investors Service.

3 Bloomberg.

insurance, senior/subordinate cash flow structure, and letter of credit—have been employed either individually or collectively to enable a large portion of HEL cash flows to obtain a triple-A rating by at least one of the top four credit agencies.

Bond Insurance

For HELBSs, the most popular form of credit enhancement is bond insurance. There are several monoline insurance companies whose only business is to insure bonds against the possible loss resulting from insufficient cash flow generated from the collateral to pay the interest and eventually to retire the bonds. (These bonds are called *surety bonds.*) When that happens, bond insurance companies provide up to as much as a 100 percent loss coverage. (For established issuers with good performance record in terms of delinquencies and defaults of their existing pools, the coverage ratio could be substantially less than 100 percent.) However, bond insurers usually require HELBSs to have a combination of a *reserve account,* a certain degree of overcollateralization (O/C), and subordinated seller interest to take the first-loss position. Bond insurers, such as MBIA, FGIC, CapMAC, and FSA, have a triple-A credit rating from at least one of the top credit agencies, and their credit quality flows through to the securities they insure.

A *reserve account* for the trust is set up by the seller. The seller makes an initial deposit on the closing date and subsequently, on a monthly basis, makes additional deposits from the *excess spread* until the account balance is built up to a predetermined percentage of the original or the outstanding balance of the entire pool or the credit enhanced class (generally referred to as Class A). The excess spread is the residual of subtracting generally three items from the monthly cash flow generated from the pool: (1) interest and principal on Class A, (2) the trust fees, and (3) the master servicer fees.

Senior/Subordinate Cash Flow Structure

Enhancing the credit of a senior class with the cash flow of a subordinate class is a more popular means of credit enhancement for credit card-backed ABSs but not for HELBSs. As an illustration of the structure, there may be a 90 percent to 10 percent split on a pro rata basis of the total cash flow generated from the pool for the senior/subordinate, or conventionally termed A/B, structure. All cash flow is to satisfy the senior class (Class A) first before the subordinate class (Class B) is paid. Class B is to absorb all losses until its balance is depleted to zero. Through this arrangement, Class A is able to obtain the triple-A rating.

In order to strengthen the subordination at a given split, a mechanism of *"shifting interest"* is developed. For example, for a lockout period of the first 5 to 7 years, this mechanism allocates all prepayments (but not amortized repayments) to Class A. As the principal balance of Class A diminishes more quickly through prepayments and that of Class B declines only marginally through amortization, the ratio of credit support rises during the lockout period. In an A/B structure, the percentage of subordination necessary for a triple-A credit for Class A is determined by the rating agencies according to their own rating criteria. Needless to say, however, the required subordination of pools of B- and C-rated loans would be significantly greater than A-rated loans.

Letter of Credit

A third alternative of credit enhancement is a letter of credit (LOC) from a commercial bank with a triple-A credit rating. Like bond insurance, LOCs usually provide loss coverage after the reserve account. Also, the credit of LOC-insured securities is reflected by the credit quality of the LOC provider.

Maturity Tranching

After credit enhancement, the triple-A-rated cash flow is often further segmented into several maturity tranches. Like multiclass mortgage pass-throughs (or simply CMOs), the cash flow segmentation allows the issuer to create securities with different expected average lives to satisfy investors with various maturity preferences. There are markedly fewer maturity tranches of HELBSs, however, than CMOs. Also, the tranches are created almost exclusively in a "sequential" (termed "sequentials") format. Thus, there are no "PACs" and "supports" as they are often created among CMOs.

The limited number of maturity tranches of HELBSs is primarily due to the shorter final maturity of HELs and the smaller size of the transaction. Additionally, and more important, HELBSs are usually offered at pricing speeds at least twice as fast as those of REMICs. With fast pricing speeds, the overall average lives of HELBSs are shortened in the first place. Usually, HELBSs are structured to have four to six maturity tranches. For fixed-rate HELBSs, the expected average lives for a five-tranche transaction (Class A1, A2, A3, A4, and A5) are around 1, 3, 5, 7, and 10 years.

For adjustable-rate HELBSs, there are also maturity tranches. However, the number of tranches is dependent on the groups of adjustable-rate loans in the pool. Each tranche is backed by a specific group whose mortgage rates are pegged to a specific index with a specific margin. The tranching in the case of adjustable-rate HELBSs is basically to match each group's underlying mortgage rates with the coupon of its corresponding tranche. The adjustable-rate tranches mostly have similar average lives.

PREPAYMENTS OF HELBSs

Prepayment rates (or speeds) of HELBSs are faster but more stable than those of conforming mortgage pools with comparable mortgage rates and maturities. This difference is more distinctive among fixed-rate than adjustable-rate pools. Generally, speeds of adjustable-rate HELBSs range between 20 percent and 30 percent CPR. This range is not much different from the normal 15 percent to 20 percent CPR of adjustable-rate conforming mortgage pools. The balance of this section focuses on fixed-rate pools.

A Typical Pattern

A newly issued fixed-rate HELBS typically can already prepay in the initial months at a speed of 2 percent to 3 percent CPR. This initial speed is 5 to 10 times as fast as current-coupon 15-year FNMAs/FHLMCs. Further, during the first 10 months or so, the HELBS speeds usually accelerate at a factor of 2 percent to 3 percent CPR per month and level off thereafter at 20 percent to 30 percent CPR.[6] This acceleration, the "seasoning" or "aging" process, is also several times as fast as that of conforming mortgages.

One generic reason for the faster prepayments of HELBSs is that HELs are primarily second-lien mortgages with an average size one-third to one-quarter that of conforming mortgages.[7] Homeowners who borrow against the equity of their homes generally have specific uses for the loan proceeds. To the extent that homeowners have the desire and the ability to lighten their debt, they are more likely to pay off the second mortgage first and the first mortgage second. This is particularly true in a stable interest-rate environment, where refinancing does not present itself as a prepayment factor.

In fact, since HELs carry a higher mortgage rate than first-lien mortgages, there is strong incentive for borrowers to prepay first HELs either partially or fully. Over time, the probability of homeowners paying off HELs becomes increasingly greater. The greater probability may explain the faster seasoning of HELs' prepayments. It may also contribute to their faster speeds after they have reached the "seasoned" stage. Further, homeowners may take out a second mortgage to remodel or upgrade their homes before selling them. After the sale, the second mortgage, along with the first, is prepaid. This phenomenon may even explain the faster prepayment behavior of open-end than closed-end HELs.[8]

Four Major Prepayment Determinants

Prepayments of all types of mortgages are primarily the result of four factors: housing turnover, refinancing, curtailments, and defaults. Over the long haul, housing turnover results in a prepayment rate of approximately 7 percent to 8 per-

---

6. Based on an extensive study of prepayment experience of HELBSs, the Financial Strategy Group of Prudential Securities developed a "HEP" curve as a yardstick to measure prepayments of HELBSs. According to the research group, the HEP curve "steps up linearly from 0% at month zero to its terminal speed in the tenth month. The HEP curve is expressed in terms of its terminal CPR percentage; thus 20% HEP is the equivalent of 2% CPR in the first month, increasing 2% [CPR] each month until 20% CPR is reached in the tenth month." See Charles Huang, *An Inside Look at Home-Equity-Loan Prepayments*, Financial Strategy Group, Prudential Securities Incorporated, January 1995.

7. The national average loan-to-value ratio of first-lien mortgages is about 80 percent. Given the $137,000 national average sales price of existing homes, the average size of first mortgages is $109,600. By comparison, the size of loans backing HELBSs ranges mostly between $25,000 and $40,000. Thus, first-lien mortgages are roughly three to four times the size of second-lien HELs. According to the Federal Reserve study, the average size of all outstanding HELs in the 1993–94 period was around $15,000.

8. According to the 1993–94 *Surveys of Consumers*, 64 percent of open-end and 38 percent of closed-end HELs are for home improvement. See footnote 3.

cent CPR for all mortgage pools.[9] Thus, variations of prepayments come from the other three factors through different underwriting criteria and credit quality of borrowers. As mentioned earlier, there are no industry-defined underwriting standards among lenders to originate HELs, and the credit quality of borrowers varies widely. As a result, for HELBSs, defaults and curtailments are relatively more important prepayment factors than refinancing.

Significance of Defaults

As mentioned earlier, HELs have a higher incidence of default than conforming mortgages. This is particularly true for loans to borrowers of lower credit quality. More important, on the basis of specific pools, the default experience of HELs can be substantially higher than that of all outstanding HELs. For pools of C-rated quality borrowers, the annual default rate could be as high as 10 percent. Technically, the default rate is derived by dividing the dollar amount of defaults by the remaining balance of the pool. For a specific pool, the remaining balance, which is the denominator of the default rate, declines over time through rapid prepayments. The numerator, however, may remain unchanged or even rise. As a result, the default rate of a specific HEL pool could be rising rapidly. By contrast, the default rate of all outstanding HELs may remain small, as the denominator expands constantly through newly originated loans, which usually have no immediate defaults.

Stability of Prepayments

Prepayments of HELBSs tend to rise more moderately in a declining interest rate environment than comparable conforming mortgages. This tendency contributes to a more stable pattern of their prepayments. When interest rates decline significantly, first mortgages with much bigger balances are always refinanced first. The best case in point is the huge refinancing wave of 1992–93, when prepayments of first mortgage pools soared to nearly 10 times their normal speeds. By contrast,

---

9. The housing turnover rate has long been recognized as one important determinant of prepayments common to all coupons, especially seasoned ones. In a stable interest-rate environment, the turnover rate can serve as a long-term prepayment rate for current and discount coupons. The 7 percent to 8 percent turnover rate is derived by dividing annual sales of existing homes by the "specified stock" of single-family owner-occupied homes. (The specified stock includes only houses on a less-than-10-acre lot with no business on the property.) In recent years, existing homes sales ranged from 3.5 to 4 million units, and the current specified stock amounts to about 50 million units. For a detailed discussion of housing turnover and prepayments, see Joseph Hu, "An Alternative Prepayment Projection Based on Housing Activity," in *The Handbook of Mortgage-Backed Securities*, revised ed., ed. Frank J. Fabozzi (Chicago: Probus Publishing, 1988). Also, see "Qualitatively Assessing Prepayments of Current- and Discount-Coupon Pass-Throughs," *Mortgage Research*, Oppenheimer & Co., Inc., October 20, 1994.

EXHIBIT 32–6

Comparison of Prepayments of Fixed-Rate HELBSs versus Conforming Mortgage Pools by the Four Major Determinants of Prepayments

	Determinants of Prepayments			
	Housing Turnover	**Refinancing**	**Curtailments**	**Defaults**
Credit Quality				
A	Indifferent	Indifferent	Indifferent	Indifferent
B	Indifferent	M lower	S higher	M higher
C	Indifferent	S lower	M higher	S higher
D	Indifferent	S lower	M higher	S higher
Loan Type				
Closed-end	Indifferent	S lower	M higher	S higher
Open-end	Indifferent	M lower	S higher	M higher
Share of First-Lien				
High	Indifferent	M lower	S higher	M higher
Low	Indifferent	S lower	M higher	S higher

Note: *M* stands for moderately, *S* for significantly.

prepayments of HELs rose only moderately. HELs are less likely to be refinanced probably because their rates usually do not move in lockstep with market interest rates. This is especially true for C- and D-rated loans, whose rates are much higher than those of first mortgages and much less responsive to a bond market rally. Also, the second mortgage balance may be too small to warrant the associated refinancing costs.

All in all, prepayment patterns of HELBSs are more complex than conforming mortgage pools. The complexity has its root in the widely different underwriting criteria and borrower credit quality of the underlying HELs. Exhibit 32–6 provides a rule-of-thumb comparison of prepayment rates between fixed-rate HELBSs and conforming mortgages due to the credit quality of borrowers, loan type, and share of first-lien loans. The comparison is made according to the four major prepayment factors.

YIELD SPREADS AND RELATIVE VALUE OF HELBSs

In a short period of just over six years, HELBSs went from being a newcomer to an established member in the family of ABSs. With intense research provided by securities dealers and rating agencies, investors have become more familiar with the idiosyncrasies of the loans underlying HELBSs. They are also increasingly comfortable with prepayments of HELBSs and can relate the unique prepayment patterns of specific issues to the type of issuers and the underlying borrowers. The annual issuance volume of $5 to $10 billion over the past six years has enhanced the liquidity of HELBSs. All this has contributed to the establishment of HELBSs as a viable asset for investors in fixed income securities.

Tightening Yield Spreads

As HELBSs become accepted among investors, their yield spreads have rapidly tightened. Not more than three years ago, 2- and 3-year average-life HELBSs traded more than 100 and 120 basis points (bps), respectively, over the 2- and 3-year Treasuries. Now the generic yield spreads for the 2- and 3-year average life HELBSs have tightened dramatically to around 75 and 90 bps, respectively. With more recent issues offering a greater variety of maturity selections, trading of longer average-life HELBSs has turned active. Currently, those with 5-, 7-, and 10-year average lives trade around 100, 115, and 135 bps over their respective comparable Treasuries. As mentioned earlier, HELBSs have relatively stable but faster speeds than conforming mortgages. This unique aspect reduces the potential fluctuation of their average lives. Relatively more stable average lives make HELBSs more comparable to PACs than to Sequentials of CMOs. But yield spreads of HELBSs are much wider than comparable average life PACs. As the HELBS market continues to grow, their generous yield spreads are expected to tighten further.

For adjustable-rate HELBSs, the index is often LIBOR, and the discount margin usually ranges between 15 and 20 bps. This margin is significantly tighter than for CMO floaters. One important reason for the tighter margins is that the stable average lives of HELBSs reduce the hedging cost of uncapping their floaters. (For example, an investor in a LIBOR floater could hedge against the possibility of the floater's coupon rate exceeding its cap by purchasing a LIBOR cap for a specified period of time with the strike equal to the floater's cap. The hedging cost is the premium of the cap. The average-life stability saves the investor from purchasing the cap for too long or too short a period, which unduly raises the hedging cost.) Additionally, HELBS floaters generally have only 2- to 3-year average lives. With the CMO issuance drought persisting over the past 18 months, there are very few triple-A-rated stable short floaters in the marketplace.

Greater Risk Weight

However, for commercial banks, HELBSs have one drawback. Commercial banks are required to maintain a minimum capital of 8 percent of risk-adjusted assets, and the risk weight of HELBSs (as well as all ABSs) is 100 percent. This weight is far greater than those of GNMAs, FNMAs/FHLMCs, and agency-guaranteed CMOs, which are 0 percent, 20 percent, and 20 percent, respectively. Thus, the capital tie-down for commercial banks investing in HELBSs is far higher than agency-guaranteed pass-throughs or CMOs. This tie-down is more expensive (or entails a greater opportunity cost) for a bank with a higher return on equity.

⑥   # MANUFACTURED HOUSING-BACKED ABS*

John N. Dunlevy, CFA, CPA
Director and Senior Portfolio Manager
Hyperion Capital Management, Inc.

Andrew Shook
Associate
NationsBanc Capital Markets, Inc.

INTRODUCTION

Manufactured housing, also referred to as mobile homes, are single-family detached homes constructed off-site and transported to a plot of land or to a manufactured housing community (park). Currently, manufactured housing is the fourth-largest sector of the asset-backed market (behind credit cards, automobiles, and home equities), with over 100 deals outstanding, totaling over $22 billion. During 1995, manufactured housing asset-backed securities (ABS) issuance totaled $5.8 billion, which represented approximately 5 percent of the $108 billion asset-backed securities issued during the year (see Exhibit 33–1).

Further, there are over eight million manufactured homes in the United States, representing 7 percent of the total housing stock.

MANUFACTURED HOUSING PRODUCT PROFILE

Product Offerings

There are two types of manufactured housing units: (1) single-section (also known as "single-wides") and (2) multisections. Single-wide units, which are transported to their site in one piece, average 1,065 square feet. Multisection units, on the other hand, which are assembled at the site after being transported in pieces, average 1,525 square feet. Exhibit 33–2 summarizes the manufactured housing loan characteristics.

---

*This chapter is reprinted from *Asset-Backed Securities,* eds. Anand K. Bhattacharya and Frank J. Fabozzi (New Hope, PA: Frank J. Fabozzi Associates, 1996). Andrew Shook was Senior Securities Analyst of Hyperion Capital Management, Inc., when this chapter was written.

E X H I B I T   33–1

1995 ABS Issuance by Sector

Sector	% Issuance
Credit cards	44%
Automobiles	24
Home equities	14
Manufactured housing	5
Other	13
	100%

Source: Prudential Securities

E X H I B I T   33–2

Manufactured Housing Loan Characteristics

	Single-Wide	Multi/Double-Wide	U.S. Avg Site-Built
Average home size	1,065 Sq Ft	1,525 Sq Ft	1,945 Sq Ft
Average sales price	$26,000	$50,000	$143,000
Loan rate vs. conventional	+338 bps.	+288 bps	—
Average loan term	200 mo.	240 mo.	360 mo.
Average monthly payment	$260	$406	$831

Source: Greentree.

Borrower Demographics

Almost 60 percent of all manufactured housing units are located in the South At-lantic or South Central (warm weather) regions of the United States. Florida has the largest single-state concentration, accounting for over 10 percent of all MH units. The demographics of the market vary by unit type. That is, multisection borrowers tend to be older and more affluent. As shown in Exhibit 33–3, 76.5 percent of multi-section borrowers are at least 35 years old. Borrowers in this category often include newly married couples who cannot yet afford a site-built home and older retired couples who no longer want to care for a home. In contrast, single-section borrow-ers are younger, have lower incomes, and are less settled into their careers.

Financing

The typical manufactured housing loan is a 15- to 20-year fully amortizing retail installment loan. Single-section units are usually financed over 15-year terms at rates between 300 bps and 350 bps above conventional 30-year rates. Multisec-

E X H I B I T   33–3

Manufactured Housing Borrower Demographics

	Single-Section	Multi/ Double-Section
Average Age (%)		
18–34	71.0	23.5
35–54	24.2	67.9
55+	4.8	8.6
Avg Years Same Job (%)		
0–5	72.3	29.1
5–10	23.4	59.5
10+	3.4	11.4
Family Income (%)		
15,000–25,000	64.7	12.8
25,000–50,000	34.5	84.6
50,000+	0.8	2.6

Source: Manufactured Home Institute.

tion units are usually financed over 20-year terms at rates between 250 bps and 300 bps over conventional 30-year rates. Currently, only 10 percent of all units financed are written as mortgage loans (i.e., financed with the unit's land).

MANUFACTURED HOUSING ABS—OVERVIEW

MH Issuers

Greentree Financial continues to dominate the issuance of securities backed by manufactured housing loans. For example, during 1995, Greentree issued $4 billion of the $5.8 billion MH securities issued. As shown in Exhibit 33–4, Greentree is dominant in both number of issues outstanding and dollar value of securities outstanding.

MH Prepayment Experience

Manufactured housing has proven to be a market that is largely interest-rate insensitive. We believe that this is the case for four reasons. First, MH loans have small balances, resulting in minimal saving from refinancings (see Exhibit 33–5).

Even a decline of 200 bps for a typical $35,000 MH loan would result in only a $44 monthly savings. Second, manufacturing housing units, like cars, are subject to depreciation. In the early years of a loan's life, depreciation exceeds

E X H I B I T   33–4

Total MH Issuance 1987–1995

Issuer	Number of Issues Outstanding	Percent	$ Value ($000) Issues Outstanding	Percent
Greentree Financial	66	77%	15,735	82%
Security Pacific	6	7	919	5
Vanderbilt	3	4	539	3
RTC	3	4	616	3
Oakwood	3	4	468	3
Others	4	4	799	4
	85	100%	19,076	100%

Source: Morgan Stanley.

E X H I B I T   33–5

MH Refinancing Incentive

	MH	Single-Family
Loan balance	35,000	150,000
Term	200 mo.	360 mo.
Current rate	11%	8%
Monthly payment	$382	$1,100
–100 b.p.		
New rate	10%	7%
New payment	$360	$998
Savings	$22	$102
–200 b.p.		
New rate	9%	6%
New payment	$338	$899
Savings	$44	$201

amortization, leaving the borrower with little equity needed to refinance. Third, few refinancing options are currently available for used manufactured housing units. This is another reason MH loans are insensitive to interest-rate movements. Finally, MH borrowers may not qualify for alternative financings because of their limited financial resources.

E X H I B I T   33–6

Prepayment Sensitivity to Rate Movements (CPR)

	+300	+200	+100	0	−100	−200	−300	+300 BP range (CPR)
Mfd housing ABS	6.0	6.0	6.0	6.0	11.3	13.4	15.8	9.8
Home equity ABS	9.0	12.0	17.0	22.0	27.0	31.0	35.0	26.0
1994 FNMA 6.5	5.0	5.9	7.0	8.6	20.6	49.1	63.1	58.1

Source: Lehman Brothers.

Exhibit 33–6 shows the interest-rate sensitivity of manufacturing housing prepayments to interest-rate movements. Manufactured housing has a CPR prepayment range (+300 to −300) of 9.8 percent CPR, which is substantially lower than the 26.0 CPR and 58.1 CPR range for home equity ABS and 30-year FNMAs, 6.5s, respectively.

MH ABS Credit Performance

In evaluating the credit performance of manufactured housing-backed ABS, it is important to consider delinquencies, loss statistics, and rating agency upgrade/downgrade data.

In terms of delinquencies, the American Bankers Association (ABA) statistics show that total delinquencies were running at around 3 percent during 1995, slightly higher than single-family mortgages but higher than the 1 percent to 1.5 percent delinquency rates for automobiles, recreational vehicles, and boat loans. According to the Manufactured Housing Institute, delinquency levels since 1990 have ranged between 2.25 percent and 3.50 percent. Based on Greentree static pool data, losses by cohort year are reported in Exhibit 33–7.

The default curve for manufactured housing starts off at a very low rate and peaks by year three. After year three, the default rate will decline gradually, leveling off at about 50 percent of its peak level in year 10. Historical experience shows that loss severity ranges between 30 percent and 60 percent (double-wide units have the highest recovery rates).

Finally, the credit record for the manufactured housing sector has been excellent. For example, as shown in Exhibit 33–8, manufactured housing-backed ABS has had more upgrades than any other ABS sector. As shown in the exhibit, the rating agency criteria for ABS appears very conservative. No MH-rated ABS has ever defaulted due to performance problems. The downgrades shown above reflect third-party credit-enhancement deterioration.

E X H I B I T   33–7

Greentree MH Static Pool Losses

Year	Orig. Pool Size ($ billion)	Pool Factor	Loss % of Orig. Pool
1991	$0.6	.47	4.55%
1992	1.4	.58	2.16
1993	2.1	.80	0.67
1994	3.2	.90	0.16
1995	4.0	.98	0.02

E X H I B I T   33–8

ABS Rating Changes

Asset Type	Number of Upgrades	Number of Downgrades	Upgrade /Downgrade Ratio
Automobiles	17	27	0.63
Credit Cards	7	14	0.50
Home Equity	4	7	0.57
Mfd Housing	38	2	19.00
Other	4	6	0.67
	70	56	1.25

Source: Moody's Investor Service

MH DEAL STRUCTURES

A typical structure, which is representative of late 1995 and 1996 deals, is shown in Exhibit 33–9. The deal outlined in the exhibit was priced at a prepayment assumption of 100 MHP. MHP is a prepayment curve used for manufactured housing collateral, which assumes that prepayments start in month one at 3.7 percent CPR and rise 0.1 percent CPR per month until they reach 6 percent CPR in month 24, then stay constant at 6 percent CPR. Therefore, if a deal is priced at a 125 MHP assumption, it is simply 1.25 times the 100 MHP vector (just described).

The deal shown in the exhibit also assumes a 10 percent clean-up call. This is the same assumption used in nonagency CMOs as well as many other ABS sectors. The investor must be sure to understand this for the longer tranches, whether the tranche is priced to maturity or to the call provision.

Third, it is important for the investor to understand the deal's waterfall or cash flow priorities. The deal in the exhibit has sequential-pay priorities for classes A1 through A5 until the first *"crossover date."* The crossover date refers to the date when the lockout period ends and the subordinated tranches (M and B1)

EXHIBIT 33–9

Greentree 1995-10 MH Structure

Class	Size ($MM)	% Deal	Rating	A/L	Window (Mos.)	Spread
A1	48.0	11.9%	AAA	1.05	1–24	+47
A2	63.0	15.5%	AAA	3.06	24–57	+48
A3	41.0	10.1%	AAA	5.07	41–73	+55
A4	33.0	8.1%	AAA	7.09	73–98	+71
A5	59.0	14.6%	AAA	10.25	98–152	+94
A6	92.0	22.7%	AAA	17.24	152–241	+145
M1	37.0	9.1%	AA–	12.57	63–241	+145
B1	16.0	4.0%	BBB+	8.30	63–143	+145
B2	16.0	4.0%	BBB+	17.20	143–241	+177
	405.0			9.25		

Collateral

Number of loans	11,805		New unit %	83%
Avg. size	$34,134		Nonpark unit%	72%
WAC	10.05%		WA LTV%	76%
WAM	280 M		Geographics:	
			10% North Carolina, 8% Michigan, 7% Texas	

begin to receive their pro rata share of principal payments. Exhibit 33–10 below shows the payment priority for Greentree 1995-10.

As previously noted, the senior bonds pay sequentially until the crossover date, which is the latter of month 49 or when the deal's "step-down" tests (discussed below) are met. Exhibit 33–11 shows how losses are allocated within the structure. If losses were to exceed the first four loss priorities, then a pro rata principal write-off would occur among the A1 to A6 tranches.

SENIOR BOND RELATIVE VALUE ANALYSIS

The structure, pricing details, Z spreads, and OAS data for a recent deal—Greentree 1996-1—are shown below:

Tranche	Size ($MM)	A/L	Window Months	Spread	Z Spread	Option Cost	OAS
A1	120	2.1	1–48	50	42	7	35
A2	50	5.2	48–78	54	40	10	30
A3	35	7.5	78–95	71	70	18	52
A4	50	11.6	95–145	93	79	17	62
A5	76	17.5	145–309	145	101	11	90

EXHIBIT 33–10

Typical Greentree MH Payment Priority

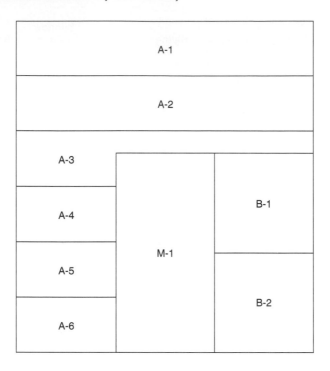

EXHIBIT 33–11

Typical Greentree MH Loss Allocation

Loss Priority	Tranche	Credit Source	Credit
5th	A1–A6	Subordination	16%
4th	M1	Subordination	8%
3rd	B1	Subordination	4%
2nd	B2	Greentree Guarantee	4%
1st	—	Excess spread	349 bps

Based on nominal spreads, Z spreads, and OAS analysis, the longer bonds in the senior structure seem to offer the best risk/return profile. The A4 bond, for example, at +93 versus the 10-year Treasury given the sectors stable prepayment profile is more attractive than the following alternative products:

Type	Spread	Z Spread	OAS
MH	+93	79	62
Credit cards	53	53	53
Corporate industrial	35	35	35
Agency PAC	90	71	56

Finally, the senior bonds of manufactured housing ABS are both SMMEA and ERISA eligible.

Mezzanine and Subordinated Bond Analysis

Before analyzing the lower-rated tranches on manufactured housing ABS, the investor must be sure to understand the priorities of cash flow that flow to these bonds. For example, the step-down tests used for the Greentree 1995-10 deal is given below:

GREENTREE 1995-10 STEP-DOWN TESTS

M-1

Principal lockout until 12/99 (48 months)
> Then must pass the following five tests:

1. Average 60-day delinquency ratio <3.5% of orig. pool balance

2. Average 30-day delinquency ratio <5.5% of orig. pool balance

3. Current losses <2.25% of orig. pool balance

4. Cumulative losses must be less than:

> 48–59 months <5.5% of orig. pool balance
> 60–71 months <6.5% of orig. pool balance
> 72–83 months <8.5% of orig. pool balance
> 84+ months <9.5% of orig. pool balance

5. Deleveraging test

$$\frac{M1 + B \text{ principal}}{Pool \text{ principal}} > 25.5\% \text{ of orig. pool balance}$$

The B1 and B2 tranches have to pass a similar series of tests in order to begin to receive principal.

The investor should know when the expected crossover date will occur. For example, Greentree 1995-10 M1, although locked out for 48 months, is not scheduled to receive any principal until month 63. This 100 MHP pricing assumption (138 MHP is needed to accelerate the principal date on M1 to month 49) is too slow to achieve step-down in month 49.

It is therefore necessary to evaluate these tranches on an OAS basis in order to capture the extension risk in the structure. The following table shows this evaluation for the subordinated tranches of Greentree 1996-1:

Tranche	Size ($MM)	A/L	Window Months	Spread	Z Spread	Option Cost	OAS
M1	36	11.9	49–309	145	124	13	111
B1	16	7.4	49–123	145	142	14	128
B2	16	20.0	123–309	175	130	13	117

Among the subordinated tranches shown above, we find the M1 bond is attractive versus alternative products:

AA Product	Spread	OAS
MH ABS	+145	111
Subordinated CMO	+150	135
CMBS	+115	90
Industrials	+50	50

Although AA-rated subordinated CMOs appear more attractive in the comparison above, MH ABS are publicly traded, increasingly more liquid, and available in bigger block sizes than subordinated CMOs. However, the intermediate-duration B1 tranche, as shown below, does not appear as attractive as alternative BBB-rated products:

BBB Product	Spread	OAS
MH ABS	145	128
Subordinated CMO	230	215
CMBS	175	135
Industrials	75	75

Finally, the current attractiveness of the AA-rated M1 tranche is a relatively recent phenomenon. That is, through the end of January 1996 only five deals have been structured with this 11- to 12-year average life AA mezzanine structure. Prior to Greentree 1995-7, the M1 tranche was a much longer bond (i.e., 17- to 19-year average life) due to a much longer principal lockout (crossover date).

CONCLUSION

Manufactured housing ABS deals offer an intriguing combination of spread, prepayment stability, and growing liquidity. In particular, the longer sectors of the AAA bonds as well as the AA-rated mezzanine tranche look more attractive than alternative products.

ⓖ CREDIT CARD ABS

David R. Howard
Senior Director, Asset Backed Securities
Fitch Investors Service, L.P.

Credit card securitization makes up the largest sector of the asset-backed market, with over $45 billion of securities issued in 1995. This chapter begins with an introduction to the credit card business, followed by the structures used to securitize these assets. Several different forms of credit enhancement are introduced, and the stress scenarios used to analyze the credit strength of the securities are analyzed. Finally, several advanced structural features are discussed, along with some of the risks associated with investing in credit card ABS.

CREDIT CARDS

The credit card market has grown significantly since 1990, increasing from $234 billion of total receivables outstanding in 1990 to $349 billion outstanding as of June 1995. This growth came from increasing reliance on credit cards by consumers, along with increasing acceptance of cards by merchants and service providers (doctors, grocery stores, etc.). Exhibit 34–1 shows the top 10 credit card issuers. In addition to growth of outstanding receivables, a wide diversity in types of cards being issued has developed. Each type is described below.

Affinity Cards

Affinity programs target members of groups who share common interests. For example, associations of medical professionals, fans of auto racing, or alumni of the same university can have the logo of their association, a picture of their favorite

EXHIBIT 34–1

Top 10 Credit Card Issuers*

Card Portfolios**	$ Billion
1 Citibank	44.80
2 Discover	27.82
3 MBNA America	25.25
4 First USA	17.45
5 First Chicago	17.21
6 AT&T Universal	14.10
7 Household Bank	12.93
8 Chase Manhattan	12.83
9 Chemical Bank	10.80
10 Capital One	10.45

* As of December 31, 1995.

** General purpose card portfolios in the United States.

Source: The Nilson Report, Oxnard, CA

Note: One exception to the list is Sears, which is not a general purpose card issuer.
The retailer has a $23.44 billion portfolio.

driver, or their school seal on credit cards. This group loyalty builds a bond to the card. MBNA is the standout issuer of affinity cards.

Low-Price Cards

This issuer's strategy is to attract an interest-rate-sensitive borrower with a low "teaser" rate offer, run up their balance quickly by offering instant and easy transfers of existing credit card balances from other banks, and keep the cardholder with competitive "go-to" rates after the introductory period has ended. To be successful in the low-price business, an issuer must have sophisticated risk-based pricing computer models to determine what rate it can offer to a particular market segment based on that segment's risk profile. ADVANTA, Capital One, and First USA have grown their portfolios dramatically using this strategy.

Co-Branded Cards

Many companies, especially automobile manufacturers, airlines, and telephone companies, have allied with card-issuing banks to jointly market cards. The intent is to promote the company's product and increase receivables for the bank. These co-branded cards reward the cardholder for usage. The rewards may be rebates on new car purchases, free airline tickets, or discounts on long-distance telephone calls. This program also provides an incentive for cardholders to pay their bills on time since the reward benefits will be revoked if the cardholder becomes delinquent. Household and General Motors, Citibank and American Airlines, and Chemical and Shell are several joint ventures in the co-branded arena. Each program has different arrangements for expense and revenue sharing.

Discover

Discover is the only significant issuer of general purpose credit cards to successfully break into the U.S. market without relying on the Visa or MasterCard associations. Discover developed its own merchant network across the country, and in the 10 years since it began, has achieved notable market penetration. The barriers to entry into this arena are high due to significant start-up costs and intense competition. Discover's card has been extremely successful because of its strategy of cash rebates for purchases and its clear and simple pricing structure.

Retail Cards

Many retail stores offer their customers the choice of using a national credit card or using the store's own card. Advantages to cardholders of using store cards are that available credit on the customer's other cards is not used up, and they can "compartmentalize" their debt burden. For example, a consumer might use a Sears card to purchase a new refrigerator and pay it off evenly over time without using up a Visa or MasterCard line. The retailer benefits because it builds customer loyalty in addition to the profitability of its lending operation.

Travel and entertainment cards, such as American Express and Diners Club, and full-service cards, such as Citibank, Chemical, and Chase, round out the spectrum of card types.

SECURITIZATION

As with credit cards, the use of securitization as a financing tool has increased in volume and importance. The first deals were done in 1987 to diversify sources of bank funding. As the banks came under pressure to free up on-balance sheet capital in 1990 and 1991, securitization filled that need. (Bank regulators treat securitization as asset sales.) More recently, securitization has been the primary funding source for specialized credit card banks. These banks, such as ADVANTA, Capital One, First USA, and MBNA, benefit from funding at AAA rates and low capital charges, and in some cases rely on off-balance-sheet treatment to meet regulatory requirements. Without securitization, some of these banks could not have grown as rapidly. As of December 1995, over $180 billion in credit card transactions have been issued. Exhibit 34–2 shows the top 10 issuers of credit card ABS.

EXHIBIT   34–2

Top 10 Credit Card ABS Issuers*

Securitizers**	$ Billion
1 Citibank	41.52
2 MBNA America	22.30
3 Sears	14.00
4 Discover	13.56
5 First USA	12.06
6 First Chicago	11.90
7 Household	10.21
8 Capital One	7.13
9 Chase Manhattan	6.02
10 ADVANTA	5.14

* As of December 31, 1995
** Total amount publicly securitized.
Source: Asset-Backed Alert.

Stand-Alone versus Master Trust

A vast majority of card securitizations have been completed using two different vehicles, the *stand-alone trust* and the *master trust*. The former is simply a single pool of receivables that is sold to a trust and used as collateral for a single security, although there may be several classes within that security. When the issuer intends to issue another security, it must designate a new pool of card accounts and sell the receivables in those accounts to a separate trust. This structure was used from the first credit card securitization in 1987 until 1991, when the master trust became the preferred vehicle.

The master trust structure allows an issuer to sell multiple securities from the same trust, all of which rely on the same pool of receivables as collateral. For example, an issuer could transfer the receivables from one million accounts (representing $1 billion of receivables) to a trust, then issue multiple securities in various denominations and sizes. When more financing is needed, the issuer transfers receivables from more accounts to the same trust. It can then issue more securities. The receivables are not segregated in any way to indicate which series of securities they support. Instead, all of the accounts support all of the securities.

This structure allows the issuer much more flexibility since the cost and effort involved with issuing a new series from a master trust is lower than creating a new trust for every issue. In addition, credit evaluation of each series in a master trust is easier since the pool of receivables will be larger and not as subject to seasonal or demographic concentrations. For example, if an issuer transferred only receivables from accounts originated in 1989 into a stand-alone trust, and the next year transferred all of the receivables from 1990 accounts into a different trust, the two would perform differently based on what underwriting standards were used, what terms (annual payment rate [APR] and minimum monthly payment) were offered, and what competing offers were out at that time.

If a master trust had been used in the same example, both series would depend on the same pool of accounts, half of which were originated in 1989 and half of which were originated in 1990. Credit differences between the two series would be contained in the structure of the deal, rather than the receivables. Investors must keep in mind, however, that the composition of accounts in a master trust pool may change dramatically over time as new accounts are added and as some existing cardholders cancel or stop using their accounts.

Other efficiencies can be included in a master trust, including sharing of principal and sharing of excess spread. These efficiencies are discussed further below.

In addition to issuing investor securities, every seller is required to maintain an ownership interest in the trust. This participation performs three critical functions. First, the participation is a buffer to absorb seasonal fluctuations in credit card receivables balance. Second, it is allocated all dilutions (balances canceled due to returned goods) and fraudulently generated receivables that have been transferred to the trust. Third, it ensures that the seller will maintain the credit quality of the pool since it owns a portion of it. To ensure that the certificateholders' invested amount is always fully invested in credit card receivables, the size of the seller's participation must remain at or above a minimum percentage of the trust receivables balance, usually 7 percent. The seller's participation does not provide credit enhancement for the investors.

The seller is obligated to add credit card accounts to the trust if the amount of its participation falls below the required minimum. If the seller cannot provide additional accounts, an amortization event will occur. (This is discussed further below.) Under most circumstances, the seller must receive rating agency approval before any accounts can be added. The seller does not need approval when the addition is a small percentage of the trust, 10 percent to 15 percent, or when the minimum seller's participation level has been breached. Of course, the rating agencies will receive notification of these events.

STRUCTURES

Regardless of whether the trust is a stand-alone or a master trust, the same general structure is used for every deal. The typical setup has three different cash flow periods: revolving, amortization (or in some cases accumulation), and early amortization. Each period performs a different function and allocates cash flows differently. This structure is designed to mimic a traditional bond, in which interest payments are made every month and principal is paid in a single "bullet" payment on the maturity date.

Since the average life of a credit card receivable is a short 5 to 10 months, an amortizing structure, like the ones used in automobile and mortgage deals, does not work very well. In this type of structure, the principal and interest collections on the pool of loans are passed directly through to investors on a monthly basis. An amortizing structure for credit card-backed securities would result in a short average life and lumpy and unpredictable repayment to investors. Use of a revolving structure gives the issuer medium- to long-term financing and gives the investor a predictable schedule of principal and interest payments.

All collections on the receivables are split into finance charge income and principal payments. Each of the three periods treats finance charge income in the same manner. Monthly finance charges are used to pay the investor coupon and servicing fees, and to cover any receivables that have been charged off in the month. Any income remaining after paying these expenses is usually called *excess spread* and is released to the seller. Principal collections, however, are allocated differently during each of the periods.

Revolving Period

During the revolving period, monthly principal collections are used to purchase new receivables generated in the designated accounts or to purchase a portion of the seller's participation if there are no new receivables. If there are not enough new receivables to reinvest in, an early amortization will be triggered because the seller's participation has fallen below the required minimum or, in some cases, the excess principal collections will be deposited in an excess funding account and held until the seller can generate more credit card receivables. The risk of early amortization gives the seller adequate incentive to maintain the seller's participation at a level well above the minimum. The revolving period continues for a predetermined length of time that has ranged from 2 to 11 years. Investors will receive only interest payments during this period.

Controlled Amortization/Accumulation

At the end of the revolving period, the controlled amortization or controlled accumulation period begins. In the case of controlled amortization, which typically runs for 12 months, principal collections are no longer reinvested but are paid to investors in 12, equal, controlled amortization payments. The payments are sized at exactly 1/12th of the invested amount so that investors can be repaid on a predetermined schedule. (Some series may have longer or shorter controlled periods and thus will have smaller or larger controlled amortization payments.) Any principal collected in excess of the controlled amount will be reinvested in new receivables, as in the revolving period. Interest will be paid only on the outstanding amount of securities as of the beginning of the monthly period.

Controlled accumulation follows a similar procedure, except that the controlled payments are deposited into a trust account, or principal funding account (PFA), every month and held until the expected maturity date. At the end of the accumulation period, the full invested amount will have been deposited into the

PFA, and the investors will be repaid their principal in a single payment. Of course, interest payments will be made each month on the total invested amount. With this structure, investors will not see any difference in monthly payments when the deal converts from revolving to accumulation.

Early Amortization

Severe asset deterioration, problems with the seller or servicer, or certain legal troubles can trigger early amortization events at any point in the deal, whether it is revolving, amortizing, or accumulating. In such cases, the deal automatically enters the early amortization period and begins to repay investors immediately. This feature helps protect investors from a long exposure to a deteriorating transaction.

All credit card transactions contain deal- and issuer-specific amortization events. The following events are basic, common triggers that are necessary for most transactions.

Seller/Servicer
1. Failure or inability to make required deposits or payments.
2. Failure or inability to transfer receivables to the trust when necessary.
3. False representations or warranties that remain unremedied.
4. Certain events of default, bankruptcy, insolvency or receivership of the seller or servicer.

Legal
5. Trust becomes classified as an "investment company" under the Investment Company Act of 1940.

Performance
6. Three-month average of excess spread falls below 0.0 percent.
7. Seller's participation falls below the required level.
8. Portfolio principal balance falls below the invested amount.

These basic triggers should address all possible worst-case scenarios as well as any unforeseen events applicable to the seller/servicer, trust, or portfolio. Some sample scenarios are listed in the table below.

Scenario	Covered by
Seller/servicer fraud	1,2,3
Default of seller/servicer	4
Taxation of trust	5, 6
Rapidly rising charge-offs	6
Federally imposed interest rate cap	6
Whipsaw interest-rate scenarios	6

Economic recession/depression	6
Spikes in dilution and/or fraudulent charges	7, 8
Declining pool balance due to competition	7, 8
Reduction in credit card usage	7, 8

In the event that an early amortization is triggered and not cured, investors will begin to be repaid immediately on a fast-pay, or uncontrolled, basis. All principal collections and any amounts in the PFA will be distributed to investors, with senior certificates being paid off first. Principal distributions will be made to subordinate investors only after senior investors are fully repaid. To help speed repayment to investors, a portion of principal collections that would normally be allocated to the seller's participation will be reallocated to investors.

In the history of credit card securitization, the only deals that have triggered early amortization events were issued by RepublicBank (Delaware), Southeast Bank, and Chevy Chase Federal Savings Bank. None was rated by Fitch. In the Chevy Chase deal, investors voted to waive the trigger event, and the transaction continued to operate normally. The securities were repaid as originally scheduled, and no investor suffered a loss. In both the Southeast Bank and RepublicBank deals, early amortization was commenced and investors were repaid without a loss, but earlier than they had expected. In modern transactions, certain features are available to protect investors from early amortization risk. (See Master Trust Features, below.)

CREDIT ENHANCEMENT

As unsecured revolving debt obligations, credit card receivables offer no collateral in the event of cardholder default. As a result, recoveries are limited. To achieve investment-grade ratings, credit enhancement is needed to insulate investors from fluctuating payment patterns and cardholder charge-offs. Common forms of credit enhancement are excess spread, cash collateral account (CCA), collateral invested amount (CIA), and subordination. Most recent transactions use a combination of enhancements, the most common being senior/sub/CIA.

Excess Spread

The yield on credit cards, which is high relative to other types of consumer loans, should cover the payment of investor interest in addition to the servicing fees and still be sufficient to reimburse the trust for any receivables charged off during the month. For example:

18%	Gross portfolio yield
−7%	Investor coupon
−2%	Servicing expense
−5%	Charge-offs
4%	Excess spread

The remaining yield, or excess spread, provides a rough indication of the financial health of a transaction. Available excess spread may be shared with other series, used to pay fees to credit enhancers, deposited into a reserve account for the benefit of the enhancers, or released to the seller.

If the deal is performing as expected, the cash flow from the pool of credit cards will be sufficient to make all principal and interest payments to investors and to pay all expenses, with plenty of excess remaining. In the example above, the 4 percent excess spread would have to be depleted (i.e., decrease in yield, increase in coupon, and/or increase in charge-offs) before there would be a cash shortfall. If, however, excess spread does fall below zero, other credit enhancements must be available to make up the shortfall.

Cash Collateral Account

A CCA is simply a segregated trust account, funded at the outset of the deal, which can be drawn upon to cover shortfalls in interest, principal, or servicing expense for a particular series if excess spread is reduced to zero. The account is funded by a loan from a third-party bank, which will be repaid only after all classes of certificates of that series have been repaid in full. Cash in the account will be invested in the highest-rated short-term securities, all of which will mature on or before the next distribution date. Draws on the CCA may be reimbursed from future excess spread.

Collateral Invested Amount

The CIA represents an uncertificated, privately placed ownership interest in the trust, subordinate in payment rights to all investor certificates. Acting like a layer of subordination, the CIA serves the same purpose as the CCA: It makes up for deficiencies if excess spread is reduced to zero. The CIA is traditionally placed with banks, who may require investment-grade ratings on the CIA as a condition to purchase. The CIA itself is protected by a spread account (which is not available to any other investors) and available monthly excess spread. If the CIA is drawn upon, it can be reimbursed from future excess spread.

This class of enhancement also goes by other names: CA investor interest, collateral interest, enhancement invested amount, or "C" tranche.

Subordination

A senior/sub structure offers two different types of investor ownership in the trust: senior participation in the form of class-A certificates and subordinate participation in the form of class B certificates. Class B will absorb losses allocated to class A that are not already covered by excess spread, the CCA, or the CIA. Like the CCA and CIA, draws on the subordinate certificates may be reimbursed from future excess spread. Principal collections will be allocated to the subordinate investors only after the senior certificates are fully repaid.

Letter of Credit

From the inception of credit card securitization until 1991, the letter of credit (LOC) was a common form of enhancement. It is an unconditional, irrevocable commitment from a bank to provide cash payments, up to the face amount of the LOC, to the trustee in the event that there is a shortfall in cash needed to pay interest, principal, or servicing. Usage as a form of enhancement was discontinued when a number of banks providing LOCs were downgraded, and the transactions they enhanced were downgraded as a result. The CCA was developed to remove downgrade risk caused by enhancer credit quality, and this marked the end of the use of LOCs in credit card transactions.

STRESS SCENARIOS

Under the most severe depression scenarios, properly structured AAA credit card ABS should repay investors 100 percent of their original investment plus interest. Securities rated in the A category (subordinated certificates) are subject to less severe recessionary scenarios than those used for AAA; however, they are considered investment-grade and of high credit quality. The trust's ability to pay interest and repay principal to class B is strong but may be more vulnerable to adverse changes in economic conditions and circumstances than class A.

Credit card ABS performance can be influenced by many variables, with both positive and negative effects. Fitch develops stress scenarios at every rating level for each ABS issuer and structure by evaluating the following performance variables:

- Underwriting standards.
- Cardholder credit scores.
- Card type: retail, low-price, affinity, co-branded, and so on.
- Fixed or floating card APR.
- Flexibility of issuer to reprice card rates.
- Frequency of floating rate resets.
- Use of teaser rates.
- Attrition.
- Geographic and demographic diversification.
- Interchange.
- Convenience usage.

- Seasoning.
- Servicing.
- Competitive position.
- Management.
- Discounting of new receivables into trust.
- Other structural features.

Current/historical performance or, if the portfolio is unseasoned, a conservative projection of performance, is used as a benchmark by which to assess future performance. The stress scenarios applied to a transaction are determined on a case-by-case basis and compared to a hypothetical industry benchmark. The major variables influencing credit enhancement levels are charge-offs, portfolio yield, monthly payment rate (MPR), and investor coupon. Exhibit 34–3 shows the benchmark stress levels used by Fitch for the first three variables for AAA and A ratings.

Charge-Offs

Credit cards are unique among loans in that the credit quality of each cardholder is reflected in their credit limit and APR, which are based on the cardholder's ability to meet debt payments (i.e., the higher the risk, the lower the credit limit and the higher the APR). Many issuers use sophisticated credit-scoring models, or well-trained credit analysts, to determine the probability of default of the cardholder. This probability dictates what credit limit should be granted and at what APR.

Examining the credit limits and APRs of a portfolio, however, does not always give a true picture of the issuer's total risk. Some issuers might be more aggressive in assigning high limits to lower credit quality borrowers. Some might not have well-developed scoring models. And, finally, some may try to gain market share by offering very low interest rates, possibly at the expense of credit quality.

All these factors must be analyzed when determining the appropriate charge-off stress to apply to a portfolio. The stress level shown in the benchmark

E X H I B I T   34–3

Fitch's Stress Benchmarks

	Triple-A Benchmark	Single-A Benchmark
Charge-offs	5x multiple	3x multiple
Portfolio yield	35% decline	25% decline
MPR	50% decline	35% decline

in Exhibit 34–3 indicates that one in every four or five cardholders defaults on their obligation to pay.

Portfolio Yield

Yield is made up of periodic APR charges, annual fees, late payment fees, overlimit fees, and in some cases, recoveries on charged-off accounts and interchange. Interchange is income from the card associations (Visa, MasterCard, Novus) that is paid to the issuing bank as compensation for taking credit risk and funding receivables, the amount of which varies from 1 percent to 2 percent per year. Most of these components are relatively stable and only comprise a small percentage of the yield. APR, on the other hand, accounts for a large majority of the yield and is the most volatile.

     In stressing a portfolio's yield, competitive position is a critical factor since a highly priced portfolio will be under pressure to reduce rates to maintain market share. Another important factor is the possibility of a federally imposed interest rate cap on credit card APRs. In November of 1991, the U.S. Senate proposed a measure to lower credit card interest rates to a cap of 14 percent. If the measure had been enacted, some portfolios would have suffered a reduction in yield of more than 30 percent.

Monthly Payment Rate

The monthly payment rate includes monthly collections of principal, finance charges, and fees paid by the cardholder and is stated as a percentage of the outstanding balance as of the beginning of the month. Reductions in MPR may come from a decrease in the number of cardholders who pay off their entire bill every month and from cardholders making smaller monthly payments.

Fitch Credit Card Default Model

When run through Fitch's default model, the benchmark scenario shown in Exhibit 34–3 gives a generic AAA level for a portfolio. However, since every credit card is not created equal, more attention must be paid to the dynamics of each variable stressed in the context of that portfolio, and how it compares to the benchmark. For example, the stress test illustrated in the table below applies to the Household Affinity Credit Card Master Trust, which is made up solely of General Motors co-branded cards:

	Current*	Benchmark	Household Affinity	Stress
Charge-offs	4.32%	5x multiple	5.25x multiple	22.68%
Portfolio yield	19.16%	35% decline	40% decline	11.50%
MPR	25.91%	50% decline	65% decline	9.07%

* As of 12/31/95.

Household's underwriting criteria is strong, and performance has been better than expected to date. However, since their portfolio is not heavily seasoned and has not been tested during a recessionary environment, Fitch imposes a slightly more conservative charge-off multiple. As the average age of the accounts increases, Fitch will revisit this stress and adjust it accordingly.

The payment rate stress on this portfolio is also very conservative. Since all the accounts are under the GM relationship, Fitch has to keep in mind what would happen if the co-branding agreement were canceled. Many cardholders using their cards to generate GM rebate points would cease making purchases, and payment rates would fall dramatically.

As another example of customizing stresses, the following table shows a scenario applied to the Sears Credit Card Master Trust:

	Current*	Benchmark	Sears	Stress
Charge-offs	5.64%	5x multiple	4.5x multiple	25.38%
Portfolio yield	19.06%	35% decline	35% decline	12.39%
MPR	6.42%	50% decline	35% decline	4.17%

* As of 12/31/95.

Since more than 60 percent of Sears' accounts are greater than five years old, portfolio statistics are very consistent, even during the 1990–1991 recession, Fitch gives Sears credit for stable underwriting and reduces the worst-case multiple. Moreover, payment rates, quite simply, cannot fall much further, even under severe economic stress.

Investor Coupon

For fixed-rate ABS, Fitch uses the expected pricing level of the securities as the investor coupon expense of the transaction. For floating-rate ABS, Fitch assumes that the investor coupon will increase dramatically. The interest-rate environment of the early 1980s, specifically the second half of 1980, is used as a stress scenario since that was the most volatile period of the last 20 years.

Additional credit enhancement is needed to cover the potential basis risk and interest-rate risk between a rapidly rising investor coupon and lagging floating-rate or low fixed-rate credit cards, where trust expenses increase faster than trust earnings. This risk is issuer- and deal-specific and is estimated based on credit card interest rates, frequency of credit card floating-rate resets, investor coupon index, frequency of investor coupon resets, and, to a limited extent, the issuer's ability to change credit card interest rates. The amount of additional enhancement required may vary from 2.5 percent to more than 4 percent.

For example, if the ABS investor's coupon floats off the one-month London Interbank Offered Rate (LIBOR), a deal with credit cards that are priced off the prime rate and reset monthly would be exposed to less interest rate risk than a deal with cards that are fixed rate or are reset quarterly. Therefore, the monthly reset portfolio would require less additional credit enhancement than the portfolio with fixed-rate cards.

Receivables Balance

An additional variable that must be examined is the receivables balance of the pool. If the outstanding principal receivables of the portfolio declines, especially during early amortization, the amount of principal collections reallocated from the seller's participation will be drastically reduced. This results in a longer pay-out period and increased exposure to a deteriorating pool. The primary concern is how cardholders will behave with regard to the solvency of the seller.

For credit cards issued by small, regional retailers, Fitch believes that if the retailer files bankruptcy under Chapter 7 of the bankruptcy code, consumers will no longer be able to use their cards since all the stores have been closed or sold, and the principal receivables balance of the trust will decline in lockstep with the amortization of the securitization. Exceptions may be made if the retailer is un-likely to file under Chapter 7.

For well-underwritten, geographically diverse, general-purpose card port-folios, insolvency of the seller will not have such a dramatic effect. Most con-sumers probably will not even know that their bank has gone into insolvency and will continue to use their cards. With the profitability of the card business, the heavy premiums at which pools of accounts are bought and sold, and the aggres-sive competition for market share, Fitch believes that portfolios such as these should continue to remain active, with consumers continuing to charge and the portfolio continuing to be serviced, even if not by the original servicer.

Some issuers fall between these two extremes. For example, a portfolio that is heavily concentrated in a single co-branding relationship or affinity group may experience heavy runoff if that relationship is canceled or becomes less of a value to cardholders. It is unlikely, however, that all cardholders would simultaneously cease using their cards, as they would for a bankrupt retailer.

MASTER TRUST FEATURES

Master trusts may be set up with one or several reallocation groups. For example, AT&T Universal Card Master Trust currently has two groups: Group I for series with fixed-rate coupons and Group II for series with floating-rate coupons. Most other trusts have only one group, in which all series are included. Depending on the structure of the trust, series within the same group may share principal and/or excess spread, have the ability to discount, or fix allocations of finance charges.

Principal Sharing

For all series in the same group, the trust allows distribution of excess principal collections to any series in its accumulation or amortization period. Since a series in its revolving period has no principal payment requirements, principal collections allocated to that series are available for reallocation. In addition, principal collections in excess of a series' controlled amount are available for reallocation. The principal reallocation feature provides investors with more assurance of timely principal repayment with no additional risk to other series.

Excess Spread Sharing

There are several ways excess spread may be shared within series of a group. Some groups may be set up as a "socialized" group, where finance charge collections are allocated to each series based on need. The interest expense for all series in the group will be the weighted average expense for each series. Thus, the highest coupon series will receive the largest allocation, and the lowest coupon will receive the smallest allocation. The excess spread for each series will be the same, since each has the same coupon expense. In effect, socialized groups share excess spread at the top of the cash-flow waterfall. AT&T Universal, Household Affinity, and Citibank Credit Card Master Trust are examples of socialized trusts.

Other trusts may allocate finance charge collections on a pro rata basis, based on size. Thus, each series will receive the same proportionate amount of finance charges, and the series with the lowest coupon expense will have the largest amount of excess spread. This amount will be available for reallocation to other series, particularly high-coupon series, if their excess spread is reduced to zero.

Discount Option

Many trusts permit the transfer of receivables to the trust at a discount, which increases the portfolio's yield by including principal collections as finance charge collections. This allows an issuer to artificially increase excess spread. A potential risk of discounting is that a deteriorating pool of assets can continue to revolve with deeper discounts, which increases potential economic exposure during early amortization. The issuer must obtain rating agency approval prior to discounting or changing the discount rate.

Fixed Allocation of Finance Charges

This innovative feature permits a larger percentage of finance charge collections to be allocated to investors after an amortization event, when cash is needed most. Before early amortization, investors receive their pro rata share of finance charge collections, and the seller receives its pro rata share. After an event is triggered, a portion of the seller's share will be made available to cover shortfalls in interest or servicing expense, or to cover charge-offs, in the investors' share. Cash flow simulations show that, even under stressful scenarios, this overallocation of finance charges provides a significant amount of support, thus reducing the need for credit enhancement.

EARLY AMORTIZATION RISK

Fitch credit ratings address the likelihood of repayment of all principal and interest in a full and timely manner, as promised. Credit card transactions, however, do not promise repayment of principal on any specific date. Instead, they define an expected payment date and advise that principal may be paid earlier or later than that date. The circumstances that would lead to earlier payment would be commencement of an early amortization. Later repayment could be caused by very low payment rates, which would mean that controlled amortization or controlled accumulation payments would not be made in full, and extra months of collection would be needed to pay off the entire invested amount. Every series defines a termination date, which is usually set 24 to 36 months after the expected payment date. All principal must be paid on or before this date. It is extremely unlikely that MPR would be so slow that principal would not be repaid by the series termination date.

The amount of enhancement any deal has does not effect the probability of early amortization. And investors must keep in mind that ratings do not reflect the likelihood of this occurrence. As a matter of fact, it is possible that a deal's AAA rating would be affirmed if an early amortization commenced.

Early amortization risk is not a focus of investors when deals perform strongly. But before consumer delinquencies and charge-offs increase, portfolio yields come down dramatically, or interest rates shoot up, investors should look very closely at their investments to determine their exposure to prepayment risk. There are many topics to consider when evaluating early amortization risk, some of which are as follows:

- Variability of charge-offs.
- APR pricing position (competitive or not).
- Fixed or floating investor coupon.
- Seller/servicer strength.
- Ability to discount new receivables into trust.
- Sharing of excess spread.
- Percent of total bank receivables that have been securitized.
- Existence of variable funding, extendible, or commercial paper series.

EVALUATING ASSET-BACKED SECURITIES: A PRIMER ON STATIC SPREAD

Anthony V. Thompson
Director of ABS Research
Goldman, Sachs & Co.

INTRODUCTION

Yield to maturity (YTM) has long been recognized as a fundamental tool for measuring relative value among traditional fixed income securities. Although certain assumptions inherent to YTM can understate or overstate actual return, these inaccuracies are often benign when comparing noncallable securities in a market such as corporates, where cash flows are relatively standardized. This, however, is not always the case within the asset-backed market, where the amortization characteristics can vary significantly from security to security.

A price calculated using yield to maturity assumes a rate of return based on the discounting of a security's interest and principal cash flows at a constant rate. For a corporate bond, the discount rate represents the yield on the Treasury benchmark nearest to maturity, plus a spread. As a measure of relative value, a price based on YTM takes into account only a security's yield, coupon, and final maturity. YTM reflects neither reinvestment nor dispersion of cash flows. When used to compare relative value among traditional corporate bonds, the assumptions inherent to YTM are less significant to the extent that all securities with similar cash flow characteristics are affected equally. However, when comparing bonds with more complex cash flow structures, what YTM offers in simplicity, it sacrifices in accuracy.

THE DRAWBACKS OF USING AVERAGE MATURITY TO DETERMINE YIELD

Certain securities in the asset-backed market, such as soft bullet credit cards, offer a single payment of principal at maturity, thus imitating the cash flow profile of a corporate bond. However, in other asset-backeds, such as retail auto loans, principal amortizes over the life of the transaction. The market convention for pricing these amortizing securities is to discount all cash flows at a rate based on the Treasury whose maturity is closest to the weighted average maturity of the security's principal cash flows. It is assumed that the impact of discounting longer cash flows at a rate that is too low relative to their maturity will equally offset the discounting of shorter cash flows at a rate that is too high. As we explain below, when cash flows are significantly dispersed, the use of an average maturity becomes an increasingly inaccurate measure of return.

Suppose an investor could own either (a) one bond with a maturity of 18 months, which we will call B18, or (b) equal amounts of two bonds, one with a maturity of 12 months (B12) and the other with a maturity of 24 months (B24), having a combined average maturity of 18 months. Assume all three bonds have the same coupon and are priced at par based on a discount rate of 6 percent. As shown in Exhibit 35–1, the price of B18 and the combination of B12 and B24 are the same. An investor should therefore be indifferent to choice (a) or (b). This method illustrates one way in which asset-backed securities with multiple principal payments are priced, i.e., based on the yield to average maturity of the underlying principal.

Now suppose the price of B12 combined with B24 was expressed as the sum of the individual prices instead of the average. For purposes of illustration, assume discount rates for B12 and B24 such that, when averaged, they equal 6 percent (see Exhibit 35–2).

This very simple example shows that the sum of the individual prices of B12 and B24 is 99.96, or .04 lower than when the Average Method is used. There is an explanation for this. In the Average Method, we calculate the price of B12+B24 using a single rate (6 percent) based on the average maturity of 18 months. Using the Individual Method, we discount B12 and B24 by separate rates, one lower (5.4 percent) and one higher (6.6 percent). Because the average

E X H I B I T   35–1

Calculation of Price Using Average Method

	B18	B12	B24	B12 + B24
Average life	18 mos.	12 mos.	24 mos.	18 mos.
Discount rate	6.0%			6.0%
Price	100.00			**100.00**

EXHIBIT 35–2

Calculation of Price Using Individual Method

	B18	B12	B24	B12 + B24
Average life	18 mos.	12 mos.	24 mos.	18 mos.
Discount rate	6.0%	5.4%	6.6%	6.0%
Price	100.00	100.12	99.73	99.96

of the individual discount rates still equals 6 percent, one would think that the two prices using either method should still be equal. But they are not. The difference in price can be explained by the effect of compounding. Because the price of the longer security (B24) is more sensitive to the higher rate than B12 is to the lower rate, their combined price is lower when using the Individual Method. In order for the sum of the prices of the individual bonds to equal the price derived using the Average Method, lower discount rates are needed. The difference between the discount rates can essentially be attributed to the difference between a security's static spread and its nominal spread.

STATIC SPREAD CREATES A LEVEL PLAYING FIELD

Static spread assumes that a given security represents a portfolio of individual securities, as if each were a zero coupon bond. Rather than discounting all cash flows by the same yield to maturity, the static spread methodology discounts each individual cash flow at a spread plus the spot rate of a zero coupon Treasury with the corresponding duration. The spread at which the sum of the discounted cash flows equals their nominal price is the static spread.

A more practical example further demonstrates how YTM based on average maturity would be misleading when comparing the three securities shown in Exhibit 35–3, each with an average life of 18 months. Security #1 pays a single "bullet" payment of principal in month 18, similar to a corporate bond or soft bullet credit card ABS. Security #2 returns principal in 24 equal installments beginning in month 7, not unlike a credit card ABS with a long controlled amortization period. Security #3 pays principal over 36 months, with a gradually declining amount of principal paid in each successive month. Security #3 approximates a short retail auto ABS. If each security trades at a price to yield of 6 percent and the yield on the 18-month Treasury benchmark is 5.45 percent, then the spread (also called the nominal spread) will be 55 bp.

The YTM derived in the example above assumes that each cash flow will be discounted at 6 percent, a rate based on the average principal maturity (18 months). If the yield curve were positively sloped, the early cash flows would be discounted at too high a rate and the later cash flows discounted at too low a rate.

EXHIBIT 35–3

Cash Flow Profiles of Three Types of Asset-Backed Securities

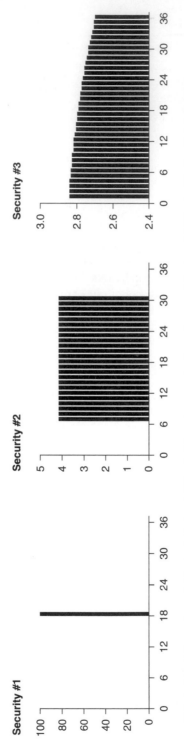

Principal cash flows shown in black, plotted on left Y axis; interest payments shown in gray, plotted on right Y axis. Months shown on X axis.

YTM based on an average maturity assumes that the two effects will equally offset each other. However, we know from the previous example that this is not the case.

To calculate static spread, assume the hypothetical yield curve shown in Exhibit 35–4. From this curve, a zero coupon curve is derived that will be used to discount each cash flow as if each were a zero coupon bond. The static spreads on the three different securities are shown in Exhibit 35–5.

Why are the nominal spreads for Security #2 and Security #3 higher than the static spreads? Their prices, when based on an average benchmark plus the nominal spread, are effectively too high. This is because the cash flows in Securities #2 and #3, which are received beyond the average maturity, are more sensitive to the average discount rate, which is too low. In order for the lower price of the sum of the individual zero coupon securities to equal the higher price of the securities using average maturity, the spread (i.e., the static spread) used to discount the series of zeros must be lower.

As one would expect, the difference between static spread and nominal spread is most significant in the case of Security #3, where the cash flows are the most dispersed. Conversely, the difference between static spread and nominal spread is the smallest in the case of Security #1, which exhibits relatively less cash flow dispersion.

EXHIBIT 35–4

Hypothetical Year Yield Curve, Maturities Three Years and Under

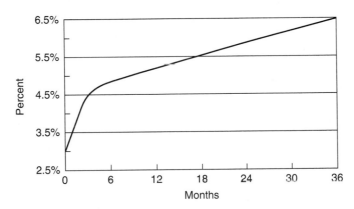

EXHIBIT 35–5

Comparison of Static and Nominal Spreads

	Security #1	Security #2	Security #3
Static Spread	55 bp	45 bp	30 bp
Nominal Spread	55 bp	55 bp	55 bp

CONCLUSION

As asset-backeds become an increasingly popular substitute for corporate bonds, investors should be aware of the subtle differences used to evaluate these securities. Yield to maturity based on a security's average maturity does not take into account the dispersion of cash flows. This is of little consequence in the corporate bond market, where securities typically have a single payment of principal at maturity. When making relative value comparisons among securities with different amortization profiles, it is more appropriate to use static spread. Static spread assumes that each cash flow is discounted individually at a rate based on the zero coupon Treasury curve. When the yield curve is upwardly sloping, static spreads on amortizing asset-backed securities will generally be lower than nominal spreads; when the yield curve is inverted, the reverse will be true. The amount that a security's static spread differs from its nominal spread will depend on the steepness of the curve and the dispersion of cash flows.

FIXED INCOME ANALYTICS AND MODELING

36

VALUATION OF BONDS WITH EMBEDDED OPTIONS

Frank J. Fabozzi, Ph.D., CFA, CPA
Adjunct Professor of Finance
School of Management
Yale University

Andrew J. Kalotay, Ph.D.
Director
Center for Finance & Technology
Polytechnic University

George O. Williams, Ph.D.
Principal
Andrew Kalotay Associates

In this chapter, we'll examine bonds with embedded options. The method described in this chapter is called the *binomial lattice model,* or simply the *binomial method.* Other methods used to value bonds with embedded options include more complicated lattice models, Monte Carlo methods, and the continuous-time diffusion method. Monte Carlo methods are addressed in the next chapter, while the continuous-time approach is applied to convertible bonds in Chapter 42.[1]

Because the most common type of option embedded in a bond is a call option, our primary focus will be on callable bonds. Although callable bonds are used to illustrate the valuation approach, these methods are applicable to all types of fixed income securities.

IMPLICATIONS OF CALLABLE BONDS

The holder of a callable bond has given the issuer the right to redeem the bond before its maturity date. A mortgage-backed security is also callable because the homeowner has the right to pay off all or part of the mortgage at any time.

---

1. The continuous-time diffusion method is explained in Frank J. Fabozzi and H. Gifford Fong, *Advanced Fixed Income Portfolio Management* (Chicago: Probus Publishing, 1994).

The call option poses two related disadvantages to the holder. First, it exposes the investor to reinvestment risk of principal because the issuer will call only when the current market rate is less than the coupon. For example, if the coupon is 13 percent and the prevailing market rate is 7 percent, the issuer will find it economical to call the 13 percent issue and refund with a 7 percent issue. In turn, the holder's reinvestment opportunities will be limited to lower rates. Second, the price appreciation potential for a callable bond is restricted. It will trade at a price below that of a comparable optionless bond.

COMPONENTS OF BONDS WITH EMBEDDED OPTIONS

We develop a valuation framework for a callable bond by decomposing the bond into parts. In effect, the holder of a callable bond has bought a noncallable bond and has sold a call option. In terms of value,

$$\text{Callable bond value} = \text{Optionless bond value} - \text{Call option value}$$

It follows that the price of a callable bond will always be less than the price of an otherwise identical optionless bond. This is shown in Exhibit 36–1. The difference between the value of the noncallable bond and that of the callable bond at any given level of interest rates is the value of the embedded call option.

E X H I B I T   36–1

Price–Interest Rate Relationship for Callable and Noncallable Bonds

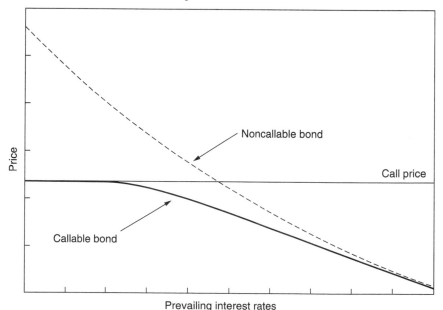

Typically, there is an initial period of call protection, after which the bond is callable at any time at a premium to par. The call price subsequently declines to par over the remaining life of the bond in a manner specified in the bond's indenture. Thus, we have an American call option whose exercise price varies over time.

The same logic applies to putable bonds; the holder has the right to sell the bond to the issuer at a designated time and price. A putable bond can likewise be broken into two separate parts, an optionless bond and a put option. The value of a putable bond is then

Putable bond value = Optionless bond value – Put option value

A GENERALIZED MODEL FOR VALUING BONDS WITH EMBEDDED OPTIONS[2]

The previous section provides a useful way to conceptualize a bond with an embedded option. Specifically, the value of a callable bond equals the value of a comparable optionless bond less the value of the call option. This insight led to the first generation of valuation models for bonds with options. These early models attempted to directly estimate the value of the embedded call option, but without explicitly incorporating the shape of the yield curve. Both the level and the shape of the yield curve affect the value of interest-rate-sensitive options.

Instead of relying on an external pricing model, the model presented in this section is based on an internally consistent framework appropriate to bonds with and without options. The difference between the values of a bond with an option and an otherwise identical bond without that option is the value of the option.

As we saw in Chapter 6, instead of discounting all cash flows at the same rate, one should discount each cash flow at its own spot rate. This is equivalent to discounting at a sequence of forward rates. Both the spot and the implied forward rates can be calculated by the bootstrapping method described in Chapter 6. However, we did not discuss how interest-rate volatility affects the value of a bond with embedded options.

VALUATION OF OPTIONLESS BONDS

We begin with a review of the valuation of optionless bonds. The value of an optionless bond is the present value of its cash flows discounted at the spot rate. One begins with the issuer's non-call-life yield curve. This is obtained by adding an

---

2. This section is adapted from Andrew J. Kalotay, George O. Williams, and Frank J. Fabozzi, "A Model for Valuing Bonds with Embedded Options," *Financial Analysts Journal,* May/June 1993, pp. 35-46.

appropriate credit spread to each on-the-run Treasury issue. The credit spreads tend to increase with maturity.

Consider a hypothetical issuer with the following non-call-life yield curve:

Maturity (yr.)	Coupon	Market Price
1	3.50%	100
2	4.00	100
3	4.50	100

For simplicity, we consider only annual-pay bonds here. The bootstrapping methodology provides the spot rates:

Year	Spot Rate
1	3.500%
2	4.010
3	4.531

The corresponding one-year forward rates are:

One-year rate today	3.500%
One-year rate one year forward	4.523
One-year rate two years forward	5.580

Now consider an optionless bond with three years remaining to maturity and a coupon of 5.25 percent. This bond's value can be determined in either of two ways; both produce the same value. First, the cash flows can be discounted at the zero-coupon or spot rates, as shown below:

$$\frac{\$5.25}{(1.03500)^1} + \frac{\$5.25}{(1.04010)^2} + \frac{\$100 + \$5.25}{(1.04531)^3} = \$102.075$$

The second way is to discount year-by-year at the forward one-year rates:

$$\frac{\$5.25}{(1.03500)} + \frac{\$5.25}{(1.03500)(1.04523)} + \frac{\$100 + \$5.25}{(1.03500)(1.04523)(1.05580)} = \$102.075$$

BINOMIAL INTEREST-RATE TREES

Exhibit 36–2 shows a binomial interest-rate tree. Each node line (vertical column of dots) is one year after the node line to its left. Each node is connected to two nodes on its right. The subscript at a particular node specifies the path followed by the one-year rate in reaching that node. L represents a path to the lower of the two subsequent one-year rates and H represents a path to the higher of the two

EXHIBIT 36–2

Three-Year Binomial Interest-Rate Tree

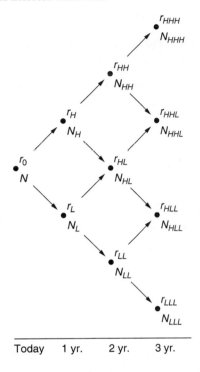

Today   1 yr.   2 yr.   3 yr.

rates. For example, N_{HH} represents a node reached in two years along a path through the higher of the two rates seen after each annual splitting.[3]

Look first at the point denoted by N in Exhibit 36–2. This is the root of the tree and is simply the current one-year rate, which we denote by r_0. In creating this tree, we have assumed that the one-year rate will take on one of two equally likely values after each one-year period elapses. We construct the tree so that the logarithm of the one-year rate obeys a binomial distribution with $p = {}^1/_2$. In this way, the limiting distribution for the one-year rate is lognormal.

We use the following notation to describe the tree in the first year. Let

σ = Assumed volatility of the one-year rate
r_L = The lower one-year rate one year forward
r_H = The higher one-year rate one year forward

The relationship between r_L and r_H is as follows:

$$r_H = r_L \, e^{2\sigma}$$

---

3. Note that N_{HL} is equivalent to N_{LH} in the second year. Similarly, in the third year N_{HLH}, N_{LHH}, and N_{HHL} are all equivalent.

where $e = 2.71828\ldots$, the base of the natural logarithm.

For example, if r_L is 4.074 percent and σ is 10 percent per year, then

$$r_H = 4.074\% \times e^{2 \times 0.10} = 4.976\%$$

In the second year, there are three possible values for the one-year rate, which we will denote as follows:

r_{LL} = The lowest one-year rate two years forward; reached by two successive lower paths

r_{HH} = The highest one-year rate two years forward; reached by two successive higher paths

r_{HL} = The middle one-year rate two years forward; reached by either the upper path followed by the lower path or the lower path followed by the upper path.

The relationship between r_{LL} and the other two rates is as follows:

$$r_{HH} = r_{LL}\, e^{4\sigma} \quad \text{and} \quad r_{HL} = r_{LL}\, e^{2\sigma}$$

For example, if r_{LL} is 4.53 percent, then with σ again being 10 percent,

$$r_{HH} = 4.53\% \times e^{4 \times 0.10} = 6.757\%$$

and

$$r_{HL} = 4.53\% \times e^{2 \times 0.10} = 5.532\%$$

Exhibit 36–3 shows the notation for the binomial tree in the third year. The notation has been simplified by letting r_t be the one-year rate t years forward reached by taking the lower path at every juncture.

Two issues must be addressed before we can value bonds using this binomial tree. What does the volatility parameter σ in the expression $e^{2\sigma}$ represent? Second, how do we find the value of a bond at each node?

Volatility and Standard Deviation

The standard deviation of the one-year rate one year forward at any node is approximately $r\sigma$.[4] The standard deviation is a statistical measure of volatility. The volatility is expressed relative to the level of the one-period rate at each node in the tree. For example, if σ is 10 percent and the current one-year rate r_0 is 4 percent, then the standard deviation of the one-year rate one year from now is 4 per-

---

4. This can be seen by noting that $e^{2\sigma} \approx 1 + 2\sigma$. Then the standard deviation of the one-period rates one period forward is

$$\frac{re^{2\sigma} - r}{2} \approx \frac{r + 2\sigma r - r}{2} = \sigma r$$

EXHIBIT 36–3

Three-Year Binomial Interest-Rate Tree Showing Volatility

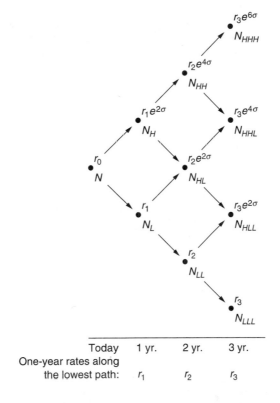

	Today	1 yr.	2 yr.	3 yr.
One-year rates along the lowest path:		r_1	r_2	r_3

cent times 10 percent, which is 0.4 percent or 40 basis points. If the current one-year rate is 12 percent, the standard deviation of the one-year rate one year forward would be 12 percent times 10 percent, or 120 basis points.

Determining the Value at a Node

A bond's value at a given node depends on the bond's value at the two nodes to its right. As seen in Exhibit 36–4, finding a bond's value at node N requires knowing its values at nodes N_L and N_H. We will discuss how one gets these two values later; as we will see, the process involves starting from the last year in the tree and working backward to get the final solution, so these two values will be known.

Thus, a bond's value at a given node depends on future cash flows. These future cash flows may be separated into the bond's value one period from now and any cash flow—like the coupon payment—that occurs at that time. The latter is known, but the former depends on which value the one-year rate takes on in the coming year.

E X H I B I T   36–4

Calculating a Value at a Node

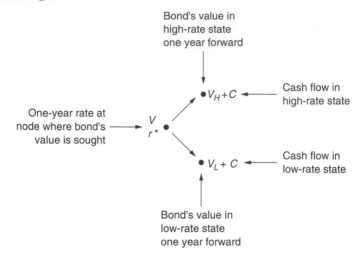

Value is expressed in present value terms at a particular time. Here, we are speaking of the present value of expected cash flows. The appropriate discount rate is the one-year rate r^* at N, the node in question. If the rate takes the upper path, we discount the sum of the two components at N_H: V_H and the coupon C. If the rate takes the lower path, we discount the components of value at N_L. Because these two outcomes are equally likely, we can simply average. This can be thought of as the average of two separate present values, or as the present value of an average. Thus with

V_H = The bond's value along the upper path
V_L = The bond's value along the lower path
C = The coupon payment

the cash flow along the upper path is $V_H + C$ and that along the lower path is $V_L + C$. These have respective present values $(V_H + C)/(1 + r^*)$ and $(V_L + C)/(1 + r^*)$. Thus, a bond's value at node N is given by

$$V = \frac{1}{2}\left(\frac{V_H + C}{1 + r^*} + \frac{V_L + C}{1 + r^*}\right)$$

Constructing a Binomial Interest-Rate Tree

We will demonstrate the construction of the tree using the same on-the-run yields as before. Using a volatility σ of 10 percent, we will construct a two-year tree that prices a two-year 4 percent bond at 100.

E X H I B I T   36–5

Find the One-Year Rates for Year 1 Using the Two-Year 4 Percent On-the-Run Issue: First Trial

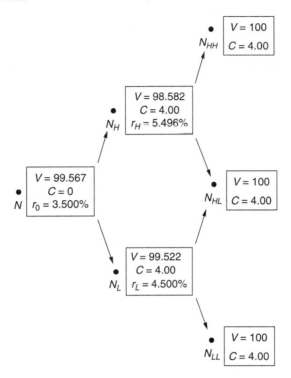

Exhibit 36–5 shows a more detailed binomial tree with the cash flow shown at each node. The root rate for the tree, r_0, is simply the current one-year rate, 3.5 percent.

There are two possible one-year rates one year forward—one along the upper path, and one along the lower. They must be consistent with the volatility assumption (that is, their ratio r_H/r_L is $e^{2\sigma}$), and the value of a 4 percent two-year bond must be 100. We can write down a simple algebraic expression for these two rates, but the formulation becomes increasingly complex beyond the first year. Furthermore, because we may want to implement this procedure on a computer, the natural approach is to find these rates by an iterative process. The steps are described below:

1. Select a value for r_1. Recall that r_1 is the one-year rate one year forward along the lower path. In this first trial, we arbitrarily selected a value of 4.5 percent.

2. Determine the corresponding value for the higher one-year rate. As explained earlier, this rate is found from the lower rate by $r_1 e^{2\sigma}$. Because r_1 is 4.5 percent, the forward one-year rate if rates rise is 5.496 percent ($= 4.5\% \times e^{2 \times 0.10}$). This value is reported in Exhibit 36–5 at node N_H.

3. Compute the bond's value in each of the two interest-rate states one year from now, using the following steps.

- Determine the bond's value two years from now. Because we are using a two-year bond, the bond's value is its maturity value of $100 plus its final coupon payment of $4, or $104.

- Calculate the bond's present value at node N_H. The appropriate discount rate is the forward one-year rate along the upper path, or 5.496 percent in our example. The present value is $98.582 (= $104/1.05496). This is the value of V_H referred to earlier.

- Calculate the bond's present value at node N_H. The appropriate discount rate is the forward one-year rate along the lower path, or 4.5 percent. The present value is $99.522 (= $104/1.045) and is the value of V_L.

- Add the coupon to both V_H and V_L to get the cash flow at N_H and N_L, respectively. In this example, these values are $102.582 along the upper path and $103.522 along the lower.

- Calculate the present value of the cash flows at N_H and N_L using the assumed value of r_0, 3.5 percent, for r^*. Thus

$$\frac{V_H + C}{1 + r^*} = \frac{\$102.582}{1.035} = \$99.113$$

and

$$\frac{V_L + C}{1 + r^*} = \frac{\$103.522}{1.035} = \$100.021$$

4. Calculate the average present value of the two cash flows obtained in the previous step using

$$V = \frac{1}{2}\left[\frac{V_H + C}{1 + r^*} + \frac{V_L + C}{1 + r^*}\right]$$

$$= \frac{\$99.113 + \$100.021}{2} = \$99.567$$

5. Compare the result obtained in step 4 with the target market value of $100. If the two values are the same, then the r_1 used in this trial is the one we seek and is the correct one-year rate to be used in the binomial tree along the lower rate path. If the value found in step 4 is not equal to the target value of $100, our assumed value is not consistent with the yield curve. In such a case, one must repeat the five steps with a different value for r_1.

When r_1 is 4.5 percent, the value obtained in step 4 is $99.567 and is smaller than the target value of $100. Therefore, 4.5 percent is too large, and the five steps must be repeated with a smaller value for r_1. It turns out that the correct value for r_1 is 4.074 percent. The corresponding binomial tree is shown in Exhibit 36–6. Steps 1 through 5, using the correct rate, are as follows.

1. Select a value of 4.074 percent for r_1.

2. The corresponding value for the forward one-year rate if rates rise is 4.976 percent $(= 4.074\% \times e^{2 \times 0.10})$.

3. The bond's value one year from now is determined from the bond's value two years from now—$104, just as in the first trial. The bond's present value at node N_H is V_H, or $99.071 (= \$104/1.04976)$. The bond's present value at node N_L is V_L, or $99.929 (= \$104/1.04074)$. With the coupons added in, we have $103.071 and $103.929 to discount back to today at 3.5 percent, giving $99.586 = \$103.071/1.035 from the upper path and $100.414 = \$103.929/1.035 from the lower path.

4. The average present value is then $(\$99.586 + \$100.414)/2 = \$100$.

5. Because the average present value is equal to the observed market price of $100, r_1 or r_L is 4.074 percent and r_H is 4.976 percent.

E X H I B I T   36–6

The One-Year Rates for Year 1 Using the Two-Year 4 Percent On-the-Run Issue

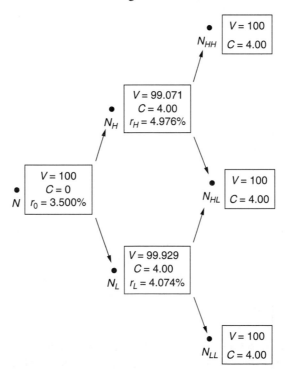

We're not done. Suppose that we want to grow this tree for one more year—that is, we want to determine r_2. We will use a three-year on-the-run 4.5 percent coupon bond to get r_2. The same five steps are used in an iterative process to find the one-year rates two years forward. Our objective now is to find the value of r_2 that will produce a value of $100 for the 4.5 percent on-the-run bond and will be consistent with (1) a volatility assumption of 10 percent, (2) a current one-year forward rate of 3.5 percent, and (3) the two possible one-year rates of 4.074 percent and 4.976 percent one year from now. The desired value of r_2 is 4.530 percent.

We explain how this is done using Exhibit 36–7, which shows the beginning of the computation. The principal payment at maturity and the final

E X H I B I T   36–7

Information for Deriving the One-Year Rates for Year 2 Using the Three-Year 4.5 Percent On-the-Run Issue

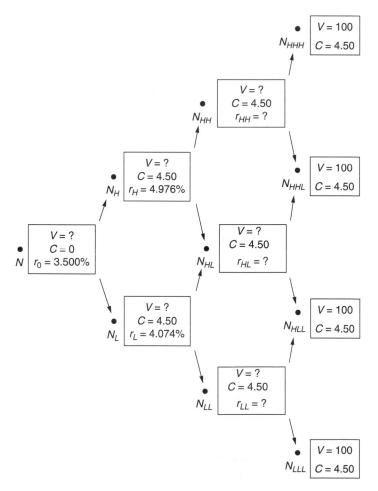

coupon payment for the three-year on-the-run bond appear in the four boxes at the end of the tree. Two years from today, the coupon payment of $4.50 is seen, but the present values of the future cash flows (from year three) are unknown. This is because the appropriate one-year discount rates are also unknown. One year from today, the coupon is again known, as are the one-year discount rates, but the present values remain unknown because the future cash flows remain unknown.

Exhibit 36–8 is the same as Exhibit 36–7, except that we have filled in the unknown values. As shown in Exhibit 36–8, the desired value of r_2 or r_{LL} is 4.530

E X H I B I T   36–8

The One-Year Rates in Year 2 Using the Three-Year 4.5 Percent On-the-Run Issue

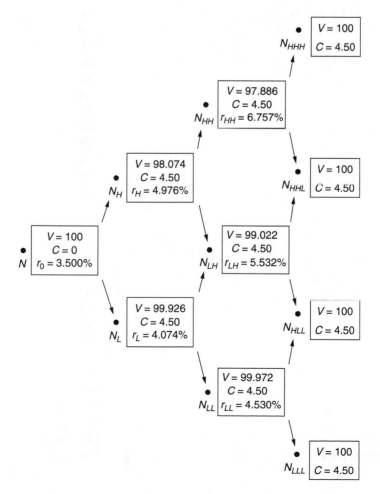

percent. Thus the other one-year rates in year two, r_{HL} and r_{HH}, are 5.532 percent and 6.757 percent, respectively.

To verify that these are the correct one-year rates to be used in year two, work backwards from the four final nodes at the right-hand end of the tree. For example, the present value of the future flows at node N_{HH} is found by discounting at 6.757 percent the (average) cash flow of $104.5 found at both of its adjacent nodes, giving $97.886.

Valuing an Optionless Bond

Exhibit 36–9 shows the resulting binomial tree that can be used to value any one-, two-, or three-year bond for this issuer. To illustrate its use, consider a 5.25 percent optionless bond with two years remaining to maturity. Also assume that the issuer's yield curve is the one corresponding to the interest rate tree in Exhibit 36–9. Exhibit 36–10 shows the various values in the discounting process. The bond's value is $102.075.

It is important to note that this value is identical to that found earlier by discounting at the spot rates or at the forward rates. Because the tree was calibrated to value the on-the-run securities, it will necessarily value any contractual set of cash flows correctly. This merely serves to demonstrate that this model is consistent with the standard valuation model for an optionless bond.

EXHIBIT 36–9

Binomial Interest-Rate Tree for Valuing up to a Three-Year Bond

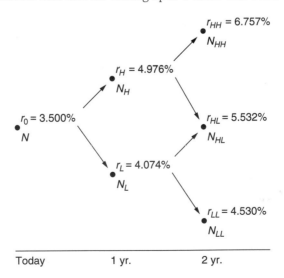

| Today | 1 yr. | 2 yr. |

E X H I B I T   36–10

Valuing an Optionless Bond with Three Years to Maturity and a Coupon of 5.25 Percent

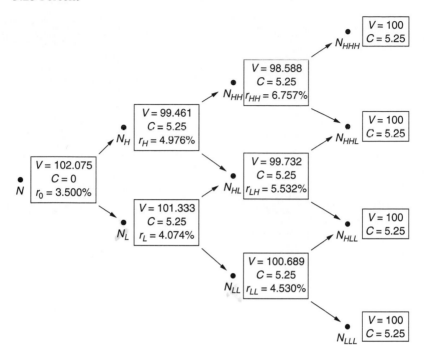

Valuing a Callable Bond

The binomial interest-rate tree can also be applied to callable bonds. The valuation process is the same as for an optionless bond, with one exception: When the call option can be exercised by the issuer, the bond's value at the node must be changed to reflect the lesser of the call price and the present value of the future cash flows.

Consider a 5.25 percent bond with three years remaining to maturity that is callable in years one and two at $100. Exhibit 36–11 shows the values at each node of the binomial tree. The discounting process is identical to that shown in Exhibit 36–10, except that at two nodes, N_L and N_{LL}, the values from the recursive valuation formula ($101.002 at N_L and $100.689 at N_{LL}) exceed the call price ($100) and therefore have been struck out and replaced with $100. These values are carried along in the discounting process, resulting in a value for this callable bond of $101.432.

In this model, the issuer calls the bond when the call price is less than the expected cost of leaving the bond outstanding to the next node, where the option

E X H I B I T   36–11

Valuing a Callable Bond with Three Years to Maturity, a Coupon of 5.25
Percent, and Callable in Years 1 and 2 at 100

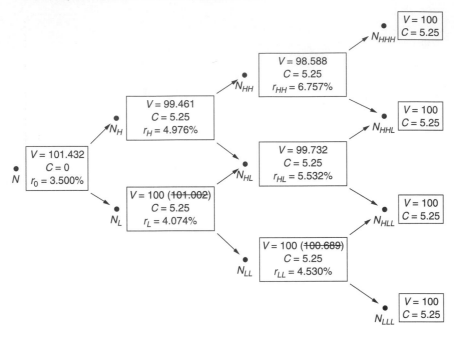

exercise decision will generally be revisited. This option exercise policy means
that a bond will be called only when the resulting net present value savings equal
the value of the call option. In other words, the option has only exercise value; it
has no time value. Actual exercise strategies may involve the sacrifice of some
time value and entail tax and accounting considerations.

Determining the Value of the Call Option

From our discussion regarding the relationship among the value of a callable
bond, the value of a noncallable bond, and the value of the call option, we know
that:

   Value of call option = Value of optionless bond – Value of callable bond.

   We have just seen how to determine the values of noncallable and callable
bonds. Their difference is just the value of the call option. In our illustration, the
noncallable bond is worth $102.075 and the callable bond is worth $101.432, so
the value of the call option is $0.643.

Extension to Other Embedded Options

The bond valuation framework presented here can be used to analyze putable bonds, options on interest-rate swaps, caps and floors on floating-rate notes, and the optional accelerated redemption granted to an issuer in fulfilling sinking-fund requirements.[5] Consider a putable bond. Suppose that a 5.25 percent bond with three years remaining to maturity is putable at par ($100) in years one and two. Assume that the appropriate binomial interest-rate tree for this issuer is the one in Exhibit 36–9. Exhibit 36–12 shows the binomial tree with the bond values altered at two nodes (N_{HH} and N_{HL}) because the bond values at these two nodes are less than $100, the value at which the bond can be put. The value of this putable bond is $102.523.

E X H I B I T   36–12

Valuing a Putable Bond with Three Years to Maturity, a Coupon of 5.25 Percent, and Putable in Years 1 and 2 at 100

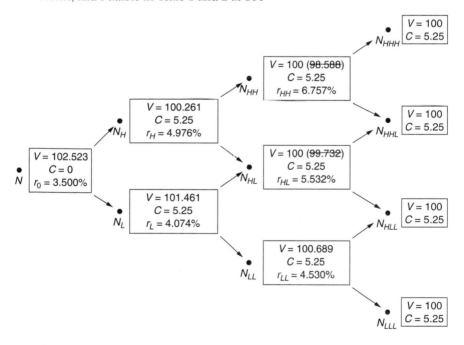

5. For a discussion of these options in a sinking-fund provision, see Chapter 5 in Richard S. Wilson and Frank J. Fabozzi, *Corporate Bonds: Structures & Analysis* (New Hope, PA: Frank J. Fabozzi Associates, 1996) pp. 188–197. The valuation of these options is explained further in Andrew J. Kalotay and George O. Williams, "The Valuation and Management of Bonds with Sinking Fund Provision," *Financial Analysts Journal*, March/April 1992, pp. 59–67.

Since the value of a putable bond can be expressed as the value of an optionless bond plus the value of a put option on that bond,

Value of put option = Value of optionless bond – Value of putable bond.

In our example, the value of the putable bond is $102.523 and the value of the corresponding nonputable bond is $102.075, so the value of the put option is –$0.448. The negative sign indicates the issuer has sold the option, or equivalently, the investor has purchased the option.

This framework can also be used to value a bond with multiple embedded options. The bond values at each node are altered to reflect the exercise of any options.

Volatility and the Theoretical Value

In our illustrations, interest-rate volatility has been set at 10 percent. The volatility assumption has an important impact on the theoretical value of option-bearing securities: the higher the volatility, the higher the value of any option,[6] including one embedded in a bond.

For a callable bond, greater volatility increases the value of a call option and so decreases the value of the bond. At the same time, greater volatility increases the value of a put option and hence increases the value of a putable bond.

Option-Adjusted Spread

This model determines the theoretical value of a bond; this value can then be compared to the observed market price. For example, if the market price of the three-year 5.25 percent callable bond is $101 and the theoretical value is $101.432, the bond is cheap by $0.432. Bond market participants, however, prefer to think not in dollar terms but rather in terms of a yield spread: A cheap bond trades at a higher spread and a rich bond at a lower spread relative to some basis.

The market convention has been to quote a yield spread as the difference between the yield-to-maturity on a particular bond and that on a Treasury bond of comparable maturity. This approach can be extended to take into account the entire yield curve, through either a set of spot rates or a set of forward rates.

We can now discuss a discounting spread over the forward-rate curve. In terms of our binomial tree, we seek the constant spread that, when added to all the forward rates on the tree, makes the theoretical value equal to the market price. This quantity is called the *option-adjusted spread* (OAS). It is option-adjusted in that a bond fairly priced relative to an issuer's yield curve will have an OAS of zero whether the bond is option-free or has embedded options.

---

6. This is explained in Chapter 59.

E X H I B I T   36–13

Demonstration of the Option-Adjusted Spread

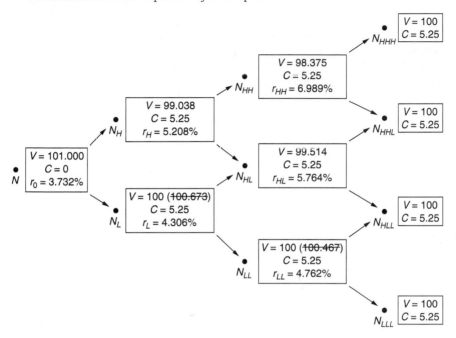

Returning to our illustration, if the observed market price is $101, the OAS would be the constant spread added to every rate in Exhibit 36–9 that will make the theoretical value equal to $101. In this case, that spread is 23.2 basis points, as can be verified in Exhibit 36–13.

Like the value of an option-bearing bond, the OAS will depend on the volatility assumption. For a given bond price, the higher the interest-rate volatility, the lower the OAS for a callable bond and the higher the OAS for a putable bond.

Effective Duration and Effective Convexity

Portfolio managers also want to know the sensitivity of a bond's price to changes in interest rates. As explained in Chapter 5, modified duration is a measure of the sensitivity of a bond's price to changes in the yield-to-maturity and is equivalent to assuming that the yield curve is flat and that future cash flows do not depend on interest rates. Consequently, modified duration is not an appropriate measure for bonds with embedded options whose cash flows can change with changing interest rates. For example, high rates change the cash flows of putable bonds, and low rates change the cash flows of callable bonds.

The correct duration measure—called *effective duration*—quantifies the price sensitivity to small changes in interest rates while simultaneously allowing for changing cash flows. In terms of our binomial interest-rate tree, price response to changing interest rates is found by shifting the tree—or, more appropriately, the yield curve from which the tree is derived—up and down by a few basis points.

Analogous to the discussion in Chapter 5, if P is the value of a bond *including accrued interest*, P_- is the value of the bond if the entire yield curve is shifted down by S basis points, and P_+ is its value when the curve is shifted up by S basis points, then

$$\text{Effective duration} = \frac{P_- - P_+}{2PS}$$

Let's return to the example of the callable 5.25 percent three-year bond. Given the yield curve and volatility assumptions we have been using, the central value P is \$101.432. Shifting the yield curve down 10 basis points, refitting the tree, and revaluing the bond gives a value for P_- of \$101.628. Similarly, shifting the curve up 10 basis points gives a value for P_+ of \$101.234. Then

$$\text{Effective duration} = \frac{\$101.628 - \$101.234}{2 \times \$101.432 \times 0.0010}$$

$$= \frac{\$0.394}{\$0.202864}$$

$$= 1.94$$

Duration is expressed in years because interest rates are expressed per year. Because the interest-rate shift (0.0010, or 10 basis points per year) appears in the denominator, the years appear in the numerator.

In the same manner, the standard convexity measure ignores the effects produced by both the shape of the yield curve and the presence of options. The applicable formula for convexity is

$$\text{Effective convexity} = \frac{P_- - 2P + P_+}{P \times S^2}$$

so that

$$\text{Effective convexity} = \frac{\$101.628 - 2 \times \$101.432 + \$101.234}{\$101.432 \times 0.0010^2}$$

Using the inserted values based on price to seven decimal places,

$$\text{Effective convexity} = \frac{\$0.0006867}{\$0.0001014}$$

$$= 6.77$$

THE CHALLENGE OF IMPLEMENTATION

For use as a practical tool, the basic interest-rate tree requires several refinements. For one thing, the spacing of the node lines in the tree must be much finer, particularly if American options are to be valued. However, the fine spacing required to value short-dated securities becomes computationally inefficient if one seeks to value, say, 30-year bonds. Although one can introduce a time-dependent node spacing, caution is required; it is easy to distort the term structure of volatility. Other practical difficulties include the management of cash flows that fall between two node lines.

SUMMARY

Many bonds are redeemable before maturity: They contain one or more embedded options. This chapter offered a framework for valuing such bonds. Our primary focus was on callable bonds. Callable bonds pose two risks to the investor in a declining-rate environment: There is reinvestment risk of principal, and there is limited upside potential relative to an optionless but otherwise similar bond.

The valuation framework presented here employs a binomial interest-rate tree based on an issuer's noncall life yield curve and an assumed interest-rate volatility. The binomial tree provides the volatility-dependent one-period rates to discount cash flows.

The option-adjusted spread is the constant spread that, when added to the rates in the interest-rate tree, produces a theoretical value for a bond equal to the market price of the bond. It is a means of expressing the difference between the theoretical value and an observed market price as a yield spread.

The archaic modified duration and convexity are inappropriate for a bond with an embedded option because these measures assume a flat yield curve and ignore the presence of any options. The appropriate measures of the response of a bond's price to changes in the yield curve are effective duration and effective convexity.

A COMPARISON OF METHODS FOR ANALYZING MORTGAGE-BACKED SECURITIES

Andrew S. Davidson
President
Andrew Davidson & Co., Inc.

Robert Kulason
Salomon Brothers Inc

Michael D. Herskovitz
Morgan Stanley

Investors that own or contemplate owning mortgage-backed securities (MBSs) need a method for valuing them. The central issue in all MBS valuation methods is the treatment of prepayment uncertainty. The homeowners' right to prepay their loans introduces a significant degree of uncertainty to the cash flows, and consequently the value, of MBSs.

The relationship between interest rates and MBS prepayment rates directly influences MBS pricing. In a bond market rally, prepayment rates rise, reducing the price gains of mortgage-backed securities. In a bear market, however, prepayment rates slow, resulting in increased price losses. This price-movement pattern is commonly referred to as "negative convexity."

The dependence of prepayment rates on interest rates affects not only MBS returns but also their interest rate risk. A traditional measure of the price sensitivity of fixed income securities, modified duration, gives the percent change in

The chapter was written when the authors were at Merrill Lynch, in the Mortgage-Backed Securities Research Department. The authors thank H. Halperin, K. Rogers, J. Van Lang, B. Starr, and N. Perrotis for their assistance. In addition, the authors acknowledge the contribution of L. Murakami.

price caused by a 100 basis point shift in the yield curve. Modified duration is a reasonable price sensitivity measure for securities with constant cash flows. It is often inadequate for MBSs, however, because prepayment rates, and consequently cash flows, vary as interest rates change.

The inadequacy of traditional fixed income analytical tools for valuing MBSs has led to the development of alternative methods. This chapter reviews four approaches to quantifying MBS return and risk characteristics. The techniques discussed are (1) static cash flow yield (SCFY) analysis, (2) total rate of return scenario analysis (SA), (3) option-adjusted spread (OAS) Monte Carlo models, and (4) the refinancing threshold pricing (RTP) model. The first three techniques constitute the currently accepted set of valuation techniques. The final method, refinancing threshold pricing, is an approach pioneered at Merrill Lynch.

Multiple approaches to valuing MBSs exist because no single methodology has been shown to explain completely the price performance of these securities. Each of the methods listed has its strengths and weaknesses. SCFY analysis is the simplest approach; however, it ignores a number of factors critical to the valuation of MBSs by assuming constant future interest rates. SA improves on the SCFY methodology by projecting MBS performance in a limited set of interest-rate scenarios. OAS Monte Carlo models extend SA by simulating MBS performance over numerous interest-rate paths. Critical to the SA and OAS approaches is the manner in which the future interest rate paths are selected and the specification of the relationship between interest rates and MBS prepayment rates. RTP is a binomial option-pricing-based methodology that differs fundamentally from the SA and OAS approaches. RTP directly models the refinancing decision of the individual mortgagor instead of attempting to specify aggregate MBS prepayment rates as a function of interest rates.

The chapter is divided into five sections. One section is devoted to each of the valuation methodologies, and a final section outlines our conclusions and recommendations. Each methodology section contains a description of the technique, the value and risk measures provided, the sensitivity of the results to input parameters, and a summary of the advantages and disadvantages of the approach. Throughout the chapter 30-year GNMA single family (SF) 8.0 percent, 9.5 percent, and 11.0 percent pass-throughs are used as examples to allow the comparison of results across methodologies. At the time the analyses were conducted, the GNMA 9.5 percent pass-through was the current coupon. The GNMA 8 percent and 11 percent pass-throughs were selected to represent the characteristics of discount and premium MBS, respectively.

STATIC CASH FLOW YIELD

The static cash flow yield (SCFY) is the discount rate that equates the value of future MBS cash flows with their market price. The future cash flows are projected based on the prepayment rate that is anticipated if interest rates remain stable for the life of the security.

SCFY is the basic measure of value in the mortgage market. Its primary advantage is its simplicity; the only required assumption is a prepayment projection. After a prepayment rate has been specified, cash flows can be generated and a yield calculated based on the security's market price. The trade-off for simplicity is that SCFY analysis ignores a number of factors critical to the valuation of MBSs, including the shape of the yield curve, the distribution and volatility of future interest rates, and the relationship between interest rates and MBS prepayment rates.

Required Assumptions

The only assumption required to compute the SCFY of MBSs is the projected prepayment rate assuming static interest rates. Typically, prepayment projections are made based on the results of a statistical analysis of historical prepayment data and are generally quoted as conditional prepayment rates (CPR) or percentages of the Public Securities Association (PSA) prepayment model. Investors should be aware that prepayment forecasts based on statistical models imply a confidence interval, which in turn implies a range of possible values for MBS.

Exhibit 37–1 illustrates the average prepayment forecast and the forecast range for seasoned GNMA pass-throughs made available by 13 firms through

E X H I B I T   37–1

Average Prepayment Forecast and Forecast Range for Seasoned GNMA Pass-Throughs

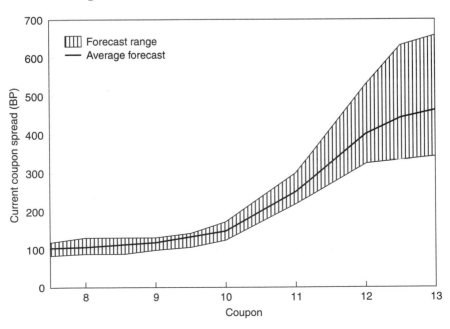

Telerate on March 15, 1988. Using the width of the range as a proxy for forecast uncertainty, it is clear that the level of uncertainty is significant for all coupons and is greatest for premium MBS.

Value Measures

Given a prepayment forecast for an MBS and its market price, its cash flow yield is uniquely determined. *The spread between the MBS static cash flow yield and either its average life or duration-matched Treasury issue has traditionally been used as a measure of value in the mortgage market.*

One way to interpret MBS static cash flow yield spreads to Treasuries is in a historical context. Based on current yield spreads, an evaluation can be made as to whether the mortgage market is historically rich or cheap relative to Treasuries. Further, spread differentials between discounts, currents, and premiums can be compared to determine intra-MBS market relative sector values.

Exhibit 37–2 shows GNMA MBS yield spreads to the 10-year Treasury bond as a function of the distance of the MBS coupon from the current coupon for selected historical dates.

Premium MBS spreads decline relative to the current coupon spread because the shorter durations of these securities cause them to trade off of the short

E X H I B I T   37–2

GNMA Yield Spreads to the 10-Year Treasury Bond for Selected Historical Dates

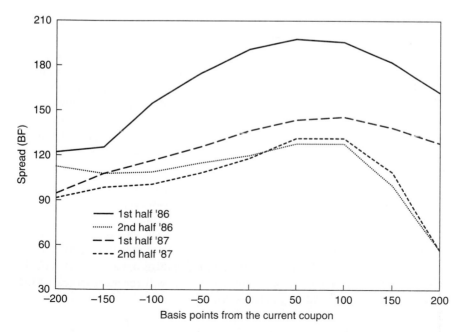

E X H I B I T   37–3

GNMA Yield Spreads to Duration-Matched Treasury Issues for Selected Historical Dates

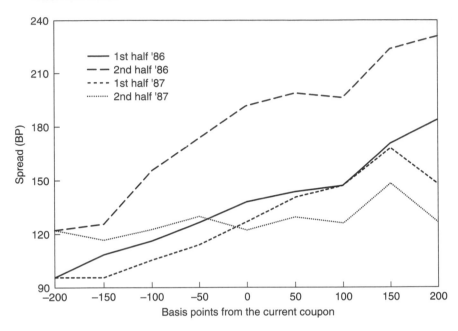

end of the yield curve. In order to adjust for the distortion introduced by mismatched durations, Exhibit 37–3 displays MBS spreads to duration-matched Treasury issues.

Exhibits 37–2 and 37–3 demonstrate that MBS spread levels have varied significantly over time. Spread-level variation can be related to changes in interest rates and corresponding changes in the option value of mortgage securities. In general, increases in interest-rate volatility will raise the value of the short option positions embedded in MBSs, which in turn reduces the prices (widens the spreads) of the securities. Conversely, lower volatility reduces the value of the short option components, thereby increasing the prices (reducing the spreads) of MBSs.

The relationship between spreads and volatility is demonstrated in Exhibit 37–4, which shows a high degree of correlation between the yield volatility of the 10-year Treasury and the spread between the current coupon GNMA and the 10-year Treasury between January 1985 and January 1988. This is strong evidence that the market uses its assessment of interest-rate volatility in pricing MBSs.

In addition to interest-rate volatility, SCFY spreads are also affected by the state of the housing market. A robust housing market will generally increase MBS supply, leading to wider MBS yield spreads.

EXHIBIT 37–4

Yield Volatility of the 10-Year Treasury Bond and the Spread between the Current Coupon GNMA and the 10-Year Treasury Bond

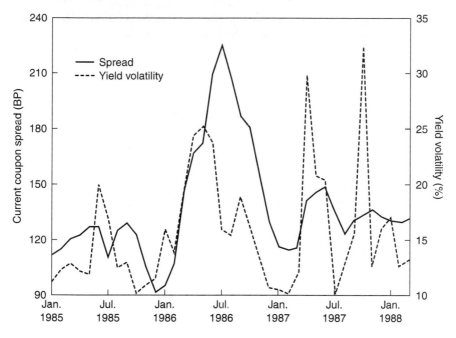

Consequently, an evaluation of MBSs based on SCFY spreads to Treasuries should incorporate current interest rate volatility levels and housing market conditions, and investors' beliefs about the future directions of these factors.

Interest-Rate Risk Measures

The weighted average life (WAL) of a MBS is used as a price risk indicator. It is the average time to receipt of the principal of the security. It is used as a measure of the effective maturity of MBS in the place of stated maturity. Stated maturity is a poor measure of effective maturity for MBSs because most principal is amortized or prepaid well before this date. Although an exact relationship between MBS WAL and MBS price sensitivity to interest rates does not exist, it is generally true that the longer the WAL, the greater the interest-rate sensitivity. Consequently, WAL can be employed as an indicator of the price risk of MBSs.

Another risk measure that can be obtained from SCFY analysis is Macaulay duration. The Macaulay duration of a security is the present value weighted average time to receipt of its cash flows. For true fixed income instruments, this measure can be shown to be equivalent to the price elasticity of the security with respect to interest rates. However, for MBSs, where cash flows are dependent on interest rates, Macaulay duration is often a poor measure of price sensitivity.

In the sections of this chapter dealing with option-adjusted spread Monte Carlo models and the refinancing threshold pricing model, MBS WALs and Macaulay durations will be compared to effective durations estimated by models that account for the dependence of MBS cash flows on interest rates.

Parameter Sensitivity

Changing the prepayment assumption can materially alter the yield, weighted average life, and duration of MBSs. Exhibit 37–5 illustrates this sensitivity, displaying static cash flow yields, weighted average lives, and Macaulay durations for GNMA 8.0 percent, 9.5 percent, and 11.0 percent pass-throughs at constant prices at three different prepayment rates: the minimum, average, and maximum forecasts depicted in Exhibit 37–1.

As prepayment rates increase, the yield on the discount increases and the yield on the premium decreases. The yield on the current coupon is insensitive to the projected prepayment rate since it is priced close to par. Weighted average lives and durations for all the pass-throughs decrease with increasing prepayment rates. Because MBS duration depends on the projected prepayment rate, the calculated yield spread to duration-matched Treasuries also depends on this assumption. This is true even for the current coupon, for which the SCFY is nearly independent of the assumed prepayment rate.

Summary

The major attractions of the SCFY methodology are its simplicity and its acceptance by the market as the standard measure of MBS value. The only assumption required is a prepayment projection. After specifying a prepayment rate and generating cash flows, a yield can be calculated based on the security's market price.

E X H I B I T   37–5

Effect of Prepayment Rate Specification on SCFY Risk and Return Measures

GNMA	Price	SCFY(%)			WA (Yrs.)			Macaulay Duration		
		Min	Avg	Max	Min	Avg	Max	Min	Avg	Max
8.0%	90–20	9.59	9.64	9.79	12.9	12.2	10.6	6.6	6.4	5.8
9.5%	99–10	9.74	9.75	9.75	12.8	10.9	9.2	6.5	5.9	5.3
11.0%	107–00	9.36	9.17	8.97	6.2	5.4	4.7	4.1	3.7	3.4

The trade-off for simplicity is that by assuming constant future interest rates, the approach ignores a number of factors critical to the valuation of MBSs, including the shape of the yield curve, the distribution and volatility of future interest rates, and the relationship between interest rates and MBS prepayment rates. Consequently, investors who rely on this methodology must subjectively decide how much spread is required to compensate them for the uncertainty introduced by these factors.

Despite these problems, a historical analysis of SCFY spreads is a useful adjunct to the other valuation methodologies presented in this chapter. In particular, the SCFY approach is most useful for the high premium and deep discount MBSs having cash flows with little sensitivity to interest rates.

SCENARIO ANALYSIS

Scenario analysis (SA) can be used to supplement SCFY analysis by examining the dynamic nature of MBSs. It consists of calculating MBS holding-period returns for a variety of possible future interest rate scenarios. For each scenario, cash flows are generated based on coupon, scheduled principal amortization, and prepayments. Cash flows that occur prior to the horizon are reinvested to the end of the holding period. At the horizon, the value of the remaining principal balance is calculated. The rate of growth necessary to equate the initial investment with the sum of the reinvested cash flows and the value of the remaining principal balance at the horizon is the total return for the scenario. The total scenario return is then converted to an annualized rate of return based on the length of the holding period.

Scenario analysis differs from the other approaches presented because it requires the use of a separate valuation model in order to arrive at the security's horizon price. Consequently, it can be employed in conjunction with OAS models or the RTP model to assess the implications of these pricing models for the dynamic performance of MBS in a holding period return context.

A simple but useful alternative horizon pricing model values the MBSs-based on SCFY spreads and projected horizon prepayment rates. The scenario horizon prepayment rate determines MBS WAL at the horizon. A MBS is then priced at a spread to its WAL-matched Treasury issue. Scenario spreads are determined by the SCFY spreads at which the same relative coupon MBS are currently trading. This approach has the advantage of investigating the implications of existing spread relationships on holding period returns. It determines the scenario holding period returns of MBSs assuming current spread relationships are maintained. Using this pricing methodology, SA can be used in conjunction with a historical analysis of SCFY spreads to make assessments of MBS relative sector values. For example, if the expected returns of discount MBSs are inordinately large relative to premium MBSs using this approach, an argument can be made that discount MBS spreads are too large relative to premium MBS spreads. Consequently, discount MBSs would be the better value.

Required Assumptions

Holding Period

The length of the holding period affects the shape of the total rate of return profile. Assuming monotonic parallel yield curve shifts, the effect of the reinvestment rate for interim cash flows will tend to offset the effect of the change in the value of the remaining principal balance at the end of the holding period. Higher interest rates imply greater reinvestment income but lower horizon prices for the remaining principal balance. For short holding periods, the price change of the security will dominate the reinvestment effect; the total scenario rate of return will decrease as interest rates increase. For sufficiently long holding periods, the reinvestment effect will dominate the impact of the horizon price, and total scenario rate of return will increase as interest rates rise.

When employing SA, the conventional practice is to evaluate MBSs based on a one-year holding period. Most investors have an opportunity to rebalance their portfolios at least this often. Further, a one-year holding period limits the effect of the reinvestment rate assumption. A short holding period, however, increases the importance of the horizon pricing model.

Prepayment Rate Function

The specification of the relationship between scenario interest rates and prepayment rates is critical. This relationship defines the embedded option in MBSs and is what differentiates MBSs from true fixed-income securities. As noted in the SCFY analysis section, the uncertainty of prepayment forecasts for MBSs assuming static interest rates is substantial. The level of difficulty associated with forecasting prepayment rates assuming nonconstant paths of future interest rates is much greater, implying even wider confidence intervals for such projections. Consequently, it is important that investors assess the sensitivity of SA risk and return measures to the prepayment rate function specification.

Interest Rate Distribution and Volatility

The type of interest-rate probability distribution and volatility level determine the weights that are assigned to each scenario. This is important when calculating the expected return and the variance of returns across all scenarios. The most popular distributions are the bell-shaped normal and the right-skewed log normal. Normal implies equal probability of equal absolute changes, while log normal implies equal probability of equal percentage changes. At low levels of volatility, the two assumptions give similar results.

Instead of selecting a probability distribution and a volatility assumption, an investor can subjectively assign probabilities to each of the scenarios. This is feasible only if a small number of scenarios are run.

Generally, the lower the volatility assumption, or for subjective probability distributions, the more heavily weighted the scenarios near the central scenario, the higher the expected return and the lower the variance of returns. The increase in expected return results from the negative convexity of MBSs.

Central Scenario

The interest-rate scenarios must be centered on a base case. Two conventional central scenarios are the unchanged market and the implied forward-rate scenarios. In the unchanged market scenario, interest rates remain unchanged over the holding period. For the implied forward scenario, interest rates follow paths described by the implied forward rates. Generally, the other scenarios selected assume parallel yield-curve shifts about the central scenario. It is also possible to specify scenarios in which yield curve rotations occur. However, the added complexity of specifying such scenarios and assigning probabilities limits their usefulness.

The implied forward scenario is generally considered to be the more theoretically sound central scenario. It also has the advantage of simplifying comparisons between different duration securities; for example, the expected returns on all Treasury bonds are equal under this scenario, independent of maturity.

Horizon Pricing Model

The horizon pricing model is another critical aspect of scenario analysis. It determines the value of the remaining principal balance of MBSs at the horizon. The shorter the horizon, the greater the impact of horizon prices on holding period returns will be.

Number of Scenarios Simulated

The number of scenarios simulated can also affect calculated expected returns and variances of returns. Generally, for MBS pass-throughs these values converge to their asymptotic values when scenarios are run at 50 basis point intervals between –400 and +400 basis point shifts in the yield curve, assuming a one-year horizon.

Reinvestment Rate

The impact of the reinvestment rate is proportional to the length of the holding period. For short holding periods, its effect is negligible. Since the standard approach is to assume a one-year holding period, the reinvestment rate assumption is relatively unimportant. If analyses are conducted employing longer holding periods, the sensitivity of the results to this assumption increases.

Value Measures

The expected return is the weighted average of the total rates of return of all the scenarios, where each scenario is weighted by its probability. The scenario weights depend on the assumed level of interest rate volatility and the probability distribution employed.

A more complete value measure is a graph of total returns versus interest rate scenarios (it could also be deemed a risk measure because the dispersion of the returns is evident). This approach has the advantage of visually displaying the dynamic performance characteristics of MBSs. However, comparisons between securities can be difficult since it is unlikely that one security will completely dominate another.

Interest-Rate Risk Measures

One of the most widely used statistical measures of dispersion is variance. The square root of variance is called *standard deviation*. This measure is particularly useful when dealing with normally distributed data. In this case, approximately 68 percent of the observations can be expected to lie within one standard deviation of the mean, and 95 percent within two standard deviations. The greater the variance and standard deviation, the wider the dispersion of scenario returns and, consequently, the riskier the security.

Parameter Sensitivity

Exhibit 37–6 demonstrates the effect of the length of the holding period on the total return profile of a GNMA 9.5 percent pass-through. As the length of the

E X H I B I T   37–6

Effect of Holding Period on the Total Return Profile of a GNMA 9.5% Pass-Through

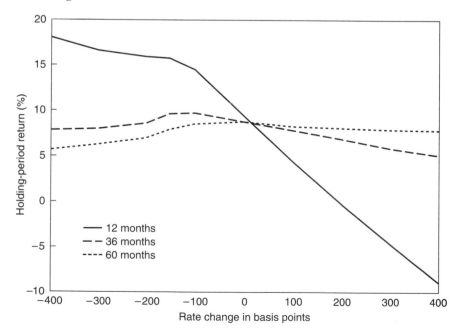

holding period increases, the profile rotates counterclockwise due to the increasing effect of the reinvestment rate and the reduced impact of the horizon price on scenario returns.

Due to their shorter durations, the corresponding return profiles for premium MBSs would be flatter for the one-year holding period and rotate further counterclockwise as the length of the holding period increased. Discount MBSs would display the opposite behavior.

Exhibit 37–7 shows the effect of the specification of the prepayment rate function on the total return profile of a GNMA 11 percent pass-through. The underlying prepayment model was shifted up and down 15 percent. A faster prepayment rate specification results in reduced holding period returns in falling interest-rate scenarios and increased returns in rising interest-rate scenarios, due to the reduction in the duration of MBS cash flows. Current and discount MBSs would behave similarly.

Exhibit 37–8 displays the effect of interest-rate volatility on the expected returns and the standard deviations of returns of GNMA 8 percent, 9.5 percent, and 11 percent pass-throughs, assuming future changes in interest rates are log-normally distributed. The base volatility level was shifted up and down 40 percent. Increased interest-rate volatility results in reduced expected returns and

EXHIBIT 37–7

Effect of Prepayment Rate Specification on the Total Return Profile of a GNMA 11% Pass-Through

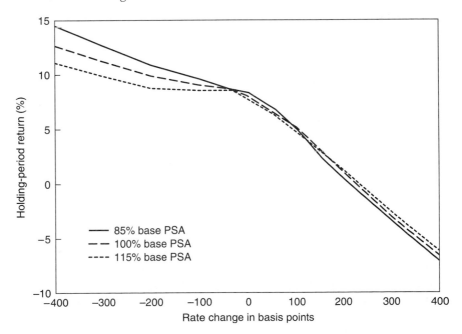

E X H I B I T   37–8

Effect of Interest-Rate Volatility on SA Risk and Return Measures

	Expected Return (%)			Standard Deviation of Returns (%)		
GNMA	**Low**	**Mid**	**High**	**Low**	**Mid**	**High**
8.0%	8.16	8.01	7.85	3.97	6.30	8.29
9.5%	8.32	7.95	7.47	3.55	5.39	6.88
11.0%	7.43	6.81	6.22	1.75	3.10	4.25

E X H I B I T   37–9

Effect of Central Yield-Curve Scenario on SA Risk/Return Measures

	Expected Return (%)		Standard Deviation of Returns (%)	
GNMA	**Implied Forward**	**Unchanged Market**	**Implied Forward**	**Unchanged Market**
8.0%	8.01	9.07	6.30	6.41
9.5%	7.95	9.00	5.39	5.50
11.0%	6.81	7.74	3.10	3.15

increased standard deviations of returns. The normal distribution would result in slightly higher expected returns, due to its symmetry.

The expected return of the GNMA 8.0 percent pass-through displays little sensitivity to interest-rate volatility because its embedded prepayment option is far out of the money. The interest rate volatility assumption is more important for current coupon and premium MBS.

Exhibit 37–9 demonstrates the effect of the central scenario yield curve on the expected returns and the standard deviations of returns for GNMA 8 percent, 9.5 percent, and 11 percent pass-throughs. The implied forward scenario shifts the return profiles downward relative to the unchanged market scenario, and consequently results in lower expected returns. This effect is due to the rising implied forward rates embedded in an upward-sloping yield curve. An inverted yield curve would cause the opposite effect. Although the choice of the central scenario yield curve has a large effect on the absolute levels of MBS expected returns, it has little impact on their relative levels.

Summary

The SA approach extends the SCFY methodology by examining the dynamic nature of MBSs. It can be used in conjunction with other MBS pricing models to assess their implications for the dynamic performance of MBSs in a holding-period-return context. If the SCFY spread-based pricing approach described in this section is employed, SA investigates the impact of existing spread relationships on MBS holding period returns. This approach can be very useful when used in conjunction with a historical analysis of SCFY spreads. Relative value between MBS market sectors can be evaluated by reviewing existing spread levels in a historical context and by assessing their impact on MBS expected returns and variances of returns. MBS value relative to other fixed income markets can be evaluated in a similar fashion through a comparison of these values to those calculated for the alternative markets. Further, the historical analysis of SCFY spreads can be used to assess likely future spread movements. This information can in turn be used when evaluating the spread sensitivity of SA results.

Ideally, an investor would like to select the security with the highest expected return and the lowest variance of returns. Usually this is not possible since it would probably indicate that the security was mispriced. Under normal circumstances, an investor must accept additional risk in order to obtain a higher expected return. SA has the advantage of delineating the available sets of MBS risk/return profiles for specific holding periods.

An additional advantage of SA is that the limited number of scenarios allows the investor to review the assumptions and results of each scenario. A relatively small set of scenarios, however, may not adequately model the effect on value of the complete distribution of future interest-rate paths.

OPTION-ADJUSTED SPREADS

In an attempt to improve on the static cash flow yield and scenario analysis measures of MBS value, mortgage market participants have begun to rely on option-adjusted spread (OAS) simulation models. The OAS simulation approach generates numerous interest-rate paths that then determine future MBS cash flows. These cash flows are discounted by the simulated interest rates plus the option-adjusted spread. The model solves for the spread that equates the market price to the average simulated price. The simulation approach provides a method for estimating MBS yields and spreads to the Treasury yield curve that are adjusted for the embedded options in these securities. In addition, these models can provide estimates of MBS option cost and effective MBS duration and convexity.[1]

---

1. Michael D. Herskovitz,"Option-Adjusted Spread Analysis for Mortgage-Backed Securities," Chap. 21 in *The Handbook of Fixed-Income Options,* ed. Frank J. Fabozzi (Chicago, IL: Probus Publishing, 1989).

Required Assumptions

Prepayment Rate Function

One of the two critical assumptions in the OAS simulation methodology is the link between interest rates and prepayment rates. If the relationship between interest rates, time, and MBS prepayments is misspecified, the calculated value and risk measures will be biased. The sensitivity of OAS model results to different prepayment function specifications is explored in the parameter sensitivity section.

Interest-Rate Diffusion Process

The second critical assumption in the OAS simulation approach is the specification of the interest-rate diffusion process. Most models assume that interest rates evolve as a log-normal random walk with a drift that centers the distribution on the implied forward rates. If the yield curve is upward sloping, the implied forward rates will indicate an upward bias to short-term interest rates. This may not reflect investors' rate expectations. However, the use of implied forward rates with the typical positively sloped yield curve builds in the requirement that longer-duration securities must yield more than shorter-duration securities in order to be fairly priced. This is necessary to price noncallable bonds correctly and is consistent with option pricing theory.

Most models diffuse a single short-term rate. In these models, the current MBS coupon, which drives the prepayment function, is assumed to shift deterministically based on the change in the short-term rate. Other models seek to introduce a greater amount of realism into the interest-rate process by diffusing both a short- and long-term rate. In this approach, the short- and long-term rate changes are less than perfectly correlated, thereby allowing for the possibility of yield-curve inversions. The long-term rate is used to drive the prepayment function, while MBS cash flows are discounted back along the short-term rate paths.

Interest-Rate Volatility

In addition to specifying an interest-rate process, an assumption about interest-rate volatility must be made. Higher volatility assumptions increase the dispersion of the simulated interest-rate paths. Since MBSs are effectively short a call option, increasing interest-rate volatility will increase calculated option cost and decrease option-adjusted spread. The sensitivity of these results to this parameter is discussed in the sensitivity section.

Number of Scenarios Simulated

The reliance of the OAS approach on a set of randomly generated interest-rate paths introduces additional uncertainty into the results of these models. The magnitude of the additional uncertainty is inversely proportional to the number of interest-rate paths simulated. Consequently, there is a trade-off between computational efficiency and the confidence intervals of the results.

Averaging Methodology

OAS values are also sensitive to the method used to aggregate the information from the individual interest-rate paths. For example, the cash flows for the paths could be averaged first and then the OAS calculated as the spread that equates this average cash flow vector with the market price of the security. Alternatively, OAS could be defined as the spread that equates the mean of the individual prices for each of the simulated interest-rate paths to the market price. Each of these methods will produce different OAS values.

The Merrill Lynch OAS model employs the latter averaging methodology. Under this approach, OAS values can be interpreted as the expected yield spreads of MBSs to Treasuries over the full range of probable interest-rate scenarios. The alternative methodology does not fully account for the relationship between scenario interest rates, prepayment rates, and MBS value.

Value Measures

Option-Adjusted Spread

Option-adjusted spread is the primary value measure produced by OAS models. Most models define OAS as the spread that equates the average simulated price to the market price. Implicit in this methodology is the assumption that the fair option-adjusted yield curve for mortgages is a fixed spread over the Treasury yield curve.

When the interest-rate diffusion process is centered on the implied forward rates, the OAS has embedded in it the requirement that different duration securities must have different yields in order to be fairly priced. Consequently, OAS values for different duration MBS should be directly comparable.

Option Cost

Spread to Treasury alone may not be a good indicator of MBS relative value. In order to compare various MBSs, the yield spreads should be benchmarked to an appropriate level, namely, the static cash flow yield. The static cash flow yield spread minus the OAS equals the implied option cost.

Interest-Rate Risk Measures

Effective Duration and Convexity

By shifting the simulated interest-rate paths up and down slightly while holding the OAS fixed, estimates of MBS price sensitivity can be calculated. The average percentage price change can be used to calculate a security's OAS effective duration. OAS effective convexity can be computed by observing the rate of change of the OAS effective duration. These price-sensitivity measures can be useful for hedging since they incorporate the effect of the prepayment option. However, OAS effective durations are measures of price sensitivity, not of maturity.

OAS Macaulay Duration

A measure of MBS maturity that is adjusted for the prepayment option is the OAS Macaulay duration. This duration measure represents the present value-weighted average time to receipt of MBS cash flow averaged across all simulation trials. Exhibit 37–10 shows the SCFY WAL, SCFY Macaulay duration, OAS Macaulay duration, and OAS effective duration of GNMA 8 percent, 9.5 percent, and 11 percent pass-throughs.

The OAS Macaulay durations of the GNMA 8.0 percent and 9.5 percent pass-throughs are shorter than their SCFY Macaulay durations. This result is consistent with expectations. Using the simulation approach, discount and current coupon securities are likely to experience an increase in prepayments relative to the static forecast, as prepayments are near their minimum based on the assumed prepayment model. The OAS effective durations of all the pass-throughs are below their SCFY Macaulay durations, reflecting the negative convexity of MBS. On a relative basis, the OAS effective duration of the GNMA 11.0 percent pass-through is depressed the most below its SCFY Macaulay duration, while the OAS effective duration of the GNMA 8.0 percent pass-through is depressed the least.

Parameter Sensitivity

Exhibit 37–11 demonstrates the effect of the specification of the prepayment-rate function on the OAS, option cost, OAS Macaulay duration, and OAS effective duration of GNMA 8 percent, 9.5 percent, and 11 percent pass-throughs. The underlying prepayment model was shifted up and down 15 percent. A faster prepayment-rate specification results in a reduction in both the OAS Macaulay and OAS effective durations of MBSs. A faster prepayment-rate specification will generally also increase the OAS of discount MBS and reduce the OAS of premium MBSs.

Exhibit 37–12 displays the effect of interest rate volatility on the OAS, option cost, OAS Macaulay duration, and OAS effective duration of GNMA 8 percent, 9.5 percent, and 11 percent pass-throughs. The base volatility level was shifted up and down 40 percent. Increased interest rate volatility results in higher

E X H I B I T   37–10

A Comparison of SCFY and OAS Risk Measures

GNMA	SCFY WAL (Yrs.)	SCFY Macaulay Duration	OAS Macaulay Duration	OAS Effective Duration
8.0%	11.5	6.1	5.5	5.8
9.5%	10.5	5.6	4.8	4.1
11.0%	5.8	3.9	3.9	2.3

E X H I B I T   37–11

Effect of Prepayment Rate on Specification OAS Risk and Return Measures

	OAS (BP)			Option Cost (BP)			OAS Macaulay Duration			OAS Effective Duration		
GNMA	Low	Mid	High	Low	Mid	High	Low	Mid	High	Low	Mid	High
8.0%	66	79	108	48	35	6	5.8	5.5	5.2	6.0	5.8	5.7
9.5%	51	60	56	67	58	62	5.1	4.8	4.6	4.3	4.1	3.9
11.0%	16	4	−13	102	114	131	4.3	3.9	3.6	2.9	2.3	1.9

E X H I B I T   37–12

Effect of Interest-Rate Volatility on OAS Risk/Return Measures

	OAS (BP)			Option Cost (BP)			OAS Macaulay Duration			OAS Effective Duration		
GNMA	Low	Mid	High	Low	Mid	High	Low	Mid	High	Low	Mid	High
8.0%	104	79	74	10	24	40	5.8	5.5	5.0	6.2	5.8	5.3
9.5%	102	60	24	16	58	94	5.1	4.8	4.4	4.5	4.1	3.7
11.0%	56	4	−41	62	114	160	3.9	3.9	3.7	2.2	2.3	2.5

option costs and lower OAS. The OAS effective duration of premium MBSs and discount MBSs is increased and decreased respectively as volatility increases.

Summary

The OAS methodology has a number of advantages over both the SCFY and SA approaches. The large number of simulated future interest-rate paths may better model the complete distribution of future rate paths and improve the statistical significance of the risk and return measures. Further, the risk measures account for the dependence of MBS prepayments on interest rates. If the interest-rate diffusion process and the relationship between interest rates and prepayment rates are correctly specified, these price-sensitivity measures should be more useful for hedging than their SCFY counterparts.

The major drawback to the OAS approach is that it is basically a black box into which an investor puts assumptions and out of which come risk/return measures. The prepayment functions and term-structure models embedded in OAS models are generally proprietary, precluding the possibility of an investor inspecting these key aspects of the model. Even if the model specifications are available, it may be difficult to evaluate them. This makes it imperative that the investor who employs these models determines their sensitivity to the required assumptions.

Because of the sensitivity of OAS results to model specification and assumptions, these values are difficult to compare on an absolute basis between models. OAS results are best employed as indicators of relative value between similar securities run under identical assumptions using a consistent methodology.

REFINANCING THRESHOLD PRICING MODEL

The refinancing threshold pricing (RTP) model is a binomial option-pricing-based methodology that differs fundamentally from the SA and OAS approaches. RTP directly models the refinancing decision of the individual mortgagor instead of attempting to specify aggregate MBS prepayment rates as a function of interest rates. This approach is based on three main concepts:

- An options approach is effective in modeling mortgage prepayments, as the mortgagor's ability to prepay the mortgage constitutes an option.

- The costs a mortgagor incurs when refinancing are not paid to the holder of the MBS.

- Mortgagors have different interest-rate levels, or thresholds, at which they prepay their mortgages. That is, different homeowners face different levels of refinancing costs.

The concept of heterogeneous mortgagors provides a fundamental and innovative insight into analyzing MBS value and serves as the starting point for the refinancing threshold pricing model. The RTP approach and models the underlying economics of MBSs by focusing on the refinancing decision of the individual mortgagor. These individual refinancing decisions are observed as prepayments. Models that estimate prepayments based on interest-rate levels, however, reverse this process. They examine the effect rather than the cause. RTP provides the potential for robust results and additional insights into MBS valuation because RTP refects the underlying process.

The process of valuing a mortgage pool begins with modeling a single mortgage loan. RTP values individual mortgagor cash flows, given their refinancing costs. This procedure, however, is not repeated for each mortgage in the pool. Instead, the pool is divided into groups of borrowers who share similar refinancing costs. Using market data, RTP endogenously determines both the costs that mortgagors face and the proportion of the pool in each refinancing cost class. This division into mortgage groups is termed *pool composition.*[2]

---

2. For a more detailed discussion of the RTP approach, refer to *The Refinancing Threshold Pricing Model: An Economic Approach to Valuing MBS,* Merrill Lynch Mortgage-Backed Securities Research, November 1987.

Required Assumptions

Interest-Rate Diffusion Process

The first assumption required is the specification of the interest-rate diffusion process. A term-structure model generates a binomial interest-rate tree. The rates at the successive branches of the tree, as well as probabilities of interest rates increasing and decreasing, are selected in a manner that is consistent with the observed prices on the current Treasury securities.

The interest-rate tree is used by a binomial option pricing model to value each of the endogenously determined refinancing classes in MBSs. When the present value of the mortgagor's cash flows exceeds the remaining principal plus refinancing costs, the mortgage is assumed to be refinanced, and the market value of the mortgage is set equal to the principal amount of the mortgage. Refinancing is not economic when the remaining principal plus refinancing costs is greater than the present value of the cash flows to be paid by the mortgagor.

Interest-Rate Volatility

In addition to specifying an interest-rate process, an assumption about interest volatility is required. Higher assumed interest-rate volatility generally results in a reduction in MBS price due to the increase in the value of the embedded short option position.

Pool Composition

The third required assumption is the pool composition and the associated thresholds. Mortgages in a pool are divided into three classes, according to interest-rate sensitivity: very sensitive, moderately sensitive, and not interest-rate sensitive. The degree of interest-rate sensitivity depends on the mortgagors' refinancing costs. Mortgagors considered very interest-rate sensitive face low refinancing costs, while mortgagors with less interest-rate sensitivity have correspondingly higher refinancing costs. While the pool could be divided into any number of classes, three captures the major implications of heterogeneous borrowers for descriptive purposes.

The model assumes that nonrefinancing prepayments occur at a constant rate over the life of the mortgage pool and are proportionally drawn from the three refinancing cost classes. At origination, the distribution of mortgagors in refinancing cost classes is assumed to be identical across all pools. This does not imply that each seasoned pool contains an equal number of high, medium, and low interest-rate-sensitive borrowers, but rather, the proportion of highly interest-rate-sensitive individuals in a GNMA 8 percent pool at origination equals the proportion of highly interest-rate-sensitive individuals in a GNMA 10 percent pool at origination. Over time, the proportions will shift as mortgagors refinance or move. Consequently, one would expect seasoned GNMA 14s to have very few highly and moderately interest-sensitive borrowers remaining in the pool, while seasoned GNMA 7s may have proportions that have not changed much since origination.

After assuming an initial pool distribution, pool composition and refinancing cost levels at origination are determined by recursively comparing market prices with model results until the difference between the two is minimized. These implied pool compositions generally remain stable over time and are consistent with prepayment expectations. Once the value of each of the refinancing classes has been determined, a weighted average is calculated based on the pool composition to determine MBS value.

Value Measures

Price
The RTP directly computes the theoretical price of MBSs. Comparisons between theoretical values and actual market prices may help investors determine MBS relative value.

Implied Spread and Implied Volatility
The term *structure model* within the RTP model creates a binomial tree of future Treasury rates based on the prices of the current Treasury securities. The RTP model discounts MBS cash flows back through this binomial lattice at the Treasury rate plus some constant spread. This spread reflects the yield premium of MBSs after accounting for the prepayment option held by the mortgagor. The implied spread and volatility are calculated by varying the respective parameter, holding the other constant, and finding the level at which the model price equals the market price. In general, the larger the implied volatility and spread, the cheaper the security.

Interest-Rate Risk Measures

By shifting the yield curve up and down slightly, estimates of MBS price sensitivity can be calculated in a manner analogous to that described in the OAS section. In addition, the price sensitivity of MBSs to changes in interest-rate volatility can be computed. Exhibit 37–13 shows the SCFY WAL, SCFY Macaulay duration, RTP effective duration, RTP effective convexity, and RTP dP/dVol[3] of GNMA 8 percent, 9.5 percent, and 11 percent pass-throughs.

Consistent with expectations, the RTP effective durations of the pass-throughs are all below their SCFY Macaulay durations, due to the negative convexity of MBSs. The convexities of the current coupon and premium pass-throughs are negative, whereas that of the discount is slightly positive. The dP/dVol estimates are consistent with the convexity estimates: The more negatively convex a security, the faster its price increases as volatility falls.

---

3. dP/dVol is defined as the price change of MBSs resulting from a 1 percent reduction in interest-rate volatility.

EXHIBIT 37–13

A Comparison of SCFY and RTP Risk Measures

GNMA	SCFY WAL (Yrs.)	SCFY Macaulay Duration	RTP Effective Duration	RTP Effective Convexity	RTP dP/dVol
8.0%	11.5	6.1	6.0	0.37	−0.02
9.5%	10.2	5.6	5.1	−0.94	0.16
11.0%	5.8	3.9	2.8	−2.48	0.62

EXHIBIT 37–14

Effect of Refinancing Cost Specification on RTP Risk/Return Measures

GNMA	RTP Price			RTP Effective Duration			RTP Duration Convexity		
	Low	Mid	High	Low	Mid	High	Low	Mid	High
8.0%	90–22	90–26	90–27	5.9	6.0	6.1	0.34	0.37	0.38
9.5%	99–00	99–10	99–15	4.8	5.1	5.4	−0.70	−0.94	−0.22
11.0%	105–12	106–29	107–27	0.9	2.8	3.2	−1.57	−2.48	−0.86

Parameter Sensitivity

Exhibit 37–14 demonstrates the effect of the refinancing cost specification on the RTP price, RTP effective duration, and RTP convexity of GNMA 8 percent, 9.5 percent, and 11 percent pass-throughs. Refinancing costs were shifted up and down 25 percent. Higher refinancing costs reduce the value of the short option position embedded in MBSs, which results in higher model prices. Higher refinancing costs also extend the duration of MBSs due to the reduction in the incentive for mortgagors to prepay their loans.

Exhibit 37–15 displays the effect of interest-rate volatility on the RTP price, RTP effective duration, and RTP effective convexity of GNMA 8 percent, 9.5 percent, and 11 percent pass-throughs. The base volatility level was shifted up and down 40 percent. Increased interest-rate volatility generally results in lower prices and shorter effective durations. The largest effects occur for the current coupon and premium pass-throughs. Discount pass-throughs are less affected by interest-rate volatility because their embedded prepayment options are far out of the money.

E X H I B I T   37–15

Effect of Interest-Rate Volatility on RTP Risk/Return Measures

GNMA	RTP Price			RTP Effective Duration			RTP Duration Convexity		
	Low	Mid	High	Low	Mid	High	Low	Mid	High
8.0%	90–22	90–26	90–27	6.1	6.0	5.6	0.53	0.37	−0.01
9.5%	99–15	99–10	98–18	5.4	5.1	4.5	−0.89	−0.94	−0.66
11.0%	107–31	106–29	105–09	3.9	2.8	2.0	−0.89	−2.48	0.57

Summary

As with the OAS approach, the RTP model provides risk/return measures that account for the dependence of MBS prepayments on interest rates. The major attraction of the RTP methodology is its independence from an exogenous prepayment function. By directly modeling the refinancing decision of mortgagors, the method provides the potential for more robust results.

Despite its conceptual relevance, RTP is still essentially a black box into which the investor puts assumptions and out of which come risk/return measures. The endogenously determined pool compositions are available for inspection, as are the parameters defining the interest-rate process. However, it may be difficult for the typical investor to assess the reasonableness of these values. As with the OAS approach, this makes it imperative that the investor assess the sensitivity of RTP results to the required assumptions.

CONCLUSIONS

Multiple techniques for valuing MBSs exist because no single technique has been shown to completely explain the price performance of these securities. All of the valuation methods discussed in this chapter are useful. However, it is critical that the results of each methodology be assessed in terms of their sensitivity to the specification of, and assumptions required for, each model. Investors should examine not only point estimates of MBS risk and return but also the confidence intervals associated with these point estimates.

SCFY analysis was the simplest approach reviewed. Although it ignores a number of factors critical to the valuation of MBSs, historical analysis of SCFY spreads is a useful check on the results of other methodologies and can provide a historical perspective on the MBS market.

SA is a valuable extension of the SCFY approach, examining the dynamic nature of MBSs in a holding-period-return context. If the spread-based horizon pricing model described in the SA section is used, SA investigates the implications of existing spread relationships for holding-period returns. Used in conjunction with a historical analysis of SCFY spreads, this can be an important tool in assessing the relative attractiveness of different MBS coupons.

OAS Monte Carlo models extend SA by simulating MBS performance over a large number of interest-rate paths. If the interest-rate diffusion process and the relationship between interest rates and prepayment rates are correctly specified, this class of model has the potential to provide MBS risk/return measures superior to those available from SCFY analysis.

The RTP model is a binomial option-pricing-based methodology that differs fundamentally from the OAS approach. RTP directly models the refinancing decision of the individual mortgagor instead of attempting to specify aggregate MBS prepayment rates as a function of interest rates. As with the OAS approach, RTP provides risk/return measures that account for the dependence of MBS prepayments on interest rates. A major attraction of the RTP methodology is that it does not depend on the specification of an exogenous prepayment function. By directly modeling the refinancing decision of mortgagors, RTP provides the potential for more robust results.

The major drawback of both the OAS and RTP approaches is that they are essentially black boxes into which an investor puts assumptions and out of which come risk/return measures. Even if model specifications are available for inspection, it may be difficult to evaluate them. Consequently, it is imperative that investors determine the sensitivity of the results of these models to the assumptions employed. OAS and RTP results should not be used in isolation but only in conjunction with the results of SCFY analysis and SA. The simpler approaches can be used as checks on the reasonableness of the results of the more sophisticated models.

⑥ NEW DURATION MEASURES FOR RISK MANAGEMENT

Thomas E. Klaffky
Managing Director
Salomon Brothers Inc

Ardavan Nozari
Vice President
Salomon Brothers Inc

Michael Waldman
Director of Fixed Income Research
MacKay-Shields Financial Corp.

INTRODUCTION

The concept of effective duration was introduced in the 1980s to allow portfolio managers to measure and control the sensitivity of their fixed income investments to changes in the level of interest rates.[1] In the 1990s, it has become standard practice for these managers to focus significant attention on their portfolios' effective duration and to express their views about the future direction of interest rates by lengthening or shortening their portfolios' effective duration relative to that of their benchmark.

Over the past few years, while interest rates have fallen, several other factors were at work that dramatically influenced performance, especially for portfolios that were designed to be market-neutral relative to their benchmark. Since 1990, the yield curve has changed from being essentially flat to being very steep (see Exhibit 38–1). Concurrently, the option-adjusted spreads (OAS) of different sectors

---

1. See Michael Waldman and Stephen Modzelewski, "A Framework for Evaluating Treasury-Based Adjustable Rate Mortgages," in *The Handbook of Mortgage-Backed Securities*, ed. Frank J. Fabozzi (Chicago: Probus Publishing, 1985); *Evaluating the Option Features of Mortgage Securities: The Salomon Brothers Mortgage Pricing Model*, Salomon Brothers Inc, September 1986; and William Boyce and Mark Koenigsberg, *Effective Duration of Callable Bonds: The Salomon Brothers Term Structure-Based Option Pricing Model*, Salomon Brothers Inc, April 1987.

EXHIBIT 38–1

The 30- to 10-Year and 10- to 2-Year U.S. Treasury Yield Spreads, January 1990–May 1993

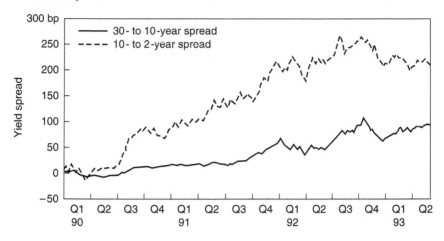

EXHIBIT 38–2

Option-Adjusted Spreads of the Corporate and Mortgage Sectors of the Salomon Brothers Broad Investment-Grade (BIG) Bond Index, January 1990–May 1993

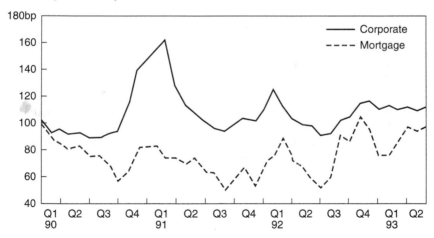

of the market have fluctuated widely (see Exhibit 38–2). In addition, in the mortgage market, prepayment projections have shifted significantly, reflecting changes in market attitudes about the relationship between prepayments and interest rates. These changes in the shape of the yield curve, OAS of different sectors, and prepayment expectations all have played key roles in determining performance.

A series of duration-like measures recently have been introduced into the fixed income markets to give investors a greater sense of how their investments should react to market forces beyond parallel shifts in the yield curve. In recent papers, we have written about these measures and have shown how different securities react to changes in OAS, the shape of the yield curve, and prepayment rates.[2] To date, however, few investors have incorporated these additional duration measures into their regular duration-control activities. In this chapter, we will review some of these findings and demonstrate how investors can integrate these concepts into the day-to-day management of their portfolios.

SPREAD RISKS

Portfolio managers often invest in a security or a market sector based on their expectation of spread movements. In essence, investors hope that a narrowing of yield spreads will boost their relative performance beyond the sector's yield advantage. To quantify the sensitivity of a portfolio to changes in spreads, we may use the concept of *spread duration*. The spread duration of a security is defined as the percentage change in its market value for a 100-basis-point change in its OAS. The spread duration of a portfolio is the market-weighted average of the spread durations of all of its securities.

Exhibit 38–3 gives the market weight and the effective and spread durations of different sectors of the Salomon Brothers Broad Investment-Grade (BIG) Bond Index.[3] With these values, we can approximate the performance of a sector for a given change in interest rate or spread. For instance, if interest rates rise by 10 basis points, by using effective duration, we can expect the market value of the mortgage sector to decline by $2.4 \times 0.10\% = 0.24\%$. If mortgage OAS narrows by 10 basis points, we use the spread duration of the mortgage sector to estimate its market value to increase by $3.4 \times 0.10\% = 0.34\%$. Overall, an increase in interest rates of 10 basis points, combined with a narrowing of OAS of 10 basis points, should be expected to lead to a $(0.34\% - 0.24\%) = 0.10\%$ increase in market value.

Exhibit 38–4 gives the market sensitivity of the entire BIG Index to spread changes of the individual sectors. These numbers are the products of the market weight of each sector and its spread duration. For example, the sensitivity of the

---

2. See Martin L. Leibowitz, William Krasker, and Ardavan Nozari, "Spread Duration: A New Tool for Bond Portfolio Management," in *Fixed-Income Portfolio Strategies*, ed. Frank J. Fabozzi (Chicago: Probus Publishing, 1989); Michael Waldman, "Beyond Duration: Risk Dimensions of Mortgage Securities," *Journal of Fixed Income*, December 1992, pp. 5–15; and Thomas E. Klaffky, Y. Y. Ma, and Ardavan Nozari, "Managing Yield Curve Exposure: Introducing Reshaping Durations," *Journal of Fixed Income*, December 1992, pp. 39–46.

3. Effective duration measures a security's sensitivity to parallel shifts in the yield curve. Spread duration, in contrast, measures the effect of a change in the security's OAS, assuming that other market rates are constant. Therefore, we would expect spread durations to differ from effective durations, especially for securities with embedded options.

EXHIBIT 38–3

Market Weight and Duration Profile of the Salomon Brothers Broad
Investment-Grade (BIG) Bond Index, May 1, 1993

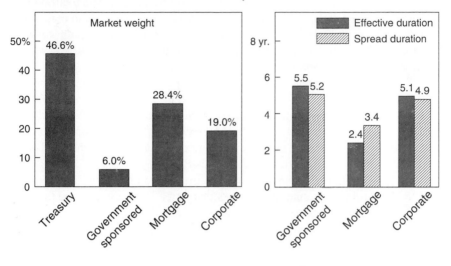

EXHIBIT 38–4

Spread Duration of the Salomon Brothers Broad Investment-Grade (BIG) Bond
Index, May 1, 1993

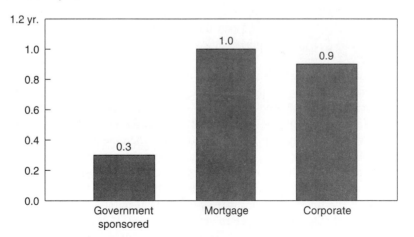

BIG Index to changes in corporate spreads (0.9 years) is the product of the market
weight of the corporate sector (19.0 percent) and its spread duration (4.9 years).
This number shows that for every 10-basis-point narrowing of corporate spreads,
the market value of corporates will rise by 0.49 percent; thus, all else being constant, the market value of the BIG Index will rise by 0.09 percent.

A portfolio manager who wants to increase the exposure of a portfolio to a particular sector should examine both the market weight and the spread duration of that sector because the portfolio's sensitivity to changes in the spreads of that sector is the product of these two values. Many portfolio managers focus only on the market weight of the sectors and overlook spread duration. To increase a portfolio's exposure to a sector, these managers will increase the sector's market weight without paying attention to how the securities in their portfolio will respond to changes in spreads.

To see how to use the concept of spread duration, consider structuring a portfolio with the objective of outperforming the BIG Index. As a matter of strategy, we may decide to overweight the corporate sector for its incremental yield and the prospect of tighter spreads. By overweighting the short-maturity corporates at the expense of short-maturity Treasuries, we can increase the yield of the portfolio and increase its corporate spread duration.

As of May 1, 1993, 14.5 percent of the market weight of the BIG Index was in U.S. Treasuries with maturities of less than three years. By shifting that 14.5 percent from Treasuries to corporate bonds with maturities of less than three years, we will increase the market weight of the corporate sector of our portfolio to 33.5 percent versus 19.0 percent for the Index. However, because the corporate sector of our portfolio is now more heavily weighted in the shorter maturities, its spread duration drops to 3.5 years versus 4.9 years for the Index (see Exhibit 38–5). At the same time, for the portfolio as a whole, by taking into account the increase in market weight and the drop in spread duration of the corporate sector, the corporate spread duration increases from 0.9 years to 1.2 years. This example shows that although the corporate sector weighting of this portfolio has increased by about 76 percent (from 19.0 percent to 33.5 percent), its corporate spread sensitivity has increased by only 0.3 years—somewhat less than a portfolio manager might have expected.

Beyond the change in spread duration, the increase in market weight of the corporate sector will bring higher yield to the portfolio and, therefore, will increase its rolling yield (one-year return assuming constant yield curve and spreads). In this example, the rolling yield is increased by 10 basis points (from 5.98 percent to 6.08 percent). Spread duration and incremental rolling yield help us to quantify the risk/reward trade-off of increasing the exposure of a portfolio to a particular sector. In this example, if the yield curve and corporate spreads remain unchanged, our portfolio will outperform the Index by its incremental rolling yield. If corporate spreads narrow by 10 basis points, we will have an additional $(0.3 \times 0.10\%) = 0.03\%$ return versus the Index. Using these measures together, we can calculate that we have a one-year cushion of an approximate $(10/0.3) = 33$-basis-point widening in corporate spreads before we underperform the Index.

This discussion demonstrates the applicability of the spread duration concept. Portfolio managers should examine not only the relative market weight of each sector in their portfolio but the portfolio's spread duration relative to differ-

EXHIBIT 38–5

A Portfolio Overweighted in Short Corporates versus the Salomon Brothers Broad Investment-Grade (BIG) Bond Index, May 1, 1993

	Market Weight	Effective Duration	Spread Duration		Rolling Yield	Yield
			Sector	Total		
BIG Index						
Treasury	46.6%	5.1 yr.	—	—	5.22%	5.87%
Government sponsored	6.0	5.5	5.2 yr.	0.3 yr.	5.89	6.06
Mortgage	28.4	2.4	3.4	1.0	5.77	5.52
Corporate	19.0	5.1	4.9	0.9	6.85	6.89
Total	100.0%	4.4 yr.			5.73%	5.98%
Portfolio						
Treasury	32.1%	6.6 yr.	—	—	5.89%	6.65%
Government sponsored	6.0	5.5	5.2 yr.	0.3 yr.	5.89	5.93
Mortgage	28.4	2.4	3.4	1.0	5.77	5.53
Corporate	33.5	3.7	3.5	1.2	5.94	6.03
Total	100.0%	4.4 yr.			5.87%	6.08%

ent sectors. By contrasting the spread duration of different sectors of their portfolio to those of the Index, they can better reflect their views about the spread prospects of a sector.

YIELD-CURVE RESHAPING RISKS

The radical change in the shape of the U.S. Treasury yield curve in the first three years of the 1990s has been an important source of return (or frustration) for fixed-income portfolios. Portfolio managers now routinely structure their portfolios with an eye toward a reshaping of the yield curve or, in some cases, try to capitalize on a yield-curve reshaping.

To quantify the yield-curve sensitivity of a portfolio, we can define a series of *partial durations* relative to specific yield-curve points.[4] The partial duration is the percentage price response per 100-basis-point movement in a particular Treasury rate, while the rest of the yield curve remains constant. By defining many points along the yield curve, partial durations will give an accurate representation

---

4. Robert R. Reitano, "Non-Parallel Yield Curve Shifts and Immunization," *Journal of Portfolio Management*, Spring 1992.

of the sensitivity of the portfolio to changes of the yield curve.[5] Partial durations
also can be used as building blocks for defining other duration-like measures relative to broader patterns of yield-curve changes.

In a recent paper, we defined two other duration measures that, along with
effective duration, can quantify the yield-curve risks of a portfolio in a broader
sense.[6] The first measure, *short-end duration* (SEDUR), assesses the sensitivity
of a portfolio to changes in the shape of the yield curve at the shorter end (represented by the spread between the yields of on-the-run U.S. Treasury 2- and 10-
year securities—that is, the 10- to 2-year spread). The second measure, *long-end
duration* (LEDUR), assesses the sensitivity of a portfolio to changes in the shape
of the yield curve at the longer end (represented by the spread between the yields
of on-the-run U.S. Treasury 30- and 10-year securities—that is, the 30- to 10-year
spread). Exhibit 38–6 shows the effective and reshaping durations for the BIG
Index and its major sectors as of May 1, 1993.

E X H I B I T   38–6

Effective and Reshaping Durations of Different Sectors of the Salomon Brothers Broad Investment-Grade (BIG) Bond Index, May 1, 1993

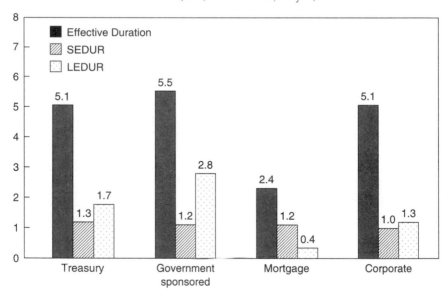

5. See Michael Waldman, "Beyond Duration: Risk Dimensions of Mortgage Securities," *Journal of
     Fixed Income*, December 1992, pp. 5-15; Brian D. Johnson and Kenneth R. Meyer, "Managing
     Yield Curve Risk in an Index Environment," *Financial Analysts Journal*, November/December
     1989; and Thomas S. Y. Ho, *Strategic Fixed-Income Investment* (Dow Jones-Irwin, Home-
     wood, IL, 1990).
6. Thomas E. Klaffky, Y. Y. Ma, and Ardavan Nozari, "Managing Yield Curve Exposure: Introducing
     Reshaping Durations," *Journal of Fixed Income*, December 1992, pp. 39–46.

To calculate the reshaping durations, we examine price changes across different yield-curve scenarios. For example, to calculate the SEDUR of a security, we calculate its price (by assuming a constant OAS equal to its current value) using two alternative yield-curve scenarios: (1) 50 basis points steeper in the short end; (2) 50 basis points flatter. Then the percentage change in price of the security under these two scenarios relative to its current price defines its short-end duration.

Reshaping durations can play a key role in portfolio management by quantifying the exposure of a portfolio to the yield curve. Using these measures, portfolio managers who deliberately want to express a view about yield-curve reshaping will structure their portfolios to have a different SEDUR and LEDUR from those of their benchmark. Of course, the magnitude of those differences depends on the convictions of the managers about their views, and the magnitude of risk they are willing to bear. Alternatively, investors who want to immunize their portfolios to yield-curve reshaping will structure a portfolio that has the same SEDUR and LEDUR as their benchmark.

To illustrate how a portfolio manager could use reshaping durations, consider a barbell portfolio of cash and a 30-year U.S. Treasury bond having the same duration as the Treasury sector of the BIG Index. This barbell portfolio will outperform the Treasury sector of the Index if the long end of the yield curve flattens. To quantify the sensitivity of the portfolio and the Index to changes in the long end of the yield curve, we may examine their respective LEDURs. This barbell portfolio has a LEDUR of 5.2 years versus 1.7 years for the Index. That is, if the 30- to 10-year yield spread were to narrow by 10 basis points, the barbell portfolio will outperform the Treasury sector of the BIG Index by $(5.2 - 1.7) \times 0.10\%$ $= 0.35\%$. Unfortunately, the barbell position also offers 103 basis points less in rolling yield than the Treasury sector of the Index. Therefore, the 30- to 10-year spread would have to narrow by at least $103/3.5 = 29$ basis points in one year before the portfolio outperforms the Index. A portfolio manager who wishes to express a view about the shape of the yield curve in this manner must examine the magnitude and the timing of a potential flattening of the yield curve.

This example illustrates the simplicity of using SEDUR and LEDUR in portfolio management. By contrasting these duration measures with those of their benchmark, portfolio managers can examine the yield-curve exposure of their portfolios and be able to quantify the risk and reward of such strategies.

PREPAYMENT RISKS

Prepayment risk can be defined as the exposure to unforeseen changes in the market's assumed long-term prepayment rates, beyond those projected to occur with movements in interest rates. These can be interpreted as errors in prepayment model forecasts, changes in housing or mortgage finance that modify prepayment prospects, or changes in market attitudes about prepayments. During the past three years, such shifts in prepayment expectations have had a dramatic impact on mortgage security performance. Thus, investment managers need to pay careful attention to the prepayment sensitivity of their portfolios and their benchmarks.

We define a security's *prepayment duration* as its percentage price change, assuming constant OAS, under a 1 percent uniform change in projected prepayment speeds across all interest-rate scenarios. Exhibit 38–7 presents the prepayment duration of selected mortgage-backed securities using the Salomon Brothers Prepayment Model. From this exhibit, we can see that some securities, such as current-coupon pass-throughs, have very low sensitivity to prepayment rates, whereas others such as interest only (IO) or principal only (PO) STRIPs have significant prepayment sensitivity. In addition, as expected, we note that an IO or a high-coupon mortgage pass-through has a positive prepayment sensitivity or exposure, indicating that its price will fall if prepayments accelerate. Conversely, a PO or a discount mortgage has a negative prepayment sensitivity, indicating that its price will rise if prepayments accelerate.

The average prepayment duration of the Mortgage Index as of May 1, 1993, was 0.025, indicating that slower-than-projected prepayment rates will benefit the Index. This should not be surprising because of the dominance of premium pass-throughs in the Index. With the prepayment duration number, we can estimate that the price risk of the Index resulting from a 10 percent increase in prepayment expectations is $0.025 \times 10\% = 0.25\%$.

E X H I B I T   38–7

Prepayment Duration of Selected Mortgage-Backed Securities, May 1, 1993

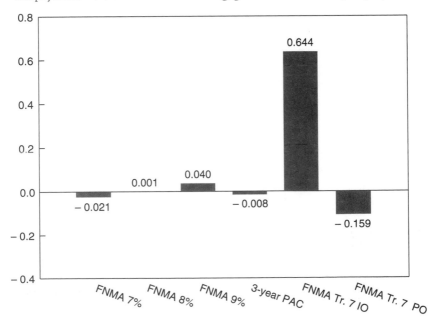

EXHIBIT 38–8

Two Mortgage Portfolios with Different Prepayment Durations, May 1, 1993

	Coupon	Term	Weight	Duration Effective	Duration Spread	Duration Prepay
Mortgage Index	8.54%	23.1 yr.	100%	2.4 yr.	3.4 yr.	0.025
Portfolio I						
30-Year GNMA	10.00%	23.2 yr.	67%	1.5	3.0 yr.	0.057
30-Year GNMA	7.00	30.0	18	7.5	6.4	−0.011
15-Year FHLMC	9.50	9.4	15	−0.2	1.6	0.049
Total	9.34%	22.4 yr.	100%	2.4 yr.	3.4 yr.	0.043
Portfolio II						
30-Year FHLMC	7.50%	29.2 yr.	26%	4.7 yr.	4.8 yr.	−0.011
15-Year FHLMC	8.00	14.2	49	1.6	3.1	0.014
15-Year FHLMC	8.00	8.6	25	1.4	2.5	0.014
Total	7.87%	16.8 yr.	100%	2.4 yr.	3.4 yr.	0.007

FHLMC: Federal Home Loan Mortgage Corporation; GNMA: Government National Mortgage Association.

As with other risk factors, we should examine the prepayment duration of the portfolio and contrast it with that of the Index to ensure that the portfolio has the desired exposure. To illustrate, consider two different portfolios, each consisting of three mortgage pass-throughs (see Exhibit 38–8). The first portfolio has a high concentration of 30-year Government National Mortgage Association (GNMA) 10s, and the second is dominated by 15-year Federal Home Loan Mortgage Corporation (FHLMC) 8s. These portfolios have the same effective duration and spread duration as the Index, but they have prepayment durations that differ sharply from that of the Index. If the prepayment expectations reflected in market prices rise, the first portfolio, with its higher prepayment duration (0.043 versus 0.025 for the Index), will underperform the Index. Conversely, faster prepayment expectations, all else being equal, will cause the second portfolio with a lower sensitivity to prepayments than the Index (0.007 versus 0.025) to outperform the Index. A 10 percent increase in assumed prepayment rates will cause the first portfolio to underperform the Index by $(0.043 - 0.025) \times 10\% = 0.18\%$, whereas the same increase will cause the second portfolio to outperform the Index by $(0.025 - 0.007) \times 10\% = 0.18\%$.

A PORTFOLIO EXAMPLE

In this final section, we illustrate how to apply the tools we have discussed to quantify and control the risks of a portfolio. Exhibit 38–9 gives the risk profile of the Salomon Brothers model portfolio versus the BIG Index as of May 1, 1993.

EXHIBIT 38–9

Risk Profile of the Salomon Brothers Model Portfolio versus the Salomon Brothers Broad Investment-Grade (BIG) Bond Index, May 1, 1993

	Market Weight	Effective Duration	Spread Duration		SEDUR	LEDUR	Prepayment Duration
			Sector	Total			
BIG Index							
Treasury	46.6%	5.1 yr.	—	—	1.3 yr.	1.7 yr.	—
Government sponsored	6.0	5.5	5.2 yr.	0.3 yr.	1.2	2.8	—
Mortgage	28.4	2.4	3.4	1.0	1.2	0.4	0.025
Corporate	19.0	5.1	4.9	0.9	1.1	1.3	—
Total	100.0%	4.4 yr.			1.2 yr.	1.3 yr.	0.007
Model Portfolio							
Treasury	50.9%	4.7 yr.	—	—	1.3 yr.	1.2 yr.	—
Government sponsored	0.0	0.0	0.0 yr.	0.0 yr.	0.0	0.0	—
Mortgage	27.1	3.2	4.1	1.1	1.3	0.6	0.028
Corporate	22.0	5.1	5.0	1.1	1.4	1.0	—
Total	100.0%	4.4 yr.			1.3 yr.	1.0 yr.	0.008

LEDUR: Long-end duration; SEDUR: Short-end duration.

In general, we have constrained the model portfolio to be duration-neutral relative to the BIG Index, but we have made choices about its exposures to various sectors, to the yield curve, and to prepayments.

In May, we structured the model portfolio to have very similar risk characteristics to those of the Index (see Exhibit 38–9). The portfolio had no market value in the government-sponsored sector, but it was modestly more sensitive than the Index to corporate and mortgage spreads. The prepayment risks of the portfolio and the Index were only marginally different from each other: The portfolio had a slightly greater exposure to prepayments. With respect to the yield curve, the portfolio had a slight bias toward steepening. The portfolio, with its longer SEDUR and shorter LEDUR, should outperform the Index if we experience a steepening at either end of the yield curve.

Our primary focus in attempting to outperform the Index was on the sector weighting and the selection of individual securities based on their perceived relative values. For example, in the corporate sector (see Exhibit 38–10), the portfolio is overexposed to the finance and utility sectors, underexposed to the industrial sector, and neutral to the Yankee sector.

Examining Exhibit 38–10, we note that the model portfolio is invested to take advantage of a realignment of spreads within the corporate market. For example, if the OAS of the utility sector narrows by 10 basis points and the OAS of the industrial sector widens by 10 basis points, the corporate sector of the portfolio can be expected to outperform the corporate sector of the BIG Index by $(1.4 - 1.1) \times (0.10\%) + (1.3 - 1.8) \times (-0.10\%) = 0.08\%$.

In Exhibit 38–11, we show a similar analysis for the mortgage sector, displaying the spread durations of the model portfolio and the BIG Index by mortgage collateral type. The portfolio's greatest concentration is in current-coupon conventional collateral. If the OAS of this sector narrows by 10 basis points relative to the rest of the mortgage index, the model portfolio will outperform the mortgage component of the Index by $(2.3 - 0.3) \times 0.10\% = 0.20\%$. By using

E X H I B I T   38–10

Spread Duration of Major Subsectors of the Corporate Sector of the Salomon Brothers Model Portfolio versus the Salomon Brothers Broad Investment-Grade (BIG) Bond Index, May 1, 1993

	Index	Portfolio	Difference
Finance	1.2 yr.	1.5 yr.	0.3 yr.
Industrial	1.8	1.3	−0.5
Utility	1.1	1.4	0.3
Yankee	0.8	0.8	0.0

E X H I B I T   38–11

Spread Duration of the Mortgage Sector of the Salomon Brothers Model Portfolio versus the Salomon Brothers Broad Investment-Grade (BIG) Bond Index by Collateral Type, May 1, 1993

Coupon Category	Index	Portfolio	Difference
GNMA			
Current (≤7%)	0.1 yr.	0.0 yr.	−0.1 yr.
Cusp (7^1/$_2$%–8^1/$_2$%)	0.6	0.6	0.0
High (≥9%)	0.7	0.0	−0.7
Conventional			
Current (≤7%)	0.3 yr.	2.3 yr.	2.0 yr.
Cusp (7^1/$_2$%–8^1/$_2$%)	1.3	0.2	−1.1
High (≥9%)	0.5	0.8	0.3

GNMA: Government National Mortgage Association.

spread duration in this way, a portfolio manager can measure exposures and express his or her views in a specific and quantifiable manner.

CONCLUSION

Portfolio managers are constantly faced with the responsibility of understanding the risks and the potential rewards of their investment decisions. Over the past few years, these investors have dramatically increased their awareness of quantitative measures and have incorporated many of these measures into their day-to-day management activities. However, as additional factors have influenced recent portfolio performance, such as changes in spreads, yield-curve shape, and prepayments, investors may wish to broaden their scope and monitor additional measures to ensure that they fully understand their exposures. Indeed, the measures reviewed in this chapter, combined with effective duration, may not be sufficient for some investors to understand the full scope of their exposures. Other measures, such as sensitivity to changes in market volatility or in currency rates, may be desirable in some situations. Overall, portfolio managers should be aware of the tools that can help them in their regular activities and should incorporate these tools into their management process to give them a better sense of their risks and potential rewards.

CHAPTER

39

⑥   # INTEREST-RATE RISK MODELS USED BY DEPOSITORY INSTITUTIONS

Elizabeth Mays, Ph.D.
Senior Economist
Federal Home Loan Mortgage Corporation

There has been an increasing emphasis on the measurement and management of interest-rate risk at depository institutions during the last decade as volatile interest rates have caused wide swings in earnings and the value of institutions' portfolios, most notably in the early 1980s. Many institutions have acquired models to measure their interest-rate risk or hired consultants to analyze their exposure. Interest-rate risk models have evolved from the simple maturity "gap" model to sophisticated measurement systems requiring detailed input data and knowledge of complex financial modeling techniques. Bank, thrift, and credit union regulators have developed policies and examination guidelines outlining the responsibilities of managers and boards of directors in the area of interest-rate risk management.

This chapter provides a primer on the four types of models most frequently used by depository institutions to measure IRR and describes some advantages and disadvantages of each type of model. In addition, it describes the model used by the Office of Thrift Supervision to measure S&Ls' interest-rate exposure.

INTEREST-RATE RISK MODELS

Interest-rate risk at depository institutions is typically defined as the sensitivity of the institution's earnings and net portfolio value to changes in interest rates. The interest-rate sensitivity of an institution's portfolio depends on the characteristics of the financial instruments that comprise the portfolio. Because deposit liabilities typically reprice faster than mortgage assets, most thrift institutions are exposed to rising interest rates; that is, their net portfolio value and earnings decline when interest rates rise and increase when interest rates fall. Because banks and credit unions typically make shorter-term loans, they are more likely to have smaller exposures to rising rates or even be exposed to falling rates. However, many banks and credit unions have increased their holdings of mortgage loans and securities and mortgage derivative products in recent years and are likely to be increasingly exposed to rising interest rates.

The interest-rate sensitivity of a financial instrument depends on many factors, including maturity, repricing characteristics, and the presence of embedded options, such as loan prepayment options, interest-rate caps on adjustable-rate loans, and deposit withdrawal options that affect the timing of the cash flows.

Net interest income (NII) and net portfolio value (NPV) are the two most common targets of IRR management. NPV is a measure of the economic value of a portfolio of financial instruments and is equal to the estimated market value of assets, less the estimated market value of liabilities, plus or minus the estimated market value of off-balance-sheet instruments.

Both the NII and NPV measures require reliable information on the amount and timing of the cash flows generated by all financial instruments in the portfolio. Because this information is frequently not known with certainty, certain assumptions must be made to perform the analysis. Depending on the type of analysis, these assumptions may include (1) how changing interest rates will affect mortgage prepayment rates and deposit withdrawal rates, (2) when issuers of debt securities with embedded call options will choose to exercise those options, (3) how management will administer interest rates that are under its control (such as rates on retail deposits) when the general level of interest rates changes, and (4) in NII simulation models, how management will reinvest interest and principal cash flows during the period of analysis.

Two types of models are commonly used by depository institutions to estimate the interest-rate sensitivity of net interest income (NII): maturity gap models and NII simulation models. Likewise, there are two types of models used to estimate the sensitivity of net portfolio value: duration gap models, and NPV simulation models.

Maturity gap and simple duration gap models are similar in that they implicitly make strict assumptions about the way interest rates and cash flows behave. For example, they assume that cash flows do not change in response to interest-rate changes so that mortgage prepayment rates do not increase even when rates at which mortgages may be financed fall, and deposit withdrawal rates do not increase when market CD rates rise. Further, maturity gap and duration gap models assume that when interest rates change, they all do so by the same amount when, in fact, rates on various assets and liabilities may change by differing amounts as a result of a shift in the term structure of interest rates.

NII and NPV simulation models, on the other hand, permit these assumptions to vary, but necessarily rely more heavily on the analyst to make choices about certain behavioral relationships incorporated into the model. Even though they rely more heavily on parameters set by analysts, NII and NPV simulation models can be much more accurate than their less sophisticated counterparts if appropriate assumptions are used.

NII SENSITIVITY ANALYSIS

Maturity Gap Models

Maturity gap models were the most widely used IRR measurement tools during the 1980s and continue to be the primary tool for IRR analysis at many institutions. Maturity gap analysis measures the difference, or "gap," between the dollar value of assets and liabilities maturing or repricing during a given time period. The dollar gap is often expressed as a percentage of assets. When multiplied by a hypothetical change in interest rates, the dollar maturity gap gives a rough estimate of the impact of such a rate change on net interest income.

To calculate the maturity gap, principal balances of interest-earning assets and interest-bearing liabilities are categorized by maturity/repricing intervals or "buckets" (e.g., under one year, one to three years), depending on when the principal cash flows will be received or when their interest rate will next be adjusted. In more sophisticated gap models, the timing of the principal cash flows are adjusted by incorporating the effects of loan amortization, mortgage prepayments, core deposit decay, and the effects of off-balance-sheet hedging instruments.

As an example of a maturity gap calculation, assume that a bank with $100 million in assets estimates that $20 million of those assets will "reprice" during the next year (by having principal mature or prepay, or by having the coupon adjust). Further, the bank estimates that $40 million of liabilities will reprice during this time. This bank is said to have a "one-year gap" equal to negative 20 percent ([$20m – $40m]/ $100m).

To estimate the effect on an institution's interest margin of a change in interest rates, the gap as a percent of assets is multiplied by the hypothetical rate change. For example, the estimated effect of a 1 percent rise in interest rates on net interest income over the next year would be a decline of .20 percent or 20 basis points. Given assets of $100 million, this decrease in interest margin would translate to a reduction in NII of $200,000 over this time period.

Although maturity gaps do provide a rough measure of NII sensitivity, they have a number of well-known shortcomings, including the following:

- The repricing intervals chosen for gap analysis are arbitrary, and there may be significant mismatches within a repricing interval. The most common repricing intervals analyzed by institutions are the one-year gap and the one-to-three-year gap. As an extreme example of a mismatch that would go undetected by the maturity gap model, consider a portfolio composed solely of liabilities that reprice in 1 month and an equal dollar value of assets that reprice in 11 months. The one-year gap of this institution would be zero, indicating no risk to net interest income. In fact, NII is significantly at risk to rising interest rates.

- Maturity gap models assume that when interest rates change they all do so by the same amount. For any given change in the general level of interest rates, however, different interest-rates may change by differing amounts. For example, rates paid on nonmaturity deposits (MMDAs, and checking and savings accounts) typically increase by a smaller amount, if at all, when other market interest rates increase. In addition, because the gap model assumes that coupons of adjustable-rate loans repricing during the period of analysis change by the full amount of the interest-rate "shock" being analyzed, the effect of interest-rate caps and floors cannot be incorporated into the gap analysis. Likewise, gap models can make no distinction between the interest-rate sensitivity of an ARM based on a lagging index such as the 11th District Cost of Funds, and an ARM repricing based on current Treasury yields even though changes in the COFI index lag behind changes in market rates.

- Maturity gap models assume that principal cash flows do not change when interest rates change. Therefore, it is not possible to incorporate properly the effect of the options embedded in many financial instruments, such as the early withdrawal option on CDs, call options on debt issues, and the mortgage prepayment option. These options have a significant impact on the rate sensitivity of a financial instrument, and neglecting to incorporate them into the analysis will misstate the exposure of institutions' NII to interest-rate changes.

The advantages of the gap model are that it is widely understood in the bank and thrift industries and it does not require knowledge of sophisticated financial modeling techniques.

NII Simulation Models

NII simulation models project interest cash flows of all assets, liabilities, and off-balance-sheet instruments in an institution's portfolio to estimate future net interest earnings over some chosen period of time. They are often referred to as "dynamic" simulation models because assumptions concerning changes in operating strategies, changes in relative interest rates, early withdrawal of deposits, and loan prepayment rates can be built into the model.

NII sensitivity is typically calculated as follows. First, "base case" NII is projected for the current interest-rate environment. Cash flows for each financial instrument are projected using assumptions about amortization characteristics; prepayment rates on loans; repricing of adjustable-rate loans, borrowings, and deposits; early withdraw of CDs; and core deposit decay rates. In addition, assumptions must be made about how the principal and interest cash flows that will be received during the period of analysis will be reinvested.

Next, various simulations are performed under alternate interest-rate scenarios. For example, many models estimate the value of NII over the next year if interest rates were to increase or decrease by 1 percent, 2 percent, 3 percent, or 4 percent. As in the base case scenario, interest cash flows are projected over the period of analysis and will depend on assumed deposit decay rates and prepayment rates, and on how rates on adjustable-rate loans and deposits are assumed to change in each interest-rate scenario. The larger the differences in projected earnings between the base case and the alternate interest-rate scenarios, the higher the exposure of an institution's NII to interest-rate changes.

NII simulation models offer the following advantages:

• NII simulation models can provide estimates of the effect on NII of changing interest rates on the future interest income of instruments with embedded prepayment options by varying prepayment rates according to the interest-rate scenario being simulated. The value of other embedded options (e.g., lifetime interest-rate caps on adjustable-rate loans) and off-balance-sheet instruments in institutions' portfolios can be similarly assessed.

• Unlike in gap analysis, interest rates on different instruments can be assumed to change by different amounts when there is a change in the general level of interest rates. For example, changes in rates on core deposits can be assumed to lag behind changes in other rates. Likewise, the effect on NII of nonparallel yield-curve shifts can be analyzed by permitting rates on short maturity instruments and long maturity instruments to change by varying amounts.

NII simulation analysis also possesses a disadvantage. Like gap analysis, NII simulation models typically only measure the effect of a change in interest rates over short periods of time, such as one year. Models that do project NII over longer periods of time sometimes aggregate these future cash flows in a manner that implies that cash flows received in the distant future are as valuable as those received in the near future. For example, a model may indicate that if rates increase by 1 percent, an institution will lose $100 during the next year but will gain $100 in year two of the analysis. In fact, the value of the $100 received in two years is less than the value of $100 received in one year. NII models that project NII over long periods should take the time value of money into account by discounting those future cash flows using appropriate discount rates.

NET PORTFOLIO VALUE SENSITIVITY ANALYSIS

Two types of models are used to analyze the sensitivity of net portfolio value: the duration gap model and the NPV simulation model. Both models require detailed information on the amount and timing of all future cash flows of all financial instruments in the portfolio as well as the specification of appropriate discount rates that reflect the current required yields of the instruments.

Duration Gap Models

Duration measures the change in the market price of a financial instrument expected to result from a given small change in interest rates. The duration gap of net portfolio value is a measure of the interest-rate sensitivity of an entire portfolio of financial instruments and is the difference between the weighted average duration of assets and liabilities, adjusted for the net duration of all off-balance sheet instruments. It measures the percentage change in the net portfolio value that would be expected to occur if interest rates were to change by 1 percent.

The net portfolio value, NPV, equals the market value of assets, A, less the market value of liabilities, L, plus or minus the market value of off-balance sheet items, O.

$$NPV = A - L \pm O \qquad (39\text{--}1)$$

To calculate the duration gap of NPV, the modified duration, D, of each item in the portfolio is separately calculated and weighted by the ratio of its market value to the net value of the portfolio. This, the weighted durations of all assets, liabilities, and off-balance-sheet instruments are summed as in equation (39–2) where D_A, D_L and D_O are the weighted average modified durations of total assets, liabilities, and off-balances sheet instruments respectively.

$$D_{\text{NPV}} = D_A(A/\text{NPV}) - D_L(L/\text{NPV}) \pm D_O(O/\text{NPV}) \qquad (39\text{--}2)$$

Modified duration indicates the expected percentage change in an instrument's price for a given change in the required yield of the instrument. For example, if a liability had a modified duration of 4, the price of the liability could be expected to decline by 4 percent for each 100 basis point increase in interest rates.

$$\Delta P = P \times - D \times \Delta r \qquad (39\text{--}3)$$

where

D = modified duration of the instrument
P = price of the instrument
r = required yield of the instrument

The duration of NPV can be used to estimate the expected change on the market value of the portfolio for a given change in interest rates, as in equation (39–4).

$$\Delta\text{NPV} = \text{NPV} \times -D_{\text{NPV}} \times \Delta r \qquad (39\text{--}4)$$

One difficulty in calculating the duration gap lies in obtaining market values for each instrument. In practice, book values are often used to calculate the duration gap when market values are not available or easily estimated. When market values diverge significantly from book values, the use of book values may result in error in the estimation of the interest-rate sensitivity of portfolio value. Other drawbacks of duration gap analysis are described below.

• Duration gap analysis typically uses modified duration to calculate the change in NPV and therefore provides accurate estimates of price sensitivities of instruments only for small changes in interest rates. It should not be used to analyze the effect of changes of more than 100 basis points. Modified duration assumes the percentage price change due to a rate change of a given magnitude will be the same when rates rise or fall (although opposite in sign). This is not, however, true when rates change by a large amount. For a simple bond with no embedded options (such as a noncallable Treasury security), a large decrease in rates will result in a larger percentage increase in price than the percentage decrease in price that would result from an equal increase in rates. The bond is said to exhibit *positive convexity*. The analysis is further complicated when analyzing financial instruments with embedded options such as mortgage loans. Because borrowers tend to prepay their loans when refinancing rates fall below the coupon on the loan, the value of the loan will not rise as much as it would have had the probability of prepayment not increased. This price behavior is referred to as *negative convexity*. However, convexity (positive or negative) is not captured by the modified duration measure and therefore typically is not captured by the duration gap approach.

• Like the maturity gap model, the duration gap model assumes all portfolio interest rates change by the full amount of the interest-rate "shock." Therefore, it is not possible to evaluate the effect of changes in the slope and curvature of the yield curve where long and short rates change by differing amounts.

• The advantages of the duration gap model are that it evaluates the impact of interest-rate changes on all future cash flows, not just near-term NII, as does the maturity gap model, and it summarizes an institution's interest-rate risk exposure in a single number.

NPV Simulation Models

Banks and thrifts began to use NPV simulation models in increasing numbers in the late 1980s and early 1990s as the knowledge of financial modeling techniques became more widespread and as regulators applied pressure on institutions to better analyze and manage their exposures.

NPV sensitivity analysis involves estimating the current market value of all financial instruments in a bank's portfolio (i.e., the portfolio is "marked to market") and analyzing how the market value of the portfolio would be expected to differ under various alternative interest-rate scenarios.

The market value of a financial instrument can be estimated using present-value analysis by projecting the amount and timing of the future net cash flows generated by the instrument and discounting those cash flows by appropriate discount rates. The familiar formula for the present value of a financial instrument is as follows:

$$PV = CF_1/(1 + r_1) + CF_2/(1 + r_2)^2 + \ldots + CF_m/(1 + r_m)^m \qquad (39\text{--}5)$$

where CF_t is the amount of the projected cash flow for period t, and r_t is the discount rate for period t. As for the NII simulation model described earlier, the NPV simulation model requires extensive date inputs. For example, to estimate the market value of an adjustable-rate mortgage, data are needed on the outstanding balance, coupon rate, index to which the loan is tied (e.g., LIBOR or CMT), margin, reset frequency, remaining maturity, amortization characteristics, any periodic and lifetime rate caps and floors, and any special features such as convertibility. The discount rate used for each projected cash flow is the yield currently available to investors from alternative instruments of comparable risk and duration.

In the alternate-rate scenarios, the discount rates of each instrument are typically adjusted by adding or subtracting the amount of the interest-rate shock, and the cash flows are recalculated for the shocked-rate environment. The percentage change from the base case value to the estimated value in the shocked-rate environment is termed the *effective duration* of the instrument.

Although many vendor models and models built in-house by depository institutions use this simple present-value approach (also referred to as *static discounted cash flow analysis*), an increasing number of these models use an option-based pricing approach to value financial instruments that contain embedded options.

The most common embedded options in thrifts' portfolios (and increasingly, in banks' and credit unions' portfolios) are the prepayment options embedded in mortgages and mortgage-derivative securities and the interest-rate caps and floors in adjustable-rate mortgages. When mortgage rates fall, mortgage prepayments typically accelerate, forcing associations to reinvest the proceeds at lower yields. Interest-rate caps and floors prevent the coupon of adjustable-rate loans and securities from moving above or below a certain level when interest rates change. Both of these types of options can have a significant impact on the interest-rate sensitivity of the instruments in which they are embedded.

Option-based pricing models are designed to provide more accurate estimates of the value of these embedded options and therefore of the mortgages themselves than the static discounted cash flow approach. In a static cash flow analysis, the mortgage prepayment option has no value unless it is "in the money" (i.e., the prepayment option is exercised because rates have fallen and the homeowner chooses to refinance). In fact, like exchange-traded options, these options have value even when they are not in the money because it is possible they will be in the money at some future date. Market participants will therefore pay more or less for the mortgage, depending on the likelihood of exercise.

On the liabilities side of the balance sheet, additional complexity is presented by the valuation of demand deposits, which have no stated maturity. For these deposits, assumptions must be made not only about how the institution will react to changes in the term structure in setting its deposit rates, but what the attrition rate of the deposits will be. The projected attrition rate depends in part on what the deposit rates are projected to be in the future.

The advantages offered by the NPV simulation over those of the duration gap model are similar to those of the NII simulation model vis-à-vis the maturity gap model. That is, the NPV simulation model may be used to analyze interest-rate shocks of more than 100 basis points and the effect of nonparallel yield-curve shifts while the duration gap model may not. In addition, the NPV simulation model provides an estimate of the current market value of the firm, itself a valuable measure for management, stockholders, and regulators. NPV simulation models can be quite complex and require extensive modeling and, as with any measure of IRR, the results are sensitive to the assumptions used.

REGULATORY ASSESSMENT OF IRR

In December 1991, Congress passed the Federal Depository Insurance Corporation Improvement Act which, in part, required all federal bank and thrift regulators to revise their risk-based capital standards to take account of interest-rate risk. During the early 1990s, the Office of Thrift Supervision (OTS) developed an NPV simulation model that estimates the market value of individual S&Ls' portfolios in a number of interest-rate scenarios. The model is used to identify highly exposed institutions for increased supervisory scrutiny. The results of the model would also be used to calculate an interest-rate risk component to be added to thrifts' risk-based capital requirements under a 1993 regulation that has yet to be implemented.[1] In 1995, the bank regulators adopted a regulation that specifies that the interest-rate risk of banks will be evaluated on an individual basis and additional capital will be required when deemed necessary.[2, 3] Unlike OTS, however, they have decided against developing a "regulatory" model to be used off-site to evaluate banks' exposure. The National Credit Union Administration currently has no plans to base capital requirements of credit unions on their interest-rate exposure.

The OTS measures thrifts' exposure using an NPV simulation model that calculates the market values of savings associations' financial instruments directly, based on their unique characteristics. The OTS model requires S&Ls to file a detailed report listing the characteristics of the financial instruments in their portfolios.[4]

---

1. The capital requirement, which was to have taken effect in December 1994, was postponed pending adoption of a system that would permit associations to appeal their interest-rate risk components.
2. The bank regulators include the Office of the Comptroller of the currency, the Federal Reserve Board, and the Federal Deposit Insurance Corporation.
3. The National Credit Union Administration has no plans to require credit unions to hold capital based on the level of their interest-rate risk exposure.
4. The OTS exempts from filing this report any savings association with less than $300 million in assets and risk-based capital ratios in excess of 12 percent. The bank regulators have proposed to exempt banks that have few off-balance-sheet positions and few long-maturity assets.

The report collects more than 600 items of information on outstanding balances, coupons, repricing characteristics, and maturities of assets, liabilities, and off-balance-sheet instruments. The most detailed information is collected on the financial instruments that comprise the largest part of S&L portfolios. For example, the reporting form collects separate information on 30-year fixed-rate mortgages, 15-year FRMs, and balloon mortgages. Data on fixed-rate mortgages are disaggregated into five coupon ranges: less than 8 percent, 8 to 9 percent, 9 to 10 percent, 10 to 11 percent, and more than 11 percent. Thirty-year fixed-rate mortgage securities that are backed by FHA or VA loans are separated from those that are backed by conventional loans so that different prepayment assumptions may be used. The form collects information on adjustable-rate mortgages by type of index and would distinguish "teaser-rate" from nonteaser-rate ARMs, disaggregates balances according to the distance between the coupon and the lifetime cap, and collects information on margins and periodic caps and floors specific to each type of ARM.

For certificates of deposit, the form collects information on original maturity, remaining maturity, early withdrawal penalties, and balances in brokered accounts. In addition, institutions may optionally report data on early withdrawals and balances deposited in new accounts during the quarter that OTS uses to estimate retail CD "rollover" rates. Data on off-balance-sheet instruments may be reported on an individual contract basis, providing OTS with information on the notional principal amount, maturity, and price or rate specified in the contract for each position held. For example, for each interest-rate swap held by an institution, the report collects the type of floating-rate index, the fixed rate, the notional principal amount, the maturity date, and the margin to be added to the floating-rate index.

The OTS model estimates the market value of each S&L's portfolio in the current interest-rate environment and in eight alternative interest-rate scenarios. The model uses interest rates at each quarter-end to estimate the current market value of all financial instruments in the portfolio and estimates what their market values would be after parallel yield-curve shocks of plus and minus 100, 200, 300, and 400 basis points. With the exception of certain off-balance-sheet instruments (for which a variant of the Black–Scholes model is used), the model uses present-value techniques to estimate market values of financial instruments. The future cash flows of each instrument are projected using the reported information on its coupon, maturity, and repricing characteristics, and making assumptions about loan prepayment rates, CD early withdrawal rates, and core deposit attrition rates. Then cash flows are discounted by discount rates that reflect the current required yield on similar instruments. The sum of an instrument's discounted cash flows is its estimated market value. In the alternative interest-rate environments, the amount of the interest-rate "shock" is added to the discount rates, and the cash flows are recalculated to account for changes in coupons, prepayment rates, and so on, that would result from the shock. OTS uses the simple present-value methodology to estimate the market values of liabilities and nonmortgage loans but uses an option-based pricing model to value mortgage loans and securities and mortgage-servicing rights.

The OTS model uses statistical models to estimate the relationship between certain variables. For example, interest rates on core deposits are assumed to adjust slowly to changes in the general level of market rates. A statistical model based on historical data is used to estimate this speed of adjustment and permits increases in core deposit rates to occur more slowly than decreases in rates. Also, the valuation of retail certificates of deposit takes into account the fact that depositors often roll over their deposits at maturity. The estimated maturity and future offered rates are based on their statistically estimated relationships to market interest rates.

To calculate the interest-rate component of the risk-based capital requirement, OTS imposes a 200-basis-point shock. Under the regulation, S&Ls with exposures in excess of 2 percent of assets would be required to hold additional capital equal to one-half the excess interest-rate risk. OTS believes it is important to simulate the effect of a 200-basis-point shock to capture the effect on S&Ls' portfolios of the prepayment options and interest-rate caps that may not come into play for smaller rate shocks and to use the option-based pricing methodology, which captures the negative convexity of mortgage loans and securities. Although the reporting form that S&Ls are required to fill out is much more extensive than that proposed by the bank regulators, OTS believes it is necessary given the industry's huge losses in the early 1980s that resulted from their interest-rate exposure and the fact that S&Ls are required by statute to hold a large portion of their assets as mortgage assets, making them more vulnerable to interest-rate swings than the typical commercial bank.

⑥ OAS AND EFFECTIVE DURATION

David Audley*
Director of Investment Systems and Technology
Tiger Management Corporation

Richard Chin*
Fixed-Income Research
Goldman Sachs & Co.

Shrikant Ramamurthy
First Vice President
Fixed-Income Research
Prudential Securities

Bonds with embedded options have uncertain maturities because the decision to exercise the option generally depends on the relationship between the level of interest rates, the exercise price of the option, and the market price of the security. Issuers of callable debt will tend to call their bonds when rates have fallen sufficiently to justify refinancing outstanding debt. However, the exact timing for the exercise of the call option is not always known because the nature of the American-style option allows issuers to exercise their call at any time between the first call date and the final maturity date. This option type is prevalent among corporate, agency, and Treasury securities. The maturities of bonds with embedded put options are known with slightly more certainty because investors will either redeem the bonds on the put date or hold them to final maturity (assuming that there are no other embedded options in addition to the one put option).

The presence of an embedded option complicates the bond-valuation process because the bond's maturity date is uncertain. It is not always clear whether the bond should be analyzed according to its final maturity, first call or

---

put date, or par call date, for example. Consider a 30-year callable utility bond with 5 years of call protection and a given level of interest-rate volatility. From a price-sensitivity standpoint, does the bond behave more like a 30-year bond, a 5-year bond, or an intermediate-maturity bond? From a compensation standpoint, are the yield spread and option-adjusted spread (OAS) commensurate with the level of interest-rate risk? The ability to quantify the price sensitivity of a particular bond is a necessary step in gauging the risk/reward trade-offs inherent in any one bond. Furthermore, the hedging of such bonds requires having the means to calculate a bond's price sensitivity to changes in interest rates.[1]

For a bond with a defined set of cash flows, such as a bullet bond, the price/ yield relationship is well understood. Consequently, the bullet bond's modified duration may be calculated easily because the amount and timing of all the cash flows are known with certainty. In this chapter, we will illustrate how the effective duration of an option-embedded bond is simply an extension of the already familiar concept used for bullet bonds. Additionally, the chapter discusses why OAS and effective duration by themselves may not provide sufficient information to completely judge the relative value between two securities.

THE PRICE/YIELD RELATIONSHIP FOR OPTION-EMBEDDED BONDS

As a starting point in the conceptual analysis of option-embedded bonds, consider the effect an embedded option has on a bond's maturity in the case of extreme interest-rate movements. If interest rates move to either very high or very low levels, the embedded option very likely will or will not be exercised (depending on whether the option is a call or a put) and, therefore, the maturity of a bond should be known with relative certainty. For example, if long-term Treasury rates drop to 2 percent and stay at that level, callable-bond issuers will probably exercise their options at the earliest possible date, whereas putable bonds will remain outstanding to final maturity as holders will not exercise their put option. On the other hand, if Treasury rates rise to 25 percent and remain at that level, putable-bond holders will exercise their options as quickly as possible in order to reinvest the proceeds at higher interest rates, whereas callable bonds will remain outstanding until final maturity because issuers will not exercise their call option. These extreme interest-rate-movement scenarios illustrate that the maturity range of most option-embedded bonds is bound by the first option-exercise date and the final maturity date. Because interest-rate movements generally are milder than those described above, the maturity of an option-embedded bond usually lies somewhere between the first option-exercise date and the final maturity date. There-

---

1. See David Audley, Richard Chin, and Shrikant Ramamurthy, *Technology and Its Effect on Valuation Metrics #17: Hedging Fixed-Income Instruments: The Basics of Cash-Market Hedging* (New York: Financial Strategies Group, Prudential Securities Incorporated, February 23, 1993).

fore, the price sensitivity of an option-embedded bond lies somewhere between that of a bond priced to final maturity and that of a bond priced to the earliest exercise date.

The following sections describe how the price/yield behavior of a bond with an embedded put or call option may be visualized in relation to the price/yield sensitivities of bonds at either end of the maturity boundaries. We will then extend the analysis to encompass put/call parity, which is helpful in understanding the effects of price/yield sensitivity on duration and OAS. As we will see, the put/call parity relationship inherent in option-embedded bonds is key to understanding the effects of interest-rate volatility on the duration and yield of option-embedded bonds.

The Price/Yield Relationship of Callable Bonds

A callable bond may be viewed as a portfolio consisting of two positions: a long position in an underlying noncallable bond and a short position in a call option. This relationship is illustrated in the following pricing equation:

$$\text{Callable bond} = \text{Underlying bond} - \text{Call option} \qquad (40\text{--}1)$$

From the equation, we can see that if interest rates fall, the price of the underlying bond increases as if it were a bullet bond. However, the magnitude of the overall price increase for the callable bond is limited by a corresponding increase in the value of the call option. If interest rates fall very far, the callable bond's price appreciation will be limited to that of a short-term bond with a maturity that is approximately equal to the option-exercise date.

Exhibit 40–1 shows how the price of a 10-year bond with 3 years of call protection is affected by changes in interest rates. For this bond, the longest possible maturity is the 10-year final maturity and the shortest term to maturity is 3 years, the earliest option-exercise date. Therefore, Exhibit 40–1 also shows price/yield curves for 3- and 10-year bullet bonds. At very high yield levels, the callable bond's price/yield curve approaches that of the 10-year bullet bond. This is because the call option's value decreases as interest rates move higher and higher. As the value of the option declines, the price behavior of the callable bond increasingly resembles that of the bullet bond with the same final maturity date as the callable bond. Conversely, if interest rates fall, the callable bond's price/yield curve becomes more like that of the 3-year bullet bond because the likelihood of option exercise increases.

Effect of Volatility on Callable-Bond Pricing

Exhibit 40–1 also indicates that the callable bond's price behavior is a function of interest-rate volatility. As volatility increases from 10 percent to 20 percent, the call option's value increases and the price of the callable bond correspondingly decreases. Thus the callable bond's price/yield curve at 20 percent volatility lies

E X H I B I T   40–1

Price Behavior of Hypothetical 10-Year Callable Bond with 3 Years of Call Protection

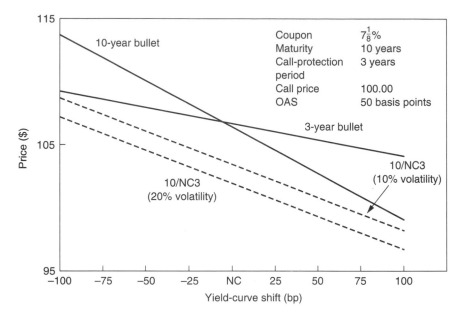

below the bond's price/yield curve at 10 percent volatility, reflecting a greater degree of negative convexity at the higher volatility levels.

At any given yield level, the vertical distance between the price/yield curves of the callable bond and the underlying noncallable 10-year bond is a reflection of the value of the call option. As volatility increases, the option value also increases, as indicated by the increasing distance between the price/yield curves.

The Price/Yield Relationship of Putable Bonds

A putable bond may be viewed as a portfolio of a long position in an underlying noncallable bond plus a long position in a put option, as shown in the following relationship:[2]

$$\text{Putable bond} = \text{Underlying bond} + \text{Put option} \qquad (40\text{–}2)$$

The equation illustrates that if interest rates rise, the price of the underlying bond decreases, but the magnitude of the overall price decrease of the put bond itself is mitigated by an increase in the value of the put option. If interest rates rise

---

2. See David Audley and Richard Chin, *Bonds with Embedded Put Options* (New York: Financial Strategies Group, Prudential Securities Incorporated, December 1990).

E X H I B I T   40–2

Price Behavior of Hypothetical 10-Year Putable Bond with Put Exercisable in 3 Years

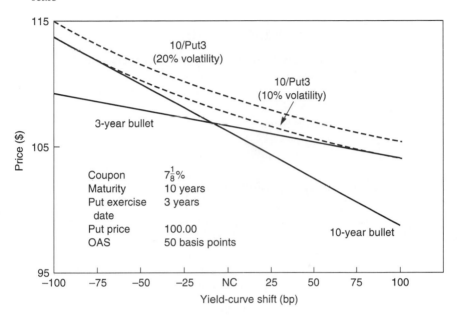

sharply, then the price depreciation of the putable bond will be limited to that of a short-term bond maturing on the putable bond's exercise date. Thus the put option cushions the putable-bond holder's downside risk.

Exhibit 40–2 shows the analogous price/yield curves of a 10-year bond with a put option that may be exercised in 3 years at two different levels of interest-rate volatility (10 percent and 20 percent). The price/yield curves for the associated 3- and 10-year bullet bonds also are shown. As yields increase, the price/yield curve for the putable bond approaches that of the 3-year bullet bond due to the growing likelihood of option exercise. Conversely, if interest rates fall, then the price/yield curve of the putable bond approaches that of the 10-year bullet because the economic incentive to exercise the put option decreases.

Effect of Volatility on Putable-Bond Pricing

As with a callable bond, the shape and level of the price/yield curve for a putable bond is a function of interest-rate volatility. Exhibit 40–2 shows that as volatility increases, the option value increases and, consequently, the price of the putable bond increases. Thus the putable bond's price/yield curve at the 20 percent volatility level lies above the bond's price/yield curve at 10 percent volatility.

The next section expands on the concept of viewing option-embedded bonds as portfolios of bonds and options by reviewing the concept of put/call parity. Put/call parity is helpful in further understanding the price/yield relationship and relative valuation of option-embedded bonds.

Put/Call Parity

Put/call parity is an important relationship in option-pricing theory that relates the price of a put option to the price of a call option. As applied to option-embedded bonds, the relationship illustrates that a position in either a callable bond or a putable bond may be viewed in two equivalent ways.[3] We will examine a callable bond first, and then a putable bond.

A callable bond may be viewed as a portfolio consisting of a long position in a bond and a short position in an option (notice that we did not specify the type of option).

For example, a 10-year callable bond with 3 years of call protection may be viewed as a portfolio consisting of a long position in a 10-year bullet bond and a short position in a call option exercisable by the issuer in 3 years. Under the principles of put/call parity, the same callable-bond position may be viewed as a long position in a 3-year bullet bond and a short position in a put option, where the issuer has the right to put a 7-year bullet bond to the investor in 3 years. Equation (40–3) reflects the duality of the option embedded in a callable bond.

Long-maturity bullet bond – Call option
$$= \text{Short-maturity bullet bond} - \text{Put option} \quad (40\text{--}3)$$

Similarly, a putable bond may be viewed as a portfolio consisting of a long position in a bullet bond and a long position in an option (notice again that we did not specify the type of option).

For example, a 10-year bond with a put option exercisable in 3 years may be viewed as a portfolio consisting of a long position in a 10-year bullet bond and a long position in a put exercisable in 3 years. (This pricing concept is similar to the one we introduced in the section on price/yield relationships of putable bonds.) Alternatively, the same putable bond may be viewed as a portfolio of a long position in a 3-year bullet bond and a long position in a call option that gives the bondholder the right to call a 7-year bullet bond away from the issuer. This pricing relationship is shown in Equation (40–4).

Long-maturity bullet bond + Put option
$$= \text{Short-maturity bullet bond} + \text{Call option} \quad (40\text{--}4)$$

---

3. See David Audley and Richard Chin, *The Internal Consistency of Option Valuation Models: The Validation of Put/Call Parity* (New York: Financial Strategies Group, Prudential Securities Incorporated, September 11, 1990).

Note that Equation (40–4) may be derived by rearranging Equation (40–3), which simply reflects the change from a short option position in a callable bond to a long option position in a putable bond.

EFFECTIVE DURATION

The objective of effective duration is to quantify an option-embedded bond's price sensitivity to changes in interest rates. If we calculate a security's price for a small change in interest rates (e.g., plus or minus 25 basis points), then the percentage change in price for this specified change in rates represents the bond's effective duration.

Effective-Duration Calculations

Described below are two methods of calculating a bond's effective duration. Both methods produce very similar results.

Constant-OAS Pricing for Yield-Curve Shifts[4]

An OAS model calculates the value of an option-adjusted spread for a given market price for a security. For small parallel shifts in the yield curve, the prices that correspond to the same OAS are the security's constant-OAS prices. The effective duration (as measured in years) is then found from the expression shown in Equation 40–5.

$$\text{Effective duration} = \frac{10,000}{\text{Price} + \text{Accrued}} \times \frac{(\text{Price up} - \text{Price down})}{(\text{Total shift in yield curve})} \quad (40\text{--}5)$$

where

$$
\begin{aligned}
\text{Price} &= \text{Market price of security} \\
\text{Accrued} &= \text{Accrued interest} \\
\text{Price up} &= \text{Constant-OAS security price for downward yield-curve shift} \\
\text{Price down} &= \text{Constant-OAS security price for upward yield-curve shift} \\
\text{Total shift} &= \text{Total range of yield-curve shift (in basis points)}
\end{aligned}
$$

The Price/Rate Derivative

For term-structure-based OAS models that use a numerical finite-difference solution to calculate the price of a bond as a function of the spot rate and time, it is possible to calculate the derivative of the price with respect to the spot rate at any time. In this case, the price derivative expresses the bond's price sensitivity to

---

4. See David Audley and Richard Chin, *Constant OAS Analysis* (New York: Financial Strategies Group, Prudential Securities Incorporated, May 14, 1990).

E X H I B I T   40–3

Effective Duration of FNMA 6.38 of 6/25/03 Callable at Par from 6/25/96

Issuer	FNMA
Coupon	6.38%
Maturity	6/26/03
Call date	6/25/96
Call price	100.000
Price[a]	100.433
Accrued interest	0.354
Yield	6.32%
OAS	48 basis points

$$\text{Effective duration using yield-curve shift} = \frac{10{,}000}{\text{Price} + \text{Accrued}} \times \frac{\text{Price up} - \text{Price down}}{\text{Total shift in yield curve}}$$

$$= \frac{10{,}000}{100.787} \times \frac{101.599 - 98.365}{50}$$

$$= 6.42$$

Effective duration using price-rate array = 6.28

[a]Price as of July 14, 1993

changes in rate. Once the current price derivative is determined, a bullet bond with the same price derivative is constructed. The modified duration of this duration-matched bullet is the effective duration.

Exhibit 40–3 shows that the effective durations that are obtained by either of these two methods are very close.

Effective Duration of Callable Bonds

Just as the slope of the tangent line to a bullet bond's price/yield curve is a measure of the bond's modified duration, the slope of the tangent line to a callable bond's price/yield curve is a measure of the callable bond's effective (modified) duration. Exhibit 40–4 illustrates that the slope of the line tangent to the callable bond's price/yield curve (Tangent Line A) is between that of the two reference noncallable bonds. This indicates that a callable bond's effective duration is bounded by the modified durations of the noncallable bonds. As interest rates either move up or down, the slope of Tangent Line A correspondingly approaches that of the appropriate noncallable bond.

The Effect of Selling Call Options on Duration

Equation 40–1 illustrates how a change in interest rates affects the duration of a callable bond. If the 10-year callable bond in Exhibit 40–4 is viewed as a portfo-

E X H I B I T   40–4

Effective Duration of Hypothetical 10-Year Callable Bond with 3 Years of Call Protection

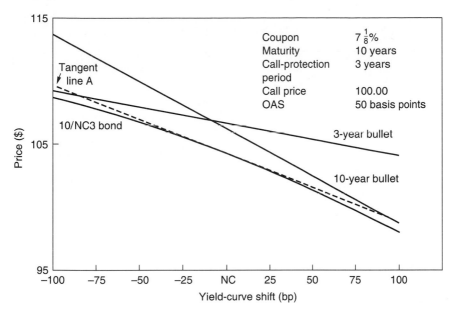

lio of a long position in a 10-year bullet bond and a short position in a call option exercisable in 3 years, the decreasing slope of Tangent Line A as interest rates fall shows that selling a call option decreases a portfolio's duration. Conversely, when rates rise, the call option is not exercised so that, in effect, the option holder (the issuer) has elected to put the bond to the bondholder. In this case, the increasing slope of Tangent Line A indicates that selling a put option increases the portfolio's duration when rates rise. In either case of extreme interest-rate movements (plus or minus 100 basis points in Exhibit 40–4), the duration of the portfolio changes in a way that is adverse to the seller of the option (the investor). Hence, the portfolio (i.e., the callable bond) is negatively convex.

Effective Duration of Put Bonds

Exhibit 40–5 illustrates that the slope of Tangent Line A, which is tangent to the putable bond's price/yield curve, also falls between the slopes of curves of the two underlying bullet bonds. Thus, the putable bond's effective duration lies between the durations of the reference bullet bonds. This indicates that, although a putable bond may be priced to the put date, its effective duration is at least as high as that of the comparable bullet bond maturing on or near the put date.

EXHIBIT   40–5

Effective Duration of Hypothetical 10-Year Putable Bond with Put Exercisable in 3 Years

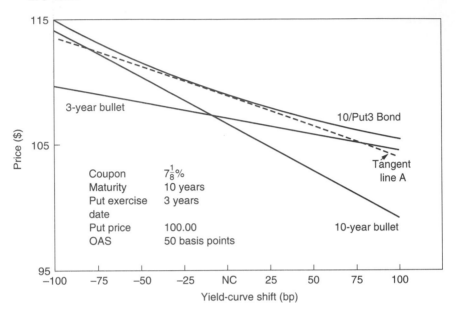

The Effect of Buying Put Options on Duration

Similar to callable bonds, the effect of interest-rate changes on a putable bond's duration is illustrated by the relationship shown in Equation 40–2. If the 10-year putable bond shown in Exhibit 40–5 is viewed as a portfolio consisting of a long position in a 10-year bullet bond plus a long position in a put option exercisable in 3 years, the decreasing slope of Tangent Line A when interest rates rise shows that buying a put option decreases a portfolio's duration. Conversely, when rates fall, the put option is not exercised, so the holder of the option (the bondholder) has essentially elected to call the bond. In this case, the increasing slope of Tangent Line A indicates that purchasing a call option increases the portfolio's duration when rates drop. In either case of extreme interest-rate movements, the duration of the portfolio changes in a way that benefits the holder of the option (the investor). Thus the portfolio (i.e., the putable bond) is positively convex.

EFFECTIVE MATURITY

Once the effective duration of an option-embedded bond is calculated, it is possible to construct a bullet bond with a modified duration equal to the effective duration of the option-embedded bond. This allows an option-embedded bond's price sensitivity to be expressed in terms of properties that are well understood for bullet bonds. The option-embedded bond's *effective maturity* is stated in terms of the maturity of the duration-matched bullet with the same coupon payments and payment dates.[5] Furthermore, if the option-embedded bond has a premium call schedule that declines to par over time, then the bullet bond's redemption value on the effective maturity date is equal to the call option's exercise price.

For example, a par-priced, 10-year bond that is callable for the last 7 years at par may have the price sensitivity of a 7-year bullet bond even though the original bond is priced relative to the 10-year Treasury note. Thus the effective maturity of this callable bond is 7 years. Bonds that are more likely to be called, perhaps due to a higher coupon or to an earlier call date, may have shorter effective maturities than bonds that are less likely to be called. Conversely, high-coupon, premium-priced putable bonds, whose put options are less likely to be exercised, may have longer effective maturities than bonds that are more likely to be put, such as deep-discount bonds.[6]

Exhibit 40–6 compares the price/yield curves of a 10-year callable bond with 3 years of call protection and its duration-matched bullet bond. For relatively

E X H I B I T   40–6

Price/Yield-Curve Comparison of Hypothetical 10/NC3 Bond and Its Duration-Matched Bullet Bond

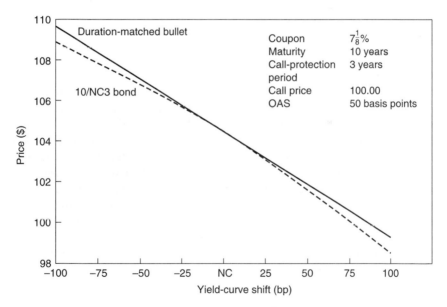

---

5. The effective maturity date is found by an iterative process in which the maturity date of the duration-matched bullet bond is varied until the modified duration of this bullet bond is equal to the original bond's effective duration.

6. Although the calculation of effective maturity takes into account the range of possible interest rates in the future, the effective maturity does not strictly equal the expected maturity, which is the probability-weighted maturity. In contrast, the effective maturity is the maturity of the duration-matched bullet.

EXHIBIT 40–7

Effective Maturity of 10/NC3 Bond as a Function of Volatility and Yield-Curve Shifts

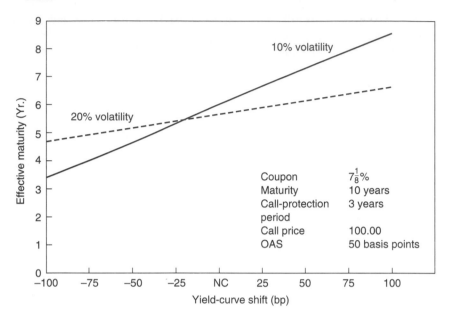

small changes in interest rates, the price/yield curves are very close to one another. For larger interest-rate movements, the two price/yield curves begin to diverge as the callable bond's negative convexity begins to dominate.

Exhibit 40–7 displays the effective maturities of a hypothetical 10-year bond, callable at par in 3 years, at two different yield volatilities. Because the value of the call option generally increases with higher volatilities, the negatively convex nature of callable securities is more apparent at 20 percent volatility than at 10 percent volatility, as shown by its lower effective maturities. Note, however, that there is a combination of interest-rate shifts and volatilities in which the two effective maturity plots cross each other. This occurs at lower interest-rate levels and reflects the situation in which a higher interest-rate volatility actually increases the likelihood that rates may increase.

OPTION-ADJUSTED SPREADS

Up to this point, our discussion has centered on using a bond's price sensitivity to interest-rate changes as one measure of risk. Now we'll switch our focus to the other side of the risk/reward equation and consider the OAS an investor receives as compensation for assuming a variety of risks. It is important to note that an

OAS value by itself does not provide sufficient information to determine whether a bond is rich or cheap. The OAS and effective duration of one security must be compared with those of another security. In the absence of such a context, it is difficult to assess accurately the relative value between two securities.

For example, a common question that arises about OAS is the point along the maturity spectrum that should be used as a reference point. Should the OAS be viewed as an adjusted yield spread relative to the option-embedded bond's maturity date or its call/put date? Should the OAS of a 10-year callable bond with 3 years of call protection be compared with the spread of a 3-year bullet bond or a 10-year bullet bond? Furthermore, if the callable bond has an effective maturity of 7 years, should the OAS be compared to the yield spread of a 7-year bullet bond? Quantitative fixed-income analysts usually say yes to all of the above because OAS is a spread to the curve.

The view that OAS is a spread over the curve is based on the definition of OAS: *OAS is the spread to short-term interest rates that equates the theoretical price of a bond to its market price.*

It can be demonstrated mathematically that the above definition of OAS results in a parallel shift of the entire zero-coupon (spot-yield) curve by an amount equal to the OAS. Thus, in a sense, the OAS is a spread over the entire curve.

A less technical, and perhaps more intuitive, way of viewing OAS as a spread to the curve is to consider the duality of embedded options in terms of put/call parity. For example, callable bonds usually are quoted either on a yield-to-maturity basis or a yield-to-call basis, depending on the level and direction of interest rates. If interest rates are high or moving higher, then the issuer is unlikely to call the bond. By electing not to exercise the call option, the issuer has effectively put the bond to the investor.

Thus, even though a bond is quoted on a yield-to-maturity basis, a corresponding yield-to-call spread exists. Because the OAS is an adjustment to the nominal yield spread, the OAS can be viewed as the result of the appropriate adjustments to *both* the yield-to-maturity and yield-to-call spreads. In this view, the OAS is an adjusted spread to both the maturity date and the call date. The following equations demonstrate this relationship:

$$\text{OAS} = \text{Yield-to-maturity spread} - \text{Call-option value in basis points} \quad (40\text{--}6)$$

or

$$\text{OAS} = \text{Yield-to-call spread} - \text{Put-option value in basis points} \quad (40\text{--}7)$$

Moreover, if the option is American-style (i.e., the option can be exercised at any time during a specified period), then the OAS may be viewed as an adjusted yield spread over an entire range of call dates.

In considering which point on the yield curve is most appropriate for comparison of OASs to bullet yield spreads, a common first approximation is that the OAS should be compared to the yield spread of the bullet bond whose final maturity is comparable to the effective maturity of the bond with embedded options.

Because OAS and effective maturity are risk/reward measures, it is reasonable to determine whether the particular value of OAS is sufficient compensation for an approximately equivalent amount of risk (when compared to the comparable bullet yield spread). For example, if the OAS of the callable 10-year bond is 100 basis points and the effective maturity is 7 years, it is reasonable to first compare the OAS to the yield spread of a 7-year bullet from the same or very similar issuer. However, this approach serves only as a general rule, and there are other important factors that enter into the determination of relative value.

Looking Beyond the OAS and Effective Duration Numbers

A common assumption is that comparable bonds with comparable effective durations should have comparable OASs. The result of this view is that bonds with higher OASs are perceived to represent better value. However, a variety of other factors should be considered before rendering a judgment about the relative richness or cheapness between the two securities.

Effect of Exogenous Factors

The technology embedded within an OAS model may be very sophisticated, but a not-too-commonly discussed point is that OAS models quantify the value of the embedded option only within the context of the model's underlying assumptions. By assuming an interest-rate process and a given randomness in interest rates, the value of the option is calculated. Then the OAS is, roughly speaking, the effective yield spread after adjusting for the value of the embedded option. Consequently, the effective yield spread implicitly reflects the host of other considerations (beyond that of the embedded option) that factor into the marketplace's pricing of the bond.

Exogenous factors such as supply and demand in particular market sectors and current investor preferences can cause one bond to be cheap to another bond on an OAS basis. Just as two comparable bullet securities can trade at different yield spread levels, comparable bonds with embedded options can trade at different OASs relative to each other or relative to equivalent-duration bullets. Thus, although there may be circumstances in which two bonds may trade at approximately the same OAS, there can be fundamental factors causing the bonds to trade at substantially different OASs.

Effect of Convexity

The comparison of the OAS versus the effective duration of two bonds provides insight into the local price sensitivities of the securities to changes in interest rates only. For relatively small changes in interest rates, two securities with similar effective durations should have similar price sensitivities. However, as interest rates move significantly, the effective durations of the two securities may no longer be comparable, so any convexity dissimilarities between the two securities begin to take effect. See Exhibit 40–6 (price/yield curve comparison between a callable bond and a bullet bond).

The effective duration number (in the absence of other information) does not highlight, for example, the possibility that a 30-year callable bond with an effective maturity of 10 years can still extend out to 30 years if interest rates rise steadily. Conversely, if interest rates decrease significantly, the effective duration continues to decrease so that the price appreciation of the callable bond is even more muted. The bond's negative convexity, which is a result of the bondholder's selling of options, reflects the potential downside of a short-option position in a volatile interest-rate environment.

Generally, the length of the investment horizon and the outlook on interest rates influence the extent to which investors may be concerned about the magnitude of the convexity effect. If the investment horizon is short and if interest rates are viewed as being stable over that time period, an investor may not be very concerned about the convexity effect. On the other hand, if the horizon spans a longer period of time, long-term price performance and convexity become larger issues. In this latter case, investors may need to be compensated for the greater exposure to negative convexity through a higher OAS, even though the two securities being compared currently may have similar effective durations.

Exhibit 40–8 illustrates such a situation in which two comparable securities do not have similar OASs. In this case, two callable Texas Utilities bonds with similar final maturities have different OASs. At a 10 percent yield volatility[7] the 9.75s have an OAS of 120 basis points, as compared to the OAS of 109 basis points for the 7.875s.

The difference in OAS can be attributed to several competing factors that act to influence the pricing of these securities. First, securities with shorter effective durations tend to have lower OASs than securities with higher effective durations, simply to reflect the trend observed for bullet securities that yield spreads increase with increasing maturities. (This OAS trend would be most evident for securities that clearly trade either to the maturity date or to the option-exercise date.) On this basis, it can be argued that the 9.75s should have the lower OAS.

On the other hand, for securities with intermediate effective durations (such as the Texas Utilities 9.75s), it is not obvious whether the security will be called or remain outstanding to final maturity. Hence, it can also be argued that as compensation for the greater degree of uncertainty, the 9.75s should have a higher OAS than do the 7.875s. In the final analysis, the higher OAS of the 9.75s indicates that the market currently demands greater compensation for the maturity uncertainty than for the duration risk.

---

7. See David Audley and Richard Chin, *Technology and Its Effect on Valuation Metrics #3: Choosing the Correct Volatility for the Valuation of Embedded Options* (New York: Financial Strategies Group, Prudential Securities Incorporated, March 1991).

EXHIBIT 40-8

OAS and Effective-Duration Comparison

Issuer	Texas Utilities	Texas Utilities
Rating (S&P/Moody's)	BBB/Baa2	BBB/Baa2
Coupon	9.75%	7.875%
Maturity	05/01/21	03/01/23
Call date	05/01/01	03/02/03
Call price	$104.87	$103.84
Issue size	$300 MM	$300 MM
Price[a]	$116.466	$99.323
OAS (10% yield volatility)	120 bp	109 bp
Effective maturity	12.3 years	24.2 years
Effective duration	7.4 years	10.5 years

[a]Prices as of June 7, 1993.

Source: Prudential Securities' IMPACT data base.

SUMMARY

Bonds with embedded options and bullet securities can respond very differently to movements in interest rates. Investors may use the analytical concepts of OAS and effective duration to help gauge the relative risk/reward trade-offs across a range of assets to determine relative value. OAS and effective duration can be useful analytical tools, but investors need to recognize that there can be a variety of fundamental and analytical reasons that may cause two comparable securities to trade at widely different OASs.

ⓖ
FIXED INCOME RISK
MODELING

Ronald N. Kahn, Ph.D.
Director of Research
BARRA

Many years ago, bonds were boring. Returns were small and steady. Fixed income risk monitoring consisted of watching duration and avoiding low qualities. But as interest-rate volatility has increased and the variety of fixed income instruments has grown, both opportunities and dangers have flourished. Accurate fixed income risk measurement has become more important and more difficult. The sources of fixed income risk have proliferated and intensified. Exposures to these risks are subtle and complex. Today's fixed income environment requires advanced multifactor techniques to adequately model the many sources of risk influencing the market, and powerful tools to compute exposures to those risks.

Duration is the traditional fixed income risk factor, and measures exposure to the risk of parallel term-structure movements. But term structures not only shift in parallel, they also twist and bend, and these movements tend to increase in magnitude as interest rates rise. In addition to interest-rate volatility, most issues are exposed to various sources of default risk, assessed by marketwide sector and quality spreads. These spreads can depend on maturity and move unpredictably over time. Beyond marketwide sources of default risk, individual issues face specific sources of default risk.

Nominal cash flows and quality ratings no longer suffice to measure risk exposures. Call and put options and sinking-fund provisions can significantly alter an instrument's risk exposures in intricate ways. Mortgage-backed securities are subject to uncertain prepayments, which influence the risk exposures of those instruments. When they are packaged as IOs, POs, or CMOs, the risk exposure accounting becomes even more difficult.

There is no question that building a fixed income risk model is complicated business. Forecasting risk factor covariance and analyzing the Byzantine provisions of today's fixed income instruments require sophisticated methods.

Using a fixed income risk model, however, should be intuitive and straightforward. Bond investors should find the risk factors sensible. Risk analysis results should be precise, but still conform to investor instincts. A good risk model should actually simplify the investment process, quantify risks, and increase investor insight.

Fixed income risk modeling plays a critical role in bond portfolio management, benchmark tracking, immunization, active strategy implementation, and performance measurement and analysis. Benchmark tracking involves comparing the risk exposures of an investment portfolio and a benchmark. Matching those exposures should lead to investment returns that accurately track benchmark returns. Immunization involves comparing the risk exposures of a portfolio and a liability stream. Matching those exposures should immunize the portfolio's liability coverage against market changes. Active strategies involve deliberate risk exposures relative to a benchmark, aimed at exceeding benchmark returns. Performance measurement and analysis involves identifying active bets and studying their past performance so as to measure bond manager skill.

This chapter describes a multifactor approach to risk modeling. This approach consists of two basic components. First, a valuation model identifies and values the many risk factors in the market. The valuation model requires the machinery to estimate exposures to these risk factors, including an option simulation to handle the wide variety of optionable fixed income securities. Second, a risk model examines the historical behavior of these risk factors to estimate their variances and covariances. The presentation here will be general, but this chapter will conclude with evidence of the performance of multifactor risk models based on their specific application to the U.S. bond market.[1]

THE VALUATION MODEL

The following multifactor valuation model is designed to identify and value risk factors in the market. This model estimates bond prices as

$$PM_n(t) = \sum_T \frac{cf_n(T) \cdot PDB(t,T)}{\exp[\kappa_n(t) \cdot T]} + \xi_n(t) \qquad (41\text{--}1)$$

$$= PF_n(t) + \xi_n(t) \qquad (41\text{--}2)$$

---

1. For a more detailed description of this application to the U.S. bond market, see Ronald N. Kahn, "Risk and Return in the U.S. Bond Market: A Multifactor Approach," in *Advances and Innovations in the Bond and Mortgage Markets,* ed. Frank J. Fabozzi (Chicago: Probus Publishing, 1989).

with

$$\kappa_n(t) = \sum_j x_{n,j} \cdot s_j(t) \tag{41-3}$$

where

PM$_n(t)$ = bond n market price at time t
Pf$_n(t)$ = bond n fitted price at time t
cf$_n(T)$ = bond n option-adjusted cash flow at time T
PDB(t,T) = price at t of default-free pure discount bond maturing at T
$x_{n,j}$ = bond n exposure to factor j
$s_j(t)$ = yield spread due to factor j at time t
$\xi_n(t)$ = bond n price error at time t
$\kappa_n(t)$ = bond n total yield spread at time t

The characteristics of the market as a whole are the term structure, represented here by the default-free pure discount bond prices PDB(t,T), and the marketwide factor yield spreads $s_j(t)$. The bond-specific exposures include the option-adjusted cash flows cf$_n(T)$ and the exposures $x_{n,j}$. These depend upon any call or put options or sinking-fund provisions embedded in bond n. The final bond-specific component of this model is the price error $\xi_n(t)$. This model clearly enumerates how a bond's total exposure to the various factors determines its price. The estimated values [PDB(t,T), $s_j(t)$, $\xi_n(t)$] result from fitting this model to actual trading prices at time t.[2] All these values change unpredictably over time.

The yield-spread factors s_j correspond to the nonterm-structure sources of risk and return identified by the model. Most of these are sources of default risk. For example, each corporate bond sector might have its own yield spread, measuring the default risk common to all AAA-rated members of the sector. Each quality rating would also have its own yield spread, measuring the additional default risk common to issues rated lower than AAA.

Beyond the factors that measure default risk, there are other factors that capture risk and return in bond markets. Benchmark factors measure the uncertain liquidity premiums afforded heavily traded issues. A current-yield factor measures the market's assessment at time t of the advantage of receiving return in the form of capital gains instead of interest, providing a possible tax advantage. A perpetual factor, appearing in markets containing perpetual bonds, measures the market's assessment at time t of the advantage or disadvantage of owning perpetual bonds.

Observed corporate bond yield spreads tend to increase with maturity, quantifying the market's perception of the increase in default risk over time. For investors, any change in the dependence of spreads upon maturity constitutes a

---

2. For more details, see Ronald N. Kahn, "Estimating the U.S. Treasury Term Structure of Interest Rates," in *The Handbook of U.S. Treasury and Government Agency Securities: Instruments, Strategies and Analysis*, Revised Edition, ed. Frank J. Fabozzi (Chicago: Probus Publishing, 1990).

source of return risk. Because these spreads appear to increase linearly with duration, a duration spread can measure the extent of this increase with duration at any given time. A risk model can then measure how this dependence changes over time.

So far, this analysis has concentrated on the estimated marketwide factors of value. Estimates of these factors rely on option-adjusted cash flows, however. Hence, the next section will describe the option adjustment procedure in more detail.

Option Adjustments

Estimating the values $[\text{PDB}(t,T), s_j(t), \xi_n(t)]$ requires market prices, cash flows, and yield-spread factor exposures. However, because embedded options alter the nominal cash flows, the final step in the valuation model involves adjusting the nominal bond cash flows accordingly.

Bonds can include call and put options and sinking-fund provisions. Mortgage-backed securities include prepayment options. These securities are portfolios containing a nonoptionable security and an option. For callable and sinkable bonds and mortgages, the issuer retains the option, and so the portfolio is long a nonoptionable security and short the option:

$$\text{Optionable bond} = \text{Nonoptionable bond} - \text{Option} \qquad (41\text{--}4)$$

and

$$\text{PF}_n(t) = \text{PFN}_n(t) - \text{PFO}_n(t) \qquad (41\text{--}5)$$

where

PFN_n = bond n nominal fitted price
PFO_n = bond n option fitted price

For putable bonds, the purchaser owns the put option, so the portfolio is long both the nonoptionable security and the option.

Viewed in this portfolio framework, the key aspect of option adjustment involves modeling the embedded option. A detailed description of option modeling is beyond the scope of this chapter, but basically it is a three-step procedure.

First, choose a model that describes the stochastic evolution of future interest rates. This model will describe the drift and, more importantly, the interest-rate volatility, of either the short interest rate or the entire term structure. It will describe a set of possible future interest-rate paths.

Second, impose a no-arbitrage condition to fairly price bonds of different maturities. This step will determine the probability weight, for valuation purposes, of each possible future interest-rate path and generate a current set of bond prices. A properly tuned model will generate prices consistent with observed bond prices.

Third, impose relevant option decision rules to apply the model to the particular option of interest. These decision rules will depend on the specific option covenants as well as the behavioral model governing the corporation or the individual mortgage holder. Imposing these rules will lead to estimated cash flows and a price for the option. The portfolio property described in Equation (41–4) dictates how the option cash flows adjust the optionable bond cash flows.

Option Adjustment Example[3]

To see this work in practice, consider a simple example of a callable zero-coupon bond. The bond nominally pays V dollars at maturity M:

$$\mathrm{PFN}_n(t) \;=\; V \cdot \mathrm{PDB}(t,M) \tag{41–6}$$

However, the traded security includes an embedded option for the issuer to call the bond at strike price K and time T, with $t < T < M$. The option model estimates the call option value as

$$\mathrm{PFO}_n(t) = -K \cdot Y \cdot \mathrm{PDB}(t,T) + V \cdot X \cdot \mathrm{PDB}(t,M) \tag{41–7}$$

where X and Y are cumulative distribution functions.[4] Equation (41–7) resembles the Black–Scholes stock option formula,[5] although X and Y are not necessarily cumulative normal distributions. They do, however, act as probabilities and range between zero and one.

Now consider the interpretation of Equation (41–7): The option involves paying the amount KY at time T, to receive VX at the later time M. With this interpretation, and with the portfolio property (Equation 41–4), the adjusted price and cash flows for the callable security are

$$\mathrm{PF}_n(t) = V \cdot \mathrm{PDB}(t,M) - [-K \cdot Y \cdot \mathrm{PDB}(t,T) + V \cdot X \cdot \mathrm{PDB}(t,M)]$$

$$= K \cdot Y \cdot \mathrm{PDB}(t,T) + V \cdot (1 - X) \cdot \mathrm{PDB}(t,M) \tag{41–8}$$

$$\mathrm{cf}_n(T) = K \cdot Y \tag{41–9}$$

$$\mathrm{cf}_n(M) = V \cdot [1 - X] \tag{41–10}$$

As Equations (41–9) and (41–10) show, the probabilities X and Y adjust the nominal cash flows. An out-of-the-money option has X, Y, and PFO all equal to zero, and the option-adjusted cash flows reduce to the nominal cash flows. For this

---

3. This section covers more details of the option adjustment process for the benefit of mathematically inclined readers.
4. These cumulative distribution functions correspond to the valuation probability—the martingale probability associated with the stochastic interest-rate model.
5. Fischer Black and Myron Scholes, "The Pricing of Options and Corporate Liabilities," *Journal of Political Economy*, May–June 1973.

callable bond example, as X and Y increase, the option will shorten the nominal cash flows. More complicated options involve more cash flows (a set of $T_1, \ldots, T_N$), more probabilities, and perhaps even more complicated numerical procedures to estimate the probabilities; but, in principle, the adjustment procedure is the same.

Remember that the true option-adjusted cash flows are still not certain. The option model chooses cash flows $-KY$ and VX to replicate the value and duration of the modeled security. Unfortunately, it is impossible to choose these cash flows to also replicate the convexity of the modeled security. The discrepancy between the convexity of the modeled security and the convexity of the replicating cash flow—the "excess convexity" of the option—is greatest when the option is at-the-money and approaches zero elsewhere. Fortunately, this discrepancy affects risk modeling only in second order, at worst—it affects only convexity, not duration. An additional yield-spread factor—an additional s_j—can account for the discrepancy.

Given a procedure for estimating these option-adjusted cash flows at time t, a set of market prices at time t will lead to estimates of $PDB(t,T)$ and $s_j(t)$, according to a procedure designed to minimize overall pricing error. The historical behavior of these market variables will then lead to the risk model itself.

THE RISK MODEL

Bond prices change over time in response to three general phenomena: shortening bond maturities, shifting term structures, and changing yield spreads. Bonds are risky because the last two phenomena are uncertain. The core of a bond risk model is, therefore, an estimate of the variances and covariances of the term structure and the yield-spread factor excess returns. The next two sections describe how to estimate these marketwide factor excess returns, and a third section describes how to estimate bond-specific risk.

Term-Structure Factor Returns

Building the risk model requires a history of the behavior of all relevant market factors, which the valuation model provides. How exactly does this work? Consider first the term-structure risk factors: the default-free pure discount bond prices. The price $PDB(t,T)$ represents the price at time t of \$1.00 paid at time T. The return to this factor between $t - \Delta t$ and t is the return to the following strategy:

> Invest \$1.00 at time $t - \Delta t$ in $PDB(t - \Delta t, T)$, a default-free pure discount bond. This bond has a maturity of $T - (t - \Delta t)$. Hold for a period Δt. Then sell the bond, now with a maturity $T - t$, for price $PDB(t, T)$.

The excess return to this factor follows by subtracting the risk-free rate of return. This risk-free rate is the return to the strategy:

Invest $1.00 at time $t - \Delta t$ in the default-free pure discount bond PDB($t - \Delta t, t$) maturing at time t. This bond has a maturity of Δt. Hold for a period Δt. Then redeem the bond, which has now matured.

The fixed holding period Δt is a defining constant of the risk model.

Yield-Spread Factor Returns

Now consider the returns associated with the yield-spread factors. The excess return to factor j at time t is the return to the following artificial strategy:

Invest $1.00 at time $t - \Delta t$ in a portfolio exposed only to factor j and to term-structure risk. The portfolio duration is set to the average market duration over the risk model history. Hold for a period Δt, *and roll down the term structure over this period.* Sell the portfolio at time t.

This strategy is artificial because it assumes a fixed term structure. The excess return to this strategy is the change in yield spread s_j over the holding period, multiplied by the average bond market duration, plus the yield spread multiplied by the holding period Δt. Duration, the fractional change in price accompanying a change in yield, enters into this formula to convert a change in yield spread into a price return.

Specific Return

Beyond the general, marketwide sources of risk discussed, individual issues also face specific risk. Factors that influence only one particular issue, or only the bonds of a particular company, generate specific risk and return. For example, LBO event risk constitutes a source of specific risk.[6] In the context of the risk model, specific returns arise because the bond pricing error $\xi_n(t)$ can change randomly over time.

The specific return to bond n at time t is the return to the following strategy:

Invest $1.00 at time $t - \Delta t$ in a portfolio long bond n, but with all marketwide sources of risk hedged. Hold for a period Δt, and then sell. The difference in pricing error will generate the specific return $[\xi_n(t) - \xi_n(t - \Delta t)]/[\ PM_n(t - \Delta t)]$.

The distinction between marketwide sources of risk and specific risk is important because investors can hedge marketwide sources of risk through other instruments exposed to those same risk sources. Specific risk is uncorrelated with marketwide risk.[7]

---

6. Ronald N. Kahn, "LBO Event Risk," in *Managing Institutional Assets,* ed. Frank J. Fabozzi (New York: Ballinger, 1990).

7. The specific risk of two different issues may be correlated, for example, if one company issued them both.

Integration

A multifactor risk model identifies the risk factors operating in a given market and then estimates their risk. Each factor generates excess returns over the model's estimation period. The risk model analyzes those return histories to forecast their variances and covariances.

Several difficult questions arise during the course of this analysis. What historical estimation period works best for covariance forecasting? Is covariance stable over time, or does it cycle or trend? These basic questions remain the subject of continual debate.

One particular question about forecasting bond market covariance concerns whether or not covariance depends on the level of rates. Does bond market risk increase as rates increase? Is volatility higher when rates are 16 percent than when rates are 8 percent? Academics have speculated that the answer is yes, and historical investigation confirms it for the U.S. bond market.

John Cox, Jonathan Ingersoll, and Stephen Ross[8] have developed a widely accepted model of the term structure, which prices bonds and bond options based on equilibrium arguments. Their model posits the stochastic evolution of the term structure, with interest-rate standard deviation and bond return standard deviation

EXHIBIT 41-1

Risk versus Level of Rates

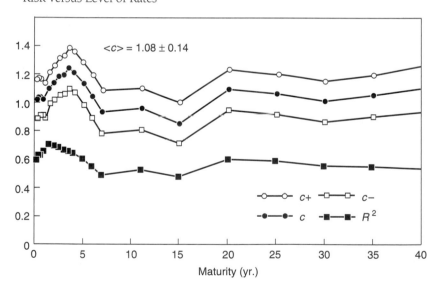

8. John C. Cox, Jonathan E. Ingersoll, Jr., and Stephen A. Ross, "A Theory of the Term Structure of Interest Rates," *Econometrica,* vol. 36, no. 2, March 1985.

both proportional to the square root of the level of rates. When rates double from 8 percent to 16 percent, volatility rises by a factor of 1.4: the square root of 2.0.

Historical investigation can probe the dependence of bond market risk on the level of rates. Exhibit 41–1 illustrates the results of a test comparing the standard deviation of monthly pure discount bond excess returns each year from 1948 to 1988, to the mean five-year spot rate observed each year. This test determined the exponent c of the relationship

$$\text{volatility} \propto (\text{rate})^c$$

If $c = 1$, then volatility is directly proportional to rates; when rates double, volatility doubles. The Cox, Ingersoll, Ross model assumes that $c = \frac{1}{2}$. The empirical results illustrated in Exhibit 41–1 demonstrate that $c = 1.08 \pm 0.14$. Within the standard errors shown in Exhibit 41–1, volatility is directly proportional to rate level. Moreover, as the R^2 statistic reveals, the level of rates explains 61 percent of the observed difference in risk from year to year. The effect is more pronounced in high-rate periods than in low-rate periods. Further study examined the dependence of yield-spread factor risk on the level of the five-year spot rate. Results were mixed, though generally consistent with direct proportionality.

Given the broad empirical and theoretical evidence supporting the dependence of covariance upon rates, forecasts of covariance based on historical data should take this effect into account.

With all this sophisticated risk model machinery now in place and integrated, how well does the resulting risk model perform?

PERFORMANCE

Multifactor risk modeling involves significant effort. Is this effort justified? Does it significantly differ from the duration approach? How well does the multifactor approach to fixed income risk modeling actually work?

To see how the multifactor approach differs from the duration and convexity approach, consider the performance of a multifactor model in the U.S. bond market. Remember that duration and convexity are both parallel yield-shift concepts. They measure the risk of parallel yield shifts. However, the term structure does not move in parallel.

The risk model views the term structure as a set of pure discount bonds of different maturities, each allowed to move independently. The covariance matrix then describes the extent to which they actually do move together. Exhibits 41–2 and 41–3 illustrate the two predominant, coherent movements of the term structure, as forecast in September 1989 based on the observed term-structure history throughout the 1980s. These *principal components* are the independent, uncorrelated collective movements of the term structure. Exhibit 41–2 illustrates the primary term-structure movement: a nonparallel shift, with short rates more volatile than long rates. A duration-based risk model would assume that a parallel shift

E X H I B I T   41–2

First Principal Component

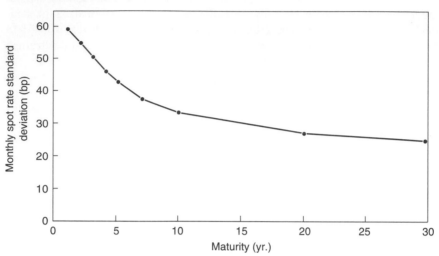

E X H I B I T   41–3

Second Principal Component

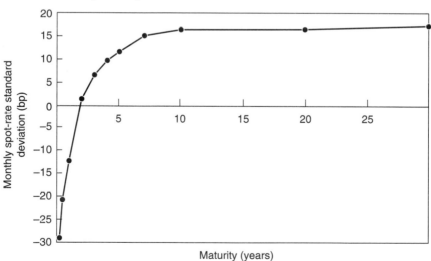

completely specified term-structure risk. This nonparallel shift accounts for 95.4 percent of modeled term-structure risk. Exhibit 41–3 illustrates the secondary term-structure movement: a twist, with short and long rates moving in opposite directions. This twist accounts for an additional 4.1 percent of modeled term-structure risk. These shapes specifically apply to the September 1989 forecast, but they have remained relatively stable from the 1950s into the 1990s, taking the level of rates into account.

To further examine how well multifactor risk modeling performs, the following test compared a simple duration model and a duration plus convexity model with a 10-factor model (pure discount bonds with maturities of 0.25, 0.5, 1, 2, 3, 4, 5, 6, 7, 10, and 30 years) in modeling noncallable U.S. Treasury security returns between January 1980 and October 1986. The noncallable U.S. Treasury market should be the simplest market to model because it requires no factors to account for default risk and no option simulation model. For demonstrating the significant enhancement resulting from the multifactor approach, this is the most difficult test. The results are as follows:

Model	Number of Factors	Percent of Explained Variance
Duration	1	75.8
Duration and convexity	2	81.1
First principal component	1	82.4
First two principal components	2	87.0
Full multifactor model	10	88.0

The full multifactor model explains significantly more of the observed variance than the simple duration model or even the duration and convexity model. The first two principal components are the optimized first two risk factors. The first principal component model employs just one factor, a nonparallel shift, and outperforms the two-factor duration and convexity model. Of course, one must construct the full multifactor risk model to identify this optimal one-factor model.

This chapter so far has described the construction of a risk model and a test of its overall performance measuring fixed income risk. How, though, does the risk model apply to a particular investment portfolio?

PORTFOLIO RISK CHARACTERIZATION

Historical analysis captures the inherent riskiness of the factors of value present in the bond market. The riskiness of a particular bond portfolio depends upon its exposure to these sources of risk.

The fraction of a portfolio's present value at each vertex measures the portfolio's exposure to term-structure risk. Two portfolios with identical distributions of present value along the vertices face identical term-structure risk. Of course, these two portfolios have identical durations. However, two portfolios can have identical durations without having identical distributions across the entire set of vertices. Such portfolios will not face identical term-structure risk.

What about yield-spread factor risk? Consider for example the risk associated with the sector yield spread. The fraction of the portfolio in each sector, multiplied by the duration of the bonds in that sector compared to bond market average duration, measures the portfolio's sector risk exposure. Risk exposures for quality factors and other factors follow analogously.

Beyond the marketwide factors of value the model identifies, there are also risk factors associated solely with individual issues. By definition, the specific risk for each issue is uncorrelated with all marketwide factor risk. It may be correlated, though, with the specific risk of other bonds of the same issuer. We can estimate this specific issue risk historically as the realized excess return risk of each specific issue not explained by the model.

Total risk follows from combining the risk exposures that characterize a given portfolio with the variances and covariances of the underlying risk factors that characterize the market, and adding in specific issue risk. This number is the predicted total variance of the portfolio excess return.

Portfolio risk analysis usually involves comparing the portfolio against a benchmark (or liability stream). Comparing risk exposures will quantify the manager's bets in relation to the benchmark. The risk model can then predict how well the portfolio will track the benchmark. For active managers, an optimizer can implement common factor and specific issue bets while still controlling risk. An active manager's utility will usually increase with expected excess return and decrease with expected tracking error. An optimizer can maximize this utility.

SUMMARY

Today's fixed income markets are characterized by complex instruments and increased volatility. In this environment, bond portfolio management must increasingly rely on sophisticated models to accurately gauge fixed income risk. Building these models requires considerable sophistication. Using them, however, should be straightforward. A good model should simplify the investment process and increase investor insight.

@ VALUATION AND
ANALYSIS OF
CONVERTIBLE
SECURITIES

Mihir Bhattacharya, Ph.D.
Managing Director, Capital Markets
UBS Securities, LLC.

Yu Zhu, Ph.D.
Director, Risk Assessment and Control
Sakura Global Capital, Inc.

Convertible bonds and convertible preferred stock are among the equity-linked products that span the spectrum from nonconvertible debt to common stock. The essential features of this class of products are as follows:

- They are convertible, usually at any time, into the underlying security, such as a common stock.
- The conversion right resides with the holder.
- The current yield or the yield-to-maturity usually exceeds the yield of the underlying security into which it is convertible.
- They sell at some premium to the underlying security.
- They are senior claims to the underlying security when issued by a primary issuer.
- They have prespecified maturity, except in the case of perpetual convertible preferred stock.

The increased volatility in the equity and debt markets, combined with the increasing sophistication of issuers and investors, has brought about several changes in the composition of convertible markets, and has given rise to the burgeoning field of equity derivatives.

Specifically, in response to the steep yield curves, the maturity of new issue convertibles has shortened. Also, step-up convertible structures have been introduced, wherein low coupons or preferred dividends are paid in the initial two to three years, and the coupon or preferred dividend rate steps up as the convertible becomes redeemable. Interest-rate volatility has focused more attention on the redemption feature in a convertible. Investors are demanding higher yield to compensate for the callability of a convertible. In other words, issuers and investors are more acutely aware of the trade-offs involved between yield and bond callability; because the investor is in effect selling back an option to the issuer, he or she is demanding a market price for it.

The notion that convertibles have options embedded in them and that option valuation is driven by, among other factors, volatility is increasingly being accepted by issuers and investors. In some situations, the embedded options can be easily separated and valued; but, as we shall see below, the embedded options usually interact with each other and are somewhat difficult to value.

This chapter focuses on the convertible valuation methodology based on the contingent claim theory. After briefly reviewing the status and growth of the convertible markets, we list the recent innovations in the product group. Then we discuss the attributes of a convertible security and the traditional valuation methods. The modern valuation methodology is introduced in its simplest form. This is followed by an outline of a more rigorous valuation model. We then discuss applications of the model for decisions faced by issuers and investors.

RECENT DEVELOPMENT IN CONVERTIBLE MARKETS

Convertible securities markets have experienced a rapid growth in recent years. A cumulative total of $164 billion of convertible securities were issued between 1980 and 1995 in the United States, far exceeding prior periods. Issuance by investment-grade companies is on the rise, as shown in Exhibit 42–1.

1991–1993 saw the largest percentage rise in the issuance of convertible preferreds, reflecting the need for balance-sheet restructuring. Equity-like securities were added to the balance sheet under threatened downgrades from rating agencies. Several very large issuers in the auto and airline industries and money center banks account for the major bulk of the issuance.

Remarkable innovations are taking place in today's convertible market. New convertible products have been brought to the market at an increasing pace. A partial list and description of these new products follows.[1,2]

---

1. A recent new product called PERCS (Preferred Equity Redemption Cumulative Stock), first developed by Morgan Stanley, is a preferred stock with mandatory conversion at maturity. Investors of this type of securities do not have any conversion options. Essentially, buying one share of PERCS can be viewed as buying one share of stock, selling an out-of-the-money call to the issuer, and receiving incremental dividends as the payment for the call sold. Because it is not a convertible security from investors' perspective, we exclude this type of security from our analysis.

2. Dividend Enhanced Convertible Stock (DECS) was introduced by Salomon Brothers in 1993. It is a convertible security that mandatorily settles, into a formula number of shares of the underlying stock, depending on the latter's stock price level on the termination date (conversion or maturity, as the case may be). It is generally issued at the same price as the underlying stock on issue date. In its simplest form, it can be viewed as a long position in a traditional convertible plus a short position in one European at-the-money put on the underlying stock.

EXHIBIT 42-1

U.S. Domestic Convertible Issuance (1980–1995) (Dollars in Million)

| | Convertible Debt | | | Convertible Preferred Stock | | Total |
	Investment Grade (1)	Noninvestment Grade (2)	Zero-Coupon (3)	Investment Grade (4)	Noninvestment Grade (5)	(1)+(2)+(4)+(5)
1980	1,435	2,924		525	761	5,645
1981	2,645	2,008		385	107	5,145
1982	1,254	1,948		100	366	3,668
1983	2,433	3,688		940	2,371	9,432
1984	2,427	1,667		356	558	5,008
1985	3,724	3,760	860	997	1,332	9,813
1986	1,777	8,339	269	1,223	3,466	14,805
1987	2,901	6,963	96	985	2,480	13,329
1988	843	2,293	1,032	103	420	3,659
1989	3,085	2,435	2,496	240	1,038	6,798
1990	3,434	1,322	2,853	162	249	5,167
1991	4,060	3,419	4,096	3,634	1,120	12,233
1992	2,461	4,576	1,546	2,148	2,889	12,074
1993	2,820	10,115	3,792	2,849	8,969	24,753
1994	1,908	4,638	566	2,315	7,327	16,188
1995	3,120	7,409	1,541	2,784	3,354	16,667
Total	40,327	67,504	19,147	19,746	36,807	164,384

Source: 1980-1992, Securities Data Corrpany; 1993-1995 UBS Securities, LLC.

Notes:

[a] Noninvestment grade includes unrated issues.

[b] 1993-95 convertible preferred includes mandatory convertibles and tax deductible convertible structures.

LYONs

One of the most significant innovations in the convertible markets is the Liquid Yield Option Note (LYON),[2] which is a zero-coupon, convertible, callable, and putable bond. From 1985 (when LYONs were developed) to 1992, more than 60 corporations, including Disney, Eastman Kodak, Motorola, Time Warner, and Waste Management, have issued LYONs or similar products in the U.S. domestic market. Total proceeds were more than $13 billion, about 28 percent of total convertible debt offered in the same period. Because they are zero-coupon bonds, they are offered at a deep discount to their face value. The maturity of LYONs is usually 15–20 years. To provide investors with more downside protection than conventional convertible bonds, the embedded put options allow LYONs holders to put the bond to the issuer on one or several predetermined put dates.[3] Exhibit 42–2 is an example of a recent LYONs issue. The issue price of $476.74 is the

E X H I B I T   42–2

Office Depot, Inc. LYONs
Accreted Value Based on 5 Percent Original Discount Convertible into 13.006 Shares of Office Depot Common Stock
Issue Date: 12/11/92

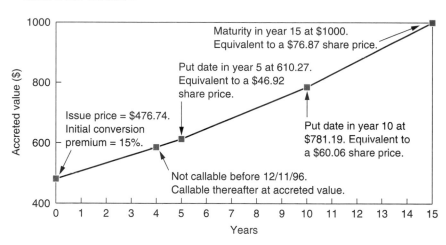

2. LYON is a service mark of Merrill Lynch & Co., and it was first developed by Merrill Lynch Capital Markets in 1985.
3. In other words, the puts are of the sequential European type. Furthermore, the puts can be *hard puts* or *soft puts*. In the former, the put obligation, which usually equals the accreted value of the bond on the put date, can only be satisfied in cash. In the latter, the obligation can be met in cash, common stock, subordinated notes, or a combination of these at the option of the issuer. Recent issues have dropped the subordinated notes alternative.

present value of the par discounted at 5 percent with semiannual compounding over the 15-year maturity of the LYON. The conversion ratio of 13.006 shares per LYON was arrived at by dividing the issue price by the initial conversion price. The initial conversion price is calculated as the stock price on issue date ($31.875 per share) multiplied by one plus the initial conversion premium (1.15).

Convertible Preferred Stock with Perpetual Provisional Calls

In June 1992, Delta Airlines (DAL) issued $1.15 billion of convertible preferred stock. This $50 preferred stock pays 7 percent dividends and can be converted into 0.7605 shares of DAL stock. The unique feature of the security is that after the initial three-year call protection period, it can be called only if DAL's share price exceeds $82.125 for at least 20 days within any consecutive 30 trading days, including the last trading day of such period. Investors will receive 0.7605 shares of stock for each preferred regardless of the stock price on the call effective date. This feature ensures ultimate conversion into common stocks with near certainty, and accordingly, the issue is given more equity credit by rating agencies than that accorded to conventional convertible preferred stock. Hence, issuers who are concerned about their credit rating may view this type of security as an attractive way to enhance their equity base. Given the motivation for issuing this security and its structure, investors should expect the security to be called for conversion as soon as the issue becomes callable.

Step-Up Convertible Securities

In the recent steep yield-curve environment, step-up callable debt has become attractive to issuers and investors alike. Following the straight debt market, step-up convertible notes and preferred stocks are gaining in popularity. The unique feature of a step-up convertible security is that it pays low coupons (or dividends) in the first two to three years, then the coupon (or dividend) rate steps up for the remaining life of the security.

For example, the 4.5 percent/ 6.5 percent of 10/15/2002 Amsco International Inc. convertible note pays 4.5 percent coupon in the first three years, and 6.5 percent for the remaining seven years to maturity. Because the bond was issued at par, the blended yield to maturity is 5.78 percent. The security is not callable for the first three years, and it is then callable at a premium such that the yield-to-call matches the yield-to-maturity on the issue date.

Because the blended yield-to-maturity of 5.78 percent is larger than the 4.5 percent initial coupon, the issuer can deduct the extra 1.28 percent as interest expense from the income statement, but it is recorded on the balance sheet as accrued liability. Note that the tax advantage of the initial three-year period is reversed when the step-up coupon becomes effective. Consequently, the issuance of a step-up convertible may suggest that the issuer expects the stock price to be above the conversion price by the time call protection expires. Failing that, the issuer will face adverse tax consequences for as long as the convertible is outstanding.

BASIC CHARACTERISTICS OF CONVERTIBLE SECURITIES

The price behavior of a convertible security can be explained by its value diagram, which describes how the value of a convertible bond is determined by its debt and equity components. Because a convertible bond can be viewed to some extent as a combination of a bond and its underlying shares, there are three lines in the value diagram representing the values of the convertible, the issuer's corresponding straight debt, and the underlying shares (Exhibit 42–3).

The horizontal axis in Exhibit 42–3 is the value of the underlying shares, which equals the stock price times the conversion ratio. This value is often called

EXHIBIT   42–3

Convertible Value Diagram

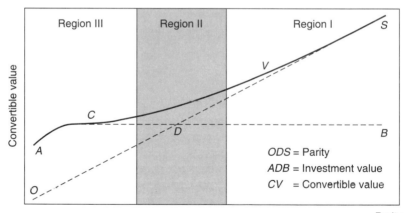

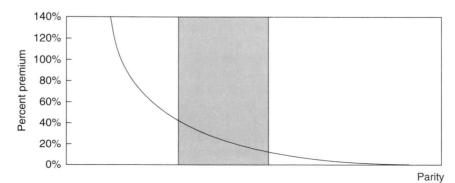

convertible's *parity value* or simply *parity*. The 45-degree line *ODS* also represents parity. *ADB* is the value of the corresponding debt, and *CV* represents the value of the convertible bond. Because a convertible bond provides the holder rights beyond those of an otherwise identical nonconvertible bond, in that it can be converted into the underlying stocks, its value should equal or exceed the larger of the value of the corresponding debt or parity. Accordingly, in the value diagram, *CV* is equal to or above the segment *AD*, where bond value exceeds parity, and is equal to or above *DS*, where parity exceeds bond value.

The vertical distance between *CV* and the parity *ODS* is called the *premium over parity*. The percent premium is defined as

$$\% \text{ Premium} = \left(\frac{\text{Convertible price}}{\text{Parity}} - 1 \right) \times 100 \qquad (42\text{--}1)$$

Percent premium, or simply premium, is a very important and commonly used parameter. It helps to segment the value of a convertible into three regions:

- *Low-premium region (Region I in Exhibit 42–3):* In this region, the underlying stock price is relatively high, and the value of the convertible responds sharply to changes in parity value and to a lesser extent to changes in interest rates.

- *Medium-premium region (Region II):* This is the hybrid region where, although parity is still the major factor, the convertible is also sensitive to interest-rate changes. Most convertible securities are issued in this region. Trading in this region is typically dominated by dedicated convertible money managers.

- *High-premium region (Region III):* If the underlying stock price falls and consequently the convertible is located in this region, its behavior would mimic that of straight nonconvertible debt. If the issuer's credit risk remains unchanged, the sensitivity of the convertible to the stock price movement would be low. On the other hand, if the default risk rises, then the issuer's common stock price and the value of its debt, convertibles included, would exhibit much higher correlation.

Needless to say, the regions do not have discrete boundaries, and depend on other parameters in addition to percent premium. Portfolio managers, however, do tend to use specified cutoff points in premium terms to invest in or out of a given convertible.

TRADITIONAL VALUATION METHOD

Traditionally, a convertible bond is viewed as an equity sold at a premium that is recouped over time due to the higher coupon of the convertible. A relevant factor in analyzing the relative attractiveness of a convertible security versus the underlying stock is its payback period. The shorter the payback period, the more attractive the convertible, especially if the payback period is shorter than the call protection period. This concept and the cash flow breakeven analysis constitute the basics of the traditional valuation method. As we shall see later, the concept of payback period is flawed, but still used by issuers and investors as a general rule. We use the following example to explain the method.

Example: Traditional Valuation Method

On July 1, 1986, Eastman Kodak (EK) issued a Eurodollar convertible bond with $6^3/_8$ percent annual coupon and 15-year maturity. Each bond has a face amount of $5,000 and can be converted into 98.6777 shares of Kodak common stock. On August 3, 1992, the bond traded at 105 (bond points, in percent of the face amount), and the EK common stock at $43.50 per share. The common stock pays $2.00 per share annual dividends.

If an investor purchased one EK $6^3/_8$ percent 7/1/2001 convertible bond instead of buying EK common shares equal to the conversion ratio of the bond, she paid a premium of $957.52 (= $5,000 × 105 percent − $43.5 × 98.6777), or 19.15 bond points per $1,000 face amount. However, this premium would be compensated for by the cash flow differential between the convertible bond and the underlying shares:

Annual cash flow differential

= Face amount × Coupon rate − Parity × Dividend yield

= $5,000 × 6.375% − $4,292.48 × 4.598%

= $121.30

This implies that, each year, the bondholder receives $121.30 more income than she would receive from dividends for buying 98.6777 shares of EK stock. Thus, the payback period should be

Premium/Annual cash flow differential

= $957.52 / 121.30

= 7.89 years

Simple derivation leads to the following formula for computing the payback period:[4]

$$\text{Payback period} = \frac{\dfrac{\% \text{ Premium}}{1 + \% \text{ Premium}}}{\text{Current yield} - \dfrac{\text{Dividend yield}}{1 + \% \text{ Premium}}} \qquad (42\text{--}2)$$

---

4. For convertibles with changing coupons or dividends such as step-up convertibles, this formula is incorrect. The payback period can be calculated by directly using its definition.

where current yield refers to that of the convertible and dividend yield to that of the underlying stock. For the EK $6^3/_8$ percent convertible bond, the percent premium was 22.31 percent, current yield was 6.071 percent, and the dividend yield was 4.598 percent. It can be easily verified that using these parameters, Equation (42–2) gives the same payback period of 7.89 years.

An alternative method of calculating payback period, although less defensible, is more commonly used. It is called the *dollar-for-dollar payback*. Under this method, the implicit question asked is: "If I were to invest the same dollar amount in buying the common shares as in buying the convertible, what would be the payback period of the premium?"

In the above example, if the same dollar amount were invested in EK stock, one could buy

$$\$5,000 \times 105\% \ / \ \$43.50 = 120.69 \text{ shares.}$$

The annual cash flow differential between the two investments is

$$\$5,000 \times 6.375\% - 120.69 \text{ shares} \times \$2.00 \text{ per share} = \$77.37$$

$$\text{Payback period} = \text{Premium/Annual cash flow differential}$$
$$= \$957.52 \ / \ \$77.37$$
$$= 12.38 \text{ years}$$

It can be shown that

$$\text{Dollar-for-dollar payback period} = \frac{\dfrac{\% \text{ Premium}}{1 + \% \text{ Premium}}}{\text{Current yield} - \text{Dividend yield}} \qquad (42\text{–}3)$$

Comparing the above two formulas, the only difference is that Equation (42–2) makes an adjustment to common dividend yield in calculating the yield advantage, whereas Equation (42–3) does not. If the underlying stock dividend yield and the convertible's percent premium are not large, the two methods would result in similar payback periods. In our example, however, the two payback periods are quite different due to the high stock dividends and the significant premium in excess of 20 percent.

Limitations of the Traditional Method

The notion of payback period is not new. Indeed, it is only an adaptation of the same method considered in capital budgeting analysis. However, in capital budgeting analysis, payback period has been supplanted to a large degree by the internal rate of return analysis and the net-present-value analysis. A pointed question for money managers then arises: Why use a method of analysis for investing millions of dollars when the same method of analysis is already considered less desirable even for much smaller purchases?

In any event, the features of the payback period are as follows:

- Dividend yield is assumed constant.
- Cash flows beyond the payback period are ignored.
- Cash flows are not discounted but subsumed in the yield advantage.
- The term structure of interest rates is assumed to be flat.

Variations on the theme include incorporating dividend growth rates and discounting the cash flow streams. Regardless of these variations, the essence of these methods is to view a convertible security as parity plus a cash flow differential with certainty. This decomposition, however, ignores a fundamental characteristic of a convertible security—the downside protection to the investors.

From the value diagram (Exhibit 42–3), we can see that the value of a convertible security is indeed equal to its parity value plus a premium. The magnitude of the premium is related to the value of the cash flow differential. However, the above analysis ignores the fact that investors have the right but not the obligation to convert the bond into its underlying shares. Because the stock price is a variable, whether investors convert or not depends on future stock prices, and cannot be predicted with certainty. If the stock price falls below the conversion price when the bond is being terminated, investors clearly would choose to receive the redemption value instead of converting. In other words, in addition to the underlying shares and the cash flow differential, convertible investors also own put options. If a convertible debt is not callable before maturity, the put option has the same maturity as the convertible and its strike price equals the redemption value plus the applicable accrued interest. When a convertible is callable, notification by the issuer to redeem it before maturity triggers another put option whose maturity equals the redemption notice period and whose strike price equals the redemption price plus the applicable accrued interest (or preferred dividend). These put options provide investors with downside protection. Not taking this feature into account would gravely underestimate the value of convertible securities.

Furthermore, for many new types of convertible securities, the significance of the payback period becomes even more questionable. For example, investors in zero-coupon convertible bonds do not receive cash income before maturity (or put date). Thus, the convertible income advantage would be zero or negative, and the payback period cannot be calculated. One may be tempted to substitute the convertible bond current yield by the yield-to-maturity or yield-to-put in the payback period calculation. However, investors will realize these yields only if they hold the bond until maturity or put date. Before maturity or put date, as the return on the corresponding straight bond varies with market conditions, the yield-to-maturity or yield-to-put of a zero-coupon convertible bond represents neither the investors' cash income nor the market returns. The payback period calculated using this parameter may not bear much practical significance.

THEORETICAL VALUATION MODEL

The modern analytic approach is to decompose a convertible bond into two parts: a corresponding straight bond and embedded options. Thus, the value of a convertible bond is equal to the sum of its investment value and the value of the embedded options. The investment value part is easy to compute. The embedded options in a convertible security are quite complicated. When they purchase a convertible bond, investors buy a bond together with a conversion option and, sometimes, a put option. At the same time, investors also sell a call option to the issuer, allowing the issuer to redeem the convertible bond before maturity. The value of all these options depends upon the future stock price, interest rates, and other market conditions. As we pointed out earlier, simple cash flow models cannot deal with valuation problems under uncertainty. Modern contingent claim theory, pioneered by Fischer Black, Myron Scholes, and Robert Merton, provides a framework to analyze convertible securities.

Example: Bond plus Warrants

XYZ Co. issued a five-year nonredeemable zero-coupon convertible bond with face value of $1,000.00 and yield-to-maturity of 6 percent. The bond can be converted into 11.905 shares of XYZ stock, but only at the maturity date. On the issue date, XYZ stock closed at $50.00 per share. The stock pays no dividends.

Clearly, this is a simple convertible bond. The only difference between this convertible bond and an ordinary five-year zero-coupon bond is that on the maturity date, investors need to decide whether to convert or redeem the bond at par. The decision rule is as follows:

> If at maturity XYZ stock price ≥ Face value/Conversion ratio = 1,000/11.905 = $84.00, then convert the bond into shares; otherwise, accept the par value.

The value of the convertible bond is equal to the value of the zero-coupon bond plus 11.905 warrants. Each warrant gives the holder the right to purchase one share of XYZ stock at $84.00 in five years. We can apply the Black-Scholes formula to calculate the warrant value.[5] If W is the warrant value, and S, K, T, σ, r, and d represent the stock price, the conversion price, time-to-maturity, stock volatility, risk-free rate, and stock dividend yield, respectively, we have

$$W(S,K,T,\sigma,r,d) = Se^{-dT}N(x) - Ke^{-rT}N\left(x - \sigma\sqrt{T}\right) \qquad (42\text{--}4)$$

---

5. See Fischer Black and Myron Scholes, "The Pricing of Option and Corporate Liabilities," *Journal of Political Economy*, May–June 1973, pp. 637–659; and Robert C. Merton, "Theory of Rational Option Pricing," *Bell Journal of Economics and Management*, Spring 1973, pp.141–183. For simplicity, we ignore the dilution factor related to warrant issuance. In general, the Black–Scholes formula should be modified to reflect the impact of dilution.

where $N(\cdot)$ is the standard normal distribution function, and

$$x = \frac{\ln\dfrac{S}{K} + \left(r - d + \dfrac{1}{2}\sigma^2\right)T}{\sigma\sqrt{T}} \qquad (42\text{--}5)$$

If XYZ stock volatility is 30 percent and the risk-free rate is 6 percent, then the theoretical value of each warrant is $9.31. The total value of warrants = $9.31 × 11.905 = $110.84. Assuming that XYZ Co. can issue a corresponding straight five-year zero-coupon bond with yield-to-maturity of 9 percent, the investment value is $643.93. Thus, the theoretical value of the above convertible bond is equal to

$$\text{Bond value} + \text{Warrant value} = \$643.93 + 110.84$$
$$= \$754.77$$

The theoretical value exceeds the issue price ($744.09) by 1.43 percent, or, as it is often said in practice, the issue price is 1.43 percent *cheaper* than the theoretical value.

The holders of the convertible bond may convert the bond into the underlying stocks only at maturity. In other words, their conversion option is a *European* option. If they have an *American conversion option*, which allows them to convert the bond into stock at any time on or before maturity, should they convert early? In this case, the answer is no. Suppose at any time t before the maturity date investor A decides to convert, and investor B does not, and will defer his decision until the maturity date. As shown in Exhibit 42–4, the terminal value of investor B's strategy is at least as large as that of investor A for all outcomes.

The above argument is valid only if the stock does not pay dividends. In fact, when investor A in the above example decides to convert at time t, the investor is voluntarily giving up her or his put option embedded in the convertible (see explanations in the previous section). If the stock pays dividends, however,

E X H I B I T   42–4

Analysis of Early Conversion (Common Stock Pays No Dividends)

	At Time t (before Maturity)	Value at Maturity T	
		Stock ≥ $84	Stock < $84
A	Converting into 11.905 shares	11.905 shares	11.905 shares (worth less than $1,000)
B	Holding convertible bond	11.905 shares	$1,000

investor A may be compensated by receiving dividends from time t to maturity T. The trade-off between the put value and the extra dividend income constitutes the so-called optimal voluntary conversion problem.[6] We will discuss this issue in more detail in a later section.

Convertible Valuation Model

In the above example, the convertible bond value is equal to the bond value plus the embedded warrants value. This type of security can be issued as a bond plus separable warrants; even if they are not separable at issue, the warrants can be stripped and traded separately. This separability makes the analysis very simple.

Most convertible securities are callable and some are also putable. When an investor purchases a convertible bond, the price includes the following four parts:

- Purchasing the issuer's corresponding straight debt.
- Purchasing the conversion option.
- Selling the early redemption option to the issuer.
- Purchasing the put option (if the bond is putable before the final maturity).

Unfortunately, these four parts are generally interrelated and can no longer be separated. For example, the conversion option is not a straightforward warrant, but a right to convert a callable/putable bond into a certain number of the underlying shares. The early redemption option is not a simple call option on a straight bond or on the underlying shares, but on a convertible bond. Consequently, we cannot directly apply the Black–Scholes formula to calculate these option values. Even if one calculates these values separately, adding them to the straight bond value would still result in an incorrect valuation of the convertible.

Although the Black–Scholes option pricing formula cannot be directly applied for evaluating convertible securities, modern convertible valuation models are based on the very same contingent claim theory. They differ in the number of stochastic variables or factors used in their construction. The simpler one-factor model assumes that the stock return is the only stochastic factor that determines the value of a convertible bond. The more complex two-factor model takes both stochastic stock returns and stochastic interest rates into account. Regardless of the number of factors in these models, almost all of them share the same basic assumptions and principles:

- Capital markets are perfect: there are no transaction costs, no taxes, all market participants are atomistic price takers, and all investors have the same information.

---

6. For more theoretical discussions on this topic, see Michael J. Brennan and Eduardo S. Schwartz, "Convertible Bonds: Valuation and Optimal Strategies for Call and Conversion," *Journal of Finance,* December 1997, pp. 1699–1715.

- Trading is continuous and no arbitrage is possible.

- Stock prices (and interest rates, as in the case of multifactor models) follow specific stochastic processes.

The one-factor convertible valuation model has been most widely applied in convertible markets. It assumes that the stochastic price movement of its underlying shares drives the value of a convertible and all other parameters (such as interest rates and volatility) are static variables. Most models make the same assumption as in the Black–Scholes model; that is, the stochastic process that governs the stock price dynamics is a geometric Wiener process.[7] The no-arbitrage conditions require that the convertible price $V(S, t)$ satisfy the following partial differential equation:

$$\frac{1}{2}\, \sigma^2\, S^2\, V_{ss} + rSV_s - rV + V_t = 0 \qquad (42\text{--}6)$$

where

V_s = the first-order partial derivative with respect to stock price.
V_{ss} = the second-order partial derivative with respect to stock price.
V_t = the first-order partial derivative with respect to time.

This equation describes how the value of a convertible moves with the stock price over time. The dynamic movement of $V(S, t)$ is restricted by the conversion feature, the issuer's early redemption rights, and investors' put options. Information and parameters of these embedded options are incorporated into the model's boundary conditions. In addition to the indicative parameters of the convertible bond, such as the maturity, coupon, conversion ratio, and call and put provisions, the most important input parameters to the model and their impact on convertible valuations are as follows:

- *The underlying stock price:* The higher the stock price, the more valuable the convertible securities, as described in Exhibit 42–3.

- *The volatility of the stock returns:* More volatile stock prices imply higher probability that the convertible will be in-the-money, thus its value is higher. However, this positive impact will be reduced when the convertible becomes callable.

- *The dividend yield of the stock:* The impact of the underlying stock's dividend yield and dividend growth rate on convertible valuation is negative because higher dividends reduce the convertible's yield advantage and act to restrain the stock price appreciation.

---

7. We assume that stock price returns over a time period Δt are normally distributed with a mean of $\mu\Delta t$ and a variance of $\sigma^2\Delta t$, where μ and σ^2 are called the instantaneous mean and variance of the stock price returns, respectively.

- *The current term structure of interest rates:* Higher interest rates reduce the value of the bond component of a convertible security. The impact on its option components is more complex: An increase in the interest rate increases the value of the holder's conversion option and the put option. From the issuer's perspective, if the convertible is out-of-the-money, the value of the issuer's call option for early redemption (via debt refinancing) decreases. At the same time, if the convertible is in-the-money, the issuer's incentive for a conversion-forcing call increases. In addition to the level of interest rates, the shape of the yield curve plays an important role in the valuation of convertible securities.

- *The issuer's straight-debt yield spreads relative to the Treasury yield curve:* A widening in the issuer's credit spreads may suggest increasing default risk, which would reduce the convertible's bond value as well as the value of any embedded put options.

Exhibit 42–5 compares the theoretical values of Motorola LYONs of 9/7/2009 with its market prices from the issue date 9/7/1989 to 3/26/1993. During that period, Motorola stock price has risen from $28^1/$_{16}$ to $65^1/$_4$, and the convertible percent premium was 15.0 percent at issue, went to as high as 43.5 percent in January 1991, and fell to below 5 percent in recent months. Exhibit 42–5 shows that the theoretical valuation tracks the market price quite well.

E X H I B I T   42–5

Motorola LYONs Convertible Price vs. Theoretical Value (9/7/89–3/26/93)

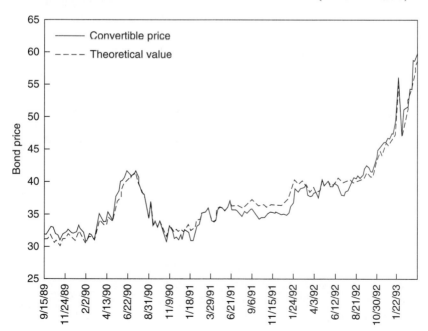

APPLICATIONS OF CONVERTIBLE VALUATION MODELS

Analytical valuation models have become increasingly important in convertible markets, both for determining terms for new issues and for secondary trading. They provide hedging, rich/cheap, and scenario analyses to investors and traders alike. Used in conjunction with fundamental analysis of the underlying stock, these analyses are indispensable in investors' investment and portfolio strategies. Throughout this section, we shall use the following hypothetical convertible bond to demonstrate the applications of a valuation model:

ABC Co. Convertible Note

Maturity	10 years
Coupon	3.0 percent semiannual on par of $1,000
Yield-to-maturity	5.5 percent
Percent premium	18.0 percent
Redemption	Not callable for five years, callable thereafter at accreted value
Stock price	$50 per share
Stock dividends	$1.75 per year (dividend yield of 3.5 percent)
Stock volatility	25 percent
ABC Co. 10-year straight debt rate	8 percent

Because the yield-to-maturity is higher than the coupon rate, the note should be issued at a discount price of $809.66 per $1,000 par value, and the conversion ratio is 13.723. This type of convertible bond is called a *deep-discount* or *partial cash pay convertible bond,* which is another innovation gaining popularity in recent years.

Parity Delta and Convertible Hedging

One of the most important results of the convertible model is the *hedge ratio,* or *parity delta,* which is defined as the ratio of the change in the convertible bond price to the change in the parity value (recall that parity equals stock price times conversion ratio):

$$\text{Parity}\Delta = \frac{\text{Change in convertible bond value}}{\text{Change in parity}} \qquad (42\text{--}7)$$

Like the equity call option delta, parity delta ranges from 0 to 1; at zero, the convertible behaves like a straight debt, and at 1, it behaves like common stock. In the case of ABC convertible, the parity delta is 0.59. It means that for a $1 increase in the parity value (corresponding to a stock price move of $1/13.723 = $0.073 per share), the bond price would move up by $0.59 or 0.059 bond points.

If an investor is holding the convertible and wants to hedge the equity risk, theoretically, the number of shares the investor needs to sell short in order to hedge each bond is equal to

$$\text{Conversion ratio} \times \text{Parity delta} = 13.723 \times 0.59$$
$$= 8.097 \text{ shares}$$

Exhibit 42–6 shows that if the stock price moves up or down by 5 percent, the hedged position would have small gains in both cases. This is because the delta of the hedged position is zero, but its gamma is positive.[8] In other words, we are long in volatility, and the volatile stock price increases the value of our position. Hedging a short position in the convertible with a long position in the underlying stock results in a negative gamma. The hedged position would have a loss whether the stock goes up or down. A better hedge would be a combination of the underlying stock and the options on it.

The middle line in Exhibit 42–7 shows the theoretical values of the ABC convertible note with respect to ABC stock price changes. The slope of the curve represents the parity delta. The curvature reflects the fact that the convertible has a positive gamma. The other two lines describe the cases when interest rates move up or down by 100 basis points in parallel. The modified duration of the convertible note is estimated at about 3.35 years, much shorter than the duration of a corresponding nonconvertible bond, even on an interest-rate option-adjusted basis. The low interest-rate sensitivity is not accidental, but due to the negative duration of the embedded conversion option. We shall discuss this later in the chapter.

EXHIBIT 42–6

Convertible Hedge Analysis

	Stock Price Changes		
	---	---	---
	−5 percent	0 percent	+5 percent
Stock price	47.50	50.00	52.00
Convertible theoretical value	796.30	816.10	837.00
Gain (loss) from convertible	(19.80)	0.00	20.90
Gain (loss) from short position	20.24	0.00	(20.24)
Net gain (loss)	0.44	0.00	0.66

---

8. Gamma is the second derivative of convertible value with respect to parity, or the rate of change in delta. Positive gamma implies that the parity delta increases with the stock price. Because delta value holds for very small changes only and not for the ± 5 percent illustration above, gamma is important when we measure the bond's sensitivity to large stock price moves.

E X H I B I T   42–7

ABC Company 10-Year Convertible Note
Equity Price and Interest Rate Sensitivity Analysis

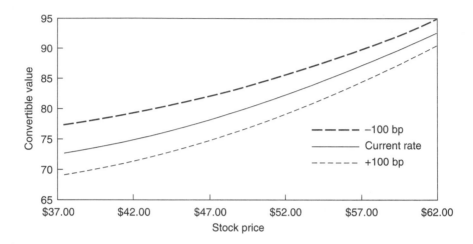

Horizon Scenario Analysis

In order to evaluate investment performance of a convertible security, investors often compare the risk/return profile of the convertible security over several time periods with that of the common stock. Exhibit 42–8 presents six-month, one-year, and two-year horizon scenario analyses of the ABC convertible note. If the stock price drops 25 percent in one year, the convertible note would have a loss of only 5.80 percent, clearly outperforming the underlying stock. In exchange for this downside protection, the convertible has to give up some of the upside gains when the stock rallies.

Premature Conversion and Critical Stock Prices

Most convertibles are converted into common shares as a result of conversion-forcing calls by the issuers. That is, if the convertible is in-the-money the instant before the convertible loses the conversion privilege following a redemption no-tice, the rational investor should convert. Occasionally, when common-stock holders are paid some form of liquidating dividend not otherwise available to the convertible holder, conversions occur without a redemption notice by the issuer. Rarely is the voting right of the common stock the chief reason to voluntarily ter-minate the life of the convertible and receive shares. There is one remaining situa-tion in which an investor might exercise the conversion option prematurely.

   Critical stock prices are the optimal stock price levels at different times at which investors should convert voluntarily, even if the issuer has not announced

E X H I B I T   42–8

Horizon Scenario Analysis of the ABC Convertible Note
(Reinvestment Rate: 3.27 Percent)

| | Total Returns in Percent | | | | | |
| | Six-Month | | One-Year | | Two-Year | |
Stock Price	Stock	Convert	Stock	Convert	Stock	Convert
–25%	–23.23	–8.27	–21.46	–5.80	–17.80	–0.62
–10	–8.24	–2.53	–6.46	–0.31	–2.80	4.23
0	1.76	2.07	3.54	4.16	7.20	8.36
+10	11.76	7.21	13.54	9.19	17.20	13.14
+25	26.76	15.82	28.54	17.70	32.30	21.39

redemption of the convertible. When investors consider converting before maturity, they evaluate the trade-off between (1) the cash income (except in the zero-coupon case) and the downside protection from the convertible security; and (2) the expected dividends from the underlying shares from the time of conversion until the maturity of the convertible. As we pointed out earlier, if the stock does not pay dividends, the convertible holder should not exercise the conversion option voluntarily before maturity. For a dividend-paying stock, on the other hand, if the stock price is high enough, the downside protection (or put) value becomes less significant, and the dividends may outweigh the income from the convertible. In this case, investors would be better off by converting before maturity. Because the convertible valuation model takes all these conditions into consideration in a uniform framework, it can be used to determine the critical stock prices. In fact, at critical stock prices, investors should be indifferent between holding the convertible and converting into shares. In mathematical terms, critical stock prices are the lower bound solution of an equation that equates convertible value to parity. Exhibit 42–9 shows the critical stock prices of ABC's 10-year convertible note.

Optimal Put Decision

For a convertible security with embedded put features, a rational investor would exercise the put option if the estimated value of the convertible immediately after the put date is below the put price. The convertible valuation model is a useful tool in helping investors make the put decision. Issuers can also apply the model to estimate the likelihood of the put being exercised, which is often an important factor in the issuer's decision.

As discussed before, the value of a convertible security depends on the future price, dividend, and volatility of the underlying stock, and the future interest rates. If the stock dividend and volatility are relatively stable, then for every interest-rate

E X H I B I T   42–9

ABC Company 10-Year Convertible Note
Critical Stock Price vs. Conversion Price per Share

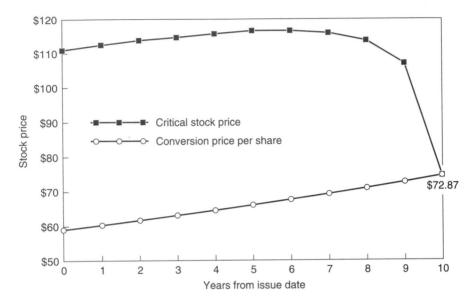

Note: Assumes a yield-to-maturity of 5.50 percent, a cash coupon of 3.00 percent, an initial conversion premium of 18 percent, and a stock price of $50.00.

scenario, we can find a critical stock price below which the put is likely to be exercised. It is important to note that the estimated theoretical value of a convertible is also dependent on the issuer's call policy, as perceived by the market.

DYNAMIC EQUITY AND BOND COMPONENTS

In order to determine whether a convertible is bond-like or equity-like, the usual practice is to use the percent premium criterion. It is commonly used as a general rule, and is often useful, but percent premium is only one of the parameters of a convertible. The following example illustrates the flaws of this method. It shows that proper valuation must take the other parameters, discussed in the previous sections, into consideration.

Suppose a zero-coupon convertible bond with three years to maturity and a conversion ratio of 10 shares per bond is not callable for life. The underlying stock pays no dividends. This convertible bond can be analyzed as a portfolio of a zero-coupon bond and a warrant. Assuming no default risk and an 8 percent interest rate, the premium and relative bond value under different scenarios can easily be calculated.

E X H I B I T   42–10

Premium of a 3-Year Zero-Coupon Convertible Bond

| | Stock | | Theoretical Value | | | |
	Price	Volatility	Warrant	Delta	p	q
(1)	$100	49.5%	$41.39	0.76	20.05%	65.50%
(2)	90	41.0	29.47	0.70	20.14	72.75
(3)	80	31.0	17.47	0.62	20.16	81.83
(4)	70	17.6	5.32	0.41	20.00	93.66
(5)	66	9.0	0.73	0.15	20.29	99.08

Exhibit 42–10 demonstrates that for nearly identical premiums, the convertible bonds can be either more equity-like, as in row (1), or more bond-like, as in row (5). It can also be shown that a convertible bond with a high premium may not indicate that it is bond-like. In fact, in-the-money convertibles with long call protection periods that are convertible into stocks with high volatility and low dividends can trade for substantial premiums.

Percent Premium and Investment Premium

Put/call parity can be applied to show that a low premium convertible is usually equity-like. Assume for simplicity that a convertible bond can be viewed as a bond plus a European warrant. From the put/call parity, the percent premium can be expressed as

$$p = \frac{\text{Convertible price}}{\text{Parity}} - 1$$

$$= \frac{\text{Put value}}{\text{Parity}}$$

(42–8)

Hence, if the percent premium is very small, it often indicates that the put is deep out-of-the-money, and the convertible is more equity-like.[9] However, as we have shown in the above examples, a high percent premium does not necessarily imply that the convertible bond is less sensitive to the underlying stock movement. In fact, when stock price volatility increases, the percent premium becomes higher, and the convertible bond becomes more sensitive to its underlying stock price movement.

---

9. Equation (42–8) is accurate only for convertible bonds with zero-coupon and zero-stock dividends, but this fact does not affect the conclusion.

Investment premium is defined as

$$\left(\frac{\text{Convertible price}}{\text{Investment value}} - 1 \right) \times 100$$

It is a more useful criterion to determine whether a convertible is more bond-like. Because a convertible bond can be valued as the sum of the investment value plus a conversion option, a small investment premium implies that its conversion option has little value. This is consistent with the notion that the convertible is more bond-like.

Convertible's Equity and Bond Components

The percent premium and the investment premium describe only the static characteristics of a convertible bond. For hedging and investment purposes, however, we need to understand the dynamics of a convertible bond. For simplicity, we assume that the convertible bond return can be explained by two factors—its underlying stock price and the yield of the corresponding straight debt—and that these two factors are not correlated. It can be shown that the dynamics of convertible bond prices is determined by the equity coefficient, β_s, and the bond coefficient, β_y. The percentage of variation in convertible returns explained by the equity component is

$$\text{Equity factor} = \frac{\beta_s^2}{\beta_s^2 + \beta_Y^2} \tag{42-9}$$

The bond component contributes the following:

$$\text{Bond factor} = \frac{\beta_Y^2}{\beta_s^2 + \beta_Y^2} \tag{42-10}$$

β_s can be calculated as

$$\beta_s = \frac{1}{1+p} \cdot \text{Parity}\Delta \cdot \sigma_s \tag{42-11}$$

where

p = the percent premium
σ_s = the stock volatility

Equation (42-11) further supports the argument that the percent premium is not the only determinant that reflects the impact of the equity factor on the convertible returns. The other two determinants are the stock price volatility and the parity delta.

β_y reflects the convertible bond's yield sensitivity:

$$\beta_y = -\text{Convertible duration} \cdot Y \cdot \sigma_Y \qquad (42\text{--}12)$$

where

Y = the corresponding straight-debt yield
σ_Y = the yield volatility

Using the same parameters as in the previous example, assuming that the bond yield volatility is 12 percent, we can compute β_s, β_Y, and the corresponding equity and bond factors. Exhibit 42–11 shows the dynamic components for the same bonds shown in Exhibit 42–10.

Because the five cases in Exhibit 42–11 are identical to those of Exhibit 42–10, their corresponding premiums are approximately 20 percent. Note that β_s decreases dramatically from row (1) to row (5), whereas the increase in β_y is relatively small. The decrease in β_s can be explained by the decreases in delta and volatility. β_y is proportional to the duration of the convertible bond, which can be viewed as a weighted average duration of the underlying bond and the related warrant, whose duration is generally negative. In row (1), for example, the duration of the underlying bond is approximately 3 years, and the duration of the warrant is –2.5 years. The weighted average duration is therefore 1.10 years. In row (5), the duration of the bond does not change. The warrant duration becomes –36.47 years, but its weight is very small, resulting in an average duration of 2.63 years and a larger β_y than in row (1).

In this example, for a wide range of parameters the convertible's equity risk is dominant, and the interest-rate risk seems much less important. This can be attributed to the convertible's short duration and the disparity between the interest-rate volatility and the stock volatility.[10]

E X H I B I T   42–11

Dynamic Components of a 3-Year Zero-Coupon Convertible Bond

| | Stock | | Convertible Dynamic Parameters | | | |
	Price	Volatility	β_s	β_y	Equity Factor	Bond Factor
(1)	$100	49.5%	0.3138	0.0106	99.89%	0.11%
(2)	90	41.0	0.2414	0.0116	99.77	0.23
(3)	80	31.0	0.1595	0.0140	99.24	0.76
(4)	70	17.6	0.0600	0.0191	90.81	9.19
(5)	66	9.0	0.0110	0.0253	16.05	83.95

10. Brennan and Schwartz compared a two-factor convertible model with a nonstochastic interest-rate model. Based on the fact that for a reasonable range of interest rates the differences between the two models are slight, they suggested that for practical purposes, it may be preferable to use a simple one-factor model. See Michael J. Brennan and Eduardo S. Schwarz, "Analyzing Convertible Bonds," *Journal of Financial and Quantitative Analysis,* November 1980, pp. 907–929.

CONVERTIBLE DEBT CALL POLICY

Because most convertible securities are callable, in order to analyze the call risk, it is important to understand the issuer's call policy. Convertible securities are called for several reasons. First, an issue may be called to force conversion into common stock. Second, in a low-interest-rate environment, if a convertible is "busted" and becomes debt-like, the issuer may also call to refinance the debt. Third, redeeming a convertible issue can also increase the earnings per share on a fully diluted basis. Finally, a convertible may be called by the issuer for strategic reasons.[11]

Theoretical Optimal Call Policy

Should or will an issuer call a convertible that is soon to be or is currently callable? This question often puzzles issuers and investors alike. In theory, at least, the *optimal call policy* answers that question. According to this theory, a convertible security should be called as soon as its parity equals the effective call price (i.e., the stated call price plus accrued interest).[12]

To arrive at this theoretical conclusion, we need to assume that the capital markets are perfect, that a firm's capital structure has no impact on the value of the firm, and that the term structure of interest rates is flat. We further assume that stocks and a convertible coupon bond form the firm's entire capital structure, that the management acts to maximize stockholder value, and that the convertible has no call notice period.

If the management policy is to call when the conversion option is in-the-money, the bond holders will not redeem but will convert instead. Because the bondholders receive higher value than what they would receive if the bond had been called earlier, this call policy is inconsistent with the management objective.

Should the convertible be called when its conversion option is out-of-the-money? The answer is no again. Suppose that when the convertible is called, the parity is below the effective call price. Because the conversion option is out-of-the-money, the bondholders now would rather redeem than convert. Assume that the redemption is financed by a straight-debt issue. This policy is less advantageous than calling later because currently the convertible coupon rate is lower than the straight-debt rate, and the call price is greater than or equal to par; delaying the call would result in net savings to the shareholders.

In summary, the convertible bond should be called when parity equals the effective call price. This is the only optimal call policy to benefit the shareholders. However, when some of the assumptions are violated, in-the-money or out-of-

---

11. Examples of the strategic reasons include maintaining voting control in the company or altering the company's capital structure and/or debt maturity structure.
12. See Jonathan Ingersoll, "An Examination of Corporate Call Policies on Convertible Securities," *Journal of Finance*, May 1977, pp. 463-478; and Brennan and Schwartz, ibid., December 1977.

the-money calls may be justified. In the following two sections, we first discuss the conversion-forcing call, then analyze the debt refinancing case when the flat-term-structure scenario is relaxed.

Forced Conversion and Call Delay

In reality, few companies follow the optimal call policy. In fact, a majority of called convertible issues were called when their conversion values far exceeded the effective call prices. In recent years, conversion-forcing calls had a call delay of 20 percent to 30 percent or more; issuers would delay calling until the underlying stock price exceeded the effective conversion price. The call delay is due to the following practical considerations.

Call Notice Period

The call notice period is usually 15 to 60 days, with a mode of 30 days. Bond-holders can redeem the bond or convert into the underlying shares any time during this period.[13] The issuer typically delays the call until the convertible is deep in-the-money so that the probability of the parity value declining below the redemption value is effectively eliminated.

Capital Structure

Under perfect markets assumptions, a firm's capital structure does not matter. In practice, however, the optimal capital structure issue is still hotly debated. When a firm calls its convertible bond to force conversion, its objective is to raise equity capital. If the forced conversion fails, the firm may have to borrow to redeem the bond. The resulting capital structure will be different from that resulting from a successful conversion. In some cases, a failed conversion may even cause financial distress to the firm.

Taxes

The existence of taxation and the asymmetry between corporate income tax and personal income tax have to be taken into account in making the call policy. Obviously, if the after-tax interest of the convertible bond is lower than the dividends on the underlying stock, keeping the convertible bond alive gives the issuer a cash flow advantage. In this case, the issuer should not call the bond to force conversion. However, it may not be optimal for individual investors to voluntarily convert because, for them, bond interests and stock dividends are taxed at the same rate.

In general, more volatile stocks require longer call delays. Suppose XYZ stock price rose to $80^3/_8$, the effective conversion price is $72, and the convert-

---

13. Sometimes, the conversion option expires before the call effective date. This is popularly termed the *screw clause* because investors could be deprived of the accreted but unpaid coupon to the conversion date. Similar screw clauses may exist for convertible preferred stocks.

ible bond mandates a 30-day call notice period. If the stock price return is lognormally distributed and the volatility is 35 percent, then one standard deviation of the stock price movement in 30 days would be

$$\$80.375 \times 0.35 \times \left(\frac{1}{12}\right)^{1/2} = \$8.12$$

This is about 10 percent of the stock price. In other words, XYZ stock may move between $72 and $88 in one month with a probability of 68 percent. If the stock price is above $72, investors will convert. Otherwise, they will redeem the bond for cash. It seems that the current cushion of 11.6 percent may not be sufficient to force conversion without high uncertainty. On the other hand, if the volatility is only 20 percent, the probability of failure in forcing conversion would be greatly reduced.

Debt Refinancing Calls

Convertible bonds pay lower coupons than concurrently issued straight debt of identical maturities. Therefore, historically it has not been common for companies to call convertible issues mainly for refinancing purposes. In the period from December 1990 to December 1992, in an attempt to fight the recession, the Federal Reserve Board lowered the discount rate seven times, and the resulting short-term interest rates were among the lowest in 30 years. The low-interest-rate environment made refinancing convertible issues a viable means of reducing debt-servicing costs. By calling convertible securities that are out-of-the-money, issuers also take out the investors' conversion options with the attendant reduction in the number of fully diluted shares for the earnings-per-share calculation.

For example, on September 21, 1992, IBM called its 7.875 percent 11/21/2004 convertible debenture, effective 11/21/1992. The bond was issued in 1984, convertible into 6.508 shares of IBM stock. On the announcement date, the bond traded at $102\frac{1}{4}$ and the stock was at $83.625 per share. Its premium was 88.1 percent; the conversion option was way out-of-the-money. This AAA/Aa1-rated bond was the biggest convertible bond in the U.S. market; it had $1.284 billion face amount outstanding, about 5.4 percent of the total market value of all investment-grade convertible bonds in the United States.

On 9/21/1992, the Treasury bond with similar maturity had a yield of 6.76 percent. Taking the corporate spread into consideration, IBM's 12-year borrowing rate was about 7.36 percent at the time. Calling the bond potentially resulted in interest savings of approximately 30 basis points to the company.[14] However, this analysis ignores the fact that this bond had a mandatory sinking-fund provision

---

14. The call price was $101.575 effective 11/21/1992, corresponding to a yield-to-maturity of 7.672 percent.

starting from 11/21/1994 to 11/21/2003 with an annual redemption amount of $96.375 million (7.5 percent of the original issue amount) with a redemption price of par plus accrued interest. Thus, the effective average maturity of the bond was not 12 years, but 7.87 years. Due to the steep upward-sloping yield curve, the savings were in fact much larger than the estimate of 30 basis points.

SUMMARY

Convertible bonds and convertible preferred stock, and, more broadly, almost all equity-linked instruments, are complicated securities with interwoven embedded options. In evaluating and analyzing these securities, the traditional cash flow analysis method is often inadequate and sometimes misleading. This chapter introduces basic principles of the modern valuation methodology. The selected applications of a simple one-factor model illustrate that the modern valuation method, applied together with fundamental analysis of the underlying equity, plays a significant role in the issuance, trading, and hedging of convertible securities. The theoretical valuation model has increasingly become an indispensable tool in convertible investment and portfolio management.

43

ⓖ THE TERM STRUCTURE OF INTEREST RATES

Richard W. McEnally, Ph.D., CFA
Meade Willis Professor of Investment Banking
University of North Carolina

James V. Jordan, Ph.D., CFA
Professor of Finance
The George Washington University

INTRODUCTION

Term-structure analysis deals with the pure price of time. Exhibit 43–1 contains a three-dimensional representation of yields on coupon-bearing U.S. Treasury securities with different terms-to-maturity for each calendar month since 1950. Even the most casual observer cannot help but notice that in most months, these yields vary with maturity and that this yield-maturity relationship itself varies from month to month. Such relationships are generally referred to as the term structure of yields. When plots of the yield-maturity relationship are examined for a single point in time, as in Exhibit 43–2, such a representation is frequently called the yield curve. When the yields-to-maturity are those of zero-coupon bonds, as Exhibit 43–3 shows, the result is the term structure of interest rates.

Regardless of how it is examined or what it is called, awareness and appreciation of the yield-maturity relationship is absolutely essential in fixed income investment analysis and management.

Some of the uses of the term structure include the following:

- *Analyzing the returns for asset commitments of different terms.* Fixed income investment managers vary their portfolios along many dimensions, including quality, coupon level, and type of issuer. No dimension is more important than the maturity dimension; it has the greatest influence on whether the portfolio will gain or lose in volatile interest-rate environments. The term structure shows the rewards that can be expected for commitments of different lengths. Properly interpreted, it can also be used to make judgments about the short-term rewards of different maturity strategies as interest rates change.

E X H I B I T   43–1a

Term Structure of Interest Rates (January 1950–March 1964)

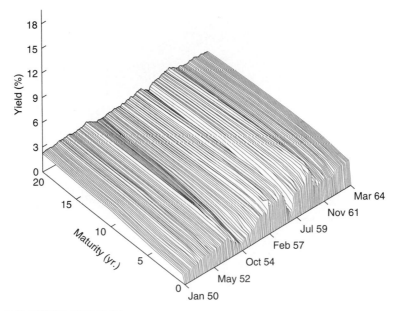

Data courtesy of Salomon Brothers, Inc.

E X H I B I T   43–1b

Term Structure of Interest Rates (May 1964–August 1978)

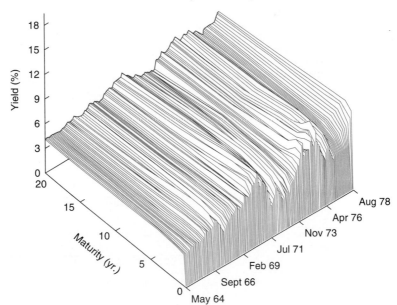

Data courtesy of Salomon Brothers, Inc.

E X H I B I T   43–1c

Term Structure of Interest Rates (October 1978–December 1992)

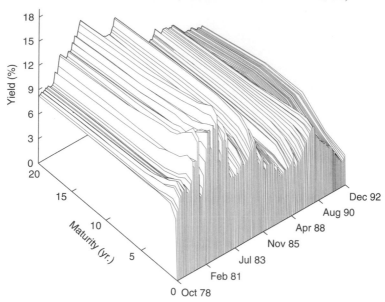

Data courtesy of Salomon Brothers, Inc.

E X H I B I T   43–2

Yields of Treasury Securities, June 30, 1992 (Based on closing bid quotations)

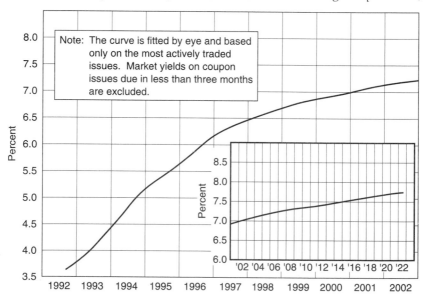

Note: The curve is fitted by eye and based only on the most actively traded issues. Market yields on coupon issues due in less than three months are excluded.

E X H I B I T   43–3

Zero-Coupon Treasury Yields (June 16, 1993)[a]

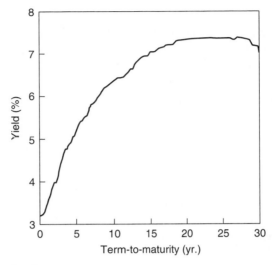

[a]Stripped interest Treasuries only.

- *Assessing consensus expectations of future interest rates.* In fixed income investment, the manager who can make better predictions of future interest rates than the consensus forecast—or even the manager who can correctly identify the direction of error in the consensus forecast—can profit immensely. A strategy based on this principle requires a knowledge of the consensus expectation of future interest rates. Analysis of the term structure may help provide this information.

- *Pricing bonds and other fixed-payment contracts.* The term structure shows the pure price of time, a price that changes from hour to hour and day to day. In pricing financial obligations, it is essential that consideration be given to the yields available on alternative investments with a similar length of commitment. The yield curve gives an idea of what these alternative yields are for coupon-bearing issues. It is common to price bonds and other contracts *off the yield curve*—that is, to set their yield equal to the yield at the same maturity point on the yield curve, with some adjustment for credit quality or other considerations.

    The pricing implications of term-structure analysis have become much more critical with the advent of zero-coupon bonds, principal-only securities, and a host of other financial instruments with nontraditional cash flow patterns. Because such securities tend to concentrate cash flows, they magnify the error from small misreadings of the price of time. Errors of this sort have accounted for large losses experienced by some investment banking firms in the past decade. An important dimension of the finance industry is the separate pricing of cash flows of different terms rather than the application of average prices with traditional yield-to-maturity.

- *Pricing contingent claims on fixed income securities.* Many conventional securities contain implicit options such as call or prepayment features, and of course a large market has developed in options on fixed income securities. The pricing of such contingent claims requires that the evolution of the term structure over time be modeled.

- *Arbitraging between bonds of different maturities.* As explained in Chapter 4, swaps between somewhat similar bonds whose prices appear to be out of line is a standard fixed income portfolio management technique. Appraising the effects of term is no problem if the maturities or durations are virtually identical. When they are not, term-structure analysis can be used to make the yields more directly comparable and thereby facilitate the analysis.

- *Forming expectations about the economy.* The shape of the term structure appears to have an impact on future real economic activity, including consumption and investment, and it may also incorporate useful forecasts of future inflation.

In this chapter, we deal principally with two questions about the term structure: What causes it to be the way it is? How can we measure, analyze, and interpret it? However, we should acknowledge at the outset that, despite the attention that has been given to the term structure (the term structure is probably the most-studied topic in financial economics), there are no firm answers to these questions. Nowhere is the well-known disagreement among economists more pronounced than in the term-structure area. Thus, the best we can hope for is more insight and understanding.

A Review of Some Basics

Chapter 4 deals with some basic aspects of bond prices and yield. At this point, it may be useful to review several of the concepts in that chapter.

Suppose that the available return on money committed for one year is 6 percent, and for two years it is 7 percent. These rates are *spot rates,* the annualized discount rates for money to be received at the end of years one and two. They would be the appropriate rates to be applied to zero-coupon bonds maturing at the end of these years.

Suppose also that we have two two-period coupon bonds: Bond A with a 10 percent coupon and Bond B with a 5 percent coupon. Assuming annual compounding, the proper prices of these bonds are

$$P_A = \frac{10}{1.06} + \frac{110}{1.07^2} = 105.512$$

$$P_B = \frac{5}{1.06} + \frac{105}{1.07^2} = 96.428$$

At these prices, the bonds will each provide the one- and two-period returns the market requires. However, the *yield-to-maturity* on these bonds—the single discount rate that equates the present value of the future flows to the price—is 6.953 percent for A and 6.975 percent for B.

$$P_A = \frac{10}{1.06953} + \frac{110}{1.06953^2} = 105.513$$

$$P_B = \frac{5}{1.06975} + \frac{105}{1.06975^2} = 96.428$$

The difference in the two bond yields arises because the yields-to-maturity are a complex average of the spot rates applied to one- and two-year money. Bond B has a somewhat greater fraction of its value tied up in more expensive year-two money, $105/(1.07)^2 = 91.711$, or 95.1 percent of its price, versus $110/(1.07)^2 = 96.078$, or 91.1 percent of the price for A, so it has the higher yield-to-maturity.

This general phenomenon, in which the yields of bonds of the same maturity depend on the patterns of their cash flows, is often referred to as the *coupon effect.* Notice that the yield-to-maturity on a pure discount or zero-coupon bond is the same as the spot-rate for money committed for the term of such a bond, provided that other factors, such as taxes, are neutral. There are no coupon effects with zeros.

In the analysis of maturity-time relationships, it is usually preferable to work with spot rates rather than yields-to-maturity because such spot rates are not tainted by coupon effects. Formally, the *term structure* deals with the relationship between spot rates and term, whereas the *yield curve* deals with yield-to-maturity and term. As this example suggests, in many instances the difference is not major, for both two-year yields are close to each other and close to the two-year spot rate. However, it could be important when the length of the commitment is long or the pattern of cash flows is unusual.

One other rate deserves mention at this point. It is the *forward rate,* the spot rate at some future point that is implicit in the existing structure of spot rates. As we will establish in the next section, spot rates of 6 percent for one-year money and 7 percent for two-year money suggest that the price of one-year money at the end of one year, or the one-year forward rate in one year, is approximately 8 percent.

THEORETICAL DETERMINANTS OF THE SHAPE OF THE TERM STRUCTURE

If buyers or issuers of fixed income securities were indifferent among securities of differing maturity, there would be no meaningful term structure; all yields would be equal. Therefore, the fact that yield curves are not perfectly horizontal suggests that some maturity preferences must exist. Reasons that have been advanced for the shape of the term structure are in effect theories or hypotheses about maturity preferences among investors. Five such theories are prominent: the market segmentation hypothesis, the expectations hypothesis, the liquidity premium hypothesis, the preferred habitat hypothesis, and the stochastic process no-arbitrage approach. Let us examine each of these in turn.

The Market Segmentation Hypothesis[1]

Suppose that buyers of fixed income securities fall roughly into two groups, one with a strong preference for short-term securities and the other with a strong preference for long-term securities. If there is little overlap in the range of maturities each group considers acceptable for portfolio investment, then the market for fixed income securities will actually be separated or segmented into two submarkets. If one group of investors gains on the other in terms of funds available for investment, then, in the absence of an offsetting response by borrowers, this group will bid up prices and thus force down security yields in its preferred submarket. The same result might occur from a relative increase in the quantity of bonds issued by borrowers in one of the maturity ranges.[2]

This, in a nutshell, is the *market segmentation, institutional,* or *hedging pressure* theory of the term structure. It appears to be particularly popular among practicing investment specialists. Commercial banks are usually the primary source of demand for short-term securities, and the demand for long-term securities is associated with life insurance companies. Advocates of this hypothesis acknowledge that these two types of institutions do not confine their investment exclusively to one end of the maturity spectrum. Moreover, they recognize the presence of other investors, including some who are comfortable operating in either maturity range. However, they also believe that banks and life insurers are so dominant and their maturity preferences are so pronounced that short- and long-term yields behave as if the markets were segmented along these lines.

It is usually asserted that life insurance company and pension fund demand for long-term bonds is stable over time. On the other hand, according to the market segmentation hypothesis, bank demand for short-term securities is more volatile. Banks prefer to lend directly to businesses and individuals when possible, putting only funds that are left over into securities. Demand for short-term loans by businesses and individuals is also quite volatile, however. In periods of strong economic activity, these borrowers demand funds for business expansion

---

1. The market segmentation hypothesis is frequently associated with John M. Culbertson. See his essay "The Term Structure of Interest Rates," *Quarterly Journal of Economics*, November 1957, pp. 485–517.
2. Borrowers might also act to offset changes in the relative position of investors in the two submarkets by shifting their borrowing to the favored, lower-interest-rate market, thereby restoring equality of interest rates. In the absence of strong maturity preferences on their part, this shifting is what we would expect rational borrowers to do, and there is evidence that some large borrowers, such as the U.S. Treasury, tend to behave in this way. However, typical formulations of the market segmentation hypothesis assume that borrower behavior is largely unaffected by interest rates or is *exogenously determined.*

and consumption, banks sell securities to accommodate their demands, and short-term yields rise relative to long-term yields. In slack periods, these borrowers pay down their loans, and banks have excess funds for which they seek an outlet in short-term securities, driving short yields downward relative to long-term yields.

Opposition to the market segmentation hypothesis is based primarily on a belief that some other hypothesis provides a better explanation for the behavior of the term structure. Advocates of other hypotheses also believe that the segmentation hypothesis understates the willingness of banks, insurance companies, and many other investors to gravitate to the segment of the maturity structure that appears to offer the highest return, thereby eliminating temporary yield differentials.

The Pure or Unbiased Expectations Hypothesis[3]

The General Idea
The expectations hypothesis stands in sharp contrast to the market segmentation hypothesis, for it is based on the assumption that fixed income investors, and possibly borrowers, collectively act to eliminate any comparative attraction of securities of a particular maturity. In effect, it acknowledges that maturity preferences may initially exist because of expectations about the future level of interest rates, but it asserts that market participants will respond in reasonable and rational ways to profit from these expectations. In the process, they neutralize maturity preferences, but they also create systematic yield differentials among securities of different maturities.

A simple example will help us understand the expectations hypothesis. Suppose that the yield curve or term structure is flat, yields are 6 percent per annum on both one-year money and two-year money, and investors are generally in agreement that these yields will increase to 8 percent in one year. Under these conditions, the term structure would not remain flat but would slope upward. Plausible equilibrium or indifference yields are 6 percent on one-year (or short-term) securities and 7 percent on two-year (or long-term) securities—the same values as the spot rates in the example of the preceding section.

To see why this is so, let us first consider an investor with a long-term, or two-year, horizon. His objective is to earn the highest possible rate of return on his money over these two years and, yield aside, he is indifferent between initially buying a two-year security and holding it for two years, or purchasing a one-year security, holding it one year, and then rolling over into another one-year security for the second year. Before yields adjust, the first alternative gives him 6 percent on his money in each year. Under the second alternative, he knows he can earn 6

---

3. The expectations hypothesis has a long history. It is frequently associated with the work of Irving Fisher, as in his "Appreciation and Interest," *Publications of the American Economic Association,* August 1986, pp. 23–39 and 88–92; and F. A. Lutz in "The Structure of Interest Rates," *Quarterly Journal of Economics,* November 1940, pp. 36–63.

percent on his money for the first year and expects that he can earn 8 percent on his money in the second year, for an average yield of approximately 7 percent per annum over the two years. Thus, he will prefer the second alternative and will buy one-year securities at 6 percent rather than two-year securities at 6 percent. As he and other like-minded investors behave in this manner, prices on two-year securities will be driven down, and their yields will be driven up. Only when two-year security yields reach 7 percent will the investors consider them as attractive as the series of two one-year security investments.[4]

We can get the same result by considering an investor who is seeking the largest total return (coupon yield plus price change) over the next year. She has a short-term horizon. Under our initial yield scenario, she knows that her total return on the one-year security will be 6 percent, for it will pay off at par in one year. On the other hand, her expected total return on the two-year security over the next year is initially only 4 percent.

To see this, assume that the two-year security has a 6 percent coupon. At the end of one year, it will be a one-year security—that is, it will have one year of life remaining. If the security is then to offer the expected yield-to-maturity of 8 percent, it must then sell for approximately 98. At this price, a purchaser will in the second year get a coupon of 6 and a capital gain of 2, for a total return of $(6 + 2)/98 \approx 8$ percent. If the two-year security sells at 98 at the end of a year, its total return over the first year is only 4 percent because of the loss of value of 2; that is, $(6 - 2)/100 \approx 4$ percent. Under these circumstances, the two-year security will be unattractive to her. Thus, she will also prefer the one-year 6 percent security and avoid the two-year 6 percent security until the price of the latter drops to 98 and its yield-to-maturity rises to 7 percent. At this point she is indifferent, as the information in the table helps to establish.

	Maturity	
	1 Year	**2 Years**
Coupon	6%	6%
Initial yield-to-maturity	6%	7%
Initial price	100	98
Capital gain, year 1	0	0
Capital gain, year 2	—	2
Return over life	6/100 = 6%	$(6 + 6 + 2)/98 \approx 14\%$
		$\approx 7\%$ per annum
Price at end of year 1 at 8%	—	98
Return, year 1	6/100 = 6%	$6/98 \approx 6\%$
Return, year 2	—	$(6 + 2)/98 \approx 8\%$

At an initial price of 98, the two-year security offers an average yield-to-maturity of 7 percent per annum, based on its 6 percent coupon each year plus a

---

4. In this example, we are requiring that equilibrium be restored by movement in the yield of the long-term security. This is purely for convenience. Restoration of equilibrium might well involve both a decrease in one-year yields and an increase in two-year yields.

capital gain of 2 in the second year on an initial investment of 98. However, if the price at the end of the first year remains at 98, consistent with a yield-to-maturity of 8 percent in the second year, then its total return in the first year is only 6 percent ($\approx 6/98$); there is no capital gain or loss. Thus, its total rate of return in the first year is exactly equal to the total rate of return on the one-year security, even though the yields-to-maturity are different. Thus, the investor doesn't care which one she buys.

This example illustrates several significant implications of the pure expectations hypothesis. First, in each period, total rates of return—coupon plus capital gain or loss—are expected to be the same on all securities regardless of their term-to-maturity. Second, forward rates or the consensus expectation of future yields can be inferred from the presently observable term structure; for example, observing a 6 percent yield-to-maturity on one-year securities and a 7 percent yield-to-maturity on two-year securities, we know that the consensus forecast of the one-year forward rate in one year must be 8 percent. Third, yields on long-term securities are equal to an average of the present yield on short-term securities plus the expected future yield or yields on short-term securities; for instance, the 7 percent price of two-year money is approximately equal to the average of the current yield on one-year money of 6 percent and the expected future yield of 8 percent.

This last implication is believed to account for the observable tendency of short-term yields to fluctuate more than long-term yields. This tendency is readily evident in Exhibit 43–1; it is also shown directly in Exhibit 43–4, which plots the mean absolute deviation (average deviation with sign ignored) of the same yields from month to month. Yields on short-term securities fluctuate considerably. Presumably, market participants regard these short rates as sometimes high and sometimes low, and expect these fluctuations to more or less average out to a "normal" level over long investment horizons.[5] This phenomenon leads to a common analogy of the yield curve with a person's waving arm: The arm is anchored to the shoulder (the long-maturity end), and the hand (short-term securities) moves up and down most as the arm is waved.

An Algebraic Formulation

It is useful to formulate the pure expectations hypothesis algebraically, and over the years a somewhat standard notation has evolved for doing this. Let $_tR_n$ be the actual, observable spot rate, with t denoting the time at which it is observed and n indicating term. In our example, we have for the one-year spot rate $_0R_1 = 6$ percent, and for the two-year spot rate after equilibrium is reached, $_0R_2 = 7$ percent, where 0 means *now*. We also need something to represent the unobservable forward rates; $_tr_{n,t}$ is used for this purpose, with the first t representing the time at which the rate goes into effect, n indicating the term to which it applies, and the second t denoting the time at which the forecast is made. In our example, rather than saying that "the currently expected price of one-year money in one year is 8 percent," we say $_1r_{1,0} = 8$ percent.

---

5. This idea about short rates is captured in stochastic models of the term structure in which the short rate is "mean-reverting;" see the subsequent discussion of stochastic models of interest rates.

EXHIBIT 43–4

Mean Absolute Deviation of Monthly Changes in U.S. Government Security
Yields and Prices (January 1950–January 1993)[a]

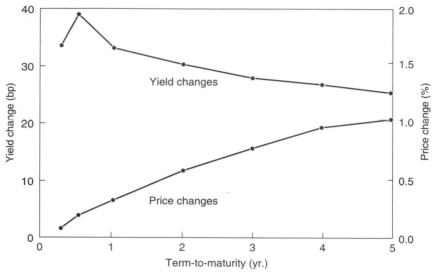

[a] Maturities of one-half year date from January 1959.

Data courtesy of Salomon Brothers Inc.

Given this notation, and acknowledging the fact that interest compounding
is ignored in our example, the proposition that long rates are an average of observable and unobservable short rates can be stated as

$$1 + {_t}R_n = [(1 + {_t}R_1)(1 + {_{t+1}}r_{1,t})(1 + {_{t+2}}r_{1,t}) \cdots (1 + {_{t+n-1}}r_{1,t})]^{1/n} \qquad (43\text{--}1a)$$

where there are n periods.

In terms of our example values,

$$(1 + {_0}R_2) = [(1 + {_0}R_1)(1 + {_1}r_{1,0})]^{1/2} \qquad (43\text{--}1b)$$

or

$$1.07 \approx [(1.06)(1.08)]^{1/2} \qquad (43\text{--}1c)$$

Notice that the average on the right side of this equation is a *geometric average,* in which we take the nth root of the product of n values, as opposed to an
arithmetic average, in which we divide the sum of n values by n. A geometric average is necessary because, with compounding, returns combine multiplicatively
rather than additively. The product of 1.06 and 1.08 is 1.1448, implying that $1
invested for one year at 6 percent and the next at 8 percent would grow in value
by 14.48 percent. Because of compounding, a yield slightly less than 7 percent
earned in each of the two years would give the same appreciation. The geometric

mean of 1.06 and 1.08 (i.e., the square root of 1.1448) is 1.06995, and this is the value that actually belongs on the left side of Equation 43–1c.[6]

We can use the same notation to derive the forward rate implicit in two observed spot rates. In general form,

$$(1 + {}_{t+m}r_{n-m,t})^{n-m} = (1 + {}_tR_n)^n / (1 + {}_tR_m)^m \tag{43–2a}$$

Thus, if we know any two points on the term structure, we can infer the yield that connects them. We can deduce the rate that is expected to prevail at the end of the shorter term-to-maturity (m) for the time interval that will be remaining ($n - m$) until the end of the longer term-to-maturity (n).

In terms of our example,

$$(1 + {}_1r_{1,0})^{2-1} = (1 + {}_0R_2)^2 / (1 + {}_0R_1)^1 \tag{43–2b}$$

or

$$1.08 \approx 1.07^2 / 1.06 \tag{43–2c}$$

Use of this relationship is not limited to one-period-ahead rates. For instance, if we know the rate on four-year obligations and five-year obligations, we can readily determine the implied rate on one-year obligations that is expected to prevail in four years; if we know the rate on one-year obligations and five-year obligations, we can obtain the rate expected on four-year securities in one year.

Alternative Statements of the Expectations Hypothesis

The pure expectations hypothesis can be stated in at least five different ways. It is useful to spell these alternatives out, both because they are often encountered and because they have different degrees of validity.[7]

> The *globally equal expected holding-period return* alternative states that expected total returns from securities of all maturities for holding periods of all lengths are equal.

> The *local expectations* version says that the expected total returns from long-term bonds over a short-term investment horizon equal today's interest rate over this horizon. Thus, the local expectations form is less comprehensive than the global version; it refers only to total returns over a horizon beginning at *present*. It corresponds to the one-period investment horizon example discussed in the beginning of this section.

---

6. With continuous compounding, the appropriate average is an arithmetic average. Letting I represent the continuous rate, where $I = \ln(1 + R)$ and $(1 + R) = e^I$, then

   ${}_0R_2 = 7\%$, ${}_0I_2 = 6.7615\%$;

   ${}_0R_1 = 6\%$, ${}_0I_1 = 5.8269\%$;

   ${}_0r_{1,0} = 8\%$, ${}_0i_{1,0} = 7.6961\%$;

   and $6.7615\% = (5.8269\% + 7.6961\%)/2$

7. These alternatives, which have many antecedents in the financial economics literature, are all summarized in John Cox, Jonathan Ingersoll, Jr., and Stephen Ross, "A Re-examination of Traditional Hypotheses about the Term Structure of Interest Notes," *Journal of Finance,* September 1981, pp. 769-99. The labels for each alternative come from Cox, Ingersoll, and Ross, except for the first, which is supplied by the authors of this chapter.

The *unbiased expectations* hypothesis states that forward rates are equal to the corresponding spot rates the market expects in the future. This is another way of saying that long-term interest rates are an average of expected future short-term rates. Both examples at the beginning of this section are consistent with this version.

The *return-to-maturity* expectations hypothesis says that the certain total return from holding a bond to maturity (a zero-coupon bond with no rein-vestment risk) is equal to the expected total return from rolling over a series of short-term bonds over the same horizon.

The *yield-to-maturity* version states that the periodic rate of return, or holding-period yield, from holding a zero-coupon bond with no reinvestment risk to maturity is equal to the expected holding-period yield from rolling over a series of short-term bonds over the same horizon. Thus, this version deals with periodic returns, such as annualized returns, whereas the return-to-maturity version is concerned with total or cumulative returns over the investment horizon. This version corresponds directly to the two-period example discussed at the beginning of this section.

In a journal article published in 1981 that created quite a stir among financial economists, Cox, Ingersoll, and Ross showed that the globally equal holding-period return variant cannot be literally valid provided there is uncertainty about future interest rates. Moreover, they also proved that the remaining four versions are *not* exact equivalents, or even consistent with each other, with uncertain interest rates.[8] According to their analysis, only the local expectations version is con-

---

8. See Cox, Ingersoll, and Ross, pages 774–77. The reason for these conclusions has to do with what is known as Jensen's inequality, which states that the expected value of the reciprocal of a variable is not the same as the reciprocal of the expected value of the variable. Because of Jensen's inequality, if expected returns on all bonds are equal for any one holding period, the expected returns on all bonds cannot also be equal for any other holding period.

   To see Jensen's inequality in an application, and to also see why the globally equal expected return variant cannot be literally valid, consider a situation in which a one-year zero-coupon bond sells for 90 and a two-year zero sells for 80, and where one year from now the two-year zero will sell for either 86.889 or 90.889 with equal probability. Thus, the total return (yield plus return of principal) on the two-year bond in the first year will be either 86.889/80 = 1.08611 or 90.889/80 = 1.13611, and the total return available on one-year bonds for the second year will be either 100/86.889 = 1.15089 or 100/90.889 = 1.10024. These prices have been chosen so that the expected return for one year on the two-year bond equals the certain return for one year on the one-year bond. The one-year zero will provide a total return of 100/90 = 1.11111 with certainty, while the expected return on the two-year zero is the same, (0.5)(86.889/80) + (0.5)(90.889/80) = (0.5)(1.08611) + (0.5)(1.13611) = 1.11111. It cannot then also be true that the certain return for two years on the two-year bond equals the expected return for two years from rolling over the one-year bond. The two-year bond guarantees a total return of 100/80 = 1.25000 over this time span. If one invests in the one-year bond for one year, earning a total return of 100/90 = 1.11111 and then rolls over into one-year bonds for the second year, the expected total return is higher, 1.11111 × [(0.5)(100/86.889) + (0.5)(100/90.889)] = 1.11111 × [(0.5)(1.15089) + (0.5)(1.10024)] = 1.11111 × 1.12557 = 1.25063. Thus, there is not equality of expected returns over all bonds for all investment horizons.

   Cox, Ingersoll, and Ross do show that in continuous time, akin to continuous compounding, the yield-to-maturity and unbiased expectations versions of the expectations hypothesis are equivalent.

sistent with equilibrium; if any of the others are valid, then there are investment strategies that will earn excess returns. Others have subsequently argued that the differences in the local expectations and unbiased expectations versions, the most popular of the five, are of second-order importance.[9] Still, in light of the findings of Cox, Ingersoll, and Ross, it is probably wise to stress the local expectations version and hence the equality of total returns over short investment horizons beginning immediately.

The Liquidity Premium or Interest-Rate Risk Hypothesis

In the expectations hypothesis, investors are assumed to act only on the basis of expected returns on bonds of different maturities; they take no notice of the possibility that actual returns (and future interest rates) may deviate from their expectations. The liquidity premium, or interest-rate risk, hypothesis considers this possibility.

Let us return to our simple situation in which there are a one-year bond and a two-year bond, each of which carries a 6 percent coupon in a 6 percent interest-rate environment. Suppose that all interest rates instantaneously go to 7 percent. What happens to the prices of these two securities?

As we have already seen, the price of the two-year security will drop to 98. At this price, it offers a capital gain of 2 spread over two years, or 1 per year, and a coupon of 6 each year. If the rate of interest remains at 7 percent, then the price at the end of the first year is 99; the return in the first year is $(6 + 1)/98 \approx 7$ percent and in the second year $(6 + 1)/99 \approx 7$ percent.

What about the one-year security? We would expect its price to drop immediately to 99. At this price, it is like the two-year security after one year has elapsed; over the year it offers a capital gain of 1, which, when added to the coupon of 6, represents a total return ≈ 7 percent on the initial investment of 99.

These price declines in response to a one-percentage-point increase in yields are 1 percent and 2 percent of the initial prices of the one- and two-year securities, respectively. For securities of even longer term, the price decline would be even larger. In reality, the price decline would not increase *quite* proportionately with the term-to-maturity. The intuition for this nonproportionality is that the more the price drops, the smaller the initial investment is, and thus the smaller the additional price decline required to raise the yield a given amount.[10]

---

9. See John Y. Campbell, "A Defense of Traditional Hypotheses about the Term Structure of Interest Rates," *Journal of Finance*, March 1986, pp. 183–193; and Miles Livingston, *Money and Capital Markets* (Englewood Cliffs, NJ: Prentice-Hall, 1990), pp. 254–56, "Appendix: Local versus Unbiased Expectations Hypotheses."

10. For example, $(6 + 1)/99$ is actually equal to 7.07 percent, and $(6 + 6 + 2)/98$ is actually equal to 14.29 percent; a price decline to 99.07 and to 98.25 are all that are necessary to give total returns of 7 percent and 14 percent, respectively.

E X H I B I T   43–5

Price of a 12 Percent Coupon Bond of Various Maturities at Yields of 10 Percent and 14 Percent

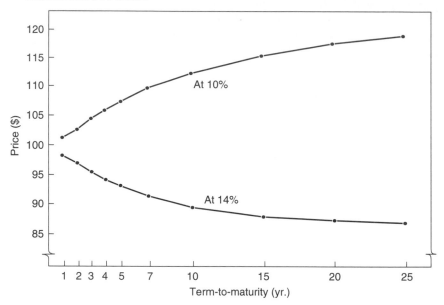

Exhibit 43–5 plots the actual prices at which a 12 percent coupon security must sell to yield 14 percent to maturity when it has a term-to-maturity of 1 to 25 years. The necessary price decline does increase with maturity, but at a decreasing rate. Exhibit 43–5 also shows the prices needed for such securities to yield only 10 percent; compared with par, these prices represent decreases or increases in price that get larger with maturity but only at a decreasing rate.

This price change/yield change relationship is purely mechanical in nature; it follows from the mathematics of bond price calculations and is frequently captured via the duration of a bond. Therefore, if all yields fluctuated by the same amount, then long bonds should fluctuate in price more than short bonds. We have already established that short-term yields fluctuate more than long-term yields; this was the message of Exhibit 43–4. Which of these influences is more important in terms of price fluctuation? That is, do short-term bonds actually vary more or less in price than long-term bonds? The answer, which can only be obtained by observation, turns out to be that longer-term bonds have greater price volatility. Exhibit 43–4 also shows mean absolute deviations of monthly bond price changes derived from yield changes for 1950 through January 1993. Here, it is evident that bond price volatility increases with maturity, first at a very rapid rate but then at a much lower rate as bond maturity lengthens.

This observation suggests a reason investors might not be indifferent among bonds of different maturities. If most investors are averse to fluctuations in the value of their portfolios, they will have some preference for short-term securities simply because their values are more stable. Therefore, in order to be willing to hold progressively longer-term bonds, investors must expect to receive higher returns.[11] Such a return increment is usually referred to as a *liquidity premium,* because shorter-term securities are more money-like; the return increment is a premium for bearing illiquidity. It might better be described as an interest-rate risk premium. Regardless of what it is called, the implication is the same: Other considerations aside, longer-term bonds should offer higher yields. In other words, longer-term bonds should on average provide higher realized total returns.

Because actual bond price fluctuations increase with maturity but at a decreasing rate, interest-rate risk premia should also increase with maturity, but at a decreasing rate. Therefore, according to the liquidity premium hypothesis, yields that would otherwise be equal regardless of term should increase, but at a decreasing rate as maturity lengthens.[12]

A formal statement of the liquidity premium, or interest-rate risk premium, hypothesis is that the market adds premia L_t to yields for term-to-maturity t that would otherwise exist, with

$$0 = L_1 < L_2 < L_3 \cdots < L_n$$

implying that these liquidity premia are positive and rise with longer maturities. Moreover,

$$(L_2 - L_1) > (L_3 > L_2) > \cdots > (L_n - L_{n-1})$$

That is, the incremental liquidity premia decrease with lengthening maturities. If the yield curve would be flat otherwise, it should rise with maturity, at first steeply but then at a continuously decreasing rate.

The Preferred Habitat Hypothesis

The liquidity premium hypothesis considers only price risk. Reinvestment risk may also be important. For example, a one-year bond may offer less price risk than a two-year bond to an investor with a two-year horizon, but it also exposes

---

11. This justification for the existence of liquidity premia is the traditional one. In recent years, the case for such premia has been made in a much more rigorous manner; for a review of such efforts, see Robert J. Shiller and J. Houston McCulloch, "The Term Structure of Interest Rates," Working Paper No. 2341, National Bureau of Economic Research, August 1987, to appear in the *Handbook of Monetary Economics.*

12. The liquidity premium hypothesis is usually attributed to J. R. Hicks. See his *Value and Capital* (Oxford: Oxford University Press, 1946). In a related vein, Reuben Kessel has argued that short yields are especially low because short securities are close substitutes for holding cash. This "money substitute" hypothesis is proposed in his essay "The Cyclical Behavior of the Term Structure of Interest Rates," in *Essays in Applied Price Theory* (Chicago: University of Chicago Press, 1965).

the investor to an uncertain reinvestment rate for the second year. The consideration of the investment horizon of investors (and borrowers) and its effect on their
maturity preferences leads to the preferred habitat hypothesis.[13]

According to this theory, investors have preferred maturities that are not
necessarily for the shortest-term securities available. Those preferences may affect the maturity pattern of yields. Pension funds, for instance, have long-term liabilities and appear to prefer long-term investments because of the reduced risk of
being forced to reinvest a large portion of their portfolios when yields are low.
They might depart from their preferred maturity range, but only for a price. With
a preponderance of such investors and no offsetting actions by bond issuers, risk
premia might actually *decrease* with maturity. The more general point of the preferred habitat hypothesis is that market participants' maturity preferences can
have a substantial but not readily predictable impact on the term structure of interest rates. Thus, the preferred habitat hypothesis can be thought of as a less rigid
version of the market segmentation hypothesis.

An Eclectic Yield-Curve Hypothesis

The market segmentation, unbiased expectations, interest-rate risk premium, and
preferred habitat hypotheses are not mutually exclusive ways of thinking about
interest rates. It is probably fair to say the majority of those who watch the money
and credit markets believe that at least two and possibly all four of these influences are present in the term structure from time to time. For example, one might
believe that relative yields are usually determined by supply/demand conditions
in the short- and long-term securities markets, with some tendency toward lower
rates in the short end, yet still believe that at some particular time the expectation
of sharply lower rates is also influencing the term structure.

One composite hypothesis, the *biased expectations hypothesis,* is particularly prominent. According to this theory, the yield curve reflects future interest-
rate expectations of the moment and also persistent (but not necessarily stable)
liquidity premia. Formally,

$$1 + {}_tR_n = [(1 + {}_tR_1)(1 + {}_{t+1}r_{1,t} + (L_2 - L_1))(1 + {}_{t+2}r_{1,t} + (L_3 - L_3)) \cdots \atop + (1 + {}_{t+n-1}r_{1,t} + (L_n - L_{n-1}))]^{1/n} \quad (43\text{--}3)$$

where the $L_t - L_{t-1}$ are incremental liquidity premia for extending maturity an additional period.

This hypothesis appeals to many because, in addition to incorporating two
elements they find intuitively appealing, it is readily able to account for humped
yield curves, which can be observed in Exhibit 43–1—situations in which rates

---

13. Franco Modigliani and Richard Sutch, "Innovations in Interest Rate Policy," *American Economic
    Review*, May 1966, pp. 178–197.

EXHIBIT 43–6

Expectations and Liquidity Effects in the Yield Curve

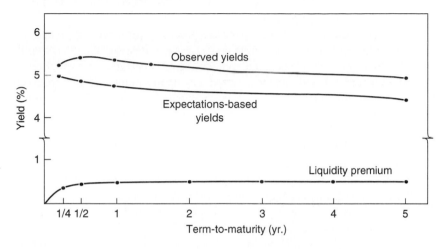

initially rise with lengthening maturity but then reach a peak and decline at the longer maturities. (Of course, rising and then declining rate expectations could also account for humped yield curves.) This pattern can be rationalized in the following way. Interest rates are expected to decline moderately, and according to the unbiased expectation hypothesis, this alone should produce a yield curve that declines over its entire length. However, liquidity premia, which have their largest marginal effects at short maturities, overpower this tendency toward a downward-sloping yield curve at the short end. Toward the middle of the yield curve and at its long end, the expectations component is dominant. Exhibit 43–6 summarizes these effects.

The Stochastic-Process No-Arbitrage Approach

In recent years, a new way of modeling the term structure has evolved; we shall refer to it as *stochastic-process equilibrium* or *no-arbitrage modeling* of the term structure. This approach has three notable characteristics or underlying assumptions.[14] First, the term structure and bond prices are related to certain stochastic factors. Second, these underlying factors are assumed to evolve over time according to a particular hypothesized stochastic process. Third, the interest rates and

---

14. See Terence C. Langetieg, "A Multivariate Model of the Term Structure," *Journal of Finance*, March 1980, p. 75.

bond prices that result must satisfy no-arbitrage or no-easy-money conditions.[15] The concept of an equilibrium term structure under uncertainty was introduced by Robert Merton in 1973.[16] Since then, a number of researchers have made significant contributions to this approach.[17]

A number of aspects of the stochastic-process equilibrium approach are worthy of comment before we examine an illustration. Possibly the most significant is that this approach is rooted in the modeling of *uncertainty*; it explicitly acknowledges that market rates are predictable only up to a point, and thus observed interest rates (or bond prices) will contain an element of surprise. With the traditional theories, this uncertainty is implicit at best, as the emphasis tends to be on expected (in a statistical sense) values.

The stochastic-process equilibrium approach is described here as an *approach* or *model* rather than as a hypothesis because the critical hypotheses involve the stochastic process or processes assumed to drive the term structure. It is at this level that the individuality and opportunity for superiority of certain models arises.

The stochastic-process equilibrium approach is not inconsistent with the more traditional approaches to the term structure. For example, the pure expectations hypothesis, liquidity premium hypothesis, and biased expectations hypotheses can all be viewed as special cases generated by certain sets of assumptions about the stochastic process underlying the term structure. This approach is better viewed as an alternative way of examining the term structure rather than as a competitor to traditional theories.

Finally, the relationship of the stochastic-process, no-arbitrage approach to contingent claims should be noted. The underlying idea of a stochastic process generating the prices of fixed income securities has a parallel in the assumed process for generating stock prices that underlies many options pricing models, such as the Black-Scholes model. Moreover, the valuation of options on fixed income securities, call provisions, prepayment features, and other contingent claims all require some assumption about the term-structure generating process. Much of the research in the term-structure area has been stimulated by the desire to value such contingent claims.

15. The actual form of the no-arbitrage condition depends on the specific model under consideration, but the bottom line is that there should be no investment strategy that can earn in excess of the risk-free rate of return on a riskless investment. For example, suppose that one-, two-, and three-year duration bonds are available. It might be possible, for example, to construct a portfolio of the one- and three-year bonds with a duration of two years and go short the two-year bond, leaving a net portfolio duration of zero. In a simple Macaulay world, such a portfolio has no interest-rate risk. Equilibrium requires that the yields on these bonds be such that the return on the net investment is equal to the riskless rate of interest.

16. Robert C. Merton, "The Rational Theory of Options Pricing," *Bell Journal of Economics and Management Science*, 1973, pp. 141–183.

17. For a useful overview of this approach and the related literature, see John Hull, *Options, Futures, and Other Derivative Securities*, second edition (Englewood Cliffs, NJ: Prentice-Hall, 1993), especially Chapter 15, "Interest Rate Derivative Securities." See also Peter A. Abken, "Innovations in Modeling the Term Structure of Interest Rates," *Economic Review* of the Federal Reserve Bank of Atlanta, July/August, 1990, pp. 2–27.

Let's look at a representative model. In an effort to analyze the yield-curve notes issued by several financial institutions, Joseph Ogden uses a model in which only one stochastic factor drives bond prices and the term structure: the instantaneous, default-free rate of interest.[18]

$$dr = \beta(\mu - r)dt + \sigma r\, dz$$

where

dr = The instantaneous change in this rate
β = A speed-of-adjustment component, > 0
$(\mu - r)$ = The extent by which the current interest rate exceeds ($r > \mu$) or falls short ($r < \mu$) of some steady-state mean level μ
dt = The passage of time
dz = A stochastic process
σ = The standard deviation of dr/r

This equation says that the change in the instantaneous rate has two components, one predictable and one unpredictable. The predictable component is equal to the extent to which the current rate differs from its long-term value, multiplied by a coefficient that measures its rate of adjustment back toward its long-term value. Thus, this component incorporates the common observation that the interest rate tends toward some normal rate and is more likely to fall when above this normal level ($\mu - r$ is negative) and rise when below ($\mu - r$ is positive). The form of this component also implies that the size of the change in the rate is greater the further the rate is from its normal level, as the predictable component is a constant *proportion* of the difference in the two. This type of model is known as a "mean-reverting" model. The predictable component of the change in the instantaneous rate is the mean of the distribution of the change. It is this mean which "reverts" to some steady-state value.

The unpredictable component is equal to the product of the standard deviation of the rate, the initial level of the rate, and some stochastic process. (Think of the stochastic process as something akin to a roulette wheel; we know a lot about how it operates but not the next value it will generate.) Thus, the unpredictable component corresponds with the commonsense notion that the interest rate is more volatile, in absolute terms, when it is high than when it is low. Because of this component, even though the rate *tends* to move toward μ due to the predictable component, the rate actually observed can move even further away from μ.

When Ogden estimated this model for the period from 1977 through July 1985, using monthly data on 90-day treasury bills, annualized values were 0.6384 for β, 0.1053 for μ, and 0.2881 for σ. The implication is that the observed rates

18. Joseph P. Ogden, "An Analysis of Yield Curve Notes," *Journal of Finance,* March 1987, pp. 99–110. The model was used in Michael J. Brennan and Eduardo S. Schwartz, "Analyzing Convertible Bonds," *Journal of Financial and Quantitative Analysis* 15, (1980), pp. 907–929 and in Georges Courtadon, "The Pricing of Options on Default-Free Bonds," *Journal of Financial and Quantitative Analysis* 17 (1982), pp. 75–100.

should have been expected to move about 64 percent of the way toward 0.1053 over the course of a year and have a standard deviation of 303 basis points per annum when $r = \mu$ (or $0.2881 \times .1053 \times 100$).

It is also possible to model the term structure by making it dependent on two stochastic factors. A popular second factor, in addition to a short rate, is a long bond rate. Michael Brennan and Eduardo Schwartz have developed such a model, which is widely used in fixed income contingent claim valuation.[19]

Both the single-factor models, such as used by Ogden, and two-factor models of the Brennan-Schwartz variety are consistent with the unbiased expectations theory. These models can be thought of as providing forecasts of the future rates that will be built into the term structure. They can generate term structures that rise with maturity and term structures that fall with maturity. Most stochastic-process no-arbitrage approaches also incorporate a risk premium factor that results from risk-averse investors and the tendency for longer bond returns to be more volatile than short ones. With such a risk premium factor, the stochastic-process, no-arbitrage approaches are consistent with the biased expectations hypothesis. These expanded approaches can generate humped term structures in addition to the standard ascending or descending term structures.[20]

CLASSIC YIELD CURVES AND THEIR RATIONALE

Exhibit 43–7 portrays four different yield curves that might be described as classics in the sense that they are prototypes of the forms into which all yield curves are supposed to fall. It is important to observe the level at which these yield curves are plotted, as well as their shape, for the level of rates plays an important role in the usual stories that are told to explain the shapes.

---

19. See Michael J. Brennan and Eduardo S. Schwartz, "An Equilibrium Model of Bond Pricing and a Test of Market Efficiency," *Journal of Financial and Quantitative Analysis*, March 1982, pp. 75–100. A reasonably straightforward presentation of the Brennan–Schwartz model accompanied by some results from using the model to price actual Treasury issues appears in Michael J. Brennan and Eduardo S. Schwartz, "Bond Pricing and Market Efficiency," *Financial Analysts Journal*, September–October 1982, pp. 49–56.

20. Another meaning of "no-arbitrage" has come into use in second generation versions of the stochastic process models. All such models are "no-arbitrage" in the sense that they produce theoretical prices ("model prices") which allow no arbitrage opportunities. However, first-generation models have no means of assuring that model prices agree with market prices. Even though model parameters, such as β and μ, can be "calibrated" based on market prices, there are not enough parameters to produce perfect pricing of actual instruments. In particular, the first-generation model cannot produce currently observed spot rates, forward rates, and zero-coupon bond prices. Although the main concern of such models is the pricing of derivative securities, users were unhappy that"plain-vanilla" securities such as zero-coupon bonds were not priced correctly. The first-generation no-arbitrage models seemed to imply arbitrage opportunities due the difference between model and market prices. Second-generation models, now known as "no-arbitrage" models, include parameters that are functions of market prices (or rates), at least for primary instruments such as zero-coupon bonds. For example, Hull and White's version of the Vasicek model, which is similar to Ogden's model, include the parameter $\theta(t) = \beta\mu$. The parameter $\theta(t)$ is computed from currently observed spot rates. The details are in Hull, *Options, Futures, and Other Derivative Securities*, chapter 15.

EXHIBIT 43–7

Alternative Classic Yield Curves and Their Explanations

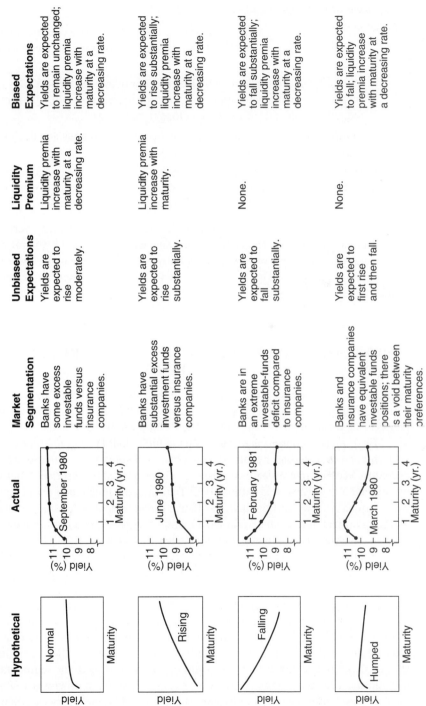

Hypothetical	Actual	Market Segmentation	Unbiased Expectations	Liquidity Premium	Biased Expectations
Normal	September 1980	Banks have some excess investable funds versus insurance companies.	Yields are expected to rise moderately.	Liquidity premia increase with maturity at a decreasing rate.	Yields are expected to remain unchanged; liquidity premia increase with maturity at a decreasing rate.
Rising	June 1980	Banks have substantial excess investment funds versus insurance companies.	Yields are expected to rise substantially.	Liquidity premia increase with maturity.	Yields are expected to rise substantially; liquidity premia increase with maturity at a decreasing rate.
Falling	February 1981	Banks are in an extreme investable-funds deficit compared to insurance companies.	Yields are expected to fall substantially.	None.	Yields are expected to fall substantially; liquidity premia increase with maturity at a decreasing rate.
Humped	March 1980	Banks and insurance companies have equivalent investable funds positions; there's a void between their maturity preferences.	Yields are expected to first rise and then fall.	None.	Yields are expected to fall; liquidity premia increase with maturity at a decreasing rate.

The four forms are these:

- *Normal.* Interest rates are at moderate levels. Yields rise continuously with increasing maturity but with a gentle and continuously decreasing slope.
- *Rising.* Interest rates are low by historical or other standards. Yields rise substantially with increasing term-to-maturity, but possibly with some reduction in the rate of increase at longer maturities.
- *Falling.* Yields are extremely high by historical standards and decline over the entire maturity range of the yield curve.
- *Humped.* This is the same as the curve in Exhibit 43–6. Interest rates are high by historical standards. The yield curve first rises with increasing maturity, but then peaks and declines at the longer maturities.

Exhibit 43–7 also summarizes the stories that can be told under a variety of term structure theories to account for these shapes. Notice that in several cases there is no adequate single explanation for the yield-curve shape under the liquidity premium hypothesis. This is consistent with the earlier observation that the liquidity premium hypothesis is most often regarded as an add-on rather than a free-standing hypothesis.

EMPIRICAL EVIDENCE ON THE TERM-STRUCTURE HYPOTHESES

In principle, it should be possible to look at the numerical record and establish which of the various hypotheses of the term structure is most nearly valid. In practice, such validation is extremely difficult for a variety of reasons.

First, market consensus expectations, which would be especially useful in verifying the expectations hypothesis, are observable only with difficulty and imperfectly. Second, interest-rate changes are characterized by surprise rather than by predictability. Thus, it is extremely difficult to conclude much about a priori expectations from ex post predictions. Third, measurement of liquidity premia is extremely difficult in an uncertain world, and liquidity premia may change over time in a manner that obscures any more basic relationships.

Finally, the two theories most at odds conceptually—the market segmentation and expectations hypotheses—often are both consistent with observed yield curves. For example, when the yield curve is low by historical standards but slopes steeply upward, the expectations hypothesis holds that yields are expected to rise. However, periods when interest rates are low also tend to be periods of slack economic activity and low short-term loan demand, so banks are in a surplus funds position compared with life insurance companies. These conditions should also produce upward-sloping yield curves according to the segmentation hypothesis. The two stories are readily reversed to explain downward-sloping yield curves. Unfortunately, if two theories predict similar yield patterns, then it is difficult to differentiate between them.

Nevertheless, it is useful to look at some of the evidence that has been brought forth on the various hypotheses.[21] This evidence does permit some very general, tentative conclusions. In a number of instances, the form of the evidence should be of interest to fixed income investors in its own right.

Interest-Rate Risk or Liquidity Premia

This is the hypothesis on which the evidence is the most unequivocal, and it tends to add up to a strong case for the presence of interest-rate risk or liquidity premia.

Possibly the most obvious evidence is the behavior of yields over long periods of time. For example, analysis of the term-structure numbers underlying Exhibit 43–1 reveals that yields on securities of the shortest term have tended to be below those on longer term securities the majority of the time over the past three decades, as shown in the following table.

	Number (Proportion) of Times	
	Short Rate ≤ Long Rate	Short Rate > Long Rate
3-month Treasury bills versus 6-month Treasury bills[a]	390 (.954)	19 (.046)
3-month Treasury bills versus 1-year bonds	481 (.930)	36 (.070)
6-month Treasury bills versus 1-year bonds[a]	357 (.873)	52 (.127)

[a]Six-month Treasury bill series commenced January 1959.

It is also useful to look at long-run total returns, which consider changes in value as well as coupon income on longer term securities. The well-known Ibbotson-Sinquefield total return series, which looks at monthly rates of return from the beginning of 1926 through the end of 1993, reveals an average annual rate of return on short-term bills (maturities of just over one month) of 3.7 percent per annum versus 5.4 percent per annum on long-term government bonds (maturities of 20 years).[22] This result occurs despite the general upward trend of interest rates over many of these years, which tended to produce capital losses on average in the long-term bond series.

Although the evidence on the existence of liquidity premia is substantial, there is no consensus on their behavior over time. Some researchers find that liquidity premia are constant over time, or at least that they do not vary with time, whereas others report time-varying liquidity premia. In the latter camp, some researchers have had limited success in relating liquidity premia to considerations such as the level of business confidence. Others have reported that liquidity pre-

---

21. A standard term-structure reference source that reviews evidence bearing on the alternative theories in much more detail is James C. Van Horne's *Financial Market Rates and Flows*, 4th edition (Englewood Cliffs, NJ: Prentice-Hall, 1994), especially Chapters 4 and 5.
22. *Stocks, Bonds, Bills, and Inflation: 1993 Yearbook* (Chicago, IL: Ibbotson Associates, 1993), Exhibit 9, p. 33.

mia vary directly with the level of interest rates, suggesting some sort of a proportional relationship or inverse relationship with the level of interest rates—which is consistent with the notion that interest rates are regarded as more likely to fall if they are high and more likely to rise if they are low.[23]

The Expectations Hypothesis

It is evident that if the liquidity premium hypothesis is valid, then the pure or unbiased expectations hypothesis cannot be. What about the biased expectations hypothesis, in which the term structure reflects expected future interest rates as well as liquidity premia?

There have been many tests of this hypothesis, and we will review some of them. However, it may be useful to keep in mind that the evidence in support of the expectations hypothesis is extraordinarily weak, to say the least. As one researcher in this area has observed, "If the attractiveness of an economic hypothesis is measured by the number of papers which statistically reject it, the expectations hypothesis is a knockout."[24]

Tests of the expectations hypothesis generally take three forms. One test is to look at the equality of realized returns on securities of different maturity through time. The examination of the Ibbotson-Sinquefield results in the previous section is representative of this type of test.

In one of the classic papers on the term structure, J. M. Culbertson examined weekly holding period returns on Treasury bills (the longest outstanding) and Treasury bonds (Culbertson used a bond of approximately 19 years' maturity) for all of 1953. Culbertson detected little evidence of parallel movements in holding period returns; as a result, he indicated, "The conclusion to which we seem forced to turn is that speculative activity (i.e., activity that should equate holding period returns), dominant though it can be in very short-run movements, does not determine the broad course of interest rates or of interest-rate relationships."[25]

In contrast, Jacob Michaelson looked at weekly holding period returns on U.S. government securities with maturities ranging from one week to more than 10 years over the 1951–1962 period.[26] He first observed a tendency for average realized total returns to increase with terms to maturity of 1 to 13 weeks over this overall period, and in a number of subperiods typified by cyclical upturns or downturns in interest rates. These results are consistent with what one would expect in a market dominated by the biased expectations theory in which realized returns on short-term securities conform closely to anticipations. He then looked

23. See Van Horne, *Financial Market Rate and Flows,* pp. 124–125, for a review of some of the studies in this area.
24. Kenneth Froot, "New Hope for the Expectation Hypothesis of the Term Structure of Interest Rates," *Journal of Finance,* June 1989, p. 283.
25. J. M. Culbertson, "The Term Structure of Interest Rates," *Quarterly Journal of Economics,* November 1957, pp. 485–517. This particular statement appears on pages 508 and 509.
26. Jacob B. Michaelson, "The Term Structure of Interest Rates and Holding Period Yields in Government Securities," *Journal of Finance,* September 1965, pp. 444–63.

at the correlation between total returns on the 13-week and the longer maturity series. The correlations obtained in this way were uniformly positive. On this basis, he concluded that the biased expectations hypothesis was supported.

Another popular test of the biased expectations hypothesis examines the pattern of revisions in yield curves with the passage of time. Such tests accept the validity of the so-called error-learning model of the formation of economic expectations. According to this model, expectations of the more distant future will be revised when expectations of the more immediate future are found to be in error, and they will be revised in the same direction. As an example of this in the present context, suppose that the market routinely forecasts some rate both three months into the future and six months into the future. If after three months have elapsed the actual rate is below the forecast made three months previously, then the market might be expected to revise downward the six-month forecast of three months ago. That is, the revision of the rate forecast implied by the term structure should be related directly to errors that are discovered in prior implicit forecasts. If this actually seems to happen, the conclusion is that (1) the error-learning model captures the way in which forecasts are made, and (2) expectations of future rates are embedded in present rates.

This test was devised by David Meiselman, and his work on the subject is a standard reference.[27] However, for our purposes, it may be more useful to look at a more recent study using a variant of this technique by Richard Worley and Stanley Diller.[28]

Their results are summarized in Exhibit 43–8. The upper panel of this figure shows the errors in forecasts of three-month rates made three months earlier; that is, the actual three-month rate is subtracted from the three-month rate that was implied by the term structure three months earlier (or $_tr_{3,t-3} - tR_3$). Notice that an inverted scale is used, so large underestimates of actual rates are near the top of the plot and large overestimates are near the bottom. The lower panel shows the coincident changes in forecasted future rates—the difference in three-month rates expected in three months and the same three-month rate that was implied by the term structure three months previously (or $_{t+3}r_{3,t} - {}_{t+3}r_{3,t-3}$). These values are plotted in the usual way so, for example, a positive number means that the forecast for rates three months out has been raised. The plotted values are based on monthly observations for 1966 through most of 1976.

It is evident from the figure that there is a close correlation between forecast errors and revisions in the forecasts. Underestimates in prior forecasts are associated with increases in forecasts of the future and, conversely, overestimates are associated with decreases in future forecasts. Although such association does not prove that the term structure is based on expectations of future interest rates,[29] it is consistent with the expectations hypothesis.

---

27. David Meiselman, *The Term Structure of Interest Rates* (Englewood Cliffs, NJ: Prentice-Hall, 1962).

28. Richard B. Worley and Stanley Diller, "Interpreting the Yield Curve," *Financial Analysis Journal*, November–December 1976, pp. 37–45.

29. As Livingston points out in *Money and Capital Markets,* such evidence simply shows that forward rates are correlated. The expectations hypothesis maintains much more than this.

E X H I B I T   43–8

Worley-Diller Analysis of the Influence of Forecast Errors on Forecast Changes

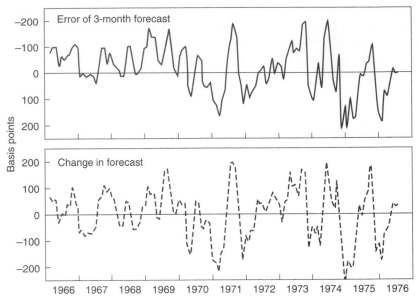

R. B. Worley and S. Diller, "Interpreting the Field Curves," *Financial Analysts Journal,* November–December 1976, p. 43.

A third approach to testing the expectations hypothesis is based on its implication that forecasts of future interest rates are embedded in the present term structure of interest rates. If the expectations considered tend to dominate the slope of the yield curve *and* if the market in the aggregate possesses adequate forecasting ability, then we should find that the term structure actually does forecast future interest rates with some degree of accuracy. This is the approach that has dominated the term-structure literature and that should be of greatest interest to persons who must actually make fixed income investment decisions. Unfortunately, the evidence in this respect is also equivocal at best.

If forecasts of future interest rates are embedded in the term structure, then long-term yields should lead short-term yields in time. For example, suppose that market participants raise their estimates of future short-term interest rates. This change should have no impact on current short rates, but according to the expectations hypothesis, it should raise current long rates. If these forecasts are correct, then in the future the actual short rate should also rise. This relationship was used by Frederick R. Macaulay in a test reported in his landmark volume *Some Theoretical Problems Suggested by the Movement of Interest Rates, Bond Yields, and Stock Prices in the United States Since 1856.*[30] Macaulay examined the relationship for the 1890–1913 period between yields on call money and on 90-day loans and found

---

30. New York: National Bureau of Economic Research, 1938.

some evidence of the latter yield series leading the former. However, he also discovered a perverse relationship at the long end of the term structure: When the yield curve was upward-sloping, long-term rates seemed to fall more often than rise.

Forecasting tests of the expectations hypothesis have become quite popular in recent years. These studies, most of which use sophisticated econometric and modeling techniques, almost always reject the expectations hypothesis in a statistical sense as a valid model of the term structure. However, their results are frequently consistent with those of Macaulay. A number of recent investigations have found returns on long bonds to be positively related to the slope of the yield curve, a result that is at odds with the expectations hypothesis but quite consistent with Macaulay's results.[31] On the other hand, several more recent studies find evidence that the term structure has some ability to predict changes in short-term interest rates. As Campbell and Shiller observe, "In a nutshell, when the spread [of long rates over short rates] is high the long rate tends to fall and the short rate tends to rise."[32]

An investigation by Eugene Fama is representative of the short-term interest rate studies.[33] Working with monthly Treasury bill data, he estimated two relationships. For the first, he began with the proposition that the observed spot rate should be equal to the associated forward rate previously embedded in the term structure. He then subtracted the one-period spot rate from both sides of the relationship and estimated, for one-month horizons and investment periods,

$$_1R_1 - {_0R_1} = a + b_a({_1r_{1,0}} - {_0R_1}) \qquad (43\text{--}4a)$$

where time is measured in months. This says that the change in one-month spot rates from one month to the next is equal to a constant plus a coefficient b_a times the amount by which the forward rate for the second month exceeded the first month's spot rate. According to the unbiased expectation hypothesis, b_a should be equal to 1.0.

Fama also related the excess of the one-month holding period return on two-month Treasury bills over the one-month rate to the right-hand side of Equation 43–4a:

$$HPR_{2,1} - {_0R_1} = a + b_b({_1r_{1,0}} - {_0R_1}) \qquad (43\text{--}4b)$$

where $HPR_{2,1}$ is the total return on two-month bills over the first month. The basis for this equation is that any excess return on two-month bills held for one month over the one-month risk-free return, the left-hand side, represents a realized liquidity premium for investing in two-month bills rather than in the risk-free asset. The equation relates this possible realized liquidity premium to the difference in the forward rate and the spot rate. If this difference is due solely to liquidity

31. For example, see John Y. Campbell and Robert J. Shiller, "Yield Spreads and Interest Rate Movements: A Bird's Eye View," *Review of Economic Studies,* May 1991, pp. 495–514; and Werner F. M. De Bondt and Mary M. Bange, "Inflation Forecast Errors and Time Variation in Term Premia," *Journal of Financial and Quantitative Analysis,* December 1992, pp. 479–496.

32. Campbell and Shiller, "Yield Spreads," p. 496.

33. Eugene Fama, "The Information in the Term Structure,"*Journal of Financial Economics*, December 1984, pp. 509–528.

premia and if these liquidity premia actually show up in realized returns, then b_b should be equal to 1.0. However, b_b should be equal to 0.0 if differences in forward and spot rates are solely due to interest-rate expectations embedded in the term structure. Thus, these two models gave Fama both the means to assess the forecasting ability of the term structure and an opportunity to gain insight into what was causing the term structure to vary in shape—either changing interest-rate expectations or changing liquidity premia.

When the two equations were estimated with monthly interest rates and investment horizons (he also extended the analysis out to six months), b_a was 0.46 with an equation R^2 of 0.13, and b_b was 0.55 with an equation R^2 of 0.17. Both b_a and b_b, although positive, were significantly less than 1.0. Fama interpreted those results as providing support for the forecasting ability of the term structure and for the proposition that variations in the term structure show up in both realized liquidity premia and changes in spot rates. Together, these two propositions lend support to the biased expectation hypothesis. Finally, Fama interpreted the fact that b_a was less than 1.0 as providing evidence that the liquidity premia varied over time.

Time variations in liquidity premia clearly reduce the forecasting efficacy of the term structure. Moreover, recent studies have suggested that the interest-rate forecasting ability of the term structure may be compromised because the interest-rate expectations it incorporates are not rational in the sense that they incorporate all available information. More specifically, it has been suggested that the forecasts of future short rates embedded in the term structure do not adequately reflect observed short-term interest rates (that is, they *underreact* to changes in short rates).[34] There is also some evidence that long-term inflation expectations and thus longer interest rates respond more sluggishly to new information than do short-term inflation expectations and interest rates.[35] These two possibilities are not inconsistent with each other, but they are consistent with a situation in which market participants are slow to adjust their expectations of inflation and interest rates to changed circumstances, which is just the pattern of behavior one might expect in a real market. In addition, there is obviously a large element of surprise in actual interest-rate changes. For all these reasons, the term structure's forecasts of interest rates may do a poor job of forecasting actual interest rates, even though the expectations hypothesis provides a valid explanation of term structure formation.

In recent years, a new round of statistical analysis of the term structure has been stimulated by interest in a concept known as *cointegration*. Cointegration may be described as a set of statistical procedures for modeling variables, such as a short rate and a long rate, that cannot diverge by too great an extent in the long run even if in the short run they can act somewhat independently. For example, a study by Michael Bradley and Stephen Lumpkin finds that rates of the term struc-

---

34. Froot, "New Hope for the Expectations Hypothesis of the Term Structure of Interest Rates."
35. De Bondt and Bange, "Inflation Forecast Errors and Time Variation in Term Premia."

ture are cointegrated, which is consistent with arbitrage acting to restrain divergences between short and long rates, and that forecasts of future rates are improved by using cointegration procedures.[36] This line of research is still in its early stages. So far, it has not materially changed our understanding of the relative roles of expectations and liquidity premia.

It is disappointing that all of this research does not yield more uniform conclusions.[37] However, it still has a number of implications that should be significant to practicing fixed income investment managers.

- The evidence in favor of positive liquidity premia is reasonably strong. Therefore, the unbiased expectations hypothesis cannot be correct. An obvious implication is that fixed income investors should expect to earn higher returns, on average, from extending maturities. This positive reward for bearing more price risk appears to be especially pronounced at the short end of the term structure.

- Another clear implication is that these liquidity premia cannot be assumed to be constant. This is unfortunate because it suggests that a change in the shape of the yield curve does not necessarily reveal a change in expected future interest rates. Yield curves might be decreasing in slope, for example, just when future rate expectations are increasing because they are more than offset by a decline in risk premia.[38]

- On the other hand, changing expectations do appear to exert some impact on the term structure. For this reason, it is not safe to attribute all change on the yield curve solely to changing liquidity premia.

- Finally, the forecasting accuracy of such expectations of future rates that are embedded in the term structure appears to be very poor. Therefore, even if one has deduced that a change in the shape of the yield curve is

---

36. See Michael G. Bradley and Stephen A. Lumpkin, "The Treasury Yield Curve as a Cointegrated System," *Journal of Financial and Quantitative Analysis,* September 1992, pp. 449–463.

37. Evidence from other countries is similarly inconclusive: Two studies reject pure expectations and find time-varying risk premia. See Tom Engsted, "The Term Structure of Interest Rates in Denmark, 1982–89," *Bulletin of Economic Research,* January 1993, pp. 19–37; Ying K. Yip, "The Information Content and Usefulness of the Term Structure of the New Zealand Bank Bill Market," *Accounting & Finance,* November 1991, pp. 1–12. Mark P. Taylor, "Modelling the Yield Curve," *Economic Journal,* May 1992, pp. 524–532, also rejects the pure expectations hypothesis but fails in an attempt to model time-varying risk premia (U.K. data). However, Taylor finds support for the market segmentation hypothesis. Finally, in another study of U.K. data—Terence C. Mills, "The Term Structure of UK Interest Rates: Tests of the Expectations Hypothesis," *Applied Economics,* April 1991, pp. 599–606—the expectations hypothesis is not rejected.

38. Because of large time-varying risk premia, at least one group of observers has dismissed the biased expectation theory as "almost vacuous" even if it is technically correct; indeed, they regard such liquidity premia as little more than a *deus ex machina* to rescue the theory. See Gregory Mankiw and Lawrence Summers, "Do Long-Term Interest Rates Overreact to Short-Term Interest Rates?" *Brooking Paper on Economic Activity,* 1984, p. 239.

caused by changing interest-rate expectations, it would be very unwise to base investment decisions on those expectations.

In sum, the expectations hypothesis as it is usually presented appears to be almost a caricature of reality, both as a description of how the term structure is formed and what future interest rates will be.

In light of this conclusion, a reasonable course of action would be the same course that a person who had never been exposed to the expectations theory might follow: Borrow long when long rates are below short ones, and borrow short when short rates are below long ones, or invest long when the yield curve is upward sloping and invest short when it is downward sloping. Indeed, this is just what the familiar yield-curve-riding operation attempts to do. However, in longer maturities, such a strategy might be quite risky; rejection of the expectation hypothesis does not imply that easy money can be made by betting against it.[39]

The Market Segmentation Hypotheses

Empirical evidence on these hypotheses is limited. One of the more relevant studies, by Michael Echols and Jan Walter Elliott,[40] was part of a larger study of term-structure influences. These authors worked with monthly data from the beginning of 1964 through the end of 1971. They first made estimates of forward rates from a model that considers macroeconomic variables, changes in the money supply, the net budgetary position, net export deficit or surplus, and the like. These estimates were refined to include the measured effects of a liquidity premium. An effort was then made to explain differences in these estimated forward rates and forward rates that were actually observed by use of a supply and a demand variable. The supply measure was the ratio of the quantity of government bonds outstanding with 5 or fewer years to maturity to the quantity of bonds with 10 or more years to maturity. The demand measure was the ratio of the stock of bank funds invested in U.S. government securities to the stock of insurance company funds invested in this way. Echols and Elliott found that an increase in bank holdings relative to insurance company holdings tended to push down forward rates, especially at shorter maturities. This result is as predicted by the segmentation hypothesis.

---

39. For example, Mankiw and Summers use their empirical results from the 1963–1983 period to analyze the strategy of going short in three-month Treasury bills in order to purchase 20-year Treasury bonds when the yields are 10 percent and 13 percent, respectively. This strategy would have generated an expected profit, before transactions cost, of $12 per $1,000 over a three-month period. However, at rate change levels observed in the 1979–1983 period, the standard deviation around this $12 profit would be $165, and the probability of a loss in any single period would be above 45 percent.

40. Michael E. Echols and Jan Walter Elliott, "Rational Expectations in a Disequilibrium Model of the Term Structure," *American Economic Review,* March 1976, pp. 28–74.

The same variables were also used in an effort to explain actual yield spreads, the excess of 12-year bond yields over the three-month Treasury bill rate. In this investigation, the spread was negatively related to relative institutional participation—more bank funds in government securities compared with insurance company funds meant *smaller* spreads. Moreover, here they found that an increase in the relative quantity of short-term bonds outstanding actually tended to *raise* the spread. Neither of these results is consistent with the segmented market hypothesis as it is usually conceived.

The Stochastic-Process No-Arbitrage Approach

Most applications of the stochastic-process no-arbitrage approach to modeling the term structure have been directed toward valuing either specific options embedded in bonds or bonds with a significant options component, such as mortgage pass-through securities; although the valuations obtained in these applications have generally been reasonable and close to observed prices, the length of the time commitment has not been the critical issue.

An interesting investigation that does address term-structure applications more directly appears in a paper by Michael Ehrhardt, David Johnson, and Joseph Odgen.[41] These authors compared the efficiency of several bond-pricing approaches by applying them to a sample of 139 Treasury bonds spread across the maturity spectrum as of July 31, 1985. Maturities ranged up to 30 years, and coupons varied from 11.465 to 16.125 and prices ranged from 88.98 to 139.42. On this date, the yield curve was upward sloping. When the stochastic-process no-arbitrage approach was used to value these bonds using historical estimates of the model inputs with no liquidity premium, the root mean squared error (RMSE, or square root of the average squared deviation of an individual bond's price from the model prediction) was 4.125 dollars per hundred dollars of par value. The introduction of a historical liquidity premium reduced the RMSE to 2.933. These values compare to an RMSE of 0.855 obtained by pricing the bonds with optimal inputs—optimal in the sense that they were chosen to fit the prices as closely as possible. The errors from this approach were of the same order of magnitude as those obtained from direct statistical term-structure estimation, a standard approach to term-structure estimation described later in this chapter.

Ehrhardt, Johnson, and Odgen then stepped ahead to August 31, 1985 and repriced the same bonds. Using the inputs that were optimal at the end of the preceding month, the RMSE was 1.125, which compares favorably with the error obtained with the then-optimal values of 0.916.

---

41. Michael C. Ehrhardt, David Johnson, and Joseph Odgen, "An Examination of Alternative Bond Pricing Models," Working Paper, The University of Tennessee, 1988. See also Michael J. Brennan and Eduardo S. Schwartz, "Bond Pricing and Market Efficiency," pp. 49–56, for results from applying a two-factor stochastic-process model to price Treasury issues.

These results, and those of other studies, are quite encouraging regarding the value of stochastic-process no-arbitrage modeling of the term structure.[42] However, much remains to be done in terms of refining and testing this approach.

ANALYZING THE TERM STRUCTURE

For many investors, an occasional rundown on yield curves as published daily by *The Wall Street Journal* and other periodicals will be sufficient to keep an eye on the term structure. Others will want to be more formal in their analysis. In this section, we review some ways of monitoring the term structure.

Published Yield Curves

Possibly the most familiar sources of term structure data are the yield curves published each month in the *U.S. Treasury Bulletin;* the yield curve in Exhibit 43–2 comes from this source. The Treasury does not release a detailed explanation of how these yield curves are generated. However, they are believed to result from application of statistical curve-fitting techniques, augmented by the judgment of Treasury analysts. As with most yield curves, the objective is to capture the yield/ maturity relationship of securities that differ only by term. Thus, Treasury issues, with no default risk and only limited call options, are especially appropriate for this purpose. In fitting these curves, only the yields on approximately current coupon bonds with no special features (e.g., flower bonds) are considered. An effort is obviously made to draw the curves smoothly so that the transition from one maturity point to another is gradual.

Yield curves are also published by a number of private sources. Some of the most accessible of these appear daily in *The Wall Street Journal.* Yield curves for the preceding day, one week prior, and four weeks prior are superimposed on a single graph; see Exhibit 43–9 for an example. As the exhibit indicates, the plotted yields reflect yields at the close of the trading day. Details of the fitting process are unavailable, but it is obvious from the abrupt discontinuities that no effort is made to smooth the data. These yield-curve plots are particularly useful for getting a snapshot view of how the term structure is evolving.

For more detailed analytical purposes, these published yield curves are not entirely satisfactory for two reasons. In the final analysis, they are subjectively de-

---

42. The comparative evaluation of various stochastic-process no-arbitrage models has also received attention. See, for example, K. C. Chan, G. Andrew Karolyi, Francis A. Longstaff, and Anthony B. Sanders, " An Empirical Comparison of Alternative Models of the Short-Term Interest Rate," *Journal of Finance,* July 1992, pp. 1209–1227. These authors conclude that the better models tend to be those that allow the conditional volatility of interest-rate changes to be dependent on the level of interest rates. The model presented earlier in this chapter has this characteristic.

EXHIBIT 43-9

Treasury Yield Curve (Yields as of 4:30 PM Eastern Time)

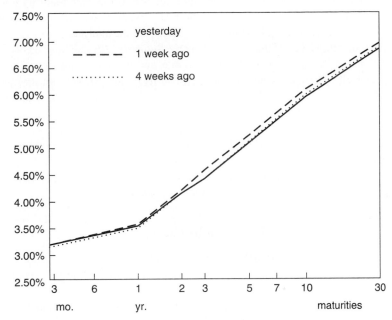

Source: *Technical Data's Bond Data* (Friday, June 25, 1993, based on yields on June 24, 1993).

rived, and there is always uncertainty about subjective numbers—it is unlikely, for example, that any two analysts would usually fit the same yield curve. Another problem arises when numerical yield values are needed for specific maturities. Such numbers must be read off the yield curve, and this is an activity of uncertain precision. It is unlikely that these are serious problems, and in fact they are present to a greater or lesser degree in almost all yield-curve analysis. However, it has become more common to work with constructed or synthetic yield-maturity data series and to statistically fit yield curves in analyzing the term structure.

Sources of Yield Maturity Series

A standard source of yields on U.S. government securities by maturity is a series published by Salomon Brothers, Inc. The Salomon Brothers yields have been used to construct many of the exhibits in this chapter. This series currently shows yields at 11 maturity points, ranging from three months to 30 years, in numerical form. It is published weekly in Salomon Brothers' *Bond Market Roundup,* and historical first-of-month (midmonth before 1959) yields are reported in Salomon Brothers' *An Analytical Record of Yields and Yield Spreads.* The Salomon Brothers data are prepared in much the same way as the *Treasury Bulletin* yield curves; that is, yield curves are fitted to actual bond yield data, following the yields of higher coupon bonds when a choice exists, and then the yields are read off at each maturity point. Thus the primary advantages of the Salomon Brothers series are its timeliness and the fact that the curve reading has already been done for the analyst.

Each monthly issue of the *Federal Reserve Bulletin* (*FRB*) contains a constant maturity yield series for U.S. government bonds and notes ranging from 1 to 30 years to maturity. These are yields at specific maturity points read off Treasury yield curves described previously. The yields are reported by calendar weeks ending on Wednesdays, by months, and by years; the weekly data represent averages of the nonreported daily values, monthly data are averages of the weeks, and so on. Therefore, the *FRB* numbers are not directly comparable with the Salomon Brothers data. Exhibit 43–10 contains the Salomon Brothers data for January 2, 1981, and the *FRB* data for the week ending January 2, 1981. Although the two series are not identical, they are quite similar, especially in the yield-curve patterns they display.

Fitting Yield Curves

These two yield series are probably more useful for investment decision making than published curves because they have been reduced to numerical terms by someone who is experienced in doing this. The numbers themselves can be examined for yield patterns, or they can be plotted to obtain yield curves such as those in Exhibit 43–1, which are of the "connect the dots" variety.

EXHIBIT 43–10

A Comparison of Salomon Brothers and Federal Reserve Bulletin Yield Data

Term-to-Maturity	Yields, Salomon Brothers, January 2, 1981	Yields, *Federal Reserve Bulletin* Week Ending January 2, 1981
3 months	15.02%	15.05%[a]
6 months	14.96	14.96
1 year	13.97	13.86
2 years	13.01	13.00
3 years	12.65	12.81
4 years	12.68	—
5 years	12.57	12.54
7 years	12.47	12.43
10 years	12.43	12.36
20 years	11.96	12.05
30 years	11.94	11.96

[a]Treasury bill discounts converted to coupon-equivalent yields.

Source: Data courtesy of Salomon Brothers Inc., and from the *Federal Reserve Bulletin*, February 1981.

Such curves are described as discontinuous. This means that they change shape at each measurement point and can do so abruptly. However, one would expect yield transitions from one maturity to another to be fairly smooth—that is, to be characterized by a continuous curve. In addition, one is often interested in maturities that are not at measurement points. Such intermediate yields could be estimated by linear interpolation, but this is clumsy and at odds with the notion of yield curves that change shape continuously. For those reasons, it is frequently desirable to fit mathematical curves to the yield points.

A number of models have been proposed for fitting such curves. Most use the method of least squares to actually fit the curve. The models differ in the form of the equation that is fitted and its number of terms. With too few terms, the estimated yield curve is excessively smooth; for example, with one term it would simply be a straight line. Too many terms will "overfit" the line; with as many terms as maturity points, the line will go precisely through each point.

One model that has proved to be particularly effective for such applications is that of Stephen Bradley and Dwight Crane.[43] The Bradley–Crane model has the form

$$\ln(1 + {}_0R_M) = a + b_1(M) + b_2 \ln(M) + e \qquad (43\text{--}5)$$

That is, values equal to the natural logarithm of one plus the observed yields for term-to-maturity of length M are regressed on two variables, the term-to-maturity and the natural log of the term-to-maturity. The last term represents the unexplained yield variation. Once the estimated values of a, b_1, and b_2 are obtained, specific maturities of interest can be substituted to obtain estimated yields at these maturity points. Exhibit 43–11 shows the Salomon Brothers yield series as of January 2, 1981, along with a yield curve fitted by this method. It can be observed that the fit is not particularly good in the shorter maturities.

Occasionally, one wishes to fit yield curves directly to yield data for individual bonds rather than to the homogenized yield series. This might be desirable as a means of avoiding possible distortions created in the process of arriving at the synthetic yield series. It might also be motivated by a particular interest in individual bonds, such as looking for arbitrage opportunities between underpriced or overpriced bonds by examining their yields in comparison with a fitted yield curve. A model for fitting such yield curves has been proposed by Elliott and Echols.[44]

The Elliott-Echols model has the form

$$\ln(1 + {}_0R_i) = a + b_1(1/M_i) + b_2(M_i) + b_3(C_i) + e_i \qquad (43\text{--}6)$$

43. Stephen P. Bradley and Dwight B. Crane, "Management of Commercial Bank Government Security Portfolios: An Optimization Approach Under Uncertainty," *Journal of Bank Research,* Spring 1973, pp. 18–30. More recent, and more complex, methods for fitting the Treasury yield curve include the methods of Nelson and Siegel, "Parsimonious Modeling of Yield Curves," *Journal of Business,* October 1987, pp.473–489, and Paul Diamant, "Semi-Empirical Smooth Fit to Treasury Yield Curve," *The Journal of Fixed Income,* July, 1996, pp. 55–70. At present no comparative studies of these methods are available.

44. Michael E. Echols and Jan Walter Elliott, "A Quantitative Yield Curve Model for Estimating the Term Structure of Interest Rates," *Journal of Financial and Quantitative Analysis,* March 1976, pp. 87–114.

E X H I B I T   43–11

Bradley-Crane Yield Curve Fitted to Salomon Brothers Yield Data for
January 2, 1981

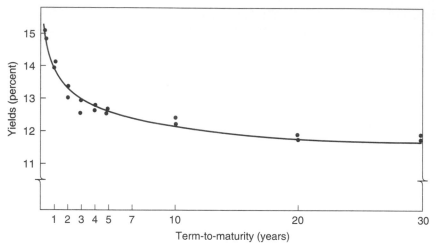

Source: Salomon Brothers Inc. Line estimated by authors.

where $_0R_i$, M_i, and C_i are the yield-to-maturity, term-to-maturity, and coupon rate
of the ith bond.

Notice that yield and maturity are related in somewhat different ways than
in the Bradley-Crane model. This representation also differs by the inclusion of
the individual bond's coupon level. Low-coupon bonds tend to have yields that
are subnormal for their term-to-maturity, presumably because of the postponable
nature of the tax of their built-in capital gain. The coupon term is intended to adjust for this effect.

Elliott and Echols suggested that for obtaining yield curves from this
model, the coupon term should be set to zero so as to avoid confounding coupon
effects and maturity effects. This approach is claimed to give the yield at which a
zero-coupon bond would sell, if one existed. An alternative (if more cumbersome) procedure is to search for the coupon rate at which the coupon rate and the
yield-to-maturity of a hypothetical bond of a given term-to-maturity would be the
same. The resulting point on the yield curve is the estimated yield at which a current coupon bond would sell if one existed. Exhibit 43–12 shows such a yield
curve fitted to individual bond and note data for this method, as of the end of
March 1977. Note that because of this coupon effect, there is no reason for the individual bonds to be scattered evenly around the line. Of course, a bond's actual
coupon should be used in estimating its appropriate yield if the objective is to determine whether it is underpriced or overpriced.

EXHIBIT 43–12

Elliott-Echols Yield Curve Fitted to Individual U.S. Government Bond and Note Yields, March 31, 1977

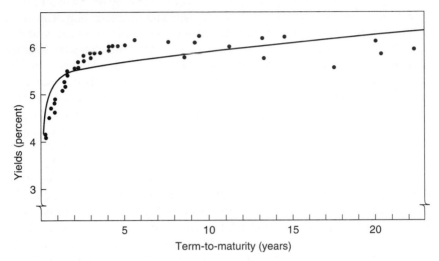

Measuring the Term Structure Directly

Recall the distinction between the yield curve and the term structure made at the beginning of this essay; the yield curve relates yields to maturity on coupon-bearing bonds to the term-to-maturity, whereas the term structure relates discount rates on single future payments to the term of the payment. For some purposes, yield curves adequately portray the price of time, but for others—such as pricing out single-payment securities or those with unusual patterns of cash flow or extracting implied forward rates—the term structure is preferred because it abstracts from coupon effects. Until recently it was impossible to observe the term structure directly, beyond the maturity range of Treasury bills, initially because there were no zero-coupon securities outstanding and later because those that were outstanding were not free from some element of default risk. However, with the advent of the STRIPS (Separate Trading of Registered Interest and Principal Securities) in 1985 via the Federal Reserve's book entry accounting system, prices and yields-to-maturity in a wide range of zero-coupon securities free from default risk have become available. Since 1989, such prices and yields at quarterly intervals for terms out to 30 years have been published in *The Wall Street Journal* on a daily basis. Such data were used to graph the term-structure relationship in Exhibit 43–3.

These discount rates change with term in a reasonably regular manner, but there are occasional jumps and dips. The usual explanation for these variations is supply-and-demand or liquidity considerations in the market for stripped securities. An analyst who wishes to smooth out these variations might find it useful to fit a curve to these data and then work with values read off the curve.

The simplicity and apparent precision of measuring the term structure with these stripped security yields is attractive. However, it may be somewhat misleading if the objective is to price future flows adjusting for their term only. The major potential problem is taxation. Stripped securities are treated as original-issue discount securities for tax purposes, and thus taxes must be paid on interest accrued under the constant or scientific yield method. If STRIPS were held only by tax-exempt investors, then their yields would be true before-tax spot rates. However, this is not so if STRIPS are not held exclusively by tax-exempt investors, and the valuations of such investors affect stripped bond prices. A taxed investor would have to make intermediate tax payments on the accrued discount; these payments would be akin to negative coupon receipts. In valuing these stripped bonds, the taxed investor would discount each cash flow to obtain the present value of the security and might apply different spot rates to each flow. The observed yields on the STRIPS would then be yields for instruments with intermediate cash flows.[45]

Possible tax effects associated with coupon bonds also create a problem for term-structure estimation and, indeed, for any use of the yield curve involving such bonds. The yield curve that we observe consists of rates that have not been explicitly adjusted for taxes. The after-tax rate for a taxed investor is not simply the observed rate times 1 minus the tax rate. It depends on the timing of the tax due to the split of dollar returns between coupon income and capital gains. Furthermore, tax rates may vary among investors in this market, and the estimation of a term structure is hampered by our not knowing which bonds are held by which investors.

Another Approach to Estimating the Term Structure

A method of term-structure analysis that was originally designed to cope with coupon effects also has promise for dealing with tax biases. This approach, like much of the contemporary analytical methodology in the fixed income area, works with discount factors rather than yields. Discount factors are values equal to $1/(1 + {_0}R_t)^t$; they are the entries found in the familiar present-value tables.

---

45. In addition, the yields on strips depend on whether a strip is created from principal payments or from coupon payments. See Phillip R. Daves and Michael C. Ehrhardt, "Liquidity, Reconstitution, and the Value of US Treasury Strips," *Journal of Finance,* March 1993, pp. 315–329. Strips created from principal payments trade at lower yields (higher prices) than strips created from coupon payments, for two reasons. First, when investors wish to reconstitute a coupon bond from a series of stripped bonds, any coupon strips can be used but only the original principal strip can be used for the principal portion of the reconstituted bond. This creates a greater demand for principal strips for the purpose of reconstitution. Secondly, principal strips have greater liquidity: Consider that when a bond is stripped, the amount of stripped principal exceeds the amount of stripped coupon on the maturity date; thus for this date, the principal strips are more liquid, and liquidity increases value.

The essence of the approach is to estimate the d coefficients in the multiple regression

$$P_{i,0} = d_1 X_{i1} + d_2 X_{i2} + \cdots + d_t X_{it} + e_i \qquad (43\text{--}7)$$

where

$P_{i,0}$ = The price of the ith bond at time zero

$X_{it}(t = 1, \ldots, T)$ = The cash flows from the bond in period t

In other words, prices of a number of bonds at a specific instant in time are related to their future coupons and maturity payments in a cross-sectional analysis. The estimated values of d are discount factors, and from them yields that are free of coupon bias can be computed. For example, d_1 is an estimate of $1/(1 + {}_0R_1)$, d_2 is an estimate of $1/(1 + {}_0R_2)^2$, and so on, so it is easy to solve for the various values of R.

The method just described can be called "discrete" estimation, since distinct discount factors at each payment date in the bond sample are estimated. Discrete estimation has its limitations. It can be applied only if at least one bond matures at each payment date, and it does not provide discount factors for maturities between those payment dates.[46] The more widely used methods of regression term structure estimation today overcome these problems by estimating a continuous discount function or, in some methods, spot or forward rate functions. In these methods, a functional form is assumed and the parameters of the function are estimated in the regression. The difficulty is that the functional form assumption affects the estimates. At last count, at least six continuous regression methods were in current use, and there seems to be little consensus regarding the best method.[47] For potential users who are not specialists in econometric methods, the simplest methods to implement are probably the McCulloch cubic spline discount function method and the Coleman-Fisher-Ibbotson forward rate estimation method (although the latter does require nonlinear least squares). To judge by recent research, there is a move toward greater rather than less

---

46. Details are in Willard T. Carleton and Ian A. Cooper, "Estimation and Uses of the Term Structure of Interest Rates," *Journal of Finance,* September 1976, pp. 1067–1083.

47. For the cubic spline discount function method, see J. Houston McCulloch, "Measuring the Term Structure of Interest Rates," *Journal of Business,* January 1971, pp. 19–31. For the Bernstein polynomial spline discount function method, see Stephen M. Schaefer, "Tax-Induced Clientele Effects in the Market for British Government Securities," *Economic Journal,* June 1981, pp. 415–438. For the exponential spline discount function method (originally developed by Oldrich Vasicek and Gifford Fong), see Frank J. Fabozzi and Gifford Fong, *Advanced Fixed Income Portfolio Management* (Chicago: Probus Publishing Company, 1994), Appendix A. For the polynomial spot rate function method, see Donald R. Chambers, Willard T. Carleton, and Donald W. Wakeman, "A New Approach to Estimation of the Term Structure of Interest Rates," *Journal of Financial and Quantitative Analysis,* September 1984, pp. 233–252. For the piecewise-constant forward rate method, see Thomas S. Coleman, Lawrence Fisher, and Roger G. Ibbotson, "Estimating the Term Structure of Interest Rates From Data that Include the Prices of Coupon Bonds," *The Journal of Fixed Income,* September 1995, pp. 85–116.

complexity, although the jury is still out on whether the more complex methods are best.[48]

If a tax adjustment is to be made, one procedure is as follows. For the entire bond sample, each coupon is stated on an after-tax basis by multiplying by 1 minus the tax rate. For a discount bond, the capital gains tax is applied to the difference between the principal and the price, and the principal repayment is reduced by this amount. For a stripped bond, the income tax on imputed interest each period is treated as a negative cash flow. For a premium bond, it is assumed that the loss will be amortized linearly over the life of the bond. After the cash flows in the bond sample are adjusted in this manner, a similar regression is run with the tax-adjusted cash flows. The discount function estimated is then an after-tax discount function. The after-tax discount factors, d_t^*, have the form

$$d_t^* = 1/[1 + {}_0R_t(1 - \text{tr})]^t$$

where

tr = The tax rate
${}_0R_t$ = The effective before-tax spot rate

All this begs the question of which tax rate to use. In several studies, different tax rates were tried until one was found to minimize the standard error of the regression.[49] This rate appears to do a good job of pricing most bonds in the sample, and in one study (Litzenberger and Rolfo) it was found to correspond to the tax rate of the major investors in several countries. Adjusting cash flows according to a particular tax specification is not the only way to go. The Schaefer, Vasicek-Fong, and Coleman-Fisher-Ibbotson term structure estimation models handle taxation differently. The differences reflect, in part, concerns about tax clienteles (investors in different tax brackets concentrating their holdings in certain types of bonds) and tax options (investors optimally trade bonds to minimize taxes).[50]

---

48. These innovations include the use of a smoothing constraint to force the estimated function to have fewer changes of curvature and cross-validation to improve the pricing of out-of-sample bonds, See Mark Fisher, Douglas Nychka, and David Zervos, "Fitting the Term Structure of Interest Rates with Smoothing Splines," Finance and Economics Division Series, Division of Research and Statistics, Division of Monetary Affairs, Federal Reserve Board, Washington, D.C., January1995. A further innovation is to force the term structure estimation method to be consistent with a stochastic model of a term structure. The Cox-Ingersoll-Ross stochastic model is incorporated into the method of Risk Metrics. See Risk Metrics Technical Document, Morgan Guaranty Trust Company, Global Research, New York, May 26, 1995.

49. This method of dealing with tax effects was developed by J. Houston McCulloch, "The Tax-Adjusted Yield Curve," *Journal of Finance,* June 1975, pp. 811–30; and further studied by Robert H. Litzenberger and J. Rolfo in "An International Study of Tax Effects on Government Bonds," *Journal of Finance,* March 1984, pp. 1–22; and by James V. Jordan in "Tax Effects in Term Structure Estimation," *Journal of Finance,* July 1984, pp. 393–406. A set of monthly term-structure estimates using McCulloch's method for the period 12/46–2/87 is published in Schiller and McCulloch, "The Term Structure of Interest Rates."

50. See Eliezer Z. Prisman, "Bond Pricing in Markets with Taxes," *Journal of Banking and Finance* 14 (1990), pp. 33–39 as well as Bradford D. and Susan D. Jordan, "Tax Options and Pricing of Treasury Bond Triplets: Theory and Evidence," *Journal of Financial Economics* 30 (1991), pp.135–164.

Estimating Implicit Forward Rates

Without Liquidity Premium Adjustment

Many uses of term structure do not require the estimation of forward rates. However, there will be occasions in which it is desirable to actually extract implicit forward rates from the yield curve or other data in order to get some idea of the interest rates the market consensus is forecasting.

If suitably spaced yields on either synthetic or actual securities are available, then forward rates can be estimated directly by the use of Equation (43–2) without the necessity for fitting yield curves. Recall that Equation (43–2) stated

$$(1 + {}_{t+m}r^b_{n-m,t})^{n-m} = (1 + {}_tR_n)^n/(1 + {}_tR_m)^m \qquad (43\text{–}2)$$

except that ^{b} has been added to r, for reasons that will be discussed shortly. Use of this formula is extremely straightforward once the data are in proper form. The equation is written on the assumption that all yields are expressed in the same units of time, per annum yields being most common. For many purposes, it will be useful to measure m and n in units that have the effect of making $n - m = 1$.

A simple example may help illustrate the process and clarify this last point. On January 2, 1981, three-month and six-month coupon equivalent Treasury bill yields as reported in *The Wall Street Journal* were 15.31 percent and 15.00 percent per annum, respectively. If we use Equation 43–2 with m and n expressed in years to estimate the three-month rate anticipated in three months, $n = 6$ months = $\frac{1}{2}$ year, $m = 3$ months = $\frac{1}{4}$ year, and

$$\left(1 + {}_{1/4}\, r^b_{1/4,0}\right)^{1/4} = \frac{(1.1500)^{1/2}}{(1.1531)^{1/4}} = \frac{1.0724}{1.0363} = 1.0349$$

This last value is for a quarter of a year because it is one plus an annual rate raised to the $\frac{1}{4}$ power. In order to make it apply to a whole year, we must raise it to the fourth power, or

$$\left[\left(1 + {}_{1/4}\, r^b_{1/4,0}\right)^{1/4}\right]^4 = 1 + {}_{1/4}\, r^b_{1/4,0}$$

When we do, we get

$$1.0349^4 = 1.1469, \text{ or } 14.69\%$$

Alternatively, we might simply express m and n in three-month periods, because we are interested in a three-month forward rate. Then $n = 6$ months = 2 and $m = 3$ months = 1, and

$$\left(1 + {}_1\, r^b_{1,0}\right)^1 = \frac{1.1500^2}{1.1531^1} = \frac{1.3225}{1.1531} = 1.1469$$

or 14.69 percent again.

Exhibit 47–13 continues the estimation of three-month forward rates as of January 2, 1981. The first rate in each series is unadjusted; the second has been adjusted

EXHIBIT 43-13

Alternative Estimates of Three-Month Forward Rates
(January 2, 1981)

Forward Rates for Three Months, Beginning	Actual Yields, Equation 43–2		Actual Yields, Equation 43–8		Fitted Yields, Equation 43–2	
	Unadjusted	Adjusted	Unadjusted	Adjusted	Unadjusted	Adjusted
April 2, 1981	14.69%	14.11%	14.69%	14.11%	13.88%	13.71%
July 2, 1981	13.02	12.76	13.01	12.77	13.40	13.19
October 8, 1981[a]	12.88	12.66	12.87	12.65	13.10	12.88
January 2, 1982					12.88	12.66
April 2, 1982					12.71	12.49
July 2, 1982					12.58	12.36
October 2, 1982					12.46	12.24
January 2, 1983					12.37	12.15
April 2, 1983					12.29	12.07
July 2, 1983					12.21	11.99
October 2, 1983					12.15	11.93

[a]October 2, 1982, for estimates based on fitted yields.

for liquidity premia, as will be discussed later. The exhibit also shows forward rates estimated using a simplified method proposed by Worley and Diller,[51,52] in which

$$_{t+m}r^b_{n-m,t} \approx \frac{(_tR_n \cdot n) - (_tR_m \cdot m)}{n-m} \tag{43-8}$$

The values n and m can be expressed in days, fractions of a year, or other convenient intervals. This equation, which does not require the use of exponents or assume compounding, is quite satisfactory provided the interval $n - m$ is not large. In terms of the preceding example,

$$_1r^b_{1,0} \approx \frac{(.1500 \cdot 2) - (.1531 \cdot 1)}{1}$$

$$\approx .1469$$

Suppose that suitably spaced yields are not available. Suppose, for example, that we want to estimate forward rates for three-month intervals beyond a year in the future. This is where curves fitted to yields or spot rates become useful. After estimating the appropriate coefficients, we can simply substitute in the appropriate values of m and n and use Equation (43-2) or (43-8) to obtain the forward rate. For example, the Bradley-Crane model equation for January 2, 1981 (Exhibit 43-13), is

$$\ln(1 + {}_0R_m) = 0.129700 + 0.000425(M) - 0.008497 \ln(M)$$

If we are interested in the three-month rate one year into the future as of the beginning of January 1982, we substitute 1.0 and 1.25 (m and n equal to 1 year and $1^1/_4$ years) in the equation, obtaining 13.8970 percent for ${}_0R_1$ and 13.6933 percent for ${}_0R_{1.25}$. Equation 43-2 gives

$$\left(_1r^b_{.25,0}\right)^{.25} = \frac{1.136933^{1.25}}{1.138970^1} = 1.030756$$

or 12.88 percent per annum.

Exhibit 43-13 contains forward rates for each three-month interval beginning three months through three years into the future estimated via the fitted curve approach, in addition to the forward rates for the first three-month intervals obtained earlier. The differences in the forward rates obtained by this approach and the forward rates computed with the actual Treasury bill yields are initially large but converge rapidly. (Recall that the Bradley-Crane model didn't fit the short maturities very well.) All these sets of numbers illustrate in striking fashion the decline in interest rates that was apparently expected as 1981 began.

---

51. Worley and Diller, "Interpreting the Yield Curve," p. 45.
52. The values in the first four columns of Exhibit 43-13 are computed by reference to the actual number of days in each period because the periods are not of equal length—principally because no Treasury bill traded on January 2 matured on October 2, making it necessary to use the bill maturing October 8.

With Liquidity Premium Adjustment

The formulas presented in the preceding discussion each had a superscript b attached to the r representing the forward rates. This superscript is intended as a reminder that these are "biased" forward rates; that is, to the extent that there are liquidity premia embedded in the term structure, forward rates are upward-biased estimates of yields the market consensus expects in the future. For many purposes, these biased forward rates are acceptable or even desirable. For example, if we wish to monitor the pattern of changes in expected forward rates from month to month and we are willing to ignore possible changes in liquidity premia, these biased forward rates tell us what we need to know. If we are attempting to price out a bond using forward rates, we might actually *prefer* rates with embedded liquidity premia.

This is fortunate because satisfactory liquidity premia estimates are impossible to obtain. Ideally, we could estimate liquidity premia in any of the following ways:

- Compute differences in yields along a long-run average yield curve or term structure.
- Compute long-run differences in average total returns on bonds of different maturities.
- Compute long-run differences in implied forward rates and actual outcomes.

Conceptually, these three approaches are not the same, and in practice none is satisfying. Other problems are those we considered when reviewing empirical evidence on the expectations hypothesis: Likely time variations in liquidity premia and actual interest rates that do not conform to expectations. In addition, the first approach assumes that yields are expected to remain unchanged.

The first approach was employed by Haim Levy in a paper that appeared in the *Financial Analysts Journal* in 1982.[53] Levy was attempting to assess the inflation expectation built into the yield curve at different times. In order to obtain a base-time yield curve, he studied the years 1961 through 1964, years he regarded as typifying low expected inflation and stable interest rates. The average real inflation-adjusted yields in these years, and the corresponding incremental liquidity premia for extending maturity an additional period, were as follows:

Years to Maturity	Average Real Yield	Incremental Liquidity Premia
1	0.80%	—
2	1.32	.52%
3	1.47	.15
4	1.65	.18
5	1.60	−.05

53. Haim Levy, "The Yield Curve and Expected Inflation," *Financial Analysts Journal*, November/
December 1982, pp. 37–42.

EXHIBIT 43-14

McCulloch Liquidity Premium Estimates, March 1951–March 1966

							$n-m$						
m	0	One Month	Two Months	Three Months	Six Months	Nine Months	1 Year	2 Years	3 Years	5 Years	10 Years	20 Years	30 Years
One month	0.17	0.13	0.11	0.09	0.05	0.04	0.03	0.01	0.01	0.01	0.00	0.00	0.00
Two months	0.28	0.22	0.17	0.14	0.09	0.06	0.05	0.02	0.02	0.01	0.00	0.00	0.00
Three months	0.34	0.27	0.21	0.17	0.11	0.07	0.06	0.03	0.02	0.01	0.01	0.00	0.00
Six months	0.41	0.32	0.26	0.21	0.13	0.09	0.07	0.03	0.02	0.01	0.01	0.00	0.00
Nine months	0.32	0.34	0.27	0.22	0.13	0.09	0.07	0.04	0.02	0.01	0.01	0.00	0.00
1 year	0.43	0.34	0.27	0.22	0.14	0.09	0.07	0.04	0.02	0.01	0.01	0.00	0.00
2 years	0.43	0.34	0.27	0.22	0.14	0.09	0.07	0.04	0.02	0.01	0.01	0.00	0.00
3 years	0.43	0.34	0.27	0.22	0.14	0.09	0.07	0.04	0.02	0.01	0.01	0.00	0.00
5 years	0.43	0.34	0.27	0.22	0.14	0.09	0.07	0.04	0.02	0.01	0.01	0.00	0.00
10 years	0.43	0.34	0.27	0.22	0.14	0.09	0.07	0.04	0.02	0.01	0.01	0.00	0.00
20 years	0.43	0.34	0.27	0.22	0.14	0.09	0.07	0.04	0.02	0.01	0.01	0.00	0.00
30 years	0.43	0.34	0.27	0.22	0.14	0.09	0.07	0.04	0.02	0.01	0.01	0.00	0.00

Source: Adapted from J. Houston McCulloch, "An Estimate of the Liquidity Premium," *Journal of Political Economy*, February 1975, p. 113. ©1975 The University of Chicago, publisher. All rights reserved.

Using the third approach, Worley and Diller estimated incremental liquidity premia for the 1966–1976 period as follows:

m	n − m	L
3 months	3 months	58 basis points
6	3	26
9	3	22
6	6	24

m = time in future when rate is effective

$n − m$ = maturity of security to which rate applies

L = liquidity premium

J. Houston McCulloch has employed a variant of this approach to make liquidity premium estimates for the largely nonoverlapping March 1951–March 1966 period contained in Exhibit 43–14.[54] Direct comparisons of McCulloch's results with those of Levy and the Worley-Diller estimates are possible. Values derived from the Levy study are well above those from McCulloch. For example, Levy's data imply that the one-year forward rate overstates the expected interest rate in one year by 52 basis points; the McCulloch results suggest that this premium is only 7 basis points. Results from the Worley-Diller and McCulloch studies are closer. For the three-month rate in three months, the estimates are dramatically different—58 basis points for Worley-Diller versus 17 basis points for McCulloch. However, premia for three-month maturities further into the future are similar—for example, 26 and 21 basis points for rates to be effective in six months, and 22 basis points for both studies for rates effective in nine months. Time variation may well account for these differences.

It is interesting that the incremental liquidity premium is for practical purposes zero for yields beyond about six months into the future in both the Worley-Diller and McCulloch studies. In the Levy study, leveling occurs only after four years out. If this property persists over time, forward rates estimated from the longer maturity portion of term structures should be unbiased.

Once one has formed some conclusions about incremental liquidity premia, adjustment of biased forward rates to unbiased market expectations of future spot rates simply involves subtracting the premia from the biased forward rates. Exhibit 43–13 uses the Worley-Diller and McCulloch liquidity premia to adjust the forward rates for January 2, 1981, obtained previously.

---

54. J. Houston McCulloch, "An Estimate of the Liquidity Premium," *Journal of Political Economy,* February 1975, pp. 95–119.

PORTFOLIO MANAGEMENT

Ⓖ

BOND MANAGEMENT: PAST, CURRENT, AND FUTURE

H. Gifford Fong
President
Gifford Fong Associates

Fixed income management has undergone a remarkable evolution. The range of portfolio strategies has expanded as the technology of portfolio analysis has developed over time. This broadened capability is permitting greater efficiency and effectiveness as well as the introduction of innovative strategies. Perhaps more remarkable is the prospect of a new dimension of fixed income portfolio strategy that dramatically goes beyond the traditional notions of management.

What follows is an overview of the changes that have occurred in fixed income portfolio strategy over the last 20 years. This historical survey will trace the emergence of various quantitative tools that have helped shape the world of modern fixed income portfolio management. After this review, a description of a representative strategy harnessing this technology will be presented.

TRADITIONAL FIXED INCOME PORTFOLIO STRATEGY[1]

The primary functional areas of modern fixed income management are shown in Exhibit 44–1, which is a triangle with three intersections representing the major strategies. At the bottom left can be found *active management,* made up of rate anticipation and/or sector management. Key to this area are expectations of interest-rate change and/or sector spread (yield difference from Treasury securities). To the lower right can be found *passive management,* where either a buy-and-hold strategy or indexing to a representative market bogey is typical.

---

1. For a more comprehensive discussion of traditional fixed income strategies, see H. Gifford Fong and Frank J. Fabozzi, *Fixed Income Portfolio Management* (Homewood, IL: Dow Jones-Irwin, 1985).

E X H I B I T   44–1

Fixed Income Management

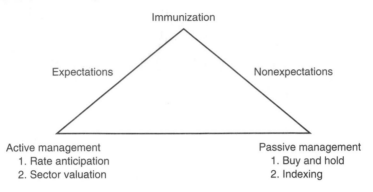

Active management
1. Rate anticipation
2. Sector valuation

Passive management
1. Buy and hold
2. Indexing

Active and passive management can be differentiated on the basis of the kinds of input necessary. For example, traditional active management is "expectationally driven"; that is, the most important set of inputs will be expectations of interest-rate and spread relationship changes. Passive management, on the other hand, is based on nonexpectational inputs; in other words, the key inputs are known at the time of the analysis. In the case of indexing, these inputs are the basic characteristics of the market index chosen.

This difference in inputs corresponds to variations in the risk-return characteristics of the alternatives. The greater the expectational inputs are, all other things being equal, the greater the return potential and the associated variability (risk) of the strategy will be. Thus, active management will have the highest expected return but the highest associated risk, and passive management will have the lowest expected return and risk on average. The emphasis in this traditional setting is to seek higher returns by managing the expectations, which in turn increase the expected returns.

In contrast to the expectational nature of active management and nonexpectational nature of passive management, the top of the triangle, *immunization*, represents a hybrid strategy. Under some circumstances, an expectational, high expected risk-return approach may be chosen, or a nonexpectational, minimum-risk posture may be assumed.

HISTORICAL PERSPECTIVE

Early quantitative tools in the 1970s were first used to support active management. Sensitivity analysis, in which the implications of the expectations on portfolio returns could be evaluated, became a fundamental tool in active strategies. Expected scenarios of interest-rate change could be applied to the current portfolio, and prospective returns could be calculated. This analysis was extended to include insights from evaluating the implications of the expected returns.[2]

This early application represents the quantification of a traditional task that was formerly done informally by the portfolio manager. With this tool, the portfolio manager could pursue a more systematic and structured approach to portfolio decision making. This was not merely a foreign step, but rather an alternative path freeing the time of the portfolio manager. In effect, a computational task became automated so more time could be devoted to tasks that could not be automated. Given the usual demands on the available time of the portfolio manager, this quantitative assistance leveraged the ability of the manager to focus on the expectational inputs that are central to the active management process.

With the approach of the 1980s, new developments encouraged the use of an old concept in a new form—immunization. Originally conceived in the 1930s, the immunization strategy awaited a series of theoretical and empirical developments before it could be put to practical use. So when relatively high interest rates prevailed (in relation to the typical actuarial assumption), and the desire to minimize pension contributions and the growth of new theoretical understanding[3] emerged at the same time, the basis for the use of immunization was laid. Moreover, the tarnished reputation of traditional active management (due to the performance of many portfolio managers in the 1970s) further confirmed the need for a new strategy.

In the 1980s, the further evolution of strategy took the direction of duration-controlled approaches. Given the aversion to unexpected exposure to changes in interest rates, reliance on interest-rate risk control by monitoring the duration of the portfolio became widespread. Out of this trend emerged indexing, which targeted the portfolio duration. Indexing is extremely quantified and minimizes the need for expectational input.

More recently, other targeted-duration strategies have emerged. These, in general, have a duration target different from the popularly followed bond indexes but serve a similar function: limiting or controlling the exposure to interest-rate changes by "targeting" the duration.

This brief history traces the changes in strategy over about the last 20 years. Concurrently, the role of quantitative methods has altered. What started out as a useful means of measuring and monitoring has developed over time as an important source of portfolio strategy.

Early applications were mere alternatives to traditional practice, and allowed the automation of basic tasks. As concern for unconstrained use of expectations increased, quantitative methods provided the means of monitoring and

---

2. See, for example, John L. Maginn and Donald L. Tuttle, eds., *Managing Investment Portfolios: A Dynamic Process* (Charlottesville, VA: The Institute of Chartered Financial Analysts, 1983), Chapter 9.
3. Important advances in the nature of immunized portfolios were made in Lawrence Fisher and Roman Weil, "Coping with Risk of Interest Rate Fluctuations: Return to Bondholders from Naive and Optimal Strategies," *Journal of Business,* October 1971; and H. Gifford Fong and Oldrich A. Vasicek, "A Risk Minimizing Strategy for Portfolio Immunization," *The Journal of Finance,* December 1984, provided explicit risk measures for immunized portfolios.

controlling risk exposure, especially the risk of interest-rate change different from a desired duration level. These applications involved the use of quantitative techniques, first to free up the time of the portfolio manager and then to help shape the appropriate policy of the portfolio management process. For example, a targeted-duration portfolio removes interest-rate forecasting from the manager's judgment but still allows expectations to be applied in sector and individual bond selection. However, as the use of quantitative methods has increased, the potential for return has decreased. The question now becomes how to expand the horizons of return in the face of qualitative control.

QUANTITATIVE INNOVATION

Exhibit 44–2 lists representative fixed income applications. Historically, the cornerstone of quantitative analysis has been the measurement of relevant factors providing analytical insight. And historically, the time demands of the traditional process of management could have been better served. More recent developments, such as indexing and immunization, suggest that quantitative innovation supplemented by traditional activities such as investment objective setting and trading can be the principal expedient of portfolio management.

Of the important contributing factors to the return of a fixed income portfolio, duration management has had the greatest impact, followed by sector selection and then individual bond selection.[4] The potential for superior performance from management contribution is therefore severely handicapped if the most important potential source is taken away.

Active duration management may not be appropriate for all investors, but the consequences and merits of the choice should be understood.

For example, targeted-duration strategies are designed to preclude large return departures from the chosen duration level. The choice of the level may be due to a number of considerations (including, importantly, the duration of the liabilities to be funded); however, whatever the level, if there is a consistent and reliable means of adding value through active duration management around the target, the potential for substantial incremental returns is achieved.

Granted, the aversion to unconstrained expectational duration management may still exist. However, if a means of active duration management could operate in a controlled, nonexpectational framework, an interesting alternative would be achieved.

Drawn from modern option valuation theory, an asset allocation analysis can provide a form of active duration management.[5] The objective is to create a syn-

---

4. This can be intuitively understood by considering the relative contribution to the variability of portfolio returns from these three sources.
5. A discussion of a specific fixed income application can be found in John L. Maginn and Donald L. Tuttle, eds., *Managing Investment Portfolios,* 2nd ed. (Charlottesville, VA: The Institute of Chartered Financial Analysts, 1990), Chapter 8; the discussion here is based on the theory discussed in H. Gifford Fong and Oldrich A. Vasicek, "Forecast-Free International Asset Allocation," *The Financial Analyst Journal,* March/April 1989, pp. 29–33.

E X H I B I T   44–2

Quantitative Applications

Active Management	
Return simulation	Predicts bond and portfolio behavior given alternative interest-rate scenario projections.
Immunization	
Immunization model	Creates and maintains a portfolio that will have an ensured return over a specified horizon, irrespective of interest-rate change.
Passive Management	
Indexing system	Creates and maintains a portfolio that will track the performance of a given bond index with a manageable set of securities.
Individual Security Analysis	
Swap systems	Allows for comparison of individual securities, with the objective of identifying historical price (or basis point spread) relationships.
Term-structure analysis	Evaluates the current level of yields by producing spot, discount, and forward-rate structures. Also values Treasury securities.
Bond valuation model	Develops a normative value for corporate and mortgage-backed securities, based on the evaluation of those characteristics of the security that contribute to overall price.
Contingent-claims model	Evaluates the embedded option in a security without forecasting interest rates.
Other	
Performance attribution system	Calculates the total return for a bond portfolio and attributes the return to its components.
Risk analysis report	Calculates option-adjusted average duration, convexity, and yield for a portfolio.

thetic call option on the best performing of the two extremes of the selected duration range. What would result would be a systematic shift within this range based on an active asset allocation between the longest and shortest duration assets.

An option valuation model used for this purpose determines the appropriate proportions of the two duration extremes. The model can systematically shift the portfolio to the highest returning asset from the lowest returning asset. A synthetic option is thereby created from this active asset allocation—an option that will achieve the returns of the best performer of the two assets. The final portfolio return will be the return of the best-performing asset less the synthetic option cost. This cost, which may be determined at the beginning of the analysis, arises from the return slippage due to the portfolio not using the best-performing asset all of the time. Because there is a gradual shift, there is a "cost" or return differential as compared to the return of the best-performing asset.

In general, the cost will vary with the number of assets, the length of the investment horizon, and the estimated risk of the assets considered (standard deviation of returns and correlation between assets). Although the cost of the strategy can vary depending on the actual outcome of the risk estimates, the strategy will still achieve the desired property of a synthetic call on the best-performing asset class.

Consider the management of an intermediate fixed income portfolio made up of high-grade government and corporate securities. Conventional indexing would target the duration of the index as the duration of the portfolio to be held. Value enhancement would take the form of a sector selection and/or individual security selection. Return differences from the most important management activity, that of active duration management, would be eliminated.

Introducing active duration management using option valuation technology can retain the most important source of management return, without the need for interest-rate forecasting. The portfolio returns would be further enhanced by using a term-structure model to value Treasury securities and a bond valuation model for the balance of the portfolio.

By harnessing the quantitative innovation of option valuation technology, a new dimension of portfolio decision making emerges. Active duration management without the need for interest-rate forecasting is made possible.

Another nonexpectational form of active duration management is tactical asset allocation. This strategy varies the duration of the portfolio based on fair value for the bond market. When the market is considered undervalued, the duration of the portfolio will be lengthened to what is considered normal; and, conversely, when the market is considered overvalued, the portfolio duration is shortened. The key is the determination of what is "fair value"; and here tactical asset allocation differs from an option valuation approach. Expectations are required in the determination of fair value for tactical asset allocation, whereas the option valuation approach does not rely upon asset valuation expectation.

What has been described is a strategy applying quantitative innovation in the management of an active intermediate portfolio. Without the additional return potential of this technology, the return prospect would be that of a conservative-duration portfolio. With the technology, the return range can be extended to longer-duration portfolios with the downside cushion of a short-duration portfolio.

SUMMARY

A review of the main functional areas of fixed income management reveal a range of risk/return potential. Over time, the popularity of strategy has shifted in recognition of the difficulty of valid and reliable interest-rate forecasts. Recent developments in option valuation technology reintroduce more active strategies, without the need for interest-rate forecasting.

⑥

THE ACTIVE DECISIONS IN THE SELECTION OF PASSIVE MANAGEMENT AND PERFORMANCE BOGEYS

Chris P. Dialynas
Advisory Managing Director
Pacific Investment Management Company

The asset allocation decision is perhaps a plan sponsor's most important decision. After the asset allocation is determined, the selection of investment managers and performance bogeys is critical. Traditional asset allocation methods are based on studies of relative returns and risk over long periods of time. Performance periods, however, both for the plan itself and the investment manager entrusted with the funds, are generally based upon relatively short time spans. As such, there is an inherent inconsistency in the investment process.

In this chapter, the active bond-management process will be explored and contrasted with the "passive management" option. We will also examine the differences in index composition. Performance inferences will be made based exclusively on the index composition and the future economic environment. We will see that successful bond management, whether active or passive, depends on good long-term economic forecasting and a thorough understanding of the mathematical dynamics of fixed income obligations. Likewise, selection of a performance bogey depends on similar considerations as well as the liability structure of the plan itself.

ACTIVE BOND MANAGEMENT

Active management of bond portfolios capitalizes on changing relations among bonds to enhance performance. Volatility in interest rates and changes in the

The author expresses his gratitude to the bond research departments at Lehman Brothers and Salomon
    Brothers for providing data.

amount of volatility induce divergences in the relative prices between bonds. Because volatility, by definition, allows for opportunity, the fact that during the years active bond managers as a class only slightly outperformed the passive indexes in one of the most volatile bond markets in the past 50 years seems counterintuitive. What went wrong then? What should we expect in the future?

Active bond managers each employ their own methods for relative value analysis. Common elements among most managers are historical relations, liquidity considerations, option-based analytical models, and market segmentation. Market segmentation allegedly creates opportunities, and historical analysis provides the timing cue. The timing of strategic moves is important because there is generally an opportunity cost associated with every strategy. Unfortunately, because the world is in perpetual motion and constant evolution, neither market segmentation nor historical analysis is able to withstand the greater forces of change. Both methods, either separately or jointly, are impotent. The dramatic increase in volatility experienced in recent years implies the world is turning and evolving more quickly. Paradoxically, many active managers are using methods voided by volatility to try to capitalize on volatility.

The mistakes of active bond managers have been costly. As a result, a significant move from active to passive (or indexed) management is in progress. Does this move make sense? To understand relative performance differentials between passive and active managers, we need to dissect the active and passive portfolios and reconstruct the macroeconomic circumstances. We will see that the compositions of the indexes and the circumstances are extremely dynamic, and given changes in either or both, the investment results are substantially affected.

MARKET INDEXES

A variety of bond market indexes are popular today, but two have been notable throughout the recent business cycles. The Lehman Government Corporate (LGC) bond index was the most popular, and the Salomon High Grade Long Term Bond Index was the traditional measure. Because the high-grade index sees little use today, the focus here will be primarily on the LGC index and the Lehman Aggregate Index (LAG), which includes mortgages. We will conclude with a comparison of the different indexes and their respective performance expectations given various interest-rate movements, as well as a review of historical performance comparisons.

The LGC Index

The LGC is primarily composed of government and agency securities. The composition of the index is detailed in Exhibit 45–1.

The LGC is constructed such that its composition is representative of the relative distribution of securities in the market exclusive of the mortgage market. Because the government issues the vast majority of debt today, it is not surprising

EXHIBIT 45-1

LGC Distribution and Reported Characteristics[a]

	6/1980	6/1984	6/1986	6/1988	6/1989	6/1990	6/1991	6/1992	6/1993
						Period Beginning			
U.S. Government	40.77	57.33	60.35	61.90	62.41	62.55	63.26	65.15	65.69
Agency	18.20	14.96	11.14	10.50	10.87	10.94	10.75	10.31	9.33
Corporates	35.74	23.85	25.10	24.52	23.39	23.08	24.26	21.33	20.91
Yankees	5.29	3.87	3.40	3.07	3.33	3.43	1.72	3.21	4.03
Duration	5.04	4.02	5.03	4.03	5.21	5.33	4.94	4.91	5.27
Yield	10.25	13.59	8.49	8.80	9.10	8.76	7.78	6.54	5.46

[a] As reported by Lehman Brothers.

that the index holds such a high and increasing proportion of government securities. The index must, by definition, "buy" the debt. With the exception of some of the 30-year government bonds issued during this period, virtually all of the government and agency debt held in the index is noncallable. Because of this, between 1980 and 1993 the index has become increasingly call-protected. We will see that the callable/noncallable distribution is an important distinguishing feature between the index and active managers.

The LAG Index

The primary difference between the LGC and the LAG is the inclusion of mortgages in the LAG. Mortgages provide the most uncertain distribution of cash flows among fixed income securities and can exhibit substantial negative convexity. The degree of convexity differential between the LGC and the LAG is largely determined by the concentration of mortgages below par. The greater the percentage of mortgages below par, the greater the relative convexity of the LAG will be. Relative index performance expectations along the yield curve spectrum are sensitive to the relative coupon distribution of mortgages in the market at any point in time. That distribution, reported in Exhibit 45–2, will largely influence subsequent duration differences between the indexes and, therefore, subsequent performance differences as well.

The Salomon Brothers High Grade Index

The Salomon Brothers high-grade, long-term bond index was a popular bond-market bogey during the 1970s and early 1980s. The index is composed primarily of high-quality (AA and AAA), long-term (10 years and longer) corporate bonds. Its reported duration approximated 8.5 years. The performance of the index was very poor during this period of increasing rates and increasing volatility in interest rates. The rate increases were so great that call options were driven well out of the money, reducing the localized cushioning effect normally associated with rate increases. The increase in volatility was tremendous, and the increased volatility also reduced the value of corporate bonds. Naturally, the high-grade index became perceived as too risky and not representative of the market's distribution of bonds. The LGC was adopted as the market index. Its shorter duration allowed it to better weather the bear market. The LAG index is most representative of the supply of bonds in the market and gained popularity during the latter half of the 1980s.

PERFORMANCE CHARACTERISTICS OF CALLABLE AND NONCALLABLE BONDS

Exhibit 45–3 characterizes the expected performance characteristics of callable and noncallable bonds under different market environments. The market environments are described by two parameters: the direction of interest rates and the volatility of rates.

EXHIBIT 45-2

LAG Distribution and Reported Characteristics

						Period Beginning				
	6/1980	6/1984	6/1986	6/1988	6/1989	6/1990	6/1991	6/1992	6/1993
U.S. Government	38.82	48.06	48.61	45.57	45.86	44.73	44.84	44.83	45.82
Agency	15.99	12.54	8.97	7.73	7.99	7.83	7.62	7.10	6.51
Corporates	31.40	19.99	20.22	18.06	17.19	16.51	17.20	14.67	14.62
Mortgages	10.14	16.18	19.46	26.35	26.52	28.48	29.13	29.25	28.57
Yankees	4.64	3.25	2.74	2.26	2.44	2.45	1.22	2.21	2.81
Asset-backed[a]						0.00	0.00	0.00	0.00
Duration	5.26	4.24	4.90	5.07	5.29	5.35	4.83	4.42	4.38
Yield	10.34	13.78	8.68	9.01	9.30	8.99	8.40	6.87	5.78

[a]Introduced to the index on December 31, 1991.

E X H I B I T   45–3

Expected Performance Characteristics of Callable and Noncallable Bonds under Different Market Environments

Direction of Interest Rates

		Increase in rates	No change	Decrease in rates
Increase	NC	+	+	(+)
	C	Amb+	–	(–)
No change	NC	*i*	*i*	(+)
	C	+	*i*	(–)
Decrease	NC	–	–*i*	+Amb
	C	(+)	+	–Amb

(Vertical axis label: Volatility Changes)

Performance Expectations
Relative to Comparable Duration
Govt. Securities Portfolios

i	Income advantage	(+)	Big winner
(–)	Big loser	–	Loser
Amb	Ambiguous	NC	Noncallable portfolio
+	Winner	C	Callable portfolio

Callable bonds do well in rising-rate environments and decreasing-volatility environments. Decreases in volatility have the profound direct effect of reducing the value of the call option embedded within the callable bond. Because the bondholder has effectively sold the option, as its value is reduced by the lower volatility, the total value of the bond increases independently of any interest-rate movement.

Callable bonds do better than noncallable bonds in increasing rate environments because the higher rates cause the option to go out of the money. As the option goes out of the money, its value diminishes and the bond's value increases. The option-value decline cushions the bond-price decline induced by higher rates, thereby reducing the *effective duration*[1] of the bond. The effective duration of the bond decreases as rates increase, and the callable bond outperforms the noncallable bond, whose duration is relatively inelastic.

Noncallable bonds perform better than callable bonds in decreasing-rate and increasing-volatility environments. Their effective duration[2] increases in

1. Effective duration refers to the call-option-adjusted duration and, as used here, is independent in durational changes induced by liquidity or credit considerations.
2. In this instance, effective duration refers to the expected percentage price change in the market. It is not used here in a volatility-adjusted duration context.

EXHIBIT 45–4

Call Features of the Bond Universe

Issue Type	Refunding Protection	Call Protection	Refunding Price	Current Call Price
Treasury	Maturity[a]	Maturity	NA	NA
Traditional agency	Maturity	Maturity	NA	NA
Traditional industrial	10 years	None	Premium	Premium
Traditional utility	5 years	None	Premium	Premium
Traditional finance	10 years[b]	None	Premium	Premium
GNMA pass-through	None	None	100	100
FNMA pass-through	None	None	100	100
FHLMC PC	None	None	100	100
CMO	None	None	100	100
Title XI	None[c]	None[c]	100[c]	100[c]
PAC CMO	Within prepayment range	None outside range	100	100
TAC CMO	Within prepayment range[d]	None outside range	100	100

[a]Some 30-year government bonds were issued with 25 years of call protection.
[b]A decline in receivables may permit an immediate par call.
[c]Default negates any refunding or call protection.
[d]Call protected within a prespecified range of payment rates on the collateral.

decreasing-rate environments because, exclusive of credit-risk considerations, the noncallable bonds are more *convex*;[3] that is, their *rate* of price increase outpaces that of the comparable-duration callable bonds. As the volatility of interest rates increases, noncallable bonds will command a premium, and because the noncallable bonds are more convex, they will appreciate exclusively because of their relative convexity advantage.

The call features of the bond universe are summarized in Exhibit 45–4.

A LOOK AT MARKET VOLATILITY

It is helpful to examine the volatility of the bond market to make inferences about performance attributes. Exhibit 45–5 displays the volatility of the bond market as

---

3. Convexity is the measure of how a bond's price change as yields change differs relative to the price change expected from its duration. Convexity is a measure of duration elasticity.

EXHIBIT 45-5

26-Week Rolling Volatility 30-Year Treasury: January 1976 through August 1993

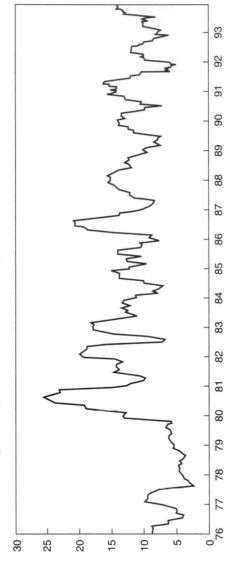

described by the 6-month moving average of the 12-month standard deviation of total return on 30-year U.S. Treasury bonds.

Unprecedented high volatility has been experienced in the bond market during the past decade. Not only has volatility been high, but the degree of variation in volatility has been high as well. It is *volatility change* that influences the value of options, which in turn cause relative performance differences between callable and noncallable portfolios.

A LOOK AT INTEREST RATES

The most important piece of the puzzle is the direction of interest rates. Exhibit 45–6 depicts the movement of rates for the period January 1, 1976, to August 1993. We observe dramatic changes in the absolute level of rates. As such changes occur, the relative values of callable and noncallable bonds change. Lower rates work to the advantage of noncallable bonds, and higher rates to the advantage of callable bonds. With extreme increases in rates, ironically, U.S. government noncallable bonds perform best. This is generally because of the importance of liquidity and credit noncallable bonds considerations to corporate bonds.

A Look at Recent History

The volatility of the bond market increased from about 4 percent in 1976 to about 20 percent in 1982. In the period from 1976 to 1982, volatility ranged between 2 percent and 20 percent. In the period from 1982 to 1993, volatility was never less than 7 percent. Over the period from 1976 to 1986, average volatility tripled. This information alone would favor bond portfolios containing the *fewest* callable securities. However, all else being equal, we would prefer noncallable portfolios during the period from 1976 to 1982 and callable ones during the 1982–1986 period. Substantial declines in volatility during the 1986–1993 period would imply a preference for callable bonds. However, the dramatic drop in rates during the period implies a preference for noncallable bonds.

Yields on long-term government bonds increased from 8 percent in 1976 to 14.5 percent in 1982. In the 1982–1986 period, rates dropped from 14.5 percent to 7.25 percent. The 1986–1989 period was one within which rates increased from 7.25 percent to 8.625 percent and long rates dropped to 6 percent by August 1993. The range in rates from 1976 to 1982 was 8 percent to 14.5 percent. The range for the middle period was 7.25 percent to 14.5 percent. Rates ranged from 7.25 percent to 10.00 percent during the 1986–1989 period and from 9.25 percent to 6 percent in the last period. We would naively expect portfolios containing callable securities to do best during the first period, portfolios containing noncallable bonds to do best during the second period, portfolios containing callable bonds to excel during the third period, and noncallable bonds to excel during the most recent period. Of course, these inferences assume constant conditions in credit, volatility, and yield-curve shape.

Yield on 30-Year Treasuries: January 1976 to June 1993

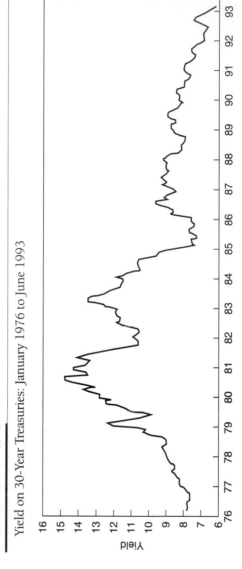

The performance differences between callable and noncallable bonds for these periods are summarized in Exhibit 45–7.

A Recent Episode

The interest-rate movement that began in 1990 continues today. For purposes of exposition, we will use June 1993 as a terminal date. This period is defined by high volatility in all segments of the bond management universe and requires a dissection into two subintervals (1990–1991 and 1991–1993) to appreciate the complexity of the bond market and the understanding required to facilitate intelligent risk-reward choices in bond-market allocations.

Interest rates approximated 8 percent across the yield curve in early 1990. Short-term rates had declined slightly from their 1989 levels as a result on the beginning of the implementation of a more liberal monetary policy aimed at countering the onset of a recession. The latter part of 1990 was marked by the Gulf War and full recession. In early 1991, one of the greatest monetary bailouts in history was in full swing as the Fed constantly slashed the discount rate in its attempt to resuscitate the economy. By June 1991, three-month Treasury Bills yielded 6 percent, and by December 1991 they yielded a mere 4 percent. The table below provides specific interest-rate details for the rate period.

	6-month	3-year	5-year	10-year	30-year	30 − 3	30 ÷ 3
1/90	7.90	7.87	7.89	7.92	7.98	.11	1.01
1/91	6.70	7.36	7.68	8.07	8.25	.89	1.21
6/91	5.93	7.28	7.91	7.92	7.98	2.05	1.35
1/92	4.00	5.05	5.93	6.70	7.40	2.35	1.47
6/93	3.24	4.33	5.05	5.78	6.68	2.35	1.54

This episode is particularly enlightening because the decline in interest rates is so substantial and the shape of the yield curve changed so dramatically. The interplay between the drop in yields and the changed yield curve illustrates the shortcoming of static duration as a risk measure and demonstrates the importance of the potential differences in duration between callable and noncallable bonds over wide interest-rate bands.

The value of callable bonds benefited considerably by the yield curve's steepening. As the call option embedded within the bond moved into the money with the drop in interest rates and started "trading to call," the bond's value was enhanced beyond what an option model would have predicted given the drop in interest rates and despite increases in volatility, because the bond was able to roll down a very steep yield curve. Despite this unexpected windfall, noncallable bonds were the preferred asset choice during this period of substantial rate reductions and limited call protection in any sector of conventional bonds. In this episode, the impact of changes in interest rate volatility was swamped by the changes in market rates and the changing of the yield-curve shape.

EXHIBIT 45-7

Performance Differences between Callable and Noncallable Bonds during Prior Periods

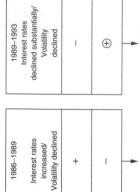

Portfolio composition	1976–1982 Interest rates increased/ Volatility increased	1982–1986 Interest rates declined/Volatility unchanged	1976–1986 Interest rates declined slightly/ Volatility increased	1986–1989 Interest rates increased/ Volatility declined	1989–1993 Interest rates declined substantially/ Volatility declined
Callable	–	(–)	–	+	–
Non-callable	–	(++)	+	–	(+)

Interest-rate change from 8% to 14.5% moved the call features out of the money. This effect swamped the increase in volatility. Thus, callable portfolios outperformed.

The steep decline in interest rates and the virtually unchanged level of high volatility favored noncallable portfolios by a wide margin. The options became in-the-money and shortened the duration of the callable portfolio, revealing the dramatic effects of negative convexity!

While interest rates declined only modestly, the tremendous increase in volatility served to make the option more valuable. A countervailing income advantage did not offset their decrease in principal value created by the option over short investment horizons.

During the first half of this period, the increase in interest rates swamped the increase in volatility. Callable bonds outperformed noncallables during this subperiod. During the second half of the period, rates declined and volatility declined. The drop in rates dominated and noncallables performed best. There were ambiguous results for the full period. Rates increased modestly and volatility was largely unchanged.

January 1990 – June 1991: The aggregate index (callable) outperformed the Lehman government corporate and the Salomon Brothers high-grade corporate index despite lower rates and higher volatility. The principal reason for the beneficial performance was the contribution of mortgage securities.

June 1991 – June 1993: The large decline in interest rates, the higher level of volatility, and the limited availability of call protection in the mortgage security universe was such a powerful combination that the performance of the call-protected government/corporate index dominated the performance of the aggregate but lagged the performance of the longer-duration Salomon Brothers index. Duration choices and yield-curve management were the two very potent sources of return.

The January 1990–June 1991 Subperiod

The aggregate index (callable) outperformed the Lehman government corporate and the Salomon Brothers high-grade corporate index despite lower rates and higher volatility. The principal reason for the beneficial performance was the contribution of mortgage securities. Mortgage securities were reasonably well call-protected at the beginning of the period and benefited from the sharp steepening that occurred at the short end of the yield curve, which more than offset the higher volatility experienced in 1990 and the general reduction in rates that occurred. The reduction in rates was not great enough or of a sufficient time to generate enough prepayments to harm the value of the mortgages substantially.

The June 1991–June 1993 Subperiod

The large decline in interest rates, the higher level of volatility, and the limited availability of call protection in the mortgage-security universe was such a powerful combination that the performance of the call-protected government/corporate index dominated the performance of the aggregate but lagged the performance of the longer-duration Salomon Brothers index. Duration choices and yield-curve management were two very potent sources of return dispersion.

THE IMPLICIT FORECASTS OF VOLATILITY AND INTEREST RATES

Most active bond managers are sector managers, or sector rotators. They hold portfolios composed of a high proportion of nongovernment securities. These portfolios are short the call options or, viewed alternatively, long portfolios of callable bonds. Combining this observation with the preceding historical analysis, it is obvious that few people seem to have anticipated the magnitude of the change in interest rates and the profound changes in realized volatility. Both of these forecast errors were important detractors from performance. Even those managers who correctly forecasted the change in interest rates terribly underestimated the combined impact of increased volatility and declining rates on the value of the option. Thus, their selection of bonds was inconsistent with their forecast.

Bond management necessarily requires a forecast of interest rates, a volatility forecast, and a set of analytical models that calculate the future value of individual securities and portfolios of securities based upon those forecasts. It is the confluence of volatility movement and interest-rate movement that largely affects bond values.

Similarly, the decision to move from active to passive management, or from passive to active, is necessarily predicated upon an implicit forecast of interest rates, volatility, and perceived investment manager consciousness. Moreover, the choice of index as a bogey for active managers or as a source of investment value contains within it an implicit forecast of both rates and volatility.

The choice of indexes in June 1993 (long government rates at 6.68 percent) is a choice of buying or selling convexity and duration. Convex portfolios, such as the LGC, hold a high percentage of noncallable bonds. Portfolios with little convexity, such as the Lehman Aggregate Index (LAG), hold many callable bonds. Thus, the durations of convex portfolios change inversely with market rates, whereas the durations of nonconvex portfolios may, perversely, change in the same direction as rates.

Simply stated, in today's world, the LGC is a convex portfolio and the LAG is not very convex.[4] As such, the LGC yields less than the LAG and is much more sensitive to changes in interest rates and changes in volatility. However, if rates decline from here, the LAG index will underperform the LGC by a significant margin because its duration will not increase and may actually decrease. Exhibit 45–8 compares the expected performance characteristics of the LGC and LAG.

The expected differences in portfolio performance are largely the result of the one-dimensional nature of duration as a descriptive risk variable. Portfolios with a high proportion of bonds containing embedded call options that are at or near the money perversely influence duration when interest rates change. Rate increases initially cause an *increase* in portfolio durations, and rate decreases cause a *decrease* in portfolio durations. The aggregate indexes today represent portfolios with this unconventional durational attribute because they contain a high proportion of callable bonds at or in the money. Portfolios described in terms of duration, convexity, and yield-curve character have greater explanatory power because their risk parameters are more fully defined. Implicit within a move to passive management is both a volatility forecast and a forecast of interest rates. The move to passive management and the adoption of market-type bogeys reinforces Say's Law, which holds that supply creates its own demand. Passive investment portfolios have done well in spite of their main investment criterion: Buy that which is produced independently of price or value considerations. Passive management relies upon the market forces to ensure that asset values are appropriate. Passive, narrow indexes, such as the LGC, have even done well recently because of the circumstances—radically lower rates and increased volatility, both of which have benefited call-protected portfolios. The past is prologue; today's investment choice will be judged by tomorrow's circumstances.

Today, the compositional and structural differences between the narrow and aggregate indexes are very pronounced. Previously, although they are compositionally distinct, their structural similarities caused highly correlated performance results. (See Exhibits 45–9 and 45–10.) The performance characteristics of the two indexes will now differ to a greater degree than has been previously experienced. In fact, the aggregate index will experience a gradual, unpredictable lengthening in duration as the high percentage of low-duration premium mortgages are prepaid and refinanced with current-coupon longer-duration mortgages. This lengthening will occur quite independently of any changes in interest rates and as long as rates do not drop considerably. A big drop in rates will most likely cause the LAG duration to decrease, and its performance would lag behind the performance of the LGC substantially. The differential would probably exceed most market participants' expectations.

---

4. The importance of coupon concentration in the relative performance of these two indexes is explained in the next section.

EXHIBIT 45-8

Comparison of the Expected Performance of the LGC and LAG

Interest rates	UNCH	Rise	Fall	UNCH	UNCH	Rise	Rise	Fall	Fall
Volatility	UNCH	UNCH	UNCH	Rises	Falls	Rises	Falls	Rises	Falls
Index that performs best	LAG	LAG	LGC	LGC	LAG	Ambiguous (LAG)[a]	LAG	LGC	Ambiguous (LAG)[a]

[a]Interest-rate movements are usually the prevailing force. The index in parentheses would therefore dominate unless the interest-rate movement was very small and the volatility movement great.

EXHIBIT 45–9

Index Performance (%) (Six-Month Periods)

End Date	LGC	LAG	LAG–LGC Difference	Ratio LGC to LAG%	Sal High Grade
12/78	.99	1.26	.27	78.57	1.00
06/79	6.62	6.50	−.12	101.85	6.16
12/79	−4.05	−4.29	−4.29	94.41	6.16
06/80	8.22	8.44	.22	97.39	−9.75
12/80	−4.77	−5.29	−5.29	90.17	7.81
06/81	.70	.15	−.55	466.67	−9.80
12/81	6.51	6.09	−.42	106.90	−2.92
06/82	6.41	6.84	.43	93.71	1.74
12/82	23.20	24.13	.93	96.15	5.91
06/83	4.82	4.91	.09	98.17	34.61
12/83	3.03	3.29	.26	92.10	5.70
06/84	−1.02	−1.68	−.48	71.43	.53
12/84	16.42	17.11	.69	95.97	−5.03
06/85	10.56	10.95	.39	96.44	23.05
12/85	9.72	10.05	.33	96.72	13.65
06/86	9.96	9.05	−.91	110.06	14.47
12/86	5.14	5.70	.56	90.18	11.52
06/87	−.44	−.17	.27	258.82	7.47
12/87	2.74	2.93	.19	93.52	−2.27
06/88	4.60	4.98	.38	93.37	2.04
12/88	2.85	2.77	−.08	102.89	6.35
06/89	9.23	9.20	−.03	100.33	11.66
12/89	4.58	4.89	.31	93.66	4.08
06/90	2.42	2.83	.41	85.51	1.85
12/90	5.73	5.96	.23	96.15	4.84
06/91	4.25	4.47	.22	95.08	5.50
12/91	11.39	11.04	−.35	3.17	13.64
06/92	2.49	2.70	.21	92.22	2.73
12/92	4.97	4.57	−.40	108.75	6.47
06/93	7.79	6.89	−.90	113.06	9.27

Those who are required to select a performance bogey for their fund have a difficult choice. The bogey performs the role of directing the risk of the assets. The choice involves a trade-off between a bogey that (1) replicates the proportional distribution of bonds in the market, (2) has risk characteristics complementary to the liability structure of the assets, and (3) has a relatively neutral market

E X H I B I T   45-10

Index Returns (%) (Two-Year Periods)

End Date	LGC	LAG	LAG–LGC Difference	Ratio LGC to LAG (%)	Sal High Grade
06/80	11.81	11.92	.11	99.08	
12/80	5.43	4.69	−.74	115.78	−6.83
06/81	−.42	−1.55	−1.03	27.10	−14.80
12/81	10.55	9.12	−1.43	115.68	−3.95
06/82	8.70	7.51	−1.19	115.85	−5.66
12/82	40.62	40.91	.29	99.29	40.80
06/83	46.37	47.61	1.24	97.40	53.31
12/83	41.58	43.71	2.13	95.13	51.48
06/84	31.45	32.25	.80	97.52	35.84
12/84	24.22	24.77	.55	97.78	24.17
06/85	31.02	31.96	.94	97.06	33.51
12/85	39.53	40.60	1.27	97.36	52.02
06/86	55.29	55.94	.65	98.84	78.51
12/86	40.25	40.74	.49	98.80	55.91
06/87	26.30	26.64	.34	98.72	34.07
12/87	18.27	18.44	.27	99.08	19.53
06/88	12.50	14.02	1.52	89.16	13.99
12/88	10.05	10.86	.81	92.54	10.41
06/89	20.73	21.25	−.48	97.55	26.16
12/89	22.89	23.56	.67	97.16	28.67
06/90	20.33	21.03	.70	96.67	23.22
12/90	23.70	24.79	1.09	95.60	24.09
06/91	18.05	19.39	1.34	93.08	17.24
12/91	25.75	26.40	.65	97.54	28.02
06/92	25.83	26.24	.41	98.44	29.12
12/92	24.93	24.59	−.34	101.38	31.14
06/93	29.18	27.48	−1.70	106.19	35.82

bias associated with it. Unfortunately, no bogey satisfies all of these require-ments, and the trade-offs can be costly.

The choices are difficult. Ultimately, correct macroeconomic forecasts will dominate the active/passive choice. Will volatility increase or diminish and when? Will rates go up or down and when? What influences volatility? How do interest rates, volatility, and yield-curve shape changes trade off? When does the volatility/interest-rate forecast favor one index over the other? These are the tough questions you should be asking your active manager or your passive index.

THE IMPORTANCE OF MORTGAGE COUPON CONCENTRATION IN RELATIVE LGC/LAG PERFORMANCE

Historically, the LAG and LGC have exhibited a high correlation. The high correlation was violated during the first half of 1986 and again in the 1990–1993 period. It is important to understand why the high correlation existed and why it diverges to better understand tomorrow's expected correlation.

It was previously noted that the major distinction between the LGC and the LAG is the inclusion of mortgages in the LAG. As such, we must determine whether these securities' options were at the money, in the money, or out of the money to establish their effect on portfolio convexity. The simplest framework we can utilize to evaluate the effect on convexity is a pricing framework. Mortgages selling at a discount exhibit positive convexity and higher durations, whereas other mortgages exhibit low or negative convexity and lower durations.

Exhibit 45–11 shows the percentage of outstanding GNMAs priced at or below par for selected time periods. We observe that in 1982 all mortgages were at par or a discount. In 1984, most mortgages were at a discount. The situation differed in June 1986 in that very few mortgages were priced at a discount. This means that the LAG exhibited a noncallable character through 1984 and most of 1985 but reversed late in 1985. The aggregate index increased its noncallable character in 1988 and declined subsequently. At that point, it took on negative convexity and a callable character. At the end of 1989, it had that callable character and therefore a shorter effective duration. In fact, under this condition, in contrast to noncallable indexes, its duration will decrease as rates *decline* and increase as rates increase. A more extreme condition now exists.

Exhibit 45–12 provides combined coupon distribution data of GNMA, FHLMC, and FNMA mortgage pass-throughs and the author's opinion about convexity characteristics.

The data in Exhibit 45–12 reveal that only 28 percent of the mortgages contained within the LAG exhibit positive convexity. In a modest bull market the LAG index duration will decline, and it will increase in a bear market. A radical

EXHIBIT   45–11

Percentage of Outstanding GNMAs Priced at or below Par

June/1978	79	*June/1980*	81	*June/1982*	83	*June/1984*	85
96.8%	100	97.4%	100	97.1%	71.6	95.7%	48.0
June/1986		*June/1987*		*June/1988*		*June/1989*	
34.9%		77%		83%		77%	
June/90		*June/91*		*June/92*		*June/93*	
62%		41%		2.6%		0%	

Source: Salomon Brothers.

EXHIBIT 45-12

Mortgage Coupon Characteristics (May 31, 1989)

Coupon	Approximate Price Range	Convexity	Percentage 6/30/93
5–6	44–99	(–)	1.01
6–7	100–104	(–)	13.01
7–8	104–107	(–)	36.18
8–9	$107-107^1/_2$	(–)	29.64
9–10	$107^1/_2-108^1/_2$	(–)	16.83
10–11	$109-112^1/_2$	(–)	2.26
11–12	113–114	(–)	.76
12–13	114+	(–)	.24
13–14		(–)	.04
>14		(–)	.03

bull or bear market in interest rates will magnify this phenomenon. The opposite response will occur with the LGC index. As such, at prevailing yield levels, the relative performance differentials between the indexes will be meaningful given some meaningful level of volatility.

Lower yields will increase performance differentials as index character diverges; higher yields will mitigate expected performance differentials because index character will merge.

THE IMPORTANCE OF CHANGES IN THE SHAPE OF THE YIELD CURVE

Changing yield-curve shapes represent the other important first-order determinant of relative performance differentials. The indexes are represented by various distributional holdings along the yield curve. Distributional differences between the LGC, the LAG,[5] and bond managers' portfolios will be important when yield-curve shapes are frequently variable and/or when changes in shape are of substantial magnitude. Yield-curve shape changes also change expected returns relative to those expected a priori because of the effects upon duration, call and put option values, prepayment behavior, and other, more subtle effects.

The yield-curve effect is not included in this analysis. Bond investment analysis is extremely complex when yield-curve shape changes are included. These complexities, including the potential correlation between interest rates and

---

5. Changes in the shape of the yield curve directly affect mortgage values. Coupon distribution relative to prevailing interest rates will influence the LAG asset distribution along the yield curve.

volatility, are beyond the scope of this chapter. Professional bond portfolio managers must understand these linkages if they hope to succeed.

Interest-Rate Volatility, Risk, and Index Choice

We will now introduce a subtle but important distinction between the indexes that is rarely noticed and almost never discussed. In Exhibit 45–13 the historical yield volatility of 5-year maturity and 30-year maturity treasuries is graphed. We ob-

E X H I B I T   45–13

Yield Volatilities, January 1980 to June 1993

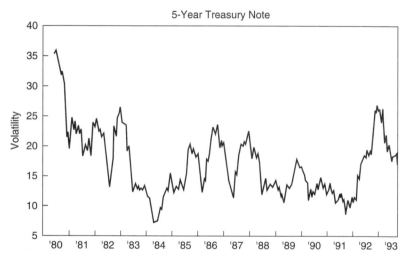

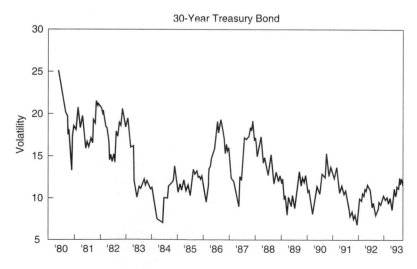

serve that the yield volatility of the 5-year is about one and one-half times more than that of the 30-year. A simple general rule is that the volatility of yields is a declining function of maturity. That is, yields on short securities are more volatile than yields on long securities.

Recall that the expected cash flow distribution is a distinguishing character-istic of the LGC and LAG. The LAG index has an expected cash flow distribution that is concentrated in the short maturity section of the yield curve much more so than the LGC. We can, therefore, infer that the LAG is a riskier bogey from an ex-pected volatility point of view when the duration of the two bogeys is equal. Al-ternatively, we can say that the LAG index is more volatile per unit of duration.

The importance of the impact of the linkage of volatility differentials to bogey risk is stronger than the mere fact that the volatility of cash flows will be different. There are other important, more subtle issues, including the impact of the volatility differentials on the value of the embedded options associated with each index, that are too complex to be examined in this chapter.

Looking Forward

Asset managers of endowments, foundations, and pension plans confront difficult choices today. We can garner sufficient insight if we focus our attention on the pension plan fixed income asset problem. The problem is significant because the amount of assets in pension plans has increased significantly during the 1980s and because the asset/liability mismatch is so great today.

In Exhibit 45–14, the differential impact of yield level on the duration of the bogeys and the pension liability is quantified. As the exhibit indicates, the du-ration mismatch between the bogeys and the pension plan liability approximates

E X H I B I T 45–14

Differential Impact of Yield Level on Duration of Bogeys and Pension Liability

		1980	1984	1988	1991	1993
O	Duration of LGC	5.04	4.02	5.03	4.94	5.27
x	Duration of LAG	5.26	4.24	5.07	4.83	4.38
◆	Approximate duration of pension liability	11.00	10.00	11.50	13.50	14.00
Z	30-year bond rate %	12.00	13.50	8.85	8.42	6.70

8.75 years (LGC) and 9.62 years (LAG) in 1993. Yet in 1984 the corresponding mismatches were only 5.98 years and 5.76 years. The dramatic drop in interest rates from 13.50 percent in 1984 to 6.70 percent in 1993 is the primary reason the mismatch increased so dramatically. This occurs because the structural character-istics between the indexes and the pension liability are so different. The indexes are intermediate and callable, whereas the pension liability is of long duration and well call protected. The mismatch would be greater if not for the fact that early re-tirement resulting from the many corporate restructurings has the effect of an ac-tive sinking fund, accelerating cash outflows and effectively shortening the duration of the liability.

What Can Be Expected If Rates Drop Another One Percent?
Cash flows with long duration and call protection are very convex in nature. The convexity implies that the duration of the flows is very sensitive to the rate to which the flows are discounted.

   The duration of long assets and liabilities is therefore very elastic with re-spect to interest rates. As previously noted, the duration of the LGC is not very sensitive and the LAG duration may, at times, even be inversely related. As a practical matter, because a plan's liabilities are long and the "market" bogeys are short, an important mismatch exists and is more pronounced today. If interest rates were to decline by 1 percent during the next few months, the value of the lia-bility stream would increase by about 15.5 percent. The assets assigned to an LGC bogey would increase by about 5.5 percent and the assets assigned to the LAG would only appreciate by about 4 percent, one quarter of the change in the value of the liability. A plan sponsor may hedge the mismatch risk through the purchase of call options on long bonds. Unfortunately, today that strategy renders a negative return to the portfolio if rates do not drop. Strangely enough, if interest rates stabilize, the duration of the LAG index will automatically increase as current-coupon mortgages are substituted for premium coupons in the refinancing process. Even with the increase in duration in the LAG, an important asset/liabil-ity duration mismatch in the pension fixed income management currently exists and must be addressed. Today's mismatch represents a very big bet against lower interest rates.

INDEX CONSCIOUSNESS

The extraordinary volatility of interest rates of the 70s and 80s continued into the 90s and has resulted in considerable volatility in returns. Durational differences between portfolios result in substantially different returns when interest rates are volatile. The historical return difference between the LGC and the Salomon High Grade Index illustrates this point. Many market participants were apparently sur-prised by the amount of price volatility that their bond portfolios experienced in the 1960s and 1970s. In an effort to control portfolio return variability relative to the "market," some bond managers have adopted portfolio constraints wherein the durational risk relative to the market index is bound. The movement to this new investment strategy should help control variability but will nullify the relative advantages achievable through expert macroeconomic analysis and interest-rate forecasting. The movement to this policy is an admission of a flawed investment theory, risk aversion, and/or an uncertain conviction in forecasting of quantitative capability. Today, given the recognition that the market bogeys are so mismatched with the expected liabilities, a thorough review of bogey selection is under way. This chapter has emphasized the importance of the contribution of good interest-rate and volatility forecasts with consistent period-dependent asset selection.

⑥ # A SPONSOR'S VIEW OF BENCHMARK PORTFOLIOS

Daralyn B. Peifer, CFA
Manager, Benefit Finance
General Mills, Inc.

THE SPONSOR'S ROLE

Today, the role of a plan sponsor in managing pension assets is a lot like that of the manager of a baseball team. A plan sponsor selects investment managers to fill assigned niches in an investment management structure in much the same manner as the baseball manager selects players to fill positions on the team roster. The baseball manager drafts and recruits players to cover the baseball field; the plan sponsor hires investment managers, both internal and external to the sponsor's organization, to cover desired portions of the capital markets.

The baseball manager has one advantage over the plan sponsor in that the team's playing field is defined by league regulations. The baseball manager does not need to worry about the size and shape of the playing field, as this responsibility resides with league officials, and thus can focus on achieving good field coverage. In contrast to the manager, the plan sponsor must first decide what the dimensions of the playing field are to be before the field can be filled with players. That is, the sponsor must decide which portions of the capital markets should be covered to meet plan objectives before a team of managers can be hired.

Defining the appropriate playing field and filling the field with superior players are two of the most critical tasks faced by the plan sponsor. The sponsor defines the playing field by specifying the long-term policy asset allocation for the pension plan. The policy allocation lists the asset classes to be included in the total pension portfolio and target weights for each of the classes. The sponsor then fills the playing field by building an investment management structure, or a configuration of investment managers who will invest the assets of the pension fund. For each asset class in the fund's policy asset mix, the structure lists the investment styles or niches to be included in the asset class program, a policy weight for each of the styles, and the investment managers who will fill the desired niches.

Plan sponsors are finding that the tasks associated with defining and covering the playing field are becoming increasingly complex. In defining the field, the sponsor may now consider for inclusion in the total pension portfolio, not only the traditional asset classes of stocks and bonds, but also the growing list of non-traditional asset classes such as real estate, energy, timberland, and private equities. To further complicate the tasks, the sponsor may also include international securities along with domestic ones in each of the asset classes represented in the policy allocation.

In covering the field, the sponsor must first determine the allocations to active and passive approaches. Today, the sponsor can choose from the extremes of purely passive and active approaches as well as a whole spectrum of structured approaches between the two extremes. Once the active/passive allocations have been established, the sponsor must select the specific investment styles and investment managers to be represented in the management structure. Here, too, the list of styles and managers available for inclusion by plan sponsors in their pension portfolios has grown tremendously in recent years. The hierarchy of sponsor decisions is detailed in Exhibit 46–1.

In this complex environment, plan sponsors have found benchmark portfolios to be very useful tools as they both define and cover their playing fields. Benchmark portfolios, also called *normal* portfolios, are quantitative descriptions of manager styles. We will focus first on the evolution of the use of benchmark portfolios by plan sponsors and the pension management trends that sparked the evolution. We will also discuss the application of benchmark portfolios to a specific portion of the sponsor's playing field, using the fixed income asset class as

E X H I B I T   46–1

Hierarchy of Sponsor Decisions

- Long-Term Investment Policy
  - Asset classes
  - Asset class weights
  - Asset class benchmarks
- Investment Management Structures
  - Active/passive management
  - Investment styles
  - Investment managers
  - Investment vehicles

an example and outlining some of the special challenges and opportunities associated with fixed income benchmarks. Finally, we will address some of the more controversial issues that plan sponsors and their consultants and investment managers face with the use of benchmark portfolios in fixed income as well as other asset class programs.

GENESIS OF BENCHMARK PORTFOLIOS

Over the past 15 years, pension plan management has been characterized by the shifting of investment responsibilities between the plan sponsor and the sponsor's investment managers. In the mid-1970s, many plan sponsors were concerned about the scope of their fiduciary responsibilities under the newly passed Employee Retirement Income Security Act (ERISA) regulations. As a result, they hired external balanced managers and turned over to these managers the responsibility for allocating pension assets among the available asset classes, emphasizing primarily stocks, bonds, and cash equivalents. In addition, they charged the managers with selecting individual securities within each of these three asset classes.

This balanced-manager approach proved to be a very frustrating one for many sponsors. The limitations of this approach are easy to see when viewed in a baseball context. A team of balanced-investment managers is much like a baseball team in which the players are allowed to choose their own positions and can change positions at any time during a game. Moreover, any number of players can cover the same position. Now, imagine a critical play-off game. The manager of the visiting team has shifted the responsibility for field coverage to the team players and is watching passively from the dugout. In the bottom of the ninth inning with the visitors one run ahead, the home team batter approaches the plate with two outs and bases loaded. The batter hits an easy fly ball to left field. However, the ball drops untouched and the winning runs score for the home team because all the visiting players are over in right field. This situation is similar to that of a plan sponsor who, having given up the responsibility for asset allocation, watches helplessly from the sidelines as stocks perform well during a period, while all of the sponsor's balanced managers are invested in bonds.

In the late 1970s, plan sponsors generally began to feel more comfortable with their fiduciary roles, and as a result, many took back the responsibility for making asset allocation decisions from their managers. These sponsors believed that they were better suited than their managers to make allocations to asset classes, because they understood the characteristics and objectives of their plans. These sponsors either terminated their balanced managers or restricted them to a single asset class and began to build configurations of multiple specialized managers within each of the asset classes represented in their pension portfolios.

There were two basic problems associated with sponsors' early attempts at building investment manager structures. First, the specialized styles of individual managers tended to be described solely in qualitative terms. For example, some common stock managers were labeled simply as "value," "growth," or "sector rotator" managers, while bond managers were often categorized as "interest-rate anticipators" or "sector selectors." Because these simple descriptions did not convey the subtleties of an investment manager's investment process, sponsors could not be sure which area of the capital markets a particular manager covered. This meant that as sponsors put together teams of investment managers, they had no way of determining whether they had achieved full coverage of their field.

The second problem resulted from the tendency of sponsors to emphasize strong recent performance as the primary manager selection criterion. Although most sponsors set out to hire managers with differing styles, their emphasis on short-term performance left them with teams of managers that were heavily weighted in the investment styles most recently in market favor. This was a lot like a team manager who recruits the strongest players from the current season, putting a team together without regard for filling all of the positions. As a result of these two problems, sponsors who adopted the multiple-specialized-manager approach instead of the balanced-manager approach were able to achieve control over the coverage among available asset classes but experienced major "gaps" or "overlaps" in the coverage within asset classes.

In the late 1970s and early 1980s, plan sponsors and their advisors began to search for better ways of defining and filling their playing fields. Benchmark portfolios began to be used for these tasks. As representations of manager styles, benchmark portfolios first served as useful tools in the evaluation of individual investment managers. However, sponsors and consultants quickly realized that benchmark portfolios could also serve as powerful tools in building manager structures. By providing more comprehensive descriptions of manager styles and quantitatively specifying managers' areas of focus, benchmark portfolios gave sponsors the means to reduce or eliminate the "gaps" and "overlaps" in their coverage of capital markets.

PENSION MANAGEMENT: EMERGING TRENDS

Plan sponsors have demonstrated increasing interest in benchmark portfolios. This attention reflects several trends in pension plan management. First, sponsors have continued to assume more active positions, taking over some of the responsibilities for plan management they relinquished to managers in previous years. These active postures reflect a heightened awareness on the part of plan sponsors of the significant impact their policy decisions have on the value of pension assets under their care. In particular, sponsors have recognized that their allocations to asset classes and manager styles have a much greater impact on their pension portfolios than do the individual security selection decisions made by investment managers.[1]

---

1. The relative impact of various portfolio decisions on the value of pension plan assets is presented in the often-quoted Gary P. Brinson, Randolph Hood, and Gilbert L. Beebower, "Determinants of Portfolio Performance," *Financial Analysts Journal,* July/August 1986, pp. 39–44.

As sponsors have assumed more responsibility for plan management, including allocations to asset classes and manager styles, they have also reassessed the allocations of resources within their own programs. Until recently, the focus of most sponsors was on the evaluation and monitoring of individual investment managers, and their staffs and budgets were devoted primarily to these functions. Today, a growing number of plan sponsors have shifted their focus from the individual manager level to the total portfolio level and have reallocated their resources accordingly. This shift is consistent with the major impact that total portfolio decisions have on plan assets.

Sponsors have also become increasingly aware of the need to clarify and prioritize plan objectives before making investment decisions. In addition, more sponsors are taking into account the unique characteristics of their own plans as well as the characteristics of their organizations in setting objectives. This new emphasis on objectives and characteristics has caused sponsors to redefine the risks relevant to their programs and to specify the tolerance of the sponsor decision makers for bearing the risks. The liability streams represented by plan obligations have received greater attention in sponsor risk discussions; as a result, risks are being defined more frequently in an asset/liability context than in an assets-only one.[2]

Along with these trends is an emphasis by plan sponsors on controlling risks at the total portfolio level. Many sponsors have acknowledged the importance of diversification in portfolio risk control and have adopted more sophisticated, quantitative approaches to diversification. As sponsors have constructed configurations of investment managers for each of their asset-class programs, they have tended to diversify along a greater number of risk dimensions or factors.

Plan sponsors have also indicated the desire for more meaningful performance evaluation. As they have taken on more responsibility for investment decisions, sponsors have expressed interest in quantifying the value added to plan assets from their own decisions and from the decisions of their investment managers, and they have begun to hold their managers accountable for their assigned roles in management structures. To this end, sponsors have worked to clarify performance expectations for themselves and their investment managers. They have also expressed interest in tying the compensation of their investment managers to

---

2. The definition of risk and the recognition of liabilities in the pension planning processes are thoughtfully addressed in Robert D. Arnott and Peter L. Bernstein, "Defining and Managing Pension Fund Risk," and Keith P. Ambachtsheer, "Integrating Business Planning with Pension Fund Planning," in *Asset Allocation: A Handbook of Portfolio Policies, Strategies, & Tactics,* eds. Robert D. Arnott and Frank J. Fabozzi (Chicago, IL: Probus Publishing, 1988), pp. 17–39 and pp. 59–85, as well as in Wayne H. Wagner, "The Many Dimensions of Risk," *Journal of Portfolio Management,* Winter 1988, pp. 35–39. An interesting approach to identifying investors' risk tolerance is presented in William F. Sharpe, "Investor Wealth Measures and Expected Return," seminar proceedings from *Quantifying the Market Risk Premium Phenomenon for Investment Decision Making,* The Institute of Chartered Financial Analysts, September 1989.

relative performance results, and this interest has been reflected in increased attention to performance-based fee systems.[3]

The shift to a total portfolio perspective, the emphasis on more sophisticated risk control, the desire for more meaningful performance evaluation, and the interest in performance-based fees have spurred pension sponsors, consultants, and investment managers alike in their quest for "perfect" benchmark portfolios.

BENCHMARK PORTFOLIOS

Controlling the risk of the total pension portfolio requires that sponsors use benchmark portfolios at two levels in their long-term policy frameworks: the asset-class level and the individual-manager level. We term benchmarks used at the asset-class level *asset-class targets* and those at the manager level *manager benchmarks*.

Asset-Class Targets

Asset-class targets are critical components of a plan sponsor's long-term policy statement. Sponsors must not only specify the asset classes to be included in the pension portfolio and appropriate weights for each of the classes; they must also define the role that each asset class is expected to play in the pension portfolio and the contribution the class is expected to make in achieving total plan objectives.

An asset-class target is a universe of securities. As the benchmark for an asset class, the target represents the set of opportunities that best achieves the purposes for which the asset class is included in the portfolio. The target reflects the trade-offs between risk and return that are associated with the class and sets forth the performance expectations for the asset-class program. By comparing the risk characteristics and the performance results of the actual asset-class program with those of the asset-class target, the sponsor ensures that the defined role of the asset class in the total portfolio will be met.

An asset-class target can be a standard broad market index, a weighted combination of components of market indexes, or a custom index. The selection of an appropriate asset-class target depends on the objectives defined for the asset class. A broad market index may be appropriate for asset classes that are included in the portfolio for total-return maximization. To the extent that the sponsor faces constraints or objectives for an asset class that differ from those of total-return maximization, some deviation from a broad market index may be necessary in the construction of the asset-class target to reflect the objectives.

---

3. Issues relating to the development and application of performance-based fee systems are discussed in Andrew Rudd and Richard C. Grinold, "Incentive Fees: Who Wins? Who Loses?" *Financial Analysts Journal,* January/February 1987, pp. 27–38, and Jeffery V. Bailey, "Some Thoughts on Performance Based Fees," *Financial Analysts Journal,* July/August 1990, pp. 31–40.

In setting asset-class targets, it is helpful to start with a broad market index as a base index and consider how that index should be altered in terms of characteristics or risk dimensions to reflect specific investment objectives. The deviations from a broad market index required to meet plan objectives may be identified by the sponsor through scenario analysis. In this type of analysis, the sponsor identifies a number of possible economic scenarios and determines which types of securities will behave in the desired manner under these scenarios to achieve plan goals. The selection of an appropriate index may involve trade-offs between investment objectives, as the deviations from a broad index required to achieve one objective may be counter to those needed to achieve another. In addition, the asset-class target must have internal consistency. Because the risk characteristics of an asset class may be interrelated, in building a target it is important to check that all of the desired characteristics are mutually achievable.

Fixed Income Targets

Fixed income asset-class targets are often more interesting to design than common-stock targets because bonds are included in pension portfolios for a variety of reasons, whereas common stocks tend to be included in pension portfolios solely for total-return purposes. As a result, sponsors tend to deviate very little from broad market indexes in setting common-stock targets. Where deviations occur, they reflect sponsors' investment constraints or opinions regarding long-term structural inefficiencies or opportunities in the stock market. Because bonds tend to be included in pension portfolios for reasons other than total-return maximization, and the reasons vary dramatically from plan sponsor to plan sponsor, the asset-class targets selected by sponsors for their fixed income programs vary as well.

In selecting a fixed income asset-class target, a sponsor might begin with one of the broad bond indexes and consider how the index would need to be altered to meet the objectives for the asset class: Exhibit 46–2 lists the characteristics of the index that need to be assessed. For example, some sponsors include bonds in their pension portfolios to provide a hedge against unexpected and severe deflation. In order to design a fixed income asset-class target to reflect this objective, the sponsor needs to consider how various fixed income securities behave in deflationary environments. The sponsor might then deviate from the broad index or "tilt" the fixed income asset-class target in favor of securities or characteristics of securities that provide the best protection against deflation. The resulting target might be weighted in favor of long-duration, high-quality securities with some additional protection against call and prepayment risks, as these kinds of securities can be expected to experience significant appreciation in declining-interest-rate environments.

Other sponsors focus on the variability of pension assets relative to liabilities and the role of fixed income securities in dampening pension surplus volatility. In establishing a fixed income asset-class target to reflect this role, a sponsor

EXHIBIT 46–2

Benchmark Portfolio Fixed Income Construction Process

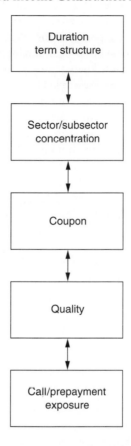

would need to begin with the pension plan liabilities as the base index and consider which types of fixed income securities would respond in a similar fashion as the liabilities and provide the best hedge for the liabilities under various economic scenarios.

Risk Control

Sponsors control the risk in their pension portfolios by comparing the risk characteristics of each asset-class target with the characteristics of the aggregate of the individual manager benchmark portfolios within the class. Ideally, the sponsor works with each investment manager to design a benchmark portfolio that reflects the manager's investment style. The sponsor then adds together the manager benchmark portfolios and compares the characteristics of the aggregate with the target. This comparison allows the sponsor to identify any mismatch or "gaps" between the aggregate manager benchmark and the target. In baseball terms, gaps in the aggregate benchmark represent areas of the playing field that are not being covered by the players on the field. In investment terms, the gaps represent unintended or inadvertent bets in the portfolio for which no reward is expected. The objective of this use of asset-class targets and manager benchmarks is to identify and eliminate all of the unintended bets, leaving only the managers' active bets, for which the sponsor expects to be rewarded.

Once gaps or unintended bets in the pension portfolio have been identified, a plan sponsor has several alternatives for reducing them. One alternative is simply to reallocate assets among the sponsor's current managers. This is equivalent to keeping the same players, but repositioning them slightly in the field. A second alternative is to add or subtract managers from the sponsor's current configuration. Yet another approach involves the addition of a completion fund, which essentially fills out the aggregate manager benchmark portfolio until it matches the asset-class target.[4] Exhibit 46–3 highlights this risk-control process.

Manager Benchmarks

In order for a sponsor to effectively control the risk of the total portfolio by monitoring the "fit" between the aggregate manager benchmark portfolio for each asset-class program and the asset-class target for the respective program, appro-

EXHIBIT   46–3

Risk Control for Asset-Class Programs

- Each manager is assigned a benchmark portfolio.
- Managers' benchmark portfolios are aggregated.
- Aggregate benchmark is compared to the asset-class target.
- "Gaps" are identified.
- Alternative actions:
  - Reallocate among current managers.
  - Add/subtract managers.
  - Add completeness or fulfillment fund.

---

4. David E. Tierney of Richards & Tierney, Inc., is often credited with the development of the concept of a completeness fund. For discussion, see William S. Gray III, "Portfolio Construction: Equity," in *Managing Investment Portfolios: A Dynamic Process,* eds. John L. Maginn and Donald L. Tuttle, sponsored by the Institute of Chartered Financial Analysts (Boston, MA: Warren, Gorham & Lamont, 1983). Also see David E. Tierney and Kenneth Winston, "Defining and Using Dynamic Completeness Funds to Enhance Total Fund Efficiency," *Financial Analysts Journal,* July/August 1990, pp. 49–60.

priate benchmark portfolios must be created for each of the individual investment managers represented in the sponsor's portfolio.

A manager benchmark is a portfolio of securities that represents a manager's investment style. Manager benchmarks describe manager styles in quantitative rather than qualitative terms. For plan sponsors, manager benchmarks represent a major improvement over the use of simple qualitative descriptors to categorize managers. Whereas qualitative descriptors tend to reflect only a single aspect of a manager's investment process and ignore others, manager benchmarks can reflect many aspects of the process. Manager benchmarks describe the varied aspects of a manager's style in terms of the manager's typical exposures along a spectrum of risk dimensions or risk factors.

A manager benchmark represents a manager's baseline position and reflects risk exposures under neutral investment conditions.[5] A neutral condition exists when the manager has no strong opinions about misvaluations of sectors and/or securities in the manager's area of expertise.

Manager Benchmark Uses

From a sponsor's perspective, the most important use of manager benchmarks is in building manager configurations. Comparing aggregate manager benchmarks with asset-class targets allows sponsors to understand and control the risk in their total portfolios. In addition to this use, however, manager benchmarks have a number of ancillary uses for sponsors as well as their investment managers.

Sponsors' expectations for portfolio risk and return can be communicated very clearly to managers using manager benchmarks. Benchmarks allow managers to better understand the assigned roles they are expected to play on the sponsor's team. They also serve to communicate the division of responsibility between the sponsor and manager. The sponsor assumes responsibility for the performance of the manager benchmark or investment style and holds the manager accountable only for the performance of the manager's actual portfolio relative to the benchmark.

Manager benchmarks help managers to understand and maintain the constraints placed on their portfolio activities by sponsor clients. In order to control portfolio risks, sponsors may place restrictions on the types of securities that managers may hold as well as on the risk exposures managers may assume. For example, to ensure that overall fixed income objectives are met, a sponsor may limit the amount of short-term securities bond managers may hold and, in addi-

---

5. One of the seminal works on common-stock risk factors and benchmark portfolios is Barr Rosenberg and Vinay Marathe, "Common Factors in Security Returns: Microeconomic Determinants and Macroeconomic Correlates," Proceedings of the Seminar on the Analysis of Security Prices, University of Chicago, May 1976, pp. 61–225. Basic fixed income benchmark concepts are presented in Martin L. Leibowitz, "Goal-Oriented Bond Portfolio Management," in *Total Return Management* (Salomon Brothers, 1979), pp. 3–20.

tion, may apply restrictions on the duration and quality of the managers' overall portfolios. By clarifying the role the manager is expected to play in a specific sponsor's portfolio and by communicating the division of responsibility, manager benchmarks facilitate adherence to sponsor constraints.

Sponsors also find manager benchmarks to provide a useful focus for reviews with managers. A sponsor can gain an understanding of a manager's current outlook for the capital markets by discussing the active "bets" or deviations in the manager's actual portfolio relative to the benchmark. Monitoring the risk exposures of a manager's actual portfolio relative to the neutral or benchmark position also enables a sponsor to gain a deeper understanding of the manager's investment processes and style. Astute sponsors can also detect shifts in a manager's style as well as identify any large and unusual "bets" present in the manager's portfolio.

Also, the identification of superior managers is aided by the use of manager benchmarks. With the randomness and uncertainty in the capital markets, it is difficult to identify with any degree of confidence the superior managers. Evaluating managers relative to appropriate benchmarks reduces some of the "noise" inherent in the performance measurement process. Manager benchmarks also enable sponsors to adopt performance-based fee systems and tie manager compensation to results relative to appropriate benchmark standards. In addition, manager benchmarks facilitate performance attribution, helping sponsors identify not only which managers are adding value to the total pension portfolios, but also the manner in which the "value added" is being generated.[6]

BENCHMARK PORTFOLIO CONSTRUCTION

The construction of a benchmark portfolio generally involves screening a broad universe for securities that represent a manager's style. For common-stock manager benchmarks, the sponsor typically begins with a broad index of 200 to 1,000 stocks that represent the manager's research universe. The sponsor then screens the universe using risk parameters that reflect the manager's neutral investment

---

6. In Jeffery V. Bailey, Thomas M. Richards, and David E. Tierney, "Benchmark Portfolios and the Manager/Plan Sponsor Relationship," *Journal of Corporate Finance,* Winter 1988, pp. 25–32, the authors present a comprehensive overview of common-stock benchmark portfolios, including a discussion of desirable properties of "correct" benchmarks and a case study of their application. An early application by a plan sponsor of common-stock benchmark portfolios is described in Walter R. Good, "Measuring Performance," *Financial Analysts Journal,* May/ June 1983, pp. 19–23. A current sponsor's approach to the construction and use of common-stock benchmark portfolios is presented in Edward P. Rennie and Thomas J. Cowhey, "The Successful Use of Benchmark Portfolios," in *Improving Portfolio Performance with Quantitative Models,* eds. H. Russell Fogler and Darwin M. Bayston (Charlottesville, VA: The Institute of Chartered Financial Analysts, April 1989), pp. 33–42.

position. The resulting manager benchmark may consist of several hundred stocks with weights assigned to each.[7]

In contrast, a cellular approach is often used in building fixed income manager benchmarks. A broad bond index can be thought of as a series of cells that exhibit certain characteristics. The screening process involves focusing on cells that are consistent with the manager's area of emphasis. If, for example, a manager ignores certain sectors or segments of the broad bond market, cells representing those segments can be eliminated from the benchmark. Cells can be defined very narrowly or very broadly. All industrial bonds of a certain maturity, coupon, and yield might define a narrow cell. Or the entire corporate segment of a published bond index might constitute a broad cell. Typically, we would expect a large number of a manager's actual holdings to be represented in the manager's benchmark portfolio. However, we would not expect all of the manager's actual holdings to be included in the benchmark, as managers are generally allowed to make bets or assume exposures that are outside their usual areas of focus.[8]

Fixed income benchmark portfolios may be very elaborate and complicated or they may be quite simple. Exhibits 46–4a and 46–4b illustrate the two extremes in benchmark building. Exhibit 46–4a depicts the more complex approach, with the manager's style being described in detailed terms of duration and sector exposure. Exhibit 46–4b, in contrast, uses a simple combination of pub-

E X H I B I T   46–4a

Fixed Income Benchmark Portfolio
Manager A

Sector	0–1	1–3	3–5	5–7	7+	Total
Governments and agencies		5%		15%	5%	25%
Mortgages			10%	15%	5%	30%
Corporate		5%	15%	10%	10%	40%
Cash equivalents	5%					5%
Total	5%	10%	25%	40%	20%	100%

---

7. Basic benchmark portfolio construction techniques for common-stock portfolios are described in Mark Kritzman, "How to Build a Normal Portfolio in Three Easy Steps," *Journal of Portfolio Management,* Summer 1987, pp. 21–23.

8. For presentations of fixed income index and benchmark portfolio construction, see Sharmin Mossavar-Rahmani, "Understanding and Evaluating Index Fund Management," and Edward A. Robie, Jr., and Peter C. Lambert, "Fixed Income Normal Portfolios and Their Application to Fund Management," in *Advances in Bond Analysis and Portfolio Strategies,* eds. Frank J. Fabozzi and T. Dessa Garlicki (Chicago: Probus Publishing, 1987), pp. 443–449 and pp. 35–48. I am also grateful to Robert C. Kuberek of Wilshire Associates for sharing his insights on bond indexing.

Fixed Income Benchmark Portfolio
Manager B

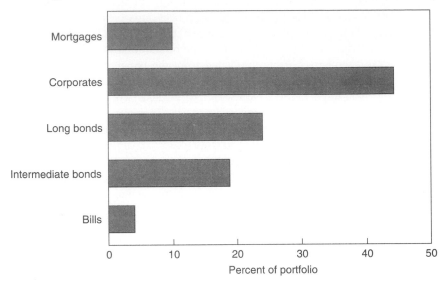

lished bond market indexes to represent the style of a second manager. Both benchmark portfolios represent significant improvements over qualitative style descriptors.

The construction process begins with a discussion of the manager's investment process and proceeds with an analysis of the risk exposures or characteristics of the manager's current portfolio. The process may also include an analysis of the characteristics of the manager's historical portfolios. The benchmark builder may examine the long-term average characteristics exhibited by the historical portfolios as well as the range and trends of characteristics to determine the appropriate manner of describing the manager's style.

Once a preliminary manager benchmark has been created, the historical performance of the benchmark versus the actual portfolio may be examined to see if the pattern of "value added" by the manager is consistent with expectations. Finally, the benchmark must be reviewed by the investment manager. Benchmark construction is an active process and often involves many trials before sponsor and manager agree that an acceptable representation of the manager's style has been reached.

Benchmark building is a creative process, with elements of both art and science. The concept of benchmark portfolios becomes more difficult to apply as one moves from common stocks to the other asset classes, with fixed income lying somewhere between common stocks and the nontraditional asset classes such as real estate and venture capital, in the degree of difficulty associated with benchmark building. Fixed income benchmarks represent several challenges not associated with the construction of common-stock benchmarks. However, offsetting these difficulties are some unique features of the fixed income markets that present opportunities for creative benchmark construction.

FIXED INCOME BENCHMARKS: CHALLENGES AND OPPORTUNITIES

The challenges of fixed income benchmark building are presented in Exhibit 46–5. One of the most significant challenges is the overwhelming size of the fixed income markets. Whereas the construction process for a common-stock benchmark portfolio may begin with a universe of only 500 to 1,000 stocks, a broad bond market index or universe may include well over 5,000 individual securities. Contributing to the complexity is the dynamic nature of the bond universes. Characterized by the continual issuance and maturity of securities, the broad bond universes that must be screened to create bond benchmark portfolios are moving targets in themselves. In addition, unlike common stocks, which tend to be "plain vanilla" in nature, there is an ever-growing array of security types represented in the fixed income markets. Compounding these challenges are the complex embedded-option features that characterize many fixed income instruments.

On the other hand, there are several characteristics of the fixed income markets that facilitate benchmark building. First is the dominance of interest-rate sensitivity as the main risk factor in the bond markets. A common-stock benchmark portfolio typically is described in terms of exposures to many different risk factors.[9] In contrast, a sponsor or manager can make a major step toward building a good fixed income benchmark simply by expressing an appropriate duration and

EXHIBIT   46–5

The Challenges of Benchmark Portfolios: Fixed Income versus Common Stock

- Dynamic universe of securities
- Great array of security types
- Complex pricing issues
- Embedded option characteristics
  - Call and put options
  - Prepayment features
- Database limitations

---

9. At present, it appears that the majority of plan sponsors use the BARRA multiple-risk factor model for common-stock benchmark portfolio construction.

term-structure exposure. The large number of published bond indexes and subindexes also facilitates the construction of fixed income benchmarks. Whereas a common-stock benchmark generally is specified in terms of individual securities, a bond benchmark may be specified in terms of components of major bond indexes and appropriate weights for the components.

Fixed income portfolios also lend themselves to consideration as distributions of expected cash inflows. As a result, sponsors have the opportunity to shape the expected cash flow distribution of a fixed income benchmark. On the asset-class target level, the benchmark can be shaped to reflect the objectives established for the fixed income asset class. This characteristic is particularly helpful in situations where the sponsor is focusing on the asset/liability relationship of the pension portfolio, as plan liabilities can be thought of as distributions of expected cash outflows. On the manager benchmark level, the benchmark can be shaped to reflect a manager's style.[10]

BENCHMARKS: CONCERNS AND ISSUES

Despite the attractive features of benchmark portfolios, most sponsors and managers have some concerns regarding their construction and use. One of the most troublesome issues involves the separation of a manager's investment style from the active management. It is difficult to analyze the risk characteristics of the manager's current and historical portfolios because the manager's active bets are reflected in the characteristics along with the manager's style. The task is to separate the manager's neutral style, for which the sponsor assumes responsibility, from the manager's proprietary "value added" processes.

There is some disagreement between sponsors and managers as to what constitutes proprietary "value added." Some managers maintain that the selection of the investment style itself represents value attributable to the manager. However, the availability of a wide variety of passive and semipassive products has made it fairly easy for sponsors to replicate managers' styles in a cost-effective manner, and therefore, sponsors have become increasingly unwilling to attribute the value added through style selection to managers. As a result, many sponsors will now pay active management fees only for the value that is added in excess of the manager's investment style.

Sponsors and consultants also express concerns about the ability of managers to game their benchmarks. Although there is no question that managers have this ability, monitoring the characteristics of the manager's actual portfolio relative to the benchmark should make this problem apparent. The processes of building and using manager benchmark portfolios involve a high degree of inter-

---

10. The mechanics of shaping the cash flow structure of a bond portfolio are addressed in Philip H. Galdi, "Indexing Fixed Income Portfolios," in *Advances in Bond Analysis & Portfolio Strategies,* eds. Frank J. Fabozzi and T. Dessa Garlicki (Chicago: Probus Publishing, 1987).

action, negotiation, and cooperation between the sponsor and investment manager. Both parties need to agree that the final benchmark to be used for evaluation, and possibly compensation, is appropriate.

Some sponsors and managers question whether the benefits of benchmark portfolios justify the related costs. Resources need to be expended for the initial construction of benchmarks as well as for their ongoing maintenance and monitoring. This issue might be debatable from the perspective of an investment manager. However, from the sponsor's perspective, benchmark portfolios are integral components of the total pension management process. For a sponsor whose investment structure includes multiple active managers, the only way that the risk of the total portfolio can be identified and managed effectively is through the use of benchmark portfolios.[11]

As indicated earlier, sponsors and consultants are finding the application of benchmark portfolios to the nontraditional asset classes particularly challenging. Conceptually, benchmark portfolios are just as valid and important for real estate, venture capital, and resource programs, for example, as for common-stock and bond programs. However, the implementation of benchmark portfolios for these asset classes has been problematic. Because investments in the nontraditional asset classes are often private ones, sponsors as well as consultants have experienced difficulty gathering enough information to form reasonable risk/return expectations for their programs and communicating their expectations to managers. Sponsors have been hampered in their efforts to establish asset-class targets and manager benchmarks by the scarcity of acceptable published indexes and the lack of formal risk models for these asset classes. This situation is improving gradually, but there is still considerable work left to be done.

SUMMARY

In the increasingly complex world of pension investing, plan sponsors are becoming more and more aware of the need to understand and control the risk of their aggregate pension portfolios. A growing number of pension sponsors are addressing this need by establishing clear objectives for their plans and translating the objectives into comprehensive policy frameworks. Benchmark portfolios have become key elements in many sponsors' policy frameworks.

Sponsors are using benchmark portfolios at both the asset class and individual-manager levels of their frameworks. In essence, sponsors are defining their playing fields through the specification of asset-class targets. Asset targets indicate those areas of the capital markets in which a sponsor intends to participate. Once the playing fields have been defined, sponsors are covering the fields with

---

11. For a more balanced treatment of the issues surrounding the use of common-stock normal portfolios including the perspectives of investment managers and consultants, see Veena A. Kutler, "Money Manager Selection: A Top-Down Perspective," Chapter 11 in *Pension Fund Investment Management,* ed. Frank J. Fabozzi (Chicago: Probus Publishing, 1990).

the use of manager benchmarks, which quantitatively describe individual investment managers' areas of specialization. Manager benchmarks are very helpful because they enable a sponsor to send a team of players out onto the playing field and know the entire field will be covered. Manager benchmarks are also proving useful to sponsors in evaluating superior managers to place on their teams.

Building and maintaining benchmark portfolios require a significant commitment of resources on the part of sponsors. However, we believe the benefits of using benchmark portfolios, particularly in managing portfolio risk, are significant and justify the attention being given them by sponsors.

47

⑥   INDEXING FIXED INCOME ASSETS*

Sharmin Mossavar-Rahmani, CFA
Partner
Goldman Sachs Asset Management

Fixed income index funds have grown dramatically since they were first introduced in 1979. Indeed, some of the nation's largest public, corporate, and multiple-employer pension plan sponsors, foundations, and insurance companies have indexed a significant portion, if not all, of their fixed income assets.

ADVANTAGES AND DISADVANTAGES

The most important factor driving the interest in indexing is the poor and inconsistent performance of active investment advisors. Historically, the returns of most active investment advisors have lagged those of market indexes. In addition, active investment advisors who have matched or outperformed market indexes have done so inconsistently when measured over 10 year periods. Investors therefore have turned to index funds to obtain both higher long-term returns as well as more consistent and reliable short-term performance.

Another key attraction of indexing is the lower advisory fee schedule for index-fund management relative to that charged for active investment management. Advisory fees for index funds range between 30 and 75 percent of advisory fees for actively managed portfolios. Fees for a $50 million index fund typically

---

*This chapter has been adapted from Sharmin Mossavar-Rahmani, *Bond Index Funds* (Chicago: Probus Publishing Company, 1991).

range between 5 and 17 basis points. The highest fees, about 20 basis points, are charged for enhanced or customized index funds, and significantly lower fees—a mere one or two basis points—are charged for very large index funds (say, in excess of $1 billion). The savings in advisory fees from indexing, therefore, can be substantial, particularly in the case of large funds.

Indexing also lowers costs (other than advisory fees) that are incurred in investing assets, including, for example, custodian and master trustee costs. Custodian costs vary in part as a function of transaction activity in a portfolio. Because index funds have lower turnover of assets and hence fewer transactions, the associated custodian costs also are lower.

Master trustee costs also vary, in part as a function of the number of portfolios that are in trusteeship. Since the size of assets given to any single advisor of an index fund is generally much larger than the size of assets given to any single advisor for active management, indexing often results in a consolidation of advisors responsible for managing a pool of assets, reducing the associated master trustee costs.

Another major advantage of indexing is the degree of control afforded the investor. When an investor hires an active investment advisor, the investor is largely at the mercy of the advisor. Although an advisor is constrained by his or her investment discipline, there is, nevertheless, tremendous latitude afforded within that discipline. As such, the investor has minimal control over the advisor's investment decisions at any point in time.

Indexing, on the other hand, allows the investor to specify both the benchmark as well as the degree of latitude allowed the index-fund advisor for deviation from the benchmark characteristics. For example, an active investment advisor may have the mandate to construct a portfolio with any average duration that he or she deems appropriate based on an interest-rate forecast, whereas an index-fund advisor may be limited to, say, a 10 percent deviation from the average duration of the index.

Finally, another advantage of indexing is the ease and precision with which the value added by the investment advisor can be measured. The performance of investment advisors is reviewed by investors and consultants on a quarterly basis. The review report includes the total return of the portfolio as well as the total return of a benchmark. To date, broad market indexes have been the most widely used benchmarks. The review process for active investment advisors, in contrast, has two shortcomings: The selected benchmarks often are not the appropriate performance benchmarks for the investment advisor; and the portfolio deviations from the benchmark characteristics, which explain relative performance, are not thoroughly examined. Indexing overcomes both shortcomings. First, establishing an index fund begins with an extensive search for the appropriate index and, hence, the appropriate performance benchmark. Second, index fund investors focus more closely on the quarterly differences in return between the portfolio and the benchmark and require investment advisors to attribute differences in return to specific deviations from the benchmark characteristics.

The rapid growth in its popularity—and its attraction—notwithstanding, indexing does have some disadvantages. In periods of rising interest rates, which characterize bear bond market cycles, index funds tracking broad market benchmarks register relatively poor or, at best, mediocre performance. Such poor performance has occurred over all recent bear market cycles. The relatively poor performance in periods of rising interest rates, however, has been offset by the relatively high total return of the benchmark in periods of falling interest rates (which characterizes a bull bond market cycle). Over complete market cycles, therefore, index funds tracking broad market benchmarks have, at best, outperformed and, at worst, matched the median active investment advisor.

Although indexing may be more attractive than traditional active management based on interest-rate anticipation, it entails a high opportunity cost, where opportunity cost is defined as the incremental returns forgone by not investing in market sectors with the highest performance. These market sectors include different maturity sectors as well as different types of securities such as Treasuries, agencies, corporates, Yankees, and mortgage-backed securities.

A few strategies have been developed over the past few years that have resulted in higher total returns than those of broad market benchmarks over a complete market cycle. Most of these strategies respond to, rather than forecast, changes in interest rates and changes in yield spreads between short-term securities and long-term securities. Examples of such strategies include (1) momentum-based strategies that use different short-term and long-term moving averages of bond prices to determine whether to invest in bonds or in short-term instruments, (2) options-based strategies that use options theory to create, synthetically, a call option on the best-performing maturity sector, (3) constant-duration strategies that assume the mean-reversion of interest rates and maintain a fixed duration over a complete market cycle of interest rates, and (4) duration-averaging strategies that also assume the mean-reversion of interest rates and extend duration as interest rates rise and shorten duration as interest rates fall.

Some of these strategies have outperformed broad market benchmarks over bull, bear, and therefore the complete interest-rate cycles. Some of the same strategies, however, have underperformed broad market benchmarks during short periods characterized by volatile interest rates and by small overall changes in interest rate from the beginning to the end of the period. Other strategies have outperformed broad market benchmarks over complete interest cycles as well as during volatile-interest-rate environments. The future long-term performance of these new strategies relative to indexing will depend on the market environment for interest rates and the actual implementation of the strategies with real assets over a market cycle.

Index funds are sometimes criticized for their rigid requirements. "True" (also called "straight," "vanilla," or "pure") index funds do not invest in instruments outside the benchmark universe, thereby forgoing the opportunities and the incremental return afforded by these instruments.

The broad market benchmarks exclude many sectors of the fixed income market including zero-coupon Treasuries, non-federal agency conventional-mortgage pass-throughs, collateralized mortgage obligations, interest-only and principal-only strips, most asset-backed securities such as CARDS and CARS, medium-term notes, and bank deposit notes and derivative instruments.

Although true index funds are constrained by the holdings of their bench-marks, this constraint can be overcome readily by enhanced index funds. Enhanced index funds have the flexibility to invest in securities outside their index universe, benefiting from the incremental return from such securities and circumventing the rigid requirements posed by true index funds.

ENHANCED INDEX FUNDS

Enhanced index funds, or "index-plus" funds, are managed with the objective of outperforming a particular index while matching the latter's major risk character-istics. Unlike pure index funds, which are passively managed portfolios, enhanced index funds are actively managed funds where trades are intended to rebalance the portfolio *and* to capture any available investment opportunities. The magnitude of outperformance depends on several factors, including the type of index fund, the strategies employed by an index-fund advisor, the latitude given to an index-fund advisor to deviate from a selected index, and the level of volatil-ity of interest rates and market-sector spreads.

Broad market index funds, for example, permit greater enhancement of total returns than do specialized market sector index funds. A specialized market sector index fund is restricted to one sector and, therefore, to investment opportu-nities in that sector only. A broad market index fund, on the other hand, can add value by allocating assets among different market sectors and by taking advan-tage of specific investment opportunities in each of those market sectors.

Similarly, the potential for enhancing total return is greatest if an index-fund advisor takes advantage of multiple investment strategies, including sector selection, yield-curve strategies, coupon selection, issuer selection, and use of de-rivative and synthetic securities. Specialization in one type of strategy limits the degree of enhancement, particularly when the prevailing market environment does not favor that strategy. It should be noted that such investment strategies are implemented while maintaining the same effective duration as that of the bench-mark. These strategies are sometimes called *duration-neutral strategies.*

The greater the latitude to deviate from certain risk and return characteris-tics of the benchmark, the greater is the potential to enhance the returns of the index fund. Of course, greater latitude to deviate means greater risk of underper-forming the benchmark.

The amount of potential enhancement also depends on the level of volatility of interest rates and market sector spreads. When volatility is low, mispricings of sectors and individual securities—and hence investment opportunities to enhance returns—are reduced. Conversely, when volatility of both interest rates and of market-sector spreads is high, an index-fund advisor can enhance returns by taking advantage of inefficiencies in the relative value of securities, changes in the shape of the yield curve, and fluctuations in yield spreads.

Notwithstanding the type of index fund, the strategies employed, the latitude given, and the level of volatility, an enhanced index fund is expected to provide at least 15 basis points of incremental value per year. Fifty basis points annually represents the maximum incremental return that typically is offered by enhanced index-fund advisors. Occasionally, an enhanced index-fund advisor may quote a multiyear target enhancement of as much as 100 basis points per year. To put this claim in perspective, it should be cautioned that such a return would require a level of performance leading to top quartile ranking among all active fixed income advisors.

Given the potential for enhancing the total return of index funds by 15— and sometimes as much as 50—basis points, the question arises as to why an index-fund investor would choose pure index funds. Two factors account for the choice. First, while enhanced index funds are expected to outperform their benchmarks over a complete market cycle, such funds may underperform during some phase of the cycle. Investment strategies may require extended periods to succeed, and sometimes they do not succeed at all. Many index-fund investors are not willing to accept the risk of interim underperformance.

Second, the fees for enhanced indexing are higher than those for pure indexing. Fees alone, however, should not deter index-fund investors from selecting enhanced indexing. The additional cost is usually less than 10 basis points. And even in cases where 10 basis points appear too high, incentive (performance-based) fees can be used such that the full additional cost is paid only when the index fund has outperformed the benchmark by a certain predetermined amount.

INDEXING METHODOLOGIES

Unlike equity index funds, bond index funds cannot purchase all securities contained in the selected index in the same proportion as that of the index itself. Most fixed income indexes contain thousands of securities; investing in all those securities in the appropriate proportion would result in an index fund whose holdings of each security are too small for portfolio rebalancing and future trading. Portfolio rebalancing is necessary as income generated by the index fund is reinvested and as securities with less than one year remaining to maturity drop out of the index. Additional trading is necessary as well since new Treasury, corporate, and mortgage-backed securities are continuously issued and added to the index. Furthermore, a significant portion of all securities contained in bond indexes are illiquid (i.e., they cannot be purchased readily in the secondary market).

The more practical approach to setting up an index fund is to select a basket of securities whose profile characteristics (such as yield, duration, and convexity) and expected total return match those of the index. Three methodologies are available for selecting and maintaining the appropriate basket: the stratified sampling approach, the optimization approach using linear programming, and the optimization approach using quadratic programming. All three methodologies are widely used.

Stratified Sampling Method

The stratified sampling method, also known as the cellular approach, is the most simple and flexible of the three approaches. In stratified sampling, an index is divided into subsectors; in other words, the index is stratified into cells. The division into subsectors is made on the basis of such parameters as sector, coupon, term-to-maturity, duration, and quality. For example, two parameters can be used to divide the index: sector and term-to-maturity (or weighted average life for mortgage-backed securities). The division by sector stratifies the market index into government, mortgage-backed, corporate, and Yankee securities. The division by term-to-maturity stratifies the market index into securities with terms-to-maturity of, say, 1 to 5 years, 5 to 10 years, and greater than 10 years.

Alternatively, a market index can be divided into detailed subsectors. Using the same parameters as before, notably sector and term-to-maturity, the division by sector could stratify the market index into Treasuries and agencies instead of government securities; Ginnie Maes, Fannie Maes, Freddie Macs, and their 15-year original-issue counterparts (Midgets, Dwarfs, Gnomes, and non-Gnome 15-year FHLMCs), and project loans instead of mortgage-backed securities; industrial, utility, telephone, finance, and transportation securities instead of corporate securities; and Canadian, World Bank, sovereign, and supranational securities instead of Yankee securities. The division by term-to-maturity could stratify the market index into, say, 2-year intervals where the first interval includes all securities with terms-to-maturity of between 1 and 3 years. A commonly used division by term-to-maturity stratifies the market index into 2- or 3-year intervals for the first 10 years (1 to 3 years, 3 to 5 years, 5 to 7 years, and 7 to 10 years), and 5-year intervals thereafter (10 to 15 years, 15 to 20 years, 20 to 25 years, and greater than 25 years).

The stratification of the index is followed by the selection of securities to represent each cell. Securities are chosen such that the profile characteristics and the expected total return of each "sample" of securities representing a particular cell match the average characteristics and expected total return of all securities in that cell. Each cell may be treated differently. In some cases, the average characteristics of the cell are matched; in other cases, cells that account for a large percentage of the index may themselves be stratified further into "subcells." And in still other cases, cells that represent a nominal percentage of the index may be omitted from the index fund altogether. Of the factors that determine the number of cells and subcategories in an index fund, the size of the fund is the most critical. A large asset size enables the index-fund advisor to divide the benchmark into a greater number of cells and to select securities to represent most of the cells in the index.

The process of setting up an index fund is complete when all cells in the index have been replicated (directly through matching average characteristics or indirectly after further stratification) or eliminated from the index fund (because they represent only a nominal percentage of the index).

As noted earlier, one of the key advantages of the stratified-sampling approach is its simplicity. Stratifying an index into cells and selecting securities to represent each cell does not require sophisticated index-related analytical systems, extensive databases on security prices and dealer inventory, or even strong quantitative expertise. And unlike the linear programming and quadratic programming approaches, stratified sampling relies on portfolio management expertise to appropriately stratify the index, to eliminate unnecessary cells, to substitute one cell for another, and to select a basket of securities that will closely track the index.

Another important advantage of stratified sampling is its flexibility. This methodology is equally effective with all types of indexes. Thus, stratified sampling is as effective with a mortgage-backed securities index fund as it is with a Treasury securities index fund.

Similarly, stratified sampling is equally useful for managing a passive "vanilla" index fund as well as for an actively managed enhanced index fund. For example, securities in an actively managed enhanced index fund are often traded on a continuous basis. In stratified sampling, securities in a cell can be easily swapped without impacting the structure of the index fund.

Finally, stratified sampling lends itself to the use of securities that are not included in the index. Securities with complex structures such as derivative mortgage-backed securities can be substituted for generic mortgage-backed securities in an enhanced index fund.

Its simplicity and flexibility notwithstanding, stratified sampling does have certain shortcomings. Stratified sampling is labor intensive. An index-fund advisor must determine the ideal cellular structure for an index based on size of portfolio and type of benchmark. The advisor must then evaluate the trade-offs between eliminating some cells and including others, and then the advisor must select securities for each cell while controlling the overall characteristics of the index fund. Such investment decisions require both time and experience in managing index funds.

Stratified sampling also may not result in an optimal portfolio. A portfolio is optimal when it achieves the highest yield and greatest convexity for a given portfolio structure with respect to parameters such as maturity, coupon, quality, sector, and call exposure. An index fund that has a higher yield and equal convexity (or equal yield and greater convexity) will outperform its benchmark over time given the same portfolio structure. But it is difficult, if not impossible, for an index-fund advisor using only stratified sampling to implement the optimal trade-offs between the yield and convexity of all securities held in the index fund (or of all those offered in the market) while maintaining the target portfolio structure.

Optimization Approach Using Linear Programming

The key shortcomings of stratified sampling can be overcome through a more systematic and mechanistic approach. The optimization approach to indexing based on linear programming is one such comprehensive technique. This optimization approach is, in fact, a more disciplined and quantitative extension of stratified sampling.

In this approach, the goal is to maximize the likelihood that an index fund will closely track an index by allocating a finite amount of dollars among the thousands of fixed income securities available in the fixed income market. The linear programming problem is formulated by specifying three components: an objective function that, when maximized, increases the likelihood that an index fund will closely track its benchmark; a set of constraints that incorporate the target cellular structure of an index fund; and a universe of securities from which a basket of securities can be selected.

The parameter represented by the objective function can vary among different optimization problems. Objective functions based on yield measures are the most widely used. In some problems, either the par or the market-value-weighted yield-to-maturity is maximized. Some optimizations may maximize the par or the market-value-weighted effective yield to account for the call/put exposure of corporate securities and prepayment exposure of mortgage-backed securities. And still in other instances, a par or alternatively a market-value-weighted adjusted yield may be maximized; the yield adjustments are designed to account for the factors specific to each security, including the amount outstanding of each security, sinking-fund or special redemption features, coupon levels, and liquidity premiums. Objective functions may also be based on the expected return of the portfolio, given a probability weighting of different interest-rate scenarios, or on the par or the market-value-weighted convexity of the portfolio. These parameters typically are used when the index-fund advisor anticipates a particular change in the level or in the volatility of interest rates.

The second component that must be specified is a set of constraints. The majority of constraints in the optimization problem define the cellular structure of the index fund. Say, for example, x percent of the index is represented by one cell containing all Treasury securities with maturities of less than three years. This percentage share is matched in the index fund by using a constraint specifying that the market-value weighting in the index fund of all Treasury securities with maturities of less than three years must equal x percent.

Because constraints with exact percentages are too restrictive, most optimization problems specify a range for the market-value weight of each cell. In the above example, two constraints can be used to specify an upper and lower bound for the range—say, y percent and z percent, respectively—such that the market value of the cell is greater than or equal to z percent and less than or equal to y percent.

Additional constraints are used to match certain portfolio parameters with those of the index. The effective duration of the portfolio is the key parameter that is constrained within a very narrow range of the effective duration of the index. Other parameters include average coupon, maturity, and quality.

Some constraints are used to implement an index-fund advisor's concerns about diversification or about extensive exposure to certain sectors of the market. For example, holdings in corporate securities from one issuer can be constrained to a certain percentage of the portfolio to minimize the index fund's exposure to any single issuer.

The third component to be specified is the universe of securities from which the optimization model can select issues. This universe is critical to the worthiness of the portfolio selected by the optimization model; if the securities selected by the optimization model are not valued correctly or cannot be found at or near prices indicated in the portfolio, the value of the results of the optimization model is significantly reduced.

Pricing and availability difficulties may be partially addressed by reducing the number of securities in the universe. For example, securities below a certain issue size or those issued before a given issue date may be eliminated from the universe. Similarly, securities that are particularly illiquid, based on recent trading volume observed by broker-dealers, also may be dropped.

The optimization approach based on linear programming offers three major advantages. First, this optimization approach is systematic and comprehensive. The optimization model can be run easily on a regular basis, using the same objective function and set of constraints. The model can ensure that all appropriate cells are filled and their characteristics matched. Second, the optimization approach searches through an entire universe of securities to select the optimal combination that will provide the highest yield and convexity for a given portfolio structure. Third, the optimization approach enables an investment advisor with little or no index-fund management expertise and resources to readily acquire some index-fund management capabilities through access to such a model.

Still, although a skillful formulation of the optimization problem overcomes some of the shortcomings of stratified sampling, the optimization approach based on linear programming has its disadvantages.

One major disadvantage of the optimization approach is the broad impact of the objective function. If an objective function is specified so as to maximize effective yield, the model will seek to maximize the effective yield of every cell, irrespective of an index-fund advisor's preference to implement a yield tilt only for particular cells.

A second disadvantage of the optimization approach is the high correlation between the quality of the portfolio selected by the model and the quality of the database specified as the universe. As mentioned earlier, most publicly available fixed income databases do not have accurate data on call, put, and sinking-fund features of particular securities or reliable prices. Furthermore, when the prices are reliable, the availability of many of the securities in the secondary market at these prices is not at all certain. Of course, one recourse would be to use as substitutes other available securities with similar characteristics; however, as an index-fund advisor starts to substitute securities and adjust prices to reflect market valuation of securities, the advisor is, in effect, moving away from a true optimization approach towards stratified sampling.

Another recourse would be to work with dealers who offer smaller databases (containing only their own inventories or securities they believe are available in the secondary market) in order to circumvent this pricing and availability problem. The key disadvantage of such databases is the requisite reliance on one dealer who offers only house inventory or securities that can be located and resold at a profit. Securities available through another dealer at lower prices are therefore excluded from the portfolio.

Finally, optimization does not lend itself to partial rebalancing of an index fund or to security swaps as readily as stratified sampling. In a true optimization, an index fund advisor cannot rebalance a particular sector of the index fund and ignore other sectors. If the mortgage-backed securities held in an index fund experience high prepayments, the additional cash generated by the mortgage-backed sector can be reinvested only by re-optimizing and rebalancing the entire portfolio. If such re-optimization is not performed, the index-fund advisor again is moving toward stratified sampling.

Optimization Approach Using Quadratic Programming

A third approach to indexing is the optimization approach using quadratic programming. This approach, also known as variance minimization, is the most complex of the three methodologies. In variance minimization, the objective is to select a basket of securities that will maximize expected return of the portfolio while minimizing the difference between the expected total return of the portfolio and that of its benchmark.

The variance minimization problem consists of three components: an objective function, a set of constraints, and a universe of securities. However, unlike linear programming, the objective function plays a far more significant role than the constraints in determining the structure of the portfolio. Also, the objective function is of quadratic rather than linear form. In variance minimization, the objective function maximizes *utility*, which is defined as the difference between the expected return of an index fund and the risk of the index fund.

In this approach, an index fund advisor determines the optimal trade-off between higher expected return and lower risk by specifying a risk-aversion factor. A low risk aversion factor reduces the importance of tracking the returns of a benchmark for the benefit of higher expected return, whereas a high risk-aversion factor trades off portfolio return for greater tracking of the returns of the benchmark.

The linchpin of the variance minimization approach is a risk-factor model that determines both the expected return of the index portfolio and the variance of expected excess return.[1] Risk-factor models consist of, among other things, a valuation model for pricing each bond in the opportunity set. Every bond is valued based on its exposure to two types of factors: (1) interest-rate and interest-rate-related factors described as term-structure factors and (2) characteristic factors such as market sector, credit quality, coupon level, issue size, and call exposure.

The most important advantage of variance minimization relative to the linear programming and stratified sampling approaches to indexing is the use of the variance-covariance matrix. Discount factors and characteristic factors are correlated, and variance minimization is the only approach that exploits this correlation in selecting a basket of securities. If two securities are highly correlated yet fall into different cells in the stratified sampling approach and satisfy different constraints in the linear programming approach, the linear programming and stratified sampling methodologies may select both securities. Variance minimization, on the other hand, is less likely to select two highly correlated securities; it is more likely to choose a second security that will diversify issue-specific risk in the index fund.

Another advantage of variance minimization is the ability to measure the contribution to tracking error of each selected security. An index-fund advisor can examine and evaluate the role each security is expected to play in minimizing tracking error and trade off the low contribution to tracking error of some selected securities for attractive features in other available securities. Of course, although securities can be substituted, it is important to note that the integrity of the initial optimal portfolio is violated; in fact, as more securities are substituted, the index-fund advisor moves increasingly away from variance minimization.

Variance minimization does have its shortcomings. One important shortcoming is the dependence of the risk-factor model on historical data. The variance-covariance matrix and the variance of the discount and characteristic factors are based on historical estimates for those factors. Often, more recent data is assigned a greater weighting than older data. Nevertheless, given the volatility and dynamic structure of the fixed income market, historical estimates are not always good indicators of the future behavior of discount and characteristic factors.

A second problem associated with variance minimization is the accuracy of the bond valuation model when data for particular characteristic factors are limited. When the market's valuation of a characteristic factor has been derived from a handful of securities, the estimate for the market's valuation may not be reliable.

---

1. Much of the early development of fixed income risk-factor models was undertaken by BARRA, a fixed income and equity consulting software firm in California.

Finally, whereas the complexities of variance minimization and its bond valuation and risk-factor model can be explained, the rationale for the selection of individual securities by the optimization model in a specific index fund is somewhat obscure. In stratified sampling, securities are selected because they fall into a particular cell and are cheaper (or have certain attributes that make them more attractive) than alternative securities that also fall into the same cell. Similarly, in the linear programming approach, if the objective function maximizes yield, securities are selected because they meet all the constraints while having the highest yield. In variance minimization, however, an intricate pattern of variances and covariances determines which security is selected. Although the value of the variances and covariances for each selected security can be examined, the selection of one security over another is a function of many relationships that an index-fund advisor cannot readily identify and isolate. Given such complexity, the ability of an index-fund advisor to measure the full implications of swapping securities in the index fund is limited to evaluating each security's contribution to tracking error.

IMPLICATIONS FOR THE FIXED INCOME MARKET

Increased use of bond indexing has had and will continue to have a far-reaching impact on the fixed income market. Wall Street broker-dealers have introduced dozens of bond indexes including broad market benchmarks and subsector benchmarks and the number of firms providing analytical systems for indexing has increased.

As indexing continues to grow, profit margins throughout the investment community will be squeezed. Investment advisors increasingly will be forced to accept lower management fees; financial consultants will be retained less frequently to conduct searches for new investment advisors; and the broker-dealer community will face the tightening of bid-ask price spreads. Ultimately, increased indexing will lead to a significant shakeout among investment advisors. The beneficiaries of such a shakeout will be firms with large assets as well as established specialty boutiques, and the casualties will be smaller organizations without extensive resources or particular niches.

☺ BOND IMMUNIZATION: AN ASSET/LIABILITY OPTIMIZATION STRATEGY

Peter E. Christensen
Managing Director
ComTech, Incorporated

Frank J. Fabozzi, Ph.D., CFA, CPA
Adjunct Professor of Finance
School of Management
Yale University

Anthony LoFaso, Ph.D.
Vice President
Union Bank of Switzerland

The purpose of this chapter is to review the mechanics and applications of the bond immunization strategy. In the first section, we define immunization as a duration-matching strategy, and then compare it to maturity-matching as an alternative approach to locking in rates. To hedge the reinvestment risk present in maturity-matching, we then explain the single-period immunization strategy and the rebalancing procedures that accompany it. Following single-period immunization, we discuss multiperiod immunization and its applications for the pension, insurance, and thrift markets. Finally, we review the recent variations on the strategy, including combination matching, contingent immunization, immunization with futures, and immunization with options.

WHAT IS AN IMMUNIZED PORTFOLIO?

Single-period immunization is usually defined as locking in a fixed rate of return over a prespecified horizon, such as locking in a 10 percent return for a five-year period. It can also be defined as generating a minimum future value at the end of a specified horizon, such as generating $100 million from a $70 million investment five years earlier. With multiperiod immunization, the horizon over which rates are locked in is extended to include multiple periods (such as a schedule of monthly payouts to retirees of a pension plan). Multiperiod immunization is a duration-matching strategy that permits funding of a fixed schedule of multiple future payouts at a minimum cost (such as funding a $500 million schedule of payouts at a cost of $200 million).

The actuary generally credited with pioneering the immunization strategy, F. M. Reddington, defined immunization in 1952 as "the investment of the assets in such a way that the existing business is immune to a general change in the rate of interest."[1] He also specified a condition for immunization: The average duration of assets must be set equal to the average duration of the liabilities. He thought that by matching the durations of assets and liabilities he would then immunize a portfolio from the effects of small changes in interest rates. By matching durations on both sides of the balance sheet, he felt that assets and liabilities would be equally price-sensitive to changes in the general level of interest rates. For any change in yield, both sides of the ledger should be equally affected; therefore, the relative values of assets and liabilities would not be changed.

Much later, Lawrence Fisher and Roman Weil defined an immunized portfolio as follows:[2]

> A portfolio of investments is immunized for a holding period if its value at the end of the holding period, regardless of the course of rates during the holding period, must be at least as large as it would have been had the interest rate function been constant throughout the holding period.
>
> If the realized return on an investment in bonds is sure to be at least as large as the appropriately computed yield to the horizon, then that investment is immunized.

Fisher and Weil demonstrated that to achieve the immunized result, the average duration of the bond portfolio must be set equal to the remaining time in the planning horizon, and the market value of assets must be greater than or equal to the present value of the liabilities discounted at the internal rate of return of the portfolio.

Before reviewing the logic of this portfolio strategy, let's look at maturity-matching as an early approach to locking in a current level of interest rates.

---

1. F. M. Reddington, "Review of the Principle of Life-Office Valuations," *Journal of the Institute of Actuaries*, vol. 78, 1952, pp. 286–340.
2. Lawrence Fisher and Roman Weil, "Coping with the Risk of Interest-Rate Fluctuations: Returns to Bondholders from Naive and Optimal Strategies," *Journal of Business*, October 1971, pp. 408–431.

MATURITY-MATCHING: THE REINVESTMENT PROBLEM

Suppose that an investor wishes to lock in prevailing interest rates for a 10-year period. Should he or she buy 10-year bonds?

By purchasing 10-year bonds and holding them to maturity, an investor can be certain of receiving all coupon payments over the 10-year period as well as the principal repayment at redemption (assuming that no default occurs). These two sources of income are fixed in dollar amounts. The third and final source of income is the interest earned on the semiannual coupon payments. "Interest on coupon" is not fixed in dollar amounts; rather it depends on the many interest-rate environments at the various times of payment.

A reinvestment problem occurs when the reinvestment of coupon income occurs at rates below the yield-to-maturity of the bond at the time of purchase. Note from Exhibit 48–1 that as interest rates shift instantaneously and remain at the new levels for a 10-year period, the total "holding period" return on a 9 percent par bond due in 10 years will vary considerably. The initial effect will appear in the value of the asset. The immediate result will be a capital gain if rates fall (or loss, if rates rise).

As the holding period increases after a change in rates, the interest-on-coupon component of total return begins to exert a stronger influence. At 10 years, we note that interest on coupon (reinvestment income) exerts a dominance over capital gain (or loss) in determining holding period returns.

Intuitively, we know that these relationships make sense. Capital gains appear instantly, whereas changes in reinvestment rates take time to exert their effect on the total holding-period return on a bond.

If rates were to jump immediately from 9 to 15 percent and a capital loss were to appear today, at what point will that capital loss be made up because the reinvestment of coupon payments is occurring at a higher (15 percent) rate? As illustrated in Exhibit 48–2, the two "offsetting forces" of market value and reinvestment return equally offset at 6.79 years. This is the duration of the 10-year, 9 percent bond. To earn the original 9 percent target return (the yield-to-maturity at the time of purchase), it is necessary to hold that bond for the period of its duration—6.79 years in our example. If we wish to lock in a market rate of 9 percent for a 10-year period, we would select a bond with a duration of 10 years (not a maturity of 10 years). The maturity for such a par bond in a 9 percent yield environment is roughly 23 years.

From Exhibit 48–1, we note that regardless of the immediate, one-time interest-rate shift, we are still able to earn a 9 percent total return if our holding period is 6.79 years—the duration of the bond. By targeting the duration of a portfolio rather than specific maturities to the prescribed investment horizon of 6.79 years, we see the equal offsets of capital gain with lower reinvestment return occurring in the portfolio. This principle of duration-matching together with rebalancing procedures that are used over time allow us to lock in rates and minimize the reinvestment risk that is associated with the maturity-matching strategy.

EXHIBIT 48–1

Total Return on a 9 Percent Noncallable $1,000 Bond Due in 10 Years and Held through Various Holding Periods

Income Source	Interest Rate at Time of Reinvestment	Holding Period in Years						
		1	3	5	6.79[a]	9	10
Coupon income	5%	$ 90	$270	$ 450	$611	$ 810	$ 900
Capital gain or loss		287	234	175	100	39	0
Interest-on-interest		1	17	54	105	191	241
Total return		$378	$521	$ 679	$816	$1,040	$1,141
(and yield)		(37.0%)	(15.0%)	(11.0%)	(9.0%)	(8.5%)	(8.2%)
Coupon income	7	$ 90	$270	$ 450	$611	$ 810	$ 900
Capital gain or loss		132	109	83	56	19	0
Interest-on-interest		2	25	78	149	279	355
Total return		$224	$404	$ 611	$816	$1,108	$1,225
(and yield)		(22.0%)	(12.0%)	(10.0%)	(9.0%)	(8.6%)	(8.5%)
Coupon income	10	$ 90	$270	$ 450	$611	$ 810	$ 900
Capital gain or loss		0	0	0	0	0	0
Interest-on-interest		2	32	103	205	387	495
Total return		$ 92	$302	$ 553	$816	$1,197	$1,395
(and yield)		(9.0%)	(9.0%)	(9.0%)	(9.0%)	(9.0%)	(9.0%)
Coupon income	10	$ 90	$270	$ 450	$611	$ 810	$ 900
Capital gain or loss		-112	-95	-75	-56	-18	0
Interest-on-interest		2	40	129	261	502	647
Total return		$ 20	$215	$ 504	$816	$1,294	$1,547
(and yield)		(2.0%)	(6.7%)	(8.5%)	(9.0%)	(9.7%)	(9.8%)

[a]Duration of a 9 percent bond bought at par and due in 10 years.

EXHIBIT 48-2

"Offsetting Forces" Principle (9 Percent Coupon, 30-Year Maturity Bond, Rates Rise Instantly from 9 Percent to 15 Percent, Reinvestment Rate Is 15 Percent)

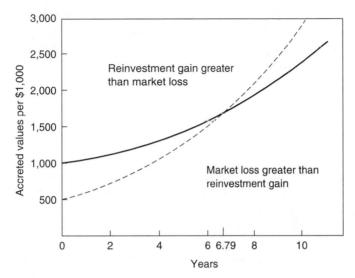

SINGLE-PERIOD IMMUNIZATION

The most straightforward approach to funding a single-period liability five years from today is to purchase a five-year, zero-coupon bond maturing on the liability payment date. Regardless of future fluctuations in interest rates, the bond, or portfolio of bonds, will be price insensitive (or immune) to changes in rates as the zero-coupon securities mature at par on the payment date. Because zero coupons have durations equal to their maturities, the five-year, zero-coupon bonds both cash-match and duration-match the single-period liability payment.

    If zero-coupon bonds have insufficient yield, a portfolio of *coupon-bearing* Treasury, agency, and corporate bonds can be immunized to fund the same single-period payment only if three conditions are met: (1) the duration of the portfolio of coupon bonds must be set equal to the five-year horizon; (2) the market value of assets must be greater than the present value of liabilities; and (3) the dispersion of the assets must be slightly greater than the dispersion of the liabilities. That is,

    1. Duration_{Assets} = $\text{Duration}_{Liabilities}$

    2. PV_{Assets} > $\text{PV}_{Liabilities}$

    3. $\text{Dispersion}_{Assets}$ > $\text{Dispersion}_{Liabilities}$

The Three Conditions for Immunization

Immunization requires that the average durations of assets and liabilities are set equal at all times. Unfortunately, simple matching of durations is not a sufficient condition.

Consider both a $200,000 par-value zero-coupon, five-year bond in a 9 percent rate environment and a $1 million five-year single-period liability. Obviously the durations of both the assets and liabilities are matched because they are both zero-coupon, five-year obligations. However, a $200,000 par-value zero-coupon, five-year bond (with a market value of $128,787) cannot realistically compound to $1 million in five years. The required annual rate to compound to $1 million in five years is almost 67 percent. In a 9 percent rate environment, $643,937 is required in market value of assets to compound to $1 million in five years.

Therefore, a second condition for immunization is necessary; the market value of assets must be greater than or equal to the present value of liabilities, using the internal rate of return (IRR) of the assets as the discount factor in present-valuing the liabilities. The assets, when compounded at the "locked-in" immunized rate of 9 percent, will grow to equal or exceed the future-value immunized target of $1 million in this example.

To understand the reasons for the third condition for immunization (that the dispersion of assets be greater than or equal to the dispersion of liabilities), it is important to understand the assumptions underlying the Macaulay measure of duration.[3] Because duration is defined as the present-value weighted average time to payment on a bond, duration must assume a discount rate (or a series of discount rates) when calculating present-value weighted time.

The discount rate assumed in the Macaulay measure of duration is the yield or internal rate of return on the bond or portfolio. By assuming only one discount rate, the Macaulay measure assumes that a flat yield curve prevails at all times, as illustrated in Exhibit 48–3. If rates shift up, say, 100 basis points, the Macaulay duration calculation assumes a parallel shift to another flat yield curve 100 basis points higher.

To meet a target duration of 6.79 years as illustrated in Exhibit 48–4(a), a portfolio could be constructed as either (1) a barbell of roughly equal amounts of zero- and 13-year-duration securities, (2) an even ladder of equal amounts of zero through 13-year duration securities, or (3) a bullet of only 6.79-year durations. Because the Macaulay duration calculation assumes that a flat yield curve connects every maturity point, the barbell structure incorporates the greatest amount of yield-curve risk by concentrating cash flows on both ends of the curve. If the yield curve is positive or inverted, the barbell structure will violate the assumption of a flat curve more than the even ladder or bullet structure. On the other

---

3. See Chapter 5 for an explanation of duration and its properties.

EXHIBIT 48-3

Present Value of Cash Flows for Macaulay Duration

Single discount rate for all cash flows

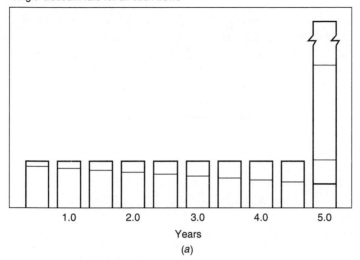

Years
(a)

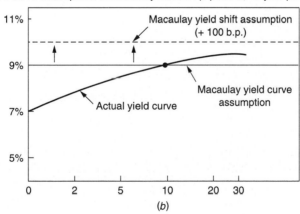

Yield curve assumptions in Macaulay duration (9 percent, 10-year par bond)

(b)

hand, the bullet structure, by concentrating cash flows at a single maturity point, incorporates a flat slope over the relevant range on the yield curve as shown in Exhibit 48–4(*b*).

For single-period immunization, a bullet maturity structure with tight cash flows around the liability date is generally preferred to an even ladder or bar-belled portfolio because of the reduced risk exposure to the yield curve becoming

E X H I B I T   48-4

Maturity Structures for Portfolios—Target Duration of 6.79 Years

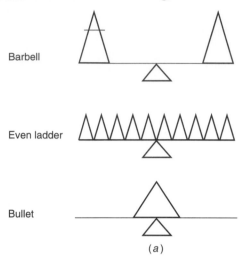

Barbell

Even ladder

Bullet

(a)

U.S. Treasury zero-coupon curve (barbell versus bullet maturity structure)

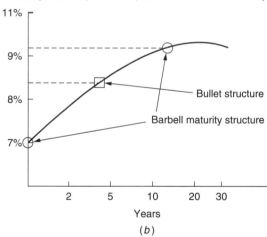

(b)

steeper or twisting. In fact, to eliminate the risk of pathological shifts in yields, the investor could tighten the cash flows still further and purchase a zero-coupon bond to cash-flow-match the single-period liability. Short of that, a bullet structure is the least risky and the barbell the most risky.

Therefore, for immunization the third condition of controlling the degree of barbelling must be incorporated into the process of structuring a portfolio. The measure used to control the barbelling is dispersion—a measure of the variance

EXHIBIT 48-5

Dispersions of Selected Issues (as of May 10, 1989)

Issuer	Coupon	Maturity	Yield	Duration	Dispersion
U.S. Treasury Strip	0	05/15/94	9.310	5.011	0.000
U.S. Treasury	9.500	05/15/94	9.186	4.047	2.330
U.S. Treasury	9.375	05/15/96	9.199	5.226	5.130
U.S. Treasury	9.125	05/15/99	9.154	6.761	11.990
U.S. Treasury	8.875	02/15/19	9.115	10.480	78.720

of cash flows around the duration date, (D), of a bond. The mathematical formula for dispersion is as follows:[4]

$$\text{Dispersion} = \frac{\sum (t_i - D)^2 \, \text{PV}(CF_i)}{\sum \text{PV}(CF_i)}$$

The dispersion of a zero-coupon bond therefore is zero, whereas the dispersion of a 30-year current-coupon U.S. Treasury bond can be 80 to 100 years squared, as illustrated in Exhibit 48–5.

REBALANCING PROCEDURES

As time passes, the single-period immunized portfolio must be rebalanced so that the duration of the portfolio is always reset to the remaining life in the planning period to ensure the offsetting effects of capital gains with reinvestment return. This rebalancing procedure requires that the coupon income, reinvestment income, matured principal, and proceeds from possible liquidation of longer bonds be reinvested into securities that maintain the duration equal to the remaining life in the planning period. Because of the multiple rebalancings required throughout the planning period, the bond portfolio is continually maintained in a duration-matched state and therefore should achieve its target return in spite of periodic shifts in rates.

An immunized bond portfolio, therefore, can be constructed once a time horizon is established. Because duration is inversely related to both the prevailing yields and the coupon rate, it may not be possible to immunize a portfolio beyond a certain number of years using only coupon-bearing securities. For example,

---

4. This measure, commonly referred to as M[2], was first developed in H. Gifford Fong and Oldrich Vasicek, "A Risk Minimizing Strategy for Multiple Liability Immunization," *Journal of Finance*, December 1984, pp. 1541–1546.

when bond market yields reached their historic highs in 1981, it was not possible to immunize a bullet liability beyond seven years in the taxable markets with current-coupon securities. In 1989, in an 8 percent rate environment, the maximum lock-up period was closer to 12 years. However, the use of zero-coupon securities with long maturities and durations can allow the investor the opportunity to lengthen the planning period over which he or she can lock in rates.

The actual targeted return on an immunized portfolio will depend on the level of interest rates at the time the program is initiated. Though bond values may, for example, decline as interest rates rise, the future value of the portfolio (or security) based on the new higher reinvestment rate and lower principal value should still correspond to the original targeted yield. As we demonstrate later in an actual simulation of an immunized portfolio, duration is the key to controlling the equal offset of reinvestment income with asset value as interest rates fluctuate.

The important point to remember is this: *The standard deviation of return on an immunized portfolio will be much lower over a given horizon than that on a nonimmunized portfolio—whether measured around a sample mean or promised yield.* With interest-rate risk minimized (when held over an assumed time horizon), the performance of the immunized portfolio is virtually ensured, regardless of reinvestment rates.

A SIMULATION OF A SINGLE-PERIOD IMMUNIZED PORTFOLIO[5]

In this section, we will illustrate the mechanics of the immunization rebalancing procedures. The parameters for the analysis are as follows:

1. $50 million is available for investment on May 10, 1989.

2. The investment horizon is five years.

3. Only Treasury notes and bonds are eligible securities for this simulation.

4. The immunized portfolio is rebalanced annually.

5. The yield-curve assumptions used in the simulation are presented in Exhibit 48–6. These yield curves do not represent interest-rate projections. They are used only to subject the immunized portfolio to a wide variety of interest-rate fluctuations over the five-year horizon.

6. A bid-ask spread of $^1/_8$ of a point is assumed on all transactions ($^1/_8$ of a point on bond sales, no transaction cost on bond purchases).

The target yield established on May 10, 1989, was 9.285 percent. Exhibit 48–7 presents the following information for the portfolio at the beginning of each year: (1) the individual issues in the portfolio, including par amount, coupon, ma-

---

5. The authors are grateful for the assistance of Susan Fox in the preparation of this analysis and for her constructive comments on the text.

EXHIBIT 48–6

Yield-Curve Assumptions

	05/10/89	05/10/90	05/10/91	05/10/92	05/10/93	05/10/94
1989	9.12	—	—	—	—	—
1990	9.21	8.00	—	—	—	—
1991	9.28	8.00	8.94	—	—	—
1992	9.23	8.00	8.96	8.75	—	—
1993	9.23	8.00	9.00	8.77	10.50	—
1994	9.22	8.00	8.98	8.85	10.42	8.00
1995	9.22	8.00	8.94	8.86	10.24	8.10
1996	9.21	8.00	8.87	8.88	9.85	8.20
1997	9.18	8.00	8.75	8.90	9.70	8.30
1998	9.15	8.00	8.62	8.93	9.60	8.40
1999	9.13	8.00	8.45	8.97	9.58	8.50
2000	9.13	8.00				
2001	9.14	8.00				
2002	9.14	8.00				
2003	9.15	8.00				
2004	9.15	8.00				
2005	9.16	8.00				
2006	9.16	8.00				
2007	9.17	8.00				

Short-term reinvestment rate

		8.55%	8.50%	8.90%	9.65%	9.25%

turity, price, and yield, (2) the duration of each security and of the portfolio, (3) the dispersion of each security and of the portfolio, and (4) the market values plus accrued interest. *Notice that the duration of the portfolio is reset each year in order to match the remaining time in the planning horizon.* Exhibits 48–8 through 48–12 summarize the actual portfolio transactions each year.

The important conclusion to draw from the simulation is that the target return for the immunized portfolio was achieved, even in the volatile-yield environment envisioned in this scenario. We note from Exhibit 48–8 that the target yield of 9.285 percent and target future value of $78,795,148 were exceeded by 5 basis points and $179,763, respectively.[6] We demonstrated in this example that targeted rates may be obtained over a predetermined immunization term, in spite of dramatic fluctuations in market yields.

---

6. Because the initial investment is $50,051,651 and the target yield is 9.285 percent, the target future value is $(1 + .09285/2)^{10} \times \$50,051,651 = \$78,795,148$.

EXHIBIT 48-7

Immunization: Proposed Portfolio of Treasury Securities on May 10, 1989[a]

| Par Value | Coupon | Maturity | Market | | Dispersion | Duration | % of Market | Market Value |
			Price	Yield				
$ 5,000,000	12.625	8/15/1994	113.46875	9.321	3.01	3.986	11.63	$ 5,821,659.19
5,000,000	11.250	2/15/1995	108.43750	9.318	3.65	4.353	11.10	5,553,953.73
8,000,000	8.875	7/15/1995	98.06250	9.289	4.19	4.737	16.13	8,072,513.81
8,000,000	8.625	10/15/1995	96.84375	9.285	4.16	5.011	15.58	7,796,516.39
9,000,000	7.375	5/15/1996	90.37500	9.272	5.77	5.301	16.90	8,458,290.75
9,000,000	7.250	11/15/1996	89.21875	9.274	6.79	5.593	16.68	8,348,727.56
6,000,000	8.500	5/15/1997	95.84375	9.245	8.14	5.674	11.99	5,999,989.64
$50,000,000	8.840	1/03/1996	97.20375	9.285	5.16	4.998	100.00	$50,051,651.06

[a]Settlement date is 5/11/89.

EXHIBIT 48–7

Continued on May 10, 1990[a]

Par Value	Coupon	Maturity	Market Price	Yield	Dispersion	Duration	% of Market	Market Value
$ 8,000,000	13.125	5/15/1994	117.29042	8.000	1.78	3.139	17.19	$ 9,896,631.39
5,100,000	9.500	5/15/1994	105.05940	8.000	1.56	3.299	9.72	5,594,925.81
5,000,000	12.625[b]	8/15/1994	116.40832	8.000	1.75	3.410	10.36	5,968,637.69
5,000,000	11.250[b]	2/15/1995	112.64256	8.000	2.23	3.794	10.01	5,764,206.73
8,000,000	8.875[b]	7/15/1995	103.63180	8.000	2.63	4.169	14.79	8,518,057.81
8,000,000	8.625[b]	10/15/1995	102.69903	8.000	2.60	4.438	14.35	8,264,938.79
9,000,000	7.375[b]	5/15/1996	97.06136	8.000	3.84	4.768	15.73	9,060,063.15
4,100,000	7.250[b]	11/15/1996	96.24896	8.000	4.65	5.092	7.11	4,091,547.83
400,000	8.500[b]	5/15/1997	102.64210	8.000	5.82	5.236	0.74	427,192.71
$52,600,000	9.740[b]	5/12/1995	106.06953	8.003	2.60	3.996	100.00	$57,586,201.90

[a]Settlement date is 5/11/90.
[b]Existing issue.

Continued on May 10, 1991[a]

Par Value	Coupon	Maturity	Market		Dispersion	Duration	% of Market	Market Value
			Price	Yield				
$ 8,000,000	13.125[b]	5/15/1994	110.72441	8.980	0.91	2.465	15.46	$ 9,371,350.59
10,000,000	13.125	5/15/1994	110.72441	8.980	0.91	2.465	19.33	11,714,188.24
5,100,000	9.500[b]	5/15/1994	101.34353	8.980	0.78	2.574	8.92	5,405,416.44
1,800,000	9.500	5/15/1994	101.34353	8.980	0.78	2.574	3.15	1,907,794.04
5,000,000	12.625[b]	8/15/1994	110.11641	8.970	0.90	2.731	9.33	5,654,042.19
5,000,000	11.250	2/15/1995	107.25195	8.930	1.24	3.123	9.07	5,494,676.23
8,000,000	8.875[b]	7/15/1995	99.79609	8.928	1.54	3.485	13.55	8,211,201.01
8,000,000	8.625[b]	10/15/1995	98.91768	8.923	1.52	3.749	13.14	7,962,430.79
5,000,000	7.375[b]	5/15/1996	95.05409	8.870	2.48	4.097	8.06	4,883,004.92
$55,900,000	10.699	12/19/1994	104.45675	8.948	1.22	2.998	100.00	$60,604,104.44

[a]Settlement date is 5/11/91.

[b]Existing issue.

EXHIBIT 48–7

Continued on May 10, 1992[a]

Par Value	Coupon	Maturity	Market Price	Yield	Dispersion	Duration	% of Market	Market Value
$18,000,000	13.125[b]	5/15/1994	107.71738	8.850	0.34	1.735	30.99	$20,544,416.86
12,300,000	13.125	5/15/1994	107.71738	8.850	0.34	1.735	21.18	14,038,684.86
6,900,000	9.500[b]	5/15/1994	101.17164	8.850	0.28	1.795	11.01	7,301,389.86
2,900,000	9.500	5/15/1994	101.17164	8.850	0.28	1.795	4.63	3,068,700.09
5,000,000	12.625[b]	8/15/1994	107.55296	8.853	0.33	1.995	8.34	5,526,789.48
5,000,000	11.250[b]	2/15/1995	105.72184	8.858	0.54	2.405	8.17	5,418,990.35
8,000,000	8.375[b]	7/15/1995	100.01049	8.863	0.75	2.761	12.41	8,229,053.49
2,200,000	7.375[b]	5/15/1996	95.01125	8.880	1.41	3.401	3.27	2,169,589.53
$60,300,000	11.565[b]	8/30/1994	104.98841	8.857	0.43	2.003	100.00	$66,297,614.52

[a]Settlement date is 5/11/92.
[b]Existing issue.

EXHIBIT 48–7

Continued on May 10, 1993[a]

| Par Value | Coupon | Maturity | Market | | Dispersion | Duration | % of Market | Market Value |
			Price	Yield				
$30,300,000	13.125[b]	5/15/1994	102.53007	10.420	0.07	0.922	46.37	$33,011,105.34
10,200,000	13.125	5/15/1994	102.53007	10.420	0.07	0.922	15.61	11,112,649.32
9,800,000	9.500[b]	5/15/1994	99.13563	10.420	0.05	0.943	14.28	10,170,504.45
5,800,000	9.500	5/15/1994	99.13563	10.420	0.05	0.943	8.45	6,019,278.14
5,000,000	12.625[b]	8/15/1994	102.56533	10.375	0.06	1.177	7.41	5,276,488.19
5,000,000	11.250[b]	2/15/1995	101.48722	10.285	0.16	1.613	7.31	5,206,439.73
400,000	8.875[b]	7/15/1995	97.48937	10.175	0.27	1.970	0.56	401,333.17
$66,500,000	12.070	6/13/1994	101.62770	10.403	0.07	1.002	100.00	$71,197,798.34

[a]Settlement date is 5/11/93.
[b]Existing issue.

EXHIBIT 48-7

Continued on May 15, 1994[a]

Par Value	Coupon	Maturity[b]	Market		Dispersion	Duration	% of Market	Market Value
			Price	Yield				
$40,500,000	13.125[c]	5/15/1994	100.05091	8.000	0.00	0.011	72.54	$43,119,694.86
15,600,000	9.500[c]	5/15/1994	100.01246	8.000	0.00	0.011	27.46	16,326,568.07
$56,100,000	12.117	5/14/1994	100.04022	8.113	0.00	0.011	100.00	$59,446,262.93

[a]Settlement date is 5/11/94.

[b]Note that on May 15, 1994, both securities mature.

[c]Existing issue.

EXHIBIT 48-8

Bond Immunization Year-End Transactions (May 10, 1990)

1. Cash Received During Year:

Coupon Income		Interest on Coupon		Matured Principal
$4,420,000	+	221,145	+	0

Plus

Cash Carryover		Interest on Cash Carryover		Total Cash Received
0	+	0	=	$4,641,145

2. Sell:

Par (000)	Coupon	Maturity	Yield	Price	Market Value
4,900	7.250	11/15/96	8.000	96.24896	$ 4,889,898
5,600	8.500	5/15/97	8.000	102.64210	5,980,698
			Less transaction costs	–	13,125
					$10,857,472

3. Available to Reinvest:

$15,498,617

4. Buy:

Par (000)	Coupon	Maturity	Yield	Price	Market Value
8,500	13.125	5/15/94	8.00	117.29042	$9,896,631
5,100	9.500	5/15/94	8.00	105.05940	5,594,926

Cash carryover = ($15,498,617 – 15,491,557) = $7,060

EXHIBIT 48–9

Bond Immunization Year-End Transactions (May 10, 1991)

1. Cash Received During Year:

Coupon Income		Interest on Coupon		Matured Principal
$5,123,250	+	264,615	+	0

Plus

Cash Carryover		Interest on Cash Carryover		Total Cash Received
7,060	+	611	=	$5,395,536

2. Sell:

Par (000)	Coupon	Maturity	Yield	Price	Market Value
4,000	7,375	5/15/96	8.870	94.05409	$3,906,404
4,100	7,250	11/15/96	8.810	93.30149	3,970,701
400	8,500	5/15/96	8.750	98.84839	412,018
				Less transaction costs −	10,625
					$8,278,498

3. Available to Reinvest: $13,674,034

4. Buy:

Par (000)	Coupon	Maturity	Yield	Price	Market Value
10,000	13.125	5/15/94	8.980	110.72441	$11,714,188
1,800	9.500	5/15/94	8.980	101.34353	1,907,794

Cash carryover = ($13,674,034 − 13,621,982) = $52,052

EXHIBIT 48–10

Bond Immunization Year-End Transactions (May 10, 1992)

				Interest on Coupon		Matured Principal
1. Cash Received During Year:	Coupon Income $5,980,500	+		334,386	+	0

Plus

			Interest on Cash Carryover		Total Cash Received
	Cash Carryover 52,052	+	4,722	=	$6,371,660

2. Sell:

Par (000)	Coupon	Maturity	Yield	Price	Market Value
8,000	8.625	10/15/95	8.868	99.28347	$ 7,991,694
2,800	7.375	5/15/96	8.880	95.01125	2,761,296
				Less transaction costs	– 13,500
					$10,739,490

3. Available to Reinvest: $17,111,150

4. Buy:

Par (000)	Coupon	Maturity	Yield	Price	Market Value
12,300	13.125	5/15/94	8.850	107.71738	$14,038,685
2,900	9.500	5/15/94	8.850	101.17164	3,068,700

Cash carryover = ($17,111,150 – 17,107,385) = $3,765

EXHIBIT 48–11

Bond Immunization Year-End Transactions (May 10, 1993)

1. Cash Received During Year:	Coupon Income		Interest on Coupon		Matured Principal	
	$6,973,875	+	463,340	+	0	
Plus	Cash Carryover		Interest on Cash Carryover		Total Cash Received	
	3,765	+	371	=	$7,441,351	

2. Sell:	Par (000)	Coupon	Maturity	Yield	Price	Market Value
	7,600	8.875	7/15/95	10.175	97.48937	$7,625,330
	2,200	7.375	5/15/96	9.850	93.68181	2,140,331
					Less transaction costs	– 12,250
						$9,753,412

3. Available to Reinvest:

4. Buy:	Par (000)	Coupon	Maturity	Yield	Price	Market Value
	10,200	13.125	5/15/94	10.420	102.53007	$11,112,649
	5,800	9.500	5/15/94	10.420	99.13563	6,019,278

Cash carryover = ($17,194,763 – 17,131,927) = $62,836

EXHIBIT 48-12

Bond Immunization Year-End Transactions (May 15, 1994)

1. Cash Received Through 5/10/94:

Coupon Income		Interest on Coupon		Matured Principal
$8,026,875	+	527,719	+	0

Plus

Cash Carryover		Interest on Cash Carryover		Total Cash Received
62,836	+	5,929	=	$8,623,359

2. Income from 5/10/94–5/15/94

Coupon Income		Interest on Coupon		Matured Principal
$3,398,812	+	0	+	$56,100,000

Total cash received (1+2) = $68,122,171

3. Sell:

Par (000)	Coupon	Maturity	Yield	Price	Market Value
5,000	12.625	8/15/94	8.025	101.13270	$ 5,204,857
5,000	11.250	2/15/95	8.075	102.28331	5,246,244
400	8.875	7/15/96	8.117	100.81621	414,640
				Less transaction costs	− 13,000
					$10,852,741

4. Mature: 5/15/94

Par (000)	Coupon		Market Value & Coupon
40,500	13.125		$43,119,695
15,600	9.500		16,326,568
$78,974,912			$59,446,263

5. Final Value:

MULTIPERIOD IMMUNIZATION

In the discussions so far, we have documented how the three conditions are required to create a single-period immunized portfolio. These conditions can be extended to create an immunized portfolio that will satisfy the funding requirements of multiple-period liabilities, such as the monthly payouts to the retired-lives portion of a pension plan.

If a liability schedule were composed of 30 annual payments, it would be possible to create 30 single-period immunized portfolios to fund that schedule. If we then analyzed the overall duration of the 30 asset portfolios, it would equal the duration of the liabilities. As long as the dispersions of assets and liabilities are closely matched and the asset value is greater than the present value of liabilities, then the liability schedule should be fully funded and the portfolio immunized.

For example, the same retired-lives payout schedule for a pension fund that will be used in the next chapter on the dedicated bond portfolio is also presented in Exhibit 48–13. The set payouts are summarized in annual amounts, but in practice they are generally converted into monthly numbers (by dividing the annual payouts into 12 equal payments).

Calculating the duration of multiperiod liabilities is not as straightforward as calculating the duration of a single-period liability, where the remaining time in the planning horizon is the liability duration. With multiple payout periods, the liability duration is derived by using, as the discount factor, the internal rate of return (IRR) on the assets. Of course, the IRR of the assets is not determinable unless we know the precise portfolio, its duration, and its dispersion.

As a result of this simultaneity problem, the construction of an immunized portfolio is an iterative process whereby an IRR guess for the portfolio is advanced; the durations and dispersion of the liabilities are then calculated based on the IRR guess; an optimal immunized portfolio is simulated to match the duration and dispersion estimates; the portfolio IRR is then compared with the estimated IRR; and, if they differ, a new IRR estimate is advanced and the procedure repeated.

Using the same portfolio constraints assumed in the dedicated portfolio,[7] a final multiperiod immunized portfolio is represented in Exhibit 48–14. Note that the 6.97-year duration of assets is equal to the 6.97-year duration of the liabilities at the portfolio IRR of 9.86 percent. Furthermore, the $110,260,534 market value of assets is greater than the $110,172,000 present value of liabilities; and the 41.42 units of asset dispersion are greater than the 40.72 units of dispersion of the liabilities.

One should also note that the market value of the immunized portfolio at $110,260,534 is considerably cheaper in funding the same schedule of retired-lives payouts with the same portfolio constraints than the market value of the ded-

---

7. See Chapter 49 for an explanation of the portfolio constraints used in the dedicated portfolio simulation.

EXHIBIT 48-13

Retired-Lives Payout Schedule for a Pension Fund: Multiperiod Immunization
Illustration

Period Ending	Liability Payments
12/31/89 (partial year @ $15MM)	$ 8,750,000
12/31/90	14,916,015
12/31/91	14,427,473
12/31/92	13,445,985
12/31/93	12,435,248
12/31/94	11,754,199
12/31/95	11,384,959
12/31/96	11,028,026
12/31/97	10,654,684
12/31/98	10,408,523
12/31/99	10,355,190
12/31/00	10,236,214
12/31/01	9,953,126
12/31/02	9,670,039
12/31/03	9,302,164
12/31/04	8,748,308
12/31/05	8,621,160
12/31/06	8,209,594
12/31/07	7,893,578
12/31/08	7,435,436
12/31/09	6,993,713
12/31/10	6,579,349
12/31/11	6,145,834
12/31/12	5,732,824
12/31/13	5,322,551
12/31/14	4,983,398
12/31/15	4,615,526
12/31/16	4,257,221
12/31/17	3,892,088
12/31/18	3,537,881
12/31/19	3,216,510
12/31/20	2,934,788
12/31/21	2,659,900
12/31/22	2,385,026
12/31/23	2,123,504
12/31/24	1,447,297
Total	$276,457,331

E X H I B I T   48–14

Multiperiod Immunization Proposed Portfolio (May 10, 1989)

Issue Name	Par Value	Credit		Coupon	Maturity	Market Price	Yield
Arkla, Inc.	$ 2,500,000	A3	/BBB+	8.900	12/15/2006	92.24200	9.83
BankAmerica	1,000,000	A3	/BBB	8.750	5/01/2001	89.15800	10.35
BankAmerica	1,000,000	A3	/BBB	8.350	5/15/2007	84.17400	10.30
Banq Nat. Paris	4,600,000	AA1	/AA	9.875	5/25/1998	99.50200	9.96
Beneficial Corp.	2,400,000	A3	/A	7.500	5/15/1998	84.98400	10.08
Beneficial Corp.	2,500,000	A3	/A	8.400	12/01/2007	86.36600	10.03
Chase Manhattan	5,000,000	BAA2	/A–	10.000	6/15/1999	99.27900	10.11
Citicorp	2,000,000	A1	/AA	8.450	3/15/2007	87.19700	10.00
Citicorp	2,000,000	A1	/AA	8.125	7/01/2007	84.42800	10.00
Fed. Home Loan	6,500,000	AGY	/AGY	8.100	3/25/1996	92.09375	9.70
FHLMC	2,400,000	AGY	/AGY	8.125	9/30/1996	91.84375	9.69
Florida Power	2,000,000	AA3	/A+	8.000	12/01/2003	86.09400	9.81
GMAC	2,700,000	AA3	/AA–	8.125	10/15/1996	89.85200	10.10
GMAC	9,900,000	AA3	/AA–	8.250	4/01/2016	85.09400	9.83
Household Fin.	2,500,000	A1	/AA–	7.500	10/01/1997	85.89200	10.03
Household Fin.	1,100,000	A1	/AA–	7.750	10/01/1999	86.06900	9.93
Household Fin.	4,800,000	A1	/AA–	8.200	9/15/2007	85.85400	9.88
Houston L & P	3,000,000	A3	/BBB+	8.125	2/01/2004	84.92000	10.11
Houston L & P	5,000,000	A3	/BBB+	8.375	10/01/2007	85.21400	10.17
Jersey Bell	2,400,000	AAA	/AAA	8.000	9/15/2016	84.43100	9.62
Nippon Tel.	1,000,000	AAA	/AAA	9.500	7/27/1998	97.82900	9.86
Oklahoma G&E	2,000,000	AA2	/AA	8.250	8/15/2016	85.57700	9.77
Pacific Gas	5,000,000	A1	/A	7.500	6/01/2004	81.99600	9.81
Penn. P&L	5,000,000	BAA3	/A–	8.250	12/01/2006	87.00400	9.82
Pub Svce E&G	5,000,000	A1	/A	8.250	6/01/2007	86.86300	9.82
Sallie Mae	1,000,000	AGY	/AGY	7.750	12/29/1996	89.50000	9.73
Sallie Mae	25,000,000	AGY	/AGY	0.000	5/15/2014	9.43750	9.67
SOC Gen.	5,000,000	AA1	/AA	9.875	7/15/2003	99.73500	9.91
Southwest Bell	5,000,000	AA3	/AA–	8.250	3/01/2014	85.88600	9.77
TSY	$22,100,000	TSY	/TSY	8.500	9/30/1990	98.81250	9.42
	$141,400,000	AA1	/AA+	6.952	8/05/2002	76.29411	9.86

[a]YTC calculation for currently callable bonds assumes call on next coupon date.
[b]Yield-to-call exceeds 100 percent.

icated portfolio discussed in the next chapter. The reason is that the onerous constraint of matching every monthly liability cash flow in a dedicated portfolio strategy is not present in the immunization strategy, allowing the duration-matched solution to be more than 1 percent cheaper in price.

However, in the absence of strict cash matching it is anticipated that some liabilities will be met through a combination of asset cash flows *and* asset sales. In this regard, immunization introduces an element of market risk into the asset/liability equation that is only minimally present under a dedicated strategy.

E X H I B I T   48–14

(Continued)

Current Yield	Duration	Call Information			% of Market	Settlement Date	Market Value
		Date	Price	YTC[a]			
9.28	8.5				2.18	5/17/89	$ 2,399,994.44
9.78	7.3	5/01/89	102.710	42.99	0.81	5/17/89	895,468.89
9.92	8.9	5/15/89	104.340	58.340	0.76	5/17/89	842,203.89
9.48	5.9				4.35	5/17/89	4,794,122.56
8.83	6.5	5/15/89	100.900	46.68	1.85	5/17/89	2,040,616.00
9.32	8.7	12/01/88	101.850	b	2.05	5/17/89	2,255,983.33
9.67	6.3				4.69	5/17/89	5,175,061.11
9.54	8.8	3/15/89	104.220	68.11	1.61	5/17/89	1,773,045.56
9.29	8.8	7/01/89	103.710	b	1.59	5/17/89	1,749,948.89
8.70	5.3				5.49	5/11/89	6,053,368.75
8.76	5.6				2.02	5/11/89	2,226,458.33
8.92	8.0	12/01/88	104.420	b	1.63	5/17/89	1,795,657.78
8.98	5.6	10/15/89	101.500	40.25	2.22	5/17/89	2,445,504.00
9.58	10.0	4/01/96	103.600	11.83	7.73	5/17/89	8,528,668.50
8.64	6.1	10/01/89	100.600	54.13	1.97	5/17/89	2,171,258.33
8.91	7.0	10/01/89	100.800	54.36	0.87	5/17/89	957,652.06
9.40	9.0	9/15/89	101.690	64.76	3.80	5/17/89	4,188,788.67
9.31	8.1	2/01/89	104.780	b	2.38	5/17/89	2,619,370.83
9.71	8.9	10/01/89	105.400	72.56	3.91	5/17/89	4,314,206.94
9.33	10.2	9/15/89	105.030	82.56	1.87	5/17/89	2,059,410.67
9.44	6.1				0.91	5/17/89	1,007,317.78
9.42	9.9	8/15/91	101.310	16.70	1.59	5/17/89	1,753,706.67
8.78	8.3	6/01/89	193.390	b	3.87	5/17/89	1,272,716.67
9.09	8.6	12/01/88	104.840	b	4.12	5/17/89	4,540,408.33
9.11	8.7	6/01/89	104.990	b	4.11	5/17/89	4,533,358.33
8.39	5.6	12/29/91	100.000	12.54	0.84	5/11/89	923,416.67
0.00	25.0	5/15/09	100.000	12.16	2.14	5/17/89	2,359,375.00
9.59	7.7				4.67	5/17/89	5,154,076.39
9.42	9.8	3/01/89	104.380	82.47	3.97	5/17/89	4,381,383.33
8.52	1.3				21.01	5/11/89	22,047,995.56
8.92	7.0	3/18/91	102.522	b	100.00		$110,260,534.26

   The degree to which market risk can be limited and the cost savings of immunization thereby justified on a risk-adjusted basis depends in large part on one's ability to characterize correctly the price response of the bonds in the portfolio to changes in interest rates. This issue is especially critical when bonds containing embedded options—such as mortgages and callable corporates—are part of the asset mix and is best resolved by appealing to option-adjusted bond analytics for the relevant bond durations.[8] The immunization simulation above, which

---

8. See Chapters 36, 38, and 40.

assumed that all bond cash flows were fixed, is justified in part by the degree of call protection on the callable corporates selected; but the inclusion of bonds with more call risk would require more finely tuned analysis.

Rebalancing Procedures for Multiperiod Portfolios

Just as with a single-period immunized portfolio, a multiperiod portfolio must be rebalanced whenever one of the three conditions is violated. If, for example, the asset and liability durations were to wander apart over time, then the portfolio must be rebalanced to return it to a duration-matched state.

In a multiperiod portfolio, the durations will tend to wander whenever a liability payment comes due. An extreme example might be a $10 million bullet liability due in one month (almost zero duration) and a $10 million bullet liability due in 10 years. The average duration of the two liabilities will be about five years.

One month from now, the one-month liability will be extinguished and the remaining liability will be 9 years and 11 months. As the asset portfolio has a duration of roughly 5 years to match what was a 5-year average duration liability, the sudden shift in liability duration from 5 years to approximately 10 years will cause a major duration mismatch and will need to be rebalanced.

APPLICATIONS OF THE IMMUNIZATION STRATEGY

The major applications of the immunization strategy have been in the pension, insurance, banking, and thrift industries.

As illustrated in Exhibit 48–15, the pension market has made widespread use of both single-period and multiperiod immunization. Single-period immunization is generally employed as an alternative to the purchase of a guaranteed

E X H I B I T   48–15

Applications for Immunization

	Market		
	Pension	**Insurance**	**Banking and Thrift**
Single period	Asset strategy (GIC alternative)		
Multiperiod	Funding retired-live payouts	Funding GIC and structured settlements	GAP management Matched growth
	Single premium buyouts Portfolio insurance	Portfolio insurance	Portfolio insurance

investment contract (GIC) from an insurance company. Both vehicles seek to lock in today's prevailing rates over a finite planning horizon. Immunization has the advantage of liquidity, as the portfolio is composed of marketable securities. GICs are privately written contracts between plan sponsor and insurance company and are not generally traded in the secondary market.

The additional benefit of an immunized portfolio is that the portfolio manager can take advantage of market opportunities in structuring and rebalancing these portfolios by including securities in the portfolio that are attractive on a relative-value basis. Investors can actively position portfolios in sectors and credits they perceive to be cheap or upgrade candidates. By actively positioning the immunized portfolio, investors can add incremental value to the portfolios and potentially outperform the illiquid GIC over a fixed planning horizon.

The pension market has also made widespread use of multiperiod immunization. Multiperiod immunization is generally employed to fund a schedule of expected benefit payouts to the retired-lives portion of a defined benefit plan. As explained in greater detail in the next chapter on cash flow matching, by matching the duration of an immunized portfolio with corresponding liabilities, the plan sponsor can lock in prevailing rates, raise its actuarial interest-rate assumption, and reduce cash contributions to the pension fund. Tens of billions of dollars in pension monies went into immunization and dedication strategies in the early and mid-1980s because of the strong incentive of cash flow savings and the reduced funding risk for the retired segment of the plan.

The insurance market has also made widespread use of the multiperiod immunization strategy for its fixed-liability insurance products such as GICs and structured settlements. Because GIC, structured settlement, and single-premium buyout assets and liabilities are generally segmented from general account assets and liabilities, the entire line of business can be immunized to minimize the interest-rate risk and lock in a spread. Again, these portfolios can be actively positioned to take advantage of market opportunities.

Lastly, banks and thrifts have made extensive use of the multiperiod immunization strategy to assist in the management of their asset/liability gap and to ensure future duration-matched growth of assets and liabilities. *Technical Bulletin 13* (TB-13) mandated for the thrift industry that the interest sensitivity of a company's assets be similar to the interest sensitivity of its liabilities. For those thrifts whose durations are not closely matched, their capital requirements will be increased.

VARIATIONS TO IMMUNIZATION

There are several variations or enhancements to the immunization strategy, including combination-matching; contingent immunization; immunization with futures, options, mortgages, or swaps; and stochastic duration matching.

The most popular variation of the immunization strategy is *combination-matching*, also called *horizon-matching*. A combination-matched portfolio is one that is duration-matched with the added constraint that it be cash-matched in the first few years, usually five years. The advantages of combination-matching over immunization are that liquidity needs are provided for in the initial cash-flow-matched period. Also, most of the positive slope or inversion of a yield curve tends to take place in the first few years. By cash flow matching the initial portion, we have reduced the risk associated with nonparallel shifts of a sloped yield curve.

The disadvantages of combination-matching over immunization are that the cost is slightly greater and the swapping discretion is constrained. The free-dom to swap a combination-matched portfolio is partially hampered not only be-cause the asset durations must be replaced in a swap but also because the cash flows in the initial five-year period must be replaced as well.

A variant strategy to immunization is *contingent immunization*. The contin-gent immunization strategy is a blend of active management with immunization such that a portfolio is actively managed with a lower floor return ensured over the horizon.[9]

The floor return, or safety net, is a rate set below the immunized rate, allow-ing managers discretion to actively position their portfolios. If managers incor-rectly position their portfolios and the market moves against them, the portfolios can still be actively managed. If the market continues to move against the portfo-lios and the floor return is violated, then managers must commit to immunized portfolios to ensure the floor return over the remainder of the horizon.

Contingent immunization requires an abrupt change in management strat-egy at the moment the floor return is violated. With dynamic asset allocation (portfolio insurance), the change in strategy is gradual. In this instance, managers gradually shift out of risky assets into riskless assets to avoid violating minimum return requirements. An actively managed bond portfolio or equity portfolio is the risky asset. An immunized portfolio, with duration matched to the holding period, can serve as the riskless asset. Overall, the performance of the portfolio of risky and riskless assets replicates the performance that would be obtained were a put option added to the risky portfolio. This synthetic put gives the portfolio maxi-mum upside potential consistent with a prespecified level of protection on the downside.

Immunized portfolios can also be created with the use of futures contracts to replicate the interest sensitivity of an immunized duration. In this form, a de-sired portfolio can be selected without regard to a target duration, and futures contracts can then be used to replicate the price sensitivity of an immunized port-folio at the desired duration.

Options can also be used with immunized portfolios to enhance returns over a specified horizon. Through the use of covered call writing or long put or call positions, managers can enhance returns over a specified horizon.

---

9. See Martin L. Leibowitz and Alfred Weinberger, "The Uses of Contingent Immunization," *Journal of Portfolio Management,* Fall 1981, pp. 51–55.

Finally, CMO PAC bonds are sometimes used in immunized portfolios to enhance returns. Though they are mortgage derivatives, their cash flows are certain across a wide band of interest-rate scenarios (prepayment speeds). As such, they can enhance performance as long as their use is actively monitored.

CONCLUSION

Bond immunization is an important risk-control strategy that is used extensively by the pension fund, insurance, banking, and thrift industries. In today's volatile markets, it is imperative that all asset/liability gaps be intentional. Immunization provides the tools to measure the interest-rate risk position an institution or a fund is taking with respect to its liabilities; it also provides the tools to minimize that risk when a minimum gap is desired.

⑥ DEDICATED BOND PORTFOLIOS

Peter E. Christensen
Managing Director
ComTech, Incorporated

Frank J. Fabozzi, Ph.D., CFA, CPA
Adjunct Professor of Finance
School of Management
Yale University

Dedication is a popular and important portfolio strategy in asset/liability management. The dedicated bond portfolio, as it is frequently called, is a strategy that matches monthly cash flows from a portfolio of bonds to a prespecified set of monthly cash requirements of liabilities. Cash matching or prefunding these liabilities leads to the elimination of interest-rate risk and defeasance of the liability.

Applications for the dedicated strategy include pension benefit funding, defeasance of debt service, municipal funding of construction take-down schedules, structured settlement funding, GIC matching, and funding of other fixed insurance products.

THE NEED FOR A BROADER ASSET/LIABILITY FOCUS

For financial intermediaries such as banks and insurance companies, there is a well-recognized need for a complete funding perspective. This need is best illustrated by the significant interest-rate risk assumed by many insurance carriers in the early years of their guaranteed investment contract (GIC) products. A large volume of compound interest (zero-coupon) and simple interest (annual pay) GICs were issued in three- through seven-year maturities in the positively sloped yield-curve environment of the mid-1970s. Proceeds from thousands of the GIC

The authors are grateful for the assistance of Anthony LoFaso of Union Bank of Switzerland for his constructive comments and contributions to the chapter.

issues were reinvested at higher rates in longer 10- to 30-year private placement, commercial mortgage, and public bond instruments. At the time, the industry expected that the GIC product would be very profitable because of the large positive spread between the higher "earned" rate on the longer assets and the lower "credited" rate on the GIC contracts.

By pricing GICs on a spread basis and investing the proceeds into mismatched assets, companies gave little consideration to the rollover risk they were assuming in volatile markets. As rates rose dramatically in the late 1970s and early 1980s, carriers were exposed to extreme disintermediation as GIC liabilities matured and the corresponding assets, with 20 years remaining to maturity, were valued at only a fraction of their original cost.

As a result of this enormous risk exposure, insurance carriers were induced to adopt a broader asset/liability focus to control the interest-rate risk associated with writing a fixed-liability product. Dedication and immunization (described in Chapter 42) have become popular matching strategies to control this market risk.

Similarly, in funding pension liabilities there is also a need for a broad asset/liability focus. Since the future investment performance of a pension fund is unpredictable, actuaries generally incorporate conservative investment return assumptions in the calculation of annual funding requirements. This conservative approach requires current contributions at much greater levels than the amounts needed under more realistic (higher) investment return assumptions. Such oversized contributions diminish both corporate cash flow and current profits for the sponsoring entity.

Through use of the dedication strategy to fund the relatively well-defined, retired-lives portion of the pension liability, some of this conservative margin can be eliminated. In the process, the plan sponsor may elect to reduce its current contributions to the pension fund or offer more generous benefits to plan participants, without increasing the current level of funding.

CASH FLOW MATCHING FOR PENSION FUNDS

The most popular application of the dedicated strategy has been to fund the payout obligations of the retired-lives portion of a pension plan. In the following simulation, we illustrate, in detail, the mechanics of this strategy as it applies to pension funds.

Determining the Liabilities

The first step in establishing a dedicated bond portfolio is to determine the schedule to be funded. For pension funds, usually it is the expected benefit payouts to a closed block of current retirees. Since the benefit payouts to active employees cannot be projected with great accuracy, they are generally not included in the analysis. Since active employees and future retirees are not included in the closed block, the schedule of benefit payments declines over time due to mortality experience. The second column of Exhibit 49–1 illustrates the annual schedule of benefit payouts that are expected to be paid to current retirees.

The forecast payouts are based on the known benefit payouts at retirement for each employee and a number of variables, including expected cost-of-living increases. As shown in Exhibit 49–1, the payouts over the 35-year time horizon for the retired employees total $283,758,000.

In addition to funding the retired-lives payouts, the dedicated strategy is frequently applied to a somewhat broader universe of participants that includes retirees plus terminated vested participants. Terminated vested participants are former employees who are vested in the pension plan and are entitled to benefit payouts commencing sometime in the future. Since these benefit amounts are relatively fixed, they can be readily match-funded. A retired plus terminated vested liability schedule is illustrated in the last column of Exhibit 49–1.

Several pension plans have extended the dedication strategy to include the funding of "anticipated retiree" pension obligations. That is, in addition to funding the retired and terminated vested liabilities, the cash flow-matched design is used to offset liabilities associated with active employees aged 50 and greater. Since these benefit payments are not fixed until the employee actually retires, the various mortality, termination, and benefit assumptions must be reviewed periodically to ensure that actual experience tracks the forecast.

Instead of a downward-sloping liability schedule, the profile of expected benefit payouts for this broad population of plan participants would increase dramatically in the first 10 to 15 years, level off for a brief period, and then begin a downward slope. The benefit schedule peaks because the active participants who will be joining the retired population over the next 10 to 15 years are generally greater in number and have higher salaries (due to inflation) compared with the population of retirees, which declines due to mortality. The percentage reduction in actuarial liability and hence in contribution requirements associated with the anticipated retirees, is frequently larger than that for the currently retired population because a higher discount rate applied to larger and longer liabilities results in a bigger savings.

Similarly, one can apply the dedication strategy to insurance company funding, where a liability schedule can represent monthly projections of fixed payouts for products such as GICs, single-premium buyouts, or structured settlements. Once that schedule is derived, the procedures for match-funding an insurance product line are similar to those for creating a dedicated portfolio for a pension fund.

Setting Portfolio Constraints

With the liability schedule determined, the next step in instituting a dedicated portfolio is to specify portfolio constraints on sector, quality, issuer, and lot sizes. To identify the cheapest portfolio possible that funds the fixed schedule of liabilities, the portfolio manager may wish to constrain the optimal or least-cost solu-

EXHIBIT 49–1

Schedule of Expected Benefit Payouts

	Retired-Lives Liabilities	Retired-Lives plus Terminated Vested
Year	Dollar Payout	Dollar Payout
1992[a]	1,250,000	2,000,000
1993	15,000,000	24,000,000
1994	14,916,015	24,519,000
1995	14,427,473	25,021,000
1996	13,445,985	25,523,000
1997	12,435,248	26,190,000
1998	11,754,199	26,809,000
1999	11,384,959	27,459,000
2000	11,028,026	28,026,000
2001	10,654,684	28,630,000
2002	10,408,523	29,221,000
2003	10,355,190	29,780,000
2004	10,236,214	30,294,000
2005	9,953,126	30,576,000
2006	9,670,039	30,312,000
2007	9,302,164	29,758,000
2008	8,748,308	29,196,000
2009	8,621,160	28,684,000
2010	8,209,594	27,992,000
2011	7,893,578	27,209,000
2012	7,435,436	26,535,000
2013	6,993,713	25,714,000
2014	6,579,349	24,996,000
2015	6,145,834	24,008,000
2016	5,732,824	23,121,000
2017	5,322,551	22,189,000
2018	4,983,398	21,076,000
2019	4,615,526	19,986,000
2020	4,257,221	18,826,000
2021	3,892,088	17,701,000
2022	3,537,881	16,589,000
2023	3,216,510	15,437,000
2024	2,934,788	14,319,000
2025	2,659,900	13,211,000
2026	2,385,026	12,098,000
2027	2,123,504	10,982,000
2028	1,337,297	9,869,000
Total	$283,758,000	

[a] Partial year @ $15 million.

tion to a universe of government and corporate securities rated single-A or better by one rating agency, as illustrated in Exhibit 49–2. In the simulation that follows, a *minimum* of 20 percent of the portfolio is constrained to be in U.S. Treasury securities, and a 30 percent *maximum* is set for the bank and finance, industrial, utility, and telephone sectors; a 30 percent *maximum* is established collectively for

E X H I B I T   49–2

Portfolio Constraints

	Minimum	Maximum
Quality[a]		
Treasury	20%	100%
Agency		100
AAA	0	100
AA	0	100
A	0	50
BBB	0	0
Sector		
Treasury	20%	100%
Agency		100
Industrial	0	30
Utility	0	30
Telephone	0	30
Bank and finance	0	30
Canadian		
Yankee	0	30
World Bank		
Euros	0	0
Concentration		
Maximum in one issue		10%
Maximum in one issuer		10
Call Constraints on Corporate		
Securities	Noncallable only	
Lot Size		
Conditional minimum	$2,000,000 (par)	
Increment	$1,000,000 (par)	
Maximum	Unlimited	

[a]Single-A split-rated securities allowed.

Yankee, Canadian, and World Bank issues; and no Euro or PAC bonds (CMOs) are allowed in this example.

As a general rule, mortgages are not desirable instruments for dedicated portfolios because uncertain prepayment rates cause uncertainty in monthly cash flows from mortgage securities. Nevertheless, some portfolio managers allow PACs because PAC cash flows are call-protected within a relatively wide band of prepayment speeds.

As seen in the protracted bull markets of the early 1990s, even wide-band PACs have become "busted" as prepayment speeds have pierced through their upper bands. As this occurs, the previously cash flow-matched portfolio becomes mismatched, compromising the integrity of the dedicated portfolio. Though the PACs can be swapped out as prepayment speeds approach the upper or lower limits of their bands, there is usually a cost associated with that swap; frequently, the plan sponsor is required to "pay in" additional funds to the program to purchase call-protected instruments. It is for these reasons that mortgages in general and PACs in particular are rarely used in the dedicated design.

It is also worth noting that the use of corporate securities, although providing higher yields, carries credit and call risks. If corporate securities are used in a dedicated portfolio, care must be taken to select call-protected securities that have a low probability of a credit downgrade. Although downgrades are always undesirable, the actual integrity of the cash flow match is still preserved with a downgrade (or even a series of downgrades) as long as the issuer does not default.

It is only when the coupon or principal payments are not made on time or in full that the cash flow match breaks down and the portfolio must be restructured.

Note also from Exhibit 49–2 that constraints on lot size are emphasized. Round-lot solutions (in lots of $2 million or more) are strongly preferred since the actual execution of the portfolio may be accomplished more efficiently without the added costs of odd-lot differentials. Also, as the dedicated portfolio is swapped or reoptimized over time, additional odd-lot premiums on the sale of such assets are avoided.

The Reinvestment Rate

Since the timing of cash receipts does not always exactly match the timing of cash disbursements, surplus funds must be reinvested at an assumed reinvestment rate until the next liability payout date. This reinvestment or rollover rate is vital because it is often preferable to prefund future benefit payments with higher-yielding securities rather than to purchase lower-yielding issues that mature closer to the liability payment dates. The more conservative the reinvestment rate, the greater the penalty for prefunding future benefit payouts and, therefore, the tighter the cash flow match. The more aggressive the reinvestment rate, the greater the prefunding in optimal portfolios but the greater the risk of not earning that aggressive short-term reinvestment rate in a future period and experiencing a shortfall of cash. Though the current actuarial rates (investment return assumptions) range from 5 percent to 8 percent, the simulation that follows assumes a short-term reinvestment rate of only 3 percent.

Selecting the Optimal Portfolio

Once the liability schedule, the portfolio constraints, and the reinvestment rate(s) are specified, an optimal (least-cost) portfolio can be structured for defeasance of the expected benefit payouts. The optimal portfolio is illustrated in Exhibit 49–3.

Assembling a dedicated portfolio that has a high probability of attaining its funding objectives over time requires restricting the universe of available issues. The fund manager must avoid questionable credits and, most important, avoid issues that may be called prior to maturity, have large sinking-fund call risk, or have significant prepayment risk. Retirement of issues prior to their stated maturity, whether through default or call, jeopardizes the funding of the liability schedule. As a result, most current coupon-callable bonds and non-PAC CMO bonds are not appropriate for matched portfolios.

The logic used to select the optimal or least-cost portfolio varies among purveyors of the cash flow-matching service. Three methods are used to identify an "optimal" portfolio. In order of sophistication, they are stepwise solutions, linear programming, and integer programming. Of the three, integer programming is the most technically advanced and is able to identify the lower-cost round-lot solution.

The Cash Flow Match

Exhibit 49–4 summarizes the cash flow match inherent in the dedicated portfolio in our example. Note that, in every year, the cash flow from the maturing principal when added to the coupon income from all securities in the portfolio and the reinvestment income will almost precisely equal the liability requirements specified by the actuary in Exhibit 49–1. Since almost all cash flow is paid out each month to fund the liability payment, the portfolio has very little cash to reinvest each period and hence assumes very little reinvestment risk. The plan can therefore lock in a rate of over 7.83 percent—the rate prevailing at the time of this writing—regardless of the future course of rates.

In this simulation, the computer model has controlled reinvestment risk by structuring relatively small surplus positions in most years. However, the model sometimes prefunds distant payouts by reinvesting the proceeds of high-yielding, shorter-maturity issues at the low reinvestment rate. This is frequently preferable to purchasing bonds with longer maturities and better matching characteristics, but with lower yields to maturity. Note from Exhibit 49–4 that the larger amount of prefunding in the years 2021 and 2022 is due to the lack of high-yielding call-protected issues in subsequent years.

Pricing the Bonds

Notice in Exhibit 49–4 that neither prices nor yields appear in the analysis. A dedicated portfolio is concerned only with cash flows. As long as all coupon payments are made in a timely fashion and every bond matures on schedule, the

EXHIBIT 49-3

Proposed Optimal Dedicated Portfolio

							Market			Duration		
Par ($000)	Moody	S&P	Security	Coupon	Maturity	Price	Yield	WAL	Nominal	Effective	Market Value ($000)
5,000	GOV	GOV	United States	5.000	12/31/1993	101.266	3.849	1.1	1.08	1.08	5,154
5,500	GOV	GOV	United States	7.625	12/31/1994	106.078	4.604	2.1	1.92	1.93	5,986
5,500	GOV	GOV	United States	11.500	11/15/1995	117.406	5.186	3.0	2.48	2.50	6,765
5,000	AGN	AGN	Federal Home L	8.600	11/13/1996	104.406	7.312	4.0	3.23	3.27	5,432
4,500	GOV	GOV	United States	8.875	11/15/1997	111.750	6.118	5.0	3.93	4.01	5,223
4,500	GOV	GOV	Resolution FDG	0.000	10/15/1998	67.753	6.676	5.9	5.74	5.91	3,049
3,000	Aaa	AAA	Southern RY CO	8.350	12/15/1999	105.411	7.356	7.1	5.18	5.30	3,263
3,500	A3	A	Shearson Lehma	9.875	10/15/2000	106.992	8.637	7.9	5.49	5.61	3,769
2,000	A3	A	Westpac BKG CO	9.125	8/15/2001	101.854	8.813	8.8	5.86	5.99	2,080
1,000	A3	A+	Firemans PD MT	8.875	10/15/2001	103.392	8.327	8.9	6.11	6.25	1,040
1,500	A3	A	Skandinaviska	8.450	5/15/2002	99.302	8.558	9.5	6.18	6.34	1,551
2,000	A3	A	Westpac BKG CO	7.875	10/15/2002	93.878	8.809	9.9	6.61	6.79	1,895
3,500	Aa2	AA–	National West M	9.375	11/15/2003	108.579	8.178	11.0	6.70	6.85	3,960
3,500	A2	A–	Svenska Handel	8.350	7/15/2004	97.306	8.719	11.7	7.10	7.26	3,504
5,000	A3	A	Shearson Lehma	11.625	5/15/2005	119.891	8.950	12.5	6.74	6.86	6,277
3,500	Aaa	AAA	General Elec	7.875	12/1/2006	100.378	7.829	14.1	8.14	8.33	3,635
4,000	Aa1	AA	Bell Tel Co PA	7.375	7/15/2007	89.569	8.640	14.7	8.29	8.47	3,677
5,000	A2	A	K Mart Corp	6.000	1/1/2008	80.752	8.893	10.6	6.94	7.08	4,145
4,000	A3	AA–	Berkley W R CO	9.875	5/15/2008	111.226	8.554	15.5	7.92	8.07	4,641
5,000	Aa1	AAA	General RE	9.000	9/12/2009	104.713	8.467	16.8	8.66	8.83	5,308

EXHIBIT 49-3

Proposed Optimal Dedicated Portfolio (*Continued*)

| Par ($000) | Moody | S&P | Security | Coupon | Maturity | Market | | | Duration | | Market Value ($000) |
						Price	Yield	WAL	Nominal	Effective	
4,500	A2	A	May Dept Store	10.625	11/1/2010	117.564	8.677	18.0	8.66	8.81	5,302
5,000	A1	A+	Hillenbrand In	8.500	12/1/2011	99.225	8.582	19.1	8.98	9.16	5,149
4,500	A3	A−	Norsk Hydro	9.000	4/15/2012	102.500	8.729	19.4	9.17	9.34	4,641
500	Aaa	AAA	General Elec	8.125	5/15/2012	99.184	8.209	19.5	9.32	9.52	514
5,000	AGN	AGN	Financing Corp	0.000	12/27/2013	16.618	8.676	21.1	20.25	22.25	831
4,000	AGN	AGN	Financing Corp	0.000	12/27/2014	15.217	8.691	22.1	21.21	23.56	609
4,000	A3	A−	NCNB Corp	10.200	7/15/2015	111.389	9.010	22.7	9.14	9.29	4,586
5,000	Aa2	AA	Southern Ind G	8.875	6/1/2016	99.740	8.901	23.6	9.43	9.61	5,183
3,000	AGN	AGN	Financing Corp	0.300	11/30/2017	11.808	8.711	25.1	24.01	27.87	354
3,500	AGN	AGN	Financing Corp	0.300	9/26/2018	11.036	8.701	25.9	24.80	29.25	386
3,000	AGN	AGN	Federal Natl M	0.300	10/9/2019	10.281	8.634	26.9	25.80	31.16	308
3,500	A2	A	Ford Hldgs	9.375	3/1/2020	105.244	8.860	27.3	9.98	10.18	3,746
5,000	A3	A	Dayton Hudson	9.700	6/15/2021	109.229	8.810	28.6	9.90	10.10	5,657
5,000	A3	AA−	Berkley W R Co	8.700	1/1/2022	97.752	8.916	29.1	10.05	10.27	5,043
2,500	GOV	GOV	Resolution FDG	0.000	10/15/2024	7.519	8.271	31.9	30.66	40.31	188
3,000	GOV	GOV	Resolution FDG	0.000	10/15/2025	7.000	8.241	32.9	31.63	41.30	210
1,500	GOV	GOV	Resolution FDG	0.000	10/15/2026	6.520	8.211	33.9	32.59	42.28	98
139,000	Aa2	AA+		6.942	16.0 years	86.213	7.835	15.8	7.14	7.37	123,160

E X H I B I T   49–4

Proposed Dedicated Portfolio: Yearly Cash Flow Summary
(Amounts in $000)

Period Ending	Beginning Balance	Maturing Principal	Coupon Income	Reinvestment Income	Cash Flow Available	Liability Schedule	Ending Balance
12/31/1992	0	0	2,740	8	2,748	1,250	1,498
12/31/1993	1,498	5,000	9,661	176	16,335	15,000	1,335
12/31/1994	1,335	5,500	9,399	169	16,403	14,916	1,487
12/31/1995	1,487	5,500	8,979	192	16,158	14,427	1,730
12/31/1996	1,730	5,000	8,347	190	15,268	13,446	1,822
12/31/1997	1,822	4,500	7,917	186	14,424	12,435	1,989
12/31/1998	1,989	4,500	7,517	197	14,204	11,754	2,450
12/31/1999	2,450	3,500	7,502	202	13,654	11,385	2,270
12/31/2000	2,270	4,000	7,222	212	13,703	11,028	2,675
12/31/2001	2,675	3,500	6,846	226	13,247	10,555	2,692
12/31/2002	2,692	4,000	6,482	232	13,406	10,409	2,998
12/31/2003	2,998	4,000	6,231	210	13,439	10,366	3,072
12/31/2004	3,072	4,000	5,873	243	13,188	10,236	2,952
12/31/2005	2,952	5,500	5,260	277	13,989	9,953	4,036
12/31/2006	4,036	4,000	4,939	218	13,193	9,670	3,523
12/31/2007	3,523	4,500	4,634	245	12,902	9,302	3,600
12/31/2008	3,600	4,500	4,111	261	12,471	8,748	3,723
12/31/2009	3,723	5,000	3,899	215	12,836	8,621	4,215
12/31/2010	4,215	4,500	3,449	199	12,363	8,210	4,153
12/31/2011	4,153	5,000	2,970	182	12,305	7,894	4,412
12/31/2012	4,412	5,000	2,323	277	12,011	7,435	4,576
12/31/2013	4,576	5,000	2,100	173	11,849	6,994	4,855
12/31/2014	4,855	4,000	2,100	181	11,136	6,579	4,557
12/31/2015	4,557	4,000	2,100	226	10,883	6,146	4,737
12/31/2016	4,737	5,000	1,470	254	11,461	5,733	5,729
12/31/2017	5,729	3,000	1,248	200	10,177	5,323	4,855
12/31/2018	4,855	3,500	1,248	194	9,797	4,983	4,814
12/31/2019	4,814	3,000	1,248	185	9,247	4,616	4,632
12/31/2020	4,632	3,500	1,084	246	9,462	4,257	5,205
12/31/2021	5,205	5,000	677	253	11,135	3,892	7,243
12/31/2022	7,243	5,000	217	377	12,837	3,538	9,299
12/31/2023	9,299	0	0	281	9,581	3,217	6,364
12/31/2024	6,364	2,500	0	208	9,072	2,935	6,137
12/31/2025	6,137	3,000	0	205	9,342	2,660	6,682
12/31/2026	6,682	1,500	0	211	8,393	2,385	6,008
12/31/2027	6,008	0	0	182	6,190	2,124	4,066
12/31/2028	4,066	0	0	123	4,189	1,337	2,852
Total		139,000	139,794	7,817		283,758	

liabilities specified by the actuary will be funded. Though credit ratings on some bonds in a portfolio may deteriorate over time and their market prices drop markedly, the integrity of the dedicated design is preserved as long as cash flow payments are complete and punctual.

Prices and yields enter the analysis only in determining the initial cost of the optimal portfolio as seen in Exhibit 49–3. In this simulation, all bonds were priced as of November 6, 1992.

The Savings to the Pension Plan

As illustrated in Exhibit 49–5, using the current actuarial investment rate assumption of 5 percent, the plan must have on hand $159,818,000 in order to fully fund the $283,758,000 of payouts to retired lives. On the basis of the November 6, 1992, pricing, the portfolio can, with a yield of 7.83 percent, fully fund the same $283,758,000 in liability payouts with an initial investment of only $123,160,000. Purchase of this portfolio would generally give the actuary the comfort level necessary to increase the assumed actuarial investment rate on the retired-lives portion of the fund. In many cases, this increase may go all the way to the funding rate of 7.83 percent.

By raising the assumed rate from 5 percent to 7.83 percent on the retired portion of the plan, the plan sponsor has reduced the present value of the accumulated plan benefits by $36,658,000. This long-term actuarial gain or potential savings of $36.7 million represents a 23 percent reduction from the higher present value required under a 5 percent actuarial assumption.

Increasing the assumed rate on the retired-lives portion of the pension fund decreases the present value of the funds promised as future payouts, thus reducing the actuarial liability. Reductions in actuarial liability usually translate into reductions in the current contribution requirements. The reduction in current contribution due to the dedicated strategy can be substantial.

In our example, the reduction in actuarial liability is $36.7 million. This amount cannot be realized in the form of a reduced contribution all in the first year. Pensions and tax legislation require that the gain be spread over 10 to 30 years. With all other factors remaining constant, the reduction in pension contribution might amount to a couple million dollars per year for each of the next 10 years. However, since every pension plan is different, and different actuarial cost methods treat gains differently, the actual savings to a plan may be of a different magnitude than represented by this example.

E X H I B I T   49–5

Reduced Funding Requirements

	Percent	Dollar Amount
1. Total liabilities	—	$283,758,000
2. Present value of total liabilities at	5.00	159,818,000
3. Portfolio cost (market value) at	7.83	123,160,000
4. Potential savings (2–3)	—	36,658,000
Percent savings (4/2)	22.94	—
Percent savings (4/3)	29.76	—

E X H I B I T   49–6

Take-Out from Reoptimizations

	Market Value (000)	Average Rating	Take-Out (000)
Original dedicated portfolio	$100,000	Aaa/AA+	—
Reoptimized dedicated portfolio (marked to market 1 year later)	99,400	Aaa/AA+	$600

Reoptimizing a Dedicated Bond Portfolio

It was originally thought that once a dedicated portfolio was structured, it should be passively managed, that is, left untouched as assets roll off in tandem with liabilities. Active management techniques can, however, be applied to dedicated portfolios. In addition to bond-for-bond swapping and active sector positioning of the portfolio, a cash-matched solution can be entirely reoptimized on a periodic basis.

For example, a portfolio that was "optimized" last year, in last year's rate environment, is not an optimal portfolio in today's rate environment, with a new yield curve, new yield spreads, and new available issues. As seen in Exhibit 49–6, a new least-cost portfolio can be created one year later to fund the same liability schedule with the same portfolio constraints. Since the new optimal portfolio will be less expensive than the old, a cash take-out can be generated by selling off a portion of the original portfolio and replacing the cash insufficiencies with a new combination of securities. When the take-out is significant, such trades are usually executed.

The take-out generated by the computer solution can be guaranteed if the reoptimization is executed through a dealer firm. Frequently, money managers and third-party software vendors work in conjunction with dealer firms to obtain a trader-priced database and guaranteed take-outs. On the other hand, if a reoptimization is simulated on a database of matrix (computer-derived) prices, the take-out may disappear when market prices are obtained in the actual execution.

Note that the new optimal portfolio will always be cheaper than the original portfolio. If the computer is not able to find a portfolio that is cheaper than the original, it will select the original portfolio again, establishing that it is still the optimum.

Active Management of Dedicated Portfolios

In addition to the use of comprehensive reoptimizations to add value, bond swaps can be undertaken to pick up yield or to swap out of an undesirable credit. To preserve the integrity of the dedicated portfolio, however, the cash flows associated with the bond being sold must be replaced with those from the bond (or bonds) being purchased. Thus bonds with identical coupons and maturities, or bonds with higher coupons and similar maturities, can be swapped. Bonds with similar coupons and slightly earlier maturities can also be swapped provided an additional cash pay-up is not required.

In addition to swapping, an active manager might add significant value by actively positioning a new dedicated portfolio in cheap sectors of the market. As spreads change, the optimized portfolio will automatically overweight the newly cheapened sectors of the market and underweight the rich ones.

For example, suppose that an existing $100 million dedicated portfolio could be reoptimized, using the same set of constraints, into a $99.4 million portfolio with a $600,000 take-out. Suppose further that the portfolio manager believes that corporate spreads will widen over the next few months. The manager might desire to temporarily upgrade the portfolio from the current average rating of double-A, await the anticipated spread changes, and then reverse the trade at a later date.

In this situation the optimal strategy is to spend the $600,000 take-out to buy a higher-quality portfolio. Rather than minimize cost, the portfolio can be optimized to maximize the quality rating, subject to the constraint of spending the full $100 million and cash flow-matching every liability payment. As shown in Exhibit 49–7, the average rating of the portfolio is increased by two rating categories, from double-A to agency.

Similarly, if rates are expected to rise, the portfolio could be positioned as short as possible by minimizing duration. In Exhibit 49–8, the duration of the portfolio has been shortened by almost six months with a cash flow match maintained. Alternatively, if rates are expected to fall, the $600,000 surplus in the portfolio could be used to maximize duration.

ROLE OF MONEY MANAGER AND DEALER FIRM

Both money managers and dealer firms have played important roles in managing and executing cash flow-matched portfolios. There are advantages to selecting a money manager over a dealer firm (and vice versa) in implementing the dedicated strategy. For example, all portfolio optimizations require a database of bonds that is both priced and sized by traders. Most money managers have access only to matrix pricing (computer-derived pricing), which is generally reliable for corporate securities within a range of plus or minus 30 basis points. When an optimizer is applied to a matrix-priced database of bonds, the optimizer will find the least-

EXHIBIT   49–7

Maximize Quality

	Market Value (000)	Average Rating	Take-Out (000)
Original dedicated portfolio	$100,000	Aaa/AA+	—
Reoptimized dedicated portfolio (minimum cost)	99,400	Aaa/AA+	$600
Reoptimized dedicated portfolio (maximum quality)	100,000	Treasury/Agency	—

EXHIBIT 49–8

Minimize Duration

	Market Value (000)	Duration (Years)	Percent Decrease
Original dedicated portfolio	$100,000	5.4	—
Reoptimized dedicated portfolio (minimum cost)	99,400	5.4	—
Reoptimized dedicated portfolio (minimum duration)	100,000	4.9	8.3

cost solution by identifying bonds that are cheap (due to mispricing) and will se-lect them in large blocks for the optimal solution. Since the computer-derived so-lution is not executable at the cheap levels specified in the database, the "least-cost" solution is not optimal when executed at market rates.

Dealer firms and software vendors with dealer connections are best posi-tioned to simulate, structure, and execute an optimal portfolio due to the accurate pricing and sizing in their databases. However, because dealer firms are not fidu-ciaries, money managers are best suited to make the active management decisions about sector positioning, call protection, credit decisions, and spread forecasts. In addition, money managers are best suited to oversee the execution of reoptimiza-tions with dealers.

In short, both dealers and money managers can add value to the process of structuring and reoptimizing dedicated portfolios.

CONCLUSION

Dedication is an important portfolio investment strategy for controlling interest-rate risk and for locking in prevailing market rates. For insurance companies with fixed liability products such as GICs or structured settlements, cash flow matching and horizon matching (duration matching with cash matching of early payouts) has been a popular approach to lock in a spread (or profit) on the entire line of business.

For pension funds, the motivation has been to control market risk by fully funding or defeasing the more quantifiable retired liabilities of a plan and locking in a market rate that is well in excess of the actuarial investment return assump-tion. By raising the actuarial rate to today's market levels on the dedicated portion of the plan, the plan sponsor may be able to reduce pension contributions (pen-sion expense) and thereby increase corporate cash flow and reported earnings.

The plan sponsor can also eliminate most funding risk (market risk) from a significant part of a plan's liability and eliminate market value fluctuations when reporting surplus asset (or unfunded liability) positions associated with that liability.

CHAPTER

50

⑥ IMPROVING INSURANCE COMPANY PORTFOLIO RETURNS

Kevin E. Grant, CFA
Portfolio Manager
Fidelity Management & Research Company

The investment utility function for a corporation is quite different from that of a pension fund or other purely investment-oriented entity. The principal difference lies in the breadth of business activities. A corporation's performance is consolidated with all business lines, creating a much more complex investment decision-making process. Pension funds adjust their portfolios in the best economic interests of the beneficiaries alone; their decisions are focused on economic factors related only to assets and liabilities.

Insurance companies and other diversified corporations operate in a highly interrelated and regulated environment; results are consolidated with business lines and are reported on a GAAP/statutory basis. This complicates the pure asset/liability economic decision-making process, requiring that corporatewide financial performance be considered. A strategic asset move may enhance investment returns but severely limit flexibility to write new insurance business. Reactions by regulators and rating agencies further complicate the process. The insurance company portfolio manager has to consider the reaction of these overseers: The proper economic decision in a pure asset/liability framework may create a temporary distortion in financial ratios and a downgrade by the rating agencies that could impair the insurance company's ability to write new business.

Thus, an insurance company portfolio manager seeking to improve portfolio investment performance has to solve a very complex problem with many con-

The author wishes to acknowledge the considerable contributions of Charles Melchreit, CFA, and David Canuel for their assistance in preparing the exhibits and sharing their insights.

flicting objectives. At first blush, the manager's objective may appear to be to maximize total return; however, it could just as easily be to minimize risk. More realistically, though, an insurance company portfolio manager's objectives involve a complex risk/return function that includes not only asset/liability management but also statutory regulations, accounting treatment, rating agencies, claims-paying abilities, new business potential, and ultimately the corporation's value to its shareholders.

SPECIAL CONSIDERATIONS FOR INSURANCE COMPANY PORTFOLIOS

The insurance company portfolio management process is not one of academic purity, with no transaction costs or taxes, with continuous prices, and with arbitrage-free markets. The capital gain/loss decision, for example, involves more than just the judgment that the asset to be purchased is better than the one to be sold. There may be insurance underwriting losses that could reduce the company's ability to take losses on the portfolio. Executing a bond swap that involves a capital loss or gain has tax and statutory implications that must be viewed in light of both the corporation's overall financial position and the portfolio's assets and liabilities. Rules requiring some bonds to be carried at market rather than book value create another set of distortions and incentives, particularly when the liabilities are carried at book and the assets at market. The key to managing around the distortions is to reduce unexpected transactions: In highly active bond management strategies, many transactions result from volatility. Active strategies require transactions, and the extent of those transactions is a positive function of volatility rather than the corporation's objectives.

The most effective approach for insurance company portfolio managers is to take a long-term view of value. This doesn't mean buy and hold, which some people interpret as buy and ignore. Rather, it means buy and incubate: Construct a portfolio that you expect will provide superior returns in many economic scenarios, and seek opportunities to improve the portfolio with asset swaps. The key is to develop the analytical tools that will identify long-term value and measure risk. The approach is not active management; rather, it's attentive management.

DON'T BUY AND HOLD, BUY AND INCUBATE

The recommended approach is to look at the assets and liabilities in a wide variety of long-run economic scenarios. The cheap bonds enhance the risk/return characteristics of the portfolio in all scenarios, whereas the rich bonds enhance the risk/return characteristics in only a few. The cheap ones should be held until they become rich. This happens much more slowly than price volatility may suggest. This realization gives the portfolio manager a tremendous advantage over the market. The manager can wait; the players showing bids and offers cannot. If you take a long-term view, you are never forced to transact.

EXISTING APPROACHES TO ASSET/LIABILITY MANAGEMENT

Fixed income portfolio management techniques have improved dramatically in the past few years. These include asset/liability techniques, which attempt to construct portfolios and control risk, and immunization, which attempts to continuously match the present value of assets to liabilities as interest rates change. The belief is that if present values (prices) are always matched, as time passes assets can be sold at their present values to fund the liabilities.

Immunization uses differential calculus to parameterize the elasticity of price to interest-rate changes. The first derivative, the modified duration, is simply the percentage change in present value (price) relative to a basis point change in interest rates. Thus, if the modified durations of the assets and liabilities are equal, as rates change their present values will change by equal proportions. This assumes that the interest-rate change on all the assets and liabilities is identical; that is, the yield curve shifts in parallel.

In general, immunization models use linear programming optimization programs to find the least-cost solution (maximize the dollar-duration-weighted internal rate of return) of the assets while matching the assets' and liabilities' modified durations. As time passes and rates change, the portfolio will become mismatched and rebalancing will become necessary. Rebalancing is most frequent when volatility is high.

Several refinements have improved immunization technology over the past few years, including the development of convexity. This is simply the second derivative of the price-yield equation; that is, it is the rate of change in modified duration due to a change in yield. Incorporating convexity into simple immunization reduces the amount of rebalancing. A convenient accidental feature of the computation is that it's a summary of the dispersion of cash flows. Matching the convexities of assets and liabilities reduces the mismatch of cash flows. Other researchers have approached cash flow dispersion mismatches more directly with other measures that have the same results as matching convexity.

Matching D3 (the sensitivity of convexity to rate changes), D4, and so on, gradually will reduce risk and rebalancing in matched portfolios. However, they have diminishing importance. When more derivatives are matched than there are cash flows, only one feasible solution exists, a dedicated portfolio having no interest-rate risk. Until this point, however, yield-curve risk remains and rebalancing is required.

Exhibit 50–1 lists several bonds and an assumed five-year bullet liability. The asset weightings were derived with the immunization model previously described. In this case, only the duration was matched. Only two bonds were required to match the liability within reasonable tolerances (±0.5%): the U.S. Treasury 6.50 percent and the Thailand 8.70 percent.

Exhibit 50–2 shows the relative present-value movement of the optimal portfolio versus the liability. Under parallel yield-curve shifts, the portfolio is matched fairly well and actually becomes modestly overfunded. When the yield curve steepens, the account is underfunded. It's overfunded when the curve flattens. Exhibit

E X H I B I T   50–1

First-Pass Immunization Noncall Assets Only[a]

Security	Coupon	Maturity	PV or Price	Yield	Duration	Dollar Allocation
Liability		8/15/1994	65.772	8.50%	4.83	($100.00)
U.S. Treasury	6.500	2/15/1990	99.250	7.96	0.50	$ 27.51
Thailand	8.700	8/1/1999	100.000	8.70	6.51	72.49
U.S. Treasury	14.250	11/15/1991	114.688	7.15	1.93	0.00
U.S. Treasury	8.625	1/15/1995	104.031	7.70	4.30	0.00
U.S. Treasury	9.125	5/15/2018	113.688	7.91	10.87	0.00
Ford Motor Credit	8.000	8/1/1994	100.000	8.00	4.00	0.00
Bowater	9.000	8/1/2009	100.000	9.00	9.12	0.00
GMAC	8.250	8/1/1996	100.000	8.25	5.17	0.00
Total assets				8.50%	4.85	$100.00

[a] Duration matched within 0.5 percent tolerance; convexity is not matched; all figures as of 8/3/89.

50–2 examines only instantaneous rate changes. Exhibit 50–3 examines the effects of time and rate changes on the portfolio. The reason mismatches are more dramatic in six months is that the assets' and liabilities' durations decay at different rates. The portfolio becomes mismatched simply because time passes. Transactions to rebalance the portfolio are necessary to maintain the match. Immunization requires frequent rebalancing due to the passage of time, without regard to value.

Immunization provides an easy way of controlling overall interest-rate risk. However, it falters because it is a static approach to dynamic yield-curve risks. Immunization exhibits several weaknesses:

1. It requires transactions. Those transactions are a result of the mathematics, not of value or opportunities in the market.

2. It overwhelmingly focuses on matching instantaneous price changes, whereas it should be concerned with the future value of the liability.

3. Transactions are a function of volatility and time, not value. This creates unpredictable capital gains and losses, which may not be appropriate for the corporation as a whole.

4. The computations assume parallel yield-curve shifts. This has been a rarity, as Exhibit 50–4 illustrates.

5. Only simply structured bonds may be used in an immunized portfolio. Bonds with variable cash flows (e.g., callables, putables, mortgage-backed securities) don't fit the model and can't be used, regardless of their value.

6. Immunization assumes reinvestment into the same security. This may not be appropriate.

Several ad hoc approaches are available to reduce transactions and yield-curve risk. Specifically, option technology attempts to broaden the universe of assets.

E X H I B I T   50–2

Effects of Yield-Curve Shifts on Immunized Portfolio (as of 8/3/89)

| | | Present Values | | |
Yield Curve	Liability	Treasury 6.5% of '90	Thailand 8.7% of '99	Overfunded (Underfunded)
Unchanged[a]	($100.00)	$27.51	$72.49	$0.00
+100 BP	(95.26)	27.37	67.92	0.04
−100 BP	(105.00)	27.65	77.52	0.17
Steeper 50 BP[b]	(99.80)	27.54	71.73	(0.53)
Flatter 50 BP[c]	(100.20)	27.48	73.30	0.59

[a] Treasury yield curve: 2-year 7.53%
                             3-year 7.58
                             4-year 7.54
                             5-year 7.56
                             7-year 7.64
                             10-year 7.74
                             30-year 7.83

[b] Steeper curve pivots counterclockwise around the 5-year. The 3-month rate falls 25 basis points, and the 30-year rate rises 25 basis points.

[c] Flatter curve pivots in the opposite direction.

E X H I B I T   50–3

Effects of Yield-Curve Shifts and Time on Immunized Portfolio (as of 2/3/90)

| | | Present Values | | | |
Yield Curve	Liability	Treasury 6.5% of '90	Thailand 8.7% of '99	Cash	Overfunded (Underfunded)
Unchanged[a]	($104.39)	$27.70	$72.49	$4.06	($0.14)
+100 BP	(99.95)	27.69	68.04	4.06	(0.16)
−100 BP	(109.04)	27.71	77.33	4.06	0.06
Steeper 50 BP[b]	(104.31)	27.70	71.74	4.06	(0.80)
Flatter 50 BP[c]	(104.46)	27.70	73.24	4.06	0.53

[a] Position becomes underfunded in unchanged rate scenario because liability rolls down the yield curve faster than the assets. Starting Treasury curve: 2-year 7.53%
                             3-year 7.58
                             4-year 7.54
                             5-year 7.56
                             7-year 7.64
                             10-year 7.74
                             30-year 7.83

[b] Steeper curve pivots counterclockwise around the 5-year. The 3-month rate falls 25 basis points, and the 30-year rate rises 25 basis points.

[c] Flatter curve pivots in the opposite direction.

EXHIBIT 50–4

Yield Curves

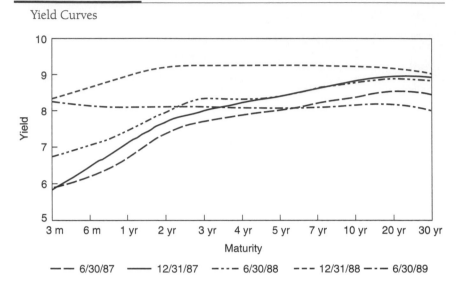

	6/30/87	12/31/87	6/30/88	12/31/88	6/30/89
3-month	5.87	5.85	6.75	8.36	8.26
6-month	6.13	6.47	7.02	8.66	8.14
1-year	6.65	7.10	7.42	9.00	8.09
2-year	7.47	7.78	7.99	9.27	8.14
3-year	7.72	8.01	8.15	9.27	8.11
4-year	7.91	8.26	8.31	9.28	8.12
5-year	8.01	8.40	8.41	9.26	8.07
7-year	8.24	8.68	8.65	9.30	8.14
10-year	8.37	8.86	8.80	9.24	8.16
20-year	8.68	9.06	8.99	9.28	8.29
30-year	8.49	8.98	8.88	9.08	8.05

Option Valuation and Immunization

Improvements in option valuation models have helped expand the asset classes
that may be included in immunized portfolios. Option-adjusted, effective, or implied durations are often substituted for modified durations. These sensitivity
measures are unstable, however, and inclusion of option-related assets in an immunized portfolio may introduce risks with which the immunization model is not
equipped to deal. Maximizing an option-adjusted yield while matching effective
duration may seem like a reasonable approach—until risk is closely examined.
Exhibit 50–5 incorporates callable corporate bonds and pass-throughs into the
immunization problem. Exhibit 50–6 shows the performance of the optimal port-

EXHIBIT 50–5

First-Pass Immunization Including Callable and Putable Assets[a]

Security	Coupon	Maturity	Call/Put Date	Call/Put Price	PV or Price	Yield	Effective Duration	Dollars
Liability		8/15/1994	—	—	64.453	8.92%	4.82	$100.00
UST	6.500	2/15/1990	—	—	99.250	7.96	0.50	21.36
Thailand	8.700	8/1/1999	—	—	100.000	8.70	6.51	0.00
UST	14.250	11/15/1991	—	—	114.688	7.15	1.93	0.00
UST	8.625	1/15/1995	—	—	104.031	7.70	4.30	0.00
UST	9.125	5/15/2018	—	—	113.688	7.91	10.87	0.00
Ford Motor Credit	8.000	8/1/1994	—	—	100.000	8.00	4.00	0.00
Bowater	9.000	8/1/2009	—	—	100.000	9.00	9.12	41.57
GMAC	8.250	8/1/1996	—	—	100.000	8.25	5.17	0.00
GNMA	8.000	1/31/2018	—	—	94.813	8.95	5.94	0.00
GNMA	9.500	1/31/2019	—	—	100.906	9.43	4.98	0.00
GNMA	10.500	7/31/2018	—	—	104.219	9.38	2.55	37.07
Xerox[b]	9.200	7/15/1999	7/15/1996	100.00	99.551	9.36	5.97	0.00
Household Finance[b]	8.875	7/5/1999	7/5/1996	100.00	98.934	9.03	5.73	0.00
ITT[c]	8.250	8/1/2001	8/1/1996	100.00	100.000	8.25	5.47	0.00
American General[c]	8.125	8/15/2009	8/15/1996	100.00	99.150	8.29	7.13	0.00
Total assets						8.92%	4.84	$100.00

[a]All figures as of 8/3/89; duration matched with 0.5 percent tolerance; convexity is not matched but is constrained to exceed 0.
[b]Callable.
[c]Putable.

E X H I B I T   50–6

Effects of Yield-Curve Shifts and Time on Immunized Portfolio (as of 2/3/90)

	Liability	UST 6.5% of '90	Bowater 9.0% of '09	GNMA 10.5%	Cash	Overfunded (Underfunded)
Unchanged[a]	($104.60)	$21.50	$41.59	$34.97	$6.13	($0.42)
+100 BP	(100.15)	21.50	38.04	34.28	5.77	(0.57)
−100 BP	(109.24)	21.51	45.67	34.98	6.58	(0.50)
Steeper 50 BP[b]	(104.51)	21.51	40.82	35.01	6.07	(1.11)
Flatter 50 BP[c]	(104.67)	21.50	42.37	34.91	6.18	0.30

[a] Position becomes underfunded in unchanged rate scenario because liability rolls down the yield curve faster than the assets. Starting Treasury curve: 2-year 7.53%
3-year 7.58
4-year 7.54
5-year 7.56
7-year 7.64
10-year 7.74
30-year 7.83

[b] Steeper curve pivots counterclockwise around the 5-year. The 3-month rate falls 25 basis points, and the 30-year rate rises 25 basis points.
[c] Flatter curve pivots in the opposite direction.

folio in several scenarios. Over the six-month period, the portfolio became heavily underfunded in all but one scenario. The degree of underfunding was worse than for a portfolio of noncall securities. It's clear that the immunization model obscured risks inherent in the new securities.

Incorporating option technology into immunization technology has all the weaknesses of pure immunization and adds risks that neither approach is capable of evaluating fully. In fact, because effective durations are unstable, incorporating option technology into immunization may exacerbate the need for rebalancing and unexpected transactions. The term *immunization* is a misnomer; there are always bets in immunized portfolios, known and unknown. The immunization model has the capacity to neither identify nor quantify those risks.

THE WISH LIST FOR PORTFOLIO MANAGEMENT

The ideal portfolio construction methodology would allow the portfolio manager to

1. Explicitly specify risk/return preferences and build them into the portfolio.
2. Never transact unless he or she wishes to (the manager should transact only when there is an opportunity to improve the risk/return profile of the portfolio and when it is in the corporation's overall best interest; transacting should be the portfolio manager's option, not the market's or the model's).

3. Always fund liabilities in any economic scenario (at the very least, the manager should be able to specify precisely what risks of underfunding liabilities he or she wishes to assume).

4. Most importantly, achieve long-run return objectives within the chosen risk and transaction tolerances.

Immunization and most other common asset/liability approaches have none of these characteristics. The total-return approach, however, begins to satisfy many of these needs.

TOTAL RETURN IN THE ASSET/LIABILITY/REGULATORY/GAAP/TAX WORLD

By examining the total returns of securities in various scenarios, many real-world constraints may be considered explicitly. Reinvestment assumptions, tax effects, regulatory restrictions, and GAAP treatment may be included in the analysis.

The total-return approach involves a lot of modeling and specification by the portfolio manager. It forces the manager to think explicitly about risk. Total return approaches examine the behavior of securities in different interest-rate environments, allowing the portfolio manager to specify tolerance for loss versus liability in each scenario and then construct a portfolio that provides superior performance over the investment horizon. The portfolio manager must specify the following:

1. An objective (he or she can maximize expected total return, maximize it in only one scenario, or minimize risk at some minimum total return level).

2. Likely and unlikely economic scenarios (the manager must specify the level of key economic variables, for example, the yield curve and credit spreads).

3. Tolerances for losses in each scenario.

4. Various portfolio parameters, such as diversification.

Models must be developed for the assets to be included:

1. For corporate bonds, all the characteristics of call and put options, sinking funds, and credit risk must be modeled.

2. For mortgage-backed securities and their various derivatives, cash flow and prepayment models must be developed. A good prepayment model may involve an econometric model with coefficients for economic refinancing, prepayment burnout, seasoning effects, and the lags in these variables.

3. Any other securities that the manager wishes to include must be modeled: for example, floating-rate notes, futures and options, swaps, and dynamic strategies.

Exhibit 50–7 shows several interest-rate scenarios specified by a portfolio manager, the assigned subjective probability, and the manager's tolerance for loss versus his liability. Exhibit 50–8 lists several assets and their modeled total return in each scenario specified by the portfolio manager. The data in Exhibits 50–7 and 50–8 are then optimized and the results reported in Exhibit 50–9. The results suggest how the manager should structure the portfolio to satisfy the risk-return objectives. As long as the specified scenarios sufficiently incorporate the actual yield-curve movement, the portfolio should not require rebalancing. However, if the manager perceives a change in value in the market, he or she has the option of taking advantage of it. The manager can also tilt the portfolio by adjusting the probabilities assigned to each scenario.

The main weakness of the total-return approach is its complexity. The investment organization must commit people, computers, and research to develop the models and educate users.

E X H I B I T   50–7

Yield Curves

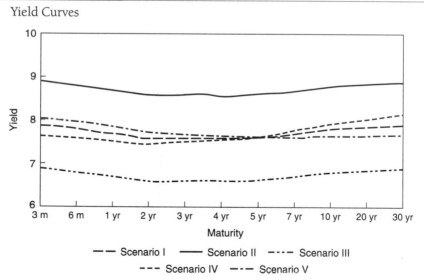

Horizon Interest Rates

Scenario	3-Month	2-Year	10-Year	Loss Tolerance Probability vs. Liability	
I	7.89	7.53	7.74	20%	0.00%
II	8.89	8.53	8.74	15	–0.10
III	6.89	6.53	6.74	10	0.00
IV	7.64	7.41	7.90	30	0.00
V	8.04	7.65	7.58	25	–0.10

EXHIBIT 50–8

Pro Forma Total Returns for Specified Assets[a]

Security	Coupon	Maturity	Scenario Total Return				
			I	II	III	IV	V
Liability	—	8/15/1994	8.77%	-0.10%	18.08%	8.61%	8.93%
UST	6.500	2/15/1990	7.95	7.89	8.02	7.97	7.94
Thailand	8.700	8/1/1999	8.87	-3.41	22.23	8.31	9.46
UST	14.250	11/15/1991	7.24	4.26	10.27	7.56	6.92
UST	8.625	1/15/1995	7.89	0.13	16.03	7.71	8.06
UST	9.125	5/15/2018	7.93	-11.92	31.76	2.64	13.42
Ford Motor Credit	8.000	8/1/1994	8.07	0.81	15.67	8.23	7.91
Bowater	9.000	8/1/2009	9.01	-8.04	28.64	6.52	11.54
GMAC	8.250	8/1/1996	9.42	-1.21	18.65	8.27	8.64
GNMA	8.000	1/31/2018	8.95	-3.19	21.08	7.13	10.74
GNMA	9.500	1/31/2019	8.42	-1.27	16.04	8.22	10.43
GNMA	10.500	7/31/2018	9.35	3.69	11.86	9.25	9.35
Xerox	9.200	7/15/1999	9.24	-1.83	20.69	8.88	9.63
Household Finance	8.875	7/15/1999	9.10	-2.15	20.73	8.71	9.51
ITT	8.250	8/1/2001	8.43	-0.47	19.33	8.28	8.67
American General	8.125	8/15/2009	8.61	-3.44	23.36	7.59	9.83

[a]Liability return assumes an initial discount rate of 8.50 percent; one-year horizon.

EXHIBIT 50–9

Suggested Portfolio for Specified Assets and Risk/Return Objectives[a]

Security	Coupon	Maturity	Weight	Scenario Total Return				
				I	II	III	IV	V
Liability	—	8/15/1994	-100%	8.77%	-0.10%	18.08%	8.61%	8.93%
UST	6.500	2/15/1990	0.0	7.95	7.89	8.02	7.97	7.94
Thailand	8.700	8/1/1999	0.0	8.87	-3.41	22.23	8.31	9.46
UST	14.250	11/15/1991	0.0	7.24	4.26	10.27	7.56	6.92
UST	8.625	1/15/1995	0.0	7.89	0.13	16.03	7.71	8.06
UST	9.125	5/15/2018	0.0	7.93	-11.92	31.76	2.64	13.42
Ford	8.000	8/1/1994	0.0	8.07	0.81	15.67	8.23	7.91
Bowater	9.000	8/1/2009	0.0	9.01	-8.04	28.64	6.52	11.54
GMAC	8.250	8/1/1996	0.0	8.42	-1.21	18.65	8.27	8.64
GNMA	8.000	1/31/2018	0.0	8.95	-3.19	21.08	7.13	10.74
GNMA	9.500	1/31/2019	0.0	9.42	-1.27	16.04	8.22	10.43
GNMA	10.500	7/31/2018	29.6	9.35	3.69	11.86	9.25	9.35
Xerox	9.200	7/15/1999	70.4	9.24	-1.83	20.69	8.88	9.63
Household Finance	8.875	7/15/1999	0.0	9.10	-2.15	20.73	8.71	9.51
ITT	8.250	8/1/2001	0.0	8.43	-0.47	19.33	8.28	8.67
AGC	8.125	8/15/2009	-0.0	8.61	-3.44	23.36	7.59	9.83
Total asset return			100.0%	9.27%	-0.19%	18.08%	8.99%	9.55%
Assets–liabilities return spread				0.50%	-0.09%	0.00%	0.38%	0.62%
Maximum permitted loss				0.00%	-0.10%	0.00%	0.00%	-0.10%
Scenario probability				20%	15%	10%	30%	25%
Expected gain			36%					

[a]Selected portfolio maximizes expected total return in five probability-weighted scenarios, subject to the loss constraints enumerated in Exhibit 50–7. The investment horizon is one year.

Long-Term Arbitrage

Market makers and traders are by definition short-term-oriented. They reduce their risk and increase their return by keeping their inventory turnover high. This creates opportunities that often persist. Total-return models are useful tools in identifying these opportunities.

Exhibit 50–10 shows an application of total-return approaches to arbitrage. The axes of the matrix list several bonds: Each column represents a bond that may be purchased; each row represents one that may be sold. The contents of the matrix are swap suggestions where the purchased combination of bonds will out-perform the one sold in each scenario.

PROBABILITY DISTRIBUTIONS: THE NEXT FRONTIER

A particularly burdensome task involved in total-return modeling is the specification of scenarios. Generally, only a small number of scenarios are specified, and it's easy to miss some important ones. This creates a potential for incomplete analysis.

One solution is to use mathematical simulations to create many scenarios. The ideal simulation is a stochastic process that simulates movement of the entire yield curve, both its position and shape. With a large number of simulated total returns, return distributions may be examined.

Exhibit 50–11 shows total-return distributions for several securities in many scenarios. They have clearly very different risk/return characteristics. Total return distributions help us to delineate clearly the risk/return characteristics of securities.

CONCLUSION

Total-return models are effective approaches to portfolio management for complex organizations. They allow their users to explicitly incorporate the realities of their businesses.

EXHIBIT 50–10

Total-Return Arbitrage Matrix[a]

Return Advantage[a]			GN30N 7.50	GN30N 8.00	GN30N 8.50	GN30N 9.00	GN30N 9.50	GN30N 10.00	GN30N 10.50	FN30N 8.00	FN30N 8.50	FN30N 9.00	FN30N 9.50	FN30N 10.00	FH30N 8.50
0 BP	GN30N	7.50	100.0	.0	.0	.0	.0	.0	.0	.0	.0	.0	.0	.0	.0
0 BP	GN30N	8.00	.0	100.0	.0	.0	.0	.0	.0	.0	.0	.0	.0	.0	.0
0 BP	GN30N	8.50	.0	.0	100.0	.0	.0	.0	.0	.0	.0	.0	.0	.0	.0
0 BP	GN30N	9.00	.0	.0	.0	100.0	.0	.0	.0	.0	.0	.0	.0	.0	.0
0 BP	GN30N	9.50	.0	.0	.0	.0	100.0	.0	.0	.0	.0	.0	.0	.0	.0
0 BP	GN30N	10.00	.0	.0	.0	.0	.0	100.0	.0	.0	.0	.0	.0	.0	.0
23 BP	GN30N	10.50	.0	.0	.0	.0	.0	.0	.0	.0	.0	24.4	.0	.0	.0
0 BP	FN30N	8.00	.0	.0	.0	.0	.0	.0	.0	100.0	.0	.0	.0	.0	.0
0 BP	FN30N	8.50	.0	.0	.0	.0	.0	.0	.0	.0	100.0	.0	.0	.0	.0
0 BP	FN30N	9.00	.0	.0	.0	.0	.0	.0	.0	.0	.0	100.0	.0	.0	.0
0 BP	FN30N	9.50	.0	.0	.0	.0	.0	.0	.0	.0	.0	.0	100.0	.0	.0
0 BP	FN30N	10.00	.0	.0	.0	.0	.0	.0	.0	.0	.0	.0	.0	100.0	.0
0 BP	FH30N	8.50	.0	.0	.0	.0	.0	.0	.0	.0	.0	.0	.0	.0	100.0
0 BP	FH30N	9.00	.0	.0	.0	.0	.0	.0	.0	.0	.0	.0	.0	.0	.0
0 BP	FH30N	9.50	.0	.0	.0	.0	.0	.0	.0	.0	.0	.0	.0	.0	.0
9 BP	FH30N	10.00	.0	.0	.0	.0	.0	.0	.0	.0	.0	.0	.0	66.4	.0
0 BP	FH30N	10.50	.0	.0	.0	.0	.0	.0	.0	.0	.0	.0	.0	.0	.0
15 BP	GN30S	8.00	.0	.0	.0	.0	.0	.0	.0	12.7	63.1	.0	.0	.0	.0
13 BP	GN30S	8.50	.0	.0	.0	.0	.0	.0	.0	.0	63.5	.0	.0	.0	.0
13 BP	GN30S	9.00	.0	.0	.0	.0	.0	.0	.0	.0	17.7	29.7	.0	.0	.0
0 BP	GN15N	8.00	.0	.0	.0	.0	.0	.0	.0	.0	.0	.0	.0	.0	.0
6 BP	GN15N	8.50	.0	.0	.0	.0	.0	.0	.0	9.8	7.4	.0	.0	.0	.0
23 BP	GN15N	9.00	.0	.0	.0	.0	.0	.0	.0	.0	23.1	.0	.0	.0	.0
0 BP	FH15N	8.00	.0	.0	.0	.0	.0	.0	.0	.0	.0	.0	.0	.0	.0
0 BP	FH15S	8.50	.0	.0	.0	.0	.0	.0	.0	.0	.0	.0	.0	.0	.0
0 BP	FH15S	8.00	.0	.0	.0	.0	.0	.0	.0	.0	.0	.0	.0	.0	.0
0 BP	UST	7.88	.0	.0	.0	.0	.0	.0	.0	.0	.0	.0	.0	.0	.0
95 BP	UST	8.25	.0	.0	.0	.0	.0	.0	.0	10.7	.0	.0	.0	.0	.0
101 BP	UST	9.88	.0	.0	.0	.0	.0	.0	.0	16.4	77.8	.0	.0	.0	.0
0 BP	UST	8.00	.0	.0	.0	.0	.0	.0	.0	.0	.0	.0	.0	.0	.0

Number of simulations evaluated = 13

Maximum allowable underperformance = 0 BP

One-year horizon scenarios:

    ± 200

    ± 150

    ± 100

    ± 50

    No change

    Steeper 50, 100

    Flatter 50, 100

[a] The column headed "Return Advantage" indicates the expected return pickup over the one-year horizon. The row headed GN30N 10.50 shows that we can expect to pick up 23 BP of total return if we sell the new GNMA 30-year 10.5% and buy a portfolio composed of 24.4% FNMA, 30-year 9.0s, 72.6% new FHLMC 30-year 10.5s, and 2.9% Gnome 8.5s.

The arbitage is evaluated over 13 scenarios encompassing a sufficient range of curve shifts and twists. The optimization finds the portfolio that shows the highest expected return advantage but that does not underperform the target security in any scenario.

EXHIBIT 50–10

(Continued)

FH30N 9.00	FH30N 9.50	FH30N 10.00	FH30N 10.50	GN30S 8.00	GN30S 8.50	GN30S 9.00	GN15N 8.00	GN15N 8.50	GN15N 9.00	FH15N 8.00	FH15S 8.50	FH15S 9.00	UST 7.88	UST 8.25	UST 8.88	UST 8.00
.0	.0	.0	.0	.0	.0	.0	.0	.0	.0	.0	.0	.0	.0	.0	.0	.0
.0	.0	.0	.0	.0	.0	.0	.0	.0	.0	.0	.0	.0	.0	.0	.0	.0
.0	.0	.0	.0	.0	.0	.0	.0	.0	.0	.0	.0	.0	.0	.0	.0	.0
.0	.0	.0	.0	.0	.0	.0	.0	.0	.0	.0	.0	.0	.0	.0	.0	.0
.0	.0	.0	.0	.0	.0	.0	.0	.0	.0	.0	.0	.0	.0	.0	.0	.0
.0	.0	.0	.0	.0	.0	.0	.0	.0	.0	.0	.0	.0	.0	.0	.0	.0
.0	.0	.0	72.6	.0	.0	.0	.0	.0	.0	.0	2.9	.0	.0	.0	.0	.0
.0	.0	.0	.0	.0	.0	.0	.0	.0	.0	.0	.0	.0	.0	.0	.0	.0
.0	.0	.0	.0	.0	.0	.0	.0	.0	.0	.0	.0	.0	.0	.0	.0	.0
.0	.0	.0	.0	.0	.0	.0	.0	.0	.0	.0	.0	.0	.0	.0	.0	.0
.0	.0	.0	.0	.0	.0	.0	.0	.0	.0	.0	.0	.0	.0	.0	.0	.0
.0	.0	.0	.0	.0	.0	.0	.0	.0	.0	.0	.0	.0	.0	.0	.0	.0
.0	.0	.0	.0	.0	.0	.0	.0	.0	.0	.0	.0	.0	.0	.0	.0	.0
100.0	.0	.0	.0	.0	.0	.0	.0	.0	.0	.0	.0	.0	.0	.0	.0	.0
.0	22.1	.0	.0	.0	.0	.0	.0	.0	.0	.0	.0	.0	.0	.0	.0	.0
.0	100.0	.0	11.5	.0	.0	.0	.0	.0	.0	.0	.0	.0	.0	.0	.0	.0
.0	.0	.0	100.0	.0	.0	.0	.0	.0	.0	.0	.0	.0	.0	.0	.0	.0
.0	.0	.0	.0	.0	.0	.0	.0	.0	.0	24.2	.0	.0	.0	.0	.0	.0
.0	.0	.0	.0	.0	.0	.0	.0	.0	.0	.0	36.5	.0	.0	.0	.0	.0
.0	.0	.0	.0	.0	.0	.0	.0	.0	.0	.0	52.6	.0	.0	.0	.0	.0
.0	.0	.0	.0	.0	.0	.0	100.0	.0	.0	.0	.0	.0	.0	.0	.0	.0
.0	.0	.0	.0	.0	.0	.0	.0	.0	.0	82.8	.0	.0	.0	.0	.0	.0
.0	.0	.0	.0	.0	.0	.0	.0	.0	.0	.0	76.9	.0	.0	.0	.0	.0
.0	.0	.0	.0	.0	.0	.0	.0	.0	.0	100.0	.0	.0	.0	.0	.0	.0
.0	.0	.0	.0	.0	.0	.0	.0	.0	.0	.0	100.0	.0	.0	.0	.0	.0
.0	.0	.0	.0	.0	.0	.0	.0	.0	.0	.0	.0	100.0	.0	.0	.0	.0
.0	.0	.0	.0	.0	.0	.0	.0	.0	.0	.0	.0	100.0	.0	.0	.0	.0
.0	.0	.0	.0	.0	.0	.0	27.9	.0	.0	61.4	.0	.0	.0	.0	.0	.0
.0	.0	.0	.0	.0	.0	.0	.0	.0	.0	5.7	.0	.0	.0	.0	.0	.0
.0	.0	.0	.0	.0	.0	.0	.0	.0	.0	.0	.0	.0	.0	.0	100.0	

EXHIBIT 50-11

Total Return Distributions: GNMAs and 5-Year Treasury

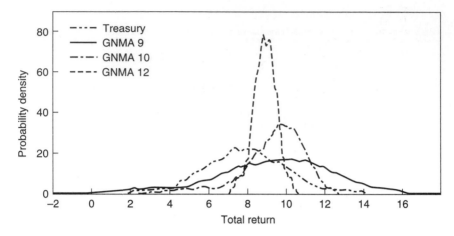

⑥ ASSET/LIABILITY MANAGEMENT FOR PROPERTY/CASUALTY INSURERS

Frank D. Campbell, CFA*
Vice President
Conning & Company

PROPERTY/CASUALTY INSURERS

Property/casualty (P/C) insurance includes a broad range of coverages: property, liability, workers' compensation, marine, surety, and health. P/C companies collect revenues, called *premiums,* in exchange for promises to indemnify the insured party for specified types of losses that may occur during the period of coverage. Some losses that occur during a policy period may not become evident until years later. In many cases, it can take years to determine the extent of loss and the liability of various parties involved. Even in lines where losses are reported quickly with no question of coverage, repair or recovery may be protracted. In the interim, inflation and judicial trends can add to the uncertainty of the ultimate costs to the insurer.

During a year, an insurer will price and write policies and collect premiums on those policies. The insurer must keep track of claims for losses that are incurred and reported during the year, and it must estimate claims for losses that were incurred during the year but that will be reported in later years. By law and regulation, the insurer must set up reserves sufficient to pay the actuarially estimated cost of those claims and any costs associated with settling those claims, usually on an undiscounted basis. In any given year, if costs of claims incurred in prior years are running above previous estimates, the insurer must add to the reserves for those prior-year claims; if costs are running below earlier estimates, reserves may be reduced. The insurer invests the funds representing claim reserves as well as the surplus of the company. Current revenue (premiums and investment income) must cover marketing

---

*This chapter was written while the author was a portfolio manager in the Investment Group of Travelers Insurance Companies.

and administrative expenses, funds to set up the reserves for new claims, any funds needed to strengthen reserves for prior-year claims, taxes, and any payments to owners. To the extent that current revenue flows are insufficient for these needs, policyholder (statutory) surplus will be drawn down; if revenue exceeds these needs, surplus is augmented. Reserves established to pay claims may be inadequate if the insurer underestimated costs of prior claims, catastrophes caused current claims to exceed levels assumed in pricing, or the insurer suffered investment losses. Surplus provides a margin to ensure that policyholders are paid for all claims. Over time, surplus growth is needed to support growth in premium volume.

Historically, insurers have attempted to price insurance products so that annual premiums would cover marketing and administrative expenses, and claim and claim adjustment expenses, perhaps even leaving a margin called an *underwriting profit*. Insurers typically report expense ratios (marketing and administrative expenses as a percentage of premium), loss ratios (claim and claim adjustment expenses as a percentage of premium), and combined ratios (the sum of expense and loss ratios). Combined ratios less than 100 (percent) indicate premium revenue exceeds general and claim expenses; that is, the company enjoys an underwriting profit. Combined ratios above 100 indicate an underwriting loss.

Before the mid-1970s, most P/C companies did manage to price for combined ratios close to 100, as shown in Exhibit 51–1. Over the 24 years from 1950 to 1973, overall industry combined ratios were above 100 in only nine years; and over the entire period, annual combined ratios averaged 98.8. Since 1974, overall industry combined ratios have been below 100 for only two years; in 1984, combined ratios reached a peak of over 120. During both periods, results varied widely among companies and among lines of insurance.

Before the 1980s, there was a tendency among P/C insurers to view insurance operations as separate from investment operations. Insurance pricing was aimed at achieving underwriting profits, or at least avoiding losses. Investment policy was aimed at providing steady growth in dividends and surplus. Often, this meant buying long-term bonds to lock in a predictable flow of investment income, supplemented with common stock investments to raise long-run returns. Investment managers needed to anticipate movements in underwriting profits and losses to adjust the tax status of the investment portfolio, but generally there was little interaction between liability (claims) management and asset management.

In the 1980s, a number of factors caused P/C insurers to focus more on coordinating management of liabilities and assets. In the high-interest-rate environment of the early 1980s, investment income began to be factored more directly into insurance pricing. In a growing number of states, insurance regulators require explicit consideration of the effect of investment income on rates of return in setting insurance prices. But competitive factors also forced pricing to reflect investment income. In the early 1980s, the industry experienced what came to be called cash flow underwriting, whereby companies would intentionally price at an underwriting loss in order to attract premium revenues that could be invested at existing high yields. Increasingly, noninsurance corporations found it attractive

EXHIBIT 51-1

Property-Casualty Combined Ratios
(Stock-Owned Companies—All Lines)

1950	93.6	1971	96.7
1951	97.8	1972	96.4
1952	94.9	1973	99.1
1953	93.7	1974	105.9
1954	94.1	1975	108.2
1955	95.5	1976	102.6
1956	101.3	1977	97.7
1957	103.5	1978	97.4
1958	100.6	1979	100.6
1959	98.3	1980	103.5
1960	99.0	1981	106.2
1961	99.9	1982	110.1
1962	99.5	1983	113.3
1963	101.5	1984	120.5
1964	102.5	1985	117.9
1965	102.5	1986	108.0
1966	98.6	1987	104.2
1967	99.5	1988	104.9
1968	100.9	1989	109.7
1969	101.5	1990	109.4
1970	100.2	1991	109.5

Source: Best's Aggregates & Averages.

to self-insure, in order to keep the high investment income, rather than paying premiums to insurers and giving them the investment opportunity.

In the high-interest-rate environment of the early 1980s, many insurance companies found themselves with large investment portfolios in old, low-coupon, long-term bonds. The bonds could not be sold without reducing reported surplus, because market values had fallen well below book. (Accounting conventions regarding statutory surplus and bonds will be discussed later.) These companies, therefore, had to attract premium revenue to meet expenses and claim payments in order to avoid selling bonds. This aggravated pressure to retain a share of market, even if it meant selling insurance products at unprofitable prices. Companies with low-coupon, long-term assets were at a disadvantage to companies unencumbered by old long-term bonds that could price low and invest premiums at existing high interest rates. This situation led to increased efforts by P/C companies to manage interest-rate risk, which in turn called for management of asset/liability durations.

There remains considerable diversity in the investment objectives among P/C companies and in the methods they use to achieve those objectives. Similarly, there are wide differences in the extent to which companies coordinate the management of liabilities and assets. The remainder of this chapter will be structured around the approach to asset/liability management taken at The Travelers Companies. We view our approach to investment management as an evolving process, and there is constant, lively, internal debate with respect to many aspects of our operating methodology. This discussion really reflects one participant's views of that process.

OVERVIEW OF THE INVESTMENT PROCESS

Within the Investment Group at Travelers, a portfolio manager is assigned to manage the portfolio representing the reserves for each business unit in the P/C companies. The portfolio manager is responsible for managing the overall characteristics of the portfolio, including interest-rate risk (duration), asset mix, liquidity, and diversification. This requires a statement of portfolio policy that establishes a normative portfolio, responsive to the characteristics of the liabilities and the needs and risk tolerance of the insurance business unit and the corporation.

The policy statement defines normal duration of assets, asset mix (for major asset classes), and cash or liquidity requirements. Policy also establishes parameters within which the portfolio manager can diverge from normal characteristics in order to take advantage of investment opportunities. A typical policy asset mix for a P/C portfolio might be as follows:

Asset Class	Normal	Range
Cash	5%	3–10%
Bonds (taxable and tax-exempt)	70	60–80
Mortgages	10	5–15
Equities	15	5–20

The portfolio manager's performance is measured by the total return of the portfolio versus a market benchmark. The benchmark is a weighted average of market indexes, where the indexes and their weights are chosen to reflect the portfolio's normative asset allocation and liquidity and duration targets.

In developing portfolio characteristics, the portfolio manager works closely with actuaries and other contacts from the insurance business unit, the client. The insurance unit will provide information on the nature of the liabilities. The insurance unit will work with the portfolio manager to develop investment strategies that meet its needs and risk tolerances.

Because Travelers is a company consisting of several business units, overall corporate investment considerations must also influence investment strategies of individual portfolios. The Investment Committee of the Board of Directors, senior management, the Corporate Finance Department, and Investment Group management all share responsibility for addressing overall corporate investment considerations.

The portfolio manager is responsible for asset allocation decisions. Much of the responsibility for management of assets within asset classes falls to specialized groups within and outside the Investment Group. Within Travelers Investment Group are specialized Private Placement, Public Bond, and Cash Management units. Travelers Real Estate Investment Company is used as a source of mortgage loans and real estate investments.

With cooperation from the insurance business unit, the portfolio manager will develop an annual investment strategy statement. The strategy statements are reviewed by senior management to ensure that portfolio strategies in aggregate are consistent with overall corporate goals and constraints. The statement will provide operating guidelines for the following investment parameters:

1. Investment goals.
2. Risk tolerances.
3. Asset-class allocations.
4. Asset diversification and characteristics.
5. Performance measurement.
6. Reporting.

The strategy statement is reviewed each year; it is revised if changes in company operations, insurance markets, financial markets, tax environment, or statutory constraints warrant changes in investment strategy. Revisions may be made within the year if conditions change significantly.

The remainder of this chapter will discuss the first four items listed above, particularly with respect to considerations specific to the P/C industry.

INVESTMENT GOALS

In general terms, the overall goal of the portfolio is to support the ongoing operations of the insurance business unit. At Travelers, the philosophy of the Investment Group is to actively manage assets to maximize total return over a multiple-year time horizon, subject to appropriate levels of risk. The portfolio manager's performance is measured on this total-return basis. However, the insurance business units have additional requirements with respect to liquidity, current income, and contribution to surplus. These represent constraints on the portfolio manager and limit freedom to manage the portfolio on a total-return basis.

A distinctive feature of the P/C industry is the cyclicality of pricing and profitability, usually referred to as the *underwriting cycles*. The cycles are not particularly regular, nor are they the same across all lines of business, in magnitude or in timing. The causes of the cycles are not well understood, but the cyclical nature of the P/C business is an important factor in companies' investment policies.

The insurance unit's needs for current income, surplus, and liquidity and its tax status may be affected by the stage of the underwriting cycle.

The cyclical nature of P/C results is evident in the combined ratios in Exhibit 51–1. Similarly, Exhibit 51–2 shows that growth in premium revenues swings widely through the cycle. When premium growth slows for the industry as a whole, premium revenue declines for many individual companies. The swings in premium growth result in dramatic shifts in the absolute level of underwriting profits/losses for the industry, as shown in Exhibit 51–3.

Combined ratios above 100 (underwriting losses) indicate that insurance underwriting operations are making a negative contribution to policyholder surplus. In P/C insurance, the ratio of premiums to surplus is viewed as an important measure of surplus adequacy. If surplus falls or does not grow fast enough, the insurer may be constrained in writing new business. This constraint may come from regulators or, more likely, from efforts to avoid a downgrade from rating agencies. Surplus constraints are most likely to be felt in the recovery stage of an underwriting cycle: Surplus has been growing slowly or even declining because of the negative contribution from underwriting; with prices firming, premium vol-

EXHIBIT 51–2

Percent Growth in Written Premium
(Stock-Owned P/C Insurance Companies)

1956	4.3	1974	6.7
1957	8.1	1975	11.1
1958	5.1	1976	21.1
1959	9.4	1977	18.6
1960	6.0	1978	12.3
1961	2.4	1979	9.8
1962	7.6	1980	6.1
1963	2.4	1981	3.5
1964	6.5	1982	3.8
1965	9.5	1983	3.8
1966	9.7	1984	8.7
1967	7.5	1985	23.5
1968	9.1	1986	24.9
1969	12.0	1987	8.4
1970	12.3	1988	3.7
1971	10.7	1989	1.7
1972	11.2	1990	3.9
1973	8.9	1991	1.4

Source: Best's Aggregates & Averages.

EXHIBIT 51–3

Underwriting Profit or Loss
(Stock-Owned P/C Insurance Companies)

1950	$0.2 Billion	1971	$.07 Billion
1951	0.0	1972	0.9
1952	0.2	1973	0.2
1953	0.3	1974	(1.8)
1954	0.4	1975	(2.9)
1955	0.3	1976	(1.4)
1956	(0.1)	1977	0.8
1957	(0.4)	1978	1.3
1958	(0.1)	1979	(0.4)
1959	0.1	1980	(2.0)
1960	0.1	1981	(3.7)
1961	0.0	1982	(6.5)
1962	0.0	1983	(9.1)
1963	(0.2)	1984	(15.7)
1964	(0.3)	1985	(17.9)
1965	(0.4)	1986	(10.4)
1966	0.1	1987	(5.5)
1967	0.0	1988	(5.8)
1968	(0.2)	1989	(12.3)
1969	(0.4)	1990	(12.6)
1970	(0.2)	1991	(12.8)

Source: Best's Aggregates & Averages.

ume is rising fast. This is precisely the time the company wants to write business, because prices are firming. Near the bottom of an underwriting cycle, the insurance operating unit will rely heavily on the investment portfolio to generate current income and add to surplus so that it can expand insurance writings as the cycle turns. When underwriting results have been strong, there will be relatively less pressure on investments to boost surplus. Therefore, the insurance business unit's expectations for income and contribution to surplus will vary depending on the strength of insurance markets.

The insurance unit's need for liquidity in the investment portfolio will also vary with conditions in insurance markets. At any time, catastrophes have the potential to cause claim and expense payments to exceed cash flow from premiums and investment income. However, negative cash flow is more likely to occur near the bottom of an underwriting cycle, when claims have been rising faster than premiums for a period of time. At such times, when insurance pricing is very competitive, the insurance unit does not want to find itself in a position in which it has to support cash flow by writing unprofitable business.

When a company's surplus position is strong, adequate liquidity may mean just having assets that are marketable. However, near the bottom of an underwriting cycle, adequate liquidity may involve having assets that can be liquidated without negatively impacting surplus. Under statutory accounting, bonds are carried at amortized cost on P/C balance sheets. If the market value of a bond drops, surplus is not affected until the bond is sold and the loss is realized. In the early 1980s, the market value of bonds in P/C portfolios was well below book values because interest rates had risen far above the levels of the previous decade. The inability to liquidate portfolios without impairing surplus probably caused many companies to continue writing business when pricing was clearly unprofitable.

RISK TOLERANCE

Marked-to-Market Exposure

Levels of risk tolerance may be developed against a number of criteria. Statutory or policyholders' surplus can affect the volume of business an insurer can write and the insurance markets that are available to that insurer. Policyholders' surplus is the difference between the statutory value of assets and liabilities; it is a margin of protection available to policyholders to ensure that all claims are paid. If surplus is too low relative to premium volume, state regulators may put pressure on the company to reduce its writings. More likely, an insurer with low surplus will restrict its premium volume to keep from incurring a downgrade on its financial ratings. Many corporate and institutional clients will only buy insurance coverage from an insurer whose A.M. Best financial rating is A +, A, or A–. Among many other factors, A.M. Best reviews financial leverage, including premiums to surplus and current liabilities to surplus.

As discussed in the previous section, growth in policyholders' surplus is depressed during periods of underwriting losses; in turn, capacity to write new business can be strained when pricing subsequently strengthens. Policyholders' surplus is also decreased by losses that are recognized on investments. For statutory and GAAP accounting, common and preferred stock are carried at market value; most bonds are carried at amortized cost (although GAAP rules for bond valuation allow use of market values). Changes in market values of stock are reflected on the balance sheet and in policyholders' surplus; changes in market values of bonds are not reflected in policyholders' surplus until the bonds are sold and the gain or loss is realized.

As shown in Exhibit 51–4, net investment income has risen through time, providing a steadily increasing contribution to earnings and to policyholders' surplus. Net investment income is defined as interest, dividends, fees, and rent received, net of investment expenses. When recognized gains and losses are added in, investment profit shows much more erratic growth. In

EXHIBIT 51–4

Net Investment Income and Profit
(Stock-Owned P/C Insurance Companies)

	Investment Income	Investment Profit
1955	$0.4 Billion	$1.1 Billion
1956	0.4	0.6
1957	0.5	(0.2)
1958	0.5	2.1
1959	0.5	1.0
1960	0.6	0.7
1961	0.6	2.5
1962	0.7	(0.2)
1963	0.7	2.0
1964	0.8	1.8
1965	0.9	1.5
1966	0.9	(0.6)
1967	1.0	2.3
1968	1.1	2.3
1969	1.2	(0.5)
1970	1.4	1.3
1971	1.8	3.4
1972	2.1	4.7
1973	2.5	(1.4)
1974	2.9	(3.3)
1975	3.1	6.6
1976	3.6	6.9
1977	4.6	4.7
1978	5.7	7.1
1979	7.6	10.8
1980	8.8	13.8
1981	10.3	8.6
1982	11.8	14.5
1983	12.4	14.8
1984	13.7	12.9
1985	15.0	22.4
1986	16.9	24.2
1987	18.8	19.8
1988	22.4	27.9
1989	25.0	35.3
1990	25.2	24.1
1991	27.1	41.0

Source: Best's Aggregates & Averages.

EXHIBIT   51–5

Policyholders' Surplus
(Stock-Owned P/C Insurance Companies)

1950	$4.2 Billion	1971	$17.3 Billion
1951	4.5	1972	21.4
1952	5.0	1973	20.1
1953	5.2	1974	14.8
1954	6.7	1975	18.5
1955	7.7	1976	23.0
1956	7.8	1977	27.1
1957	7.1	1978	32.5
1958	8.6	1979	39.2
1959	9.4	1980	47.5
1960	9.5	1981	47.5
1961	11.7	1982	53.3
1962	11.1	1983	56.4
1963	12.6	1984	53.3
1964	13.7	1985	64.4
1965	13.7	1986	81.8
1966	12.0	1987	89.9
1967	13.6	1988	102.3
1968	14.9	1989	117.7
1969	12.7	1990	122.9
1970	14.0	1991	140.8

Source: Best's Aggregates & Averages.

1957, 1969, and 1974, recognized losses on investments created overall investment losses at the same time the industry was incurring underwriting losses. The combined effect was large declines in surplus. Policyholder surplus is shown in Exhibit 51–5.

The willingness of a P/C insurer to recognize investment losses will vary over time, in part depending on current levels of policyholders' surplus and current and projected underwriting results. The company's risk tolerance is likely to be stated in terms of a maximum acceptable aggregated recognized capital loss at year-end, or perhaps a minimum acceptable investment contribution to surplus (net investment plus recognized gains or losses). The risk tolerance for recognizing investment losses will influence the portfolio manager's allocation between assets that are marked to market on the balance sheet and assets that are carried at other than market value.

Interest-Rate Risk

The P/C industry's emphasis on policyholders' surplus has sometimes diverted attention from management of owners' equity. Due to numerous aspects of industry accounting, these concepts are not equal and are not impacted symmetrically by various types of risk. In calculating policyholders' surplus, liabilities for claim and claim adjustment expense are carried at estimated ultimate cost; most bonds are carried at amortized cost on the asset side of the calculation. Therefore, the balance sheet carrying values of major items in the calculation of policyholders' surplus are unaffected by changes in interest rates. In calculating the economic value of owners' equity, liabilities are converted to present value, and all assets are valued at market; therefore, both the liability and the asset sides of the owners' equity calculation are affected by changes in interest rates.

Over the past decade, most financial institutions have paid increasing attention to interest-rate risk and management of asset/liability duration mismatch. The P/C industry has been somewhat slow to accept the importance of asset/liability duration management. At least in part, this is due to the emphasis on policyholders' surplus and statutory accounting. Many P/C managers have doubted that investors rewarded them for managing interest-rate risk. It was never clear that investors had sufficient information to evaluate the relative interest-rate risk exposure among P/C insurers. P/C insurers publish enough data to allow calculation of reasonable estimates of market values of assets, present values of liabilities, and durations for both; however, the estimation process is cumbersome.

Duration as used here will refer to modified duration. Modified duration gives the approximate percentage change in the market or economic value of an asset or liability for a 100-basis-point movement in interest rates.

Using economic values (market or present values) for assets (A), liabilities (L), and owners' equity (S),

$$S = A - L$$

Because surplus is the difference between asset and liability portfolios with predominantly fixed income characteristics, surplus too may have predominantly fixed income characteristics.[1] Because duration is linear in the weights of component assets or liabilities, it follows that the duration of surplus (Ds) can be defined as follows:

$$S \times Ds = (A \times Da) - (L \times Dl) \tag{51–1}$$

$$Ds = Dl + (A/S) \times (Da - Dl) \tag{51–2}$$

$$Ds = Dl + (\text{Leverage}) \times (\text{Mismatch})$$

The duration of surplus equals the duration of the liabilities plus a term that is the product of asset leverage times the asset/liability duration mismatch. For the pe-

---

1. The discussion of surplus duration is taken from Thomas Messmore, "The Duration of Surplus," *The Journal of Portfolio Management,* Winter 1990.

riod 1984 to 1988, the ratio of P/C industry assets to policyholders' surplus averaged 4.1. This tends to overstate asset leverage to the extent that statutory liabilities are undiscounted (reducing surplus). Discounting loss and loss adjustment expenses, based on past payout patterns and using approximate portfolio yields as discount factors, indicates that asset leverage based on economic values was closer to 2.6.

Equation (51–2) can be manipulated to show that a P/C company that wishes to minimize the interest-rate risk of its economic surplus should invest for an asset duration (Da) that is less than the liability duration (Dl). Setting duration of surplus equal to zero in Equation (51–2) yields

$$0 = Dl + (A/S) \times (Da - Dl)$$

$$Da = Dl \times [1 - (S/A)] = Dl \times (L/A) \qquad (51-3)$$

For a typical P/C company, with an asset-to-surplus ratio of 2.6, minimizing interest-rate risk of economic surplus (duration of surplus close to zero) would require an asset duration less than two-thirds of the liability duration—a significant short mismatch.

Estimating Interest-Rate Risk

The major components of P/C company liabilities are "loss and loss-adjustment reserves" (more accurately described as claim and claim-adjustment reserves) and "unearned premium reserves." To some extent, these liabilities may be thought of as fixed income obligations. The loss and loss-adjustment reserves have been set up for claims that have already occurred; the ultimate amount of the claim cost is uncertain, but insurers estimate these amounts in establishing the reserve. In addition, based on past payout patterns, insurers can estimate the timing of payouts for existing claim obligations.

Using appropriate discount rates (based on market or company-specific yields), present values can be calculated for expected payouts of claims and adjustment expenses. This would be the amount that needs to be invested to meet the expected amount and timing of claim obligations. For sensitivity analysis, the calculations could be repeated for more or less conservative assumptions of ultimate claim amounts and payout patterns. Similarly, estimates of duration of the liabilities can be calculated, based on expected claim amounts and payout patterns. These calculations can be carried out by the actuarial staff and provided to the portfolio manager.

Insurers report historical payout patterns for loss and loss-adjustment expenses in statutory statements that must be filed annually with state insurance commissions. Schedule O shows the payout of incurred losses by calendar year for property coverages; Schedule P does the same for liability and related coverages. These data can be used to make useful estimates of present values of liabilities for other insurers and for the industry as a whole.

Schedule P liabilities tend to have the longest average lives and account for about 85 percent of P/C loss and loss-adjustment liabilities. For industry Schedule P losses incurred in 1982–83, about one-third were paid within the same year the loss was incurred; 86 percent were paid within five years of the year in which the losses were incurred. Of course, these percentages are estimates because it is not certain what the ultimate loss payments for these years will be until the last claim is paid.

Assuming that industrywide loss payout patterns from earlier years continue, Schedule P losses incurred in a given calendar year have an average life (to payment) of about 2.8 years. Schedule P loss and loss-adjustment expenses on P/C balance sheets at the end of 1988 had an estimated average life of 3.4 years (payouts slow after the first one to two years) and a duration of about 2.5. These estimates would vary among individual companies depending on the mix of business. For instance, auto liability claims have a shorter average life than workers' compensation claims, which in turn have a shorter average life than medical malpractice claims.

Schedule O liabilities have a shorter duration than Schedule P liabilities. Roughly two-thirds of Schedule O losses are paid in the year in which they are incurred; the average life of these losses is between one and two years.

Unearned premium reserves are set up to allow for premiums that have been booked but for which the period of coverage has not been completed. Unearned premium represents obligations for claims that will be incurred in the remainder of the policy period. The liabilities represented by these future claims have a duration near 2.0, depending on the mix of premium between Schedule O and P lines. The loss and loss-adjustment expense and "unearned premiums" account for 85–90 percent of P/C liabilities. Most other liabilities on P/C balance sheets are short-term in nature. Estimates prepared at Travelers indicate that for the industry as a whole P/C liabilities had durations of about 2.0–2.2 over the period 1984–1987.

The duration of P/C assets appears to be much longer than the duration of liabilities. Bonds constitute almost 60 percent of P/C admitted assets. P/C companies report the distribution of bond holdings across maturity class in Schedule D of the annual filings to state insurance commissions. At the end of 1991, those bonds had an average reported maturity of over 10 years, essentially unchanged from the late 1980s. Estimates made by Travelers indicate that for the industry as a whole, P/C asset durations averaged close to 5.0–5.5 over the period 1984–1987. (These estimates assumed common stock had a duration of 4.0 and preferred stock a duration of 10.) Because the estimation process did not adjust for bond call features, these estimates should be viewed only as a rough indication of the duration of P/C assets. However, it clearly appears that P/C asset durations exceed liability durations.

Putting estimates of liability duration (2.0–2.2), asset duration (5.0–5.5), and asset-to-surplus ratio (2.6) into Equation (51–2), the duration of owners' equity for the P/C industry as a whole is estimated to be close to 10. At year-end 1987, the duration of 30-year U.S. Treasury bonds was also about 10. This suggests substantial interest-rate risk for owners' equity. In general, if all interest rates were to rise one percentage point, economic surplus of P/C insurers would drop by roughly 10 percent.

Although these estimates should be viewed as illustrative only, they are consistent with work carried out by David Babbel and Kim Staking and described in a Goldman Sachs research report.[2] Babel and Staking estimated the duration of surplus for 25 P/C writers over the period 1981–1987 and they reported the average surplus duration to be 9.7 years.

Why So Much Interest-Rate Risk?

Being invested long allows P/C companies to take advantage of the positive slope of yield curves that exists much of the time. It is not clear, however, how large this payoff is. Managing the interest-rate exposure of owners' equity does not necessarily mean buying bills instead of bonds; it may mean buying more 5- to 10-year bonds and fewer 20-year bonds. During the 1980s, the Treasury yield curve had an average slope from 1 year to 30 years of 84 basis points; however, the average slope from 5 years to 30 years was only 15 basis points. P/C companies have traditionally owned large holdings of tax-exempt bonds; in that market the reward for going long appears larger. During the 1980s, the municipal debt yield curve from 1 year to 30 years averaged 300 basis points, with 197 basis points of that slope between 5 years and 30 years.[3]

Moreover, P/C companies may not view interest-rate risk symmetrically because of book accounting and concern for statutory surplus. For statutory purposes most bonds are carried at amortized cost. (FASB has adapted standards to encourage insurers to mark more bonds to market for GAAP.) If interest rates are unchanged, investing long usually offers the highest yield. If interest rates go down, P/C companies can sell bonds and realize gains and higher surplus or just keep the higher-than-market book yields. If interest rates go up, statutory bond valuations do not change, and reported surplus is not affected, unless the insurer is forced to sell the bonds.

Companies may not even view the duration of liabilities on their balance sheet at any one time as reflecting their liabilities as an ongoing concern. In general, a P/C company is constantly renewing a share of its old business and writing new business. At any time, a company can expect to write business in the future that will generate a stream of claim liabilities further into the future. Rather than considering duration of existing liabilities, P/C companies manage to a liability stream that assumes some continuing level of future insurance writings. These

---

2. David F. Babbel and Kim B. Staking, *The Market Reward for Insurers That Practice Asset/Liability Management* (New York: Goldman, Sachs & Co., November 1989).

3. Based on weekly averages of quotes for high-grade municipal bonds and notes. The source of the yield data is Bank of America.

companies may invest long to lock in an investment yield on future business. As claims are settled, they are largely paid out of current premium and investment income flows. To adopt this view, a company should be relatively sure that it can maintain new business at adequate volumes and prices. Locking into long-term bonds may put insurers at a pricing disadvantage if interest rates subsequently rise.

Management of stock-owned P/C companies must balance regulators' concern for statutory surplus with the need to maximize shareholder wealth. Management has often questioned whether investors pay attention to interest-rate risk of P/C insurers. Investors seem to recognize that the P/C industry is subject to interest-rate risk, but investors may be unable to distinguish relative interest-rate exposure of individual companies.

At Travelers, we attempted to study this issue. We estimated duration of owners' equity for a group of 10 P/C companies. We then compared the interest sensitivity of the stock returns of these companies with the estimates of duration of the economic value of owners' equity. For the group as a whole, the interest sensitivity of stock returns was very close to the estimate of duration of owners' equity. However, looking among individual companies there was little correlation between estimated interest sensitivity of stock returns and the estimated duration of owners' equity. There could be several explanations: Estimates of duration of owners' equity are subject to error; the sample was too small; other factors influenced specific stock returns. On the other hand, it may be that investors have enough information to recognize that the P/C industry is exposed to interest-rate risk, but not enough to distinguish relative exposure among companies. This would suggest that a manager who is concerned with performance of his company's stock may not see much advantage to managing interest-rate exposure. His company will just be categorized with the rest of the industry.

The recent study by David Babbel and Kim Staking cited earlier, however, indicates that investors do recognize differences in interest-rate risk between P/C companies. Further, their work indicates that investors attach higher value to firms that control interest-rate risk. Their study of 25 P/C companies showed that market valuation of owners' equity (called liquidation value in their study) tended to be highest for firms with surplus duration near 0.0.

Travelers adopted asset/liability management techniques in the early 1980s. Today, tolerance for interest-rate risk is measured in terms of duration of owners' equity or economic surplus. Duration of liabilities is estimated two ways: looking only at liabilities currently on the balance sheet or arising from current-year business; and assuming the level of new business shown in the three-year business plan. Duration of surplus assuming no new business gives an extreme view of the interest-rate exposure of the company if it cannot write business at prices deemed profitable. On a normal basis, the risk strategy calls for minimizing the interest-rate risk of economic surplus (i.e., duration near 0.0). However, risk tolerance allows for some interest-rate risk, depending on the interest-rate forecast, the slope of yield curves, and conditions in insurance markets.

ASSET-CLASS ALLOCATION

At the end of 1991, bonds constituted 77 percent of the investment portfolios of P/C companies. Common stock accounted for 12 percent of investments, while cash and short-term assets made up an additional 6 percent. Small shares of the portfolios were devoted to preferred stock, mortgages, real estate, and other assets. The industry's asset mix is shown in Exhibit 51–6. Most types of bonds are utilized by P/C companies, including Treasuries, agencies, municipals, corporates, mortgage-backed, and foreign issues.

In making asset allocation decisions, the portfolio manager will take into account the investment goals and risk tolerance of the insurance business unit and the overall corporation. The portfolio manager will consider expected returns, risks or volatility, and covariances among asset classes. In addition, the portfolio manager's decisions will be influenced by regulatory and tax considerations that are specific to the P/C industry. Finally, it must be realized that P/C liabilities are not certain. The number and size of claims and the timing of their payouts may be affected by such factors as the state of the economy, inflation, and interest rates; these same factors can affect the returns and risks of investment assets. This suggests the need to take into account the cross-correlations among P/C liabilities and various classes of investment assets in making asset allocation decisions.

The portfolio manager must also take into account the current portfolio allocations in setting target allocations. Selling assets that are held with unrecognized losses may be in conflict with the company's needs for statutory surplus. Cash flow may limit how rapidly some asset classes can be built up if other asset classes cannot be sold off.

E X H I B I T   51–6

Cash and Invested Assets: Year-End 1991
(All P/C Companies—Statutory Values)

Bonds	$368.0 Billion
Common stock	58.1
Preferred stock	9.8
Mortgages	6.2
Real estate	1.7
Cash and equivalents	30.9
Other	5.3

Source: Best's Aggregates & Averages.

Regulatory Influence on Asset Allocation

State regulations address investment policy by setting minimum standards for quality and diversification. These regulations generally are intended to prevent speculative investment activity. These standards vary among states, and some companies that operate in a number of states comply by adopting the tightest limitation (among all the states in which they operate) for each type of standard. Some of the major limitations on P/C investments include the following:

- New York requires that unsecured debt of U.S. corporations, joint stock associations, and business trusts must meet certain fixed-charge coverage tests, generally 1.5 times fixed charges. Secured debt of U.S. corporations must be of investment grade and meet fixed-charge coverage tests.

- Illinois limits the percentage of an insurer's admitted assets that may be held in various types of obligations of states, political subdivisions, or public instrumentalities in aggregate. For example, not more than 2 percent of admitted assets may be held in the direct, general obligations of any one political subdivision of a state.

- The lesser of surplus or 10 percent of admitted assets may be held in common stock of U.S. corporations. Common stock of U.S. corporations traded over the counter is not to exceed 15 percent of surplus or 1.5 percent of admitted assets. Common stock must be traded on a national securities exchange or over the counter with a nationwide automated quotations system, and the issues must meet specific net income, total asset, and minimum number of shareholder tests (New York standards).

- Not more than 50 percent of admitted assets may be held in obligations secured by first or second mortgages on U.S. real estate (New York standard).

- Not more than 12.5 percent of admitted assets may be held in U.S. real property (New York standard).

- Not more than 10 percent of admitted assets may be held in investments issued by a Canadian entity and not more than 1 percent of admitted assets may be held in other foreign investments (New York standard).

To provide more flexibility, P/C companies are allowed to put some percentage of admitted assets into investments that do not meet regulatory standards (or that exceed regulatory limits); this percentage is an aggregate over all investment restrictions. These exception percentages are commonly referred to as *basket* limitations. In practice, regulatory limits probably have had their greatest impact on junk bond allocations. Most noninvestment-grade bonds will not meet the coverage tests set out by many state regulators; therefore, most noninvestment-grade bonds would be counted in the basket limitation. This has effectively limited P/C purchases of noninvestment-grade bonds. At the end of

1991, only 1 to 2 percent of the bonds in P/C portfolios were below investment grade (as designated by NAIC classifications).

A feature of regulation that probably has been more important in shaping P/C asset allocations is differential valuation methods among asset classes under statutory accounting. For purposes of measuring statutory surplus, bonds generally are carried at amortized cost, and mortgages are carried at the principal amount. In contrast, common and preferred stock are carried at market values, as determined by the Securities Valuation Office (SVO) of the National Association of Insurance Commissioners (NAIC). Preferred stock in good standing and subject to a 100 percent mandatory sinking fund is carried at cost.

A drop in the market value of a stock holding reduces statutory surplus through an unrealized loss. A decline in the market value of bonds, due to a change in the general level of interest rates or to other market conditions, does not affect statutory surplus. For P/C insurers, stocks expose statutory surplus to market risk to a greater extent than bonds. This different treatment of market value risk has tended to bias P/C investments toward bonds.

Over time, regulation that shifts portfolio investment toward bonds from stock can adversely affect the performance of P/C investments. Numerous historical studies show that stocks outperform bonds over long periods of time. Statutory accounting and surplus concerns force many insurers to pay added attention to the short-term volatility of stock.

Taxes and Asset Allocation

For institutions engaged in spread lending, tax preferred investment assets are of limited usefulness in their asset portfolios; for these companies, the bulk of investment income has an offsetting interest expense. For P/C insurers, because a larger share of investment income flows to net income, the tax status of investment income has a greater impact on P/C companies' bottom lines. For stock-owned P/C companies, investment profit (net income plus realized gains or losses) totaled $237 billion over the ten years 1982–1991; this was partially offset by a cumulative underwriting loss of $109 billion. This indicates that over half of investment income was exposed to income tax. This calculation understates the percentage of investment income that is potentially exposed to corporate income tax; P/C investment income in the 1980s had an implied tax payment built in, from large holdings of tax-exempt bonds. Before the 1980s, virtually all of investment income was exposed to corporate income tax, because on average the industry ran underwriting profits.

Not only is P/C investment income highly exposed to corporate income tax, but the exposure varies widely with the underwriting cycle. In the 1980s, on a calendar-year basis, underwriting losses varied from as much as 122 percent (1984) of investment profit to as little as 14 percent (1980). This cyclicality can be smoothed for tax purposes by tax rules that allow profit and loss to be matched across time. Still, the cyclicality increases the value of tax planning in investment decisions.

Traditionally, the tax exposure of investment income has caused P/C companies to hold a large share of their portfolios in tax-exempt bonds. Tax preferences (lower capital gains tax rates and the corporate dividend exclusion) also increased the relative attraction of stock. P/C companies would shift investments toward tax-preferenced assets when underwriting losses declined, and away from tax-preferenced assets when underwriting losses were rising. According to Federal Reserve Flow of Funds data, tax-exempt bonds accounted for an average of 56 percent of all bonds in P/C portfolios over the period 1964 to 1991. (See Exhibit 51–7.) The percentage varied from 36 percent to 68 percent, and the dollar holdings of tax-exempt bond holdings actually fell in 1983 and 1984, when underwriting losses were very large. For individual companies, shifts in and out of tax-exempt bonds were much larger. Shifts in the tax value of preferenced assets add to the need to maintain liquidity in the portfolio. As underwriting losses rise, P/C companies want to be able to move out of tax-exempt securities into taxable bonds with higher nominal yields, but at that stage of the underwriting cycle, they may have the least appetite for recognizing losses that drain statutory surplus.

The Tax Reform Act of 1986 increased the effective tax rates of P/C insurers, even though it cut the highest marginal tax rate from 46 percent to 34 percent. The Tax Reform Act accelerated the timing for recognizing taxable income by re-

E X H I B I T   51–7

Tax-Exempt Bonds as a Percentage of Total Bond Holdings—At Year-End (Portfolios of Non–Life Insurers)

1964	56.5	1979	64.4
1965	55.6	1980	65.7
1966	55.0	1981	64.2
1967	58.1	1982	64.2
1968	57.1	1983	63.6
1969	57.8	1984	57.4
1970	55.6	1985	51.0
1971	59.5	1986	47.5
1972	65.1	1987	49.2
1973	68.4	1988	47.5
1974	66.3	1989	43.3
1975	62.2	1990	40.6
1976	58.7	1991	37.3
1977	59.3	1992	35.6
1978	63.0		

Source: Federal Reserve, Flow of Funds.

quiring adjustments for unearned premium reserves and discounting of claim reserves. It also reduced the tax benefit of tax-exempt interest and stock dividends; a new Alternative Minimum Tax further reduced the tax benefit of preferenced investment income.

Tax changes related to tax-preferred assets are very important for asset allocation decisions. For corporations, the Tax Reform Act (and a follow-up bill in 1987) reduced the dividends-received deduction to 70 percent from 85 percent. For securities acquired after August 7, 1986, it also reduced P/C insurers' deductions for losses by 15 percent of the sum of tax-exempt interest and dividends-received deduction; the decrease in deduction is called *proration*. In general, 15 percent of interest on tax-exempt bonds purchased after August 7, 1986, is included in taxable income; this implies a tax rate of 5.1 percent ($34\% \times 15\%$). The effective tax rate on tax-exempt bonds bought before that date remains 0 percent. For stock acquired after August 7, 1986, the percentage of dividends included in taxable income is 40.5 percent ($30\% + (15\% \times 70\%)$); the effective tax rate is 13.77 percent ($34\% \times 40.5\%$). These rates involve some simplification, but they are approximately valid when the insurer is not in an Alternative Minimum Tax (AMT) situation.

Corporations pay the larger of their regular corporate tax or AMT. AMT is 20 percent of Alternative Minimum Taxable Income (AMTI); AMTI equals regular taxable income plus certain preference items and adjustments. As preference items become larger, AMTI and AMT become larger, and the likelihood of being in an AMT-paying situation increases.

For purposes of portfolio allocation decisions, the most important preference items relate to the dividends-received deduction, 100 percent of interest on municipal bonds purchased prior to August 7, 1986, and 85 percent of interest on non-grandfathered municipal bonds. As of 1990, 75 percent of this "tax-exempt" income is included as a preference item. If a bond is a private-activity bond issued after August 7, 1986 (referred to as an AMT bond), 100 percent of its tax-exempt income is included as a preference item.

Exhibit 51–8 compares effective tax rates for income (interest and dividends) from various types of securities under regular tax and under AMT.

After-tax returns on each asset class will depend on whether or not the company finds itself in an AMT position. To optimize asset allocation decisions, it is important to know what the insurer's tax situation will be. This, in turn, requires coordinated planning among the corporate finance unit, the insurance business unit, and the investment unit.

The larger preference items are relative to regular taxable income, the more likely the company will be required to pay the AMT. For any given mix of investment assets, a P/C insurer's regular taxable income will decline (rise) as underwriting losses expand (shrink). Therefore, the likelihood of being in an AMT situation will depend on the stage of the underwriting cycle and on the number and severity of large catastrophe losses during the year. The income effects of underwriting cycles and large catastrophes tend to be widespread across the P/C industry. There-

EXHIBIT 51–8

Comparison of Tax Rates

	Tax Mode	
Security	Regular Tax	AMT
Taxable bonds	34.00%	20.00%
Municipal bonds		
Purchased before 8/7/86	0.00	15.00[a]
Purchased after 8/7/86	5.10	15.75[b]
Private-activity bonds		
Purchased before 8/7/86	0.00	20.00
Purchased after 8/7/86	5.10	20.00
Stocks		
Purchased before 8/7/86	10.20[c]	16.50[d]
Purchased after 8/7/86	13.77	17.025[e]

[a](20% × 75%)
[b](20% × 15%) + (20% × 85% × 75%)
[c](34% × 30%)
[d](20% × 30%) + (20% × 70% × 75%)
[e](20% × 30%) + (20% × 70% × 75%) + (20% × 70% × 75% × 85%)

fore, many insurers are likely to find themselves moving toward (or away from) an AMT situation and trying to move out of (into) tax-preferenced investment assets at the same time. On the margin, this may affect spreads between tax-preferenced and fully taxable investment assets. An asset manager who is able to anticipate shifts in insurance underwriting results may be able to make portfolio adjustments ahead of competitors. Large catastrophes are not predictable, but the insurance business unit can give useful input on the direction of underwriting cycles.

In general, if a P/C insurer expects to pay AMT, it can increase after-tax income by buying more taxable bonds. If the insurer expects to pay regular tax, buying more tax-preferenced bonds can increase after-tax income. The asset mix that maximizes after-tax income will depend on relative yields among tax-preferenced and fully taxable assets, underwriting results, and availability of tax carryovers. To maximize after-tax income over a multiple-year horizon, it is necessary to forecast all these factors.

Liability/Asset Correlations

At any time, P/C insurers have estimates of the number of claims that have been incurred, costs of settling those claims, and the timing of payouts to settle those claims. The present value of those estimated claim payouts varies inversely with investment yields, due to the discounting effect. However, even on an undiscounted basis, the timing and amount of the liabilities remain uncertain until they are finally settled. The size of the ultimate claim payment may be affected by the level of inflation between occurrence and settlement. A plaintiff in a personal injury claim may be willing to settle more quickly if interest rates are high (and settlement amounts can be invested at high yields) than if interest rates are low. Looking at current business, auto claims may increase in number during periods of strong economic activity when both personal and commercial vehicles are driven more.

It seems very reasonable to assume that the P/C liabilities are a function of general economic activity, inflation, interest rates, and numerous other factors. These factors can also affect returns and risks of investment assets. Asset/liability management in P/C companies should take into account the variability of P/C liabilities and their correlations with major classes of investment assets.

A great deal of work has been done in tracking historical returns, volatility, and cross-correlations among major classes of investment assets. Various analyses have also attempted to relate asset performance and risk to various concepts such as economic activity, inflation, and interest rates. Less progress has been made in understanding the variability of P/C liabilities, the factors causing that variability, and the relationship with investment asset performance. This work will go forward as the payoffs to improved asset/liability management are recognized.

Research is under way to develop models that will provide a framework to optimize investment asset allocation taking into account many of the considerations discussed here. Such models may be based on maximizing total return on the investment assets, but constraints could be applied for current income, surplus adequacy, risk tolerance, and asset diversification. The models would include tax effects and underwriting results. The models would allow the user to include factors such as economic activity, inflation, and interest rates that affect both assets and liabilities, and therefore, the correlations among asset classes and liabilities. Travelers is participating in research along these lines. At present, work is proceeding to improve the inputs to models, especially behavior and interrelationships of asset classes and liabilities. It is hoped that this type of tool will eventually allow improved business performance, by more closely coordinating the management of assets and liabilities.

ASSET DIVERSIFICATION

The previous section discussed factors affecting the allocation of portfolios among asset classes. The issue of what defines an asset class was intentionally avoided. Taxable bonds may be considered a separate asset class from tax-exempts, but taxable bonds may be further divided among government, corporate, and mortgage-backed bonds. Bonds may be divided by investment and noninvestment grade, or broken down even more finely by quality rating. The appropriate definition of asset classes really depends on how many classes the portfolio manager wants to consider in making gross allocations and how correlated the manager perceives asset performance to be within and among asset groupings.

Regardless of how asset classes are defined, there may remain a need to look beyond the asset-class allocations to ensure that the portfolio is adequately diversified against all identifiable sources of risk. Managing asset/liability duration mismatch may minimize interest-rate risk, but protecting against credit risk and spread risk requires making sure the portfolio is diversified over sectors, industries, and credit qualities.

For P/C insurers, assets and liabilities are often exposed to the same types of diversification risks. Therefore, there is a need to manage the diversification of assets and liabilities in a coordinated process.

Natural catastrophes can generate huge and sudden losses for P/C companies. In 1989, Hurricane Hugo, an earthquake in the Oakland-San Francisco area, and a chemical plant explosion in Texas caused billions of dollars of insured losses all within a month's time. An insurer can minimize the expected impact from any catastrophe by spreading its writings across many geographic areas, limiting the business it writes in hazard-prone areas, and by reinsuring. Investments should be reviewed on a similar basis to be sure that they are not concentrated in geographic areas prone to natural catastrophes. A company's exposure to a geographic region may not look excessively large when looking separately at assets and liabilities; however, the combined asset and liability exposure may be excessive.

Economic conditions can also vary on a regional basis. In a region where unemployment is rising, insurers are likely to see a rise in theft and arson claims, and workers' compensation claims may also rise, as workers file claims for treatment they postponed when work was plentiful. This same economic weakness is likely to hurt mortgage and real estate investments, as well as performance of municipal bonds. The value of debt and stock of companies located in the region will also be affected. Liabilities and assets need to be diversified geographically, even for regions not identified with natural catastrophes. This may be difficult for regional insurance companies. Their insurance exposure will be concentrated geographically, and they may face regulatory and political pressure to keep investment funds in the region.

The liabilities of commercial insurers can be very vulnerable to the fortunes of individual industries. Asbestos manufacturers were a relatively small industrial group that generated billions of dollars of claims for P/C insurers. A prudent diversification program would require that the mix of insurance liabilities associated with particular industries (or the distribution of premium volume by industry) be compared with the distribution of bond and stock holdings across industries, to ensure that the insurer is not inadvertently doubling its bets.

Some insurers have started to look at whether assets can be found that are inversely correlated with various types of claim liabilities. It has been suggested that investments in contracting companies and building supply firms might perform well following natural catastrophes. With large exposure to toxic waste cleanup, some insurers have looked at investments in companies that clean up toxic waste sites. Health care insurers may look for investments that either help control health care costs or benefit directly from rising health care costs. This type of diversification effort may grow as insurers better understand the factors affecting their liabilities and more closely coordinate the management of assets and liabilities.

SUMMARY

Traditionally, P/C companies held a bond portfolio to fund insurance reserves while investing surplus largely in common stock. P/C insurers have accepted a great deal of interest-rate risk, because insurance pricing was viewed as insensitive to investment results. Statutory accounting methods often provided disincentives to economically efficient investment decisions. With the high interest rates of the 1980s, there has been an increased recognition of the need for asset/liability management. Asset/liability management in the P/C industry involves more than just managing interest-rate risk. P/C liabilities are affected by many of the same factors that affect asset performance: economic activity, inflation, and interest rates, as well as regional and industry factors. Management of assets and liabilities should be coordinated to improve asset allocation and ensure diversification across all identifiable sources of risk.

⑥ GLOBAL CORPORATE BOND PORTFOLIO MANAGEMENT

Jack Malvey, CFA
Managing Director
Lehman Brothers

INTRODUCTION

The corporate bond market is the most fascinating subset of the global capital markets. Beyond the abstractions of rating symbols, reports of new issues each day in the financial media, and portfolio performance measurement, thousands of real organizations with different credit stories sell debt to finance their expansion. These real organizations range from Canadian provinces, development banks such as the Asian Development Bank, and sovereigns such as Italy, Poland, Malaysia, and Sweden to corporations in North America, Europe, and Asia; their credit quality spans from impeccable to defaulted. These corporate borrowers use dozens of types of debt instruments (first mortgage bonds, debentures, equipment trust certificates, subordinated debentures, medium-term notes, floating-rate notes, private placements, preferred stock) in multiple currencies (dollar, yen, mark, Swiss franc, pound) at any maturity, ranging from one year to one hundred years. Sometimes, these debt structures carry embedded options, which may allow for full or partial redemption prior to maturity at either the option of the corporate borrower or the issuer. Sometimes, the coupon payment floats every quarter with short-term interest rates or resets to a higher rate after a fixed interval or a rating change.

Each day, hundreds of corporate bond portfolio managers face thousands of choices in the primary (new issue) and secondary markets. These portfolio managers consist of individuals in the pursuit of high yields, commercial banks arbitraging the difference between the higher yields on floating-rate notes and their lower cost of funding, mutual funds attempting to maximize both yield and total return, insurers and state pension funds seeking to fund their projected long-term liabilities, and "pure" total-return maximizers competing against each other on a monthly, quarterly, and annual basis to please their clients or risk losing them. These choices are partially driven by the existing security population of the corporate market (sectoral, issuer, structural, and currency) and partially by the psychology of the portfolio managers (overall risk tolerance, shortfall risk aversion, career risk, and internal politics of the investment-management institution).

Borrowers and investors intersect mainly through dealers. Each day, a few dozen corporate bond dealers relay information about secondary positions and new issue offerings from any of the thousands of corporate borrowers to the hundreds of corporate bond portfolio managers. Through their investment banking and syndicate operations, dealers also advise issuers on when and how to sell new debt. Through their fixed income research, sales, and trading arms, dealers convey investment recommendations to portfolio managers.

The task of global corporate bond portfolio management is to process all of this rapidly changing information about the corporate bond market (issuers, issues, dealers, and competing managers) and to construct the portfolio with the best risk-adjusted return. This discipline combines the excitement and qualitative tools of equity analysis with the quantitative precision of fixed income analysis. This chapter provides a guide to methodologies that may help portfolio managers meet this formidable challenge.

CORPORATE RELATIVE-VALUE ANALYSIS

How should portfolio managers in Tokyo decide how many and which floating-rate notes to purchase? Should U.S. investors add Eurobonds of non-U.S. issuers? Should London portfolio managers buy fixed-rate U.S. industrial paper and swap into floating-rate notes? Should U.S. insurers buy perpetual floaters issued by British banks and swap back into fixed-rate corporates? Should U.S. mutual funds purchase a new 10-year bullet offering of Viacom and, if so, on swap or for cash? When should investors fade the corporate sector and increase allocation to governments, pursue the "strategic upgrade trade," rotate from industrials into Yankees, and deploy a credit derivative (i.c., short the high-yield index) to hedge their portfolios? To respond to such questions, investors need to begin with an analytical framework (relative-value analysis) and to develop a strategic outlook for the global corporate market.

Economists have long debated the concept and measurement of "value." But fixed-income practitioners, perhaps because of the daily pragmatism enforced by the markets, have developed a consensus about the definition of value. In the bond market, "relative value" refers to the ranking of fixed income investments by sectors, structures, issuers, and issues in terms of their expected performance during some future interval.

For the day trader, relative value may carry a maximum horizon of a few minutes. For a large insurer, relative value may have a multiyear horizon. Accordingly, "relative-value analysis" refers to the methodologies used to generate such rankings of expected returns.

The practice of relative-value analysis has improved greatly during the past decade. This methodological evolution has been spurred by the widespread availability of inexpensive technologies that facilitate multihorizon and comparative analyses of portfolios and individual securities, the introduction of quantitative techniques to evaluate embedded options and risk-return trade-offs, new indices (i.e., Eurobond and high-yield) that gather pricing and market composition data, and the proliferation of new fixed income products such as credit derivatives. As a result, back-of-the-envelope methodologies have given way to more rigorous techniques that allow comparisons of relative value throughout the global fixed income markets.

Within the global corporate market, "classic" relative-value analysis is a dialectical process combining the best of top-down and bottom-up approaches. This method picks the sectors with the most potential upside, populates these favored sectors with the best representative issuers, and selects the structures of the designated issuers at the curve points that match the investor's outlook for the benchmark curve.

For many corporate investors, the use of classic relative-value analysis has been sufficient to ensure a measure of portfolio success. Although sector, issuer, and structural analyses remain the core of superior relative-value analysis, the increased availability of information and technology has transformed the analytical process into a complex discipline. To assist their endeavors, corporate portfolio managers in the 1990s have far more data than ever on the total returns of sectors, issuers, and structures, quantity and composition of new-issue flows, distribution of product demand by investor classes, aggregate credit-quality movements, multiple sources of credit analyses on individual issuers, and spreads.

Investors are badly in need of technological help and new processes to sort through the proliferation of market data. At the same time, the global corporate market has been broadened by waves of new issuers. At year-end 1995, about 20,000 corporate debt securities issued by 4,000 different issuers were sloshing around the global capital markets. Altogether, this pool of debt securities amounted to about $3 trillion of dollar and nondollar securities issued in both fixed-rate and floating-rate form. Derivative corporate securities, ranging from index swaps to structured notes, added another $500 billion to $1 trillion to the corporate debt universe.

STRATEGIC OUTLOOK: PERSISTENCE OF "CAPITAL-MARKET CAMELOT"?

The early to mid-1990s have been the best of times for most corporate issuers, investors, and dealers. In this "Age of Capital-Market Camelot," global inflation has calmed. Yield curves in almost all currencies have fallen. Except in Japan, equity valuations have skyrocketed to new altitudes. Corporate profitability has soared. The rating agencies have even been forced to reward corporate borrowers with higher ratings on average, especially in the high-yield market. With loftier corpo-

EXHIBIT 52–1

Lehman Brothers Indices
Fixed Income Asset Total Returns: 1973 through 1995

		Investment-Grade Corporate	High-Yield Corporate	Eurobond	Government	Mortgage	Global Gov't	S&P500
1973	Oil embargo &	1.51%	N/A	N/A	3.08%	N/A	N/A	−14.77%
1974	recession	−5.86	N/A	N/A	6.57	N/A	N/A	−26.39
1975	Economic	16.70%	N/A	N/A	8.38%	N/A	N/A	37.16%
1976	rebound	19.34	N/A	N/A	12.36	16.31%	N/A	23.84
1977		3.16	N/A	N/A	2.80	1.89	N/A	−7.18
1978	Inflation,	0.35%	N/A	N/A	1.80%	2.41%	N/A	6.56%
1979	oil price hike,	−2.10	N/A	N/A	5.41	0.13	N/A	18.44
1980	recession	−0.29	N/A	N/A	5.19	0.65	N/A	32.42
1981		2.95	N/A	N/A	9.36	0.07	N/A	−4.91
1982	The "Golden Age"	39.20%	N/A	N/A	27.75%	43.04%	N/A	21.41%
1983		9.27	5.84% (a)	N/A	7.39	10.13	N/A	22.51
1984		16.62	9.70	N/A	14.50	15.79	N/A	6.27
1985		24.06	25.64	N/A	20.43	25.21	N/A	32.16
1986		16.53	17.45	N/A	15.31	13.43	N/A	18.47
1987		2.56	4.99	1.35%	2.20	4.29	15.93%	5.23
1988		9.22	12.53	9.12	7.03	8.72	4.49	16.81
1989	Slowdown &	14.09%	0.83%	13.54%	14.23%	15.35%	6.67%	31.49%
1990	recession	7.05	−9.59	8.84	8.72	10.72	12.70	−3.15
1991	Slow rebound &	18.51%	46.08%	16.49%	15.32%	15.72%	15.34%	30.45%
1992	refunding blitz	8.69	15.75	8.17	7.23	6.95	4.51	7.61
1993		12.16	17.12	10.30	10.66	6.84	12.30	10.08
1994	Strong economic growth, higher inflation expectations, & higher rates	−3.93%	−1.03%	−2.41%	−3.37%	−1.61%	1.56%	1.32%
Jan. 95		2.12%	1.36%	1.68%	1.86%	2.14%	2.09%	2.59%
Feb. 95		2.88	3.43	2.31	2.15	2.55	2.41	3.90
Mar. 95	More moderate	0.82	1.08	0.54	0.63	0.47	4.61	2.95
Apr. 95	economic & profit	1.69	2.54	1.36	1.31	1.42	1.60	2.95
May. 95	growth, descending	4.71	2.80	3.49	4.03	3.15	2.81	4.00
Jun. 95	interest rates	0.90	0.64	0.66	0.77	0.57	0.69	2.32
July. 95		−0.44	1.26	−0.47	−0.37	0.17	0.71	3.32
Aug. 95		1.61	0.31	1.06	1.17	1.04	−2.30	0.25
Sep. 95		1.18	1.23	0.87	0.96	0.88	2.26	4.22
Oct. 95		1.30	0.62	1.55	1.52	0.89	1.25	−0.36
Nov. 95		1.91	0.88	1.58	1.56	1.14	1.07	4.39
Dec. 95		1.65	1.57	1.17	1.42	1.25	1.48	1.93
1995		**22.25%**	**19.17%**	**16.91%**	**18.34%**	**16.80%**	**20.18%**	**37.58%**

(a) Half-year number only; high-yield index began on 7/1/1983.

E X H I B I T   52–1

(Continued)

TOTAL RETURN EXPECTATIONS

	Investment-Grade Corporate	High-Yield Corporate	Eurobond	Government	Mortgage	Global Gov't	S&P500
Mean (1973–1995)	10.09%	12.65% (1)	9.14% (3)	9.60%	N/A	10.41% (3)	13.19%
Mean (1976–1995)	10.98	N/A	N/A	10.13	10.64%	N/A	15.37
Mean (1973–1979)	4.73	N/A	N/A	5.77	5.19	N/A	5.38
Mean (1980–1989)	13.42	11.00% (2)	8.00% (4)	12.34	13.67	9.03% (4)	18.19
Mean (1990–1995)	10.79	14.58%	9.72%	9.48	9.24	11.10%	13.98
StDv (1973–1995)	10.51%	13.35% (1)	6.06% (3)	6.86%	N/A	5.98% (3)	16.89%
StDv (1976–1995)	10.37	N/A	N/A	7.15	10.25%	N/A	13.31
StDv (1973–1979)	8.84	N/A	N/A	3.44	6.48	N/A	21.03
StDv (1980–1989)	11.17	7.80% (2)	5.04% (4)	7.32	12.18	4.96% (4)	12.04
StDv (1990–1995)	8.44	17.55%	6.43%	6.89	6.19	6.31%	14.93
Coeff. Var (1973–1995)	104%	106% (1)	66% (3)	71%	N/A	57% (3)	128%
Coeff. Var (1976–1995)	94	N/A	N/A	71	96	N/A	87
Coeff. Var (1973–1979)	187	N/A	N/A	60	125	N/A	391
Coeff. Var (1980–1989)	83	71% (2)	63% (4)	59	89	55% (4)	66
Coeff. Var (1990–1995)	78	120%	66%	73	67	57%	107

(1) 1983 through 1995.
(2) 1983 through 1989.
(3) 1987 through 1995.
(4) 1987 through 1989.

rate bond prices and tighter spreads, the corporate asset class has outperformed all other fixed-income categories during the 1990s as shown in Exhibit 52–1. And issuers have enjoyed the lowest debt-capital costs since the early to mid-1960s.

Hopefully, this global capital-market celebration of equities and corporate debt will extend unabated well into the next decade. But as the remainder of the 1990s unfold and the global capital markets inevitably descend from their current cyclical summit, reservations reminiscent of the mid–to–late 1980s are likely to resurface. "Economic unease" (less euphemistically, "How long until the next recession?") will rank at the top of the list of strategic concerns of many corporate investors. From time to time, the "recessionists" will air their economic indictments to talk down central bankers and the yield curves.

The growth of corporate profitability also will slow during the late 1990s. In turn, rating-agency analysts, now cloaked in equity analyst garb in some groups, are poised to pounce on earnings offenders and to drive up their downgrade ratios (total downgrades/total upgrades) from cyclical troughs. Aside from the occasional rating nicks, slower earnings growth will not prove greatly offensive to the global corporate market. Historically, general credit-quality deterioration and weaker corporate-debt valuations have been associated with earnings declines, not leaner growth rates.

More intense global competition, swifter technological change, slower profitability growth, lower capital costs, and philosophical shifts on regulation, public asset ownership, and industry concentration have spurred a global merger and acquisition boom in the 1990s. Indeed, the current scale of corporate issuer transformation is unprecedented in the history of the global capital markets. From 1995 through the first two months of 1996, 34 percent of Lehman Brothers investment-grade index and 11 percent of its high-yield index merged, bought, sold, restructured, or privatized. With the "positive event risk" of equity-financed, strategic mergers dominant, investor anxiety has been limited so far in the investment-grade corporate market. In high-yield corporates, where positive event risk reigns, event risk presents more strategic upside than downside.

Geopolitical risk also is moving into the strategic foreground. Washington, Moscow, London, Bejing, Madrid, and Tokyo have either changed or may change political administrations during the late 1990s. In some cases, these new political winds ripple into the global capital markets.

With these mounting strategic risks, the global corporate asset class likely will have to adjust to leaner absolute and relative returns during the late 1990s.

RELATIVE-VALUE METHODOLOGIES

In this section, several relative-value methodologies are reviewed.

Total Return Analysis

Corporate relative-value analysis begins with a detailed dissection of past returns and a projection of expected returns. Capital markets have regular rhythms. For instance, the economic cycle is the major determinant of overall corporate spreads as shown in Exhibit 52–2. During recessions, the escalation of default risk widens spreads (risk premiums over presumably default-free government securities of similar maturity). Conversely, economic prosperity reduces bankruptcies and tightens corporate spreads.

Thanks to the development of corporate indices (effectively databases of prices, spreads, issuer, and structure composition), analysis of monthly, annual, and multiyear total returns has uncovered numerous patterns (i.e., seasonality, election-cycle effects, and auction effects) in the global corporate market (some are detailed below). Admittedly, these patterns do not always reoccur. But an awareness and understanding of these total-return patterns are essential to optimizing portfolio performance. For example, investors can examine the performance of utilities versus industrials during recessions, compare bullets to callables when the Fed raises rates, and test the efficacy of option-adjusted spread (OAS) analysis.

EXHIBIT 52-2

30-Year Baa Industrial Spreads 1945–1995

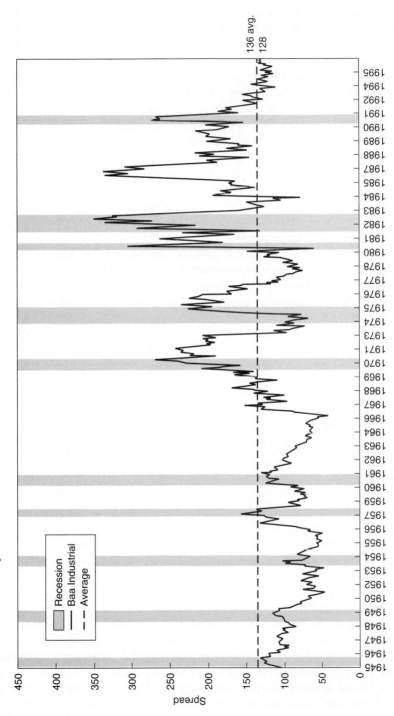

Sources: Moody's Investors Service and Lehman Brothers Fixed Income Research.

Benchmark Treasuries: 10-year until 1954; 20-year until 1977; 30-year thereafter.

Historical analogies can be taken to extremes. The U.S. stock market does not tumble every October. The "fourth-quarter effect" (the underperformance of low-quality corporates compared with high-quality corporates in the fourth quarter) does not occur every year. Nonetheless, portfolio strategy is difficult to chart unless these technical patterns are taken into account. Frequently, technical prophecies become self-fulfilling during periods of below-average liquidity.

Total return analysis also justifies portfolio objectives and constraints. After years of admonitions by various academics, market analysts, and consultants, total return data have been used to justify the relaxation of credit-quality constraints for many U.S. corporate portfolios during the 1990s. Consistent index outperformance is impossible without utilization of the entire index. And on a risk-adjusted basis, lower-quality corporates have provided a competitive advantage for investors. Based on this information, many A-constrained investors now have permission from their clients to use Baa/BBB's; many investment-grade constrained investors are now authorized to use crossovers (BB/Ba2 to Baa3/BBB–); and some crossover investors are able to move into B's and even CCC's. For example, BB's outperformed BBB's by five basis points (bp) per month from 1987 through 1995. On a cumulative basis over this period, the BB asset class gained 14.21 percent over BBB's. As measured by standard deviation of total return, BBB and BB nominal returns each have a monthly standard deviation of 1.46 percent.

During the next decade, the set of corporate bond indices will be extended to cover the private placement, preferred stock, and nondollar corporate markets. Although the dream of daily pricing of issuer-term structures for every corporate issuer does not seem achievable in an over-the-counter market, the enhancement of corporate pricing models by the index-reporting firms will lead eventually to the daily reporting of more–accurate index returns instead of the current monthly version. Moreover, the implementation of rigorous return-attribution models will improve the understanding of the sources of total return among such factors as curve, spread, sector, structure (issue size, coupon, embedded options), and currency.

Primary Market Analysis

Supply is often a misunderstood variable in the tactical relative-value calculus. Prospective new supply induces many traders, analysts, and investors to advocate a defensive stance toward the overall corporate market as well as toward individual sectors and issuers. Yet the premise, "supply will hurt spreads" is more cliché than fact. In the first quarters of 1991, 1992, 1993, and the first two months of 1996, origination bursts were associated with market spread contraction and strong relative returns for corporates. In contrast, the sharp supply decline during the first quarter of 1994 was accompanied by spread expansion and a major decline in both relative and absolute returns for corporates.

In the investment-grade corporate market, heavy supply often helps spreads/returns as the new primary valuations validate and enhance secondary valuations. When primary origination declines sharply, secondary traders lose re-inforcement from the primary market and tend to raise their bid spreads. In effect, Say's Law (supply creates its own demand) appears to hold during some intervals in the corporate market. Counter to intuition and cliché, relative corporate returns often perform best during periods of heavy supply.

In fairness, Say's Law does not always hold. Supply surges in September 1993 and May–June 1995 were associated with spread weakness. But other factors, such as concern about the state of the U.S. economy, affected valuations. And for a single issuer, a huge slug of potential new supply will almost always affect secondary valuations *prior* to the new offering as traders automatically raise spreads. If the new offering is well received, the issuer's spreads usually tighten.

Primary-market myopia has intensified during the 1990s. The sharp descent of global yield curves generated a global refunding blitz that spawned gross origination records in 1991 through 1993 that may not be topped for a generation. The upward rotation of global yield curves choked supply in 1994. But with curve relief, the origination spigot reopened in 1995 and 1996.

Given their immediate focus on the deals of the day and week, portfolio managers often overlook market-structure dynamics in making portfolio decisions. Because the pace of change in market structure is gradual, market dynamics have less effect on short-term tactical investment decision making than on long-term strategy. To optimize long-term strategic decisions, investors must take into account changes in the structure of the global capital markets.

The composition of the global corporate bond market has shifted markedly during the 1980s and 1990s. Medium-term note (MTN) origination has come to dominate the front end of the corporate curve. Rule 144A bonds (quasi-private placement bonds) have captured a growing share of Yankee, high-yield, and emerging-market debt. Structured notes and index swaps have heralded the introduction of derivative instruments into the mainstream of the corporate market. The high-yield corporate sector has become just another asset class after having been stress tested in 1989–1990. Global origination has become a more popular technique for agencies, supranationals, sovereigns, Canadians, and some large corporate borrowers.

Although the growth of derivatives and high-yield instruments stands out during the past decade, the globalization of the corporate market has been the most profound development. The rapid growth of the Eurobond market since 1975 and the emergence of the Dragon bond market (dollar offerings initially made only in Asia) in the early 1990s have led to the proliferation of truly transnational corporate portfolios. From a broad viewpoint, the rapid development of the emerging-market debt may be seen as a subset of this globalization process. Globalization will accelerate during the next decade as many high-quality European and Asian issuers, especially newly privatized entities, join the ranks of global borrowers.

In the U.S. investment-grade corporate market, the dominance of capital-intensive utilities has been replaced by a more balanced distribution of issuers. At the end of 1995, utilities accounted for 18 percent of outstanding public corporate debt, down from 62 percent in 1973. Financial institutions held a 26 percent market share, up from 13 percent in 1973. From 1973 through 1995, industrials climbed from 25 percent to 36 percent. From a zero index representation in 1973, Yankees surged to 20 percent at year-end 1995.

Partially offsetting this proliferation of issuers, the global corporate market has become structurally more homogeneous during the past decade for three reasons. First, there has been a continued shift away from utility issuers, who had preferred long-dated maturities to fund long-term capital assets. Second, new origination has been less costly at the front of very steep yield curves. Moreover, many issuers have sought to minimize interest expense and to maximize earnings, fixed-charge coverages, and ratings. Third, the emergence and tremendous growth of the swap market made intermediate origination more convenient.

As the shape of the yield curve inevitably changes through time, more structural diversification may again become fashionable. Nevertheless, the supremacy of bullets in the global high-grade markets is unlikely to change during the next decade.

The trend toward bullet securities does not pertain to the high-yield market, where callables remain the structure of choice. With the hope of credit-quality improvement, many issuers expect to refinance prior to maturity at lower rates.

There are three strategic portfolio implications for this structural evolution. First, scarcity value must be considered in corporate relative-value analysis. The dominance of bullet structures translates into scarcity value for structures with embedded call and put features. This aspect is not captured by option-valuation models. For example, the steady decline in the percentage of electric utilities in the investment-grade corporate market helps to explain their robust valuations in the face of growing competition.

Second, long-dated maturities will decline as a percentage of outstanding corporate debt, especially if Congress ever enacts some form of the U.S. Treasury's 1995 proposal to eliminate the tax deductibility of interest expense on new structures of U.S. corporate borrowers with maturities greater than 40 years. All else being equal, this change will lower the effective duration of all outstanding corporate debt and reduce aggregate sensitivity to interest-rate risk. The possible overall dampening of interest-rate sensitivity should also ripple through to reduce spread volatility. For asset/liability managers with long horizons, this shift of the maturity distribution suggests a rise in the value of long corporates and helps to explain the warm reception afforded to every new Century offering (100-year maturity) to date.

Third, corporate derivatives are in their adolescence. The maturation of corporate bond derivatives, whether on a stand-alone basis or embedded in structured notes, will give rise to new strategies for investors and issuers.

Demand Analysis

Naturally, demand plays a major role in corporate relative-value analysis. With some lags, U.S. demand can be analyzed for corporate product for the four main investor classes (insurers, state pension funds, mutual funds, and total-return investors). In the mid-1990s, corporate product has been elevated to "pedestal status" by U.S. insurers and "semi-pedestal status" by U.S. pension funds and mutual funds. Total-return managers are more wary, but they do not want to risk a significant underweighting after, in some cases, missing the corporate rallies of 1991–1995. This is the most powerful factor supporting valuations in the corporate market. During the late 1990s, total-return investors will converge to a "neutral-plus allocation." Severe underweighters need to boost their allocation as the share of corporate product in the Lehman Aggregate index creeps toward 20 percent from 17 percent at year-end 1995. Heavy overweighters in the 35 percent and above neighborhood will slim down with the escalation of cyclical risk.

Global corporate demand flows are difficult to track formally. Based on direct observation, many European and Asian investors are underweighted in their corporate holdings. Many of these international investors have their hands full dealing with a dozen major government yield-curve movements in a dozen currencies. There is little time and less appetite for sorting out credit risks. During the next decade as more non-U.S. investors become beholden to performance measurement versus some indices and as the global asset management business becomes more competitive, such corporate underweightings (unless warranted by the economic/credit cycle) will become less common among non-U.S. investors. In particular, European investors are expected to boost their demand for corporates with Currency Union in 1999. Over the same interval, U.S. investors will boost their dollar and nondollar holdings in non-U.S. corporate issuers because of the same competitive pressures. Barring unforeseen political/economic developments such as an eruption of trade and capital-market protectionism, the corporate bond markets should become truly globalized during the next 10 years.

Liquidity and Trading Analysis

Short-term and long-term liquidity influence portfolio management decisions. Some investors are reluctant to purchase equipment trust certificates, Rule 144As, private placements, MTNs, and nonlocal corporate issuers. Other investors gladly exchange a potential liquidity disadvantage for incremental yield. For investment-grade issuers, these liquidity concerns often are exaggerated. Liquidity poses more of an issue for the credit derivatives and high-yield markets.

Trading has boomed across the global capital markets during the past decade. This has amplified the provision of liquidity in the corporate bond market.

This expansion in secondary trading stems from an accumulation of factors: the great refunding blitz of the early 1990s; the resulting multiplier effect of record origination as most new issues were sold partially on swap against existing issues; the market volatility triggered by the 1990–1991 recession; a variety of secular sector opportunities (such as buying U.S. bank debt in the early 1990s); the effects of the descent of the yield curve as investors sought call protection in bullets, some defense against the yield curve in put structures in 1994, and short-term yield maximization in high-coupon callables in 1992–1993; the cyclical steepening of the yield curve, which facilitated the expansion of dealer inventories to take advantage of the "positive carry trade"; the entrants of new dealers into the corporate bond market, especially from the ranks of commercial banks; the conversion of some total-return managers to an equity-style approach; and the conversion of some insurers to a total-return style approach.

Secondary Trade Rationales

Capital-market and issuer expectations constantly change. Recession may arrive sooner rather than later. The yield curve may have steepened instead of flattened. Instead of descending, the yield curve may have retreated. The auto and paper cycles may be moving down from their peaks. An industrial may have announced a large debt-financed acquisition, earning an immediate ratings rebuke from the agencies. A major bank may plan to repurchase 20 percent of its outstanding common stock, great for shareholders but leading to higher financial leverage for debtholders. In response to daily information flows, portfolio managers amend their portfolios. To understand trading flows and the real dynamics of the corporate market, investors should consider the most common rationales for trading and not trading. There are dozens of rationales to execute secondary trades. Several of the most popular are discussed below.

Yield/Spread Pickup Trades

These trades represent the most common secondary transaction across all sectors of the global corporate market. Based on our observation, 60 percent of all secondary swaps reflect investor intentions to add additional yield within the duration and credit-quality constraints of a portfolio. If five-year, A3/A– GMAC paper trades at 60 bp, 10 bp behind five-year, A1/A+ Ford Motor Credit at 50 bp, some investors will deem the rating differential irrelevant and swap into GMAC for a spread gain of 10 bp per annum. This "yield-first psychology" mirrors the institutional yield needs of long-term asset/liability managers, commercial banks, and mutual funds. Despite the passage of two decades, this investor bias toward yield maximization also may be a methodological relic left over from the era prior to the introduction and market acceptance of total-return indices in the mid-1970s. There is empirical support for the effectiveness of yield-first psychology. Baa-rated corporates (11.01 percent) outperformed A-rated securities (10.09 percent) by 92 bp from 1973 through 1995, according to Lehman indices. But this tactic is not without risk. As measured by the standard deviation of total return, Baa-rated returns (11.91 percent) have been considerably more volatile than A-rated returns (10.62 percent). In general, yield/spread maximization works reasonably during periods of economic growth. But as shown from 1989 through stretches of 1992, yield maximization can be highly hazardous to optimization of portfolio return.

Credit-Upside Trades

Credit-upside trades are closely related to yield/spread maximization transactions. In the illustration of the GMAC and Ford Motor Credit trade described above, some investors may swap based on their view of potential credit-quality improvement for GMAC. Credit-upside trades are particularly popular in the crossover sector (securities with ratings between Ba2/BB and Baa3/BBB–, by either rating agency), and for good reason. From the early 1990s through the mid-1990s, such notable issuers as Chrysler, McDonnell Douglas, and Transco Energy regained investment-grade status and produced exceptional relative returns for investors. In the mid-1990s, crossovers with investment-grade potential include such major issuers as Delta Airlines, Digital Equipment, and Time Warner Inc.

Credit-Defense Trades

Credit-defense trades become more popular with the gathering of economic storm clouds. Secular sector transformations often generate uncertainties and induce defensive repositioning by investors. In anticipation of greater competition, some investors have reduced their portfolio exposures in the mid-1990s to sectors such as electric utilities and telecommunication firms. Unfortunately, because of yield-maximization needs and a general reluctance to realize losses by some institutions (i.e., insurers), many investors tend to react more slowly to credit-defense propositions. Ironically, once a credit sours sufficiently to invoke the wrath of the rating agencies, internal portfolio guidelines often dictate security liquidation immediately after the loss of single-A or investment-grade status. This is usually the worst possible time to sell a security, and doing so maximizes the harm incurred by the portfolio. For example, some A-rating constrained investors were forced to sell General Motors/GMAC positions following the loss of A ratings in the fall of 1992. Many investors understood that their collective actions largely were responsible for the temporary ballooning of GM/GMAC's spreads (i.e., five-year paper peaked at about 250 bp). But investment policies, sometimes legislated in certain U.S. states, had to be honored to the delight of some total-return investors on the other side of the trade ledger.

New-Issue Swaps

New-issue swaps contribute to secondary turnover. Because of perceived superior liquidity, many portfolio managers prefer to rotate their portfolios gradually into more current, on-the-run issues. This disposition, reinforced by the usually superior market behavior of newer issues in the U.S. Treasury market, has become a self-fulfilling prophecy for some corporate issues. In addition, some portfolio managers buy certain new issues to generate sufficient commissions to pay vendors through soft dollars. Rarely, an underwriter may insist on cash-only purchases for "hot" transactions. As a result of these practices, investors usually pay for their new-issue purchases through some combination of cash and swap of an existing security in their portfolio.

Sector-Rotation Trades

Sector-rotation trades, within corporates and among fixed-income asset classes, have become more popular during the 1990s but do not rival the activity in the equity market. As soon as the Fed launched its preemptive strike against inflation in February 1994, some investors exchanged fixed-rate corporates for floating-rate corporates. In 1995, the specter of U.S. economic weakness prompted some investors in high-yield corporates to rotate from consumer-cyclical sectors such as autos and retailing into consumer noncyclical sectors such as food, beverage, and health care. The weakness of the U.S. dollar in late 1994 and early 1995 triggered a rotation from dollar-denominated corporate debt by some non-U.S. investors. And after trailing index benchmarks during the first half of 1995 because of an underweighting of corporate exposure, some total-return investors boosted allocation to the global corporate asset class and traded out of governments and MBS.

Curve-Adjustment Trades

These trades are undertaken to reposition overall portfolio duration. The portfolio duration of most corporate investors resides within a range from 25 percent below to 25 percent above the index duration. If corporate investors could have predicted yield-curve movements perfectly in 1994 and 1995, they would have lowered their portfolio duration at the beginning of 1994 and extended their duration in late 1994. Although most fixed-income investors prefer to reconfigure the duration of their aggregate portfolios in the more liquid Treasury market, strategic portfolio duration tilts also can be implemented in the corporate market. As discussed under curve analysis below, corporate investors also trade to concentrate their exposure on curve areas that appear to offer the promise of greater short-term return. With the steepening of the underlying yield curve between 10 years and 30 years during 1995 and early 1996, 20-year securities, for example, developed greater appeal for investors seeking higher yields than in the 10-year sector and lower duration than in the 30-year sector.

Structure Trades

These trades also gain appeal with movements in volatility and the shape of the yield curve. As shown during the second quarter of 1995, the rapid descent of the yield curve contributed to underperformance of callable structures. With curve stabilization during the third quarter of 1995, investors were more willing to trade into an extra 35 bp of spread for high-quality callables compared to bullets of similar quality and were less put off by the possible cost of negative convexity.

Cash Flow Reinvestment

Cash flow reinvestment needs force investors into the secondary market on a regular basis. Some cash flows arrive during interludes in the primary market. And sometimes the composition of recent primary supply may not be compatible with portfolio objectives. Two weeks of heavy, long-dated crossover supply will not help A-rated, barbelling mutual funds with 10-year maturity constraints. Based on the year-end 1995 investment-grade index, corporate investors needed to reinvest about $40 billion of cash flow in 1996 alone. In the absence of defaults, high-yield investors will have another $15 billion to reinvest in 1996.

Bias for Activity

Bias for activity affects both passive (indexers) and active managers as well as dealers. Referring to the overall capital markets, the late Fisher Black perfectly characterized some of this activity as "noise trading." Dealers closely monitor the aging of their security inventories. Stale positions, usually on the books for more than 90 days, justifiably are viewed with suspicion by risk managers. Ancient holdings may be worth less than their marks, otherwise they would have been purchased by investors. Accordingly, all corporate traders seek to limit their stale positions. At the same time in their quest for portfolio optimization, indexers are rebalancing their portfolios to conform with the ever-shifting composition of indices. And active managers are surfing among primary and secondary flows for the slightest glimmer of incremental value. The sum total of dealer activity, indexer realignments to cut tracking error, and active managers searching for valuation nuances breeds a natural bias for activity in the global corporate market.

Trading Constraints

Market analysts should also track the main rationales for not trading.

Portfolio Constraints

Collectively, these inhibitions are the single biggest contributor to the persistence of market inefficiency across the global corporate markets. Many U.S. state pensions cannot purchase corporate securities with ratings below A3/A– and Rule 144As under administrative and legislative guidelines. Some pension funds also have limitations on MTNs and non-U.S. corporations. Regulators have limited the exposure of U.S. insurers to high-yield corporates. At the same, many European investors are restricted to issues, rated at least single-A and sometimes Aa, manufactured originally in annual-pay Eurobond form. Such European investors often cannot purchase securities of an identical credit issued in the U.S. Yankee market. Globally, many commercial banks must operate exclusively in the floating-rate realm; all fixed-rate securities, unless swapped, are out of bounds.

"Story" Disagreement

Traders, salespersons, sell-side analysts and strategists, and buy-side colleagues have dozens of potential trade rationales that will supposedly benefit portfolio performance. The proponents of the secondary trade may have a legitimate point, but the portfolio manager may be unwilling to accept the "shortfall" risk if the investment recommendation does not pan out in the immediate future. Portfolio managers will reject such trade propositions by claiming to be "full in the name." That means the portfolio already is at its limits with respect to exposure to a credit/sector. Alternatively, "full in the name" can be viewed as market colloquialism to politely say no to the proposed swap.

Buy-and-Hold

Although many long-term asset/liability managers claim to have become more total-return focused in the 1990s, accounting constraints (i.e., cannot sell positions at a loss compared to book cost or take too extravagant a gain compared to book cost) limit the ability of these investors to transact. Effectively, these investors are traditional "buy-and-hold" investors.

Administrative Burdens

Compliance and accounting demands have soared during the 1990s. Many portfolio managers spend almost 50 percent of their schedule on these administrative chores. Moreover, some investors are burdened with multiple functions: analysis, portfolio management, and marketing. In particular, portfolio managers with heavy marketing obligations to existing and potential clients may be limited in their capability to react to short-term valuation anomalies in the corporate bond market.

Seasonality

Secondary trading slows at month ends, more so at quarter ends, and the most at the conclusion of calendar years. Dealers often prefer to reduce balance sheets at year-end. And portfolio managers take time to mark their portfolios, prepare reports for their clients, and chart strategy for the next period. During these intervals, some of the most compelling secondary offerings can languish.

SPREAD ANALYSIS

By custom, some segments of the high-yield and Eurobond markets still prefer to measure value by bond price or bond yield rather than spread. But for the rest of the global corporate market, nominal spreads (the yield difference between corporate and government bonds of similar maturities) have become the basic units of both price and relative-value analysis. Eventually, the Eurobond and high-yield markets also will switch to spreads to be consistent with other markets.

Unlike the mortgage-backed securities market, the corporate market has not adopted and is not likely to adopt option-adjusted spreads or zero-volatility spreads as measures of price/value for two reasons. First, almost all Eurobonds and MTNs as well as a growing percentage of public investment-grade corporate debt (87 percent in 1995) are bullet securities that do not feature embedded options. Second, the standard one-factor binomial models in use do not take into account credit-spread volatility.

Although spreads are the mainstay of corporate relative-value analysis, corporate investors should avoid spread myopia when making relative-value decisions. Spread movements are a key but not the exclusive determinant of relative returns. Coupon, maturity, and structural differentials often can more than counter spread movements, even general movements in the entire corporate market. For example, in April 1993, the nominal total return difference between investment-grade corporates and governments was zero thanks to the negative effects of a rising benchmark curve on the longer-duration corporate market versus the shorter-duration government market. In August 1993, the exact converse occurred. Spreads widened in some sectors, but corporates outperformed governments because of the sharp descent of the yield curve.

Investors should develop a rigorous understanding of the strengths and weaknesses of spread tools. The most common technique for analyzing spreads among individual securities and across industry sectors is mean-reversion analysis. Buy this *cheap* (wide spread) sector or issuer because the spread used to be much tighter. Sell this *rich* (tight spread) sector or issuer because the spread used to be much wider.

Mean-reversion analysis can be instructive as well as misleading for several reasons. First, the mean is highly dependent on the interval selected. And there is no market consensus on the appropriate interval. Some investors use 1, 3, 5, 10, and even 50-year means to judge relative value. For traders, the mean may be one week to three months. Second, it is uncertain why a somewhat arbitrary mean should exert a mysterious gravitational effect on current spreads in the near future. Third, the timing of supposed reversion is uncertain. In the absence of macroeconomic changes or sector/issuer-specific fundamental developments, spread persistence often rules. Rich sectors/issues tend to remain rich for long intervals, and cheap sectors/issues tend to remain cheap for long intervals.

Quality-spread analysis examines the spread differentials between low- and high-quality credits. Not surprisingly based on the satisfactory global economic environment at the end of 1995, Exhibit 52–3 shows that industrial quality spreads (Baa–Aaa yields) stabilized and were near their lowest ebb since the mid-1970s. This analysis may tempt some investors to upgrade the quality of their portfolios in anticipation of the next recession. As highlighted by this chart, an upgrade trade does not make sense unless a recession is fairly imminent. Moreover, Baa/BBB industrial spreads have been tighter for extended stretches at many intervals during the post-World War II era, as shown in Exhibit 52–2.

EXHIBIT 52-3

30-Year Industrial Quality Spreads 1945–1995

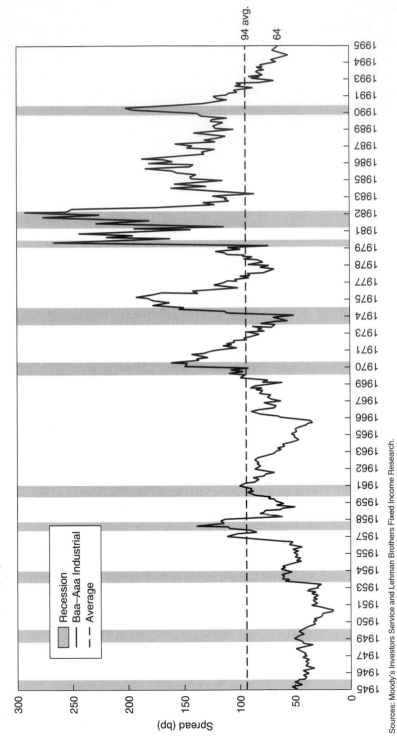

Sources: Moody's Investors Service and Lehman Brothers Fixed Income Research.

Benchmark Treasuries: 10-year until 1954; 20-year until 1977; 30-year thereafter.

"Percent yield spread" analysis (the ratio of corporate yields to government yields for securities of similar duration), shown in Exhibit 52–4, is another popular technical tool with some investors. This methodology has serious drawbacks that undermine its usefulness. Percent yield spread is more a derivative than an explanatory or predictive variable. Our data show that yields and spreads do not always move in the same direction. The economic cycle is the main determinant of overall spreads. A recession in a low-yield environment may precipitate high-percent yield spreads. Strong economic growth accompanied by inflation, indicating a higher benchmark Treasury curve, would generate low-percent yield spreads.

Sector Rich/Cheap Analysis

Exhibit 52–5 displays a sector rich/cheap analysis for the investment-grade corporate market on December 31, 1995. These sector rankings are calculated through the use of a multiple-regression equation. The independent variables are credit quality (average of the agencies' ratings, watchlist adjustment, Lehman analyst rankings), issuer investment ranking (1=buy, 3=hold, 5=sell), relative market risk (subjective score from 5 percent through 95 percent to reflect any possible operating, financial, regulatory, or merger and acquisition event that would adversely affect value), macro sector (i.e., utilities versus industrials), micro sector (i.e., chemicals versus airlines), and structure (coupon, maturity, embedded options). The dependent variable is spread, expressed in OAS terms in the investment-grade market and price in the high-yield market (not shown here). The relative rich/cheap score for each issue is calculated by comparing its expected spread with its actual spread. Sector scores are the market-weighted average of every issue in the sector.

Sector rich/cheap analysis has been fairly effective in anticipating sector movements. For example, at the beginning of 1995, this model accurately showed insurers and brokers to be among the cheapest sectors in the investment-grade corporate market. Both sectors subsequently outperformed.

Despite its apparent success in 1995, the limitations of rich/cheap analysis should be understood. This methodology provides valuation rankings based on static snapshots of market valuations. As with spread mean/reversion analysis, such rankings do not necessarily indicate when a sector/security will become richer or cheaper. Rich/cheap analysis should be viewed as a useful empirical guide, not a final arbiter of sector value.

Structure Analysis

Leaving aside credit, issue structure analysis and structural allocation decisions usually hinge on yield-curve and volatility forecasts as well as interpretation of option-valuation model outputs (see the discussion below). In the short run, these factors largely will influence structural performance. But investors should also take into account long-run market dynamics.

EXHIBIT 52–4

30-Year Baa Industrial Percent Yield Spread 1945–1995

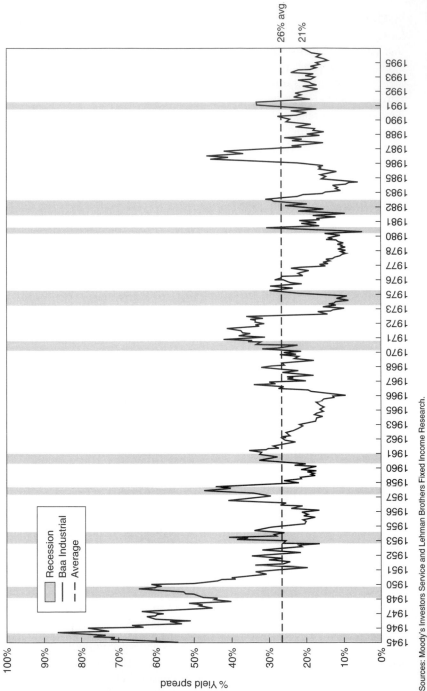

Sources: Moody's Investors Service and Lehman Brothers Fixed Income Research.

Benchmark Treasuries: 10-year until 1954; 20-year until 1977; 30-year thereafter.

EXHIBIT   52–5

Corporate Bond Index Statistics for December 1995

	Duration to Worst	Mod. Adj Duration	Mkt Wgtd Rating	Invest Trend	Rel Mkt Risk	Rich/ Cheap (OAS bp)	Price	YTW	Market Value	% of Sector	% of Corp
Corporate Bond Index	6.34	5.90	A2/A3	2.71	51.61	−1.65	107.55	6.34	793,223	100.00	100.00
Industrial	*6.68*	*6.37*	*A2/A3*	*2.69*	*62.73*	*−5.67*	*109.85*	*6.43*	*283,400*	*100.00*	*35.73*
Basic industry	*6.79*	*6.53*	*A2/A3*	*2.74*	*68.65*	*2.01*	*110.96*	*6.37*	*39,628*	*13.98*	*5.00*
Chemicals	6.44	6.31	A2/A3	2.72	67.47	0.60	110.42	6.26	18,021	45.48	2.27
Metals	6.24	6.19	BAA1/BAA2	2.86	63.25	−4.58	109.35	6.12	3,364	8.49	0.42
Paper	7.24	6.80	A3/BAA1	2.74	70.81	4.62	111.80	6.46	18,243	46.04	2.30
Other	0.00	0.00	0	0.00	0.00	0.00	0.00	0.00	0	0.00	0.00
Capital goods	*6.98*	*6.62*	*A2/A3*	*2.81*	*66.23*	*−7.06*	*109.58*	*6.33*	*44,167*	*15.58*	*5.57*
Aerospace	7.81	7.58	A2/A3	2.97	58.63	−16.18	113.65	6.29	6,674	15.11	0.84
Building materials	7.07	6.85	A3/BAA1	3.00	60.59	−0.71	108.26	6.46	1,674	3.79	0.21
Conglomerates	6.15	5.85	A3/BAA1	2.86	68.78	−5.14	109.22	6.32	17,133	38.79	2.16
Constr. machinery	8.36	8.07	A2/A3	1.66	66.92	−8.27	114.18	6.47	3,638	8.24	0.46
Packaging	6.43	6.58	A3/BAA1	3.00	74.97	2.95	108.12	6.31	1,431	3.24	0.18
Defense	8.12	7.04	A2/A3	2.84	73.69	3.61	107.43	6.51	5,582	12.64	0.70
Environmental	6.30	6.22	A1/A2	3.00	63.57	−13.50	107.73	6.13	4,154	9.40	0.52
Others	7.11	6.75	A2/A3	3.00	58.74	−13.61	106.69	6.20	3,882	8.79	0.49
Consumer cyclical	*6.83*	*6.51*	*A2/A3*	*2.47*	*63.29*	*−4.03*	*109.72*	*6.62*	*74,644*	*26.34*	*9.41*
Automotive	6.67	6.54	A1/A2	2.86	41.25	−13.22	118.00	6.33	16,489	22.09	2.08
Entertainment	9.39	8.95	BAA2/BAA3	1.32	87.11	−10.56	108.64	7.27	5,070	6.79	0.64
Gaming	5.15	4.97	BAA2/BAA3	3.00	80.00	7.66	97.34	6.72	544	0.73	0.07
Home construction	6.56	6.34	BAA3/BAA3	3.00	75.00	2.26	104.65	7.01	681	0.91	0.09
Lodging	5.62	5.44	BAA1/BAA2	3.55	70.85	1.11	103.42	6.66	1,762	2.36	0.22
Media—cable	7.68	7.07	BAA2/BAA3	2.18	91.42	7.84	108.66	7.15	7,243	9.70	0.91
Media —noncable	6.98	6.95	BAA1/BAA2	2.95	72.17	−16.06	110.66	6.62	10,659	14.28	1.34
Retailers	6.57	6.08	A1/A2	2.12	58.89	2.92	106.81	6.65	24,550	32.89	3.09
Services	7.46	6.50	AA3/A1	2.64	51.16	−4.42	105.37	6.23	1,964	2.63	0.25
Textile	5.60	5.62	BAA1/BAA2	3.00	73.08	25.40	106.33	5.91	1,753	2.35	0.22
Others	4.95	4.80	BAA1/BAA2	2.86	70.56	−7.66	106.68	6.29	3,929	5.26	0.50
Consumer Noncyclical	*6.31*	*5.98*	*A2/A3*	*2.91*	*61.00*	*−6.47*	*107.53*	*6.34*	*61,194*	*21.59*	*7.71*
Beverage	6.49	6.01	A1/A2	2.65	45.99	−12.41	108.77	6.09	10,693	17.47	1.35
Consumer products	7.97	7.36	AA2/AA3	2.73	40.66	−15.43	114.72	6.28	4,277	6.99	0.54
Food	6.84	6.42	A2/A3	2.95	64.03	−2.55	106.62	6.38	12,980	21.21	1.64
Health care	6.81	6.66	A2/A3	2.68	61.66	−20.66	107.92	6.26	10,559	17.25	1.33
Pharmaceuticals	6.91	6.77	AA2/AA3	3.00	42.02	−16.97	106.80	6.04	5,787	9.46	0.73
Supermarkets	4.92	4.87	BAA1/BAA2	2.50	69.46	−5.03	107.77	6.45	1,869	3.05	0.24
Tobacco	4.89	4.58	A3/BAA1	3.29	81.68	11.87	105.23	6.72	14,321	23.40	1.81
Others	4.02	3.90	AA2/AA3	3.00	59.65	−11.51	111.67	5.95	708	1.16	0.09
Energy	*6.33*	*5.96*	*A2/A3*	*2.68*	*50.28*	*−8.63*	*112.35*	*6.33*	*34,849*	*12.30*	*4.39*
Independent	6.01	5.92	A3/BAA1	3.00	66.16	−18.08	108.67	6.27	3,894	11.17	0.49
Integrated	6.31	5.91	A1/A2	2.60	44.46	−9.23	113.52	6.23	25,937	74.43	3.27
Oil field services	6.95	6.30	A3/BAA1	2.85	66.55	−5.34	111.49	6.40	1,813	5.20	0.23
Refining	5.87	5.64	BAA1/BAA2	2.76	65.77	−6.54	112.33	6.47	2,133	6.12	0.27
Others	7.71	7.39	BAA3/BAA3	3.00	75.00	30.30	101.10	8.57	1,072	3.08	0.14

EXHIBIT 52–5

(Continued)

	Duration to Worst	Mod. Adj Duration	Mkt Wgtd Rating	Invest Trend	Rel Mkt Risk	Rich/ Cheap (OAS bp)	Price	YTW	Market Value	% of Sector	% of Corp
Technology	6.75	6.61	A1/A2	2.70	61.34	–21.36	107.49	6.14	10,775	3.80	1.36
Transportation	7.03	6.75	A3/BAA1	2.39	69.46	–8.17	113.58	6.69	18,143	6.40	2.29
Airlines	7.43	7.16	BAA2/BAA3	1.70	86.26	–4.69	116.66	7.26	5,323	29.34	0.67
Railroads	7.50	7.07	A2/A3	2.84	62.64	–9.93	113.66	6.52	7,401	40.79	0.93
Services	6.00	5.89	A3/BAA1	2.44	62.28	–9.19	110.60	6.35	5,419	29.87	0.68
Others	0.00	0.00	0	0.00	0.00	0.00	0.00	0.00	0	0.00	0.00
Utilities	7.43	6.07	A2/A3	2.61	41.75	9.00	105.59	6.62	146,201	100.00	18.43
Electric	7.23	5.68	A2/A3	2.59	39.47	13.88	104.94	6.76	76,404	52.26	9.63
Telecommunication	8.03	6.64	AA3/A1	2.61	40.08	5.13	105.27	6.45	52,601	35.98	6.63
Natural gas	6.49	6.00	BAA1/BAA2	2.69	57.01	–0.83	109.66	6.50	17,196	11.76	2.17
Distributors	8.10	7.09	A3/BAA1	2.57	49.55	0.50	105.31	6.72	2,351	13.67	0.30
Pipelines	6.23	5.83	BAA1/BAA2	2.71	58.19	–1.04	110.38	6.47	14,844	86.33	1.87
Water	0.00	0.00	0	0.00	0.00	0.00	0.00	0.00	0	0.00	0.00
Finance	4.84	4.70	A1/A2	2.91	45.99	1.59	105.10	6.07	206,850	100.00	26.08
Banking	5.27	5.18	A2/A3	2.98	44.38	0.42	107.33	6.10	75,476	36.49	9.52
Brokerage	4.71	4.56	A2/A3	3.02	57.96	3.94	104.74	6.25	23,692	11.45	2.99
Financial Cos.	4.25	4.08	A1/A2	2.84	41.09	1.25	102.91	5.92	88,741	42.90	11.19
Captive	4.41	4.24	A1/A2	2.73	42.48	1.84	99.32	5.97	34,569	38.95	4.36
Noncaptive	4.14	3.98	AA3/A1	2.90	40.20	0.87	105.34	5.89	54,172	61.05	6.83
Consumer	4.30	4.23	A1/A2	2.88	42.23	–0.82	105.36	5.92	24,092	44.47	3.04
Diversified	4.01	3.77	AA3/A1	2.92	38.57	2.23	105.32	5.87	30,081	55.53	3.79
Insurance	6.36	6.08	A2/A3	2.74	57.84	5.37	107.55	6.38	16,038	7.75	2.02
Others	4.88	4.72	A3/BAA1	3.00	74.43	2.79	106.73	6.39	2,903	1.40	0.37
Yankees	6.66	6.48	AA3/A1	2.58	48.14	–8.57	108.67	6.26	156,772	100.00	19.76
Canadians	7.18	6.99	A1/A2	2.15	45.50	–14.86	111.74	6.29	50,720	32.35	6.39
Corporates	6.60	6.48	A1/A2	2.84	57.09	–3.54	107.78	6.34	57,800	36.87	7.29
Supranationals	7.09	6.70	AAA/AA1	2.26	11.11	–11.11	109.03	6.01	11,451	7.30	1.44
Sovereigns	5.92	5.71	AA3/A1	2.87	49.26	–6.99	105.94	6.16	36,802	23.47	4.64

Specifically, callable structures have become a rare species in the investment-grade corporate bond market as the positively–sloped U.S. yield curve shifted downward during the 1990s. In turn, the composition of the public U.S. corporate bond market has been converging toward its intermediate-bullet Eurobond cousin. Bullets climbed from 24 percent of Lehman's investment-grade index at the start of 1990 to 76 percent at year-end 1995. Over the same interval, callables declined at an astounding rate from 72 percent to an 18 percent index share. Sinking-fund structures, once the structural mainstay of natural-gas pipelines and many industrial sectors, are on the "structural endangered species list," with a drop from 32 percent of the public bond market in 1990 to only 4 percent in 1995. Despite a flurry of origination in 1994 and early 1995, put market share also has fallen from 5 percent in 1990 to 3 percent in 1995. Pure corporate zeros are in danger of extinction, with a fall from 4 percent market share in 1990 to negligible in 1995 (only 12 bonds left).

These percentages actually understate the diminution of embedded options in the global corporate market. Currently, corporate bond indices omit MTNs, 144As, and private placements. With most outstanding MTNs and 144As in bullet form and including the near unanimous use of the bullet form in the dollar and nondollar Eurobond markets, the embedded-option share of the global, fixed-rate corporate market is approximately half of its share in the U.S. public market. Overall, callable structures constituted only about 9 percent to 10 percent of the global corporate bond market in early 1996.

Bullets

As noted above, these plain-vanilla, optionless instruments have become more popular among issuers and investors. Front-end bullets (one- to five-year maturities) have great appeal to the growing cadre of barbellers (who use corporates at the front of the curve and Treasuries in longer maturities) and asset swappers (non-U.S. institutions who convert short bullets into floating-rate products). Intermediate corporates (5–12 maturities), especially in the 10-year neighborhood, have become the most popular segment of the U.S. investment-grade and high-yield corporate markets. Fifteen-year maturities are comparatively rare and have been favored by banks that occasionally uncover arbitrages in the asset-swap market. Because 15-year structures take five years to roll down a positively sloped yield curve, these structures frequently have held less appeal for many investors.

In contrast, 20-year structures are favored by many investors. Spreads for these structures are benched off the 30-year Treasury. With a positively sloped yield curve, the 20-year structure provides higher yield than a 10-year or 15-year security and less vulnerability (lower duration) than a 30-year security.

The 30-year maturity is the most popular form of long-dated security in the global market. But in 1992, 1993, and late 1995, there was a minor rush to issue 50-year (half-Centuries) and 100-year (Centuries) securities. These longer-dated securities provide investors with extra positive convexity for only a modest increase in modified-adjusted duration.

Callables

Typically, after a 5-year or 10-year wait, these structures are callable at the option of the issuer at any time. Call prices usually are set at a premium above par (par + the initial coupon) and decline linearly on an annual basis to par 5–10 years prior to final scheduled maturity. The ability to refinance debt in a potentially lower-interest rate environment is extremely valuable to issuers. Conversely, the risk of earlier-than-expected retirement of an above-current market coupon is bothersome to investors. To place callables, issuers pay investors an annual spread premium (about 30 bp to 40 bp for high-quality issuers) for being short the call option. This call premium varies through time. During 1993, some high-quality issuers sold new 30-year callable structures at market-clearing spread premiums of only about 20 bp over a bullet to the same maturity. In 1994, callable spread premiums rose with rates. By the second quarter of 1995, callable spread premiums for some high-quality issuers such as DuPont, Wal-Mart, and Wisconsin Power & Light had risen to 40 bp to 45 bp over a bullet to the same maturity.

Investors devote considerable attention to the callable component of their portfolio and to the comparative analysis of individual callable structures. At the portfolio level, corporate callables have gone out of fashion in the 1990s for four reasons. First, many corporate investors saw sizable portions of their callable holdings liquidated during the great-refunding blitz of 1991–1993. To the dismay of some investors, this forced reinvestment into lower-yielding securities and hurt annual portfolio yields. To protect against a reoccurrence of this "yield-reduction calamity," some corporate investors have steered toward a greater bullet concentration. Second, fixed income generalists had an even rougher time coping with the callability of MBS during the 1990s. These generalists often prefer to concentrate on credit risk alone in the corporate asset class and relegate the callability/negative convexity problem exclusively to MBS. Third, the rating agencies have warned U.S. insurers about excessive callability exposure. To stave off potential downgrades, some insurers already have retreated from MBS. Some insurers also may develop a shyness toward callable corporates. Fourth, the main manufacturers of new callable debt, electric utilities and telephones, are in the midst of enormous secular industry change. Based on growing fundamental uncertainty, some investors want to trim their exposure to any type of electric and telephone structure. Finally, and most important, callables have not fared well during the 1990s. On a duration-adjusted basis, callables outdistanced the Lehman investment-grade index in 1992 (14 bp) and 1994 (11 bp). Tethered to their redemption prices, callable prices were not able to rise as high or as quickly as their bullet counterparts in an environment of falling rates as in 1993 and 1995.

Like any sector or issuer out of fashion, callable structures eventually will rebound. If interest rates remain static or reverse, the current class of outstanding callable corporates (typically trading in the neighborhood of their call prices) will outperform the overall corporate bond market. Unfortunately, if interest rates descend rapidly, as was the case during the second quarter of 1995, callable structures will trail bullets.

In view of their growing scarcity value alone, diversified investors should consider at least a neutral weighting to callable corporate structures.

As discussed below (Corporate Option Valuation Analysis) the comparative analysis of callable structures often consists exclusively of an OAS calculation. But OAS calculations vary widely, depending on the selection of the volatility parameter and the use of an issuer-specific curve or Treasury curve. For example, in

February 1996, the OAS of Consolidated Edison $7^1/_2$s of 2023, callable in 2003, was either 102 bp with a Treasury curve input or –2 bp with an issuer-bullet curve input. In any case, as also discussed below, ex ante OAS may not be helpful in predicting ex post total return. In addition to OAS, investors should examine the nominal spread premium for the option over the underlying bullet and review weighted-average horizon returns under multiple scenarios. For example, Con Ed $7^1/_2$s were trafficking at 121 bp in early 1996 compared to 85 bp for an estimated Con Ed bullet to 2023. For being vulnerable to call exercise beginning seven years out, investors could add an annual spread premium of approximately 36 bp. For an A1/A+ issuer, this premium appeared attractive. Using a six-month horizon, 12 percent volatility, five yield-curve scenarios from down 100 bp to up 100 bp, and assuming equal probability of horizon outcome, a weighted-average horizon return of 3.80 percent can be calculated for this Con Ed security.

Rather than merely looking at OAS in callable analysis, investors should compare the nominal spread premium over the underlying bullet and weighted-average horizon return of baskets of callable and bullet securities to determine relative value. Although OAS is less helpful in the corporate bond market, option-valuation models remain essential to the calculation of more realistic horizon prices.

Sinking Funds

This structure allows an issuer to execute a series of partial calls (annually or semi-annually) prior to maturity. There is also usually a provision to retire an additional portion of the issue on the sinking fund date (accelleration option), typically ranging from one to two times the mandatory sinking fund obligation. Considering their advantages as a liability-management tool, the greater decline in sinking-fund origination relative to callables during the 1990s is somewhat puzzling. For investors, sinking fund structures are extremely valuable during periods of rising interest rates. Sinkers restrain the potential price fall if rates climb because issuers must execute a partial par call. Like callables, sinkers do not fully benefit as much as bullets when rates fall. During the 1990s, sinkers outperformed the Lehman investment-grade index on a duration-adjusted basis in 1992 (18 bp) and led the investment-grade market when rates soared in 1994 (50 bp). Conversely, with rate declines, sinker performance trailed the overall market during the rest of the 1990s.

Putables

Put structures are simpler than callables. Unlike American-option callables (which allow call at any time at the designated call price after expiration of the noncallable/nonredemption period), puts typically feature a single one-time, one-date put option (European option). Less frequently, put bonds offer a second or third put option. With falling rates, issuers have shied away from new put structures during the 1990s. Rather than run the risk of refunding the put bond in 5 years or 10 years at a higher cost, many issuers would prefer to pay an extra 10 bp to 20 bp for the privilege of issuing a longer-term liability. Put structures provide investors with a partial defense against sharp increases in interest rates. The price of a put structure cannot fall as quickly or as far below par as a bullet; after all, the investor can return the security to the issuer at par on the put date.

Despite the greater simplicity of put bonds, there is a seemingly never-ending debate about their proper evaluation. There are two basic schools. Neither methodology should be used exclusively; both approaches have merit. First, "volatility traders" insist on the merits of buying puts with low volatilities. This school believes that the ultimate arrival of higher volatility parameters will lead to outperformance. Unfortunately, low-volatility parameters (often in the 3 percent to 6 percent range) are associated with premium put structures with prices way above par. Effectively, these structures are so far "out of the money" that a very low likelihood of put exercise exists. In turn, the put option has very little value and its low-implied volatility is unlikely to budge much.

The second put school examines the "yield sacrifice" compared to bullets and views the put option as an "extension option." For example, a new 10-year security putable in five years will trade at a tighter spread off the 5-year Treasury and at a tighter spread than a regular 5-year security of the same issuer. If the yield sacrifice seems slight (i.e., 10 bp to 20 bp), this school would consider the structure attractive given the investor's ability to roll into another 5-year structure at the end of five years.

Step-Ups

After a designated interval, the coupon of an issue "steps up" to a higher rate. Usually, the issuer also has the option to retire the security at par on the coupon step-up rather than incur the additional interest expense. These structures have become more popular with agency issuers and often are intended for smaller institutional and retail investors seeking to maximize short-term yield. Step-ups have been seldom used in the investment-grade corporate market. But step-ups are a regular feature of the high-yield market (typically a zero coupon for several years, followed by the arrival of a cash coupon). Step-up evaluation is nearly identical to callable analysis. If rates rise, then the structure will remain outstanding, and investors will gain an extra coupon flow after the step-up date. If rates fall, this structure has a high probability of retirement.

Zeros

As noted above, these structures have nearly vanished from the corporate bond market. Unless the tax code changes, their revival seems unlikely during the remainder of the 1990s. Most corporate investors, especially at taxable institutions, prefer real semiannual or annual cash flows. And duration-hungry investors can turn to long-dated, cash-paying bullets.

Globals

An invention of the 1990s, "global" securities are underwritten simultaneously in the North American, European, and Asian capital markets. To appeal to non-U.S. investors, credit quality is very high, usually single-A or better. And to ensure liquidity, issue size typically begins at $500 million, with many issues above $1.0 billion.

By the beginning of 1996, global corporate bonds had risen to 5.3 percent of Lehman's investment-grade, 24.8 percent of the Yankee, and 15.3 percent of the Eurobond indices. Assuming constant market growth rates, global index share on December 31, 2000 may represent 11.4 percent of investment-grade corporates, 48.8 percent of Yankees, and 32 percent of Eurobonds. As global market share climbs, portfolio exclusion will become increasingly difficult for all classes of investors.

Given the lower underwriting costs and capability to tap investors throughout the world at the time of issuance, more U.S. and non-U.S. corporate issuers will utilize global issuance to shave costs. Most globals will be priced at tighter spreads than Yankees for the same issuer thanks to a broader universe of potential buyers and the influence of conservative investors who assign a premium to liquidity.

Global issuance will branch out beyond sovereigns. Among the 29 outstanding issues simultaneously warehoused in the investment-grade and Eurobond indices, only five currently are pure corporate issuers.

On a duration-adjusted basis versus Aa corporates, Globals outperformed in 1993, 1994, and early 1996. Each new issue alters the composition of indices. This forces investors with allocation targets (all indexers and most total-return managers) to consider portfolio adjustments.

Rule 144As

Because of their lower administrative costs, these are quasi-private placements that have gained favor among non-U.S. issuers, high-yield borrowers, and U.S. insurers issuing surplus notes. There is little difference between 144As and public corporates. New-issue announcements, subsequent visibility, and pricing are indistinguishable from their public counterparts. Most corporate investors are now authorized to include 144As in their portfolios.

Further boosting their market visibility for issuers and investors, 144As may join the corporate bond indices at the end of 1996. Historically, the exclusion of all privates from corporate indices made sense. Many total-return, state pension fund, and mutual-fund managers were unable to use privates in accordance with their investment policies. Corporate index producers could not gather information on every new private placement on a timely basis. Pricing proved an even greater obstacle in this less-liquid market.

Classic private placement indices arrived in July 1996. Portfolio management targets and market analysis, which fail to account for this growing subset of the global corporate market, will become increasingly flawed over time.

Floating-Rate Notes

The floating-rate note market, populated by securities whose coupons reset after quarterly or semiannual intervals at some specified spread over a reference rate such as LIBOR, Prime, Fed Funds, or three-month Treasury bills, remains the main hunting ground for U.S. and non-U.S. banks in the corporate bond market. Consistent with stable-to-improved credit quality for most U.S. and non-U.S. banks over the past five years (except for Japan and France) and concurrent with limited loan growth at many banks in Asia and Europe (a function of economic malaise, cash-rich corporate borrowers, and over-capitalized banks), global floater demand has outstripped floater supply. With short-term rates descending in the mid-1990s, a resurgence in floater supply does not appear in the offing until the global rate cycle reverses course. Many borrowers prefer to lock in comparatively low fixed rates available in multiple currencies. Moreover, floater redemptions/maturities rose in 1996. Through the asset-swap market, floater demand also has contributed to the tremendous spread compression at the front end of the fixed-rate corporate curve.

For pure total-return investors, the floating-rate market holds greater appeal when short-term rates begin to climb. As shown during 1994, floating-rate vehicles provided better total returns than even short-dated fixed rate product. And as shown during 1989–1990, floater valuations become extremely attractive during periods of global economic weakness. The perception of credit risk varies throughout the world. And the estimation and portfolio tolerance of default risk covers a wide global range. Accordingly given its quasi-money market nature, the floater market is hypersensitive to credit risk. For total-return investors with horizons beyond a quarter, these episodic eruptions of distress in the floater market typically provide some of the best bargains in the global corporate market.

Corporate Option Valuation Analysis

All fixed-income investors should have a firm grasp of the strengths and weakness of corporate option-valuation models.

Volatility Parameters

A decade after the introduction of option-valuation models to corporate structures, there is still no consensus on the proper selection of the volatility parameter. In looking at the A1/A+ Consolidated Edison $7^1/_2$s of 2023, callable in 2003, trading at 121 bp over the long bond, investors must select a volatility parameter. In the late 1980s and early 1990s, the market convention was to select a range of volatilities (typically 8 percent, 10 percent, and 12 percent) to calculate the embedded option value and OAS. Beginning in the early 1990s, volatility fashion partially switched to using daily implied volatilities imported from the Treasury curve or the swaps/caps markets. In our view, corporate volatilities should be less than Treasury volatilities. In reality, the single factor, corporate option-valuation model is being asked to undertake double duty: account for curve and for spread volatility in valuing an option. Both curve and spread movements will influence the likelihood of option exercise. Treasury curve volatility is much higher than corporate spread volatility. During the mid-1990s, the combination of spread volatility (either range or standard deviation over some interval) in the 5 percent to 6 percent area for high-quality corporates and long Treasury volatility in the 12 percent to 20 percent area points to a reasonable range of about 10 percent to 13 percent for the corporate volatility parameter. As a check, implied volatilities can be derived for any corporate security. Like in the mid-1980s, the best advice is to test the evaluation of the corporate option under a range of volatility assumptions.

Treasury Curve versus Issuer-Specific Curve

There is also a lack of market consensus on the curve parameter, when calculating option-adjusted spreads. Some practitioners only use the current Treasury curve. The Treasury curve has the advantage of ready availability and the production of a larger OAS. Other practitioners prefer an issuer specific curve. The use of issuer-specific curves facilitates the comparison of corporate securities of varying credit qualities. But this technique requires the correct input of an issuer bullet curve and generates lower OASs, which may not appeal to some buyers of OAS. Despite the extra effort, issuer-specific curves produce more impartial and realistic OASs. And as discussed above under callable structures, issuer-specific curves should be referenced in studying option values.

Role of "OAS Analysis" in Corporate Relative-Value Analysis

In the corporate bond market, some practitioners appear to confuse option valuation with "relative-value analysis." Since the introduction of option valuation (usually expressed in terms of option-adjusted spread [OAS]) in the mid-1980s, it has been fashionable in some circles to advocate OAS maximization as a path to superior total return in the corporate bond market. Usually, such OAS advocates hope to find a single numerical shortcut that will eliminate the need to be conversant with the issuer's fundamentals and issue's technicals. Unfortunately, OAS is not that magical shortcut to relative value.

At first, the newness of this technology and the widespread inability to back-test over an extended period contributed to the presumed efficacy of OAS maximization as a valid portfolio strategy. But in the corporate bond market, ex ante OAS rankings of securities do not necessarily correlate well with ex post total return rankings.

As shown in Exhibit 52–6, baskets of structurally homogeneous utility securities were ranked by OAS at the end of 1987 and compared to subsequent returns over the next five years. The correlations were very weak and exhibited a negative tendency. In other words, OAS minimization proved more effective than OAS maximization.

This result should not be a total surprise. A one-factor model of interest rates should have limited efficacy in attempting to cope simultaneously with changes in three variables: curve, volatility, and credit spreads. Each of these factors changes through time. Most practitioners now acknowledge that forward rates are not necessarily a good predictor of future interest rates. Just as forward rates and inherent credit quality vary, OAS rankings also will shift through time.

E X H I B I T   52–6

Ex Ante OAS Rankings vs. Ex Post Total Return Rankings

			Cumulative Total Return Analysis from January 1, 1988											
Issuer	**Coupon**	**Maturity**	**1-Year**	**Rank**	**2-Year**	**Rank**	**3-Year**	**Rank**	**4-Year**	**Rank**	**5-Year**	**Rank**		
Aa's														
Duke Power	9.000	5/1/16	9.26%	3	24.31%	3	30.50%	7	51.51%	3	62.27%	3		
Potomac Elec Power	9.250	3/1/16	9.76	2	25.75	1	31.15	5	50.55	6	61.37	6		
Florida Power + Light	9.125	5/1/16	9.18	5	23.97	5	30.83	6	50.70	5	61.54	5		
Delmarva Power + Light	9.250	6/1/15	8.34	7	23.65	7	31.15	4	49.44	7	Called			
Southern Calif Edison	9.250	3/1/16	9.77	1	24.16	4	32.94	1	52.79	1	61.93%	4		
Pub Svc Electric + Gas	9.125	3/1/16	9.18	4	24.46	2	31.30	3	50.76	4	62.86	1		
Pub Svc Co of Oklahoma	9.000	5/1/16	8.78	6	23.75	6	31.98	2	51.59	2	62.78	2		
A's														
Atlantic City Electric	8.875	5/1/16	8.49%	11	23.03%	11	30.66%	10	51.62%	11	63.48%	9		
Alabama Power	9.375	5/1/16	10.36	7	25.38	6	31.50	8	53.12	7	62.20	11		
Carolina Power + Light	8.875	3/1/16	9.43	10	24.55	8	33.44	3	52.13	10	64.00	8		
Pennsylvania Pwr + Light	9.000	4/1/16	10.97	4	25.76	5	32.45	5	54.22	6	64.64	6		
Virginia Electric Power	8.500	4/1/16	9.56	8	24.45	9	30.67	9	52.41	9	62.90	10		
South Carolina E + G	8.750	2/1/17	10.75	5	24.86	7	32.84	4	52.98	8	64.82	5		
Houston Lighting + Power	9.000	3/1/17	9.55	9	24.19	10	32.44	6	54.49	5	64.53	7		
Pacific Gas + Electric	8.625	5/1/19	10.64	6	27.36	3	31.66	7	54.56	4	65.15	4		
Illinois Power	9.375	9/1/16	12.95	1	27.70	2	30.02	11	55.81	3	67.36	2		
Commonwealth Edison	9.125	4/1/15	12.89	2	29.95	1	36.26	1	59.95	1	66.93	3		
Texas Utilities Ele Co	9.375	3/1/16	12.17	3	27.12	4	35.37	2	57.11	2	69.46	1		
Baa's														
Cincinnati Gas + Elec	9.250	4/1/16	10.72%	8	26.26%	7	32.76%	6	51.74%	6	65.22%	7		
New York State Elec Gas	9.250	4/1/16	14.07	3	27.97	4	31.47	8	53.39	5	66.58	6		
Northern Indiana Pub Ser	9.250	12/1/16	12.14	6	27.24	6	34.31	4	54.00	4	67.20	5		
Pub Svc Co Of Indiana	9.600	8/1/05	14.65	1	27.34	5	33.96	5	51.20	8	Called			
Arizona Public Service	9.000	2/1/17	12.35	4	21.18	8	31.49	7	51.23	7	69.63%	2		
Duquesne Light	9.500	2/1/16	14.20	2	30.63	1	35.86	3	58.34	2	69.24	4		
Cleveland Electric Illum	9.375	3/1/17	11.71	7	29.32	2	36.78	2	57.84	3	64.92	1		
Detroit Edison	9.375	4/15/16	12.18	5	29.03	3	37.27	1	60.73	1	69.49	3		
TELCO's														
New Jersey Bell	9.375	2/15/26	9.55%	4	24.90%	10	32.00%	3	52.22%	7	Called			
New England Tel	9.000	3/1/26	8.74	11	24.78	11	30.03	11	50.64	12	61.02%	8		
Mountain States Tel	9.000	4/1/26	9.00	9	25.26	6	31.23	6	52.01	9	62.70	3		
Illinois Bell Tel	8.500	4/22/26	8.33	12	25.54	5	30.34	10	51.60	10	60.56	9		
General Tel (Ca)	9.375	6/15/26	9.88	3	25.17	7	32.11	2	51.22	11	60.35	11		
Southern Bell Tel	8.625	9/1/26	10.49	2	26.67	1	33.03	1	52.80	3	63.58	2		
New York Tel	5.625	5/15/24	5.76	13	17.41	13	18.83	13	37.46	13	44.67	12		
Bell Tell of Pa	8.750	4/1/26	9.07	8	25.02	9	30.70	7	52.08	8	61.55	6		
Pacific Bell	8.625	4/15/23	8.76	10	24.76	12	30.70	8	52.44	6	60.45	10		
American Tel & Tel	8.625	4/1/26	9.44	6	26.17	3	29.97	12	53.29	2	63.75	1		
S'western Bell Tel	8.625	4/15/20	9.34	7	25.61	4	30.63	9	52.66	4	61.09	7		
General Tel (Northwest)	8.750	4/15/16	9.49	5	25.07	8	31.50	5	52.59	5	61.98	5		
GTE Corp	9.125	12/1/16	11.07	1	26.34	2	31.86	4	53.46	1	62.36	4		

EXHIBIT 52–6

(Continued)

	OAS	Rank	1988	Rank	1989	Rank	1990	Rank	1991	Rank	1992	Rank
							Annual Total Return Analysis from January 1, 1988					
Aa's												
Duke Power	18	1	9.26%	3.00	15.03%	4	6.36%	6	20.61%	1	10.50%	5
Potomac Elec Power	18	2	9.76	2	15.95	1	5.67	7	19.07	6	10.61	3
Florida Power + Light	17	3	9.18	5	14.79	6	6.98	5	19.51	2	10.60	4
Delmarva Power + Light	17	4	8.34	7.00	15.37	2	7.58	3	18.00	7	Called	
Southern Calif Edison	17	5	9.77	1.00	14.37	7	8.80	1	19.33	3	9.13	6
Pub Svc Electric + Gas	16	6	9.18	4.00	15.27	3	6.98	4	19.07	5	11.70	1
Pub Svc Co of Oklahoma	15	7	8.78	6.00	14.98	5	8.27	2	19.11	4	10.87	2
A's												
Atlantic City Electric	16	1	8.49%	11.00	14.55%	9	7.70%	5	20.49%	9	11.42%	3
Alabama Power	16	2	10.36	7.00	14.96	4	6.33	9	21.22	5	9.09	10
Carolina Power + Light	14	3	9.43	10.00	15.09	3	8.90	1	18.07	11	11.42	2
Pennsylvania Pwr + Light	13	4	10.97	4.00	14.68	7	6.86	6	21.10	6	10.18	7
Virginia Electric Power	12	5	9.56	8.00	14.82	5	6.38	8	21.09	7	10.17	8
South Carolina E + G	12	6	10.75	5.00	14.00	11	8.03	4	19.44	10	11.34	4
Houston Lighting + Power	11	7	9.55	9.00	14.61	8	8.30	3	21.37	4	9.86	9
Pacific Gas + Electric	11	8	10.64	6.00	16.56	2	4.70	10	22.12	3	10.24	6
Illinois Power	10	9	12.95	1.00	14.57	10	2.90	11	25.49	1	11.19	5
Commonwealth Edison	8	10	12.89	2.00	16.78	1	6.60	7	22.50	2	7.36	11
Texas Utilities Ele Co	8	11	12.17	3.00	14.81	6	8.33	2	20.91	8	11.84	1
Baa's												
Cincinnati Gas + Elec	13	1	10.72%	8.00	15.45%	4	6.70%	6	18.51%	7	12.91%	2
New York State Elec Gas	12	2	14.07	3.00	13.68	6	4.00	8	21.46	3	12.62	3
Northern Indiana Pub Ser	11	3	12.14	6.00	14.94	5	7.25	4	19.05	6	12.60	4
Pub Svc Co Of Indiana	10	4	14.65	1.00	12.55	7	6.84	5	16.87	8	Called	
Arizona Public Service	9	5	12.35	4.00	8.83	8	10.27	1	19.27	5	17.14%	1
Duquesne Light	9	6	14.20	2.00	16.12	3	5.68	7	21.58	2	10.64	5
Cleveland Electric Illum	8	7	11.71	7.00	17.43	1	7.64	3	20.13	4	7.45	7
Detroit Edison	8	8	12.18	5.00	16.65	2	8.35	2	22.27	1	8.86	6
TELCO's												
New Jersey Bell	24	1	9.55%	4	15.34%	11	7.24%	1	19.81%	10	Called	
New England Tel	19	2	8.74	11	16.07	5	5.48	9	20.27	9	10.18%	3
Mountain States Tel	19	3	9.00	9	16.26	3	6.18	5	20.30	8	10.44	1
Illinois Bell Tel	18	4	8.33	12	17.23	1	5.08	11	20.67	6	8.87	9
General Tel (Ca)	18	5	9.88	3	15.26	10	7.08	2	18.74	12	9.14	7
Southern Bell Tel	17	6	10.49	2	16.04	6	6.56	4	19.02	11	10.42	2
New York Tel	17	7	5.76	13	11.64	13	1.66	13	18.39	13	6.99	12
Bell Tell of Pa	17	8	9.07	8	15.92	8	5.90	7	20.85	5	9.34	5
Pacific Bell	16	9	8.76	10	15.99	7	6.13	6	21.14	3	8.08	11
American Tel & Tel	16	10	9.44	6	16.66	2	4.19	12	22.75	1	10.14	4
S'western Bell Tel	15	11	9.34	7	16.21	4	5.30	10	21.43	2	8.44	10
General Tel (Northwest)	14	12	9.49	5	15.53	9	6.60	3	20.47	7	9.27	6
GTE Corp	11	13	11.07	1	15.15	12	5.79	8	21.06	4	8.92	8

Source: Lehman Brothers Fixed Income Research.

EXHIBIT 52–7

Correlation Matrix of Cumulative and Annual Total
Return Rankings and OAS Results

**Correlation Matrix of Cumulative Total Return Rankings
and OAS Results**

Electrics	1-Year	2-Year	3-Year	4-Year	5-Year
Aa	0.32	0.36	0.86	−0.39	−0.63
A	−0.75	−0.69	−0.39	−0.89	−0.88
BBB	−0.12	−0.60	−0.79	−0.62	−0.85
Telephones	−0.30	−0.32	0.07	−0.66	−0.25

**Correlation Matrix of Annual Total Return Rankings and
OAS Results**

Electrics	1988	1989	1990	1991	1992
Aa	0.32	0.29	−0.79	−0.71	−0.50
A	−0.75	−0.12	0.09	−0.51	0.02
BBB	−0.12	−0.52	−0.57	−0.62	0.70
Telephones	−0.30	0.16	0.25	−0.60	0.39

Source: Lehman Brothers Fixed Income Research.

This test of OAS efficacy in the corporate market has some admitted flaws. It is somewhat unfair to expect OAS rankings at one point in time to map total returns for the next five years. Moreover, the option models of 1987 were not as refined as the models of the mid-1990s. Other models and other corporate sectors were also unsuccessful in predicting subsequent total return. Accordingly, investors should exercise caution in using OAS as a guide to expected total return. A one-factor model does not offer much help in predicting spread/return volatility in the subsequent year or two.

Although the OAS output from an option-valuation model is not necessarily a useful guide to relative value in the corporate bond market, option-valuation models are essential to the development of better horizon prices and horizon total returns for corporate securities under multiple scenarios. Rather than relying on OAS, investors should use multiple-horizon analysis to help judge relative value among corporate securities.

Multifactor option valuation will eventually mitigate these weaknesses. In the interim, investors are forced to rely on heuristic techniques such as variation of issuer-specific spread curves to gauge modified-adjusted duration, convexity, and OAS.

Corporate Curve Analysis

The rapid development of credit derivatives in the mid-1990s has inspired a groundswell of academic interest in the development of more rigorous techniques to analyze the term structure of corporate spread curves. Conversely, the fledgling credit-derivative business may not have taken off by now without the earlier efforts of academics studying the dynamics of corporate curves. More practically, spread compression in the mid-1990s and the continued likelihood of low-spread volatility have also boosted investor interest in term-structure analysis of corporate-spread curves. In an attempt to locate the "cheapest" areas of the corporate curve, which presumably will provide the greatest subsequent total return over subsequent short-term intervals, some total-return investors have deployed their government-curve tools in the corporate bond market. This search for corporate-curve cheapness seems to be less prevalent among mutual funds (who often have maturity constraints, no holdings greater than 10 years in some funds) and asset/liability managers (insurers and pension funds, who have long horizons). The asset/liability investor class, the real controllers of market valuation for investment-grade corporates, appears content to balance yield optimization with targeted credit-risk tolerances and durations. Moreover, even if such long-term investors seek to emulate the market nimbleness of short-term total-return maximizers, the constraining combination of portfolio size, accounting adjustments, and transactions costs restrain their ability to curve hopscotch within the corporate market.

For the less-constrained, total-return manager, there are numerous techniques to evaluate corporate spreads and the shape of generic and individual issuer curves. Some of these techniques (mean-reversion analysis, quality spreads, and percent yield spreads) were discussed under spread analysis. Other techniques include the calculation of spread ranges by credit-quality category (i.e., maximum/minimum range for long AA corporates 1945–1995) and the standard deviation of spreads for sectors and issues. In turn, both generic and specific credit term structures can by analyzed by movement, range, and standard deviation analysis.

There also has been growing interest in the interaction between the benchmark Treasury curve and the corporate spread curve. In early 1994, some market observers claimed that the flattening of the benchmark curve (i.e., between 10-year and 30-year Treasuries) implied a steepening of generic and individual issuer yield curves between the same curve points. Corporate investors presumably would demand a higher risk premium (more long spread) to extend from 10 years to 30 years with a flatter underlying yield curve. Otherwise, investors should accept a similar spread for less interest-rate risk in a 10-year maturity. Conversely, a steepening of the yield curve between 10 years and 30 years supposedly would lead to a flattening of corporate curves between these two points. In this case, some of the extra compensation for duration extension was provided by the benchmark curve. Moreover, greater investor preference for higher yield would bid down 30-year corporate spreads.

These premises about the interaction between the benchmark and corporate curves were not borne out during 1994 and 1995. In contrast to the expectations of some investors and in the midst of the highest percentage change in rates in six decades during 1994, the generic corporate spread curve of the 20-largest issuers in the investment-grade corporate bond market proved highly inelastic to changes in the shape and altitude of the benchmark curve.

Why such inelasticity? First, there has been more rapid growth of mutual fund and total-return barbellers than longer-term, insurance and pension fund managers. The barbell cohort seldom modifies investment policy to surf among ripples in the underlying benchmark curve. Second, spread duration has become a more popular methodology to measure risk. In the current compressed spread milieu, the arrival of a spread wave would prove more injurious to portfolio performance for holders of long corporates. Third, trading conventions limit movements of corporate spreads. Some dealers configure the corporate trading function by industry grouping (i.e., all utilities, all industrials), some prefer curve segmentations (i.e., all longs, all intermediates, and all shorts), and some use a blend of the industry grouping/curve segmentation. The net effect is that the main areas of the corporate curve (short, intermediate, and long) tend to trade in their own universes over short intervals. Although arbitrage opportunities may seem evident, the lack of subsequent performance gratification often reinforces the underlying spread indifference to gyrations along the entire benchmark curve.

Corporate portfolio managers should reconsider the efficacy of portfolio tactics tied to gyrations in the benchmark curve. During 1994 and 1995, these reservations were well-founded. If the corporate market continues to operate within a tight spread, low-volatility framework, dealers and investors will be forced to devote more effort to extract relative value from the interaction between corporate spread curves and the benchmark-Treasury curves. But it is difficult to predict which strategies will produce the optimal payoffs for investors. Seasonality, supply, recessions, and individual issuer developments, such as event risk, will override the efficacy of generic curve strategies.

Credit Analysis: Cornerstone of Corporate Portfolio Analysis

Not surprisingly for this quasi-equity asset class, superior credit analysis has been and will remain the most important determinant of the relative performance of corporate bond portfolios. For too many years, investors and dealers have had to relearn the hard way that credit analysis has no shortcuts or model magic. Specifically, variables such as interest-rate volatility and binomial processes imported from option-valuation techniques are not especially helpful in ranking the expected performance of a pool of individual credits such as British Gas, Commonwealth Edison, Motorola, Pohang Iron & Steel, and Tenneco.

Credit analysis is both nonglamorous and arduous for many top-down port-folio managers and strategists, who focus primarily on macro variables. Genuine credit analysis encompasses actually studying issuers' financial statements, inter-viewing issuers' management, evaluating industry issues, reading indentures and charters, and developing an awareness of (not necessarily concurrence with) the views of the rating agencies about various industries and issuers.

Aside from the explicit incorporation of equity-market signals in analysis (already a standard in the high-yield market), the art of analyzing an individual credit is unlikely to change substantively during the next decade. No new finan-cial ratios are expected that will enhance the predictive capabilities of analysts and portfolio managers. The rigor of the analysis, especially at institutions at-tempting to outperform others with similar portfolio objectives and constraints, should vastly improve. Instead of merely relying on the rating agencies and a cur-sory glance at the historic financial ratios, top-notch corporate bond analysts will develop their own operating and financial forecasts in the same manner as their equity and high-yield analytical colleagues.

Unfortunately, the advantages of such analytical rigor may clash with the rapid expansion of the universe of global bond credits. At the beginning of 1996, there were 4,000 different credits in the dollar-denominated corporate bond mar-ket. With continued privatization of state enterprises, new entrants to the high-yield club, and the rapid growth of the developing markets, the global roster of issuers could reach 5,000 by 2000.

Historically, many institutional participants in the corporate market have underallocated resources to credit evaluation. Often, credit positions are viewed as a stepping-stone to portfolio management. Sometimes, portfolio managers rel-egate their responsibility to the rating agencies and to sell-side analysts. Such ab-dication of credit responsibilities will eventually undermine portfolio success. Credit calamities are regular events. Ultimately, such credit calamities neutralize the benefits of allocations to the riskier corporate asset class. Hopefully, the cor-porate marketplace will not soon forget the painful lessons of the great credit crunch of the late 1980s and early 1990s. Given the increasing competitiveness of the asset-management business, the goal of consistent returns will demand the greater use of talented credit professionals.

Asset Allocation/Sector Rotation

Sector rotation strategies have long been popular with equity investors. During the fourth quarter of 1995, a proclaimed change in sector leadership from tech-nology (for a day or two, anyway) and financial institutions toward more defen-sive, noncyclical sectors helped power the U.S. equity market to multiple new highs.

In the corporate bond market, "macro" sector rotation strategies also have a long history. During the past two decades, there have been major shifts in in-vestor sentiment toward the four major sectors: utilities (wariness of nuclear exposure in the early to mid-1980s); financial institutions (concern about asset quality in the late 1980s and early 1990s); industrials (event risk in the late 1980s and recession vulnerability during 1990–1992); and Yankees (periodic wariness about the implications of sovereignty for Quebec and political risk for sovereigns).

But compared to the equity market, the effectiveness of corporate micro-sector asset allocation recommendations, as illustrated in Exhibit 52–8, and rotation strategies have been poorly researched and documented because of a lack of data. Ibbotson data start in 1926 but do not have any sector detail. Moody's and S&P have yield averages (not total returns) for Aaa, Aa, A, and Baa categories back to the Great Depression in the 1930s, but only for the industrial and utility sectors. Lehman Brothers introduced monthly total returns for utilities, industrials, and financial institutions in 1973 and added Yankees in 1976, but an unbundling into detailed subsectors was not available until 1993.

With the extension of detailed sector analysis back to 1989, researchers now have only a single economic/credit cycle to study the efficacy of sector rotation strategies. For example during 1995, the timing and efficacy of a rotation from cyclical to noncyclical sectors became a very popular strategic question for corporate investors, especially in the high-yield market.

Based on analysis of these data, the investment-grade corporate market was a poor predictor of the "official" recession from July 1990 through March 31, 1991. During the nine months prior to the real start of recession, the performance of supposed defensive sectors was ambiguous relative to more cyclical sectors. Effectively, corporate investors did not consistently gain from a defensive tilt well ahead of recession.

Despite their greater vulnerability, industrials posted higher returns than overall corporates in seven of the nine months (October 1989 through June 1990) leading to recession and for the first three months of recession (July through August 1990). During recession, industrial performance was sloppier, with outperformance in only four of nine months. And the meager economic recovery of 1991 tempered subsequent industrial performance to only four outperformance months of nine.

The long-held notion of utilities and Yankees as defensive sectors needs to be reexamined in the corporate bond market. Overall, utilities fared better prior to (five months) and after recession (five months) than during recession (four months). Canadians and Yankee corporates were outdistanced by supranationals and sovereigns during this period.

Asset allocation/sector rotation strategies also beg the nature/nurture question of corporate portfolio management: What's more important for performance, sector selection or issuer selection?

There is no single answer. The efficacy of sector selection versus issuer selection on relative performance depends on portfolio objectives/constraints and varies over time with the stage of the economic/credit cycle. For example, from 1991 through 1993, sector selection generally contributed more as the global economy regained momentum. With increased spread compression in the mid-1990s, optimal issuer selection became more important.

In an attempt to empirically respond to this question, the "maximum potential performance" of an investment-grade corporate portfolio versus the Lehman index was measured from 1976 through January 31, 1996. Optimal allocation was defined as a 50 percent overweighting to the best performing of four main sectors (financial institutions, industrials, utilities, and Yankees), a 25 percent overweighting to the second best performing sector, a 25 percent underweighting to the third best sector, and a 50 percent underweighting to the worst performing sector.

Given these assumptions, optimal portfolio allocation would have delivered an average annual gain of 145 bp over the Lehman index during the past 20 years. The asset allocation advantage seems to have dissipated over the past half decade. After delivering a 172 bp gain over the index in 1990, this advantage has contracted to only 80 bp in 1995. The corporate investment-grade market has become more efficient. The rating agencies have become more proactive. There are more sell-side and buy-side analysts. Most importantly, the corporate market has been operating at the crest of the economic/credit cycle. In turn, performance differentiation has become more difficult.

Using a more detailed analysis of 45 industry sectors for 1995 and January 1996, the case for asset allocation gains strength. On a cumulative basis over 13 months, optimal asset allocation among 45 sectors generated a 290 bp gain.

This methodology is imperfect. The drag of transaction costs would have tempered the "maximum potential realized return." But this realized return still would have been positive.

Based on market surveys, many corporate investors pay less attention to sector allocation than their equity counterparts. Corporate debt investors will converge to equity-market allocation styles. In the increasingly competitive asset management business, investors need to examine and to act upon every potential edge.

Additional Portfolio Tactics

Using the analytical techniques of choice, investors hunt for the optimal securities in the primary and secondary corporate markets. Performance is usually defined in reference to a public index like the Lehman Aggregate index or the government/corporate index. Sometimes, clients and sponsors will accept a customized index. Often, the best technique of all to outperform an index is to use securities outside an index. For example, investor use preferred stock, MTNs, private placements, 144As, nondollar corporates swapped into dollars, floaters, and credit derivatives to achieve their goals. The following examples illustrate the best areas for investors to search for incremental portfolio value.

Geographic/Yield Extension

As issuers diversify internationally, global fixed income portfolio diversification has accelerated. This diversification also has been driven by the quest to meet yield/return targets in a spread-compressed market. U.S. investors have become more interested in the "same name/more spread trade." For example, in February 1996, U.S. investors could have purchased Ford $6^{1}/_{2}$s of 2000 (a Dragon issue) at a five-bp spread premium over five-year Ford paper trading in the U.S. market. U.S. investors also have added more non-U.S. credit to their portfolios, such as a triple-A equivalent Nestle $7^3/_8$s of 2005 trading at 36 bp in February 1996. More slowly, non-U.S. investors have stepped up their involvement in U.S.-based issuers. In particular, non-U.S. investors have incurred a great portfolio sacrifice by generally ignoring the U.S. high-yield market. Ironically, many of these same non-U.S. investors are more comfortable holding a very low-rated sovereign with a history of default in the past 15 years than holding a blue-chip "crossover" credit in the U.S. market, such as Time Warner. During the next decade, non-U.S. investors will climb the credit-learning curve and become more involved in the U.S. high-yield market. During the next decade, U.S. investors will climb the currency and asset-swap learning curve to become more involved in the nondollar corporate market.

Credit Extensions

In most calendar years, investors are rewarded early in the year by extension of portfolio credit quality into lower-quality tiers ("first-quarter effect" reviewed below). Over longer intervals and except during recessions, lower-quality corporates provide investors with consistently higher returns. For this reason, credit-quality constraints have been falling in the United States during the 1990s. Non-U.S. investors will follow during the next decade.

Asset-Swap Extensions

Already more popular among floating-rate and non-U.S. investors, asset-swap extensions should become a major area of investment emphasis for U.S. investors. During the mid-1990s, some U.S. investors already have sought to boost their front-end returns/yields by deploying asset swaps (buying a floater and converting into a fixed-rate spread). The asset-swap market has become more efficient during the 1990s. But for investors content to live with their credit selection for a one- to five-year term (for a cost, swaps can be unwound prior to expiration), spread premiums can be gained. There are minimal spread pickups available from swapping short-dated floaters into fixed-rate product. Natural floater buyers already have bought up this comparatively scarce product. Conversion of "quasi-perpetuals" from floaters into fixed-rate products with terms out to 10 years offers the maximum spread gain. For example, a NatWest step-up variable-rate note could have been asset-swapped into a spread of 180 bp to the 1999 coupon reset date. These trades are not without risk. If the value of the underlying floater falls and if the floater is not retired at the expiration of the swap, an investor could be left with a perpetual floater that may be trading below purchase cost.

Callable asset swaps also have become popular in Europe. For example, an investor can add spread by shorting a quarterly call option. In the case of a A1/AA-Korea floater trading to a March 1998 maturity, an investor can boost quarterly yield by 4 bp to LIBOR plus 29 bp. Until maturity or call, such investors have boosted spread at the risk of an early call, perhaps in a tighter spread environment. For many investors, the short-term yield gain offsets the medium-term replacement risk.

Preferred Extensions

During the past decade, some of the best total returns have been garnered in the preferred stock market. Investors can add yield/expected return by moving down in issuer capitalization structures. At the height of the economic/credit cycle, this strategy is low risk. The converse also applies.

The preferred stock market tends to lag most other capital-market sectors for three reasons. First, preferred mutual funds have become less popular over the last half-decade. Retail investors use equity, high yield, emerging market, and even investment-grade corporate funds more than preferred funds. Second, the preferred market has become more dependent on direct investments from individual investors. In turn, this investor class is less schooled in the valuation of callable fixed income securities and the arbitrages available relative to other debt instruments. Third, the preferred market garners less strategist/analyst focus. Even large institutional investors can become less comfortable with a higher allocation to this security class.

These constraints will not be overcome immediately. But with more attention, we expect a decline in the "preferred arbitrage" over conventional debt alternatives. For example, a Texas Utility perpetual preferred traded at 180 bp over the long bond in February 1996 versus 115 bp for a similar structure in the corporate bond market.

Credit Derivative Extensions: New Tools for Risk Management/Return Enhancement

Credit derivatives, a rapidly growing subset of the estimated $20 trillion global derivative marketplace, are neither new nor especially novel. Among its exhibits, the Museum of American Financial History in New York includes a Massachusetts Bay Colony debt instrument parable in either currency or produce dating from 1780. In June 1863, the Confederate States of America issued a dual currency loan, payable in Sterling or French Francs, with the coupon linked to the price of cotton. And the Blue Ridge Railroad issued a Sterling/dollar pay security in 1869.

The corporate bond market has been the slowest to develop derivative product for investors. The interest-rate swap market skyrocketed in the early 1980s to serve mainly issuers' needs. The Chicago Board of Trade (dealer's index) and the Comex (Moody's index) launched futures contracts in 1987 based on corporate indices. Both contracts failed. In retrospect, the timing (week of October 19, 1987) could not have been less opportune. Moreover, the contracts allowed investors and dealers to take a position on the overall investment-grade corporate market as measured differently by two 100-bond samples. The merits of these contracts were never clear to users.

During the 1980s and early 1990s, limited attempts were undertaken by several dealers to allow investors to write covered call options on individual high-coupon, high-grade issues. But this business suffered from the decline in interest rates and ensuing spread compression. Structured notes, in some cases a form of credit derivative, enjoyed greater success during the early 1990s. Unfortunately, several notable derivative mishaps tarnished the luster of structure notes during 1994.

Several market and institutional forces impeded the development of a corporate derivative market over the past decade. First, fixed income investors had to reckon with a cyclical peak in credit risk within the global corporate market during 1989–1991. This cyclical peak monopolized investor attention during the past half-decade given rolling shocks from event risk in the industrial sector, asset quality and credit-quality meltdowns in the financial-institution sector, and the effects of recession and prolonged economic malaise through the global corporate market. Second, most corporate-market participants have been trained to reckon only with fundamental and technical factors and their translation into valuation adjustment in the cash corporate market.

Despite some negative publicity about derivatives in 1994 and 1995, the austerity of value differentiation among traditional high-quality cash credit instruments has stimulated investor interest in the development of the embryonic credit derivative markets. More simply, in the mid-1990s it has become more difficult for total-return investors to stand above the crowd.

With the proliferation of the derivative markets, many corporate investors have developed derivative expertise in other areas. And younger portfolio managers have had more rigorous training in business schools.

The ongoing expansion of fixed income products also fosters the development of credit derivatives. In addition to corporates, generalist portfolio managers simultaneously may be dealing with U.S. Treasury, MBS, nondollar, and other derivative markets. This does not allow much time for the assimilation of credit analysis. In what may be a dangerous practice if handled carelessly, corporate derivatives might allow the generalist portfolio manager to take a long or short position in a corporate sector without plowing through all the underlying credit differentials for each issuer within the sector.

What types of credit derivatives are currently available? For the past eight years, investors have been able to execute outright swaps tied to fixed income indices. Usually, an index swapper will agree to exchange a cash flow tied an Aa bond index (MBS, corporates, high-yield) offset by a floating-rate cash flow, typically linked to LIBOR. In the United States, where most portfolio managers bench their total returns to some index, index swaps have become increasing popular as a hedging tool. For example, an investor with a heavy overweighting in high-yield corporates may prefer to short the high-yield index for some interval rather than sell favorite high-yield positions. In Europe, where return comparisons to bond indices remains less common, index swaps are less popular.

"Spread options" represent a second form of credit derivatives. Currently, two-way markets are limited. For example, it is difficult for an investor to easily execute an option (either call or put) on the direction of the spreads on five-year General Motors debt. And transactions for highly volatile credits undergoing negative fundamental perceptions—for example, Kmart 7.95s of 2023 (spread from 170 bp to 700 bp to 490 bp over late 1995 and early 1996)—are even more difficult. With further market development, these transactions will become more commonplace by the end of the 1990s.

The third generic form of credit derivatives are basket or exotic options. In these forms, an investor takes a stand on a basket of credits. Option values depend on the number of defaults in the basket. These "basket" options are more popular with large institutions such as commercial banks and insurers who want to hedge their default risk on subsets of their credit exposures.

Much work needs to be done on the construction of credit-derivative models. So far, most academic efforts have extended the one-factor option-valuation models in use in the derivative market to the credit sectors. These early models ultimately will be superseded by richer models that incorporate a more precise credit parameter. As shown in a rich academic literature, credit risk is partially systematic, with spreads/default-risk premiums adhering to a well-defined pattern. Credit spreads rise during periods of economic distress and contract during robust economic periods. More cyclical industries, sectors undergoing secular change, and more-complex, less-liquid structures are more sensitive to the state of the economic/credit cycle. Second and much more difficult, credit models need to account for the discontinuous, nonlinear jumps that affect individual sectors/issuers/issues after a "paradigm strip" (e.g., Kmart's tumble from market favor in the fall of 1995). This task requires the incorporation of specific issuer credit/market valuation risks obtained from superior credit analysis directly into the credit derivative model.

SOME USEFUL EMPIRICAL FINDINGS
Annual Seasonal Effects

The global corporate asset class tends to provide its comparative advantage over credit-risk-free Treasuries during the first half of the year, especially for lower-quality credits. A defensive shift regularly takes place across the entire credit-quality spectrum in the corporate market during the second half of most years. In the investment-grade corporate market, this phenomenon regularly shows up during the fourth quarter. The high-yield market reacts in the third quarter. The converse occurs at the beginning of each new calendar year. Lower-quality securities outperform during the first quarter. As a nearly annual supplement to the longer-term credit cycle, annual seasonality has been the best technical technique to add incremental value to the corporate portfolios during the past two decades. Based on Lehman's investment-grade index since its inception on January 1, 1973, through December 31, 1995, Baa-rated corporates underperformed A's by 22 bp during the fourth quarter (investors/dealers became more defensive) and then outperformed A's by 71 bp during the first quarter (investors/dealers became more adventurous with the beginning of a new performance campaign). On average over the past 23 years, the simple upgrade trade (out of Baa's by the start of the fourth quarter and back into Baa's by the end of the fourth quarter) produced a 93 bp total-return advantage before transaction costs. This "fourth-quarter effect" has been evident in 14 of the past 23 years (60.9 percent). The exception years are 1974, 1977, 1980, 1981, 1982, 1984, 1988, 1993 (anticipation of this effect contributed to its arrival in the third quarter), and 1994 (strong economy and RJR debt tender). The "first-quarter effect" has shown up in 18 of the past 23 years (78.3 percent) and every year since 1986. The exception years are 1974, 1979, 1980, and 1986.

Reflecting greater market awareness of this seasonality, the fourth-quarter effect (underperformance of Baa's to A's) has materialized in various forms (70 percent) during the past decade. The first-quarter effect has been even more regular with a 90 percent appearance rate during the past decade.

A similar pattern appears in the high-yield corporate market. This effect has less empirical support given the more recent origin of Lehman's high-yield database on July 1, 1983, the rapid development of this embryonic market over the past 15 years, and the distortion from the 1989–1990 implosion. The first-quarter effect holds in the high-yield market; CCC (7.57 percent). B (5.17 percent), and BB (4.58 percent) securities posted total returns during the first quarter of 1984 through 1995 consistent with the risk assumed. But instead of a fourth-quarter effect, there is more of a third-quarter effect with BB's (2.32 percent) faring much better than B's (1.48 percent).

The investment implications are that within the corporate bond realm, long-term investment actions should be driven more by fundamental than technical factors. But for shorter horizons, these seasonal patterns should be useful. Until these effects are arbitraged out of the global corporate market (investors may have a long wait), corporate investors should consider the "upgrade trade" at the start of every fourth quarter and the "yield maximization/downgrade trade" at the beginning of every nonrecessionary first quarter.

Election-Cycle Effects

Based on Ibbotson and Lehman data, the U.S. Presidential election cycle appears to exert a weak influence on relative corporate returns. A shift in political/economic gears often leads to frictions manifest in a slower economy during the early stages of a new administration in Washington. During the post–World War II era, real corporate returns relative to Treasuries peaked in the year prior to election at 1.36 percent, decreased during election to 0.84 percent, and fell further in the year after election to –0.42 percent. From 1972 through 1993, the peak real advantage for corporates shifted to the election year (1.47 percent compared to 1.13 percent in the year prior to an election and –0.44 percent in the year after an election). Congressional midterm elections since 1930 do not appear to have consistently affected relative corporate returns.

The investment implications are that asset allocators should consider overweightings of the corporate asset class in the year prior and for most of the Presidential election year. A reduction in corporate exposure should be considered immediately prior to Presidential elections.

Treasury Auction-Noise Effects

U.S. Treasury auctions have exerted a regular influence on relative corporate returns. Except for the first quarter, when the first-quarter effect (defined above) dominates, relative corporate returns peak in the auction month as benchmarks tend to shift. From 1973 through 1995, relative investment-grade corporate returns were –3 bp in April. This advantage climbs during the May auction month to 29 bp and then swings back to –15 bp during the post-auction month of June. This cycle repeats during the third and fourth quarters: July (–6 bp) to August refunding (20 bp) to September (–23 bp); October (10 bp) to November refunding (15 bp) to December (–15 bp).

Weekday Effects

New corporate supply and origination are clustered on Tuesdays, Wednesdays, and Thursdays. Mondays are reserved for strategy meetings, new-issue preparation, and administrative chores. In the absence of daily corporate returns, anecdotal evidence points to the superiority of transacting midweek.

Holiday Effects

Major holidays dampen primary and secondary trading activity, especially at year-end. Peak vacation season in August also limits activity across the global corporate market. Given the slight reduction in liquidity during these periods, active managers should attempt to transact prior to or after peak holiday periods.

SUMMARY

Abetted by the persistence of outmoded portfolio constraints for many institutional investors, the development of a suitable relative-value methodology for intermarket and intramarket analysis is the major challenge for the global fixed income markets. Analysis, technology, and data have improved greatly during the 1990s. But regional and product biases persist. Some European strategists and managers ignore U.S. spread products. More commonly, some U.S. portfolio managers do not follow nondollar products. Because of either internal constraints or the absence of an analytical framework, many investors restrict their search for relative value to varying subsets of the global bond markets.

During the past two decades, competition has been the great leveler of a diverse array of industries, from autos, consumer electronics, and financial services, to manufacturing. The escalation of competition among the stewards of fixed income assets also promises to level anachronistic methodologies. In this ever more efficient and difficult milieu, corporate portfolio managers will use every quantitative and qualitative tool, explore every macro and micro strategic technique, and deploy every type of security in most currencies to deliver the very best performance for their clients. Investor resisters, who cling to the limitations of the past, will enjoy an early retirement with the captains of past protocols in other industries.

E X H I B I T   52–8

Lehman Brothers Recommended Fixed Income Asset Allocation for Total Return
Investors as of December 31, 1995

	Outperformance List		Corporate Index		Relative Weighting %	
Industrials		**33%**		**36%**		**92%**
Basic industry		12%		14%		86%
Chemical	43%		46%		93%	
Metals	9%		8%		113%	
Paper	48%		46%		104%	
Other industrial	0%		0%		0%	
Capital goods		13%		15%		87%
Aerospace	15%		15%		100%	
Building materials	5%		3%		167%	
Conglomerates	34%		38%		89%	
Construction machinery	10%		8%		125%	
Defense	4%		3%		133%	
Environmental	12%		13%		92%	
Packaging	10%		10%		100%	
Other capital goods	10%		9%		111%	
Consumer cyclical		28%		26%		108%
Automotive	20%		23%		87%	
Entertainment	15%		7%		214%	
Gaming	1%		1%		100%	
Home construction	1%		1%		100%	
Lodging	3%		2%		150%	
Media—cable	12%		10%		120%	
Media—noncable	12%		14%		86%	
Retailers	32%		34%		94%	
Services	1%		3%		33%	
Textile	1%		2%		50%	
Other consumer cyclical	2%		4%		50%	
Consumer noncyclical		21%		22%		95%
Beverage	21%		17%		124%	
Consumer	7%		7%		100%	
Food	23%		21%		110%	
Healthcare	15%		17%		88%	
Pharmaceuticals	9%		9%		100%	
Supermarkets	3%		3%		100%	
Tobacco	22%		25%		88%	
Other consumer noncyclical	0%		1%		0%	
Energy		12%		13%		92%
Independent	13%		11%		118%	
Integrated	76%		75%		101%	
Oil field service	6%		5%		120%	

Bold =Key decision sectors during 1996

E X H I B I T   52–8

(Continued)

	Outperformance List	Corporate Index	Relative Weighting %
Refining	5%	6%	83%
Other energy	0%	3%	0%
Technology	5%	4%	125%
Transportation	9%	6%	150%
Airlines	40%	29%	138%
Railroads	30%	41%	73%
Services	30%	30%	100%
Other transportation	0%	0%	0%
Utilities	17%	18%	94%
Electric	55%	53%	104%
Telephone	31%	37%	84%
Natural gas	14%	10%	140%
Gas distributors	5%	14%	36%
Gas pipelines	95%	86%	110%
Water	0%	0%	
Financial Institutions	28%	26%	108%
Banking	40%	37%	108%
Brokerage	14%	12%	117%
Finance companies	34%	43%	79%
Captive	39%	39%	100%
Noncaptive	61%	61%	100%
Consumer	40%	45%	89%
Diversified	60%	55%	109%
Insurance	12%	8%	150%
Other finance	0%	1%	0%
Yankees	22%	20%	110%
Canadians	29%	32%	91%
Corporates	40%	37%	108%
Supranationals	5%	7%	71%
Sovereigns	26%	24%	108%

⑥ THE MANAGEMENT OF HIGH-YIELD BOND PORTFOLIOS

Howard S. Marks, CFA
Chairman
Oaktree Capital Management

Portfolio management consists of selecting individual securities and allocating differing amounts of investment capital to those securities. Quite aside from the isolated analysis of individual securities against some standard of acceptability, portfolio management consists of attempting to assemble a combination of securities, the holding of which will result in the attainment of the investor's objectives.

There are a number of questions that must be answered relating to managing portfolios of high-yield bonds. Some of the most important concern the identification of acceptable classes of bonds, selection of individual securities, diversification versus concentration, and attitude toward turnover. Perhaps the most important, however, is one that sets the scene for all the others: the matter of one's philosophy on *trying to be right versus avoiding being wrong*—toward winning versus not losing.

In discussing each of these subjects, I will attempt to describe the available alternatives. However, I have my own biases and I have made my choices. I am sure those biases will show through clearly. They will affect what I say here, and I will be much more articulate in defending my choices than in supporting the alternatives.

Before I discuss the choices, however, I wish to lay out the investment philosophy that guides my own high-yield bond management activities. I do so both to indicate my own predisposition and to provide an example of the type of personal philosophy necessary to undertake portfolio management in a rational manner.

I have elected to participate in high-yield bonds because of my conviction that these bonds suffer as a class from severe bias on the part of traditional investors. This bias causes the bonds to offer promised yields so high that they incorporate an excessive premium for risk bearing relative to the actual risks I believe are involved. Since the principal attraction applies to the sector in general, and not just to a few bonds, it is my objective to participate in the sector in general, and to enjoy the excessive rewards without bearing unnecessary risk.

THE BASIC APPROACH: OFFENSE OR DEFENSE?

In every investment decision, as in many other choices, we must decide whether to place primary emphasis on going aggressively for a win or on acting conservatively to avoid a loss. Approaching a water hazard on the golf course, you must decide between going over the water to try for a very good score or going safely around the water to avoid a bad score and a ruined round. Such a choice of mindset is fundamental in the investment process and, because the conscious bearing of risk is at the core of high-yield bond investing, essential in the area of high-yield bonds.

The long-term return on any high-yield bond portfolio will be determined by a simple formula:

Riskless return + Yield spread – Credit losses

A riskless return such as the yield on Treasury bonds provides the foundation. We add to that the yield spread we are paid to bear credit risk, and then we subtract the losses due to credit problems that we actually incur. When there are no credit problems, the yield spread is realized; only credit difficulties can keep us from receiving the contractual, promised return.

Anyone can achieve average performance simply by buying the same securities as everyone else—or some of each. The money manager who is forever average, however, adds no value. The task of assembling an average portfolio could easily be turned over to a computer, and thus the average manager does not deserve much compensation. Above-average performance must be the aim of active portfolio management and, given the above formula, there are two basic ways to achieve it: increase the yield spread or reduce the credit losses. The choice between the two hinges on whether one prefers to be very right or to avoid being very wrong.

In a typical high-yield bond market there is a fairly broad range of "promised yields" available on bonds of going concerns. However, if the market's operations are at all "efficient," the risk of default will rise along with the promised yields. (Otherwise, the buyers of the higher-yielding bonds would be getting something—the additional yield—for nothing, a condition the market strives to prevent.)

Trying to increase returns by way of wider spreads raises the starting point—the promised yield—but also increases the risk that problems will be encountered. You must have access to credit research in order to be a high-yield bond investor, but the key question is: How much do you want to bet on being right in the more uncertain situations?

CHOOSING AMONG THE HIGH-YIELD BOND CATEGORIES

Within the framework provided by investment objectives and personal philosophy regarding risk, a high-yield bond portfolio manager must decide which classes of bonds to purchase. This decision hinges largely on the above-mentioned attitude toward risk. First, do you wish to invest in the safer and lower-yielding classes or in the riskier opportunities with their potential for top-of-the-chart returns? Second, do you wish to spread the risk by investing in many sectors? Or do you prefer to specialize in fewer sectors, attempting to add value by focusing your analytical efforts and acquiring above-average expertise, but also accepting the increased risk associated with concentration?

I have chosen to concentrate on what I consider to be the safer bonds selling near the bottom of the yield spectrum. Obviously, to the extent that I am able accurately to identify the less risky bonds, I can reduce the total risk in my portfolios (although at the cost of forgoing the higher available yields). I also feel that doing so permits me to develop a competitive knowledge advantage through concentrating my credit analysis. And, perhaps most important in my view, it allows me to avoid the need to make judgments on the hard-to-predict factors that will determine the survival or demise of issues in the more risky classes.

I feel the safest bonds are those of companies that

- Receive low ratings because of the lack of a record rather than a record of actual problems.
- Are riding positive fundamental trendlines rather than declining trends that must be arrested.
- Are likely to survive in their present form without having to pass any make-it-or-break-it trial.
- Do not require unrealistic levels of prosperity and growth, major corporate restructurings, or successful turnarounds for survival.

To help sharpen my focus, I sorted the high-yield bond universe into four major types and developed a general view concerning each in the context of my investment approach. This enabled me to make a "first cut" on most high-yield bonds according to the safety standards listed above.

Fallen Angels

The initial decision concerned the "fallen angels," or former high-grade bonds that have experienced operating difficulties and thus fallen into the lower-rated high-yield bond universe. The issuers of such bonds are prime examples of companies riding negative trends that will have to be reversed in order for them to survive and service their debt. I have not used them for this reason.

Emerging Credits

In contrast to fallen angels are the "emerging credits," the first companies to issue high-yield bonds receiving low credit ratings at the time of issue (rather than being downgraded to those ratings). I feel these bonds' low ratings stem from inexperience rather than poor experience—from a lack of years and "critical mass." I have chosen to invest in them, however, because of my conviction that most of them can look forward to stability, and perhaps improvement, and will survive in their present form.

Leveraged Buyouts and Recapitalizations

In the mid-1980s, major new groups of high-yield bond issuers appeared: the leveraged buyouts and recapitalizations. These companies often have decades-long histories and sales in the billions of dollars. On the other hand, they receive their low ratings because they have been leveraged up to extremely high debt/equity ratios and low, uncertain interest coverage ratios. In addition, they often depend heavily on restructuring and asset sales. The conclusion here is not black or white. I have chosen to invest in what I consider to be the best of these bonds, emphasizing those that have shown stable cash flow and that I feel can prosper essentially as they are, without benefit of massive managerial action or need for a uniformly favorable economic environment.

Divisional Divestitures

Finally, I have found that the "divisional divestitures," which result primarily from the breakup of LBOs, have performance prospects similar to those of the emerging credits. These smaller units have to date been burdened with corporate overhead and bureaucracy and have often been lost as unrelated "orphan" businesses within corporate giants. Freed of these disadvantages and motivated through management ownership, in general they face excellent prospects and are low in risk.

For the above reasons, I have chosen to emphasize the emerging credits and divisional divestitures and to buy the best of the LBOs and recapitalizations. Other professional investors have chosen basic strategies quite different from that.

Some investors concentrate on the high end of the risk and yield spectrum, which is populated by bonds that scare away most investors and thus may languish at prices affording truly excessive promised yields. Prominent here are the less certain of the non-cash-paying bonds, the junior subordinated issues, and the bonds of distressed and bankrupt companies. Other managers limit themselves to a small number of industries, bearing the risk of concentration in exchange for the chance to apply their specialized expertise and what they consider to be the strong outlook for these groups. Still others are willing to hold bonds in all categories and move from group to group as they perceive the shifts in relative value.

I feel strongly that none of these strategies is right or wrong. Any strategy can be viable if it is well thought out, within the capabilities of the organization in terms of execution, and designed so that it fits the client's or employer's attitude toward risk and return. If so, it can satisfy investment objectives, which is the goal of portfolio management.

SELECTING INDIVIDUAL SECURITIES

Within the categories of bonds that have been chosen, a major task consists of selecting the individual securities that will make up the portfolio. Of course, the most important task is the approval or disapproval of companies for investment. It is also the subject about which I will say the least, hinging as it does on credit analysis, a subject on which other contributors will write extensively.

It is my view that the task of populating a high-yield bond portfolio with individual securities consists primarily of taking the credit analyst's reports and deciding whether the risk level indicated in each case is

1. Within the risk tolerance of the portfolio.

2. Fully compensated by the promised yield.

This is not something you can be told how to do. It requires experience, objectivity, cynicism, and judgments concerning both qualitative and quantitative factors. (It is to be hoped that the difficulty of passing on this skill will safeguard today's portfolio managers, including myself, from being entirely replaced by readers of books like this!) There are, however, certain topics under this broad heading about which a few pointers can be given.

Position in the Capital Structure

The accepted risk and the promised yield can be greatly influenced by the choice of location in the issuer's capital structure. *Priority* refers to the order of claim in case of bankruptcy, and the priority of unsecured creditors ranges from senior at the top, down through senior subordinated and subordinated, to junior subordinated. In the case of many companies, prospective bond buyers face a choice between various levels of priority; of course, each step upward in terms of priority brings with it a decrease in promised yield.

Two things must be borne in mind in this context. The first is that, except in those few cases where the market is making a glaring mistake, there is no single correct choice. The decision in each case will properly be a function of

• The ratio of yield forgone to priority gained.

- The relative riskiness of the issuer (that is, it seems illogical to give up yield to gain seniority in the case of a company perceived to be extremely creditworthy).
- The attitude of the investor toward risk and return.

Second, note that high priority is not a substitute for creditworthiness. When a company defaults, it ceases to service *all* of its unsecured debt. Greater seniority will help to limit the losses, but not to avoid the problem.

Secured versus Unsecured

Analogously, it's possible to purchase debt securities that are secured by a lien against specific assets. In such cases the investment is protected up to the value of those assets. Unlike the case for unsecured debt, the law generally causes interest on secured debt to accrue after a bankruptcy petition has been entered, as long as the value of the collateral exceeds the amount of the debtholders' legal claim. Additionally, secured debtholders may enjoy the current payment of interest in bankruptcy or, less frequently, the compounding of interest on any unpaid interest.

The caveats regarding priority apply here as well. Deciding between secured and unsecured debt will generally be a subjective matter, will hinge on the factors discussed under the topic of priority, and will not enable a creditor of a company falling into distress to avoid the associated travails.

Non-Cash-Paying Securities

Increasingly of late, and especially in connection with leveraged buyouts and recapitalizations, non-cash-paying securities have come to make up a significant portion of the high-yield bond universe. They are often employed in highly leveraged transactions to bridge the funding gap when a company is incapable of paying cash interest on all of the debt being created. Companies issuing non-cash-paying securities plan to sell off assets or improve profitability and cash flow before zero-coupon, payment-in-kind, or deferred-interest bonds mature (and before current interest payments come due on deferred-interest bonds).

The choice here is also subjective and must be made on a case-by-case basis. Generally speaking, the compensation in terms of increased yield for accepting non-cash-paying securities is substantial. But the investor receives nothing as time passes, instead merely compounding the amount he or she is owed by the issuer. A holder of the current-pay bonds of a company that defaults in the fifth year will already have "taken a lot of cash off the table," but a zero-coupon bondholder will have taken none. I feel that a great deal of the attraction of high-yield bonds lies in the way substantial interest received today cushions against difficulties arising tomorrow. In non-cash-paying securities, the promise grows, but no cash is pocketed.

Covenants

The attractiveness and subsequent performance of individual high-yield bonds can be greatly influenced by the covenants they bear. Rather than carrying the fiduciary duty they do to stockholders, with regard to bondholders managements can do almost anything they wish that is legal and not strictly prohibited in the indenture that serves as the contract between issuer and buyer. Thus covenants are inserted by investment bankers during the issuance process to provide the buyer protections needed to make bonds salable.

Most of these covenants are designed to prevent the paying out of excess dividends, overleveraging, and other actions on the part of management that would lead to the deterioration of credit quality. Bondholders have in recent years grown increasingly concerned about "event risk," the possibility that management will take voluntary actions that result in the transfer of wealth from bondholders to stockholders (perhaps including themselves). It is at event risk that most covenants are directed.

Covenants are not a solution to business difficulties, but they may help protect against actions that increase companies' susceptibility to problems or accentuate the impact on bondholders. In addition, tight covenants often prove to be of value to bondholders in that managements may later pay to have their restrictions lifted. Covenants constitute a specialized and somewhat esoteric aspect of high-yield bond portfolio management, but a very important one.

Overall, the great variety of securities and their features permits managers of high-yield bond portfolios to "dial their risk" according to risk/return attitudes and the peculiarities of individual securities. No one can be categorical about how best to do it, but I hope I have highlighted some of the important considerations.

HOW MUCH DIVERSIFICATION?

I have touched on the trade-off between the risks and benefits to be derived from concentrating versus diversifying in deciding which bond classes to buy. Further consideration must be given to this subject at the level of individual securities.

A principle in statistics called the "law of large numbers" states that as the size of a sample increases, the likelihood decreases that the mean of the sample will vary greatly from the mean of the universe from which it is drawn. This principle is applied in investment management (sometimes unconsciously) in the form of something called diversification. Clearly, the larger the number of securities a portfolio holds, everything else being equal, the higher the probability that the portfolio's return will resemble the return on the entire asset class.

At the lowest level, we can see that holding a portfolio consisting of only one security is very risky. First, the holder would be entirely exposed to individual events taking place at that one company or in the market for its securities. Second, there is a good possibility that the investor, by holding only one security, could miss out on a major move in the general market. In theoretical terms, the portfolio is overexposed to the nonsystematic, diversifiable risks attached to the one security and underexposed to the nondiversifiable risk and general market dynamics attached to a portfolio more reflective of the broad universe of securities.

At the other extreme, however, it is equally clear that an active manager would not want to own everything. Doing so would ensure performance that is average, no more and no less. If the manager or the manager's organization possesses any superior insight concerning the outlook, its value will be fully diluted by the failure to act accordingly—that is, to eliminate some securities from the portfolio and emphasize others. Such totally diversified portfolios are called index funds. They offer a low-cost way to ensure "market performance" and total surrender on the subject of trying to add value and achieve above-average performance.

Clearly, the answer for most portfolio management applications must lie somewhere between holding one security and holding every security. The question is, where? The answer takes us back to the choice between trying to be right and avoiding being wrong.

Remember, it is my objective to enjoy the benefits of high-yield bond investing with strictly limited risk. I strive to employ the knowledge that results from credit analysis to avoid mistakes, not to try for a *tour de force*. That is, I want to have a high batting average and to avoid hitting into inning-ending double plays; I do not try to hit home runs.

I choose to hold a large number of bonds (70–100) in my portfolios, and the reasoning goes like this: There are 500 bonds out there with yields of 10 percent. I assemble 100 of them in a portfolio, which then has an average promised yield of 10 percent. I normally expect on average to suffer a 1 percent default rate, with one of the 100 bonds defaulting each year, and to lose 60 percent of the amount I invested in that one bond (or 0.6 percent of my total principal) in its default. Thus my net return (ignoring price fluctuations) will be 9.4 percent.

Suppose I choose instead to buy only 10 bonds. The fact that they are 10 percent bonds is unchanged, so the promised yield on the portfolio will still be 10 percent. However, if the one defaulting bond I bought in the 100-bond portfolio makes it through to the 10-bond portfolio, my default rate will be 10 percent. In such a case I will lose 6 percent of my principal, and my net return will be only 4 percent.

Because of the way this example is constructed, concentration is shown to add to risk but not return. Obviously, however, those who concentrate do so in the belief that they can add to return in a way that more than offsets the increase in risk. That is, they view concentration as a chance to put their knowledge of credits to its best use.

This issue ultimately comes down to the reliability of opinions concerning future developments. Anyone who is sure he or she knows what lies ahead should put all of his or her capital into the one asset with the best outlook. Although no professional investors hold only one security, those who feel they know a great deal about the future generally hold fewer securities (or should) than those who do not.

My portfolios are positioned toward the higher end of the diversification spectrum. Although I work hard through credit analysis to know as much as I can about each company's future, I remain concerned about the amount I cannot know. Going back to the example, I do not feel that I (or anyone else) can tell with a high degree of accuracy which of the 10 percent bonds will turn out to provide more than just the promised return (through capital gains) and which will depreciate or default. Clearly, there will be some of each, but which will be which usually comes as a surprise. From this stems my conviction that high diversification is an attractive way to increase safety and that concentration would not predictably increase my returns.

One last word on diversification: A large number of securities alone will not result in low risk. The key word is *covariance,* and there should not be much of it. That is, the securities should not co-vary, or move together. A portfolio of 100 leveraged buyout bonds of wallboard companies should not be considered diversified. Instead, holdings should represent a variety of classes of bonds, broad economic sectors (such as heavy industry or consumer), industries, companies, and perhaps maturities. Only in this way can avoidable risk be reduced.

THE ROLE OF TRADING

The last topic for consideration is that of turnover: how much to trade and when. This is yet another subject on which there is a difference of opinion. Some investors feel that superior knowledge of companies and the market can be used to reliably add a further component, short-term trading profits, to the formula for total return shown earlier.

My view, on the other hand, is that the principal purpose is to participate in the long-term, big-picture benefits afforded by the high-yield sector. Trading undertaken for short-term reasons might result in being either in or out of the market or an individual security at the wrong time. It might present an undesirable distraction from the major mission. And it might prove expensive, given the significant transaction costs and limitations on liquidity in the high-yield market.

On the subject of market timing, though it should be possible to gain an advantage through hard work in terms of knowledge of individual companies, it is less likely that anyone can do an above-average job of forecasting interest rates and broad bond market movements and thus of knowing when to be in or out of the market. For this reason, my portfolios are fully invested all of the time; the benefit in the long term comes from the bonds' high yields, and I live with what I consider to be the unpredictable and unavoidable short-term market fluctuations.

With regard to individual securities, rather than engage in short-term trading, which amounts to little more than a guess at the direction of the next fluctuation, I restrict sales to those that are fundamentally motivated.

1. If ongoing credit analysis indicates that a company is undergoing fundamental deterioration that threatens its survival, I will usually sell.

This is doubly true if I feel the analysis is early, and thus the market has yet to get wind of the negative developments and reflect them in the bond's price.

2. If a company shows improvement in creditworthiness (or if improvement is perceived by the market), such that the price rises and the yield falls significantly, I will also sell. Though the bond has probably become a safer holding, it may fail to satisfy the portfolio's yield criterion.

3. Finally, it is the portfolio manager's ultimate responsibility to examine each security's *balance between risk and return* (and its contribution to the overall portfolio in both regards). If these two elements get out of line—most importantly, if the risk is perceived to rise relative to the prospective return—the holding should be reviewed for sale.

Overall, as was stated earlier, much of a manager's approach to portfolio management will depend on his or her fundamental stance regarding being right versus not being wrong, aggressiveness versus defensiveness. Aggressive portfolio managers might long for the opportunity to show how much they know about the future. Thus they might concentrate their portfolios in a relatively small number of higher-yielding (and riskier) bonds and emphasize short-term trading, market timing, or movements from one sector to another.

More defensive managers would be more concerned about avoiding mistakes than about pulling off a major coup. They might tend to hold more diversified portfolios drawn from the less risky portion of the high-yield universe, and trade infrequently and only as demanded by significant changes in fundamentals or security prices.

It is most important to note, once again, that neither approach is right or wrong. The aggressive manager's actions might lead to excessive risks and losses. The cautious manager might either assume so little risk as to produce inadequate returns or be wrong in picking the low-risk bonds and walk into a minefield. Either strategy can produce above-average or below-average returns, either one can be executed well or poorly, and either can be appropriate or inappropriate depending on whose money is being managed.

SURVIVING MARKET FLUCTUATIONS

Finally, I want to touch on the subject of preparing for the regular fluctuations that are a normal part of every portfolio manager's existence. Much is expected of portfolio managers, especially in the area of knowing what the future holds, which I feel is unreasonable. There is one thing, however, that managers should be able to do for their clients: stand against the extreme ebbs and flows of psychology. Put more simply, they should refuse to join the buyers who make the market's tops and the sellers who make its bottoms.

High-yield bonds are as attractive as they are, offering yield spreads that are excessive relative to the risks involved, primarily for one reason: They are controversial and less than fully understood. These same attributes, however, leave the market subject to significant fluctuations.

External developments have regularly buffeted this market. In addition, exaggerated fear of widespread recession-related defaults rears its head whenever a business cycle reaches old age. The sector finds few friends or defenders among nonparticipants, journalists, politicians, or regulators. Finally, as an inefficient market, high-yield bonds are subject to fluctuation whenever most of the participants want to either buy or sell in amounts that exceed the market's liquidity.

The swirl of controversy and the excessively harsh reaction to adverse developments have from time to time produced significant price declines, such as when LTV went bankrupt, when Ivan Boesky was exposed, and when Drexel Burnham, the principal market maker in this sector, was put out of business. They also explain the enactment of a law prohibiting high-yield investment by savings and loan associations despite the total lack of loss experience to support such a ban. Finally, they explain the rash of press reports that cited "crash" and "collapse" when the average high-yield bond lost 7 percent in 1990, the kind of negative return that is experienced often and greeted much more calmly in the stock market.

It is a fact of life in all markets that fluctuations come and go. They are regularly overblown in the controversial high-yield bond market, however, and they cause great concern. Every portfolio manager should be equipped with a well-thought-out philosophy and strategy to stand by, should be backed by an organization with a strong execution capability, and should be operating under a game plan that incorporates the economic, psychological, and political realities of client or employer. If all of these requirements have been met, the portfolio and its manager should have the staying power needed to get through the rough spots. In the end, the generous returns in high-yield bonds should make all of the effort worthwhile.

⑥ # INTERNATIONAL BOND INVESTING AND PORTFOLIO MANAGEMENT

Christopher B. Steward, CFA
Vice President
Scudder, Stevens and Clark

Adam M. Greshin, CFA
Principal
Scudder, Stevens and Clark

INTRODUCTION

The communications revolution has had a profound impact on the world at large, but it is the capital markets that have come closest to fulfilling Marshal McLuhan's vision of a "global village." International capital markets enjoy practically instantaneous communication on a scale that was nearly unimaginable a decade ago. Faxes, market information systems such as Reuters and Bloomberg, and the internet, have created a seamless flow of investment information that functions as well across borders as it does across the street. This increased flow of information, combined with the removal of capital controls in most developed markets during the 1980s, has resulted in a dramatic increase in cross-border investment flows. Between 1981 and 1994, holdings of foreign assets by the G7 countries grew 3.4 times to $10.1 trillion, a compound annualized growth rate of 12 percent.[1] At the same time, household savings have been increasingly invested with professional fund managers through mutual funds and pension funds. By one estimate, U.S. and European fund managers alone control over $8 trillion in assets.[2] Reduced transactions costs and greater liquidity in the asset markets,

---

1. *OECD Economic Outlook,* no. 58, Paris (December 1995).
2. Michael Mussa and Morris Goldstein, "The Integration of World Capital Markets," in *Changing Capital Markets: Implications for Monetary Policy* (Federal Reserve Bank of Kansas, 1993).

especially in the derivatives markets, has enabled these professional investors to shift large amounts of capital across borders more freely. These flows can quickly overwhelm national authorities, as, in 1992, George Soros's Quantum hedge fund was able to force a devaluation of the British pound in a matter of days. A market-forced devaluation of the British pound in 1967 required several years of specula-tive pressure.

Institutional investors have been active in the international bond markets for a long time, but the amount of insitutional assets invested in international bonds is tiny relative to the available pool of assets. Only 7 percent of the assets of the world's 300 largest pension funds are estimated to be invested in foreign bond and equity securities.[3] Retail investment in international bonds, primarily through mutual funds, is a much more recent phenomenon. In 1990, Lipper Ana-lytical Services, which tracks U.S. Mutual Funds, counted only 32 funds in its General World Income category with total net assets of $6 billion. By 1995, that had grown to 157 funds, with nearly $20 billion in assets.

Questions remain as to the appropriateness of international bonds in U.S. dollar portfolios, particularly in light of the volatility in the foreign exchange mar-kets in the past two decades. Should international bonds be a core holding in U.S. portfolios, or should they be used on an occasional basis when foreign interest rate and currency levels appear attractive? This chapter will examine the reasons for in-vesting in international bonds and will touch on some of the more interesting is-sues in constructing a global bond portfolio. First, the historical data regarding the return enhancement and diversification, or risk-reduction, benefits of international bond investments are examined. Next, the impact of including foreign-pay interna-tional bonds in a U.S. bond portfolio is discussed. Finally, techniques for manage-ment of foreign-pay international bond portfolios are addressed, with emphasis on the question of whether or not to hedge currency exposures.

THE RATIONALE FOR INTERNATIONAL BOND INVESTING

Risk and return are the universal yardsticks applied to any potential investment as rational investors are always seeking the highest return for the lowest level of risk. Wall Street firms hire Ph.D. mathematicians to seek out correlations between markets that can be exploited to either tailor risk management products (such as exotic options or structured notes) or to uncover anomalies that can be used for arbitrage. Under the standard Markowitz mean-variance framework, any asset class with a less than perfect correlation to another will provide some diversifica-tion benefit in reducing portfolio risk. Many investors are attracted to interna-tional bonds by the higher returns that they have historically provided, the components of which will vary among income, domestic price change, and for-eign currency change. However, for some investors, the potential for a reduction

---

3. See Mussa and Goldstein.

in the risk or volatility of return relative to a portfolio invested solely in U.S. fixed income securities will be more important.

In analyzing the case for international bonds, there is no a priori reason why one rationale for international bond investing should receive more emphasis than another. The relative emphasis on these rationales is properly a function of the investment objectives of the investor, and these objectives should be reflected in the guidelines for and composition of an international bond portfolio. To certain investors, especially those with long-term time horizons, return enhancement may be paramount, and the impact of international bonds on interim volatility of returns is relatively unimportant. For these investors, embarking on a program of international bond investing is not appropriate unless international bonds can be expected to improve the rate of return. To others, particularly investors with shorter time horizons who have been concerned by the occasional roller-coaster ride in the U.S. fixed income markets, the attraction of international bonds may be their potential for reducing the volatility of overall portfolio returns.

Superior Rates of Return

A very powerful fundamental argument can be made for the inclusion of international equities as a separate asset class in domestic portfolios. Since many areas of the world are growing more rapidly than the United States and are experiencing higher rates of investment spending and productivity growth, a portfolio of foreign equities should, over time, provide a higher return than a portfolio of U.S. equities. No such strong fundamental arguments exist, however, for international bonds. Whatever their currency denomination, all bonds are influenced by the same factors: coupon income, interest-rate movements, and changes in credit risk. Unlike equities, which can theoretically rise in price indefinitely, bond prices are effectively capped, as their yields will never fall to zero.[4] The addition of currency exposure allows for significantly greater returns but also greater losses, as currency movements are notoriously difficult to forecast.

There have been long periods (throughout much of the late 1960s and 1970s and again from 1985–1987) when international bonds provided superior returns to U.S. instruments, and long periods (from 1981 to 1984 and from 1988 to 1989) when the reverse was true. In the former case, foreign bonds benefited both from higher yields than in the United States and strengthening currencies. This, coupled with the higher unanticipated inflation rates in the United States compared with other industrialized countries, led to lackluster domestic U.S. bond returns relative to those abroad. The 1985–1987 period is most memorable for the downward spiral in the U.S. dollar, which produced windfall currency gains for holders of foreign-pay instruments. In the 1981–1984 period, U.S. bonds benefited from income streams much higher than in other markets coupled with an improvement in the inflation outlook, which resulted in generous capital

---

4. Historically, the floor for nominal bond yields has been around 2.5 percent.

gains as interest rates declined. In 1988 and 1989, renewed confidence in the U.S. dollar and lower-than-expected inflation in the U.S. economy led to the superior performance of U.S. bonds relative to most foreign-pay alternatives.

These results strongly suggest that potential returns from international bonds relative to U.S. bonds must be carefully analyzed by the three components: income advantage, expected relative domestic price movements, and prospective currency changes.

The best case for ongoing observance of international bonds lies in the continual array of opportunities and risks provided by the constant shifting of international exchange rate and interest rate relationships. The range of starting yields is continuously changing; some foreign rates provide a yield advantage against a U.S. interest rate bogey, and others provide a disadvantage. At any time, different countries will be at different points in their economic and interest rate cycles. Similarly, foreign currency relationships are continuously shifting, sometimes moving with interest rates and sometimes moving against them. Over time, it should be possible to capitalize on these shifting relationships, which will, in the aggregate, supply a greater number of opportunities than any one individual and relatively homogeneous market could. This rationale is an opportunistic and selective one, which has at its heart the cyclicality of economic behavior worldwide.

In the analysis that follows, the eight foreign bond markets in the Salomon Brothers World Bond Market Performance Index[5] are analyzed in relation to the U.S. market. Included are the government bond markets of Australia, Canada, France, Germany, Japan, Netherlands, Switzerland, and the United Kingdom. The analysis focuses on the 1978–1995 period due to the availability of reliable data and a sufficient amount of time for interest rate and currency cycles to work their way through the markets.

A comparison of the eight foreign bond markets with the U.S. market shows that over the period 1978–1995, U.S. bonds provided a slightly inferior rate of return of 10.42 percent compared to a 11.80 percent rate of return produced by a market-weighted index of foreign-pay bonds. The superior performance of the international bond index during this period is largely a function of the time period chosen, since there is no a priori reason to expect international bond returns, over the long run, to be any better or worse than domestic returns. Furthermore, the result is largely influenced by the very strong Japanese returns, which represents roughly one third of the market-weighted index. An index equally weighted in the seven foreign bond markets without Japan would have produced a return only 20 to 30 basis points higher than that of the United States.

---

5. Exhibits 54–1 through 54–8, and 54–10 through 54–12, use the Salomon Brothers World Bond Market Performance Index (WBMPI) because it has seven years of data more than the World Government Bond Index (WGBI). The WBMPI differs from the WGBI in that it has only 9 countries (plus ECU denominated bonds), compared with the WGBI's 14. The WBMPI also includes Euro and foreign bonds, whereas the WGBI includes only domestic government debt. For the analysis of individual country returns, we look only at the domestic government debt component of the WBMPI. Returns for Australia are from October 1984.

Exhibit 54–1 shows total returns from nine bond markets in U.S. dollar terms over the 1978–1995 period. It is interesting to note that foreign-exchange movements added to returns in half the countries, and it subtracted from returns in the other half. Also note that domestic returns were higher than U.S. domestic returns in only half the markets studied. Japan was the best-performing bond market during that period due primarily to the strength of the yen. The strong performance of Australia was due to extraordinary returns in the domestic market, more than 200 basis points above any of the other markets. The United States ranked sixth, toward the middle of the range of returns. Switzerland lagged behind the other countries due to its historically low yields, which more than counteracted the 3 percent per annum appreciation of the Swiss franc versus the U.S. dollar over the 18-year period.

The total return figures in Exhibit 54–1 mask significant disparities in annualized total returns among bond markets. In Exhibit 54–2, the 1978–1995 period is broken down into annual return data for a better look at short-run changes. Notice the large disparity between the best- and worst-performing bond markets in each year. The smallest difference in total returns was recorded in 1995, when the 27.8 percent return in Switzerland was 14.2 percent, better than the 13.6 percent return in the United Kingdom. The largest difference in returns appeared in 1985, when France had a 52.7 percent return and Australian bonds lost 12.4 percent—a 65 percent return differential. These wide disparities are far greater than the re-

E X H I B I T   54–1

International Bond Market Annualized Rates of Return—1978–1995

	Total Return in U.S. Dollars	Return vs. U.S.	Components of Return	
			Total Domestic Return	Foreign Exchange Change
Australia	13.16%	2.74%	14.30%	−0.99%
Canada	9.82	−0.60	11.17	−1.22
France	11.14	0.71	11.43	−0.26
Germany	9.81	−0.61	7.52	2.13
Japan	12.99	2.57	7.84	4.78
Netherlands	10.56	0.13	8.46	1.93
Switzerland	8.01	−2.41	4.80	3.06
United Kingdom	10.71	0.29	12.04	−1.18
United States	10.42	−	10.42	−
International index	11.80	1.38	9.04	2.53

EXHIBIT 54–2

U.S. Bonds and Non-U.S. World Index (Unhedged) vs. Best and Worst Performing Markets

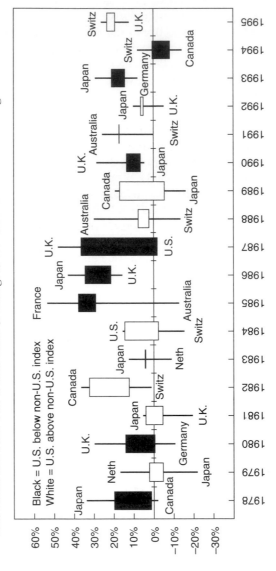

turn differentials in Exhibit 54–1, which have been smoothed out with the passage of time. Also note that the range of variation among bond market returns, and between the U.S. bond market and the non-U.S. government bond index, has narrowed significantly in the past 5 to 6 years. Exhibit 54–2 also shows that it is unusual for countries to appear in the best or worst column in consecutive years. Japan was the best performing market in 1992–93 but was also the worst performing market in 1989–90. Switzerland was the best performer in both 1994 and 1995. All of the countries except Germany had at least one year at the top of the performance ranking, and every country except France was the worst performer for at least one of the 18 years. This reinforces the idea mentioned earlier that value added from opportunistic international bond investing can be great, but over time government policies and market forces tend to correct the economic disparities that lead to large short run gains or losses.

The rates of return experienced by each of the nine countries have no necessary repetitive significance. The 1978–1995 period was unique in many respects. In the late 1970s an acceleration in U.S. inflation and a widening gap in economic growth between the United States and Europe caused U.S. interest rates to rise relative to those in Europe and Japan. The Soviet invasion of Afghanistan and the Iran hostage crisis helped lead to a loss of confidence in the Carter administration and a weakening in the dollar. The second oil shock in 1979 was the reason for the strong performance of the United Kingdom's bond market from 1979 to 1980 and the negative returns in Japan and Germany, two oil-importing countries. The 1981–1984 period was characterized by strong relative returns of U.S. and Canadian bonds due to high income levels and renewed confidence in the dollar. Japanese bonds also performed well due to Japan's success at combating global inflation and the emergence of the yen as the world's strongest currency. The 1985–1986 period experienced one of history's great bond market rallies, with interest rates retreating from the record levels reached earlier in the decade. The dollar's decline from its 1984 peak meant that foreign bond markets were once again in favor among U.S. investors. The 1988–1989 period witnessed a return to dollar strength and declining interest rates in the United States relative to other countries. The political liberalization of Eastern Europe in 1989 had a negative impact on European bond markets as interest rates rose to reflect the unanticipated growth and inflation potential of a more integrated European market. In the early 1990s, concerns over the political fate of European Monetary Union, which led to the United Kingdom and Italy suspending their participation in the European Monetary System, and the eventual widening of the currency fluctuation bands from $2^1/_4$ to 15 percent caused significant European bond and currency market volatility.

Exhibit 54–3 shows the contribution of currency movements to returns. The 1978–1995 period has been divided into three 6-year subperiods to illustrate the impact of a shorter time horizon on foreign currency returns. For each of the 6-year periods, the impact of currency on return has been much higher than for the 18-year period as a whole. This is not surprising given the wide swings in foreign

EXHIBIT 54–3

Average Annual Contribution of Foreign Currency Changes to International Bond Returns

	1978–95	1978–83	1984–89	1990–95
Australia	−0.99%		−1.01%	−0.98%
Canada	−1.22	−2.13%	1.19	−2.68
France	−0.26	−9.18	6.24	2.83
Germany	2.13	−4.31	8.25	2.83
Japan	4.78	0.51	8.25	5.72
Netherlands	1.93	−4.92	8.18	2.97
Switzerland	3.06	−1.52	5.86	5.00
United Kingdom	−1.18	−4.59	1.75	−0.60
International index	2.53	−2.09	6.37	3.50

currency values that can occur in the short term. Over time, as the economic imbalances that caused the currency movements have adjusted, currency prices have readjusted toward previous levels. However, it should be remembered that looking at changes over a long period can mask significant shorter-term volatility. For example, the U.S. dollar appreciated a modest 3.5 percent against the yen during calendar 1995, yet, at one point the dollar had fallen by as much as 20 percent from year-end 1994 levels. A similar caveat should be mentioned in regard to analysis of cyclical data. Applying a long-term average to a study of the cycles of the sun would lead one to conclude that dusk is the normal state, when night and day account for the vast majority of the hours in a day.

A second challenge involving foreign currency exposure relates to the fact that foreign currency adds to the volatility of foreign bond returns. On a market-by-market basis, this has been true. Exhibits 54–4 and 54–5 show the standard deviation of monthly total returns in nine bond markets in both local currency and dollar-denominated terms. The data are presented for the 1978–1995 period and are also broken down into 6-year segments. For the 18-year period as a whole, the volatility of returns in the United States was greater than the volatility of local currency returns in any other market except Canada. Exhibit 54–4 also reflects the fact that volatility has decreased in some countries and increased in others. When foreign exchange movements are factored in, the volatility of foreign bond returns in U.S. dollar terms increases substantially, as shown in Exhibit 54–5. Thus, for the 1978–1995 period, and for each of the subperiods, the United States had the lowest standard deviation of return when all returns were converted to U.S. dollars.

EXHIBIT 54-4

Annualized Standard Deviations of Monthly Domestic Local Bond Market Total Returns

Local Currency	1978–95	1978–83	1983–89	1990–95
Australia	7.7%		7.7%	7.8%
Canada	11.0	13.1%	8.7	10.7
France	6.0	5.7	5.8	6.5
Germany	5.4	6.8	4.0	4.9
Japan	6.2	5.8	6.2	6.5
Netherlands	5.2	6.5	3.7	5.0
Switzerland	4.1	4.6	2.5	4.7
United Kingdom	9.6	11.7	8.4	8.4
United States	9.7	11.8	9.5	6.8
International index	5.1	5.8	4.8	4.8

EXHIBIT 54-5

Annualized Standard Deviations of Monthly Bond Market Total Returns Converted to U.S. Dollars

U.S. Dollars	1978–95	1978–83	1984–89	1990–95
Australia	15.3%		19.0%	11.0%
Canada	12.9	15.2%	10.9	12.0
France	13.5	13.7	14.3	11.7
Germany	14.7	16.2	15.4	11.8
Japan	16.0	17.1	16.4	14.0
Netherlands	13.9	14.8	14.9	11.4
Switzerland	14.7	16.2	15.4	11.9
United Kingdom	16.5	17.6	18.2	13.3
United States	9.6	11.8	9.5	6.8
International index	12.3	13.2	13.7	9.7

The additional volatility associated with foreign currency instruments has led to the development of *currency-hedged* investments, which neutralize the currency component of international bonds while maintaining exposure to local bond price movements. This will be addressed later in the chapter. As discussed in the next section, although foreign exchange rate movements greatly increase the volatility of individual market returns, the overall impact of the currency movements on a diversified international bond portfolio in far less. Importantly, as Exhibit 54–5 shows, the standard deviation of the unhedged International Index in U.S. dollar terms, although higher than the U.S. market, is lower than that of most of the individual markets. This is because the correlations of return between the individual foreign markets and currencies are less than perfect.

Diversification

A second rationale for international bond investing is diversification. The inclusion of foreign bonds in a portfolio should reduce the risk or volatility of returns of a portfolio otherwise invested solely in U.S. fixed income securities. This is because foreign bond markets do not move with, or are not perfectly correlated with, the U.S. bond market. Intuitively this is obvious. The dynamics of the business cycle, and the role of monetary policy in dealing with the business cycle, differ by country. Institutional or structural forces, government financing practices, and tradition mean that the role of buyers and sellers varies among fixed income markets. The trend of inflation, a country's tolerance of inflation, and the sources of inflationary pressure differ among countries, as does the impact of inflation on the trend and structure of interest rates. Finally, a host of geopolitical, foreign policy, and societal forces ensure that the movements of foreign bond prices are not perfectly correlated. Consequently, when foreign currency bonds are added to a portfolio of U.S. fixed income securities, the price movements often offset each other, and the overall volatility of returns can be reduced.

Exhibit 54–6 shows the correlation coefficients of monthly changes in total returns (bond prices plus income) in local currency terms among nine major bond markets over the 1978–1995 period. The bond market with the highest correlation to the U.S. market is Canada's—not a surprising occurrence in view of the bilateral relationships between the two economies. The lowest correlations are between Japanese bonds and some of the European bond markets, which once again is reasonable in view of the lesser interdependence between these economies. In most cases, the correlation among the continental European bond markets is higher than that between those markets and the United States, reflecting the high degree of interdependence between the European economies, and the existence of formal trading and currency relationships.

Exhibit 54–7 shows the correlation coefficients of monthly domestic total returns between the United States and foreign markets broken down by 6-year time periods. In all cases except Canada, the degree of correlation or interdependence rose over the 18-year period or remained roughly unchanged. This is one more statistical manifestation of the degree to which the world is getting smaller,

EXHIBIT 54-6

Correlation Coefficients of Domestic Total Returns in Foreign Bond Markets, 1978–1995 (Based on Monthly Data)

	U.S.	Aus.	Can.	Fra.	Ger.	Jap.	Net.	Swi.	U.K.
United States	1.00								
Australia	.32	1.00							
Canada	.71	.20	1.00						
France	.34	.23	.38	1.00					
Germany	.50	.26	.50	.57	1.00				
Japan	.38	.15	.32	.34	.52	1.00			
Netherlands	.52	.28	.47	.64	.82	.44	1.00		
Switzerland	.36	.23	.33	.41	.55	.39	.57	1.00	
United Kingdom	.39	.29	.38	.38	.43	.36	.44	.37	1.00

EXHIBIT 54-7

Correlation Coefficients between U.S. and Foreign Bond Market Domestic Total Returns (Based on Monthly Data)

	1978–95	1978–83	1984–89	1990–95
Australia	.32		.03	.68
Canada	.71	.76	.83	.51
France	.34	.13	.51	.49
Germany	.50	.54	.47	.51
Japan	.38	.34	.44	.43
Netherlands	.52	.56	.49	.53
Switzerland	.36	.35	.36	.46
United Kingdom	.39	.40	.34	.49
International index	.59	.61	.55	.64

and of the increased synchronization of economic behavior resulting from freer global capital movements. Increased bond market correlation also reflects the more uniform impact on the industrialized countries of a number of significant economic events during the period, notably the second oil shock in 1979–1980, which led to inflation and higher interest rates in all industrialized countries; the global recession that ended in 1982; the economic expansion throughout the remainder of the 1980s; and the crash and quick recovery of global stock markets from 1987 to 1988. The economic policy coordination that began in the postwar era with Bretton Woods accelerated rapidly in the 1970s and 1980s. To the extent that this trend continues, increased interdependence among bond markets is to be expected. For reasons discussed above, however, international bond price trends should remain less than perfectly correlated.

Exhibit 54–8 shows the correlation coefficients of monthly total returns converted to U.S. dollars for the 1978–1995 period overall, again broken down into 6-year segments. A comparison of Exhibits 54–7 and 54–8 shows that the impact of currency movements on the correlation of returns with the United States over the 18 years resulted in substantially smaller correlations for all countries. In the German bond market, changes in the deutschemark/U.S. dollar exchange rate markedly reduced the domestic bond market correlation coefficient from .50 to .33. Over shorter periods, where exchange rate movements are more marked, domestic total return and converted U.S. dollar total return correlations can diverge more substantially. For example, in the 1984–1989 period, the correlation coefficient of German bond market returns with U.S. returns was .47 in local currency terms and only .21 in U.S. dollar terms. Similarly, the correlation coefficient between Japanese and U.S. returns in 1984–1989 was reduced from .44 to .21 when the currency factor was added.

Exhibits 54–7 and 54–8 lead to the conclusion that while local bond price movements among countries are becoming more correlated, currency volatility has continued to reduce the correlation among international bond markets as measured in U.S. dollar terms. This supports the use of international bonds for portfolio diversification.

Another driving force behind the increased correlation of global bond markets has been the convergence of inflation rates at relatively low levels. As Exhibit 54–9 shows, G7 inflation rates rose into double digits following the 1973 and 1979 OPEC

E X H I B I T   54–8

Correlation Coefficients between U.S. and Foreign Bond Market Total Returns Converted to U.S. Dollars (Based on Monthly Data)

	1978–95	1978–83	1984–89	1990–95
Australia	.11		−.04	.42
Canada	.64	.68	.71	.49
France	.29	.25	.27	.38
Germany	.33	.42	.21	.33
Japan	.26	.31	.21	.26
Netherlands	.36	.48	.20	.35
Switzerland	.28	.38	.16	.26
United Kingdom	.34	.44	.18	.39
International index	.40	.50	.25	.44

EXHIBIT 54-9

G7 Inflation Rates (1974–1995, year-on-year changes, smoothed)

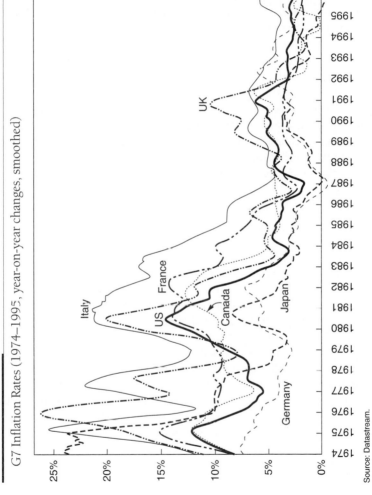

Source: Datastream.

oil price shocks. Bond investors, who had misjudged the inflationary impact during the first OPEC oil price shock in 1973, drove bond prices sharply higher to keep real yields positive. The deflationary policies pursued by the Federal Reserve under Chairman Volker, especially the shift to targeting money supply growth rather than interest rates, also pushed short-term interest rates into uncharted territory. Hence, by 1980, both bond yields and inflation were at extraordinarily high levels, providing opportunities for exceptional bond market returns as central banks waged war on inflation.

In recent years, nearly all central banks have accepted price stability as their primary goal. Central banks in eight countries (Australia, Britain, Canada, Finland, Italy, New Zealand, Spain, and Sweden) have adopted, at least temporarily, explicit inflation targets. An additional four (France, Germany, Switzerland, and Denmark) have medium-term inflation objectives. Some central banks, such as the Bank of England, the Bank of Canada, and Sweden's Riksbank, also publish regular reports on the inflationary outlook. In and of itself, convergence of inflation rates at low levels tends to increase correlations of bond markets and to reduce currency volatility since changes in purchasing power parity are reduced. However, given the increase in cross-border investment flows relative to trade flows, the potential impact on currency volatility is not readily apparent.

THE IMPACT OF INTERNATIONAL BONDS ON A U.S. BOND PORTFOLIO: THE CASE FOR INTERNATIONAL BOND INVESTING

The above analysis demonstrates that a market-weighted portfolio of foreign-pay bonds over the 18-year period from 1978 to 1995 had a U.S. dollar average annual total return of 11.80 percent, slightly higher than the 10.42 average annual return of a U.S.-pay portfolio. Over shorter periods of time, however, foreign-pay bonds occasionally offered better returns, and occasionally worse. Volatility in the individual foreign markets and the aggregate markets in an international index measured in U.S. dollar terms was shown always to be greater than U.S. bond volatility, due to fluctuations in exchange rates. Finally, the correlation of foreign-pay bonds with U.S. bonds was shown to be relatively low, supporting the diversification benefits of international bonds in a U.S. portfolio. Given these risk/return characteristics, it is possible to examine the impact of foreign bonds on a U.S. fixed income portfolio.

Exhibit 54–10 shows a comparison of the compound rates of return of three portfolios: an international bond index market-weighted in the eight foreign markets studied above; the U.S. bond market; and two diversified portfolios. One portfolio is assumed to be invested 80 percent in the U.S. market average and 20 percent in the international index; the second has a 70 percent U.S. weighting.

For the period as a whole, the U.S. bond market underperformed the international index by a margin of 138 basis points (1.38 percent) per annum. The U.S. portfolio return was augmented by 28 basis points when a 20 percent commit-

E X H I B I T   54–10

Compound Annual Rates of Return

	1978–95	1978–83	1984–89	1990–95
International index	11.80%	6.09%	15.78%	13.77%
United States	10.42	6.20	14.26	10.96
Portfolio 1 (80% United States, 20% international index)	10.70	6.18	14.56	11.52
Portfolio 2 (70% United States, 30% international index)	10.84	6.17	14.72	11.80

ment to the international bond index was made, as illustrated by portfolio 1. In portfolio 2, the return was boosted by 42 basis points through a 30 percent commitment to international bonds. The results are magnified if the period is divided into three six-year segments. In 1984–1989, and again in 1990–1995, international bonds outperformed U.S. bonds by a large margin, and a 20 percent commitment to the international bond index added 30 basis points to total return in the 1984–1989 period and 56 basis points to total return in the 1990–1995 period. From 1978 to 1983, U.S. bonds had better returns than the international index, and the net result of a 20 percent commitment to international bonds subtracted only 2 basis points from returns. The 30 percent allocation to international bonds in portfolio 2 provided even better returns for the last two subperiods, adding 46 basis points in the 1984–1989 period and 84 basis points in the 1990–1995 period. The underperformance of portfolio 2 in the 1978–1983 period was only one basis point worse than that of portfolio one, underperforming the U.S. by 3 basis points. Exhibit 54–10 is intuitively obvious from a total return standpoint. International bonds will add to the total returns of a U.S.-based portfolio when the foreign bond markets or currencies outperform the U.S. market, and they will be a drain on returns when the reverse is true.

Exhibit 54–11 shows the effect of international diversification on the standard deviation of a portfolio. Despite the substantially higher volatility of the international bond index relative to the U.S. market, a weighting in international bonds can lower the overall volatility of a U.S. portfolio because the correlation between U.S. bonds and international bonds is relatively low. Over the 1978–1995 period, a 20 percent weighting in international bonds added 28 basis points to total return while lowering the annual standard deviation of the portfolio from 9.64 percent to 8.17 percent. A 30 percent allocation to international bonds results in an even lower standard deviation of 7.80 percent. This supports the theory that international bonds have some diversification characteristics. Even during the 1978–1983 period, when international bonds had a lower return and higher volatility than U.S. bonds, a 20 percent weighting in international bonds

EXHIBIT 54–11

Annualized Standard Deviations of Monthly Returns (in U.S. Dollars)

	1978–95	1978–83	1984–89	1990–95
International index	12.34%	13.17%	13.57%	9.60%
United States	9.64	11.83	9.45	6.77
Portfolio 1 (80% United States, 20% international index)	8.17	9.93	8.09	5.81
Portfolio 2 (70% United States, 30% international index)	7.80	9.32	7.84	5.63

lowered the annualized standard deviation of the portfolio by 1.90 percent, a reduction of nearly one-sixth, at a cost of only 2 basis points in foregone return.

During shorter periods of time, or during different time periods, the internationally diversified portfolio may have a higher volatility than the U.S. market average. For example, in the 1986–1989 period, coinciding with strong returns in the foreign bond markets and sharp fluctuation in exchange rates, international bonds increased portfolio volatility slightly, but added 95 basis points to total return. During this period, correlations of returns to the U.S. market remained relatively low although somewhat higher than in previous periods. However, the fluctuations of the currency markets added significantly to the volatility (and return) of foreign bonds relative to U.S. bonds, which were enjoying a period of relative stability. The net effect was that a combination of 20 percent international bonds and 80 percent U.S. bonds was slightly more volatile than a U.S. portfolio.

The trade-off between low correlations of international returns with U.S. returns but higher volatility compared with U.S. returns also explains why most long-run studies of the appropriate mix of international bonds in an overall portfolio is in the 20 to 40 percent range. This is illustrated in Exhibit 54–12 using the data from Exhibits 54–10 and 54–11. A portfolio of 100 percent U.S. government bonds resulted in a return of 10.42 percent and a standard deviation of 9.66 percent. As international bonds were initially added to the portfolio, volatility declined and returns increased. A portfolio of 60 percent U.S. bonds and 40 percent international bonds had the lowest overall volatility. Beyond this point, an investor could still have added to total returns by increasing the portfolio weighting in international bonds, but only at the cost of higher overall portfolio volatility. At the upper end of this range, the higher volatility of foreign bonds in U.S. dollar terms relative to U.S. bonds, despite the low correlation of foreign bonds and U.S. bonds, meant that the combined volatility of foreign and U.S. bonds was higher than for U.S. bonds alone.

EXHIBIT 54–12

Historical Risk/Return Trade-Off of International Diversification (1978–1995 Monthly Data)

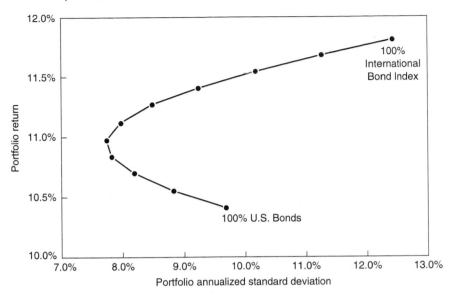

As discussed above, the rationale behind foreign-pay bond investing is twofold: the opportunity for superior returns resulting from changes in relative interest rates and exchange rates, and a reduction in long-term portfolio volatility for a given return. The objectives and requirements of each different portfolio will determine which of these considerations has greater sway over the decision to invest overseas. Although return enhancement and lower volatility are both important considerations in portfolio management, the evidence suggests that the potential for enhanced returns through active management should be the primary motive for international bond investing since the reduction in volatility of a combined U.S. and foreign portfolio is relatively small.

As the currency component of unhedged foreign-pay international bonds results in substantially more volatility for U.S. dollar-based investors than domestic bonds, it seems reasonable to question how it impacts a portfolio's risk/return characteristics relative to other asset classes, especially domestic equities and hedged foreign-pay bonds.[6] Exhibit 54–13 shows that for the period 1985–1995, the risk/return profile for a portfolio with varying percentages allocated to the

---

6. We return to the Salomon Non-U.S. World Government Bond Index which includes a currency-hedged index assuming rolling one-month forward foreign exchange contracts. The equity series used is a Standard & Poor's equity composite total return index from Datastream.

EXHIBIT 54-13

U.S. Bonds versus U.S. Equities and Hedged and Unhedged International Bonds (1985–1995 Monthly Data)

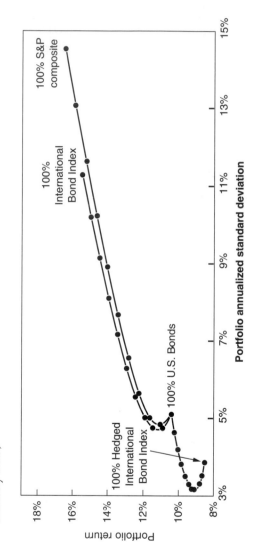

Standard & Poor's 500 Composite Index and U.S. bonds was very similar to the profile of international bonds and U.S. bonds. The chart also shows that for the 1985–1995 period hedged international bonds provided much better risk reduction than either U.S. equities or international bonds alone, but at a significant cost in total return. Hedge costs and a declining dollar produced a return for the hedged non-U.S. bond index that was 7 percent lower than the unhedged non-U.S. index and 1.9 percent lower than U.S. returns.

The conclusion to be drawn from this analysis is that unhedged foreign-pay international bonds are a very different animal from most other bond products. The impact of unhedged international bonds on the risk/return profile of a domestic bond portfolio for the 1985–1995 period is very similar to the addition of domestic equities. Hedged non-U.S. bond returns historically have reduced the standard deviations of returns, but at a significantly lower return than those available from either U.S. bonds or unhedged non-U.S. investments. This has led some studies to conclude that a partially hedged portfolio of non-U.S. bonds provides a better portfolio diversifier than either a completely hedged or completely unhedged portfolio. While the diversification benefits are likely to remain, it is not clear that there is any ongoing reason why hedged international bonds should routinely underperform U.S. bonds.

ACTIVE INTERNATIONAL BOND MANAGEMENT

Thus far, the discussion has centered on passive allocations to either hedged or unhedged foreign-pay international bonds. But what of active international bond management? There is little question that, with the benefit of hindsight, a strategy of active international bond investing over the 18-year period from 1978 to 1995 could have provided enhanced returns to a U.S.-based investor. Exhibit 54–2 showed the best- and worst-performing bond markets for each of the 18 years. In only one of the 18 years, 1984, was the U.S. market the best performer. In 1987, for example, a U.S. investor could have realized almost a 50 percent return enhancement by investing in United Kingdom long bonds. Although choosing the best market is always difficult, *any* of the foreign bond markets in 1987 would have provided more attractive returns in dollar or local currency terms than the U.S. market. Against the U.S., the unhedged international bond index outperformed in 8 years, underperformed in 8 years, and had the same total return in 2 years, with an annualized outperformance of 1.38 percent. The crucial question, of course, is whether, without such hindsight, a portfolio manager can provide incremental return through active international investing without incurring a commensurate degree of risk. The wide disparity of returns in Exhibit 54–2 illustrates the significant opportunities in foreign-pay bonds but also points to the pitfalls of adopting an inappropriate investment strategy.

At the heart of the case for active international bond management is the ability to profit from inefficiencies in international markets. Inefficiencies arise from capital controls, restricted information flows, or simply differences in how market participants use similar information. Differences in tax treatment by countries, legal impediments that restrict the free flow of capital across borders, and differences in national character and institutions all create disparities in national investment postures. Although there is evidence to suggest that the international bond and currency markets are becoming more efficient, they are still a long way from the efficiency of the U.S. market, which benefits from the homogeneity of rules and regulations governing the investment community. In the international markets, the availability of information, particularly with regard to central bank policies, is much improved over earlier years, but a variety of impediments prevent market information from being used in a similar fashion.

A classic example of the inefficiency of international bond markets arising from differences in investment objectives is the case of Switzerland. For years, the Swiss capital markets benefited from the country's reputation as a safe haven from the Cold War, and from strict secrecy laws that emphasized anonymity. The demand among private investors for Swiss franc-denominated assets and bank accounts meant Swiss interest rates were far lower than they otherwise would have been had investors been making the same analytical decisions regarding Swiss bonds as they were making regarding other international bonds. This is one reason for the unattractive total returns on Swiss bonds in the 1978–1989 period. In the late 1980s, as the Cold War wound down and the secrecy laws that attracted dubious cash to Switzerland came under fire, Swiss interest rates rose to levels more in line with economic fundamentals.

The foreign exchange markets do compensate over time for inefficiencies noticeable in various domestic bond markets, but in the short term currencies can actually magnify total return discrepancies. Economic theory teaches that interest rate differentials and currency changes reflect differential inflation rates so that currency changes equal the difference in income factors. Historically, high-inflation countries, such as Australia, with generous domestic bond returns due to high nominal income streams, have experienced a loss in the value of their currency relative to moderate-inflation countries with lower domestic nominal bond returns. Exhibit 54–14 shows that there has been a strong correlation between the change in exchange rates relative to the dollar since the demise of fixed exchange rates in the early 1970s and changes in the price level relative to the United States. The currencies of Japan, Germany, Switzerland, and the Netherlands, whose price levels grew during the 24-year period only 60 to 80 percent as much as in the United States, all appreciated significantly against the U.S. dollar, from 100 to 240 percent.

Over shorter periods of time, however, foreign exchange movements often act counter to what theory would dictate. This is most apparent in the huge total return differentials in Exhibit 54–2. A myriad of special factors determine exchange rate movements in the short term; inflation differentials is only one of these factors. Official foreign exchange intervention and different perceptions of political forces are among the many factors that distort fundamental exchange rate relationships. In view of these inefficiencies and the investment opportunities

Exchange Rates and Inflation Relative to U.S. 1972–1995

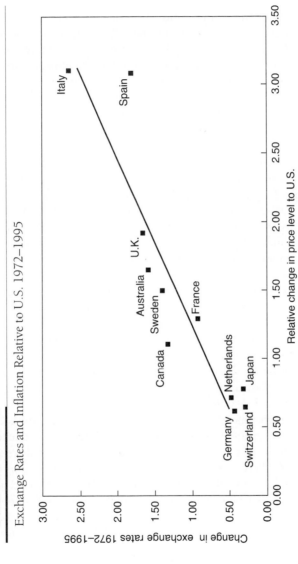

Source: Datastream

they present, active international bond investment can use active currency management to add incremental value to a U.S.-based portfolio.

THE TOOLS OF ACTIVE MANAGEMENT

Of the three components of international bonds returns: income, capital change, and currency, only income in local currency terms, and hence the initial margin over the income bogey provided by U.S. alternatives, are known with certainty. However, even this income cushion will be subject to change as exchange rates fluctuate; and the shorter the investment time horizon, the less important the yield relationship with U.S. bonds. Yield spreads are measured in annual terms, so that a 2 percent yield advantage of French franc bonds over U.S. bonds shrinks to a mere 0.5 percent cushion if the investment time horizon is three months. A margin of 50 basis points is practically insignificant in the international bond markets in light of the potential volatility in currencies and relative interest rates that can occur over three months.

A simple, long-term strategy of investing in the highest-yielding international bond markets normally is not appropriate for total-return-oriented investors. This is true for two reasons. First, high interest rates usually reflect domestic economic imbalances, such as inflation (real or perceived) or strong growth in the money supply, which can lead to an erosion in local bond prices. Second, high yields often are necessary to compensate investors for an expected decline in the relative value of the local currency. Those countries with the highest income streams—such as Australia, the United Kingdom, and Canada—have experienced a weakening of their currencies versus the U.S. dollar. Over shorter periods of time, when foreign exchange movements and bond prices are not directly linked to domestic economic fundamentals but are a response to managed rates, a yield-oriented investment strategy may be appropriate. This proved to be the case in 1988 in Australia, where high yields and a strengthening currency led to generous converted U.S. dollar returns.

The factors that have a bearing on currency fluctuation, the second component of return, have been reviewed earlier. By and large, they relate to fundamental economic and political trends.[7] From a practical viewpoint, there are two main problems in using these factors to project currency movements. One relates to the analyst's ability to accurately perceive trends not already reflected in the present currency price. The second relates to the interaction of these factors and the ability to project which factors will dominate. As pointed out earlier, the component of return provided by currency changes for an international bond index over long

---

7. For a complete discussion of the fundamental and technical factors influencing exchange rates, see Michael Rosenberg, *Currency Forecasting: A Guide to Fundamental and Technical Models of Exchange Rate Determination* (Burr Ridge, IL: Irwin, 1993) and Roger G. Clarke and Mark P. Kritzman, *Currency Management: Concepts and Practices* (Charlottesville, VA: The Research Foundation of the Institute of Chartered Financial Analysts, 1996).

time periods has not been large. In Exhibit 54–1, the currency contribution to the index's total return for the 1978–1995 period was shown to be 2.53 percent per annum. As can be seen in Exhibit 54–2, currency becomes increasingly important, however, as the time period is shortened; and changes can be even more significant for individual markets.[8] Thus the international bond investor must be willing to make judgments on foreign exchange.

The third component of return, domestic price movements, must be analyzed both absolutely and relative to expected U.S. movements. There are substantial differences between various markets regarding the extent of government influence on the level of interest rates. However, the common key variables affecting interest rate movements are generally viewed to be the following:

1. Monetary policy, particularly with regard to exchange rates.

2. The level and direction of domestic inflation rates.

3. Demand for funds, which is often related to real GNP growth.

4. Supply of funds.

5. Fiscal policy and budget deficits.

6. Social and political developments.

These variables must be analyzed to assess their likely impact on the direction of interest rates in each country. As in the United States, this analysis must distinguish between movements in short rates and long rates, which most often are in the same direction but not usually of equal magnitude. When the potential shape and movement of the yield curve in each country is projected, judgments on the appropriate maturity structure can be made.

Gone are the days when interest rate projections could be made on a country-by-country basis, with no regard to the impact of international economic developments on domestic bond prices. In the early 1980s, for example, domestic economic trends and apparent government desires would have suggested lower interest levels in a number of foreign economies, but record-high U.S. interest rates precluded lower rates abroad without precipitating even further foreign exchange deterioration versus the U.S. dollar. In 1989, the surging deutschemark forced many European countries to keep short-term rates high relative to Germany to guard against currency volatility in the closely aligned European economies. This divergence of policy objectives led to intense pressures within the European Monetary System, which resulted in the United Kingdom and Italy leaving the EMS in 1992 and the widening of the fluctuation bands from $2^1/_4$ percent to 15 percent in 1993. Today, few projections of foreign interest rate levels are made without reference to expectations for German, Japanese, and United States interest rate levels. In fact, some systems, such as J.P. Morgan's RiskMet-

---

8. Exhibit 6 of Chapter 17 shows that the contribution of currency to annual international bond returns ranged from –6.3 percent to +25.6 percent over an 11-year period.

rics™, use correlations between markets to arrive at a measure of value at risk for global bond portfolios.

Clearly, then, international bond portfolio management requires ongoing economic analysis and judgment to assess the prospective exchange rate and domestic price components of return. It is important to distinguish between these two components when making judgments about prospective total returns. Whereas the income component of return is predictable, exchange rates and domestic bond prices will change, and they may not change in the same direction and with the same magnitude. Active international investment requires separate judgments to be made about the attractiveness of each country's interest rates and currency. There may be times when a bond market is attractive for interest-rate reasons and unattractive for currency reasons. Whereas one option in such a scenario would be to avoid foreign-pay investment until currency risk is deemed appropriate, another option would be to purchase the foreign bond and eliminate the foreign exchange risk by hedging the currency exposure in the forward currency markets. Currency-hedged bond investments are examined later in the chapter.

MANAGING AN INTERNATIONAL BOND PORTFOLIO

The foregoing analysis detailing the advantages of including foreign-pay international bonds in a domestic bond portfolio still leaves many questions unanswered about how such a portfolio should be structured. Should the portfolio be global, or international (excluding the United States)? If it is international, can U.S. bonds be held opportunistically, or not at all? Can the portfolio invest in emerging markets? Can it use futures and options? For currencies, or for interest rates also? Should the portfolio be completely hedged? Should proxy hedging (hedging a cash bond exposure in one currency with a short derivatives position in another currency) be allowed? Should duration or maturity limitations be imposed? Should a maximum country allocation be imposed? If so, on an absolute basis or relative to a benchmark?

Guidelines and Benchmarks

As a global bond portfolio can be many things, a clear set of guidelines is essential for effective management. As part of the guidelines, the selection of an appropriate benchmark is desirable. Many benchmark indexes are available for global bond markets with subindexes in many permutations: ex-U.S., currency-hedged, G7 only, 1–3 year, 3–5 year, 7–10 year, emerging markets, Brady bonds, and so on. Although some clients may only wish to outperform a U.S. benchmark, an international benchmark should be selected for both measuring performance and quantifying risk.

The benchmark, with its weightings and durations for each market, serves as the baseline portfolio and the performance bogey. The portfolio manager may choose to over- or underweight a particular market based upon a favorable or unfavorable outlook in one of three ways. Hold a smaller (or even zero) percentage in the portfolio than is contained in the index; reduce the duration of the holdings in that country to below the duration of the index; or hedge out the currency risk back into dollars or into another currency expected to provide better performance, or some combination of the above.

Exhibit 54–15 displays the composition of two of the most widely used global government bond indices: the Salomon Brothers World Government Bond Index and the J.P. Morgan Global Government Bond Index.

As you can see, the two indexes differ somewhat in the weightings they give to different markets. The largest difference is in the weight given to Japan, which accounts for 31.73 percent of the Salomon index but only 24.82 percent of the J.P. Morgan index. The J.P. Morgan index also has a duration of almost one-half year longer than the Salomon Brothers index in both Japan and Italy. The reason for these differences is that the Salomon index is market-weighted, based on the total outstandings of each bond market, whereas the J.P. Morgan index purports to use only actively traded bonds within each market. Of the universe of non-U.S. fixed income domestic government securities, J.P. Morgan considers only 60 percent to be "investable," that is, tradeable and redeemable for cash and not appealing exclusively to domestic investors for tax or regulatory reasons.

EXHIBIT 54–15

Comparison of J.P. Morgan and Salomon Brothers Non-U.S. Government Bond Indexes (December 1995)

Country	J.P. Morgan Global Government Bond Index—Excluding U.S.		Salomon Brothers Non-U.S. World Government Bond Index	
	Weight	Duration	Weight	Duration
Japan	24.82%	6.14	31.73%	5.65
Germany	16.22	4.61	16.03	4.42
France	12.34	5.19	10.37	5.46
U.K.	9.43	5.99	7.83	6.03
Italy	7.29	3.71	8.78	3.23
Holland	6.51	5.76	5.25	5.61
Belgium	5.51	4.91	4.12	4.87
Spain	4.63	3.81	3.54	3.72
Canada	4.61	5.24	4.42	5.46
Sweden	3.55	4.00	2.73	4.01
Denmark	3.12	4.76	2.47	4.69
Australia	1.99	4.49	1.46	4.58
Austria	—	—	1.26	4.51

Thus, care should be taken to select a benchmark that most closely matches the objectives of the client or fund.

The selection of a benchmark is only part of establishing an appropriate set of guidelines. The guidelines should also be explicit on what markets or securities may be purchased (by region, credit rating, etc.), any maturity or credit-quality targets or constraints, the use of derivatives in either foreign exchange or interest rate instruments, hedging policy, and so on.

Portfolio Allocation: Selecting Markets

Actively managed portfolios (i.e., those not attempting to replicate the performance of an index) need a discipline for deciding which markets to over- or underweight within the portfolio at any one time. Loosely speaking, international bonds trade within four blocs: the dollar bloc (the United States, Canada, Australia, and New Zealand); the European, or deutschemark bloc; Japan (which stands alone); and the emerging markets. The deutschemark bloc is often further subdivided into a core group (Germany, France, Holland, and Belgium) and a peripheral group (Italy, Spain, the United Kingdom, Denmark, Sweden, Finland, and Portugal). These groupings are only approximate, as many might create a different division between the European core and periphery.

The trading bloc construct is useful because each bloc has a benchmark market that greatly influences price movements in the other markets. Investors are often more focused on the spread level of, say, Denmark to Germany, than the absolute level of yields in Denmark. Generally speaking, when bond markets are rallying, spreads within each bloc tend to narrow, much as corporate bond spreads tend to tighten in the United States when yields on Treasuries are falling. In Europe, the peripheral markets tend to outperform the core markets in a bond market rally, much like a high beta stock will outperform during a stock market rally. However, just like high beta stocks in the equity market, peripheral bond markets will tend to underperform in a bear market. Thus, international bond portfolio managers tend to add risk relative to the benchmark (lengthen duration, overweight higher-yielding markets) if they are bullish and to reduce risk if they are bearish.

As bond markets within each trading bloc tend to trade in a similar fashion, international bond portfolio managers can try to outperform the index without incurring excessive additional risk by over- and underweighting selected markets within a bloc while keeping their bloc-by-bloc allocations close to the benchmark. For example, during 1995, many portfolio managers were concerned over political developments in Italy but felt that the peripheral group as a whole would outperform the core. Thus, they chose to increase their holdings of Spanish and Swedish government bonds at the expense of their Italian holdings. International bond portfolio managers can also sometimes outperform their benchmarks by investing in markets outside of the index (provided that such investments are permissible under the portfolio's guidelines). For example, one of the best performing bond markets in dollar terms for 1995 was Finland, which was not contained in either the Salomon or J.P. Morgan government bond indexes. The downside of this strategy can be seen in those portfolios that had a significant exposure to emerging markets during the Mexican crisis in the first quarter of 1995.

CURRENCY-HEDGED BOND INVESTMENT

Foreign-pay bonds incorporate two kinds of risks: interest rate risk, which is a part of all fixed income securities; and currency risk, which is unique to foreign currency-denominated securities. Once the decision is made to purchase foreign-pay bonds, the investor must decide whether the expected return from the foreign currency component of the bond is sufficient to compensate for the additional volatility inherent in a foreign currency instrument. The decision whether or not to adopt an open foreign currency position is easier to make if incremental return is the sole reason for international bond investing. However, international bonds also have important diversification benefits that result from both foreign interest-rate and currency exposure. Because foreign currency movements are a major factor behind the lower correlation of foreign-pay bonds with domestic bonds, a decision to eliminate currency risk based on a pessimistic foreign currency projection will almost certainly increase the correlation of the non-dollar bond returns with the U.S. returns relative to the correlation of unhedged returns with the U.S. returns. While highly correlated, the volatility of hedged bonds, especially a diversified group of hedged bonds, may be sufficiently lower than the U.S. market to provide a significant diversification benefit (see Exhibit 54–13).

In the early 1990s, a new subset of international bond funds experienced explosive growth: short-term global income funds. These funds were designed to generate high-coupon income while maintaining a fairly stable net asset value. Three factors in particular motivated the creation of these funds. First, relatively high interest rates abroad, especially in the peripheral European countries, which allowed for generous coupon income. Second, a stable European Monetary System, which, outside of infrequent devaluations, held currencies within a narrow $2^{1}/_{4}$ percent, or wide 6 percent, band. This allowed for proxy hedging of peripheral currency exposure with core market currencies where interest rates, and hence hedging costs, were significantly lower. Third, a plan for European Monetary Union that would replace national currencies with a single pan-European currency by 1999 led to increased optimism about the prospects for capital gains in the peripheral bond markets. This is because, with the adoption of a single currency, the devaluation risk component of interest rates, which was substantial in some markets, would be eliminated, allowing for significantly lower interest rates. Also, although most of the short-term global income funds were run on a currency-hedged basis, a downward trending dollar also enhanced returns.

The short-term global income funds enjoyed several years of generous returns with relative price stability. However, with the breakdown of the European Monetary System in 1992, which led to the exit of the British pound and Italian lira from the system and devaluations by most of the other EMS participants relative to the deutschemark, many funds experienced losses and far more volatility than their shareholders were comfortable with. Many short-term global income funds have closed or changed to full-duration global bond funds, as investors moved to other types of funds.

Mechanics of Currency-Hedged Bond Investing

To purchase a foreign-pay bond, two separate transactions must be made. The bond must be purchased, and then the currency in which the bond is denominated must be purchased to pay for the bond. If the decision is made to hedge the foreign currency component of the bond, a simultaneous sale of the currency purchased is transacted through the forward currency market.[9] In practice, the forward sale of a currency entails no money changing hands between the currency dealer and the investor. Instead, a sale price for the currency at some point in the future is agreed upon, and the investor commits to deliver the currency at that future point and at that price. The currency dealer commits to delivering dollars in return. In other words, the investor has locked in a sale price for the foreign currency, thereby eliminating practically all exposure to currency volatility in the interim.

Currency exposure can be fully hedged using a series of forward exchange contracts matching each of the coupon payments and the final principal repayment when the foreign bond matures. Fully hedged investment is relatively unusual, mostly because investors rarely purchase a bond with the intention of holding it to maturity, but also because the liquidity of the forward currency markets beyond one or two years is fairly limited. The most common practice is to use rolling forward contracts from one month to one year in duration, which may be renewed at the expiration date. Rolling forward contracts are not perfect hedges because the price of the bond is difficult to predict at some point in the future, but the amount of residual foreign exchange exposure generally is quite small and has little impact on total return.

Hedged foreign bond investment reduces the currency volatility involved with international investing. Two components of return, income and currency gain or loss, become known quantities.[10] The only unknown is the local price change of the foreign bond. An investor can compare the foreign-pay bond yield combined with the known currency gain or loss embodied in the forward discount or premium with yields available on straight domestic bonds. This differential can then be incorporated into projections for foreign interest rate changes relative to

---

9. Several currency-hedging alternatives, including currency swaps or options, are available, although the forward markets combine the most widely used for hedged global bond investing.
10. For a more detailed analysis of forward currency contracts and the foreign exchange markets, see Roger M. Kubarych, *Foreign Exchange Markets in the United States*. Rev. ed. (Federal Reserve Bank of New York, 1983).

domestic interest rate changes. If expected foreign bond market returns are greater than both the yield give-up (if any) required to buy the foreign bond and the forward currency discount (if any), then the hedged foreign bond is an attractive investment from a total return point of view. A simple example illustrates this relationship.

Assume that 10-year yields on United Kingdom (U.K.) bonds are 9.0 percent and 10-year U.S. bond yields are 8.0 percent. Further assume that the spot rate for sterling is 1.600 dollars per one pound sterling and that the three-month forward rate is 1.595 dollars per pound—a 0.33 percent discount over three months.[11] The hedged U.K. bond return over a three-month period is as follows:

$$\text{Income} + \frac{\text{Forward discount}}{\text{or premium}} + \frac{\text{U.K. bond}}{\text{price change}^{12}}$$

$$2.25\ \% = {}^9\!/_4 + (-0.33\%) + \text{U.K. bond price change}$$
$$= 1.92\% + \text{U.K. bond price change}$$

The 1.92 percent known return from income and currency in U.K. bonds can then be compared to the 2.0 percent known income return from U.S. bonds (8 percent/4) over three months. The differential of 0.08 percent must be made up by price appreciation of the U.K. bond relative to the U.S. bond. If the U.K. bond appreciates by more than 0.08 percent on a relative basis, the currency-hedged investment earns a superior return.

Currency-hedged international bond investment reduces the decision to buy foreign-pay bonds to a projection of relative interest rate spreads. If foreign interest rates are expected to decline relative to U.S. rates sufficiently to offset the net of the income advantage or disadvantage versus the hedge gain or cost, then

---

11. The discount or premium for the currency in the forward market is closely aligned with the yield spread on Eurodeposits of the same duration as the forward contract. In this example, three-month Eurosterling deposits are assumed to be 8.8 percent, and three-month Eurodollar deposits are 7.5 percent. The discount is computed as follows:

$$\text{Spot rate} \times 1 + \frac{(\text{Eurodollar rate} - \text{Eurosterling rate})}{4}$$
$$= 1.600 \times 1 + \frac{(.075 - .088)}{4}$$
$$= 1.600 \times .99675$$
$$= 1.5948$$

Therefore, $1.5948/1.6000 = .9967$ or a discount of .0033.

12. These three components are not really additive since currency gain or loss should be applied to the income and local price change as well. Nonetheless, both these effects generally are quite small. More specifically, the actual formula is as follows:

$$\frac{\text{Forward discount}}{\text{or premium}} + (\text{Income} + \text{U.K. bond price change}) \times 1 + \frac{(\text{forward discount or premium})}{100}$$

hedged investment will augment total returns regardless of the course of the U.S. dollar over the holding period. The cost of the currency hedge generally is of only minor import in making total return projections, particularly over the short term.[13] In the above example, U.K. 10-year interest rates have to decline only 2 basis points relative to U.S. rates to compensate for the cost of the hedge, an insignificant movement considering the lack of correlation between U.K. and U.S. local bond markets.

Rolling Hedged Yields

When currency-hedged investment first became popular in the mid-1980s, reference occasionally was made to computing so-called rolling hedged yields on foreign bonds as a basis of comparison with U.S. bond yields. Rolling hedged yields are computed by adding the *annualized* discount or premium for the currency hedge to the yield-to-maturity of the foreign bond for an "all-in yield." In the above example using a U.K. 10-year bond, the rolling hedged yield is calculated as follows:

Yield-to-maturity of foreign bond + Annualized discount or premium

$$= 9.0\% + -(0.33\% \times 4) = 9.0\% - 1.3\%$$
$$= 7.7\%$$

The rolling hedged yield of 7.7 percent on the U.K. bond could then be used as a measure of relative value versus the 8.0 percent yield available in the United States.

The problem with using rolling hedged yields as yield-to-maturity equivalents is that rolling hedged yield calculations assume that the cost of the hedge (i.e., the discount or premium) will not change over the life of the bond. This is almost assuredly not the case. Hedge costs vary directly with U.S. and foreign short-term interest rate spreads. When the currency hedge is rolled out after each expiration date, the new hedge cost will reflect the prevailing short-term interest rate spread, which may be very different from what it was when the hedge was last rolled. A rolling hedged yield is better used as a measure of the shape of the

---

13. Occasionally, hedge costs can be fairly high, particularly when short-term interest rates in the United States are low relative to foreign rates. In December 1989, three-month Eurosterling deposits were 15.2 percent and three-month Eurodollar deposits were 8.5 percent. A three-month sterling hedge back into dollars would have cost 1.7 percent. Nonetheless, this is relatively unusual and generally coincides with a time when the yield advantage of the foreign bond in question exceeds the U.S. rate by a large amount. In December 1989, 10-year U.K. government bonds yielded 10.5 percent, and U.S. Treasuries yielded 7.9 percent.

14. This is true because hedge costs are a function of relative short rates, and the yield spread between two 10-year bonds is a function of relative long rates. High-rolling hedged yields reflect more positively shaped foreign yield curves, which, taken alone, say little about prospective total returns.

foreign yield curve relative to the U.S. yield curve than as a measure of prospective total returns.[14]

To restate, with currency-hedged investment, the cost of the hedge and the income advantage or disadvantage of the foreign bond is known from the outset. The investor is left with the decision of whether the foreign bond market will have better local price appreciation relative to the U.S. market and whether the expected marginal appreciation will be enough to compensate for any income or hedge costs that may accompany the foreign bond purchase.

Hedged versus Unhedged Foreign Bonds

The ability to participate in foreign interest-rate cycles without the added volatility of currency movements is appealing from both a theoretical and a practical standpoint. Many analysts and portfolio managers have argued that currency-hedged investing is a priori superior to unhedged investing because of the former's more favorable risk/return characteristics over the long term. There is some theoretical justification to this argument for dollar-based investors. If forward exchange rates, which govern hedge costs, accurately reflect the expected average movement of foreign currencies versus the dollar (i.e., forward rates do not include an embedded risk premium or discount), then hedged foreign bond returns will be equivalent to unhedged returns over time. Research tends to support this theory, although, as was mentioned earlier, total return comparisons between foreign and domestic bonds, hedged or unhedged, are somewhat beholden to the time period chosen. For example, for the period 1985–1995, the Salomon Non-U.S. World Government Bond Index returned 15.44 percent in U.S. dollar terms, 7 percentage points more than the hedged Non-U.S. World Government Bond Index. However, if we exclude the first three years of the index, 1985–1987 when the dollar was declining sharply against all currencies from its 1984 peak and currencies contributed more than 23 percent on average to index returns, the picture changes dramatically. Over the last eight years of the index, 1988–1995, the return differential between the hedged and unhedged indexes narrowed to 1.52 percent in favor of the unhedged Non-U.S. World Government Bond Index.

The theoretical debate over the superiority of hedged or unhedged investment has little practical significance. In fact, the historical attractiveness of one form of investment over the other varies considerably with the base currency of the investor and the time period studied.[15] From a practical standpoint, the choice between currency-hedged and unhedged foreign bonds depends on the priorities of the international bond investor. For total-return investors, whether or not to

15. Hedged foreign bonds have been attractive from a risk/return standpoint for U.S.-based investors due to the high volatility of the U.S. bond market. For investors based in Switzerland or Japan, however, hedged investing has been considerably less attractive because of the historically low volatility of Swiss and Japanese bonds. For a more complete discussion, see Chapter 55, "International Fixed Income Investing: Theory and Practice."

hedge is a function of the outlook for the currency in which the foreign bond is denominated. For long-term investors interested in lowering the overall volatility of a U.S. dollar portfolio, and only a small overall allocation to international bond portfolios, unhedged foreign bonds can be used to good effect. This is true because the currency component of unhedged bonds, which is eliminated in hedged bond portfolios, means that unhedged bonds have a lower correlation with dollar-denominated instruments. When small amounts of international bonds are added to a predominantly U.S. dollar bond portfolio, unhedged bonds are effective diversifiers. For investors unable or unwilling to take currency risk but still interested in diversification, hedged bonds are an appropriate substitute. In addition, the larger the commitment to international bonds relative to U.S. bonds or equities, the greater the case for hedging, as the low volatility of hedged bonds in and of themselves becomes more important than their correlations to other asset classes.

CONCLUSION

International bonds have historically provided both superior returns and a risk-reduction benefit when added to portfolios of U.S. Treasuries. Active management of an international bond portfolio offers the possibility of further enhancing returns as market inefficiencies and varying economic cycles result in imperfectly correlated bond market movements. However, a thorough understanding of capital flows, economic fundamentals, and local market structure is required to anticipate changes in bond and currency prices and to outperform the international index over time.

Some investors have turned to currency-hedged international bond investment to participate in foreign interest rate cycles without taking currency risk. Hedged investment is appropriate when the prospects for foreign bond markets are attractive relative to the prospects for U.S. bonds, irrespective of potential currency movements. Although hedged international bonds have a greater correlation with U.S. bonds due to the lack of currency fluctuation, evidence suggests that hedged bonds can reduce the volatility of a U.S.-based portfolio and occasionally augment portfolio returns.

There is no a priori reason to expect international bonds, hedged or unhedged, to provide superior long-term returns relative to U.S. bonds. To the extent that governments continue to remove the remaining barriers to world capital flows, fixed income returns and interest-rate volatility in the major markets can be expected to converge. In the meantime, the variance of monetary, fiscal, and political trends and policies among countries suggest that, from time to time, particular markets will offer better investment value than the U.S. market.

INTERNATIONAL FIXED INCOME INVESTING: THEORY AND PRACTICE

Michael R. Rosenberg, Ph.D.
First Vice President and Manager
International Fixed Income Research
Merrill Lynch Capital Markets

In a recent Greenwich Associates study of institutional bond buying in the United States, two emerging trends appeared significant to the future direction of the fixed income investment business. According to the study, the primary trend emerging among U.S. bond buyers is the increasing globalization of bond portfolios. The secondary trend, which is directly related to the primary trend, is the greatly increased use of risk management instruments to deal with the risk and volatility of U.S. portfolio managers' increasingly diversified international bond portfolios.

These trends toward globalization and the more sophisticated use of risk management tools are growing at an increasingly rapid pace among European and Japanese investors as well and have caused a need for more detailed information on the theory and practice of global bond portfolio management. The purpose of this chapter is to address that need by critically analyzing the case for international fixed income diversification from a risk/return and active-management standpoint, and by providing internationally minded investors with the basic tools to actively manage their global bond portfolios.

The chapter is divided into six sections. The first section examines the contribution that international bonds can make to the risk/return profile of a broadly diversified portfolio. Contrary to the generally accepted notion that substantial risk reduction opportunities are available, the evidence suggests that only a modest reduction in portfolio risk can be achieved through international diversification on an unhedged basis. The second section analyzes whether a stronger case can be made for international diversification on a hedged basis. Once again, contrary to the growing belief that hedged diversification guarantees investors less risk without sacrificing portfolio return, it can be demonstrated that if transaction costs and other fees associated with hedging are taken into consideration, international diversification on a currency hedged basis may prove to be more expensive than not hedging at all.

The third section focuses on whether there are unique "free-lunch" strategies that investors can exploit. One favorite strategy has been to favor markets that offer relatively high yields. We show that high-yield strategies can prove to be quite risky and are by no means a free lunch.

The fourth section attempts to salvage the case for international fixed income investment by directing the focus away from purported free-lunch strategies and toward tactical asset allocation considerations. Sizable differences in total return exist among the domestic and overseas markets that, if exploited, can substantially enhance the total-return prospects of an otherwise purely domestic bond portfolio. Thus, domestic investors will profit by viewing foreign bonds not as a *separate* asset class for *all* seasons, but as a *tactical* asset for *selected* seasons.

The fifth section provides internationally minded investors with general guidelines for setting up and constructing a global bond portfolio. The sixth and final section provides both a general framework for designing an active global bond portfolio strategy and a disciplined approach to assess the key decision criteria—the currency, market, and bond selection decisions—that global bond investors must address.

THE CASE FOR INTERNATIONAL FIXED INCOME DIVERSIFICATION

Proponents of international fixed income diversification quite often point to reams of charts and tables that purport to show significant risk-reduction possibilities from combining U.S. and foreign bonds in a passively managed diversified portfolio. Unfortunately, our research does not corroborate that evidence. Although portfolio risk reduction is possible through international diversification, our research indicates that the extent of risk reduction from passive management is fairly modest.

Exhibit 55–1 plots the cumulative total returns on U.S. and foreign dollar-denominated bonds from March 1973 (the beginning of floating exchange rates) to December 1995. U.S. bonds are represented by the Merrill Lynch Domestic Master Index, which includes government and corporate debt and, since 1975, mortgage securities. The foreign bond market performance index splices two international bond indexes together: the InterSec Research Non-North American Bond Index from 1973 to 1984 and the Salomon Brothers World Bond Index from 1985 to 1995, both measured in U.S. dollar terms. Note that in Exhibit 55–1 the performance of the U.S. and overseas markets differed widely over interim periods: The foreign markets were stronger in the late 1970s, the U.S. market was stronger in the early 1980s, and the foreign markets regained superiority during

EXHIBIT 55–1

Total Return Performance of the Non-U.S.$ and the U.S. Bond Market since 1973 (in U.S. Dollar Terms)

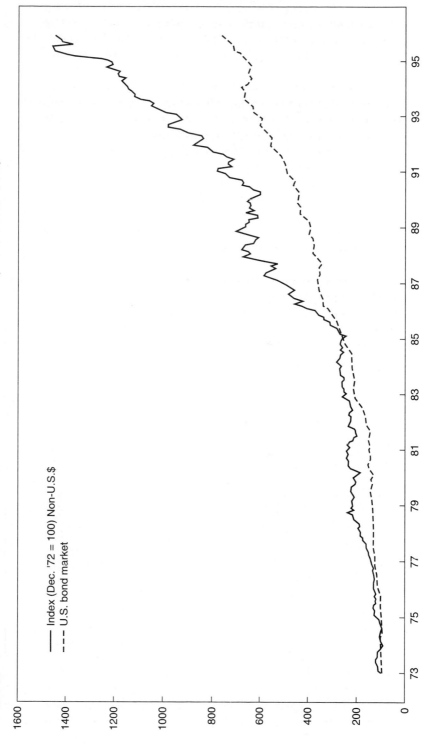

1985–95. Over the entire period, the evidence shows that the average annualized return in U.S. dollar terms was 12.2 percent on foreign bonds and 9.2 percent per annum on U.S. domestic bonds. We attribute that disparity to sampling error over the time period chosen for study. In the long run, there is no a priori reason why the expected return on foreign bonds in U.S. dollar terms should be higher or lower than the expected return on U.S. domestic bonds. Indeed, as Exhibits 55–2 and 55–3 show, the cumulative returns on U.S. and foreign bonds were the same over the 1973–85 period, and were also quite similar over the 1988–94 period.

The evidence shows that the volatility of foreign bond market returns in U.S. dollar terms has been considerably greater than the volatility of U.S. domestic bond market returns. Between March 1973 and December 1995, the standard deviation of monthly returns was 12.2 percent on foreign bonds in U.S. dollar terms, whereas it was 6.1 percent on U.S. domestic bonds. The roughly 100 percent difference in volatility was due entirely to the impact of the dollar's volatility; in fact, foreign bond market returns in local currency terms were, on average, less volatile than U.S. bond market returns.

Although foreign bonds in U.S. dollar terms were more volatile than U.S. domestic bonds, it was still possible to combine foreign bonds with U.S. domestic bonds in a diversified bond portfolio to reduce overall portfolio risk, because the returns on U.S. and foreign bonds are not highly positively correlated. The evidence shows that the average correlation of monthly U.S. and foreign bond returns for the 1973–95 period was only 0.34.

Exhibit 55–4 shows how much portfolio risk could have been reduced through passive international diversification on an unhedged basis. This graph demonstrates how an investor could have varied the allocation of an internationally diversified bond portfolio between dollar and nondollar bonds from March 1973 to December 1995 to achieve a certain level of return for a given level of risk. For example, if a U.S. investor had committed 100 percent of his or her funds to the U.S. domestic bond market, the average annual return would have been 9.2 percent and the annualized standard deviation of monthly returns would have been 6.1 percent. Allocating 10 percent of his or her funds to foreign bonds and leaving the balance in U.S. domestic bonds would have yielded a slightly higher annual return of 9.6 percent, with a portfolio standard deviation of 6.0 percent. That constitutes a 0.1 percent reduction in portfolio volatility from the 100 percent U.S. allocation case. At that allocation, overall portfolio risk would have been minimized. Any commitment to foreign bonds beyond 10 percent would have increased portfolio risk.

The extent of risk reduction from passive international fixed income diversification appears quite modest, so much so that it hardly seems worthwhile. In fact, one major U.S. pension consultant, after examining the historical evidence, concluded that "nondollar bond investment is a diversification opportunity that U.S. investors can afford to pass up, especially those with smaller funds and limited resources for the conduct of their investment program."

EXHIBIT 55-2

Total Return Performance: U.S. & Foreign Bonds 1973–1985 (in U.S. Dollar Terms)

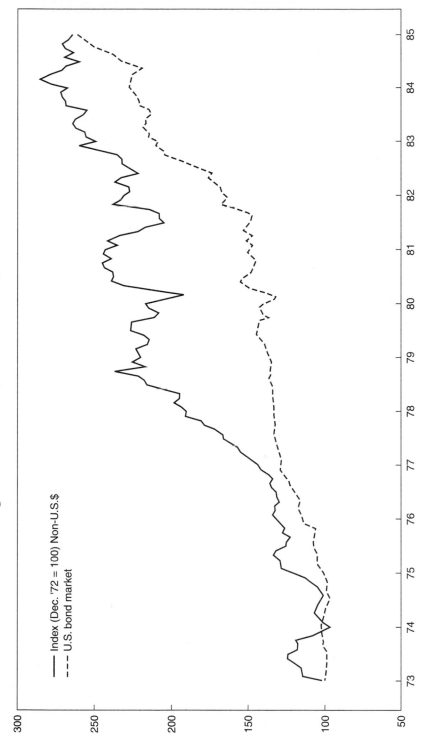

Total Return Performance: U.S. & Foreign Bonds 1988–1995 (in U.S. Dollar Terms)

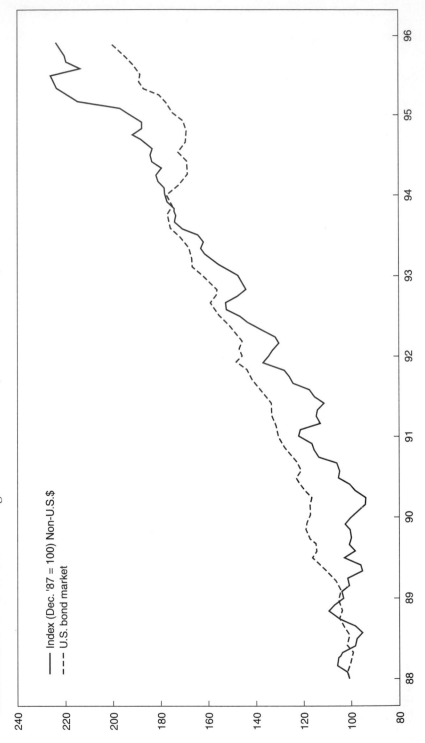

— Index (Dec. '87 = 100) Non-U.S.$

- - - U.S. bond market

EXHIBIT 55-4

Risk/Return Profile of Passively Managed International Fixed Income Portfolios (1973–1995)

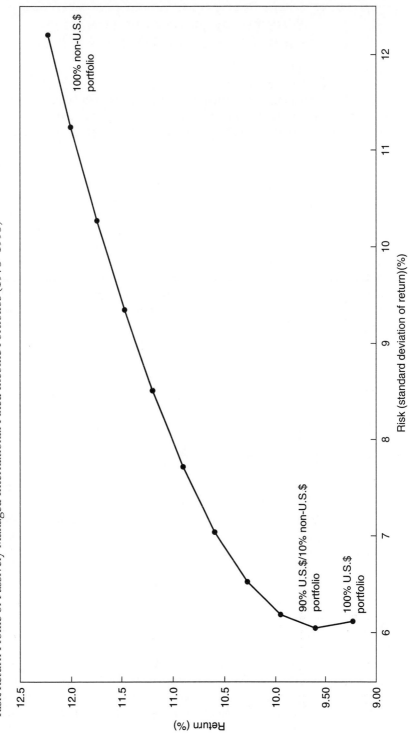

WHY THERE IS NO FREE LUNCH IN
CURRENCY-HEDGED FOREIGN BONDS

In order to salvage the case for nondollar bonds, a number of analysts have argued for hedged rather than unhedged foreign bonds in U.S. portfolios. Those analysts contend that because currency volatility adds to the volatility of a foreign bond portfolio, hedging away currency risk in the forward exchange market should render hedged foreign bonds less volatile than unhedged foreign bonds. At the same time, currency hedging should not involve any loss of long-term expected return, assuming no risk premium is embedded in forward exchange rates. Taken together, a policy of purchasing hedged foreign bonds should offer greater risk reduction with no loss of expected return compared to traditional unhedged international diversification. That assessment has led a number of observers to conclude that hedged foreign bonds offer U.S. investors a free lunch.

Had U.S. investors bought the idea of currency-hedged foreign bonds during the 1978–87 period, they would indeed have received a free lunch, as the historical evidence clearly shows (see Exhibit 55–5a). The return on hedged nondollar bonds (11.0 percent per annum) over the 1978–87 period closely matched the return on unhedged nondollar bonds (10.9 percent per annum), but the monthly annualized standard deviation of return on hedged foreign bonds was significantly lower than the comparable volatility of unhedged foreign bonds (5.9 percent vs. 13.6 percent). As Exhibit 55–5a shows, had U.S. investors diversified into nondollar bonds, they could have reduced portfolio risk by purchasing either hedged or unhedged nondollar bonds, but the extent of available risk reduction was much more dramatic for diversification into hedged nondollar bonds. In the case of unhedged nondollar bond diversification, the modestly lower overall portfolio risk was due to the low average monthly correlation between U.S. and unhedged foreign bonds (0.42). In contrast, in the case of hedged nondollar bond diversification, the dramatically lower overall portfolio risk was due largely to the low volatility of hedged foreign bonds (5.9 percent) compared to U.S. bond market volatility (10.6 percent).

Although the historical evidence indicates that a free lunch existed during the the 1978–87 period, we were never comfortable with the idea that this free lunch would persist indefinitely. After all, one of the first basic principles we learn in introductory economics courses is that there is no such thing as a free lunch. We questioned the validity of the free-lunch hypothesis, largely because it cannot hold for all investors. Exhibit 55–5(b) looks at the risk/return trade-off that would have faced Japanese fund managers had they invested in hedged nonyen bonds during the 1978–87 period. The evidence clearly shows that hedged nonyen bonds fared poorly compared to yen domestic bonds in terms of both risk and return, which is opposite to the case for U.S. investors. The reason is fairly straightforward: U.S. domestic bonds were more volatile than their foreign counterparts over the 1978–87 period, whereas Japanese domestic bonds were less volatile than their foreign counterparts. However, there is no reason why either of those trends must persist.

EXHIBIT 55–5

(*a*) Historical Risk/Return Trade-Off: U.S. Domestic Bonds versus Hedged and Unhedged Nondollar Bonds (Annualized Monthly Returns and Standard Deviations)

(*b*) Historical Risk/Return Trade-Off: Yen Bonds versus Hedged and Unhedged Nonyen Bonds (Annualized Monthly Returns and Standard Deviations)

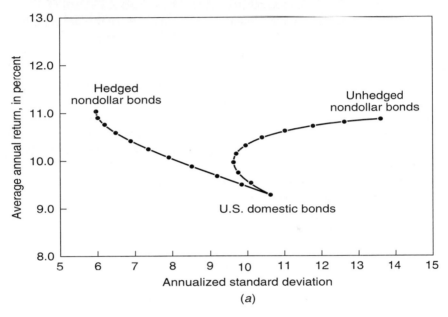

(*a*)

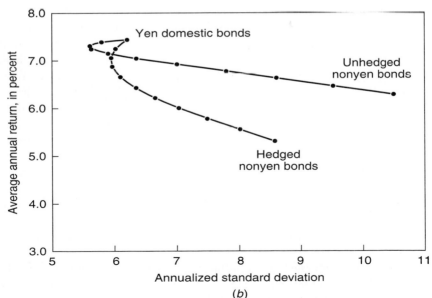

(*b*)

In fact, we attributed the lower average volatility of hedged foreign bonds relative to U.S. bonds to two factors that we felt would not likely recur in the future: (1) institutional rigidities such as capital flow restrictions and heavily regulated capital markets in a number of key overseas financial centers, which may have limited their volatility, at least artificially, and (2) monetary policies in the late 1970s and early 1980s in the United States that were more unstable than in Germany or Japan, which accentuated the U.S. bond market's volatility.

Indeed, changes on both counts are now taking place that are contributing to a worldwide convergence in bond market volatilities. Regarding the first point, we are presently witnessing a major liberalization and deregulation of many of the overseas markets. Regarding the second point, we see growing evidence of a convergence of world inflation rates and macroeconomic policies. As a result, the evidence now shows that had U.S. investors shifted funds from U.S. to hedged foreign bonds over the more recent 1988–1995 period, they would have had to sacrifice considerable return in order to achieve any meaningful reduction in portfolio risk (see Exhibit 55–6). In other words, the free lunch that was available in 1978–87 is now gone.

Theoretically, it is more reasonable to assume not only that long-term expected returns should be the same across markets, but that their expected risks should be the same as well. If we make the assumption that both the expected returns and expected volatilities will be the same on U.S. and hedged foreign bonds, it can be shown that it makes no difference in terms of long-term risk reduction whether or not a foreign bond portfolio is hedged.

Consider the assumptions outlined in Exhibit 55–7. The table shows that the return on U.S. bonds and unhedged foreign bonds was 9.3 percent per annum over the 1973–85 period. We also show the historical volatilities of U.S. and unhedged foreign bonds (10.6 percent and 13.6 percent, respectively) for the 1973–85 period. Now let's make the assumption that the return on hedged foreign bonds and the volatility of hedged foreign bonds just matches the U.S. historical average return and volatility. It is really not important to this exercise which level of volatility is assumed as long as the volatilities of U.S. and hedged foreign bonds are assumed to be the same. Finally, lets assume that the average historical correlations between U.S. bonds and hedged and unhedged foreign bonds will continue to prevail. Note that the monthly correlation of U.S. bond returns with unhedged foreign bond returns was 0.42, which was significantly lower than the 0.54 correlation of U.S. bond returns with hedged foreign bond returns. This is because currency fluctuations reduce the co-movement of U.S. and foreign bonds. This suggests that although unhedged foreign bonds will tend to be more volatile than their hedged counterparts, because of currency volatility, unhedged foreign bonds have the upper hand over hedged foreign bonds because they are more efficient diversifiers when a combined U.S.–foreign bond portfolio is created.

If these assumptions are plausible, then the diversification benefits derived from portfolio combinations of U.S. and hedged foreign bonds can be shown to be the same as those derived from portfolio combinations of U.S. and unhedged

EXHIBIT 55-6

U.S. vs. Hedged Foreign Bonds: Historical Risk/Return Trade-Offs—1978–87 and 1988–95

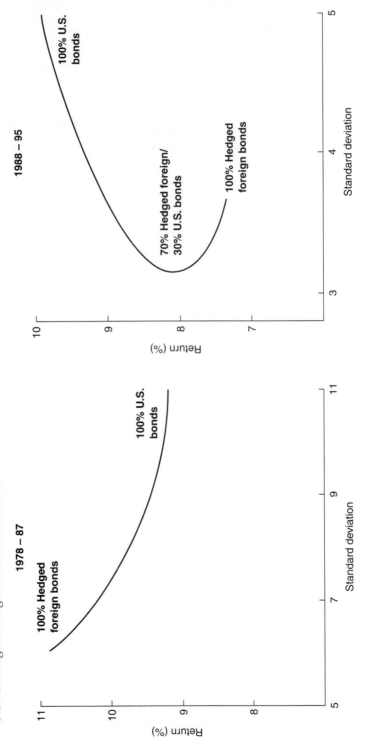

E X H I B I T   55–7

Theoretical Long-Run Expected Returns, Standard Deviations, and
Correlations for U.S. Domestic, Hedged Nondollar, and Unhedged Nondollar
Bonds

	Expected Return	Expected Standard Deviation	Correlation with U.S. Bonds
U.S. domestic bonds	9.3[a]	10.62[a]	1.00[a]
Hedged nondollar bonds	9.3	10.62	0.54[a]
Unhedged nondollar bonds	9.3	13.57[a]	0.42[a]

[a]Historic average.

foreign bonds. This is demonstrated in Exhibit 55–8: Whichever diversification
route is taken, the same minimum risk portfolio results. Hedged foreign bonds
have an advantage over their unhedged counterparts in that they are less volatile,
but unhedged foreign bonds have an advantage over their hedged counterparts in
that they are more efficient diversifiers. When combined with U.S. bonds, both
advantages cancel each other out, such that hedged and unhedged foreign bonds
offer the same long-term risk-reduction benefits.

That analysis leads to what I humbly term *Rosenberg Proposition I.*

Rosenberg Proposition I

In a world free of transaction costs, the amount of risk reduction available from in-
ternational bond diversification in the long run is independent of whether or not
currency risk is hedged.

Followers of finance theory will recognize this to be a paraphrase of the famous
Modigliani–Miller proposition that the value of the firm is independent of its capital structure (debt/equity mix). The conclusion from Rosenberg Proposition I is
that hedged international fixed income diversification offers no advantage over
unhedged international fixed income diversification in the long run. Unfortunately, the story does not end there; there are transaction costs and other fees associated with continuously hedging a foreign bond portfolio. Exhibit 55–9 lists
the extra costs and fees associated with always hedging an otherwise passively
managed foreign bond portfolio. Those include (1) the execution costs of buying
and selling forward exchange (in terms of bid-ask spreads); (2) additional settlement costs in the form of custodial fees; and (3) additional management fees, because a continuously hedged foreign bond portfolio, unlike a passively managed
unhedged foreign bond portfolio, requires constant rollover of short-term hedges.
Clarke and Kritzman estimate the additional cost to be 20–30 basis points if the
forward hedges are rolled over on a monthly basis. Those additional costs and

EXHIBIT 55–8

Alternative Paths to Achieve the Minimum Risk Portfolio through Diversified Combinations of U.S. and Hedged/Unhedged Foreign Bonds

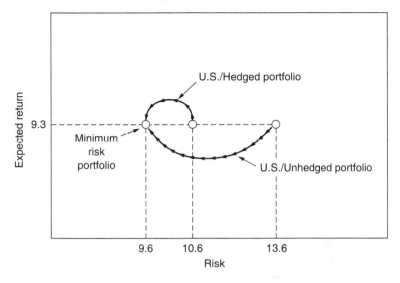

EXHIBIT 55–9

Additional Costs Associated with Managing a Continuously Hedged Foreign Bond Portfolio

	Cost in Basis Points
Execution costs	5
Settlement costs	5
Management fees	10–20
Total	20–30

Source: Roger G. Clarke and Mark P. Kritzman, *Currency Management: Concepts and Practices* (AIMR, 1996).

fees must then be subtracted from the expected return on hedged foreign bonds, and the resulting net return can then be compared to U.S. and unhedged foreign bond market returns. If we factor that lower expected return into the theoretical diversification exercise described in Exhibit 55–8, it becomes evident that the unhedged foreign bond diversification route will yield a higher expected return for the same level of risk than the hedged foreign bond diversification route.

That leads to what I have termed *Rosenberg Proposition II*.

Rosenberg Proposition II

In a world where transaction costs and management fees are not insignificant, hedged foreign bonds will be a more expensive means than unhedged foreign bonds to achieve risk reduction.

Thus, our findings suggest that from a long-term perspective, instead of offering a free lunch, currency hedging may prove to be a more expensive lunch than if one never hedged at all. This does not mean that we do not favor hedging at all. What it does mean is that we favor hedging only on a selective basis when conditions warrant it. Pursuing an alternative policy of continuously hedging will prove to be a costly means to achieve guaranteed long-term risk reduction.

WHY THERE IS NO FREE LUNCH IN HIGH-YIELD FOREIGN BONDS

Ever-eager to build a case for international fixed income diversification, a number of analysts have suggested that investors may be able to earn excess returns by overweighting high-yield markets and underweighting low-yield markets in a diversified international bond portfolio. The rationale for implementing such a strategy is to exploit what appears to be persistent departures from uncovered interest-rate parity. The theory of uncovered interest-rate parity (UIP) states that the return on high-yield markets should match the return on low-yield markets when the returns are expressed in a common currency. UIP will be valid if high-yielding markets have depreciating currencies and low-yielding markets have appreciating currencies, with the loss or gain on the exchange rate offsetting, on average, the yield differential between the high- and low-yielding markets.

While sensible in theory, the UIP hypothesis does not hold up to empirical verification. Indeed, the evidence shows that currencies with relatively high interest rates normally do not depreciate as much as interest-rate differentials predict, while currencies with relatively low interest rates do not rise in value as much as interest-rate differentials anticipate. If such departures from UIP can be counted on to persist in the future, investors would, over time, be able to earn higher average returns by overweighting the high-yield bond markets.

The problem with adopting a strategy that favors the high-yield markets is that it can be extremely risky. While it is true that most empirical studies find evidence of persistent departures from UIP in the past, one cannot guarantee that the departures from UIP will continue in the future. There is no agreement among economists as to what led to the departures from UIP in the past. Several analysts contend that high-yield markets offer higher average returns because they are perceived to be riskier assets. Other analysts contend that the marketplace systematically overpredicts the potential weakness of high-yield "soft" currencies and at the same time overpredicts the potential strength of the low-yield "hard" currencies. Still others contend that interest-rate differentials between high- and low-yielding markets embody, in part, the market's anticipation of a possible dramatic event that may upset the currency markets. If that dramatic event fails to take place during the sample period that UIP is tested, high-yield markets may appear to offer higher average returns than low-yield markets over that period. A dramatic event, such as a speculative attack, normally has a small probability of occurring, but as long as there is some possibility of a crisis occurring, this possibility will be reflected in yield spreads. Over a sufficiently long period, a speculative attack may eventually take place, thereby validating UIP as a long-run proposition. But over short- and even medium-term horizons when no such attack takes place, it may appear that yield spreads overpredict the underlying weakness of high-yield currencies.

Consider the case of the ERM collapse in 1992–93 and the subsequent weakness in many of the European currencies versus the deutsche mark. Prior to the ERM collapse, the cumulative return on high-yield European currencies substantially exceeded the cumulative return on DM-denominated investments. For example, in the case of the Italian lira, the cumulative return on lira money market investments, when expressed in DM terms, far exceeded the cumulative return on deutsche mark money market investments over the January 1987 to August 1992 period (see Exhibit 55–10). That outperformance was due largely to a comfortably wide yield spread between Italian and German money market investments that was not completely offset by the lira's modest depreciation versus the deutsche mark over that period. Italian investments offered a large yield pickup over German investments because the market perceived that there was significant risk in owning lira assets and that at some point a dramatic event might cause the lira to come under heavy downward pressure versus the deutsche mark. Since no dramatic event took place over the January 1987 to August 1992 period that upset the lira/DM crossrate, the cumulative return on lira-denominated investments far exceeded the cumulative return on deutsche mark-denominated investments over that period.

However, market perceptions about the potential riskiness of lira investments eventually proved to be correct. The lira came under heavy downward pressure in September 1992 and was first devalued and then permitted to float freely. The lira remained under heavy downward pressure for the next $2^{1}/_{2}$ years, with the net decline in the lira far exceeding the Italian–German yield spread. In fact, as shown in Exhibit 55–10, the cumulative excess returns available on lira denominated assets were completely erased in 1992–95.

To put it simply, what goes around comes around—UIP appears to be valid over very long-run periods, although significant departures will exist over short- and medium-term periods. This example demonstrates that one should be skeptical of strategies that purportedly guarantee investors a free lunch. The foreign exchange and international bond markets are among the most actively traded markets in the world. It is highly unlikely that these markets could be so inefficient as to generate unexploited profit opportunities from purported free-lunch strategies.

EXHIBIT 55-10

Total Return Performance of Italian and German Money-Market Investments
(In Deutsche mark Terms)

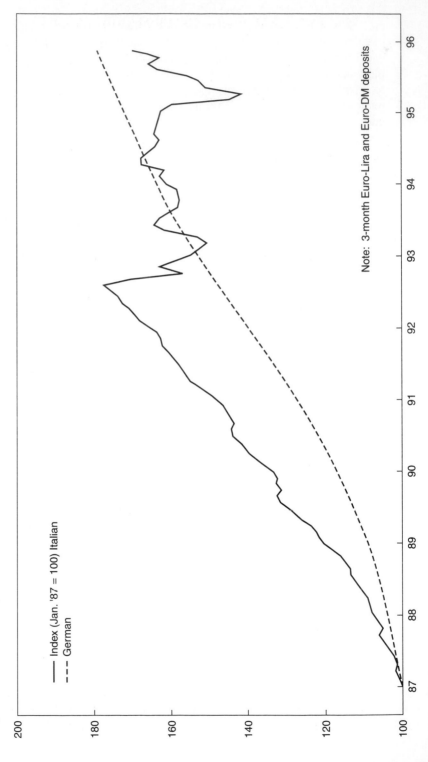

Note: 3-month Euro-Lira and Euro-DM deposits

— Index (Jan. '87 = 100) Italian
--- German

THE CASE FOR ACTIVE MANAGEMENT

If a strong case cannot be made for currency-hedged foreign bonds or high-yield foreign bonds, can the case for international fixed income diversification be salvaged? The answer to that question is an emphatic yes. If we are to build a case for nondollar bonds, we must admit that, in terms of reducing portfolio risk, the benefits of passive international fixed income diversification are limited, whether or not the underlying foreign currency exposure is hedged. Instead, the case for international fixed income diversification needs to be directed away from risk-reduction considerations and toward total-return-enhancement considerations. Foreign bonds offer U.S. investors a unique opportunity to enhance the return on their U.S. fixed income portfolios, but that return enhancement opportunity is available only through successful active management, not through purported free-lunch strategies. It is widely recognized that the differences in total-return performance among the competing subsectors of the U.S. domestic bond market are relatively small when compared to the sizable differences in performance that exist between the U.S. and overseas markets. If U.S. fund managers can exploit such differences by correctly shifting their portfolios from U.S. to foreign bonds and then back when conditions warrant, there will be great interest in the use of foreign bonds, not as a separate asset class for all seasons, but as a tactical asset for selected reasons.

One way of measuring the total-return opportunity set available to international investors is to examine the total-return spread between the best- and worst-performing markets over time. The difference between the best and worst performers gives some indication of the return that could have been earned if an investor had correctly underweighted the weak markets and overweighted the strong markets. Another way of measuring the total-return opportunity set is to examine the total-return spread between the strongest market and the investor's homebase market.

Exhibit 55–11 shows the total-return spread between the best- and worst-performing markets over the 1973–95 period, as well as the U.S. domestic bond market's total return over the same period. On average, there has been a 33 percent per annum difference (that is, 3300 basis points) in total return performance between the strongest- and weakest-performing markets during that period. That suggests that there have been substantial opportunities to increase total return by correctly overweighting the strong markets and underweighting the weak. The U.S. domestic bond market was the best-performing market only twice, in 1982 and 1984. On four occasions—1977, return performance 1978, 1987, and 1990—it was at or near the bottom of the international bond total return performance list. On average, the spread between the best-performing market and the U.S. market has been about 15 percent per annum. Thus, U.S. investors who could correctly forecast relative market performance could have significantly enhanced their total-return performance had they taken a global perspective in their bond investment decisions.

If U.S. bond investors accept the notion that the tactical use of foreign bonds can help boost the performance of their domestic portfolios, then we

Total Return Performance of Major Gov't. Bond Markets in U.S. Dollar Terms
Best, Worst, and U.S. Market Total Returns

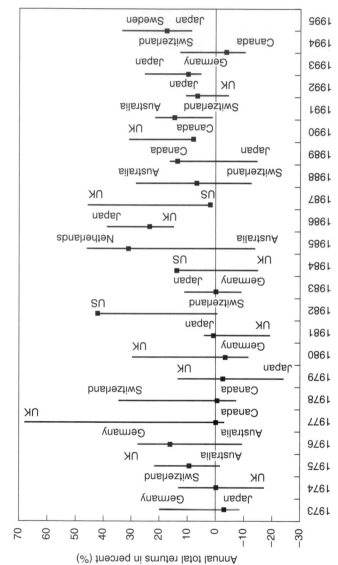

should expect to see a growing number of U.S. fund managers selectively adding foreign bonds in an aggressive manner to help them outperform their domestic benchmark, such as the Merrill Lynch Domestic Master Index or the Lehman Government Corporate Bond Index. In fact, we believe that the way the international fixed income investment game is played in the U.S. will change radically in the coming years, from a dedicated international bond management strategy that treats foreign bonds as a *separate* asset class to one that treats foreign bonds as a tactical asset to help domestic-oriented investors outperform their domestic benchmark and competition. To get an idea of how U.S. fund managers may use foreign bonds on a tactical basis, let's consider the following exercise.

Consider a hypothetical U.S. domestic bond fund that establishes internal investment policy guidelines in the following manner: The fund will allocate 20 percent of its portfolio to foreign bonds and the remainder to U.S. domestic and corporate bonds when it is believed that the dollar is trending lower. When it is believed that the dollar is trending higher, the fund will allocate 100 percent to U.S. domestic bonds (see Exhibit 55–12). To determine whether the dollar's trend is up or down, a simple trading rule is followed. If the dollar's trade-weighted value on a monthly average basis lies below its 12-month moving average, the dollar's trend is considered to be down, and vice versa. Hence the crossover of the 1- and 12-month averages in the dollar's value is used as the criterion to adjust the domestic/foreign mix. Exhibit 55–13 shows that the dollar has had several major cycles in the past 23 years. The 1- and 12-month moving average trading rule defines those broad cycles fairly clearly, although several moving average crossovers have proved to be false signals.

We have simulated the total-return outcome (excluding transaction costs) that could have been achieved had a U.S. bond manager followed our trading rule over the 1973–95 period. Exhibit 55–14 shows the cumulative differences in total return performance between the Merrill Lynch Domestic Master Index and the active domestic/foreign bond strategy. It is assumed that a U.S. bond manager starts out owning 100 percent of the Merrill Lynch Domestic Master Index; then,

EXHIBIT 55–12

Investment Policy Guidelines—Hypothetical U.S. Domestic Bond Portfolio

Recommended Allocation to Domestic and Foreign Bonds		
	Bearish on the Dollar	**Bullish on the Dollar**
U.S. domestic bonds	80%	100%
Foreign bonds	20	0

Long-Run Trend in the U.S. Dollar Index

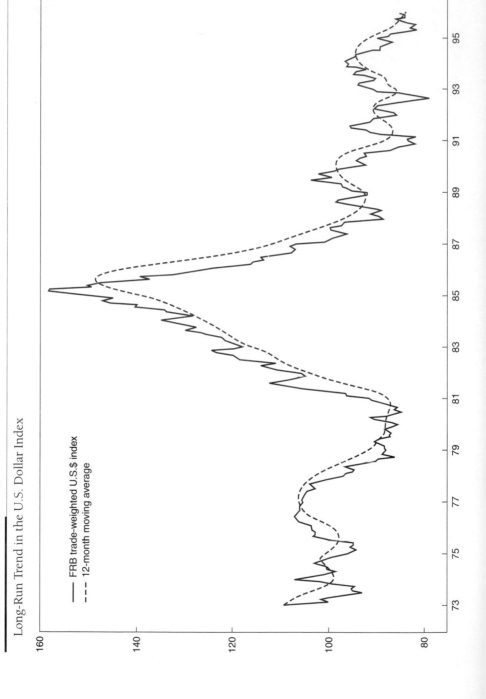

EXHIBIT 55-14

Total Return Performance of an Actively-Managed Global Bond Portfolio vs. a 100% U.S. Treasury Portfolio

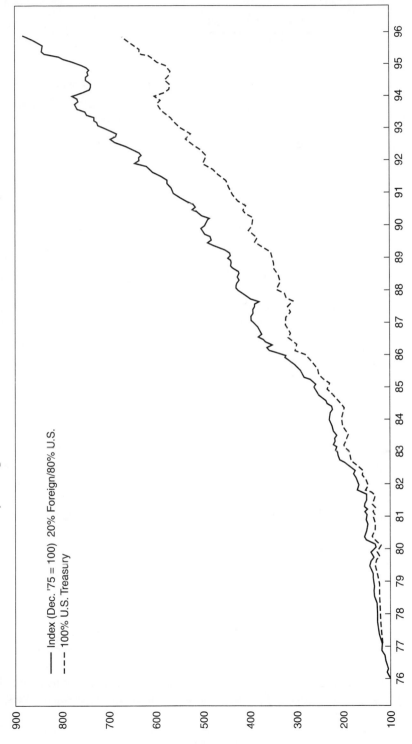

EXHIBIT 55–15

Total Returns of Alternate Strategies

Strategy	Total Return per Annum
Active 80/20—100/0 mix	10.7%
Passive 80/20 mix	9.9%
100% U.S. passive	9.2%

when the trading signal indicates the dollar is heading lower, the manager cuts that position to 80 percent, with the remaining 20 percent allocated to the foreign bond index. When the trading signal indicates the dollar is headed higher, the foreign bond position is liquidated, returning the portfolio to the original 100 percent domestic bond allocation. Implementing that active domestic/foreign bond strategy on an ongoing basis for the period 1973–95 yielded a total return of 10.7 percent per annum, which amounts to a 150-basis-point per annum total-return pickup over the 9.2 percent per annum return on the Merrill Lynch Domestic Master Index for the same period. The 10.7 percent per annum return also compares favorably to the 9.9 percent average annual return that could have been earned on an 80 percent U.S./20 percent foreign *passively* managed global bond portfolio (see Exhibit 15–15).

The preceding analysis was conducted for illustrative purposes only. In no way are we suggesting we have uncovered a new free-lunch trading strategy. The analysis simply highlights the importance of taking an active management approach to international fixed income investment and shows why total-return enhancement issues will eventually dominate risk-reduction considerations in decisions about involvement in the overseas bond markets. The next two sections provide internationally minded investors with general guidelines for setting up and constructing a global bond portfolio and a comprehensive framework for designing an active global bond portfolio strategy.

GENERAL GUIDELINES FOR CONSTRUCTING A GLOBAL BOND PORTFOLIO

Managing a global bond portfolio is more complex than managing a domestic bond fund. Variations in government regulations, market practices, settlement procedures, yield conventions, and secondary market liquidity mean that the international investment manager must be thoroughly knowledgeable about numerous institutional details. Moreover, transaction costs in the form of commissions, taxes, bid-ask spreads, custody fees, and settlement charges differ widely among markets, so the international investment manager must have a thorough understanding of trading, regulatory, and accounting practices as well. Finally, and perhaps most important, the international fixed income strategy process requires that the investment manager evaluate the complex interaction of currency movements, interest-rate changes, inter- and intramarket yield-spread developments, and yield-curve shifts in all of the major markets.

The investor's first step in setting up an international bond portfolio is to determine financial objectives. Some managers seek to maximize total return, whereas others seek to maximize income. Time horizons also differ widely among investment managers; some global bond investors may select a short-term time horizon to capture short-run swings in exchange rates or interest rates, whereas others may adopt a longer term to capture broad trends in currency and bond market movements. Management styles also differ regarding the level of portfolio turnover and the use of derivative products. Finally, investors with different base currencies may face different constraints on the investments they can make in other currencies.

The U.S. institutional investor market for nondollar bonds can be broken down into 11 investor types: (1) dedicated international bond mutual funds, (2) internationally dedicated accounts of U.S. pension funds, (3) active managers of U.S. domestic bond portfolios, (4) high-yield (junk) domestic bond funds, (5) the treasury departments of U.S. banks, (6) the treasury/cash management departments of U.S. corporations, (7) international property and casualty insurance companies, (8) global equity funds, (9) individuals, (10) hedge funds, and (11) general investment managers.

In the initial stages of setting up an international bond portfolio, the investment manager should draw up a delegation-of-authority list that indicates which foreign markets and credits will be approved for purchase. Based on an assessment of country and credit risk, as well as an assessment of tax and liquidity considerations, an approved list of issuers should be drawn up. Names can be added and dropped as conditions warrant.

For example, a risk-averse fund manager may choose to invest only in government and government-guaranteed issues. Another manager may approve the purchase only of AAA and AA corporate issues, and so forth. The delegation-of-authority list should also detail what percentage of the fund's assets can be assigned to any single credit.

Once it is clear which markets and credits will be approved for purchase, the international investor should select a global custody service (usually a large international bank with an extensive overseas branch and correspondent banking network) to arrange for the delivery and settlement of traded securities and foreign exchange, the collection of coupon income, the reclamation of any coupon tax due the investor because of double-taxation treaties, the maintenance of cash balances in various markets on deposit, the receipt of comprehensive and timely reports on portfolio activities, and the valuation of total assets under management. It would be wise for the investment manager to set up an internal bond operations unit to review all trade details (e.g., price, settlement date, and accrued interest), specify delivery instructions, and contact the global custody service to arrange for settlement and safe custody.

Once those housekeeping duties are fulfilled, the international investment manager should attend to the establishment of portfolio management guidelines for the distribution of the global bond fund's assets. Those self-imposed asset allocation guidelines should assign minimum, normal, and maximum positions that can be held in any single currency block or market. The purpose of the guidelines is to underscore the desire for diversification yet provide ample latitude for active management. For example, Exhibit 55–16 highlights the asset distribution guidelines for a hypothetical global bond fund. The guidelines define the proportion of the portfolio's funds that can be assigned to the major currency blocks: U.S. dollar, Canadian dollar, German mark, French franc, Japanese yen, British pound, and Australian/New Zealand dollars.

The weights chosen as "normal" should reflect the approximate relative current market value of each of the major markets in the total world bond market, or perhaps even better, the relative liquidity and tradeability of each market. If investors use a widely followed external benchmark for performance evaluation, such as the Merrill Lynch Global or Salomon Brothers World Bond Index, they might want to use the benchmark's fixed weights as the normal weights. The normal weights shown in Exhibit 55–16 are the market capitalization weights of all the key markets in the Merrill Lynch Global Government/Eurobond Index as of April 1989 (see Exhibit 55–17).

EXHIBIT 55–16

Asset Allocation Guidelines for Structuring a Global Bond Portfolio (Percent Breakdown)

Currency Block	Minimum Position	Normal Position	Maximum Position
U.S.$	23.5	47.0	73.5
Yen	11.5	23.0	46.0
DM, Dfl, SFr	6.5	13.0	33.0
Sterling	3.5	7.0	25.0
FFr, ECU	2.0	4.0	20.0
C$	2.0	4.0	20.0
A$, NZ$	1.0	2.0	10.0

By assigning minimum and maximum guidelines in the manner shown in Exhibit 55–16, the investment manager places certain operational constraints on the asset allocation decisions. Within the limits defined by these guidelines, the investment manager is free to allocate funds among currencies and markets. Those markets and/or currencies expected to perform relatively favorably should be assigned portfolio weights in the normal-maximum range, whereas those markets and/or currencies expected to perform relatively poorly should be assigned weights in the minimum-normal range. The stronger an investor's conviction about currency and interest-rate trends, the more the assigned weight may lean toward the extreme end of the min-norm or norm-max range. Because the risk of being wrong must be factored into each investment decision, in times of uncertainty there is likely to be a tendency for the recommended portfolio weights to move closer to the market norm. That is consistent with the risk-averse behavior of most individual investors and portfolio managers.

A FRAMEWORK FOR FORMULATING INTERNATIONAL FIXED INCOME STRATEGY

This section describes a unique framework to assist investors in their formulation of a global bond portfolio strategy. The framework revolves around a strategy table, depicted in Exhibit 55–17, that highlights the key decision criteria that global bond investors must address. The strategy table breaks down the global fixed income investment process into three key decision criteria—currency, market, and bond selection. Each of those decision criteria can and should be treated separately in a forecasting context, but they need to be integrated in a portfolio construction context. In the analysis that follows, we show how to accomplish this integration process.

The strategy table shows how an investor's desired exposure to the individual currencies, markets, maturity categories, sectors, and market durations compares with the broad market capitalization and individual maturity category, sector, and duration weights of the Merrill Lynch Global Government/Eurobond Index. The recommended portfolio weights are in standard type and the weights of the Merrill Lynch Global Bond Index are shown in boldface. How far investment managers will allow their portfolio stances to deviate from market capitalization weights will depend not only on their confidence about the general direction that currencies and interest rates may take, but on their outlook for yield-curve slope and sector-spread changes as well. We begin our analysis by focusing on the factors that determine an investor's optimal net currency position. We then focus on those factors that determine the level of exposure to interest-rate risk that an investor will desire across a wide range of markets. We conclude by showing how to combine currency and bond investment decisions in the portfolio construction process.

EXHIBIT 55–17

International Fixed Income Strategy Table—Recommended Asset Mix (Percent Breakdown)

Currency Block	Currency Decision		Market Decision			Bond Selection Decision — Maturity Structure					Sector Breakdown		Portfolio Duration	Portfolio Risk	
	Net Currency Position	Currency Hedge	Gross Currency Position	Cash Equivalent	Bonds	1–3 Years	3–5 Years	5–7 Years	7–10 Years	Long	Government	Euro/Foreign		Currency Risk	Interest-Rate Risk
U.S.$	49	0	49	24	25	0	0	0	21	4	25	0	3.3	1.04	0.76
	47		**47**		**47**	**17**	**9**	**5**	**5**	**11**	**41**	**6**	**4.5**		
C$	6	0	6	2	4	2	0	0	2	0	4	0	2.3	1.50	0.77
	4		**4**		**4**	**1**	**1**	**0**	**0**	**1**	**3**	**1**	**4.5**		
A$/NZ$	8	0	8	0	8	4	0	0	4	0	8	0	3.8	4.00	5.07
	2		**2**		**2**	**1**	**1**	**0**	**0**	**0**	**1**	**1**	**3.0**		
Yen	20	0	20	8	12	0	0	0	12	0	12	0	4.5	0.87	0.80
	23		**23**		**23**	**5**	**5**	**5**	**7**	**1**	**20**	**3**	**4.9**		
European STG	7	0	7	4	3	0	0	0	0	3	3	0	4.1	1.00	0.73
	7		**7**		**7**	**1**	**1**	**1**	**2**	**2**	**6**	**1**	**5.6**		
DM, DFl and SF	8	0	8	0	8	4	0	0	3	1	8	0	5.7	0.62	0.80
	13		**13**		**13**	**2**	**4**	**3**	**3**	**1**	**8**	**5**	**4.4**		
FFr, ECU	2	0	2	0	2	0	0	0	1	1	2	0	8.8	0.50	1.00
	4		**4**		**4**	**1**	**1**	**1**	**1**	**0**	**3**	**1**	**4.4**		
Total	100	0	100	28	62	10	0	0	43	9	62	0	3.9		0.84
	100		**100**		**100**	**38**	**22**	**16**	**18**	**16**	**82**	**18**	**4.6**		

Note: Recommended portfolio weights are shown in standard type and the weights of the Merrill Lynch Global Government/Eurobond Index are shown in boldface.

Currency Decision

In a global bond portfolio context, currency and interest-rate decisions should be treated separately. In the strategy table, the currency and market decisions are clearly separated, with currency hedging driving a wedge between the two key decision criteria. By means of the currency hedge, an investor can simultaneously overweight (underweight) a market and underweight (overweight) the underlying currency.

The purpose of the currency decision section of the strategy table is to draw an investment manager's attention to his or her portfolio's net currency position or exposure. A portfolio's net currency exposure in a particular market equals the actual gross allocation to that market, adjusted for any currency hedges. From the strategy table, this is shown simply as

Net currency position = Gross currency position – Currency hedge

The net currency position of a global bond portfolio will be tilted in favor of one currency depending on the portfolio manager's opinion about the trend in exchange rates. To get a quick reading of how far each currency bet deviates from market norms, we introduce a summary risk measure called *currency risk*, which we define as the ratio of the portfolio's (recommended) net currency position to the benchmark index's market capitalization weight (see Exhibit 55–18). A reading above 1.0 for the currency risk measure indicates a willingness to bear more currency risk than that to which a global bond market performance index would be exposed.

By undertaking currency exposure that exceeds or falls short of market norms, investors are making relative value judgments, namely, whether one currency will do better or worse than another. In the aggregate, the composite currency risk of a global bond portfolio must equal 1.0, with those currencies

E X H I B I T   55–18

Calculation of Currency Risk

Currency Decision	*Portfolio Risk*
Net Currency Position	**Currency Risk**
49	1.04
47	
Currency risk = $\dfrac{\text{Net currency position}}{\text{Market capitalization weight}}$	

enjoying a currency risk objective greater than 1.0 offset by those currencies with a currency risk objective less than 1.0.

The decision to set a currency risk objective at any particular level for any single currency depends on your outlook and conviction regarding the future path of exchange rates. There are essentially three inputs that investors need to determine their own optimal net currency exposures: (1) the projected change in currency values, (2) the projected local returns in each bond market, and (3) the levels of short-term forward premiums, which are known at the outset. To help explain how an investor can set optimal net currency exposures, let's assume a two-bond-market world consisting of the U.S. and German markets, where each makes up 50 percent of the global bond market. We will wish to have a 25 percent minimum exposure to each currency and a 75 percent maximum exposure. With two markets and the use of forward currency hedges, an investor can create four asset categories. (In an N-market world, an investor can create N^2 asset categories.) Those asset categories are listed in Exhibit 55–19, along with their projected total returns for a given investment horizon expressed in U.S. dollar terms.

Given the four asset categories shown in Exhibit 55–19, there are two asset categories that allow an investor to have a net exposure to dollars: U.S. dollar bonds and German bonds hedged into dollars. Likewise, there are two categories that allow an investor to have a net exposure to deutsche marks: German bonds and U.S. dollar bonds hedged into deutsche marks. If an investor wanted to make a currency bet in favor of the dollar (i.e., have a dollar currency risk objective greater than 1.0), two conditions would have to be met:

1. The projected return on U.S. bonds must exceed the projected return on German bonds (unhedged) in U.S. dollar terms; that is

$$R_{U.S.} > R_G + DM$$

E X H I B I T   55–19

Asset Choices in a Two-Market World

Asset Choices	Projected Total Return in U.S. Dollar Terms
U.S. Dollar Bonds	$R_{U.S.}$
German Bonds	$R_G + DM$
German Bonds Hedged into U.S.$	$R_G + FP_{DM}$
U.S. Dollar Bonds Hedged into DM	$R_{U.S.} - FP_{DM} + DM$

$R_{U.S.}$ = U.S. local bond market return

R_G = German local bond market return

FP_{DM} = Short-term forward premium on deutsche marks

DM = Appreciation/depreciation of DM versus U.S. dollar

2. The projected return on German bonds hedged into U.S. dollars on a rolling basis must exceed the projected return on German bonds (unhedged) in U.S. dollar terms; that is

$$R_G + \text{FP}_{DM} > R_G + \text{DM}$$

If either of those conditions is not met, an investor would do better by making a currency bet in favor of the deutsche mark, either by buying DM bonds outright or by buying U.S. bonds hedged into deutsche marks. Let's assume that both conditions are met, and thus, in terms of setting strategy, we adopt a U.S. dollar currency risk objective equal to 1.5 and a deutsche mark currency risk objective equal to 0.5. Because an overweight net U.S. dollar position can be detained by being long U.S. dollar bonds or by being long German bonds hedged into U.S. dollars, it becomes evident that a variety of gross currency position/hedging schemes can satisfy those single-currency risk objectives. This is demonstrated in Exhibit 55–20.

A net U.S. dollar currency position of 75 percent (i.e., a currency risk objective equal to 75 percent/50 percent = 1.5) can be arrived at by having a gross currency position or allocation in U.S. bonds of 75 percent; by having a 50 percent allocation to U.S. bonds and a 25 percent allocation to German bonds hedged into U.S. dollars; by having a 25 percent allocation to U.S. bonds and a 50 percent al-

E X H I B I T   55–20

How a Variety of Gross Allocation/Hedging Schemes Can Satisfy a Single-Currency Risk Objective[a]

| Market | Currency Decision | | Market Decision | Portfolio Risk |
	Net Currency Position (%)	Currency Hedge (%)	Gross Currency Position (%)	Currency Risk
U.S.	75.0	+50.0	25.0	1.5
	75.0	+37.5	37.5	1.5
	75.0	+25.0	50.0	1.5
	75.0	+12.5	62.5	1.5
	75.0	0.0	75.0	1.5
Germany	25.0	−50.0	75.0	0.5
	25.0	−37.5	62.5	0.5
	25.0	−25.0	50.0	0.5
	25.0	−12.5	37.5	0.5
	25.0	0.0	25.0	0.5
Total	100.0	0.0	100.0	1.0

[a]Assumption: U.S. and Germany make up 50 percent of the world bond market.

location to hedged German bonds; and so forth. Is there a difference in terms of total-return outcome between choosing one particular gross allocation/hedging scheme over another, when the net currency exposure is the same? The answer is "sometimes." Remember that the decision to have an overweight U.S. dollar position depends upon the following:

$$R_{U.S.} > R_G + DM \qquad \text{Acquire U.S. dollar bonds}$$

and

$$R_G + FP_{DM} > R_G + DM \qquad \text{Acquire hedged German bonds}$$

If both conditions are satisfied, the appropriate method to obtain an overweight dollar position will depend on the relationship between $R_{U.S.}$ and (R_G + FP_{DM}). If the projected return on U.S. dollar bonds exceeds the projected return on hedged German bonds, that is, if

$$R_{U.S.} > R_G + FP_{DM}$$

then the optimal allocation will be a 75 percent exposure (our maximum required exposure) in U.S. bonds with nothing hedged. If the projected return on hedged German bonds exceeds the projected return on U.S. dollar bonds, that is, if

$$R_{U.S.} < R_G + FP_{DM}$$

then the optimal allocation will be a 25 percent exposure in U.S. dollar bonds (our minimum required exposure) and a 50 percent exposure in German bonds hedged into U.S. dollars. If the projected return on U.S. dollar bonds equals the projected return on hedged German bonds, that is, if

$$R_{U.S.} = R_G + FP_{DM}$$

then all gross allocation/hedging schemes will yield the same expected return, and thus, everything else being equal, investors who seek a certain currency risk objective will be indifferent as to allocation schemes.

In the final analysis, either the allocation/hedging scheme is irrelevant, or the optimal allocation scheme is actually a corner solution, where nothing or everything is hedged.

Market Decision

The purpose of the market decision section of the strategy table is to draw an investment manager's attention to his or her gross currency position, or to the total allocation to each market and how that allocation is divided between cash and bonds. To get a more complete reading of a global bond portfolio's price sensitivity to changes in interest rates, we introduce a summary risk measure we call *interest-rate risk*. We define interest-rate risk in a given market as the ratio of the recommended gross currency position to the market capitalization weight multiplied by the ratio of the recommended portfolio duration to the market's average duration (see Exhibit 55–21).

EXHIBIT 55–21

Calculation of Interest-Rate Risk

	Market Decision		*Portfolio Risk*
Currency Block	**Gross Currency Position**	**Portfolio Duration**	**Interest-Rate Risk**
U.S.$	49	3.3	0.76
	47	4.5	
C$	6	2.3	0.77
	4	4.5	
A$/NZ$	8	3.8	5.07
	2	3.0	
Yen	20	4.5	0.80
	23	4.9	
STG	7	4.1	0.73
	7	5.6	
DM	8	5.7	0.80
	13	4.4	
FFr	2	8.8	1.00
	4	4.4	

$$\text{Interest-rate risk} = \frac{\text{Gross currency position}}{\text{Market capitalization weight}} \times \frac{\text{Portfolio duration}}{\text{Market duration}}$$

By defining interest-rate risk in this manner, we highlight the fact that a global bond portfolio can achieve greater exposure to an anticipated interest-rate decline in a particular market in two ways: (1) by increasing the size of either the gross currency position or allocation relative to market norms, leaving the portfolio's duration unchanged, or (2) by raising the portfolio's duration relative to the market's average duration, leaving the gross allocation unchanged. Likewise, a global bond portfolio can achieve a reduced exposure to an anticipated interest-rate rise in a particular market both by cutting back the size of either the gross currency position or allocation relative to the market norm, and by lowering the duration of the existing holdings relative to the market's average duration. For an entire portfolio, the composite interest-rate risk is a weighted average of the interest-rate risks of the individual markets.

The decision to set an interest-rate-risk objective at any particular level for an individual market or for an entire multimarket portfolio depends on opinions regarding the future trend in interest rates. A reading above 1.0 for interest-rate risk indicates a willingness to bear more interest-rate risk than that to which a global benchmark index would be exposed.

An investor can obtain a desired interest-rate risk through a variety of gross allocation/duration schemes simply by altering the gross currency position and the portfolio's average duration in an inverse manner. To see that more clearly, assume that an investor wishes to have an overweight exposure to a projected decline in U.S. bond yields equal to 1.5 times the U.S. market's average exposure to yield changes; that is, the investor desires a U.S. bond interest-rate risk equal to 1.5. Assume that the U.S. bond market makes up 50 percent of the world bond market and that the average duration of the U.S. bond market is four years.

As illustrated in Exhibit 55–22, a variety of gross allocation/duration schemes can satisfy the 1.5 interest-rate risk for the U.S. bond market. For example, a 75 percent allocation to U.S. bonds, with the average duration of the U.S. bond holdings equal to four years (75 percent/50 percent × 4.0/4.0 = 1.5) satisfies the 1.5 interest-rate risk objective, or a gross allocation of 50 percent to U.S. bonds, with the average duration of the U.S. bond holdings equal to six years (50 percent/50 percent × 6.0/4.0 = 1.5) achieves this objective, and so forth.

If a variety of gross allocation/duration schemes generate the same interest-rate risk, is there a difference in terms of total-return outcome between one particular allocation scheme and another? As was true in the case of currency risk, the answer is "sometimes." The interest-rate risk as we defined it relies on duration being a reliable proxy measure of the price sensitivity of a bond portfolio to a given change in yield. Duration is widely viewed as a reliable measure of interest-rate risk if it is assumed that the yield curve is flat and that any yield changes that do occur are small and uniform across the entire yield curve, that is, parallel. If those conditions are met, then it does not matter which gross allocation/duration scheme is adopted, because the total-return outcome from the competing allocation schemes will be the same. If the yield curve is assumed to be flat (with yields

EXHIBIT 55–22

How a Variety of Gross Allocation/Duration Schemes Can Satisfy a Single Interest-Rate-Risk Objective[a]

Market	Gross Currency Position	Portfolio Duration	Interest-Rate Risk
U.S.	25.0	12.0	1.5
	37.5	8.0	1.5
	50.0	6.0	1.5
	62.5	4.8	1.5
	75.0	4.0	1.5

[a]Assumption: (1) U.S. makes up 50 percent of the world bond market; (2) U.S. bond market average duration = four years.

unchanged) the same standstill yield will be earned along the entire maturity/duration spectrum. Thus, a small-allocation/long-duration scheme will yield the same return as a large allocation/short duration scheme.

However, if the assumption of a flat yield curve is relaxed, the standstill yield on various gross allocation/duration schemes will differ. Consider an unchanging, upward-sloping yield curve where the standstill yield on long-duration bonds exceeds the standstill yield on short-duration notes. In that instance, the standstill yield on a small-allocation/long-duration scheme will exceed the standstill yield on a large-allocation/short-duration scheme, even though both allocation schemes generate the same interest-rate risk. Thus, investors who expect an upward-sloping yield curve to exhibit little change should use small-allocation/long-duration schemes to meet interest-rate risk objectives. The opposite would be the case for a downward-sloping yield-curve environment.

Now consider the implications of a large parallel shift of a flat or upward-sloping yield curve. As was true in the case of an unchanging upward-sloping yield curve, the return on small-allocation/long-duration schemes will once again exceed the return on large-allocation/short-duration schemes, because small-allocation/long-duration schemes offer greater positive convexity than do large-allocation/short-duration schemes. Thus, assuming yield changes are large and yields move in a parallel fashion, the greater positive convexity of small-allocation/long-duration schemes will lead to greater upside performance in a declining-yield environment and less downside risk in a rising-yield environment.

Let's now consider the possibility of nonparallel shifts. If the yield curve flattens because short-term interest rates rise relative to long-term interest rates or steepens because short-term interest rates decline relative to long-term interest rates, then the relative performance of competing gross allocation/duration schemes may differ considerably, even though they may generate the same interest-rate risk. In the case of a flattening yield curve, small-allocation/long-duration schemes should outperform large-allocation/short-duration schemes, whereas in the case of a steepening yield curve the opposite should be true.

The Bond Selection Decision

When nonparallel shifts of the yield curve are anticipated, neither duration nor our summary measure of interest-rate risk may be adequate indicators of a bond portfolio's price sensitivity to changes in interest rates. In such cases, it may be more important to manage the maturity structure of the portfolio correctly than to get the portfolio's duration or interest-rate risk right. Therefore, in any bond investment decision, the summary measure of interest-rate risk—which considers only the gross allocation and the portfolio's relative duration—must be supplemented by comparing the portfolio's recommended maturity structure to the maturity mix of the benchmark index. That is why the strategy table breaks down the bond selection decision into component sources of bond investment risk. The bond selection section of the strategy table draws an investment manager's attention not only to his or her portfolio's average duration and how that compares to market norms, but also to the portfolio's maturity structure and how that compares with the maturity mix of the benchmark index and to the portfolio's sector breakdown (governments versus Euros) and how that compares to market norms.

Tying the Pieces Together

In the preceding sections, we described the steps that investors should take in formulating their currency, market, and bond selection decisions. The strategy table helps investors formulate a global investment decision process by allowing them to assess just how far their currency, market, and bond selection decisions deviate from market norms. In this section, we show how those individual decision criteria can be integrated into the construction of a global bond portfolio.

An investor begins the process of assigning portfolio weights by setting out desired currency and interest-rate risk objectives for each market, with allowances made for any maturity or sector adjustments if changes are expected in yield-curve slope or intramarket spread. How far the bets on currency and interest-rate risk will be allowed to deviate from market norms will depend on the investor's outlook and conviction regarding the future direction of exchange rates and interest rates.

The precise assignment of portfolio weights across currencies and markets must satisfy both the currency risk and the interest-rate risk objectives. The problem for portfolio managers is that a variety of portfolio schemes can jointly satisfy any set of currency and interest-rate risk objectives. That is shown in Exhibit 55–23, which plots a range of currency risk and interest-rate risk measures between 0 and 1.5 for the U.S. dollar and the U.S. bond market on the horizontal axes and various gross currency positions or allocations consistent with those risk objectives on the vertical axis. Given a U.S. dollar currency risk objective of 1.5, for example, it is evident that a variety of gross allocation/hedging schemes can satisfy that objective—for example, a 75 percent allocation to U.S. dollar bonds with nothing hedged satisfies it, as does a 50 percent allocation to U.S. dollar bonds with an additional 25 percent coming from hedged foreign bonds, and so forth. Likewise, a variety of gross allocation/duration schemes can satisfy an interest-rate risk objective of 1.5—for example, a 75 percent U.S. allocation, with the portfolio's duration equal to the market's average duration, or a 50 percent U.S. allocation, with the portfolio's duration equal to 1.5 times the market's average duration, and so forth. As the shaded area in the graph indicates, a variety of allocations to the U.S. dollar bond market, coupled with selective currency hedges and adjustments to portfolio duration, can jointly satisfy both the 1.5 currency risk objective and 1.5 interest-rate risk objectives. Which gross allocation/hedging/duration scheme should be selected in constructing a global bond portfolio? The answer is fairly straightforward: the optimal allocation scheme is one that maximizes portfolio return while satisfying the investor's currency and interest-rate risk objectives.

EXHIBIT 55–23

Integrating Currency and Market Decisions

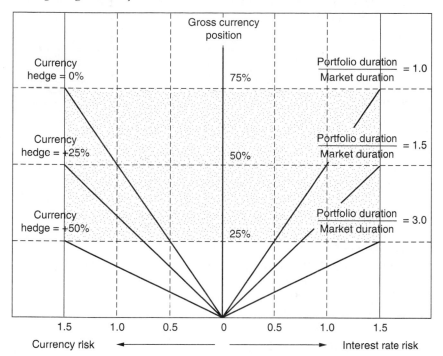

There are two important steps in deriving the optimal allocation scheme: the gross allocation/hedging decision and the gross allocation/duration decision. As we previously discussed, under certain assumptions it makes no difference which gross allocation hedging/duration scheme is selected to satisfy a desired set of currency and interest-rate risk objectives, because they all should yield the same return. However, once those assumptions are relaxed, certain allocation schemes may yield higher expected returns than others, even though they may satisfy the same currency and interest-rate risk objectives.

The best way to describe how an optimal portfolio allocation can be selected from a range of competing risk allocation schemes is through a simple illustration. As before, let's assume a universe consisting of the U.S. and German bond markets, where each makes up 50 percent of the global bond market. We wish to have a 25 percent minimum exposure to each currency and market and a 75 percent maximum exposure. Let's assume that, given our assessment and conviction of likely currency changes and local market return outcomes, we adopt a U.S. dollar currency risk objective equal to 1.5 and a deutsche mark currency risk objective of 0.5. Let's assume further that interest-rate risk objectives of 1.0 are sought for both the U.S. and German bond markets. The projected local market returns for the U.S.

E X H I B I T   55–24

Projected Total Returns on U.S. and Hedged German Bonds under Hypothetical Alternative Allocation Schemes

Asset Allocations		Projected Total Return When U.S. and German Total-Return Curves Are Flat				Projected Total Return When German Total-Return Curve is Upward Sloping	
U.S.	Germany	$R_{U.S.}$	R_G	FP_{DM}	$R_G + FP_{DM}$	R'_G	$R'_G + FP_{DM}$
25.0%	75.0%	10%	5%	6%	11%	5%	11%
37.5	62.5	10	5	6	11	6	12
50.0	50.0	10	5	6	11	7	13
62.5	37.5	10	5	6	11	8	14
75.0	25.0	10	5	6	11	9	15

($R_{U.S.}$) and German (R_G) bond markets are shown in Exhibit 55–24 along with the known 6 percent short-term forward premium on deutsche marks (FP_{DM}).

It is expected that the returns earned on U.S. and German bonds in local currency terms will amount to 10 percent and 5 percent, respectively. For now, let's assume that those returns will be invariant to the particular gross allocation/duration scheme selected; that is, we assume flat total-return curves for both markets.

Given the 6 percent short-term forward premium on deutsche marks, the projected return on German bonds hedged into U.S. dollar terms is 11 percent (5 percent + 6 percent = 11 percent). Assuming that the dollar is projected to rise by 5 percent against the deutsche mark over the investment horizon, the projected return on unhedged German bonds in U.S. dollar terms will be equal to zero (5 percent – 5 percent = 0 percent). As shown in the total-return analysis section of Exhibit 55–25, assuming flat U.S. and German total-return curves and a minimum 25 percent exposure to both the U.S. market and the German bond market on an unhedged basis, the desired currency risk and interest-rate risk objectives are satisfied, and total return is maximized by having a 25 percent allocation to U.S. bonds and a 50 percent exposure to German bonds hedged into U.S. dollars. That follows from the analysis described earlier, when we noted that hedged German bonds would be preferred over U.S. dollar bonds outright if

$$R_G + FP_{DM} > R_{U.S.}$$

whereas U.S. dollar bonds outright would be preferred over hedged German bonds if

$$R_{U.S.} > R_G + FP_{DM}$$

EXHIBIT 55-25

Asset-Weighted Total-Return Analysis

Assumptions	Total Return from U.S. Assets		+ Return from Unhedged German Assets		+ Return from Hedged German Assets		= Total Return
	Asset Weight	Total Return (%)	Asset Weight	Total Return (%)	Asset Weight	Total Return (%)	(%)
U.S. and Germany	.250	(10)	.25	(5-5)	.500	(11)	8.00
have flat total-return	.375	(10)	.25	(5-5)	.375	(11)	7.88
curves	.500	(10)	.25	(5-5)	.250	(11)	7.75
	.625	(10)	.25	(5-5)	.125	(11)	7.63
	.750	(10)	.25	(5-5)	0	(11)	7.50
Germany has an	.250	(10)	.25	(5-5)	.500	(11)	8.00
upward-sloping	.375	(10)	.25	(6-5)	.375	(12)	8.50
total-return curve	.500	(10)	.25	(7-5)	.250	(13)	8.75
	.625	(10)	.25	(8-5)	.125	(14)	8.75
	.750	(10)	.25	(9-5)	0	(15)	8.50

Given that the projected return on hedged German bonds equals

$$R_G + FP_{DM} = 0.05 + 0.06 = 0.11$$

whereas the projected return on U.S. dollar bonds outright equals

$$R_{U.S.} = 0.1$$

it is clear that

$$R_G + FP_{DM} > R_{U.S.}$$

Thus, the optimal allocation should be a corner solution in favor of hedged German bonds.

In this example, the specific allocation scheme that maximized total return was determined by focusing only on the optimal gross allocation/hedging scheme, because all the competing gross allocation/duration schemes must yield the same return if flat total-return curves are assumed. However, if we relax the assumption that the projected local returns on U.S. and German bonds are invariant to the particular gross allocation/duration scheme selected, a different total-return ranking among the competing allocation schemes will arise. Consider the case where, as before, the U.S. local bond market return (10 percent) is invariant to the gross allocation/duration scheme selected, but the German total-return curve is positively sloped; that is, the projected return on small-allocation/long-duration schemes will yield a higher projected return than large-allocation/short-duration schemes, even though the same interest-rate risk objective is satisfied. In Exhibit 55–24, the projected local return on German bonds (R'_G) is shown to vary from 5 percent for large-allocation (75 percent)/short-duration schemes to 9 percent for small-allocation (25 percent)/long-duration schemes. As shown in the total-return analysis section of Exhibit 55–25, the desired currency risk and interest-rate risk objectives are satisfied and total return is maximized by having a U.S. dollar bond allocation equal to 50–62.5 percent and a hedged German bond allocation of 12.5–25.0 percent. This more balanced allocation contrasts to the corner solution allocation (a 25 percent U.S. dollar bond allocation and a 50 percent allocation to hedged German bonds) in the previous example, because even though hedged German bonds have a higher expected return than U.S. dollar bonds under all allocation schemes, that is,

$$R'_G + FP_{DM} > R_{U.S.}$$

smaller hedged German bond allocations (with larger portfolio durations) have a comparative advantage over larger hedged German bond allocations (with smaller portfolio durations) in an upward-sloping total-return-curve environment. Thus, investors would do better to exploit the higher projected returns on such schemes. Although the projected 10 percent return on U.S. dollar bonds is lower than the projected returns on hedged German bonds (11 percent–15 percent) for all allocations shown, the portfolio weight assigned to U.S. dollar bonds (50.0 percent–62.5 percent) turns out to be larger than the 25 percent U.S. dollar bond allocation when flat U.S. and German bond total-return curves were assumed. The allocation to U.S. dollar bonds is larger because the currency risk and interest-rate risk objectives can both be satisfied with a higher expected return if a small rather than a large hedged German bond allocation is chosen.

CONCLUSION

A global bond portfolio's currency and interest-rate exposure will be dictated by the investment manager's currency risk and interest-rate risk objectives. Although various portfolio weighting schemes simultaneously can satisfy both risk objectives, they may yield quite different returns. The analysis presented here reveals how a portfolio manager can find the particular weighting scheme that both maximizes total return and satisfies the investor's currency risk and interest-rate risk objectives.

DERIVATIVE INSTRUMENTS AND THEIR PORTFOLIO MANAGEMENT APPLICATIONS

⑥ # INTRODUCTION TO INTEREST-RATE FUTURES AND OPTIONS CONTRACTS

Mark Pitts, Ph.D.
Principal
White Oak Capital Management Corp.

Frank J. Fabozzi, Ph.D., CFA, CPA
Adjunct Professor of Finance
School of Management
Yale University

With the advent of options, futures, and forwards on interest-rate instruments, proactive fixed income risk management, in its broadest sense, assumes a new dimension. Investment managers and traders can achieve new degrees of freedom. It is now possible to alter the interest-rate sensitivity of a fixed income portfolio economically and quickly. *Derivative contracts,* known as such because they derive their value from an underlying instrument, offer investment managers and traders risk and return patterns that were previously either unavailable or too costly.

The purpose of this chapter is twofold. First, we explain the basic characteristics of options, futures, and forward contracts. Second, we review the most actively traded and most representative over-the-counter (OTC) and listed contracts. We omit from our discussion the use of futures for hedging; this topic will be explained in more detail in Chapter 60.

BASIC CHARACTERISTICS OF DERIVATIVE CONTRACTS

Futures Contracts

A *futures contract* is an agreement between a buyer (seller) and an established futures exchange or its clearinghouse in which the buyer (seller) agrees to take (make) delivery of a specific amount of a valued item such as a commodity, stock, or bond at a specified price at a designated time. For some futures contracts, settlement at expiration is in cash rather than actual delivery.

When an investor takes a position in the market by buying a futures contract, the investor is said to *be long the futures* or have a *long position in the futures*. If, instead, the investor's opening position is the sale of a futures contract, the investor is said to *be short the futures* or have a *short position in the futures*.

Futures contracts based on a financial instrument or a financial index are known as *financial futures*. Financial futures can be classified as interest-rate futures, stock index futures, or currency futures. This chapter focuses on interest-rate futures and includes a description of the most important interest-rate futures contracts currently traded.

To illustrate how financial futures work, suppose that X buys a futures contract and Y sells a futures contract on an 8 percent 5-year Treasury note for settlement one year from now. Suppose also that the price at which X and Y agree to transact one year from now is $100. This is the futures price. This means that one year from now Y must deliver an 8 percent 5-year Treasury note and will receive $100. X will take delivery of an 8 percent 5-year Treasury note and will pay $100.

The profit or loss realized by the buyer or seller of a futures contract depends on the price and interest rate on the delivery date. For example, if the market price of an 8 percent 5-year Treasury note at the settlement date is $110, because rates have declined, the buyer profits, paying $100 for a security that is worth $110. In contrast, the seller loses, because an instrument worth $110 must be delivered in exchange for $100. If interest rates rise on 8 percent 5-year Treasury notes so that the market price is $90, the seller of the futures contract profits and the buyer loses.

When the investor first takes a position in a futures contract, he must deposit a minimum dollar amount per contract as specified by the exchange. Futures brokers can, and often do, ask for more than the exchange minimums. As the price of the futures contract fluctuates, the value of the investor's equity in the position changes. At the close of each trading day, any market gain results in an increase in the investor's equity, whereas any market loss results in a decrease. This process is referred to as *marking to market*. Should an investor's equity position fall below an amount determined by the exchange, he must provide additional margin. On the other hand, if an investor's equity increases, he or she may withdraw funds. Consequently, a futures position frequently involves substantial cash flows before the delivery date. Margin is described in more detail later in this chapter.

Forward Contracts

A *forward contract* is much like a futures contract. A forward contract is an agreement for the future delivery of some amount of a valued item at a specified price at a designated time. Futures contracts are standardized agreements that define the delivery date (or month) and quality and quantity of the deliverable. Futures contracts are traded on organized exchanges. A forward contract is, in contrast, usually nonstandardized, and is traded over the counter by direct contact between buyer and seller.

Although both futures and forward contracts set forth terms of delivery, futures contracts are not intended to be settled by delivery. In fact, generally less than 2 percent of outstanding futures contracts are delivered or go to final settlement. However, forward contracts *are* intended to be held to final settlement. Many of the most popular forward contracts, however, settle in cash rather than actual delivery.

Forward contracts may or may not be marked to market. Consequently, there is no interim cash flow on forwards that are not marked to market.

Finally, both parties in a forward contract are exposed to credit risk because either party may default on its obligation. In contrast, credit risk for futures contracts is minimal because the clearing corporation associated with the exchange guarantees the other side of each transaction.

Options

An *option* is a contract in which the seller of the option grants the buyer of the option the right to purchase from, or sell to, the seller a designated instrument at a specified price within a specified period of time. The seller (or *writer*) grants this right to the buyer in exchange for a certain sum of money, called the *option price* or *option premium.*

The price at which the instrument may be bought or sold is called the *exercise* or *strike price.* The date after which an option is void is called the *expiration date.* An *American option* may be exercised any time up to and including the expiration date. A *European option* may be exercised only on the expiration date.

When an option writer grants the buyer the right to purchase the designated instrument, it is called a *call option.* When the option buyer has the right to sell the designated instrument to the writer, the option is called a *put option.* The buyer of an option is said to be *long the option;* the writer is said to be *short the option.*

Consider, for example, an option on an 8 percent 5-year Treasury note with one year to expiration and an exercise price of $100. Suppose that the option price is $2 and the current price of the Treasury note is $100 with a yield of 8 percent. If the option is a call option, then the buyer of the option has the right to purchase an 8 percent 5-year Treasury note for $100 within one year. The writer of the option must sell the Treasury note for $100 to the buyer if he or she exercises the option. Suppose that the interest rate on the Treasury note declines and its price rises to $110. By exercising the call option, the buyer realizes a profit, paying $100 for a Treasury note that is worth $110. After considering the cost of buying the option, $2, the net profit is $8. The writer of the option loses $8. If, instead, the market interest rate rises and the price of the Treasury note falls below $100, the call option buyer will not exercise the option, losing the option price of $2. The writer will realize a profit of $2. Thus, the buyer of a call option benefits from a decline in interest rates (a rise in the price of the underlying fixed income instrument) and the writer loses.

If the option is a put rather than a call, and the interest rate on Treasury notes declines and the price rises above $100, the option buyer will not exercise the option. The buyer will lose the entire option price. If, on the other hand, the interest rate on Treasury notes rises and the note's price falls below $100, the option buyer will profit by exercising the put option. In the case of a put option, the option buyer benefits from a rise in interest rates (a decline in the price of the underlying fixed income instrument) and the option seller loses.

The maximum amount that an option buyer can lose is the option price. The maximum profit that the option writer (seller) can realize is the option price. The option buyer has substantial potential upside return, whereas the option writer has substantial downside risk. The risk/reward relationships for option positions are investigated in Chapter 53.

Options can be written on cash instruments or futures. The latter are called *futures options* and are traded only on the exchanges. Options on cash instruments are also traded on the exchanges, but have been much more successfully traded over the counter. These *OTC,* or *dealer, options* are tailor-made options on specific Treasury issues, mortgage securities, or interest-rate indexes. Option contracts are reviewed later in this chapter.

Differences between Option and Futures (or Forward) Contracts

Unlike a futures or forward contract, an option gives the buyer the *right* but not the *obligation* to perform. The option seller has the obligation to perform. In the case of a futures or forward contact, both the buyer and seller are obligated to perform. In addition, the buyer of a futures or forward contract does not pay the seller to accept the obligation, whereas in the case of an option, the buyer pays the seller an option premium.

Consequently, the risk/reward characteristics of the two contracts also differ. In a futures or forward contract, the long position realizes a dollar-for-dollar gain when the price of the futures or forward increases and suffers a dollar-for-dollar loss when the price of the futures or forward decreases. The opposite holds for a short position. Options do not provide such a symmetric risk/reward relationship. The most a long position may lose is the option premium, yet the long retains all the upside potential. However, the gain is always reduced by the price of the option. The maximum profit the short position may realize is the option price, but the short position has substantial downside risk.

REPRESENTATIVE EXCHANGE-TRADED INTEREST-RATE FUTURES CONTRACTS

Interest-rate futures contracts can be classified by the maturity of their underlying security. Short-term interest rate futures contracts have an underlying security that matures in less than one year. The maturity of the underlying security of long-term futures exceed one year. Below we describe the specifications of the more commonly used futures contracts.

The Treasury Bond Futures Contract

The T-bond futures contract is the most successful interest-rate (or commodity) futures contract. Prices and yields on the T-bond futures contract are quoted in terms of a (fictitious) 20-year 8 percent Treasury bond, but the CBT allows many different bonds to be delivered in satisfaction of a short position in the contract. Specifically, any Treasury bond with at least 15 years to maturity or to first call, if callable, qualifies for delivery. Consequently, there are usually at least 20 outstanding bonds that constitute good delivery.

The T-bond futures contract calls for the short (i.e., the seller) to deliver $100,000 face value of any one of the qualifying Treasury bonds. However, because the coupons and maturities vary widely, the price that the buyer pays the seller depends on which bond the seller chooses to deliver. The rule used by the Chicago Board of Trade is one that adjusts the futures price by a conversion factor that reflects the price the bond would sell for at the beginning of the delivery month if it were yielding 8 percent. Using such a rule, the conversion factor for a given bond and a given delivery month is constant through time and is not affected by changes in the price of the bond or the price of the futures contract.

To illustrate, consider the delivery price for the Treasury 12 percent bonds of 8/15/13, callable 8/15/08, if they had been delivered on the June 1988 contract. At the beginning of June 1988, this bond had 20 years, $2^{1}/_{2}$ months to call. To calculate the conversion factor, the term-to-call is rounded down to the nearest quarter year, in this case giving an even 20 years to call. Because a 20-year 12 percent bond yielding 8 percent sells for 139.59, the conversion factor for the 12 percent bond for the June 1988 contract was 1.3959 (i.e., 139.59 divided by 100).

The seller has the right to choose which qualifying bond to deliver and when during the delivery month delivery will take place. When the bond is delivered, the buyer is obligated to pay the seller the futures price times the appropriate conversion factor, plus accrued interest on the delivered bond.

Paradoxically, the success of the CBT Treasury bond contract can in part be attributed to the fact that the delivery mechanism is not as simple as it may first appear. There are several options implicit in a position in bond futures. First, the seller chooses which bond to deliver. Thus, the seller has an option to swap between bonds. If the seller is holding bond A for delivery, but bond B becomes cheaper to deliver, she can swap bond B for bond A and make a more profitable delivery. Second, within some guidelines set by the CBT, the seller decides when during the delivery month delivery will take place. She thus has a timing option that can be used to her advantage. Finally, the short retains the possibility of making the wildcard play. This potentially profitable situation arises from the fact that the seller can give notice of intent to deliver for several hours after the exchange has closed and the futures settlement price has been fixed. In a falling market, the seller can use the wildcard option to profit from the fixed delivery price.

The seller's options tend to make a contract a bit more difficult to understand, but at the same time they make the contract more attractive to speculators, arbitrageurs, dealers, and anyone else who understands the contract better than other market participants. Thus, in the case of the Treasury bond futures contract, complexity has helped provide liquidity.

Because of the importance of this contract, it is discussed in more detail in Chapter 58.

Treasury Note Futures

There are three Treasury note futures contracts: 10-year, 5-year, and 2-year. All three contracts are modeled after the Treasury bond futures contract and are traded on the CBT. The underlying instrument for the 10-year Treasury note futures contract is $100,000 par value of a hypothetical 10-year, 8% Treasury note. There are several acceptable Treasury issues that may be delivered by the short. An issue is acceptable if the maturity is not less than 6.5 years and not greater than 10 years from the first day of the delivery month. The delivery options granted to the short position and the minimum price fluctuation are the same as for the Treasury bond futures contract.

For the 5-year Treasury note futures contract, the underlying is $100,000 par value of a U.S. Treasury note that satisfies the following conditions: (1) an original maturity of not more than five years and three months, (2) a remaining maturity not more than five years and three months, and (3) a remaining maturity not less than four years and three months. The minimum price fluctuation for this contract is one 64th of a percent. The dollar value of one 64th for a $100,000 par value is $15.625 and is therefore the minimum price fluctuation.

The underlying for the 2-year Treasury note futures contract is $200,000 par value of a U.S. Treasury note with a remaining maturity of not more than two years and not less than one year and nine months. Moreover, the original maturity of the note delivered to satisfy the 2-year futures cannot be more than five years and two months. The minimum price fluctuation for this contract is one 128th of a percent. The dollar value of one 128th for a $200,000 par value is $15.625 and is therefore the minimum price fluctuation.

The Treasury Bill Futures Contract

The IMM's futures contract on Treasury bills was the first contract on a short-term debt instrument, and has been the model for most subsequent contracts on short-term debt. The contract is based on three-month Treasury bills with a face value of $1 million.

The contract is quoted and traded in terms of a futures "price," but the futures price is, in fact, just a different way of quoting the futures interest rate. Specifically, the futures price is the annualized futures rate subtracted from 100.

For example, a futures price of 92.25 means that Treasury bills are trading in the futures market at a rate of 7.75 percent. The actual price that the buyer pays the seller is calculated using the usual formula for Treasury bills:

$$\text{Invoice price} = \$1,000,000 \times \left[1 - \text{Rate} \times \left(\frac{\text{Days to maturity}}{360} \right) \right]$$

where the rate is expressed in decimal form. As this formula shows, each basis-point change in the interest rate (or each .01 change in the futures price) leads to a $25 change in the invoice price for a 90-day bill. Consequently, the value of a .01 change in the futures contract is always $25.

The Treasury bill futures contract is considerably simpler than the T-bond and T-note futures contracts. First, because all Treasury bills of the same maturity are economically equivalent, there is effectively only one deliverable issue, namely, Treasury bills with three months to maturity. The fact that the three-month bills may be either new three-month bills or older bills that currently have three months of remaining life makes little difference because the new and old issues will trade the same in the cash market. Thus, all the subtleties surrounding conversion factors and most deliverable issues are absent from the Treasury bill futures market. Furthermore, there is little uncertainty or choice involved in the delivery date, because delivery must take place during a very narrow time frame, usually a three-day period. The rules of the exchange make clear well in advance the exact dates on which delivery will take place. Finally, because there are no conversion factors, there is no wildcard play in the Treasury bill futures market.

Although the Treasury bill futures contract is simple and thus may not provide as many speculative and arbitrage opportunities as the more complex long- and intermediate-term futures contracts, it does provide a straightforward means of hedging or speculating on the short end of the yield curve. Because the Treasury bill rate is a benchmark off which other short-term rates may be priced, the bill contract fills a well-defined need of many market participants.

The Eurodollar Time Deposit Futures Contract

As the Eurodollar and LIBOR sectors of the fixed income market have grown substantially in recent years, so has volume in the IMM's Eurodollar time deposit futures contract. Unlike most other fixed income futures contracts, the Eurodollar contract does not allow actual delivery. Instead, settlement is made in cash. The final settlement price is determined by the three-month Eurodollar deposit rate when trading on the contract is concluded. Although this mechanism does not allow delivery of an actual instrument, the cash flow from a futures position is such that the contract provides a very good vehicle for hedging or speculating on short-term Eurodollar and LIBOR-based debt.

Like the Treasury bill contract, the quoted futures price for Eurodollar time deposits is equal to 100 minus the annualized yield. Also, each .01 change in the futures price (1-basis-point change in yield) carries a value of $25. Settlement on Eurodollar futures takes place on a single day during the delivery month.

The yield on the Eurodollar futures contract is quoted in terms of an add-on, or simple, interest rate. Rates on Eurodollar contracts are thus directly comparable to the rates on domestic CDs or interbank deposits. However, to compare the Eurodollar rate to the Treasury bill rate, one of the rates must be converted so that both rates will be in the same terms.

The Eurodollar futures contract is one of the most heavily traded contracts. It is frequently used to trade the short end of the yield curve, and many hedgers have found the Eurodollar contract to be the best hedging vehicle for a wide range of hedging situations.

The Municipal Bond Futures Contract

Because there are risks unique to the municipal bond market, the Treasury bond futures contract has not been particularly effective in managing the risk of municipal bonds. Proposed and actual changes in tax laws and changing economic conditions that might be expected to increase the likelihood of defaults are examples of factors that might affect the municipal bond market but not the Treasury market. The CBT's municipal bond futures contract was designed to give participants in the municipal bond market a more effective means of controlling such risks.

The municipal bond futures contract is based on the value of the Bond Buyer Index (BBI). The BBI consists of 40 actively traded general obligation and revenue bonds. To be included in the BBI, the issue must be rated at least single A and the size of the term portion of the issue must be at least $50 million ($75 million for housing issues). No more than two bonds of the same issuer are included in the BBI. In addition, for an issue to be considered, it must meet the following three conditions: It must have at least 19 years remaining to maturity, a first call date between 7 and 16 years, and at least one call at par before redemption.

The Bond Buyer serves as the index manager for the contract, and prices each issue in the index based on prices received daily from five dealer-to-dealer brokers. After the highest and lowest price obtained for each issue are dropped, the average of the three remaining prices is computed. The average price is then multiplied by a conversion factor designed to equate the bond to an 8 percent issue, just as in the cases of the Treasury bond and note futures contracts. This gives an average converted price for each bond in the BBI. These prices are then summed and divided by 40, giving an average converted price for the BBI.

The BBI is revised bimonthly when new issues are added and older issues, or issues that no longer meet the criteria for inclusion in the index, are dropped. A smoothing coefficient is calculated on the index revision date so that the value of the BBI will not change merely because of the change in its composition. The average converted price for the BBI is multiplied by this coefficient to get the value of the BBI for a particular date.

Mechanics of Futures Trading

Types of Orders

When a trader wants to buy or sell a futures contract, the price and conditions under which the order is to be executed must be communicated to the futures brokers. The simplest type of order, yet potentially the most perilous from the trader's perspective, is the *market order.* When a market order is placed, it is executed at the best price available as soon as the order reaches the trading pit, the area on the floor of a futures exchange where all transactions for a specific contract are made. The danger of market orders is that an adverse move may take place between the time the trader places the order and the time the order reaches the trading pit.

To avoid the dangers associated with market orders, the trader can place a *limit order* (or *resting order*) that designates a price limit for the execution of the transaction. A *buy limit order* indicates that the futures contract may be purchased only at the designated price or lower. A *sell limit order* indicates that the futures contract may be sold only at the designated price or higher.

The danger of a limit order is that there is no guarantee that it will be executed at all. The designated price may simply not be obtainable. Even if the contract trades at the specified price, the order may not be filled because the market does not trade long enough at the specified price (or better) to fill all outstanding orders. Nevertheless, a limit order may be less risky than a market order. The trader has more control with a limit order, because the price designated in the limit order can be revised based on prevailing market prices as long as the order has not already been filled.

The limit order is a conditional order: It is executed only if the limit price or a better price can be obtained. Another type of conditional order is the *stop order.* A stop order specifies that the order is not to be executed until the market reaches a designated price, at which time it becomes a market order. A *buy stop order* specifies that the order is not to be executed until the market rises to a designated price (i.e., trades at or above, or is bid at or above, the designated price). A *sell stop order* specifies that the order is not to be executed until the market price falls below a designated price (i.e., trades at or below, or is offered at or below, the designated price). A stop order is useful when a futures trader already has a position on but cannot watch the market constantly. Traders can preserve profits or minimize losses on open positions by allowing market movements to trigger a closing trade. In a sell (buy) stop order, the designated price is less (greater) than the current market price of the futures contract. In a sell (buy) limit order the designated price is greater (less) than the current market price of the futures contract.

There are two dangers associated with stop orders. Because futures markets sometimes exhibit abrupt price changes, the direction of the change in the futures price may be very temporary, resulting in the premature closing of a position. Also, once the designated price is reached, the stop order becomes a market order and is subject to the uncertainty of the execution price noted earlier for market orders.

A *stop-limit order,* a hybrid of a stop order and a limit order, is a stop order that designates a price limit. Thus, in contrast to the stop order, which becomes a market order if the stop is reached, the stop-limit order becomes a limit order if the stop is reached. The order can be used to cushion the market impact of a stop order. The trader may limit the possible execution price after the activation of a stop. As with a limit order, the limit price might never be reached after the order is activated, and therefore the order might not be executed. This, of course, defeats one purpose of the stop order—to protect a profit or limit a loss.

A trader may also enter a *market-if-touched order.* A market-if-touched is like a stop order in that it becomes a market order if a designated price is reached. However, a market-if-touched order to buy would become a market order if the market *falls* to a given price, whereas a stop order to buy becomes a market order if the market *rises* to a given price. Similarly, a market-if-touched order to sell becomes a market order if the market rises to a specified price, whereas the stop order to sell becomes a market order if the market falls to a given price. One may think of the stop order as an order designed to exit an existing position at an acceptable price (without specifying the exact price), and the market-if-touched order as an order designed to enter a position at an acceptable price (also without specifying the exact price).

Orders may be placed to buy or sell at the open or the close of trading for the day. An *opening order* indicates that a trade is to be executed only in the opening range for the day, and a *closing order* indicates that the trade is to be executed only within the closing range for the day.

Futures brokers may be allowed to try to get the best possible price for their clients. The *discretionary order* gives the broker a specified price range in which to fill the order. For example, a discretionary order might be a limit order that gives the broker a one-tick (i.e., one-basis-point or one-32nd) discretion to try to do better than the limit price. Thus, even if the limit price is reached and the order could be filled at that limit, the broker can wait for a better price. However, if it turns out that the market goes in the wrong direction, the broker must fill the order but at no worse than one tick from the limit price. A *not held order* gives the broker virtually full discretion over the order. The not held order may be placed as any of the orders mentioned so far (market, stop, limit, etc.), but if the broker believes that filling the orders is not advisable, he or she need not fill them.

A client may enter orders that contain order cancellation provisions. A *fill-or-kill* order must be executed as soon as it reaches the trading floor or it is immediately canceled. A *one-cancels-other order* is a pair of orders that are worked simultaneously, but as soon as one order is filled the other is automatically canceled.

Orders may designate the time period for which the order is effective—a day, week, or month, or perhaps by a given time within the day. An *open order,* or *good-til-canceled order,* is good until the order is specifically canceled. If the time period is not specified, it is usually assumed to be good only until the end of the day. For some orders, like the market order, a specific time period is not relevant, because they are executed immediately.

Upon execution of an order, the futures broker is required to provide confirmation of the trade. The confirmation indicates all the essential information about the trade. When the order involves the liquidation of a position, the confirmation shows the profit or loss on the position and the commission costs.

Taking and Liquidating a Position

Once an account has been opened with a broker, the futures trader may take a position in the market. If the trader buys a futures contract, he is said to have a long position. If the trader's opening position is the sale of the futures contract, the trader is said to have a short position.

The futures trader has two ways to liquidate a position. To liquidate a position before the delivery date, he must take an offsetting position in the same contract. For a long position, this means selling an identical number of contracts; for a short position, this means buying an identical number of contracts.

The alternative is to wait until the delivery date. At that time, the investor liquidates a long position by accepting the delivery of the underlying instrument at the agreed-upon price, or liquidates a short position by delivering the instrument at the agreed-upon price. For interest-rate futures contracts that do not call for actual delivery (e.g., Eurodollar and municipal bond futures), settlement is in cash at the settlement price on the delivery date.

The Role of the Clearing Corporation

When an investor takes a position in the futures market, there is always another party taking the opposite position and agreeing to satisfy the terms set forth in the contract. Because of the *clearing corporation* associated with each exchange, the investor need not worry about the financial strength and integrity of the party taking the opposite side of the contract. After an order is executed, the relationship between the two parties is severed. The clearing corporation interposes itself as the buyer for every sale and the seller for every purchase. Thus the investor is free to liquidate a position without involving the other party to the original transaction and without worry that the other party may default. However, the investor *is* exposed to default on the part of the futures broker through which the trade is placed. Thus, each institution should make sure that the futures broker (and specifically the *subsidiary* that trades futures) has adequate capital to ensure that there is little danger of default.

Commissions

Commissions on futures contracts have been fully negotiable since 1974. Futures commissions are usually quoted on the basis of a *round-turn,* meaning a price that includes the opening and closing out of the futures contract. In most cases, the commission is the same regardless of the maturity date or type of the underlying instrument traded.

Commissions for institutional accounts vary enormously, ranging from a low of about $11 to a high of about $30. As with any service, the price that a broker charges a particular client is based on many factors, including volume of business, amount of value added by the broker, strength of the relationship (or desire to create a relationship), cost of providing the service, and related transactions. To create a good working relationship for both parties, an account manager should consider all of these factors when negotiating commissions.

Margin Requirements

When first taking a position in a futures contract, an investor must deposit a minimum dollar amount per contract as specified by the exchange. (A broker may ask for more than the exchange minimum, but may not require less than the exchange minimum.) This amount is called the *initial margin,* and constitutes a good faith deposit. The initial margin may be in the form of Treasury bills. As the price of the futures contract fluctuates, the value of equity in the position changes. At the close of each trading day, the position is marked to market, so that any gain or loss from the position is reflected in the equity of the account. The price used to mark the position to market is the settlement price for the day.

Maintenance margin is the minimum level to which an equity position may fall as a result of an unfavorable price movement before additional margin is required. The additional margin deposited, also called *variation margin,* is simply the amount that will bring the equity in the account back to its initial margin level. Unlike original margin, variation margin must be in cash. If there is excess margin in the account, that amount may be withdrawn.[1]

If a variation margin is required, the institution is contacted by the brokerage firm and informed of the additional amount that must be deposited. A margin notice is sent as well. Even if futures prices subsequently move in favor of the institution such that the equity increases above the maintenance margin, the variation margin must still be supplied. Failure to meet a request for variation margin within a reasonable time will result in the closing out of a position.

Margin requirements vary by futures contract and by the type of transaction; that is, whether the position is an outright long or short, or a spread (a long together with a short), and whether the trade is put on as a speculative position or as a hedge. Margins are higher for speculative positions than for hedging positions and higher for outright positions than for spreads. Margin requirements also vary between futures brokers. Exchanges and brokerage firms change their margin requirements as contracts are deemed to be more or less risky, or as it is felt that certain types of positions (usually speculative positions) should be discouraged.

---

1. Although there are initial and maintenance margin requirements for buying stocks and bonds on margin, the concept of margin differs for futures. When securities are bought on margin, the difference between the price of the security and the initial margin is borrowed from the broker. The security purchased serves as collateral for the loan and interest is paid by the investor. For futures contracts, the initial margin, in effect, serves as good faith money, indicating that the investor will satisfy the obligation of the contract. No money is borrowed by the purchaser. Similarly, the seller of futures borrows neither money nor securities.

REPRESENTATIVE EXCHANGE-TRADED FUTURES OPTIONS CONTRACTS

Although futures contracts are relatively straightforward financial instruments, options on futures (or *futures options,* as they are commonly called) deserve extra explanation. Options on futures are very similar to other options contracts. Like options on cash (or spot) fixed income securities, both put and call options are traded on fixed income futures. The buyer of a call has the right to buy the underlying futures contract at a specific price. The buyer of a put has the right to sell the underlying futures contract at a specific price. If the buyer chooses to exercise the option, the option seller is obligated to sell the futures in the case of the call, or buy the futures in the case of the put.

An option on the futures contract differs from more traditional options in only one essential way: The underlying instrument is not a spot security, but a futures contract on a security. Thus, for instance, if a call option buyer exercises her option, she acquires a long position in futures instead of a long position in a cash security. The seller of the call will be assigned the corresponding short position in the same futures contract. For put options the situation is reversed. A put option buyer exercising the option acquires a short position in futures, and the seller of the put is assigned a long position in the same futures contract. The resulting long and short futures positions are like any other futures positions and are subject to daily marking to market.

An investor acquiring a position in futures does so at the current futures price. However, if the strike price on the option does not equal the futures price at the time of exercise, the option seller must compensate the option buyer for the discrepancy. Thus, when a call option is exercised, the seller of the call must pay the buyer of the call the current futures price minus the strike price. On the other hand, the seller of the put must pay the buyer of the put the strike price minus the current futures price. (These transactions are actually accomplished by establishing the futures positions at the strike price, then immediately marking to market.) Note that, unlike options on spot securities, the amount of money that changes hands at exercise is only the difference between the strike price and the current futures price, not the whole strike price. Of course, an option need not be exercised for the owner to take her gains; she can simply sell the option instead of exercising it.

We now turn to the options contracts themselves. We describe two of the most important contracts, the CBT's option on the long-term bond futures contract and the IMM's option on the Eurodollar contract. There are also options on the 5-year and 10-year note futures contracts, but because they are both very similar in structure to options on Treasury bond futures, they are not included in this section.

Options on Treasury Bond Futures

Options on CBT Treasury bond futures are in many respects simpler than the underlying futures contracts. Usually, conversion factors, most deliverables, wildcard plays, and other subtleties of the Treasury bond futures contract need not concern the buyer or seller of options on Treasury bond futures. Although these factors affect the fair price of the futures contract, their impact is already reflected in the futures price. Consequently, they need not be reconsidered when buying or selling an option on the futures.

The option on the Treasury bond futures contract is in many respects an option on an index; the "index" is the futures price itself, that is, the price of the fictitious 20-year 8 percent Treasury bond. As for the futures contract, the nominal size of the contract is $100,000. Thus, for example, with futures prices at 95, a call option struck at 94 has an intrinsic value of $1,000 and a put struck at 100 has an intrinsic value of $5,000.

In an attempt to compete with the OTC option market, in 1994 the CBT introduced the *flexible Treasury futures options*. These futures options allow counterparties to customize options within certain limits. Specifically, the strike price, expiration date, and type of exercise (American or European) can be customized subject to CBT constraints. One key constraint is that the expiration date of a flexible contract cannot exceed that of the longest standard option traded on the CBT. Unlike an OTC option, where the option buyer is exposed to counterparty risk, a flexible Treasury futures option is guaranteed by the clearinghouse. The minimum size requirement for the launching of a flexible futures option is 100 contracts.

The premiums for options on Treasury bond futures are quoted in terms of points and 64ths of a point. Thus, an option premium of 1-10 implies a price of $1^{10}/_{64}$ percent of face value, or $1,156.25 (from $100,000 \times 1.15625\%$). Minimum price fluctuations are also $^1/_{64}$ of 1 percent.

Although an option on the Treasury bond futures contract is hardly identical to an option on a Treasury bond, it serves much the same purpose. Because spot and futures prices for Treasury bonds are highly correlated, hedgers and speculators frequently find that options on bond futures provide the essential characteristics needed in an options contract on a long-term fixed income instrument.

Options on Eurodollar Futures

Options on Eurodollar futures fill a unique place among exchange-traded hedging products. These options are currently the only liquid listed option contracts based on a short-term interest rate.

Options on Eurodollar futures (traded on the IMM) are based on the quoted Eurodollar futures price (i.e., 100 minus the annualized yield). Like the underlying futures, the size of the contract is $1 million and each .01 change in price carries a value of $25. Likewise, the option premium is quoted in terms of basis points. Thus, for example, an option premium quoted as 20 (or .20) implies an option price of $500; a premium of 125 or (1.25) implies an option price of $3,125.

Like other debt options, buyers of puts on Eurodollar futures profit as rates move up and buyers of calls profit as rates move down. Consequently, institutions with liabilities or assets that float off short-term rates can use Eurodollar futures options to hedge their exposure to fluctuations in short-term rates. Consider institutions that have liabilities that float off short-term rates. These include banks and thrifts that issue CDs and/or take deposits based on money market rates. Also included are industrial and financial corporations that issue commercial paper, floating-rate notes, or preferred stock that floats off money market rates. Likewise, those who make payments on adjustable-rate mortgages face similar risks.[2] In each instance, as short-term rates increase, the liability becomes more onerous for the borrower. Consequently, the issuers of these liabilities may need a means of capping their interest-rate expense. Although options on Eurodollar futures do not extend as far into the future as many issuers would like, they are effective tools for hedging many short-term rates over the near term. Consequently, an institution with floating-rate liabilities can buy an interest-rate *cap* by buying puts on Eurodollar futures. As rates move up, profits on the put position will tend to offset some or all of the incremental interest expense.

On the other side of the coin, and facing opposite risks, are the purchasers of floating-rate instruments—that is, investors who buy money market deposits, floating-rate notes, floating-rate preferred stock, and adjustable-rate mortgages. Investors who roll over CDs or commercial paper face the same problem. As rates fall, these investors receive less interest income. Consequently, they may feel a need to buy interest-rate *floors,* which are basically call options. As rates fall, calls on debt securities increase in value and will offset the lower interest income received by the investor.

In conclusion, options on Eurodollar futures can be used to limit the risk associated with fluctuations in short-term rates. This is accomplished by buying puts if the exposure is to rising rates, or by buying calls if the exposure is to falling rates.

Mechanics of Trading Futures Options

To take a position in futures options, one works with a futures broker. The types of orders that are used to buy or sell futures options are generally the same as the orders discussed for futures contracts. The clearinghouse associated with the exchange where the futures option is traded once again stands between the buyer and the seller. Furthermore, the commission costs and related issues that we discussed for futures also generally apply to futures options.

There are no margin requirements for the buyer of futures options, but the option price must be paid in full when the option is purchased. Because the option price is the maximum amount that the buyer can lose regardless of how adverse the price movement of the underlying futures contract, there is no need for margin.

Because the seller has agreed to accept all of the risk (and no reward other than the option premium) of the position in the underlying instrument, the seller is

---

2. To the extent that the interest-rate payment on an adjustable-rate mortgage has an upper and lower bound, the risk to issuers and investors is limited by the nature of the instrument.

generally required to deposit not only the margin required for the underlying futures contract but, with certain exceptions, the option price as well. Furthermore, subsequent price changes adversely affecting the seller's position will lead to additional margin requirements.

OTC CONTRACTS

There is a substantial over-the-counter market for fixed income options and forwards. (Forward contracts are the over-the-counter equivalent of futures contracts.) For example, in the OTC market, one can easily buy or sell options on LIBOR, commercial paper, T-bill, and prime rates. One can buy and sell options on virtually any Treasury issue. One can buy and sell options on any number of mortgage securities. One can buy and sell options with expirations ranging from as short as one day to as long as 10 years. In the OTC market, one can easily take forward positions in 3- and 6-month LIBOR going out to about 2 years.

In the options market in particular, a natural division has evolved between the OTC market and the listed market. Given the relatively small number of futures contracts, the exchanges' need for standardization, and the synergy created by the futures options contract trading side by side with the underlying futures contract, the exchanges have been most successful with options on futures contracts. Because off-exchange options on futures are prohibited, futures options cannot be traded over the counter. On the other hand, because the OTC market is very good at creating flexible structures and handling a diversity of terms, the OTC market has been more successful than the exchanges in trading options on cash securities and on cash market interest rates.

In the following sections, we discuss the structure of the OTC fixed income derivative markets and their advantages and disadvantages relative to the exchange-traded markets. We also discuss the most important contracts traded in the OTC market. These are options on mortgage securities, options on cash Treasuries, caps and floors on LIBOR, and forward rate agreements on LIBOR.

The Structure of the OTC Market

As in other OTC markets, there is no central marketplace for OTC fixed income options and forward contracts. A transaction takes place whenever a buyer and seller agree to a price. Unlike an exchange transaction, the terms, size, and price of the contract generally remain undisclosed to other market participants. Accordingly, the OTC market is much less visible than the exchange markets and it is more difficult to ascertain the current market price for a given option or forward contract. Two groups, however, help to alleviate this problem. First, there are the OTC market makers. Market makers in OTC fixed income options and forwards are typically large investment banks and commercial banks. A market maker, by definition, stands ready to buy or sell a given option or forward contract to accommodate a client's needs. To be effective, the market maker must be willing and able to handle large orders and must keep the bid-ask spreads reasonably narrow.

The other group that helps bring order to the OTC market is the brokers. The sole job of the brokers is to bring together buyers and sellers; it is not the brokers' job to take positions in option and forward contracts. The buyers and sellers that the brokers bring together can be market makers or the end users of the contracts. To do their job, the brokers must distribute information about the prices where they see trades taking place and the prices at which they believe further trades can be completed. This information is distributed to potential buyers and sellers over the phone and over publicly available media such as Telerate pages.

Because there is no central market for OTC fixed income options and forwards, there can be no clearinghouse. Consequently, those who position OTC contracts may have to give considerable weight to the creditworthiness of their counterparty. For example, entities that sell options or position forward rate agreements (FRAs) can have potential liabilities equal to several times their net worth. Furthermore, there is no guarantee that these counterparties have effective hedges against their positions, or in fact, that they are hedging at all. Furthermore, financial problems on the part of the counterparty can jeopardize the ability or willingness of the counterparty to make good on the terms of a contract even if it is hedged. Consequently, unlike the exchange-traded markets where one neither knows nor cares who is on the other side of a trade, in the OTC market it is usually very important to know who is on the other side. Creditworthiness can be one of the most important considerations in the trade.

The potential credit problems associated with OTC trades are mitigated in a number of ways. First, some institutions will not buy options from or take either side of an FRA contract with any party other than a major entity with a sound credit rating. Secondly, some institutions require their counterparty to post collateral immediately after the transaction is completed. This collateral serves much the same purpose as initial margin in the futures and futures options market. Finally, some institutions reserve the right to call for additional collateral from their counterparties if the market moves against the counterparty. This is analogous to variation margin in the exchange-traded markets. Although these provisions may not be as good as a central clearinghouse, they are apparently good enough for a very large number of institutions and good enough for a very large market to develop.

Liquidity, in terms of being able to easily close out an existing position, can be a constraint in the over-the-counter market. OTC options and forwards are generally not assignable transactions. Thus, for example, if one sells an option, the contingent liability associated with that option cannot be transferred to a third party without the express permission of the option buyer. If an option seller wants to cover a short option position, often the best strategy is to buy a similar option from a third party to offset the risks of the original option. However, if the credit of the offsetting party is in question, or the offsetting option is not identical, risks will remain for the option seller. The option buyer can face similar problems if closing out the option before expiration. Credit considerations and the fact that the option buyer may not be able to sell an identical option to offset the first option make it more difficult to effectively close out the long option position. Because FRAs involve contingent liabilities for both sides of the transaction, similar problems exist for both buyers and sellers of FRAs.

Some of the problems associated with the OTC market arise from the fact that the contracts are not standardized. However, nonstandardization leads to many benefits as well. As indicated above, OTC contracts can be specified in virtually any terms that are acceptable to both buyer and seller. A potential buyer or seller can thus approach a market maker with whatever structure is needed and in many (but certainly not all) cases obtain the desired structure at a reasonable price. Compared to the very rigid structure of the exchange-traded markets, this is a remarkable advantage.

The OTC Contracts

Options on Mortgages

The over-the-counter market for options on fixed income instruments began in the mid-1970s with *standby* commitments. Standbys were essentially put options on mortgages that allowed the holder (usually a mortgage banker) to sell mortgages at a given price during a given period of time. Although standbys were popularized by the Federal National Mortgage Association, other institutions soon got into the business of selling options. Thrift institutions, in particular, soon became sellers of puts, as well as calls, on mortgages. The thrift would typically sell out-of-the-money puts (struck at a yield that seemed attractive relative to current yields) and out-of-the-money calls (often struck at the thrift's cost of the underlying securities). Until the early 1980s, there were no real market makers in the OTC mortgage options market. Thus, a trade typically did not occur until an end-user who wanted to buy an option could be paired with an end-user who wanted to sell the very same option. The intermediary who stood in between these two parties was usually not willing to position one side without the other.

Today, the market for options on mortgages includes many more participants, although the original standby commitments no longer exist. Investment banks and commercial banks now play a major role in the mortgage options market. Many of the large investment and commercial banks are now willing to position mortgage options without having the other side of the trade. This makes the market much more liquid and flexible than it would be otherwise. The end-users of options on mortgages have not changed greatly, but the number of users has increased greatly. Mortgage bankers continue to buy puts on mortgages. Thrifts continue to sell both puts and calls. As some thrifts now play the role of mortgage banker, they too have become buyers of puts on mortgages. Money managers have also become a part of the market, usually as sellers of call options against mortgages in their portfolios.

The market for mortgage options today is composed almost entirely of options on the standard agency pass-through mortgage securities. Options on CMO tranches, IOs, POs, and the like are not a significant part of the OTC mortgage options market. The majority of the options traded are on 30-year mortgages, but options on 15-year products are also readily available. In terms of expiration, trading in mortgage options tends to be concentrated in the shorter expirations, with most of the options expiring within 60 days, and the vast majority expiring within one year. In terms of strike price, most of the trading is in at the money and out of the money options.

Given the willingness of OTC market makers to position options, a client can easily trade options on $25 million of underlying securities with little or no prior notice. Some firms will position $100 million or more of mortgage options on the wire. Thus, the OTC options market can be as liquid as the exchange-traded options markets.

Options on Treasury Securities

Although not as old as the OTC options market for mortgages, the OTC options market for Treasury securities is now just as large and liquid. As in the mortgage options market, investment banks and commercial banks play major roles as market makers, frequently standing ready to buy or sell options on $100 million (or more) of Treasury securities. Most of the action is in options expiring within 60 days, written at the money or out of the money. Options on Treasuries are concentrated in the on-the-run issues, with most of the remaining business being done in the off-the-run issues.

Except for the mortgage bankers, who have considerably less interest in options on Treasuries, the end-users of options on Treasuries mirror the market for options on mortgages. Thrifts tend to be writers of out-of-the-money puts and calls, and money managers and mutual funds tend to be covered call writers.

Caps and Floors on LIBOR

The primary OTC options covering the short end of the yield curve are the caps and floors on 3- and 6-month LIBOR. A cap on LIBOR is, in essence, a series of puts on LIBOR-based debt, whereas a floor on LIBOR is, in essence, a series of calls on LIBOR-based debt.

The buyer of a cap or floor holds most of the rights in the contract, as with other options. The seller of a cap or floor will of course receive an options premium from the buyer but is then obligated to perform on the contract.

To see how these contracts work, consider a 5-year, $100 million cap on 3-month LIBOR struck at 11 percent. Such a contract will specify reset dates occurring every three months for a total of 20 resets. The first reset will usually occur immediately or within a couple of weeks of the trade date, and the last reset will usually be about three months before the stated maturity of the contract. To determine what the payoff to the cap buyer will be, on every reset date one compares the 3-month LIBOR (taken from a predetermined source) with the 11 percent strike rate. If the 3-month LIBOR is at or below 11 percent, nothing is owed to the cap buyer. However, if the 3-month LIBOR is above 11 percent, the cap seller must pay the cap buyer the monetary value of the amount by which 3-month

LIBOR exceeds 11 percent. In this case, for a 90-day interest accrual period, the value of each basis point is $2,500 (from .0001 × $100,000,000 × 90/360). Thus, for example, if 3-month LIBOR on a particular reset date is 11.50 percent, the cap seller owes the cap buyer $125,000 for that reset. If, on the next reset date, 3-month LIBOR is 13 percent, the cap seller owes the cap buyer $500,000 for that reset. If, on the next reset date, 3-month LIBOR is 10.50 percent, the cap seller owes nothing to the cap buyer for that reset. In most cases, the cap seller pays the cap buyer the amount of money owed for a particular reset at the end of the interest accrual period—in this case, three months after the reset date.

The mechanics of floors are similar, except that the payoff comes when rates fall below a given level, instead of when they rise above a given level. For example, if one buys a $25 million 7-year 6.50 percent floor on 6-month LIBOR, there are a total of 14 reset dates. On each of these reset dates, one compares 6-month LIBOR to 6.50 percent. If 6-month LIBOR is above 6.50 percent, nothing is owed to the buyer of the floor for that reset. However, if 6-month LIBOR is below 6.50 percent, for a 180-day interest accrual period the floor seller owes the floor buyer $1,250 for every basis point by which 6-month LIBOR is below 6.50 percent (from .0001 × $25,000,000 × $^{180}/_{360}$).

Like other OTC options markets, the cap and floor market is composed of market makers, end users, and brokers. The market makers are once again the large investment banks and commercial banks. However, there are fewer market makers and generally wider spreads in the cap and floor market than there are in the options market for mortgages or Treasury securities. Nonetheless, there is an active market out to 10 years, particularly for out-of-the-money caps, and to a lesser degree, out-of-the-money floors.

The end user buyers of caps and floors are primarily institutions with risks that they need to cover. For example, institutions that fund short and lend long will tend to have losses as short-term rates rise. Similarly, businesses that fund by rolling over short-term obligations such as commercial paper or by bank borrowings tied to LIBOR or the prime rate will tend to have losses as short-term rates rise. These institutions, which include many thrifts, banks, and finance companies, as well as industrial and construction companies, can protect themselves against rising short-term rates by buying caps. End-user buyers of floors tend to be firms that face losses if rates fall. Such a case might occur, for example, if an institution borrows at a floating rate with a built-in floor. Such an institution may be structured so that floating rates, per se, pose no problem; the problem arises when the floating rate at which they borrow is no longer really floating because the floor has been hit. This institution may buy a floor so that it will receive monetary compensation from the floor seller whenever the floating rate falls below the floor rate, thus covering the risks of lower rates.

The sellers of caps and floors, other than the market makers, are quite varied. In some cases, sellers sell caps or floors outright to bring in premium income. Others sell caps and/or floors to smooth out the cash flows on other fixed income instruments, such as certain derivative mortgage products. In other cases, sellers only implicitly sell the caps or floors. The following example illustrates both kinds of sellers.

When the cap market was developing, it quickly became obvious that there were many natural buyers of caps, but few natural sellers of caps. One successful effort to create sellers of caps occurred when investment bankers, who had many potential buyers of caps, realized that caps could be created as a derivative of the floating-rate note (FRN) market. Issuers of FRNs routinely issue notes reset off LIBOR. Furthermore, there were known buyers of *capped* FRNs; but of course, capped FRNs must have a higher coupon than uncapped FRNs to compensate the FRN buyer for the cap risk. If an issuer sells capped floating-rate notes, the issuer, in effect, buys a cap on LIBOR from the buyer of the FRN. This cap can then be sold to the investment banker, who in turn sells it to cap-buying clients. The deals that took place took exactly this form. The investment bankers underwrote capped FRNs for certain FRN issuers who agreed to make caplike payments to their investment banker. The banker then sold caps to another client but did not incur any market risks, because the two sets of potential payments offset one another. Using part of the proceeds of the sale of the cap, the investment bank agreed to make payments to the issuer to bring the cost of the floating-rate debt down to a level below that of uncapped floating-rate notes. Thus the investment bankers, the issuers of the FRNs, the buyers of the FRNs, and the ultimate cap-buying clients all walked away with a satisfactory transaction.

Such a transaction illustrates how creative financing can be used to create a seller of an instrument when no obvious seller exists. In this example, the issuers of the FRNs are willing to sell caps, given the fact that they, in turn, find someone willing to sell the caps to them. The ultimate seller of caps is the buyer of the capped FRNs. The buyers of the FRNs are, however, only implicit sellers of caps in the sense that they never explicitly have a position in caps on their books.

This example, which is just one of dozens, shows how market makers explicitly and implicitly induce end-users of financial products to buy or sell the instruments that allow the market makers to cover their positions in the OTC market. This is not to say that the market makers are taking advantage of the other parties to their trades. As is often the case, all parties to a transaction can come out ahead.

Forward Rate Agreements (FRAs)

The FRA market represents the over-the-counter equivalent of the exchange-traded futures contracts on short-term rates. FRAs are a natural outgrowth of the interbank market for short-term funds. However, unlike the interbank market, virtually any creditworthy entity can buy or sell FRAs.

The liquid and easily accessible sector of the FRA market is for 3- and 6-month LIBOR. Rates are widely quoted for settlement starting one month forward, and settling once every month thereafter out to about six months forward. Thus, for example, on any given day forward rates are available for both 3- and 6-month LIBOR one month forward, covering, respectively, the interest period starting in one month and ending in four months, and the interest period starting in one month and ending in seven months. These contracts are referred to as 1×4 and 1×7 contracts. On the same day, there will be FRAs on 3- and 6- month LIBOR for settlement two months forward. These are the 2×5 and 2×8 contracts. Similarly, settlements occur three months, four months, five months, and six months forward for both 3- and 6-month LIBOR. These contracts are also denoted by the beginning and end of the interest period they cover.

On each subsequent day, contracts with the same type of structures, that is, contracts with one month, two months, and so on, to settlement date, are offered again. Thus, although on any given day a relatively limited number of structures are widely quoted, new contracts with new settlement dates are offered at the beginning of each day. This is quite different from the futures market, where the same contracts with the same delivery dates trade day after day.

As for other OTC debt instruments, there are market makers and brokers who make the market work. However, unlike the other OTC derivative instruments, in the FRA market the commercial banks are clearly the dominant force among the market makers. This dominance is due to the ability of the banks to blend their FRA transactions into their interbank transactions and overall funding operations. Consequently, many banks are willing to quote on a much wider variety of structures than the standard structures explained above. One can choose maturities other than 3- and 6-month LIBOR, and one can choose many settlement dates other than at an even number of months in the future.

In most cases, FRAs are written so that no money changes hands until the settlement date. To determine the cash flows on the settlement date, LIBOR taken from some predetermined source is compared to the LIBOR rate specified in the FRA contract. The actual dollar amount that changes hands is the dollar value of the difference between the two rates, *present valued* for a period equal to the maturity of the underlying LIBOR, either three or six months. The rationale behind present valuing is that if an FRA is used to hedge the rate on a deposit (or other short-term instrument), the loss (gain) due to a change in interest rates will be paid (saved) at the maturity of the deposit, not at the issue date. Thus, because cash payments on the FRA are made on the settlement date (which presumably is the same as the issue date of the deposit) the present value of the interest expense (or saving) on the deposit will equal the amount of money actually received or paid on the FRA.

Finally, one peculiarity of the FRA market deserves note. If one *buys* an FRA, one profits from an *increase* in rates, and if one *sells* an FRA, one profits from a *decline* in rates.

SUMMARY

In this chapter, we have examined several of the most important and representative exchange-traded and OTC interest-rate futures and options contracts. In the next chapter, we discuss the pricing of futures contracts and the applications of futures to portfolio management.

⑥   # PRICING FUTURES
AND PORTFOLIO
APPLICATIONS

Frank J. Fabozzi, Ph.D., CFA, CPA
Adjunct Professor of Finance
School of Management
Yale University

Mark Pitts, Ph.D.
Principal
White Oak Capital Management Corp.

One of the primary concerns most traders and investors have when taking a position in futures contracts is whether the futures price at which they transact will be a fair price. Buyers are concerned that the price may be too high and that they will be picked off by more experienced futures traders waiting to profit from the mistakes of the uninitiated. Sellers worry that the price is artificially low and that savvy traders may have manipulated the markets so that they can buy at bargain-basement prices. Furthermore, prospective participants frequently find no rational explanation for the sometimes violent ups and downs that occur in the futures markets. Theories about efficient markets give little comfort to anyone who knows of or has experienced the sudden losses that can occur in the highly leveraged futures markets.

Fortunately, the futures markets are not as irrational as they may at first seem; if they were, they would not be so successful. The interest-rate futures markets are not perfectly efficient markets, but they probably come about as close as any market. Furthermore, there are very clear reasons why futures prices are what they are, and there are methods by which traders, investors, and borrowers will quickly eliminate any discrepancy between futures prices and their fair levels.

In this chapter, we will explain how the fair or theoretical value of an option is determined. We then explain some of the more important portfolio applications of interest-rate futures.

PRICING OF FUTURES CONTRACTS

There are several different ways to price futures contracts. Fortunately, all lead to the same fair price for a given contract. Each approach relies on the *Law of One Price*. This law states that a given financial asset (or liability) must have the same price regardless of the means by which one goes about creating that asset (or liability). In this section, we will demonstrate one way in which futures contracts can be combined with cash market instruments to create cash flows that are identical to other cash securities.[1] The Law of One Price implies that the synthetically created cash securities must have the same price as the actual cash securities. Similarly, cash instruments can be combined to create cash flows that are identical to futures contracts. By the Law of One Price, the futures contract must have the same price as the synthetic futures created from cash instruments.

Illustration of the Basic Principles

To understand how futures contracts should be priced, consider the following example. Suppose that a 20-year, 100 par value bond with a coupon rate of 12 percent is selling at par. Also suppose that this bond is the deliverable for a futures contract that settles in three months. If the current 3-month interest rate at which funds can be loaned or borrowed is 8 percent per year, what should be the price of this futures contract?

Suppose the price of the futures contract is 107. Consider the following strategy:

Sell the futures contract at 107.

Purchase the bond for 100.

Borrow 100 for three months at 8 percent per year.

The borrowed funds are used to purchase the bond, resulting in no initial cash outlay for this strategy. Three months from now, the bond must be delivered to settle the futures contract and the loan must be repaid. These trades will produce the following cash flows:

From settlement of the futures contract	
Flat price of bond	107
Accrued interest (12% for 3 months)	+ 3
Total proceeds	110
From the loan	
Repayment of principal of loan	100
Interest on loan (8% for 3 months)	+ 2
Total outlay	102
Profit	8

---

1. For other ways to price futures contracts, see Chapter 5 in Mark Pitts and Frank J. Fabozzi, *Interest Rate Futures and Options* (Chicago: Probus Publishing, 1990).

This strategy will guarantee a profit of 8. Moreover, the profit is generated with no initial outlay because the funds used to purchase the bond are borrowed. The profit will be realized *regardless of the futures price at the settlement date*. Obviously, in a well-functioning market, arbitrageurs would buy the bond and sell the futures, forcing the futures price down and bidding up the bond price so as to eliminate this profit.

In contrast, suppose that the futures price is 92 instead of 107. Consider the following strategy:

> Buy the futures contract at 92.
>
> Sell (short) the bond for 100.
>
> Invest (lend) 100 for 3 months at 8 percent per year.

Once again, there is no initial cash outlay. Three months from now a bond will be purchased to settle the long position in the futures contract. That bond will then be used to cover the short position (i.e., to cover the short sale in the cash market). The outcome in three months would be as follows:

From settlement of the futures contract	
Flat price of bond	92
Accrued interest (12% for 3 months)	+ 3
Total outlay	95
From the loan	
Principal received from maturing investment	100
Interest earned from the 3-month investment (8% for 3 months)	+ 2
Total proceeds	102
Profit	7

The 7 profit is a pure arbitrage profit. It requires no initial cash outlay and will be realized regardless of the futures price at the settlement date.

There is a futures price that will eliminate the arbitrage profit, however. There will be no arbitrage if the futures price is 99. Let's look at what would happen if the two previous strategies were followed and the futures price were 99. First, consider the following strategy:

> Sell the futures contract at 99.
>
> Purchase the bond for 100.
>
> Borrow 100 for 3 months at 8 percent per year.

In three months the outcome would be as follows:

From settlement of the futures contract	
Flat price of bond	99
Accrued interest (12% for 3 months)	+ 3
Total proceeds	102

From the loan

Repayment of principal of the loan	100
Interest on the loan (8% for 3 months)	+ 2
Total outlay	102
Profit	0

There is no arbitrage profit.

Next, consider the following strategy:

Buy the futures contract at 99.

Sell (short) the bond for 100.

Invest (lend) 100 for 3 months at 8 percent per year.

The outcome in three months would be as follows:

From settlement of the futures contract

Flat price of bond	99
Accrued interest (12% for 3 months)	+ 3
Total outlay	102

From the loan

Principal received from maturing investment	100
Interest earned from the 3-month investment (8% for 3 months)	+ 2
Total proceeds	102
Profit	0

Thus, neither strategy results in a profit. The futures price of 99 is the equilibrium price, because any higher or lower futures price will permit arbitrage profits.

Theoretical Futures Price Based on Arbitrage Model

Considering the arbitrage arguments just presented, the equilibrium futures price can be determined on the basis of the following information:

- The price of the bond in the cash market.
- The coupon rate on the bond. In our example, the coupon rate was 12 percent per annum.
- The interest rate for borrowing and lending until the settlement date. The borrowing and lending rate is referred to as the *financing rate*. In our example, the financing rate was 8 percent per annum.

We will let

r = financing rate
c = current yield, or coupon rate divided by the cash market price

P = cash market price
F = futures price
t = time, in years, to the futures delivery date

and then consider the following strategy that is initiated on a coupon date:

Sell the futures contract at F.

Purchase the bond for P.

Borrow P until the settlement date at r.

The outcome at the settlement date is as follows:

From settlement of the futures contract

Flat price of bond	F
Accrued interest	$+ ctP$
Total proceeds	$F + ctP$

From the loan

Repayment of principal of loan	P
Interest on loan	$+ rtP$
Total outlay	$P + rtP$

The profit will equal

$$\text{Profit} = \text{Total proceeds} - \text{Total outlay}$$
$$\text{Profit} = F + ctP - (P + rtP)$$

In equilibrium, the theoretical futures price occurs where the profit from this strategy is zero. Thus, to have equilibrium, the following must hold:

$$0 = F + ctP - (P + rtP)$$

Solving for the theoretical futures price, we have

$$F = P + Pt(r - c) = P(1 + t(r - c)) \tag{57-1}$$

Alternatively, consider the following strategy:

Buy the futures contract at F.

Sell (short) the bond for P.

Invest (lend) P at r until the settlement date.

The outcome at the settlement date would be as follows:

From settlement of the futures contract

Flat price of bond	F
Accrued interest	$+ ctP$
Total outlay	$F + ctP$

From the loan

Proceeds received from maturing of investment	P
Interest earned	$+\ rtP$
Total proceeds	$P + rtP$

The profit will equal

$$\text{Profit} = \text{Total proceeds} - \text{Total outlay}$$
$$\text{Profit} = P + rtP - (F + ctP)$$

Setting the profit equal to zero so that there will be no arbitrage profit and solving for the futures price, we obtain the same equation for the futures price as Equation (57–1).

Let's apply Equation (57–1) to our previous example in which

$r = .08$
$c = .12$
$P = 100$
$t = .25$

Then, the theoretical futures price is

$$F = 100 + 100 \times .25(.08 - .12)$$
$$= 100 - 1 = 99$$

This agrees with the equilibrium futures price we derived earlier.

The theoretical futures price may be at a premium to the cash market price (higher than the cash market price) or at a discount from the cash market price (lower than the cash market price), depending on the value of $(r - c)$. The term $r - c$ is called the *net financing cost* because it adjusts the financing rate for the coupon interest earned. The net financing cost is more commonly called the *cost of carry*, or simply *carry*. *Positive carry* means that the current yield earned is greater than the financing cost; *negative carry* means that the financing cost exceeds the current yield. The relationships can be expressed as follows:

Carry	**Futures Price**
Positive $(c > r)$	Will sell at a discount to the cash price $(F < P)$
Negative $(c < r)$	Will sell at a premium to the cash price $(F > P)$
Zero $(r = c)$	Will be equal to the cash price $(F = P)$

In the case of interest-rate futures, carry (the relationship between the short-term financing rate and the current yield on the bond) depends on the shape of the yield curve. When the yield curve is upward-sloping, the short-term financing rate will generally be less than the current yield on the bond, resulting in positive carry. The futures price will then sell at a discount to the cash price for the bond. The opposite will hold true when the yield curve is inverted.

A Closer Look at the Theoretical Futures Price

To derive the theoretical futures price using the arbitrage argument, we made several assumptions. We will now discuss the implications of these assumptions.

Interim Cash Flows   No interim cash flows due to variation margin or coupon interest payments were assumed in the model. However, we know that interim cash flows can occur for both of these reasons. Because we assumed no variation margin, the price derived is technically the theoretical price for a forward contract (which is not marked to market at the end of each trading day). If interest rates rise, the short position in futures will receive margin as the futures price decreases; the margin can then be reinvested at a higher interest rate. In contrast, if interest rates fall, there will be variation margin that must be financed by the short position; however, because interest rates have declined, the financing can be done at a lower cost. Thus, whichever way rates move, those who are short futures gain relative to those who are short forwards. Conversely, those who are long futures lose relative to those who are long forwards. These facts account for the difference between futures and forward prices.

Incorporating interim coupon payments into the pricing model is not difficult. However, the value of the coupon payments at the settlement date will depend on the interest rate at which they can be reinvested. The shorter the maturity of the futures contract and the lower the coupon rate, the less important the reinvestment income is in determining the futures price.

The Short-Term Interest Rate (Financing Rate)   In deriving the theoretical futures price, it is assumed that the borrowing and lending rates are equal. Typically, however, the borrowing rate is greater than the lending rate.

We will let

r_B = borrowing rate
r_L = lending rate

Consider the following strategy:

Sell the futures contract at F.

Purchase the bond for P.

Borrow P until the settlement date at r_B.

The futures price that would produce no arbitrage profit is

$$F = P + P(r_B - c) \tag{57–2}$$

Now consider the following strategy:

Buy the futures contract at F.

Sell (short) the bond for P.

Invest (lend) P at r_L until the settlement date.

The futures price that would produce no profit is

$$F = P + P(r_L - c) \tag{57-3}$$

Equations (57–2) and (57–3) together provide boundaries for the futures price equilibrium. Equation (57–2) provides the upper boundary and Equation (57–3) the lower boundary. For example, assume that the borrowing rate is 8 percent per year, or 2 percent for three months, and the lending rate is 6 percent per year, or 1.5 percent for three months. Then, using Equation (57–2) and the previous example, the upper boundary is

$$F \text{ (upper boundary)} = \$100 + \$100 \,(.02 - .03)$$
$$= \$99$$

The lower boundary using Equation (57–3) is

$$F \text{ (lower boundary)} = \$100 + \$100 \,(.015 - .03)$$
$$= \$98.50$$

In calculating these boundaries, we assumed no transaction costs were involved in taking the position. In actuality, the transaction costs of entering into and closing the cash position as well as the round-trip transaction costs for the futures contract must be considered, and do affect the boundaries for the futures contract.

Deliverable Bond and Settlement Date Unknown In our example, we assumed that only one bond is deliverable and that the settlement date occurs three months from now. As explained earlier in this chapter, futures contracts on Treasury bonds and Treasury notes are designed to allow the short position the choice of delivering one of a number of deliverable issues. Also, the delivery date is not known.

Because there may be more than one deliverable, market participants track the price of each deliverable bond and determine which is the cheapest to deliver. The futures price will then trade in relation to the bond that is cheapest to deliver. The cheapest to deliver is the bond or note that will result in the smallest loss or the greatest gain if delivered by the short futures position.[2]

In addition to the reasons we have already discussed, there are several reasons why the actual futures price will diverge from the theoretical futures price based on the arbitrage model. First, there is the risk that although an issue may be the cheapest to deliver at the time a position in the futures contract is taken, it may not be the cheapest to deliver after that time. Thus, there will be a divergence between the theoretical futures price and the actual futures price. A second reason

---

2. An alternative procedure is to compute the implied (breakeven) repo rate. This rate is the yield that would produce no profit or loss if the bond were purchased and a futures contract were sold against the bond. The cheapest-to-deliver bond is the one with the highest implied repo rate. For a further discussion, see Chapter 58.

for this divergence is the other delivery options granted the short position. Finally, there are biases in the CBT conversion factors.

Deliverable Is a Basket of Securities   The municipal index futures contract is a cash settlement contract based on a basket of securities. The difficulty in arbitraging this futures contract is that it is too expensive to buy or sell every bond included in the index. Instead, a portfolio containing a smaller number of bonds may be constructed to track the index. The arbitrage, however, is no longer risk-free, because there is the risk that the portfolio will not track the index exactly. This is referred to as *tracking error risk*. Another problem in constructing the portfolio so that the arbitrage can be performed is that the composition of the index is revised periodically. Therefore, anyone using this arbitrage trade must constantly monitor the index and periodically rebalance the constructed portfolio.

APPLICATIONS TO PORTFOLIO MANAGEMENT

This section describes various ways in which a money manager can use interest-rate futures contracts.

Changing the Duration of the Portfolio

Money managers who have strong expectations about the direction of interest rates will adjust the duration of their portfolio to capitalize on their expectations. Specifically, if they expect interest rates to increase, they will shorten the duration of the portfolio; if they expect interest rates to decrease, they will lengthen the duration of the portfolio. Also, anyone using structured portfolio strategies must periodically adjust the portfolio duration to match the duration of some benchmark.

Although money managers can alter the duration of their portfolios with cash market instruments, a quick and less expensive means for doing so (especially on a temporary basis) is to use futures contracts. By buying futures contracts on Treasury bonds or notes, they can increase the duration of the portfolio. Conversely, they can shorten the duration of the portfolio by selling futures contracts on Treasury bonds or notes.

Asset Allocation

A pension sponsor may wish to alter the composition of the pension fund's assets between stocks and bonds. An efficient means of changing asset allocation is to use financial futures contracts: interest-rate futures and stock index futures.

Creating Synthetic Securities for Yield Enhancement

A cash market security can be synthetically created by using a position in the futures contract together with the deliverable instrument. The yield on the synthetic security should be the same as the yield on the cash market security. If there is a difference between the two yields, it can be exploited so as to enhance the yield on the portfolio.

To see how, consider an investor who owns a 20-year Treasury bond and sells Treasury futures that call for the delivery of that particular bond three months from now. The maturity of the Treasury bond is 20 years, but the investor has effectively shortened the maturity of the bond to three months.

Consequently, the long position in the 20-year bond and the short futures position are equivalent to a long position in a 3-month riskless security. The position is riskless because the investor is locking in the price that he or she will receive three months from now—the futures price. By being long the bond and short the futures, the investor has synthetically created a 3-month Treasury bill. The return the investor should expect to earn from this synthetic position should be the yield on a 3-month Treasury bill. If the yield on the synthetic 3-month Treasury bill is greater than the yield on the cash market Treasury bill, the investor can realize an enhanced yield by creating the synthetic short-term security. The fundamental relationship for creating synthetic securities is as follows:

$$RSP = CBP - BFP \qquad (57-4)$$

where

CBP = cash bond position
BFP = bond futures position
RSP = riskless short-term security position

A negative sign before a position means a short position. In terms of our previous example, CBP is the long cash bond position, the negative sign before BFP refers to the short futures position, and RSP is the riskless synthetic 3-month security or Treasury bill.

Equation (57–4) states that an investor who is long the cash market security and short the futures contract should expect to earn the rate of return on a risk-free security with the same maturity as the futures delivery date. Solving Equation (57–4) for the long bond position, we have

$$CBP = RSP + BFP \qquad (57-5)$$

Equation (57–5) states that a cash bond position equals a short-term riskless security position plus a long bond futures position. Thus, a cash market bond can be synthetically created by buying a futures contract and investing in a Treasury bill.

Solving Equation (57–5) for the bond futures position, we have

$$BFP = CBP - RSP \qquad (57-6)$$

Equation (57–6) tells us that a long position in the futures contract can be synthetically created by taking a long position in the cash market bond and shorting the short-term riskless security. Shorting the short-term riskless security is equivalent to borrowing money. Notice that it was Equation (57–6) that we used in deriving the theoretical futures price when the futures was overpriced. Recall that when the futures price was 107, the strategy to obtain an arbitrage profit was to sell the futures contract and create a synthetic long futures position by buying the bond with borrowed funds. This is precisely what Equation (57–6) states. In this case, instead of creating a synthetic cash market instrument as we did with Equations (57–4) and (57–5), we have created a synthetic futures contract. The fact that the synthetic long futures position was cheaper than the actual long futures position provided an arbitrage opportunity.

If we reverse the sign of both sides of Equation (57–6), we can see how a short futures position can be synthetically created.

In an efficient market, the opportunities for yield enhancement should not exist very long. Even in the absence of yield enhancement, however, synthetic securities can be used by money managers to hedge a portfolio position that they find difficult to hedge in the cash market either because of lack of liquidity or because of other constraints.

Hedging

Hedging[3] with futures involves taking a futures position as a temporary substitute for transactions to be made in the cash market at a later date. If cash and futures prices move together, any loss realized by the hedger from one position (whether cash or futures) will be offset by a profit on the other position. When the net profit or loss from the positions are exactly as anticipated, the hedge is referred to as a *perfect hedge.*

In practice, hedging is not that simple. The amount of net profit will not necessarily be as anticipated. The outcome of a hedge will depend on the relationship between the cash price and the futures price when a hedge is placed and when it is lifted. The difference between the cash price and the futures price is called the *basis*. The risk that the basis will change in an unpredictable way is called *basis risk.*

In most hedging applications, the bond to be hedged is not identical to the bond underlying the futures contract. This kind of hedging is referred to as *cross hedging*. There may be substantial basis risk in cross hedging. An unhedged position is exposed to price risk, the risk that the cash market price will move adversely. A hedged position substitutes basis risk for price risk.

A short (or sell) hedge is used to protect against a decline in the cash price of a fixed income security. To execute a short hedge, futures contracts are sold. By establishing a short hedge, the hedger has fixed the future cash price and transferred the price risk of ownership to the buyer of the futures contract. As an example of why a short hedge would be executed, suppose that a pension fund manager knows that bonds must be liquidated in 40 days to make a $5 million payment to

---

3. Hedging is discussed in more detail in Chapter 60.

the beneficiaries of the pension fund. If interest rates rise during the 40-day period, more bonds will have to be liquidated to realize $5 million. To guard against this possibility, the manager would sell bonds in the futures market to lock in a selling price.

A long (or buy) hedge is undertaken to protect against an increase in the cash price of a fixed income security. In a long hedge, the hedger buys a futures contract to lock in a purchase price. A pension fund manager may use a long hedge when substantial cash contributions are expected and the manager is concerned that interest rates will fall. Also, a money manager who knows that bonds are maturing in the near future and expects that interest rates will fall can employ a long hedge to lock in a rate.

SUMMARY

In this chapter, we have explored the cash and futures arbitrage and equilibrium futures pricing. The theoretical futures price is determined by the net financing cost, or carry. Carry is the difference between the financing cost and the cash yield on the underlying cash instrument. The basic futures pricing model presented in this chapter must be modified to account for nuances of specific futures contracts. In the next chapter, the basic pricing model is extended to the Treasury bond futures contract.

Some of the important uses of futures contracts by portfolio managers—altering a portfolio's duration, the potential to create synthetic securities with enhanced returns, and hedging—are discussed. Probably the most common application is hedging a portfolio. The details of how to do this with interest rate futures (and futures options) are explained in Chapter 60.

ⓖ   # TREASURY BOND
FUTURES MECHANICS
AND BASIS VALUATION*

David T. Kim
Odyssey Partners, L.P.

INTRODUCTION

Since its inception in 1977, the bond futures contract has been the grandfather of the family of financial futures contracts. It is the primary vehicle for hedging an investor's Treasury cash positions and is easily the most liquid Treasury futures contract. It has become so successful, in fact, that it is often the driving force of the Treasury market.

An investor owning or long a bond futures contract can expect the delivery of one of a group of bonds within a certain time. Conversely, an investor who is short that contract is expected to make that delivery. However, the belief that the bond futures contract is simply a substitute for the current cash long bond is potentially a very costly one. The bond future may have the trading characteristics of many different bonds. Depending on the current yield environment, shape of the yield curve, and other factors, some bonds will obviously have a much greater impact on the pricing and consequent movement of the futures contract. One should never assume that only one bond controls its price.

The futures contract is like a large station wagon carrying a group of bonds. The bonds that are most important sit in the front and have the most impact on its direction and speed, but during some instances, the forgotten bonds in the back can grab control of the steering wheel. The true essence of basis pricing is determining how likely certain bonds are to gain control and how long they will drive. Frequently, the car that seemed to be driving straight on the expected route can

* The author would like to thank Pierre Wolf, George Batjiaka, and Joon Lee for their helpful comments and suggestions.

lurch right through a trader's P and L and sometimes right over the trader. Thus, it is of paramount importance to comprehend fully the different dimensions of the contract and its deliverability options.

MECHANICS OF THE FUTURES CONTRACT

Conversion Factor

The Chicago Board of Trade (CBT) was initially a place where participants in the agricultural market (e.g., farmers) went to protect themselves against inclement weather and other factors that could cause wide price and delivery swings. Thus, the CBT made a number of bonds deliverable because it was well-steeped in agricultural futures and wanted to ensure ease in delivering bonds if there was a large open interest at settlement. The conversion factor helps in that regard. In fact, if only one bond were eligible for delivery, the open interest or total number of positions in the bond future would be lower. Because most traders never involve themselves in the delivery process, there can obviously be positions before the last day of trading of that futures contract that are much larger than the deliverable bond.[1] However, such positions would still curtail activity in bond futures because there would be no more delivery games, which would be the antithesis of what the Board desires—the largest volume of trading and positioning possible. Undoubtedly, it is cynical to claim that this was the Board's main reason for allowing a group of bonds to be delivered, because most of the ideas that have come out of basis trading originated far after the contract's introduction. It was most likely an effort to stop a squeeze on any one deliverable bond.

For that reason, the CBT established a delivery factor algorithm to approximately equalize the cost of delivering a host of eligible bonds. Certainly, the factor does not make all bonds equally profitable to deliver. In fact, it is one of the main reasons why they are not. Without a factor system, the contract would simply be a futures contract on the lowest coupon bond with the longest maturity, because this would obviously have the lowest dollar price and, thus, be the cheapest security to deliver.

The factor rate the CBT uses is 8 percent. That is, when calculating conversion factors (CF), these bonds are all priced to yield 8 percent. The resulting price is then divided by 100 and rounded off to the nearest ten thousandth (four decimal places). A 20-year bond with a 12 percent coupon to yield 8 percent should be

---

1. The amount outstanding of each issue in the basket of deliverable bonds varies from $4.75 billion of both the $13^{1}/_{4}\%$ 5/15/14 and the $12^{1}/_{2}\%$ 8/15/14 to $32 billion of the thrice-opened 8% 11/15/21. The open interest on bond futures is typically between 300,000 and 400,000, whereas the number delivered is much smaller. For the June 1993 contract, only 13,383 contracts were delivered.

priced at $139.58. The conversion factor is simply 1.3958 (price/100). Keep in mind that the CF is roughly the price of the security to yield 8 percent.

This, however, is not precisely correct. To calculate the CF exactly, one must take the first day of the delivery month of the futures contract as the settlement date and the first day of the last delivery month as its maturity (the contract month that is closest to the maturity without being longer than the maturity). In other words, whatever the length of the bond, one would simply round down to the nearest quarter. For example, if the bond were maturing on 5/31/16, the maturity date used to calculate the CF would be 3/01/16. Even though June 1 is an eligible date and only one day from the actual maturity, it falls *after* the bond matures. One must remember to always go back to the last contract month passed. Thus, for both maturity and settlement, there can only be four days used: March 1, June 1, September 1, and December 1, for these are the four contract months for bonds on the CBT. The CF for the $10^5/_8$ percent of 8/15/15 for the September 1994 contract is determined as follows:

Settlement date	9/01/94
Maturity date	6/01/15
Priced to yield	8% (as always)
To price	$126.342
CF	1.2634

Invoice Price

The futures contract trades in increments of $100,000 per contract. Thus, for every contract a trader is long and involved in delivery, he will receive $100,000 par amount of an eligible bond. The one defining characteristic of an eligible bond is that it must be 15 years or longer to maturity or to call. The trader long the futures and short the cash bond must pay, upon being delivered the bond, the following invoice price per contract:

$$\text{Invoice price} = \text{Futures settlement price} \times \text{Conversion factor}$$
$$\times \$1,000 + \text{Accrued interest}$$

Accrued interest is simply the amount of interest earned on a bond from the last coupon payment to the settlement date. The futures settlement price is the official closing price determined by the CBT at the end of each trading day. If one makes delivery after the contract has stopped trading, the settlement price is the price at which the contract stopped trading.

To illustrate the calculation of the invoice price, consider the $7^1/_8$ percent of 2/15/23 for delivery into the September 1994 contract if delivery is made on September 30, 1994, and the futures settlement price (price at which the contract ceases to trade) is $104^8/_{32}$.

$$CF = .9024$$

$$\text{Futures settlement price} = 104.25$$

$$\text{Accrued interest per contract}^2 = \$890.63$$

Then,

$$\text{Invoice price} = 104.25 \times .9024 \times \$1,000 + \$890.63$$
$$= \$94,966$$

Implied Repo Rate

Simply looking at the bond with the highest conversion factor will not identify which bond is cheapest to deliver (CTD). It is necessary to take into account that if a bond has a conversion factor greater than one, it is a premium bond, and must be purchased at a premium.

The best instrument with which to gauge cheapness should incorporate the *relative* cost of delivering, and that is precisely what the implied repo rate indicates. The implied repo rate is the return received by going long the basis. This involves buying the cash bond, financing it at the current borrowing or repo rate to term, and then delivering those bonds to satisfy the short futures obligation. Therefore, the bond with the highest implied repo rate is the one that is cheapest to deliver; the higher the implied repo rate, the cheaper the bond is to deliver.

The implied repo rate is simply

$$\frac{\text{Cash in} - \text{Cash out}}{\text{Cash out}} \times \frac{60}{n}$$

where

n = number of days involved in the trade

We must annualize the return by multiplying the cash flow quotient by $360/n$ because other money market rates are also quoted using this convention.

For the exact return, the formula is as follows:

$$\frac{[(FP \times CF) + Ae + IC - (\text{Price of bond} + Ab)] \times 360}{d1 \times (\text{Price of bond} + Ab) - (IC \times d2)}$$

where

FP = Futures price
Ab = Accrued interest of bond at beginning or inception of trade

---

2. Accrued interest is calculated by simply dividing the coupon rate by 2 and multiplying that quotient by the number of days elapsed since the last coupon payment divided by the total number of days in that six-month period. In this case, the total number of days between the coupon payment on August 15 and the settlement date of September 30 is 46 days. Therefore, the accrued interest is simply $(7.125/2) \times (46/184)$.

Ae = Accrued interest of bond at end of trade (delivery to cover short)

IC = Interim coupon (any coupon that falls between settlement date and delivery date)

d1 = Number of days between settlement and actual delivery

d2 = Number of days between interim coupon and bond delivery

For example, the implied repo rate of the $8\frac{1}{2}$ percent of 2/15/20 with settlement on 7/14/94, delivery on 9/30/94, a futures price of $112^{16}/_{32}$, and a bond price of $119^{22}/_{32}$ is calculated as follows:

$$FP = 112.50$$

$$CF = 1.0537$$

$$Ae = \frac{8.5}{2} \times \frac{46}{184} = 1.0625$$

$$IC = \frac{8.5}{2} = 4.25$$

$$\text{Bond price} = 119.6875$$

$$Ab = \frac{8.5}{2} \times \frac{149}{181} = 3.499$$

$$d1 = 9/30/94 - 7/14/94 = 78 \text{ days}$$

$$d2 = 9/30/94 - 8/15/94 = 46 \text{ days}$$

Thus, the implied repo rate is

$$\frac{[(112.50 \times 1.0537) + 1.0625 + 4.25 - (119.6875 + 3.499)] \times 360}{78 \times (119.6875 + 3.499) - (4.25 \times 46)}$$

$$= .0255 \text{ or } 2.55\%$$

The Delivery Procedure

The vast majority of people who trade bond futures never involve themselves in the process of delivery because of its complexities. Instead, they either liquidate the futures position completely with an offsetting transaction or roll forward into the next contract, which is more liquid. If an investor is long a future after it has ceased trading, she can expect to be delivered a Treasury bond, and if an investor is short a future after it has stopped trading, she will be required to deliver a Treasury bond to fulfill the obligation required of her position. The short would adhere to the following three-day procedure.

1. *Position Day*: The day in which the CBT is given notice by the futures short that he plans to make delivery of a certain amount of bonds in two business days. This intention can be made any time before 8:00 P.M. central standard time (CST). The first eligible intention day is the

second-to-last business day of the month before the delivery month. If the investor has not informed the Board of intention to deliver by the second-to-last day of the delivery month, then the Board automatically assumes that he will be delivering at the end of the month.

2. *Notice Day*: The day in which the CBT is given notice about which particular issue he intends to deliver and then matches the short with the futures long who has had the longest outstanding position. The Board then informs the long that she will be delivered to the next day. Notice must occur before 2:00 P.M. CST unless it is the last notice day of the month, in which case notice must be made before 3:00 P.M. The party long the futures is notified by 4:00 P.M. which bond she will be receiving.

3. *Delivery Day*: The short must have in his account by 10:00 A.M. CST the bonds he has specified he would deliver and must actually deliver them by 1:00 P.M. CST to the long party the Board has assigned to him. The long pays the short the invoice price for that particular bond only after being delivered the bonds.

The short may not promise to deliver a certain bond and then deliver another one; there is a one point per contract penalty for not delivering the bonds specified on notice day. The advantage gained by switching bonds will seldom ever offset the one point penalty.

THE BASIS

As mentioned earlier, the best measure of what is cheapest to deliver is the implied repo rate. However, this is not the way most people determine which issue is the cheapest or whether the futures contract is over- or undervalued. That is done through following the basis because, computationally, the implied repo rate is considerably more difficult and because the basis is derived from price, which is what traders deal in when they trade cash bonds and futures.

The basis is simply the difference between the cash bond price and the converted futures price. The converted futures price is the product of the futures price and the conversion factor. To place the figure in 32ds, multiply the basis by 32.

$$\text{Basis} = (\text{Bond price} - \text{Futures price} \times \text{Conversion factor}) \times 32$$

A long basis trade involves the purchase of a deliverable cash bond and sale of a factor-weighted amount of futures contracts. Going short the basis means selling a deliverable cash bond and buying a factor-weighted number of futures contracts.

It should be recognized that the basis on the cheapest-to-deliver bond (CTD) must converge to zero by the end of the delivery month. Riskless money could be made if this were not the case. For example, if the basis were still worth something on the last day of the month, a trader could do the following: (1) sell the basis and then effectively "buy" the bond upon delivery and (2) sell the futures position to fulfill his short basis obligation. The trader is synthetically selling the cash bond at a level higher than it is delivered to him. This difference is the positive value of the basis on that last day.

Many people believe that the basis can never be negative. This is simply not true. The *net* basis can never be negative because an option can never have a negative value because it only provides one with the *opportunity* to transact at a certain price, not an obligation. The gross basis may be negative before the delivery month if there is an inverted curve and if the value of the delivery options granted to the short is low. (This is a rare occurrence.) However, during the delivery month, the basis cannot be negative at any time because one could simply buy the basis (buy bonds, sell futures) and subsequently unwind it by selling cash bonds at the higher current market price while being able to buy futures at the same level.

The most famous blunder in basis trading occurred at the end of 1987. In the middle of December, a primary dealer who was long 5,500 December bond futures contracts was delivered $550 million par amount of the $10^3/_8$ percent 11/15/12 to satisfy the short's obligation. Even though this issue was the cheapest, the basis on the bond was trading in the marketplace at around $10,000 per $1 million. Of course, the dealer congratulated itself on its serendipity. The firm had fallen quite unexpectedly into a cash pool of about $5.5 million. This present was known on Wall Street as the Christmas gift; the deliverer should not have handed those bonds over until the last day because it could have at least made positive carry by holding them, and, conversely, the Wall Street firm could now forgo the cost of being short the cash bonds. That bond was trading in the cash market at approximately $109.30; however, the firm received bonds at an effective cost of $108.30, which is $87^{25}/_{32}$ (contract price) multiplied by a conversion factor of 1.2336. As soon as the firm was delivered these bonds, it turned around and sold them back out to complete every trader's fantasy—a huge profit with no risk.

The early delivery in this case was not only excruciatingly painful for the deliverer but also uncommon. However, even discounting this example as a fluke, one might still wonder why anyone would be content in buying the basis and earning a lower return or implied repo rate than could be obtained from simply investing money at current short-term interest rates.[3] The discrepancy exists because the basis long has several deliverability options that could increase his or her return, sometimes dramatically. These options, combined with carry, comprise the value of the basis. Both will be discussed in the next two sections.

CARRY

Carry is a Wall Street term used to describe the amount of money made or lost by holding, or carrying, a bond. The ownership of the bond provides interest income, which is offset by the financing charge one must pay to borrow the money

---

3. If we were to look at an implied repo table, we would see that all eligible bonds have a lower return or implied repo rate than the present money market rates.

to purchase the bond. Obviously, with an upward-sloping yield curve, there is positive carry when one is long a bond whereas an inverted curve burdens the long with negative carry (i.e., a daily loss).

For basis trades, most people calculate carry until the last possible delivery date, which is usually the best time for delivery with a normal yield curve. An inverted curve is more complex, as one has to determine whether the negative carry (money lost by financing a bond purchase, or the bond yield minus the financing or repo rate) is greater than the value of the options.

An ideal example is Paul Volcker's monetarist experiment between 1979 and 1981, when the curve twisted and often was inverted. Initially, traders automatically delivered their bonds on the first eligible delivery date to avoid the negative carry. As time passed, the deliveries began to take place later in the month. This occurred because some traders began to realize that it was advantageous to deliver later in the month, retain the options, and suffer through the negative carry. Early delivery in this scenario should be based solely on whether the exercising of the option is more valuable than the money forgone in financing. Thus, it is crucial to value those options accurately.

However, one should be cautious in dismissing the importance of carry. The simplicity of its calculation can and often does belie its ability to damage a trader's P&L. There is no question that with a certain term repo rate (financing rate to a certain date—in this case, that date is usually the end of the delivery month), figuring the amount of carry for that period is quite easy. However, as any repo desk will attest, those financing rates do not stay very constant and can often swing dramatically.

For example, assume that a bond is currently yielding 8 percent and the repo rate to the end of the delivery month is 3 percent. If there are 30 days left, the amount of money made per million by carrying the bond is $4,075.[4] However, if a dealer or a big hedge fund decided to squeeze[5] or tighten an issue in the financing market or if there are simply too many shorts in that issue and the rate drops to 2

---

4. A relatively precise and fairly common estimation of carry is as follows:

$$(\text{Coupon rate}/365) - (\text{Repo rate}/360 \times \text{Price}/100)$$

In this case, because the yield is also 8 percent, the price is 100. Thus, the calculation is $(.08/365) - (.03/360) \times 100/100 = .0001358$. Per million, the carry is $135.84. For 30 days, this totals $4,075.

5. A squeeze in the repo market occurs when there are too many traders short a particular issue and not enough lenders of that security. The most famous example of this was the squeeze of the April and May 1993 two-year notes. Many traders were short the issue during the when-issued period in hopes of purchasing them cheaper during the auction. Unfortunately for them, most were unable to buy them from the Treasury in the auction. Consequently, desperate shorts who needed to make delivery or fail, and effectively lend money at 0 percent in the finance market, were often willing to lend money at exactly that level. Large regional banks are frequently mentioned as creating a tight repo rate in an issue when they buy a large amount of an issue and keep it in their portfolio instead of lending it out. The Fed has now established a policy that if an issue becomes remarkably or "unnaturally" tight, they will reopen that issue to mitigate the shortage.

percent, then the carry increases quickly to $4,908 per million. On the surface, this does not appear to be a substantial amount, but for a basis position of $500 million, quite an ordinary position for many basis traders, this translates into a difference of $416,500—quite a large payout.

This variability can be avoided by simply locking up, or lending (borrowing), money at the current term rate. In this case, the trader who is short the bonds and has cash available to borrowers could lend money at the fixed rate of 3 percent for the duration of her expected holding, which appears to be 30 days. Unfortunately, this act of prudence is often overlooked for several reasons. In some cases, the trader may not know how long she will keep the trade alive, or she may predict that the term rate will rise in the future. However, the reason could also be appetite for risk, ignorance, or sloth. Regardless of the reason, this oversight can prove to be very volatile. However, these concerns do not affect the true value of the basis, because one can always be assured of a certain financing rate. The key to rewards lies in valuing the deliverability options.

OPTIONS

The true essence of determining basis richness or cheapness is in the valuation of the net or option-adjusted basis, which is the gross basis minus carry. This value is comprised of the value of the different deliverability options. The mathematics of calculating those different options is highly complex, not only because of the inherent difficulty associated with valuing any derivative with multiple pricing constraints, but also because many of these constraints, and hence the effect on the option prices, are interdependent. Even if a trader were to correctly value each delivery option, he may not obtain the value of the net basis simply by summing them because some options are mutually exclusive. For example, if the trader exercises the wildcard, he cannot exercise the switching option.

For the sake of clarity, each option will be explained independently. It is beyond the scope of this chapter to derive precise values for each option. Although the following explanations omit the exact mathematical derivations, they should prove helpful in understanding the skeleton of basis valuation. The five different deliverability options are the yield shift option, yield spread option, new-auction option, wildcard option, and switching option.

Yield-Shift Option

Because the conversion factor is the price of the bond at 8 percent divided by 100, there is a general bias toward delivering bonds with higher durations when yields are above 8 percent and with lower durations when yields are below 8 percent.

The logic behind this idea is rather simple. Consider that the converted cash price equals the bond price divided by the CF. Assuming that there is no severe penalty for high-coupon bonds (that is, they do not trade substantially cheaper), all bonds would be almost equally deliverable if yields are at 8 percent. However, if rates are below 8 percent and an investor uses an 8 percent factor to discount, then she is underestimating the value of the subsequent coupon and principal receipts. Likewise, if the trader uses 8 percent as the discount rate when rates are above 8 percent, she is overvaluing those future payments. Now, the low-coupon, long-maturity bonds have a higher CF than they should, and that makes them more attractive to deliver.

For a different perspective, suppose that yields are rising above 8 percent and are now pushing up against 10 percent. Obviously, the higher duration bonds drop more in price than the shorter durations when yields rise. Because the CF is constant, the flat price (price/CF) is lower. The price of the higher duration issue goes down more than the lower duration bond, and this leads to a lower converted price. If yields are moving down through 8 percent and to almost 7 percent, for example, then the higher duration bond will rise in price faster. This is not what traders want if they are short because this will increase the converted price. The low-duration bond is preferable because its price rises more slowly in both relative and absolute terms.

It has been proven that when yields are above 8 percent, it is generally cheaper to deliver bonds with higher duration, and when they are below 8 percent, it is generally cheaper to deliver bonds with lower duration.

The 8 percent mark is the general cutoff, but it is not the precise point at which all the breakeven prices of the eligible bonds are equal. This is because the CF truncates the actual maturity of the bond: It is rounded down to the last contract month, and the first deliverable date is used as the settlement date. Also, there is a slight difference because it is assumed that all callable bonds will be called at the first call date, which is obviously not necessarily true. After the bond auction in November 1984, the Treasury discontinued the issuance of callable bonds, which effectively added five years to the maturity of post-1984 bonds in determining the factors.

To see how the cutoff ultimately affects deliverability, consider that if carry is ignored, then the converted cash price (CC) of any given Treasury issue is the price of the bond divided by its conversion factor. That is,

$$CC = \frac{\text{Bond price}}{CF}$$

Remember that the basis at the end of the delivery month has to be zero. Obviously, the bond price must equal, by that last day, the futures settlement price multiplied by the CF. Thus, if one can sell a bond at the market price and buy futures at a price less than the CC, then a profit will be locked in. Also, by definition, the most deliverable bond is the one with the lowest CC price. Exhibit 58–1 shows the group of bonds that we will consider to be the entire eligible basket for delivery.

The bonds are all yielding less than 8 percent, and thus the market favors those issues with lower durations; clearly, the $12^{1}/_{2}$ and $13^{1}/_{4}$ have the lowest durations of the four. This can be verified by observing the CCs. The lowest CC, 113.42, belongs to the $13^{1}/_{4}$ and the highest CC belongs to the $7^{1}/_{8}$, which has the highest duration. However, as Exhibit 58–2 shows, if bond yields rise above 8 percent, the basket instantly inverts as the higher duration bonds put a sparkle in the deliverer's

EXHIBIT 58-1

Deliverability Analysis of Yields below 8 Percent

Issue		Price	Yield	CF	CC
$13^1/_4$%	5/15/09–14	166.19	6.53%	1.4652	113.42
$12^1/_2$	8/15/09–14	159.11	6.54	1.4022	113.47
$7^1/_4$	5/15/16	104.75	6.84	.9218	113.64
$7^1/_8$	2/15/23	104.19	6.79	.9014	115.59

EXHIBIT 58-2

Deliverability Analysis of Yields above 8 Percent

Issue		Price	Yield	CF	CC
$7^1/_8$%	2/15/23	82.38	8.80%	.9014	91.39
$7^1/_4$	5/15/16	84.36	8.85	.9218	91.52
$12^1/_2$	8/15/09–14	138.58	8.53	1.4022	98.83
$13^1/_4$	5/15/09–14	146.12	8.50	1.4652	99.73

eye. The $7^1/_8$ and the $7^1/_4$ are now several points more deliverable than the 2014 bonds. In general, one can assume that when yields rise, higher duration issues (low-coupon, long-maturity) become more deliverable, and when yields decline, lower duration issues (high-coupon, short-maturity) become more deliverable.

It is easier to observe this characteristic by simply looking at a graph of converted cash prices versus different bond yields. As shown in Exhibit 58–3, as bond yields rise through 8 percent, the higher duration $7^1/_8$ has a lower converted or breakeven futures price than the lower duration $12^1/_2$ and the $13^1/_4$, and is thus cheaper to deliver. The converse is also true—the further bond yields fall below 8 percent, the cheaper the $12^1/_2$ and the $13^1/_4$ is to deliver. Note that although there is very little difference in deliverability between the two high coupons because their durations are so similar, there is a significant difference between the $7^1/_8$ and the $7^1/_4$. This is because not only does the $7^1/_8$ have a lower coupon, its maturity is 6.75 years longer. Consequently, between those two issues, the $7^1/_4$ is cheaper if yields are below 8 percent, and the $7^1/_8$ is cheaper when yields are over 8 percent.

The value of the yield shift option is clearly correlated with the proximity of current rates to the switchover point (the yield level at which it becomes more profitable to deliver opposite duration bonds).[6] If rates are relatively stable and

---

6. This point is generally around 8 percent, but as discussed before, this is not the precise level. In this
  case, it appears to be closer to 7.85 percent.

E X H I B I T   58–3

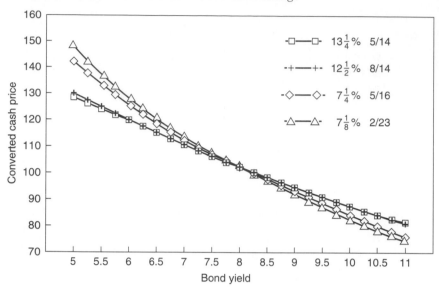

Attractiveness of Market Basket Due to Yield Change

-□——□-	$13\frac{1}{4}$% 5/14
-+——+-	$12\frac{1}{2}$% 8/14
-◇——◇-	$7\frac{1}{4}$% 5/16
-△——△-	$7\frac{1}{8}$% 2/23

long bond yields are hovering around 10 percent, the probability of rates breaking through the switchover point is very low, and thus the value of the yield change option is also very low. Conversely, if bond yields are fluctuating wildly around the 8 percent level, the option can be quite valuable.

One would probably imagine that if yields at the beginning of a delivery month were 10 percent, for example, and gradually declined 5 basis points every trading day for the next couple of weeks, the value of the option would increase as it slowly approached 8 percent. This is not necessarily true because, like an ordinary option, the value of the yield-change option suffers from time decay or theta. This is simply the daily decline in an option's value due strictly to the passage of time. The theta as we approach the expiration date of the option (which is, in this case, the eighth-to-the-last business day of the delivery month) does not increase linearly but rather almost exponentially. Therefore, if the aforementioned scenario occurred, the March yield-shift option would approach being worthless while the June yield-shift option would increase in value. This is not only because the June contract still has months before expiration, but also because the rate of time decay is different for the two contract months.

Yield-Spread Option

The basket of bonds is affected not only by the general yield movements but also by the yield spread between the different bonds in the basket. Clearly, bonds that are more expensive in the cash bond market relative to their neighbors are usually more expensive to deliver. Several factors can affect these yield spreads, including the stripping of a bond, tightening in the repo markets, or simply buying or selling of a certain issue by a large hedge fund.

This also explains why the cheapest to deliver (CTD) is not always the bond that is delivered. The CTD is only the cheapest up to a certain point. If everyone who intended to deliver bought the CTD and its price rose, it probably would not remain the cheapest. Exhibit 58–4 shows this clearly.

At the time of this writing, for the September 1994 contract, the $11^1/_4$ was the CTD, followed by the $10^5/_8$ and the $11^3/_4$. Notice how close the implied repo rates of these three issues are. This implies that even a small change in price between the issues can easily change the profitability landscape. If the price of the $11^1/_4$ increases by only .008 percent or $^4/_{32}$ while the other two bonds stay unchanged, the implied repo rate of the $11^1/_4$ decreases to 2.72 percent, which makes the issue the most expensive out of this basket.

Clearly, if the CTD can change with seemingly minor moves, upon large shifts in the yield curve, the basis can move dramatically. Inherent in every basis trade is a yield-curve bet. For example, consider the basis move in late July–early August of 1993. Interest rates were well below 8 percent, making the lower duration bonds cheaper to deliver, and that was indeed the case with the $11^3/_4\%$ 11/15/14, which was the CTD. The current long bond at the time was the $7^1/_8$ percent 2/15/23. A trader long that basis would, in effect, be long the $7^1/_8$ and short the $11^3/_4$. This basis was at $^{93}/_{32}$ on July 29. By August 10, it had risen all the way to $^{136}/_{32}$. Many observers attributed the move to the purchase of large strips, but it had much more to do with the flattening of the curve.

The basis is often market directional: As the market trades up with an even yield move, the basis will increase because of the differing durations. In this case, the rally was coupled with the aforementioned flattening, especially between the 10-year note and the long bond, which flattened from 77.5 bp to 64 bp during that interim. Thus, in this instance, it really was not due to any of the other complicated options but rather a simple yield-curve play.

E X H I B I T   58–4

Yield-Spread Effects on Implied Repo Rates for the September 1994 Contract

Issue		Price	Yield	CF	Implied Repo Rate
$11^1/_4\%$	2/15/10–15	155.52	6.45%	1.3230	2.79%
$10^5/_8$	8/15/10–15	148.44	6.47	1.2634	2.75
$11^3/_4$	11/15/09–14	156.30	6.21	1.3242	2.74
$11^1/_4$[a]	2/15/10–15	155.64	6.44	1.3230	2.72[a]

[a]Former CTD, now most expensive to deliver.

E X H I B I T   58–5

Breakeven Prices of the Deliverable Basket

Issue		Price	Yield	CF	CC(Price/CF)
$9^1/_4$%	2/15/16	126.86	6.89%	1.1295	112.32
9	11/15/18	124.70	6.93	1.1075	112.60
12	8/15/08–13	152.13	6.55	1.3458	113.04
$7^1/_8$	2/15/23	103.42	6.85	.9014	114.74

New-Auction Option

The new-auction option's value is derived from the possibility that a new bond may be auctioned with a different coupon or maturity than any bond in the current basket and thus be a candidate for the exalted station of cheapest to deliver.

Look at the basket of bonds in Exhibit 58–5. Assuming that the prices and the different bases listed are typical of those currently in the marketplace, the calculations of CC prices are shown in Exhibit 58–5. As can be seen, the $9^1/_4$ is the cheapest and the $7^1/_8$ is the most expensive.

Let us see how a newly auctioned issue can change the profitability of delivering the new bond. First, understand that bond yields must move from the current yields for the new bond to be attractive. For example, if the CTD is currently the most recently auctioned bond ($7^1/_8$ percent 2/15/23) and bond yields move to 7.23 percent, the new bond will still have a $7^1/_8$ percent coupon. Second, realize that under the current environment of rates well below the 8 percent level, the probability that a newly auctioned bond will become the cheapest is very low. This is because this environment favors a low-duration bond. Because of the wide disparity of bond maturity dates in the market basket (from 2/16 to 2/23), it is difficult for a move in the yields to compensate for the difference in the lengths of maturities.

To prove this, assume the bond auction in May of 1993 was for a new bond maturing in May of 2023.[7] If bond yields move up to 7.75 percent right before the auction of the new 5/15/23 bond, the CF for this $7^3/_4$ percent bond for June delivery would be .9716. This implies a CC of 102.92 (100/.9716). The CC of the $9^1/_4$ percent would be 102.616 (115.905/1.1295), assuming that the yield of the $9^1/_4$ is about even to the new bond so that 115.905 is the price of the $9^1/_4$ at 7.75 percent. This means that the $9^1/_4$ would remain the CTD. If yields rose over 8 percent, the value of delivery would change, but this would be due to the passing of the 8 percent mark.

---

7. Of course, this was not true. This auction was a reopening of the previous bond—the $7^1/_8$ % of 2/23.

Therefore, consider a case in which the newly issued bond is the CTD and there is an auction that would compete with it. These conditions suggest an environment of yields over 8 percent (remember that over 8 percent, the CTD usually tracks the highest duration bond). If the current bond is the 9.5 percent of 2/15/23 (for simplicity's sake, assume that it is the only bond deliverable into the June 1993 contract), and yields decrease to 8.5 percent before the May 1993 auction, the profit scenario would be as follows:

Issue		Price	Yield	Factor	CC
$9^1/_2\%$	2/15/23	110.75	8.5%	1.1690	94.74
$8^1/_2$	5/15/23	100.00	8.5	1.0562	94.68

The simple addition of an extra deliverable should not have an impact on the price of the $9^1/_2$, but notice how this affects the *basis* of the one previously deliverable bond. For example, assume that the basis of that bond was $^{5.5}/_{32}$ before the new bond auction and that the futures price was $94^{19}/_{32}$. The newly auctioned bond is more deliverable than the old bond by $^2/_{32}[94.74 - 94.68]$. This means that the bond future price will fall by just that amount because that is now the new CC price (remember that CC does not include carry). This would occur as arbitrageurs bought the new bond and sold the futures price down to the CC. If the cash bond prices remained constant and the futures price fell by $^2/_{32}$, the basis on that old bond would increase by $^{2.25}/_{32}$ to $^{7.75}/_{32}$. Thus, as expected, the investor who is long the basis of the $9^1/_2$ profits by the introduction of the newly auctioned bond.

Notice that if the new bond does not create a potentially profitable switching opportunity, the trader long that basis loses only the value of the auction option. As with any other option, the largest amount of money an investor can lose is the value of that option, which in this case is worth very little, if anything.

It is evident that the new-auction option is most valuable when yields are above the switchover point and move down or when yields are below the switchover point and rise. The yield increase, however, must produce a coupon that compensates for the extra six months on the next bond auctioned.

The new-auction option is in effect before the respective refundings, which until August 1993 were in February, May, August, and November. With the move to have larger semiannual auctions in February and August, the value of this option has lessened. Consider a situation in late April 1993 when yields were well above 8 percent yet falling rapidly. For the June 1993 futures contract, there was no longer a new-auction option because there was no bond auction in May. However, there would still remain an auction option for the September 1993 futures.

If there are two auctions before the delivery month, then there are two possibilities of the auction yielding a bond whose coupon can be profitably switched into. The value of this option theoretically ends immediately after the bond auction results are posted, which is around 2:00 P.M. eastern time—approximately an hour after the auction itself. The bond futures price should adjust immediately, or there is ample room for arbitrage. However, one should not be misled into thinking that traders are on the edge of their seats waiting for the auction results to see if there will be a cheaper-to-deliver bond. Clearly, they are aware if there is a potential for the creation of a more profitable delivery, and the future's price will hover accordingly.

Also, reconsider the first instance of yields below 8 percent. If the auction results in a bond with a lower coupon, then the new bond could prove profitable to deliver if rates rise through 8 percent. Even though it was the new auction that created the issue, the potential option value would then be attributed to the yield change option, because it was not the auction itself that created the opportunity, but rather the yield shift. However, there also would be no opportunity to switch into the new, cheaper bond if the bond is never created in an auction. Regardless, the categorization is a simple matter of semantics.

The Wildcard Options

The CF creates tails in one's position. If a trader is long $50 million of the bond basis, he is required to deliver $50 million in eligible bonds. If the bond has a coupon other than 8 percent, he will have a tail of some sort. For example, the $7^1/_8$ percent 2/15/23 has a CF of .9024 for the June 1994 contract. Thus, if a trader is long $50 million of this basis, he would be short 451 contracts. After he delivers the bonds to cover his 451 short in the futures, he would still be long $4.9 million cash bonds, which is his tail.

This wildcard or late-day option comes into play because of the tail and because the futures markets and cash markets do not trade simultaneously at all times. The CBT stops trading at 2:00 P.M. CST, whereas the cash market is open almost the entire day.[8] The short has until 8:00 P.M. CST to give notice of intention to deliver, but the futures price is stuck at the 2:00 P.M. close. This allows the short to buy the bond tail short after 2:00 if the market dips and allows the short to sell the bond tail long after 2:00 if the market rallies.

Although this option is available on many consecutive days, it does not cover those entire trading days but rather only the six-hour time frame between 2:00 P.M. and 8:00 P.M. If the short fails to give notice of intent to deliver by 8:00, that day's wildcard option expires worthless.

Wildcard Call Option
The call is in effect if the hedge ratio is less than one. In this instance, the trader who is long the basis is also long the bond tail, which she will try to sell before delivering. Therefore, if the market rises after the 2:00 futures close, she will be able to sell that tail at a high price although the futures price is frozen at the 2:00

---

8. The only exception is on weekdays between 4:30 P.M. and 5:30 P.M. CST, which is the time between the close of the cash bond market in the United States and its opening in Tokyo, and on the weekends up until 5:30 P.M. CST Sunday.

settlement price. However, not all rallies will do. The rally should be looked at as just a rally of the tail, as the remainder is hedged and must be delivered. The size of the tail is obviously very important because the larger it is, the smaller the movement has to be to reach a profitable switching point or strike price. Remember that the tail is simply the CF minus one. The formula for how much it should rally is as follows:

$$S(\text{call}) = BP + \frac{(BS \times CF)}{1 - CF}$$

where

   S = Strike or breakeven price
   BP = Bond price at 2:00 P.M. CST
   BS = Basis
   CF = Conversion factor

Wildcard Put Option

This option is in effect if the hedge ratio is greater than one. The short holds an implicit out-of-the-money put option on the bond. A hedge ratio greater than one means that the long basis trader possesses a futures tail that she must cover in the cash market. If the market falls after 2:00, the trader can buy back her cash at a lower price and still use the higher futures close to calculate her invoice price. However, this does not imply that any drop in the cash market will make it profitable to deliver. The strike price is determined by the following formula:

$$S(\text{put}) = BP - \frac{(BS \times CF)}{(CF - 1)}$$

The following illustrates the wildcard put option scenario. Suppose it is 4:25 on a Thursday afternoon. The market has begun to suspect that the Federal Reserve may begin an aggressive easing campaign due to recent economic weakness. According to Federal Reserve chairman Greenspan's testimony before a congressional body the previous day, the Fed will now focus mainly on money supply growth, which has shown signs of weakness. Money supply is released at 4:30, and M2 is so strong that it places the yearly growth rate above the upper band. The ease hopes vanish quickly and the market plummets. The calculation to determine how much it has to drop before the wildcard option is profitable is shown below:

Issue	Price	Futures Settlement	Basis	CF
13$^1/_4$% 5/15/14	164$^{18}/_{32}$	112–07	$^{4.5}/_{32}$	1.4652

$$S(\text{put}) = 164.5625 - \frac{.1396 \times 1.4652}{.4652}$$

$$= 164.123$$
$$= 164^4/_{32}$$

The issue has to drop $^{14}/_{32}$ ($164^{18}/_{32}$ − $164^{4}/_{32}$) before it is profitable to exercise this option. Certainly, this does not imply that a trader should buy the tail at 164-03. If he thinks the market will decline further, he should wait before purchasing the tail. If the market begins to rise after the initial decline, the trader has missed an opportunity for profit but he has not lost any money. It is the asymmetric profit profile of not being able to lose any money besides the value of that day's wildcard option, which is usually infinitesimally small, and of having a large upside potential that makes this wildcard an option. If the market falls anywhere short of the 164-04 level, it would not be profitable to cover and give notice to deliver.

The wildcard option is enhanced by a few characteristics of the specific bond and the market in general. If the bond's coupon is significantly different from 8 percent, then the CF will be greatly different from one. This leaves a larger tail with which to cover the basis loss a trader gives up by exercising his option early. It should then be obvious that the smaller the basis at the time of exercise, the easier it is to cover the loss. So if financing rates are close to the bond's yield (i.e., a relatively flat yield curve), the carry is small if positive at all, and thus the wildcard's strike price is not as far out of the money. Lastly, if the market is very volatile, that increases the value of the option because there is a greater potential for price jumps after 2:00 P.M.

The wildcard option in the environment at the time of this writing usually does not come into play very often for a few reasons.

The first is that the market has to rise (or fall) enough to cover the value of the basis. The time frame in which a wildcard option can come into play is from the first notice day, which is two business days before the start of the delivery month, to the day before the last trading day. Also, remember that the theoretical value of the basis must converge to zero by the end of the month. But because the basis stops trading eight days before the end of the month, and because the switching option is usually the most valuable, the basis on that eighth day is usually considerably more than zero. Consequently, it would take a substantial rise (or fall) to cover the value of the remaining basis.

The second reason is that the market generally tends to quiet down after the close of the futures market because of lack of liquidity (which can sometimes be the impetus of precipitous declines and explosive rallies) and lack of interest. The only news that comes out after 2:00 P.M., besides those occasional breaking world events, are the money supply announcement at 3:30 P.M. CST and sometimes a late Johnson Redbook report (a report on retail sales), which is usually released to its subscribers around 1:45 P.M. CST. Money supply is not the earthshaker it used to be even as recently as 1992,[9] and even though the Redbook reports have found

---

9. Financial numbers tend to fall in and out of favor with Wall Street. Money supply, once considered by many to be the preeminent predictor of future economic strength, has been recently frowned upon by some who question its true correlation with the growth rate. As recently as 1989, the release of merchandise trade figures used to move markets like nothing else. It now comes and goes with barely a whisper.

a following, they are not usually impressive enough to move the market substantially. This is partly because both numbers generally have more relevance (in terms of yield) for the short end of the yield curve.

Switching Option

After the last day of the futures trading, the deliverer has the option to deliver another bond if it becomes more deliverable. In other words, he is looking to switch or change the bond he has currently taken with him "off the board" for a more profitable bond. This option, often referred to as the *end-of-the-month option,* is similar to the wildcard option in that much of the potential profitability depends on the futures settlement price being frozen on the last trading day's settlement at 1:00 P.M. while the cash prices are free to fluctuate. Thus, he is guaranteed a fixed invoice price (the price he is paid to deliver those particular bonds) and will only "lose" the value of that basis if he delivers it, and less than that if he delivers a cheaper bond. Like any other option, then, the maximum loss is the value of the net basis or the value of the option premium.

The switching option is different from the wildcard option in that if the trader is positioned in the basis when it goes "off the board" or stops trading, he will guarantee himself either of having to make delivery or of being delivered to. In fact, at 1:00 P.M. on that eighth-to-last business day, he should position himself to face amounts because that is what is required in delivery. Therefore, it is not as if there is a one-week option on the tail, because the tail should be covered when the contracts go off the board. For example, assume that a trader is long $10 million of the $13^1/_4$ percent $^5/_{14}$ basis and is short 146 contracts against the amount as a factor weight. He must either buy back 46 contracts right before they close or sell $4.6 million $13^1/_4$s. No tail means no wildcard.

Return back to Exhibit 58–1, the original basket of deliverable bonds. Because yields are far below the 8 percent mark, the lower durations are clearly the CTDs. Now assume that the futures stopped trading at 120.50 and yields fall 50 basis points during the seven-day window. This is obviously a hefty change in yields during a relatively short time span. As shown in Exhibit 58–6, however unlikely, the move is both possible and elucidating.

E X H I B I T   58–6

Analysis of Deliverability with Yields Falling Roughly 50 Basis Points

Issue		Price	Yield	CF	CC
$13^1/_4$%	5/15/09–14	184.87	6.03%	1.4652	126.17
$12^1/_2$	8/15/09–14	176.35	6.00	1.4022	125.76
$7^1/_4$	5/15/16	110.88	6.34	.9218	120.29
$7^1/_8$	2/15/23	111.14	6.29	.9014	123.30

The switching profitability can be easily calculated to determine which issue should be swapped into and delivered. A trader should just follow the logical procession of switching by totaling the different cash flows involved and subtracting the value of the old invoice price, that is, the money forgone by switching to another bond.

1. Sell the old (previous) deliverable—Receive money (+).

2. Buy the new (cheaper) deliverable—Expend money (–).

3. Lose potential money on old deliverable—Money forgone (–).

4. Deliver the new bond at new invoice price—Receive money (+).

This analysis is shown in Exhibit 58–7. When calculating the profitability of swapping into different issues after the move in yields, it can be seen that the $7^1/_4$ is now the most profitable to switch into. The long basis trade in this case has resulted in a whopping $8.51 profit minus the value of the original basis. If the basis minus carry had been greater than $8.51, then the entire trade would not have been profitable.

In the above scenario, every issue provides the opportunity for a profitable switch. If, for example, the $12^1/_2$'s yield decreased more than 50 basis points because of large hedge fund buying, and the price rose to $177.35, there would be a loss of $0.07 in switching to the $12^1/_2$. Thus, if this were the case and the $12^1/_2$ were the only other deliverable bond, the trader should simply keep and deliver the $13^1/_4$ and just realize the switching option loss. This should illuminate the fact that the yield spread option is extremely important during this end-of-the-month period.

Now view the trade from the basis short's perspective. The trader was hoping to make the premium of the option or the net basis. But the large and sudden drop in yields has netted him ownership of the $7^1/_4$ and a loss of $8.51 minus the value of the outstanding basis.

Notice that there is no change if the trader stays with the $13^1/_4$ as expected. This implies that the maximum loss associated with not switching is zero. In other words, it has the same profit profile as an option. If the market rallies, and there

E X H I B I T   58–7

Profitability of Switching Issues to Deliver

Issue		1. Sell Old	2. Buy New	3. Lose Potential	4. Deliver New	5. Net Gain (Loss)
$13^1/_4$%	5/15/09–14	+ $184.87	– $184.87	– $176.56	+ $176.56	= $0.00
$12^1/_2$	8/15/09–14	+ $184.87	– $176.35	– $176.56	+ $168.97	= $0.93
$7^1/_4$	5/15/16	+ $184.87	– $110.88	– $176.56	+ $111.08	= $8.51
$7^1/_8$	2/15/23	+ $184.87	– $111.14	– $176.56	+ $108.62	= $5.79

exists a profitable swap opportunity, then the basis long owns an implied out-of-the-money call option, and if the market declines and there exists a profitable swap opportunity, then the trader owns an implied out-of-the-money put option. Both options have implied strikes at where the market must move to execute a profitable swap.

The degree to which the bonds are out of the money depends on the difference in deliverability of the bonds in the basket. If one bond is clearly the most deliverable under almost any circumstance, then both options are considerably out of the money. If the basket is tightly bunched as to profitability, and thus as to possibility of delivery, then the strikes are closer to the current market price. The aforementioned rally clearly shows that the basis long owns an out-of-the-money call option. However, notice that the $7^1/_8$ does not become the best switching candidate because the dramatic rally could not compensate for the difference in profitability to deliver the original basket. Remember that the $7^1/_8$ was originally a couple of points more expensive to deliver than any other bond in that basket. Much of this was due to the fact that the $7^1/_8$ has a 7.5-year-longer maturity than the $7^1/_4$.

In the case of neither of the two strikes being touched, the basis long loses the premium or the basis. If the basis long does indeed profit from both a market decline and rally, it is, in effect, long a strangle. However, even if it is a true strangle, that is, the out-of-the-money factor is the same for both the put and the call, equal price moves both up and down are still significant because, unlike an ordinary bond strangle, the payoff can often have an asymmetric profitability profile. Therefore, one should be careful to ascertain not only the probability of yields moving to a certain level, but also the profitability once through there.

To fully understand the risk inherent in any basis position, one must not only be able to calculate the profitability of switching but also ascertain at what point the profitable switch can occur. To determine exactly how far out of the money those strike prices are, that is, how much the yield curve has to move to enable a profitable switch (assuming a parallel yield move), one has to first observe the relative dollar durations (DD) of the two issues. Dollar duration is the *dollar* value change per 100-basis-point change in yield, or approximately the present value of a basis point multiplied by 100. It is also the key to determining the profitability of switching because one should be more concerned with the *dollar* amount involved in switching than with the change as a percentage of price, which is what is measured by Macaulay's duration and modified duration.

Clearly, if two bonds are of equal maturity, the bond with the higher coupon will have the higher price. Thus, by definition, the higher coupon bond will often have the higher dollar duration. Thus, if yields decline, the higher coupon bond will jump in price more than the lower coupon bond, and on a yield rise, the lower coupon bond will lose more money. During the switching period, the implication is clear—on a rally, one can sell the higher coupon bond and, with that money, buy the lower coupon. The converse is also true: If yields rise, the higher dollar duration bond will decline in price more and thus make it cheaper to deliver.

Because the price/yield relationship is not linear for larger price moves, convexity can play a major role. Convexity, the second derivative of the price/yield function, simply implies that for equal yield movements, the price will increase more than it will decline. Thus, any formula that measures price change by simply using duration will be inaccurate for large yield shifts. Of course, this problem can be at least partially rectified by simply including convexity in the calculation. For simplicity's sake, we will assume the prices are very good approximations, and thus omit the effect of convexity.

Therefore, the formula to find the strike price of the implied option would simply equal the low and high coupons' DD multiplied by the yield shift. Obviously, only a small yield change is required to make it profitable to switch into another bond if the new bond's basis (BS) is only $^2/_{32}$ more expensive than the previous CTD. Consequently, one must also consider the two bonds' basis to determine how much the move must compensate. The following formula gives the strike price:

$$\text{Basis of high coupon} - (\Delta r \times DD_H) = \text{Basis of low coupon} - (\Delta r \times DD_L)$$

where

Δr = parallel rate change required for the two issues to be equally deliverable

This reduces to

$$BS_H - BS_L = \Delta r(DD_H - DD_L)$$

Solving for Δr,

$$\Delta r = BS_H - BS_L / DD_H - DD_L$$

The following example shows how to determine the movement required for a profitable switch. Suppose that there are only two deliverable bonds—the $11^1/_4$ percent 02/15/15, which is currently the cheapest, and the $8^1/_2$ percent 2/15/20, which is the potential switching candidate. Also assume that the futures went "off the board" at $116^{19}/_{32}$. The yield shift required to make the two issues equally deliverable is calculated as follows.

Issue	Price	Yield	Dollar Duration	CF	Basis
$11^1/_4$% 2/15/15	155.25	6.46%	16.16	1.3293	$^8/_{32}$
$8^1/_2$ 2/15/20	123.35	6.62	14.65	1.0543	$^{13+}/_{32}$

$$\Delta r = \frac{8/32 - 13.5/32}{16.16 - 14.65} = \frac{.25 - .42}{16.16 - 14.65} = -0.1125$$

Therefore, a profitable switch can be executed if yields fall more than 11.25 basis points. The further the rally, the greater will be the profit in switching and delivering the $8^1/_2$s. Also remember, however, that the larger the shift, the greater is the error due to convexity.

EXHIBIT 58-8

Calendar of Delivery Month

June 1994

Sunday	Monday	Tuesday	Wednesday	Thursday	Friday	Saturday
May 29	May 30	May 31	1	2	3	4
	First Position Day	*First Notice Day*[b]	*First Delivery Day*			
	Wildcard option	Wildcard option	Wildcard option	Wildcard option	Wildcard option	Wildcard option
Yield shift option[a]	Yield shift option	Yield shift option	Yield shift option	Yield shift option	Yield shift option	Yield shift option
5	6	7	8	9	10	11
Wildcard option	Wildcard option	Wildcard option	Wildcard option	Wildcard option	Wildcard option	Wildcard option
Yield shift option	Yield shift option	Yield shift option	Yield shift option	Yield shift option	Yield shift option	Yield shift option
12	13	14	15	16	17	18
Wildcard option	Wildcard option	Wildcard option	Wildcard option	Wildcard option	Wildcard option	Wildcard option
Yield shift option	Yield shift option	Yield shift option	Yield shift option	Yield shift option	Yield shift option	Yield shift option
19	20	21	22	23	24	25
		Last Trading Day				
Wildcard option	Wildcard option	Switching option				
Yield shift option	Yield shift option	Yield shift option	Switching option	Switching option	Switching option	Switching option
26	27	28	29	30		
		Last Position Day	*Last Notice Day*	Last		
				Delivery Date		
Switching option	Switching option	Switching option				

[a] *Yield shift option* here also encapsulates the yield spread option. It is in effect much before May 29 as it is the only option affected by a change in the overall yield environment, and this, obviously, can occur considerably before the month of June. The new-auction option is similar in that it is applicable any time before the auction of a new bond.

[b] Do not confuse the terminology. Some people refer to position day as first notice day. *First notice day* here refers to the first day the basis short can inform the CBT which bond is to be delivered.

CONCLUSION

As stated before, the value of the basis cannot be derived simply by adding all the deliverability options, because some are mutually exclusive and some are interdependent. Accurate valuation is immensely difficult because of the many parameters that must be considered. Among them are market volatility, potential change in the financing rate, time to first and last delivery dates, the shape of the yield curve, whether or not an auction will be held in the interim, yield spreads between the deliverable bonds, and how they all interact with each other. The delivery process and options for the June 1994 contract shown in Exhibit 58–8 should prove helpful in conceptualizing the sequence of events in a delivery month.

A beginning in valuing the basis through a simplified approach is to take the expected value of the futures at the different stages of the delivery process and calculate the value of the basis at each final outcome. One first has to make an assumption about whether the future distribution of bond prices is normal, lognormal, or any other shape. Then, by creating numerous scenarios of yield moves in both directions, one can observe which bond's net basis appears to be cheapest.

☺ THE BASICS OF INTEREST-RATE OPTIONS

William J. Gartland, CFA
Vice President
Bloomberg Financial Market

Nicholas C. Letica
Associate Director
Bear Stearns & Co.

As the sophistication and diversity of investors have grown, the need for derivative instruments such as options has increased accordingly. Knowledge of option strategies, once the province of a few speculators, is now necessary for everyone who wishes to maintain a competitive edge in an increasingly technical market. Moreover, the new options technology has been applied with increasing success to securities with optionlike characteristics such as callable bonds and mortgage-backed securities.

In Chapter 56, option contracts were described: exchange-traded options on physical securities, exchange-traded options on futures, and over-the-counter options. In this chapter, we will review how options work, their risk/return profiles, the basic principles of option pricing, and some common trading and portfolio strategies. A more detailed discussion of hedging strategies is provided in Chapter 60.

Throughout most of the discussion, our focus will be on options on physicals. The principles, however, are equally applicable to options on futures or futures options.

HOW OPTIONS WORK

An *option* is the right but not the obligation to buy or to sell a security at a fixed price. The right to buy is called a *call,* and the right to sell is called a *put;* a call makes money if prices rise and a put makes money if prices fall.

If the owner of an option used the option to buy or to sell the underlying security, we say that the option has been *exercised.* Because the holder is never required to exercise an option, the holder can never lose more than the purchase price of the option—an option is a limited-liability instrument.

An option on a given security can be specified by giving its strike price and its expiration date. The *strike price* is the price on the optional purchase. For example, a call with a strike price of par is the right to buy that security at par. The *expiration date* is the last date on which the option can be exercised: After that, it is worthless, even if it had value on the expiration date. If an option is allowed to expire, it is said to be *terminated*. On or before the expiration date, the option holder may decide to sell the option for its market value. This is called a *pair-off*.

Some options can be exercised at any time until expiration: They are called *American* options. On the other hand, some options can only be exercised at expiration and are called *European* options. Because it is always possible to delay the exercise of an American option until expiration, an American option is always worth at least as much as its European counterpart. In practice there are only a limited number of circumstances under which early exercise is advantageous, so the American option rarely costs significantly more than the European.

The easiest way to analyze a position in a security and options on that security is with a *profit/loss graph*. A profit/loss graph shows the change in a position's value between the *analysis date* ("now") and a *horizon date* for a range of security prices at the horizon.

Suppose a call option struck at par is bought today for 1 point. At expiration, if the security is priced below par, the option will be allowed to expire worthless; the position has lost 1 point. If the security is above par at expiration, the option will be exercised; the position has made 1 point for every point the security is above par, less the initial 1-point cost of the option. Exhibit 59–1 shows the resulting profit/loss graph.

Note that if the price of the underlying increases by 1 point, the option purchase breaks even. This happens because the value of the option at expiration is equal to the initial purchase price. A price of 101 is the breakeven price for the call: The call purchase will make money if the price of the underlying exceeds 101 at expiration.

A put is the reverse of a call. Look at Exhibit 59–2, which is the profit/loss graph of a put option struck at par bought for 1 point. At expiration, the put is worth nothing if the security's price is more than the strike price and is worth one point for every point that the security is priced below the strike price. The breakeven price for this trade is 99, so the put purchase makes money if the underlying is priced below 99 at expiration.

Put/Call Parity

A put and a call struck at the money split up the profit/loss diagram of the underlying security into two parts. Consider the position created by buying a call and selling a put such that the strike price of the two options is equal to the price of the

EXHIBIT 59-1

Long Call vs. Underlying Security Price
Call Struck at Par, at Expiration, with 1-Point Premium

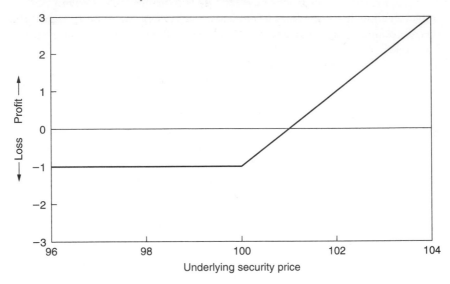

EXHIBIT 59-2

Long Put vs. Underlying Security Price
Put Struck at Par, at Expiration, with 1-Point Premium

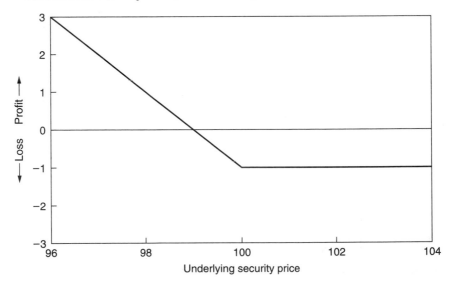

underlying. If the price of the security goes up, the call will be exercised; if the price of the security goes down, the put will be exercised. In either case, at expiration the underlying is delivered at the strike price. So in terms of profit and loss, owning the call and selling the put is the same as owning the underlying.

Exhibit 59–3 divides the profit/loss graph of the underlying security into graphs for a long call and a short put, respectively. The following three facts can be deduced.

Long security	=	Long call	+	Short put	(Exhibit 59–3)
Long call	=	Long security	+	Long put	(Exhibit 59–4)
Long put	=	Short security	+	Long call	(Exhibit 59–5)

This relationship is called *put/call parity*; it is one of the foundations of the options markets. Using these facts, a call can be created from a put by buying the underlying, or a put made from a call by selling the underlying. This ability to convert between puts and calls at will is essential to the management of an options position.

Valuing an Option

The first fact to determine about an option is its worth. There are many option valuation models for each class of options, each of which uses different parameters

E X H I B I T   59–3

Long Security = Long call + Short Put

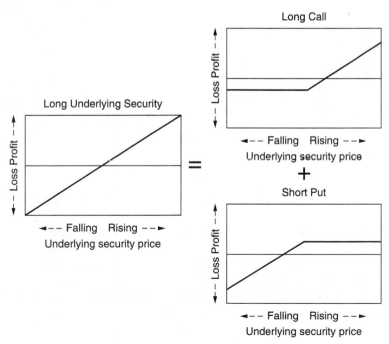

E X H I B I T   59–4

Long Call = Long Security + Long Put

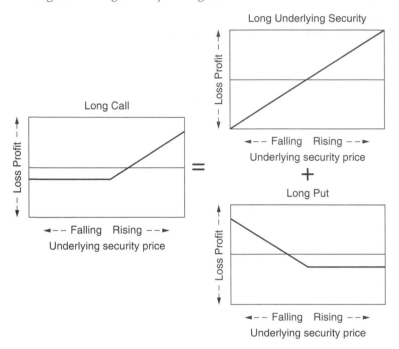

and returns slightly different values. However, the five main determinants of option value are the price of the underlying, the strike price of the option, the expiration of the option, the volatility of the underlying, and the cost of financing the underlying.

The most apparent component of option value is intrinsic value. The *intrinsic value* of an option is its value if it were exercised immediately. An option with intrinsic value is an *in-the-money* option. When the underlying security trades right at the strike price, the option is called *at the money*. Otherwise, an option with no intrinsic value is called *out of the money*.

An option has no value over and above its intrinsic value, called *time value*. The intrinsic value is the value of the option if exercised immediately, whereas the time value is the remaining value in the option due to time expiration. Clearly, the more time there is to expiration, the greater the time value.

Exhibit 59–6 graphs the value of an option as time to expiration increases. Exhibit 59–7 compares the value of an option at expiration with the values of options with one and three months to expiration. There is a sharp corner in the graph at the strike price that becomes more pronounced as the time to expiration decreases. This sharp corner makes an at-the-money option increasingly difficult to hedge as expiration approaches.

E X H I B I T 59–5

Long Put = Short Security + Long Call

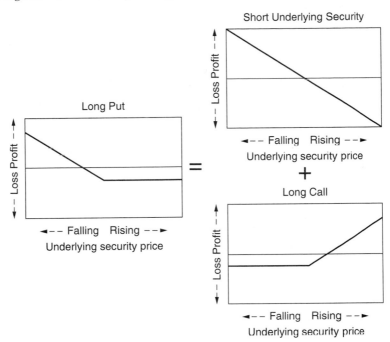

If the option is out of the money, it has some time value because there is a chance that the option will expire in the money; as it gets further out of the money, this is less likely and the time value decreases.

If the option is in the money, its time value is due to the fact that it is better to hold the option than the corresponding position in the underlying security because if the security trades out of the money the potential loss on the option is limited to the value of the option; as the option gets further in the money, this possibility becomes more farfetched and the time value decreases.

Either way, the time value depends on the probability that the security will trade through the strike price. In turn, this probability depends on how far from the strike price the security is trading and how much the security price is expected to vary until expiration.

Volatility measures the variability of the price or the yield of a security. It measures only the magnitude of the moves, not the direction. Standard option pricing models make no assumptions about the future direction of prices, but only about the distribution of these prices. Volatility is the ideal parameter for option pricing as it measures how wide this distribution will be. We discuss volatility in more detail at the end of this chapter.

EXHIBIT 59–6

Call Option Value vs. Time until Expiration
Three Calls: At the Money, 1 Point in the Money, 1 Point out of the Money

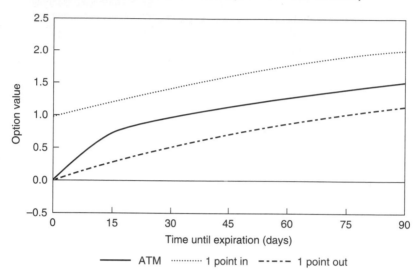

EXHIBIT 59–7

Call Option Value vs. Underlying Security Price
Call Struck at Par with 1 and 3 Months to Expiration

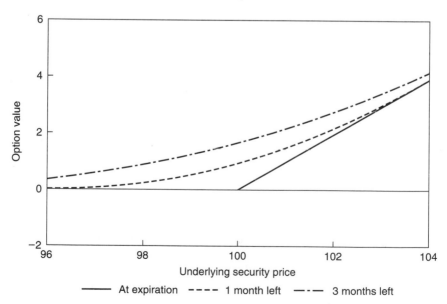

The higher the volatility of a security, the higher is the price of options on that security. If a security had no volatility, for example, that security would always have the same price at time of purchase of an option as at its expiration, so all options would be priced at their intrinsic value. Increasing the volatility of a security increases the time value of options on that security as the chance of the security price moving through the strike price increases. Increases in the value of an at-the-money option are approximately proportional to increases in the volatility of the underlying. Exhibit 59–8 shows how the price of an option behaves as the volatility of the underlying security increases.

The final factor that influences options prices is the *carry* on the underlying security. Carry is the difference between the value of the coupon payments on a security and the cost of financing that security's purchase price. With the usual upward-sloping yield curve, most securities have a positive carry.

The effect of the carry can be seen by comparing the price of an at-the-money call with an at-the-money put where the underlying security has a positive carry. The writer of the call anticipates the chance of being required to deliver the securities and thus buys the underlying as a hedge; the put writer hedges by selling the underlying. The call writer earns the carry while the put writer loses the carry, so the call should cost less than the put. When the yield curve inverts and short-term rates are higher than long-term rates, carry becomes negative and calls cost more than puts.

By put/call parity, selling an at-the-money call and buying an at-the-money put is equivalent to shorting the underlying security. The cash taken out of the

E X H I B I T   59–8

Call Option Value vs. Percent Price Volatility
Three Calls: At the Money, 1 Point in the Money, 1 Point out of the Money; Three
Months from Expiration

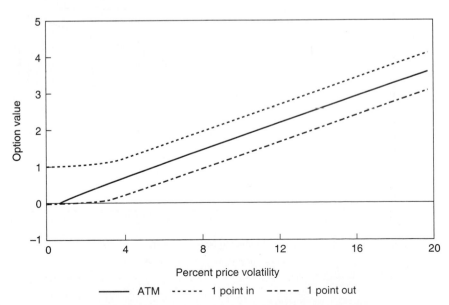

option trade, accounting for transaction costs, compensates the option holder for the carry on the position in the underlying until expiration. This trade is called a *conversion,* and it is frequently used to obtain the effect of a purchase or sale of securities when buying or selling the underlying is impossible for accounting reasons.

Exhibit 59–9 compares the cost of an at-the-money call and put for a range of financing rates. The two graphs intersect where the call and the put have the same value: This happens when the cost of financing the underlying is equal to the coupon yield on the security, so the carry is zero and there is no advantage to holding the underlying over shorting it.

Exhibit 59–10 summarizes the parameters that affect the value of an option and how much raising each parameter affects that value.

Delta, Gamma, and Theta: Hedging an Option Position

More precise quantitative ways to describe the behavior of an option are needed to manage an option position. Options traders have created the concepts of delta, gamma, and theta for this purpose. Delta measures the price sensitivity of an option, gamma the convexity of the option, and theta the change in the value of the option over time.

E X H I B I T   59–9

Treasury Option Value vs. Financing Rate
Long Call, Long Put Struck at Par, 3 Months to Expiration

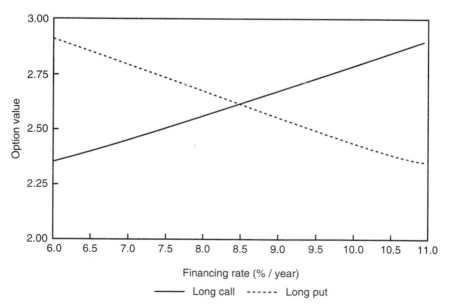

E X H I B I T   59–10

The Effect of an Increase of a Factor on Option Values

	Call	Put
Underlying price	Increase	Decrease
Strike Price	Decrease	Increase
Carry	Decrease	Increase
Time to expiration	Increase	Increase
Volatility	Increase	Increase

For a given option, the *delta* is the ratio of changes in the value of the option to changes in the value of the underlying for small changes in the underlying. A typical at-the-money call option would have a delta of 0.5; that means for a 1-cent increase in the price of the underlying the value of the call would increase by 0.5 cents. On the other hand, an at-the-money put would have a delta of –0.5; puts have negative deltas because they decrease in value as the price of the underlying increases (see Exhibit 59–10).

The standard method of hedging an options position is called *delta hedging,* which unsurprisingly makes heavy use of the delta. The idea behind delta hedging is that for small price moves, the price of an option changes in proportion with the change in price of the underlying, so the underlying can be used to hedge the option. For example, 1,000,000 calls with a delta of 0.25 would for small price movements track a position of 250,000 of the underlying bonds, so a position consisting of 1,000,000 of these long calls and 250,000 of the security sold short would be delta hedged. The total delta of a position shows how much that position is long or short. In the example above, the total delta is

$$0.25 \times 1,000,000 - 1 \times 250,000 = 0$$

so the position is neither long nor short.

Intuitively, the delta of an option is the number of bonds that are expected to be delivered into this option. For example, an at-the-money call has a delta of 0.5, which means that one bond is expected to be delivered for every two calls that are held. In other words, an at-the-money call is equally as likely to be exercised as not. An option that is deeply out of the money will have a delta that is close to 0 because there is almost no chance that the option will ever be exercised. An option that is deeply in the money will almost certainly be exercised. This means that a deeply in the money put has a delta of –1 because it is almost certain that the holder of the option will exercise the put and deliver one bond to the put writer.

Put/call parity tells us that a position in the underlying security may be duplicated by buying a call and selling a put with the same strike price and expiration date. Thus, the delta of the call less the delta of the put should be the delta of the underlying. The delta for the underlying is 1, so we get the following equation:

$$\text{delta}(call) - \text{delta}(put) = 1$$

where call and put are options on the same security with the same strike price and expiration date. This says that once the call is bought and the put sold, the bond is certain to be delivered; if the call is out of the money, the put is in the money. Moreover, as the chance of having the underlying delivered into the call becomes smaller, the chance of having to accept delivery as the put is exercised becomes larger. Exhibit 59–11 compares the deltas for a long and a short put.

Making the position delta neutral does not solve all hedging problems, however. This is demonstrated in Exhibit 59–12. Each of the three positions shown is delta neutral, but position 1 is clearly preferable to position 2, which is in turn better than position 3. The difference between these three positions is *convexity*. A position such as position 1 with a profit/loss graph that curves upward has a positive convexity, whereas position 3 has a graph that curves downward and thus has negative convexity.

Gamma measures convexity for options; it is the change in the delta for small changes in the price of the underlying. If a position has a positive gamma, then as the market goes up the delta of the position increases and as it declines the delta increases. Such a position becomes longer as the market trades up and

E X H I B I T   59–11

Option Delta vs. Underlying Security Price
Long Call, Short Put Struck at Par, 3 Months to Expiration

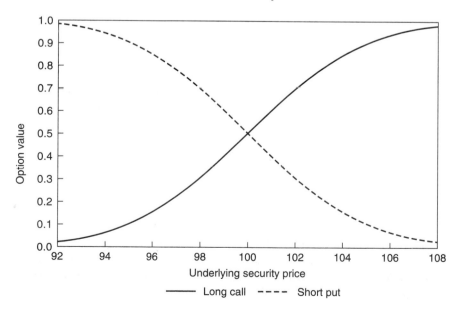

EXHIBIT 59–12

Delta-Neutral Positions with Different Gamma

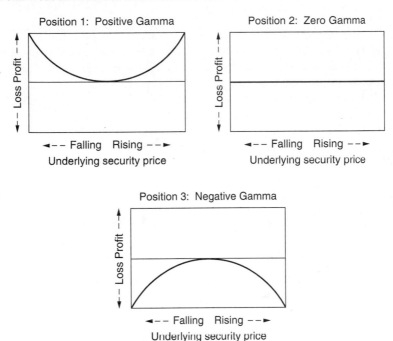

shorter as the market trades down. A position like this is called *long convexity* or *long volatility.* These names come from the fact that if the market moves in either direction this position will outperform a position with the same delta and a lower gamma. Exhibit 59–13 shows this phenomenon.

A long option always has a positive gamma. The delta of a call increases from 0 to 1 as the security trades up and the delta of a put increases also, moving from –1 to 0. Exhibits 59–1 and 59–2 show that the profit/loss graph of options curves upward. Because of this, options traders often speak of buying or selling volatility as a synonym for buying or selling options.

A position with a zero gamma is called *flat convexity* or *flat gamma.* Here, a change in the underlying security price does not change the delta of the position. Such a position trades like a position in the underlying with no options bought or sold. If the position has in addition a delta of zero, then its value is not affected by small changes in the price of the underlying security in either direction. Position 2 in Exhibit 59–12 is a profit/loss graph for a position with no delta or gamma.

A position with negative gamma is called *short volatility* or *short convexity.* The profit/loss curve slopes downward in either direction from the current price on the underlying; thus the position gets longer as the market trades down and

E X H I B I T   59–13

Profit/Loss Diagram with Convexity
Long Security with Flat and Long Convexity

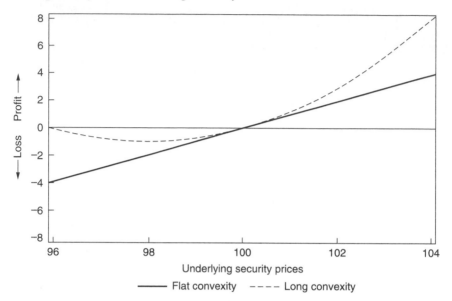

shorter as the market trades up. Either way, this position loses money if there are significant price movements. Position 3 demonstrates this behavior.

A position that is long volatility is clearly preferable to an otherwise identical position that is short volatility. The holder of the short-volatility position must be compensated for this. In order to create a position that is long volatility it is necessary to purchase options and spend money; moreover, if the market does not move, the values of the options will decrease as their time to expiration decreases, so the position loses money in a flat market.

Conversely, creating a position that is short volatility involves selling options and taking in cash. As time passes the value of these options sold decreases because their time value falls, so the position makes money in a flat market. Large losses could be sustained in a volatile market, however.

To describe the time behavior of options, there is one last measure called *theta*. The theta of an option is the overnight change in value of the option if all other parameters (prices, volatilities) stay constant. This means that a long option has a negative theta, because as expiration approaches the time value of the option will erode to zero. For example, a 90-day at-the-money call that costs 2 points might have a theta of –0.45 ticks per day.

Exhibit 59–14 shows the effects of different volatility exposures.

EXHIBIT 59–14

Comparison of Different Volatility Positions (All Positions Are Delta Neutral)

	Short Volatility	Flat Volatility	Long Volatility
Convexity	Position has negative convexity: gamma < 0	Position has no convexity: gamma = 0	Position has positive convexity: gamma > 0
Options purchased	More sold than bought	Sold as many as bought	More bought than sold
Time value	Position earns value as time passes: theta > 0	Position stays flat as time passes: theta = 0	Position loses value as time passes: theta < 0
Market moves	Position loses money if the market moves in either direction	Position is invariant with respect to market moves	Position makes money if the market moves in either direction

OPTIONS STRATEGIES—REORGANIZING THE PROFIT/LOSS GRAPH

Investors have many different goals; reducing risk, increasing rates of return, or capturing gains under expected market moves. Often, these objectives are simply to rearrange the profit/loss graph of a position in accordance with the investor's expectations or desires. By increasing the minimum value of this graph, for example, the investor reduces risk.

Options provide a precise tool to accomplish this rearrangement. Because it is impossible to replicate the performance of an option position using just the underlying, options allow a much broader range of strategies to be used. The following characteristics of options provide an explanation.

Directionality

Both a put and a call are directional instruments. A put, for example, performs only in a decreasing market. This property makes options ideal for reducing directional risk on a position. Take, for example, a position that suffers large losses in a downward market and makes a consistent profit if prices rise. By purchasing a put option, some of these profits are given up in exchange for dramatically increased performance if the market declines.

Convexity

Buying and selling options makes it possible to adjust the convexity of a position in almost any fashion. Because OTC options can be purchased for any strike price and expiration, convexity can be bought or sold at any place in the profit/loss graph. For example, an investor holding mortgage-backed securities priced just over par might anticipate that prepayments on this security would start to increase dramatically if the market traded up, attenuating possible price gains. In other words, the investor feels that the position is short convexity above the market. To adjust the profit/loss graph, calls could be purchased with strike prices at or above the market. This trade sells some of the spread over Treasuries in exchange for increased performance in a rising market.

Fee Income

An investor who wishes to increase the performance of a position in a stable market can sell convexity by writing options and taking in fees. This increases the current yield of the position, at the cost of increasing volatility risk in some area of the profit/loss graph. A typical example of this is the venerable covered call strategy, where the manager of a portfolio sells calls on a portion of the portfolio, forgoing some profits in a rising market in exchange for a greater return in a stable or decreasing market.

Leveraged Speculation

Investors with a higher risk/reward profile wish to increase their upside potential and are willing to accept a greater downside risk. In this case, options can be used as a highly leveraged position to capture windfall profits under a very specific market move. A strongly bullish investor might purchase 1-point out-of-the-money calls with 30 days to expiration for $1/2$ point. If the market traded up 2 points by expiration the option would then be worth 1 point and the investor would have doubled the initial investment; a corresponding position in the underlying would have appreciated in value by only about 2 percent. Of course, if the market did not trade up by at least 1 point the calls would expire worthless.

CLASSIC OPTION STRATEGIES

The following section gives a brief explanation of some of the simplest pure options strategies.

Straddle

The most pure convexity trade is called a *straddle*, composed of one call and one put with the same strike price. Exhibit 59–15 shows the profit/loss graph of a straddle struck at the money at expiration and with 3 months to expiration.

EXHIBIT 59-15

Profit/Loss Diagram for a Long Straddle
Struck at Par, at Expiration, and 3 Months Out

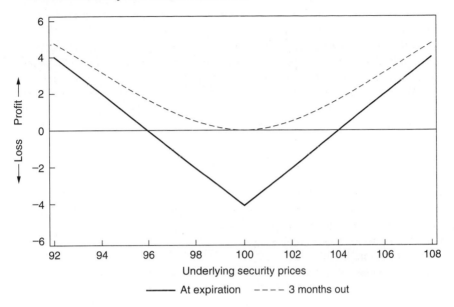

—— At expiration   – – – – 3 months out

This position is delta neutral, as it implies no market bias. If the market stays flat, the position loses money as the options' time value disappears by expiration. If the market moves in either direction, however, either the put or the call will end up in the money and the position will make money. This strategy is most useful for buying convexity at a specific strike price. Investors who are bearish on volatility and anticipate a flat market could sell straddles and make money from time value.

Strangle

A *strangle* is the more heavily leveraged cousin of a straddle. An at-the-money strangle is composed of an out-of-the-money call and an out-of-the-money put. The options are struck so that they are both equally out of the money and the current price of the security is halfway between the two strikes. The profit/loss graph is found in Exhibit 59–16.

Just like a straddle, a strangle is a pure volatility trade. If the market stays flat, the position loses time value, whereas if the market moves dramatically in either direction the position makes money from either the call or the put. Because the options in this position are both out of the money, the market has to move significantly before either option moves into the money. The options are much cheaper, however, so it is possible to buy many more options for the same money.

EXHIBIT 59–16

Profit/Loss Diagram for a Long Strangle
Struck at Par, at Expiration, and 3 Months Out

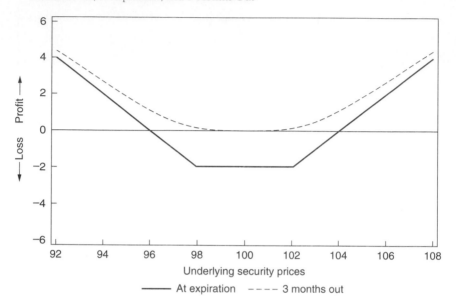

— At expiration   – – – 3 months out

This is the ideal position for the investor who is heavily bullish on volatility and wants windfall profits in a rapidly moving market.

Writing strangles is a very risky business. Most of the time the market will not move enough to put either option much into the money and the writer of the strangle will make the fee income. Occasionally, however, the market will plummet or spike and the writer of the strangle will suffer catastrophic losses. This accounts for the picturesque name of this trade.

Spread Trades

Spread trades involve buying one option and funding all or part of this purchase by selling another. A *bull spread* can be created by owning the underlying security, buying a put struck below the current price, and selling a call above the current price. Because both options are out of the money, it is possible to arrange the strikes so that the cost of the put is equal to the fee for the call. If the security price falls below the put strike or rises above the call strike, the appropriate option will be exercised and the security will be sold. Otherwise, any profit or loss will just be that of the underlying security. In other words, this position is analogous to owning the underlying security except that the final value of the position at expiration is forced to be between the two strikes. Exhibit 59–17 shows the profit/loss graph of this position at expiration and with three months left of time value.

E X H I B I T   59–17

Profit/Loss Diagram for a Bull Spread
Struck at Par, at Expiration, and 3 Months Out

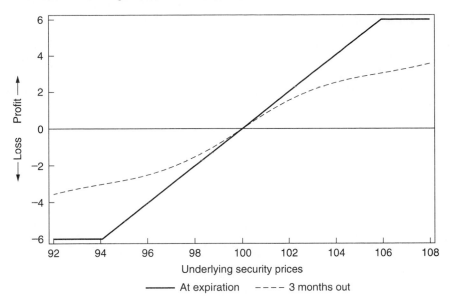

The other spread trade is a *bear spread:* It is the reverse of a bull spread. It can be created by selling a bull spread. Using put/call parity, it can also be set up by holding the underlying security, buying an in-the-money put, and selling an in-the-money call. A bear spread is equivalent to a short position in the underlying, where the position must be closed out at a price between the two strike prices. Exhibit 59–18 shows the profit/loss graph of a bear spread.

PRACTICAL PORTFOLIO STRATEGIES

The strategies discussed in the previous section are the basic techniques used by speculators to trade options. The usual fixed income investor has a lower risk/reward profile than the speculator and specific objectives that must be accomplished; a floor on rate of return or an increase in current yield, for example. Such investors need a class of strategies different from that needed by speculators; even though the same strategies are often used, the risk is carefully controlled.

Portfolio Insurance

This is the most obvious and one of the most commonly used options strategies. An investor with a portfolio of securities who fears a decreasing market buys puts on some or all of the portfolio; if the market falls, the puts are exercised, and the

E X H I B I T   59–18

Profit/Loss Diagram for a Bear Spread
Struck at Par, at Expiration, and 3 Months Out

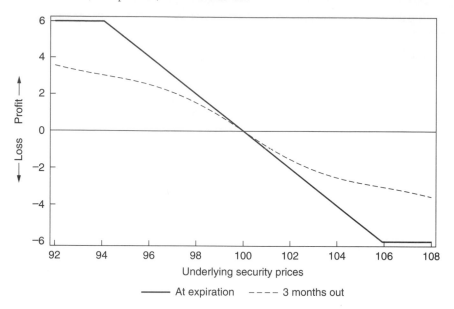

securities are sold at the strike price. Alternatively, the investor may keep the underlying security and pair off the in-the-money puts, receiving cash in compensation for the decreased value of the security. Either way, the investor has limited losses on the portfolio in exchange for selling off return in a stable or rising market.

As the strike price of the put increases, so does its cost and the resultant impact on the stable market rate of return. Often, out-of-the-money options are used; the floor on returns is lower because the strike price is lower, but the lower cost of the options means that less return is given up if the market is flat or rises. By put/call parity, such a position is equivalent to holding a call option struck at or in the money.

Another popular strategy is to buy at-the-money options on a portion of the portfolio. This reduces but does not eliminate downside risk: Exhibit 59–19 shows the profit/loss graphs at expiration for positions with different percentages of the portfolio hedged with an at-the-money put. Note that all the graphs intersect at a single point. This is the point where the initial cost of the option is equal to the value of the option at expiration, which is the breakeven price for this trade.

It is not possible to buy options on many classes of securities that may well be held in a portfolio. Perfect insurance for such securities is unattainable, but cross-market hedging will often permit a reduction in downside risk to acceptable levels. This is discussed further in Chapter 60.

EXHIBIT 59–19

Hedged Underlying Security with Puts
Long Puts Struck at Par, at Expiration

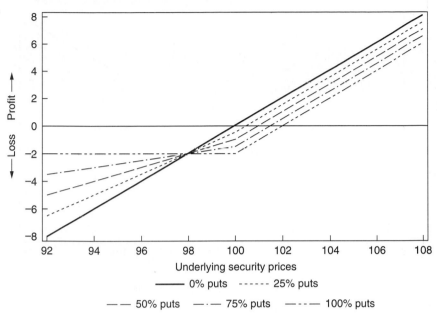

Covered Calls

Writing covered calls is a strategy that sells volatility in return for fees. An investor who holds a portfolio sells calls on some or all of the portfolio in return for fees. If the market stays the same or falls, the investor pockets the option fees. If the market increases until the calls are in the money, the investor is called out by the option holder. In other words, possible gains on the portfolio are sold for fee income.

Often the investor wishes to preserve some upside potential. Just as in the portfolio insurance example, there are two different ways to do this. The calls can be struck out of the money, that is, above the current market price. This strategy allows all gains up to the strike price to be captured. If the bonds in the portfolio are currently trading below the original purchase price, a popular strategy is to sell calls struck at this purchase price. This provides fee income and increased current yield but prevents the possibility that the bonds will be called at a price below the original purchase price and the portfolio will book a capital loss.

Otherwise, calls can be sold on a portion of the portfolio. This allows unlimited price gains to be captured on the remainder. Exhibit 59–20 shows the profit/loss graph of a covered call program where different portions of the portfolio have calls sold against them.

E X H I B I T   59–20

Covered Call Writing Program
Short Calls Struck at Par, at Expiration

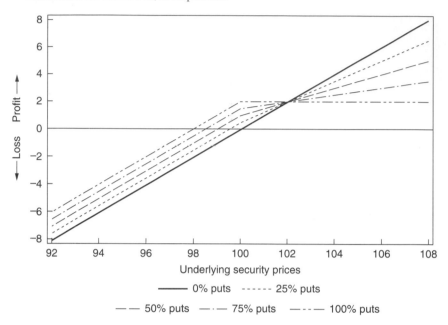

---- 0% puts   - - - - - - 25% puts

— — 50% puts   — · — 75% puts   — - - — 100% puts

Buy-Writes and Writing Puts

Buy-writes and writing puts are two very closely related strategies for selling volatility that most investors think of as entirely different. To execute a buy-write, a bond is purchased, and simultaneously a call is written on this bond to the same dealer for the fee income. If the security is trading above the strike price at expiration, the security is called and the investor is left with just the option fee. If the price of the security has fallen, the investor is left holding the security but the total cost of the security is reduced by the fee from the call. By put/call parity, this trade is identical to writing a put struck at the money. In both cases, the investor is delivered the security only if the price of the security is lower than the price of the original sale.

In the MBS market, a buy-write is composed of forward purchases and short calls on forward delivery contracts (standard TBA transactions). If the call is exercised, it offsets the forward sale and the buyer never takes delivery of the security, keeping the fee income. Otherwise, the buyer will receive the security on the forward settlement date for the original forward sale price, although the total price is decreased by the value of the option fee.

Put writing is a more general strategy that applies to all fixed income options markets. The investor writes a put fee for the income and receives the underlying instrument at expiration if the security trades below the strike price. This can be a very effective strategy if carefully structured. An investor may feel that a security offers real value if bought at a certain price below the market. The investor could then write puts struck at that price. If the security falls below the strike, it is delivered at a price that is more agreeable than the current price. Otherwise, the investor simply pockets the fee income.

Volatility

Volatility plays a key role in the valuation of options and in option strategies. In this section, we focus on methods for estimating volatility.

Statistically, volatility is a measure of the dispersion or spread of observations around the mean of the set of observations. If volatility seems strangely like a standard deviation, then you remember your statistics. When people speak of volatility, all they really are talking about is a standard deviation.

For fixed income securities, volatility is expressed in yield or price units, either on a percentage or on an absolute basis. Price volatilities can be computed for any security. Yield volatilities should be computed only for those securities with a consistent method for computing yield. Given the complexity of calculating a yield on a MBS and the variation of results, the predominant volatility measure in the MBS market is price volatility. The government bond market, where yields are easily calculated, favors yield volatility.

There are two types of volatility: empirical volatility and implied volatility. Each is described below.

Empirical Volatility

Empirical volatility is the actual, historical market volatility of a specific security. These numbers are typically calculated for various time periods (10 days, 30 days, 360 days) and are usually annualized.[1] Calculating an empirical volatility is nothing more than calculating the standard deviation of a time series. Thus, an absolute volatility is the annualized standard deviation of daily price or yield changes, assuming a normal distribution.

Percentage volatility is the annualized standard deviation of the daily change in the log of prices or yields, assuming a lognormal distribution of prices or yields. Similar to the daily absolute yield changes, the logs of the daily yield changes have a slight bias toward lower yields. The intuitive approach to calculating a percentage volatility is to find the standard deviation of daily *returns,* assuming a normal

---

1. When annualizing a volatility, certain assumptions are inherent to the calculation. To convert from daily to yearly volatility, for example, the daily volatility is multiplied by the square root of the number of business days in the year, approximately 250.

distribution. This approach is equivalent to the lognormal assumption as long as the distribution can be characterized as being equally normal and lognormal and the changes in prices are taken on a small interval, such as daily.

As previously mentioned, empirical volatility can be measured over various time periods. The most common interval on which the standard deviation is taken is 30 days; other common intervals are 10 days and 360 days. The choice of interval determines how quickly and to what degree an empirical volatility responds to deviations. As the time period shortens, volatility increasingly reflects current conditions but is more unstable as each sample asserts greater influence in the deviation. Conversely, as the interval increases, more of a lag and a smoothing are introduced into the calculation.

The interval used to calculate an empirical volatility should be chosen to match the length of the option contract. This provides the investor with an indication of how volatile the underlying security has been recently and how this relates to the volatility employed to price the option.

With no industry standard for volatility units, converting between the price and yield expression of absolute or percentage volatility is a useful skill. The path to follow to convert from one unit to the next is shown in Exhibit 59–21. The modified duration of a security provides the link between price and yield volatilities. Modified duration is defined as the percentage change in price divided by the absolute change in yield.

Implied Volatility

Implied volatility is merely the market's expectation of future volatility over a specified time period. An option's price is a function of the volatility employed, so where an option's price is known the implied volatility can be derived. Although it sounds straightforward, calculating an implied volatility is far more complicated than calculating an empirical volatility, because expectations cannot be observed directly. An option pricing model along with a mathematical method to infer the volatility must be employed. The result of this calculation is a percentage price volatility that can be converted to the various types of volatility measures discussed previously (see Exhibit 59–21).

Owing to the existence and liquidity of fixed income options, proxies for implied volatilities can be derived from Treasuries. Options on Treasury futures listed on the Chicago Board of Trade (CBT) are often the best vehicles for implied volatility calculations. Of these, the bond contract provides the best information necessary to calculate an implied volatility. The resultant implied volatility provides a good indication of the market's expected volatility for the Treasuries with maturities similar to that of the particular bond futures contract in question. The implied volatility on the 20-year bond future contract, for example, is a useful proxy for the market's expected volatility on long-term Treasury securities.

Exhibit 59–22 shows implied percentage prices and absolute yield volatilities for calls and puts on the bond futures contract of March 1990 over a range of

EXHIBIT 59–21

Converting Volatility Measures

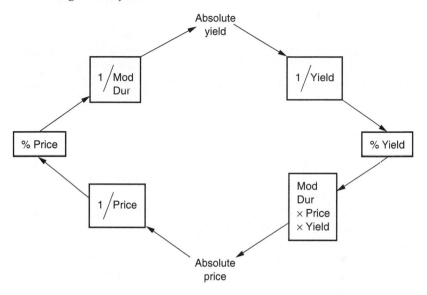

EXHIBIT 59–22

Implied Volatilities for Options on Bond Futures
(Based on Closing Prices for January 18, 1990)

March 1990 Bond Contract Closing @ 95 $^8/_{32}$ (Modified Duration = 8.61)				
	Strike Price[a]			
	92	**94**	**96**	**98**
Closing call option price	3:21	1:45	0:38	0:12
Closing put option price	0:07	0:27	1:21	2:59
	Percentage Price Volatilities			
Implied call volatility	9.28	9.34	8.90	9.82
Implied put volatility	9.71	8.94	8.78	9.76
	Absolute Yield Volatilities			
Implied call volatility	108	109	103	114
Implied put volatility	113	104	102	113

[a] Option prices are quoted in points and 64ths (i.e., 3:21 = 3.00 + $^{21}/_{64}$).

Sample Calculation of Converting from Percentage Price Volatility to Absolute Yield Volatility for Bond Futures Calls Struck at 92

$$\text{Modified duration} = \frac{\text{\% Change in price}}{100 \text{ bp change in yield}} \qquad (59\text{–}1)$$

$$\text{Absolute yield volatility} = \text{Percentage price volatility} \times \frac{1}{\text{Modified duration}} \times 100.00 \qquad (59\text{–}2)$$

$$\text{Absolute yield volatility} = 9.28 \times \frac{1}{8.61} \times 100 = 107.8 \text{ basis points} \qquad (59\text{–}3)$$

strike prices. Exhibit 59–23 provides a specific example of how an implied percentage price volatility can be converted into an implied absolute yield volatility (from Exhibit 59–22). In particular, the absolute yield volatility for calls on the March 1990 bond contract with a strike price of 92 is derived from this option contract's percentage price volatility.

CONCLUSION

Options are no longer merely toys for speculators and dealers. Any investor with specific goals can use option strategies to tailor the performance of a portfolio. Because it is impossible to obtain the effects of options by using only the underlying securities, a whole new universe of strategic possibilities is opened up. In particular, investors with contingent liabilities cannot create an adequate hedge without the use of options.

Increased liquidity in the options markets and a better understanding of the properties of options make option strategies more accessible to the average investor and allow these strategies to be used for a wider range of securities. In particular, the over-the-counter options markets allow the purchase and sale of options with any desired strike price and expiration date.

In the future, options and option valuation technology will be used increasingly often for cross-market arbitrage trades where securities and options in one market will be used to duplicate securities in another. As options trading removes the arbitrages, the relationships between the various markets will become reinforced.

⑥   # HEDGING WITH FUTURES AND OPTIONS

Mark Pitts, Ph.D.
Principal
White Oak Capital Management Corp.

Frank J. Fabozzi, Ph.D., CFA, CPA
Adjunct Professor of Finance
School of Management
Yale University

This chapter addresses a primary concern of many portfolio managers: how the futures and options markets can be used to hedge fixed income portfolios.

We begin by discussing the prerequisites for creating an effective hedge. We then show how to derive the hedge ratio and the target rate, or price, for a hedge. For each case that we cover, examples demonstrate the performance of hedging strategies under various scenarios.

HEDGING WITH FUTURES

The Preliminaries

Before a hedge is ever initiated, there are several steps that the prudent manager should take in order to be completely comfortable with the hedging process. By taking these steps before the hedge is set, the potential hedger gains an understanding of what a hedge can and cannot accomplish and ensures that, if the hedge is set, it is set in the proper manner. Briefly, the preliminary steps are as follows:

1. Determine which futures contract is the most appropriate hedging vehicle.

2. Determine the target for the hedge, that is, the effective rate or price most likely to result from the hedge.

3. Estimate the effectiveness of the hedge, that is, the risk of a hedged position relative to an unhedged position.

4. Estimate the absolute (as opposed to relative) risk of the hedged position.

5. Determine the proper hedge ratio, that is, the number of futures contracts needed to hedge the underlying risk.

A primary factor in determining which futures contract will provide the best hedge is the degree of correlation between the rate on the futures contract and the interest rate that creates an unwanted underlying risk. For example, it is preferable to hedge a long-term corporate bond portfolio with Treasury bond (T-bond) futures than with Treasury bill (T-bill) futures, because long-term corporate bond rates are more highly correlated with T-bond rates than with T-bill rates. Similarly, an anticipated sale of short-term liabilities tied to the T-bill rate would generally be more effectively hedged using T-bill futures than Eurodollar time deposit futures. Using the right delivery month is also important. A manager trying to lock in a rate or price for June should use June futures contracts because June contracts would give the highest degree of correlation. Correlation is not, however, the only consideration if the hedging program is of significant size. If, for example, a manager wanted to hedge $500 million of short-term liabilities in a distant delivery month, liquidity in the futures market would be an important consideration. In such a case, it might be necessary to spread the hedge across two or more different contracts. Consequently, a hedger of liabilities tied to the T-bill rate might hedge by selling some T-bill futures and some Eurodollar time deposit futures, eventually rolling the position entirely into T-bill futures.

Having determined the right contract and the right delivery months, the risk manager should then determine what is expected of the hedge. Obviously, if this *target rate* is too high (if hedging a sale) or too low (if hedging a purchase), hedging is perhaps not the right strategy for dealing with unwanted risk. Determining what to expect (i.e., calculating the target rate for a hedge) is not always simple. This chapter explains how the risk manager should approach this problem for both simple and complex hedges.

Hedge effectiveness tells the risk manager what percentage of risk is eliminated by hedging. Thus, if the hedge is determined to be 90 percent effective, over the long run a hedged position will have only 10 percent of the risk (that is, standard deviation) of an unhedged position. However, for any particular hedge, the hedged position can have more variation than the unhedged position.

The *residual hedging risk*—the absolute level of risk in the hedged position—tells us how much risk remains after hedging. Although it may be comforting to know, for example, that 90 percent of the risk is eliminated by hedging, without additional statistics the hedger still does not know how much risk remains. The residual risk in a hedged position is expressed most conveniently as a standard deviation. For example, it might be determined that the hedged position has a standard deviation of 15 basis points. Assuming a normal distribution of hedging errors, the hedger will then obtain the target rate plus or minus 15 basis points two times out of three. The probability of obtaining the target rate plus or minus 30 basis points is 95 percent, and the probability of obtaining the target rate plus or minus 45 basis points is greater than 99 percent.

The target rate, the hedge effectiveness, and the residual hedging risk determine the basic trade-off between risk and expected return. Consequently, these statistics give the risk manager facts essential to making a decision with regard to hedging. Using these figures, he or she can construct confidence intervals for hedged and unhedged positions. Comparing these confidence intervals, he or she can then determine whether hedging is the best alternative. Furthermore, if hedging is the right decision, the level of confidence in the hedge is defined in advance.

The risk manager should also be aware that the effectiveness of a hedge and the residual hedging risk are not necessarily constant from one hedge to the next. Hedges for dates near a futures delivery date will tend to be more effective and have less residual risk than those lifted on other dates. The life of the hedge, that is, the amount of time between when the hedge is set and when it is lifted, also generally has a significant impact on hedge effectiveness and residual hedging risk. For example, a hedge held for six months might be 90 percent effective, whereas a hedge held for one month might be only 25 percent effective. This is because the security to be hedged and the hedging instrument might be highly correlated over the long run, but only weakly correlated over the short run. On the other hand, residual hedging risk usually increases as the life of the hedge increases. The residual risk on a six-month hedge may be 85 basis points, whereas the residual risk for a one-month hedge may be only 35 basis points. It may seem surprising that it is possible for the longer hedges to have more risk and also be more effective. However, hedge effectiveness is a measure of *relative* risk, and because longer time periods exhibit greater swings in interest rates, the greater percentage reduction in risk for longer hedges does not mean that there is less remaining risk.

The target rate, the residual risk, and the effectiveness of a hedge are relatively simple concepts. However, because these statistics are usually estimated using historical data, the hedger should be sure that these figures are estimated with care. Statistics can be a tricky business. Well-intentioned amateurs and not-so-well-intentioned professionals have been known to produce statistics that lead to overly optimistic estimates of what a hedge can do. Consequently, the hedger should not necessarily judge the skill of a broker by how much the broker promises to accomplish with a hedge.

The final factor that must be determined before the hedge is set is the *hedge ratio*, or the number of futures contracts needed for the hedge. Usually the hedge ratio is expressed in terms of relative face amounts. Accordingly, a hedge ratio of 1.20 means that for every $1 million face value of securities to be hedged, one needs $1.2 million face value of futures contracts to offset the risk. As the following pages demonstrate, hedge ratio calculations run the gamut from trivial to esoteric.

The Hedging Principle

Hedging is one of the primary ways that managers use interest-rate futures contracts. It is difficult to state concisely the general principle that underlies futures hedging, but a one-line attempt might be as follows: Do in the futures market today what you anticipate needing (or wanting) to do on a future date. For instance, if a portfolio manager owns a long bond that he anticipates selling in six months, he hedges today by selling bond futures for delivery six months hence. If the same manager does not anticipate an actual sale but wants to hedge the value of the bond six months forward, then he would, in a sense, like to sell the bond (as evidenced by the fact that he no longer wants the volatility of a long bond position) but is constrained from doing so. His course of action should be the same; he sells bond futures to hedge his position.

Similarly, an asset manager can use futures to hedge the rate at which anticipated cash flows will be invested. A manager expecting a cash inflow in one year might plan to buy long bonds when the cash is available, but she would like to hedge the rate at which that investment will be made. Anticipating a future purchase of bonds, the manager could hedge by buying bonds in the futures market today. If, on the other hand, the manager planned to invest the cash in short-term securities, she would hedge by buying short-term debt futures instead of bond futures.

Liability managers can apply the same hedging principle. The liability manager who funds operations by continually rolling over short-term debt faces substantial interest-rate risk arising from the uncertainty of future rate levels. Because the manager anticipates having to sell new short-term debt in the future, a proper hedge would be to sell futures on short-term debt.[1]

The liability manager who plans to sell long-term debt to fund operations faces the risk that long-term rates will rise before the anticipated bond issuance. To hedge, the liability manager will enter into a trade in the futures market to mirror the trade anticipated for a future date. The manager thus sells futures on long-term debt to hedge the subsequent sale of long-term debt.

Some managers are responsible for both the asset and liability side of the balance sheet. Frequently, one side of the balance sheet is more sensitive to interest-rate fluctuations than the other and managers find themselves managing an interest-rate gap. Usually, this occurs because the assets are of much longer maturities than the liabilities. Consequently, as interest rates rise, interest expense increases while interest income stays constant. To make matters worse, as rates rise long-term assets fall below their purchase price. Because a sale of assets would then result in realized losses, managers often have few choices for correcting the imbalance.

Asset and liability managers can, however, control this exposure by combining the techniques used by asset managers and the techniques used by liability managers. Instead of reducing the interest-rate sensitivity of their assets by trading into shorter maturity securities (and booking a loss), the managers can sell intermediate- or long-term debt futures and accomplish the same end. Alternatively (or concurrently), the managers can increase the interest-rate sensitivity of

---

1. A manager who funds with floating-rate debt does not actually roll over short-term debt, but his or her interest-rate expense is determined by future short-term rates. Consequently, the best hedge will also be to sell short-term debt futures.

their liabilities by lengthening their effective maturity. This is accomplished by selling short-term debt futures.

In each of the foregoing examples, the risk managers follow essentially the same rule. Whatever action they expect or want to take but are constrained from taking in the cash market, they take instead in the futures market. At the risk of oversimplification, this rule can be followed by most, if not all, asset and liability managers.

Risk and Expected Return in a Hedge

When one enters into a hedge, the objective is to "lock in" a rate for the sale or purchase of a security. However, there is much disagreement about what rate or price a hedger should expect to lock in when futures are used to hedge. One view is that the hedger should, on average, lock in the current spot rate for the security. The opposing view is that the hedger should, on average, lock in the rate at which the futures contracts are bought or sold. As it turns out, the right answer usually lies somewhere in between these two positions. However, as the following examples illustrate, each view is entirely correct in certain situations.

The Target for Hedges Held to Delivery

Risk-minimizing hedges that are held until the futures delivery date provide examples of hedges that lock in the futures rate of interest. A hedge with T-bill futures contracts is the most straightforward illustration of this. Suppose an investor buys a $1 million six-month T-bill at 8.5 percent and expects to sell it three months hence, at which time the bill will have three months of remaining life. To hedge this sale, the investor sells one $1 million three-month T-bill contract for delivery in three months. Suppose further that when the hedge is set, spot three-month bills are at 8.18 percent and three-month T-bill futures are at 9 percent. What rate does the hedger lock in for the sale of the T-bill three months hence (i.e., on the futures delivery date)?

The process of *convergence* guarantees that the hedger locks in 9 percent (the futures rate) for his sale, while the spot rates of 8.18 percent and 8.5 percent are all but irrelevant. Convergence refers to the fact that at delivery there can be no discrepancy between the spot and futures price for a given security (or commodity).[2] If the futures price were higher than the spot price, an investor could buy in the cash market, immediately sell in the futures market, and take out money at no risk. If the futures price were lower than the spot price, an investor could buy in the futures market and immediately sell in the cash market, again taking out cash at no risk. Thus, arbitrage between the cash and futures market forces the cash and futures prices to converge on the delivery date.

To see how convergence guarantees the hedger a price equal to the futures price on the day the hedge is set, consider the cash flows associated with a T-bill

---

2. In the case of more than one deliverable, this is true only for the one cheapest to deliver.

contract sold at 9 percent (quoted as 91.00). For each basis-point increase in the futures rate above 9 percent (or .01 decrease in the quoted futures price below 91.00), the investor receives a margin inflow of $25. Now, if the investor targets 9 percent as the expected sale rate for the T-bill (which will then have three months to maturity), every basis point above 9 percent at which the investor sells the T-bill will cost him exactly $25 (from $1,000,000 × .0001 × 90/360). Thus, ignoring transaction costs, any shortfall relative to the targeted rate is exactly offset by gains on the futures contract. Conversely, if the hedger is able to sell the T-bill at a price higher (or yield lower) than the target, losses on the futures contract offset any windfall the hedger experiences in the cash market. This guarantees that the investor does no worse and no better than the target.[3]

The Eurodollar time deposit futures work in much the same fashion as the T-bill contracts. Using the Eurodollar contract, the hedger can lock in a rate or price for an anticipated purchase or sale. If the hedge is held until delivery, the only rate that the hedger can lock in with certainty is the rate prevailing in the futures market. As the previous example shows, the rate on the securities in the cash market does not determine the rate that can be locked in.

The same principles hold true in the market for intermediate- and long-term debt, except that the hedge is a little more complicated because the hedger does not know for sure when delivery will take place or which bond will be delivered. However, for the sake of simplicity, consider the T-bond contract and assume that the hedger knows which bond will be delivered and that delivery will take place on the last day of the delivery month (which is frequently the most advantageous day to make delivery). Consider the $7^5/_8$ T-bonds maturing on February 15, 2007. For delivery on the June 1985 contract, the conversion factor for these bonds was .9660, implying that the investor who delivers the $7^5/_8$s would receive from the buyer .9660 times the futures settlement price, plus accrued interest. Consequently, at delivery, the (flat) spot price and the futures price times the conversion factor must converge. Otherwise, arbitrageurs would buy at the lower price and sell at the higher price and earn risk-free profits. Accordingly, a hedger could lock in a June sale price for the $7^5/_8$s by selling T-bond futures contracts equal to .9660 times the face value of the bonds. For example, $100 million face value of $7^5/_8$s would be hedged by selling $96.6 million face value of bond futures (966 contracts).

The sale price that the hedger locks in would be .9660 times the futures price. Thus, if the futures price is 70 when the hedge is set, the hedger locks in a sale price of 67.62 for June delivery, regardless of where rates are in June. Exhibit 60–1 shows the cash flows for a number of final prices for the $7^5/_8$s and illustrates how cash flows on the futures contracts offset gains or losses relative to the target price of 67.62. In each case, the effective sale price is very close to the target price (and,

---

3. For this to be exactly true, one must ignore the fact that net margin inflows from the futures contract can be invested over the life of the hedge, and net margin outflows must be borrowed (or paid out at an opportunity loss) over the life of the hedge.

EXHIBIT 60–1

T-Bond Hedge Held to Delivery

Instrument to be hedged: $7\,^5/_8\%$ T-bonds of 2/15/07 Conversion factor for June 1985 delivery = .9660 Price of futures contracts when sold = 70 Target price = .9660 × 70 = 67.62			
Actual Sale Price for $7\,^5/_8\%$ T-Bonds	**Final Futures Price[a]**	**Gain(Loss) on 966 Contracts ($10/.01/Contract)[b]**	**Effective Sale Price[c]**
62-0	64.182	$5,620,188	$67,620,118
63-0	65.217	4,620,378	67,620,378
64-0	66.253	3,619,602	67,619,602
65-0	67.288	2,619,792	67,619,792
66-0	68.323	1,619,982	67,619,982
67-0	69.358	620,172	67,620,172
68-0	70.393	(379,638)	67,620,362
69-0	71.429	(1,380,414)	67,619,586
70-0	72.464	(2,380,224)	67,619,776
71-0	73.499	(3,380,034)	67,619,966
72-0	74.534	(4,379,844)	67,620,156
73-0	75.569	(5,379,654)	67,620,346
74-0	76.605	(6,380,430)	67,619,570
75-0	77.640	(7,380,240)	67,619,760

[a] By convergence, must equal bond price divided by the conversion factor.
[b] Bond futures trade in even increments of 32nds. Accordingly, the futures prices and margin flows are only approximate.
[c] Transaction costs and the financing of margin flows are ignored.

in fact, would be exact if the calculations were carried through to the required decimal places). However, the target price is determined by the futures price, so the target price may be higher or lower than the cash market price when the hedge is set.

When we admit the possibility that bonds other than the $7^5/_8$s of 2007 can be delivered, and that it might be advantageous to deliver other bonds, the situation becomes somewhat more involved. In this more realistic case, the hedger may decide not to deliver the $7^5/_8$s, but if she does decide to deliver them, the hedger is still assured of receiving an effective sale price of approximately 67.62. If the hedger chooses not to deliver the $7^5/_8$s, it would be because another bond could be delivered more cheaply, and thus the hedger would be able to do better than the targeted price.

In summary, if an investor sets a *risk-minimizing* futures hedge *that is held until delivery*, he or she can be assured of receiving an effective price dictated by the *futures* rate (*not* the spot rate) on the day the hedge is set.

The Target for Hedges with Short Holding Periods

Now let us return to our original example of purchasing a $1 million, six-month T-bill at 8.5 percent. What if the investor has no intention of holding the T-bill for three months, as in the original example, but intends to sell it in the very next term, say within a day? The investor still faces the risk that rates will rise and the sale price of the T-bill will fall. To hedge this risk the investor would sell two of the nearby T-bill futures contracts, currently trading at 9 percent and calling for delivery in three months. (Two three-month T-bill contracts are required because at the time of sale the T-bill will be approximately twice as volatile as a three-month T-bill.) What rate should the hedger expect to lock in—the futures rate of 9 percent or the spot rate of 8.5 percent?

Because the hedge is lifted before delivery, the hedger can no longer be assured of locking in any particular rate, spot or future. However, the effective rate that one obtains in this example is much more likely to approximate the current spot rate of 8.5 percent interest than the futures rate of 9 percent.

The critical difference between this hedge and the example in the last section is that the hedge is not held until delivery and, therefore, convergence will generally not take place by the termination date of the hedge. In fact, because the futures delivery date is three months from the day the hedge is set and the hedge will be lifted in one day, it is much more realistic to assume that the difference between the rates on the spot six-month T-bill and the three-month T-bill future will not change over the life of the hedge, much less converge.

This example is not unique to T-bills. Whether the hedger is hedging with one of the other short-term contracts or hedging longer-term instruments with the intermediate- and long-term contracts, he should expect the hedge to lock in the spot rate rather than the futures rate for very short-lived hedges. To illustrate, returning to the simplified example in which the $7^5/_8$ percent of 2007 were the only deliverable bonds on the T-bond futures contract, suppose that the hedge is set three months before delivery date and the hedger plans to lift the hedge after one day. It is much more likely that the spot price of the bond will move parallel to the converted futures price (that is, the futures price times the conversion factor) than that the spot price and the converted futures price will converge by the time the hedge is lifted.

A one-day hedge is, admittedly, an extreme example. Other than underwriters, dealers, and traders who reallocate assets very frequently, few hedgers are interested in such a short horizon. The very-short-term hedge does, however, illustrate a very important point: The hedger should *not* expect to lock in the futures rate (or price) just because he is hedging with futures contracts. The futures rate is locked in *only if the hedge is held until delivery*, at which point convergence must take place. If the hedge is held for only one day, the hedger should expect to lock in the one-day forward rate, which will very nearly equal the spot rate. Generally hedges are held for more than one day, but not necessarily to delivery. The proper target for these cases is examined in the next two sections.

The Basis

The basis is a concept used throughout the futures markets. The *basis* is simply the difference between the spot (cash) price of a security (or commodity) and its futures price:

$$\text{Basis} = \text{Spot price} - \text{Futures price}$$

In the fixed income markets, two problems can arise when one tries to make practical use of the concept of the basis. First, the quoted futures price does not equal the price that one receives at delivery. For intermediate- and long-term contracts, the actual futures price equals the quoted futures price times the appropriate conversion factor. In the case of the short-term contracts, the quoted futures price is actually 100 minus the annualized futures interest rate. The actual invoice price must be derived using the applicable yield-to-price conventions for the instrument in question. Consequently, to be useful the basis in the fixed income markets should be defined using actual futures delivery prices rather than quoted futures prices. Thus, the price basis for fixed income securities should be redefined as follows:

$$\text{Price basis} = \text{Spot price} - \text{Futures delivery price}$$

Unfortunately, problems still arise due to the fact that fixed income securities (unlike most other securities and commodities) age over time. Thus, it is not exactly clear what is meant by the "spot price." Does spot price mean the current price of the actual instrument that can be held and delivered in satisfaction of a short position, or does it mean the current price of an instrument that currently has the characteristics called for in the futures contract? For example, when the basis is defined for a three-month T-bill contract maturing in three months, should spot price refer to the current price of a six-month T-bill, which is the instrument that will actually be deliverable on the contract (because in three months it will be a three-month T-bill), or should spot price refer to the price of the current three-month T-bill? In most cases the former definition of the spot price makes the most sense.

For hedging purposes it is also frequently useful to define the basis in terms of interest rates rather than prices. The *rate basis* is defined as follows:

$$\text{Rate basis} = \text{Spot rate} - \text{Futures rate}$$

where *spot rate* refers to the current rate on the instrument that can be held and delivered on the contract, and the *futures rate* is the interest rate corresponding to the futures delivery price of the deliverable instrument.

The rate basis is particularly useful for analyzing hedges of short-term instruments because it nets out all effects due solely to the aging process. For instance, if spot one-year T-bills and three-month T-bill futures for delivery in nine months are both trading at 12 percent, the rate basis is zero because cash (that is, the 1-year T-bill) and futures are at the same interest rate. However, a one-year

T-bill at 12 percent has a price of 88, while a three-month T-bill at 12 percent has a price of 97, giving a price basis of –9. Furthermore, because the cash security ages, a change in the price basis does not necessarily imply that there has been a change in the rate basis, or vice versa. Accordingly, the relationship between the price basis and the rate basis is not always an obvious one.

A More General Approach to the Target

Both rate and price bases are helpful in explaining the two kinds of hedges examined in the preceding sections. The first hedge was a hedge of six-month T-bills for a sale date three months in the future. By selling three-month T-bill futures for delivery in three months, the hedger was able to lock in a rate equal to the rate at which the contract was sold (9 percent in the example). The second hedge was a hedge of the same T-bill for a sale date only one day in the future. In this case, the hedger sells the same T-bill futures contract and expects to lock in a rate approximately equal to the current rate on the six-month T-bill (8.5 percent in the example). To illustrate why the two hedges are expected to lock in such different rates, we must consider the *target basis*. The target rate basis is defined as the expected rate basis on the day the hedge is lifted. In the first example, a hedge lifted on the delivery date is expected to have, and by convergence will have, a zero rate basis when the hedge is lifted. Thus, the target rate for the hedge should be the rate on the futures contract plus the expected rate basis of zero, or in other words, just the futures rate. In the latter case, one would not expect the basis to change very much in one day, so the target rate basis equals the futures rate plus the current difference between the spot and futures rate (i.e., the current spot rate).

The hedger can set the target rate for any hedge equal to the futures rate plus the target rate basis. That is,

$$\text{Target rate for hedge} = \text{Futures rate} + \text{Target rate basis}$$

The next section shows how this definition can be used to set a target for almost any hedge.

If projecting the basis in terms of price rather than yield is more manageable (as is often the case for intermediate- and long-term futures), we can work with the *target price basis* instead of the target rate basis. The target price basis is just the projected price basis for the day the hedge is to be lifted. For a deliverable security, the target for the hedge then becomes[4]

$$\text{Target price for hedge} = \text{Futures delivery price} + \text{Target price basis}$$

The idea of a target price or rate basis explains why a hedge held until the delivery date locks in a price with certainty, and other hedges do not. As is often

---

4. It should be noted that for the intermediate- and long-term instruments, the target price for the hedge does not exactly equal the price corresponding to the target rate for the hedge, or vice versa. This follows from the nonlinearity of price-to-yield functions. The expected price of a bond on a future date does *not* exactly equal the price associated with its expected yield.

said, hedging substitutes basis risk for price risk, and the examples illustrate this principle. For the hedge held to delivery, there is no uncertainty surrounding the target basis; by convergence, the basis on the day the hedge is lifted is certain to be zero. For the short-lived hedge, the basis will probably approximate the current basis when the hedge is lifted, but its actual value is not known. For hedges longer than one day but ending prior to the futures delivery date, there can be considerable risk because it is possible for the basis on the day the hedge is lifted to be anywhere within a wide range. Thus, the uncertainty surrounding the outcome of a hedge is directly related to the uncertainty surrounding the basis on the day the hedge is lifted, that is, the uncertainty surrounding the target basis.

The discussion so far has, of course, centered on two special cases, the very short-term hedge and the hedge held to delivery. Most hedges fall somewhere between these two extremes. The problem then is to define the target rate for hedges that are held for more than a few days, but are closed out prior to delivery. This is essentially a question of calculating a target basis because, as before, the target rate for the hedge should equal the futures rate plus the target basis.

To show how the target basis is used for these hedges, let us examine a simplified case in which we believe that the rate basis will decline linearly over time. The basis is thus expected to change by the same amount each day until, at delivery, the basis is zero. To show how this assumption affects the target rate for the hedge, assume that the hedger who bought six-month T-bills at 8.5 percent plans to resell the T-bills in 30 days, that is, one-third of the way between the purchase date and the futures delivery date.[5] To account for the relative volatility of five-month T-bills and three-month T-bill futures, the investor should sell 1.67 contracts per $1 million invested. In these circumstances, what rate should the hedger target if the nearby T-bill contract is selling at 9.00 percent?

The rate basis at the outset of the hedge is –.50 percent. Assuming a linear decline in the basis, after 30 days the rate basis will equal –.33 percent. The target basis for the hedge is therefore –.33 percent. Using the formula for the target rate given in the last section, we have

$$\text{Target rate for hedge} = \text{Futures rate} + \text{Target rate basis}$$
$$= 9.00\% - .33\%$$
$$= 8.67\%$$

Because the hedge is lifted closer to the day the hedge is set than to the delivery date, the target rate is closer to the spot rate of 8.5 percent than to the futures rate of 9 percent.

The actual outcome of the hedge will be determined by how closely the target rate basis approximates the actual basis on the day the hedge is lifted. However, if the projection is accurate, the target rate and price will be locked in by the hedge.

---

5. Five-month T-bills are not liquid instruments, but they do provide a good example of the hedging technique.

In the intermediate- and long-term markets it is somewhat easier (but not necessarily more accurate) to define the target for the hedge in terms of a price rather than an interest rate. Accordingly, in a hedge one might assume that the price basis, rather than the rate basis, will decline linearly over time. For example, suppose that 80 days before the assumed delivery date for the June 1985 T-bond futures contract a hedger wants to lock in a sale price for $100 million face value of $7^5/_8$s of 2007, for a sale date 20 days in the future. (To simplify, assume the $7^5/_8$s are the only deliverable bond.) The bonds may be selling at 67 in the cash market while the bond futures contract is at 68. Because the conversion factor for these bonds for the June 1985 contract was .9660, the price basis is calculated as

$$67 - (.9660 \times 68) = 67 - 65.688 = 1.312$$

If the price basis declines linearly through time, on the day the hedge is lifted the basis will equal .9840. Thus, the target basis, in terms of price rather than yield, is .9840. Using a formula similar to the earlier one, the target price for the hedge is given by

$$\text{Target price for hedge} = \text{Futures price} \times \text{Conversion factor} \\ + \text{Target price basis}$$

Or, in this example,

$$\text{Target price} = 65.688 + .984$$
$$= 66.672$$

As in the earlier example, if the actual price basis on the day the hedge is closed out equals the target price basis, and the hedger shorts the appropriate number of futures contracts (966 in this case), the effective sale price for the hedged security will, except for rounding, equal the targeted price. Exhibit 60–2 demonstrates this fact.

Basis Risk

As illustrated in the previous sections, for a given investment horizon, hedging substitutes basis risk for price risk. Thus, one trades the uncertainty of the price of the hedged security for the uncertainty of the basis. Consequently, when hedges don't produce the desired results, it is customary to place the blame on "basis risk." However, basis risk is the real culprit only if the target for the hedge is properly defined. Basis risk should refer only to the *unexpected* or *unpredictable* part of the relationship between cash and futures. The fact that this relationship changes over time does not in itself imply that there is basis risk. If, for example, the rate basis between a T-bill futures contract and the deliverable T-bill is 1 percent, we know for certain that the basis will decline to virtually 0 percent on the delivery date. Thus, with respect to delivery date, there is no basis risk. The basis will change by 1 percent, but this change is *completely predictable*, so there is no basis risk associated with the delivery date.

Basis risk, properly defined, refers only to the uncertainty associated with the target rate basis or target price basis. Accordingly, in order to correctly assess

EXHIBIT 60–2

T-Bond Hedge Held for 20 Days

> Instrument to be hedged: $7^5/_8$% T-bonds of 2/15/07
> Conversion factor = .09660
> Price of futures contracts when sold = 68
> Target price = (.9660 × 68) + .984 = 66.672

Actual Sale Price of Bonds	Futures Price When Hedge Is Closed Out[a]	Gain (Loss) on 966 Contracts ($10/.01/Contract)[b]	Effective Sale Price[c]
60-0	61.093	$6,672,162	$66,672,162
61-0	62.128	5,672,352	66,672,352
62-0	63.164	4,671,576	66,671,576
63-0	64.199	3,671,766	66,671,766
64-0	65.234	2,671,956	66,671,956
65-0	66.269	1,672,146	66,672,146
66-0	67.304	672,336	66,672,336
67-0	68.340	(328,440)	66,671,560
68-0	69.375	(1,328,250)	66,671,750
69-0	70.410	(2,328,060)	66,671,940
70-0	71.445	(3,327,870)	66,672,130
71-0	72.480	(4,327,680)	66,672,320
72-0	73.516	(5,328,456)	66,671,511

[a] By assumption, when closed out, the futures price equals (cash price − target basis) ÷ conversion factor.

[b] Bond futures trade in even 32nds. Thus, the futures prices and the gains and losses are approximate.

[c] Transaction costs and the financing of margin flows are ignored.

the risk and expected return in a hedge, it is imperative that the target basis be properly defined.

Hedges That Do Not Minimize Risk

We have, until now, taken the risk-minimizing hedge as our point of departure and assumed that it is the desired hedge. In so doing, we have ignored expected return in our desire to minimize risk. A different approach can be taken to achieve different targets (that is, different expected returns), but only at the cost of increasing risk.

An extreme example is when the hedge ratio is set equal to zero, that is, when there is no hedge. The risk is then the risk of holding an unhedged cash security, and the target is the expected price of the security on the anticipated sale date. Futures prices in this case are irrelevant.

Alternatively, it is possible to define the target and then work backward to find the hedge ratio that gives this desired target. A typical example is that of a hedger who wants the target to be the current price of the security. This is not totally unreasonable because there is frequently some hedge ratio that on average (at least, historically) offsets changes in cash prices with changes in futures prices. However, if the hedger uses a hedge ratio that makes the current price the target price, he must generally take on more risk than if he chooses a hedge ratio that equates the target price to the implied futures price.

The important point here is that both the target and the risk level depend on the hedge ratio. If the manager uses the risk-minimizing hedge ratio, the target and risk level are determined as described in earlier sections. If, on the other hand, the target is set equal to the current price, a hedge ratio can usually be found to give this result on average, but the hedge will not generally be the risk-minimizing hedge. The hedger may thus obtain a more desirable target rate for the hedge, but only by assuming incremental risk.

In subsequent sections, we will continue to assume that risk minimization is the primary concern of the hedger and set up hedges accordingly.

Cross Hedging

Previously, we defined a cross hedge in the futures market as a hedge in which the security to be hedged is not deliverable on the futures contract used in the hedge.[6] For example, an investor or issuer who wants to hedge the sale price of long-term corporate bonds might hedge with the T-bond futures contract, but because corporate bonds cannot be delivered in satisfaction of the contract, the hedge would be considered a cross hedge. Similarly, on the short end of the curve, a hedger might want to hedge a three-month rate that does not perfectly track the T-bill rate or the Eurodollar rate. A hedger might also want to hedge a rate that is of the same quality as the rate specified in one of the contracts, but that has a different maturity. For example, one must cross hedge to hedge a Treasury bond, note, or bill with a maturity that does not qualify for delivery on any futures contract. Thus, when the security to be hedged differs from the futures contract specification in terms of either quality or maturity, one is led to the cross hedge.

Conceptually, cross hedging is somewhat more complicated than hedging deliverable securities, because it involves two relationships. First, there is the relationship between the most deliverable security and the futures contract. This relationship was addressed in the foregoing sections. Secondly, there is no relationship between the security to be hedged and the most deliverable security. Practical considerations may at times lead us to shortcut this two-step relationship and focus directly on the relationship to the security to be hedged and the futures contract, thus ignoring the deliverable security altogether. However, in doing so, one runs the risk of miscalculating the target rate and the risk in the hedge. Fur-

---

6. Because there is never actual delivery on the Eurodollar time deposit contract, a cross hedge is defined as one in which the rate to be hedged does not perfectly correspond to the three-month LIBOR rate underlying the futures contract.

thermore, if the hedge does not perform as expected, the shortcut makes it difficult to tell why the hedge went awry.

The Hedge Ratio

The key to minimizing risk in a cross hedge is to choose the right hedge ratio. The
hedge ratio depends on *volatility weighting*, or weighting by relative changes in
value. The purpose of an asset hedge is to have gains or losses from a futures position to offset any difference between the target sale price and the actual sale
price of the asset. Accordingly, the hedge ratio is chosen with the intention of
matching the volatility (dollar change) of the futures contract to the volatility (i.e.,
dollar deviation from the target price) of the asset. The purpose of a liability
hedge is to use futures gains or losses to offset any discrepancy between the target
interest expense and the actual interest expense. In summary, then, the hedge ratio
is determined by the volatility of the instrument to be hedged relative to the
volatility of the hedging instrument. Consequently, the hedge ratio is given by

$$\text{Hedge ratio} = \frac{\text{Volatility of hedged security}}{\text{Volatility of hedging instrument}}$$

As the formula shows, if the instrument to be hedged is more volatile than
the hedging instrument, more of the hedging instrument will be needed.

Although it might be fairly clear why volatility is the key variable in determining the hedge ratio, "volatility" has many definitions. For hedging purposes,
however, we are concerned with volatility in absolute dollar terms.[7] To calculate
the dollar volatility of a fixed income security, one must know the precise point in
time that volatility is to be calculated (because volatility generally declines as a
security ages) and the price or yield at which to calculate volatility (because
higher yields generally lower dollar volatility for a given yield change). The relevant point in the life of the security for calculating volatility is the point at which
the hedge will be lifted. Volatility at any other point is essentially irrelevant because the goal is to lock in a price or rate only on that particular day. Similarly, the
relevant yield at which to initially calculate volatility is the target yield. Consequently, the "volatility of the hedged security" referred to in the formula is the
price value of a basis point for the security on the hedge lift date, calculated at its
current implied forward rate.

An example shows why volatility weighting leads to the correct hedge
ratio. Suppose that on April 19, 1985, an investor owned the Southern Bell $11^{3}/_{4}$
percent bonds of 2023 and sold June 1985 T-bond futures to hedge a future sale of
the bonds. Because the telephone bonds are not deliverable, the investor must
cross hedge. Suppose that (a) the Treasury $7^{5}/_{8}$s of 2007 were the most deliverable

---

7. Duration and volatility in terms of percentage change in value may be helpful in deriving the hedge
   ratio, but offsetting actual dollars is always the bottom line.

bond on the contract and that they were trading at 11.50 percent, (b) the Southern Bell bonds were at 12.40 percent, and (c) the T-bond futures were at a price of 70. To simplify, assume also that the yield spread between the two bonds remains at .90 percent and that the anticipated sale date was the last business day in June 1985.

The sale date corresponds to the final futures delivery date, so the target basis for the deliverable $7^5/_8$s is zero, by convergence. Because the conversion factor for the $7^5/_8$s for the June 1985 contract was .9660, the target price for hedging the $7^5/_8$s would be 67.62 (from $70 \times .9660$) and the target yield would be 11.789 percent (the yield at a price of 67.62). The yield on the telephone bonds is assumed to stay at .90 percent above the yield on the $7^5/_8$s, so the target yield for the Southern Bell bonds would be 12.689 percent with a corresponding price of 92.628. At these target levels, the price values of a basis point (PVBP) for the $7^5/_8$s and telephone bonds are, respectively, .056332 and .072564. As indicated earlier, all of these calculations are made using a settlement date equal to the anticipated sale date, in this case the end of June 1985. Thus, the relative price volatilities of the hedged security and the deliverable security are easily obtained from the assumed sale date and target prices.

However, in the formula for the hedge ratio we need the volatility not of the deliverable security but of the hedging instrument, that is, of the futures contract. Fortunately, knowing the volatility of the hedged security relative to the most deliverable security and the volatility of the most deliverable security relative to the futures contract, the relative volatilities that define the hedge ratio can be easily obtained as follows:

$$\text{Hedge ratio} = \frac{\text{Volatility of hedged security}}{\text{Volatility of futures contract}}$$

$$= \frac{\text{Volatility of hedged security}}{\text{Volatility of most deliverable}} \times \frac{\text{Volatility of most deliverable}}{\text{Volatility of futures contract}}$$

Or, more concisely, assuming a fixed yield spread between the security to be hedged and the most deliverable bond,

$$\text{Hedge ratio} = \frac{\text{PVBP of hedged security}}{\text{PVBP of most deliverable}} \times \frac{\text{Conversion factor}}{\text{for most deliverable}}$$

where PVBP stands for the price value of a basis point.

The hedge ratio in the example at hand is therefore approximately 1.24 (from $(.072564/.056332) \times .9660$). Exhibit 60–3 shows that if the simplifying assumptions hold, a futures hedge using the recommended hedge ratio very nearly locks in the target price for $10 million face value of the telephone bonds. (Furthermore, most of the remaining error could be eliminated by frequent adjustments to the hedge ratio to account for the fact that the price values of a basis point change as rates move up or down.)

EXHIBIT 60–3

Hedging a Nondeliverable Bond to a Delivery Date with Futures

Instrument to be hedged: Southern Bell $11^3/_4$% of 4/19/23
Hedge ratio = 1.24
Price of futures contract when sold = 70
Target price for Southern Bell bonds = 92.628

Actual Sale Price of Telephone Bonds	Yield at Sale	Yield of Treas. $7^5/_8$[a]	Price of Treas. $7^5/_8$	Futures Price[b]	Gain (Loss) on 124 Contracts ($10/.01/ Contract)	Effective Sale Price[c]
$7,600,000	15.468%	14.568%	54.590	56.511	$1,672,636	$9,272,636
7,800,000	15.072	14.172	56.167	58.144	1,470,144	9,270,144
8,000,000	14.696	13.796	57.741	59.773	1,268,148	9,268,148
8,200,000	14.338	13.438	59.313	61.401	1,066,276	9,266,276
8,400,000	13.996	13.096	60.887	63.030	864,280	9,264,280
8,600,000	13.671	12.771	62.451	64.649	663,524	9,263,524
8,800,000	13.359	12.459	64.018	66.271	462,396	9,262,396
9,000,000	13.061	12.161	65.580	67.888	261,888	9,261,888
9,200,000	12.776	11.876	67.134	69.497	62,372	9,262,372
9,400,000	12.503	11.603	68.683	71.100	(136,400)	9,263,600
9,600,000	12.240	11.340	70.233	72.705	(355,420)	9,264,580
9,800,000	11.988	11.088	71.773	74.299	(533,076)	9,266,924
10,000,000	11.745	10.845	73.312	75.892	(730,608)	9,269,392
10,200,000	11.512	10.612	74.839	77.473	(926,652)	9,273,348
10,400,000	11.287	10.387	76.364	79.052	(1,122,448)	9,277,552
10,600,000	11.070	10.170	77.884	80.625	(1,317,500)	9,282,500
10,800,000	10.861	9.961	79.394	82.188	(1,511,312)	9,288,688
11,000,000	10.659	9.759	80.899	83.746	(1,704,504)	9,295,496
11,200,000	10.463	9.563	82.403	85.303	(1,897,572)	9,302,428

[a] By assumption, the yield on the $7^5/_8$s is 90 basis points lower than the yield on the Southern Bell bond.
[b] By convergence, the futures price equals the price of the $7^5/_8$s divided by .9660 (the conversion factor).
[c] Transaction costs and the financing of margin flows are ignored.

Although the example in Exhibit 60–3 is constructed for a hedge held to the futures delivery date, the technique is equally valid for hedges lifted prior to delivery. The primary difference is that if the hedge is lifted before delivery, the target basis for the deliverable issue will not generally be zero; thus, the target will be different.

Changing Yield Spreads

Another refinement in the hedging strategy is usually necessary for hedging nondeliverable securities. This refinement concerns the assumption about the relative yield spread between the most deliverable security and the security to be hedged.

In the last section, it was assumed that the yield spread was constant over time. However, yield spreads are not constant over time and vary with the maturity of the instruments in question, the level of rates, and with many unpredictable and nonsystematic factors.

Regression analysis is a simple technique that allows the hedger to capture the relationship between yield levels and yield spreads and use it to his advantage.[8] The regression is a statistical technique that uses historical data to model the imperfect relationship between two variables. For hedging purposes, the variables are the yield on the security to be hedged and the yield on the most deliverable security. The regression equation takes the following form:

$$\begin{matrix} \text{Yield on security} \\ \text{to be hedged} \end{matrix} = a + b \times \begin{matrix} \text{Yield on most} \\ \text{deliverable security} \end{matrix} + \text{Error}$$

The regression procedure provides an estimate of b (the *yield beta*), which is the expected relative yield change in the two securities. The error term accounts for the fact that the relationship between the yields is not perfect and contains a certain amount of "noise." The regression will, however, give an estimate of a and b so that over the sample period the error is on average zero. The example in the previous section that used constant spreads implicitly assumes that the yield beta in the regression equals 1.0 and a equals .90 (because .90 was the assumed spread).

For the two issues in question, that is, the Southern Bell $11^3/_4$s and the Treasury $7^5/_8$s, the estimated yield beta over a recent period was 1.05. Thus, yields on the corporate issue are expected to move 5 percent more than yields on the Treasury issue. To calculate the relative volatility of the two issues correctly, this fact must be taken into account; thus, the hedge ratio derived in the last section is multiplied by the factor 1.05. Consequently, instead of shorting 124 T-bond futures contracts to hedge $10 million of telephone bonds, the investor would short 130 contracts.

The formula for the hedge ratio is revised as follows to incorporate the impact of the yield beta:

$$\text{Hedge ratio} = \text{Yield beta} \times \frac{\begin{matrix} \text{PVBP of the} \\ \text{hedged security} \end{matrix}}{\begin{matrix} \text{PVBP of the} \\ \text{most deliverable} \end{matrix}} \times \text{Conversion factor}$$

where beta is derived from the yield of the hedged security regressed on the yield of the most deliverable security. As before, PVBP stands for the change in price for a single basis-point change in yield, calculated at the forward prices, for settlement on the day the hedge is to be lifted.

---

8. The regression is useful for noncallable bonds and bonds that are very unlikely to be called. However, the regression will not capture the effects of a call on yield spreads. Strategies for hedging callable instruments can be found in Mark Pitts and Frank J. Fabozzi, *Interest Rate Futures and Options* (Chicago: Probus Publishing, 1990), Chapters 11 and 12.

The hedging strategy can also be applied to hedges of short-term assets or liabilities. However, there are no conversion factors for short-term futures, so the hedge ratio for the short-term contracts simplifies to

$$\text{Hedge ratio} = \text{Yield beta} \times \frac{\text{PVBP of the hedged security}}{\text{PVBP of the futures contract}}$$

Deriving the Target for a Cross Hedge

It was shown earlier that the target rate for a hedge of a deliverable security should be defined as the sum of the futures rate and the target basis. That is,

$$\text{Target rate for hedge} = \text{Futures rate} + \text{Target-rate basis}$$

The target-rate basis is determined by the projected path of the basis through time. For simplicity, a linear decline in the basis was used in the examples.

When the discussion turned to cross hedging, the relationship between the security to be hedged and the deliverable security was modeled using the regression equation:

$$\begin{array}{c}\text{Yield on security} \\ \text{to be hedged}\end{array} = a + b \times \begin{array}{c}\text{Yield on most} \\ \text{deliverable security}\end{array} + \text{Error}$$

On average, the error term is equal to zero. Combining these two equations, the target for a cross hedge is easily derived.[9]

$$\text{Target rate} = a + b \times (\text{Futures rate} + \text{Target basis})$$

Cross Hedging Summarized

A cross hedge is more complicated than a hedge of a deliverable security because the security to be hedged is not directly tied to the futures contract, even on the delivery date. However, the deliverable security and the futures contract are directly linked (at least at delivery). The cross hedger bridges the gap by estimating the relationship between the security to be hedged and the deliverable security (via the regression procedure) and estimating the relationship between the deliverable security and the futures contract (by projecting the future course of the basis). Combining these two estimates results in a forecast of the relationship between the security to be hedged and the futures contract. The combined estimates also forecast what the hedger can expect from the hedge (i.e., the target rate). Exhibit 60–4 shows these relationships schematically.

---

9. Because a regression of the deliverable security on itself would result in an intercept term equal to
   0.0 and a yield beta equal to 1.0, this formulation includes the target rate for a deliverable security as a special case. Consequently, the original formula is derived when the cross hedge formula is applied to the deliverable security. The formula is also applicable if the hedger chooses to assume the yield spread will stay constant: setting the intercept (a) equal to the assumed yield spread and b equal to 1.0, the formula will give the correct target rate for constant yield spreads.

E X H I B I T   60–4

A Schematic of the Relationships in a Cross Hedge

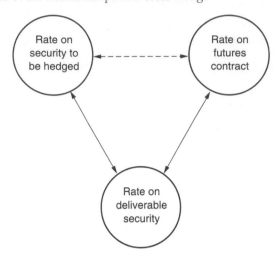

In a cross hedge it is sometimes necessary to take a shortcut by focusing on the relationship between the security to be hedged and the futures contract, leaving out the deliverable security. This relationship is the convolution of the two relationships mentioned earlier—the relationship between the security to be hedged and the deliverable security, and the relationship between the deliverable security and the futures contract. The shorter route is sometimes the only practical approach, either because data are not available for the relevant regressions or because there is a need to simplify.

HEDGING WITH OPTIONS

In this section, three of the most widely used options hedging strategies are examined. These examples show how options hedges are constructed and illustrate the basic principles of hedging with options. We also show how hedge ratios should be calculated for options hedges.

Basic Hedging Strategies

Protective Puts

Consider first an investor who has a portfolio of fixed income securities and wants to hedge against rising interest rates. The most obvious options hedging strategy is to buy puts on fixed income instruments. These *protective puts* are usually out-of-the-money puts and may be either puts on cash instruments or puts on fixed income futures. If interest rates rise, the puts will increase in value (holding other factors constant), offsetting some or all of the loss on the cash instruments in the portfolio.

This strategy is a simple combination of a long put option with a long position in a spot security. The result is a payoff pattern resembling a long position in a call option alone. Such a position has limited downside risk but large upside potential. However, if rates fall, the price appreciation on the securities in the portfolio will be diminished by the amount paid for the puts.

The protective put strategy is very often compared to purchasing insurance. Like insurance, the premium paid for the protection is nonrefundable and is paid before the coverage begins. The degree to which a portfolio is protected depends upon the strike price of the options; thus, the strike price is often compared to the deductible on an insurance policy. The lower the deductible (that is, the higher the strike on the put), the greater the level of protection and the more the protection costs. Conversely, the higher the deductible (the lower the strike on the put), the more one can lose, but the cost of the insurance is lower. No one strike price dominates any other, in the sense of performing better at all possible rate levels. Consequently, it is impossible to say that one strike price is necessarily the "best" strike price, or even that buying protective puts is necessarily better than doing nothing at all.

Covered Call Writing

Another options hedging strategy used by many portfolio managers is to sell calls against their fixed income portfolios; that is, to do *covered call writing*. The calls that are sold are usually out-of-the-money calls and can be either calls on cash securities or calls on fixed income futures. Covered call writing is just an outright long position combined with a short call position. The strategy thus results in a payoff pattern that resembles a short position in a put option alone. Obviously, this strategy entails much more downside risk than buying a put to protect the value of the portfolio. In fact, many portfolio managers do not consider covered call writing a hedge.

Regardless of how it is classified, it is important to recognize that although covered call writing has substantial downside risk, it has less downside risk than an unhedged long position alone. On the downside, the difference between the long position alone and the covered call writing strategy is the premium received for the calls that are sold. This premium acts as a cushion for downward movements in prices, reducing losses when rates rise. There is a cost associated with obtaining this cushion: The bond holder gives up some of the potential on the upside. When rates decline, the call options become greater liabilities for the covered call writer. These incremental liabilities decrease the gains the portfolio manager would otherwise have realized on the portfolio in a declining-rate environment. Thus, the covered call writer gives up some (or all) of the upside potential of the portfolio in return for a cushion on the downside. The more upside potential that is forfeited (that is, the lower the strike price on the calls), the more cushion there is on the downside. Like the protective put strategy, there is no "right" strike price for the covered call writer.

Selecting the "Best" Strategy

Comparing the two basic strategies for hedging with options—the protective put strategy and the covered call writing strategy—it is impossible to say which is necessarily the better or more correct options hedge. An individual manager's view of the market determines the best strategy (and the best strike prices). Purchasing a put and paying the required premium is appropriate if the manager is fundamentally bearish. If, on the other hand, one is neutral to mildly bearish, it is better to take in the premium on the covered call writing strategy. If a manager has no set view on the market and prefers as little risk as possible, then the futures hedge discussed earlier in this chapter is most appropriate. If the manager is fundamentally bullish, then no hedge at all is probably the best strategy.

Collars

There are, of course, many options hedging strategies used by portfolio managers. For example, many managers combine the protective put strategy and the covered call writing strategy. By combining a long position in an out-of-the-money put and a short position in an out-of-the-money call, the portfolio manager creates a long position in a *collar*. The manager who uses the collar eliminates part of the portfolio's downside risk by giving up part of its upside potential. The collar has many facets. It bears a resemblance to the protective put, covered call writing, an unhedged position, and a futures or forward hedge. The collar resembles the protective put strategy in that it limits the possible losses on the portfolio if interest rates go up. It resembles the covered call writing strategy in that the portfolio's upside potential is limited. It resembles an unhedged position in that the value of the portfolio varies with interest rates, within the range defined by the strike. On the other hand, if the put strike price and the call strike price are both equal to the forward price, the collar resembles a forward hedge in that the effective sale price is not dependent upon interest rates.

Options Hedging Preliminaries

In a manner comparable to the strategies used by the futures hedgers, there are certain preliminaries that options hedgers should consider before setting their hedges. The options hedging preliminaries include these steps:

1. Determine the options contract that is the best hedging vehicle.
2. Find the appropriate strike price. For a cross hedge, the hedger will want to convert the strike price on the options that are actually bought or sold into an equivalent strike price for the actual securities being hedged.
3. Estimate the relative and absolute risk in the hedge (not necessarily a simple matter for a cross hedge).
4. Determine the hedge ratio, that is, the number of options to buy or sell. (If not a cross hedge, the hedge ratio will usually be 1.0.)

The best options contract to use (item 1 above) depends upon several factors. These include price, liquidity, and correlation with the instrument(s) to be hedged. In imperfect markets, price is important because all options will not be priced in the same manner or with the same volatility assumption. Consequently, some options may be overpriced and some underpriced. Obviously, other factors being equal, it is better to use the underpriced options when buying and the overpriced options when selling. Whenever there is a possibility that the option position may be closed out prior to expiration, liquidity is an important consideration. If the particular option is illiquid, closing out a position may be prohibitively expensive, and the manager loses the flexibility of closing out positions early, or rolling into other positions that may become more attractive. Correlation with the underlying instrument(s) to be hedged is another factor in selecting the right contract. The higher the correlation, the more precisely the final profit and loss can be defined as a function of the final level of rates. Poor correlation leads to more uncertainty.

While most of the uncertainty in an options hedge usually comes from the uncertainty of interest rates themselves, slippage between the securities to be hedged and the instruments underlying the options contracts adds to that risk. Thus, the degree of correlation between the two underlying instruments is one of the determinants of the risk in the hedge.

The two remaining items in the list of preliminaries, determining the hedge ratio and the strike price, can best be explained with examples. Thus, the balance of this chapter is devoted to examples of options hedges. Our focus will be on hedging a long-term bond position with futures options.

Hedging with Puts on Futures

Investors in corporate and government notes and bonds often want to hedge their positions against a possible increase in interest rates. Buying puts on futures is one of the easiest ways to purchase protection against rising rates. To illustrate the strategy of buying puts on futures in order to guard against rising interest rates, we can use the utility bond example used earlier in this chapter. (The strategy for hedging Treasury bonds is similar.) In that example, an investor held $11^3/_4$ percent bonds of 2023 and used futures to lock in a sale price for those bonds on a futures delivery date. At this point we want to show how the hedger could have used futures options instead of futures to protect against rising rates.

In the example, rates were already high; the hedged bonds were selling at a yield of 12.40 percent and the Treasury $7^5/_8$ percent of 2007 (the most deliverable bond at the time) were at 11.50 percent. For simplicity, we assumed that the yield spread would remain at 90 basis points. In terms of a yield regression, this would be equivalent to a regression in which the beta equals 1.0 and the intercept term is 0.90 percent.

From Exhibit 60–3, we can see that the current price on the bonds to be hedged is roughly equivalent to a futures price of 71–24. Thus, if the hedger wants to buy out-of-the-money puts, a futures strike price of, say, 66 might be appropriate. To see what a futures price of 66 translates into in terms of yield and price for the hedged bonds, we have to work through the most deliverable bond. Exhibit 60–5 illustrates this process schematically. We start with the 66 strike price for the options. Using the conversion factor of 0.9660 for the most deliverable bond (the $7^5/_8$ percent of 2007), and assuming complete convergence, a futures price of 66 implies a price of 63.756 and a yield of 12.51 percent for the Treasury $7^5/_8$ percent interest bonds.[10] Having assumed a constant yield spread of 0.90 percent between the most deliverable bond and the hedged bonds, we arrive at an equivalent yield of 13.41 percent for the bonds to be hedged. A yield of 13.41 percent for these bonds corresponds to a price of 87.668. Consequently, buying a T-bond futures option struck at 66 is roughly equivalent to buying an option struck at 87.668 on the bonds that we want to hedge.

As explained earlier in this chapter, the futures (and futures options) hedge ratio is derived from the following formula:

$$\text{Hedge ratio} = \text{Yield beta} \times \frac{\text{PVBP of the hedged security}}{\text{PVBP of the most deliverable}} \times \text{Conversion factor}$$

Because we are assuming a constant yield spread between the security to be hedged and the most deliverable bond, the beta is set equal to 1.0. For increased accuracy, we calculate the price values of a basis point at the option expiration date (assumed for simplicity to be June 28, 1985) and at the yields corresponding to the futures strike price of 66 (12.51 percent for the most deliverable bond and 13.41 percent for the hedged bond). The respective price values of a basis point are 0.065214 and 0.050969. This results in a hedge ratio of 1.236 for the options hedge, or 1.24 with rounding.[11]

To create a table for the protective put hedge for $10 million in underlying bonds, we can use some of the numbers from Exhibit 60–3. Everything will be the same except the last two columns. For the put option hedge we must insert the value of the 124 futures put options in place of the 124 futures contracts in the next-to-last column. This is easy because the value of each option at expiration is just the strike price of the futures option (66) minus the futures price (or zero if that difference is negative), all multiplied by $1000. The effective sale price for

---

10. Options on T-bond and T-note futures expire in the month preceding the futures settlement month. Thus, complete convergence is not ensured. However, to keep the example simple and make the options and futures hedges directly comparable, we are treating the option as if it expired on the last day of the futures settlement month.

11. For an option on a cash market instrument, there is only one deliverable, so there is no conversion price. The hedge ratio is then

$$\text{Hedge ratio} = \text{Yield beta} \times \frac{\text{PVBP of the hedged security}}{\text{PVBP of the underlying security}}$$

EXHIBIT 60–5

Calculating Equivalent Prices and Yields

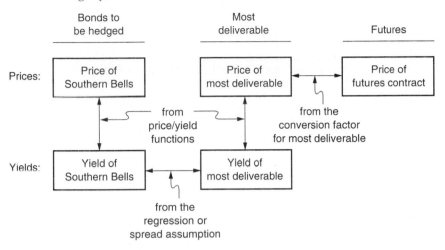

the hedged bonds is then just the actual market price on the sale date, plus the value of the options at expiration, minus the cost of the options.

A reasonable price for the 66 put options would have been in the neighborhood of $^{24}/_{64}$, or $375 per options contract. With a total of 124 options, the cost of the protection would have been $46,500 (not including financing or commissions). This cost, together with the final value of the options, is combined with the sale price for the hedged bonds to arrive at the effective sale price for the hedged bonds. These final prices are shown in the last column of Exhibit 60–6. The effective price is never less than 87.203. This equals the price of the hedged bonds equivalent to the futures strike price of 66 (i.e., 87.668), minus the cost of the puts (i.e., $0.4650 = 1.24 \times {}^{24}/_{64}$). This minimum effective price is something that can be calculated before the hedge is ever initiated. (As prices decline, the effective sale price actually exceeds the projected effective minimum sale price of 87.203 by a small amount. This is due to rounding and the fact that the hedge ratio is left unaltered although the relative price values of a basis point that go into the hedge ratio calculation do change as yields change.) As prices increase, however, the effective sale price of the hedged bonds increases as well. Unlike the futures hedge shown in Exhibit 60–3, the options hedge protects the investor if rates rise but allows the investor to profit if rates fall.

Covered Call Writing with Futures Options

Covered call writing is a strategy used by many investors. Unlike the protective put strategy, covered call writing is not used for the sole purpose of protecting a portfolio against rising rates. The covered call writer, believing that the market

EXHIBIT 60–6

Hedging a Nondeliverable Bond to a Delivery Date with Puts on Futures

Instrument to be hedged: 11³/₄% Utility Bonds of 2023				
Hedge ratio = 1.24				
Strike price for puts on futures = 66				
Target minimum price for hedged bonds = 87.203				
Actual Sale Price of Hedged Bonds	**Futures Price**[a]	**Value of 124 Put Options**[b]	**Cost of 124 Put Options**	**Effective Sale Price**[c]
$ 7,600,000	56.511	$1,176,636	$46,500	$ 8,730,136
7,800,000	58.144	974,144	46,500	8,727,644
8,000,000	59.773	772,148	46,500	8,725,648
8,200,000	61.401	570,276	46,500	8,723,776
8,400,000	63.030	368,280	46,500	8,721,780
8,600,000	64.649	167,524	46,500	8,721,024
8,800,000	66.271	0	46,500	8,753,500
9,000,000	67.888	0	46,500	8,953,500
9,200,000	69.497	0	46,500	9,153,500
9,400,000	71.100	0	46,500	9,353,500
9,600,000	72.705	0	46,500	9,553,500
9,800,000	74.299	0	46,500	9,753,500
10,000,000	75.892	0	46,500	9,953,500
10,200,000	77.473	0	46,500	10,153,500
10,400,000	79.052	0	46,500	10,353,500
10,600,000	80.625	0	46,500	10,553,500
10,800,000	82.188	0	46,500	10,753,500
11,000,000	83.746	0	46,500	10,953,500
11,200,000	85.303	0	46,500	11,153,500

[a] These numbers are approximate because futures trade in even 32nds.

[b] From 124 × $1000 × {(66 − Futures Price), 0}.

[c] Does not include transaction costs or the financing of the options position.

will not trade much higher or much lower than its present level, sells out-of-the-money calls against an existing fixed income portfolio. The sale of the calls brings in premium income that provides partial protection in the event that rates increase. The premium received does not provide the kind of protection that a long put position provides, but it does provide additional income that can be used to offset declining prices. If, on the other hand, rates fall, portfolio appreciation is limited because the short call position constitutes a liability for the seller, and this liability increases as rates go down. Consequently, there is limited upside potential for the covered call writer. Of course, this is not so bad if prices are going nowhere, in which case the added income from the sale of options is obtained without sacrificing any gains.

To see how covered call writing with futures options works for the bond used in the protective put example, we construct a table much as we did before. With futures selling around 71–24 on the hedge initiation date, a sale of a 78 call option on futures might be appropriate. As in the earlier examples, it is assumed that the hedged bond will remain at a 90-basis-point spread off the most deliverable bond, the U.S. $7^5/_8$ percent of 2007. We let the price of the 78 calls be $^{24}/_{64}$. The number of options contracts sold will be the same, namely 124 contracts for $10 million face value of underlying bonds. Exhibit 60–7 shows the results of the covered call writing strategy given these assumptions.

To calculate the effective sale price of the bonds in the covered call writing strategy, the premium received from the sale of calls is added to the actual sale price of the bonds, while the liability associated with the short call position is subtracted from the actual sale price. The liability associated with each call is the futures price minus the strike price of 78 (or zero if this difference is negative) multiplied by $1,000. The middle column in the exhibit is just this value multiplied by 124, the number of options sold.

Just as the minimum effective sale price could be calculated beforehand for the protective put strategy, the maximum effective sale price can be calculated beforehand for the covered call writing strategy. The maximum effective sale price will be the price of the hedged security corresponding to the strike price of the option sold, plus the premium received. In this case, the strike price on the futures call option was 78. A futures price of 78 corresponds to a price of 75.348 for the underlying Treasury (from 78 times the conversion factor), and a corresponding yield of 10.536 percent for the most deliverable bond, the $7^5/_8$ percent of 2007. The equivalent yield for the hedged bond is 90 basis points higher, or 11.436 percent, for a corresponding price of 102.666. Adding on the premium received, 0.465 points, the final maximum effective sale price will be about 103.131.[12] As we can see in Exhibit 60–7, if the hedged bond does trade at 90 basis points over the most deliverable bond as expected, the maximum effective sale price for the hedged bond is, in fact, slightly over 103. (The discrepancies shown in the exhibit are due to rounding and the fact that the position is not adjusted even though the relative price values of a basis point change as yields change.)

The Futures Options Collar

The final strategy that we will illustrate for futures options is the *long collar*. As explained earlier, the collar is a combination of the examples in the previous two sections. That is, to create a long collar, the bondholder would buy protective puts

---

12. As in the protective put example, we assume for simplicity that the option expires on the futures expiration date and that the most deliverable bond does not change over the life of the hedge.

EXHIBIT   60–7

Writing Calls on Futures against a Nondeliverable Bond

Instrument to be hedged: $11^3/_4$ % Utility Bonds of 2023
Hedge ratio = 1.24
Strike price for call on futures = 78
Expected maximum effective price for bonds = 103.131

Actual Sale Price of Bonds	Futures Price[a]	Liability of 124 Call Options[b]	Premium from 124 Call Options	Effective Sale Price[c]
$ 7,600,000	56.511	$ 0	$46,500	$ 7,646,500
7,800,000	58.144	0	46,500	7,846,500
8,000,000	59.773	0	46,500	8,046,500
8,200,000	61.401	0	46,500	8,246,500
8,400,000	63.030	0	46,500	8,446,500
8,600,000	64.649	0	46,500	8,646,500
8,800,000	66.271	0	46,500	8,846,500
9,000,000	67.888	0	46,500	9,046,500
9,200,000	69.497	0	46,500	9,246,500
9,400,000	71.100	0	46,500	9,446,500
9,600,000	72.705	0	46,500	9,646,500
9,800,000	74.299	0	46,500	9,846,500
10,000,000	75.892	0	46,500	10,046,500
10,200,000	77.473	0	46,500	10,246,500
10,400,000	79.052	130,448	46,500	10,316,052
10,600,000	80.625	325,500	46,500	10,321,000
10,800,000	82.188	519,312	46,500	10,327,188
11,000,000	83.746	712,504	46,500	10,333,996
11,200,000	85.303	905,572	46,500	10,340,928

a These numbers are approximate because futures trade in even 32nds.

b From 124 × $1,000 × Max{(Futures price – 78), 0}

c Does not include transaction costs or the interest earned on the options premium.

and simultaneously sell covered calls. Usually, both options are out of the money and the manager chooses the strike prices so that the premiums net out as nearly as possible. This strategy alters the risk/return profile of the bond portfolio, but it does so without any net payment or receipt of options premiums. This strategy eliminates the portfolio's downside risk by forfeiting its upside potential.

To see how the strategy works we need only combine numbers from Exhibits 60–6 and 60–7. Exhibit 60–8 shows the actual sale price of the bond to be hedged, the value of 124 long put options on futures struck at 66, and the liability

EXHIBIT   60–8

Hedging a Nondeliverable Bond to a Delivery Date with Futures Options Collars

	Instrument to be hedged: $11^3/_4$ % Utility Bonds of 2023 Hedge ratio = 1.24 Strike price for puts on futures = 66 Target minimum price for hedged bonds = 87.203 Strike price for calls on futures = 78 Expected maximum price for bonds = 103.131			
Actual Sale Price of Bonds	**Futures Price[a]**	**Value of 124 Put Options**	**Liability of 124 Call Options**	**Effective Sale Price[b]**
$ 7,600,000	56.511	$1,176,636	$ 0	$ 8,776,636
7,800,000	58.144	974,144	0	8,774,144
8,000,000	59.773	772,148	0	8,772,148
8,200,000	61.401	570,276	0	8,770,276
8,400,000	63.030	368,280	0	8,768,280
8,600,000	64.649	167,524	0	8,767,524
8,800,000	66.271	0	0	8,800,000
9,000,000	67.888	0	0	9,000,000
9,200,000	69.497	0	0	9,200,000
9,400,000	71.100	0	0	9,400,000
9,600,000	72.705	0	0	9,600,000
9,800,000	74.299	0	0	9,800,000
10,000,000	75.892	0	0	10,000,000
10,200,000	77.473	0	0	10,200,000
10,400,000	79.052	0	130,448	10,269,552
10,600,000	80.625	0	325,500	10,274,500
10,800,000	82.188	0	519,312	10,280,688
11,000,000	83.746	0	712,504	10,287,496
11,200,000	85.303	0	905,572	10,294,428

[a] Because futures trade in even 32nds, these numbers are approximate.

[b] Does not include transaction costs or the financing of the options positions.

of 124 call options on futures struck at 78. Because both the puts and the calls sold at $^{24}/_{64}$, there is no net premium on the options positions. The effective sale price for the hedged bond is given in the last column of Exhibit 60–8.

The heart of the collar is that it allows prices to vary only within a range. Because this example was constructed using puts with strike prices roughly equivalent to a price of 87.668 on the hedged bond, and calls with strike prices equivalent to a price of about 102.666 for the hedged bond, and because there was

E X H I B I T   60–9

Alternative Strategies

Actual Sale Price of Bonds	Effective Sale Price with Futures Hedge	Effective Sale Price with Protective Puts	Effective Sale Price with Covered Calls	Effective Sale Price with Collar
$ 7,600,000	$9,272,636	$ 8,730,136	$ 7,646,500	$ 8,776,636
7,800,000	9,270,144	8,727,644	7,846,500	8,774,144
8,000,000	9,268,148	8,725,648	8,046,500	8,772,148
8,200,000	9,266,276	8,723,776	8,246,500	8,770,276
8,400,000	9,264,280	8,721,780	8,446,500	8,768,280
8,600,000	9,263,524	8,721,024	8,646,500	8,767,524
8,800,000	9,262,396	8,753,500	8,846,500	8,800,000
9,000,000	9,261,888	8,953,500	9,046,500	9,000,000
9,200,000	9,262,372	9,153,500	9,246,500	9,200,000
9,400,000	9,263,600	9,353,500	9,446,500	9,400,000
9,600,000	9,264,580	9,553,500	9,646,500	9,600,000
9,800,000	9,266,924	9,753,500	9,846,500	9,800,000
10,000,000	9,269,392	9,953,500	10,046,500	10,000,000
10,200,000	9,273,348	10,153,500	10,246,500	10,200,000
10,400,000	9,277,552	10,353,500	10,316,052	10,269,552
10,600,000	9,282,500	10,553,500	10,321,000	10,274,500
10,800,000	9,288,688	10,753,500	10,327,188	10,280,688
11,000,000	9,295,496	10,953,500	10,333,996	10,287,496
11,200,000	9,302,428	11,153,500	10,340,928	10,294,428

no net options premium, the resulting collar allows prices to vary only between these ranges. As always, however, some discrepancy results from rounding and the static hedge ratio.

SUMMARY

In this chapter, we have covered five basic hedging strategies. For the holder of bonds, these include (1) an unhedged position, (2) a hedge with futures, (3) a hedge with out-of-the-money protective puts, (4) covered call writing with out-of-the-money calls, and (5) hedging with long collars. Similar strategies exist for those whose risks are that rates will decrease. As might be expected, there is no "best" strategy. Each strategy has its advantages and its disadvantages, and it is impossible to get something for nothing. To get anything of value, something of value must be forfeited.

In order to make a choice among strategies, it helps to lay the alternatives side by side. Using the futures and futures options examples from this chapter, Exhibit 60–9 shows the final values of the portfolio for the various alternatives. (These are the unhedged values together with the final columns from Exhibits 60–3, 60–6, 60–7, and 60–8.) It is easy to see from Exhibit 60–9 that if one strategy is superior to another at one level of rates, it is inferior at some other level of rates. Consequently, we cannot conclude that any one strategy is the best strategy.

The manager who makes the strategy decision effectively makes a choice among probability distributions. Except for the perfect hedge, there is always a range of possible final values of the portfolio. Of course, exactly what that range is, and the probabilities associated with each possible outcome, is a matter of opinion. Yet given a probability distribution of prices or rates, corresponding probability distributions for each hedging alternative can be created.[13]

---

13. For a further discussion, see Pitts and Fabozzi, *Interest Rate Futures and Options*, pp. 379–386.

61

⑥ INTEREST-RATE SWAPS*

Anand K. Bhattacharya, Ph.D.
Managing Director
Head of Fixed Income Research
Prudential Securities Inc.

Frank J. Fabozzi, Ph.D., CFA, CPA
Adjunct Professor of Finance
School of Management
Yale University

In recent years, significant increases in interest rates and their volatility have resulted in a substantially higher exposure to interest-rate risk for market participants. This risk is especially severe for financial institutions that show a mismatch between the average duration of their assets and liabilities. In such cases, because the interest-rate sensitivity of assets and liabilities is not synchronized, any changes in market interest rates will have a disproportionate effect on the net worth of the institution. Given that direct restructuring of the asset and liability mix, which essentially involves changes in the contractual characteristics of such instruments, may not always be possible, institutions increasingly have to rely on synthetically managing the interest-rate exposure of the firm. This chapter and Chapter 62 examine the role of capital market innovations such as interest-rate swaps, interest-rate caps and floors (and derivatives such as interest-rate collars and corridors), and compound options in asset/liability management. The focus in this chapter is on interest-rate swaps.

There has already been widespread use of swaps, caps, and floors in the management of taxable institutions, and increased use by pension funds, endowment funds, and other tax-exempt investors is expected as a result of an important Internal Revenue Service regulation in July 1992. Specifically, under section 512 of the Internal Revenue Code, income from contracts such as swaps, caps, and floors (called *notional principal contracts*) is excluded from the Unrelated Business Income Tax. Prior to this ruling, there was concern that the income realized

---

*The version of this chapter that appeared in the third edition was coauthored with Dr. John Breit.

by tax-exempt investors using these contracts would be treated as Unrelated Business Income Tax and therefore taxed.

INTEREST-RATE SWAPS

An interest-rate swap is an agreement whereby two parties (called *counterparties*) agree to exchange periodic interest payments. The dollar amount of the interest payments exchanged is based on some predetermined dollar principal, which is called the *notional principal amount*. The dollar amount each counterparty pays to the other is the agreed-upon periodic interest rate multiplied by the notional principal amount. The only dollars that are exchanged between the parties are the interest payments, not the notional principal amount (or simply *notional amount*). The notional amount also provides important documentation for corporate financial statements and helps determine the contingent liability of swap market makers in the event that the market maker is a regulated financial institution, such as a bank. The notional amount of swaps is also relevant for determining capital requirements.

FEATURES OF A GENERIC SWAP

In the most common type of swap, one party agrees to pay the other party fixed interest payments at designated dates for the life of the contract. This party is referred to as the *fixed-rate payer*. The other party agrees to make interest-rate payments that float with some index and is referred to as the *floating-rate payer*.

For example, suppose that for the next five years party X agrees to pay party Y 10 percent per year, while party Y agrees to pay party X six-month LIBOR. Party X is a fixed-rate payer/floating-rate receiver, while party Y is a floating-rate payer/fixed-rate receiver. Assume that the notional amount is $50 million, and that payments are exchanged every six months for the next five years. This means that every six months, party X (the fixed-rate payer/floating-rate receiver) will pay party Y $2.5 million (10 percent times $50 million divided by 2). The amount that party Y (the floating-rate payer/fixed-rate receiver) will pay party X will be six-month LIBOR times $50 million divided by 2. For example, if six-month LIBOR is 7 percent, party Y will pay party X $1.75 million (7 percent times $50 million divided by 2). Note that we divide by two because a half-year's interest is being paid.

The interest-rate benchmarks that are commonly used for the floating rate in an interest-rate swap are those on various money market rates such as London Interbank Offered Rate (LIBOR), Treasury bills, commercial paper composite, prime rate, certificate of deposit composite, federal funds rate, J. J. Kenney, or the Eleventh District cost of funds. Although the fixed rate at which the cash flows are determined is fixed over the life of the swap, the floating-rate cash flows vary based on the periodic valuation of the index at the swap reset date. Swaps may be structured so that the floating rate resets on a daily, weekly, monthly, quarterly, or semiannual basis for either monthly, quarterly, semiannual, or annual settlement.

INTERPRETING A SWAP POSITION

There are two ways that a swap position can be interpreted: (1) as a package of forward/futures contracts and (2) as a package of cash flows from buying and selling cash market instruments.

Package of Forward Contracts

Interest-rate swaps can be viewed as a package of more basic interest-rate control tools, such as forwards. The pricing of an interest-rate swap will then depend on the price of a package of forward contracts with the same settlement dates and in which the underlying for the forward contract is the same index. Although an interest-rate swap may be nothing more than a package of forward contracts, it is not a redundant contract for several reasons. First, for forward or futures contracts, the longest maturity does not extend out as far as that of an interest-rate swap; an interest-rate swap with a term of 15 years or longer can be obtained. Second, an interest-rate swap is a more transactionally efficient instrument; in one transaction an entity can effectively establish a payoff equivalent to a package of forward contracts. The forward contracts would each have to be negotiated separately. Third, the liquidity of the interest-rate swap market has grown since its beginning in 1981; it is now more liquid than forward contracts, particularly long-dated (i.e., long-term) forward contracts.

Package of Cash Market Instruments

To understand why a swap can also be interpreted as a package of cash market instruments, consider the following. Suppose that an investor enters into the following transaction:

- Buys $50 million par of a five-year floating-rate bond that pays six-month LIBOR every six months.
- Finances the purchase of the five-year floating-rate bond by borrowing $50 million for five years with the following terms: 10 percent annual interest rate paid every six months.

The cash flow of the above transaction is presented in Exhibit 61–1. The second column of the exhibit sets out the cash flow from purchasing the five-year floating-rate bond. There is a $50 million cash outlay and then cash inflows. The amount of the cash inflows is uncertain because they depend on future LIBOR. The third column shows the cash flow from borrowing $50 million on a fixed-rate basis. The last column shows the net cash flow from the entire transaction. As can be seen in the last column, there is no initial cash flow (no cash inflow or cash outlay). In all 10 six-month periods the net position results in a cash inflow of LIBOR and a cash outlay of $2.5 million. This net position, however, is identical to the position of a fixed-rate payer/floating-rate receiver.

It can be seen from the net cash flow in Exhibit 61–1 that a fixed-rate payer has a cash market position that is equivalent to a long position in a floating-rate bond and borrowing the funds to purchase the floating-rate bond on a fixed-rate basis. But the borrowing can be viewed as issuing a fixed-rate bond, or equivalently, being short a fixed-rate bond. Consequently, the position of a fixed-rate payer can be viewed as being long a floating-rate bond and short a fixed-rate bond.

What about the position of a floating-rate payer? It can be easily demonstrated that the position of a floating-rate payer is equivalent to purchasing a fixed-rate bond and financing that purchase at a floating rate, with the floating rate being the reference interest rate for the swap. That is, the position of a floating-rate payer is equivalent to a long position in a fixed-rate bond and a short position in a floating-rate bond.

EXHIBIT 61–1

Cash Flow for the Purchase of a Five-Year Floating-Rate Bond Financed by Borrowing on a Fixed-Rate Basis

Transaction: Purchase for $50 million a five-year floating-rate bond: floating rate = LIBOR, semiannual payments

Borrow $50 million for five years: fixed rate = 10% semiannual payments

Six-Month Period	*Cash Flow (in Millions of Dollars) from:*		
	Floating-Rate Bond[a]	**Borrowing Cost**	**Net**[a]
0	−$50	+$50.0	$0
1	+(LIBOR$_1$/2) × 50	−2.5	+(LIBOR$_1$/2) × 50 − 2.5
2	+(LIBOR$_2$/2) × 50	−2.5	+(LIBOR$_2$/2) × 50 − 2.5
3	+(LIBOR$_3$/2) × 50	−2.5	+(LIBOR$_3$/2) × 50 − 2.5
4	+(LIBOR$_4$/2) × 50	−2.5	+(LIBOR$_4$/2) × 50 − 2.5
5	+(LIBOR$_5$/2) × 50	−2.5	+(LIBOR$_5$/2) × 50 − 2.5
6	+(LIBOR$_6$/2) × 50	−2.5	+(LIBOR$_6$/2) × 50 − 2.5
7	+(LIBOR$_7$/2) × 50	−2.5	+(LIBOR$_7$/2) × 50 − 2.5
8	+(LIBOR$_8$/2) × 50	−2.5	+(LIBOR$_8$/2) × 50 − 2.5
9	+(LIBOR$_9$/2) × 50	−2.5	+(LIBOR$_9$/2) × 50 − 2.5
10	+(LIBOR$_{10}$/2) × 50 + 50	−52.5	+(LIBOR$_{10}$/2) × 50 − 2.5

[a]The subscript for LIBOR indicates six-month LIBOR as per the terms of the floating-rate bond at time *t*.

TERMINOLOGY, CONVENTIONS, AND MARKET QUOTES

Here we review some of the terminology used in this market and explain how swaps are quoted.

The date that the counterparties commit to the swap is called the *trade date*. The date that the swap begins accruing interest is called the *effective date*, and the date that the swap stops accruing interest is called the *maturity date*. The *settlement date* refers to the actual date on which cash flows are exchanged.

Although our illustrations assume that the timing of the cash flows for both the fixed-rate payer and floating-rate payer will be the same, this is rarely the case in a swap. In fact, an agreement may call for the fixed-rate payer to make payments annually but the floating-rate payer to make payments more frequently (semiannually or quarterly). Also, the way interest accrues on each leg of the transaction differs, because there are several day-count conventions in the fixed income markets.

The terminology used to describe the position of a party in the swap markets is a blend of cash market jargon and futures jargon. The obvious reason as we just explained is that a swap position can be interpreted as a position in a package of cash market instruments or a package of futures/forward positions. The counterparty to an interest-rate swap is either a fixed-rate payer or floating-rate payer. There are a number of ways to describe these positions:

Fixed-Rate Payer
- Is short the bond market.
- Has bought a swap.
- Is long a swap.
- Has established the price sensitivities of a longer-term liability and a floating-rate asset.

Floating-Rate Payer
- Is long the bond market.
- Has sold a swap.
- Is short a swap.
- Has established the price sensitivities of a longer-term asset and a floating-rate liability.

To understand why the fixed-rate payer is viewed as short the bond market and the floating-rate payer is viewed as long the bond market, consider what happens when interest rates change. Those who borrow on a fixed-rate basis will benefit if interest rates rise because they have locked in a lower interest rate. But those who have a short bond position will also benefit if interest rates rise. Thus, a fixed-rate payer can be said to be short the bond market. A floating-rate payer benefits if interest rates fall. Because a long position in a bond benefits if interest rates fall, terminology describing a floating-rate payer as long the bond market has been adopted. From the discussion of both the interpretation of a swap as a package of cash market instruments above and the duration of a swap discussed later in this chapter, the description of a swap in terms of the sensitivities of long and short cash positions follows accordingly.

The convention that has evolved for quoting swaps levels is for a swap dealer to set the floating rate equal to the index and then quote the fixed rate that will apply. To illustrate this convention, consider the following 10-year swap offered by a dealer to market participants.

> *Floating-rate payer:*
>   Pay floating rate of 6-month LIBOR
>   Receive fixed rate of 8.75%

> *Fixed-rate payer:*
>   Pay fixed rate = 8.85%
>   Receive floating rate = 6-month LIBOR

The offer price that the dealer would quote the fixed-rate payer would be to pay 8.85 percent and receive LIBOR flat. (The term *flat* means with no spread.) The bid price that the dealer would quote the floating-rate payer would be to pay LIBOR flat and receive 8.75 percent. The bid-offer spread is 10 basis points.

The fixed rate is some spread above the Treasury yield curve with the same term-to-maturity as the swap. In our illustration, suppose that the 10-year Treasury yield is 8.35 percent. Then the offer price that the dealer would quote to the fixed-rate payer is the 10-year Treasury rate plus 50 basis points versus receiving LIBOR flat. For the floating-rate payer, the bid price quoted would be LIBOR flat versus the 10-year Treasury rate plus 40 basis points. The dealer would quote the swap above as 40–50, meaning that it is willing to enter into a swap to receive LIBOR and pay a fixed rate equal to the 10-year Treasury rate plus 40 basis points; it would be willing to enter into a swap to pay LIBOR and receive a fixed rate equal to the 10-year Treasury rate plus 50 basis points. The difference between the Treasury rate paid and received is the bid-offer spread.

APPLICATIONS

Here we describe how interest-rate swaps can be used in asset/liability management.

Converting Floating-Rate Debt to Fixed-Rate Debt Using Swaps

Fixed-rate payer/floating-rate receiver swaps can be used to convert floating-rate liabilities synthetically to fixed-rate liabilities, because the floating cost of liabilities is "counterbalanced" by floating-rate receipts associated with the swap. Any increase or decrease in liability costs is matched by a similar change in the floating-rate inflows, as long as the notional amount of the swap is equal to the principal amount of the liability. The net effect of this strategy is to lock in the liability cost at a fixed rate.

As an example, consider the case of a financial institution issuing floating-rate liabilities that are priced at a spread of 10 basis points over three-month LIBOR at a rate of 9.10 percent. The preponderance of the institution's assets, however, are fixed-rate instruments. As long as interest rates either remain stable or fall, the institution will be able to earn a spread over its floating-rate funding costs. However, if interest rates increase, the institution's spread will decrease. In order to synthetically convert the floating liability cost to fixed debt expense, the institution enters into an interest-rate swap for five years with another entity paying fixed and receiving floating cash flows. Suppose that the fixed-rate side of the swap is priced at a spread of 80 basis points over the five-year Treasury rate at a rate of 9.40 percent and that the floating side of the swap is three-month LIBOR at 9.00 percent. The funding cost to the institution in various interest-rate scenarios is illustrated in Exhibit 61–2.

In this example, if the institution had not swapped the floating-rate debt cost for fixed-rate cash flows, the liability rate would have repriced in every interest-rate scenario at a spread of 10 basis points over three-month LIBOR, assuming parallel shifts in the yield curve. By entering into the interest-rate swap, the floating outflow of the liability is partially canceled by the floating inflow from the swap in all interest-rate scenarios. The net funding cost is determined as follows:

Floating-rate liability cost + Fixed rate of swap − Floating rate of swap

The effectiveness of this strategy will depend on the extent of basis risk between the liability rate and the swap floating-rate index (usually LIBOR). In the previous example, because the liability rate and the floating side of the swap are both based on three-month LIBOR, there is no basis risk. However in other in-

E X H I B I T   61–2

Converting Floating-Rate Debt to Fixed-Rate Debt Using Interest-Rate Swaps

		Swap Cash Flows		
Interest-Rate Scenario	Liability Cost	Fixed Outflow	Floating Inflow (LIBOR)	Net Funding Cost
+300 bp	12.10%	9.40%	12.00%	9.50%
+200	11.10	9.40	11.00	9.50
+100	10.10	9.40	10.00	9.50
Stable	9.10	9.40	9.00	9.50
−100	8.10	9.40	8.00	9.50
−200	7.10	9.40	7.00	9.50
−300	6.10	9.40	6.00	9.50

stances, where the liability rate is keyed off another indicator, such as the Treasury bill index or the prime rate, the existence of basis risk may mitigate the swap's effectiveness. For instance, if the liability rate increases by 1 percent and LIBOR increases by only 0.85 percent, the synthetic fixed rate will be 0.15 percent higher than it would have been in the absence of such imperfect correlation. Conversely, if the liability rate increases by 0.85 percent and LIBOR by 1 percent, the synthetic liability rate will be 0.15 percent lower than the swap fixed rate. The synthetic funding rate will also be affected by any discrepancies in the repricing frequency of the liability and the reset period of the swap. Ideally, close synchronization between these dates will minimize the deviation of the synthetic liability cost from the swap fixed rate that occurs because of reset date mismatch.

Converting Fixed-Rate Debt to Floating-Rate Debt Using Reverse Swaps

A similar strategy using reverse swaps, where the financial institution receives fixed-rate cash flows and pays floating-rate cash flows, is used to convert the fixed cost of liabilities to a synthetic floating rate. In this case, the fixed-rate interest cost of the liability is offset by the fixed-rate inflow of the swap. If the liability rate is higher (lower) than the swap fixed rate, then the synthetic floating rate will be higher (lower) than the swap floating rate. A financial institution that has fixed-rate debt and a preponderance of floating-rate assets, such as adjustable-rate mortgages, collateralized mortgage obligation (CMO) floater bonds, or floating-rate notes, may adopt this strategy to better match the average duration of their assets and liabilities.

As an example, consider the case of an institution that has three-year fixed-rate debt at a coupon rate of 8.85 percent. In order to convert this fixed-rate debt into floating-rate liabilities, the institution enters into a reverse swap (floating-rate payer/fixed-rate receiver) for three years. The terms of the swap involve paying three-month LIBOR and receiving fixed-rate cash flows at a spread of 65 basis points over the three-year Treasury yield at a rate of 8.70 percent. An illustration of this example is presented in Exhibit 61–3. An analysis of this illustration reveals that the effective funding cost is determined as follows:

Fixed-rate liability cost – Fixed-rate of swap + Floating-rate of swap

The institution has converted fixed-rate debt to LIBOR-based debt at a spread of 15 basis points over LIBOR. A schematic of the cash flows involved in synthetically converting floating-rate liability costs to fixed-rate funding and vice versa is presented in Exhibit 61–4. Although the dynamics of the cash flow are essentially reversed, most dealers will charge a higher spread (offer side) for fixed-rate-paying swaps than fixed-rate-receiving swaps (bid side). This bid-ask differential, which is a function of variables such as hedging costs, dealer inventory, relative supply of fixed- and floating-rate payers in the market, conditions in the Treasury market, and quality spreads in the domestic and international bond markets, is used to compensate the dealers for the market-making function.

EXHIBIT 61–3

Converting Fixed-Rate Debt to Floating-Rate Debt Using Interest-Rate Swaps

	Swap Cash Flows			
Interest-Rate Scenario	Liability Cost	Fixed Outflow	Floating Inflow (LIBOR)	Net Funding Cost
+300 bp	8.85%	8.70%	12.00%	12.15%
+200	8.85	8.70	11.00	11.15
+100	8.85	8.70	10.00	10.15
Stable	8.85	8.70	9.00	9.15
−100	8.85	8.70	8.00	8.15
−200	8.85	8.70	7.00	7.15
−300	8.85	8.70	6.00	6.15

EXHIBIT 61–4

Synthetic Conversion of Interest-Rate Liability

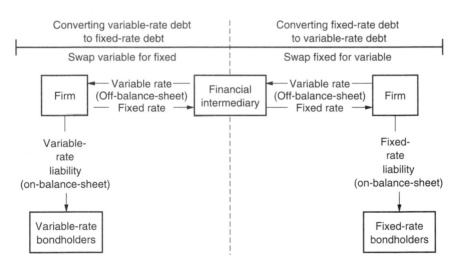

In the foregoing discussion, it has been tacitly assumed that the payment frequencies and the payment basis of the fixed and floating legs of the swap and the liability being swapped are identical. Any differences in the frequencies or basis will change the net spread calculations. This observation also applies to asset swaps (discussed later). For example, in swapping a fixed liability to a floating-rate obligation, the net spread over LIBOR usually will be slightly different from the spread between the liability coupon and the coupon of the swap. This difference arises because swaps usually pay fixed on an actual/365 or 30/360 basis and floating on an actual/360 basis. Hence, the net spread over LIBOR will be 360/365 of the nominal spread between coupons.

DOLLAR DURATION OF A SWAP

As with any fixed income contract, the value of a swap will change as interest rates change. As explained in Chapter 5, dollar duration is a measure of the change in the dollar value of an asset due to a change in interest rates. From our earlier discussion of how to interpret an interest-rate swap, it was explained that from the perspective of the party who pays floating and receives fixed, the position can be viewed as follows:

Long a fixed-rate bond + Short a floating-rate bond

This means that the dollar duration of an interest-rate swap from the perspective of a floating-rate payer is just the difference between the dollar duration of the two bond positions that constitute the swap. That is,

Dollar duration of a swap = Dollar duration of a fixed-rate bond
− Dollar duration of a floating-rate bond

Most of the interest-rate sensitivity of a swap will result from the dollar duration of the fixed-rate bond because the dollar duration of the floating-rate bond will be small. It will always be less than the length of time to the next reset date. Therefore, the dollar duration of a floating-rate bond for which the coupon rate resets every six months will be less than six months. The dollar duration of a floating-rate bond becomes smaller as the swap gets closer to its reset date.

INNOVATIONS IN SWAP MARKETS

In addition to allowing a firm to issue debt for which it has a comparative relative advantage and then swapping the cash flows to fine-tune the asset/liability gap, interest-rate swaps also serve other useful purposes, especially because of the off-balance-sheet treatment accorded them. It often has been argued that swaps are preferable to refunding because the latter often is constrained by restrictive covenants. Periodically, firms may want to make adjustments in the capital structure with respect to the composition of debt by refinancing longer-term debt with short-term debt at lower interest costs. In certain instances, this may not be easy to accomplish, especially if the debt is noncallable. Swaps provide an effective means to alter the covenants of a debt issue to accomplish asset/liability objectives without incurring the administrative, legal, and underwriting costs of issuing additional debt. In this case, the firm may swap the higher-coupon debt to a cheaper floating-rate liability based on a variety of indexes, such as the Treasury bill index, prime rate, and LIBOR.

In order to address such specific investor needs, several innovations, such as basis swaps, yield-curve swaps, amortizing swaps, asset swaps, forward swaps, equity swaps, and swaptions have been developed over the last several years to further expand the degree of flexibility provided by generic swaps. A discussion of the salient features of these capital market innovations is presented in this section.

Basis Swaps

Basis swaps are designed to manage the basis risk inherent in a balance sheet where the asset returns and liability costs are based on different indexes. For instance, a financial institution that invests in a CMO floater with a return of 60 basis points over one-month LIBOR funded by six-month certificates of deposit at an interest cost of prime less 200 basis points is subject to basis risk, despite the minimal duration mismatch. This risk arises because the asset resets monthly off LIBOR, whereas the liability resets every six months based on movements in the prime rate. To alleviate this risk, the institution could enter into a floating-to-floating basis swap, where the institution receives cash flows that are reset every six months at a rate of prime less 150 basis points and pays swap cash flows on a monthly basis indexed off one-month LIBOR. The basis risk will be controlled for the *tenor*, or time period, of the swap.

As an illustration, assume one-month LIBOR is 9 percent and the prime rate is 10 percent. Without the basis swap, the spread earned by the institution is defined as the difference between the asset return and the liability cost, 1.60 percent (9.60 percent − 8.00 percent) in our illustration. (For the sake of simplicity, it is assumed that the asset returns are not constrained by caps inherent in CMO floaters.[1]) Assuming that the correlation between the prime rate and one-month LIBOR is imperfect, in that a 1 percent change in the prime results in less or more than a 1 percent change in one-month LIBOR, the spread will not be maintained in all interest-rate scenarios. As previously indicated, the institution enters into a basis swap to lock in the spread over funding costs without incurring the basis risk between the prime rate and LIBOR. Although basis swaps are used most often to refine the interest-rate sensitivity of assets and liabilities, these swaps can also be used to arbitrage spreads between various funding sources. The dynamics of the basis swap are illustrated in Exhibit 61–5.

Yield-Curve Swaps

In a yield-curve swap, the counterparties agree to exchange payments based on the difference between interest rates at two points on a given yield curve. These swaps are therefore an example of a floating-rate for floating-rate swap, or basis swap.

To illustrate a yield-curve swap, suppose party A agrees to receive six-month Treasury bill rate and to pay party B the yield on a 10-year Treasury minus

---

1. A discussion of synthetically "stripping" these caps is in Chapter 62.

EXHIBIT 61–5

Locking in a Floating Spread over Funding Costs Using Basis Swaps

				Swap Cash Flows		
LIBOR	Asset Return[a]	Prime	Liability Costs[b]	Floating Inflows[c]	Floating Outflows[d]	Net Spread[e]
7.0%	7.60%	9.5%	7.5%	8.00%	7.00%	1.10%
9.0	9.60	10.0	8.0	8.50	9.00	1.10
11.0	11.60	12.0	10.0	10.50	11.00	1.10

[a] Asset return = LIBOR + 60 basis points.
[b] Liability costs = Prime – 200 basis points.
[c] Swap floating inflows = Prime – 150 basis points.
[d] Swap floating outflows = LIBOR.
[e] Net spread = Asset return + Swap inflows – Liability costs – Swap outflows.

200 basis points, with the rate on both reset every six months. If at a reset date the six-month T-bill rate is 3.5 percent and 10-year Treasury yield is 6 percent, party A receives 3.5 percent and pays party B 4 percent. If the yield curve flattens such that the six-month Treasury bill rate is 5 percent and the 10-year Treasury is 6.5 percent, then party A receives 5 percent and pays 4.5 percent.

Amortizing and Accreting Swaps

In the preceding discussion, it was implicitly assumed that the notional amount does not change over the life of the swap. However, with respect to amortizing assets such as mortgage loans and other mortgage-backed instruments such as CMO bonds and automobile receivables, the spread over funding costs will not be maintained because of the asset principal balance declining over time. This declining spread is especially critical for assets whose average life and duration may exhibit dramatic changes due to the possibility of prepayments. In such instances, if bullet swaps with the same notional amount are used, there is the risk of being either underhedged or overhedged with respect to liability costs. If interest rates decrease and prepayments increase substantially, the average life of the asset will shorten. In such instances, the asset may not generate funds sufficient to earn a positive spread. On the other hand, if interest rates rise and prepayments slow down, resulting in an extension of the average life of the asset, the swap may have to be extended or additional swap coverage obtained (at higher cost, owing to bearish interest-rate conditions[2]) to maintain a positive spread.

---

2. A bearish interest-rate scenario refers to one in which rates are rising and market prices are falling (a bearish market). In a bullish interest-rate scenario, rates are falling and market prices are rising.

In such instances, the institution may enter into an amortizing swap, which permits the notional amount of the swap, and hence the exchange of the cash flows, to change in accordance with the amortization rate of the asset. Note that the amortization rate of the notional amount cannot usually be changed over the life of the swap. Because the amortizing swap can be replicated by using a strip of swaps, the swap rate is determined as a blended rate of individual bullet swap rates. This feature of amortizing swaps also provides a market participant with the choice of entering into a series of swaps to match the amortization rate of assets or entering into an amortizing swap at an annual blended rate.

Although amortizing swaps improve the match between the asset and hedged liability cash flows, such swaps do not completely alleviate the risk of being overhedged with respect to liability costs. A major portion of this risk is mitigated for assets such as Planned Amortization Class (PAC) CMO bonds, which provide for a specified amortization rate within a wide band of prepayment scenarios. For assets that exhibit a higher degree of prepayment volatility, if falling interest rates lead to an increase in prepayments and an attendant shortening of average life, the firm may have to continue exchanging swap cash flows for a period longer than the average life of the asset, unless the swap can be terminated.

In instances where the liability schedule is expected to increase, an interest-rate swap with an accreting balance may be used to fix the interest cost of the liabilities. Perhaps the most common example of this type of swap application is found in the construction industry, where accreting swaps may be used to fix the rate on a project funded with a floating-rate drawdown facility.

Forward Swaps

A forward swap allows a market participant to initiate a swap with a specified delayed start. Such swaps can be used to hedge debt refinancings or anticipated debt issuance in conjunction with expenditures expected in the future. For instance, suppose a firm has $200 million of noncallable fixed-rate debt maturing in three years. In order to lock in anticipated funding requirements three years hence for a period of five years at current rates, the firm could enter into a forward swap to pay fixed and receive floating cash flows starting three years from now. If rates have increased at the time of issuance, the firm would issue floating-rate debt and effectively convert the floating-rate funding to a fixed-rate liability, because the firm would be a floating-rate receiver.

Equity Swaps

In recent years, the concept of swapping cash flows has been applied to the equity area. In an *equity swap*, the cash flows that are swapped are based on the total return on some stock market index and an interest rate (either a fixed rate or a floating rate). Moreover, the stock market index can be a non-U.S. stock market index and the payments could be non-dollar denominated. For example, a money manager can enter into a two-year quarterly reset equity swap based on the German DAX market index versus LIBOR in which the money manager receives the market index in deutsche marks and pays the floating rate in deutsche marks.

Swaptions

Swaptions are representative of the new class of second-generation derivative products that have developed around the swaps, caps, and floor markets. Swaptions can take many forms, but typically they are options to pay or receive a predetermined fixed rate in exchange for LIBOR at some time in the future. As the market develops, it is likely that additional variable-rate indexes will be used to determine floating-rate cash flows. Alternatively, swaptions can contain an option to cancel an existing swap. The second structure is essentially the same as the first, because a swap can be canceled by entering into a new swap in the opposite direction.

In view of this overlap between options to enter swaps and options to cancel swaps, the usual shorthand terminology of puts and calls is rarely used for swaptions. Rather, the option characteristic is spelled out in more detail, for instance, an option to receive fixed at 9 percent for three years, starting two years hence. Swaption exercise can be European (exercisable on only one date in the future) or American (exercisable on any date up to and including the expiration date), with the bulk of the interbank market for European exercise. A typical American swaption structure would be to enter into, say, a seven-year swap paying fixed at 9 percent at any time before maturity. As an example, if the option is exercised after one year, the option holder will pay 9 percent and receive LIBOR for six years.

In terms of flexibility and costs, swaptions lie between swaps and customized interest-rate protection instruments, such as caps and floors. If LIBOR increases, the fixed payer of a swap, the holder of an option to pay fixed, and the cap buyer all benefit equally. If LIBOR decreases, the fixed payer of a swap incurs an opportunity loss and the holder of the swaption or cap loses only the upfront premium. The premium for a cap is greater than that for a swaption because the buyer of the cap essentially has purchased a strip of options, whereas the holder of a swaption owns only one option. If rates increase and the swaption is exercised, the owner of the swaption is exposed to the risk of a fall in interest rates. However, the holder of the cap can still take advantage of the beneficial movement in rates. In view of this observation, swaptions can be viewed as instruments that provide some of the protection and flexibility afforded by caps and floors.

The pricing of swaptions is still somewhat of an art. The development of models for pricing and hedging swaptions is on the cutting edge of options theory. Dealers differ greatly in the models they use to price such options, and the analytical tools range from modified Black-Scholes models to binomial lattice versions to systems based upon Monte Carlo simulations. As a result, bid-ask spreads are wide, and it pays to shop around, particularly for more complicated structures that cannot be backed off in the interbank markets.

Swaptions provide the sophisticated firm with an additional, flexible tool for asset/liability management. On the liability side, the primary uses of swaptions have been in hedging uncertain funding requirements and issuing synthetically callable debt. With respect to fixing liability costs, a corporation can lock in coupon rates for future funding by paying fixed in a forward swap. However, the firm may desire to preserve the opportunity to save on these funding costs in the event that rates decline in the future by purchasing a swaption, despite the attractiveness of the current interest-rate structure. In the event that funding requirements are uncertain, the flexibility of these instruments really comes into play as swaptions can lock in current rates without committing the firm to future borrowing.

Much of the current activity in swaptions has been fueled by an arbitrage between the swaption and callable bond markets. Historically, investors have not demanded full compensation for call options embedded in corporate bonds. Hence, corporations can issue callable debt and then effectively strip off the embedded call option by writing a swaption, thereby lowering the all-in cost of the debt. On the asset side, the primary use of swaptions has been in hedging prepayable swapped assets, such as mortgage-backed instruments. An investor may purchase fixed-rate mortgage-backed securities, swap the fixed rate to floating, and earn an attractive spread over LIBOR. However, this spread is subject to erosion if the asset balance declines because of high prepayments. By giving up some of this spread and purchasing swaptions, the investor can reduce prepayment risk exposure.

ASSET SWAP

Our earlier applications focused exclusively on the use of interest-rate swaps and associated issues in swap-based liability hedging. Such swaps are referred to as *liability-based swaps*. *Asset-based swaps*, which use principles involved in liability hedging, are becoming increasingly popular to customize asset coupons and maturities, thereby expanding the asset universe available to portfolio managers. Asset swaps serve several useful functions, such as facilitating yield enhancement, creating assets that are not available in the marketplace, and changing the interest-rate sensitivity of the portfolio, without actually trading the securities.

Similar to the use of swaps in converting fixed-rate debt to floating-rate debt and vice versa, interest-rate swaps also can be used to accomplish the same objective with fixed- and floating-rate assets. For instance, floating-rate notes (FRNs) can be converted synthetically to fixed-rate assets using a receive fixed-rate and pay floating-rate swap. Similarly, fixed-rate assets such as mortgage-backed securities (especially certain types of CMO bonds such as PAC classes) and receivable-backed securities (such as manufactured housing, credit card, and automobile loan collateralized bonds) can be converted to floating-rate instruments by using a receive floating-rate and pay fixed-interest-rate swap. Asset-based swaps can also be used to alter the duration characteristics and, hence, the interest-rate sensitivity of an asset portfolio. For instance, a financial institution that has a predominance of long-term fixed-rate assets can reduce the duration of its portfolio, thereby increasing the interest-rate sensitivity of the assets by creating synthetic floating-rate assets. Characteristics of interest-rate swaps, such as amortizing features and option covenants, can be used to customize and reasonably ensure a particular yield level.

The flexibility afforded by swaps in the design of such synthetic assets becomes apparent when it is realized that investors seeking a particular type of asset, say, a floating-rate asset, can evaluate traditional floating-rate instruments, such as FRNs and CMO floaters as well as fixed-rate assets, by using interest-rate swaps to synthetically convert them to floating-rate assets. Asset-based swaps can also tailor the maturity (tenor) of the swap without having to depend on conditions in the debt markets. The latter feature is especially important for institutions that have "underwater" assets. With recent developments in the asset securitization market, which portend increased securitization of a gamut of assets, firms can always use a collateralized financing structure to raise funds and then reinvest the proceeds in assets of desired maturity and coupon. However, this option, besides being time-consuming, involves administrative, legal, and investment banking costs. Also, assets of particular maturity and coupon may not always be traded in the markets. Asset-based swaps fulfill this particular need in the market mainly because of ease of execution, customization features, and flexibility of swap termination.

TERMINATION OF INTEREST-RATE SWAPS

There are two ways to terminate a swap: (1) a reverse swap and (2) a swap sale.

Reverse Swap

The simplest way to terminate an interest-rate swap is to enter into an offsetting position. For illustrative purposes, assume that a firm entered into a five-year swap, paying fixed at a rate of 9.40 percent and receiving three-month LIBOR. After two years, the firm decides to terminate the swap by entering into a reverse swap, paying floating rate and receiving fixed rate. By matching the reset and settlement periods of the *reverse swap* to those of the original swap, the floating-rate payment of the reverse swap is counterbalanced by the floating-rate inflow from the original swap.

E X H I B I T   61–6

Termination of Interest-Rate Swaps

| | Termination Interest-Rate Scenario | |
	Bearish	Bullish
Swap		
Pay fixed (5-year original maturity/ 3-year remaining maturity)	9.40%	9.40%
Receive 3-month LIBOR	LIBOR	LIBOR
Reverse Swap		
Receive fixed (3-year remaining maturity)	10.40%	8.40%
Pay 3-month LIBOR	LIBOR	LIBOR
Profit (Loss)	1.00%	(1.00%)

Two cases are illustrated in Exhibit 61–6—a bearish scenario and a bullish scenario. In a bearish interest-rate scenario, the new fixed rate on the reverse swap is likely to be higher than the fixed rate on the original swap. The new fixed rate in Exhibit 61–6 is assumed to be 10.40 percent. In this bearish scenario, there will be a profit associated with the reverse swap. The firm has effectively created an annuity of 1 percent of the notional amount for the remaining period of the swap.

In a bullish interest-rate scenario, rates are falling and market prices are rising. In the illustration in Exhibit 61–6, the new fixed rate is assumed to be 8.40 percent, resulting in a loss on the reverse swap. In this illustration, the firm has created a reverse annuity of 1 percent per annum for three years.

In either case, because the closing transaction involves receiving the fixed side of a swap, the spread over Treasury is based on the bid side of the market, whereas the original swap involves payment of the swap at the offer spread.

Swap Sale

Instead of managing the cash flows of two swaps and the credit risk of two counterparties, the firm may sell the swap for either a profit or loss in the secondary market. In the event that current market swaps with a maturity equal to the remaining maturity of the swap to be terminated are being offered at a higher fixed rate, the swap could be sold for a fee. On the other hand, if current market swaps with a maturity similar to the swap to be liquidated are being originated at lower rates, then an exit fee may have to be paid for terminating the swap. Formally, the termination value of a swap is determined as the present value of an annuity discounted for the remaining term-to-maturity at the current swap rate. The periodic value of the annuity payments is determined as the difference between the old fixed swap rate and the new fixed swap rate multiplied by the remaining notional amount of the original swap. Formally, this is stated as

$$\text{Termination value of swap} = \text{PV of Annuity at } r_s t$$

where

$$\text{Annuity payments} = (r_s - r_m) \times \text{Notional amount}$$
$$r_s = \text{Original swap fixed rate}$$
$$r_m = \text{Current swap fixed rate}$$
$$t = \text{Time remaining to maturity of swap}$$

SUMMARY

In the management of interest-rate volatility and associated asset/liability structural decisions, customized risk-management instruments such as swaps, caps and floors, and split-fee options provide a high degree of coverage flexibility and customization. Interest-rate swaps can be used either to synthetically extend or to shorten the duration characteristics of any asset or liability. The benefit of swaps is that direct changes in the contractual characteristics of either assets or liabilities are associated with administrative, legal, and investment banking costs. Additional swaps covenants, such as amortizing and accreting features and option riders, can be included in the contractual agreement either to better match the funding of an asset or to lock in the return of a synthetic asset.

⑥ # INTEREST-RATE CAPS AND FLOORS AND COMPOUND OPTIONS*

Anand K. Bhattacharya, Ph.D.
Managing Director
Head of Fixed Income Research
Prudential Securities Inc.

Interest-rate caps and floors provide asymmetric interest-rate risk management capabilities similar to those provided by options, except that protection can be customized to a much greater degree. As indicated by the nomenclature, *interest-rate caps,* also referred to as *interest-rate ceilings,* allow the purchaser to "cap" the contractual rate associated with a liability. Alternatively, interest-rate floors allow the purchaser to protect the total rate of return of an asset. The seller of the cap pays the purchaser any amount above the periodic capped rate on the settlement date. Conversely, the purchaser of the floor receives from the seller any amount below the periodic protected rate on the relevant date. The protection provided by caps and floors is asymmetric, in that the purchaser is protected from adverse moves in the market but maintains the advantage of beneficial moves in market rates. In this respect, caps and floors differ from interest-rate swaps. Recall that interest-rate swaps seek to insulate the user from the economic effects of interest-rate volatility, regardless of the direction of interest rates.

Interest-rate protection obtained by purchasing caps and floors can be customized by selecting various contractual features. The following decision variables are commonly used in determining the parameters of either interest-rate caps or floors.

FEATURES OF INTEREST-RATE CAPS AND FLOORS

The *underlying index* from which the contractual payments will be determined can be chosen from a set of indexes based on LIBOR, commercial paper, prime

---

*The version of this chapter that appeared in the third edition was coauthored with Dr. John Breit.

rate, Treasury bills, or certificates of deposit. Because these instruments are originated along several maturities, an additional variable associated with the index concerns the maturity of the index.

The *strike rate* is the rate at which the cash flows will be exchanged between the purchaser and seller of the customized interest-rate protection instrument. Caps with a higher strike rate have lower up-front premiums, although the trade-off between the premium and the strike rate is not directly proportional. Similarly, floors with a lower strike rate have a lower up-front premium. Increasing (decreasing) the strike rate does not result in a proportionate decrease in the up-front fee for interest-rate caps (floors).

The term of the protection may range from several months to about 30 years, although the liquidity of longer dated caps is not sufficiently high.

The *settlement frequency* refers to the frequency with which the strike rate will be compared to the underlying index to determine the periodic contractual rate for the interest-rate protection agreement. The most common frequencies are monthly, quarterly, and semiannually. At settlement, the cash flows exchanged could be determined on either the average daily rate prevalent during the repricing interval or the spot rate on the settlement date.

The *notional amount* of the agreement on which the cash flows are exchanged is usually fixed, unless the terms of the agreement call for the amortization of the notional amount. For instance, in "spread enhancement" strategies, which involve the purchase of an amortizing asset, such as a fixed-rate mortgage-backed security funded by floating-rate capped liabilities, amortization of the cap notional amount may be necessary in order to maintain the spread. Unless the amortization feature is included in the design of the cap, the spread between the asset cash flows and the liability costs will be eroded.

PRICING OF CAPS AND FLOORS

The *up-front premium* is the fee paid by the purchaser to the seller of the interest-rate agreement at the inception of the contract. This fee is similar to the premium paid to purchase options and is determined by factors such as the strike rate, volatility of the underlying index, the length of the agreement, the notional amount, and any special features, such as amortization of the notional principal.

The pricing of both caps and floors draws heavily on option pricing theory; for instance, an increase in market volatility results in a higher premium for both the cap and the floor. The strike rate for a cap is inversely related to the premium paid for the cap because rates have to advance before the cap is in the money or the payoff is positive. On the other hand, the strike rate for interest-rate floors is directly related to the up-front premium. A higher strike indicates that the likelihood of the index falling below this rate is greater, which indicates a higher likelihood of positive payoff from the floor. The longer the term-to-maturity, the greater the premium because optional protection is available for a longer period of time. Hence, there is a higher probability that the payoff associated with these instruments will be positive. With respect to the payment frequency, the agreement with a shorter payment frequency will command a higher premium because there is a greater likelihood of payoff and the payments are determined only on the settlement date. This may be an important determinant of cash flows, especially in highly volatile markets. Any advantageous changes in market volatility for interest-rate agreements with longer settlement frequencies may not result in a payoff for the purchaser of the agreement because the option-like characteristics of caps and floors are European rather than American in design.

There also may be additional contractual features, such as variable premiums, cost of termination options prior to stated maturity, conversion privileges from one program to another, and purchase of a combination of programs, such as *interest-rate collars* and *corridors*.

INTEREST-RATE CAPS

As noted above, an interest-rate cap can be used to create an upper limit on the cost of floating-rate liabilities. The purchaser of the cap pays an up-front fee to establish a ceiling on a particular funding rate. If the market rate exceeds the strike rate of the cap on the settlement date, the seller of the cap pays the difference. As an illustration, consider the following example, where an institution purchases an interest-rate cap to hedge the coupon rate of LIBOR-indexed liabilities, which reprice every three months.

Notional amount:	$10,000,000
Underlying index:	3-month LIBOR
Maturity:	3 years
Cap strike level:	10%
Premium:	145 basis points or 1.45% of $10,000,000 = $145,000
Settlement frequency:	Quarterly
Day count:	Actual/360

The up-front premium can be converted to an annual basis-point equivalent by treating $145,000 as the present value of a stream of equal quarterly payments with a future value of zero at the maturity of the cap. Ideally, this should be computed at the rate at which the up-front premium can be funded for three years. Assuming that this premium can be funded at a rate of 9 percent and the cap has 12 reset periods, the annual basis-point equivalent of the up-front premium is 56 basis points.[1]

In this example, the payments to the purchaser of the cap by the seller can be determined as the quarterly difference between the three-month LIBOR index

---

1. This represents the annuity over three years, which when discounted quarterly at an annual rate of 9 percent equals the up-front premium of 145 basis points.

and the cap strike rate of 10 percent times the notional amount of the agreement. Specifically, the cap payments are computed as follows:

$$\text{(Index rate} - \text{Strike rate)} \times \text{(Days in settlement period/360)}$$
$$\times \text{Notional amount}$$

For instance, where three-month LIBOR is 11 percent, the payments made by the cap seller, assuming 90 days in the settlement period, would be determined as follows:

$$(11\% - 10\%) \times (90/360) \times 10{,}000{,}000 = \$25{,}000$$

The purchaser does not receive any payments when the reference rate, as indicated by the value of three-month LIBOR, is below the strike rate of 10 percent. The payoff profile of this capped liability is illustrated in Exhibit 62–1. Because the annual amortized premium of the cap is 56 basis points, the maximum rate associated with the capped liability at a strike of 10 percent is 10.56 percent. In interest-rate scenarios where the value of three-month LIBOR is below 10 percent, the interest expense of the capped liability is higher than the unhedged interest expense by the amount of the amortization of the up-front premium. Given that the maximum risk exposure associated with the purchase of the cap is limited to the up-front premium, the dynamics of caps are similar to those of debt options. On a more specific basis, because the purchaser of the cap benefits in rising rate scenarios, the conceptual options analog is a strip of put options. However, caps can be purchased for maturities longer than those associated with a strip of

E X H I B I T   62–1

Effective Interest Expense of a Capped Liability

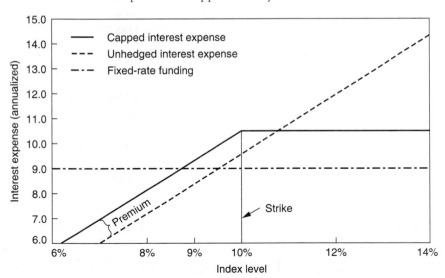

E X H I B I T   62–2

Effective Interest Cost under Two Cap Levels

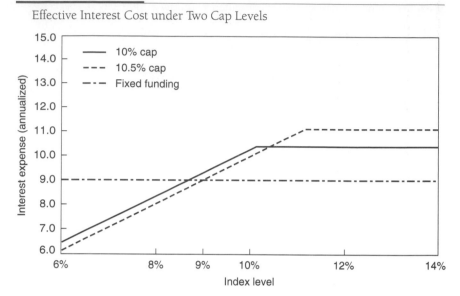

puts. By increasing the strike rate of the cap, say, from 10 percent to 10.5 percent, the up-front premium (and hence the annual amortized premium) can be reduced. However, as illustrated in Exhibit 62–2, the maximum interest expense of the capped liability increases with a higher cap strike rate.

There are several advantages associated with the use of the cap in protecting the interest expense of a floating-rate liability. The purchaser of the cap can obtain protection against higher rates and also fund the liabilities at a floating rate to take advantage of lower interest rates. In this respect, the capped liability strategy can result in a lower cost of funds than certain fixed-rate alternatives.

In addition to capping the cost of liabilities, interest-rate caps can also be used to synthetically strip embedded caps in floating-rate instruments such as CMO floaters and adjustable-rate mortgages. For instance, consider the case of an institution owning a CMO floater bond that reprices monthly at a spread of 60 basis points over LIBOR, with a cap of 600 basis points over the initial coupon rate. If the initial coupon rate is 9.60 percent, the coupon is capped at 15.60 percent. Because the only sources of cash flow available to CMO bonds are the principal, interest, and prepayment streams of the underlying mortgages, CMO floaters are by definition capped. In this respect, CMO floaters are different from other LIBOR-indexed bonds, such as floating-rate notes. The institution could strip off the embedded cap in the CMO floater by buying a cap at a strike rate of 15 percent or 16 percent. With a strike rate about 600 to 700 basis points out of the money, the cap could be purchased quite inexpensively. As interest rates increase, the loss in coupon by the embedded cap feature of the CMO bonds would be compensated by the cash inflows from the cap. The same strategy could be applied to strip caps inherent in adjustable-rate mortgages. However, the exercise of stripping caps associated with adjustable-rate mortgages is somewhat more difficult because of the existence of periodic and lifetime caps.

PARTICIPATING CAPS

It is difficult to pinpoint the exact nature of financial instruments labeled as participating caps. A common theme in the definition of such instruments is the absence of an up-front fee used to purchase the cap. The confusion in definition arises from the variations of the term *participating*. One type of participating cap involves the purchase of cap protection where the buyer obtains full protection in the event that interest rates rise. However, in order to compensate the seller of the cap for this bearish protection, the buyer shares a percentage (the participation) of the difference between the capped rate and the level of the floating-rate index in the event that interest rates fall.

For illustrative purposes, assume that a firm purchases a LIBOR participating cap at a strike rate of 10 percent with a participation rate of 60 percent. If LIBOR increases to levels greater than 10 percent, the firm will receive cash flows analogous to a nonparticipating cap. However, if LIBOR is below the capped rate, say 8 percent, then the firm gives up 60 percent of the difference between LIBOR and the capped rate, that is, $(10\% - 8\%) \times 0.6 = 1.2$ percent. In this case the effective interest expense would be 9.20 percent ($8.00\% + 1.20\%$) instead of LIBOR plus the annual amortized premium, as in a nonparticipating cap. In bullish interest-rate scenarios, the effective interest expense using a participating cap would be higher than a nonparticipating cap owing to the participation feature. However, in bearish interest-rate scenarios, the effective interest cost of the floating-rate liability would be higher for a nonparticipating cap owing to the annualized cost of the up-front premium. An illustration of the effective interest costs using both hedging alternatives is presented in Exhibit 62–3.

Other participating caps, also known as *participating swaps,* combine the analytical elements of interest-rate swaps and caps to create a hedge for floating-rate liability costs. In a participating cap structure, the firm uses interest-rate swaps to convert the floating liability rate to a fixed rate and uses caps to create a maximum upper limit on the remainder of the interest expense of the floating-rate liability. However, what distinguishes this structure is that the caps are purchased without paying an up-front fee. The purchase is funded by executing the swap (fixed-rate payer/floating-rate receiver) at an off-market rate involving a higher spread than the current market rate for equivalent maturity swaps. Such participations can be structured in one of the following ways.

- The buyer decides the maximum rate on the floating-rate liability, which leads to the problem of determining the mixture of notional amounts of caps and swaps.

EXHIBIT 62–3

Effective Interest Expense for Participating Cap

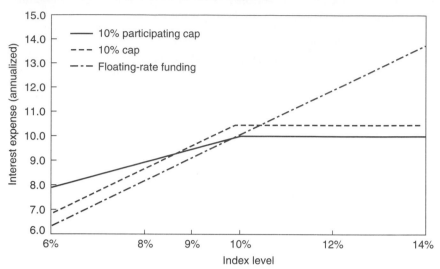

- The buyer decides on the relative mix of swaps and caps, which leads to the problem of determining the maximum rate level that can be attained with this combination.

Regardless of the choice by the buyer, the following relationship should hold in this type of participating structure:

$$\text{(Present value of annuity at } r_o - r_m, t) \times (\% \text{ of swap}) = \text{Cap premium} \times (\% \text{ of cap})$$

or

$$\text{(Present value of annuity at } r_o - r_m, t) \times (\% \text{ of swap})$$
$$= \text{Cap premium} \times (1 - \% \text{ of swap})$$

or

$$\% \text{ of cap} = \frac{\text{Present value of annuity at } r_o - r_m, t}{\text{Cap premium} + \text{Present value of annuity at } r_o - r_m, t}$$

where

r_m = Current market swap fixed rate for t periods
r_o = Off-market swap fixed rate for t periods

As an example, consider the case of an institution desiring to cap a floating-rate liability expense that floats at a spread of 10 basis points over three-month LIBOR at a maximum rate of around 10 percent for a period of five years using this type of participating cap structure. The current market rate on a five-year pay-

EXHIBIT 62–4

Effective Interest Expense Using Participating Cap Structure

LIBOR	Unhedged	Capped Rate 46% Caps	Synthetic Fixed Rate 54% Swaps	Blended Rate
11.0%	11.10%	10.10%	10.00%	10.046%
9.0	9.10	10.10	9.00	9.506
7.0	7.10	10.10	7.00	8.426

fixed and receive-floating (three-month LIBOR) swap is 80 basis points over the five-year Treasury yield at a rate of 9.40 percent. The current level of LIBOR is 9 percent and off-market five-year swaps are priced at a fixed rate of 10 percent. The cap premium for a five-year cap indexed off three-month LIBOR at a strike rate of 10 percent is 200 basis points, or 2 percent of notional amount.

The value of the annuity for five years is the difference between the off-market and the current market swap rate (that is, 10% − 9.40% = 0.60%). The present value of this annuity for five years at a discount rate of 9.4 percent (current swap rate) is 2.37185 percent. Therefore, using the above equation for participating structures, the amount of the caps is defined as [2.37185/(2.37185 + 2.0000)] = 54 percent. Hence, the amount of swaps is (1 − 0.54) = 0.46, or 46 percent. Using this structure, the effective liability expense in various interest-rate scenarios is presented in Exhibit 62–4. In this example, the synthetic fixed rate using swaps is based on the higher off-market rate, whereas the blended rate is determined as a weighted average of the cap and the swap fixed rate.

In bullish interest-rate scenarios, the blended rate is higher than the unhedged expense owing to the existence of the swap. The full benefit of the fall in rates is attained only partially by the portion of the liability mix that is capped. As interest rates increase, the blended rate is also higher than current market swaps owing to the existence of the higher-priced off-market swap that is used to fund the cap premium.

INTEREST-RATE FLOORS

Interest-rate floors are used to protect the overall rate of return associated with a floating-rate asset. As an example, consider the case of a financial institution that owns adjustable-rate mortgages in its portfolio. In the event that interest rates decrease, the coupon payments on floating-rate assets will be lower, because the repricing of variable-coupon assets is based on a floating-rate index. In order to protect the asset rate of return in bullish interest-rate scenarios, the firm could purchase an interest-rate floor. Analogous to caps, the protective features of a floor can be customized by choosing various attributes of interest-rate protection.

As an illustration, consider the following interest-rate floor purchased by an institution to protect the return on Treasury bill–indexed floating-rate assets:

Notional amount:	$10,000,000
Underlying index:	3-month Treasury bill
Maturity:	3 years
Floor strike level:	8%
Premium:	85 basis points or 0.85% of $10,000,000 = $85,000
Settlement frequency:	Quarterly
Day count:	Actual/360

The cash flow dynamics of interest-rate floors are opposite to those of interest-rate caps, as illustrated in Exhibit 62–5. As can be seen in this illustration, a floor is beneficial in bullish interest-rate scenarios. Hence, purchasing a floor is analogous to buying a strip of call options. In bearish interest-rate scenarios, the floating-rate asset earns returns constrained only by the contractual features of such instruments (if any), such as embedded caps. However, the asset return is reduced marginally by the amortization of the floor premium. In bullish interest-rate scenarios, where the asset returns are subject to erosion, the seller of the floor pays the buyer the difference between the strike rate of the floor and the value of the underlying index, adjusted for the days in the settlement period to compensate for the loss in asset coupon.

E X H I B I T   62–5

Effective Return of a Floored Asset

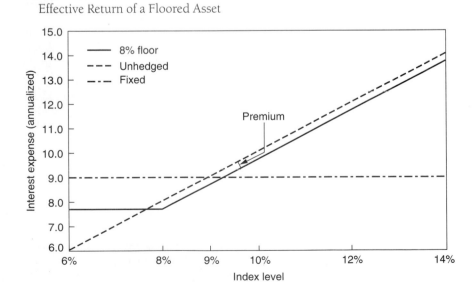

INTEREST-RATE COLLARS

Interest-rate collars involve the purchase of a cap to hedge a floating-rate liability at a higher strike rate and the sale of a floor at a lower strike rate to offset the cost of purchasing the cap. If the underlying index rate exceeds the capped rate on the reference date, the seller of the cap pays the firm the amount above the capped rate; if the market rate is less than the floor strike rate, the firm pays the buyer the difference between the floor rate and the index level. If the market rate is between the strike rate of the cap and the strike rate of the floor, the effective interest costs of the firm are normal floating-rate funding costs plus the amortized cap premium (outflow) less the amortized floor premium (inflow). The net effect of this strategy is to limit the coupon rate of the floating-rate liability between the floor strike rate and the cap strike rate. The coupon liability rate is adjusted by the net amount of the amortized cap premium paid and the amortized floor premium received to determine the effective interest cost.

For example, assume that a firm has floating-rate liabilities that are indexed at three-month LIBOR. In order to cap this floating-rate liability for one year, the firm purchases an interest-rate floor at a strike rate of 11 percent for a premium of 85 basis points. In order to offset this cost, the firm sells a floor at a strike rate of 8 percent for a premium of 60 basis points. The profit and loss profile of this strategy is presented in Exhibit 62–6. As interest rates rise above the cap strike rate, the firm receives cash flows from the seller of the cap offsetting the higher outflow on the floating-rate liability. As interest rates fall below the floor strike rate,

E X H I B I T   62–6

Interest-Rate Collar

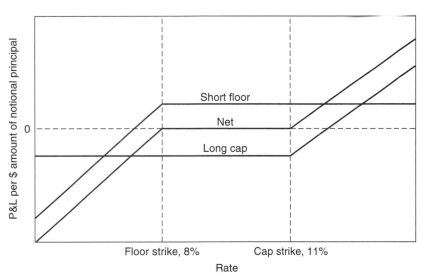

the falling interest expenses associated with the floating-rate liability are offset by the cash outflows to the buyer of the floor. In interest-rate scenarios between the floor and cap strike rate, there are no cash outflows or inflows associated with the hedges. This results in interest expenses associated with the floating-rate liability equal to normal borrowing costs. However, effective interest costs will be slightly higher to account for the net cap less floor premium, unless the collar is structured with a zero premium.

The main benefit from an interest-rate collar is that the firm obtains protection from interest-rate increases at a considerably lower cost than with the purchase of a cap. However, in return for the benefit of lower-cost interest-rate protection, the firm gives up the benefit from market rallies below the floor strike rate. Because the interest-rate protection is obtained without fixing rates, interest-rate collars are sometimes also described as *swapping into a bond*. However, this is an inefficient form of creating a collar because of the bid-ask volatility spread[2] associated with the structure. Given that the strategy involves buying a cap and selling a floor, the premium paid for the cap is based on a higher offer volatility, whereas the premium received for the floor is based on a lower bid volatility.

INTEREST-RATE CORRIDORS

An alternative strategy to reduce the cost of the cap premium is to buy a cap at a particular strike rate and sell a cap at a higher strike rate, reducing the cost of the lower strike cap and hedging the interest expense of a floating-rate liability. In contrast to an interest-rate collar, the firm maintains all the benefit of falling interest rates, because there is no sale of a floor. As long as rates are below the strike rate of the lower strike cap, the effective interest expense of the firm is limited to normal borrowing cost plus the amortized net cap premium. As interest rates increase above the lower strike rate, the interest cost to the firm is capped until market rates are above the higher strike cap. As interest rates rise above the strike rate of the second cap, interest costs increase by the amount of the outflow of the cap.

As an illustration, consider the case of a firm that purchases a cap at a strike rate of 11 percent and sells a cap at a strike rate of 15 percent to offset the cost of the first cap. The profit and loss profile of this strategy is presented in Exhibit 62–7. At market rates below 11 percent, the caps are out of the money, and the firm's effective interest cost floats at normal borrowing costs plus the net amortized cap premium. As interest rates increase above 11 percent, the first cap is in the money and starts paying cash flows to the firm to offset the higher coupon associated with the floating-rate liability. This allows the firm to cap the effective interest expense at a rate of 11 percent plus the net amortized cap premium. However, at rates higher than 15 percent, the second cap becomes in the money, and the firm has to start paying cash flows to the cap buyer. The net effect of this development is to increase the liability costs by the amount of cash outflows associated with the second cap.

---

2. See the discussion on termination of caps and floors later in this chapter.

EXHIBIT 62–7

Interest-Rate Corridor

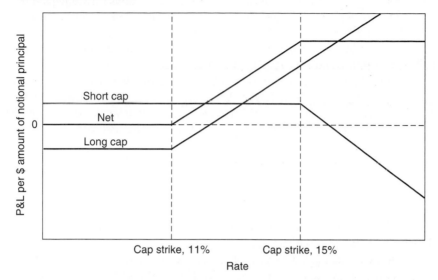

Although interest-rate collars allow the firm to offset the cost of capping floating-rate liabilities, a word of caution is in order, especially if the caps are struck under the auspices of a zero-premium strategy. Cap premiums are determined by principles of option pricing theory; consequently, the premium received for a 15 percent cap will be less than the premium paid for the 11 percent cap because of the higher strike rate and bid-offer volatility spreads. Therefore, in a zero-premium strategy, to equate the premium received for the higher strike cap to that paid for the lower strike cap, the notional amount of caps sold must be larger than the notional amount of caps purchased. Although this allows the firm to cap the liability rate at zero cost up to the strike rate of 15 percent, the firm is exposed to tremendous risk in a high-interest-rate, or "doomsday," scenario. As market interest rates increase to over 15 percent, the cash outflows paid to the buyer of the higher-strike cap may negate any cash flows received from the lower-strike cap and result in much higher interest costs than the lower-strike cap rate. The extent of this offsetting effect will be an inverse function of the ratio of the notional amount of higher-strike to lower-strike caps—the greater this ratio, the smaller will be the effect of the cash inflows of the lower-strike cap and the higher will be the effective interest cost.

CAP/FLOOR PARITY

Similar to put/call parity for options, which essentially specifies the relationship between these types of options and the price of the underlying security, caps and floors are related to interest-rate swaps. As an example, consider a strategy that involves buying a cap at 9.50 percent and selling a floor at 9.50 percent, both based off the same index, for example, LIBOR. This is equivalent to entering into an interest-rate swap, paying fixed at 9.5 percent, and receiving floating payments based on LIBOR. If interest rates increase to above the cap level, say 11 percent, the cap will pay 1.5 percent. At the same level, the holder of the swap will receive LIBOR at 11 percent. This translates into a positive cash flow of the difference between LIBOR and the fixed rate of the swap, that is, 11 percent − 9.5 percent = 1.5 percent. If interest rates decrease to below the floor level, say 7.5 percent, the holder of the floor pays the difference between the index and the floor strike rate, that is, 9.5 percent − 7.5 percent = 2 percent. At the same level, the swap holder loses the difference between the swap fixed rate and LIBOR, that is, 2 percent. Therefore, the cap/floor swap parity may be stated as

Long cap + Short floor = Fixed swap

However, for cap/floor swap parity to hold, the fixed rate of the swap should be paid on the same basis (actual/360 days, 30/360 days, or actual/365 days) as the floating rate, not a varying basis on the two rates. A graphical illustration of cap/floor swap parity is presented in Exhibit 62–8.

The cost of a market swap is zero because no premium cash flows are exchanged at inception. Therefore, using cap/floor swap parity, the cost of a cap should be the same as the cost of a floor struck at the same rate on an identical index. This relationship should hold irrespective of the pricing model used to value the caps and floors. Unless this relationship is true at every point, an arbi-

E X H I B I T   62–8

Synthetic Swap Cap/Floor Swap Parity

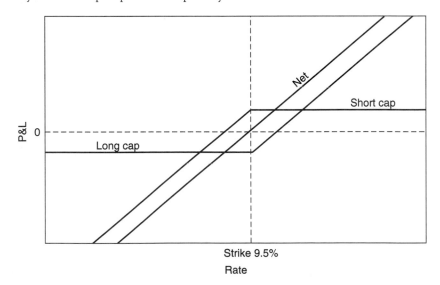

Strike 9.5%

Rate

trage exists in these markets that could be used to emulate the characteristics of the overpriced instrument. For instance, if caps are overpriced, a synthetic cap could be created by buying a floor and entering into an interest-rate swap, paying fixed at the floor strike rate and receiving floating using the same underlying index as the floor. Such arbitrage possibilities due to deviation from cap/floor swap parity also ensure efficient pricing in these markets.

TERMINATION OF CAPS AND FLOORS

As is apparent from the discussion on the characteristics of caps (floors), these instruments are essentially a strip of put (call) options on forward interest rates. Hence, caps and floors are priced using the same theoretical and analytical concepts involved in pricing options. The termination value of caps and floors can be determined using concepts similar to those involved in determining the market value of options (premium) prior to expiration; in interest-rate swaps, where the termination of swaps is based on the bid-ask spread to the Treasury yield, the bid-ask spread for caps and floors is stated in terms of volatility. On a practical basis, this is a much "cleaner" method of determining bid-ask spreads in the cap and floor market than deriving forward curves using bid and ask yield spreads. In order to compensate the financial intermediary for the market-making function, the offer volatility is higher than the bid volatility. Because option premiums are directly related to volatility, the difference between the offer premium and bid premium for either a cap or floor prior to maturity will be directly related to the magnitude of the spread between bid and offer volatility.

COMPOUND OPTIONS

Interest-rate protection provided by conventional options, such as puts and calls, and derivative optionlike instruments, such as caps and floors, extends over a specified period of time. During this time period, the option may be either "exercised," terminated prior to maturity, or allowed to expire worthless. The exercise (or lack thereof) is triggered by movements either in the price of the underlying security (as in the case of debt options) or in the underlying index (as in the case of caps and floors). However, any termination of the optional contract prior to maturity is incurred at the expense of the bid-offer spread. Given that swaps, caps, and floors are usually longer in maturity than conventional put and call options, termination costs are likely to be higher for such instruments. Additionally, the interest-rate protection provided by swaps, caps, and floors falls more in the category of passive hedging because, with the exception of the exchange of cash flows, there is no ongoing active management of the hedge.

For a shorter time horizon where the holding (outstanding) period of the asset (liability) is subject to change, firms can use interest-rate debt options. Such options can be used to manage asset/liability spreads or offset short-term opportunity losses associated with long-term interest-rate protection instruments. For instance, in rising interest-rate scenarios, where liability costs rise more quickly than the return on assets or the return on assets is fixed, put options can be used to offset the erosion in spread. The benefit of falling rates is still maintained as the loss on puts is limited to the up-front premium. Entities paying fixed in an interest-rate swap would be able to offset the opportunity loss in falling-rate scenarios by purchasing calls on Treasuries. In recent years, an important innovation known as *compound options* or *split-fee options* has allowed investors to limit losses of such short-term option strategies by permitting them to assess market conditions before purchasing additional optional coverage.

Compound options, which are essentially options on options, allow the firm to purchase a window on the market by paying a premium that is less than the premium on a conventional option on the same underlying instrument. The optional coverage can be extended at expiration of the window period by paying another premium. In essence, compound options provide an additional element of risk management by providing the opportunity to further limit downside losses associated with asymmetric coverage without sacrificing the essential ingredients of optional coverage.

Compound options allow the investor to purchase an option to exercise another option by paying a fee known as the *up-front premium* for a specified period of time. At the end of this period, known as the *window date*, the investor may exercise the option on the option by paying another fee known as the *back-end fee*. Therefore, the label *split-fee* stems from the dichotomous nature of the fees paid for the combined option. Split-fee options also have been labeled *up and on* options; this terminology refers to the up-front fee and the back-end fee paid on the window date.

Comparison with Conventional Option Strategies

Compound options offer several advantages over conventional options, such as additional leverage and greater risk-management capabilities. This point is illustrated by contrasting the coverage provided by compound puts and calls with conventional options. The graphical representation of the profit profile of a long put versus a compound put is illustrated in Exhibit 62–9. As indicated in the graph, the net profit profile of a long put is the standard textbook representation. As interest rates decline, causing increases in the value of the underlying security, the losses associated with the purchase of an at-the-money conventional put are limited to the up-front premium (*CE*). As interest rates increase, resulting in a fall in the price of the underlying security, the option can be exercised and the underlying security sold at the higher strike price. The net profit from exercising the option is the difference between the strike price and the value of the underlying security less the cost of the option. The net profit profile of the conventional put option in bullish and bearish interest-rate scenarios is denoted by *HEA*.

However, with the compound put option, the same degree of protection afforded by the conventional put is available in bullish interest-rate scenarios at a

E X H I B I T   62–9

Long Put vs. Split-Fee Option

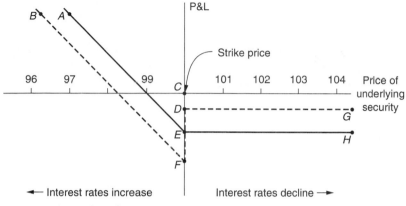

CE = Conventional put option premium
CD = Front-end fee for compound put option
DF = Back-end fee for compound put option

much lower cost, as indicated by the up-front premium of *CD* in Exhibit 62–9. In the event that interest rates continue to decline, the compound option can be allowed to expire unexercised. On the other hand, if interest rates are expected to increase, the optional coverage can be extended by exercising the second leg of the compound option. The total profit from the exercise of the compound option may be less than that obtained from exercising the conventional put if the sum of the up-front fee and the back-end fee is greater than the up-front put premium. In the event that the compound option is not exercised at the window date, the profit profile of the split-fee option strategy will be discontinuous, as indicated by *GD* in the graph. If the back-end fee is paid and the option exercised on the window date, the profit profile of the compound put is *HEFB*.

Portfolio managers frequently will purchase call options to profit from impending bullish changes in the market. The rationale underlying this strategy is based on the expectation that if interest rates decline, leading to an increase in the price of the underlying security, the portfolio manager will be able to purchase the asset at the lower strike price. The profit profile of this conventional call option is compared to that of a compound call in Exhibit 62–10. As indicated in the illustration, if interest rates remain unchanged or increase, the losses of a conventional call strategy are limited to the up-front call premium. The profit profile of the call is labeled *QNJ* in the graph; the call strategy is profitable in bullish interest-rate scenarios. In bearish interest-rate scenarios, the use of split-fee options results in losses lower than those associated with the conventional call strategy because of the lower up-front premium. However, if at the window date interest rates are

EXHIBIT 62-10

Long Call vs. Split-Fee Option

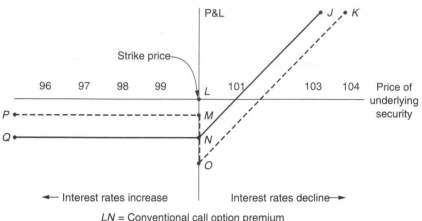

LN = Conventional call option premium
LM = Front-end fee for compound call option
MO = Back-end fee for compound call option

lower, resulting in the exercise of the compound option, the profit profile of the compound call is denoted by *PMOK*. If the compound call is not exercised, the profit profile of the split-fee option will be denoted by *PM*.

Uses of Compound Options

Compound options have been used mainly to hedge mortgage pipeline risk, especially the risk of applicants seeking alternative sources of financing or canceling the loan. This risk, known as *fallout risk*, is usually hedged by purchasing put options. The ramifications of fallout risk are especially severe if the expected mortgage production has already been sold forward. If interest rates fall and mortgage loans fall out of the pipeline, the mortgage lender can let the option expire unexercised. On the other hand, if rates increase, the lender can participate in the upside movement of the market by selling originated loans at the higher put strike price. With a compound put option, the mortgage lender can obtain the same optional protection at a much lower cost and retain the flexibility of extending the protection after assessing market conditions. If at the window date there is no need for put protection, the loss is lower than that of the premium of a conventional put. On the other hand, if additional protection is required, it can be purchased by either extending the compound option or by purchasing a conventional put option. For instance, it is possible that if forward market prices are higher (lower) on the window date, the purchase of a put (call) may be cheaper than exercising the option on the option.

Portfolios using active call-buying programs as yield-enhancement vehicles may purchase compound calls when there is uncertainty regarding an impending fall in interest rates. Instead of purchasing a higher-premium conventional call, the compound call allows the portfolio manager to purchase a window on the market for a lower cost. At the window date, if there is a greater degree of certainty regarding bullish market conditions, the compound options can be extended. However, if the degree of uncertainty increases, the loss is limited to the lower up-front premium.

Compound options, such as calls, can also be used in conjunction with longer-term instruments, such as fixed interest-rate swaps, to offset short-term opportunity losses caused by a fall in interest rates. However, perhaps the largest potential use of compound option technology lies in the application of these concepts to the cap and floor market in designing long-term options on options. Recall that caps (floors) are essentially a package of European puts (calls) on forward interest rates. The market for options on caps and floors, which allow the buyer to either cancel or initiate customized interest-rate protection, is still fairly undeveloped, but the potential uses of such instruments are enormous. As with any optional coverage, the development of such options on a series of options will add another element of flexibility provided by customized risk-management instruments.

CONCLUDING COMMENTS

Swaps, floors, and compound options are customized risk-management instruments. Whereas interest-rate swaps are intended to insulate the user from changes in interest-rate volatility, caps and floors are designed to provide asymmetric coverage in capping liability costs and protecting the rate of return on assets. In either case, the user retains the right to participate in upside movements of the market. In order to reduce the up-front cost of purchasing caps and floors, the user can either enter into participating agreements that involve giving up a proportional share of beneficial market moves or enter into agreements, such as collars and corridors, that are analogous to option spread strategies.

Because the termination of such agreements involves exit costs, these instruments may prove beneficial for passive hedging where interest-rate protection is desired for longer periods of time. By the same token, these agreements also should not be used if the holding period of either the asset or liability is flexible or subject to change. For shorter periods of time, the user may decide to use split-fee options, which provide greater leverage and risk-management capabilities similar to conventional options, although contemporary use of split-fee options has been mainly in mortgage pipeline hedging. However, compound option technology can be applied readily to develop options on caps and floors, thereby adding an additional element of flexibility for these instruments in designing customized interest-rate protection.

QUESTIONS

⑥

PART 1: BACKGROUND

1. The indenture for most fixed income securities has a provision that grants to either the issuer/borrower or the investor the right to alter the security's cash flow.

   a. What are these provisions?

   b. Which provision(s) grant the issuer/borrower the right to alter the security's cash flow?

   c. Which provision(s) grant the investor the right to alter the security's cash flow?

2. In what way can interest-rate risk and reinvestment risk offset each other?

3. **a.** What is event risk?

   b. Give two examples of event risk.

4. A pension fund manager invests $20 million in a debt obligation that promises to pay 6.4 percent per year for four years. What is the future value of the $20 million?

5. Suppose that a life insurance company has guaranteed a payment of $14 million to a pension fund 4.5 years from now. If the life insurance company receives a premium of $10.4 million from the pension fund and can invest the entire premium for 4.5 years at an annual interest rate of 6.25 percent, will it have sufficient funds from this investment to meet the $14 million obligation?

6. Suppose that a portfolio manager purchases $24 million of par value of a 10-year bond that has a coupon rate of 6 percent and pays interest once per year. The first annual coupon payment will be made one year from now. How much will the portfolio manager have if he (1) holds the bond until it matures 10 years from now and (2) can reinvest all the annual interest payments at an annual interest rate of 5 percent?

7. If the discount rate that is used to calculate the present value of a debt obligation's cash flow is decreased, what happens to the price of that debt obligation?

8. The pension fund obligation of a corporation is calculated as the present value of the actuarially projected benefits that will have to be paid to

beneficiaries. Why is the interest rate used to discount the projected benefits important?

9. A pension fund manager knows that the following liabilities must be satisfied:

Years from Now	Liability
1	$6.0 million
2	4.0
3	9.1
4	4.3

Suppose that the pension fund manager wants to invest a sum of money that will satisfy this liability stream. Assuming that any amount that can be invested today can earn an annual interest rate of 4.2 percent, how much must be invested today to satisfy this liability stream?

10. **a.** Why will a bond sell below par value?

b. What is the maximum price of a bond?

11. Calculate for each of the bonds below the price per $100 of par value assuming semiannual coupon payments.

Bond	Coupon Rate	Years to Maturity	Required Yield
A	8%	9	7%
B	9	20	9
C	6	15	10
D	0	14	8

12. Consider a bond selling at par ($100) with a coupon rate of 6 percent and 10 years to maturity.

a. What is the price of this bond if the required yield is 15 percent?

b. What is the price of this bond if the required yield increases from 15 percent to 16 percent, and by what percentage did the price of this bond change?

c. What is the price of this bond if the required yield is 5 percent?

d. What is the price of this bond if the required yield increases from 5 percent to 6 percent, and by what percentage did the price of this bond change?

e. From your answers to parts (b) and (d), what can you say about the relative price volatility of a bond in high compared to low interest-rate environments?

13. Suppose you are reviewing a price sheet for bonds and see the following prices (per $100 par value) reported. You observe what seem to be several errors. Without calculating the price of each bond, indicate which bonds seem to be reported incorrectly and explain why.

Bond	Price	Coupon Rate	Required Yield
U	90	6%	9%
V	96	9	8
W	110	8	6
X	105	0	5
Y	107	7	9
Z	100	6	6

14. What is the difference between the dirty (or full) price and the clean (or flat) price of a bond?

15. A money manager is considering buying two bonds. Bond X matures in three years and has a coupon rate of 10 percent payable semiannually. Bond B, of the same credit quality, matures in 10 years and has a coupon rate of 12 percent payable semiannually. Both bonds are priced at par.

a. Suppose the manager plans to hold the bond that is purchased for three years. Which would be the best bond for the manager to purchase?

b. Suppose the manager plans to hold the bond that is purchased for six years instead of three years. In this case, which would be the best bond for the manager to purchase?

c. Suppose that the manager is managing the assets of a life insurance company that has issued a five-year guaranteed investment contract (GIC). The interest rate that the life insurance company has agreed to pay is 9 percent on a semiannual basis. Which of the two bonds should the manager purchase to ensure that the GIC payments will be satisfied and that a profit will be generated by the life insurance company?

16. What is meant by a bond-equivalent yield?

17. a. What are the two methods used to calculate a portfolio yield?

b. What are the limitations of these two methods?

18. a. What is the total return for a 10-year zero-coupon bond selling to offer a yield-to-maturity of 6 percent if the bond is held to maturity?

b. Explain why the total return from holding a bond to maturity will be between the yield-to-maturity and reinvestment rate.

    c. For a long-term, high-coupon bond, do you think that the total return from holding a bond to maturity will be closer to the yield-to-maturity or the reinvestment rate?

19. a. Often, the duration of a bond is referred to as some type of weighted average time of the cash flows of the bond. What is a better interpretation of duration?

    b. What is the difference between modified duration and effective duration, and which is the appropriate measure for bonds with embedded options?

    c. If two bonds have the same dollar duration, yield, and price, their dollar price sensitivity will be the same for a given change in interest rates. Is this true? Why or why not?

20. Calculate the requested measures for bonds A and B (assume each bond pays interest semiannually):

	A	B
Coupon	8%	9%
Yield-to-Maturity	8%	8%
Maturity (in Years)	2	5
Par	100.00	100.00
Price	100.000	104.055

    a. Price value of a basis point.

    b. Macaulay duration.

    c. Modified duration.

    d. Convexity.

    e. Calculate the actual price of the two bonds for a 100-basis-point increase in interest rates.

    f. Using duration, estimate the price of the bonds for a 100-basis-point increase in interest rates.

    g. Using both duration and convexity, estimate the price of the bonds for a 100-basis-point increase in interest rates.

    h. Comment on the accuracy of your results in (f) and (g), and state why one approximation is closer to the actual price than the other.

    i. Without working through calculations, indicate whether the duration of the two bonds would be higher or lower if the yield-to-maturity were 10 percent rather than 8 percent.

21. The following excerpt is taken from an article entitled "Denver Investment to Make $800 Million Treasury Move" that appeared in the December 9, 1991, issue of *BondWeek,* p. 1:

Denver Investment Advisors will swap $800 million of long-zero coupon Trea-
suries for intermediate Treasuries . . . The move would shorten the duration of
its $2.5 billion fixed-income portfolio . . .

Why would the swap described above shorten the duration of the portfolio?

22. Suppose that you are given the following information about two
callable bonds that can be called immediately:

	Estimated Percentage Change in Price If Interest Rates Change by	
	−100 basis points	+100 basis points
Bond ABC	+15%	−20%
Bond XYZ	+22%	−16%

You are told that both of these bonds have the same maturity and the
coupon rate of one bond is 7 percent and the other 13 percent. Suppose
that the yield curve for both issuers is flat at 8 percent. Based on this information, which bond is the lower-coupon bond and which is the
higher-coupon bond? Explain why.

23. *(This question is adapted from CFA Examination II, June 1, 1991,
Morning Section, Question 2):*

a. Calculate the two-ycar spot rate implied by the U.S. Treasury yield-
curve data given below. Assume interest is paid annually for
purposes of this calculation. Show all calculations.

Years to Maturity	Current Coupon (Yield-to-Maturity)	Spot Rate
1	7.5%	7.5%
2	8.0	?

b. Explain why a spot-rate curve can be derived entirely from the
current-coupon (yield-to-maturity) yield curve.

c. Given a U.S. Treasury one-year spot rate of 9.0 percent and U.S.
Treasury two-year spot rate of 9.5 percent, calculate the implied one-
year forward rate for the two-year U.S. Treasury security with one
year remaining to maturity. Explain why a one-year forward rate of
9.6 percent would not be expected to prevail in a market given these
spot rates.

d. Describe *one* practical application of the spot-rate concept and *one*
practical application of the forward rate concept.

24. *(This question is adapted from CFA Examination II, June 2, 1990, Morning Section, Question 2):*

The following are average yields on U.S. Treasury bonds at two different points in time:

	Yield-to-Maturity	
Term-to-Maturity	**January 15, 19XX**	**May 15, 19XX**
1 year	7.25%	8.05%
2 years	7.50	7.90
5 years	7.90	7.70
10 years	8.30	7.45
15 years	8.45	7.30
20 years	8.55	7.20
25 years	8.60	7.10

a. Assuming a pure expectations hypothesis, define a forward rate. Describe how you would calculate the forward rate for a three year U.S. Treasury bond two years from May 15, 19XX, using the actual term structure above.

b. Discuss how *each* of the *three* major term-structure hypotheses could explain the January 15, 19XX term structure shown above.

c. Discuss what happened to the term structure over the time period and the effect of this change on the U.S. Treasury bonds of 2 years and 10 years.

d. Assume that you invest solely on the basis of yield spreads, and in January 19XX acted upon the expectation that the yield spread between 1-year and 25-year U.S. Treasuries would return to a more typical spread of 170 basis points. *Explain* what you would have done on January 15, 19XX, and *describe* the result of this action based upon what happened between January 15, 19XX, and May 15, 19XX.

25. In the May 19, 1992, *Weekly Market Update* published by Goldman Sachs & Co., the following information was reported in various exhibits for the Treasury market as of the close of business Thursday, May 28, 1992:

On-the-Run-Treasuries	
Maturity	**Yield**
3-Mo.	3.77%
6-Mo.	3.95
1-Yr.	4.25

2-Yr.	5.23
3-Yr.	5.78
5-Yr.	6.67
7-Yr.	7.02
10-Yr.	7.37
20-Yr.	7.65
30-Yr.	7.88

Key Off-the-Run Treasuries

Issue	Yield
Old 10-Yr.	7.42%
Old 30-Yr.	7.90

a. What is the credit risk associated with a Treasury security?

b. Why is the Treasury yield considered the base interest rate?

c. What is meant by *on-the-run Treasuries*?

d. What is meant by *off-the-run Treasuries*?

e. What is the yield spread between (i) the off-the-run 10-year Treasury issue and the on-the-run 10-year Treasury issue, and (ii) the off-the-run 30-year Treasury issue and the on-the-run 30-year Treasury issue?

f. What does the yield spread between the off-the-run Treasury issue and the on-the-run Treasury issue reflect?

26. In the May 29, 1992, *Weekly Market Update* published by Goldman Sachs & Co., the following information was reported in various exhibits for certain corporate bonds as of the close of business Thursday, May 28, 1992:

Issuer	Rating	Yield	Spread	Treasury Benchmark
General Electric Capital Co.	Triple A	7.87%	50	10
Mobile Corp.	Double A	7.77	40	10
Southern Bell Tel & Teleg	Triple A	8.60	72	30
Bell Tell Co Pa	Double A	8.66	78	30
AMR Corp	Triple B	9.43	155	30

a. What is meant by *Rating*?

b. Which of the five bonds has the greatest credit risk?

c. What is meant by *Spread*?

d. What is meant by *Treasury Benchmark*?

    e. Using the information for the Treasury market reported for May 29, 1992, in the previous question, explain how each of the spreads reported above was determined.

    f. Why do each of the spreads reported above reflect a risk premium?

27. For the corporate bond issues reported in the previous question, answer the following questions:

    a. Should a triple-A-rated bond issue offer a higher or lower yield than a double-A-rated bond issue of the same maturity?

    b. What is the spread between the General Electric Capital Co. issue and the Mobile Corp. issue?

    c. Is the spread reported in (b) consistent with your answer to (a)?

    d. The yield spread between these two bond issues reflects more than just credit risk. What other factors would the spread reflect?

    e. The Mobil Corp. issue is not callable. However, the General Electric Capital Co. issue is callable. How does this information help you in understanding the spread between these two issues?

28. For the corporate bond issues reported in question 26, answer the following questions:

    a. What is the yield spread between the Southern Bell Telephone and Telegraph bond issue and the Bell Telephone Company (Pennsylvania) bond issue?

    b. The Southern Bell Telephone and Telegraph bond issue is not callable, but the Bell Telephone Company (Pennsylvania) bond issue is callable. What does the yield spread in (a) reflect?

    c. AMR Corp. is the parent company of American Airlines and is therefore classified in the transportation industry. The issue is not callable. What is the yield spread between AMR Corp. and Southern Bell Telephone and Telegraph bond issues, and what does this spread reflect?

29. In the May 29, 1992, *Weekly Market Update* published by Goldman Sachs & Co., the following information was reported in an exhibit for high-grade, tax-exempt securities as of the close of business Thursday, May 28, 1992:

Maturity	Yield	Yield as a Percentage of Treasury Yield
1-Yr.	3.20%	76.5%
3-Yr.	4.65	80.4
5-Yr.	5.10	76.4
10-Yr.	5.80	78.7
30-Yr.	6.50	82.5

a. What is meant by a *tax-exempt security*?

b. What is meant by a *high-grade* issue?

c. Why is the yield on a tax-exempt security less than the yield on a Treasury security of the same maturity?

d. What is meant by the *equivalent taxable yield*?

e. Also reported in the same issue of the Goldman Sachs report is information on "Intra-market Yield Spreads." What is an intramarket yield spread?

30. a. Explain why it is inappropriate to use one yield to discount all the cash flows of a financial asset.

b. Explain why a financial asset can be viewed as a package of zero-coupon instruments.

c. Would a tax-exempt yield ever be greater than the same maturity Treasury yield? Why or why not?

31. Here are comments made by your clients at different times. Respond to each one.

a. "The yield curve is upward sloping today. This suggests that the market consensus is that interest rates are expected to increase in the future."

b. "I can't make any sense out of today's term structure. For short-term yields (up to three years), the spot rates increase with maturity; for maturities greater than three years but less than eight years, the spot rates decline with maturity; and for maturities greater than eight years, the spot rates are virtually the same for each maturity. There is simply no theory that explains a term structure with this shape."

c. "When I want to determine the market's consensus of future interest rates, I calculate the implied forward rates."

32. How are spot rates related to forward rates?

33. What characteristics are critical in judging or comparing bond indexes?

34. What are the three broad-based market indexes?

PART 2: GOVERNMENT AND PRIVATE DEBT OBLIGATIONS

1. Calculate the dollar price for the following Treasury coupon securities:

	Price Quoted	Par
a.	95–4	$ 100,000
b.	87–16	1,000,000
c.	102–10	10,000,000
d.	116–30	10,000
e.	102–4+	100,000

2. The bid and ask yields for a Treasury bill maturing on January 16, 1992, were quoted by a dealer as 5.91 percent and 5.89 percent, respectively. Shouldn't the bid yield be less than the ask yield, because the bid yield indicates how much the dealer is willing to pay, and the ask yield is what the dealer is willing to sell the Treasury bill for?

3. The following is from the March 1991 monthly report published by Blackstone Financial Management:

   The Treasury also brought $34.5 billion in new securities to the market in February as part of the normal quarterly refunding . . . the auctions went slightly better than expected given the significant size and the uncertainties surrounding the duration of the war. The 3-year was issued at a 6.98 percent average yield, the 10-year at a 7.85 percent average yield, and the 30-year at a 7.98 percent average yield. All bids were accepted at the average yield or better (i.e., with no tail), indicating ample demand for the securities.

   a. What is meant by the *average yield* and the *tail*?

   b. Why does the absence of a tail indicate ample demand for the Treasuries auctioned?

4. a. What is the difference between a STRIP, a trademark Treasury zero-coupon security, and a Treasury receipt?

   b. What is the most common type of Treasury zero-coupon security?

5. a. What is the difference between a government sponsored enterprise security and a federally related institution?

   b. Are government sponsored enterprise securities backed by the full faith and credit of the U.S. government?

6. a. What is the difference between a general obligation bond and a revenue bond?

   b. Which type of bond would an investor analyze using an approach similar to that for analyzing a corporate bond?

7. Explain why you agree or disagree with the following statements:

   a. "All municipal bonds are exempt from federal income taxes."

   b. "All municipal bonds are exempt from state and local taxes."

   c. "An insured municipal bond is safer than an uninsured municipal bond."

8. If congress changes the tax law so as to increase marginal tax rates, what will happen to the price of municipal bonds?

9. a. Explain the different types of refunded bonds.

   b. Identify two reasons why an issuing municipality would want to refund an outstanding bond issue.

10. What can you say about the typical relationship between the yield on short-term and long-term municipal bonds?

11. **a.** Why is commercial paper an alternative to short-term bank borrow-
       ing for a corporation?

    b. What is the difference between directly placed paper and dealer-
       placed paper?

    c. What does the yield spread between commercial paper and Treasury
       bills of the same maturity reflect?

12. **a.** How can a repurchase agreement be used by a dealer firm to finance
       a long position in a Treasury security?

    b. One party in a repo transaction is said to "buy collateral," the other
       party to "sell collateral." Why"

    c. When there is a shortage of a specific security for a repo transaction,
       will the repo rate increase or decrease?

13. Explain whether the rate on an overnight repurchase agreement would
    be higher or lower than the rate on overnight federal funds.

14. **a.** Why is a bank that creates a BA called an *accepting bank*?

    b. How is this related to an acceptance's credit risk?

    c. Why is the "eligibility" of a bankers acceptance important?

15. Indicate whether you agree or disagree with the following statements:

    a. "A sinking-fund provision in a bond issue benefits the investor."

    b. "A guaranteed bond is safer than a debenture bond."

16. What is the difference between refunding protection and call
    protection?

17. **a.** Who are the four nationally recognized statistical rating
       organizations?

    b. What is meant by an investment-grade bond?

18. Describe the general characteristics of a medium-term note.

19. Explain how the emergence of the medium-term note market has trans-
    formed the way corporations raise funds.

20. Describe the general characteristics of a floating-rate note.

21. "A floating-rate note will always trade in the market at par value." Do
    you agree with this statement?

22. **a.** Describe the different types of preferred stock.

    b. What was the most popular type of preferred stock in the 1980s?

    c. What is the most popular type of preferred stock today, and why?

23. Why are corporate treasurers the main buyers of preferred stock?

24. Consider the following convertible bond:

    Par value = $1,000
    Coupon rate = 9.5%
    Market price of convertible bond = $1,000

Conversion ratio = 37.383
Estimated straight value of bond = $510
Yield-to-maturity of straight bond = 18.7%

Assume that the price of the common stock is $23 and that the dividend per share is $0.75 per annum.

a. Calculate each of the following:

   (i) Conversion value
   (ii) Market conversion price
   (iii) Conversion premium per share
   (iv) Conversion premium ratio
   (v) Premium over straight value
   (vi) Yield advantage of bond
   (vii) Premium payback period

b. Suppose that the price of the common stock increases from $23 to $46.

   (i) What will be the approximate return realized from investing in the convertible bond?
   (ii) What would be the return realized if $23 had been invested in the common stock?
   (iii) Why would the return be higher by investing in the common stock directly rather than by investing in the convertible bond?

c. Suppose that the price of the common stock declines from $23 to $8.

   (i) What will be the approximate return realized from investing in the convertible bond?
   (ii) What would be the return realized if $23 had been invested in the common stock?
   (iii) Why would the return be higher by investing in the convertible bond rather than by investing in the common stock directly?

25. The following excerpt is taken from an article entitled "Caywood Looks for Convertibles" that appeared in the January 13, 1992, issue of *BondWeek*, p. 7:

Caywood Christian Capital Management will invest new money in its $400 million high-yield portfolio in "busted convertibles," double- and triple-B rated convertible bonds of companies whose stock . . . said James Caywood, ceo. Caywood likes these convertibles as they trade at discounts and are unlikely to be called, he said.

a. What is a *busted convertible?*

b. What is the premium-over-straight value at which these bonds would trade?

c. Why does Mr. Caywood seek convertibles with higher investment-grade ratings?

d. Why is Mr. Caywood interested in call protection?

e. Explain the limitation of using premium-over-straight value as a measure of the downside risk of a convertible bond.

26. The following excerpt is taken from an article entitled "Bartlett Likes Convertibles" that appeared in October 7, 1991, issue of *BondWeek*, p. 7:

> Bartlett & Co. is selectively looking for opportunities in convertible bonds that are trading cheaply because the equity of the issuer has dropped in value, according to Dale Rabiner, director of fixed income at the $800 million Cincinnati-based fund. Rabiner said he looks for five-year convertibles trading at yields comparable to straight bonds of companies he believes will rebound.

Discuss this strategy for investing in convertible bonds.

27. What is a high-yield bond?

28. Why has the issuance of securities pursuant to SEC Rule 144A become a popular financing technique for the high-yield market in recent years?

29. a. What is a split-coupon security?

b. What is a payment-in-kind security?

30. How does a bank loan differ from the typical high-yield security?

31. a. What is the difference between a Eurobond and a foreign bond?

b. What is a global bond?

c. What is a Yankee bond?

32. What are the components of return when investing in non-U.S. pay securities?

33. What are the factors generally regarded as affecting foreign currency movements?

34. a. What is a Brady bond?

b. What are the two types of principal Brady bonds?

35. How do stable value contracts differ from traditional fixed income instruments?

36. What factors are important in selecting the type of stable value products to use?

PART 3: CREDIT ANALYSIS

1. Traditionally, credit analysis for corporate bonds has focused almost exclusively on the default risk of the bond. Explain another purpose of credit analysis for investors who actively trade corporate bonds.

2. What are the variables an analyst should consider in reviewing an industry?

3. Describe the following ratios traditionally used in financial analysis:

   a. Pretax interest coverage ratios

   b. Leverage ratios

   c. Cash flow/spending ratio

   d. Cash flow/capital ratio

4. Describe several nonfinancial factors that an analyst should consider in evaluating a company.

5. What areas of analysis should be expanded in evaluating high-yield bonds?

6. What is the difference between a liquidation and a reorganization?

7. What is the difference between a Chapter 7 and Chapter 11 bankruptcy filing?

8. What is meant by a *debtor-in-possession*?

9. What is meant by the principle of *absolute priority*?

10. What are the different approaches that can be used to evaluate Chapter 11 companies?

11. What are the most important documents for the analysis of bankrupt securities?

12. What is meant by *fraudulent conveyance*?

13. Why have ongoing concerns developed among many investors and underwriters about the potential default risks of municipal bonds?

14. What is the role of the legal opinion in a municipal bond issue?

15. What is meant by the *flow-of-funds structure* of a municipal revenue bond issue?

16. a. When assessing the creditworthiness of a general obligation, what factors should investors consider?

    b. When assessing the creditworthiness of a revenue bond, what factors should investors consider?

17. In rating sovereign debt, why do rating companies rate both local currency debt and foreign currency debt rather than assign just one rating to a country?

18. What are the three factors that determine values of emerging market debt?

19. a. What is meant by cross-border risk?

    b. What is sovereign risk?

20. What are foreign exchange reserves?

21. a. What is meant by a quasi-sovereign?

    b. Why are foreign banks difficult to value?

22. Explain each of the following relationships:

   a. interest rate parity

   b. purchasing power parity

   c. international Fisher effect

PART 4: MORTGAGE-BACKED AND ASSET-BACKED SECURITIES

1. What is a *mortgage*?

2. What are the two primary factors in determining whether funds will be lent to an applicant for a mortgage loan?

3. What is meant by *conforming mortgage* and *noncomforming mortgage*?

4. Why is the interest rate on a mortgage loan not necessarily the same as the interest rate that the investor receives?

5. a. What are the three components of the cash flow of a mortgage loan?

   b. Why is the cash flow of a mortgage unknown?

6. In what sense has the investor in a mortgage loan granted the borrower (homeowner) a call option?

7. Consider the following fixed-rate level-payment mortgage:

Maturity = 360 months
Amount borrowed = $200,000
Annual mortgage rate = 8%

   a. What is the monthly mortgage payment?

   b. Construct an amortization schedule for the first eight months.

8. a. In adjustable-rate mortgages, what are the two types of reference rates used?

   b. What types of restrictions are imposed on the reference rate at a reset date?

9. What is a *balloon mortgage* and how does it differ from a *fixed-rate level-payment mortgage*?

10. a. What are the different types of agency pass-through securities?

   b. Which type of agency pass-through carries the full faith and credit of the U.S. government?

11. Why is it necessary to forecast prepayments to value a mortgage-backed security?

12. What is the current industry standard to describe prepayment behavior?

13. What is meant by the a*verage life* of a pass-through?

14. What are the limitations of yield measures for a mortgage pass-through security?

15. Explain why in general prepayment volatility is greatest for mortgage-backed securities whose underlying mortgages have coupons between 100 and 300 basis points above current mortgage rates.

16. Explain why effective duration and effective convexity are more appropriate measures of price volatility when rates change than modified duration and convexity.

17. In calculating the total return from holding a pass-though security, what assumptions are required?

18. How does a collateralized mortgage obligation alter the cash flow from mortgages so as to shift the prepayment risk across various classes of bondholders?

19. "By creating a CMO, an issuer eliminates the prepayment risk associated with the underlying mortgages." Do you agree with this statement?

20. What is a *sequential-pay CMO tranche*?

21. What is the characteristic of an accrual CMO tranche?

22. a. What is a *planned amortization class band*?

    b. Indicate why you agree or disagree with the following statement: "A PAC band is not exposed to prepayment risk."

    c. What is meant by the *PAC band*?

    d. Does the PAC band change over time or does it stay constant?

23. a. What is a *principal-only security*? An *interest-only security*?

    b. How is the price of an interest-only security expected to change when interest rates change?

24. A broker showed a money manager a stripped mortgage-backed security and recommended the purchase of the interest-only security. The broker stated that since the stripped MBS is created from a Ginnie Mae pass-through, the principal and interest are guaranteed. Therefore, the broker told the money manager that the interest-only security is guaranteed. Comment.

25. Suppose you are told that the yield of a pass-through security is 8.5 percent and that you are seeking to invest in a security with a yield greater than 8 percent.

    a. What additional information would you need to know before you might acquire this pass-through security?

    b. What are the limitations of the yield for assessing the potential return from investing in a mortgage-backed security?

26. **a.** What is a *support bond*?

   b. What is its role in a CMO structure with PAC bonds?

   c. What happens to a PAC bond if the support bonds are paid off?

27. What factors should be considered in analyzing a CMO?

28. What is a nonagency CMO?

29. In a nonagency CMO deal, what is compensating interest?

30. Why should investors in nonagency mortgage-backed securities be more concerned with current loan-to-value ratios rather than original loan-to-value ratios?

31. Describe the structural call protection provided for in a commercial mortgage-backed security.

32. What are the five types of deal structures for a commercial mortgage-backed security?

33. **a.** What types of credit enhancement are used in asset-backed securities and nonagency mortgage-backed securities?

   b. What is the difference between internal and external credit enhancements?

34. What are the factors that determine the amount of credit enhancement needed in structuring an asset-backed security?

35. Explain each of the following forms of credit enhancement:

   a. Third-party guarantees

   b. Reserve funds or cash collateral

   c. Recourse to the issuer

   d. Overcollateralization

   e. Senior/subordinated structures

36. An asset-backed security has been credit enhanced with a letter of credit from a bank with a double A credit rating. If this is the only form of credit enhancement, explain whether this issue can be assigned a triple A credit rating.

37. An issuer is considering two possible credit enhancement structures backed by a pool of automobile loans. Explain which structure would probably receive the higher credit rating:

Total principal value of asset-backed security: $300 million

Principal value for	Structure I	Structure II
Pool of automobile loans	$304 million	$301 million
Senior class	250	270
Subordinated class	50	30

38. In asset-backed securities, why are defaults considered prepayments?

39. a. What are the cash flow characteristics of auto loan-backed securities?

b. How sensitive are auto loans to prepayments as a result of declining interest rates?

40. a. What are the two types of home equity loans?

b. What three ratios are analyzed by originators of home equity loans?

c. Why are borrowers categorized by credit quality?

41. What are the four major determinants of prepayments for home equity loan-backed securities?

42. a. What are manufacturing housing loans?

b. What has been the historical prepayment experience of manufactured housing loan-backed securities?

43. What are the different types of credit cards?

44. a. What are the cash flows for a credit card receivable-backed security?

b. What is meant by a controlled amortization in a credit card receivable structure?

c. What can trigger an early amortization in a credit card deal?

d. What does the monthly payment rate mean?

45. What is meant by the static spread?

PART 5: ADVANCED ANALYTICS AND MODELING

1. In Robert Litterman, Jose Scheinkman, and Laurence Weiss, "Volatility and the Yield Curve," *The Journal of Fixed Income,* Premier Issue, 1991, p. 49, the following statement was made:

> Many fixed income securities—e.g. callable bonds—contain embedded options whose prices are sensitive to the level of volatility. Modeling the additional impact of volatility on the value of the coupons allows for a better understanding of the price behavior of these securities.

Explain why.

2. Explain how volatility is introduced in the binomial method for valuing bonds with embedded options.

3. a. Explain how the binomial interest-rate tree is constructed.

b. If an on-the-run issue for an issuer is evaluated using the binomial method, how would the theoretical value compare to the actual market price?

4. Given the following information, determine the theoretical value of the call option:

Theoretical value of noncallable bond = $103
Theoretical value of callable bond = $101

5. Explain why you agree or disagree with the following statement: "The value of a putable bond is never greater than the value of an otherwise comparable option-free bond."

6. a. What is meant by the *option-adjusted spread*?

b. What is the spread relative to?

7. What is the effect of greater expected interest-rate volatility on the option-adjusted spread of a security?

8. In an article entitled "CUNA Mutual Looks for Noncallable Corporates" that appeared in the November 4, 1991, issue of *BondWeek*, p. 6, Joe Goglia, a portfolio manager for CUNA Mutual Insurance Group, stated that he invests in "planned amortization class tranches, which have less exposure to prepayment risk and are more positively convex than other mortgage-backeds." Is this true?

9. The following excerpt is taken from an article entitled "Call Provisions Drop Off" that appeared in the January 27, 1992, issue of *BondWeek*, p.2:

> Issuance of callable long-term bonds dropped off further last year as interest rates fell, removing the incentive for many issuers to pay extra for the provision, said Street capital market officials. . . . The shift toward noncallable issues, which began in the late 1980s, reflects the secular trend of investors' unwillingness to bear prepayment risk and possibly the cyclical trend that corporations believe that interest rates have hit all time lows. . . .
>
> Though investors are more aware of the value of call protection, the price of a 10-year call provision has dropped to 13–15 basis points from 25–30 a few years ago, investment bankers said . . . Junk bond issuers have not given up on calls. . . .

a. What "incentive" is this article referring to in the first sentence of the excerpt?

b. Why would issuers not be willing to pay for this incentive if they feel that interest rates will continue to decline?

c. Why has the value of call protection decreased?

d. Why do you think issuers of junk (high-yield) bonds have not eliminated call provisions?

10. What are the methodologies used to value mortgage-backed securities?

11. Explain the required assumptions of each methodology used to value mortgage-backed securities?

12. **a.** Explain how effective duration is calculated.

   b. What is assumed about the OAS in calculating effective duration?

13. **a.** What is meant by *spread duration*?

   b. What is meant by *partial durations*?

14. What is meant by *yield-curve reshaping risk*?

15. How can the exposure of a portfolio to changes in the shape of the yield curve be estimated?

16. What is meant by *prepayment duration*?

17. The current on-the-run yields for the Ramsey Corporation are given below:

Maturity	Yield-to Maturity	Market Price
1 year	7.5%	100
2 years	7.6	100
3 years	7.7	100

   Assume that each bond is an annual-pay bond. Since each bond is trading at par, its coupon rate is equal to its yield-to-maturity.

   a. Using the bootstrapping methodology, complete the following table:

Year	Spot Rate	One-Year Forward Rate
1		
2		
3		

   b. Using the spot rates, what would be the value of an 8.5 percent option-free bond of this issuer?

   c. Using the one-year forward rates, what would be the value of an 8.5 percent coupon option-free bond of this issuer?

   d. Using the valuation model explained in the binomial model described in Chapter 36 (which assumes that one-year rates undergo a lognormal random walk with volatility σ), show that if σ is assumed to be 10 percent, the lower one-year forward rate one year from now *cannot* be 7 percent.

   e. Demonstrate that if σ is assumed to be 10 percent, the lower one-year forward rate one year from now is approximately 6.944 percent.

   f. Demonstrate that if σ is assumed to be 10 percent, the lower one-year forward rate two years from now is approximately 6.437 percent.

g. Show the binomial interest-rate tree that should be used to value any bond of this issuer.

h. Determine the value of an 8.5 percent coupon option-free bond for this issuer using the binomial interest-rate tree given in part (g).

i. Determine the value of an 8.5 percent coupon bond that is callable at part (100) assuming that the issue will be called if the price exceeds par.

18. The following information was reported in William M. Boyce, Webster Hughes, Peter S. A. Niculescu, and Michael Waldman, "The Implied Volatility of Fixed-Income Markets," in Frank J. Fabozzi (ed.), *Advances and Innovations in the Bond and Mortgage Markets* (Chicago: Probus Publishing, 1989) for two issues of CommonWealth Edison bonds as of December 31, 1987:

Issue	Next Call Date	Call Price	Market Price	Effective Duration*
14.375 of 1994	7/15/89	104.11	111.30	1.7
10.625 of 1995	9/1/90	102.86	104.12	3.4

*Evaluated at 16% volatility

a. What is meant by *effective duration*?

b. Why is it necessary to make an interest-rate volatility assumption to calculate effective duration?

19. a. Suppose that a 7 percent coupon corporate bond is immediately callable. Also suppose that if this issuer issued new bonds the coupon rate would be 12 percent. Why would the modified duration be a good approximation for the effective duration for this bond?

b. In calculating the effective duration for a mortgage-backed security, a prepayment model is needed to determine what would happen to the cash flows if interest rates change. Why?

20. The following excerpt is taken from an article entitled "Denver Investment to Make $800 Million Treasury Move" that appeared in the December 9, 1991, issue of *BondWeek*, p. 1:

Denver Investment Advisors will swap $800 million of long zero-coupon Treasuries for intermediate Treasuries. . . . The move would shorten the duration of it's $2.5 billion fixed-income portfolio.

Why would the swap described above shorten the duration of the portfolio?

21. Why are the net interest income and net-present-value simulation models preferable to maturity gap and simple duration models in assessing interest-rate risk for a depository institution?

22. How can option-based analysis be used in net-present value simulation models?

23. a. What are the limiting assumptions in the maturity gap and simple duration gap models?

  b. What are some limitations of duration gap analysis?

24. a. Explain the features of a multifactor bond valuation model.

  b. What are the factors used in such models?

  c. Explain how historical analysis captures the inherent riskiness of the factors of value present in the bond market.

25. Indicate why you agree or disagree with the following statement: "The traditional measures of risk in the context of a single market—duration and convexity in both their standard and option-adjusted forms—lose all meaning in the context of an international portfolio."

26. What has been empirically observed to be the largest component of risk in bond markets throughout the world?

27. The put provision for two zero-coupon convertible bonds is given below:

W. R. Grace due 5/16/06: Putable on 5/16/96 at 67.557. Put payable in cash, common stock, or a combination.
Bershire Hathaway due 9/28/04: Putable on 9/28/94 at 58.125, on 9/28/99 at 76.24. Put payable in cash.

  a. Which issue has a soft put?

  b. Which issue has a hard put?

28. a. What is a *LYON*?

  b. Explain the options embedded in a LYON.

  c. Describe the complexities in valuing a LYON.

29. Briefly describe the option approach to the valuation of convertible bonds.

30. Explain how to evaluate the investment performance of a convertible bond.

31. Describe several applications of term-structure modeling.

32. The pure expectations hypothesis can be stated in at least five different ways. Describe each.

33. Several models have been proposed for fitting yield curves. Briefly describe each.

PART 6: PORTFOLIO MANAGEMENT

1. What are the features that distinguish an active strategy from a passive strategy?

2. Describe the more popular bond indexes used today.

3. How will the performance of a bond index consisting of only government bonds differ from that of a bond index consisting of both government and corporate bonds during a period of declining and volatile interest rates?

4. What is meant by a *normal portfolio*?

5. Explain why the risk of the total pension portfolio requires that sponsors use benchmark portfolios at two levels in their long-term policy frameworks.

6. What is meant by a *manager benchmark*?

7. a. What is *tracking error*?

    b. Why does tracking error occur in an indexing strategy?

8. Why are typical custodian costs and master trustee costs lower with indexed funds than actively managed funds?

9. Why does indexing give the investor a greater degree of control over an actively managed fund?

10. Comment on the precision that can be reached in evaluating an investment advisor employing an indexing strategy compared with an active portfolio manager. Why is the former more precise and easier to measure?

11. What are the factors that determine the magnitude of outperformance of an enhanced index fund? Explain each.

12. Why are enhanced index-fund strategies sometimes referred to as a *duration-neutral strategy*?

13. Briefly describe the three methodologies for setting up an index fund, pointing out the advantages and disadvantages of each.

14. What is meant by *immunizing* a bond portfolio?

15. What is the basic underlying principle in an immunization strategy?

16. Why may the matching of the maturity of a coupon bond to the maturity of a liability fail to immunize a portfolio?

17. Why must an immunized portfolio be rebalanced periodically?

18. *(The following question is adapted from CFA Examination III, June 1, 1991, Morning Session, Question 5):*

Global Foundation has recently hired Strategic Allocation Associates (SAA) to review and make recommendations concerning allocation of its $5 billion endowment portfolio. Global has indicated an interest in introducing a structured approach (where structured management is broadly defined as indexing, immunization, dedication, etc.) to at least a portion of the fund's fixed income component.

After analysis of Globals's current asset mix, investment objectives, international exposure, and cash flow data, SAA has recommended that the overall asset mix be 50 percent equity, 5 percent real estate, and 45 percent fixed income securities. Within the fixed income component, SAA further recommended the following allocation:

- 50% Structured management
- 40% Specialty active management (20% Market timing, 10% High-yield, 10% Arbitrage)
- 10% Non dollar/international active management

Global's investment committee has asked you, as a senior partner in SAA, to address several issues.

   a. Compare structured management to active management with specific focus on *each* of the following aspects:

- Predictability of returns
- Level of return
- Cash flow characteristics

   b. Explain the potential impact on the active managers' strategies and freedoms of action resulting from the introduction of a structured portfolio component.

19. Explain why "the total-return approach involves a lot of modeling and specification by the portfolio manager." Explain why "it forces the manager to think explicitly about risk."

20. In managing a high-yield bond portfolio, a manager must decide which classes of bonds to purchase. What are some of the factors that the manager should consider in making this decision?

21. What are some of the factors to consider in selecting particular high-yield issues?

22. a. What is a *fallen angel*?

   b. What is an *emerging credit*?

23. a. What arguments have been put forth for investing in foreign bonds?

   b. What does the empirical evidence suggest regarding the benefits of investing internationally?

24. The quotation following is from an article entitled "Spanish Bonds to be Tops" that appeared in the March 4, 1991, issue of *BondWeek:*

The Spanish bond market will be one of the best performing European markets this year due to its relatively high yields, a strong peseta (the Spanish currency) and moves by the Spanish government to liberalize the market, according to analysts. The Spanish government's recent move to lower short-term rates from 14.7% to 14.5%, hold monthly auctions and abolish the 25% withholding tax

on bonos (government bonds) for non-residents has also helped increase liquidity in the market, they said.

Explain why the relatively high yields, a strong peseta, and the government's liberalization policies will contribute to the projected favorable
performance of the Spanish bond market cited in this quotation.

25. A U.S. portfolio manager is considering investing in 10-year
government bonds of several countries. In addition to looking at the
yield of each government bond, the manager has determined the modified duration for all 10-year issues.

  a. Explain why the yield measure may not be a good indication of the
  relative return from investing in a non-U.S. government bond.

  b. What is the problem of using modified duration as a measure of the
  price volatility of a non-U.S. government bond relative to changes in
  interest rates in the foreign market?

PART 7: DERIVATIVE INSTRUMENTS AND THEIR
PORTFOLIO MANAGEMENT APPLICATIONS

1. **a.** What is the difference between a forward and a futures contract?

   b. What is the difference between options and forward or futures contracts?

2. **a.** When does convergence take place on a futures contract?

   b. Why is convergence guaranteed to take place?

3. Describe the options embedded in the Treasury bond futures contract.

4. **a.** Describe the types of orders that can be used when trading futures
   contracts.

   b. How can a limit order be used to preserve profits or minimize losses
   on open positions?

5. Describe two ways of liquidating a futures position.

6. **a.** Why is margin not required for the buyer of a futures option?

   b. Why is it required for sellers of futures options?

7. How can a LIBOR cap be viewed as a series of puts on LIBOR-based
   debt?

8. How can an issuer protect itself against rising short-term rates by using
   caps?

9. What is the *Law of One Price*?

10. How are cash flows on floating-rate agreements at settlement date
    determined?

11. **a.** When will a futures contract trade at a discount to the cash market price?

   b. When will it trade at a premium to the cash market price?

12. How does arbitrage ensure that the observed futures price does not depart from its theoretical price?

13. Why do interim cash flows (variation margin) account for differences between forward and futures pricing?

14. What factors affect the theoretical upper and lower boundaries on futures contracts?

15. Why is the cheapest-to-deliver important in pricing Treasury bond and note futures contracts?

16. Describe the way interest-rate futures can be used to adjust the duration of a portfolio.

17. **a.** How can an investor synthetically create a short-term bond position using long cash bonds and futures contracts?

   b. What return will be received on this position?

18. Suppose that bond ABC is the underlying asset for a futures contract with settlement six months from now. You know the following about bond ABC and the futures contract:

   1. In the cash market ABC is selling for $80 (par value is $100).

   2. ABC pays $8 in coupon interest per year in two semiannual payments of $4, and the next semiannual payment is due exactly six months from now.

   3. The current six-month interest rate at which funds can be loaned or borrowed is 6 percent.

   a. What is the theoretical (or equilibrium) futures price?

   b. What action would you take if the futures price were $83?

   c. What action would you take if the futures price were $76?

   d. Suppose that bond ABC pays interest quarterly instead of semiannually. If you know that you can reinvest any funds you receive three months from now at 1 percent for three months, what would the theoretical futures price for a six-month settlement be?

   e. Suppose that the borrowing rate and lending rate are not equal. Instead, suppose that the current six-month borrowing rate is 8 percent and the six-month lending rate is 6 percent. What is the boundary for the theoretical futures price?

19. What is meant by basis trading in the Treasury bond futures contract?

20. Why is an American option always worth at least as much as its European counterpart?

21. Using a profit/loss graph, explain why a position of a long call and a short put is equivalent to owning the underlying security.

22. a. Why do options trade above their intrinsic value when there is time remaining to expiration?

  b. Why, if there is no volatility in the market, would the option be priced at its intrinsic value?

23. a. Why is a position in an option with negative gamma considered to be short volatility or convexity?

  b. What happens to this position as the price of the underlying changes?

24. Why is a long position in a straddle considered to be a pure convexity trade?

25. How is implied volatility determined?

26. What is a *covered call strategy,* and why would this be used?

27. What is meant by *hedge effectiveness*? How is it measured? What factors influence hedge effectiveness?

28. Would the rate locked in on a one-day hedge be closer to the spot or 3-month futures rate? How can one lock in a futures rate?

29. What factors affect a cross hedge?

30. How can relative yield volatilities be accounted for in determining the number of futures contracts to hedge a position when cross hedging?

31. You work for a conservative investment management firm. You recently asked one of the senior partners for permission to open up a futures account so that you could trade interest trade futures as well as cash instruments. He replied, "Are you crazy? I might as well write you a check, wish you good luck, and put you on a bus to Las Vegas. The futures markets are nothing more than a respectable game of craps. Don't you think you're taking enough risk trading bonds?" How would you try to persuade the senior partner to allow you to use futures?

32. a. What are the risks associated with hedging?

  b. Why is hedging considered to substitute basis risk for price risk?

33. a. How can a protective put strategy be compared to buying insurance?

  b. Explain the covered call writing strategy, pointing out risk and return implications.

34. a. How could a money manager use a Treasury bond futures contract to hedge against increased interest rates over the next quarter?

  b. Suppose an institutional investor wants to hedge a portfolio of mortgage pass-through securities using Treasury bond futures contracts. What are the risks associated with such a hedge?

35. "There's no real difference between options and futures. Both are hedging tools, and both are derivative products. It's just that with options you have to pay an option premium, while futures require no upfront payment except for a "good faith" margin. I can't understand why anyone would use options." Do you agree with this statement?

36. a. What is the motivation for the purchase of an over-the-counter option?

    b. Does it make sense for an investor who wants to speculate on interest-rate movements to purchase an over-the-counter option on Treasury securities?

37. Suppose that a life insurance company has issued a three-year GIC with a fixed rate of 10 percent. Under what circumstances might it be feasible for the life insurance company to invest the funds in a floating-rate security and enter into a three-year interest-rate swap in which it pays a floating rate and receives a fixed rate?

38. How can the duration of an interest-rate swap be calculated?

39. What is meant by *counterparty risk* in a swap transaction?

40. Unlike interest-rate swaps, which are designed to insulate the user from changes in interest-rate volatility, caps and floors are designed to provide asymmetric coverage in capping liability costs and protecting the return on assets. How do caps and floors provide this coverage?

INDEX